Contents

The National Garden Scheme

A company limited by guarantee. Registered in England & Wales.
Charity No. 1112664. Company No. 5631421

Registered & Head Office: Hatchlands Park, East Clandon,
Guildford, Surrey, GU4 7RT. 01483 211535 www.ngs.org.uk

© The National Garden Scheme 2017

Published by Constable, an imprint of Little, Brown Book Group,
Carmelite House, 50 Victoria Embankment, London EC4Y 0DZ

An Hachette UK Company
www.hachette.co.uk www.littlebrown.co.uk

CLARENCE HOUSE

The National Gardens Scheme celebrates the remarkable milestone of its 90th anniversary this year, in confident style. A concept that has enabled generous and hospitable gardeners to raise more than £45 million over that period for nursing charities is more successful than ever. At the same time, as you will see from this handbook and the excellent website, the look and feel of the organization has been carefully updated. It seems to me that this has been done in the same way that some of us make changes in our gardens – with loving care, attention to detail and an awareness of what works well and should be left alone. The result appears to have character and to be warm and welcoming, just like the National Gardens Scheme itself.

As the charity announces record donations this year, it is worth reflecting that it has grown from 600 gardens opening in 1927, and raising £8,000, to providing the most significant charitable funding of nursing in the country. Along the way, in a manner that I would venture very few other charities can match, it has given joy, interest and inspiration to millions of people.

For me, as Patron, the wonderful thing about the National Gardens Scheme is its unique blend of Britishness – the marriage of nursing and gardens; the exemplary role of volunteers; the cumulative fundraising power of small events; the championing of local community activity and the celebration of what gardens can do for the benefit of us all. So I can only wish you all another very happy year of garden visiting.

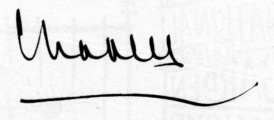

Who's Who

Chairman's Message

2017 is a momentous year for us all at the National Garden Scheme as it is our 90th anniversary. It is an opportunity to celebrate our wonderful gardens, our unique charitable contribution to nursing, and our endlessly generous volunteers and garden owners.

We started the year with the exciting news that 2016 had been a record year with our 3,800 gardens raising £3.5 million. It is a remarkable achievement that makes me reflect on how far we have come since our first year in 1927 when the original 600 gardens raised £8,000 for district nurses. Ninety years later supporting nurses is still our mission, so that today - little known to most – we are the most substantial charitable funder of nursing in the country.

We are also launching new branding. I am very excited about our new look because I think it really portrays who we are in a suitably engaging and characterful manner and will raise public awareness of us.

We were delighted when Mary Berry agreed to become our President. Mary opened her garden in support of the National Garden Scheme for over 20 years and has a personal commitment to the principle of sharing your garden with visitors.

We are fortunate in having many loyal supporters among whom I would particularly mention our core sponsor Investec Wealth & Investment. And we depend on your support as visitors, for which a hearty thanks from me, and do help celebrate our 90th.

Martin McMillan, OBE

"Investec congratulates the National Gardens Scheme on their milestone 90th anniversary."

Jonathan Wragg
Chief Executive, Investec Wealth & Investment

Private Clients \ International Clients \ Charities \ Financial Advisers

Offices at: Bath Belfast Birmingham Bournemouth Cheltenham Edinburgh Exeter Glasgow Guildford Leeds Liverpool London Manchester Reigate Sheffield

Some tips on using your handbook

This book lists all the gardens opening for the National Garden Scheme between January 2017 and early 2018. It is divided up into county sections, each including a calendar of opening dates and details of each garden, listed alphabetically.

Symbols explained

NEW Gardens opening for the first time this year or re-opening after a long break.

◆ Garden also opens on non-NGS days. (Gardens which carry this symbol contribute to the NGS either by opening on a specific day(s) and/or by giving a guaranteed contribution.)

♿ Wheelchair access to at least the main features of the garden.

🐕 Dogs on short leads welcome.

❀ Plants usually for sale.

NPC Plant Heritage National Plant Collection.

🛏 Gardens that offer accommodation.

☕ Refreshments are available, normally at a charge.

D Garden designed by a Fellow, Member or Pre-registered Member of The Society of Garden Designers.

🚌 Garden accessible to coaches. Coach sizes vary so please contact garden owner or County Organiser in advance to check details.

Group Visits Group Organisers may contact the County Organiser or a garden owner direct to organise a group visit to a particular county or garden. See the front of each county section for County Organiser contact details, or visit www.ngs.org.uk

Children must be accompanied by an adult

Photography is at the discretion of the garden owner; please check first. Photographs must not be used for sale or reproduction without prior permission of the owner.

Donation To indicates that a proportion of the money collected will be given to the nominated charity.

Toilets are not usually available at private gardens.

If you cannot find the information you require from a garden or County Organiser, call the NGS office on 01483 211535

Celebrating our 90th year

For 90 years the National Garden Scheme has been offering people access to many of the most beautiful private gardens in England and Wales. This in itself has provided constant memorable experiences as visitors have discovered the unique blend of garden quality, the welcome and community atmosphere and, of course, the famous teas.

But as they have explored the gardens, visitors have made another discovery, that they are contributing to a remarkable charitable programme which has made the National Garden Scheme the most significant charitable funder of nursing in this country. Founded in 1927 to raise money for district nurses, today it continues to give its money to a group of nursing charities — which you can read about individually on pages 8–20. The fundraising mechanism is impressive; each year the total net income that the charity has raised is given away in full to the beneficiaries and this includes more than 80% of all the money raised at the gardens.

This constant annual flow of significant grants has enabled the National Garden Scheme to make a substantial contribution to the work of its beneficiaries; whether funding for a new Macmillan cancer centre, paying for Marie Curie nurses, supporting the QNI's team of community nurses or helping Carers Trust develop their network of support for carers of all ages. At a time of unprecedented challenges for health and social care the combined efforts of the National Garden Scheme and its nursing beneficiaries is a shining example of what can be achieved.

As a group we are also pooling our resources and experience to spread the important message of the benefits of gardens for people's health and wellbeing. This took a significant step forward in 2016 with the publication of a new report Gardens and Health: Implications for Policy and Practice, which was commissioned by the National Garden Scheme. The report was produced by The King's Fund and has become the benchmark for the increasing media interest in this area.

The challenge for an organisation with a long heritage is to remain relevant in changing times. As the National Garden Scheme announces record donations of £3 million this year I am proud that it is increasingly relevant and committed to its cause.

Below 70 Queen's nurses attended the Frogmore Gardens open day in 2016, shown here with George Plumptre and Head Gardener at Frogmore, Neil Dodds

George Plumptre

George Plumptre, Chief Executive

QNI The Queen's Nursing Institute

"2017 is a landmark year for both the Queen's Nursing Institute and the National Garden Scheme. The QNI celebrates the 130th anniversary of its foundation and it is 90 years since the NGS was established to fundraise for our work.

The money raised today by the NGS for nursing and caring in the community is as important today as it was in 1927. There is an increasing need for compassionate and skilled nursing care in people's homes and communities, where 90% of all clinical contact takes place.

Our Queen's Nurses are champions of excellent patient care and they are also regular visitors to NGS gardens. By visiting a garden you too are contributing to high quality nursing care in the community for everyone who needs it."

**Dr Crystal Oldman,
Chief Executive**

The Queen's Nursing Institute founded the National Garden Scheme in the 1920s, to raise money to support district nursing and the two charities have developed strong ties and a shared heritage ever since. As the Scheme grew through the post-war years it continued to be run directly as part of the Queen's Nursing Institute until it was set up as an independent charity in 1980.

Today the Queen's Nursing Institute works to improve nursing services for patients in their own homes and communities. We believe that skilled and compassionate nursing should be available to everyone, where and when they need it. We achieve this through our network of Queen's Nurses who are experts in delivering care, benefiting the patients and the communities they serve.

WE ARE MACMILLAN.
CANCER SUPPORT

" We are extremely proud of our longstanding partnership with the National Garden Scheme which has raised a fantastic £15.7 million since it began in 1985. This has been achieved with the support of the committed NGS garden owners and volunteers, who have given their time and passion to make a difference to the lives of people affected by cancer.

I am delighted that the NGS is currently helping to fund the new NGS Macmillan Unit at the Chesterfield Royal Hospital which will be opening to patients in 2017. The new NGS Macmillan Unit is a purpose-built facility which will provide treatment, care, information and support for people affected by cancer. Thanks to the new unit we will be able to provide the people of North Derbyshire with the very best care.

The National Garden Scheme is Macmillan's largest single donor having donated over £16 million since the partnership first took root in 1985. Since then, the NGS has funded 147 Macmillan professional posts, this and the NGS's funding of Macmillan services has helped Macmillan ensure that no one has to face cancer alone.

There are more than 2.5 million people living with or beyond cancer in the UK today, rising to 4 million by 2030. At Macmillan we want to make sure we can provide support to everyone who needs it, to help people affected by cancer feel more in control of their lives.

We are grateful to the NGS for the outstanding contribution they have made to Macmillan over the years. I hope that you enjoy reading Garden Visitor's Handbook, and spend many happy hours visiting these stunning gardens around the country."

Lynda Thomas,
Chief Executive

Marie Curie

Care and support
through terminal illness

" We are so proud to have such a fantastic partnership with the National Garden Scheme (NGS) which continues to go from strength to strength. The NGS is Marie Curie's biggest corporate sponsor, donating nearly £8 million to the charity since 1997, and their support has helped Marie Curie to provide more care to people with a terminal illness and their families.

Our nurses often talk about the importance of gardens for people being looked after at home, and consider this as part of their care. Keen gardeners are brought out into their gardens to enjoy them when they are no longer able to manage this and Marie Curie's hospice gardens provide tranquillity for patients. The support we receive from the NGS makes this possible for thousands of people each year and we look forward to celebrating their 90th anniversary with them this year."

**Dr Jane Collins,
Chief Executive**

Marie Curie was founded in 1948 and today provides a lifeline for people living with any terminal illness and for their families. We offer expert care, guidance and support to help them get the most from the time they have left. Marie Curie nurses work day and night supporting people in their own homes, while their hospices offer the reassurance of specialist round-the-clock care and support both for people who stay and for others who visit on a day basis.

Marie Curie nurses are one of the most recognised and respected of all nursing groups in the UK and their addition to the group of charities supported annually by the National Garden Scheme was a significant milestone for both charities.

hospice UK

Hospice UK believes hospice care should be available for every person in need. Hospice UK supports more than 220 hospices across the UK, so that they can deliver high quality care to 360,000 children, young people, adults and their families every year.

The National Garden Scheme has raised over £4 million for hospice care since 1996 and is the largest single supporter of Hospice UK. Their annual funding supports all of our vital projects and directly helps individual hospices all over the country. As the challenge to improve end of life care for all grows Hospice UK will work tirelessly to support communities and extend our reach so that hospice care can be delivered to more people when and where they need it.

Providing expert, compassionate care, tailored to the needs of the individual, however long it may be needed, is why hospices exist and this is why the constant support of everyone involved in the National Garden Scheme is so important.

" *2017 marks the 50th anniversary of the modern hospice movement and there has never been such an important time to support our cause. Around 100,000 people who require palliative care are not getting the support they need, and the demand is rapidly increasing as our population ages. The funding Hospice UK receives from the NGS means that Hospice UK are able to change this.*

Gardens provide a peaceful location for everyone and horticulture is an important feature of the care delivered in hospices.

We want to thank everyone who opens their garden and all those who take the time to visit one during the Anniversary Weekend. "

Tracey Bleakley,
Chief Executive

Blickling Hall

SAVE up to 25%
when you subscribe
to COUNTRY LIFE

Credit Country Life Picture Library/Val Corbett

Not only will you have the very best of British life delivered to your door every week, you will also receive your personal copy of our international property and schools supplements.

Every print subscription comes complete with a free trial digital edition and all of our subscribers are entitled to join Rewards for free and take advantage of our hand-picked offers, unique giveaways and unmissable prizes.

carerstrust
action · help · advice

"*Carers Trust is extremely proud of our partnership with The National Garden Scheme. Over the years they have raised much needed funds to help support some of the UK's seven million unpaid carers. This has been achieved with the support of the wonderful garden owners and volunteers who so generously give up their time, as well as everyone who visits the thousands of gardens which open every year. Thank you for your generous support.*

With The National Garden Scheme's support, Carers Trust helps unpaid carers manage the stress of their caring roles, which includes hosting activities such as gardening and visits to gardens. Some of our local support services have gardens which give unpaid carers respite from their caring role. We know that even one hour away from caring can make a huge difference.

Carers Trust celebrates our 5th year in April 2017, and the support of The National Garden Scheme has been instrumental in helping us grow to the point that Carers Trust and our network support more than 500,000 carers across the UK.

NGS is one of our longest standing supporters and we are extremely grateful for the tremendous difference their support allows us to make to carers lives."

Gail Scott Spicer
Chief Executive

The National Garden Scheme first funded carers in 1996 when it began annual support for Crossroads Care. In 2012 Crossroads Care merged with Princess Royal Trust for Carers to form Carers Trust which the NGS has funded ever since.

Carers Trust works to improve support, services and recognition for anyone living with the challenges of caring, unpaid, for a family member or friend who is ill, frail, disabled or has mental health or addiction problems.

The photograph above shows HRH The Princess Royal, Patron of Carers Trust, visiting an NGS garden in Gloucestershire in July 2015.

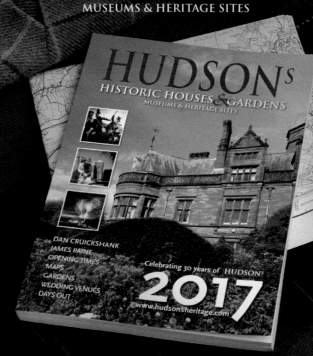

PERENNIAL

GARDENERS' ROYAL BENEVOLENT SOCIETY

Helping Horticulturists In Need Since 1839

"*On behalf of Perennial, I would like to congratulate the NGS on its 90th anniversary. Thank you to all the NGS garden owners who have put so much effort and enthusiasm into opening their wonderful gardens over the past 90 years as well as those who visit the gardens each year and in so doing, support the valuable work of the beneficiary charities.*

As the single largest supporter of Perennial, the NGS has made a massive difference to the lives of thousands of current, former and retired horticulturists, and their families.

With your help we are able to fund our nationwide team of trained professional Caseworkers and Debt Advisers, who travel the length and breadth of the UK, dealing with problems such as debt, homelessness, illness, poverty, disability and workplace accidents. Our free and confidential services can be life changing, and they help their clients for as long as they need us, sometimes for years.

In this anniversary year, we look back with pride on our long association with the NGS, following the merging of our own Gardeners' Sunday open garden scheme with the NGS in 1986.

By showing and sharing the beauty of gardens, NGS garden owners and visitors are helping to keep Britain beautiful, and play their part in helping us to find self-employed gardeners who are in need of our help, clients that can be hard for us to reach. Their fundraising activities ensure that gardeners and horticulturists across the country can count on Perennial for many years to come."

Dougal Philip,
Chairman

Perennial combines two charities which have been supported annually by the National Garden Scheme since 1986, the Gardeners' Royal Benevolent Society and the Royal Fund for Gardeners' Children. Through Perennial, the National Garden Scheme helps horticulturists who are facing difficulties.

The NGS donation is invaluable to the charity's on-going work to help individuals and families and also supports gardeners' children by providing ongoing support for families when one or both parents have died as well as for children who are disadvantaged by other circumstances.

Perennial owns two outstanding gardens, York Gate in Yorkshire and Fullers Mill in Suffolk, both of which open in support of NGS.

COBRA

The UK's largest range of lawnmowers

Create a lawn that is the envy of your neighbours with a new lawnmower from Cobra. At the heart of these powerful, stylish mowers is a choice of either electric, cordless or petrol engines powered by Briggs & Stratton, Honda and Subaru.

Cobra have over 45 lawnmowers in their range including rear roller, 4 wheeled and professional models and are sure to have a lawnmower to suit your specific gardening needs.

Promo prices start from just £84.99 inc VAT

COBRA
For a Great British striped lawn

COBRA PRO

LI-ION
40v Lithium-ion

For your nearest dealer visit: **www.cobragarden.co.uk** or call: **0115 986 6646**

Promotional prices only at participating dealers

PARKINSON'S^{UK}
CHANGE ATTITUDES.
FIND A CURE.
JOIN US.

❝ It has been an absolute pleasure to see our partnership with the National Garden Scheme grow and flourish year on year. Since we joined forces, Parkinson's UK has contributed to more than 40 new nursing posts – an incredible achievement which just wouldn't be possible without funding from significant donors like the National Garden Scheme.

Parkinson's UK first became a guest charity of the National Garden Scheme in 2013. After three years in partnership, we were honoured to be the first guest in their incredible 90-year history to become a permanent beneficiary. To date, our blossoming relationship has raised an incredible £622,000 – enabling us to fund specialist Parkinson's nurses and give a lifeline to thousands of people across the UK.

People like Alan, (pictured above) who first opened his garden for the NGS with his wife Lynn 13 years ago. When Parkinson's UK became a guest charity, Alan hadn't heard of us – but just a year later he was diagnosed with Parkinson's – a progressive, neurological condition. Our partnership allows us to reach families like Alan and Lynn's, and fund vital care so they don't have to face Parkinson's alone.

A personal highlight for me, was attending the launch of the "Gardens and Health" report in May 2016, and learning about the huge impact gardening can have on the nation's health. We know many people with Parkinson's find gardening a therapeutic escape from daily life with the condition, and hope to increase awareness of this health benefit through our partnership.

We're incredibly grateful to be united with such an innovative organisation. In 2017, we're looking forward to working together to drive change in health policy, and continue our partnership legacy – improving care for everyone affected by Parkinson's."

Steve Ford, Chief Executive

BEDFORDSHIRE

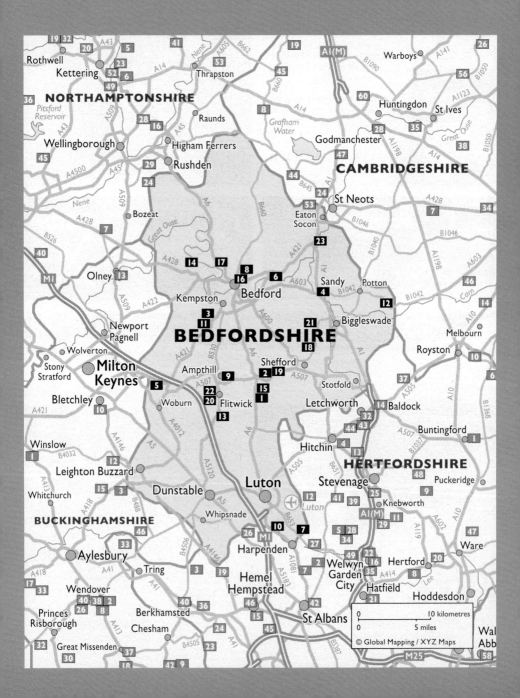

The Birthplace of John Bunyan, it is little wonder the county of Bedfordshire inspired the author of Pilgrim's Progress.

Running North to South through scenic countryside, a number of National Garden Scheme gardens lie along the John Bunyan Trail, from Stevington and Clapham, through Bedford, Ampthill, Steppingley to Westoning and Barton-le-Clay.

Bedfordshire also boasts a trio of 18th century gardens designed by Capability Brown, two of which open for the National Garden Scheme. First, Southill Park, an imposing country house with rolling lawns, flanked by belts, lakes and a Tuscan temple. It is also a founding garden which first opened its gates toNational Garden Scheme visitors in 1927. Second, Luton Hoo, where, wrote Samuel Johnson, "magnificence is not sacrificed to convenience, nor convenience to magnificence".

Once celebrated for its market gardens, many of the county's garden owners are as enthusiastic about their edibles as they are of their flowers. From the historic to the contemporary and from the village to the town, a warm welcome awaits you at a National Garden Scheme open garden in Bedfordshire. Join us for a truly British experience of garden, tea and well-being.

Volunteers

County Organiser
Indi Jackson
01525 713798
indi.jackson1@gmail.com

County Treasurer
Colin Davies
01525 712721
colin.davies@which.net

Publicity
Doug Copeland
01799 550553
dougcopeland@btinternet.com

Facebook
Richard Hall
richh17@aol.com

Newsletter
Kate Gardner
07725 307803
kgardner287@gmail.com

Booklet Co-ordinator
Indi Jackson
(as above)

Talks
Victoria Diggle
01767 627247
victoria@diggledesign.com

Assistant County Organisers
Geoff & Davina Barrett
01908 585329
geoffanddean@gmail.com

Mary Marshall
marybmarshall@hotmail.co.uk

Brenda Hands
brenda.iris@hotmail.co.uk

Left: Dragon's Glen

OPENING DATES

All entries subject to change. For latest information check www.ngs.org.uk

Map locator numbers are shown to the right of each garden name.

Your support helps Carers Trust to provide more help to unpaid carers

Flaxbourne Farm

THE GARDENS

1 NEW 10 ALDER WYND

Silsoe, Bedford, MK45 4GQ.
David & Frances
Hampson, 01525 861356,
mail@davidhampson.com. *From
Barton Road, turn into the estate on
Obelisk Way. At end of Obelisk Way
turn R at school, then 1st L into Alder
Wynd and bear R.* 10 Alder Wynd
is the 1st house on R. Sat 15, Sun
16 July (2-5). Adm £3, chd free.
Home-made teas. **Visits also
by arrangement June to Sept.**
One of four finalists in the 2016
Daily Mail National Garden
Competition, the garden
demonstrates what can be achieved
in a relatively small space, 10m
x 11m. Created from scratch in
the Autumn of 2014, the garden
is roughly courtyard in style and
formed from a series of raised beds
and oak structures. Lush plantings
of banana, tree ferns, hostas,
bamboos and colourful herbaceous
perennials. This small area has a
wide selection of plants, tetrapanax,
roses, wisteria, clematis, a variety of
grasses and traditional perennials.
A water feature provides a subtle
background noise. The pathways are
narrow and made of slate chippings,
there are two shallow steps to the
decked area, both are wheelchair
accessible with care.
♿ ❉ ⛳

2 DRAGONS GLEN

17 Great Lane, Clophill, Bedford,
MK45 4BQ. Kate & Andy Gardner.
*Great Lane is situated approx
halfway along the high st almost
opp the Village Primary School. The
house is approx. 500m up the lane
on the L.* Mon 29 May (1.30-5).
Combined adm with Speeds
Dairy Farmhouse £6, chd free.
Sun 10 Sept (2-5). Adm £4,
chd free. Home-made teas.
Gluten and dairy free cakes are
available at all garden openings.
Single adm £4.
This contemporary garden takes full
advantage of the sloped landscape
and dry conditions of its Greensand
Ridge location to great effect. Dry
woodland, herbaceous borders,
waterfall and wildlife pond create
distinct spaces that are linked
together by the oriental influences
that run throughout the garden.
Large decked areas, unusual
water feature. Featured on and
in BBC Gardeners World, BBC 3
Counties Radio and Garden News.
Partial wheelchair access due to
steep slopes and steps around
the garden.
❉ ⛳

3 22 ELMSDALE ROAD

Wootton, Bedford, MK43 9JN. Roy
& Dianne Richards, 07733 222495,
roy.richards60@ntlworld.com. *4m
from J13 M1. Join old A421 towards
Bedford, follow signs to Wootton.
Turn R at The Cock PH follow Rd
to Elmsdale Rd.* Sat 8, Sun 9 July
(12.30-5.30). Combined adm
with The Old Post Office £5,
chd free. Home-made teas and
cakes, tea and coffee **Visits also
by arrangement June to Sept
for groups 8+.**
Topiary garden greets visitors before
they enter a genuine Japanese Feng
Shui garden incl bonsai every plant
is strictly Japanese, large Koi pond
with bog garden and Tea House.
The garden was created from
scratch by the owners and has
many interesting features. Japanese
lanterns and a large collection
of Japanese plants and bonsai.
From China the Kneeling Archer
terracotta soldier pond and sunken
bog garden. Partial wheelchair
access. The Garden is on 2 levels
and has gravel type paths but some
of the garden can be viewed from
the lower level.
♿ 🐗 🚐 ⛳

4 THE FIRS

33 Bedford Road, Sandy,
SG19 1EP. Mr & Mrs D
Sutton, 01767 227589,
d.sutton7@ntlworld.com. *7m E of
Bedford. On B1042 between Sandy
town centre & A1.* On-road parking.
Sun 30 July (2-5). Adm £3.50,
chd free. Home-made teas,
cakes and jams. **Visits also
by arrangement May to Sept
home made cakes/tea for
groups of 10+, by request.**
Price on application.
¼-acre town garden surrounding
a Victorian Gentleman's residence.
Designed and created from scratch
since 2000 this garden has many
individual garden rooms and ideas
that could be included into anyone's
garden - large or small. The garden
provides food for the kitchen,
flowers for the table and features
modern sculpture and railway
memorabilia. Money raised from the
refreshments will go to the Need
Project, providing food parcels in
Bedfordshire. One gravel path, but
otherwise wheelchair accessible to
all parts.
♿ ❉ ⛳

5 FLAXBOURNE FARM

Salford Road, Aspley Guise,
MK17 8HZ. Paul & Denise Meads,
info@ukeventsandtents.co.uk.
*5m W of Ampthill. 1m S of J13 of
M1. Turn R in village centre, 1m over
railway line.* Sun 7 May, Sun 13
Aug (2-5.30). Adm £5, chd free.
Home-made teas. **Visits also
by arrangement May to Aug
conducted tours for groups 12+.**
A beautiful, entertaining and
fun garden of 3 acres, lovingly
developed with numerous water
features, a windmill, modern arches
and bridges, a small moated castle,
lily pond, herbaceous borders and
a Greek temple ruin. A recently
established jungle garden complete
with a three way bridge, planted
up with Japanese acers, tree ferns,
hostas, gunneras and large bamboos.
An orchard garden with oriental
features with a flyover walkway,
an inspirational woodland setting.
Crow's nest, crocodiles, tree house
with zip wire for children. Huge
Roman arched stone gateway.
An ideal garden for coach tours.
Conducted tours, tea and coffee
available on request. Wheelchair
access is available to all the main
parts of the garden.
♿ 🐗 🚐 ⛳

GREYWALLS
See Northamptonshire

6 NEW HOWBURY HALL GARDEN
Howbury Hall Estate, Renhold, Bedford, MK41 0JB. Julian Polhill & Lucy Copeman. *2m E of Bedford. Off A421 A1 - M1 link. Leave A421 at the A428/Gt Barford exit, take A428 to Bedford. Entrance to house & gardens ½m on R. Parking in field. Short walk to garden.* Sun 25 June, Sun 27 Aug (12-5). Adm £5, chd free. Home-made teas.
A late Victorian garden designed with mature trees, sweeping lawns, wonderful colour themed herbaceous borders. In the woodland area, walking towards the large pond, the outside of a disused ice house can be seen. There is a large walled garden for vegetables and cut flowers and a comprehensive collection of apple varieties of Bedfordshire ❀ ☕

7 THE HYDE WALLED GARDEN
East Hyde, Luton, LU2 9PS. D J J Hambro Will Trust. *2m S of Luton. M1 exit/10a Exit to A1061 towards Harpenden take 2nd on L signed East Hyde. From A1 exit J4 follow A3057 N to r'about 1st L to B653 follow road to Wheathampstead/ Luton to East Hyde.* Sun 11 June, Sun 2 July (2-5). Adm £4.50, chd free. Home-made teas.

Walled garden adjoins the grounds of The Hyde (not open). Extends to approx 1 acre and features rose garden, seasonal beds and herbaceous borders, imaginatively interspersed with hidden areas of formal lawn. An interesting group of Victorian greenhouses, coldframes and cucumber house are serviced from the potting shed in the adjoining vegetable garden. Gravel paths. ఉ ❀ ☕

8 192 KIMBOLTON ROAD
Bedford, MK41 8DP. Tricia Atkinson. *On B660 between Brickhill Drive & Avon Drive nr pedestrian crossing.* Sat 10 June (1.30-4.30). Adm £3.50, chd free. Home-made teas.
A third of acre cottage garden. Grape vine, vegetable and soft fruit patch and orchard. Garden incl over 60 roses. Featured in Bedfordshire Clanger. Wheelchair access with care. Some gravel. ఉ ❀ ☕

9 ◆ KING'S ARMS GARDEN
Ampthill, MK45 2PP. Ampthill Town Council, 01525 755648, bryden.k@ntlworld.com. *8m S of Bedford. Free parking in town centre. Entrance opp Old Market Place, down King's Arms Yard.* For NGS: Sun 29 Jan, Sun 29 Oct (2-4). Adm £3, chd free. Light refreshments. For other opening times and information, please phone or email.

Small woodland garden of about 1½ acres created by plantsman the late William Nourish. Trees, shrubs, bulbs and many interesting collections throughout the yr. Maintained since 1987 by 'The Friends of the Garden' on behalf of Ampthill Town Council. See us on Facebook Kings Arms Garden. Wheelchair access to most of the garden. ఉ ❀ ☕

10 LUTON HOO HOTEL GOLF & SPA
The Mansion House, Luton Hoo, Luton, LU1 3TQ. Luton Hoo Hotel Golf & Spa, 01582 734437, www.lutonhoo.co.uk. *Approx 1m from J10 M1, take London Rd A1081 signed Harpenden for approx ½m - entrance on L for Luton Hoo Hotel Golf & Spa.* Sun 23 July (11-4). Adm £5, chd free. Light refreshments. Visitors wishing to have lunch/formal afternoon tea at the hotel must book in advance directly with the hotel.
The gardens and parkland designed by Capability Brown are of national historic significance and lie in a conservation area. Main features - lakes, woodland and pleasure grounds, Victorian grass tennis court and late C19 sunken rockery. Italianate garden with herbaceous borders and topiary garden. Gravel paths. ఉ 🛏 ☕

11 NEW THE OLD POST OFFICE
Church Road, Wootton, Bedford, MK43 9EU. Carol Bishop. *From A421 take signs to Wootton. Go along Fields Rd, L turn at the end (by the garage) and then immed turn R onto Church Rd. The Old Post Office is half way up Church Rd.* Sat 8, Sun 9 July (11-4). Combined adm with 22 Elmsdale Road £5, chd free. Home-made teas.
There are large front and rear gardens, the front primarily a restored Georgian box-edged layout with cottage style planting. The rear garden is totally walled, divided into packed 'rooms' with path terrace and pergola, a well, fruit trees, apple, mulberry, medlar, pear, fig, grapevine and peach. Gravel pathway and drive. ఉ ❀ ☕

Luton Hoo Golf Spa

The National Garden Scheme is Hospice UK's largest single funder

12 THE OLD RECTORY
Church Lane, Wrestlingworth, Sandy, SG19 2EU.
Mrs Josephine Hoy, 01767 631204, hoyjosephine@hotmail.co.uk. *5m E of Sandy, 5m NE of Biggleswade. Wrestlingworth is situated on B1042. 5m from Sandy & 6m from Biggleswade. The Old Rectory is at the top of Church Lane, which is well sign posted, behind the church.* Sun 21, Sun 28 May (2-6). Adm £5, chd free. Home-made teas. **Visits also by arrangement Apr to June groups are welcome with prior appointment.**
4 acre garden full of colour and interest. The owner has a free style of gardening sensitive to wildlife. Beds overflowing with tulips, alliums, bearded iris, peonies, poppies, geraniums and much more. Beautiful mature trees and many more planted in the last 30 years. Incl a large selection of betulas. Gravel gardens, box hedging, woodland garden and wild flower meadows. Wheelchair access maybe limited on grass paths.
&♿ ⚘ ✿ 🚌 ☕ ♥

13 THE OLD VICARAGE
Church Road, Westoning, MK45 5JW. Ann & Colin Davies. *2m S of Flitwick. Off A5120, 2m N of M1 J12. ¼m up Church Rd, next to church.* Sun 2 Apr, Sun 18 June (2-5.30). Adm £4, chd free. Cream teas in C14 church next door.
A traditional 2-acre vicarage garden on sandy soil with box and laurel hedges, a formal lawn and many mature shrubs and trees. The colour co-ordinated herbaceous beds have been further expanded. There is also a romantic cornfield meadow, fruit trees, an English rose garden, pond, rockery and small vegetable garden. There should be a good show of hellebores and daffodils for the spring opening. Wheelchair access generally good.
&♿ ✿ ☕

14 PARK END THATCH
58 Park Road, Stevington, Bedford, MK43 7QG. Susan Young, www.susanyoungdesign.co.uk. *5m NW of Bedford. Off A428, through Bromham.* Sun 25 June (12-5). Adm £4, chd free. Light refreshments.
½ acre cottage garden set within old orchard and designed by the owner, Professional Gardeners' Guild Member and Society of Garden Designers Pre-Registered Member. Sunny borders of flowering shrubs with herbaceous planting. Fragrant roses and climber covered pergola. Winding grass paths shaded by trees. Trellis border featuring colour and texture. Garden cultivated to be drought tolerant. Wildlife friendly. Fruit production and herbs. Small plant nursery. View of Stevington windmill. Outside WC, regret cannot be accessed by wheelchair. Main path is gravel on a slight slope, grass paths. Most of garden is accessible by wheelchair.
&♿ ✿ D ☕ ♥

15 NEW THE ROUND COTTAGE
36 Ampthill Road, Silsoe, Bedford, MK45 4DX. Peter & Jane Gregory. *Within Silsoe village on Ampthill Road. From A6 enter Silsoe village, from Bedford direction take the 1st R after The George PH. From Luton direction take 1st L after the village shop. Garden is 200m on R.* Sat 17, Sun 18 June (2-5.30). Home-made teas. Evening opening Thur 27 July (7-9). Wine. Adm £3, chd free. Savoury nibbles with wine on 27 July.
This is a small garden surrounding a 1820's thatched cottage. Traditional style flower beds with perennials mixed with exotics from around the world and a sprinkling of annuals. Large Koi pond with waterfall, greenhouse and summer house. Vegetable and fruit area and small shady walkway. The cottage has a deep lit well. Two classic cars on display. The vegetable area and shady walk are inaccessible by wheelchair.
&♿ ✿ ☕ ♥

16 1A ST AUGUSTINE'S ROAD
Bedford, MK40 2NB. Chris Damp, 01234 353465/01234 353730. *St. Augustine's Rd is on L off Kimbolton Rd as you leave the centre of Bedford.* Sat 5 Aug (12-4.30). Adm £2.50, chd free. Home-made teas. **Visits also by arrangement Apr to Sept for groups of 6+.**
A colourful suburban garden, comprising of herbaceous boarders, climbers, plum trees and a pretty terrace lined with pots. There are also sweet peas, salvias, a small collection of vegetables, a pond and green house. The garden is wheelchair accessible.
&♿ ✿ ☕

Howbury Hall Garden

Park End Thatch

sharp bend. Signed Sandy Smith &
Shefford. Mon 29 May (1.30-5).
Combined adm with Dragons
Glen £6, chd free. Home-made
teas at Dragons Glen. Single
adm £4.

The front garden is laid mainly
to mature trees, a pond that was
completed in 2015 and fruit trees. The
back garden was landscaped 5 years
ago and comprises of a gravel path
meandering through borders with a
mixture of shrubs and perennials. At
the bottom of the rear garden is a
vegetable patch and wooden framed
greenhouse. Wheelchair access via a
gravel driveway.

&. ❋ ☕

GROUP OPENING

20 NEW STEPPINGLEY VILLAGE GARDENS

Steppingley, Bedford, MK45 5AT.
*Follow signs to Steppingley, pick up
yellow signs at Fordfiled Road r'about
between Ampthill & Flitwick. Lindy
Lea next to Hospital and village
centre for West Oak & Townsend
Farmhouse.* Sat 3, Sun 4 June
(2-5). Combined adm £5, chd
free. Home-made teas in Village
Pavilion.

NEW LINDY LEA
Roy & Linda Collins.

TOWNSEND FARMHOUSE
Hugh & Indi Jackson.
(See separate entry)

WEST OAK
John & Sally Eilbeck.

Steppingley is a picturesque
Bedfordshire village on the
Greensand ridge, close to Ampthill,
Flitwick and Woburn. Although few
older buildings survive, most of
Steppingley was built by 7th Duke
of Bedford between 1840 and 1872.
Set within an acre, Lindy Lea is a
haven for wildlife with two water
features, informal perennial plantings,
variety of shrubs and mature trees.
There is also a vegetable garden and
a sunny terrace furnished with pots
and climbers. Townsend Farmhouse
is medium sized country garden
with tree lined driveway, herbaceous

17 SECRET GARDEN

4 George Street, Clapham,
Bedford, MK41 6AZ. Graham
Bolton, 07746 864247,
bolton_graham@hotmail.com.
*3m N of Bedford (not the bypass).
Clapham Village High St. R into
Mount Pleasant Rd then L into
George St. 1st white Bungalow
on R.* Sat 6 May (12.30-5.30).
Adm £2.50, chd free. Light
refreshments. **Visits also by
arrangement Apr & May.**
Alpine lovers can see a wide
variety of alpines in two small
scree gardens, front and back of
bungalow plus pans, dwarf Salix,
rhododendron, daphnes. Dwarf
acers conifers and pines hellebores
epimediums. Two small mixed
borders of herbaceous salvias,
lavenders and potentillas. Alpine
greenhouse plus one greenhouse
and cold frames with plants for sale.
Featured in RHS The Garden. Partial
wheelchair access. No access at the
rear of property due to narrow
gravel paths but garden can be
viewed from the patio.

&. ❋ ☕

18 SOUTHILL PARK

Southill, nr Biggleswade, SG18 9LL.
Mr & Mrs Charles Whitbread.
*3m W of Biggleswade. In the village
of Southill. 3m from A1 junction at
Biggleswade.* Sun 28 May (2-5).
Adm £5, chd free. Home-made
teas.
Southill Park is one of the founder
gardens which first opened its gates
to NGS visitors in 1927. In the
ornamental garden, there is a formal
rose garden, a sunken garden and a
pond. Directly in front of the main
facade are four herbaceous flower
beds designed by Tom Stuart-Smith.
The parkland was designed by
Lancelot 'Capability' Brown and
a large conservatory houses the
tropical collection. A number of
books have been written about
Southill Park.

&. ❋ ☕

19 SPEEDS DAIRY FARMHOUSE

Beadlow, Shefford, Bedfordshire,
SG17 5PL. Martin & Sarah Hind.
*A507, turning opposite Beadlow
Manor Golf Club, Farmhouse at
the end of a dead end road on the*

The Round Cottage

borders, flowering shrubs and pretty courtyard. West Oak is an informal garden of approx ¾ acre with open countryside on two sides. It consists of lawns and shrubs with perennial planting including some mature trees. There is a herb garden, greenhouse, vegetable gardens with soft fruit, and small orchard with chickens. The garden has been developed over nearly 30 years by the present owners from a completely bare plot. Some gravel paths and steps.
&. ✳ ☕ 🍷

21 THE SWISS GARDEN

Old Warden Aerodrome, Old Warden, Biggleswade, SG18 9ER. The Shuttleworth Trust in Partnership with Central Beds Council, www.shuttleworth. org/the-swiss-garden/. *2m W of Biggleswade. Signed from A1 & A600.* **Sat 22 Apr (9.30-5). Adm £8, chd free. The Shuttleworth Restaurant - open all day.** This enchanting garden was created in the 'Swiss Picturesque' style for the 3rd Lord Ongley in the early C19 and reopened in July 2014 after a major HLF-funded restoration. Serpentine paths lead to cleverly contrived vistas, many of which focus on the thatched Swiss Cottage. Beautiful wrought-iron bridges, ponds, sweeping lawns and the magnificent Pulhamite-lined Grotto Fernery have all been given a new lease of life by this landmark restoration. The pathways in the Swiss Garden are firm and even, with minimal gradients, and most are suitable for access by wheelchair users.
&. ✳ 🚗 ☕ 🍷

22 TOWNSEND FARMHOUSE

Rectory Road, Steppingley, Bedford, MK45 5AT. Hugh & Indi Jackson, 01525 713798, indi.jackson1@gmail.com. *In Steppingley Village. Follow directions to Steppingley village and pick up yellow signs from village centre.* **Sun 9 Apr, Mon 1 May (2-5). Adm £4, chd free. Home-made teas. Opening with Steppingley Village Gardens on Sat 3, Sun 4 June. Visits also by arrangement Mar to Sept for groups of 6+.** A medium sized country garden with tree lined driveway, cottage garden style herbaceous borders, flowering shrubs, box hedging, natural pond, vegetable beds, wildlife friendly areas and pretty courtyard. Swathes of spring bulbs including, narcissi, fritillaria, muscari, scilla and tulips are complemented by Hellebores and cherry blossoms in the spring. Wheelchair access - gravelled driveway and paths.
&. ✳ ☕ 🍷

23 WALNUT COTTAGE

8 Great North Road, Chawston, MK44 3BD. D G Parker. *2m S of St Neots. Between Wyboston & Blackcat r'about on S-bound lane of A1. Turn off at McDonalds, at end of filling station forecourt turn L. Off rd parking.* **Sat 22, Sun 23 July (2-6). Adm £4.50, chd free. Home-made teas.** Once a land settlement. 4 acre smallholding. 1 acre cottage garden. Over 2000 species give year round interest. Bulbs, herbaceous, water, bog plants, ferns, grasses, shrubs, trees, coppiced paulownias. Rare, exotic and unusual plants abound. Large pond, level grass paths. 1 acre young trees and shrubs. 2500sq metre glasshouse growing Chinese vegetable. 1½-acre picnic and party zone. Level grass paths.
&. 🐎 ✳ 🚗 ☕ 🍷

BERKSHIRE

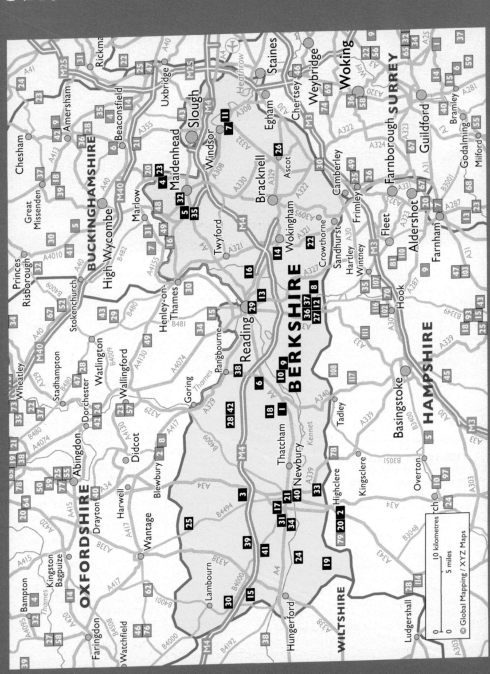

The Royal County of Berkshire offers a wonderful mix of natural beauty and historic landmarks that are reflected in the portfolio of gardens opening for the National Garden Scheme.

The Thames flows right through the county, passing picturesque towns and villages, many of which have beautiful gardens opening in 2017. Private gardens at famous places such as Windsor Castle and Eton College offer rare opportunities for visitors to enjoy gardens not normally open to the public. All are generously opened to raise funds for the nursing and caring charities we support.

With 2017 marking the 90th anniversary of the National Garden Scheme we are also proud to have three of the founding gardens which first opened in 1927 – Englefield House, Stubbings House and Welford Park – still generously opening their garden gates to our visitors.

Our gardens come in every shape, size and style, great examples of which are reflected in the group openings in Cookham and Swallowfield. We also offer a new group of village gardens in Beenham and are delighted to welcome back the lovely waterside garden at The Mill House, Donnington.

If you are organising a group visit, please see our gardens open 'by arrangement', or if you would like someone locally to give a talk about the National Garden Scheme, contact Angela at angela. oconnell@icloud.com. Some gardens may capture your interest due to their designers or their historic setting, while most have evolved thanks to the efforts of their enthusiastic owners. We think they all offer moments of inspiration and look forward to welcoming you at a garden soon.

Below: St Timothee

Volunteers

County Organiser
Heather Skinner
01189 737197
heatheraskinner@aol.com

County Treasurer
Hugh Priestley
01189 744349 Fri – Mon
hughpriestley@aol.com

Publicity
Claire Fletcher
07709 905908
cfletcher7@sky.com

Booklet Co-ordinator
Heather Skinner
(as above)

Assistant County Organisers
Gill Cheetham
01344 423440
gillcheetham@btopenworld.com

Ron Cummings
01488 608124,
ron@roncummings.co.uk

Cathie Davies
07718 589347
cathieldavies@gmail.com

Carolyn Foster
01628 624635
candrfoster@btinternet.com

Angela O'Connell
01252 668645
angela.oconnell@icloud.com

Graham O'Connell
01252 668645
graham.oconnell22@gmail.com

Deborah Padwick
07824 999002
debspadwick@yahoo.co.uk

Charlotte Stacey
07785 308109
charlotte_stacey@hotmail.co.uk

OPENING DATES

All entries subject to change. For latest information check **www.ngs.org.uk**

Map locator numbers are shown to the right of each garden name.

February

Snowdrop Festival

Wednesday 8th
◆ Welford Park 39

Sunday 19th
Oak Cottage 22

March

Saturday 18th
Stubbings House 35

Sunday 19th
Stubbings House 35

April

Sunday 23rd
The Old Rectory, Farnborough 25

Wednesday 26th
Inholmes 15
Rooksnest 30

Saturday 29th
Stubbings House 35

Sunday 30th
Malverleys 20
Rookwood Farm House 31
Stubbings House 35

May

Monday 1st
Stubbings House 35

Sunday 14th
Sandleford Place 33

Sunday 21st
The Old Rectory, Farnborough 25

90th Anniversary Weekend

Saturday 27th
Cookham Gardens 4
The RISC Roof Garden, Reading 29

Sunday 28th
St Timothee 32

June

Sunday 4th
Swallowfield Inner Village Gardens 36

Tuesday 6th
◆ Frogmore House Garden 11

Saturday 10th
Canje Grove 2

Eton College Gardens 7

Sunday 11th
Canje Grove 2
Chieveley Manor 3
Sandleford Place 33
Stockcross House 34
The Tithe Barn 38

Sunday 18th
NEW Beenham Village Gardens 1
Kirby House 19
The Mill House Donnington 21
The Old Rectory Inkpen 24

Wednesday 21st
Inholmes 15
Rooksnest 30

Sunday 25th
The Old Rectory, Farnborough 25
Pyt House 28
Willow Tree Cottage 42

July

Saturday 1st
The RISC Roof Garden, Reading 29

Sunday 2nd
Swallowfield Outlying Village Gardens 37
West Mills Allotments & Island Cottage 40

Sunday 9th
The Harris Garden 13
Jannaways 17

Tuesday 11th
Wickham House 41

Sunday 16th
Odney Club 23

Sunday 23rd
Farley Hill Place Gardens 8
Ivydene 16

Sunday 30th
Deepwood Stud Farm 5
Malverleys 20

Monday 31st
Deepwood Stud Farm 5

August

Sunday 13th
King's Copse House 18

By Arrangement

Deepwood Stud Farm 5
Farley Hill Place Gardens 8
Field Farm Cottage 9
Handpost 12
Hogarth Hostas 14
Island Cottage, West Mills Allotments & Island Cottage 40
Ivydene 16
Old Waterfield 26
The Priory 27
Rooksnest 30
St Timothee 32
Sandleford Place 33
Stockcross House 34
Stubbings House 35

Deepwood Stud Farm

The National Garden Scheme is the largest single funder of Macmillan

THE GARDENS

GROUP OPENING

1 NEW BEENHAM VILLAGE GARDENS

The Green, Beenham, Reading, RG7 5NX. *From M4 J12 take A4 W towards Newbury. After 3½m turn R to Beenham for 1½m. Follow signs to car parking at Awberry Farm.* **Sun 18 June (11-5). Combined adm £6, chd free. Home-made teas at Awberry Farm.**

NEW AWBERRY FARM
Pauline & Freddie Brown.

NEW BROOKFIELD
Pauline Stares.

NEW FERNWOOD
Nola Rice-Wood.

NEW RUSSETTS
Chris & Mary Bosworth.

NEW ST MARY'S FARM HOUSE
Dick Russell.

Beenham village sits in an attractive rural setting. It has an C18 church and several Grade II listed houses. To help us celebrate 90 yrs of the NGS raising funds for nurses, we are delighted to welcome a selection of five varied and interesting gardens, four within walking distance and one requiring transport. There will also be a flower arranging demonstration and an exhibition of work by the Beenham Art Group in the Tithe Barn at Awberry Farm.
✿ 🚗 🍵

2 CANJE GROVE

Church Road, Woolton Hill, Newbury, RG20 9XQ. Yvonne & Simon Sonsino. *12 mins S of M4 J13, follow A34 to Winchester. A34 exit for Highclere & Wash Common A343. At end of slip road go R on A343. Approx ½m turn R at Xrds. Take 3rd L onto Church Rd with NGS signs. Street parking.* **Sat 10, Sun 11 June (2-5). Adm £3.50, chd free. Home-made teas.**

An artist and flower arrangers garden of just over ⅓ acre. The garden features multiple colour and plant themed rooms, ranging from cool shady impact planting, courtyard styling near the house and art studio, raised ponds, a wooden Shepherd's hut, a small orchard, rose hedges, peonies, topiary and picket fences, to a gated vegetable garden at the rear complete with hens. Art studio open with botanical art and calligraphy. Featured in Country Homes & Interiors (Mar 2016).
🍵

3 CHIEVELEY MANOR

Chieveley, Nr Newbury, RG20 8UT. Mr & Mrs CJ Spence. *5m N of Newbury. Take A34 N, pass under M4, then L to Chieveley. After ½m L up Manor Lane.* **Sun 11 June (2-5). Adm £5, chd free. Home-made teas. *Donation to St Mary's Church, Chieveley.***

Large garden surrounding listed house (not open) in the heart of Chieveley village. Attractive setting with fine views over stud farm. Walled garden containing lovely borders, shrubs and rose garden, evolving every year. Box parterre filled with alliums, white geraniums and lavender. Many viticella clematis growing through shrubs.
♿ ✿ 🍵

GROUP OPENING

4 COOKHAM GARDENS

Cookham, SL6 9QD. *3½m N of Maidenhead. All within ½m of each other in Cookham, nr the train station. Please park your car at the NT car park at Cookham Moor, street parking or nr station. Tickets & map available at any garden.* **Sat 27 May (2-5). Combined adm £5.50, chd free. Home-made teas at Hunters Lodge.**

2 BELLE VUE COTTAGES
Liz & William Wells.

HUNTERS LODGE
Daphne Wardell-Yerburgh.

2 VICARAGE CLOSE
Sue Yerburgh.

Three contrasting gardens in the beautiful Thameside village of Cookham, all within ½m walk and close to the Stanley Spencer Gallery. Two showcase innovative use of limited spaces. A small stunning modern garden, 2 Bellevue Cottages has a curving walkway that weaves through arbours bordered by lush, exotic and evergreen planting, punctuated by dabs of intense colour. Sorry not suitable for children. 2 Vicarage Close is a small contemporary water garden with a structured pool and waterfall surrounded by simplistic planting. A series of floating steps lead to an overhanging deck and a small grass area. The third, Hunters Lodge is a country style garden with a series of rooms leading to a summerhouse and a newly created wildlife pool surrounded by aquatic plants. Filled with herbaceous and climbing plants, lawned areas and set behind Edwardian house (not open) in heart of village, it is a lovely place to enjoy afternoon tea.
✿ 🍵

5 DEEPWOOD STUD FARM

Henley Road, Stubbings, Nr Maidenhead, SL6 6QW. Mr & Mrs E Goodwin, 01628 822684, ed.goodwin@deepwood properties.com. *2m W of Maidenhead. M4 J8/9 take A404M N. 2nd exit for A4 to Maidenhead. L at 1st r'about on A4130 Henley, approx 1m on R.* **Sun 30, Mon 31 July (2-5). Adm £4.50, chd free. Home-made teas on lawn or in conservatory. Visits also by arrangement Apr to Aug for groups of 10-40.**

4 acres of formal and informal gardens within a stud farm, so great roses! Small lake with Monet style bridge and 3 further water features. Several neo-classical follies and statues. Walled garden with windows cut in to admire the views and horses. Woodland walk and enough hanging baskets to decorate a pub! Partial wheelchair access.
♿ 🍵

6 ◆ ENGLEFIELD HOUSE GARDEN

Englefield, Theale, Reading, RG7 5EN. Mr & Mrs Richard Benyon, 01189 302221, peter.carson@englefield.co.uk, www.englefieldestate.co.uk. *6m W of Reading. M4 J12. Take A4 towards Theale. 2nd r'about take A340 to Pangbourne. After ⅙m entrance on the L.* **For opening times and information, please phone, email or visit garden website.**

The 12 acre garden descends dramatically from the hill above the historic house through woodland where mature native trees mix with Victorian conifers. Drifts of spring and summer planting are followed by striking autumn colour. Stone balustrades enclose the lower terrace, with wide lawns, roses, mixed borders and topiary. Open every Monday from Apr-Sept (10-6) and Oct-Mar (10-4). Please check Englefield website for any changes before travelling. Group bookings by arrangement from Apr-Sept with option of refreshments and tour with gardener. Partial access to parts of the gardens.

♿ 🚌 🍂

7 ETON COLLEGE GARDENS

Eton, Nr Windsor, SL4 6DB. *½m N of Windsor. Parking signed off B3022, Slough Rd. Walk from car park across playing fields to entry. Cars with disabled badges will be directed closer. Tickets & maps sold at entrance.* **Sat 10 June (2-5). Adm £5, chd free. Home-made teas in the Fellows garden.**

A rare chance to visit a group of central College gardens surrounded by historic school buildings, including Luxmoore's garden on a small island in the Thames reached across two attractive bridges. Also an opportunity to explore the fascinating Eton College Natural History Museum and a small group of other private gardens. Wheelchair access limited to three central gardens and over grass to Luxmoores (sorry, no access to the Museum or further gardens in Eton town).

♿ 🍂

8 FARLEY HILL PLACE GARDENS

Church Road, Farley Hill, Reading, RG7 1TZ. Tony & Margaret Finch, 01189 762544, tony.finch7@btinternet.com. *From M4 J11, take A33 S to Basingstoke. At T-lights turn L for Spencers Wood, B3349. Go 2m turn L, through Swallowfield towards Farley Hill. Garden ½m on R.* **Sun 23 July (2-5). Adm £4.50, chd free. Home-made teas. Visits also by arrangement Mar to Oct for groups of 15+. Please mention NGS.**

A 4 acre, C18 cottage garden. 1½ acre walled garden with yr-round interest and colour. Well stocked herbaceous borders, large productive vegetable areas with herb garden, dahlia and cutting flower beds. Victorian glasshouse recently renovated and small nursery. Plants, lovely cut flowers and produce for sale. The garden is used by several magazines as a photo location, and was featured in Country Living (Nov 2016). Partial wheelchair access.

❄ 🚌 🍂

9 FIELD FARM COTTAGE

Sulhamstead Hill, Sulhamstead, RG7 4DA. Mrs Anne Froom, 01189 302735, anne.froom@knowall.it, www.bandbwestberkshire.co.uk. *From A4 take lane by The Spring Inn for 1m. Garden is on L, 150yds past 2 LH turns.* **Visits by arrangement May to Sept for groups of 10+. Refreshments available on request. Adm £4, chd free.**

A pretty ¾ acre cottage garden planted with a wide variety of herbaceous perennials, set in a series of garden rooms. Lovely borders spill over the lawn and there is a large pond which is fed by a natural spring. Wild garden, small white garden and a variety of trees planted by the owner. Small vegetable garden and greenhouse. The terrain is rather uneven but most of the garden can be viewed from a wheelchair.

♿ 🛏 🍂

10 FOLLY FARM

Sulhamstead Hill, Sulhamstead, RG7 4DG. *7m SW of Reading. From A4 between Reading & Newbury (2m W of M4 J12) take road marked Sulhamstead at The Spring Inn. Restricted car parking.* **Visits by arrangement Tue 13, Wed 14 June for private tours for groups of 12 only. Limited availability. Adm £25. Pre-booking essential, please phone 01483 211535. Tea & home-made pastries.**

Gardens laid out in 1912 by Sir Edwin Lutyens and Gertrude Jekyll. Garden designs evolved during culmination of their partnership and considered one of their most complex. Extensively restored and replanted by current owners assisted by Dan Pearson. Recently reopened for private group visits which include 1½ hour guided tour and refreshments. Please note paths are uneven and there are many sets of steps between areas of the garden. Sorry no dogs.

🕶 🍂

11 ◆ FROGMORE HOUSE GARDEN

Windsor, SL4 1LB. Her Majesty The Queen. *1m SE of Windsor. Entrance via Park St gate into Long Walk.* **For NGS: Tue 6 June (10-5.30). Adm £6.50, chd free. Light refreshments. Picnics welcome. Pre-booking recommended. For advance tickets please go to Shop at www.ngs.org.uk or phone 01483 211535.**

The private royal garden at Frogmore House on the Crown Estate at Windsor. This landscaped garden set in 30 acres with notable trees, lawns, flowering shrubs and C18 lake, is rich in history. It is largely the creation of Queen Charlotte, who in the 1790s introduced over 4,000 trees and shrubs to create a model picturesque landscape. The historic plantings, incl tulip trees and redwoods, along with Queen Victoria's Tea House, remain key features of the garden today. Please note the Royal Mausoleum is closed due to long term restoration. To book optional garden history tours (approx 45 mins) with limited availability, please go to Shop at www.ngs.org.uk or phone 01483 211535. Tickets for garden and to visit the house are also available on the day by cash payment only. Last entry 4pm.

🚗 ☕

12 HANDPOST

Basingstoke Road, Swallowfield, Reading, RG7 1PU. Faith Ramsay, faith@mycountrygarden.co.uk, www.mycountrygarden.co.uk. *From M4 J11, take A33 S. At 1st T-lights turn L on B3349 Basingstoke Rd. Follow road for 2¾ m, garden on L.* **Visits by arrangement May to July for groups of 12+. Adm £6. Light refreshments.**
4 acre designer's garden with many areas of interest. Features incl two lovely long borders attractively and densely planted in six colour sections, a formal rose garden, old orchard with a grass meadow, pretty pond and peaceful wooded area. Large variety of plants, trees and a productive fruit and vegetable patch.
✿ Ⓓ ☕

13 THE HARRIS GARDEN

Whiteknights, Pepper Lane, Reading, RG6 6AS.
The University of Reading, www.friendsoftheharrisgarden. org.uk. *1½ m S of Reading. Off A327 Shinfield Rd. From Pepper*

Lane entrance to campus, turn R to car park. **Sun 9 July (2-5). Adm £3.50, chd free. Home-made teas.**
Described as 'a real gem', the Harris Garden at the Whiteknights campus of Reading University is a 12 acre haven of peace and tranquillity. Planting provides yr-round interest including notable trees, stream, pond and herbaceous borders. With lots to enjoy it is an important amenity for University visitors, as well as for teaching and research. National Plant Heritage collection of Digitalis.
♿ ✿ ☕

14 HOGARTH HOSTAS

25 Simons Lane, Wokingham, RG41 3HG. Jonathan Hogarth, 01189 776879, ahogie25@aol.com, www.small-hostas.com. *1 m W of Wokingham. Take A329 W towards Reading after Woose Hill r'about. ¼ m take 2nd L. On corner of Walter Rd.* **Visits by arrangement Apr to July on various weekend dates for groups of 6+. Refreshments on request. Adm £4, chd free.**
This is a great opportunity for hosta enthusiasts to view a large private collection of new and old hosta varieties. All specimens displayed in pots and on shelves in a courtyard setting. Owner is a National Collection Holder of Small and Miniature Hostas. RHS gold medal winner at Hampton Court Flower Show 2015 & 2016.

Happy to provide information and advice. Ideal visit for gardening clubs. Hostas, hand-made cards and jewellery for sale. Seen on BBC Gardeners' World (July 2016). Partial wheelchair access over grass.
♿ ✿ 🚗 NPC ☕

15 INHOLMES

Woodlands St Mary, RG17 7SY.
3m SE Lambourn. M4 J14, take A338 N, take 1st L onto B4000. After 1½ m Inholmes signed on L. **Wed 26 Apr, Wed 21 June (11-4). Adm £4.50, chd free. Home-made teas. Last entry 3.30pm. Combined adm with Rooksnest £6.50, chd free.**
Set in 10 acres with wonderful views over parkland. A wide variety of different areas to enjoy such as a walled garden, many spring bulbs, inspirational herbaceous borders and rose beds. Walks to the lake and through the meadow. Most areas accessible by wheelchair over grass, gravel and paving.
♿ 🐐 🚗 ☕

16 IVYDENE

283 Loddon Bridge Road, Woodley, Reading, RG5 4BE. Janet & Bill Bonney, 01189 697591, billabonney@aol.com. *3½ m E of Reading. Loddon Bridge Rd is main road through Woodley. Garden approx 100yds S of Just Tiles r'about. Parking in adjacent roads.* **Sun 23 July (10-5). Adm £4, chd free. Light refreshments. Visits also by arrangement June to Aug for groups of 10-25. Please mention NGS.**
Small urban gardeners' garden with mature tree fern walkway and many unusual hostas, ornamental grasses and plants. Overflowing herbaceous borders and rose bed, using mainly patio roses. New and developing are the vertical garden and the Heuchera Tapestry bed. The garden also features stained glass and ceramic art to complete the picture. Owner is a previous BBC Gardener of the Year finalist. Featured in Garden News and Garden of the Week.
🐐 ✿ ☕

The Harris Garden

Chieveley Manor

17 JANNAWAYS

Bagnor, Newbury, RG20 8AH. Mr
& Mrs Sharples. *3m W of Newbury.
From M4 J13, S on A34. Take A4 exit
towards Newbury. 1st L to Station
Rd. Turn L to Lambourn Rd. 1st R
to Bagnor, past Watermill Theatre,
then follow NGS signs.* Sun 9 July
(2-5.30). Adm £5, chd free. Teas
& biscuits included.

This 5 acre garden encompasses
a lake naturally fed by springs. A
circular walk from formal beds near
the house, leads along a woodland
path, crossing a weir to wild flowers
and specimen trees. A pitch perfect
lawn, fish pond, pagodas and many
hidden gems provide visitors with a
rich panoply of vistas round every
corner. Children's jungle gym and
trampoline.

18 KING'S COPSE HOUSE

Bradfield Gate, Nr Reading,
RG7 6JR. Mr & Mrs J Wyatt. *M4
J12, A4 to Theale. At 2nd r'about take
3rd exit A340 towards Pangbourne,
then soon 1st L. After 1¼m turn L
to Bradfield Southend. In village turn
R on Hungerford Lane, after ½m L
on Cock Lane.* Sun 13 Aug (2-5).
Adm £4.50, chd free. Home-
made teas.

A beautiful and formal landscaped
garden set in 4 acres, recently

renovated to a high standard to
incorporate some original and
rare specimens together with new
plantings. Orchard, large fish pond,
secret rose garden, herbaceous
borders, and spectacular views over
the Pang Valley. Walks through 40
acre SSSI ancient woodland.

19 KIRBY HOUSE

Upper Green, Inkpen, RG17 9ED.
Mrs R Astor. *5m SE of Hungerford.
A4 to Kintbury. At Xrds by Corner
Stores take Inkpen Rd. Follow road
into Inkpen. Pass common on L. Just
past Crown & Garter PH, turn L (to
Combe & Faccombe), at T-junction
turn L, house on R.* Sun 18 June (2-
5). Adm £4, chd free. Combined
adm with The Old Rectory
Inkpen £7, chd free.

7 acres in beautiful setting with
views of South Berkshire Downs
and historical Combe Gibbet, across
lawn with ha-ha and parkland. C18
Queen Anne House (not open).
Formal borders, lily pond garden
and terraces laid out by Harold Peto.
Reflecting pond with fountain, lake,
walled garden and contemporary
sculptures. Refreshments available
at The Old Rectory, Inkpen. Some
uneven paths.

20 MALVERLEYS

Fullers Lane, East End, Newbury,
RG20 0AA. *A34 S of Newbury,
exit signed for Highclere. Follow
A343 for ½m, turn R to Woolton
Hill. Pass school & turn L to East
End. After 1m R at village green,
then after 100 metres, R onto
Fullers Lane.* Sun 30 Apr, Sun 30
July (2-5). Adm £10, chd free.
Pre-booking essential, please
visit www.ngs.org.uk or phone
01483 211535 for information
& booking. Tea & cake and tour
with Head Gardener included.
Ticket availability is limited
so please book early to avoid
disappointment.

10 acres of dynamic gardens which
have been developed over the last
5 yrs to include magnificent mixed
borders and a series of contrasting
yew hedged rooms, hosting flame
borders, a cool garden, a pond
garden and new stumpery. A
vegetable garden with striking fruit
cages sit within a walled garden,
also encompassing a white garden.
Meadows open out to views over
the parkland.

21 THE MILL HOUSE
DONNINGTON

Oxford Road, Donnington,
RG14 2JD. Dr & Mrs Jane Vaidya.

1m N of Newbury on B4494. From M4 J13, follow signs to Donnington. Approx 2m (B4494 Oxford Rd) pass Castle PH on L. Mill House 50yds on R. Please park with consideration in Donnington village. **Sun 18 June (2-5). Adm £5, chd free. Home-made teas.**
The Mill House has a large and verdant garden with many trees and waterside plants. Enticing paths follow its streams and the R Lambourn running through. In summer it is like a secret garden with overhanging trees and the sound of running water. Herbaceous borders surround the central lawn with vivid splashes of colour. A haven for birds and quiet reflection for people. Art studio open particularly featuring the garden as a subject.

22 OAK COTTAGE
99B Kiln Ride, Finchampstead, Wokingham, RG40 3PD.
Ms Liz Ince. *2½m S of Wokingham. Off B3430 Nine Mile Ride between A321 Sandhurst Rd & B3016 Finchampstead Rd.* **Sun 19 Feb (2-4.30). Adm £3.50, chd free. Light refreshments.**
¼ acre garden with woodland feel. Mature trees underplanted with several thousand snowdrops and other spring flowering bulbs. Several unusual winter flowering plants and many hellebores. Collection of unusual varieties of snowdrops. Main paths offer partial wheelchair access, but others are chipped bark and unsuitable.

23 ODNEY CLUB
Odney Lane, Cookham, SL6 9SR.
John Lewis Partnership. *3m N of Maidenhead. Off A4094 S of Cookham Bridge. Signs to car park in grounds.* **Sun 16 July (2-6). Adm £5, chd free. Light refreshments served 2pm-5pm.** *Donation to Thames Valley Adventure Playground.*
This 120 acre site is beside the Thames with lovely riverside walks. A favourite with Stanley Spencer who featured our magnolia in his work. Lovely wisteria, specimen trees, herbaceous borders, side

gardens, summer bedding and ornamental lake. The John Lewis Partnership Heritage Centre will be open, showcasing the textile archive and items illustrating the history of John Lewis and Waitrose. Some gravel paths. Dogs on leads please.

THE OLD MILL
See Wiltshire

24 THE OLD RECTORY INKPEN
Lower Green, Inkpen, RG17 9DS.
Mrs C McKeon. *4m SE of Hungerford. From centre of Kintbury at the Xrds, take Inkpen Rd. After ½m turn R, then go approx 3m (passing Crown & Garter PH, then Inkpen Village Hall on L). Nr St Michaels Church, follow car park signs.* **Sun 18 June (2-5). Adm £4, chd free. Home-made teas. Combined adm with Kirby House £7, chd free.**
On a gentle hillside with lovely countryside views, the Old Rectory offers a peaceful setting for this pretty 2 acre garden. Enjoy strolling through the formal and walled gardens, herbaceous borders, pleached lime walk and wild flower meadow (some slopes).

25 THE OLD RECTORY, FARNBOROUGH
Nr Wantage, Oxon, OX12 8NX.
Mr & Mrs Michael Todhunter, 01488 638298. *4m SE of Wantage. Take B4494 Wantage-Newbury road, after 4m turn E at sign for Farnborough. Approx 1m to village, Old Rectory on L.* **Sun 23 Apr, Sun 21 May, Sun 25 June (2-5.30). Adm £5, chd free. Home-made teas.** *Donation to Farnborough PCC.*
In a series of immaculately tended garden rooms, incl herbaceous borders, arboretum, boules, roses, vegetable and new bog garden, there is an explosion of rare and interesting plants, beautifully combined for colour and texture. With stunning views across the countryside, it is the perfect setting for the 1749 rectory (not open), once home of John Betjeman, in memory of whom John Piper

created a window in the local church. Awarded Finest Parsonage in England by Country Life and The Rectory Society. Plants and home-made preserves for sale. Some steep slopes and gravel paths.

26 OLD WATERFIELD
Winkfield Road, Ascot, SL5 7LJ.
Hugh & Catherine Stevenson, catherine.stevenson@ oldwaterfield.com. *6m SW of Windsor to E of Ascot Racecourse. On E side of A330 midway between A329 & A332.* **Visits by arrangement for groups of 10-25. Light refreshments on request. Adm £4.50, chd free.**
Set in 4 acres between Ascot Heath and Windsor Great Park, the original cottage garden has been developed and extended over the past few years. Herbaceous borders, meadow with specimen trees, large productive vegetable garden, orchard, and mixed hedging. Winter bed with dogwoods and snowdrops at its best in late February.

27 THE PRIORY
Beech Hill, RG7 2BJ. Mr & Mrs C Carter, 01189 883146, tita@getcarter.org.uk. *5m S of Reading. M4 J11, A33 S to Basingstoke. At T-lights, L to Spencers Wood. After 1½m turn R for Beech Hill. After approx 1½m, L into Wood Lane, R down Priory Drive.* **Visits by arrangement June to Aug for groups of 10+. Teas on request. Adm £4.50, chd free.**
Extensive gardens in grounds of former C12 French Priory (not open), rebuilt 1648. The mature gardens are in a very attractive setting beside the R Loddon. Large formal walled garden with espalier fruit trees, lawns, mixed and replanted herbaceous borders, vegetables and roses. Woodland, fine trees, lake and Italian style water garden. A lovely garden for group visits.

Pyt House

28 PYT HOUSE

Ashampstead, RG8 8RA.
Hans & Virginia von Celsing,
www.Vvcgardendesign.com. *4m W
of Pangbourne. From Yattendon head
towards Reading. Road forks L into a
beech wood towards Ashampstead.
Keep L & join lower road. ½ m turn L
just before houses.* **Sun 25 June (2-
5). Combined adm with Willow
Tree Cottage £5, chd free.
Home-made teas.**
A 4 acre garden planted over
the last 10 yrs by designer owner,
around C18 house (not open).
Mature trees, yew, hornbeam and
beech hedges, pleached limes,
modern perennial borders, pond,
orchard and vegetable garden. New
iris beds. Broadly organic, a haven
for bees and butterflies, and we also
have chickens.

✿ ⓓ ☕

29 THE RISC ROOF GARDEN, READING

35-39 London Street, Reading,
RG1 4PS. Reading International
Solidarity Centre,
www.risc.org.uk/gardens. *Central
Reading. 5 mins walk from Oracle
Shopping Centre. 10 mins from
station. Park in Queens Rd or Oracle
car parks. Disabled parking at rear
of building.* **Sat 27 May, Sat 1 July
(12-4). Adm £3.50, chd free.
Light refreshments at RISC
Global Cafe.** *Donation to RISC.*
Small edible roof forest garden
developed to demonstrate
sustainability and our dependence
on plants. All plants in the garden
have an economic use for food,
clothing, medicine etc, and
come from all over the world.
Demonstration of renewable energy,
water harvesting and irrigation
systems. Garden accessed by
external staircase. Regular tours of
garden.

✿ ☕

30 ROOKSNEST

Ermin Street, Lambourn
Woodlands, RG17 7SB. Dame
Theresa Sackler, 01488 71678,
garden@rooksnest.net. *2m S of
Lambourn on B4000. From M4 J14,
take A338 Wantage Rd, turn 1st L
onto B4000 (Ermin St). Rooksnest*

signed after 3m. **Wed 26 Apr, Wed 21 June (11-4). Adm £4.50, chd free. Light refreshments. Last entry 3.30pm. Combined adm with Inholmes £6.50, chd free. Visits also by arrangement Mar to June for groups of 15+.** Approx 10 acre exceptionally fine traditional English garden. Rose garden (under renovation), herbaceous garden, pond garden, herb garden, vegetables and glasshouses. Many specimen trees and fine shrubs, orchard and terraces. Garden mostly designed by Arabella Lennox-Boyd. Light refreshments incl teas, coffees, home-made cakes and light lunches. Plant sale at June opening only. All areas have step-free access, although surface consists of gravel and mowed grass.

31 ROOKWOOD FARM HOUSE

Stockcross, RG20 8JX. The Hon Rupert & Charlotte Digby, 01488 608676, charlotte@ rookwoodfarmhouse.co.uk, www.rookwoodfarmhouse.co.uk. *3m W of Newbury. M4 J13, A34(S). After 3m exit for A4(W) to Hungerford. At 2nd r'about take B4000 towards Stockcross, after approx ¾ m turn R into Rookwood.* **Sun 30 Apr (1-5). Adm £5, chd free. Home-made cakes & teas.** This exciting valley garden, a work in progress, has elements all visitors can enjoy. A rose covered pergola, fabulous tulips, giant alliums, a kitchen garden featuring a parterre of raised beds, as well as bog gardens and colour themed herbaceous planting, all make Rookwood well worth a visit. Gravel paths, some steep slopes.

32 ST TIMOTHEE

Darlings Lane, Maidenhead, SL6 6PA. Sarah & Sal Pajwani, 07976 892667, pajwanisarah@gmail.com. *1m N of Maidenhead. M4 J8/9 to A404M. 2nd exit onto A4 to Maidenhead. L at 1st r'about to A4130 Henley Rd. After ½ m turn R onto Pinkneys Drive. At Pinkneys Arms PH, turn L into Lee*

Lane, follow NGS signs. **Sun 28 May (11-4.30). Adm £4, chd free. Home-made teas. Visits also by arrangement Sept & Oct for groups of 10+.** A recently created 2 acre garden adjacent to Pinkneys Green. Deep, gently flowing, colour themed borders planted for yr-round interest with a wide range of attractive grasses and perennials. Other features incl a box parterre, wildlife pond, rose terrace and wild areas all set around established trees and a 1930s family home (not open).

33 SANDLEFORD PLACE

Newtown, Newbury, RG20 9AY. Mel Gatward, 01635 40726, melgatward@btinternet.com. *1½ m S of Newbury on A339. House on NW side of Swan r'about at Newtown on A339 1½ m S of Newbury.* **Sun 14 May, Sun 11 June (2-5.30). Adm £5, chd free. Home-made teas. Visits also by arrangement Feb to Oct. For bookings more than a month in advance pre-payment requested.** A plantswoman's 4 acres, more exuberant than manicured with R Enborne flowing through. Various areas of shrub and mixed borders create a romantic, naturalistic effect. Wonderful old walled garden. Long herbaceous border flanks wild flower meadow. Yr-round interest from early carpets of snowdrops and daffodils, crocus covered lawn, to autumn berries and leaf colour. A garden for all seasons. Previously featured in Country Gardens & Interiors magazine. Wheelchair access to most areas. Guide dogs only.

34 STOCKCROSS HOUSE

Church Road, Stockcross, Newbury, RG20 8LP. Susan & Edward Vandyk, 07765 674863, dragonflygardens@btinternet. com. *3m W of Newbury. M4 J13, A34(S). After 3m exit A4(W) to Hungerford. At 2nd r'about take B4000, 1m to Stockcross, 2nd L into Church Rd.* **Sun 11 June (10-4). Adm £5, chd free. Refreshments**

& light lunches. **Visits also by arrangement May to July for groups of 10+.** A delightful two acre garden set around a Grade II listed former vicarage (not open) with an emphasis on naturalistic planting, colour combinations and plant partnerships. Romantic wisteria and clematis covered pergola, reflecting pond with folly, rich variety of roses, vegetable and cutting garden. Pond with cascade and duck house. Small stumpery with ferns. Sculptural elements by local artists. Partial wheelchair access with some gravelled areas.

35 STUBBINGS HOUSE

Henley Road, Maidenhead, SL6 6QL. Mr & Mrs D Good, 01628 825454, info@stubbingsgroup.com, www.stubbingsnursery.co.uk. *2m W of Maidenhead. From A4130 Henley Rd follow signed private access road opp Stubbings Church. See website for further directions.* **Sat 18 Mar (10-4.30); Sun 19 Mar (10-4); Sat 29 Apr (10-4.30); Sun 30 Apr (10-4); Mon 1 May (10-4.30). Adm £3.50, chd free. Visits also by arrangement Apr to Sept for groups of 10-20.** Parkland garden accessed via adjacent retail nursery. Set around C18 house (not open), home to Queen Wilhelmina of Netherlands in WW2. Large lawn with ha-ha and woodland walks. Notable trees incl historic cedars and araucaria. March brings an abundance of daffodils and in May a 60 metre wall of wisteria. Attractions include a C18 icehouse and access to adjacent NT woodland. A level site with firm gravel paths for wheelchair access.

The National Garden Scheme is Marie Curie's largest single funder

GROUP OPENING

36 SWALLOWFIELD INNER VILLAGE GARDENS

Swallowfield Street, Swallowfield, RG7 1QX. *5m S of Reading. From M4 J11 take A33 S. At 1st T-lights turn L on B3349 signed Swallowfield. On entering the village follow signs for parking, & purchase of tickets & gardens map.* **Sun 4 June (2-6). Combined adm £6, chd free. Home-made teas.**

APRIL COTTAGE
Linda & Bill Kirkpatrick.

BIRD IN HAND HOUSE
Margaret & John McDonald.

BRAMBLES
Sarah & Martyn Dadds.

NEW **BRIARWOOD**
Mrs Jenny Burnett.

5 CURLYS WAY
Carolyn & Gary Clark.

PRIMROSE COTTAGE
Hilda & Eddie Phillips.

RUSSETTS
Roberta Stewart.

This year the lovely gardeners in Swallowfield are offering two different NGS open days. The first on 4th June involves the inner village gardens which are all within walking distance. They showcase a variety of beautiful well stocked gardens of all shapes and sizes. The garden owners, many of whom are members of the local Horticultural Society, are always happy to chat and share their enthusiasm and experience. Plants for sale.

Your visit has already helped 600 more people gain access to a Parkinson's nurse

GROUP OPENING

37 SWALLOWFIELD OUTLYING VILLAGE GARDENS

The Street, Swallowfield, RG7 1QY. *5m S of Reading. From M4 J11 take A33 S. At 1st T-lights turn L on B3349 signed Swallowfield. On entering the village follow signs for parking, & purchase of tickets & gardens map.* **Sun 2 July (2-6). Combined adm £6, chd free. Home-made teas.**

5 BEEHIVE COTTAGES
Ray Tormey.

THE FIELD HOUSE
Marguerite & Robin Bradley.

GREENWINGS
Liz & Ray Jones.

LAMBS FARMHOUSE
Eva Koskuba.

LODDON LOWER FARM
Mr & Mrs J Bayliss.

NORKETT COTTAGE
Jenny Spencer.

THREE GABLES
Sue & Keith Steptoe.

WESSEX HOUSE
Val Payne.

This year the lovely gardeners in Swallowfield are offering two different NGS open days. The second is on 2nd July and involves the outlying village gardens that can be visited by car. Whilst each provides its own character and interest, they all nestle amongst rural countryside by the Whitewater, Blackwater and Loddon rivers which create an abundance of wildlife and lovely views. The garden owners, many of whom are members of the local Horticultural Society, are always happy to chat and share their enthusiasm and experience. Plants for sale.

---

38 THE TITHE BARN

Tidmarsh, RG8 8ER. Frances Wakefield. *1m S of Pangbourne, off A340. In Tidmarsh, turn by side of Greyhound PH, over bridge, R into Mill Corner field for car park. Short walk over field to garden.* **Sun 11 June (2-5). Adm £3.50, chd free. Home-made teas.**
This is a delightful ¼ acre village garden within high brick walls around The Tithe Barn (not open) dating from 1760. Formally laid out with parterres of box and yew. There are roses, hostas, delphiniums and lavender as well as interesting vintage pots and containers. Previous winner of the English Garden magazine Gardener's Garden competition and featured in Homes & Gardens magazine.

39 ◆ WELFORD PARK

Welford, Newbury, RG20 8HU. Mrs J H Puxley, www.welfordpark.co.uk. *6m NW of Newbury. M4 J13, A34(S). After 3m exit for A4(W) to Hungerford. At 2nd r'about take B4000, after 4m turn R signed Welford. Entrance on Newbury-Lambourn road.* **For NGS: Wed 8 Feb (11-4). Adm £6, chd free. For other opening times and information, please visit garden website.**
One of the finest natural snowdrop woodlands in the country approx 4 acres, along with a wonderful display of hellebores throughout the garden and winter flowering shrubs. This is an NGS 1927 pioneer garden on the R Lambourn set around Queen Anne House (not open). Also the stunning setting for BBC Great British Bake Off 2014, 2015 & 2016. Dogs welcome on leads. Coach parties please book in advance. Refreshments available.

GROUP OPENING

40 WEST MILLS ALLOTMENTS & ISLAND COTTAGE

West Mills, Newbury, RG14 5HT. *In centre of Newbury nr the canal. Park in town centre car parks. Walk either side of St Nicholas Church or between Cote Restaurant & Holland & Barrett to canal. 100yds to Swing Bridge & follow signs. Limited side road parking.* **Sun 2 July (2-5).**

Combined adm £5, chd free. Home-made teas at Island Cottage (weather permitting).

ISLAND COTTAGE
Karen & Roger Swaffield, karen.swaffield@btinternet.com.
Visits also by arrangement Apr to Oct for small groups.

WEST MILLS ALLOTMENTS
Newbury Town Council (local contact Alison Martin).

Allotments and small town garden in the centre of Newbury. You are welcome to visit the allotments on our 120 plot site and the opportunity to talk to some of the plot holders about their methods. A variety of fruit, vegetables and flowers to see, some in greenhouses and polytunnels. Island Cottage is a small town garden set between a backwater of the R Kennet and the Kennet and Avon Canal. You will find interesting combinations of colour and texture to look at rather than walk through, although you can do that too! A deck overlooks a sluiceway towards a lawn and border. Started from scratch in 2005, and mostly again after the floods of 2014. Plants for sale at the allotments.

41 WICKHAM HOUSE
Wickham, Newbury, RG20 8HD. Mr & Mrs James D'Arcy, www.wickhamhouse.com. *7m NW of Newbury or 6m NE of Hungerford. From M4 J14, take A338(N) signed Wantage. Approx ¾m turn R onto B4000 for Wickham & Shefford Woodlands. Through Wickham, entrance 100yds on R. From Newbury take B4000, house on L just before Wickham.* **Tue 11 July (11-4). Adm £5, chd free. Home-made teas & home cooked gammon rolls.**
In a beautiful country house setting, this exceptional ½ acre walled garden was created from scratch in 2008. Designed by Robin Templar-Williams, the different rooms

Farley Hill Place Gardens

have distinct themes and colour schemes. Delightful arched clematis and rose walkway. Wide variety of trees, planting, pots brimming with colour and places to sit and enjoy the views. Separate cutting and vegetable garden. Gravel paths.

42 WILLOW TREE COTTAGE
Ashampstead, RG8 8RA. Katy & David Weston. *4m W of Pangbourne. From Yattendon head towards Reading. L fork in beech wood to Ashampstead, keep L, join lower road, ½m turn L before houses.* **Sun 25 June (2-5). Combined adm with Pyt House £5, chd free. Home-made teas at Pyt House.**
Small pretty cottage garden surrounding the house that was originally built for the gardener of Pyt House. Substantially redesigned and replanted in recent yrs. Perennial borders, vegetable garden, pond with ducks and chickens. Most of the garden is accessible by wheelchair.

BUCKINGHAMSHIRE

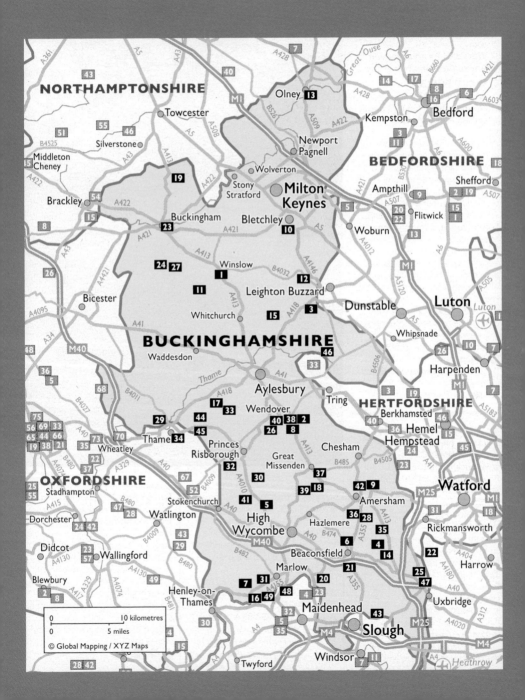

Buckinghamshire has a beautiful and varied landscape; edged by the River Thames to the south, crossed by the Chiltern Hills, and with the Vale of Aylesbury stretching to the north.

This year Buckinghamshire will hold five group openings, many of which can be found in villages of thatched or brick and flint cottages.

If you are looking for an interesting afternoon visit Little Missenden village, featured in Midsummer murders, with nine different gardens open including the village school.

Many Buckinghamshire gardens have been used as locations for films and television, with the Pinewood Studios nearby and excellent proximity to London.

We also boast historical gardens including Ascott, Stoke Poges Memorial Gardens (Grade 1 listed), and Cowper and Newton Museum Gardens.

Most of our gardens offer homemade tea and cakes to round off a lovely afternoon, visitors can leave knowing they have enjoyed a wonderful visit and helped raise money for nursing and caring charities at the same time.

Volunteers

County Organiser
Maggie Bateson
01494 866265
maggiebateson@gmail.com

County Treasurer
Tim Hart
01494 837328
timgc.hart@btinternet.com

Publicity
Sandra Wetherall
01494 862264
sandracwetherall@gmail.com

Social Media
Lisa Wilhelmy
07493 442641
lisa.wilhelmy@yahoo.co.uk

Booklet Co-ordinator
Maggie Bateson
(as above)

Assistant County Organisers
Janice Cross
01494 728291
gwendalice@aol.com

Judy Hart
01494 837328
judy.elgood@gmail.com

Margaret Higgins
01844 347072
jhiggins816@btinternet.com

Mhairi Sharpley
01494 782870
mhairisharpley@btinternet.com

Left: Turn End

OPENING DATES

All entries subject to change. For latest information check **www.ngs.org.uk**

Map locator numbers are shown to the right of each garden name.

Ascott

© Neil Campbell-Sharp

THE GARDENS

1 ABBOTS HOUSE

10 Church Street, Winslow, MK18 3AN. Mrs Jane Rennie, 01296 712326, jane@renniemail.com. *9m N of Aylesbury. A413 into Winslow. From town centre take Horn St & R into Church St, L fork at top. Entrance 20 metres on L. Parking in town centre & adjacent streets.* **Sun 4 June (12.30-5.30). Adm £3, chd free. Home-made teas. Visits also by arrangement Apr to July for groups of 20 max.**
Garden on different levels divided into four; courtyard near house with arbour, pond with waterfall and pots; woodland garden with rose gazebo and swimming pool; garden with grasses; walled Victorian kitchen garden with glasshouses, potager, fruit pergola, wall trained fruit, many Mediterranean plants and recent meadow planting. Late spring bulbs and many pots. Experimental wild areas. Some sculptures. Partial wheelchair access, garden levels accessed by steps only.

  ♿ ❀ ☕

2 ACER CORNER

10 Manor Road, Wendover, HP22 6HQ. Jo Naiman, 07958 319234, jo@acercorner.com, www.acercorner.com. *3m S of Aylesbury. Follow A413 into Wendover. L at clock tower r'about into Aylesbury Rd. R at next r'about into Wharf Rd, continue past schools on L, garden on R.* **Fri 23, Sat 24 June, Sat 14, Sun 15 Oct (2-5). Adm £2.50, chd free. Home-made teas. Visits also by arrangement May to Oct for groups of 20 max.** *Donation to South Bucks Jewish Community Charity.*
Garden designer's garden with Japanese influence and large collection of Japanese maples. The enclosed front garden is Japanese in style. Back garden is divided into three areas; patio area recently redesigned in the Japanese style; densely planted area with many acers and roses; and the corner which includes a productive greenhouse and interesting planting.

  🐕 ❀ ☕ ▣

3 ◆ ASCOTT

Ascott, Wing, Leighton Buzzard, LU7 0PR. The National Trust, 01296 688242, JNash@ascottestate.co.uk, www.nationaltrust.org.uk/ascott. *2m SW of Leighton Buzzard, 8m NE of Aylesbury. Via A418. Buses: 150 Aylesbury - Milton Keynes, 100 Aylesbury & Milton Keynes.* **For NGS: Mon 1 May, Mon 28 Aug (2-6). Adm £5, chd £2.50. Light refreshments. (NT members are required to pay to enter the gardens on NGS days). For other opening times and information, please phone, email or visit garden website.**
Combining Victorian formality with early C20 natural style and recent plantings to lead it into the C21, with a recently completed garden designed by Jacques and Peter Wirtz who designed the gardens at Alnwick Castle, and also a Richard Long Sculpture. Terraced lawns with specimen and ornamental trees, panoramic views to the Chilterns. Naturalised bulbs, mirror image herbaceous borders, impressive topiary incl box and yew sundial. Ascott House is closed on NGS Days. Outdoor wheelchairs available from car park. Mobility buggy, prior booking advised.

  ♿ ❀ 🚗 ☕ ▣

4 BEECH HOUSE

Long Wood Drive, Jordans, Beaconsfield, HP9 2SS. Sue & Ray Edwards, raybcm@tiscali.co.uk. *From A40, L to Seer Green & Jordans for approx 1m. Turn into Jordans Way on L. Longwood Drive 1st L. From A413 turn into Chalfont St Giles. Straight ahead until L signed Jordans. 1st L Jordans Way.* **Visits by arrangement Mar to Nov for groups of 2-30. Adm £3, chd free.**
2 acre plantsman's garden built up over the last 29 yrs, with a wide range of plants aimed at providing yr-round interest. Many shrubs, roses, grasses, ferns, perennials and trees planted for their ornamental bark and autumnal foliage. A particular feature is the meadow in the back garden with numerous bulbs and wild flowers in spring and early summer. Wheelchair access dependent upon weather conditions.

  ♿ 🐕

5 BRADENHAM MANOR

Bradenham, High Wycombe, HP14 4HF. National Trust & Grant Thornton UK, www.nationaltrust.org.uk. *2½m NW of High Wycombe, 5m S of Princes Risborough. On A4010, turn by Red Lion PH, car park signed on village green.* **Sun 25 June (12.30-4). Adm £4, chd free. Home-made teas in the cricket pavillion on the village green.**
C17 yew trees line a unique wilderness garden cut into a steep hill, offering stunning views of the Chilterns and a haven for wildlife. NT restoration reinstated Victorian parterres, summer borders, and rejuvenated 100 yr old orchard. New guardians are in the process of restoring the Walled Garden, cut flower borders, the Gardeners Cottage Garden, and a Secret Garden overlooking a Medieval church. Share our plans and progress in our third yr, chat with our beekeeper and try locally made organic apple juice in the orchard.

  🐕 ▣

The Manor House

6 18 BROWNSWOOD ROAD

Beaconsfield, HP9 2NU. John & Bernadette Thompson. *From New Town turn R into Ledborough Lane, L into Sandleswood Rd, 2nd R into Brownswood Rd.* **Sat 10, Sun 11 June (1.30-5.30). Adm £3.50, chd free. Home-made teas & gluten free options.**
A plant filled garden designed by Barbara Hunt. A harmonious arrangement of arcs and circles introduces a rhythm that leads through the garden. Sweeping box curves, gravel beds, brick edging and lush planting. A restrained use of purples and reds dazzle against a grey and green background.

7 BURROW FARM

Hambleden, RG9 6LT. David Palmer, 01491 571256. *1m SE of Hambleden. On A4155 between Henley & Marlow, turn N at Mill End. After 300yds, R onto Rotten Row. After ½m, Burrow Farm entrance on R.* **Sun 28 May, Sun 18 June (1-5). Adm £5, chd free. Home-made teas. Visits also by arrangement May & June.**
Burrow Farm and the adjacent cottages (not open) are part Tudor and part Elizabethan, set in the Chilterns above Hambleden Valley where it meets the Thames. Views of pasture and woodlands across the ha-ha greatly enhance the setting. Special features are the parterre, arboretum and C15 barn, where home-made teas will be served.

8 CEDAR HOUSE

Bacombe Lane, Wendover, HP22 6EQ. Sarah Nicholson, 01296 622131, jeremynicholson@btinternet.com. *5m SE Aylesbury. From Gt Missenden take A413 into Wendover. Take 1st L before row of cottages, house at top of lane.* **Visits by arrangement May to Sept for groups of 10+. Adm £3.50, chd free. Tea.**
A chalk garden in the Chiltern Hills with a steep sloping lawn leading to a natural swimming pond with aquatic plants. Wild flowers with native orchids. Shaped borders hold a great variety of trees, shrubs and perennials. A lodge greenhouse and a good collection of half hardy plants in pots. Steep, sloping lawn.

Burrow Farm

9 CHESHAM BOIS HOUSE

85 Bois Lane, Chesham Bois, HP6 6DF. Julia Plaistowe, 01494 726476, julia.plaistowe@yahoo.co.uk, cheshamboishouse.co.uk. *1m N of Amersham-on-the-Hill. Follow Sycamore Rd (main shopping centre road of Amersham) which becomes Bois Lane. Do not use SatNav once in lane as you will be led astray.* **Sun 26 Mar, Sun 14 May (2-5); Sun 9 July (11-5). Adm £4, chd free. Home-made teas. Visits also by arrangement Mar to Sept.**
3 acre plantswoman's garden with primroses, daffodils and hellebores in early spring. Interesting for most of the yr with lovely herbaceous borders, rill with small ornamental canal, walled garden, old orchard with wildlife pond, and handsome trees of which some are topiaried. It is a peaceful oasis. During the Sunday openings, the nearby 800 yr old church will be open. Incl in Buckinghamshire Garden Trust. Gravel in front of the house.

10 126 CHURCH GREEN ROAD

Bletchley, Milton Keynes, MK3 6DD. David & Janice Hale. *13m E of Buckingham, 11m N of Leighton Buzzard. Off B4034 into Church Green Rd, take L turn at mini-r'about.* **Sun 25 June (2-6); Tue 27 June (2-5). Adm £3, chd free. Home-made teas.**
A gentle sloping mature garden of ½ acre is a plant lover's delight, which incl a small formal garden, shady areas and mixed borders of shrubs, perennials and roses. Features incl a thatched wendy house, pergola, formal pond, wildlife pond, productive fruit and vegetable garden, two greenhouses and patio.

Donations from the NGS enable Perennial to care for horticulturalists

GROUP OPENING

11 THE CLAYDONS

East Claydon, MK18 2ND. *1½m SW Winslow. In Winslow turn R off High St, by the Bell PH & follow NT signs towards Claydon House & The Claydons.* **Mon 29 May (2-6). Combined adm £5, chd free. Home-made teas in the village hall.**

CLAYDON COTTAGE
Mr & Mrs Tony Evans.

THE OLD RECTORY
Mrs Jane Meisl.

THE OLD VICARAGE
Nigel & Esther Turnbull.

Three small villages, originally part of the Claydon Estate with typical north Buckinghamshire cottages and two C13 churches. The Old Vicarage, a large garden on clay with mixed borders, scented garden, dell, shrub roses, vegetables and a natural clay pond. Small meadow area and planting to encourage wildlife, and beehives. A free children's quiz. Access via gravel drive. Claydon Cottage has many quirky features and surprises. The Old Rectory is a large garden with a wildflower meadow, herbaceous borders, a woodland walk and cloud hedging. Partial wheelchair access.

&. ✿ ☕

12 CLOSE COTTAGE

Church Lane, Soulbury, Leighton Buzzard, LU7 0BU. Rachel Belsham & Daniel Storey, belshamstorey@btinternet.com. *Approx 3m NW of Leighton Buzzard. In centre of village, next to field below church, on narrow country lane leading uphill from The Boot PH. Parking in field, clearly signed.* **Sun 30 Apr, Sun 18 June (1.30-5.30). Adm £4.50, chd free. Home-made teas. Visits also by arrangement Apr to Aug for groups of 10+.**
The 3 acre garden at Close Cottage is 15 yrs old and encompasses a formal terraced garden, orchard and paddock. The garden is laid to lawn and planted with a wide variety

of shrubs, bulbs and perennials. The orchard incl an avenue of cherry trees, various fruit trees, a wild flower meadow, woodland area, vegetable beds and a cutting garden.

🐕 ✿ ☕

13 ♦ COWPER & NEWTON MUSEUM GARDENS

Market Place, Olney, MK46 4AJ. Mrs E Knight, 01234 711516, www.cowperandnewtonmuseum. org.uk. *5m N of Newport Pagnell. 12m S of Wellingborough. On A509. Please park in public car park in East St.* **For NGS: Sat 10, Sun 11 June (10.30-4.30). Adm £3, chd free. Home-made teas. For other opening times and information, please phone or visit garden website.**
The Flower Garden of C18 poet William Cowper, who said 'Gardening was of all employments, that in which I succeeded best', has plants introduced prior to his death in 1800, many mentioned in his writings. The Summer House Garden, with Cowper's 'verse manufactory', now a Victorian Kitchen Garden, has new and heritage vegetables organically grown, also a herb border and medicinal plant bed. Features incl lacemaking demonstrations and local artists painting live art.

&. ✿ ☕

14 CRAIGLEA HOUSE

Austenwood Lane, Chalfont St Peter, Gerrards Cross, SL9 9DA. Jeff & Sue Medlock, 01753 884852, suemedlock@msn.com, *6m SE Amersham. From Gerrards Cross take B416 to Amersham. Take L fork after ½m into Austenwood Lane, garden is ⅓m on R. Park at St Joseph's Church or Priory Rd.* **Visits by arrangement May to Sept for groups of 8+. Adm £4.50, chd free. Home-made teas.**
Delightful 1 acre garden complements the Arts and Crafts House which it surrounds. The planting ranges from the formal rose garden, lawns, herbaceous borders and pergola, to the natural planting around wildlife ponds, and fruit

trees. Garden contains a wide range of plants, incl many hostas, a small vegetable and cutting garden and many seats affording lovely views of garden.

&. ✿ 🚌 ☕

GROUP OPENING

15 CUBLINGTON GARDENS

Cublington, Leighton Buzzard, LU7 0LF. *5m SE Winslow, 5m NE Aylesbury. From Aylesbury take A413 Buckingham Rd. After 4m, at Whitchurch, turn R to Cublington.* **Sun 28 May (2-5.30). Combined adm £5, chd free.**

CHERRY COTTAGE, 3 THE WALLED GARDENS
Gwyneira Waters.

LARKSPUR HOUSE
Mr & Mrs S Jenkins, 01296 682615, gstmusketeers3@aol.com. **Visits also by arrangement June & July for groups of 16 max.**

THE OLD STABLES
Mr & Mrs S George.

1 STEWKLEY ROAD
Tom & Helen Gadsby.

A group of diverse gardens in this attractive Buckinghamshire village listed as a conservation area. Cherry Cottage is adapted for wheelchair gardening with raised beds and artificial grass. Larkspur House is a beautifully maintained modern garden with hostas and alliums being firm favourites. It has a large, newly planted orchard and wild flower meadow. The Old Stables is a large garden divided into areas of different character, both formal and informal, featuring a revolving summerhouse and a circular hornbeam maze. 1 Stewkley Road has a strong focus on home grown food with an idyllic organic kitchen garden, small orchard and courtyard garden. Partial wheelchair access to some gardens.

&. 🐕

16 DANESFIELD HOUSE

Henley Road, Marlow,
SL7 2EY. Danesfield House
Hotel, 01628 891010,
ksmith@danesfieldhouse.co.uk,
www.danesfieldhouse.co.uk. *3m
from Marlow. On the A4155 between
Marlow & Henley-on-Thames. Signed
on the LH-side Danesfield House
Hotel and Spa.* **Wed 9 Aug (10.30-4.30). Adm £4.50, chd free.
Pre-booking essential for lunch
and afternoon tea.**
The gardens at Danesfield were
completed in 1901 by Robert
Hudson, the Sunlight Soap magnate
who built the house. Since the
house opened as a hotel in 1991,
the gardens have been admired by
several thousand guests each yr.
However, in 2009 it was discovered
that the gardens contained
outstanding examples of pulhamite
in both the formal gardens and
the waterfall areas. The 100 yr old
topiary is also outstanding. Part of
the grounds incl an Iron Age fort.
Guided tours welcome on NGS
open days. You may wander the
grounds on your own or there
will be two 1hr tours offered by
our Head Gardener at 10.30am
and 1.30pm for 30 max per tour.
Pre-booking essential due to high
demand. The gardeners will be
available for questions after each
tour. Restricted wheelchair access to
the gardens due to gravel paths.

  ♿ 🛏 ☕

GROUP OPENING

17 DINTON VILLAGE GARDENS

Dinton, HP17 8UN. *4m SW
Aylesbury, 4m NE Thame. For
SatNavs enter HP17 8UQ. ¼m off
A418. Please only use turning signed
Ford & Dinton for free car park,
clearly signed.* **Sun 30 Apr (2-6).
Combined adm £4, chd free.
Sun 25 June (2-6). Combined
adm £5, chd free. Cream teas in
village hall.**

GREENDALE
S A Eaton.
Open on Sun 30 Apr

HERMIT'S COTTAGE
Mr & Mrs M Usherwood.
Open on all dates

HONEYSUCKLE COTTAGE
Mr & Mrs W Lee.
Open on Sun 25 June

INNISFREE
David & Rosemary Jackson.
Open on Sun 25 June

LAVENDER COTTAGE
Sara & Trevor Hopwood.
Open on Sun 25 June

WESTLINGTON FARM
Shaun & Catherine Brogan.
Open on all dates

WILLOW COTTAGE
Philip & Jennifer Rimell.
Open on Sun 30 Apr

Dinton is a very picturesque,
secluded, historic village, set in
countryside with views to the
Chiltern Hills. A conservation
area, it has many pretty, thatched,
whitewashed, old cottages and has
been featured in the Midsomer
Murders TV series. The 7 colourful
and very interesting gardens range
from small, informal cottages
through to medium and larger
country house styles, each one with
a strikingly different character and
purpose. All are within easy and
peaceful walking distance of the
car park and village hall. The lovely
C11/12 Norman church, a Grade
I listed building, has an outstanding
south doorway and a 800 yr old
font (open to visitors). Wheelchair
access and dogs allowed to 5
gardens. WC at village hall.

  ♿ 🐕 ❀ ☕

> The National Garden
> Scheme is the
> largest single funder
> of the Queen's
> Nursing Institute

18 FRESSINGWOOD

Hare Lane, Little Kingshill, Great
Missenden, HP16 0EF. John &
Maggie Bateson. *1m S of Gt
Missenden, 4m W of Amersham.
From the A413 at Chiltern Hospital,
turn L signed Gt & Lt Kingshill. Take
1st L into Nags Head Lane. Turn R
under railway bridge, then L into New
Rd & continue to Hare Lane.* **Sun 21
May (2-5.30). Adm £4, chd free.
Home-made teas.**
Thoughtfully designed garden
with yr-round colour and many
interesting features. Shrubbery with
ferns, grasses and hellebores. Small
formal garden, herb garden, pergolas
with roses and clematis. Topiary
and landscaped terrace. Newly
developed area incorporating water
with grasses. Herbaceous borders
and bonsai collection.

  ❀ ☕

19 GLEBE FARM

Lillingstone Lovell, Buckingham,
MK18 5BB. Mr David Hilliard,
01280 860384,
thehilliards@talk21.com,
www.glebefarmbarn.co.uk.
*Lillingstone Lovell. Off A413, 5m N of
Buckingham & 2m S of Whittlebury.
From A5 at Potterspury, turn off A5 &
follow signs to Lillingstone Lovell.* **Sun
25 June (1.30-5). Adm £3, chd
free. Home-made teas.**
A large cottage garden with an
exuberance of colourful planting and
winding gravel paths amongst lawns
and herbaceous borders on two
levels. Ponds, a wishing well, vegetable
beds, a knot garden, a small walled
garden and an old tractor feature.
Everything combines to make a
beautiful garden full of surprises.

  ♿ 🐕 ❀ 🛏 ☕

GROUP OPENING

20 GRANGE DRIVE WOOBURN

Wooburn Green, HP10 0QD.
Alan & Elaine Ford, 01628 525818,
lanforddesigns@gmail.com. *On
A4094, 2m SW of A40, between
Bourne End & Wooburn. From
Wooburn Church, direction
Maidenhead, Grange Drive is on L
before r'about. From Bourne End, L*

Baker's Close, Long Crendon Gardens

© Fiona McLeod

at 2 mini-r'abouts, then 1st R. **Visits by arrangement Feb to Sept to Magnolia House & The Shades. Combined adm £3.50, chd free.** *Light refreshments.*

MAGNOLIA HOUSE
Alan & Elaine Ford.

THE SHADES
Pauline & Maurice Kirkpatrick.

2 diverse gardens in a private tree lined drive which formed the entrance to a country house now demolished. Magnolia House is a ½ acre garden with many mature trees incl magnificent copper beech and magnolia reaching the rooftop, a small cactus bed, fernery, stream leading to pond and greenhouses with 2 small aviaries. Front garden now has natural pond and bees. The Shades drive is approached through mature trees and beds of herbaceous plants and 60 various roses. A natural well is surrounded by shrubs and acers. The garden was developed in 2010 to incl a natural stone lawn terrace and changes made to the existing flower beds. A green slate water feature with alpine plants completes the garden. Child friendly. Partial wheelchair access.

21 HALL BARN
Windsor End, Beaconsfield, HP9 2SG.
The Hon Mrs Farncombe, jenefer@farncombe01.demon.co.uk.
½ m S of Beaconsfield. Lodge gate 300yds S of St Mary & All Saints' Church in Old Town centre. Please do not use SatNav. **Visits by arrangement Feb to Sept. Home-made teas & tour on request for groups of 10+ only. Adm £4, chd free.**
Historical landscaped garden laid out between 1680-1730 for the poet Edmund Waller and his descendants. Features 300 yr old cloud formation yew hedges, formal lake and vistas ending with classical buildings and statues. Wooded walks around the grove offer respite from the heat on sunny days. One of the original NGS garden openings of 1927. Gravel paths.

GROUP OPENING

22 HIGHER DENHAM GARDENS
Higher Denham, UB9 5EA. *6m E of Beaconsfield. Turn off the A412 about ½ m N of junction with A40 into Old Rectory Lane. After 1m enter Higher Denham straight ahead. Tickets for all gardens available at the community hall 70yds into the*

village. **Sun 12 Mar (2-5). Sun 11 June (1-5). Home-made teas in the community hall. Combined adm £5, chd free.** *Donation to Higher Denham Community CIO.*

9 LOWER ROAD
Ms Patricia Davidson.
Open on Sun 11 June

11 LOWER ROAD
Anne Ling.
Open on Sun 12 Mar

5 SIDE ROAD
Jane Blythe.
Open on Sun 11 June

WIND IN THE WILLOWS
Ron James, 07740 177038, r.james@company-doc.co.uk.
Open on all dates
Visits also by arrangement Mar to Sept for groups of 10+.

In March, Wind in the Willows and 11 Lower Road will have spring bulbs in flower, Wind in the Willows also has a large collection of mature hellebores and early flowering shrubs. In June, 3 gardens incl 1 reopening after a break, in the delightful chalk stream Misbourne Valley. Wind in the Willows has over 350 shrubs and trees, informal woodland and wild gardens incl riverside and bog plantings and a collection of 80 hostas and 12 striped roses in 3 acres. 'Really

different' and 'stunning' are typical visitor comments. The garden in 9 Lower Road is a medium size garden backing onto the river and recently professionally redesigned and highly praised by visitors last yr. Compare the design with the outcome and see how existing shrubs and trees have been integrated into the now maturing design. The garden at 5 Side Road is medium sized with lawns, borders and shrubs, and many features which children will love incl a competition to find hidden objects! In June the owner of Wind in the Willows will lead optional guided tours of the garden starting at 2pm and 4pm. Tours last approx 1 hour. Wind in the Willows is featured as a case study in Carol Klein's recent book 'Making a Garden'. Partial wheelchair access to some gardens
&. ✿ ☕ ☕

23　HILL HOUSE, BUCKINGHAM

Castle Street, Buckingham, MK18 1BS. Leonie & Peter Thorogood, 07860 714758, leonie@pjtassociates.com. *By parish church in Buckingham town centre. Signed Tingewick Road*

Industry, off Buckingham bypass. **Visits by arrangement June to Sept. Home-made teas on request. Adm £3.50, chd free.** ⅓ acre town garden on old castle walls by parish church in Buckingham conservation area. Designed for ease of maintenance, yr-round interest and colour. Good roses, hostas and herbaceous, a gardener's garden. Slight slopes to some areas of the garden.
&. ☕ 🚗 ☕

24　HILLESDEN HOUSE

Church End, Hillesden, MK18 4DB. Mr & Mrs R M Faccenda, 01296 730451, suef@faccenda.co.uk. *3m S of Buckingham through Gawcott. Next to church in Hillesden.* **Sun 18 June (2-5). Adm £5, chd free. Home-made teas. Visits also by arrangement June & July for groups of 20+.**
By superb church Cathedral in the Fields. Carp lakes, fountains and waterfalls with mature trees. Rose, alpine and herbaceous borders, 5 acres of formal gardens with 80 acres of deer park and parkland. Wild flower areas and extensive lakes developed by the owner. Lovely walks and plenty of wildlife.

Also a newly created woodland and vegetable garden. An orchard was planted 2 yrs ago. No wheelchair access to lakes.
&. ☕ ✿ ☕

25　HILLS HOUSE

Village Road, Denham Village, UB9 5BH. Mr & Mrs B Savory. *Turn off M40 J1A towards London. Turn L at T-lights, stay in middle lane, turn L at r'about & stay in RH lane. Follow sign Village Only & follow road ¼m. Turn L over bridge, next to St Mary's Church.* **Sun 23 Apr, Sun 25 June (2-5). Adm £4, chd free. Home-made teas.**
A C16 3 acre garden in Denham Village with an impressive collection of majestic specimen trees, walled garden and designated shrub borders. A large rose garden and perennial border frame a sunken buxus parterre, and annual display of baskets that flow to an orchard on long gravel paths. Walk through serene areas and woodland plantings, with a spring display of bulbs underneath mature trees. No wheelchair access to sunken parterre. Gravel paths.
&. ☕ ☕

The Shades, Grange Drive Wooburn

26 HOMELANDS

Springs Lane, Ellesborough, Aylesbury, HP17 0XD. Jean & Tony Young, 01296 622306, young@ellesborough.fsnet.co.uk. *6m SE of Aylesbury. On the B4010 between Wendover & Princes Risborough. Springs Lane is between village hall at Butlers Cross & the church. Narrow lane with an uneven surface.* **Visits by arrangement May to Aug. Adm £4, chd free. Light refreshments.**

Secluded ¾ acre garden on difficult chalk, adjoining open countryside. Designed to be enjoyed from many seating positions. Progress from semi-formal to wild flower meadow and wildlife pond. Deep borders with all season interest, and gravel beds with exotic late summer and autumn planting.

&. 🐕 ☕ ♿

27 KINGSBRIDGE

Steeple Claydon, MK18 2EJ. Mr & Mrs T Aldous, 01296 730224. *3m S of Buckingham. Halfway between Padbury & Steeple Claydon. Xrds with sign to Kingsbridge Only.* **Visits by arrangement for groups of 8+. Home-made teas.**

Stunning and exceptional 6 acre garden imaginatively created over last 26 yrs. Main lawn is enclosed by softly curving colour themed herbaceous borders, many roses and shrubs interestingly planted with cleverly created landscaping features. Clipped topiary yews, pleached hornbeams lead out to the ha-ha and countryside beyond. A natural stream with bog plants, nesting kingfishers, meanders serenely through woodland gardens with many walks. A garden to visit again and again. .

&. ☕ ♿

GROUP OPENING

28 LITTLE MISSENDEN GARDENS

Amersham, HP7 0RD. *2½m NW of Old Amersham. On A413 between Great Missenden & Old Amersham.* **Sun 2 July (1-6). Combined adm £6, chd free. Home-made teas.**

NEW **BOURN'S MEADOW**
Roger & Sandra Connor.

HOLLYDYKE HOUSE
Bob & Sandra Wetherall, 01494 862264, sandracwetherall@gmail.com. **Visits also by arrangement June & July for groups of 10+.**

NEW **LITTLE MISSENDEN CE INFANT SCHOOL**
Laura Lees.

MANOR FARM HOUSE
Evan Bazzard.

NEW **THE MANOR HOUSE**
Hayley & Hugh Karseras.

MILL HOUSE
Terry & Eleanor Payne.

MISSENDEN LODGE
Rob & Carol Kimber.

TOWN FARM COTTAGE
Mr & Mrs Tim Garnham.

THE WHITE HOUSE
Mr & Mrs Harris.

A variety of gardens set in this attractive Chiltern village in an area of outstanding natural beauty. The first episode of the new series of Midsomer Murders was set in the village. You can start off at one end of the village and wander through stopping off halfway for tea at the beautiful Anglo-Saxon church built in 975. The gardens reflect different style houses including several old cottages, a Mill House and a more modern house. There are herbaceous borders, shrubs, trees, old fashioned roses, hostas, topiary, koi and lily ponds, kitchen gardens, play areas for children and the R Misbourne runs through a few. Some gardens are highly colourful and others just green and peaceful. Beekeeper at Hollydyke House. Partial wheelchair access to some gardens due to gravel paths and steps.

&. 🐕 ❀ ☕ ♿

GROUP OPENING

29 LONG CRENDON GARDENS

Long Crendon, HP18 9AN. *2m N of Thame. Long Crendon village is situated on the B4011 Thame-Bicester road. Maps showing the*

---

location of the gardens will be available on the day at each garden & at Church House in the High St. **Sun 23 Apr, Sun 4 June (2-6). Combined adm £5, chd free. Home-made teas at Church House, High St.** *Donation to Long Crendon Day Centre & Community Library.*

BAKER'S CLOSE
Mr & Mrs Peter Vaines.
Open on Sun 23 Apr

BARRY'S CLOSE
Mr & Mrs Richard Salmon.
Open on Sun 23 Apr

48 CHILTON ROAD
Mr & Mrs M Charnock.
Open on Sun 4 June

COP CLOSE
Sandra & Tony Phipkin.
Open on Sun 4 June

25 ELM TREES
Carol & Mike Price.
Open on Sun 4 June

MANOR HOUSE
Mr & Mrs West.
Open on Sun 23 Apr

MULBERRY HOUSE
Ken Pandolfi & James Anderson.
Open on Sun 23 Apr

TOMPSONS FARM
Mr & Mrs T Moynihan.
Open on Sun 4 June

Four gardens open on Sun 23 April. Two large gardens, Baker's Close, partly walled with terraced lawns, rockery, shrubs and wild area. A spring planting of thousands of daffodils, narcissi and tulips. Barry's Close has a collection of spring flowering trees forming a backdrop to borders, pools and water garden. Along the High St, Mulberry House, a restored vicarage garden which incl a formal knot garden, a wooded walkway, pond and Zen area; and Manor House, a large garden with views towards the Chilterns, two ornamental lakes and a large variety of spring bulbs and shrubs. Four gardens open on Sun 4 June incl two cottage style gardens, 25 Elm Trees, with a terrace and small orchard area, wildlife pond, rockery and deep borders; and 48 Chilton Rd with perennial borders and summerhouse. Along the High St, Tompsons Farm, a large woodland garden with mature trees and shrubs sweeping down to a lake. Cop Close, 1⅓ acre garden with vegetable and cutting garden and borders. Partial wheelchair access to some gardens.

30 NEW **LOOSLEY DENE**
Lower Road, Loosley Row, Princes Risborough, HP27 0PE. Tim & Sarah Halliday. *7m W of High Wycombe, 2m E of Princes Risborough off the A4010. From Princes Risborough, take L onto Woodway to Lacey Green. Up the hill after 1m take R fork into Lower Rd. After ⅓m turn R at small Xrds down into Loosley Hill, park in field on R (signed).* **Sat 3 June (1.30-5); Sat 8 July (10.30-12.30). Adm £4, chd free. Home-made teas.**
Within 4½ acres, set into hillside, the garden has panoramic views of the Chiltern landscape. Well established trees and shrubs with yr-round interest has been redesigned in the last 6 yrs maintaining some original features dating to C19. Yorkstone terrace retained by Cotswold stone walls overlook lawns, steps, and paths lead to small parterre, mixed borders with lavenders and roses. Chickens, ducks and pigs.

31 LORDS WOOD
Frieth Road, Marlow Common, SL7 2QS. Mr & Mrs Messum. *1½m NW Marlow. From Marlow turn off the A4155 at Platts Garage into Oxford Rd, towards Frieth for 1½m. Garden is 100yds past the Marlow Common turn, on the L, opp Valley View Stables.* **Fri 23 June, Fri 8 Sept (11-4). Adm £4.50, chd free. Home-made teas.**
Lords Wood was built in 1899 and has been the Messum's family home since 1974. 5 acres of garden features extensive and mature borders in varying styles. Vegetable, flower and herb gardens, large water gardens, rockery, orchard and woodland walks. There are two wildflower meadows with fantastic views over the Chilterns. The gardens are always

changing with something new to delight and inspire at every visit. Partial wheelchair access; gravel paths and steep slopes.

32 THE MANOR HOUSE
Church End, Bledlow, Nr Princes Risborough, HP27 9PB. The Lord Carrington. *9m NW of High Wycombe, 3m SW of Princes Risborough. ½m off B4009 in middle of Bledlow village. SatNav directions HP27 9PA.* **Sun 21 May (2-5). Adm £5, chd free. Light refreshments.**
Paved garden, parterres, shrub borders, old roses and walled kitchen garden. Water garden with paths, bridges and walkways fed by 14 chalk springs, plus 2 acres of landscaped planting with sculptures. Partial wheelchair access as there is stepped access or sloped grass to enter the gardens.

33 MOAT FARM
Water Lane, Ford, Aylesbury, HP17 8XD. Mr & Mrs P Bergqvist, 01296 748560, patricia@quintadelarosa.com. *Turn up Water Lane by Dinton Hermit in the middle of Ford village, after approx 200yds, turn L over cattle grid between beech hedges into Moat Farm.* **Visits by arrangement Apr to Sept for groups of 8+. Home-made teas.**
A country garden with herbaceous borders, roses, hostas, trees and water. A moat that flows through the garden and a blind moat through the arboretum. Small walled garden and some vegetables.

34 ◆ NETHER WINCHENDON HOUSE
Nether Winchendon, Thame, Aylesbury, HP18 0DY. Mr Robert Spencer Bernard, 01844 290101, Contactus@netherwinchendon house.com, www.netherwinchendonhouse. com. *6m SW of Aylesbury, 6m from Thame. Approx 4m from Thame on A418, turn 1st L to Cuddington, then L at Xrds, downhill turn R & R again to parking by house.* **For NGS: Sun**

30 Apr, Sun 28, Mon 29 May, Sun 27, Mon 28 Aug (2-5.30). Adm £4, chd free. Cream teas at the church (2.30-5). For other opening times and information, please phone, email or visit garden website.
Nether Winchendon House is set in 7 acres of garden with fine and rare trees, surrounded by parkland. A Founder Garden (1927). Medieval and Tudor house set in stunning landscape. The South Lawn runs down to the R Thame. Picturesque village with interesting church. Conducted tours of the house (additional adm of £4, not to NGS).

35 NORTH DOWN
Dodds Lane, Chalfont St Giles, HP8 4EL. Merida Saunders, 01494 872928. *4m SE of Amersham, 4m NE of Beaconsfield. Opp the green in centre of village, at Costa turn into UpCorner onto Silver Hill. At top of hill fork R into Dodds Lane. North Down is 7th on L.* **Visits by arrangement May to Aug for groups of 2-36. Adm £4, chd free. Light refreshments.**
A passion for gardening is evident in this plantswomans lovely ¾ acre garden which has evolved over the yrs with scenic effect in mind. Colourful and interesting throughout the yr. Large grassed areas with island beds of mixed perennials, shrubs and some unusual plants. Variety of rhododendrons, azaleas, acers, clematis and a huge Kiftsgate rose. Displays of sempervivum varieties, alpines, grasses and ferns. Small patio and water feature, greenhouse and an Italianate front patio to owner's design.

36 ORCHARD HOUSE
Tower Road, Coleshill, Amersham, HP7 0LB. Mr & Mrs Douglas Livesey, 01494 432278, jane.livesey88@btinternet.com. *From Amersham Old Town take the A355 to Beaconsfield. Appox ¾m along this road at top of hill, take the 1st R into Tower Rd. Parking in cricket club grounds.* **Sun 18 June (2-5). Adm £5, chd free. Home-made teas in the barn. Visits**

The White House, Little Missenden Gardens

© Ellen Rooney

also by arrangement June & July for groups of 10+. **Adm incl refreshments.**
The 5 acre garden is made up of two wooded areas with eco hedges for wildlife. Two ponds with wild flower planting, large avenues of silver birches, a bog garden with board walk running through, and a wild flower meadow. There is a raised garden area with numerous raised beds used as a cutting garden for flowers and some vegetables. Bees. Rear garden lawn slopes down.

♿ 🐕 ❄ ☕

37 OVERSTROUD COTTAGE
The Dell, Frith Hill, Gt Missenden, HP16 9QE. Mr & Mrs Jonathan Brooke, 01494 862701, susanmbrooke@outlook.com. *½m E Gt Missenden. Turn E off A413 at Gt Missenden onto B485 Frith Hill to Chesham Rd. White Gothic cottage* set back in lay-by 100yds uphill on L. Parking on R at church. **Sun 16 Apr, Sun 7, Sun 28 May, Sun 11 June (2-5). Adm £3.50, chd free.** Cream teas at parish church. **Visits also by arrangement Apr to July for groups of 15-30.**
Artistic chalk garden on two levels. Collection of C17/C18 plants incl auriculas, bulbs, hellebores, pulmonarias, geraniums, herbs, succulents and peonies. Many antique, species and rambling roses. Potager and lily pond. Cottage was once C17 fever house for Missenden Abbey. Features incl a garden studio with painting exhibition (share of flower painting proceeds to NGS).

❄ ☕

38 11 THE PADDOCKS
Wendover, HP22 6HE. Mr & Mrs E Rye, 01296 623870, pam.rye@talktalk.net. *5m from Aylesbury on A413. From Aylesbury* turn L at mini-r'about onto Wharf Rd. From Gt Missenden turn L at the Clock Tower, then R at mini-r'about onto Wharf Rd. **Sat 24, Sun 25 June, Sat 1, Sun 2 July (2-5). Adm £2.50, chd free. Visits also by arrangement June & July for groups of 30 max.** *Donation to Bonnie People in South Africa.*
Small peaceful garden with mixed borders of colourful herbaceous perennials, a special show of David Austin roses and a large variety of spectacular named Blackmore and Langdon delphiniums. A tremendous variety of colour in a small area. The White Garden with a peaceful arbour, The Magic of Moonlight created for the BBC. Most of the garden can be viewed from the lawn.

♿ ❄

39 PETERLEY CORNER COTTAGE

Perks Lane, Prestwood, Great Missenden, HP16 0JH. Dawn Philipps, 01494 862198, dawn.philipps@googlemail.com. *Turn into Perks Lane from Wycombe Rd (A4128), Peterley Corner Cottage is the 3rd house on the L.* **Visits by arrangement May to Aug for groups of 10+. Adm £4.50, chd free. Tea.**

A 3 acre mature garden, incl an acre of wild flowers and indigenous trees. Surrounded by tall hedges and a wood, the garden has evolved over the last 30 yrs. There are many specimen trees and mature roses incl a Paul's Himalaya Musk and a Kiftsgate. A large herbaceous border runs alongside the formal lawns with other borders like heathers and shrubs. The most recent addition is a potager.

40 THE PLOUGH

Chalkshire Road, Terrick, Aylesbury, HP17 0TJ. John & Sue Stewart. *2m W of Wendover. Entrance to garden & car park signed off B4009 Nash Lee Rd. 200yds E of Terrick r'about. Access to garden from field car park.* **Sun 14, Mon 29 May (1-5). Adm £4, chd free. Home-made teas.**

Formal garden with open views to the Chiltern countryside. Designed as a series of outdoor rooms around a listed former C18 inn, incl border, parterre, vegetable and fruit gardens, and a newly planted orchard. Delicious home-made teas and jams for sale made with fruits from the garden.

41 RED KITES

46 Haw Lane, Bledlow Ridge, HP14 4JJ. Mag & Les Terry, 01494 481474, les.terry@lineone.net. *4m S of Princes Risborough. Off A4010 halfway between Princes Risborough & West Wycombe. At Hearing Dogs sign in Saunderton turn into Haw Lane, then ¾m on L up the hill.* **Tue 16 May, Tue 4 July (2-5). Adm £4, chd free. Home-made teas. Visits also by arrangement May to Sept for groups of 15+.**

This much admired 1½ acre Chiltern hillside garden is planted for yr-round interest and is lovingly maintained with mixed and herbaceous borders, wild flower orchard, established pond, vegetable garden, managed woodland area and a lovely hidden garden. Many climbers used throughout the garden which changes significantly through the seasons. Sit and enjoy the superb views from the top terrace.

42 RIVENDELL

13 The Leys, Amersham, HP6 5NP. Janice & Mike Cross. *Off A416. Take A416 N towards Chesham. The Leys is on L ½m after Boot & Slipper PH. Park at Beacon School, 100yds N.* **Mon 17 Apr (2-5). Adm £3.50, chd free. Home-made teas.**

S-facing garden comprising a series of different areas, incl a woodland area, gravel area with grasses and pond, fruit and vegetable garden, bug hotels, herbaceous beds containing a wide variety of shrubs, bulbs and perennials, all surrounding a circular lawn with a rose and clematis arbour.

43 ◆ STOKE POGES MEMORIAL GARDENS

Church Lane, Stoke Poges, Slough, SL2 4NZ. South Bucks District Council, 01753 523744, memorial.gardens@southbucks. gov.uk, www.southbucks.gov.uk/stokepogesmemorialgardens. *1m N of Slough, 4m S of Gerrards Cross. Follow signs to Stoke Poges & from there to the Memorial Gardens. Car park opp main entrance, disabled visitor parking in the gardens. Weekend disabled access through churchyard.* **For NGS: Sun 21 May (1.30-4.30). Adm £5, chd free. Home-made teas. For other opening times and information, please phone, email or visit garden website.**

Wind in the Willows, Higher Denham Gardens

© Ellen Rooney

Unique 20 acre Grade I registered garden constructed 1934-9. Rock and water gardens, sunken colonnade, rose garden, 500 individual gated gardens. Spring garden with bulbs, wisteria and rhododendrons. Guided tours every half hour. Guide dogs only.

& ✿ 🚗 ☕

44 TURN END

Townside, Haddenham, Aylesbury, HP17 8BG. Peter Aldington, turnendtrustevents@gmail.com, www.turnend.org.uk. *3m NE of Thame, 5m SW of Aylesbury. Turn off A418 to Haddenham. Turn at Rising Sun to Townside. Please park at a distance with consideration for neighbours.* **Mon I May (2-5.30). Adm £4.50, chd free. Home-made teas.**
Intriguing series of garden rooms each with a different planting style enveloping architect's own post-war 2* listed house (not open). Dry garden, small woodland, formal box garden, sunken gardens, mixed borders around curving lawn, framed by ancient walls and mature trees. Bulbs, irises, wisteria, roses, ferns and climbers. Courtyards with pools, pergolas, secluded seating, Victorian Coach House. Open studios with displays and demonstrations by creative artists. Steps, narrow archways, stone pathways.

🐄 ✿ ☕

National Garden Scheme support helps raise awareness of unpaid carers

45 TYTHROP PARK

Kingsey, HP17 8LT. Nick & Chrissie Wheeler. *2m E of Thame, 4m NW of Princes Risborough. Via A4129, at T-junction in Kingsey turn towards Haddenham, take L turn on bend. Parking in field on L.* **Sun I I June (2-5.30). Adm £6, chd free. Home-made teas.** *Donation to St Nicholas Church, Kingsey.*
10 acres of gardens surrounding C17 Grade I listed manor house. In the past 9 yrs the grounds at Tythrop have undergone some major changes and now blend traditional styles with more contemporary planting. Features incl large intricate parterre, deep mixed borders, water features, large greenhouse, kitchen and cut flower garden, wild flower meadow, many old trees and shrubs.

☕

46 WESTEND HOUSE

Cheddington, Leighton Buzzard, LU7 0RP. His Honour Judge & Mrs Richard Foster, 01296 661332, westend.house@hotmail.com, www.westendhousecheddington. co.uk. *5m N of Tring. From double mini-r'about in Cheddington take turn to Long Marston. Take I st L & Westend House is on your R.* **Sun 2 July (2-5). Adm £3.50, chd free. Home-made teas.**
A country garden of 2 acres restored and developed in recent yrs featuring herbaceous and shrub borders, a formal rose garden with swags, wild flower areas adjacent to the pond and in the orchard, a natural wildlife pond and stream with recently extended planting, potager with vegetables and picking flowers. Wood and metal sculptures. Rare breed hens, sheep and pigs in field next to garden. All cakes are home-made and tea is served in bone china with waitress service. Some bespoke sculptures and seasonal vegetables for sale. Wheelchair access to far side of pond restricted.

& 🐄 ✿ 🚗 🚌 ☕

47 THE WHITE HOUSE

Village Road, Denham Village, UB9 5BE. Mr & Mrs P G Courtenay-Luck. *3m NW of Uxbridge, 7m E of Beaconsfield.*

Signed from A40 or A412. Parking in village road. The White House is in centre of village. **Sun I I June (2-5). Adm £5, chd free. Cream teas.**
Well established 6 acre formal garden in picturesque setting. Mature trees and hedges with R Misbourne meandering through lawns. Shrubberies, flower beds, rockery, rose garden and orchard. Large walled garden and laburnum walk. Herb garden, vegetable plot and Victorian greenhouses. Gravel entrance and path to gardens.

& 🐄 ✿ ☕

48 WHITEWALLS

Quarry Wood Road, Marlow, SL7 1RE. Mr W H Williams, 01628 482573. *½m S Marlow. From Marlow crossover bridge. I st L, 3rd house on L with white garden wall.* **Visits by arrangement Mar to Oct. Adm £2.50, chd free.**
Thames side garden, approx ½ acre, with spectacular views of the weir. Large water lily pond, interesting planting of trees, shrubs, herbaceous perennials and bedding, and a large conservatory. Many chairs to sit by the river and view the weir.

& 🐄 🚗

49 WITTINGTON ESTATE

Henley Road, Medmenham, Marlow, SL7 2EB. SAS Institute *The Wittington Estate is located off r'about approx I ½m from Marlow on the A4155 Henley Rd.* **Sun 25 June (10.30-4.30). Adm £5, chd free. Light refreshments.**
Situated on the banks of the Thames, between Marlow and Henley is SASUK and the Wittington Estate. Built in 1898 for Hudson Ewbank Kearley, later Viscount Devonport. Stunning viewpoints, rose garden, court garden, herbaceous borders, flash-lock capstan wheel, boat house, pump house and arboretum (under restoration). Wood tree sculpture.

& ☕

CAMBRIDGESHIRE

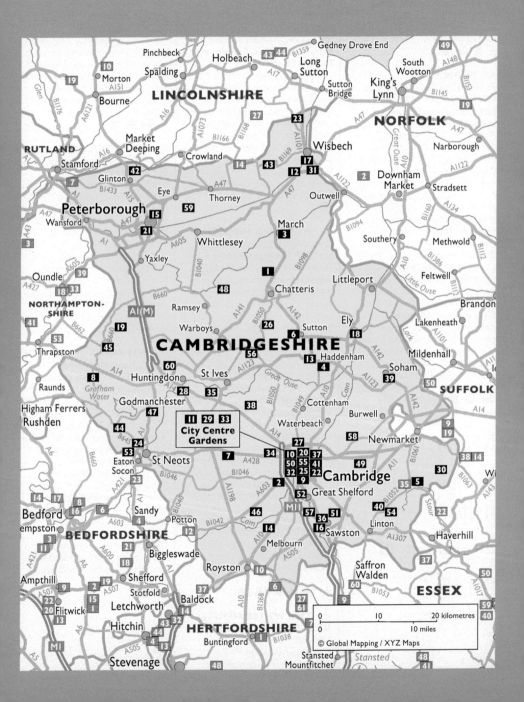

The low-lying flat lands of Cambridgeshire offer many diverse and interesting gardens.

The Cambridge University gardens are well worth a visit, and people interested in urban gardens can find plenty in the city of Cambridge - these smaller gardens are ideal for giving inspiration for back garden planting and design.

Peterborough has gardens showing an innovative approach to designing for smaller spaces. Ely has a delightful group of varied gardens in this historic Cathedral City.

The whole county embraces many delightful gardens, from former rectory gardens to very small urban gardens. There are many surprises waiting to be discovered in Cambridgeshire, and our generous garden owners invite you to come and take a closer look.

Volunteers

County Organiser
George Stevenson
01733 262698
chrisgeorge1a@aol.com

County Treasurer
Nicholas Kyberd
01954 200568
n.kyberd@ntlworld.com

Booklet Coordinator
Robert Marshall
01733 555978
robfmarshall@btinternet.com

Assistant County Organisers
Pam Bullivant
01353 667355
pbu1@hotmail.co.uk

Patsy Glazebrook
01799 541180
glazebro@doctors.org.uk

Angie Jones
01733 222367
janda.salix@gmail.com

Nicholas Kyberd
(as above)

Dulce Threlfall
01638 508470
dulce.quercus6065@btinternet.com

Annette White
01638 730876
annette323@btinternet.com

© Howard Rice

Left: 5 The Crescent, Impington Gardens

OPENING DATES

All entries subject to change. For latest information check www.ngs.org.uk

Extended openings are shown at the beginning of the month.

Map locator numbers are shown to the right of each garden name.

January

Robinson College
(Daily)   50

February
Snowdrop Festival

Robinson College
(Daily)   50

March

Robinson College
(Daily)   50
Sunday 26th
Kirtling Tower   30
NEW 2a Nine Chimneys
Lane   40

April

Robinson College
(Daily until Friday
21st)   50
Sunday 2nd
Barton Gardens   2
Netherhall Manor   39
Sunday 9th
Churchill College   10
Fitzwilliam College   20
Kirtling Tower   30
Trinity College,
Fellows' Garden   55
Sunday 23rd
◆ Docwra's Manor   14
Sunday 30th
Chaucer Road Gardens   9
Leckhampton   32
Lucy Cavendish College   33
Netherhall Manor   39

May

Monday 1st
Chaucer Road Gardens   9
Sunday 14th
◆ Ferrar House   19
Saturday 20th
Bell Gables   4
NEW High Bank
Cottage   23
Sunday 21st
Bell Gables   4

© Fiona Lea

Docwra's Manor

NEW High Bank Cottage 23

90th Anniversary Weekend

Saturday 27th
109 High Street   24
The Old Vicarage   44
Sunday 28th
Cambourne Gardens   7
College Farm   13
289 Dogsthorpe Road   15
Duxford Gardens   16
Island Hall   28
Willow Holt   59
Monday 29th
289 Dogsthorpe Road   15
NEW Northborough
Gardens   42
Willow Holt   59

June

Robinson College
(Every Monday to
Friday from
Monday 19th)   50
Sunday 4th
Barton Gardens   2
The Burystead   6
Catworth, Molesworth &
Brington Gardens   8
Madingley Hall   34
Saturday 10th
Clear View   12
Staploe Gardens   53
Sunday 11th
Clear View   12
Ely Gardens   18
Highsett Cambridge   25
Mary Challis Garden   36
The Old Rectory   43
Stapleford Gardens   52
Staploe Gardens   53
Sunday 18th
NEW Alderley   1
Streetly End & West
Wickham Gardens   54
Whittlesford Gardens   57
Saturday 24th
45 Beaver Lodge   3
NEW Impington
Gardens   27
Robinson College   50
Sunday 25th
45 Beaver Lodge   3

NEW Impington Gardens 27
Kirtling Tower   30
NEW 2a Nine
Chimneys Lane   40
Orwell Gardens   46
Ramsey Forty Foot   48

July

Robinson College
(Daily)   50
Saturday 1st
Burrough Green
Gardens   5
10 Gwydir Street   22
Norfolk Terrace Garden 41
Sunday 2nd
Burrough Green
Gardens   5
Clare College Fellows'
Garden   11
10 Gwydir Street   22
55 Milton Road   37
Norfolk Terrace
Garden   41
Sawston Gardens   51
Wytchwood   60
Saturday 15th
Twin Tarns   56
Sunday 16th
◆ Ferrar House   19
King's College Fellows'
Garden   29
Twin Tarns   56
Sunday 30th
NEW 5 Leach Close   31

August

Robinson College
(Daily)   50
Sunday 6th
◆ Elgood's Brewery
Gardens   17
Netherhall Manor   39
Robinson College   50
Sunday 13th
Netherhall Manor   39
Saturday 19th
45 Beaver Lodge   3
Sunday 20th
45 Beaver Lodge   3
Tuesday 29th
Robinson College   50

Reed Cottage

THE GARDENS

1 NEW ALDERLEY

Benwick Road, Doddington, March,
PE15 0TU. Jill Vaughan & John
Overvoorde. 1m W of Doddington
on Benwick Road (B1093). Use
entrance for Delfland Nurseries and
park in shop car park. Sun 18 June
(1.30-5.30). Adm £2.50, chd
free. Home-made teas.
¾ acre garden with areas
professionally designed and
replanted in 2012. Summer border
features grasses and perennials in
pastels and silver with burgundy
accents; courtyard contains plants
which will tolerate dry shade
including ferns. A woodland area has
informal paths which wind between
specimen trees. Organic kitchen
garden with vegetables, soft fruit and
small orchard. The Delfland Shop
will be open on the day with a wide
range of organic vegetable plugs
plus bedding and container plants
(not organic); nearly all are grown
on the nursery. Most of the garden
is level paving or grass. No disabled
WC. Assistance dogs welcome.

GROUP OPENING

2 BARTON GARDENS

High Street, Barton, Cambridge,
CB23 7BG. 3½m SW of Cambridge.
Barton is on A603 Cambridge to Sandy
Rd, ½m for J12 M11. Sun 2 Apr,
Sun 4 June (2-5). Combined adm
£5, chd free. Home-made teas
in Barton Church (April) Village
Hall (June).

NEW BRYGHT BARN, 48 HIGH STREET
Jenny Robson Platt.
Open on Sun 4 June

FARM COTTAGE
Dr R M Belbin.
Open on all dates

GLEBE HOUSE
David & Sue Rapley.
Open on Sun 4 June

114 HIGH STREET
Meta & Hugh Greenfield.
Open on all dates

31 NEW ROAD
Drs D & M Macdonald.
Open on Sun 4 June

THE SIX HOUSES
Perennial.
Open on all dates

Varied group of large and small
gardens reflecting different
approaches to gardening.
Farm Cottage: large landscaped
cottage garden with herbaceous
beds and themed woodland walk.
Glebe House is a 1 acre mature,
partly wooded and walled garden
with large (unfenced) duck pond.
Italiante style courtyard garden.
Landscaped secret garden with
gazebo. 114 High Street: small
cottage garden with an unusual
layout comprising several areas incl
vegetables, fruit and a secret garden.
31 New Road: large, wildlife friendly
cottage garden with a good show
of spring flowers, mature shrubs,
trees and a kitchen garden. The Six
Houses: recently renovated gardens,
incl winter and dry gardens, lovely
spring bulbs and a small wood.
Bryght Barn: a charming small
garden being developed by new
owner. The White Horse Inn (118
High Street) serves meals. Some
gardens have gravel paths.

3 45 BEAVER LODGE
Henson Road, March, PE15 8BA.
Mr & Mrs Maria & Paul
Nielsen Bom, 01354 656185,
beaverbom@gmail.com. *A141 to
Wisbech rd into March, turn L into
Westwood Ave, follow rd leading to
Henson Rd, turn R. Property opp
school playground.* Sat 24, Sun 25
June, Sat 19, Sun 20 Aug (11-4).
Adm £3, chd free. Home-made
teas. **Visits also by arrangement
June to Sept small groups
welcome.**
A delightful town garden divided
into several rooms. A pergola
leads to an ornamental pond with
koi carp, surrounded by borders
with a large variety of plants and
ornamental trees. Fern area with
ornamental waterfall. The whole
garden has an Oriental theme
with bonsais and statues. Also a
corner with a fountain that has a
Mediterranean feel. Large variety of
bonsai trees and acers of different
types have been added to a new
part of the garden. Featured in
Garden News, Fenland Advertiser
and Cambridgeshire Times.

4 BELL GABLES
Church Lane, Wilburton, Ely,
CB6 3RQ. Shona Mckay & William
Bertram. *Church Lane is off A1123
between Stretham & Haddenham
behind the parish church in
Wilburton.* Sat 20, Sun 21 May
(11-5). Adm £3.50, chd free.
Home-made teas in St Peter's
Church, opp garden 2 - 5pm.
Approx one acre of garden with a
large natural pond with moorhens,
grass snakes and other pond life. A
small walled garden and formal fruit
and flower parterre. Wheelchair
access - level drive but with gravel
finish. There is a concrete ramp
down to the lawn.

*Visit a garden and
support hospice
care in your local
community*

GROUP OPENING

5 BURROUGH GREEN GARDENS
Burrough Green, Newmarket,
CB8 9NH. *5m S of Newmarket.
Take B1061 out of Newmarket, &
Burrough Green is signed to L 1m
after Dullingham.* Sat 1, Sun 2 July
(1-6). Combined adm £5, chd
free. Home-made teas at Village
Hall.

ACORN HOUSE
Mr & Mrs David Swanney.

7 ELIZABETH WAY
Mr & Mrs Robert King.

NEW QUERCUS
Dulce Threlfall, 01638 508470,
dulce.quercus6065@btinternet.
com.
**Visits also by arrangement
Apr to Oct for groups of 10+**

New modern, contemporary and
evolving 1½ acre garden on clay
with 'English' planting, Quercus has
espaliered plums, roses, iris and
variety of screening shrubs in front.
To the rear a large rose garden leads
to 2 large mirrored mixed borders.
Arboretum, orchard, soft fruit,
vegetable and cutting gardens and
large greenhouse. 7 Elizabeth Way is
an Aladdin's Cave of plants, tucked
away in a corner of a conservation
village. Being small, the garden has
been interestingly designed to make
maximum use of space, with over
50 varieties of clematis, and many
varieties of heuchera. Also found
in the terraced borders are a huge
variety of herbaceous perennials
shrubs and other plants, which add
colour and interest throughout the
garden. Acorn House is an elegant
two-acre garden, only ten years
old, offering many areas of interest.
These include herbaceous borders,
a mini arboretum with many unusual
trees, a shady woodland walk,
an orchard, and a vegetable plot.
Seating throughout the garden.

---

6 THE BURYSTEAD
Bury Lane, Sutton, Ely, CB6 2BB.
Sarah Cleverdon & Stephen
Tebboth. *6m W of Ely. Drive through
Sutton towards Earith. Turn R, signed
'Sutton Gault' & 'Anchor Inn', Bury
Lane. Our house is 1st on L, approx
300 metres.* Sun 4 June (12-5).
Adm £3.50, chd free. Home-
made teas. Refreshments and
home-made cakes.
½ acre walled courtyard garden of
formal design, set against a backdrop
of a restored C16 thatched barn.
Orchard and sculpture at front of
house. Also a cottage garden and a
new vegetable plot.

GROUP OPENING

7 CAMBOURNE GARDENS
Great Cambourne, CB23 6AH.
*8m W of Cambridge on A428. From
A428: take Cambourne junction into
Great Cambourne. From B1198,
enter village at Lower Cambourne &
drive through to Great Cambourne.
Follow NGS signs via either route to
start at any garden.* Sun 28 May
(11-5). Combined adm £5.50,
chd free. Light refreshments.
Teas and cakes at 128
Greenhaze Lane.

14 GRANARY WAY
Mrs Jackie Hutchinson.

128 GREENHAZE LANE
Fran & John Panrucker.

22 JEAVONS LANE
Mr Sheppard.

5 MAYFIELD WAY
Debbie & Mike Perry.

14 MILLER WAY
Geoff Warmington.

43 MONKFIELD LANE
Tony & Penny Miles.

A unique and inspiring modern
group, all created from new build in
just a few years. This selection of six
demonstrates how imagination and
gardening skill can be combined in
a short time to create great effects
from unpromising and awkward
beginnings. The grouping includes
a garden inspired by the French
Riviera complete with a miniature

meadow, a foliage garden, and many other beautiful borders showing their owners' creativity and love of growing fine plants well. Cambourne is one of Cambridgeshire's newest communities, and this grouping showcases the happy, vibrant place it has become. No garden is more than 15 years old, and most are much younger. Featured on Cambridge TV and Cambridge News.

&. ☕

GROUP OPENING

8 CATWORTH, MOLESWORTH & BRINGTON GARDENS

Huntingdon, PE28 0PF. *10m W of Huntingdon. A14 W for Catworth, Molesworth & Brington exit at J16 onto B660.* **Sun 4 June (2-6). Combined adm £4, chd free. Home-made teas at Molesworth House and Yew Tree Cottage.**

32 HIGH STREET
Colin Small.

MOLESWORTH HOUSE
John Prentis.

YEW TREE COTTAGE
Christine & Don Eggleston.

3 varied gardens showing the best of planting, design and creativity. 32 High Street is a long narrow garden with many rare plants including ferns, herbaceous borders, woodland area and wildlife pond. Molesworth House is an old rectory garden with everything that you'd both expect and hope for, given its Victorian past. There are surprising corners to this traditional take on a happy and relaxed garden. Yew Tree Cottage, informal garden approx 1 acre, complements the C17 building (not open) and comprises flower beds, lawns, vegetable patch, boggy area, copses and orchard. Plants in pots and hanging baskets. Partial wheelchair access.

&. ✿ ☕

GROUP OPENING

9 CHAUCER ROAD GARDENS

Cambridge, CB2 7EB. *1m S of Cambridge. Off Trumpington Rd (A1309), nr Brooklands Ave junction. Parking available at MRC Psychology Dept on Chaucer Rd.* **Sun 30 Apr, Mon 1 May (2-5). Combined adm £6, chd free. Home-made teas at Upwater Lodge.**

NEW 11 CHAUCER ROAD
Mark & Jigs Hill.

16 CHAUCER ROAD
Mrs V Albutt.

UPWATER LODGE
Mr & Mrs George Pearson, 07890 080303, jmp@pearson.co.uk. **Visits also by arrangement Apr to Sept wine can be offered by arrangement.**

11 Chaucer Road is a ¾ acre Edwardian garden that has changed rapidly over the ensuing 110 yrs. A rock garden with pond and large weeping Japanese maple dates from about 1930. 16 Chaucer Road is a ½-acre garden, divided by arches and hedges into separate areas, each with its own character. Front rose garden. Unusual hawthorn and late summer borders. Blackberries and apple trees. Wildlife area with new sculpture. Waterproof footwear advised. Upwater Lodge is an Edwardian academic's house with 7acres of grounds. It has mature trees, fine lawns, old wisterias, and colourful borders. There is a small, pretty potager with vegetables and autumn fruits, and a well maintained grass tennis court. A network of paths through a wooded area lead down to a dyke, water meadows and a small flock of rare breed sheep. Enjoy a walk by the river and watch the punts go by. Buy home-made teas and sit in the garden or take them down to enjoy a lazy afternoon with ducks, geese, swans and heron on the riverbank. Cakes made with garden fruit where possible. Swings and climbing ropes. Stalls selling cards, prints and fabric crafts. Plant stall possible but please email to check. Some gravel areas and grassy paths with fairly gentle slopes.

&. ☕

Madingley Hall

10 CHURCHILL COLLEGE

Storey's Way, Cambridge, CB3 0DS. University of Cambridge, www.chu.cam.ac.uk. *1m from M11 J13. 1m NW of Cambridge city centre. Turn into Storeys Way from Madingley Rd (A1303), or from Huntingdon Rd (A1307). Parking on site.* Sun 9 Apr (2-5). Combined adm with Fitzwilliam College £5, chd free. Home-made teas.

42 acre site designed in 1960s for foliage and form, to provide year round interest in peaceful and relaxing surrounds with courtyards, large open spaces and specimen trees. 10m x 5m orchid house, herbaceous plantings. Beautiful grouping of Prunus Tai Haku (great white cherry) trees forming striking canopy and drifts of naturalised bulbs in grass around the site. The planting provides a setting for the impressive collection of modern sculpture. Orchid house, Sculptures. The greenhouse is restricted in size.
&♿ ☕ 🌷

11 CLARE COLLEGE FELLOWS' GARDEN

Trinity Lane, Cambridge, CB2 1TL. The Master & Fellows, www.clare.cam.ac.uk. *Central to city. From Queens Rd or city centre via Senate House Passage, Old Court & Clare Bridge.* Sun 2 July (2-5.30). Adm £4, chd free. Home-made teas. Tea; Coffee; Juice and Cakes.

2 acres. One of the most famous gardens on the Cambridge Backs. Herbaceous borders; sunken pond garden, fine specimen trees and tropical garden. Gravel paths.
♿ ☕ 🌷

12 CLEAR VIEW

Cross Lane, Wisbech St Mary, PE13 4TX. Margaret & Graham Rickard, 01945 410724, magsrick@hotmail.com. *3m SW of Wisbech. Approach village via Barton Rd from Wisbech. Leverington Common into Station Rd, or Sandbank & from Guyhirn. Yellow signs at most junctions.* Sat 10, Sun 11 June (10.30-5.30). Adm £4, chd free. Home-made teas. All cakes, jams, preserves

etc are home made. Visits also by arrangement May to July please telephone a week before your intended arrival. Small coaches welcome.

Approx 1½ acre with lake incorporating large wildlife area, and wildlife meadow. Secluded cottage garden with many old fashioned plants, herbaceous border, gravel garden with raised bed and pond. Allotments and small orchard. Plenty of secluded seating. Gravel paths in cottage garden are too narrow but it can be viewed from the picket fencing and the grass.
♿ ✿ 🚗 ☕ 🌷

13 COLLEGE FARM

Station Road, Haddenham, Ely, CB6 3XD. Sheila & Jeremy Waller, www.primaveragallery.co.uk. *From Stretham & Wilburton, at Xrds in Haddenham, turn R, past the church. Exactly at the bottom of the hill, turn L down narrow drive, with a mill wheel on R of the drive.* Sun 28 May (1-5). Adm £5, chd free.

40 acres around an intact Victorian farm. New walks, gallery and sculpture cattle yard. Further walks by ponds and through meadows. Roses, wild flowers, new water plants, foxgloves and new plantings of trees add colour and shape. Splendid fen views, lovely water features and ancient ridge and furrow pasture land with interesting wild flowers, original farm buildings and abundant wildlife. Amongst the farm buildings an outside gallery, and inside the house another gallery full of extraordinary paintings, art and craft. Wheelchair access is only possible around the garden near the house, but not through the gallery, farm, milking parlour and many of the walks.
♿ 🐎

14 ◆ DOCWRA'S MANOR

2 Meldreth Road, Shepreth, Royston, SG8 6PS. Mrs Faith Raven, 01763 260677, www.docwrasmanorgarden.co.uk. *8m S of Cambridge. ½m W of A10. Garden is opp the War Memorial in Shepreth. King's Cross-Cambridge train stop 5 min walk.* For NGS: Sun 23 Apr (2-5). Adm £5, chd free. Home-made teas. For other opening times and information,

please phone or visit garden website.

2½ acres of choice plants in a series of enclosed gardens. Tulips and Judas trees. Opened for the NGS for more than 40yrs. The garden is featured in great detail in a book published 2013 'The Gardens of England' edited by George Plumptre. Wheelchair access to most parts of the garden, gravel paths.
♿ ☕ 🌷

15 289 DOGSTHORPE ROAD

Peterborough, PE1 3PA. Michael & Julie Reid, www.facebook.com/AnArtistsGarden?ref=stream. *1m N of city centre. A47 Paston turn. Exit r'about South. Down Fulbridge rd to end & turn L into St Paul's Rd. Turn R at end down Dogsthorpe Rd. Garden 600 metres on R.* Evening opening Sun 28 May (5-8). Adm £6, chd free. Wine and nibbles. Mon 29 May (12-6). Adm £3.50, chd free. Home-made teas.

A 'peaceful' urban garden designed by Fine Artist, Julie Reid. Divided into rooms using layers and texture from brave use of trees, shrubs and year round perennial planting including ferns, bamboos and Acers. Subtle structural and sculptural additions including our new water features and Japanese inspired garden. Social and intimate seating areas allow guests and gardeners to relax and enjoy. Open Artists Studio and Fine Art Exhibition. 'Pop-up tea shop. Wine and nibbles incl in adm (Sun). Home-made teas, cakes and savouries available to buy (Mon). Nene Valley Living, Radio Cambridgeshire,.
✿ 🌷

GROUP OPENING

16 DUXFORD GARDENS

Mill Lane, Cambridge, CB22 4PT. *Entrance to Mill Lane is opposite the John Parleycorn PH. Temple Farmhouse is at end of lane.* Sun 28 May (2-6). Combined adm £5, chd free. Home-made teas at United Reformed Church, Chapel Street a short walk from all the open gardens. WC.

2 THE BIGGEN
Mr & Mrs Derek & Judy Chamberlain.

6 THE BIGGEN
Mrs Bettye Reynolds.

BUSTLERS COTTAGE
John & Jenny Marks.

31 ST PETER'S STREET
Mr David Baker.

TEMPLE FARMHOUSE
Peter & Jenny Shaw.

These gardens are an extremely interesting mix, ranging from very large to very small. The gardens are all examples of what can be easily grown in Duxford. 2 The Biggen created in 9 yrs from an overgrown plot of greenery, has mixed borders, small stumpery and alpine area. 6 The Biggen a ¼ acre plants women's garden with unusual perennials, charming places to sit and enjoy. 31 St Peter's Street the garden slopes down to a rockery and circular stone steps leading to a secluded patio. Bustlers Cottage is a traditional Cambridgeshire cottage garden extending over 1 acre with old roses, herbaceous borders, vegetables and an old fig tree. Temple Farmhouse the R Cam flows gently through the 3½ acre rural garden with majestic trees, informal flowerbeds, vegetable garden enclosed with mature box hedges.

✿ ☕

17 ◆ ELGOOD'S BREWERY GARDENS
North Brink, Wisbech, PE13 1LW. Elgood & Sons Ltd, 01945 583160, info@elgoods-brewery.co.uk, www.elgoods-brewery.co.uk. *1m W of town centre. Leave A47 towards Wisbech Centre. Cross river to North Brink. Follow river & brown signs to brewery & car park beyond.* For NGS: Sun 6 Aug (11.30-4.30). Adm £4, chd free. Light refreshments. For other opening times and information, please phone, email or visit garden website.
Approx 4 acres of peaceful garden featuring 250 yr old specimen trees providing a framework to lawns, lake, rockery, herb garden, dipping pool and maze. Wheelchair access to Visitor Centre and most areas of the garden.

& ✿ 🚗 ☕

GROUP OPENING

18 ELY GARDENS
Chapel Street, Ely, CB6 1AD. *14m N of Cambridge. Parking at Barton Rd car park, Tower Road or the Grange Council Offices. (Also, disabled parking only at Deanery.). Map given at first garden visited.* Sun 11 June (2-6). Combined adm £5, chd free. Cream teas at 42 Cambridge Road.

THE BISHOPS HOUSE
The Bishop of Ely.

42 CAMBRIDGE ROAD
Mr & Mrs J & C Switsur.

12 & 26 CHAPEL STREET
Ken & Linda Ellis, www.simplygardeningofely.co.uk.

THE DEANERY
Very Rev & Mrs Mark Bonney.

50A PRICKWILLOW ROAD
Ms Hunter.

A delightful and varied group of gardens in an historic Cathedral city. The Bishop's house and the Deanery are monastic buildings. The Bishop's garden adjoins Ely Cathedral and has mixed planting with a formal rose garden, wisteria and more. The Deanery, with lawns, an orchard, lavender hedge, developing borders and shrubs, has views over the Dean's meadow and towards the Cathedral. 12 & 26 Chapel Street: the former a small town garden reflecting the owners eclectic outlook, from alpine to herbaceous, all linked with a model railway! The latter a green oasis of peace in the city. 42 Cambridge Road is a secluded town garden with interesting herbaceous borders, roses, shrubs and trees. A vegetable garden with raised beds. 50 A Prickwillow Rd is a small walled garden with the emphasis on texture and foliage. Wheelchair access to areas of most gardens.

& ✿ ☕

FENLEIGH
See Lincolnshire

19 ◆ FERRAR HOUSE
Little Gidding, Huntingdon, PE28 5RJ. Mrs Susan Capp, 01832 293383, info@ferrarhouse.co.uk, www.ferrarhouse.co.uk. *Take Mill Rd from Great Gidding (turn at Fox & Hounds) then after 1m turn R down single track lane. Car Park at Ferrar House.* For NGS: Sun 14 May, Sun 16 July (10-5). Adm £3, chd free. Cream teas. For other opening times and information, please phone, email or visit garden website.
A peaceful garden of a Retreat House with beautiful uninterrupted views across meadows and farm land. Adjacent to the historic Church of St John's it was here that a small religious community was formed in the C17. The poet T. S. Eliot visited in 1936 and it inspired the 4th of his Quartets named Little Gidding. Lawn and walled flower beds with a walled vegetable garden. WC accessible at Ferrar House.

& 🛏 ☕

20 FITZWILLIAM COLLEGE
Storey's Way, Cambridge, CB3 0DG. Master & Fellows, www.fitz.cam.ac.uk. *1m NW of Cambridge city centre. Turn into Storey's Way from Madingley Rd (A1303) or from Huntingdon Rd (A1307). Free parking on site.* Sun 9 Apr (2-5). Combined adm with Churchill College £5, chd free. On-site cafe for drinks and snacks.
Traditional topiary, borders, woodland walk, lawns from the Edwardian period and specimen trees are complemented by modern planting and wild meadow. The avenue of limes, underplanted with spring bulbs, leads to The Grove, the 1813 house once belonging to the Darwin Family (not open). Some ramped pathways.

& ✿ ☕

21 39 FOSTER ROAD

Campaign Ave, Sugar Way, Woodston, PE2 9RS. Robert Marshall & Richard Handscombe, 01733 555978, robfmarshall@btinternet.com. *1m SW of Peterborough City Centre. A605 Oundle Rd, at T.L. turn N into Sugar Way. Cross 1st r'bout, L at 2nd r'bout to Campaign Ave. R at next r'bout on Campaign Ave. 2nd R to Foster Rd. Continue until very end. L into cul-de-sac.* **Visits by arrangement Feb to Sept weekends & weekdays possible, groups very welcome. Adm incl tea/coffee/biscuits (cake for groups). Adm £4, chd free. Light refreshments in garden pergola or indoor lounge, weather depending.**

Plantsman's garden in compact, new estate plot. Mixed borders; woodland/shade; 'vestibule' garden; exotics and ferns; espaliered fruit; pergola; patio; pond; parterre; many pots; octagonal greenhouse; seating and sculpture. Uncommon snowdrops, over 250 hostas, plus daphnes, acers and other choice/ unusual cultivars. Trees and hedges create enclosure and intimacy. 4 x British Shorthair cats. Compact 'town garden' conceals many design ideas to maximise planting - without grass to cut. See how trees (x12) and hedges can be used in a small garden. Large collection, approaching 250 cultivars, of Hostas. Uncommon and some very rare snowdrops. Featured in Mail on Saturday, Garden News, Modern Gardens. All viewings accompanied by garden owner(s). Main garden and WC accessible by wheelchair.

🚻 ✿ 🚪 ☕

22 10 GWYDIR STREET

Cambridge, CB1 2LL. Mrs Rosemary Catling. *A603 East Rd, R into St Matthews St, L into Norfolk Terrace then R at junction with Gwydir St.* **Sat 1, Sun 2 July (11-5). Combined adm with Norfolk Terrace Garden £4, chd free. Light refreshments at Norfolk Terrace.**

L shaped town garden, paved with some raised beds. The formal structure is informally planted with perennials, shrubs and small trees. Many in pots. There is a sitting area under a mature fig tree and small pond. An artist's garden with attention to form and colour combination. Some artwork also for sale. Some unusual plants and shrubs. Access for small wheelchair down narrow side passage.

🚻 ✿ ☕

23 NEW HIGH BANK COTTAGE

Kirkgate, Tydd St. Giles, Wisbech, PE13 5NE. Mrs F Savill. *Heading from Wisbech, North Cambs. B1101 take turn signed Tydd St Giles. Parking at Tydd St Giles golf & country club, a few minutes walk from the garden. www.pure-leisure.co.uk/parks/tydd-st-giles/overview/.* **Sat 20, Sun 21 May (10.30-4). Adm £3.50, chd £1.50. Home-made teas.**

The garden is a tranquil oasis from the hurry of life. A cottage garden, mainly, but has many mature trees and shrubs. It is seperated into different areas with seating so that the views of the garden can be appreciated. Two ponds, one of which has fish. River bank with areas for wildlife, and, also an allotment. There will be coffee/tea and homemade cakes and biscuits available to purchase. Plants and garden related craft items, homemade cards and craft items. There are gravelled areas, and some steps.

✿ ☕

24 109 HIGH STREET

Hail Weston, PE19 5JS. Dawn Isaac, www.dawn-isaac.com. *1m W of St Neots. Take 1st R signed Hail Weston & follow High St round. 109 is opp church & village hall.* **Sat 27 May (1-5). Combined adm with The Old Vicarage £3, chd free. Home-made teas.**

Set in 1/3 acre, this space has been designed to show that a practical family garden can still be beautiful. There is a large lawn with a sunken trampoline surrounded by mixed borders, ornamental vegetable and cutting garden, clematis-covered gazebo dining space, teenager-friendly area with fire pit and mini beach plus garden house.

🐑 🅳 ☕

GROUP OPENING

25 HIGHSETT CAMBRIDGE

Cambridge, CB2 1NZ. 40, 49, 50, 53, 59, 70, 73, 82 & 85. *Centre of Cambridge. Via Station Rd, Tenison Rd, 1st L Tenison Ave, entrance ahead. SatNav CB1 2DX.* **Sun 11 June (2-5.30). Combined adm £5, chd free. Home-made teas at 82 & 83 Highsett.**

9 delightful town gardens within Central Cambridge. Set in large communal grounds with fine specimen trees and lawns. A haven for children and wildlife. Architect Eric Lyons planned the whole estate in the late 1950's with a mixture of flats, small houses and large town houses, the very ethos of tranquil living space for all generations. Several of the Open Gardens have been skilfully modernised by garden designers.

🚻 ☕

26 HORSESHOE FARM

Chatteris Road, Somersham, Huntingdon, PE28 3DR. Neil & Claire Callan, 01354 693546, nccallan@yahoo.co.uk. *9m NE of St Ives, Cambs. Easy access from the A14. Situated on E side of B1050, 4m N of Somersham Village. Parking for 8 cars in the drive.* **Visits by arrangement May to July groups up to 20. Adm £4, chd free. Home-made teas.**

This 3/4 acre plant-lovers' garden has a large pond with summer-house and decking, bog garden, alpine troughs, mixed rainbow island beds with over 25 varieties of bearded irises, water features, a small hazel woodland area, wildlife meadow, secret corners and a lookout tower for wide fenland views and bird watching. Featured in WI Life and Amateur Gardening magazines.

✿ 🚗 ☕

GROUP OPENING

27 NEW IMPINGTON GARDENS
Cambridge, CB24 9NU.
www.impingtonmill.org. *Just over 2m N of Cambridge. Off A14 at J32. B1049 to Histon. L into Cambridge Rd at T-lights, follow Cambridge Rd round to R, the Windmill is approx 400 yds on L.* Sat 24, Sun 25 June (11-6). Combined adm £6, chd free. Home-made teas at 5 The Crescent.

Alderley

NEW 3 COOKE WALK
Trevor & Philippa Smith.

NEW 5 THE CRESCENT
Joanne Bishop & David Pountney, 01223 232888, joanneeferg@yahoo.co.uk.

THE WINDMILL
Pippa & Steve Temple, 07775 446443, mill.impington@ntlworld.com, www.impingtonmill.org.
Visits also by arrangement Apr to Oct by arrangement.

A charming and contrasting group of gardens. The Windmill is a previously romantic wilderness of 1½ acres surrounding windmill, now filled with bulbs, perennial beds, pergolas, bog gardens, grass bed and herb bank, secret paths, wild areas, an amazing compost site! - and much more! 3 Cooke Walk is a little gem recently designed with a distinctive oriental character, making the best use of the limited space. Water features, swing seat, bridge and room spaces for both dining and relaxing. 5 The Crescent has large impact cottage-style herbaceous borders that wrap around the house. Interest throughout the year, herbs, unusual perennials and in particular plants for dry sun/shade. Back garden designed to create a 'wow' factor in mid- summer borders. The Windmill - open for viewing. Featured in Daily Mail - local press and radio. some paths gravel - but access otherwise pushable. Guide dogs only welcome.

28 ISLAND HALL
Godmanchester, PE29 2BA. Mr Christopher & Lady Linda Vane Percy, www.islandhall.com. *1m S of Huntingdon (A1). 15m NW of Cambridge (A14). In centre of Godmanchester next to free car park.* Sun 28 May (11-4.30). Adm £4, chd free. Home-made teas. 3-acre grounds. Tranquil riverside setting with mature trees. Chinese bridge over Saxon mill race to embowered island with wild flowers. Garden restored in 1983 to mid C18 formal design, with box hedging, clipped hornbeams, parterres, topiary, good vistas over borrowed landscape and C18 wrought iron and stone urns. The ornamental island has been replanted with Princeton elms (ulmus americana). Mid C18 mansion (not open).

29 KING'S COLLEGE FELLOWS' GARDEN
Queen's Road, Cambridge, CB2 1ST. Provost & Scholars of King's College. *In Cambridge, the Backs. Entry by gate at junction of Queen's Rd & West Rd. Parking at Lion Yard 10mins walk, or some pay & display places in West Rd & Queen's Rd.* Sun 16 July (2-6). Adm £3.50, chd free. Cream teas.
Fine example of a Victorian garden with rare specimen trees. With a small woodland walk and a kitchen/allotment garden created in 2011 and 1 new rose pergola and herbaceous border created in 2013. Gravel paths.

30 KIRTLING TOWER
Newmarket Road, Kirtling, Newmarket, CB8 9PA. The Lord & Lady Fairhaven. *6m SE of Newmarket. From Newmarket head towards village of Saxon Street, through village to Kirtling, turn L at war memorial, signed to Upend, entrance is signed on the L.* Sun 26 Mar, Sun 9 Apr, Sun 25 June (11-4). Adm £5, chd free. Light refreshments at the Church. Selection of hot & cold food, sandwiches & cakes, tea & coffee.
Surrounded by a moat, formal gardens and parkland. In the spring swathes of daffodils, narcissi, crocus, muscari, chionodoxa and tulips. Closer to the house vast lawn areas, Secret and Cutting Gardens. In the summer the Walled Garden has superb herbaceous borders with anthemis, hemerocalis, geraniums and delphiniums. The Victorian Garden is filled with peonies. Views of surrounding countryside. Display of stonemasonry from Lady Fairhaven's stone yard. Collection of Classic Cars on display. Plants and crafts on sale. Live music in the walled garden. Hot and cold food for sale in the church. Many of the paths and routes around the garden are grass - they are accessible by wheelchairs, but can be hard work if wet.

31 [NEW] 5 LEACH CLOSE

Wisbech, PE13 2QQ. Alan & Sandra Wheeldon. *Weasenham Lane runs between Cromwell Rd B198 & Churchill Rd B1101. Leach Close is down New Drove on L. Please Park in New Drove & walk into Leach Close, follow signs and enter through the gate.* Sun 30 July (10-4). Adm £2.50, chd free. Home-made teas.

Garden contains unusual mix of shrubs, perennials, summer bedding and some exotics. Heavy use of pots to extend garden onto patio. Many interesting statues and garden features. Separate vegetable garden with distinct beds for each type of produce. Two greenhouses with tomatoes, cucumbers and exotics. Several ornamental and fruit trees. Several places to sit and enjoy the view. Featured in Wisbech Standard and Citizen.

🐕 ✿ ☕

32 LECKHAMPTON

37 Grange Road, Cambridge, CB3 9BJ. Corpus Christi College. *Runs N to S between Madingley Rd (A1303) & A603. Entrance opp Selwyn College. No parking available on site.* Sun 30 Apr (2-6). Adm £4, chd free. Home-made teas.

10 acres comprising formal lawns and extensive wild gardens, featuring walkways and tree-lined avenues, fine specimen trees under-planted with spring bulbs, cowslips, anemones, fritillaries and a large area of lupins. Gravel and grass paths.

♿ ☕

Macmillan and the National Garden Scheme, partners for more than 30 years

33 LUCY CAVENDISH COLLEGE

Lady Margaret Road, Cambridge, CB3 0BU. Lucy Cavendish College. *1m NW of Gt St Mary. College situated on corner of Lady Margaret Rd & Madingley Rd (A1303). Entrance off Lady Margaret Rd.* Sun 30 Apr (2-5). Adm £3.50, chd free.

The gardens of 4 late Victorian houses have been combined and developed over past 25yrs into an informal 3 acre garden. Fine mature trees shade densely planted borders. An Anglo Saxon herb garden is situated in one corner. The garden provides a rich wildlife habitat.

♿

34 MADINGLEY HALL

Cambridge, CB23 8AQ. University of Cambridge, 01223 746222, reservations@madingleyhall.co.uk, www.madingleyhall.co.uk. *4m W of Cambridge. 1m from M11 J13.* Sun 4 June (2.30-5.30). Adm £5, chd free. Home-made teas at St Mary Magdalene Church adjacent to Madingley Hall Drive.

C16 Hall (not open) set in 8 acres of attractive grounds landscaped by Capability Brown. Features incl landscaped walled garden with hazel walk, alpine bed, medicinal border and rose pergola. Meadow, topiary, mature trees and wide variety of hardy plants. St Mary Magdalene Church open throughout the event. Featured on BBC Look East & Cambridge TV.

✿ 🚌 ☕

35 ◆ THE MANOR, HEMINGFORD GREY

Hemingford Grey, PE28 9BN. Mrs D S Boston, 01480 463134, diana_boston@hotmail.com, www.greenknowe.co.uk. *4m E of Huntingdon. Off A14. Entrance to garden by small gate off river towpath. Limited parking on verge halfway up drive, parking near house for disabled. Otherwise park in village.* For opening times and information, please phone, email or visit garden website.

Garden designed and planted by author Lucy Boston, surrounds

C12 manor house on which Green Knowe books based (house open by appt). 3 acre 'cottage' garden with topiary; snowdrops, old roses, extensive collection of irises incl Dykes Medal winners and Cedric Morris varieties, herbaceous borders with mainly scented plants. Meadow with mown paths. Enclosed by river, moat and wilderness. Late May splendid show of Irises followed by the old roses. Care is taken with the planting to start the year with a large variety of snowdrops and to extend the flowering season right through to the first frosts. The garden is interesting even in winter with the topiary. Gravel paths but wheelchairs are encouraged to go on the lawns.

♿ ✿ ☕

36 MARY CHALLIS GARDEN

High Street, Sawston, Cambridge, CB22 3BG. A M Challis Trust Ltd. *7m SE of Cambridge. Entrance via lane between 60 High St & 66 High St (Billsons Opticians).* Sun 11 June (2-6). Adm £4, chd free. Home-made teas.

Given to Sawston in 2006 this 2 acre garden is being restored by volunteers: Pond with jetty, formal flower garden, pretty shaded pathway, vegetable beds with vine house, meadow and woodland, with concern for the flora and fauna – and the village children. Featured in the Cambridge Magazine (Cambridge Newspapers). Paths and lawns should be wheelchair accessible from car-park.

♿ 🐕 ✿ ☕

37 55 MILTON ROAD

Cambridge, CB4 1XA. Richard & Pauline Freeman. *No 55 lies approx halfway between Gilbert Rd & Ascham Rd.* Sun 2 July (2-6). Adm £3, chd free.

Our garden is divided into 2 main areas separated by a beech hedge. One has a lawn surrounded by herbaceous and shrub beds, a small vegetable and cutting area and a shady wildlife area. The other consists of 4 large beds and a long border filled with shrubs and herbaceous plants divided by gravel paths. We aim for colour and interest all yr round, each of us managing one half of the garden. Shallow steps in several areas.

🐄

38 5 MOAT WAY
Swavesey, CB24 4TR. Mr & Mrs N Kyberd, 01954 200568, n.kyberd@ntlworld.com. *Off A14, 2m beyond Bar Hill. Look for School Lane/Fen Drayton Rd, at mini r'about turn into Moat Way, no.5 is approx 100 metres on L. Visits by arrangement June to Aug. Adm £3, chd free.*
Colourful garden filled with collection of trees, shrubs and perennials. Large patio area displaying many specimen foliage plants in planters, incl pines, hostas and acers.

39 NETHERHALL MANOR
Tanners Lane, Soham, CB7 5AB. Timothy Clark, 01353 720269. *6m Ely, 6m Newmarket. Enter Soham from Newmarket, Tanners Lane 2nd R 100yds after cemetery. Enter Soham from Ely, Tanners Lane 2nd L after War Memorial. Sun 2, Sun 30 Apr, Sun 6, Sun 13 Aug (2-5). Adm £3, chd free. Visits also by arrangement Mar to Aug (March, early May, August.).*
An elegant garden 'touched with antiquity' Good Gardens Guide. An unusual garden appealing to those with an historical interest in the individual collections of genera and plant groups: March – old primroses, daffodils and Victorian double flowered hyacinths. May – old English tulips. Crown Imperials. Aug – Victorian pelargonium, heliotrope, calceolaria, dahlias. Author of Margery Fish's Country Gardening and Mary McMurtrie's Country Garden Flowers. Historic Plants 1500-1900. The only bed of English tulips on display in the country. Author's books for sale. Flat garden with two optional steps. Lawns.

♿ ☕

40 NEW 2a NINE CHIMNEYS LANE
Balsham, CB21 4ES. Mr & Mrs Jim & Hilary Potter, 01223 891211, hppotter@btinternet.com. *In centre of Balsham just off High St. 3m E of A11, 12m S of Newmarket & 10m SE of Cambridge. Car parking in the High St or the Church car park. Sun 26 Mar, Sun 25 June (1-5). Adm £3, chd £1. Home-made teas. Visits also by arrangement Mar to Sept for groups of 8+*
Two acres of garden with spring bulbs, herbaceous border, raised vegetable beds, large duck pond, wild flower meadow, an orchard and modern sculptures. A Music Maze was planted in 1993 and has two types of trees in ½m of hedge; green yew (Taxus baccata) and golden yew (Taxus elegantissima) in the shape of a treble clef with viewing hill. Gravel garden, human sundial. Mature and new trees. Including the maze there are over 1500 trees in total and two paved areas form the shape of French horns incl an alpine garden. Hard paths around formal garden area. Limited wheelchair access to grassland areas. Fine in dry weather with a good driver.

♿ ☕

41 NORFOLK TERRACE GARDEN
38 Norfolk Terrace, Cambridge, CB1 2NG. John Tordoff & Maurice Reeve. *Central Cambridge. A603 East Rd turn R into St Matthews St to Norfolk St, L into Blossom St & Norfolk Terrace is at the end. Sat 1, Sun 2 July (11-5). Combined adm with 10 Gwydir Street £4, chd free. Light refreshments.*
A small, paved courtyard garden in Moroccan style. Masses of colour in raised beds and pots, backed by oriental arches. An ornamental pool done in patterned tiles offers the soothing splash of water. The owners' previous, London garden, was named by BBC Gardeners' World as 'Best Small Garden in Britain'. There will also be a displays of recent paintings by John Tordoff and handmade books by Maurice Reeve.

☕

GROUP OPENING

42 NEW NORTHBOROUGH GARDENS
Peterborough, PE6 9BN. *From A15, take B1162 to Northborough, then 1st R into Lincoln Rd, then L into Church St by Packhorse PH. Parking at Northborough School. Mon 29 May (1-5). Combined adm £4, chd free. Home-made teas in church next door.*

> NEW **11 CHURCH STREET**
> Clare & John Strak.
> NEW **9 CHURCH STREET**
> Gillian Hazlerigg.

Cottage garden with great views of the C12 church. Vegetables, fruit trees, chickens, borders and lawn, And a mature family garden of the old vicarage with intimate views of Northborough church. Lawns, borders, vegetables, herbs and fruit trees. Plenty of places to sit and contemplate. Accessible with a good pusher - access via gravel and lawns.

🌼 ☕

43 THE OLD RECTORY
312 Main Road, Parson Drove, Wisbech, PE13 4LF. Helen Roberts. *SW of Wisbech. From Peterborough on A47 follow signs to Parson Drove L after Thorney Toll. From Wisbech follow the B1166 through Levrington Common. Sun 11 June (11-4). Adm £4, chd free. Home-made teas.*
Walled Georgian cottage garden of 1 acre, opening into wild flower meadow and paddocks. Long herbaceous border, 2 ponds and unusual weeping ash tree. Terraced areas and outdoor kitchen! No hills but lovely open Fen views . New for 2017 bridge over wildlife dyke (Monet!) and par3 golf hole come and have a putt!

♿ 🌼 ☕

44 THE OLD VICARAGE

Causeway, Great Staughton, St Neots, PE19 5BF. Mr & Mrs Richard Edmunds, 01480 860397, elizabeth.edmunds4@btinternet.com. *5m off A1, 8m from St Neots. Take the B645 to Great Staughton.* Sat 27 May (2-5.30). Combined adm with 109 High Street £3, chd free. Home-made teas in the kitchen or the garden by summer houses. A nice place to have a picnic. Visits also by arrangement Apr to Oct groups of 10+.

A good Old Vicarage garden, redesigned in 2008/9 to enhance original plan. A Natural Swimming Pond which has pretty rockery planting with ferns and a man made waterway running into it over rocks. Also, a Wendy house on a platform with swings and slide off it. natural swimming pond, great garden for children and nice layout. Some gravel paths easily negotiable by wheelchair.

&. 🐄 ✿ 🚗 ☕

109 High Street

45 OLD WESTON GARDEN FARM

High Street, Old Weston, Huntingdon, PE28 5LA. Sylvia & John Younger, 07814 449799, owgardenfarm@hotmail.co.uk, www.oldwestongardenfarm.weebly.com. *Between Huntingdon and Oundle. Coming from Old Weston Village, with PH on R take next R into High St (a country rd), go past the chicken farm on R, we are within 500 meters.* Sun 10 Sept (1-4.30). Adm £4, chd free. Home-made teas. Visits also by arrangement.

This 9 acre smallholding offers plenty of interest. The 2 acre Kitchen Garden has been laid out in an intricate 'Potager' design mixing flowers for cutting (available as 'Pick Your Own') and companion planting among the wide range of fruit, vegetables and herbs. Hens range freely in the orchard, turkeys and geese are raised for Christmas along with rare-breed pigs. Grass paths throughout which can be uneven and bumpy for wheelchairs.

✿ ☕

GROUP OPENING

46 ORWELL GARDENS

Orwell, Royston, SG8 5QN. *8m SW of Cambridge. Meadowbank 34 High Street is between the village hall & thatched wall. For 57 Cakebreade Cottage, Town Green Road, park at recreation ground & walk up gravel drive opp.* Sun 25 June (2-5). Combined adm £4, chd free. Home-made teas.

CAKEBREADE COTTAGE
Mrs Verity Tilleard-Haines, 01223 208605 or 07805 857550, verity_haines@yahoo.com.
🛏

MEADOWBANK
Sue and Paddy Ward, 01223 208852 or 07969554069, Sue.paddy@btinternet.com. Visits also by arrangement June & July.

Two very different country gardens. Cakebreade Cottage C16 is a small intimate cottage garden on an old orchard footprint, and is a charming informal organic secluded garden planted mostly within the last three years. Containing a large range of herbaceous plants in soft colours. Climbing roses, fruit trees, herbs and a small meadow area surrounded by some mature trees. Meadowbank is a large 2 acre garden with lovely views across the fields, and has been mostly replanted within the last 6 years on a mature site. Rose garden, herbaceous borders and herb garden, vegetable patch, extensive wild flower meadow, stream with bog plants, and a newly planted grove of trees. Art studio open at Cakebreade Cottage with art work for sale. Cakebreade Cottage uneven lawn area, side access. Meadowbank access for wheelchairs down the right side of the house.

&. ☕

47 23a PERRY ROAD

Buckden, St. Neots, PE19 5XG. David & Valerie Bunnage, 01480 810553, d.bunnage@btinternet.com. *5m S of Huntingdon on A1. From A1 Buckden r'about take B661, Perry Rd approx 300yds on L.* Visits by arrangement Apr to Oct. Adm £4, chd free.

Approx 1 acre garden consisting of many garden designs incl Japanese interlinked by gravel paths. Large selection of acers, pines, rare and unusual shrubs. Also interesting features, a quirky garden. Plantsmans garden for all seasons new wildlife pond with small stumpery and woodland plus small seaside garden with beach hut. WC. Coaches welcome.

🚗

GROUP OPENING

48 RAMSEY FORTY FOOT

Ramsey, PE26 2YA. *3m N of Ramsey. From Ramsey (B1096) travel through Ramsey Forty Foot, just before bridge over river, turn into Hollow Rd at The George PH and carry on for 300m.* Sun 25 June (2-6). Combined adm £3, chd free. Home-made teas.

THE ELMS
Mr R Shotbolt.

FIRST COTTAGE
Kevin Brown.

LAKE VIEW HOUSE
Sir John & Lady O'reilly.

THE WILLOWS
Jane & Andrew Sills.

Four interesting and contrasting gardens in the village of Ramsey Forty Foot. The Elms is a 1½ acre informal garden with ancient water-filled clay pits teeming with wildlife and backed by massive elms. Large collection of shrubs, perennials, bog and aquatic plants. Woodland and arid plantings. The Willows is a cottage garden with riverside location filled with old roses, herbaceous beds; shrubs, ferns, pond and vegetable garden. First Cottage is a rural cottage garden full of colour, with long herbaceous borders, shrub beds and terraces with a natural pond. A rockery hosts a miniature steam railway. Lake View House is a garden of mixed beds and borders with some specimen trees, running down to a lake. A good place to finish your visit with tea/coffee and cake, accompanied by gentle background music. Some wheelchair access.
& 🐕 🍵 ☕

49 NEW REED COTTAGE

Rectory Farm Road, Little Wilbraham, Cambridge, CB21 5LB. Mr Robert Turner, rj-turner@hotmail.co.uk. *5m S of Newmarket, 5m E of Cambridge. In centre of village on corner opp grass triangle.* Visits by arrangement Apr to July visit April to see

5000 tulips and spring bulbs. Visit July to see the garden in full flower. Adm £5, chd free. Light refreshments. Sandwiches, tea, coffee, wine..
A delightful traditional cottage garden with stunning borders of many mature herbaceous perennials. 5000 bulbs in spring, and full colour in summer. A garden pond adds to the enjoyment and brings wildlife benefits. A well stocked vegetable garden makes us 60% self efficient. A shaded area hosts ferns and hostas.
✿ ☕

50 ROBINSON COLLEGE

Grange Road, Cambridge, CB3 9AN. Warden and Fellows, www.robinson.cam.ac.uk/about-robinson/gardens/national-gardens-scheme. *Garden at main Robinson College site, report to Porters' Lodge. There is only on-street parking.* Every Mon to Fri 2 Jan to 21 Apr (10-4). Every Sat and Sun 7 Jan to 16 Apr (2-4). Every Mon to Fri 19 June to 11 Aug (10-4). Every Sat and Sun 24 June to 6 Aug (2-4). Every Mon to Fri 29 Aug to 29 Dec (10-4). Every Sat and Sun 2 Sept to 31 Dec (2-4). Adm £4, chd free.
10 original Edwardian gardens are linked to central wild woodland water garden focusing on Bin Brook with small lake at heart of site. This gives a feeling of park and informal woodland, while at the same time keeping the sense of older more formal gardens beyond. Central area has a wide lawn running down to the lake framed by many mature stately trees with much of the original planting intact. More recent planting incl herbaceous borders and commemorative trees. Please report to Porters' Lodge on arrival to pay for entry and guidebook. No picnics. Children must be accompanied at all times. NB from time to time some parts, or occasionally all, of Robinson College gardens may be closed for safety reasons involving work by contractors and our maintenance staff. Please report to Porters' Lodge on arrival for information. Ask at Porters' Lodge for wheelchair access.
& ☕

GROUP OPENING

51 SAWSTON GARDENS

Sawston, Cambridge, CB22 3HY. *5m SE of Cambridge. Halfway between Saffron Walden & Cambridge on A1301.* Sun 2 July (1-6). Combined adm £5, chd free. Cream teas at Sweet Tea cafe, High St.

BROOK HOUSE
Mr & Mrs Ian & Mia Devereux.

DRIFT HOUSE
Mr Alan & Mrs Jean Osborne.

11 MILL LANE
Tim & Rosie Phillips.

35 MILL LANE
Doreen Butler.

22 ST MARY'S ROAD
Ann & Mike Redshaw.

VINE COTTAGE
Dr & Mrs Tim Wreghitt.

6 varied gardens. Brook House has many lovely recently designed and planted features set in 1½ acres. One of the highlights is an impressive large walled garden. Drift House has ⅓ acre mature mixed planting, lawns, fish pond, kitchen garden and a cloud-pruned Juniper tree. 35 Mill Lane has colourful massed annual and perennial floral displays and fascinating water features. See immaculate lush lawns, roses, delightful mature mixed borders and a newly designed sun dappled secluded haven in the back garden at 11 Mill Lane. 22 St Mary's Road has views over SSSI meadows, wildlife friendly planting and colour-themed contemporary borders. Vine Cottage's large mature garden incorporates a secret Japanese courtyard. Many other features to be seen, something for everyone. Great value for £5. Enjoy a cream tea at 'Sweet Tea', or take up the discounts on offer for garden visitors at the Jade Fountain Chinese restaurant. With such a variety of gardens, wheelchair access is variable.
& 🐕 ✿ ☕

GROUP OPENING

52 STAPLEFORD GARDENS

Stapleford, Cambridge, CB22 5DG. *4m S of Cambridge on A1301. In London Rd next to Church St. Parking available on site.* Sun 11 June (2-6). Combined adm £5, chd free. Home-made teas at 59-61 London Road.

NEW **6 HAVERHILL ROAD**
Mr & Mrs John & Joan King.

59-61 LONDON ROAD
Dr & Mrs S Jones.

57 LONDON ROAD
Mrs M Spriggs.

5 PRIAMS WAY
Tony Smith.

Contrasting gardens showing a range of size, planting and atmosphere in this village just S of Cambridge. The London Road and Priam's Way gardens form an interlocking series of garden rooms incl herbaceous beds, kitchen garden, pit and summer houses with sculptures set around.
 ♿ 🍵

GROUP OPENING

53 STAPLOE GARDENS

Staploe, St. Neots, PE19 5JA. *Great North Rd in western part of St Neots. At r'about just N of the Coop store, exit westwards on Duloe Rd. Follow this under the A1, through the village of Duloe & on to Staploe.* Sat 10, Sun 11 June (1-5). Combined adm £4, chd free. Home-made teas.

FALLING WATER HOUSE
Caroline Kent.

OLD FARM COTTAGE
Sir Graham & Lady Fry.

Old Farm Cottage: flower garden surrounding thatched house (not open), with 3 acres of orchard, grassland, young woodland and pond maintained for wildlife.
Falling Water House: a mature woodland garden, partly reclaimed from farmland 10yrs ago, it is constructed around several century

old trees incl three Wellingtonia. Kitchen garden potager, courtyard and herbaceous borders, planted to attract bees and wildlife, through which meandering paths have created hidden vistas. Old Farm Cottage has rough ground and one steep slope.
♿ 🐕 ❀ 🍵

GROUP OPENING

54 STREETLY END & WEST WICKHAM GARDENS

West Wickham, CB21 4RP. *3m from Haverhill & 3m from Linton. From the A1307 between Linton & Haverhill. Turn N at Horseheath towards West Wickham, from Horseheath turn L at triangle of grass & trees, well signed.* Sun 18 June (11-5). Combined adm £4.50, chd free. Light refreshments at Clover Cottage.

CLOVER COTTAGE
Mr Paul & Mrs Shirley Shadford, 01223 893122, shirleyshadford@live.co.uk.
Visits also by arrangement in June adm incl tea or coffee & biscuits.

NEW **25 HIGH STREET**
Mrs Jane Scheuer.

New this year 25 High Street, West Wickham is a charming informal cottage garden to ramble and wander in with many routes through borders and pathways. Plants are allowed to self-seed and hybridise freely. Several interesting and unusual shrubs and herbaceous perennials from many continents. Find arches of roses and clematis at Clover Cottage in Streetly End and many varieties of hardy geraniums, and raised fruit and vegetable beds. Delightful pond and borders of English roses, climbers and herbaceous plants. Ferns and shade plants under an old tree, and views over open countryside from the summerhouse in the sunken white garden. NO ACCESS FOR WHEELCHAIRS, PUSHCHAIRS, WHEELED WALKERS OR DOGS TO GARDENS.
❀ 🚗 🍵

55 TRINITY COLLEGE, FELLOWS' GARDEN

Queens Road, Cambridge, CB3 9AQ. Master and Fellows' of Trinity College, www.trin.cam. ac.uk/about/gardens. *Short walk from city Centre. At the Northampton St/Madingley Rd end of Queens Rd close to Garrett Hostel Lane.* Sun 9 Apr (1-4). Adm £3.50, chd free. Home-made teas. Special dietary requirements are usually catered for.
Interesting historic garden of about 8 acres with impressive specimen trees, mixed borders, drifts of spring bulbs, and informal lawns with notable influences throughout from Fellows over the years. Across the gently flowing Bin Brook to Burrell's Field you will find some modern planting styles and plants nestled amongst the accommodation blocks in smaller intimate gardens. Members of the Gardening staff will be on hand to answer any queries. The teas and cakes are provided, and served, by a local Girl Guide unit. Wheelchair access - some gravel paths.
♿ ❀ 🍵

56 TWIN TARNS

6 Pinfold Lane, Somersham, PE28 3EQ. Michael & Frances Robinson, 01487 843376, mikerobinson987@btinternet.com. *Easy access from the A14. 4m NE of St Ives. Turn onto Church St. Pinfold Lane is next to the church. Please park on Church Street as access is narrow and limited.* Sat 15, Sun 16 July (1-5). Adm £4, chd free. Cream teas. **Visits also by arrangement May to Sept any size group.**
One-acre wildlife garden with formal borders, kitchen garden and ponds, large rockery, mini woodland, wild flower meadow (June/July), topiary, rose walk, willow sculptures. Character oak bridge and tree-house. Adjacent to C13 village church.
❀ 🍵

GROUP OPENING

57 WHITTLESFORD GARDENS

Whittlesford, CB22 4NR. *7m S of Cambridge. 1m NE of J10 M11 & A505. Parking nr church.* Sun 18 June (2-6). Combined adm £5, chd free. Home-made teas at the church.

THE GUILDHALL
Professor Peter Spufford.

5 PARSONAGE COURT
Mrs L Button.

11 SCOTTS GARDENS
Mr & Mrs M Walker.

15 WEST END
Mr & Mrs A Watson.

WHITBY COTTAGE
Mrs Laura Latham.

Find a variety of country, formal and modern gardens here. Returning this year 15 West End is a small garden with an ornamental pond and herbaceous borders. Whitby Cottage is a small claybat walled pretty cottage garden with an interesting water feature and large koi carp. Parsonage Court has an arched walkway, shrubs, raised fish pond and delightful seating area around an old tree. 11 Scotts Gardens is a small walled cottage garden with sunny and shady areas, and a variety of shrubs and large perennials. A knot garden, large fig tree and a lovely water feature can be found at the C16 timber framed Guildhall (house not open).
&♿ 🐕 ❀ ☕

58 WILD ROSE COTTAGE

Church Walk, Lode, Cambridge, CB25 9EX. Mrs Joy Martin, 01223 811132, joymartin123@btinternet.com. *From A14 take the rd towards Burwell turn L in to Lode & park on L. Walk straight on between cottages to the archway of Wild Rose Cottage.* Visits by arrangement Mar to Sept please email or phone in advance if possible. Groups welcome by arrangement. Adm £3.

A real cottage garden overflowing with plants. Gardens within gardens of abundant vegetation, roses climbing through trees, laburnum tunnel, a daffodil spiral which becomes a daisy spiral in the summer. Circular vegetable garden and wildlife pond. Described by one visitor as a garden to write poetry in! It is a truly wild and loved garden where flowers in the vegetable circle are not pulled up! Chickens ducks and dog, circular vegetable garden, wild life pond, and wild romantic garden! Lots of little path ways.

59 WILLOW HOLT

Willow Hall Lane, Thorney, PE6 0QN. Angie & Jonathan Jones. *4m E of Peterborough. From A47, between Eye & Thorney turn S into Willow Hall Lane. 1.6m on R. NOT in Thorney Village.* Sun 28, Mon 29 May (11-5). Adm £4, chd free. Home-made teas.

An intriguing natural garden developed over 24 years from impenetrable undergrowth on a base of rubbish. Hundreds of plants hide strange sculpted creatures alongside meandering paths. 2 acres with ponds, woodland and meadow. A garden to get lost in. 75% accessible by wheelchair users with a good pusher.
❀ ☕

60 WYTCHWOOD

7 Owl End, Great Stukeley, Huntingdon, PE28 4AQ. Mr David Cox. *2m N of Huntingdon on B1043. Parking available at Great Stukeley Village Hall in Owl End.* Sun 2 July (1.30-5.30). Adm £3.50, chd free. Home-made teas. Cream teas and home made cakes.

A 2 acre garden with borders of perennials, annuals and shrubs, lawns, fish pond and a larger wildlife pond. The garden includes 1 acre for wildlife with grasses set among rowan, birch, maple and field maple trees, foxgloves, ferns and bulbs. Roses are a special feature in June. Enjoy home made and cream teas, plenty of seats. Short gravel drive at the garden entrance.
♿ ❀ ☕

Elgood's Brewery Gardens

Your visit helps Marie Curie work night and day in people's homes

CHESHIRE & WIRRAL

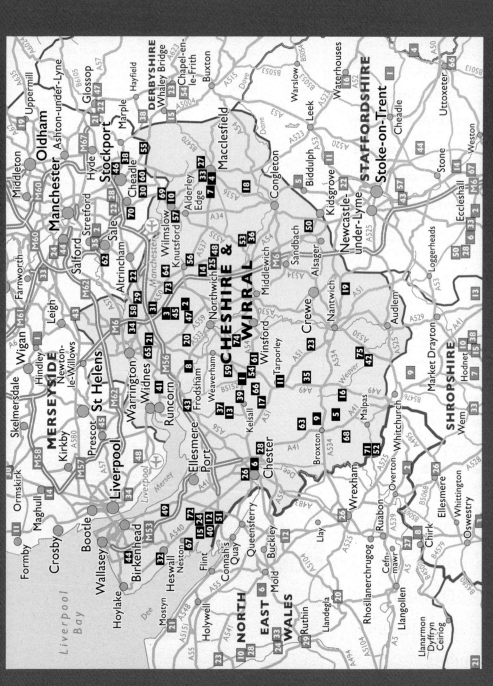

The area of Cheshire and Wirral comprises what are now the four administrative regions of West Cheshire and Chester, East Cheshire, Warrington and Wirral, together with gardens in the south of Greater Manchester, Trafford and Stockport.

The perception of the area is that of a fertile county dominated by the Cheshire Plain, but to the extreme west it enjoys a mild maritime climate, with gardens often sitting on sandstone and sandy soils and enjoying mildly acidic conditions.

A large sandstone ridge also rises out of the landscape, running some 30-odd miles from north to south. Many gardens grow ericaceous-loving plants, although in some areas, the slightly acidic soil is quite clayey. But the soil is rarely too extreme to prevent the growing of a wide range of plants, both woody and herbaceous.

As one travels east and the region rises up the foothills of the Pennine range, the seasons become somewhat harsher, with spring starting a few weeks later than in the coastal region.

As well as being home to one of the RHS's major shows, the region's gardens include two National Garden Scheme 'founder' gardens in Arley Hall and Peover Hall, as well as the University of Liverpool Botanic Garden at Ness.

Volunteers

County Organiser
John Hinde
0151 353 0032
john.hinde@maylands.com

County Treasurer
Andrew Collin
01513 393614
andrewcollin@btinternet.com

Social Media
Janet Bashforth
01925 349895
janbash43@sky.com

Graham Beech
01625 402946
gb.ngs@talktalk.net

Publicity
Linda Enderby
07949 496747
lmaenderby@outlook.com

Booklet Co-ordinator
John Hinde
(as above)

Assistant County Organisers
Sue Bryant
0161 928 3819
suewestlakebryant@btinternet.com

Jean Davies
01606 892383
mrsjeandavies@gmail.com

Sandra Fairclough
0151 342 4645
sandra.fairclough@tiscali.co.uk

Juliet Hill
01829 732804
t.hill573@btinternet.com

Romy Holmes
01829 732053
romy@bowmerecottage.co.uk

Left: Rowley House

OPENING DATES

All entries subject to change. For latest information check **www.ngs.org.uk**

Extended openings are shown at the beginning of the month.

Map locator numbers are shown to the right of each garden name.

February
Snowdrop Festival

Sunday 19th
West Drive Gardens   70

Saturday 25th
Briarfield   12

Sunday 26th
Briarfield   12
Bucklow Farm   14
◆ Dunham Massey   22

April

Saturday 15th
Bank House   5

Sunday 16th
All Fours Farm   2
Bank House   5

Saturday 22nd
Poulton Hall   49

Sunday 23rd
Briarfield   12
Long Acre   35
Poulton Hall   49

Sunday 30th
◆ Mount Pleasant   39

May

Monday 1st
All Fours Farm   2
Framley   24
◆ Mount Pleasant   39

Saturday 6th
Hathaway   27

Sunday 7th
Hathaway   27
Tirley Garth Gardens   66

Wednesday 10th
◆ Tatton Park   64

Thursday 11th
◆ Cholmondeley Castle
Garden   16

Sunday 14th
◆ Abbeywood Gardens   1
◆ Ness Botanic Gardens   40
◆ Stonyford Cottage   59
Tirley Garth Gardens   66

Friday 19th
10 Statham Avenue   58

Saturday 20th
Inglewood   32

Sunday 21st
◆ Dunham Massey   22
Inglewood   32
Sandymere   54
Tirley Garth Gardens   66

90th Anniversary Weekend

Sunday 28th
All Fours Farm   2
73 Hill Top Avenue   30
Manley Knoll   37
Rowley House   53
Tattenhall Hall   63

June

Saturday 3rd
Brooklands   13
Hatton House
Gardens   28
The Old Parsonage   45
◆ Peover Hall Gardens   48
Sun House   60
Sycamore Cottage   62

Sunday 4th
Brooklands   13
Free Green Farm   25
Hatton House
Gardens   28
◆ Norton Priory
Museum & Gardens   41
NEW 24 Old
Greasby Road   44
The Old Parsonage   45
◆ Peover Hall Gardens   48
Sun House   60
West Drive Gardens   70

Saturday 10th
Bank House   5
Bowmere Cottage   11

Sunday 11th
Bank House   5
Bowmere Cottage   11
Winterbottom House   73

Wednesday 14th
◆ Tatton Park   64

Friday 16th
Twin Gates   67

Saturday 17th
NEW 61 Birtles Road   7
The White Cottage   71

Sunday 18th
NEW 61 Birtles Road   7
Bucklow Farm   14
NEW 60 Kennedy
Avenue   33
Long Acre   35
The White Cottage   71

Wednesday 21st
Clemley House   17
Oakfield Villa   42
Wren's Nest   75

Friday 23rd
Winterbottom House   73

Saturday 24th
All Fours Farm   2
Ashmead   4
150 Barrel Well Hill   6
Willaston Grange   72

Sunday 25th
Ashmead   4
150 Barrel Well Hill   6
Burton Village Gardens   15
51 Garth Drive   26
Well House   69

Wednesday 28th
51 Garth Drive   26

July

Dingle Farm (Every Saturday and Sunday from Saturday 22nd)   21

Saturday 1st
◆ Bluebell Cottage
Gardens   8
Clemley House   17
The Rowans   52
10 Statham Avenue   58

Sunday 2nd
◆ Bluebell Cottage
Gardens   8
218 Marple Road   38
The Rowans   52
10 Statham Avenue   58

Thursday 6th
5 Cobbs Lane   19

Saturday 8th
NEW 181a Higher Lane   29
Rowley House   53

Sunday 9th
NEW 181a Higher Lane   29
Rowley House   53
68 South Oak Lane   57

Wednesday 12th
5 Cobbs Lane   19

Friday 14th
Somerford   56

Saturday 15th
Sunnyside Farm   61

Sunday 16th
Sunnyside Farm   61
Tattenhall Hall   63

Saturday 22nd
NEW Thorncar   65

Sunday 23rd
Somerford   56

Friday 28th
NEW The Homestead   31

Saturday 29th
The Firs   23

Sunday 30th
The Firs   23
68 South Oak Lane   57
◆ Stonyford Cottage   59

August

Saturday 5th
Clover Bank Organic
Farm   18
21 Scafell Close   55

Sunday 6th
◆ Arley Hall & Gardens   3
Clover Bank
Organic Farm   18
Cogshall Grange   20
Dingle Farm   21
73 Hill Top Avenue   30
21 Scafell Close   55

Saturday 12th
Laskey Farm   34

Sunday 13th
◆ Abbeywood Gardens   1
Laskey Farm   34

Sunday 20th
NEW 24 Old Greasby
Road   44

Your visit to a garden will help more people be cared for by a Parkinson's nurse

---

THE GARDENS

1 ◆ ABBEYWOOD GARDENS

Chester Road, Delamere, Northwich, CW8 2HS. The Rowlinson Family, 01606 889477, info@abbeywoodestate.co.uk, www.abbeywoodestate.co.uk. *11m E of Chester. On the A556 facing Delamere Church.* **For NGS: Sun 14 May, Sun 13 Aug (9-5). Adm £5, chd free. Restaurant in garden. For other opening times and information, please phone, email or visit garden website.**
Superb setting near Delamere Forest. Total area 45 acres incl mature woodland, new woodland and new arboretum all with connecting pathways. Approx 4½ acres of gardens surrounding large Edwardian House. Vegetable garden, exotic garden, chapel garden, pool garden, woodland garden, lawned area with beds.
ᴥ 🐴 ❀ 🚐 ☕

2 ALL FOURS FARM

Colliers Lane, Aston by Budworth, Northwich, CW9 6NF. Mr & Mrs Evans, 01565 733243. *M6 J19, take A556 towards Northwich. Turn immed R, past The Windmill PH. Turn R after approx 1m, follow rd, garden on L after approx 2m. We're happy to allow direct access for drop off & collection for those with limited mobility.* **Sun 16 Apr, Mon 1, Sun 28 May, Sat 24 June (10-4). Adm £5, chd free. Home-made teas. Visits also by arrangement parties of 16 or more by arrangement. Please contact Hazel.**
A traditional and well established country garden with a wide range of roses, hardy shrubs, bulbs, perennials and annuals. You will also find a small vegetable garden, pond and greenhouse as well as vintage machinery and original features from its days as a working farm. The majority of the garden is accessible by wheelchair.
ᴥ ❀ 🚐 ☕

3 ◆ ARLEY HALL & GARDENS

Northwich, CW9 6NA. Viscount Ashbrook, www.arleyhallandgardens.com. *10m from Warrington. Signed from J9 & 10 (M56) & J19 & 20 (M6) (20 min from Tatton Park, 40 min to Manchester). Please follow the brown tourist signs.* **For NGS: Sun 6 Aug (11-5). Adm £8, chd £3.50. All refreshments available. For other opening times and information, please visit garden website.**
One of Britain's finest gardens, Arley has been lovingly created by the same family over 550yrs and is famous for its double herbaceous border, thought to be the oldest in Europe, avenue of ilex columns, walled garden, pleached lime avenue and Victorian Rootree. A garden of great atmosphere, interest and vitality throughout the seasons.
ᴥ 🐴 ❀ 🚐 ☕

4 ASHMEAD

2 Bramhall Way, off Gritstone Drive, Macclesfield, SK10 3SH. Peter & Penelope McDermott, 01625 434200, penelope.mcdermott@pmsurveying.plus.com. *1m W of Macclesfield. Turn onto Pavilion Way, off Victoria Rd , then immediate L onto Gritstone Drive. Bramhall Way first on R.* **Sat 24, Sun 25 June (12-5). Adm £3.50, chd free. Home-made teas. Visits also by arrangement May to Sept groups 10 + or less by appointment, teas £2.50.**
⅛ acre suburban cottage garden, featuring plant packed mixed borders, rock gardens, kitchen garden, island beds, water feature, pond. The garden demonstrates how small spaces can be planted to maximum effect to create all round interest. Extensive range of plants favoured for colours, texture and scent. Pots used in a creative way to extend and enhance borders.
ᴥ ❀ ☕

Cogshall Grange

5 BANK HOUSE
Goldford Lane, Bickerton,
SY14 8LL. Dr & Mrs M
A Voisey, 01829 782287,
voisey598@btinternet.com. *4m
NE of Malpas. 11m S of Chester
on A41 turn L at Broxton r'about
to Nantwich on A534. Take 5th R
(1¾m) to Bickerton. Take 2nd R
into Goldford Lane. Bank House is
approx 1m on L. Field parking.* **Sat
15, Sun 16 Apr, Sat 10, Sun 11
June (1.30-5). Adm £5, chd free.
Home-made teas. Visits also
by arrangement Apr to July
10 - 40.**
1¾ acre garden at the foot of
Bickerton Hill, in area of outstanding
beauty, with extensive views to the
East and South. Sheltered, terraced
borders stocked with a wide range
of shrubs, trees and herbaceous
plants; established wild garden,
Millennium garden with water
features and productive vegetable
garden. Unfenced swimming pool
and ponds. Parts of garden too
steep for chairs.

6 150 BARREL WELL HILL
Boughton, Chester,
CH3 5BR. Dr & Mrs John
Browne, 01244 329988,
john.browne@jwbcatalyst.co.uk.
*On riverside ¾m E of Chester
off A5115. No parking at garden.
Preferred access via Chester Boats,*

*on the hour from the Groves, central
Chester. Cost £3.50 one way. Or bus
to St Pauls Church. Parking 100m at
Boughton Health Centre CH2 3DP.*
**Sat 24, Sun 25 June (11-5). Adm
£4, chd £2. Home-made teas.
Visits also by arrangement Apr
to July groups of 10+.**
Spectacular terraced garden with
views over the R Dee to the
Meadows and Clwyd Hills. Uniquely,
preferred method of arrival is by
leisurely river cruiser from Chester.
Informal cottage style garden
on historic site by the Martyrs
Memorial. Lawns running down to
the river, prolific shrub and flower
beds, productive vegetable patch
and soft and hard fruit areas, springs,
stream and lily pond. River cruisers
leave the centre of Chester regularly
and arrangements have been made
that they will drop off and pick up
garden visitors on their way up river.
Not suitable for wheelchairs or
children under eight due to steps
and unprotected drop into river.

THE BEECHES
See North East Wales

7 NEW 61 BIRTLES ROAD
Macclesfield, SK10 3JG. Kate
& Graham Tyson. *Close to
Macclesfield Leisure Centre &
Macclesfield Hospital. Follow NGS
signs from Priory Road & A537*

junction with Whirley Lane. **Sat 17,
Sun 18 June (1-5). Adm £3, chd
free. Light refreshments.**
The rear garden of this south facing
semi has been developed over the
past five years, mixed herbaceous
borders and island beds packed with
a wide variety of planting to give
year round interest, new last year, a
fragrant Rose Garden. A rockery has
a waterfall which falls to the wildlife
pond. There is seating around the
garden. Regret no wheelchair access.
✿ ☕

8 ◆ BLUEBELL COTTAGE GARDENS
Lodge Lane, Dutton,
WA4 4HP. Sue & Dave
Beesley, 01928 713718,
info@bluebellcottage.co.uk,
www.bluebellcottage.co.uk. *5m
NW of Northwich. From M56 (J10)
take A49 to Whitchurch. After 3m
turn R at T-lights towards Runcorn/
Dutton on A533. Then 1st L. Signed
with brown tourism signs from
A533.* **For NGS: Sat 1, Sun 2
July (10-5). Adm £4, chd free.
Home-made teas. For other
opening times and information,
please phone, email or visit garden
website.**
South facing country garden
wrapped around a cottage on a
quiet rural lane in the heart of
Cheshire. Packed with thousands of
rare and familiar hardy herbaceous

perennials, shrubs and trees. Unusual plants available at adjacent nursery. The opening dates coincide with the peak of flowering in the herbaceous borders. Some gravel paths. Wheelchair access to 90% of garden. WC is not fully wheelchair accessible.

&. ❀ � ☕

9 BOLESWORTH CASTLE

Tattenhall, CH3 9HQ. Mrs Anthony Barbour, 01829 782210, dcb@bolesworth.com. *8m S of Chester on A41. Enter by Lodge on A41.* **Visits by arrangement Apr & May groups of 10+. Light Refreshments by arrangement. Adm £6, chd free.**
Rock Walk above castle with one of the finest collections of rhododendrons, camellias and acers in any private garden in the NW. Set on a steep hillside accessed by a gently rising woodland walk and overlooking spectacular view of the Cheshire plain. Formal lawns beside and below castle with well stocked shrub borders. Regret no wheelchair access.

🐕 ☕

10 BOLLIN HOUSE

Hollies Lane, Wilmslow, SK9 2BW. Angela Ferguson & Gerry Lemon, 07828 207492, fergusonang@doctors.org.uk. *From Wilmslow past the Station & proceed to T-junction & turn L onto Adlington Rd. After ½ m turn R into Hollies Lane. Go to turning circle at end & take 2nd exit to Bollin House.* **Visits by arrangement June & July groups 8-25. If more than 10 cars anticipated please let us know. Adm £4, chd free. Home-made teas. Tea and cake or scones £3.50 per person..**
There are two components to this garden, the formal garden and the wild flower meadow. The garden contains richly planted, deep, herbaceous borders with a wide plant variety. Also an orchard, wild flower area and vegetable garden. The meadow contains both cornfield annuals and perennial wild flower areas which are easily accessible with meandering mown paths. Ramps to gravel lined paths to most of the garden. Some narrow paths through borders. Mown pathways in the meadow.

&. ❀ ☕

11 BOWMERE COTTAGE

5 Bowmere Road, Tarporley, CW6 0BS. Romy & Tom Holmes, 01829 732053, romy@bowmerecottage.co.uk. *10m E of Chester. From Tarporley High St (old A49) take Eaton Rd signed Eaton. After 100 metres take R fork into Bowmere Rd, Garden 100 metres on LH-side.* **Sat 10, Sun 11 June (1-5). Adm £4, chd free. Home-made teas. Visits also by arrangement June & July.**
A mature 1-acre country style garden around a Grade II listed house with well stocked mixed shrub and herbaceous borders, pergolas, two plant filled courtyard gardens and a small kitchen garden. Shrub and rambling roses, clematis, hardy geraniums and a wide and colourful range of hardy plants make this a very traditional English garden. Cobbled drive and courtyard. Tea/coffee and home made cakes.

❀ ☕

12 BRIARFIELD

The Rake, Burton, Neston, CH64 5TL. Liz Carter, 0151 336 2304, carter.burton@btinternet.com. *9m NW of Chester. Turn off A540 at Willaston-Burton Xrds T-lights & follow rd for 1m to Burton village centre.* **Sat 25, Sun 26 Feb (1-4). Adm £3, chd free. Sun 23 Apr (1-5). Adm £4, chd free. Home-made teas in St Nicholas' Church (April only), close to the garden. Opening with Burton Village Gardens on Sun 25 June. Visits also by arrangement Mar to Oct.**
Tucked under the S-facing side of Burton Wood the garden is home to many specialist and unusual plants, some available in plant sale. This 2-acre garden is on two sites, a couple of minutes along an unmade lane. Shrubs, colourful herbaceous, bulbs, alpines and water features compete for attention as you wander through four distinctly different gardens. Always changing, Liz can't resist a new plant! Rare and unusual plants sold (70% to NGS) in Neston Market each Friday morning. Featured in Cheshire Life

❀ � ☕

13 BROOKLANDS

Smithy Lane, Mouldsworth, CH3 8AR. Barbara & Brian Russell-Moore, 01928 740413, ngsmouldsworth@aol.co.uk. *1½ m N of Tarvin. 5½ m S of Frodsham. Smithy Lane is off B5393 via A54 Tarvin/Kelsall rd or the A56 Frodsham/Helsby rd.* **Sat 3, Sun 4 June (2-5). Adm £4, chd free. Home-made teas and cakes using eggs from our own hens. Visits also by arrangement May to July for groups of 10+.**
A lovely country style, ¾ acre garden with backdrop of mature trees and shrubs. The planting is based around azaleas, rhododendrons, mixed shrub and herbaceous borders. There is a small vegetable garden, supported by a greenhouse and hens providing eggs for all the afternoon tea cakes!!

&. ❀ � ☕

14 BUCKLOW FARM

Pinfold Lane, Plumley, Knutsford, WA16 9RP. Dawn & Peter Freeman. *2m S of Knutsford. M6 J19, A556 Chester. L at 2nd set of T-lights. In 1¼ m, L at concealed Xrds. 1st R. From Knutsford A5033, L at Sudlow Lane. becomes Pinfold Lane.* **Sun 26 Feb (1-3). Adm £3.50, chd free. Mulled Wine and Light refreshments. Sun 18 June (2-5). Adm £4, chd free. Cream teas in June. 2018: Sun 25 Feb.** *Donation to Knutsford Methodist Church.*
Country garden with shrubs, perennial borders, rambling roses, herb garden, vegetable patch, wildlife pond/water feature and alpines. Landscaped and planted over the last 30yrs with recorded changes. Free range hens. Carpet of snowdrops and spring bulbs. Leaf, stem and berries to show colour in autumn and winter. Featured in Cheshire Life. Cobbled yard from car park, but wheelchairs can be dropped off near gate.

&. 🐕 ❀ ☕

GROUP OPENING

15 BURTON VILLAGE GARDENS

Burton, Neston, CH64 5SJ. *9m NW of Chester. Turn off A540 at Willaston-Burton Xrds T-lights & follow rd for 1m to Burton. Maps given to visitors. Buy your ticket at first garden.* **Sun 25 June (11-5). Combined adm £5, chd free. Home-made teas.** In the Sports and Social Club behind the village hall.

BRIARFIELD
Liz Carter.
(See separate entry)

◆ BURTON MANOR WALLED GARDEN
Burton Manor Gardens Ltd, 0151 345 1107, www.burtonmanorgardens.org.uk.

LYNWOOD
Pauline Wright.

NEW TRUSTWOOD
Peter & Lin Friend.

Burton is a medieval village built on sandstone overlooking the Dee estuary. Four gardens are open. Trustwood (new) is a country wildlife garden with fruit, flowers and vegetables in raised beds at the front; at the back a more formal garden blends into the wood where the hens live. Lynwood has superb views of the Clwydian hills across the Dee; set on a sandstone outcrop enclosing a sunken pond, the garden is divided into 'rooms', each with its own collection of colourful herbaceous plants. Briarfield's sheltered site, on the south side of Burton Wood (NT), is home to many specialist and unusual plants, some available in the plant sale at the house. The 1½ acre main garden invites exploration not only for its huge variety of plants but also for the imaginative use of ceramic sculptures. Period planting with a splendid vegetable garden surrounds the restored Edwardian glasshouse in Burton Manor's walled garden. Plants for sale at most gardens. Well signed free car parks. Maps available. Featured in Cheshire Life.

&. ❀ 🚗 ☕

16 ◆ CHOLMONDELEY CASTLE GARDEN

Cholmondeley, nr Malpas, SY14 8AH. Marquess of Cholmondeley, 01829 720383, www.cholmondeleycastle.com. *4m NE of Malpas. Signed from A41 Chester-Whitchurch rd & A49 Whitchurch-Tarporley rd.* **For NGS: Thur 11 May (11-5). Adm £7, chd £4. Light lunches & home-made teas.** For other opening times and information, please phone or visit garden website.

Over 20 acres of romantically landscaped gardens with fine views and eye-catching water features, but still manages to retain its intimacy. Beautiful mature trees form a background to spring bulbs, exotic plants in season incl magnolias, rhododendrons, azaleas and camellias and many other, particularly *Davidia Involucrata* which will be in flower in late May. Magnificent magnolias. One of the finest features of the gardens are its trees, many of which are rare and unusual and Cholmondeley Gardens is home to over 35 county champion trees. Partial wheelchair access.

&. ❀ 🚗 ☕

17 CLEMLEY HOUSE

Well Lane, Duddon Common, Tarporley, CW6 0HG. Sue & Tom Makin. *8m S.E of Chester, 3m W of Tarporley. A51 from Chester towards Tarporley. 1m after Tarvin turnoff, at bus shelter, turn L into Willington Rd. After community centre, 2nd L into Well Lane. Third house.* **Evening opening Wed 21 June (6-9). Sat 1 July (1.30-5.30). Adm £5, chd free. Home-made teas.** Home grown organic fruits used in jams & cakes. Gluten free & Vegan cakes usually available. 2 acre organic, wildlife friendly, gold award winning cottage garden. Orchard, 3 wildlife ponds, wild flower meadow, fruit and vegetable areas, badger sett, rose pergola, gazebo, summer house, barn owl and many other nest and bat boxes. Drought tolerant gravel garden and shade garden, shepherd's hut and poly tunnel. Year round interest. 'Frogwatch' charity volunteers transport migrating amphibians to the safety of these ponds when they are found on the roads in early spring. Features regularly in the N.W. Cottage Garden Society Magazine, Cheshire Life Magazine, Cheshire Wildlife Trust 'The Grebe' & RSPB Magazine ' Nature's Home'. Gravel paths may be difficult to use but most areas are flat and comprise grass paths or lawn.

&. 🐕 ❀ ☕

18 CLOVER BANK ORGANIC FARM

Shellow Lane, North Rode, Congleton, CW12 2NX. Brian & Jane Clarkson. *Approx 4m S Macclesfield, 4m N Congleton. From Macclesfield A523 turn R before Bosley T-lights - Bullgate Lane - Cloverbank drive signed on R. From Congleton A536 turn R into Shellow Lane. Cloverbank drive signed on L.* **Sat 5, Sun 6 Aug (11-4). Adm £5, chd free. Home-made teas.** Started 2011, garden complements stunning modern house above large pond with bridge and surrounding plantings of roses. dahlias, herbaceous, raised vegetable beds, marginal and wetland planting, woodland, Remembrance Garden, wild rose and soft fruit hedging and fruit trees, large wild flower areas. Shady area with new water feature and underplanting. Spectacular views to Pennines. A 'must see' garden. Winner of the Cheshire Farm Garden Competition, finalist in the Daily Mail National Garden Competition. Mainly gravel paths, some grass areas could be difficult to manage.

&. ❀ ☕

The National Garden Scheme and Perennial, helping gardeners when they are in need

19 5 COBBS LANE

Hough, Crewe, CW2 5JN. David & Linda Race. *4m S of Crewe. M6 J16 r'about take A500 towards Nantwich. At next r'about take 1st exit Keele/Nantwich (not the bypass). Next r'about straight on Hough/Nantwich. After 1m turn L into Cobbs Lane. From the W A51 Nantwich bypass to A500 r'about 3rd exit signed Shavington, continue 3m passing White Hart PH, then R into Cobbs Lane. Pass No. 5, parking 300m at Village Hall, no parking on Lane* **Thur 6, Wed 12 July (11-5). Adm £5, chd free. Home-made teas at Village Hall 300m up Cobbs Lane.**

A plant person's ⅔ acre garden with island beds, wide cottage style herbaceous borders with bark paths. A large variety of hardy and some unusual perennials. Interesting features, shrubs, grasses and trees, with places to sit and enjoy the surroundings. A water feature runs to a small pond, wildlife friendly garden containing a woodland area. Finalists in Daily Mail Garden Competition.

20 COGSHALL GRANGE

Hall Lane, Antrobus, Northwich, CW9 6BJ. Anthony & Margaret Preston. *3m NW of Northwich. Take A559 Northwich to Warrington. Turn into Wheatsheaf Lane or Well Lane. Head S on Sandiway Lane to grass triangle & then R into Hall Lane.* **Sun 6 Aug (11-5). Adm £6, chd free. Light refreshments.**

Set in the historic landscape of a late Georgian country house this is a contemporary garden, designed by the internationally renowned garden designer, Tom Stuart-Smith. The gardens contain a mixture of both informal and formal elements, modern herbaceous plantings, a walled garden, wild flower meadows, an orchard and woodland borders with views to parkland and the surrounding countryside.

21 DINGLE FARM

Dingle Lane, Appleton, Warrington, WA4 3HR. Robert Bilton, www.dinglefarmonline.co.uk. *2m N from M56 J10. A49 towards Warrington, R at T-lights onto Stretton Rd, 1m turn L at The Thorn PH, after 1m turn L into Dingle Lane. Plenty of parking.* **Every Sat and Sun 22 July to 6 Aug (10-5). Adm £4, chd free. Cream teas.**

The garden features include a large pond, an array of ornamental grasses, wild flower meadows, orchard, vegetable patch, newly planted woodland area and manicured lawns. The garden is overlooked and accessed through the Dingle Farm Tea Rooms. Lunches and cream teas served all day. Art Studio and Gift Shop. Set in the beautiful Cheshire countryside. There are woodland walks adjacent to the site. Also the Dingle Farm Tea Room overlooks the main garden and has it own Tea Garden, where you can enjoy morning coffee, lunches and afternoon tea.

22 ◆ DUNHAM MASSEY

Altrincham, WA14 4SJ. National Trust, 0161 941 1025, www.nationaltrust.org.uk/dunhammassey. *3m SW of Altrincham Off A56; M6 exit J19; M56 exit J7. Foot: close to Trans-Pennine Trail & Bridgewater Canal. Bus: Nos 38 & 5* **For NGS: Sun 26 Feb, Sun 21 May, Sun 17 Sept (11-5.30). Adm £8.60, chd £4.30. For other opening times and information, please phone or visit garden website.**

Enjoy the elegance of this vibrant Edwardian garden. Richly planted borders packed with colour and texture, sweeping lawns, majestic trees and shady woodland all await your discovery. Explore the largest Winter Garden in Britain and marvel at the colourful, scent-filled Rose Garden. Water features. C18 Orangery, rare Victorian Bark House. Visitors to the garden, incl NT members, should collect ticket from Visitor Reception at Visitor Centre

23 THE FIRS

Old Chester Road, Barbridge, Nantwich, CW5 6AY. Richard & Valerie Goodyear. *3m N of Nantwich on A51. After entering Barbridge turn R at Xrds after 100 metres. The Firs is 2nd house on L.* **Sat 29, Sun 30 July (1-5). Adm £4, chd free. Light refreshments.**

Canal side garden set idyllically by the Shropshire Union Canal. Approx 0.4 acre of varied trees, shrubs and herbaceous beds, with some wild areas. All leading down to an observatory at the bottom of garden.

24 FRAMLEY

Hadlow Road, Willaston, Neston, CH64 2US. Mrs Sally Reader, 07496 015259, sllyreader@yahoo.co.uk. *½ m S of Willaston village centre. From Willaston Green, proceed along Hadlow Rd, crossing the Wirral Way. Framley is the next house on R.* **Mon 1 May (10.30-4). Adm £4, chd free. Home-made teas. Visits also by arrangement May & June please contact by email as early in year as possible.**

This 5 acre garden holds many hidden gems. Comprising extensive mature wooded areas, underplanted with a variety of interesting and unusual woodland plants - all at their very best in spring. A selection of deep seasonal borders surround a mystical sunken garden, planted to suit its challenging conditions. Wide lawns and sandstone paths invite you to discover what lies around every corner. Please phone ahead for parking instructions for wheelchair users - access around much of the garden although the woodland paths may be challenging.

25 FREE GREEN FARM

Free Green Lane, Lower Peover, WA16 9QX. Sir Philip & Lady Haworth. *3m S of Knutsford. Near A50 between Knutsford & Holmes Chapel. Off Free Green Lane.* **Sun 4 June (2-6.30). Adm £5, chd free. Home-made teas.**

2-acre garden with pleached limes, herbaceous borders, ponds, parterre, garden of the senses, British woodland with fernery, quasi jungle area with Banana. Topiary. Wildlife friendly. Assortment of trees, and ten different forms of hedging. Ponds and underplanted woodland. Wheelchair access not easy in the wood.

26 51 GARTH DRIVE

Chester, CH2 2AF. Mrs Heather Redhead, 01244 370227, redheadh@aol.com. *Bache railway station with parking is 10 min walk away. Bus stop on Liverpool Rd close to its junction with Lumley Rd, buses from Wirral & Chester. At the far end of Garth Drive. Limited parking in Garth Dr.* **Sun 25, Wed 28 June (1-5). Adm £3, chd free. Home-made teas. A selection of home made scones and cakes. Tea, coffee and chilled water. Visits also by arrangement May to July refreshments by prior arrangement.**
A suburban garden a mile from Chester city centre packed with a variety of herbaceous borders, a pond, and productive areas which is set over several levels. Additional cakes and scones may be available to purchase - please enquire. Not suitable for wheelchairs.
✿ ☕

27 HATHAWAY

1 Pool End Road, Tytherington, Macclesfield, SK10 2LB. Mr & Mrs Cordingley. *2m N of Macclesfield, ½m from The Tytherington Club. Stockport: follow A523 to Butley Ash, R on A538 Tytherington. Knutsford: follow A537 at A538, L for Tytherington. Leek: follow A523 at A537 L & 1st R A53.* **Sat 6, Sun 7 May (10-5). Adm £4, chd free. Home-made teas.**
Garden of approx ⅓ acre. SW facing. Garden laid out in two parts. Large lawn area surrounded by mature, colourful perennial borders. Rose arbour, small pond with koi, patio, raised fruit and cut flower bed. Small mature wooded area with winding paths on a lower level. Front, laid to lawn with two main borders separated by a small grass area. Good wheelchair access to most of garden except wood area.
♿ ☕

28 HATTON HOUSE GARDENS

Hatton Heath, Chester, CH3 9AP. Judy Halewood, basebotanics@hotmail.com. *4m SE of Chester. From Chester on A41 2km past The Black Dog PH. From Whitchurch on A41 7km past the Broxton r'about.* **Sat 3, Sun 4 June (11-4). Adm £5, chd free. Light refreshments. Great tea, coffee and homemade cakes/ sandwiches. Visits also by arrangement Apr to July for groups of 5+.**
Approx 8 acres of beautifully landscaped gardens both formal and natural. Pathways leading through extensive herbaceous borders and rose garden give way to lawns, azalea rock gardens, waterfalls and wild flowers. The 2 acre lake is rich in wildlife and flanked by woodland, wild flowers, bulbs, bridges and follies. All of the gardens are wheelchair friendly apart from the Sunken Garden.
♿ ✿ 🚗 ☕

29 NEW 181a HIGHER LANE

Higher Lane, Lymm, WA13 0RF. Melanie Farrow, 07803 079495, mguest@tektura.com. *M6 signed Lymm approx 2m T-junction turn R. Follow rd approx 2m house on R. From M56 one straight rd. Follow Lymm approx. ¾m house on R ½m after T-lights.* **Sat 8, Sun 9 July (12-5). Adm £5, chd free. Home-made teas and cakes, coffees and juices. Visits also by arrangement June & July.**
A structured garden, backing on to open fields with garden room. Clipped Box and Yew Hedges and Balls and Pleached trees. Colour scheme of Purples and Lime Greens with pops of colour. Herbaceous borders. Vegetable garden and greenhouse. Various seating areas.
♿ ✿ ☕

30 73 HILL TOP AVENUE

Cheadle Hulme, Stockport, SK8 7HZ. Mrs Land, 0161 486 0055. *4m S of Stockport. Turn off A34 (new bypass) at r'about signed Cheadle Hulme (B5094). Take 2nd turn L into Gillbent Rd, signed Cheadle Hulme Sports Centre. Go to end, small r'about, turn R into Church Rd. 2nd rd on L is Hill Top Ave. From Stockport or Bramhall turn R or L into Church Rd by The Church Inn. Hill Top Ave is 1st rd on R.* **Sun 28 May, Sun 6 Aug (2-6). Adm £3.50, chd free. Tea. Visits also by arrangement May to Aug, 5+ Refreshments by prior arrangement.** *Donation to Arthritis Research UK.*
⅙-acre plantswoman's garden. Well stocked with a wide range of sun-loving herbaceous plants, shrub and climbing roses, many clematis varieties, pond and damp area, shade-loving woodland plants and

Sandymere

some unusual trees and shrubs, in an originally designed, long narrow garden.

✿ 🚗 ☕

31 NEW THE HOMESTEAD

2 Fanners Lane, High Legh, Knutsford, WA16 0RZ. Janet Bashforth. *J20 M6/J9 M56 at Lymm interchange take A50 for Knutsford,' after 1m turn R into Heath Lane then 1st R into Fanners Lane. Follow parking signs.* **Evening opening Fri 28 July (6-9.30). Adm £5, chd free. Wine. Adm incl glass of wine, cup of tea or coffee.** Nestled in the Cheshire countryside this compact gem of a garden has been created over the last 2½ yrs by a keen gardener and plants woman. Enter past groups of Liquidamber and White Stemmed Birch, visit shaded nooks with their own distinctive planting. Past topiary nestled in grasses, enjoy the exuberant colours of the hot area. Greenhouse and a small pond. Further on there is a small pond with water lilies and Iris. Many types of roses and clematis adorn the fencing along the paths and into the trees.

♿ ✿ ☕

32 INGLEWOOD

4 Birchmere, Heswall, CH60 6TN. Colin & Sandra Fairclough, www.inglewood-birchmere. blogspot.co.uk. *6m S of Birkenhead. From A540 Devon Doorway/Clegg Arms r'about go through Heswall. ¼ m after Tesco, R into Quarry Rd East, 2nd L into Tower Rd North & L into Birchmere.* **Sat 20, Sun 21 May (1.30-4.30). Adm £4, chd free. Home-made teas.** Beautiful ½ acre garden with stream, large koi pond, 'beach' with grasses, wildlife pond and bog area. Brimming with shrubs, bulbs, acers, conifers, rhododendrons, herbaceous plants and new hosta border. Interesting features including hand cart, antique mangle, wood carvings, bug hotel and Indian dog gates leading to a secret garden. Lots of seating to enjoy refreshments.

♿ 🐕 ✿ ☕

33 NEW 60 KENNEDY AVENUE

Macclesfield, SK10 3DE. Bill North, 01625 266032 / 078573 17227, julie.north3@ntlworld.com. *5min NW of Macclesfield Town Centre. Take A537 Cumberland St, 3rd r'bout (West Park) take B5087 Prestbury Rd. Take 5th turn on L into Kennedy Ave, last house on L before Brampton Ave opp Belong Care Home.* **Sun 18 June (1-5). Adm £3.50, chd free. Home-made teas. Visits also by arrangement June to Aug groups 5 upwards. Adm incls a glass of wine.** Small suburban garden designed to provide Al Fresco Dinning and relaxed entertaining, also providing relaxing Cottage Garden tranquility which includes display of 60 Hanging Baskets. A Bee Keepers Garden. Unusually front garden set out in Cottage Garden style. Seating. Not suitable for disabled access. Winner of Chelsea Flower Show Sponsor M&G, My Little Garden Photographic competition.

☕

34 LASKEY FARM

Laskey Lane, Thelwall, Warrington, WA4 2TF. Howard & Wendy Platt, 07740 804825, wendy.platt1@gmail.com, www.laskeyfarm.com. *2m From M6/M56. From M56/M6 follow directions to Lymm. At T-junction turn L onto the A56 in Warrington direction. Turn R onto Lymm Rd. Turn R onto Laskey Lane.* **Sat 12, Sun 13 Aug (11-5). Adm £5, chd free. Home-made teas. Visits also by arrangement June to Aug groups of 12+.** 1½ acre garden packed with late summer colour including herbaceous and rose borders, vegetable area, parterre and a maze showcasing grasses and prairie style planting. Interconnected pools for wildlife, fish and terrapins form an unusual water garden and there are also a greenhouse and treehouse to explore. Live music and an exhibition of the work of Lymm Artists will take place over the weekend. Exhibition of the work of Lymm Artists and live music between 1pm and 3pm both days.

Featured in Cheshire Life and on BBC Radio Manchester. Most areas of the garden may be accessed by wheelchair.

♿ 🐕 ✿ 🚗 ☕

35 LONG ACRE

Wyche Lane, Bunbury, CW6 9PS. Margaret & Michael Bourne, 01829 260944, mjbourne249@tiscali.co.uk. *3½ m SE of Tarporley. In Bunbury village, turn into Wyche Lane by Nags Head PH car park, garden 400yds on L.* **Sun 23 Apr, Sun 18 June (2-5). Adm £4.50, chd free. Home-made teas. Visits also by arrangement Apr to June groups of 10+. Donation to St Boniface Church Flower Fund.** Plantswoman's garden of approx 1 acre with unusual and rare plants and trees, pool garden, exotic conservatory, herbaceous, S African bulbs, disa orchids and clivia. Spring garden with camellias, magnolias, bulbs.

✿ ☕

36 ◆ THE LOVELL QUINTA ARBORETUM

Swettenham, CW12 2LD. Tatton Garden Society, 01565 831981, admin@ tattongardensociety.org.uk, www.tattongardensociety.co.uk. *4m NW of Congleton. Turn off A54 N 2m W of Congleton or turn E off A535 at Twemlow Green, NE of Holmes Chapel. Follow signs to Swettenham. Park at Swettenham Arms PH.* **For NGS: Sun 1 Oct (1-4). Adm £5, chd free. For other opening times and information, please phone, email or visit garden website.** The 28-acre arboretum has been established since 1960s and contains around 2,500 trees and shrubs, some very rare. Incl National Collections of Pinus and Fraxinus, a large collection of oak, a collection of hebes and autumn flowering and colouring trees and shrubs. A lake and way-marked walks. Autumn colour. Care required but wheelchairs can access much of the arboretum on the mown paths.

♿ 🐕 🚗 NPC

The Queen's Nursing Institute founded the National Garden Scheme exactly 90 years ago

37 MANLEY KNOLL
Manley Road, Manley, WA6 9DX. Mr & Mrs James Timpson, www.manleyknoll.com. *3m N of Tarvin. On B5393, via Ashton & Mouldsworth. 3m S of Frodsham, via Alvanley.* **Sun 28 May (12-5). Adm £5, chd free. Home-made teas.**
Arts and Crafts garden created early 1900s. Covering 6 acres, divided into different rooms encompassing parterres, clipped yew hedging and ornamental ponds. Banks of rhododendron and azaleas frame a far-reaching view of the Cheshire Plain. Also a magical quarry/folly garden with waterfall.
🐾 ✿ ▼

38 218 MARPLE ROAD
Offerton, Stockport, SK2 5HE. Barry & Pat Hadfield. *3½m E of Stockport leave M60 J27 at the r'about take 5th exit onto A626 signed for Marple, follow the A626, parking on L at Offerton Sand & Gravel. Disabled drop off only at the house.* **Sun 2 July (11-4.30). Adm £4, chd free. Home-made teas. and cakes.**
This secret south facing garden approx 1 acre, full of herbaceous plants, vegetable plot, plant growing area, topiary, unfenced ponds/water features, fun areas, developed from paddock to garden over 20yrs by current owners. We are trying to encourage children of all ages in this fun garden. There will be a quiz. Wheelchair access to most areas.
& ✿ ▼

39 ◆ MOUNT PLEASANT
Yeld Lane, Kelsall, CW6 0TB. Dave Darlington & Louise Worthington, 01829 751592, louisedarlington@btinternet.com, www.mountpleasantgardens.co.uk. *8m E of Chester. Off A54 at T-lights into Kelsall. Turn into Yeld Lane opp Farmers Arms PH, 200yds on L. Do not follow SatNav directions.* **For NGS: Sun 30 Apr, Mon 1 May, Sat 2, Sun 3 Sept (12-5). Adm £5, chd £2. Cream teas.**
For other opening times and information, please phone, email or visit garden website.
10 acres of landscaped garden and woodland started in 1994 with impressive views over the Cheshire countryside. Steeply terraced in places. Specimen trees, rhododendrons, azaleas, conifers, mixed and herbaceous borders; 4 ponds, formal and wildlife. Vegetable garden, stumpery with tree ferns, sculptures, wild flower meadow and Japanese garden. Bog garden, tropical garden. Sculpture trail. Sculpture Exhibition. Featured in Cheshire Life. Please ring prior to visit for wheelchair access.
✿ 🚗 ▼

40 ◆ NESS BOTANIC GARDENS
Neston Road, Ness, Neston, CH64 4AY. The University of Liverpool, 0151 795 6300, nessgdns@liverpool.ac.uk, www.nessgardens.org.uk. *10m NW of Chester. Off A540. M53 J4, follow signs M56 & A5117 (signed N Wales). Turn onto A540 follow signs for Hoylake. Ness Gardens is signed locally.* **For NGS: Sun 14 May (10-5). Adm £7.50, chd £3.50.**
For other opening times and information, please phone, email or visit garden website.
Looking out over the dramatic Dee Estuary from a lofty perch of the Wirral peninsula, Ness Botanic Gardens boasts 64 spectacular acres of landscaped and natural gardens overflowing with horticultural treasures. With a delightfully peaceful atmosphere, a wide array of events taking place, plus a cafe and gorgeous open spaces it's a great fun-filled day out for all. National Collection of Sorbus. Herbaceous borders, Rock Garden, Mediterranean Bank, Potager and conservation area. Mobility scooters and wheelchairs are available free to hire [donations gratefully accepted] but advance booking is highly recommended.
& ✿ 🚗 [NPC] ▼

41 ◆ NORTON PRIORY MUSEUM & GARDENS
Tudor Road, Manor Park, Runcorn, WA7 1SX. Norton Priory Museum Trust, 01928 569895, info@nortonpriory.org, www.nortonpriory.org. *2m SE of Runcorn. If using Sat-Nav try WA7 1BD and follow the brown Norton Priory signs.* **For NGS: Sun 4 June (10-5). Adm £3.50, chd £2.70.**
For other opening times and information, please phone, email or visit garden website.
Beautiful 2½-acre Georgian Walled Garden, with fruit trees, herb garden, colour borders and rose walk. Home to the National Collection of Tree Quince (Cydonia Oblonga) and surrounded by historic pear orchard and wild flower meadow. Tea room and plant sales in the courtyard. Norton Priory is also home to medieval ruins and a brand new museum. Featured on BBC's Countryfile Garden paths are gravel but there is level access to the whole garden site.
& ✿ 🚗 [NPC] ▼

42 OAKFIELD VILLA
Nantwich Road, Wrenbury, Nantwich, CW5 8EL. Carolyn & Jack Kennedy, 01270 781106. *6m S of Nantwich & 6m N of Whitchurch. Garden on main rd through village next to Dairy Farm. Parking in field between Oak Villas & School 1min walk to garden.* **Wed 21 June (10-5). Combined adm with Wren's Nest £6, chd free. Home-made teas. Visits also by arrangement July & Aug max 15, between 10am and 5pm, teas by arrangement.**
Romantic S-facing garden of densely planted borders and creative planting in containers, incl climbing roses, clematis and hydrangeas. Divided by screens into rooms, the garden incl a small fishpond and water feature. Pergola clothed in beautiful climbers provides relaxed sheltered seating area. Small front garden, mainly hydrangeas and

clematis. 50+ clematis and many hydrangeas. Some gravelled areas.
& ☕

The Firs

43 THE OLD COTTAGE
44 High Street, Frodsham, WA6 7HE. John & Lesley Corfield, 07591 609311, corfield@rock44.plus.com. *DO NOT FOLLOW SATNAV - no parking at garden. On A56 close to Frodsham town centre. Follow signs from town centre to railway car park, garden signed from there (short walk). Or park in town centre and follow signs uphill N to cottage.* **Visits by arrangement June to Aug for groups of 6+. Adm £4.50, chd free.** At the rear of the Grade II listed C16 cottage (not open) are ⅔ acre, organic and wildlife friendly garden featuring many aspects that support various forms of wildlife. Steps lead up to a large vegetable and herb garden, with further mixed planting in herbaceous borders. Wildlife pond and bog garden. Further areas of fruit trees and shady woodland borders. Extensive views over Mersey estuary. Partial wheelchair access - please ring for details.
& 🐕

44 NEW 24 OLD GREASBY ROAD
Upton, Wirral, CH49 6LT. Lesley Whorton & Jon Price, 07905 775 750, wlesley@hotmail.co.uk. *Approx 1m from J2A on M53 (Upton Bypass). M53 J2; follow Upton sign. At r'about (J2A) straight on to Upton Bypass. At 2nd r'about, turn L by Upton Cricket Club. 24 Old Greasby Rd on L.* **Sun 4 June, Sun 20 Aug (11-5). Adm £3.50, chd free. Home-made teas. Visits also by arrangement May to Sept groups of 10 or more (max 30). Tel Lesley 07905 775 750.** A multi-interest and surprising suburban garden. Both front and rear gardens incorporate innovative features designed for climbing and rambling roses, clematis, under-planted with cottage garden plants with a very productive kitchen garden. Unfortunately, due to narrow access and gravel paths, there is no wheelchair access.
✿ ☕

45 THE OLD PARSONAGE
Arley Green, Via Arley Hall and Gardens, Northwich, CW9 6LZ. The Viscount & Viscountess Ashbrook, 01565 777277, ashbrook@ arleyhallandgardens.com, www.arleyhallandgardens.com. *5m NNE of Northwich. 3m NNE of Great Budworth. M6 J19 & 20 & M56 J10. Follow signs to Arley Hall & Gardens. From Arley Hall notices to Old Parsonage which lies across park at Arley Green (approx 1m).* **Sat 3, Sun 4 June (2-5.30). Adm £5, chd free. Home-made teas. Visits also by arrangement May & June for 10-30. Teas at Gardener's Kitchen, Arley Hall. For conducted tours, check availability of guide.** *Donation to Save The Children Fund (3 & 4 June).* 2-acre garden in attractive and secretive rural setting in secluded part of Arley Estate, with ancient yew hedges, herbaceous and mixed borders, shrub roses, climbers, leading to woodland garden and unfenced pond with gunnera and water plants. Rhododendrons, azaleas, meconopsis, cardiocrinum, some interesting and unusual trees. Used as set by Disney for film 'Evermoor' and possibly 'Peaky Blinders'. Wheelchair access over mown grass, but some slopes and bumps and rougher grass further away from the house.
& 🐕 ✿ ☕

46 39 OSBORNE STREET
Bredbury, Stockport, SK6 2DA. Geoff & Heather Hoyle, Geoff.hoyle@btinternet.com, www.youtube.com/user/ Dahliaholic. *1½m E of Stockport, just off B6104. Follow signs for Lower Bredbury/Bredbury Hall. Leave M60 J27 (from S & W) or J25 (from N & E). Osborne St is adjacent to pelican crossing on B6104.* **Sat 9, Sun 10 Sept (1-5). Adm £4, chd free. Light refreshments. Teas, coffees, and cakes. Visits also by arrangement in Sept for groups of 10+.** This dahliaholic's garden contains over 350 dahlias in 150+ varieties, mostly of exhibition standard. Shapely lawns are surrounded by deep flower beds that are crammed with dahlias of all shapes, sizes and colours, and complemented by climbers, soft perennials and bedding plants. An absolute riot of early autumn colour. The garden comprises two separate areas, both crammed with very colourful flowers. The dahlias range in height from 18 inches to 8 feet tall, and are in a wide variety of shapes and colours. They are interspersed with salvias, fuchsias, argyranthemums, and bedding plants. The garden is on YouTube: search for Dahliaholic. Featured in The Garden (RHS) magazine.
☕

47 PARM PLACE

High Street, Great Budworth, CW9 6HF. Peter & Jane Fairclough, 01606 891131, janefair@btinternet.com. *3m N of Northwich. Great Budworth on E side of A559 between Northwich & Warrington, 4m from J10 M56, also 4m from J19 M6. Parm Place is W of village on S side of High St.* **Visits by arrangement Apr to Aug between 10 and 40. Tea/coffee and biscuits provided for donation. Adm £4, chd free.** *Donation to Great Ormond Street Hospital.*

Well-stocked ½ acre plantswoman's garden with stunning views towards S Cheshire. Curving lawns, parterre, shrubs, colour co-ordinated herbaceous borders, roses, water features, rockery, gravel bed with some grasses. Fruit and vegetable plots. In spring large collection of bulbs and flowers, camellias, hellebores and blossom.

48 ♦ PEOVER HALL GARDENS

Over Peover, Knutsford, WA16 9HW. Randle Brooks, 01565 757980, bookings@peoverhall.com, www.peoverhall.com. *4m S of Knutsford. A50/Holmes Chapel Rd/Whipping Stocks PH turn onto Stocks Lane. Approx 0.9m turn onto Grotto Lane. ¼m turn onto Goostrey Lane. Main entrance on bend.* **For NGS: Sat 3, Sun 4 June (2-5). Adm £5, chd free. Home-made teas in Park House Tea Room & Paddock. For other opening times and information, please phone, email or visit garden website.**

The gardens to Peover Hall are set in 15 acres and feature a number of 'garden rooms' filled with clipped box, topiary, roses, a lily pond, a walled garden, Romanesque loggia, C19 dell, rhododendrons and pleached limes. There are Grade I listed Carolean Stables which are of significant architectural importance. Partial wheelchair access to garden.

49 POULTON HALL

Poulton Lancelyn, Bebington, CH63 9LN. The Lancelyn Green Family, www.poultonhall.co.uk. *2m S of Bebington. From M53, J4 towards Bebington; at T-lights R along Poulton Rd; house 1m on R.* **Sat 22, Sun 23 Apr (1.30-4.30). Adm £4.50, chd free. Home-made teas.**

3 acres; lawns fronting house, wild flower meadow. Surprise approach to walled garden, with reminders of Roger Lancelyn Green's retellings, Excalibur, Robin Hood and Jabberwocky. Scented sundial garden for the visually impaired. Memorial sculpture for Richard Lancelyn Green by Sue Sharples. Rose, nursery rhyme, witch, herb and oriental gardens and new Memories Reading room. There are often choirs or orchestral music in the garden. Level gravel paths. Separate wheelchair access (not across parking field).

50 ♦ RODE HALL

Church Lane, Scholar Green, ST7 3QP. Randle & Amanda Baker Wilbraham, 01270 873237, enquiries@rodehall.co.uk, www.rodehall.co.uk. *5m SW of Congleton. Between Scholar Green (A34) & Rode Heath (A50).* **For opening times and information, please phone, email or visit garden website.**

Nesfield's terrace and rose garden with view over Humphry Repton's landscape is a feature of Rode, as is the woodland garden with terraced rock garden and grotto. Other attractions incl the walk to the lake with a view of Birthday Island complete with heronry, restored ice house, working 2 acre walled kitchen garden and Italian garden. Fine display of snowdrops in Feb and Bluebells in May. Snowdrop Walks 4 Feb - 5 March 11-4 pm Tues - Sat (Closed Mons) Bluebell Walks 29 Apr - 6 May Summer: Weds and Bank Hol Mons 11-5. Partial wheelchair access, some steep areas with gravel and woodchip paths, access to WC, kitchen garden and tearooms.

51 ROSEWOOD

Old Hall Lane, Puddington, Neston, CH64 5SP. Mr & Mrs C E J Brabin, 0151 353 1193, angela.brabin@btinternet.com. *8m N of Chester. From A540 turn down Puddington Lane, 1½m. Park by village green. Walk 30yds to Old Hall*

Tirley Garth

Lane, turn L through archway into garden. **Visits by arrangement individuals, medium or large groups. Adm £3, chd free. Tea.** All yr garden; thousands of snowdrops in Feb, Camellias in autumn, winter and spring. Rhododendrons in April/May and unusual flowering trees from March to June. Autumn Cyclamen in quantity from Aug to Nov. Perhaps the greatest delight to owners is a large Cornus capitata, flowering in June. Bees kept in the garden. Honey sometimes available.

52 THE ROWANS
Oldcastle Lane, Threapwood, nr Malpas, SY14 7AY. Paul Philpotts & Alan Bourne. *3m SW of Malpas. Leave Malpas on B5069 for Wrexham, after 3m, take 1st L after Threapwood Shop/PO into Chapel Lane, L into Oldcastle Lane, garden 1st Bungalow on R.* **Sat 1, Sun 2 July (1.30-5.30). Adm £5, chd free. Home-made teas.**
This 1-acre multi-award winning garden, featured in Cheshire Lifes 2016 list of top ten secret NGS Gardens. It has an Italianate theme, divided into numerous formal and natural areas, in which to sit and enjoy the views and feature statuary. Many mature and unusual trees, several ponds, herbaceous borders, vegetable plots, greenhouse, and an extensive Hosta collection. A tranquil haven for visitors.

53 ROWLEY HOUSE
Forty Acre Lane, Kermincham, Crewe, CW4 8DX. Tim & Juliet Foden. *3m ENE from Holmes Chapel. J18 M6 to Holmes Chapel, take A535 Macclesfield Rd, 1½m turn R towards Swettenham at Twemlow, by Yellow Broom restaurant into Forty Acre Lane, Rowley House ½m on L.* **Sun 28 May, Sat 8, Sun 9 July (1-4.30). Adm £5, chd free. Light refreshments. Teas & home made cakes.**
Our aim is to give nature a home and create a place of beauty. There is a formal courtyard garden and informal gardens featuring rare trees, and herbaceous borders, a pond

with swamp cypress and woodland walk with maples, rhododendrons, ferns and shade loving plants. Beyond the garden there are wild flower meadows, natural ponds and wood with its ancient oaks. There are also wood sculptures.

54 SANDYMERE
Middlewich Road, Cotebrook, CW6 9EH. John Timpson, 07900 567944, rme2000@aol.com. *5m N of Tarporley. On A54 approx 300yds W of T-lights at Xrds of A49/A54.* **Sun 21 May (12-5). Adm £6, chd free. Home-made teas. Visits also by arrangement May to July for groups of 5+.**
16 landscaped acres of beautiful Cheshire countryside with terraces, walled garden, extensive woodland walks and an amazing hosta garden. Turn each corner and you find another gem with lots of different water features including a new rill built in 2014, which links the main lawn to the hostas. Partial wheelchair access.

55 21 SCAFELL CLOSE
High Lane, Stockport, SK6 8JA. Lesley & Dean Stafford, 01663 763015, lesley.stafford@live.co.uk. *High Lane is on A6 SE of Stockport towards Buxton From A6 take Russel Ave then Kirkfell Drive. Scafell Close on R.* **Sat 5, Sun 6 Aug (1-4.30). Adm £3, chd free. Light refreshments. Visits also by arrangement July & Aug one group per day, wander round at your leisure.**
⅓ acre landscaped suburban garden. Colour themed annuals border the lawn featuring the Kinder Ram statue in a heather garden, passing into vegetables, soft fruits and fruit trees. Returning perennial pathway leads to the fishpond and secret terraced garden with modern water feature and patio planting. Finally visit the blue front garden. Featured in Amateur Gardening. Partial wheelchair access.

56 SOMERFORD
19 Leycester Road, Knutsford, WA16 8QR. Emma Dearman & Joe Morris. *1m from centre of Knutsford. Take A50 direction of Holmes Chapel. Sharp L after Esso garage into Leycester Rd. Cross Legh Rd. Somerford is opp Leycester Close. Park on rd.* **Evening opening Fri 14 July (6-8.30). Adm £6, chd free. Wine. Sun 23 July (12-6). Adm £4, chd free. Tea.**
Majestic trees surround this 1½ acre garden which has been designed and planted over the past 7 years. Hard landscaping and sculptures complement lush herbaceous and perennial borders. Lawns are separated by a magnificent oak pergola. Cube-headed hornbeams lead into the snail-trail walk and informal lawn and fernery. Back after a year off. Come and see the new child friendly water feature! Sculpture. The garden featured as an inspiration garden in Love Your Garden with Alan Titchmarsh. Most of the garden is accessible by wheelchair. Ring 01565 621095 for further information.

57 68 SOUTH OAK LANE
Wilmslow, SK9 6AT. Caroline & David Melliar-Smith, 01625 528147, caroline.ms@btinternet.com. *¾m SW of Wilmslow. From M56 (J6) take A538 (Wilmslow) R into Buckingham Rd. From centre of Wilmslow turn R onto B5086, 1st R into Gravel Lane, 4th R into South Oak Lane.* **Sun 9, Sun 30 July (11-4.30). Adm £4, chd free. Visits also by arrangement June to Aug max group 25.**
With year-round colour, scent and interest, this attractive, narrow, hedged cottage garden has evolved over the years into 5 natural 'rooms'. These Hardy Plant Society members passion for plants, is reflected in the variety of shrubs, trees, flower borders and pond, creating havens for wildlife. Share this garden with its' varied history from the 1890's. Some rare and unusual hardy, herbaceous and shade loving plants and shrubs. Featured in the Wilmslow Guardian.

58 10 STATHAM AVENUE

Lymm, WA13 9NH. Mike & Gail Porter. *Approx 1m from J20 M6 / M56 interchange. Follow B5158 signed Lymm. Take A56 Booth's Hill Rd, towards Warrington, turn R on to Barsbank Lane, after passing under the Bridgewater canal turn R (50m) onto Statham Ave. No 10 is 100 metres on R.* **Evening opening Fri 19 May (6-9). Adm £7, chd free. Wine and cheese. Sat 1, Sun 2 July (11-5). Adm £4, chd free. Home-made teas and Gail's famous meringues with fresh fruit (July).**
Described as peaceful, pastel shades in early summer. Beautifully structured ¼ acre south facing plot, carefully terraced and planted as it rises to the Bridgewater towpath. Hazel arch opens to formal clay paved courtyard with cordoned peach trees. Working greenhouse. Rose pillars lead to established herbaceous beds, quiet shaded areas, bordered by azaleas and rhododendrons. Interesting outhouses. Featured in Amateur Gardening. Short gravel driveway and some steps to access the rear garden. The rear garden is sloping.

&. ☞ ☕

59 ♦ STONYFORD COTTAGE

Stonyford Lane, Oakmere, CW8 2TF. Janet & Tony Overland, 01606 888970, info@ stonyfordcottagegardens.co.uk, www.stonyfordcottagegardens. co.uk. *5m SW of Northwich. From Northwich take A556 towards Chester. ¾m past A49 junction turn R into Stonyford Lane. Entrance ½m on L.* **For NGS: Sun 14 May, Sun 30 July (11-4). Adm £4.50, chd free. Home-made teas. Lunches and cream teas available. For other opening times and information, please phone, email or visit garden website.**
Set around a tranquil pool this Monet style landscape has a wealth of moisture loving plants, incl iris and candelabra primulas. Drier areas feature unusual perennials and rarer trees and shrubs. Woodland paths meander through shade

and bog plantings, along boarded walks, across wild natural areas with views over the pool to the cottage gardens. Unusual plants available at the adjacent nursery. Open Tues - Sun & BH Mons Apr - Oct 10-5pm. Cottage Tea Room. Plant Nursery. Some gravel paths.

&. ✿ 🚗 ☕

60 SUN HOUSE

66 Bridge Lane, Bramhall, Stockport, SK7 3AW. Peter & Susan Hale, 0161 439 1519, susan.hale1@btopenworld.com. *3½m S of Stockport. Sun House is on Bridge Lane (A5143) between junction with A5102 at the Bramall Hall r'about & Bramhall Moor Lane.* **Sat 3, Sun 4 June (1.30-5.30). Adm £4, chd free. Home-made teas. Gluten free cakes available on open day. Visits also by arrangement May & June no plant sales available until after the open day.**
Sun House garden is quirky and romantic, full of interest and colour all year round. The garden is surrounded by mature trees with dry, shady, acid soil addressed by building numerous ponds and bog areas which are at their best in Spring. It has a wide range of herbaceous plants, mosaic and ceramic decorations, gravel garden, vegetable plot, chickens and two life-sized terracotta warriors. Display and sale of ceramics and crafts. New exploration trail for children each year. Featured in Amateur Gardener magazine and recently in BBC 2's The Great British Garden Revival. Some paths need care, unfenced ponds.

&. ✿ 🚗 ☕

61 SUNNYSIDE FARM

Shop Lane, Little Budworth, CW6 9HA. Mike & Joan Smeethe, 01829 760618, joan.ann.smeethe@btinternet.com. *4m NE of Tarporley. Signed field parking reached directly off A54 approx 1m E of T-lights at A54/ A49 Xrds. Take track opp Longstone Lane 250yds W of Shrewsbury Arms. Ignore SatNav.* **Sat 15, Sun 16 July (2-5.30). Adm £4, chd free. Home-made teas. Visits also**

by arrangement June to Aug groups of 10+.
A plant lover's and beekeeper's atmospheric country garden. Wildlife and child friendly the five acres encompass oak woodland, wildflower meadow, pool garden, potager and fruit garden, orchard with beehives, long border with naturalistic planting and cottage garden. With a wealth of unusual plants and interesting colour schemes this is a constantly evolving garden. Wheelchair access to most parts of the garden. Please phone for disabled parking at house.

&. ☞ 🐴 ✿ ☕

62 SYCAMORE COTTAGE

Manchester Road, Carrington, Manchester, M31 4AY. Mrs C Newton, cottonandrose@gmail.com. *From M60 J8 take Carrington turn (A6144) through 2 sets of T-lights. Garden approx 1m after 2nd set of T-lights on R. From M6 J20 signed for Partington/Carrington garden approx 1m on L.* **Sat 3 June (12-5). Adm £4, chd free. Light refreshments. Visits also by arrangement for groups of 10+.**
Approx ⅕ acre cottage garden split into distinct areas, with woodland banking, natural spring, well and ponds. Also features decking with two seating areas and summer house. Garden featured on Cupranols TV advert.

✿ ☕

63 TATTENHALL HALL

High Street, Tattenhall, CH3 9PX. Jen & Nick Benefield, Chris Evered & Jannie Hollins, 01829 770654, janniehollins@gmail.com. *8m S of Chester on A41. Turn L to Tattenhall, through village, turn R at Letters PH, past war memorial on L through Sandstone pillared gates. Park on rd or in village car park.* **Sun 28 May, Sun 16 July (2-5.30). Adm £4.50, chd free. Home-made teas. Visits also by arrangement Mar to Oct any size of group, limited parking facilities.**
Plant enthusiasts garden around Jacobean house (not open). 4½ acres, wild flower meadows, interesting trees, large pond, stream,

walled garden, colour themed borders, succession planting, spinney walk with shade plants, yew terrace overlooking meadow, views to hills. Glasshouse and vegetable garden. Wildlife friendly sometimes untidy garden, interest throughout the year, continuing to develop. Articles in Gardenista, online magazine. Gravel paths, cobbles and some steps.

♿ ✵ ☕

64 ◆ TATTON PARK

Knutsford, WA16 6QN. National Trust, leased to Cheshire East Council, 01625 374400, www.tattonpark.org.uk. *2½ m N of Knutsford. Well signed on M56 J7 & from M6 J19.* **For NGS: Wed 10 May, Wed 14 June (10-6). Adm £7, chd £5. For other opening times and information, please phone or visit garden website.** Features incl orangery by Wyatt, fernery by Paxton, restored Japanese garden, Italian and rose gardens. Greek monument and African hut. Hybrid azaleas and rhododendrons; swamp cypresses, tree ferns, tall redwoods, bamboos and pines. Fully restored productive walled gardens. Wheelchair access apart from rose garden and Japanese garden.

♿ ✵ 🚘 🛌 ☕

65 NEW THORNCAR

Windmill Lane, Appleton, Warrington, WA4 5JN. Mrs Kath Carey. *South Warrington. From M56 J10 take A49 towards Warrington for 1½ m. At 2nd set of T-lights turn L into Quarry Lane, as the road swings R it becomes Windmill Lane. Thorncar is 4th house on R.* **Sat 22 July (12.30-4.30). Adm £3.50, chd free. Light refreshments. Refreshments provided by WI.** A one third acre plantwoman's suburban garden planted since 2011 within the framework of part of an established garden. It is not planted for aesthetics but to give some colour 12 months of the year and to require no watering even in dry spells.

♿ ✵ ☕

51 Garth Drive

66 TIRLEY GARTH GARDENS

Mallows Way, Willington, Tarporley, CW6 0RQ. Tirley Garth. *2m N of Tarporley. 2m S of Kelsall. Entrance 500yds from village of Utkinton. At N of Tarporley take Utkinton rd.* **Sun 7, Sun 14, Sun 21 May (1-5). Adm £5, chd free. Home-made teas.**
40-acre garden, terraced and landscaped, designed by Thomas Mawson (considered the leading exponent of garden design in early C20), it is the only Grade II* Arts and Crafts garden in Cheshire that remains complete and in excellent condition. The gardens are an important example of an early C20 garden laid out in both formal and informal styles. By early May the garden is bursting into flower with almost 3000 Rhododendron and Azalea many 100 years old. Exhibition by local Artists. Very limited wheelchair access to tea rooms.

67 TWIN GATES

3 Earle Drive, Parkgate, Neston, CH64 6RY. John Hinde & Lilian Baker. *Approx ½m N of Neston town centre. From Neston (Tesco/Brown Horse PH), N towards Methodist Church. At church (Brewers Arms on L), take L fork into Park St, becomes Leighton Rd. Continue for approx ½m, L into Earle Drive.* **Evening opening Fri 16 June (6-10). Adm £5, chd free. Glass of wine incl in adm. Additional glass by donation.**
Garden developed over last 3 to 4 years and now beginning to mature. Mixed herbaceous and shrub borders, with some choice small trees all set in fully stocked sinuous borders. In June, peaonies and roses come to the fore, but there are plenty of other genus, too. Join us for wine and music on a hopefully balmy evening! Weather not guaranteed!

68 THE WELL HOUSE

Wet Lane, Tilston, Malpas, SY14 7DP. Mrs S H French-Greenslade, 01829 250332. *3m NW of Malpas. On A41, 1st R after Broxton r'about, L on Malpas Rd through Tilston. House on L.* **Visits by arrangement Apr to Sept not open Aug. Open Feb for snowdrops. Refreshments by arrrangement for small groups but not coaches. Adm £5, chd free.**
1-acre cottage garden, bridge over natural stream, spring bulbs, perennials, herbs and shrubs. Triple ponds. Adjoining ¾-acre field made into wild flower meadow; first seeding late 2003. Large bog area of kingcups and ragged robin. February for snowdrop walk.

69 WELL HOUSE

Dean Row Road, Wilmslow, SK9 2BU. Steven & Jill Kimber. *2m N of Wilmslow. On Dean Row Rd (B 5358), at junction with Adlington Rd (A5102). Park at the Unicorn PH 300 yds, from the house. Next to Shell garage. Less able visitors can drop off at house limited space.* **Sun 25 June (10.30-4.30). Adm £4.50, chd free. Home-made teas.**
Familiar to many gardening friends this happily maturing 3 acre garden, tended with a gentle hand offers; a shady woodland, formal borders and imaginative landscaping. Featuring lush herbaceous planting, wild flowers are a particular passion. Both naturalised and planted they are managed, cultivated and encouraged wherever possible. Especially within the meadow which now boasts many wild orchids. Wheelchair access through the main gate.

The Homestead

GROUP OPENING

70 WEST DRIVE GARDENS

6, 9 West Drive, Gatley, Cheadle, SK8 4JJ. Mr & Mrs D J Gane, Thelma Bishop & John Needham, 0161 4 280204, Davidjgane@btinternet.com. *4m N of Wilmslow on B5166. 4 m N of Wilmslow on B5166. From J5 (M56) drive past airpt. to B5166 (Styal Rd).L to Gatley. Go over T-lights at Heald Green. West Drive is last turn on R before Gatley(approx.1½ m from T-lights).* **Sun 19 Feb (11-2). Combined adm £3, chd free. Light refreshments. Sun 4 June (10.30-5). Combined adm £5, chd free. Home-made teas. and WC at No 6. Visits also by arrangement Feb to Sept.**
Cul-de-sac, do not park beyond notice. Here are two gardens of very different character, reflecting their owner's gardening style. Although suburban , they are surrounded by mature trees and have a secluded feel. Rich variety of planting incl. ferns, hostas and herbaceous borders. with clematis,roses,foxgloves,aquilegias at their best. Wild life pond at no.6 and other water features.Ceramics and containers with alpines complete the picture. Home-made teas, no.6. Opening in February for displays of hellebores and snowdrops. Access to top of gardens giving general overview, with shallow step leading onto gravel at no.6 and several steps and narrow paths at no.9.

71 THE WHITE COTTAGE

Threapwood, Malpas, Cheshire, SY14 7AL. Chris & Carol Bennion. *3m W of Malpas. From Malpas take Wrexham Rd B5069 W for 3m. From Bangor on Dee take B5069 E to Threapwood. Car Park in field opp shop & garage.* **Sat 17, Sun 18 June (1-5). Adm £4, chd free. Home-made teas.**
An interesting and relaxing country garden containing mature trees and shrubs, topiary and meandering herbaceous borders brimming with soft romantic planting. An orchard area contains mature and young fruit trees, raised beds and greenhouse. Several distinct areas provide a variety of vistas. Features include a dovecote, pergola, horseshoe garden, statuary, topiary, countryside views.

72 WILLASTON GRANGE

Hadlow Road, Willaston, Neston, CH64 2UN. Mr & Mrs M Mitchell. *Willaston. On the A540 (Chester High Rd) take the B5151 into Willaston. From the Village Green in the centre of Willaston turn onto Hadlow Rd, Willaston Grange is ½m on your L.* **Sat 24 June (1-5). Adm £5, chd free. Home-made teas.**
Willaston Grange was part of Cheshire NGS and after a 20 year break, appears in 2017 as a 'work in progress'.The gardens extend to almost 6 acres with a small lake, wide range of mature and rare trees, herbaceous borders, woodland and vegetable gardens, orchard and magical tree house. After a full restoration, the Arts and Crafts house provides the perfect backdrop, along with afternoon tea and live music. Most areas accessible by wheelchair.

73 WINTERBOTTOM HOUSE

Winterbottom Lane, Mere, Knutsford, WA16 0QQ. Neil & Verona Stott, thestotts@btinternet.com. *Half way between Mere T-lights & High Legh. Signed off A50. From A50 opp Kilton Inn turn into Hoo Green Lane, in ½m bear L down Winterbottom Lane (narrow lane - take care!). Winterbottom House at end . Follow signs for ample parking with wheelchair access.* **Sun 11 June (1-5). Adm £5, chd free. Home-made teas. Evening opening Fri 23 June (6-9). Adm £7, chd free. Wine. A glass of wine incl on 23 June. Visits also by arrangement June to Aug 10 -20.**
A large garden developed over many years with two distinct areas. One mainly trees, grasses and woodland planting with natural koi pond leading to vegetable garden and greenhouse. The other more formal area with lots of herbaceous borders and shrubs to give year round interest. This area incl period summer house, ornamental rill and extensive lawns with plenty of seating areas. Some gravel paths but no steps.

74 WOOD END COTTAGE

Grange Lane, Whitegate, Northwich, CW8 2BQ. Mr & Mrs M R Everett, 01606 888236, woodendct@supanet.com. *4m SW of Northwich. Turn S off A556 (Northwich bypass) at Sandiway T-lights; after 1¾ m, turn L to Whitegate village; opp school follow Grange Lane for 300yds.* **Visits by arrangement May to July. Adm £4.50, chd free. Home-made teas.**
Plantsman's ½ acre garden in attractive setting, sloping to a natural stream bordered by shade and moisture-loving plants. Background of mature trees. Well stocked herbaceous borders, trellis with roses and clematis, magnificent delphiniums, many phlox, meconopsis and choice perennials. Interesting shrubs and flowering trees. Vegetable garden.

75 WREN'S NEST

Wrenbury Heath Road, Wrenbury, Nantwich, CW5 8EQ. Sue & Dave Clarke, 07855 398803, wrenburysue@gmail.com. *Nantwich 12m from M6 J16. From Nantwich signs for A530 to Whitchurch, reaching Sound school turn 1st R Wrenbury Heath Rd, across the Xrds and bungalow is on L, telegraph pole right outside.* **Wed 21 June (10-5). Combined adm with Oakfield Villa £6, chd free. Visits also by arrangement May to July phone or email. Refreshments on request.**
Set in a semi-rural area, this bungalow has a Cottage Garden Style of lush planting and is 80ft x 45ft. The garden is packed with unusual and traditional perennials and shrubs incl over 100 hardy geraniums, campanulas, crocosmias, iris and alpine troughs. Plants for sale. Proceeds from this garden will be for the NGS. National collection of Hardy Geranium sylvaticum and renardii.

CORNWALL

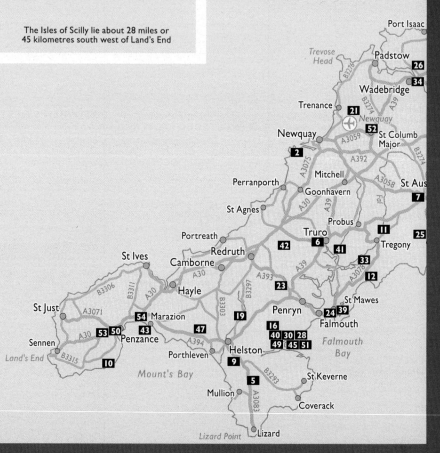

ISLES OF SCILLY

Tresco
St Martin's
Bryher
Hugh Town
St Mary's
St Agnes

The Isles of Scilly lie about 28 miles or
45 kilometres south west of Land's End

Port Isaac

Trevose
Head

Padstow

26

Wadebridge

34

Trenance

21

Newquay

52

St Columb
Major

Newquay

2

Perranporth

Mitchell

Goonhavern

St Aus

St Agnes

Probus

7

Portreath

Truro

11

Redruth

42

6

Tregony

25

Camborne

41

St Ives

33

Hayle

23

12

St Just

St Mawes

Marazion

19

Penryn

24 39

Sennen

54

47

16

Falmouth

53 50

43

40 30 28

Land's End

Penzance

49 45 51

10

Porthleven

Falmouth
Bay

Helston

9

Mount's Bay

5

St Keverne

Mullion

Coverack

Lizard Point

Lizard

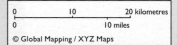

Cornwall has some of the most beautiful natural landscapes to be found anywhere in the world.

Volunteers

County Organisers
Bryan Coode
01726 882488
bhcoode@btconnect.com

Christopher Harvey Clark
01872 530165
suffree2012@gmail.com

County Treasurer
Andrew Flint
01726 879336
flints@elizaholidays.co.uk

Publicity
Nutty Lim
01726 815247
christianne.gf.lim@gmail.com

Booklet Co-ordinator
Peter Stanley
01326 565868
stanley.m2@sky.com

Assistant County Organisers
Ginnie Clotworthy
01208 872612
giles.clotworthy@btopenworld.com

Sarah Gordon
01579 362076
sar.gordon@talktalk.net

Katie Nichols
01872 275786
katherinemlambert@gmail.com

Alison O'Connor
01726 882460
tregoose@tregoose.co.uk

Marion Stanley
01326 565868
stanley.m2@sky.com

Ian Wright
ian.wright@nationaltrust.org.uk

Here, you will discover some of the country's most extraordinary gardens, a spectacular coastline, internationally famous surfing beaches, windswept moors and countless historic sites. Cornish gardens reflect this huge variety of environments particularly well.

A host of National Collections of magnolias, camellias, rhododendrons and azaleas, as well as exotic Mediterranean semitropical plants and an abundance of other plants flourish in our acid soils and mild climate.

Surrounded by the warm currents of the Gulf Stream, with our warm damp air in summer and mild moist winters, germination continues all year.

Cornwall boasts an impressive variety of beautiful gardens. These range from coastal-protected positions to exposed cliff-top sites, moorland water gardens, Japanese gardens and the world famous tropical biomes of the Eden Project.

Right: St Michael's Mount

OPENING DATES

All entries subject to change. For latest information check www.ngs.org.uk

Extended openings are shown at the beginning of the month.

Map locator numbers are shown to the right of each garden name.

March

Sunday 5th
Ince Castle 20

Sunday 26th
Ince Castle 20

April

Waye Cottage
(Every day from
Saturday 1st) 55

Saturday 8th
♦ Trewidden Garden 53

Sunday 9th
Ince Castle 20

Saturday 15th
NEW Bodwannick
Manor Farm 4

Sunday 16th
NEW Bodwannick
Manor Farm 4

Monday 17th
Riverside Cottage 41

Sunday 23rd
♦ Lamorran House 24
Meudon Hotel 28

Monday 24th
♦ Pencarrow 35

Saturday 29th
♦ Chygurno 10

Sunday 30th
♦ Chygurno 10
Ince Castle 20

May

Waye Cottage
(Every day) 55

Monday 1st
♦ Chygurno 10
♦ Moyclare 29

Sunday 7th
♦ Boconnoc 3
East Down Barn 14
Ethnevas Cottage 16
Navas Hill House 30

Sunday 14th
Byeways 8
♦ The Japanese
Garden 21

Monday 15th
♦ The Japanese
Garden 21

Saturday 20th
♦ Pinsla Garden &
Nursery 38

Sunday 21st
♦ Pinsla Garden &
Nursery 38
Riverside Cottage 41
Trebartha 46

90th Anniversary Weekend

Sunday 28th
NEW Bodwannick Manor
Farm 4
Lower Amble Gardens 26
♦ St Michael's Mount 43

June

Waye Cottage
(Every day) 55

Sunday 11th
Creed House & Creed
Lodge 11
♦ The Homestead
Woodland Garden 19
Mary Newman's
Garden 27

Friday 16th
♦ Trematon Castle 48

Saturday 17th
Carminowe Valley
Garden 9
Half Acre 17

Sunday 18th
Arundell 2
Carminowe Valley
Garden 9
Half Acre 17
Penheale Manor 36

Friday 23rd
Dye Cottage 13

Saturday 24th
Dye Cottage 13
♦ Roseland House 42

Sunday 25th
Anvil Cottage 1
Dye Cottage 13
♦ Roseland House 42
Trenarth 49
Trewan Hall 52
Windmills 56

July

Waye Cottage
(Every day) 55

Sunday 2nd
Anvil Cottage 1
Trerose Manor 51
Windmills 56

Saturday 8th
The Old Watermill 32
Poldarian 39

Sunday 9th
♦ Bosvigo House 6
Mary Newman's
Garden 27
Poldarian 39

Sunday 16th
Arundell 2
Brookvale 7

Saturday 22nd
♦ Chygurno 10
Tregonning 47

Sunday 23rd
♦ Chygurno 10
Tregonning 47

Friday 28th
♦ Hidden Valley
Gardens 18

Saturday 29th
♦ Hidden Valley
Gardens 18
Kennall House 23
♦ Roseland House 42

Sunday 30th
Byeways 8
♦ Roseland House 42

August

Waye Cottage
(Every day) 55

Saturday 5th
♦ Pinsla Garden &
Nursery 38

Sunday 6th
♦ Pinsla Garden &
Nursery 38

Wednesday 9th
♦ Bonython Manor 5

Sunday 27th
Crugsillick Manor 12

September

Waye Cottage
(Every day) 55

Sunday 24th
Trebartha 46

By Arrangement

Anvil Cottage 1
Arundell 2
Carminowe Valley
Garden 9
Creed House &
Creed Lodge 11
Crugsillick Manor 12
East Down Barn 14
Ethnevas Cottage 16
Kennall House 23
Mary Newman's
Garden 27
Meudon Hotel 28
Navas Hill House 30
The Old Rectory 31
Parc-Lamp 33
Pencarn 34
Riverside Cottage 41
NEW Sea View 44
Tregonning 47
Trenarth 49
Trereife Park 50
Waye Cottage 55

THE GARDENS

I   ANVIL COTTAGE
South Hill, PL17 7LP.
Geoff & Barbara Clemerson,
01579 362623,
geoff@south-hill.co.uk. *3m NW
of Callington. Head N on A388 from
Callington centre. After ½ m L onto
South Hill Rd (signed South Hill),
straight on for 3m. Gardens on R just
before St Sampson's Church.* **Sun
25 June, Sun 2 July (1.30-5).
Combined adm with Windmills
£5, chd free. Cream teas. Visits
also by arrangement June to
Sept.**
Essentially a plantsman's garden.
Winding paths take you through a
series of themed rooms housing
some both familiar and rare and
unusual plants. Higher up, a wild
flower garden leads through a formal
rose garden to a raised viewpoint
with spectacular views of Caradon
Hill and Bodmin Moor. Very limited
wheelchair access due to steps.

2   ARUNDELL
West Pentire, Crantock,
TR8 5SE. Brenda & David Eyles,
01637 831916,
david@davideyles.com. *I m W of
Crantock. From A3075 take signs to
Crantock. At junction in village keep
straight on to West Pentire (Im). Park
in field (signed) or public car parks
at W Pentire.* **Sun 18 June, Sun
16 July (1-5). Adm £5, chd free.
Home-made teas. Visits also
by arrangement May to Aug on
Thursdays.**
A garden where no garden should
be! - on windswept NT headland
between 2 fantastic beaches. I acre
packed with design and plant interest
round old farm cottage. Front:
cottage garden. Side: Mediterranean
courtyard. Rear: rockery and
shrubbery leading to stumpery and
fernery and on to stream and pond,
Cornish Corner, herbaceous borders,
Beth Chatto dry garden, small
pinetum and jungle garden. Appeared
on Gardeners' World; articles in Coast
magazine, Garden News, Cornwall
Today, Cornish Life. Wheelchair access

Chygurno

© Carole Drake

from public car park with entrance via rear gate. 14 shallow steps in centre of garden useable with care.

 ♿ 🐑 ❀ ☕

3 ◆ BOCONNOC
Lostwithiel, PL22 0RG. Elizabeth Fortescue, 01208 872507, office@boconnoc.com, www.boconnoc.com. *Off A390 between Liskeard & Lostwithiel. From East Taphouse follow signs to Boconnoc. (SatNav does not work well in this area).* **For NGS: Sun 7 May (2-5). Adm £5.50, chd free. Home-made teas in Stable Yard. For other opening times and information, please phone, email or visit garden website.**
20 acre gardens surrounded by parkland and woods with magnificent trees, flowering shrubs and stunning views. The gardens are set amongst mature trees which provide the backcloth for exotic spring flowering shrubs, woodland plants, with newly-planted magnolias and a fine collection of hydrangeas. Bathhouse built in 1804, woodland gardens, obelisk built in 1771, house dating from Domesday, deer park, C15 church.

 ♿ 🐑 🛏 🚌 ☕

4 NEW BODWANNICK MANOR FARM
Nanstallon, Bodmin, PL30 5LN. Gaia Trust. *From A30, take A389 signed to Lanivet and Bodmin. 1m after Lanivet turn L (signed to Nanstallon). From Bodmin, take A389 signed for A30. After 1½m turn R at Jim's hardware store.* **Sat 15, Sun 16 Apr, Sun 28 May (11-4). Adm by donation. Light refreshments in old farmhouse conservatory and on terrace.**
1½-acre plantsman's garden with fern-rich rockery, water and kitchen gardens, daffodils, roses and shrubs. It is remarkable for its aura of peace and tranquillity, but its air of antiquity is deceptive as it was the lifetime creation of Martin Appleton and his family. Now in the care of the Gaia Trust, it has particular features of interest and is full of yr-round interest. Wheelchair access possible to much but not all of the garden.

 ♿ 🐑 ❀ ☕

5 ◆ BONYTHON MANOR
Cury Cross Lanes, Helston, TR12 7BA. Mr & Mrs Richard Nathan, 01326 240550, sbonython@gmail.com, www.bonythonmanor.co.uk. *5m S of Helston. On main A3083 Helston to Lizard Rd. Turn L at Cury Cross Lanes (Wheel Inn). Entrance 300yds on R.* **For NGS: Wed 9 Aug (2-4.30). Adm £8, chd £2. Home-made teas. For other opening times and information, please phone, email or visit garden website.**
Magnificent 20-acre colour garden incl sweeping hydrangea drive to Georgian manor (not open). Herbaceous walled garden, potager with vegetables and picking flowers; 3 lakes in valley planted with ornamental grasses, perennials and South African flowers. A 'must see' for all seasons colour.

 ♿ 🐑 ❀ 🚌 🛏 ☕

6 ◆ BOSVIGO HOUSE
Bosvigo Lane, Truro, TR1 3NH. Wendy Perry, 01872 275774, www.bosvigo.com/. *Truro City Centre. At Highertown, nr Sainsbury r'about, turn down Dobbs Lane. After 500yds, entrance to house is on L, after sharp LH-bend.* **For NGS: Sun 9 July (2-6). Adm £5, chd free. Home-made teas in the Servants Hall. For other opening times and information, please phone or visit garden website.**
Created by artist owner, the 2 acre garden surrounding the Georgian house has been designed to create dazzling displays of vivid colour and plant harmonies. Each garden room is designed with a different palette of colour. For the opening in July the Vean garden and walled garden will be looking their best. Very limited wheelchair access.

 🚌 ☕

7 BROOKVALE
Gover Valley, St. Austell, PL25 5RA. Leslie & Myrna Baker. *1m from the town centre, close to the Gover Viaduct.* **Sun 16 July (2-6). Adm £4, chd free. Cream teas.**
Brunel's GWR viaduct is a magnificent backdrop to this all year round garden created by the current owners over the past 30 years. Both sun and shade plantings with significant herbaceous borders and an extensive rockery.

 ❀ ☕

With your support we can help raise awareness of Carers Trust and unpaid carers

8 BYEWAYS
Dunheved Road, Launceston, PL15 9JE. Tony Reddicliffe. *Launceston town centre. 100yds from multi-storey car park past offices of Cornish & Devon Post into Dunheved Rd, 3rd bungalow on R.* **Sun 14 May, Sun 30 July (1-5). Adm £4, chd free. Home-made teas.**
Small town garden developed over 5yrs by enthusiastic amateur gardeners. Herbaceous borders, rockery. Tropicals incl bananas, gingers and senecio. Stream and water features. Many areas to sit and view.

 🐑 ☕

9 CARMINOWE VALLEY GARDEN
Tangies, Gunwalloe, TR12 7PU. Mr & Mrs Peter Stanley, 01326 565868, stanley.m2@sky.com, www.carminowevalleygarden.co.uk. *3m SW of Helston. A3083 Helston-Lizard rd. R opp main gate to Culdrose. 1m downhill, garden on R.* **Sat 17, Sun 18 June (1.30-4.30). Adm £5, chd free. Visits also by arrangement Apr to Aug.**
Overlooking the beautiful Carminowe Valley towards Loe Pool this abundant garden combines native oak woodland, babbling brook and large natural pond with more formal areas. Wild flower meadow, mown pathways, shrubberies, orchard, nectar beds, cutting garden, kitchen garden, summerhouse. Enclosed cottage garden, tulips in spring and roses early summer provide huge contrast. Gravel paths, slopes.

 ♿ 🐑 ❀ 🚌 🛏 ☕

10 ◆ CHYGURNO

Lamorna, TR19 6XH. Dr & Mrs
Robert Moule, 01736 732153,
rmoule010@btinternet.com. *4m S
of Penzance. Off B3315. Follow signs
for The Lamorna Cove Hotel. Garden
is at top of hill, past Hotel on L.* **For
NGS: Sat 29, Sun 30 Apr, Mon
1 May, Sat 22, Sun 23 July (2-5).
Adm £5, chd free. For other
opening times and information,
please phone or email.**
Beautiful, unique, 3-acre cliffside
garden overlooking Lamorna Cove.
Planting started in 1998, mainly
S-hemisphere shrubs and exotics
with hydrangeas, camellias and
rhododendrons. Woodland area
with tree ferns set against large
granite outcrops. Garden terraced
with steep steps and paths. Plenty of
benches so you can take a rest and
enjoy the wonderful views. Featured
on BBC Gardeners World.
🐕

11 CREED HOUSE & CREED LODGE

Creed, Grampound, Truro,
TR2 4SL. The Croggon
family, 01872 530372,
www.creedhouse.co.uk. *9m W of
Truro. From the centre of Grampound
on A390, take rd signed to Creed.
After 1m turn L opp Creed Church,
garden is on L.* **Sun 11 June
(11-5). Adm £4.50, chd free.
Home-made teas. Visits also by
arrangement Apr to June.**
5-acre landscaped Georgian rectory
garden; tranquil rural setting;
spacious lawns. Tree collection;
rhododendrons; sunken cobbled yard
and formal walled rose garden. Trickle
stream to ponds and bog. Natural
woodland walk together with
recently planted small garden around
new house. Herbaceous beds, shrubs
and large terrace with rose bed
below. Dogs welcome on leads.
🐕 🛏 ☕

12 CRUGSILLICK MANOR

Ruan High Lanes, Truro,
TR2 5LJ. Dr Alison Agnew &
Mr Brian Yule, 01872 501972,
alisonagnew@icloud.com. *On
Roseland Peninsula. Turn off A390
Truro-St Austell rd onto A3078
towards St Mawes. Approx 5m after*
*Tregony turn 1st L after Ruan High
Lanes towards Veryan, garden is
200yds on R.* **Sun 27 Aug (11-5).
Adm £4, chd free. Home-made
teas. Visits also by arrangement
June to Sept for groups of 15+
only.**
2 acre garden, substantially relandscaped and planted - mostly
over last 4 yrs. To the side of the
C17/C18 house, a wooded bank
drops down to walled kitchen
garden and hot garden. In front,
sweeping yew hedges and paths
define oval lawns and broad mixed
borders. On a lower terrace, the
focus is a large pond and the
planting is predominantly exotic
flowering trees and shrubs. Partial
wheelchair access. Garden is on
several levels connected by fairly
steep sloping gravel paths.
♿ 🐕 ✿ ☕ ☕

13 DYE COTTAGE

St Neot, PL14 6NG. Sue & Brian
Williams. *Opp The London Inn in
centre of St Neot village. Turn off A38
to St Neot. Street parking.* **Fri 23,
Sat 24, Sun 25 June (2-5). Adm
£3.50, chd free. Home-made
teas.**
⅓ acre cottage garden, designed
and completely maintained by the
owners over the past 23 yrs. Many
seating areas - down by the river,
in courtyard garden, fire pit corner,
and on rose terrace. Wisteria
walk, potting shed, greenhouse,
summerhouse, office (once the tree
house!), fruit cage, mature borders,
and roses everywhere. Regret no
wheelchair access.
🐕 ✿ ☕

14 EAST DOWN BARN

Menheniot, Liskeard, PL14 3QU.
David & Shelley Lockett,
07803 159662. *S side of village
near cricket ground. Turn off A38 at
Hayloft restaurant/railway station
junction and head towards Menheniot
village. Follow NGS signs from sharp L
hand bend as you enter village.* **Sun
7 May (1-5). Adm £3, chd free.
Home-made teas. Visits also by
arrangement Apr & May.**
Garden laid down between 1986-
1991 with the conversion of the
Barn into a home and covers almost
½ acre of East sloping land with
stream running North - South acting
as the Easterly boundary. 3 terraces
before garden starts to level out at
stream. Garden won awards in the
early years under the stewardship of
the original owners. Steep slopes.
☕

15 ◆ EDEN PROJECT

Bodelva, PL24 2SG. The
Eden Trust, 01726 811911,
www.edenproject.com. *4m E of
St Austell. Brown signs from A30
& A390.* **For opening times and
information, please phone or visit
garden website.**
Described as 8th wonder of the
world, the Eden Project is a global
garden for the C21. Discover the
story of plants that have changed
the world and which could change
your future. The Eden Project is
an exciting attraction where you
can explore your relationship with
nature, learn new things and get
inspiration about the world around
you. Yr-round programme of talks,
events and workshops. Wheelchairs
available - booking of powered
wheelchairs is essential; please call
01726 818895 in advance.
♿ 🐕 ✿ 🚌 🛏 ☕

16 ETHNEVAS COTTAGE

Constantine, Falmouth, TR11 5PY.
Lyn Watson & Ray Chun,
01326 340076. *6m SW of Falmouth.
Nearest main rds A39, A394. Follow
signs to Constantine. At lower village
sign, at bottom of winding hill, turn off
on private lane. Garden ¾m up hill
(single lane track with few passing
spaces, please drive very slowly).* **Sun
7 May (1-4). Adm £4, chd free.
Light refreshments. Visits also
by arrangement for groups of
20 max.**
Isolated granite cottage in 2 acres.
Intimate flower and vegetable
garden. Bridge over stream to large
pond and primrose path through
semi-wild bog area. Hillside with
grass paths among native and
exotic trees. Many camellias and
rhododendrons. Mixed shrubs and
herbaceous beds, wild flower glade,
spring bulbs. A garden of discovery
of hidden delights.
✿ ☕

17 HALF ACRE

Mount Pleasant, Boscastle,
PL35 0BJ. Carole Vincent,
www.carolevincent.org. *5m N of
Camelford. Park at doctors' surgery at
top of village (clearly signed). Limited
parking for disabled at garden.* **Sat
17, Sun 18 June (1.30-5.30).
Adm £4, chd free. Home-made
teas.**
Old stone cottage with 2 studios
overlooking cliffs and sea, set in
1½ acres of gardens - cottage,
small wood and Blue Circle garden
(RHS Chelsea 2001) constructed
in colour concrete. Owner has a
national reputation for her sculpture
in concrete, and sculptures all
around occupy small spaces or
command a view. Mid-June should
see the flowering of the roses and
echiums. Studio open. Painting
exhibition. Regret no dogs.

18 ◆ HIDDEN VALLEY GARDENS

Treesmill, Par, PL24 2TU.
Tricia Howard, 01208 873225,
hiddenvalleygardens@yahoo.co.uk,
www.hiddenvalleygardens.co.uk.
*2m SW of Lostwithiel. Yellow
sign directions on A390 between
Lostwithiel (2m) & St Austell (5m),
directing onto B3269 towards Fowey,
followed by a R turn. From Fowey,
take B3269 and turn L at yellow
sign.* **For NGS: Fri 28, Sat 29
July (10-5). Adm £4.50, chd
free. Cream teas and home-
made cakes in tea hut. For other
opening times and information,
please phone, email or visit
garden website.**
Award-winning 3-acre colourful
garden in hidden valley with
nursery. Cottage-style planting with
herbaceous beds and borders,
grasses, ferns and fruit. Gazebo with
country views. Iris fairy well and
vegetable potager. July opening for
special displays of herbaceous plants
including collections of crocosmia,
agapanthus and dahlias and many
other colourful flowers. Children's
quiz. Dogs on lead. In Feb Tricia has
a collection of some 70+ named
snowdrops as well as hellebores
and early flowering daffodils. Please
ring to visit. Special drop off parking
for wheelchair access directly into
garden area. Mainly wheelchair
accessible, some gentle slopes.

19 ◆ THE HOMESTEAD WOODLAND GARDEN

Crelly, Trenear, Wendron,
TR13 0EU. Shirley Williams &
Chris Tredinnick, 01326 562808,
homesteadholidays@btconnect.
com, www.the-homestead-
woodland-garden.com. *3m N
of Helston. From Helston B3297
towards Redruth, 3m. Entrance 3rd
on R 200 metres past Crelly/Bodilly
sign & bus shelter.* **For NGS: Sun
11 June (1-4). Adm £5, chd free.
Light refreshments. For other
opening times and information,
please phone, email or visit garden
website.**
3 acres of divided gardens giving
all-yr round interest and 3 acres
of wildlife habitat and deciduous
woodland with primroses in spring.
Cornish variety apple orchard
where chickens, ducks and geese
roam free. Vegetable garden,
mature garden with pond and
mixed borders. Archways, pergolas,
seating, water features, hot and
shady areas, walled garden, Japanese
and Moroccan area. Sculptures
sited throughout. Unfenced ponds,
uneven paths (which may be
slippery when wet) and some steps.

Riverside Cottage

20 INCE CASTLE

Saltash, PL12 4RA. Lord & Lady Boyd, 01752 842672, www.incecastle.co.uk. *3m SW of Saltash. From A38 at Stoketon Cross take turn signed Trematon, then Elmgate. No large coaches.* **Suns 5, 26 Mar, 9, 30 Apr (2-5). Adm £4, chd free. Home-made teas.** Romantic garden at the end of winding lanes, surrounding C17 pink brick castle on a peninsula in R Lynher. Old apple trees with bulbs, woodland garden with fritillaries, camellias and rhododendrons. Extraordinary 1960s shell house on edge of formal garden. Partial wheelchair access.

21 ◆ THE JAPANESE GARDEN

St Mawgan, TR8 4ET. Natalie Hore & Stuart Ellison, 01637 860116, www.japanesegarden.co.uk. *6m E of Newquay. St Mawgan village is directly below Newquay Airport. Follow brown & white road signs on A3059 & B3276.* **For NGS: Sun 14, Mon 15 May (10-6). Adm £4.50, chd £2.** For other opening times and information, please phone or visit garden website. East meets West in a unique garden for all seasons. Spectacular Japanese maples and azaleas, symbolic teahouse, koi pond, bamboo grove, stroll, woodland, zen and moss gardens. An oasis of tranquillity. Adm free to gift shop, bonsai and plant areas. Some gravel paths.

22 ◆ KEN CARO

Bicton, Liskeard, PL14 5RF. Mr & Mrs K R Willcock, 01579 362446. *5m NE of Liskeard. From A390 to Callington turn off N at St Ive. Take Pensilva Rd, follow brown tourist signs, approx 1m off main rd. Plenty of parking. (SatNav is misleading).* For opening times and information, please phone. Connoisseurs' garden full of interest all yr round. Lily ponds, panoramic views, plenty of seating, picnic area, in all 10 acres. Garden started in 1970, recently rejuvenated. Woodland walk, which has one of the largest beech trees. Good collection of yellow magnolias and herbaceous plants. Large collection of hydrangeas. Over 200 camellias, large collection of ilex, day lilies with iris. Full of spring bulbs. Daily 5 Mar to 30 Sept (10-5), adm £5, chd free. Featured in Cornwall Today. Partial wheelchair access.

23 KENNALL HOUSE

Ponsanooth, TR3 7HJ. Nick & Mary Wilson-Holt, 01872 870557, kennallvale@hotmail.com. *4m NW of Falmouth. Off A393 Falmouth-to-Redruth rd. Turn L at Ponsanooth PO for ⅓m. Garden at end of drive marked Kennall House.* **Sat 29 July (1.30-5). Adm £5, chd free. Light refreshments. Visits also by arrangement May to Nov.** The 12-acre garden-cum-arboretum, beautifully situated in the Kennall Valley, is an intriguing combination of typical British species and exotics, sympathetically laid out in a variety of spacious settings, incl walled garden and fast-flowing stream with ponds. Wide variety of trees incl new plantings of rare specimens.

Penheale Manor

An unusual Cornish garden with yr-round interest. Limited access.

&. 🐄 ☕

24 ◆ LAMORRAN HOUSE

Upper Castle Road, St Mawes, Truro, TR2 5BZ. Robert Dudley-Cooke, 01326 270800, info@lamorrangarden.co.uk, www.lamorrangarden.co.uk. *A3078, R past garage at entrance to St Mawes. ¾m on L. ¼m from castle if using passenger ferry service.* **For NGS: Sun 23 Apr (11-4). Adm £6.50, chd free. Home-made teas. For other opening times and information, please phone, email or visit garden website.**

4-acre subtropical garden overlooking Falmouth bay. Designed by owner in an Italianate/Cote d'Azur style. Extensive collection of Mediterranean and subtropical plants incl large collection of palms Butia capitata/Butia yatay and tree ferns. Reflects both design and remarkable micro-climate. Beautiful collection of Japanese azaleas and tender rhododendrons. Large collection of S-hemisphere plants. Italianate garden with many water features. Champion trees.

🐄 🦽 ☕

25 ◆ THE LOST GARDENS OF HELIGAN

Pentewan, St Austell, PL26 6EN. Heligan Gardens Ltd, 01726 845100, info@heligan.com, www.heligan.com. *5m S of St Austell. From St Austell take B3273 signed Mevagissey, follow signs.* **For opening times and information, please phone, email or visit garden website.**

Lose yourself in the mysterious world of The Lost Gardens where an exotic sub-tropical jungle, atmospheric Victorian pleasure grounds, an interactive wildlife project and the finest productive gardens in Britain all await your discovery. Wheelchair access to Northern gardens. Armchair tour shows video of unreachable areas. Wheelchairs available at reception free of charge.

&. 🐄 ✿ 🦽 NPC ☕

GROUP OPENING

26 LOWER AMBLE GARDENS

Chapel Amble, Wadebridge, PL27 6EW. *3m N of Wadebridge. Take lane signed Middle & Lower Amble opp PO. 1m to L turn by pond. Parking in field beyond farmhouse.* **Sun 28 May (2-6). Combined adm £5, chd free. Home-made teas at Millpond Cottage. Picnic site at Lower Amble Farmhouse wood.**

LOWER AMBLE COTTAGE
Mr & Mrs C Burr.

LOWER AMBLE FARMHOUSE
Mr & Mrs Laurence Grand.

MILLPOND COTTAGE
Sheilagh Lees.

Peaceful hamlet with wide valley and moorland views, developed from mill farm buildings of early 1800s. Lower Amble Cottage: 1-acre garden of 13 years' development, with lawns, mixed beds, sculptures, small pond and trees. Lower Amble Farmhouse: 1-acre garden divided into varied spaces, plus 4 acres of deciduous woodland, pond and wild flower orchard. Millpond Cottage: large 20-yr-old garden with orchard, pond, vegetable garden and mixed herbaceous borders with many roses, geraniums and interesting perennials. Disabled parking in Millpond Cottage drive or access through side gate.

&. 🐄 ✿ ☕

27 MARY NEWMAN'S GARDEN

48 Culver Road, Saltash, PL12 4DT. Tamar Protection Society, 01579 384381/01752 842132, brigettedixon481@btinternet.com, www.tamarprotectionsociety. *200yds down from railway station. Lower end of Culver Rd near to Waterside of Saltash, ¼m from Saltash Fore St. Plenty of parking in adj streets.* **Sun 11 June, Sun 9 July (12-4). Adm by donation. Cream teas. Light refreshments. Visits also by arrangement 15 Apr to 30 Sept on specific days agreed by the Trustees of the Tamar Protection Society.**

Mary Newman's is a delightful Elizabethan cottage and garden - reputedly the home of Sir Francis Drake's first wife, Mary Newman. The garden is laid out in authentic Elizabethan style, showcasing the plants and herbs vital to a household of the period, and has the feeling of being a very secret garden which is a shelter from the humdrum of the busy world we live -in. Plants for sale cultivated within garden. Also open 15 April to end Sept Wed, Thurs, Sat, Sun (12-4) by donation in aid of Tamar Protection Society. Ramp can be requested at reception for main access. Wheelchair access to ground floor of cottage.

&. ✿ ☕

28 MEUDON HOTEL

Maenporth Road, Mawnan Smith, Falmouth, TR11 5HT. Tessa Rabett, 01326 250541, wecare@meudon.co.uk, www.meudon.co.uk. *Follow signs for Mabe, then Mawnan Smith.* **Sun 23 Apr (1-5). Adm £7, chd free. Home-made teas. Bar drinks, snacks, cream teas. Visits also by arrangement Mar to May.**

Meudon has 9 acres of sub-tropical valley garden created by the Fox family in 1800. Wealthy Quakers and shipping agents, their Packet ships provided transport for Meudon's wonderful collection of rare and exotic trees and shrubs from around the world. Terraces, pathways, meander down to Bream Cove (private beach). Formal garden, herbaceous borders, indigenous plants, and sunken pond area. Brazilian Gunnera manicata, Japanese banana trees Musa basjoo, Wollemia pine, Dicksonia antarctica, rhodendendrons, camellias, magnolia, Trachycarpus fortunei. Wheelchair access limited to upper terrace and ponds (although they take a little longer to get to).

&. 🐄 🛏 ☕

29 ◆ MOYCLARE
Lodge Hill, Liskeard,
PL14 4EH. Elizabeth & Philip
Henslowe, 01579 343114,
elizabethhenslowe@btinternet.
com, www.moyclare.co.uk. *1m S of
Liskeard centre. Approx 300yds S of
Liskeard railway stn on St Keyne-
Duloe rd (B3254).* **For NGS: Mon
1 May (2-5). Adm £3.50, chd
free. Home-made teas. For other
opening times and information,
please phone, email or visit garden
website.**
Gardened by one family for
over 80yrs; mature trees, shrubs
and plants (many unusual, many
variegated). Once most televised
Cornish garden. Now revived and
rejuvenated and still a plantsman's
delight, full of character. Camellia,
brachyglottis and astrantia (all Moira
Reid) and cytisus Moyclare Pink
originated here. Meandering paths
through fascinating shrubberies,
herbacious borders and sunny
corners. Wellstocked pond.
Wildlife habitat area. Quite a lot
of the garden can be enjoyed by
wheelchair users.
&. ❄ 🚗 ☕

Gardens are at the heart of hospice care

30 NAVAS HILL HOUSE
Bosanath Valley, Mawnan Smith,
Falmouth, TR11 5LL. Aline &
Richard Turner, 01326 251233,
alineturner@btinternet.com.
*1½m from Trebah & Glendurgan
Gdns. Head for Mawnan Smith,
pass Trebah and Glendurgan Gdns
then follow yellow signs.* **Sun 7
May (2-5). Adm £4, chd free.
Home-made teas. Visits also by
arrangement May & June.**
8½-acre garden divided into
various zones; kitchen garden with
greenhouses, potting shed, fruit cages,
orchard; 2 plantsman areas with
specialist trees and shrubs; walled
rose garden; ornamental garden with
water features and rockery; wooded
areas with bluebells and young large
leafed rhododendrons. Seating areas
with views across wooded valley,
not a car in sight! Partial wheelchair
access, some gravel and grass paths.
&. 🐕 ❄ ☕

31 THE OLD RECTORY
Trevalga, Boscastle, PL35 0EA.
Jacqueline M A Jarvis,
01840 250512, jacqueline@
jacquelinejarvis.co.uk. *Coastal rd
between Tintagel & Boscastle. At
Trevalga Xrds turn inland away from
hamlet. Garden ½m up narrow,
steep hill. Limited parking.* **Visits
by arrangement Apr to June.
Parking limited, larger groups
would need to share cars
and notify owner in advance.
Adm £4, chd free. Light
refreshments.**
On N Cornish coast, a challenging,
exposed, NW-facing garden with
panoramic sea views, ½m inland,
elevation 500ft. 'From Field to
Garden' a 30 yr project by artist
owner. Informal incl woodland,
perennial borders, sunken and
walled areas. Lookout at front of
garden (4 step spiral stair access)
with stunning views across circa
50m of coastline - Hartland Point
to Pentire Point. Gravel drive and
partial wheelchair access to garden.
&. ☕

32 THE OLD WATERMILL
St. Mabyn, Bodmin, PL30 3BX. Mr
& Mrs E R Maunsell. *SE edge of
St Mabyn on rd to Helland. Approx
1m from B3266, 2m from A39.* **Sat
8 July (1.30-5.30). Adm £4, chd
free. Cream teas.** *Donation to
South West Equine Protection.*
A 2-acre garden in the making -
started about 6 years ago, creating
a new garden out of wilderness.
Two ponds, one stream, several
springs. Mature trees and fantastic
Alice in Wonderland walk on top
of ancient Cornish hedge. Varied
plantings, characterful woodland
beds, interlinking paths and bridges.
Orchard, lawns and sitting areas.
Plentiful wildlife. Gravel paths.
&. 🐕 ❄ ☕

33 PARC-LAMP
Ruan Lanihorne, Truro, TR2 5NX.
Kathleen Ward, 01872 501530.
*2½m W of Tregony. Truro to Tregony:
A390 E to St Austell. Turn R on
A3078 to St Mawes Rd. In Tregony
cross bridge then 1st R to Ruan
Lanihorne. Garden 1st L after bend.
Next to award winning The Kings
Head PH.* **Visits by arrangement
June to Sept, max 12. Adm £4,
chd free. Tea.**
Small, intensively-planted, terraced
Mediterranean style garden with
travertine paving and gravelled areas.
The sheltered site has a micro-
climate which allows many unusual
tender trees and plants to thrive.
Enjoy the garden from various
seating places. Entry is by steep
steps. Featured in Garden News and
Cornwall Today.
☕

34 PENCARN
Gonvena, Wadebridge,
PL27 6DL. Mr Trevor Wiltshire,
01208 814631/ 07796 184506,
trevordwiltshire@gmail.com,
www.pencarn.org.uk. *Central
Wadebridge. Follow Gonvena
Hill (B3314) past Wadebridge
comprehensive school; shortly
afterwards (at postbox in wall) turn
R into Gonvena and St Giles Follow
lane right down, last house at bottom
on R.* **Visits by arrangement Feb
to Oct (11-5). Adm £4.50, chd
free. Home-made teas.**
Sited on a tree-covered, SW-facing
hillside, a 1-acre plantsman's garden
par excellence (owner worked
at RHS Wisley). Mediterranean-
themed section, two large ponds
and rock garden. Plant collections
and unusual plants abound: in
raised beds, small cliffs and stone
hedges smothered with alpines.
3 greenhouses in a productive
vegetable garden. Sitting areas, and
decks over ponds. Childrens play
area. All except vegetable garden
accessible to wheelchair users.
&. 🐕 ❄ ☕

Byeways

35 ◆ PENCARROW
Washaway, Bodmin,
PL30 3AG. Molesworth-St
Aubyn family, 01208 841369,
info@pencarrow.co.uk,
www.pencarrow.co.uk. *4m NW of
Bodmin. Signed off A389 & B3266.*
**For NGS: Mon 24 Apr (10-5.30).
Adm £5.75, chd free. Cream
teas. For other opening times and
information, please phone, email or
visit garden website.**
50 acres of tranquil, family-owned
Grade II* listed gardens. Superb
specimen conifers, azaleas, magnolias
and camellias galore. 700 varieties of
rhododendron give a blaze of spring
colour; blue hydrangeas line the
mile-long carriage drive throughout
the summer. Discover the Iron
Age hill fort, lake, Italian gardens
and granite rockery. Free parking,
dogs welcome, café and children's
play area. Gravel paths, some steep
slopes.
  ♿ 🐄 ❀ 🚐 ☕ 🌱

36 PENHEALE MANOR
Egloskerry, Launceston, PL15 8RX.
Mr & Mrs James Colville. *SX26
88; 3½ m NW of Launceston. Take
rd from St Stephen's, Launceston, to
Egloskerry. From centre of village to
Penheale entrance is ½ m on R.* **Sun
18 June (2-5). Adm £6, chd £2.
Home-made teas.**

A rare opportunity to enjoy
midsummer in the secluded peace
and tranquility of the walled gardens
surrounding this Jacobean manor
house which was extended so
distinctively by Lutyens in the 1920s.
Gatehouse and courtyard pavilions
frame the rose gardens, and
impressive yew hedges shelter drifts
of herbaceous colour, extending to
the more familiar Cornish style of
beautiful woodland areas beyond.
Partial wheelchair access due to
stony paths.
  ♿ 🚐 ☕

37 ◆ PINETUM PARK &
PINE LODGE GARDENS
Holmbush, St Austell, PL25 3RQ.
Mr Chang Li, 01726 73500,
office@pinetumpark.com,
www.pinetumpark.com. *1m E of St
Austell. On A390 between Holmbush
& St Blazey at junction of A391.* **For
opening times and information,
please phone, email or visit garden
website.**
Hidden gem on S coast of Cornwall
and a must visit for garden lovers.
From serious plant hunters
interested in rare plants to those
seeking a tranquil day out, the 30
acre park has colour for all seasons.
Discover 6000 plants, trees and
flowers with 23 champion trees.
Pinetum Park has 10 individual

gardens to explore throughout
every season. Gardens easily
accessible but with no wheelchair
access to Japanese garden.
  ♿ 🐄 ❀ 🚐 ☕ 🌱

38 ◆ PINSLA GARDEN &
NURSERY
Cardinham, PL30 4AY. Mark &
Claire Woodbine, 01208 821339,
cwoodbine@btinternet.com,
www.pinslagarden.net. *3½ m E of
Bodmin. From A30 or Bodmin take
A38 towards Plymouth, 1st L to
Cardinham & Fletchers Bridge, 2m on
R.* **For NGS: Sat 20, Sun 21 May,
Sat 5, Sun 6 Aug (9-5). Adm
£3.50, chd free. Home-made
teas. For other opening times and
information, please phone, email or
visit garden website.**
Romantic 1½ -acre artist's
garden set in tranquil woodland.
Naturalistic cottage garden planting
surrounds our C18 fairytale cottage.
Imaginative design, intense colour
and scent, bees and butterflies.
Unusual shade plants, acers and
ferns. Fantastic range of plants and
statues on display and for sale.
Friendly advice in nursery. Featured
in Country Homes and Interiors.
Wheelchair access limited as some
paths are narrow and bumpy.
  ♿ 🐄 ❀ ☕

39 POLDARIAN

12 Carrick Way, St. Mawes, Truro, TR2 5BB. Brian & Valerie Willis. *From A390 St Austell to Truro, turn onto A3078 to St Mawes. Leave water tower and disused garage on R and ignore rd to St Mawes Castle on R. Continue ¼ m until yellow NGS signs. Parking by direction.* **Sat 8, Sun 9 July (10.30-4.30). Adm £5, chd free. Home-made teas. Cream teas.**
Beautiful well-structured ¾ acre terraced plantsman's garden of trees, shrubs and perennials with yr-round colour and harmony and lovely sea and harbour views. Sorry, no wheelchair access; some steps to terraces.

40 ◆ POTAGER GARDEN

High Cross, Constantine, Falmouth, TR11 5RF. Mr Mark Harris, 01326 341258, enquiries@potagergarden.org, www.potagergarden.org. *5m SW of Falmouth. From Falmouth, follow signs to Constantine. From Helston, drive through Constantine and continue towards Famouth.* **For opening times and information, please phone, email or visit garden website.**
Potager has emerged from the bramble choked wilderness of an abandoned plant nursery. With mature trees which were once nursery stock and lush herbaceous planting interspersed with fruit and vegetables Potager Garden aims to demonstrate the beauty of productive organic gardening. There are games to play, hammocks to laze in and boule and badminton to enjoy. Featured in The Observer & Cornwall Life.

41 RIVERSIDE COTTAGE

St. Clement, Truro, TR1 1SZ. Billa & Nick Jeans, 01872 263830, billajeans@gmail.com. *1½ m SE of Truro. From Trafalgar r'about on A39 in Truro, follow signs for St Clement, up St Clement Hill. R at top of hill, continue to car park by river.* **Mon 17 Apr, Sun 21 May (2-5). Adm £4, chd free. Cream teas and home-made cakes. Visits also by arrangement Apr & May.**
Small garden on beautiful Tresillian River Estuary. Small Victorian orchard and nut walk with wild flower areas, wildlife pond, borders and vegetable patch. Steep paths and steps but plenty of seats. Walk through to C13 St Clement Church and 'Living Churchyard'. Apart from numerous seats and benches, affording places of rest and views down the river, there's a swing for the children, and the best cream teas in the parish.

42 ◆ ROSELAND HOUSE

Chacewater, TR4 8QB. Mr & Mrs Pridham, 01872 560451, charlie@roselandhouse.co.uk, www.roselandhouse.co.uk. *4m W of Truro. At Truro end of main st. Park in village car park (100yds) or on surrounding rds.* **For NGS: Sat 24, Sun 25 June, Sat 29, Sun 30 July (1-5). Adm £4, chd free. Home-made teas. For other opening times and information, please phone, email or visit garden website.**
The 1-acre garden is a mass of rambling roses and clematis. Ponds and borders alike are filled with plants, many rarely seen in gardens. National Collection of clematis viticella cvs can be seen in garden and display tunnel, along with a huge range of other climbing plants. Featured in Garden News, Cornwall Today and The Garden. Some slopes.

Trerose Manor

43 ◆ ST MICHAEL'S MOUNT

Marazion, TR17 0HS. James & Mary St Levan, 01736 710507, mail@stmichaelsmount.co.uk, www.stmichaelsmount.co.uk. 2½ m E of Penzance. ½ m from shore at Marazion by Causeway; otherwise by motor boat. **For NGS: Sun 28 May (10-5). Adm £7, chd £3.50. For other opening times and information, please phone, email or visit garden website.**

Infuse your senses with colour and scent in the unique sub-tropical gardens basking in the mild climate and salty breeze. Clinging to granite slopes the terraced beds tier steeply to the ocean's edge, boasting tender exotics from places such as Mexico, the Canary Islands and South Africa. Laundry lawn, mackerel bank, pill box, gun emplacement, tiered terraces, well, tortoise lawn. Walled gardens, seagull seat. The garden lawn can be accessed with wheelchairs although further exploration is limited due to steps and steepness.

44 🆕 SEA VIEW

Treligga, Delabole, PL33 9EE. Duncan Scott, 01840 211033, seaview.treligga@gmail.com. Hamlet 1m W of Delabole, approached via no-through-rd signed to Treligga from B3314 at Westdowns. Turn L at noticeboard; house is end-on to rd at bottom of narrow lane. **Visits by arrangement June & July afternoons only, max group size 10. Adm £4, chd free. Light refreshments.**

Imaginative garden in a remote coastal hamlet, designed as a series of varied, colourful and naturalistic enclosures - with flowers, vegetables, meadow and orchard. Although just a few fields away from the cliff edge with the sea 400 feet below, the feeling is more countryside than seaside and the garden sits sympathetically within the wider environment of its coastal setting. Sorry, not currently suitable for wheelchair users owing to steps.

45 ◆ TREBAH

Mawnan Smith, TR11 5JZ. Trebah Garden Trust, 01326 252200, mail@trebah-garden.co.uk, www.trebah-garden.co.uk. 4m SW of Falmouth. Follow tourist signs from Hillhead r'about on A39 approach to Falmouth or Treliever Cross r'about on junction of A39-A394. Parking for coaches. **For opening times and information, please phone, email or visit garden website.**

26-acre S-facing ravine garden, planted in 1830s. Extensive collection rare/mature trees/shrubs incl glades; huge tree ferns 100yrs old, subtropical exotics. Hydrangea collection covers 2½ acres. Water garden, waterfalls, rock pool stocked with mature koi carp. Enchanted garden for plantsman/artist/family. Play area/trails for children. Use of private beach. Steep paths in places. 2 motorised vehicles available, please book in advance.

46 TREBARTHA

Trebartha, nr Launceston, PL15 7PD. The Latham Family. 6m SW of Launceston. North Hill, SW of Launceston nr junction of B3254 & B3257. No coaches. **Sun 21 May, Sun 24 Sept (2-5). Adm £5, chd free. Home-made teas.**

Historic landscape gardens featuring ponds, streams, cascades, rocks and woodlands, including fine American trees, bluebells in spring, ornamental walled garden and private garden at Lemarne (best seen in autumn). Allow at least 1 hour for a circular walk. Some steep and rough paths, which can be slippery when wet. Stout footwear advised. Interesting garden project in progress.

47 TREGONNING

Carleen, Breage, Helston, TR13 9QU. Andrew & Kathryn Eaton, 01736 761840, alfeaton@aol.com, tregonninggarden.co.uk. 1m S of Godolphin Cross. From Xrds in centre of Godolphin Cross head S towards Carleen. In ½m at fork signed Breage 1¼ turn R up narrow lane marked no through rd. After ½m parking on L opp Tregonning Farm. **Sat 22, Sun 23 July (1-4.30). Adm**

£4, chd free. Home-made teas. **Visits also by arrangement Apr to Sept for groups.** Located 300ft up NE side of Tregonning Hill this small (less than 1 acre) maturing garden will hopefully inspire those thinking of making a garden from nothing more than a pond and copse of trees (in 2009). With the ever present challenge of storm force winds, garden offers yr round interest and a self-sufficient vegetable and soft fruit paddock. Sculpted grass meadow, with panoramic views from Carn Brea to Helston. A section of the garden is designed in the form of a plant (incorporating a deck, leaf shaped beds, a stream and large pond). Also cottage/small parterre garden, spring garden, Mediterranean patio. Carp pond and fernery. Featured in Cornwall Life, Cornwall Today & Amateur Gardening Magazine.

48 ◆ TREMATON CASTLE

Castle Hill, Trematon, Saltash, PL12 4QW. Bannerman, info@bannermandesign.com, www.bannermandesign.com/trematon. 2m SW of Saltash. Lanes surrounding the castle are very narrow, please approach from Trematon and Trehan. **For NGS: Fri 16 June (11-4.30). Adm £7, chd free. Home-made teas. For other opening times and information, please email or visit garden website.**

Property of Duchy of Cornwall since the Conquest, Trematon is a perfect miniature motte and bailey castle. On R Lynher estuary, '... one of the superb views of Cornwall .... all the more romantic for being still a private residence' (John Betjeman). Julian and Isabel Bannerman have begun to create a garden playing on its pre-Raphaelite glories, wild flowers, orchard, woodland, scented borders, seaside and exotic planting. Featured in Isabel & Julian Bannerman's new book Landscape of Dreams. Regrettably not suitable for wheelchair users, pea gravel throughout.

49 TRENARTH

High Cross, Constantine, TR11 5JN. Lucie Nottingham, 01326 340444, lmnottingham@btinternet.com, www.trenarthgardens.com. *6m SW of Falmouth. Main rd A39/A394 Truro to Helston, follow Constantine signs. High X garage turn L for Mawnan, 30yds on R down dead end lane, Trenarth is ½m at end of lane.* **Sun 25 June (2-5). Adm £4, chd free. Cream teas. Visits also by arrangement Mar to Oct garden clubs and groups especially welcome, tour and teas provided.**

4 acres round C17 farmhouse in peaceful pastoral setting. Yr-round interest. Emphasis on tender, unusual plants, structure and form. C16 courtyard, listed garden walls, yew rooms, vegetable garden, traditional potting shed, orchard, new woodland area with childrens' interest, palm and gravel garden. Circular walk down ancient green lane via animal pond to Trenarth Bridge, returning through woods. Abundant wildlife. Bees in tree bole, lesser horseshoe bat colony, swallows, wild flowers and butterflies. Family friendly, children's play area, the Wolery, and plenty of room to run, jump and climb. Featured in WI magazine and Cornwall Wildlife Trust publication.

🐄 ✿ 🚗 ☕

Funds from NGS gardens help Macmillan support thousands of people every year

50 TREREIFE PARK

Penzance, TR20 8TJ. Mr & Mrs T Le Grice, 01736 362750, trereifepark@btconnect.com, www.trereifepark.co.uk. *2m W of Penzance on A30 on Lands End rd. Garden and house signed R through estate gates.* **Visits by arrangement May to Sept, garden and house tours available. Adm £6, chd free. Cream teas.**

Mature gardens undergoing restoration in the historic setting of Trereife Park. Established specimen camellia, rhododendron, azalea walk under mature beech trees. Modern parterre, sculptural yew hedge, S-facing walled terrace with wisteria and magnolia. New hot border with unusual Mediterranean planting. Medlar collection around events lawn and old kitchen garden awaiting restoration.

🐄 ✿ 🚗 🚌 ☕

51 TREROSE MANOR

Old Church Road, Mawnan Smith, Falmouth, TR11 5HX. Mrs P Phipps, 01326 250784, info@trerosemanor.co.uk, www.trerosemanor.co.uk. *Some parking at house, otherwise on rd or field if signed. From Mawnan Smith bear L at Red Lion. ½m turn R into Old Church Rd. After ½m garden is immed after Trerose Farm.* **Sun 2 July (2-5). Adm £5, chd free. Home-made teas.**

Old Cornish Manor House. An acre of garden planned for all seasons. Various rare and tender plants. Camelias in winter. Akebia, pink wisteria, cassia in spring. Poppies, alstroemerias, hollyhocks, echiums, cornus giving way to agapanthus, purple and pink passion flowers, salvias, campsis, tibouchinas, clerodendrums and dahlias including dahlia imperialis.

♿ ✿ 🚌 ☕

52 TREWAN HALL

St Columb, TR9 6DB. Mrs Jo Davies, www.trewan-hall.co.uk. *6m E of Newquay. N of St Columb Major, off A39 to Wadebridge. 1st turning on L signed to St Eval & Talskiddy. Entrance ¾m on L in woodland. Map on website.* **Sun 25 June (2-5). Adm £4, chd free. Home-made teas.**

Set within 36 acres of parkland, fields and broadleaved woodland, with features incl flower borders, rose beds, kitchen garden enclosed by restored cob wall and traditional orchard with beehive. Driveway bordered by mature rhododendrons and hydrangeas leading to Grade II star listed C17 manor house (not open). Children's play area. Long-standing David Bellamy Gold Conservation Award. Disabled WC.

♿ 🐄 ☕

53 ◆ TREWIDDEN GARDEN

Buryas Bridge, Penzance, TR20 8TT. Mr Alverne Bolitho - Richard Morton, Head Gardener, 01736 364275/363021, contact@trewiddengarden.co.uk, www.trewiddengarden.co.uk. *2m W of Penzance. Entry on A30 just before Buryas Bridge. SatNav TR19 6AU.* **For NGS: Sat 8 Apr (10.30-5.30). Adm £6.50, chd free. Light refreshments. For other opening times and information, please phone, email or visit garden website.**

Historic Victorian garden with magnolias, camellias and magnificent tree ferns planted within ancient tin workings. Tender, rare and unusual exotic plantings create a riot of colour thoughout the season. Water features, specimen trees and artefacts from Cornwall's tin industry provide a wide range of interest for all.

🐄 ✿ 🚌 NPC ☕

54 ◆ VARFELL FARM

Long Rock, Penzance, TR20 8AQ. Mr M Mann, 01736 339276, mike.mann@national-dahlia-collection.co.uk, www.nationaldahliacollection.co.uk. *3m N of Penzance. Turn off A30 near Long Rock r'about, signed Varfell.* **For opening times and information, phone, email or visit garden website.**

National Dahlia Collection growing in 2 acre field of riotous colour which delights the eye. All types of dahlias are exhibited from dainty pompoms to huge decoratives amounting to 1600 named varieties bred and grown here. Displayed in ordered rows, fully labelled for identification in mail order sales. Open to the public free of charge from Aug to mid Oct, donations to NGS welcomed. Come

and see the extraordinary show.
Coach parties welcome by prior
arrangement. In dry conditions with
some wheelchairs it is possible to
move around the field or possible to
view the field as a whole from road.

55 WAYE COTTAGE

Lerryn, nr Lostwithiel, PL22 0QQ.
Malcolm & Jennifer Bell,
01208 872119. *4m S of Lostwithiel.
Village parking, garden 10min, level
stroll along riverbank/stepping stones.
Open most days but do ring first -
best after 6pm.* **Daily Sat 1 Apr to
Sat 30 Sept (11-5). Adm £4, chd
free. Visits also by arrangement
Apr to Sept with garden clubs
welcome at reduced rate.**
Never immaculate but abundantly-
planted, this 1-acre cottage garden
has a large and interesting collection
of plants, some rare and unusual,
together with delightful bonsai theatre.
Wander along the meandering
paths, sit on the many benches and
enjoy stunning river views. Attractive
riverside village with PH and shop
supplying picnics to eat on trestle
tables on village green. New tearoom
in converted boathouse. Featured
in Cornwall Today & Cornwall Life.
Steep paths and steps sadly make it
impossible for the disabled.

56 WINDMILLS

South Hill, Callington, PL17 7LP. Mr
& Mrs Peter Tunnicliffe. *3m NW of
Callington. Head N from Callington
A388, after about ½m turn L onto
South Hill Rd (signed South Hill).
Straight on for 3m, the gardens are on
R just before church.* **Sun 25 June,
Sun 2 July (1.30-5). Combined
adm with Anvil Cottage £5, chd
free. Home-made teas.**
Next to medieval church and on the
site of an old rectory and there are
still signs in places of that long gone
building. A garden full of surprises,
formal paths and steps lead up
from the flower beds to extensive
vegetable and soft fruit area. More
paths lead to water feature with
rustic stone bridge, past a pergola,
and down into large lawns with trees
and shrubs. Limited wheelchair access.

Sea View

CUMBRIA

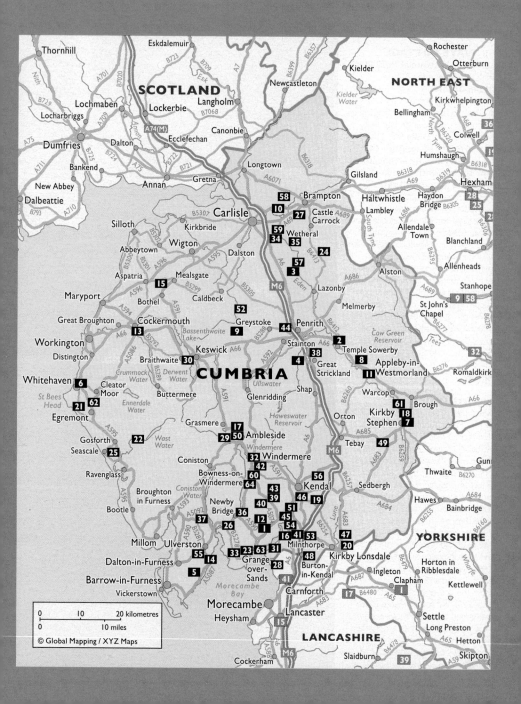

Venture into Daniel Defoe's "... County eminent only for being the wildest, most barren and frightful of any that I have passed over in England, or even in Wales itself..." and be amazed by the gardens and horticultural excellence that Cumbria can offer.

From Rydal Hall's 17th century Picturesque Viewing Room, through the 19C planting of Dora's Field (Wordsworth's remembrance of his dead daughter) and the founding of the British Pteridological Society, to the 21C gardens created by Chelsea Gold Medal winners – for more than 300 years Cumberland and Westmorland (now Cumbria) have provided England with gardens and scenery second to none.

Considered by the knowledgeable to be worth the journey over 300 years ago, it is still a county to visit for gardens that encompass all gardening traditions. From real cottage gardens providing produce for the family to the set piece gardens of the great estates – all can be found in the far north west of England.

Below: **Station Master's House**

Volunteers

County Organiser
Diane Hewitt
01539 446238
dhewitt.kinsman@gmail.com

County Treasurer
Derek Farman
01539 444893
derek@derejam.myzen.co.uk

Publicity –
Publications & Special Interest
Carole Berryman
01539 443649
Carole.Berryman@student.sac.ac.uk

Publicity – Social Media
Gráinne Jakobson
01946 813017
gmjakobson22@gmail.com

Booklet Co-ordinator
Diane Hewitt (as above)

Assistant County Organisers

Central
Carole Berryman (as above)

East
Sue Sharkey
07811 710248
bsjsewebank@btinternet.com

North
Alannah Rylands
01697 320413
alannah.rylands@me.com

North East
Cate Bowman
01228 573903
catebowman@icloud.com

North East
Grace Kirby
01228 670076
gracekirby03@gmail.com

South East
Linda & Alec Greening
01524 781624
lindagreening48@gmail.com

West
Gráinne Jakobson (as above)

OPENING DATES

All entries subject to latest information check www.ngs.org.uk

Extended openings are shown at the beginning of the month.

Map locator numbers are shown to the right of each garden name.

February
Snowdrop Festival

Sunday 19th
Lower Rowell Farm & Cottage — 41
Summerdale House — 53

Friday 24th
Summerdale House — 53

March

Summerdale House (Every Friday and Saturday) — 53

April

Summerdale House (Every Friday and Saturday) — 53

Sunday 2nd
◆ Dora's Field — 17
◆ High Close Estate and Arboretum — 29
High Moss — 30
◆ Holehird Gardens — 32
◆ Rydal Hall — 50

Sunday 9th
Fern Bank — 21

Saturday 22nd
◆ Conishead Priory and Buddhist Temple — 14

Sunday 23rd
◆ Conishead Priory and Buddhist Temple — 14
Orchard Cottage — 45

Sunday 30th
Low Fell West — 40

May

Summerdale House (Every Friday and Saturday) — 53

Monday 1st
Low Fell West — 40

Friday 5th
Chapelside — 9

Saturday 6th
Chapelside — 9

Sunday 7th
Chapelside — 9
NEW Cherry Cottage — 10
Dallam Tower — 16
Hayton Village Gardens — 27
Windy Hall — 60

Thursday 11th
◆ Rydal Hall — 50

Saturday 13th
Highlands — 31

Sunday 14th
Highlands — 31

Friday 19th
Chapelside — 9

Saturday 20th
◆ Acorn Bank — 2
Chapelside — 9
Langholme Mill — 37

Sunday 21st
Chapelside — 9
Fell Yeat — 20
Langholme Mill — 37
Matson Ground — 42

90th Anniversary Weekend

Saturday 27th
NEW Armathwaite Gardens — 3

Sunday 28th
Orchard Cottage — 45

June

Summerdale House (Every Friday and Saturday) — 53

Friday 2nd
Chapelside — 9

Saturday 3rd
Chapelside — 9
Church View — 11

Galesyke — 22

Sunday 4th
Chapelside — 9
Galesyke — 22
Tenter End Barn — 56
Windy Hall — 60
Yewbarrow House — 63

Wednesday 7th
Larch Cottage Nurseries — 38

Sunday 11th
NEW Armathwaite Gardens — 3
Crookdake Farm — 15
Hazelwood Farm — 28
Low Blakebank — 39
Middle Blakebank — 43
8 Oxenholme Road — 46
Wetheral Gardens — 59
Yews — 64

Thursday 15th
◆ Rydal Hall — 50

Friday 16th
Chapelside — 9

Saturday 17th
Broom Cottage — 8
Chapelside — 9

Sunday 18th
Askham Hall — 4
Chapelside — 9
Ivy House — 35
Summerdale House — 53
NEW Tithe Barn — 58

Thursday 22nd
Haverthwaite Lodge — 26
Lakeside Hotel & Rocky Bank — 36

Saturday 24th
◆ Acorn Bank — 2
Boxwood House — 7

Sunday 25th
Boxwood House — 7
Orchard Cottage — 45

July

NEW Beckside Farm (Every Saturday from Saturday 15th) — 5
Summerdale House (Every Friday and Saturday) — 53

Saturday 1st
Ravenstonedale Village

Gardens — 49

Sunday 2nd
Ewebank Farm — 19
Park House — 47
Ravenstonedale Village Gardens — 49
Stewart Hill Cottage — 52
Yewbarrow House — 63

Thursday 6th
◆ Rydal Hall — 50

Sunday 9th
NEW Abi and Tom's Garden Plants — 1
NEW The Coach House — 12
NEW Cockermouth Gardens — 13

Thursday 13th
◆ Holehird Gardens — 32
Newton Rigg College Gardens — 44

Sunday 16th
Holme Meadow — 34

Sunday 23rd
Eden Place — 18
Greenfield House — 24
Woodend House — 62

Sunday 30th
Winton Park — 61

August

NEW Beckside Farm (Every Saturday) — 5
Summerdale House (Every Friday and Saturday to Saturday 26th) — 53

Sunday 6th
Fell Yeat — 20
Park House — 47
Yewbarrow House — 63

Sunday 13th
Berriedale — 6

Thursday 17th
Haverthwaite Lodge — 26
Lakeside Hotel & Rocky Bank — 36

Sunday 20th
Grange Fell Allotments — 23

Thursday 24th
◆ Holker Hall Gardens — 33

Your visit helps fund 389 Marie Curie Nurses

THE GARDENS

1 NEW ABI AND TOM'S GARDEN PLANTS
Halecat, Witherslack, Grange-Over-Sands, LA11 6RT. Abi & Tom Attwood, 015395 52946, info@halecatplants.co.uk, www.halecatplants.co.uk. *20 mins from Kendal. From A950 turn N to Witherslack. Follow brown tourist signs to Halecat. Rail Grange-over-sands 5m, Bus X6 2m, NCR 70.* **Sun 9 July (10-4.30). Combined adm with The Coach House £3.50, chd free. Tea. Visits also by arrangement Mar to Oct. 48-seater coaches have to park at the bottom of the main drive where we will meet you.**
The 1 acre nursery garden is a fusion of traditional horticultural values with modern approaches to the display, growing and use of plant material. Our full range of perennials can be seen growing alongside one another in themed borders be they shady damp corners or south facing hot spots. The propagating areas, stock beds and family garden, normally closed to visitors, will be open on the NGS day. More than 1,000 different herbaceous perennials are grown on the nursery, many that are excellent for wildlife. Featured in Gardens Illustrated, Homes and Garden Magazine, Lancashire Life and Cumbria Life. Sloping site that has no steps but steep inclines in places.
  ♿ 🐄 ❀ 🚌 ☕

2 ◆ ACORN BANK
Temple Sowerby, CA10 1SP. National Trust, 017683 61893, acornbank@nationaltrust.org.uk, www.nationaltrust.org.uk. *6m E of Penrith. Off A66; ½m N of Temple Sowerby. Bus: Penrith-Appleby or Carlisle-Darlington; alight Culgaith Rd end.* **For NGS: Sat 20 May, Sat 24 June (10-5). Adm £7, chd £3.50. Light refreshments. For other opening times and information, please phone, email or visit garden website.**
Sheltered and tranquil, walled gardens contain a herb garden with more than 250 medicinal and culinary plants. Traditional apple orchards and mixed borders. Beyond the walls lie woodland walks with a wonderful display of snowdrops, daffodils and wild flowers in spring. Dogs welcome on leads on woodland walks. 20 May and 24 June, herb garden tours with Gardener, 11am numbers limited, additional charge. Tearoom offering light lunches and a selection of scones and cakes. Walled gardens accessible with grass and firm gravel paths, woodland paths have steep gradients and some steps. Access map and information available.
  ♿ ❀ ☕

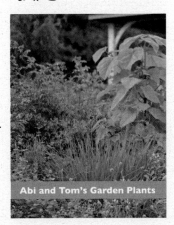
Abi and Tom's Garden Plants

GROUP OPENING

3 NEW ARMATHWAITE GARDENS

Armathwaite, Carlisle, CA4 9PG.
Turn off A6 just S of High Hesket signed Armathwaite, after 2m Coombe House is on R & Hazel Cottage is at the junction. Turn R at junction to Armathwaite - 2 The Faulds is in the village. **Sat 27 May, Sun 11 June (12-5). Combined adm £5, chd free. Home-made teas at Hazel Cottage.**

NEW COOMBE EDEN

Belinda & Mike Quigley.

HAZEL COTTAGE

Mr D Ryland & Mr J Thexton.

NEW 2 THE FAULDS

Mr & Mrs Phil & Jane Dutton.
(See separate entry)

Coombe Eden is approx 1 acre Victorian garden renovation project of traditional and contemporary beds. Steeply banked to a Japanese style bridge over the stream to a woodland area. Contemporary mixed beds, large rhododendrons give a breathtaking display in May. Hazel Cottage is a flower arranger's and plantsman's garden extending to 5 acres. Mature herbaceous borders with many unusual plants. Planted for a ll seasons. 2 The Faulds is a compact garden with rare and unusual trees, shrubs and herbaceous perennial. Collection of trees grown from seed. Art work and stained glass on display. 2 The Faulds has featured in Cumbria Life.
☕

4 ASKHAM HALL

Askham, Penrith, CA10 2PF. Countess of Lonsdale, 01931 712350, enquiries@askhamhall.co.uk, www.askhamhall.co.uk. *5m S of Penrith. Turn off A6 for Lowther & Askham.* **Sun 18 June (10-5). Adm £5, chd free. Home-made teas.** *Donation to Askham and Lowther Churches.*

Askham Hall is a Pele Tower incorporating C14, C16 and early C18 elements in a courtyard plan.

Recently opened with luxury accommodation, a restaurant, spa and wedding barn. Splendid formal garden with terraces of herbaceous borders and topiary, dating back to C17. Meadow area with trees and pond, kitchen gardens and animal trails. Cafe serving tea, coffee, cake, lunch and ice-cream. Combined with Summer Fair.
✿ 🚍 🛏 ☕

5 NEW BECKSIDE FARM

Little Urswick, Cumbria, nr Ulverston, LA12 0PY. Anna Thomason, 01229 869151, anna@becksidefarm.eclipse.co.uk. *On outskirts of village - good off road parking. A590 towards Barrow. S off A590 to Urswick. Go through Great Urswick & Little Urswick. Park at T-junction. Rail Ulverston 4m, NCR 70 & 700 ½m.* **Every Sat 15 July to 23 Sept (12-5). Adm £3.50, chd free. Visits also by arrangement June to Sept. Teas need to be pre-booked.**
Organic cottage garden with raised beds, herbaceous borders. Many unusual\new varieties of tender perennials and annuals, raised from seed and cuttings each year. Several interesting patio/seating areas. Productive greenhouse, again with unusual varieties. Ferns and summer flowering bulbs in pots. Ulverston is a pretty market town that has many tea shops and several PHs serving food. Featured in Cumbria Life.
✿ ☕

6 BERRIEDALE

15 Loop Road South, Whitehaven, CA28 7TN. Enid & John Stanborough, 01946 695467. *From S, A595 through T-lights onto Loop Rd approx 150yds on R. From N, A595 onto Loop Rd at Pelican Garage, garden approx 1½m on L. Whitehaven rail stn 20 mins brisk walk, mainly up hill.* **Sun 13 Aug (2-5). Adm £3.50, chd free. Cream teas. Visits also by arrangement May to Sept any number.**
Suburban garden, surprisingly large with different areas and levels. Incl large vegetable plot (with award winning onions and leeks), pond, Japanese inspired border and many seating areas around the garden.

Children love the fairy dell and mini trail. The owners raise over 1000 bedding plants which give riotous colour around the garden in mid to late summer. John wins prizes with his fuchsias at local shows and has many for sale. Partial wheelchair access to most of flower garden. Vegetable garden can be accessed by separate entrance with prior notice.
♿ 🐕 ✿ 🚍 ☕

7 BOXWOOD HOUSE

Hartley, Kirkby Stephen, CA17 4JH. Colin & Joyce Dirom, 01768 371306, boxwoodhouse@hotmail.co.uk. *In the centre of Hartley approx, 1m from Kirkby Stephen. Exit M6 J38. Follow A685, R in Kirkby Stephen for Hartley. From A66 exit at Brough onto A685, 1st L in Kirkby St for Hartley. Kirkby Stephen Station approx. 2m. KS on Coast to Coast Walk.* **Sat 24, Sun 25 June (11-5). Adm £3.50, chd free. Visits also by arrangement June & July for groups of 10-30, adm £6 includes Home-made teas.**
A peaceful natural garden. Packed herbaceous borders, shrubberies, herb, hosta and heuchera beds plus the tranquil pond are all designed to be wildlife friendly. The summer house provides one of the many seating areas around the garden overlooking a productive vegetable plot and fruit trees, whilst a meadow walk leads to a stunning view of the whole garden and the fenced off chicken area. Featured in Cumbria Life magazine.
🐕 ✿ ☕

8 BROOM COTTAGE

Long Marton, Appleby-In-Westmorland, CA16 6JP. Mr & Mrs Peter & Janet Cox. *From A66 1m E of Kirkby Thore, take turn signed Long Marton. From Appleby, follow signs to Long Marton (2m), L at church. Car parking signed. Short walk to house with 3 disabled spaces.* **Sat 17 June (1-4.30). Adm £4, chd free. Light refreshments made with garden produce.**
Peaceful 2 acre wildlife garden set around C18 former farmhouse. Wildlife pond with ducks and

Church View

© Val Corbett

moorhens, stream, wild copse and wildflower hay meadow with mown paths. Beautiful views of the Pennines and surrounded by pastures. A haven for birds. Large productive organic fruit and vegetable garden. Bee friendly walled herb garden, shrub and cottage garden borders. Surfaces are tarmac, cobbles, slate chippings and mown grass which may be wheelchair accessible. An area of pebbles in the walled herb garden is not.

♿ ☕

9 CHAPELSIDE
Mungrisdale, Penrith, CA11 0XR. Tricia & Robin Acland, 017687 79672. *12m W of Penrith. On A66 take minor rd N signed Mungrisdale. After 2m, sharp bends, garden on L immed after tiny church on R. Park at foot of our short drive. On C2C Reivers 71, 10 cycle routes.* **Fri 5, Sat 6, Sun 7, Fri 19, Sat 20, Sun 21 May, Fri 2, Sat 3, Sun 4, Fri 16, Sat 17, Sun 18 June (1-5). Adm £3, chd free. Visits also by arrangement. Refreshments for groups by arrangement.**
1 acre organic windy garden below fell, around C18 farmhouse and outbuildings, latter mainly open. Fine views. Tiny stream, large pond. Alpine, herbaceous, raised, gravel, damp and shade beds, bulbs in grass. Extensive range of plants, many unusual. Relaxed planting regime. Art constructions in and out, local stone used creatively. Featured in 'Country Homes and Interiors'.

🐔 ❄

10 NEW CHERRY COTTAGE
Crosby Moor, Crosby-On-Eden, Carlisle, CA6 4QX. Mr & Mrs John & Lesley Connolly, 01228 573614, jtlaconnolly@aol.com. *Off A689 midway between Carlisle & Brampton. Take turn signed 'Wallhead'. Cherry Cottage is on the corner of junction on R. Park in the lane.* **Sun 7 May (11-5). Adm £3.50, chd free. Light refreshments. Visits also by arrangement Apr to Sept max 20.**
Relaxed country garden surrounding an C18 cottage on an approx. 1/3 acre site. It has a wide range of habitats incl herbaceous borders, wildlife pond, bog garden, shady woodland, productive fruit and vegetable area, 2 greenhouses and summer house. Various seating areas connected by grass and gravel paths. Not suitable for wheelchairs.

❄ ☕

11 CHURCH VIEW
Bongate, Appleby-in-Westmorland, CA16 6UN. Mrs H Holmes, 017683 51397, engcougars@btinternet.com, www.engcougars.co.uk/church-view. *0.4m S of Appleby town centre. A66 N take B6542 for 2m St Michael's Church on L garden opp. A66 S take B6542 & continue to Royal Oak Inn, garden next door, opp church.* **Sat 3 June, Sat 30 Sept (12-4.30). Adm £3.50, chd free. Visits also by arrangement May to Oct.**

A modern cottage garden with coherent layers of colour, texture and interest. From spring bulbs, through the lushness of summer roses and herbaceous plants galore, to the inherent richness of late perennials and graceful grasses well into late autumn. Plants occupy every inch of this garden for all seasons! Also vegetables in a raised bed system. Approx 2/5 acre. Garden featured in Period Homes and Interiors. Partial wheelchair, main garden is on a sloping site with gravel paths.

❄ ♿

12 NEW THE COACH HOUSE
Bleacragg Road, Fern Hill, Witherslack, Grange-Over-Sands, LA11 6RX. Adele & Mike Walford, 015395 52102, mwandaj@btinternet.com. *From A950 turn North to Witherslack. Follow brown signs to Halecat, continue on lane for 1/2m. Rail Grange-over-sands 5m, Bus X6 2m, NCR 70.* **Sun 9 July (10-4.30). Combined adm with Abi and Tom's Garden Plants £3.50, chd free. Home-made teas. Coach House apple juice. Visits also by arrangement July to Sept.**
An acre garden - a riot of chaotic exuberance. From a stable yard, old tip and remnants of an orchard - six years of hard work appear to have resulted in a garden. Mixed borders, lots of vegetables, greenhouse, polytunnel, ponds and lots and lots of roses. Members of the South Lakes Orchard Group, we have a young orchard and Northern and Heritage apple trees. Enthusiastic volunteers from Wwoof provide help. Wheelchair access is limited to the flower garden only. Paths are uneven and on sloping ground.

🐔 ❄ ☕

Donations from the National Garden Scheme help Parkinson's UK care for more people

GROUP OPENING

13 NEW COCKERMOUTH GARDENS

Brigham Road, Cockermouth, CA13 0AX. *All gardens are within the Cumbrian market town of Cockermouth. Heading west on A66, turn R at Travel Lodge r'about into C'mouth. 3rd L into Brigham Rd; parking in the area. Three gardens nearby.(NB-Foot access only up lane to The White House-no cars please).* **Sun 9 July (11-5). Combined adm £4.50, chd free. Homemade teas at The White House, Brigham Road. Home-made cakes, tea, coffee and cold drinks available.**

NEW **HIGH MOOR**
Gloria & Tony Edwards.

NEW **8 HOLMEWOOD AVENUE**
Anne & Roger Asquith.

NEW **RUBBY BANKS COTTAGE**
Margaret Thurm.

NEW **2 SUNSCALES HOUSE**
George & Margaret Peacock.

NEW **145 THE PARKLANDS**
Alison Skelton.

NEW **THE WHITE HOUSE**
Jean & John Jowsey.

Different sized gardens varying from an acre in size to an idyllic cottage styled garden all featuring a variety of garden designs and hard landscaping such as pergolas, arches and seating areas. Cottage garden planting, formal and informal arrangements, herbaceous borders, roses, shrubs, topiary, large trees, acers, oriental inspired areas, espalier fruit trees, orchards, ponds and other water features as well as fruit and vegetables. Greenhouses and extensive use of containers for specimen plants and areas for bees and chickens. Wheelchair access in most gardens but there are gravelled and narrow paths at some locations which may prove difficult for some users.

❀ 🍵

14 ♦ CONISHEAD PRIORY AND BUDDHIST TEMPLE

A5087 Coast Road, Ulverston, LA12 9QQ. Manjushri Kadampa Meditation Centre, 01229 584029 Ext 234, visits@manjushri.com, www.manjushri.org. *2m S of Ulverston. 30 mins from M6 J36, follow A590 to Ulverston then S onto A5087 Coast Rd signed Croftlands, Bardsea & 'Coastal route to Barrow'. Rail 2 m, Bus 11, NCR 700.* **For NGS: Sat 22, Sun 23 Apr (11-5). Adm £3.60, chd free. Light refreshments. For other opening times and information, please phone, email or visit garden website.**

Conishead Priory was founded by Augustinian monks in 1160. 70 acres of gardens and woodland surround the Temple and Romantic Gothic mansion. Temple garden an oasis of peace, arboretum, wildlife and cottage gardens. Map of woodland walks to beach on Morecambe Bay. Free simple 15 minute Guided Meditations at 12.30, 2 and 3.30 and guided tours of Temple and part of the mansion at 1 and 2.30.

&. 🐾 🍵

15 CROOKDAKE FARM

Aspatria, Wigton, CA7 3SH. Kirk & Alannah Rylands, 016973 20413, alannah.rylands@me.com. *3m NE of Aspatria. Between A595 & A596. From A595 take B5299 at Mealsgate signed Aspatria. After 2m turn sharp R in Watch Hill signed Crookdake. House 1m on L.* **Sun 11 June (1-5). Adm £3.50, chd free. Home-made teas. Visits also by arrangement in June 10+ Refreshments by arrangement.**

Windswept informal farmhouse (not open) garden with a careful colour combination of interesting planting sympathetic to the landscape incl various different areas with densely planted herbaceous borders, fenced vegetable patch, wild meadow and large pond area home to moisture-loving plants, hens, ducks and moorhens. Opening supported by old vehicle enthusiasts. All types of old vehicles encouraged to attend.

❀ 🍵

16 DALLAM TOWER

Milnthorpe, LA7 7AG. Mr & Mrs R T Villiers-Smith. *7m S of Kendal. 7m N of Carnforth. Nr J36 off M6. A6 & B5282. Stn: Arnside, 4m; Lancaster, 15m.* **Sun 7 May (2-5). Adm £4, chd free. Cream teas.**

Large garden; natural rock garden, water garden; wood walks, lawns, shrubs. C19 cast iron orangery. Limited wheelchair access Deep gravel paths.

&. ❀ 🍵

Askham Hall

17 ◆ DORA'S FIELD

Rydal, Ambleside, LA22 9LX. National Trust, www.nationaltrust.org.uk. 1½m N of Ambleside. Follow A591 from Ambleside to Rydal. Dora's Field is next to St Mary's Church. **For NGS: Sun 2 Apr (11-4). Adm by donation. Also open High Close Estate.** For other opening times and information, please visit garden website.

Named for Dora, the daughter of the poet William Wordsworth. Wordsworth planned to build a house on the land but, after her early death, he planted the area with daffodils in her memory. Now known as Dora's field the area is renowned for its spring display of daffodils and Bluebells. 2 April; Wordsworth's Daffodil Legacy.

18 EDEN PLACE

Kirkby Stephen, CA17 4AP. J S Parrot Trust. ½m N of Kirkby Stephen. A685 Kirkby Stephen to Brough. **Sun 23 July (11-5). Adm £3.50, chd free. Tea.**

3 acre garden with many large perennial borders and island beds enclosed by tall hedges. Part of the garden is made over to aviaries with exotic birds, some are free - flying. Also a lake and a woodland walk. Free-flying parrots.

19 EWEBANK FARM

Old Hutton, Kendal, LA8 0NS. Sue & Barry Sharkey. 3m NE of Kendal. Oxenholme Stn - B6254 - Old Hutton. 3rd turning on L. R turns at next 2 junctions. M6 take J37 A684 Sedbergh. 1st R & R again. After 3m turn L. Ewebank. From Oxenholme Station, bikes take (70)68. **Sun 2 July (1-5). Adm £4, chd free. Home-made teas.**

Relaxing, rural, wildlife friendly garden. New 'green roof" and sink garden. Welcoming hens and suggestions of music. Large lawn slopes down to a stream where curved decking follows the gentle contours of the land. Areas of shade for ferns, moisture-loving plants and over 60 hostas . Mixed borders, statues, topiary, raised vegetable

beds, orchard and espaliered apples. Visitors from an Owl Sanctuary. Featured in 'Lancashire Life'.

57 NEW 2 THE FAULDS

Front Street, Armathwaite, Carlisle, CA4 9PB. Mr & Mrs Phil & Jane Dutton, www.thebuzzshelter.wordpress.com. Central to the village of Armathwaite, 10m SE of Carlisle. Turn off A6 just S of High Hesket signed Armathwaite. After 2m turn R at T-junction. Proceed under bridge to Armathwaite village. The garden is on the R, a short distance past Eden Stores. **Sat 2 Sept (12-5). Adm £3.50, chd free. Opening with Armathwaite Gardens on Sat 27 May, Sun 11 June.**

Featured in Cumbria Life, a compact garden accessed via sandstone steps is divided into 3 distinct areas. Rare and unusual trees, shrubs and herbaceous perennials, a collection of trees in pots grown from seed, raised beds, wild- life pond and Bantam run. Art work and stained glass are on display. Nearby church with stained glass by Burne-Jones/William Morris and recent window by the garden owner. For refreshments there are 2 PHs and a village shop all within a short walking distance. Featured in Cumbria Life.

20 FELL YEAT

Casterton, Kirkby Lonsdale, LA6 2JW. Mrs A E Benson, 01524 271340. 1m E of Casterton Village. On the rd to Bull Pot. Leave A65 at Devils Bridge, follow A683 for 1m, take the R fork to High Casterton at golf course, straight across at two sets of Xrds, house on L, ¼m from no-through-rd sign. **Sun 21 May, Sun 6 Aug (1-5). Adm £4, chd free. Home-made teas. Visits also by arrangement May to Aug groups up to 30. No coaches. Refreshments by arrangement.**

1 acre country garden with mixed planting, incl unusual trees, shrubs and some topiary. Small woodland garden and woodland glades. 2 ponds which encourage dragonflies. Several arbours where you can sit and relax. New paved topiary

garden. Many ferns in a designated area; old roses in mixed borders and a large collection of hydrangeas. A garden to explore. Metal sculptures in various areas. Adjoining nursery specialising in ferns, hostas, hydrangeas and many unusual plants. Wheelchair access - slight rises between different areas.

21 FERN BANK

High House Road, St. Bees, CA27 0BZ. Chris & Charm Robson. At the edge of the village going out towards A595. 2m from A595 down road signed St Bees unsuitable for long vehicles (or something like that), or B5345 from Whitehaven. **Sun 9 Apr (12-5.30). Adm £3.50, chd free. Home-made teas.**

Located in St Bees village, this is a spring garden on different levels with natural planting. Nearest the house lawns and borders lead down to the 'secret' garden via a pergola clad with roses, wisteria and clematis. Hidden away are 5 ponds surrounded by trees and boardwalks, a haven for wildlife. In Spring this area is lit up by snowdrops, leucojum, marsh marigolds and daffodils. Poetry trail through the garden. The entrance level where teas are served is wheelchair accessible but because of the steep slopes the rest of the garden is not accessible.

22 GALESYKE

Wasdale, CA20 1ET. Christine & Mike McKinley. From Gosforth, follow signs to Nether Wasdale & then to Lake, approx 5m. From Santon Bridge follow signs to Wasdale then to Lake, approx 2¼m. **Sat 3, Sun 4 June (10.30-5). Adm £4, chd free. Cream teas.**

4 acre woodland garden with spectacular views of the Wasdale fells. The R Irt runs through the garden and both banks are landscaped, you can cross over the river via a picturesque, mini, suspension bridge. The garden has an impressive collection of rhododendrons and azaleas that light up the woodlands in springtime.

ALLOTMENTS

23 GRANGE FELL ALLOTMENTS

Fell Road, Grange-Over-Sands, LA11 6HB. Mr Bruno Gouillon, 01539 532317, brunog45@hotmail.com. *Opposite Grange Fell Golf Club. Rail 1.3 m, Bus 1m X6, NCR 70.* **Sun 20 Aug (11-5). Adm £3, chd free. Visits also by arrangement June to Sept groups no more than 30.**
The allotments are managed by Grange Town Council. Opened in 2010, 30 plots are now rented out, offering a wide selection of gardening styles and techniques. The majority of plots grow a mixture of vegetables, fruit trees and flowers. There are a few communal areas where local fruit tree varieties have been donated by plot holders with herbaceous borders and annuals. Featured in and on Grange Now, Lakeland Radio, Westmorland Gazette.
🐕 ✿ 🚌

24 GREENFIELD HOUSE

Newbiggin, nr Cumrew, Brampton, CA8 9DH. Emma & Chris Gray. *8m S of Brampton. Located between the villages of Cumrew & Croglin off B6413. Armathwaite train station, Leeds/Settle line, 5.2m.* **Sun 23 July (1-5). Adm £3.50, chd free. Home-made teas.**
A village garden set on the edge of the Pennines comprising of a series of garden rooms and lawn areas divided by beech and yew hedges. Contained within are richly planted shrub and herbaceous borders in colour themed planting schemes, roses, a box parterre, an orchard area with espalier apple trees and a productive vegetable garden. Approx 1 acre of gardens and grounds. The garden is mainly level, however there are some steps which make smaller parts of the garden inaccessible by wheelchair.
♿ ✿ 🍵

25 HALL SENNA

Hallsenna, Gosforth, Holmrook, CA19 1YB. Chris & Helen Steele, 01946 725436, helen.steele5@btinternet.com. *2m SW of Gosforth. Follow main A595 either N or S. 1m S of Gosforth turn down lane opp Seven Acres Caravan Park, proceed for approx 1m.* **Visits by arrangement May to Sept access via bridleway, no coaches. Adm £7, chd free. Home-made teas. Teas by prior arrangement. Contact Helen to discuss..**
Tucked away within the hamlet of Hallsenna close to the West Cumbrian coast this garden provides the visitor with many different aspects of gardening. The 1.3 acre site includes borders fully planted for year round colour and many delightful structures built to provide interest and punctuate your journey through the garden. Teas can be provided by prior arrangement. Partial wheelchair access due to steep slopes on entry into the garden.
♿ 🐕 ✿ 🍵

26 HAVERTHWAITE LODGE

Haverthwaite, LA12 8AJ. David Snowdon, 015395 39841, sheena. taylforth@lakesidehotel.co.uk. *100yds off A590 at Haverthwaite.*

© Val Corbett
Crookdake Farm

Turn S off A590 opp Haverthwaite railway stn. Bus 6, NCR 70. **Thur 22 June, Thur 17 Aug (11-4). Combined adm with Lakeside Hotel & Rocky Bank £7.50, chd free. Single adm £3.50. Refreshments - 20% discount from Lakeside Hotel Conservatory Menu on the Open Day. Visits also by arrangement Mar to Sept.**
Traditional Lake District garden that has been redesigned and replanted. A wonderful display of hellebores and spring flowers. Gardens on a series of terraces leading down to the R Leven and incl: rose garden, cutting garden, dell area, rock terrace, herbaceous borders and many interesting mature shrubs. In a stunning setting the garden is surrounded by oak woodland and was once a place of C18 and C19 industry.
🐕 🚌 🍵 ✿

GROUP OPENING

27 HAYTON VILLAGE GARDENS

Hayton, Brampton, CA8 9HR. *7m E of Carlisle. 5m E of M6 J43. ½m S of A69, 3m W of Brampton signed to Hayton. Map of gardens with tickets, narrow road, please park on one side only.* **Sun 7 May (12-5). Combined adm £4, chd free. Home-made teas at Hayton Village Primary School with live music. Usually Pimms/ Cava or warmer equivalent in the Conservatory at Millbrook.** *Donation to Hayton Village Primary School.*

CHESTNUT COTTAGE
Mr Barry Bryan.

HAYTON C OF E PRIMARY SCHOOL
Hayton C of E Primary School, www.hayton.cumbria.sch.uk.

KINRARA
Tim & Alison Brown, 01228 670067 (Ashton Design), tim@tjbgallery.com.
Visits also by arrangement Apr to Oct architect/Artists' garden. Interest all yr. Back garden developing as Jungle open for private visits.

LITTLE GARTH
Dugald Campbell.

MILLBROOK
Emily & Angus Dawson.

NEW THE PADDOCK
Phil & Louise Jones.

SOUTH VIEW COTTAGE
Mrs Anita Laird.

WEST GARTH COTTAGE
Debbie Jenkins, 01228 670430,
debbiejenkins.art@gmail.com,
www.westgarth-cottage-gardens.
co.uk.
**Visits also by arrangement
Apr to Aug tea/coffee and
biscuits available for pre-
arranged visits.**

NEW SEASON - we are opening in
spring for the first time to share our
many rhododendrons, magnolias,
camellias and spring flowers and
foliage.... A valley of gardens of
varied size and styles all within
½ m, mostly of old stone cottages.
Smaller and larger cottage gardens,
courtyards and containers, steep
wooded slopes, sweeping lawns,
exuberant borders, frogs, pools
and poultry, colour and texture
throughout. Home-made teas and
live music at the school. Often an
informal treasure hunt for children
young and old. Gardens additional
to those listed also generally open
and there are views into numerous
others of very high standard. Two
of the gardens; Westgarth Cottage
and Kinrara are designed by artist/s
and an architect with multiple
garden design experience. Featured
in Carlisle 'News and Star'. Varying
degrees of wheelchair access from
full to minimal.

♿ ✿ ☕

28 HAZELWOOD FARM
Hollins Lane, Silverdale,
Carnforth, LA5 0UB. Glenn &
Dan Shapiro, 01524 701276,
glenn@hazelwoodfarm.co.uk,
www.hazelwoodfarm.co.uk. *4m
NW of M6 J35. From Carnforth
follow signs to Silverdale, after
1m turn L signed Silverdale, after
level Xing turn L then 1st L into
Hollins Lane. Farm on R.* **Sun 11
June (11-5). Adm £4, chd free.**

Home-made teas. Visits also by
arrangement in June groups of
20+.
A theatre of light curtained by
backdrops of woodland. Steep paths
winding up and through natural
limestone cliff, intersected by a
tumbling rill joining ponds, provide
staging for alpine gems and drifts of
herbaceous, prairie and woodland
planting. Old and English roses,
bulbs and the National Collection
of Hepatica. Wildlife friendly garden
surrounded by NT access land. New
bird, bee and butterfly garden, rock
garden, Hepatica collection, well-
stocked plant sale. Features in new
Timber Press book, 'Rock Gardening:
Reimagining classic style', Joseph
Tychonievich. Partial wheelchair
access - lower level only.

✿ ♿ NPC ☕ 🍽

**29 ♦ HIGH CLOSE ESTATE
AND ARBORETUM**
Loughrigg, Ambleside, LA22 9HH.
National Trust, 015394 37623,
neil.winder@nationaltrust.org.uk,
www.nationaltrust.org.uk.
*10 min NW from Ambleside.
Ambleside (A593) to Skelwith Bridge
signed for High Close, turn R &
head up hill until you see a white
painted stone sign to 'Langdale',
turn L, High Close on L.* **For NGS:
Sun 2 Apr (11-4). Adm by
donation. Light refreshments.
Small cafe in house part of the
YHA. For other opening times and
information, please phone, email or
visit garden website.**
Originally planted in 1866 by
Edward Wheatley-Balme, High
Close was designed in the fashion
of the day using many of the
recently discovered 'exotic' conifers
and evergreen shrubs coming into
Britain from America. Today the
garden contains a variety of tree
species many of which are the
remains of the original Victorian
plantings. Tree trail.

🐒 🍽

30 HIGH MOSS
Portinscale, Keswick, CA12 5TX.
Christine & Peter Hughes,
christine_hug25@hotmail.com.
*1m W of Keswick. Enter village off
A66, take 1st turning R through white*

gates, on R of rd after ⅓ m. **Sun 2
Apr (2-5). Adm £5, chd free.**
*Visits also by arrangement Apr to
Oct on Thursdays only. Donation to
Hospice at Home.*
Lakeland Arts and Craft house
(not open) and garden (mentioned
in Pevsner). 4½ acres of formal
and informal S-facing terraced
gardens. Magnificent views of the
fells. Many fine trees and shrubs,
rhododendrons and azaleas. Spring
meadow planted with daffodils
and camassia. Old tennis court
converted into vegetable/flower
parterre for the Diamond Jubilee
with rose garden and sun dial
by Joe Smith. Open as part of
Cumbria Daffodil Day. The garden
is not suitable for wheelchair users
because of the sloping ground and
steps.

31 HIGHLANDS
High Knott Road, Arnside,
Carnforth, LA5 0AW. Judith &
Stephen Slater, 01524 761535,
judithslater@rocketmail.com.
*12m J35 & J36 M6. M6. From A6
Milnthorpe T-lights take B5282 to
Arnside. Follow signs in village.* **Sat
13, Sun 14 May (10.30-5). Adm
£4, chd free. Home-made teas.
Home made soups available.**
**Visits also by arrangement May to
Sept for groups of 10+.**
1½ acre gently terraced garden
including 3 types of rockery. Well-
stocked herbaceous borders leading
to a tranquil woodland garden.
Raised vegetable beds and orchard
with mistletoe. Secluded and secret
areas. Courtyard garden with water
feature and beech tunnel exit.
Extensive hosta collection. Various
unique sculptures with a twist.
Wildlife friendly. New additions for
this year. Steps or steep incline to
rear garden.

🐒 ✿ ♿ ☕ 🍽

Perennial, supporting
horticulturalists
since 1839

Boxwood House

32 ◆ HOLEHIRD GARDENS

Patterdale Road, Windermere,
LA23 1NP. Lakeland Horticultural
Society, 015394 46008,
enquiries@holehirdgardens.org.
uk, www.holehirdgardens.org.uk.
*1m N of Windermere. On A592,
Windermere to Patterdale rd.* For
NGS: Sun 2 Apr, Thur 13 July
(10-5). Adm £4, chd free. Self-
service hot drinks available.
For other opening times and
information, please phone, email or
visit garden website.
Run by volunteers with the aim
of promoting knowledge of the
cultivation of plants particularly
suited to Lakeland conditions. One
of the best labelled gardens in the
UK. National Collections of *astilbe*,
daboecia, *polystichum* (ferns) and
meconopsis. Set on the fellside with
stunning views over Windermere.
The walled garden gives protection
to mixed borders whilst alpine
houses display an always colourful
array of tiny gems. Wheelchair
access limited to walled garden and
beds accessible from drive.
♿ ✿ NPC ☕

33 ◆ HOLKER HALL GARDENS

Cark-in-Cartmel, Grange-
over-Sands, LA11 7PL.
The Cavendish Family,
015395 58328, info@holker.co.uk,
www.holker.co.uk. *4m W of
Grange-over-Sands. 12m W of M6
(J36) Follow brown tourist signs. Rail
1m, NCR 700 ½m.* For NGS: Thur
24 Aug (10.30-5). Adm £8.50,
chd free. For other opening times
and information, please phone,
email or visit garden website.
25 acres of romantic gardens, with
peaceful arboretum, inspirational
formal gardens, flowering meadow
and Labyrinth. Summer brings
voluptuous mixed borders and
bedding. Discover unusually large
rhododendrons, magnolias and
azaleas, and the National Collection
of Styracaceae. Discover our latest
garden feature - The Pagan Grove,
designed by Kim Wilkie. Guided tour
of the gardens with our experienced
guide. Donation required.
♿ ✿ 🚌 NPC ☕

34 HOLME MEADOW

1 Holme Meadow, Cumwhinton,
Carlisle, CA4 8DR. John &
Anne Mallinson, 01228 560330,
jwai.mallinson@btinternet.com.
*2m S of Carlisle. From M6 J42 take
B6263 to Cumwhinton, in village take
1st L then bear R at Lowther Arms,
Holme Meadow is immed on R.* Sun
16 July (11-4). Adm £3, chd free.
Light refreshments. Visits also
by arrangement June to Aug for
groups of 10+.
Village garden developed and
landscaped from scratch by owners.
Incl shrubbery, perennial beds
supplemented by annuals; gazebo,
pergola and trellis with climbers,
slate beds and water feature,
ornamental copse, pond, wild
flower meadow and kitchen garden.
Designed, planted and maintained to
be wildlife friendly.
✿ ☕

35 IVY HOUSE

Cumwhitton, Brampton, CA8 9EX.
Martin Johns & Ian Forrest. *6m E
of Carlisle. At the bridge at Warwick
Bridge on A69 take turning to Great
Corby & Cumwhitton. Through Great
Corby & woodland until you reach a
T-junction Turn R.* Sun 18 June
(1-5). Adm £4, chd free.
Home-made teas in
Cumwhitton village hall.
Approx 2 acres of sloping fell-side
garden with meandering paths
leading to a series of 'rooms': pond,
fern garden, gravel garden with
assorted grasses, vegetable and herb
garden. Copse with meadow leading
down to beck. Trees, shrubs, ferns,
bamboos and herbaceous perennials
planted with emphasis on variety of
texture and colour. Steep slopes.
🐕 ☕

36 LAKESIDE HOTEL & ROCKY BANK

Lake Windermere, Newby Bridge,
Ulverston, LA12 8AT. Mr N
Talbot, 015395 39841, sheena.
taylforth@lakesidehotel.co.uk,
www.lakesidehotel.co.uk. *1m N
of Newby Bridge. Turn N off A590
across R Leven at Newby Bridge
along W side of Windermere.*
Thur 22 June, Thur 17 Aug
(11-4). Combined adm with

Haverthwaite Lodge £7.50, chd free. Light refreshments. Single adm to Lakeside and Rocky Bank £5. Refreshments - 20% discount from Hotel Conservatory menu on the Open Day. **Visits also by arrangement Mar to Sept.**
Two diverse gardens on the shores of Lake Windermere. Lakeside has been created for year round interest, packed with choice plants, incl some unusual varieties. Main garden area with herbaceous borders and foliage shrubs, scented and winter interest plants and seasonal bedding. Roof garden with lawn, espaliered local heritage apple varieties and culinary herbs. Lawn art on front lawn. Rocky Bank is a traditional garden with rock outcrops. Planted with unusual specimen alpines. Herbaceous borders, shrubs and ornamental trees. Woodland area with species rhododendrons. Working greenhouse and polytunnels. Wild flower garden and cut flower garden. Wheelchair access not available at Rocky Bank.

37 LANGHOLME MILL
Woodgate, Lowick Green, LA12 8ES. Judith & Graham Sanderson, 01229 885215, judith@themill.biz. *7m NW of Ulverston. West on A590. At Greenodd, N on A5902 towards Broughton. Langholme Mill is approx 3m along this road on L as road divides on the hill.* **Sat 20, Sun 21 May (11-5). Adm £5, chd free. Home-made teas. Visits also by arrangement Apr to Sept please phone Judith 01229 885215.**
Approx 1 acre of mature woodland garden with meandering lakeland stone paths surrounding the mill race stream which can be crossed by a variety of bridges. The garden hosts well established bamboo, rhododendrons, hostas, acers and astilbes and a large variety of country flowers. Featured in Amateur Garden.

38 LARCH COTTAGE NURSERIES
Melkinthorpe, Penrith, CA10 2DR. Peter Stott, www.larchcottage.co.uk. *From N leave M6 J40 take A6 S. From S leave M6 J39 take A6 N signed off A6.* **Wed 7 June, Wed 4 Oct (1-4). Adm £4, chd free.**
For 2 days only Larch Cottage Nurseries are opening the new lower gardens and chapel for NGS visitors. The gardens include lawns, flowing perennial borders, rare and unusual shrubs, trees, small orchard and a kitchen garden. A natural stream runs into a small lake - a haven for wildlife and birds. At the head of the lake stands a chapel, designed and built by Peter for family use only. Larch Cottage has a Japanese Dry garden, ponds and Italianesque columned garden specifically for shade plants, the Italianesque tumbled down walls are draped in greenery acting as a backdrop for the borders filled with stock plants. Newly designed and constructed lower gardens and chapel. Larch Cottage Nurseries Founder awarded Fellowship - Hort Week One of top 50 plant nurseries in the UK Gardens Illustrated Garden of Eden - Lancashire Life. The gardens are accessible to wheelchair users although the paths are rocky in places.

39 LOW BLAKEBANK
Underbarrow, Kendal, LA8 8BN. Mrs Catherine Chamberlain. *Lyth Valley between Underbarrow & Crosthwaite. East off A5074 to Crossthwaite. Signed Red Scar & Broom Farm off the main rd between Crosthwaite & Underbarrow. 1st drive on R off Broom Lane.* **Sun 11 June (10.30-4.30). Combined adm with Middle Blakebank £5, chd free. Home-made teas at Middle Blakebank.**
Charming and secluded 3 acre garden surrounding C17 Lakeland farmhouse (not open) and bank barn. Plenty of seating to enjoy beautiful views of the Lyth Valley and Scout Scar. Garden under development. Mixed borders, ponds, lawned areas, topiary, small bluebell wood and vegetable garden. Uneven ground, slopes and steps.

40 LOW FELL WEST
Crosthwaite, Kendal, LA8 8JG. Barbie & John Handley, 015395 68297, barbie@handleyfamily.co.uk. *4½m S of Bowness. Off A5074, turn W just S of Damson Dene Hotel. Follow lane for ½m.* **Sun 30 Apr (2-5.30); Mon 1 May (10.30-2); Sun 8 Oct (11-4). Adm £4, chd free. Home-made teas. Visits also by arrangement nearest access for large coaches ½m away.**
This 2 acre woodland garden in the tranquil Winster Valley has extensive views to the Pennines. The four season garden, restored since 2003, incl expanses of rock planted sympathetically with grasses, unusual trees and shrubs, climaxing for autumn colour. There are native hedges and areas of plant rich meadows. A woodland area houses a gypsy caravan and there is direct access to Cumbria Wildlife Trust's Barkbooth Reserve of Oak woodland, blue bells and open fellside. Featured in Cumbria Life. Wheelchair access to much of the garden, but some rough paths, steep slopes.

41 LOWER ROWELL FARM & COTTAGE
Milnthorpe, LA7 7LU. John & Mavis Robinson & Julie & Andy Welton, 015395 62270. *Approx 2m from Milnthorpe, 2m from Crooklands. Signed to Rowell off B6385, Milnthorpe to Crooklands Rd. Garden ½m up lane on L.* **Sun 19 Feb (10-4). Adm £3.50, chd free. Tea. Visits also by arrangement Feb to July groups of 10+, refreshments by arrangement.**
Approx 1¼ acre garden with views to Farleton Knott and Lakeland hills. Unusual trees and shrubs, plus perennial borders; architectural pruning; retro greenhouse; polytunnel with tropical plants; cottage gravel garden and vegetable plot. Fabulous display of snowdrops in spring followed by other spring flowers, with colour most of the year. Wildlife ponds and 2 friendly pet hens.

42 MATSON GROUND

Windermere, LA23 2NH.
Matson Ground Estate
Co Ltd, 015394 47892,
info@matsonground.co.uk.
⅔m E of Bowness. Turn N off B5284 signed Heathwaite. From E 100yds after Windermere Golf Club, from W 400yds after Windy Hall Rd. Rail 2½m; Bus 1m, 6, 599, 755, 800; NCR 6. **Sun 21 May (1-5). Adm £3.50, chd free. Home-made teas. Visits also by arrangement for gardening groups of 4+.**
2 acre formal garden with a mix of established borders, wild flower areas and stream leading to a large pond and developing aboretum. Rose garden, rockery and topiary terrace borders; white garden. Walled kitchen garden with raised beds, fruit trees and greenhouse. Previous visitors will notice changes to the garden as a new gardener started in June 2016.
& 🐄 🌼 🚌 🍵

43 MIDDLE BLAKEBANK

Underbarrow, Kendal, LA8 8HP.
Mrs Hilary Crowe, 015395 68959,
hfcmbb@aol.com. *Lyth Valley between Underbarrow & Crosthwaite. East off A5074 to Crosthwaite. The garden is on Broom Lane, a turning between Crosthwaite & Underbarrow signed Red Scar & Broom Farm.* **Sun 11 June (10.30-4.30). Combined adm with Low Blakebank £5, chd free. Home-made teas. Visits also by arrangement May to Sept we are happy to open for small groups.**
The garden extends to 4½ acres and overlooks the Lyth Valley with extensive views south to Morecambe Bay and east to the Howgills. We have orchards, wild flower meadow and more formal garden with a range of outbuildings. Over the last 5 years the garden has been developed with plantings that provide varying colour and texture all year. We enjoy providing home made cakes and sandwiches - under cover if necessary!
🐄 🍵

44 NEWTON RIGG COLLEGE GARDENS

Newton Rigg, Penrith, CA11 0AH.
Newton Rigg College,
www.newtonrigg.ac.uk. *1m W of Penrith. 3m W from J40 & J41 off M6. ½m off the B5288 W of Penrith. We have The Coast to Coast cycle route (Route 7) & public pathway approx 500 metres from the garden entrance gates.* **Thur 13 July (1-8). Adm £4.50, chd free. Tea. Visits also by arrangement 15+.**
Our Educational Gardens have much of horticultural interest incl herbaceous borders, ten ponds, decorative and productive organic garden, woodland walk, seasonal borders, Pictorial Meadows, Pleached Hornbeam Walkway and extensive range of ornamental trees and shrubs. Our Horticultural, Floristry and Forestry staff and students will give informative tours and a variety of demonstrations.
& 🐄 🌼 🚌 🍵

45 ORCHARD COTTAGE

Hutton Lane, Levens,
Kendal, LA8 8PB. Shirley & Chris Band, 015395 61005,
chrisband67@gmail.com. *6m S of Kendal. Turn N off A590 or A6 signed Levens. From Xrds by Methodist Church, 300 metres down Hutton Lane. Park near this Xrds. Garden access via 'The Orchard'.* **Sun 23 Apr, Sun 28 May, Sun 25 June (1-5). Adm £3.50, chd free. Light refreshments at Sizergh Castle (2m). Visits also by arrangement Mar to Sept any from 1 to 60.**
¾ acre sloping garden in old orchard. Plantsperson's paradise. Winding paths, diverse habitats, secret vistas. All yr interest and colour. Collections of ferns (100+ varieties), hellebores (70+), grasses, cottage plants, geraniums, Acers (25) Hostas. Auricula theatres, 'imaginary' stream, bog garden. Trees support clematis, roses and honeysuckle. Wildlife friendly. Featured in 'Lancashire Magazine' & Pteridologist - The Fern Magazine'.
🌼 🚌 🍵

46 8 OXENHOLME ROAD

Kendal, LA9 7NJ. Mr & Mrs John & Frances Davenport, 01539 720934,
frandav8@btinternet.com. *SE Kendal. From A65 (Burton Rd, Kendal/Kirkby Lonsdale) take B6254 (Oxenholme Rd). No.8 is 1st house on L beyond red post box.* **Sun 11 June (10-4.30). Adm £3.50, chd free. Home-made teas. Visits also by arrangement Apr to Oct for groups of 10+.**
Artist and potters garden of approx ½ acre of mixed planting designed for year-round interest, incl two linked small ponds. Roses, grasses and colour themed borders surround the house, with a gravel garden at the front, as well as a number of woodland plant areas, vegetable and fruit areas and sitting spaces. John is a ceramic artist and Frances is a painter. Paintings and pots are a feature of the garden display. Garden essentially level, but access to WC is up steps.
& 🐄 🌼 🚌 🍵

47 PARK HOUSE

Barbon, Kirkby Lonsdale,
LA6 2LG. Mr & Mrs P Pattison.
2½m N of Kirkby Lonsdale. Off A683 Kirkby Lonsdale to Sedburgh rd. Follow signs into Barbon Village. **Sun 2 July, Sun 6 Aug (10.30-4.30). Adm £4, chd free. Cream teas.**
Romantic Manor House (not open). Extensive vistas. Formal tranquil pond encased in yew hedging. Meadow with meandering pathways, water garden filled with bulbs and ferns. Formal lawn, gravel pathways, cottage borders with hues of soft pinks and purples, shady border, kitchen garden. An evolving garden to follow.
🐄 🌼 🍵

48 PEAR TREE COTTAGE

Dalton, Burton-in-Kendal,
LA6 1NN. Linda & Alec Greening, 01524 781624,
lindagreening48@gmail.com. *5m from J35 & J36 of M6. From northern end of Burton-in-Kendal (A6070) turn E into Vicarage Lane & continue approx 1m.* **Visits by arrangement June & July groups of 15+. Refreshments by arrangement.**
⅓ acre cottage garden in a delightful

rural setting. A peaceful and relaxing garden, harmonising with its environment and incorporating many different planting areas, from packed herbaceous borders and rambling roses, to wildlife pond, bog garden, rock garden and gravel garden. A plantsperson's delight, incl over 200 different ferns, and many other rare and unusual plants.

✿ 🚗 ☕ ♨

GROUP OPENING

49 RAVENSTONEDALE VILLAGE GARDENS

Kirkby Stephen, CA17 4NQ. *8m E J38 M6 (Tebay), 4m W Kirkby Stephen. From A685, follow signs for Ravenstonedale, into village.* Sat 1, Sun 2 July (11-5). Combined adm £6, chd free. Home-made teas in High Chapel Community and Heritage Centre, Ravenstonedale. Pimms & Prosecco in gardens.

THE CHANTRY
Joan & John Houston, 01539 623468, joanbarnard@btinternet.com. Visits also by arrangement May to Sept for groups of 10 - 25. Refreshments by arrangement.

NEW HIGH CHAPEL HOUSE
Dave & Jackie Wedd.

NEW LOW THACKTHWAITE
David & Vivien Caldow, 015396 23027.
🛏

NEW RAVENSTONEDALE ALLOTMENTS
Sue Richardson.

NEW WYEGARTH RIGG
Sue & Chris Richardson.

'Ravenstonedale is one of Westmorland's loveliest villages … the whole place has a most delightful air of rural serenity and dignity' (Wainwright). There is an almost unique church, with collegiate pews and a three tier pulpit, various buildings and structures of historical interest and two excellent pubs. Good starting point for walks of varying distance – short to hay meadows, longer to the top of Green Bell and the Howgills. The four gardens and the allotments show very different ways of battling the challenges of strong winds, lots of rain, 800ft elevation and a very short growing season, and of encouraging wildlife, including red squirrels. The garden opening is part of a Ravenstonedale Village Festival, celebrating its history, heritage and creativity. Lots of activities for children and adults, including treasure hunt, walking tours, art exhibition, plant and produce sale.. Delicious homemade teas in Heritage Centre (50% sales to NGS) and other refreshments in gardens.

✿ ☕

50 ◆ RYDAL HALL

Ambleside, LA22 9LX. Diocese of Carlisle, 01539 432050, www.rydalhall.org. *2m N of Ambleside. E from A591 at Rydal signed Rydal Hall. Bus 555, 599, X8, X55; NCR 6.* For NGS: Sun 2 Apr, Thur 11 May, Thur 15 June, Thur 6 July (11-4). Adm by donation. Light refreshments in tea shop on site. For other opening times and information, please phone or visit garden website.

Formal Italianate gardens designed by Thomas Mawson in 1911; the gardens have recently been restored to their former glory. Formal garden with fountain and croquet lawn, C17 viewing station, fine herbaceous planting, informal woodland garden, community vegetable garden, orchard and apiary. Magnificent views across Windermere and the Lakeland Fells. Limited Wheelchair access, top terrace only.

♿ 🐎 ✿ 🚗 🛏 ☕ ♨

51 ◆ SIZERGH CASTLE

Sizergh, Kendal, LA8 8DZ. National Trust, 015395 60951, www.nationaltrust.org.uk. *3m S of Kendal Approach rd leaves A590 close to & S of A590/A591 interchange* For NGS: Sat 9 Sept (10-5). Adm £6.47, chd £3.24.

For other opening times and information, please phone or visit garden website.
⅔ acre limestone rock garden, largest owned by National Trust; collections of Japanese maples, dwarf conifers, hardy ferns; Wild flower areas, hot wall and herbaceous borders, Kitchen garden and fruit orchard with spring bulbs. Terrace garden and lake. National Collections of *Asplenium scolopendrium, Cystopteris, Dryopteris, Osmunda* in new Stumpery garden. National Trust members are admitted free with an opportunity to donate to the good causes the NGS supports. Non Trust members entrance fees are donated to the NGS. Featured in The Times in their 20 best Great British gardens to visit this summer.

♿ ✿ 🚗 NPC ☕ ♨

52 STEWART HILL COTTAGE

Hesket Newmarket, CA7 8HX. Mr & Mrs D Scott, 01768 484841, ardrannoch@hotmail.com. *7m W of Penrith. From S leave A66 at Sportsman's Inn – drive 5m Haltcliffe Bridge. Turn before Haltcliffe Bridge signed Newsham 2m garden 200yds on R.* Sun 2 July (2-5). Adm £5, chd free. Home-made teas. Visits also by arrangement July to Dec. *Donation to Community Action Nepal.*

8yr old garden comprising mainly roses, courtyard newly designed, organic vegetable garden incl walled kitchen garden, potager, ornamental pool and croquet lawn.

✿ ☕ ♨

Your visit helps the Queen's Nursing Institute to champion excellence in community nursing

53 SUMMERDALE HOUSE

Nook, Lupton, LA6 1PE.
David & Gail Sheals,
www.summerdalegardenplants.
co.uk. *7m S of Kendal, 5m W of
Kirkby Lonsdale. From J36 M6 take
A65 towards Kirkby Lonsdale, at
Nook take R turn Farleton. Location
not always signed on highway.
Detailed directions available on our
website.* Sun 19 Feb (11-4.30).
Home-made teas. Every Fri and
Sat 24 Feb to 26 Aug (11-4.30).
Sun 18 June (11-4.30). Home-
made teas. Adm £4, chd free.
Refreshments on Suns only.
Home-made soups & bread
(Feb only).
1½ acre part-walled country garden
set around C18 former vicarage.
Several defined areas have been
created by hedges, each with its
own theme and linked by intricate
cobbled pathways. Beautiful setting
with fine views across to Farleton
Fell. Traditional herbaceous borders,
ponds, woodland and meadow
planting provide year round interest.
Large collections of auricula,
primulas and snowdrops. Adjoining
specialist nursery growing a wide
range of interesting and unusual
herbaceous perennials. Home made
jams and chutneys for sale.

🐾 ✿ ☕ ▶

54 SUNNYSIDE

Woodhouse Lane, Heversham,
Milnthorpe, LA7 7EW. Anita
Gott, 015395 63249. *1½m N
of Milnthorpe. From A6 turn into
Heversham, then R at church signed
Crooklands. In ½m turn L down lane.*
Visits by arrangement June to Aug
groups of 15-25. Refreshments by
arrangement.
½-acre country cottage garden with
a well at the bottom, 3 greenhouses,
pond and mixed borders. Large,
immaculate vegetable garden.
Orchard with hens. Area to attract
bees and butterflies. Prizewinner in
local garden competition 2016.

☕

55 ◆ SWARTHMOOR HALL

Swarthmoor Hall Lane,
Ulverston, LA12 0JQ. Jane
Pearson, Manager, 01229 583204,
info@swarthmoorhall.co.uk,
www.swarthmoorhall.co.uk. *1½m
SW of Ulverston. A590 to Ulverston.
Turn off to Ulverston railway stn.
Follow Brown tourist signs to Hall.
Rail 0.9m. NCR70 & 700 1m.* For
opening times and information,
please phone, email or visit garden
website.
Wild purple crocus meadow in
early spring: late February or early
March depending on weather, earlier
if mild winter later if cold and frosty.
Also, good displays of snowdrops,
daffodils and tulips.

👤 ✿ 🛏 ☕ ▶

56 TENTER END BARN

Docker, Kendal, LA8 0DB. Mrs
Hazel Terry, 01539 824447,
hnterry@btinternet.com. *3m N
Kendal. From Kendal take A685
Appleby rd. Then 2nd on R to Docker.
At the junction bear L.* Sun 4 June
(11-4.30). Adm £3.50, chd free.
Home-made teas. Visits also
by arrangement Apr to Sept for
groups of 4+.
3 acres of cultivated and natural
areas, in a secretive rural setting.
A patio garden, large lawns,
herbaceous borders and a small
vegetable patch. Walks on the wild
side around a mere and woodlands.
Many birds can be seen at various
feeding stations, also waterfowl on
the mere. All managed by one OAP.
Wheelchair access - rather uneven
around the woodland paths. Could
be difficult around mere in wet
weather.

👤 🐾 ✿ ☕ ▶

58 NEW TITHE BARN

Laversdale, Irthington, Carlisle,
CA6 4PJ. Mr & Mrs Gordon &
Christine Davidson. *8m N E of
Carlisle. Laversdale, N. Cumbria, ½m
from Carlisle Airport. From 6071 turn
for Laversdale, from M6 J44 follow
A689 Hexham. Follow NGS signs.*
Sun 18 June (1-5). Adm £4, chd
free. Home-made teas.
Set on a slight incline, the thatched
property has stunning views of
the Lake District, Pennines and
Scottish Border hills. Planting
follows the cottage garden style,
the surrounding walls, arches,
grottos and quirky features have
all been designed and created by
the owners. There is a peaceful
sitting glade beside a rill and pond.
Wheelchairs unable to view the
small 'shaded woodland area' down
steep steps.

👤 � ☕

GROUP OPENING

59 WETHERAL GARDENS

Carlisle, CA4 8JG. *4m E of Carlisle.
The village of Wetheral is situated
2m from both J42 & J43 off the M6
motorway or approx 1m off the A69
Carlisle to Newcastle Rd. Wetheral
is on the Carlisle to Newcastle
train line.* Sun 11 June (12-5).
Combined adm £5, chd free.
Home-made teas in Wetheral
Community Hall.

ACORN BANK
Isabel Ferguson.

EDEN CROFT
Jack & Ali Spedding.

HILLCREST
Joyce Johnston.

NEW **THE METHODIST CHURCH**
Allotment holders,
01228 560118.
Visits also by arrangement in
June.

ROTHAY
John & Heather Park.

STATION MASTER'S HOUSE
Judith Jansen.

NEW **TAVISTOCK HOUSE**
John Shaw.
A selection of gardens around
Wetheral including cottage,
herbaceous, kitchen, vegetable, and
the local allotments. To include
Acorn Bank a medium sized garden
with herbaceous borders, gravel
garden, orchard and vegetable
patch. Eden Croft a large children
friendly garden with sweeping
lawns and fantastic views. Hillcrest
has a small garden with open
views clipped shrubs and trees,
stone toughs, small pond and
interesting plants. Rothay traditional
country garden with lawns and

mixed borders comprising colour and textured planting with an assortment of container plants. Station Master House has perennial cottage style planting, vegetable plots and small orchard, walled patio area with stone steps. The village allotments which grow a large selection of vegetables are also open for those interested in allotment growing. Station Master House has received both local and national press coverage. Partial wheelchair access for some areas.

✿ ☕ ▱

Your support helps
Carers Trust to
provide more help
to unpaid carers

---

60 WINDY HALL

Crook Road, Windermere, LA23 3JA. Diane & David Kinsman, 015394 46238, dhewitt.kinsman@gmail.com, windy-hall.co.uk. *½m S of Bowness-on-Windermere. On western end of B5284, pink house up Linthwaite Hotel driveway. Rail 2.6m; Bus 1m, 6, 599, 755, 800; NCR 6.* Sun 7 May, Sun 4 June (10-5). Adm £4.50, chd free. Home-made teas.
Visits also by arrangement. Guided tours & home-made Lunch or Teas for groups of 8+.
'A masterclass in gardening with nature, not against it, making the most of plants that thrive in the wet climate and acid soil'. 35 gardening years by 2 people on 4 hillside acres with 6ft of rain. Woodland with rhododendrons, camellias, magnolias, hydrangeas, bluebells and foxgloves. Extensive moss and Japanese influenced gardens, ponds, meadows, stewartias, gunneras large and small, alpine and Best gardens. And much much more. Plant Heritage Aruncus

collection. Rare Hebridean sheep, exotic waterfowl and pheasants.

✿ 🚗 NPC 🛏 ☕

61 WINTON PARK

Appleby Road, Kirkby Stephen, CA17 4PG. Mr Anthony Kilvington. *2m N of Kirkby Stephen. On A685 turn L signed Gt Musgrave/ Warcop (B6259). After approx 1m turn L as signed.* Sun 30 July (11-5). Adm £6, chd free. Light refreshments.
4 acre country garden bordered by the banks of the R Eden with stunning views. Many fine conifers, acers and rhododendrons, herbaceous borders, hostas, ferns, grasses and several hundred roses. Four formal ponds plus rock pool. Partial wheelchair access.

♿ ☕

62 WOODEND HOUSE

Woodend, Egremont, CA22 2TA. Grainne & Richard Jakobson, 019468 13017, gmjakobson22@gmail.com. *2m S of Whitehaven. Take the A595 from Whitehaven towards Egremont. On leaving Bigrigg take 1st turn L. Go down hill, garden at bottom on R opp Woodend Farm. Close to cycleways & Coast to Coast route.* Sun 23 July (11-5.30). Adm £3.50, chd free. Home-made teas. Visits also by arrangement Apr to Oct.
An interesting garden tucked away in a small hamlet. Meandering gravel paths lead around the garden with imaginative, colourful planting and lots of interest throughout the year. Take a look around a productive, organic potager, shady walk, wildlife pond, mini spring and summer meadows and a pretty summer house. Wildlife friendly. Plant sale, home-made teas, mini-quiz for children. Featured in local newpapers. The gravel drive and paths are difficult for wheelchairs but more mobile visitors can access the main seating areas in the rear garden.

✿ 🚗 ☕

63 YEWBARROW HOUSE

Hampsfell Road, Grange-over-Sands, LA11 6BE. Jonathan & Margaret Denby, 015395 32469, jonathan@bestlakesbreaks.co.uk,

www.yewbarrowhouse.co.uk. *¼m from town centre. Proceed along Hampsfell Rd passing a house called Yewbarrow to brow of hill then turn L onto a lane signed 'Charney Wood/ Yewbarrow Wood' & sharp L again. Rail 0.7m, Bus X6, NCR 70.* Sun 4 June, Sun 2 July, Sun 6 Aug, Sun 3 Sept (11-4). Adm £4.50, chd free. Cream teas. Visits also by arrangement May to Oct morning coffee, tea with biscuits for groups £2.50 a head. Cream teas £5 a head.
'More Cornwall than Cumbria' according to Country Life, a colourful 4 acre garden filled with exotic and rare plants, with dramatic views over the Morecambe Bay. Outstanding features include the Orangery, the Japanese garden with infinity pool, the Italian terraces and the restored Victorian kitchen garden. Dahlias, cannas and colourful exotica are a speciality. www.youtube.com/watch?v=v--VH2cLG18. There is limited wheelchair access owing to the number of steps.

🐐 ✿ 🚗 ☕

64 YEWS

Middle Entrance Drive, Storrs Park, Bowness-on-Windermere, LA23 3JR. Sir Christopher & Lady Scott. *1m S of Bowness-on-Windermere. On A5074, W on Middle Entrance Drive. About 0.3m N of Blackwell, The Arts & Crafts House. Rail Windermere 3m, Bus 1m, 6, 599, 755, 800; NCR 6.* Sun 11 June (11.30-5). Adm £3.50, chd free. Home-made teas.
Medium-sized formal Edwardian garden; fine trees, ha-ha, herbaceous borders; greenhouse (by Messenger). Bog area with bamboos, primuli, hostas. Young yew maze and vegetable garden. Designed by H. Avary Tipping in 1912. Rose garden under reconstruction. Wheelchair access is reasonable given the private nature of the garden.

♿ 🐐 ✿ ☕

DERBYSHIRE

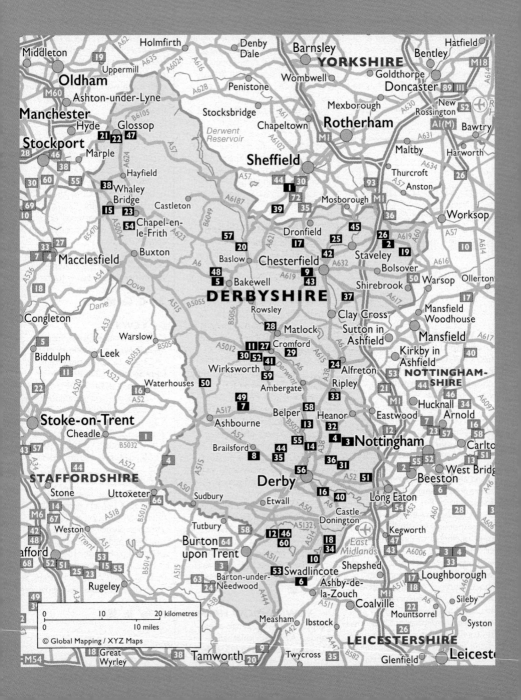

Derbyshire is the county where the Midlands meets the North, and visitors are attracted to the rugged hills of the High Peak, the high moorlands near Sheffield and the unspoilt countryside of the Dales.

There are many stately homes in the county with world famous gardens, delightful private country gardens, and interesting small cottage and town gardens.

Some of the northern gardens have spectacular views across the Peak District; their planting reflecting the rigours of the climate and long, cold winters. In the Derbyshire Dales, stone walls give way to hedges and the countryside is hilly with many trees, good agricultural land and very pretty villages.

South of Derby the land is much flatter, the architecture has a Midlands look with red brick replacing stone and softer planting in the gardens.

The east side of Derbyshire is different again, reflecting the recent past with small pit villages, and looking towards the rolling countryside of Nottinghamshire. There are fast road links with other parts of the country via the M1 and M6, making a day trip to a Derbyshire garden a very easy choice.

Volunteers

County Organiser
Irene Dougan
01335 370958
irene.dougan@ngs.org.uk

County Treasurer
Robert Little
01283 702267
robert.little@ngs.org.uk

Publicity
Roger Roberts
01332 841905
roger.roberts@ngs.org.uk

Booklet Co-ordinator
Dave Darwent
01142 665881
dave.darwent@ngs.org.uk

Assistant County Organisers
Dave Darwent
(as above)

Gill & Colin Hancock
01159 301061
gillandcolin@tiscali.co.uk

Jane Lennox
01663 732381
jane@lennoxonline.net

Pauline Little
01283 702267
plittle@hotmail.co.uk

Christine Sanderson
01246 570830
christine.r.sanderson@uwclub.net

Kate & Peter Spencer
01629 822499
pandkspencer@yahoo.co.uk

Left: **Holme Point**

OPENING DATES

All entries subject to change. For latest information check www.ngs.org.uk

Map locator numbers are shown to the right of each garden name.

February
Snowdrop Festival

Saturday 18th
The Dower House   18

Sunday 19th
The Dower House   18

Saturday 25th
10 Chestnut Way   12
NEW The Old Vicarage   41

Sunday 26th
10 Chestnut Way   12
NEW The Old Vicarage   41

April

Sunday 2nd
Chevin Brae   13

Sunday 9th
122 Sheffield Road   47

Wednesday 19th
◆ Bluebell Arboretum and Nursery   6

Sunday 23rd
334 Belper Road   4

Saturday 29th
NEW Treetops Hospice Care   51

Sunday 30th
12 Ansell Road   1
◆ The Burrows Gardens   8

May

Monday 1st
12 Ansell Road   1

Sunday 7th
Coxbench Hall   14
Moorfields   37
122 Sheffield Road   47
Tilford House   49

Sunday 14th
◆ Cascades Gardens   11
Locko Park   31
The Paddock   42

Tuesday 16th
◆ Renishaw Hall & Gardens   45

Wednesday 17th
◆ Bluebell Arboretum and Nursery   6

Saturday 20th
12 Water Lane   52

Sunday 21st
334 Belper Road   4
Fir Croft   20
Repton NGS Village Gardens   46
12 Water Lane   52

90th Anniversary Weekend

Saturday 27th
12 Ansell Road   1
◆ Melbourne Hall Gardens   34

Sunday 28th
12 Ansell Road   1
228 Belper Road   3
Gamesley Fold Cottage   21
Highfield House   24
The Hollies   26
The Holly Tree   28
◆ Melbourne Hall Gardens   34
Rectory House   44

Monday 29th
12 Ansell Road   1
Brick Kiln Farm   7
◆ The Burrows Gardens   8
The Holly Tree   28
◆ Tissington Hall   50

June

Sunday 4th
334 Belper Road   4
Fir Croft   20

Sunday 11th
NEW Higher Crossings   23
Hollies Farm Plant Centre   27
16 Monarch Drive   36

Saturday 17th
9 Newfield Crescent   39

Renishaw Hall

Sunday 18th
Fir Croft   20
9 Newfield Crescent   39
Westgate   54

Tuesday 20th
◆ Renishaw Hall & Gardens   45

Wednesday 21st
◆ Bluebell Arboretum and Nursery   6

Saturday 24th
◆ Calke Abbey   10
The Dower House   18
Elmton Gardens   19

Sunday 25th
12 Ansell Road   1
◆ Cascades Gardens   11
The Dower House   18
Elmton Gardens   19
Gamesley Fold Cottage   21
High Roost   22
Highfield House   24
◆ Meynell Langley Trials Garden   35

July

Saturday 1st
Craigside   15
NEW The Old Vicarage   41

Sunday 2nd
Craigside   15
The Lilies   30
Moorfields   37
NEW The Old Vicarage   41
Park Hall   43
13 Westfield Road   53

Saturday 8th
New Mills School and Sixth Form   38

Sunday 9th
◆ The Burrows Gardens   8
New Mills School and Sixth Form   38

Saturday 15th
2 Manvers Street   33
26 Windmill Rise   58

Sunday 16th
8 Curzon Lane   16
Hollies Farm Plant Centre   27
2 Manvers Street   33
◆ Meynell Langley Trials Garden   35
16 Monarch Drive   36
Repton NGS Village Gardens   46
26 Windmill Rise   58

Wednesday 19th
◆ Bluebell Arboretum and Nursery   6

Thursday 20th
26 Windmill Rise   58

Sunday 23rd
◆ Cascades Gardens   11
8 Curzon Lane   16

Thursday 27th
Thornbridge Hall Gardens   48

Saturday 29th
Barlborough Gardens   2
Wild in the Country   57

THE GARDENS

1 12 ANSELL ROAD
Ecclesall, Sheffield, S11 7PE.
Dave Darwent, 0114 2 665881,
dave@poptasticdave.co.uk,
www.poptasticdave.co.uk/_/
Horticulture.html. *Approx 3m SW of City Centre. Travel to Ringinglow Rd (88 bus), then Edale Rd (opp Ecclesall C of E Primary School). 3rd R - Ansell Rd. No 12 on L ¾ way down, solar panel on roof.* Sun 30 Apr, Mon 1 May (10.30-4.30); Sat 27, Sun 28, Mon 29 May, Sun 25 June, Sun 30 July (12-6); Sun 27 Aug (10.30-4.30). Adm £2.50, chd free. Light refreshments. **Visits also by arrangement May to Sept, groups 20 max. No parking for large coaches. Afternoon teas available on request when booking.**
Established 1930s, the garden contains many original plants maintained in the original style. Traditional rustic pergola and dwarf wall greenhouse. Owner (grandson of first owner) aims to keep the garden as a living example of how interwar gardens were cultivated to provide decoration and produce. More detail online. Afternoon Teas available during the 90th Anniversary Weekend openings: cucumber sandwiches, strawberries and cream, selection of dainties and unlimited tea or coffee. Then and now pictures of the garden in 1929 and 1950's Vs present. Map of landmarks up to 55m away which can be seen from garden.
✿ ☕

The National Garden Scheme is Hospice UK's largest single funder

12 Ansell Road

GROUP OPENING

2 BARLBOROUGH GARDENS

Barlborough, Chesterfield, S43 4ER. Christine Sanderson, http://wwwfacebook.com/barlboroughgardens. *7m NE of Chesterfield. Off A619 midway between Chesterfield & Worksop. ½m E M1, J30. Follow signs for Barlborough then yellow NGS signs. Parking available in village. Coach parking available at Royal Oak PH.* Sat 29, Sun 30 July (1-6). Combined adm £6, chd free. Home-made teas at Stone Croft and The Hollies.

CLARENDON
Neil & Lorraine Jones.

GOOSE COTTAGE
Mick & Barbara Housley.

GREYSTONES BARN
Jenny & Ernie Stamp.

THE HOLLIES
Vernon & Christine Sanderson.
(See separate entry)

LINDWAY
Thomas & Margaret Pettinger.

Barlborough is an attractive historic village and a range of interesting buildings can be seen all around the village centre. The village is situated close to Renishaw Hall for possible combined visit. Map detailing location of all the gardens is issued with admission ticket, which can be purchased at any of the gardens listed. For more information checkout our Facebook page (details above). Featured in the Daily Telegraph's NGS Gardens to visit. Partial wheelchair access at The Hollies. Access to rear of Clarendon via stone slabs.

3 228 BELPER ROAD

Stanley Common, Ilkeston, DE7 6FT. John & Rosina Osborn. *Approx 3m W of Ilkeston on A609. From Derby: Follow A608 (from the Meteor Centre). Turn R onto A609 at the Rose & Crown PH at Smalley Xrds. Garden approx 1m on L just* after church. Parking on rd. Sun 28 May (1-5). Adm £3, chd free. Home-made teas.
Garden borders green belt land. Current layout is about 8yrs old. Site previously dominated by old Leylandii hedge cut back to about 15ft high. This has now transformed into colourful hedge of many climbers and shrubs. Plants mostly herbaceous perennial and shrubs. Collections of hosta, tree peonies, acers, a magnificent wisteria and some unusual shrubs.

4 334 BELPER ROAD

Stanley Common, DE7 6FY. Gill & Colin Hancock, 01159 301061, www.hamescovert.com. *7m N of Derby. 3m W of Ilkeston. On A609, ¾m from Rose & Crown Xrds (A608). Please park in field up farm drive or Working Men's Club rear car park if wet.* Sun 23 Apr (12-4.30). Light refreshments. Sun 21 May, Sun 4 June (12-4.30). Home-made teas. Adm £3.50, chd free. April highlight - home-made soup, bread & cakes. **Visits also by arrangement Apr to June adm £6 incl tea/coffee/cake and our personal attention.**
Now in our 20th year of opening and still an evolving country garden. Plenty of seating to enjoy our highly recommended home-made cakes. New greenhouse with Streptocarpus. Take a scenic walk to a 10 acre wood with glades and ½ acre lake. April: cowslips. May: laburnum tunnel and wisteria. June: wild flowers, hostas, ferns and roses. Children welcome with plenty of activities to keep them entertained. Featured on Love your Garden with Alan Titchmarsh. Paths round wood and lake not suitable for wheelchairs.

5 BIRCHFIELD

The Dukes Drive, Ashford in the Water, Bakewell, DE45 1QQ. Brian Parker, 01629 813800. *2m NW of Bakewell. On A6 to Buxton between New Bridge & Sheepwash Bridge.* Visits by arrangement, adm £3 April - Sept, £2 Oct - March. Please leave message if no answer. **Donation to Thornhill Memorial Trust.**
Beautifully situated ¾ acre part terraced garden with pond and a 1¼ acre arboretum and wildflower meadow. An extremely varied collection of trees, shrubs, climbers, colourful perennials, bulbs and bamboos, all designed to give yr-round colour and interest. Many overgrown shrubs have been removed allowing for much new planting. Featured in Reflections.

6 ♦ BLUEBELL ARBORETUM AND NURSERY

Annwell Lane, Smisby, Ashby de la Zouch, LE65 2TA. Robert & Suzette Vernon, 01530 413700, sales@bluebellnursery.com, www.bluebellnursery.com. *1m NW of Ashby-de-la-Zouch. Arboretum is clearly signed in Annwell Lane (follow brown signs), ¼m S, through village of Smisby off B5006, between Ticknall & Ashby-de-la-Zouch. Free parking.* For NGS: Weds 19 Apr, 17 May, 21 June, 19 July, 16 Aug, 13 Sept, 18 Oct (9-5). Adm £5, chd free. Tea/coffee available on request. For other opening times and information, please phone, email or visit garden website.
Beautiful 9 acre woodland garden with a large collection of rare trees and shrubs. Interest throughout the yr with spring flowers, cool leafy areas in summer and sensational autumn colour. Many information posters describing the more obscure plants. Bring wellingtons in wet weather. Adjacent specialist tree and shrub nursery. Please be aware this is not a wood full of bluebells, despite the name. The woodland garden is fully labelled and the staff can answer questions or talk at length about any of the trees or shrubs on display. Rare trees and shrubs. Educational signs. Woodland. Arboretum. Please wear sturdy, waterproof footwear during or after wet weather! Full wheelchair access in dry, warm weather however grass paths can become wet and inaccessible in snow or after rain.

7 BRICK KILN FARM

Hulland Ward, Ashbourne,
DE6 3EJ. Mrs Jan Hutchinson,
01335 370440, robert.
hutchinson123@btinternet.com.
*4m E of Ashbourne (A517). 1m S
of Carsington Water. From Hulland
Ward take Dog Lane past church
2nd L. 100yds on R. From Ashbourne
A517 Bradley Corner turn L follow
sign for Carsington Water 1m on L.*
Mon 29 May (2-5). Adm £3.50,
chd free. Home-made teas.
**Visits also by arrangement
May to Aug (am, pm and
evening visits), £5 adm incl
refreshments.** *Donation to Great
Dane Adoption Society.*
A small country garden which wraps
around an old red brick farmhouse
accessed through a courtyard with
original well. Irregularly shaped
lawn bounded by wide herbaceous
borders leading to duck pond
and pet's memorial garden. Small
holding. Cattle and horses grazing.
www.youtube.com/watch?v=G-
nk3hZ6Pmo. Level garden, some
uneven flagstones, gravel drive
plenty of parking.

8 ♦ THE BURROWS GARDENS

Burrows Lane, Brailsford,
Ashbourne, DE6 3BU. Mrs
N M Dalton, 01335 360745,
enquiries@burrowsgardens.com,
www.burrowsgardens.com. *5m
SE of Ashbourne; 5m NW of Derby.
A52 from Derby: turn L opp sign
for Wild Park Leisure 1m before
village of Brailsford. ¼ m.* **For NGS:**
Sun 30 Apr, Mon 29 May, Sun
9 July, Mon 28 Aug (11-4.30).
Adm £5, chd free. Home-made
teas. **For other opening times and
information, please phone, email or
visit garden website.**
5 acres of stunning garden set
in beautiful countryside where
immaculate lawns show off exotic
rare plants and trees, mixing with
old favourites in this outstanding
garden. A huge variety of styles
from temple to Cornish, Italian and
English, gloriously designed and
displayed. This is a must see garden.
Non NGS: Open every Tues, Fri,
and Sun from April - August incl.
Look out for Special events such
as Shakespeare productions and
wine tasting. Refreshments can be
provided for pre-booked groups.
Most of garden accessible to
wheelchairs.

9 BYWAYS

7A Brookfield Avenue, Brookside,
Chesterfield, S40 3NX. Terry
& Eileen Kelly, 01246 566376,
telkel1@aol.com. *1½ m W of
Chesterfield. Follow A619 from
Chesterfield towards Baslow.
Brookfield Av is 2nd R after
Brookfield Sch. Please park on
Chatsworth Rd (A619).* Sat 5, Sun
6 Aug (1-4.30). Adm £3, chd
free. Home-made teas. **Visits
also by arrangement July & Aug
adm £5.50 incl tea and cakes.**
Donation to Ashgate Hospice.
Previous winners of the Best Back
Garden over 80sq m, Best Front
Garden, Best Container Garden and
Best Hanging Basket in Chesterfield
in Bloom. Well established perennial
borders incl helenium, monardas,
phlox, penstemon, grasses, acers
(30+), giving a very colourful
display. Rockery and many planters
containing hostas, fuchsia, ferns and
roses. 5 seating areas. Featured in
Derbyshire Times.

10 ♦ CALKE ABBEY

Ticknall, DE73 7LE. National
Trust, 01332 865587,
www.nationaltrust.org.uk. *10m
S of Derby. On A514 at Ticknall
between Swadlincote & Melbourne.*
**For NGS: Sat 24 June, Sat 16
Sept (10-5). Adm £9.70, chd
£4.80. Light refreshments.**
**For other opening times and
information, please phone or visit
garden website.**
Late C18 walled gardens gradually
repaired over the last 25yrs. Flower
garden with summer bedding,
herbaceous borders and the
unique auricula theatre. Georgian
orangery, impressive collection of
glasshouses and garden buildings. Ice
house, grotto and gardeners' tunnel.
Vegetable garden growing unusual
varieties of fruit and vegetables,
often on sale to visitors. Restaurant
at main visitor facilities for light
refreshments and locally sourced
food. Electric buggy available for
those with mobility problems.

Cascades Gardens

11 ◆ CASCADES GARDENS

Clatterway, Bonsall, Matlock, DE4 2AH. Alan & Alesia Clements, 01629 822813, cascadesgardens@gmail.com, www.cascadesgardens.com. *5m SW of Matlock. From Cromford A6 T-lights turn towards Wirksworth. Turn R along Via Gellia, signed Buxton & Bonsall. After 1m turn R up hill towards Bonsall. Cascades on R at top of hill before village.* **For NGS: Sun 14 May, Sun 25 June, Sun 23 July, Sun 6 Aug (1-5). Adm £5, chd free. Home-made teas. For other opening times and information, please phone, email or visit garden website.**
Fascinating 4 acre garden in spectacular natural surroundings with woodland, high cliffs, stream, pond, a ruined corn mill and old lead mine. Secluded garden rooms provide peaceful views of the extensive collection of unusual plants, shrubs and trees. Good range of home-made cakes. Mostly accessible. Gravel paths, some steep slopes.

& 🐄 ❀ 🚘 🛏 🍵

12 10 CHESTNUT WAY

Repton, DE65 6FQ. Robert & Pauline Little, 01283 702267, rlittleq@gmail.com, www.littlegarden.org.uk. *6m S of Derby. From A38/A50, S of Derby, follow signs to Willington, then Repton. In Repton turn R at r'about. Chestnut Way is ¼m up hill, on L.* **Sat 25, Sun 26 Feb (11-3). Adm £3, chd free. Home-made soup (Feb). Home-made teas (all dates). Opening with Repton NGS Village Gardens on Sun 21 May, Sun 16 July, Sun 24 Sept. Visits also by arrangement Feb to Oct for groups of 10+ (adm incl home-made tea and guided tour).**
Wander through an acre of sweeping mixed borders, spring bulbs, mature trees to a stunning butterfly bed, maturing arboretum, established prairie. Meet a pair of passionate, practical, compost loving gardeners who gently manage this plantsman's garden. Designed and maintained by the owners. Expect a colourful display throughout the yr. Plenty of seats, conservatory if wet. Thousands of snowdrops. Excellent plant stall in Spring. Special interest in viticella clematis, organic vegetables and composting. Featured on Radio Derby and in The Derbyshire. Level garden, good solid paths to main areas. Some grass/bark paths.

& 🐄 ❀ 🚘 🍵

13 CHEVIN BRAE

Milford, Belper, DE56 0QH. Dr David Moreton, 01332 843553, david.moreton@lubrizol.com. *1½m S of Belper. Coming from S on A6 turn L at Strutt Arms & cont up Chevin Rd. Park on Chevin Road. After 300 yds follow arrow to L up Morrells Lane. After 300 yds Chevin Brae on L with silver garage.* **Sun 2 Apr (1-5). Adm £2.50, chd free. Home-made teas. Visits also by arrangement Feb to Nov, please leave message on answer phone.**
A large garden, with swathes of daffodils in the orchard a spring feature. Extensive wild flower planting along edge of wood features aconites, snowdrops, wood anemones, fritillaries and dog tooth violets. Other parts of garden will have hellebores and early camelias. Tea and home-made pastries, many of which feature fruit and jam from the garden, served from the summer house in the middle of the orchard.

🐄 ❀ 🍵

14 COXBENCH HALL

Alfreton Road, Coxbench, Derby, DE21 5BB. Mr Brian Ballin. *4m N of Derby close to A38. After passing through Little Eaton, turn L onto Alfreton Rd for 1m, Coxbench Hall is on L next to Fox & Hounds PH between Little Eaton & Holbrook. From A38, take Kilburn turn & go towards Little Eaton.* **Sun 7 May, Sun 10 Sept (2.30-4.30). Adm £3, chd free. Home-made teas (incl diabetic and gluten free).**
Formerly the ancestral home of the Meynell family, the gardens reflect the Georgian house standing in 4½ acres of grounds most of which is accessible and wheelchair friendly. The garden has 2 fishponds connected by a stream, a sensory garden for the sight impaired, a short woodland walk through shrubbery, rockery, raised vegetable beds and seasonal displays in the mainly lawned areas. As a Residential Home for the Elderly, our Gardens are developed to inspire our residents from a number of sensory perspectives - different colours, textures and fragrances of plants, growing vegetables next to the C18 potting shed. There is also a veteran (500 - 800 yr old) Yew tree. Most of garden is lawned or block paved. Regret no wheelchair access to woodland area.

& 🐄 🍵

15 CRAIGSIDE

Reservoir Road, Whaley Bridge, SK23 7BW. Jane & Gerard Lennox, 07939 012634, jane@lennoxonline.net, www.craigside.info. *11m SE of Stockport. 11m NNW of Buxton. Turn off A6 onto A5004 to Whaley Bridge. Turn R at train station 1st L under railway bridge onto Reservoir Rd. Park on roadside or in village. Garden ½m from village.* **Sat 1, Sun 2 July (1-5). Adm £3.50, chd free. Light refreshments. Visits also by arrangement Apr to July.**
1 acre garden rising steeply from the reservoir giving magnificent views across Todbrook reservoir into Peak District. Gravel paths, stone steps with stopping places. Many mature trees incl 500+yr old oak. Spring bulbs, summer fuchsias, herbaceous borders, alpine bed, steep mature rockery many heucheras and hydrangeas. Herbs, vegetables and fruit trees. Gluten free cakes available also savoury alternatives. Refreshments also available for 4 legged visitors with a selection of home-made dog biscuits! These are also edible for humans and were tested by some of the volunteers. Featured on High Peak Radio and Radio Tameside. Also featured in Amatuer Gardener.

🐄 🍵

16 8 CURZON LANE

Alvaston, Derby, DE24 8QS. John & Marian Gray, 01332 601596, maz@curzongarden.com, www.curzongarden.com. *2m SE of Derby city centre. From city centre take A6 (London Rd) towards Alvaston. Curzon Lane on L, approx ½m before Alvaston shops.* Sun 16, Sun 23 July, Sun 13 Aug (12-5). Adm £2.50, chd free. Tea. **Visits also by arrangement July & Aug.** Mature garden with lawns, borders packed full with perennials, shrubs and small trees, tropical planting and hot border. Ornamental and wildlife ponds, greenhouse with different varieties of tomato, cucumber, peppers and chilies. Well stocked vegetable plot. Gravel area and large patio with container planting.

17 DAM STEAD
3 Crowhole, Barlow, Dronfield, S18 7TJ. Derek & Barbara Saveall, 01142 890802, barbarasaveall@hotmail.co.uk. *Chesterfield B6051 to Barlow. Tickled Trout PH on L. Springfield Rd on L then R on unnamed rd. Last cottage on R.* **Visits by arrangement May to Sept. Adm £3, chd free. Light refreshments.**
Approx 1 acre with stream, weir, fragrant garden, rose tunnel, orchard garden and dam with an island. Long woodland path, alpine troughs, rockeries and mixed planting. A natural wildlife garden large summerhouse with seating inside and out. 3 village well dressings and carnival over one week mid August.

18 THE DOWER HOUSE
Church Square, Melbourne, DE73 8JH. William & Griselda Kerr, 01332 864756, griseldakerr@btinternet.com. *6m S of Derby. 5m W of exit 23A M1. 4m N of exit 13 M42. In Church Square, turn R at board giving church service times just before church, gates then 50 yds ahead.* Sat 18, Sun 19 Feb (10-4). Adm £3, chd free. Sat 24, Sun 25 June (10-5). Adm £3.50, chd free. Light refreshments. **Visits also by arrangement, max group size for refreshments 26.**
Beautiful view of Melbourne Pool from balustraded terrace running length of 1831 house. Garden

drops steeply by paths and steps to lawn with herbaceous border and bank of roses best in June with late summer beds good in August and September. Rose tunnel, glade, orchard, hellebores and small woodland lovely in early spring, bog planting, rockery, herb garden, other small lawns and vegetable garden. Children can search for a bronze crocodile, a stone pig and a metal bug. They might also see a huge iron sunflower hanging in a tree and a bronze girl doing cartwheels. There are many seats around the garden where visitors can sit while keeping an eye on their children as they do the searching. Featured in Derbyshire Life and on Radio Derby. Wheelchair access only to the top half of the garden.

GROUP OPENING

19 ELMTON GARDENS
Elmton, Worksop, S80 4LS. *2m from Creswell, 3m from Clowne, 5m from J30, M1. From M1 take A616 to Newark. Follow approx 4m. Turn R at Elmton signpost. At junction turn R.* Sat 24, Sun 25 June (1-5). Combined adm £5, chd free. Cream teas.

NEW ASH LEA
Jane & Graham Cooper.
ELM TREE COTTAGE
Dianne & Chris Illsley.
ELMWOOD HOUSE
Ian & Liz Chapman.
PEAR TREE COTTAGE
Geoff & Janet Cutts.
PINFOLD
Nikki Kirsop.

Elmton has 5 gardens. Elm Tree Cottage has a ¼ acre garden with mixed borders, a rose garden, lawn, a wildlife pond and chickens. It is full of colour. Pinfold has a pretty ⅓ acre garden encouraging wildlife. Once a farmyard it is now a mature garden full of trees and plants, themed borders and lots of roses and perennials. It is designed to have rooms with different styles of planting. Elmwood House is a

½ acre S-facing garden overlooking rolling farmland. It has mature trees and shrubs, a large pond, water features and colourful borders. It has a lovely open feel. Ash Lea is a newly acquired garden with great potential and super views. It has raised beds, vegetables and a fruit cage. Two of the greenhouses have grape vines. Trees incl heritage apples and medlar. Pear Tree Cottage has a cottage style garden designed to be easily maintained. A vegetable patch shares the front garden. The back has views over fields. Small areas of the garden have different planting themes. Food and drink is available throughout the day at the Elm Tree PH. Cream Teas are available from the School House next to the church.

20 FIR CROFT
Froggatt Road, Calver, S32 3ZD. Dr S B Furness, www.alpineplantcentre.co.uk. *4m N of Bakewell. At junction of B6001 with A625 (formerly B6054), adjacent to Power Garage.* Sun 21 May, Sun 4, Sun 18 June (2-5). Adm by donation.
Massive scree with many varieties. Plantsman's garden; rockeries; water garden and nursery; extensive collection (over 3000 varieties) of alpines; conifers; over 800 sempervivums, 500 saxifrages and 350 primulas. Many new varieties not seen anywhere else in the UK. Huge new tufa wall planted with many rare Alpines and sempervivums.

The National
Garden Scheme
is the largest
single funder of
Macmillan

21 GAMESLEY FOLD COTTAGE

Gamesley Fold, Glossop, SK13 6JJ.
Mrs G Carr, 01457 867856,
gcarr@gamesleyfold.co.uk,
www.gamesleyfold.co.uk. *2m W of
Glossop. Off A626 Glossop - Marple
Rd nr Charlesworth. Turn down lane
directly opp St. Margaret's School,
white cottage at bottom.* Sun 28
May, Sun 25 June (1-4). Adm
£2.50, chd free. Home-made
teas. Visits also by arrangement
May & June (Suns only 1-4), any
number welcome.
Old fashioned cottage garden with
rhododendrons, herbaceous borders
with candelabra primulas, flowers
and herbs. Vegetable garden and a
water feature. Plant nursery selling
wild flowers and cottage garden
plants. Featured in local press.

22 HIGH ROOST

27 Storthmeadow Road,
Simmondley, Glossop,
SK13 6UZ. Peter & Christina
Harris, 01457 863888,
peter-harris9@sky.com. *¾m SW
of Glossop. From Glossop A57 to M/
CL at 2nd r'about, up Simmondley
Ln nr top R turn. From Marple A626
to Glossop, in Chworth R up Town Ln
past Hare & Hound PH 2nd L.* Sun
25 June (12-4). Adm £3, chd
free. Light refreshments. Visits
also by arrangement June to
Aug. *Donation to Manchester Dogs
Home.*
Garden on terraced slopes, views
over fields and hills. Winding paths,
archways and steps explore different
garden rooms packed with plants,
designed to attract wildlife. Alpine
bed, vegetable garden, water
features, statuary, troughs and
planters. A garden which needs
exploring to discover its secrets
tucked away in hidden corners.
Craft stall, children's garden quiz and
lucky dip.

23 NEW HIGHER CROSSINGS

Crossings Road, Chapel-en-le-
Frith, High Peak, SK23 9RX.
Malcolm & Christine Hoskins. *Turn
off B5470 N from Chapel-en-le-Frith*
on Crossings Rd signed Whitehough/
Chinley. Higher Crossings is 2nd
house on R beyond 1st Xrds with
Eccles Rd. Best park L on Eccles Rd.
Sun 11 June (1.30-5). Adm £4,
chd free. Light refreshments.
2 acres of formal terraced country
garden, sweeping lawns and
magnificent Peak District views.
Rhododendrons, acers, azaleas,
hostas herbaceous borders. Mature
specimen trees and shrubs. Beautiful
stone terrace and sitting areas.
Garden gate leading into meadow.
Featured in Pure Buxton magazine.

24 HIGHFIELD HOUSE

Wingfield Road, Oakerthorpe,
Alfreton, DE55 7AP. Paul
& Ruth Peat and Janet &
Brian Costall, 01773 521342,
highfieldhouseopengardens@
hotmail.co.uk,
www.highfieldhouse.weebly.com.
*Rear of Alfreton Golf Club. A615
Alfreton-Matlock Rd.* Sun 28 May,
Sun 25 June (10.30-5). Adm
£3, chd free. Home-made teas.
Visits also by arrangement
Feb to July Please note:18 - 28
Feb only (not March & Apr)
then May - July. Adm £6 incl
refreshments. Groups 15+.
Lovely country garden of approx 1
acre, incorporating a shady garden,
woodland, tree house, laburnum
tunnel, orchard, herbaceous borders
and vegetable garden. Reopening in
2017 after work to our house and
garden; come and visit us! Fabulous
AGA baked cakes and lunches.
Groups welcome by appointment -
12th -28th February for Snowdrops
(refreshments inside by the fire) and
May - July. Lovely walk to Derbyshire
Wildlife Trust nature reserve to see
Orchids in June. Some steps, slopes
and gravel areas.

25 HILLSIDE

286 Handley Road,
New Whittington, Chesterfield,
S43 2ET. Mr E J Lee,
01246 454960,
eric.lee5@btinternet.com. *3m
N of Chesterfield. Between B6056
& B0652 N of village. SatNav
friendly.* Visits by arrangement,
groups and individual visitors.
Adm £2.50, chd free. Light
refreshments.
⅓ acre sloping site. Herbaceous
borders, rock garden, alpines,
streams, pools, bog gardens, asiatic
primula bed, and alpine house.
Acers, bamboos, collection of
approx 150 varieties of ferns,
eucalypts, euphorbias, grasses,
conifers, Himalayan bed. 1000+
plants permanently labelled. Yr
round interest.

26 THE HOLLIES

87 Clowne Road, Barlborough,
Chesterfield, S43 4EH. Vernon
& Christine Sanderson. *7m NE
of Chesterfield. Off A619 midway
between Chesterfield & Worksop.
½ m E M1, J30. Follow signs for
Barlborough then yellow NGS signs.
Parking available along Clowne Road.*
Sun 28 May (2-6). Adm £2.50,
chd free. Home-made teas.
Opening with Barlborough
Gardens on Sat 29, Sun 30 July.
The Hollies maximises the unusual
garden layout and incl a shade area,
patio garden, cottage border and
a fruit and vegetable plot. Enjoy a
trip back to the 1920s at the 90th
Anniversary Weekend opening. A
wide selection of home made cake
on offer incl gluten free and vegan
options plus tea and coffee. Home-
made tombola stall plus Whitwell
Brass Band playing during the
afternoon. Partial wheelchair access.

27 HOLLIES FARM PLANT CENTRE

Uppertown, Bonsall, Matlock,
DE4 2AW. Robert & Linda Wells,
www.holliesfarmplantcentre.co.uk.
*From Cromford turn R off A5012
up The Clatterway. Keep R past
Fountain Tearoom to village cross,
take L up High St, then 2nd L onto
Abel Lane. Garden straight ahead.*
Sun 11 June, Sun 16 July, Sun 13
Aug (11-3). Adm £3, chd free.
Home-made teas.
The best selection in Derbyshire
with advice and personal attention
from Robert and Linda Wells at
their family run business. Enjoy a visit
to remember in our beautiful display

garden - set within glorious Peak District countryside. Huge variety of hardy perennials incl the rare and unusual. Vast selection of traditional garden favourites. Award winning hanging baskets. Ponds, herbaceous borders and glorious views.

🐐 ✿ 💺

28 THE HOLLY TREE

21 Hackney Road, Hackney, Matlock, DE4 2PX. Carl Hodgkinson. *½m NW of Matlock, off A6. Take A6 NW past bus stn & 1st R up Dimple Rd. At T-junction, turn R & immed L, for Farley & Hackney. Take 1st L onto Hackney Rd. Continue ¾m.* **Sun 28, Mon 29 May (11-4.30). Adm £3, chd free. Home-made teas.**
The garden is in excess of 1½ acres and set on a steeply sloping S-facing site, sheltering behind a high retaining wall and incl a small arboretum, bog garden, herbaceous borders, pond, vegetables, fruits, apiary and chickens. Extensively terraced with many paths and steps and with spectacular views across the Derwent valley to Snitterton and Oker.

🐐 ✿ 💺

29 ♦ LEA GARDENS

Lea, Matlock, DE4 5GH. Mr & Mrs J Tye, 01629 534380, www.leagarden.co.uk. *5m SE of Matlock. Off A6 & A615.* **For opening times and information, please phone or visit garden website.**
Rare collection of rhododendrons, azaleas, kalmias, alpines and conifers in delightful woodland setting. Gardens are sited on remains of medieval quarry and cover about 4 acres. Specialised plant nursery of rhododendrons and azaleas on site. Open daily 1 March to 31 July (9-5). Plant sales by appointment out of season. Visitors welcome throughout the yr. Coffee shop noted for home baked cakes and light refreshments. Gravel paths, steep slopes. Free access for wheelchair users.

♿ 🐐 ✿ 🚌 💺

30 THE LILIES

Griffe Grange Valley, Grangemill, Matlock, DE4 4BW.

Chris & Bridget Sheppard, www.thelilies.com. *4m N Cromford. On A5012 Via Gellia Rd 4m N Cromford. 1st house on R after junction with B5023 to Middleton. From Grangemill 1st house on L after Prospect Quarry (IKO Permatrack).* **Sun 2 July, Sun 3 Sept (11.30-5). Adm £3.50, chd free. Home-made teas.**
1 acre garden gradually restored over the past 10yrs situated at the top of a wooded valley, surrounded by wildflower meadow and ash woodland. Area adjacent to house with seasonal planting and containers. Mixed shrubs and perennial borders many raised from seed. 3 ponds, vegetable plot, barn conversion with separate cottage style garden. Natural garden with stream developed from old mill pond. Walks in large wildflower meadow and ash woodland both SSSI's. Handspinning demonstration and natural dyeing display using materials from the garden and wool from sheep in the meadow. Light lunches served 11:30am to 3:00pm, home-made teas all day. Locally made crafts for sale. Partial wheelchair access. Steep slope from car park, limestone chippings at entrance, some boggy areas if wet.

♿ ✿ 💺

31 LOCKO PARK

Spondon, Derby, DE21 7BW. Mrs Lucy Palmer, www.lockopark.co.uk. *6m NE of Derby. From A52 Borrowash bypass, 2m N via B6001, turn to Spondon. More directions on www.lockopark. co.uk. NB. SatNav use DE21 7BW via Locko Rd.* **Sun 14 May (2-5). Adm £3.50, chd free. Home-made teas.**
An original 1927 open garden for the NGS. Large garden; pleasure gardens; rose gardens designed by William Eames. House (not open) by Smith of Warwick with Victorian additions. Chapel (open) Charles II, with original ceiling. Tulip tree in the arboretum purported to be the largest in the Midlands. Large collection of rhododendron and azalea. Featured in Derby Telegraph and on BBC Radio Derby.

🐐 ✿ 💺

32 9 MAIN STREET

Horsley Woodhouse, DE7 6AU. Ms Alison Napier, 01332 881629, ibhillib@btinternet.com. *3m SW of Heanor. 6m N of Derby. Turn off A608 Derby to Heanor rd at Smalley, towards Belper, (A609). Garden on A609, 1m from Smalley turning.* **Sat 5, Sun 6 Aug (1.30-4.30). Adm £3, chd free. Cream teas. Visits also by arrangement Apr to Sept. Refreshments by prior arrangement.**
⅓ acre hilltop garden overlooking lovely farmland view. Terracing, borders, lawns and pergola create space for an informal layout with planting for colour effect. Features incl large wildlife pond with water lilies, bog garden and small formal pool. Emphasis on carefully selected herbaceous perennials mixed with shrubs and old fashioned roses. Gravel garden for sun loving plants and scree garden, both developed from former drive. Wide collection of home grown plants for sale. All parts of the garden accessible to wheelchairs. Wheelchair adapted WC.

♿ 🐐 ✿ 🚌 💺

33 2 MANVERS STREET

Ripley, DE5 3EQ. Mrs D Wood & Mr D Hawkins, 01773 743962, d.s.Hawkins@btinternet.com. *Ripley Town centre to Derby rd turn L opp Leisure Centre onto Heath Rd. 1st turn R onto Meadow Rd, 1st L onto Manvers St.* **Sat 15, Sun 16 July (1.30-5). Adm £3, chd free. Home-made teas. Visits also by arrangement July & Aug, refreshments on request when booking.**
Summer garden with backdrop of neighbouring trees, 10 borders bursting with colour surrounded by immaculate shaped lawn. Perennials incl 26 clematis, annuals, baskets, tubs and pots. Ornamental fish pond. Water features, arbour and summerhouse. Plenty of seating areas to take in this awe inspiring oasis.

✿ 🚌 💺

Hillside

34 ♦ MELBOURNE HALL GARDENS

Church Square, Melbourne, Derby, DE73 8EN. Melbourne Gardens Charity, 01332 862502, Melbhall@globalnet.co.uk, www.melbournehallgardens.com. *6m S of Derby. At Melbourne Market Place turn into Church St, go down to Church Sq. Garden entrance across visitor centre next to Melbourne Hall tea room.* For NGS: Sat 27, Sun 28 May (1.30-5.30). Adm £5, chd free. For other opening times and information, please phone, email or visit garden website.
A 17 acre historic garden with an abundance of rare trees and shrubs. Woodland and waterside planting with extensive herbaceous borders. Meconopsis, candelabra primulas, various Styrax and Cornus kousa. Other garden features incl Bakewells wrought iron arbour, a yew tunnel and fine C18 statuary and water features. 300yr old trees, waterside planting, feature hedges and herbaceous borders. Fine statuary and stonework. Recently featured in Derbyshire Life. Gravel paths, uneven surface in places, some steep slopes.
&. ✿ 🚗 🍴

35 ♦ MEYNELL LANGLEY TRIALS GARDEN

Lodge Lane (off Flagshaw Lane), Kirk Langley, Ashbourne, DE6 4NT. Robert & Karen Walker, 01332 824358, enquiries@meynell-langley-gardens.co.uk, www.meynell-langley-gardens.co.uk. *4m W of Derby, nr Kedleston Hall. Head W out of Derby on A52. At Kirk Langley turn R onto Flagshaw Lane (signed to Kedleston Hall) then R onto Lodge Lane. Follow Meynell Langley Gardens signs.* For NGS: Sun 25 June, Sun 16 July, Sun 20 Aug, Sun 17 Sept, Sun 15 Oct (10.30-4.30). Adm £3, chd free. For other opening times and information, please phone, email or visit garden website.
Formal ¾ acre Victorian style garden established over 20yrs, displaying and trialling new and existing varieties of bedding plants, herbaceous perennials and vegetable plants grown at

the adjacent nursery. Over 180 hanging baskets and floral displays. 45 varieties of apple, pear and other fruit. Summer fruit pruning demonstrations on July NGS day and apple tasting on October NGS day. Adjacent tea rooms serving light lunches and refreshments daily. Level ground and firm grass. Full disabled access to tea rooms.

& ♞ ❀ ⛟ ☕

36 16 MONARCH DRIVE

Oakwood, Derby, DE21 2XW. Gary & Gill Stillwell. *3m NE of Derby. Nr A52 & A38. From A38 take A61 to Derby, at island take 1st L to Breadsall village. Turn R onto Brookside Rd, at junction R & immed L onto Lime Lane. Sun 11 June, Sun 16 July (12-4). Adm £2.50, chd free. Light refreshments.*
A lovely plantaholic cottage style garden, with curved lawns, island gravel beds, small ornamental ponds. Large collection of perennials, displayed in curved borders. Many grasses, acers, bamboos and palms. 3 patios with container planting. Cakes and biscuits for sale. Wheelchair users to negotiate small step via ramp, garden totally flat after step.

& ❀ ☕

37 MOORFIELDS

257/261 Chesterfield Road, Temple Normanton, Chesterfield, S42 5DE. Peter, Janet & Stephen Wright, 01246 852306, peterwright100@hotmail.com. *4m SE of Chesterfield. From Chesterfield take A617 for 2m, turn on to B6039 through Temple Normanton, taking R fork signed Tibshelf, B6039. Garden ¼m on R. Limited parking. Sun 7 May, Sun 2 July (1-5). Adm £3, chd free. Light refreshments.*
Visits also by arrangement May to July groups 10+ (afternoons or evenings preferable).
Two adjoining gardens each planted for seasonal colour. The larger one has mature, mixed island beds and borders, a gravel garden to the front, a small wild flower area, large wildlife pond, orchard and soft fruit, and vegetable garden. Show of late flowering tulips. The smaller gardens of No. 257 feature herbaceous borders and shrubs. Extensive views

across to mid Derbyshire. Free range eggs for sale.

❀ ☕

38 NEW MILLS SCHOOL AND SIXTH FORM

Church Lane, New Mills, High Peak, SK22 4NR. Mr Craig Pickering, 07833 373593, cpickering@newmillsschool.co.uk, www.newmillsschool.co.uk/ngs. html. *12m NNW of Buxton. From A6 take A6105 signed New Mills, Hayfield. At C of E Church turn L onto Church Lane. School on L. Parking on site. Sat 8 July (10-5); Sun 9 July (1-5). Adm £3, chd free. Light refreshments in School Library.* **Visits also by arrangement June & July for groups 10+.**
Mixed herbaceous perennials/shrub borders, with mature trees and lawns and gravel border situated in the semi rural setting of the High Peak incl a Grade II listed building with 4 themed quads. The school was awarded a distinction for their first garden at Tatton RHS Flower Show 2015. Hot and Cold Beverages and a selection of sandwiches, cream teas and home-made cakes available. Article in In and Around Glossop and High Peak. Ramps allow wheelchair access to most of outside, flower beds and into Grade II listed building and library.

& ❀ ☕ ☕

39 9 NEWFIELD CRESCENT

Dore, Sheffield, S17 3DE. Mike & Norma Jackson, 01142 366198, mandnjackson@googlemail.com. *Dore - SW Sheffield. Turn off Causeway Head Rd on Heather Lea Av. 2nd L into Newfield Crescent. Parking on roadside. Sat 17, Sun 18 June (2-6). Adm £3.50, chd free. Light refreshments.* **Visits also by arrangement Apr to Sept.**
Mature, wildlife friendly garden planted to provide all yr interest. Upper terrace with alpines in troughs and bowls. Lower terrace featuring pond with cascade and connecting stream to second pond. Bog garden, rock gardens, lawn alpine bed, wilder areas,

mixed borders with trees, shrubs and perennials. Featuring azaleas, rhododendrons, camellias, primulas. Wheelchair access without steps to top terrace offering full view of garden.

& ♞ ☕

Your visit has already helped 600 more people gain access to a Parkinson's nurse

40 ◆ OLD ENGLISH WALLED GARDEN, ELVASTON CASTLE COUNTRY PARK

Borrowash Road, Elvaston, Derby, DE72 3EP. Derbyshire County Council, 01629 533870, www.derbyshire.gov.uk/elvaston. *4m E of Derby. Signed from A52 & A50. Car parking charge applies.* **For NGS: Sat 12 Aug (12-4). Adm £2.50, chd free. Home-made teas. For other opening times and information, please phone or visit garden website.**
Come and discover the beauty of the Old English walled garden at Elvaston Castle. Take in the peaceful atmosphere and enjoy the scents and colours of all the varieties of trees, shrubs and plants. Summer bedding and large herbaceous borders. After your visit to the walled garden take time to walk around the wider estate featuring romantic topiary gardens, lake, woodland and nature reserve. Estate gardeners on hand during the day. Delicious home-made cakes available.

& ♞ ❀ ☕

41 NEW THE OLD VICARAGE

The Fields, Middleton by Wirksworth, Matlock, DE4 4NH. Jane Irwing, 01629 825010, irwingjane@gmail.com. *Garden located behind church on Main St & nr school. Travelling N on A6 from Derby turn R at Cromford, turn R onto Porter Lane, then R again onto Main St at Xrds. Park in Village Hall. Walk through churchyard. No parking at house.* **Sat 25, Sun 26 Feb (11-4); Sat 1, Sun 2 July, Sat 26, Sun 27, Mon 28 Aug (11-5). Adm £3.50, chd free. Home-made teas. Visits also by arrangement Feb to Oct.**
Traditional front garden with lawn and mixed summer borders in gentle valley overlooking Black Rocks. To the side a courtyard garden and fernery where acid loving plants and ferns are grown. Beyond is the orchard, fruit garden, vegetable patch and greenhouse, the home of honey bees, doves and hens. Spectacular Rambling Rector rose over front of house in late June early July. Cakes, some gluten free, various hot and cold drinks served in the garden or in fernery if wet (limited space).
☕

42 THE PADDOCK

12 Manknell Rd, Whittington Moor, Chesterfield, S41 8LZ. Mel & Wendy Taylor, 01246 451001, debijt9276@gmail.com. *2m N of Chesterfield. Whittington Moor just off A61 between Sheffield & Chesterfield. Parking available at Victoria Working Mens Club, garden signed from here.* **Sun 14 May, Sun 6 Aug (11-5). Adm £3.50, chd free. Cream teas. Visits also by arrangement Apr to Aug.**
½ acre garden incorporating small formal garden, stream and koi filled pond. Stone path over bridge, up some steps, past small copse, across the stream at the top and back down again. Past herbaceous border towards a pergola where cream teas can be enjoyed.
&. 🐾 ✿ ☕

43 PARK HALL

Walton Back Lane, Walton, Chesterfield, S42 7LT. Kim & Margaret Staniforth, 01246 567412, kim.staniforth@btinternet.com. *2m SW of Chesterfield centre. From town on A 619 L into Somersall Lane. On A632 R into Acorn Ridge. Park on field side only of Walton Back Lane.* **Sun 2 July (2-5.30). Adm £5, chd**
free. Home-made teas. **Visits also by arrangement Apr to July for groups 20+.** *Donation to Bluebell Wood Childrens Hospice.*
Romantic 2 acre plantsmans garden, in a stunningly beautiful setting surrounding C17 house (not open) 4 main rooms, terraced garden, parkland area with forest trees, croquet lawn, sunken garden with arbours, pergolas, pleached hedge, topiary, statuary, roses, rhododendrons, camellias, several water features. Two steps down to gain access to garden.
&. 🚐 ☕

44 RECTORY HOUSE

Kedleston, Derby, DE22 5JJ. Helene Viscountess Scarsdale. *5m NW Derby. A52 from Derby turn R Kedleston sign. Drive to village turn R. Brick house standing back from rd on sharp corner.* **Sun 28 May (2-5.30). Adm £4, chd free. Home-made teas.**
The garden is next to Kedleston Park and is of C18 origin. Many established rare trees and shrubs also rhododendrons, azaleas and unusual roses. Large natural pond with amusing frog fountain. Primulas, gunneras, darmeras and lots of moisture loving plants. The winding paths go through trees and past wild flowers and grasses. New fernery with rare plants. An atmospheric garden. Delicious teas and cakes available. Soft drinks. Featured in Derbyshire Countryside and Derby Evening Telegraph. Wheelchair access possible with care. Uneven paths.
&. ✿ ☕

45 ♦ RENISHAW HALL & GARDENS

Renishaw, Sheffield, S21 3WB. Alexandra Hayward, 01246 432310, enquiries@renishaw-hall.co.uk, www.renishaw-hall.co.uk. *10m from Sheffield city centre. By car: Renishaw Hall only 3m from J30 on M1, well signed from junction r'about.* **For NGS: Tue 16 May, Tue 20 June (10.30-4). Adm £5.50, chd free. Light refreshments at The Cafe.** For other opening times and information, please phone, email or visit garden website.

Dam Stead

Renishaw Hall and Gardens boasts 7 acres of stunning gardens created by Sir George Sitwell in 1885. The Italianate gardens feature various rooms with extravagant herbaceous borders. Rose gardens, rare trees and shrubs, National Collection of Yuccas, sculptures, woodland walks and lakes create a magical and engaging garden experience. The Cafe will be open for light meals, hot and cold drinks and cakes. Winner of HHA Garden of the Year. Wheelchair route around garden.

& 🐴 ✿ 🏠 NPC ☕ 🍷

GROUP OPENING

46 REPTON NGS VILLAGE GARDENS
Repton, Derby, DE65 6FQ. *6m S of Derby. From A38/A50, S of Derby, follow signs to Willington, then Repton.* **Sun 21 May, Sun 16 July, Sun 24 Sept (1.30-5.30). Combined adm £6, chd free. Home-made teas at 10 Chestnut Way.**

ASKEW COTTAGE
Louise Hardwick,
www.hardwickgardendesign.co.uk.
Open on Sun 24 Sept
D

10 CHESTNUT WAY
Robert & Pauline Little.
Open on all dates
(See separate entry)

HOLME POINT
Mrs Janet Holmes,
01283 707445.
Open on all dates
Visits also by arrangement
May to Sept.

22 PINFOLD CLOSE
Mr & Mrs O Jowett.
Open on Sun 21 May

REPTON ALLOTMENTS
Mr O Jowett.
Open on Sun 16 July

WOODEND COTTAGE
Wendy & Stephen Longden.
Open on Sun 16 July
(See separate entry)

Repton is a thriving village dating back to Anglo Saxon times and was where Christianity was first preached in the Midlands. In the crypt of the church there are still well preserved remains of Saxon architecture. The village gardens are all quite different ranging from the very small to very large several of them have new features for 2017. Askew cottage is a professionally designed garden and has many structural features linked together by curving paths. 10 Chestnut Way is a plantoholic's garden often likened to a tardis - be prepared to be surprised. Holme Point is an exquisitely designed small garden, formal beds are overflowing with perennial plants, 22 Pinfold Close is the smallest garden but is packed full with a special interest in tropical plants. Repton allotments is a small set of allotments currently undergoing a revival, with attractive views across Derbyshire. Woodend Cottage is an organic garden with stunning views from the grass labyrinth. All gardens have plenty of seats. Some gardens have grass or gravel paths but most areas accessible.

& ✿ 🏠 ☕

47 122 SHEFFIELD ROAD
Glossop, SK13 8QU. Simon Groarke. *From Glossop town centre take A57 Snake Pass Sheffield. Cont on A57 3rd exit rdbt cont ¾m. House on R. Park on Shirebrook Drive. From Sheffield take A57 Glossop. After long descent, house on L.* **Sun 9 Apr, Sun 7 May (12.30-4.30). Adm £3.50, chd free. Cream teas.**
A woodland garden with an array of spring bulbs and a host of bluebells in May. Pathways meander through the garden and down to the brook. Nearer the house the garden opens up to perennial borders and lawns. There are plenty of seats to sit and enjoy the garden but please note there are several steps and uneven paths. Bluebell woodland garden with a babbling brook running through. Attractive perennial borders. Camellias, azaleas and rhododendrons are focal

points. Featured on BBC Radio Manchester's Becky Want Show.

✿ ☕

48 THORNBRIDGE HALL GARDENS
Ashford in the Water, DE45 1NZ. Jim & Emma Harrison, www.thornbridgehall.co.uk. *2m NW of Bakewell. From Bakewell take A6, signed Buxton. After 2m, R onto A6020. ½m turn L, signed Thornbridge Hall.* **Thur 27 July (9-5). Adm £6, chd free. Light refreshments.**
A stunning C19, 12 acre garden, set in the heart of the Peak District overlooking rolling Derbyshire countryside. Designed to create a vision of 1000 shades of green, the garden has many distinct areas. These incl koi lake and water garden, Italian garden with statuary, grottos and temples, 400ft herbaceous border, kitchen garden, scented terrace, hot border and refurbished glasshouses. Contains statuary from Clumber Park, Sydnope Hall and Chatsworth. Tea, coffee, sandwiches and cakes available. Gravel paths, steep slopes, steps.

🐴 ✿ 🏠 ☕

49 TILFORD HOUSE
Hognaston, Ashbourne, DE6 1PW. Mr & Mrs P R Gardner, 01335 372001, peter.rgardner@mypostoffice.co.uk. *5m NE of Ashbourne. A517 Belper to Ashbourne. At Hulland Ward follow signs to Hognaston. Downhill (2m) to bridge. Roadside parking 100 metres.* **Sun 7 May (2-5). Adm £4, chd free. Home-made teas. Visits also by arrangement May to July, groups of 10+. Adm £5.**
A 1½ acre streamside english country garden. Woodland, wildlife areas and ponds lie alongside colourful borders. Extensive collections of primulas, hostas, iris and clematis as well as many unusual plants and trees. Sit and relax in a magical setting to enjoy listening to the continuous sounds of the birds. Featured in Derby Evening Telegraph, Ashbourne Telegraph, The Derbyshire Magazine and Derbyshire Life Magazine.

🐴 ✿ ☕

50 ◆ TISSINGTON HALL
Tissington, Ashbourne,
DE6 1RA. Sir Richard & Lady
FitzHerbert, 01335 352200,
tisshall@dircon.co.uk,
www.tissingtonhall.co.uk. 4m N of
Ashbourne. E of A515 on Ashbourne
to Buxton Rd in centre of the
beautiful Estate Village of Tissington.
**For NGS: Mon 29 May, Mon 28
Aug (12-3). Adm £6, chd free.
Cream teas at Herbert's Fine
English Tearooms. For other
opening times and information,
please phone, email or visit garden
website.**
Large garden celebrating over 75yrs
in the NGS, with stunning rose
garden on west terrace, herbaceous
borders and 5 acres of grounds.
Refreshments available at the award
winning Herberts Fine English
Tearooms in village (Tel 01335
350501). Wheelchair access advice
from ticket seller.

& 🛏 ✿ 🛏 ☕

51 NEW TREETOPS HOSPICE CARE
Derby Road, Risley, Derby,
DE72 3SS. Treetops Hospice Care,
www.treetopshospice.org.uk. On
main rd, B5010 in centre of Risley
village. From J25 M1 take road
signed to Risley. Turn L at T-lights,
Treetops Hospice Care on L approx
½ m through village. From Borrowash
direction Treetops is on R just
after church. **Sat 29 Apr (10.30-
4). Adm £3, chd free. Light
refreshments.**
Beginning with a modest appeal
for spring bulbs, the 12 acre site of
woodland and grounds now has
thousands of daffodils. It has been
developed over the last 10yrs taking
into consideration the needs and
fundraising activities of the hospice.
Raised wheelchair walkways allow
guests to access the woodland
areas plus a 20 minutes circular walk
on bark chipped paths and raised
walkways. Refreshments incl teas
and coffees, cakes and light lunches
available. Wheelchair access along
raised walkways through part of the
woods and along some tarmacked
paths, forming circular walk.

🛏 ✿ ☕

52 12 WATER LANE
Middleton, Matlock,
DE4 4LY. Hildegard
Wiesehofer, 01629 825543,
wiesehofer@btinternet.com.
Approx 2½ m SW of Matlock. 1½ m
NW of Wirksworth. At A6 & B5023
intersection take rd to Wirksworth.
R to Middleton. Follow NGS signs.
From Ashbourne take Matlock rd
& follow signs. Park on main rd. Ltd
parking in Water Lane. **Sat 20, Sun
21 May, Sun 27, Mon 28 Aug
(11-5.30). Adm £3.50, chd free.
Home-made teas. Visits also
by arrangement Apr to Aug for
groups 10+.**
Small, eclectic hillside garden on
different levels, created as a series
of rooms over the last 15yrs. Each
room has been designed to capture
the stunning views over Derbyshire
and Nottinghamshire and incl a
woodland walk, ponds, eastern and
infinity gardens. Glorious views and
short distance from High Peak Trail,
Middleton Top and Engine House.
Light wheelchair access only to front
terrace and conservatory, views
over some of garden possible.

& 🛏 ✿ ☕

53 13 WESTFIELD ROAD
Swadlincote, DE11 0BG. Val
& Dave Booth, 01283 221167
or 07891 436632,
valerie.booth@sky.com. 5m E of
Burton-on-Trent, off A511. Take A511
from Burton-on-Trent. Follow signs for
Swadlincote. Turn R into Springfield
Rd, take 3rd R into Westfield Rd.
**Sun 2 July, Sun 6 Aug (1-5).
Adm £3, chd free. Home-made
teas. Visits also by arrangement
June to Aug adm £5 incl tea and
cake.**
A garden on 2 levels of approx
½ acre. (7 steps with handrail).
Redesigned top area to incl a new
summerhouse. Packed herbaceous
borders designed for colour. Roses
and clematis scrambling over
pergolas. A passion of ours are roses
(over 60). Shrubs, baskets and tubs.
Greenhouses, raised bed vegetable
area, fruit trees and 2 ponds. Free
range chicken area. Plenty of seating.

🛏 ✿ ☕

54 WESTGATE
Combs Road, Combs,
Chapel-en-le-Frith, High
Peak, SK23 9UP. Maurice &
Chris Lomas, 07854 680170,
ca-lomas@sky.com. N of Chapel-
en-le-Frith off B5470. Turn L immed
before Hanging Gate PH, signed
Combs Village. ¾ m on L by railway
bridge. **Sun 18 June (1-5). Adm
£3, chd free. Home-made teas.
Visits also by arrangement Apr
to July for groups 10+.**
Large sloping garden in quiet village
with beautiful views. Features incl
mixed borders and beds containing
many perenials, hosta and heuchera.
Large rockery. Vegetable and fruit
beds. Wild flower area, grasses and
fernery. Natural pond and stream
with bog area. 3 formal ponds.
Chicken area. Lots of places to sit
and enjoy the views. Featured in
Amateur Gardening.

✿ ☕

55 WHARFEDALE
34 Broadway, Duffield, Belper,
DE56 4BU. Roger & Sue
Roberts, 01332 841905,
rogerroberts34@outlook.com,
www.garden34.co.uk. 4m N
of Derby. Turn onto B5023 to
Wirksworth (Broadway) off A6 at
T-lights midway between Belper &
Derby. **Sat 26, Sun 27, Mon 28
Aug (10-5). Adm £3.50, chd
free. Home-made teas. Visits
also by arrangement in Aug for
between 4 - 25 visitors. Adm £7
incl beverage and cake.**
Garden design enthusiast with over
500 varieties and rare specimens
planted for late summer show.
Eclectic yet replicable. 12 distinct
areas incl naturalistic, tropical and
single colour borders. Italian walled
garden. Woodland with pond and
walkway. Japanese landscape with
stream, moon gate and pavilion.
Front cottage garden with winter
shrubs and meadow planting.
Stone, wire and wood sculptures.
Fully labelled. Comfortable seating
around the garden. 100's of plants
for sale. Close to Kedleston Hall
and Derwent Valley World Heritage
Site. Home-made produce and take
home delicacies available. Feature in
Garden News magazine.

✿ 🚗 ☕

2 Manvers Street

© Fiona Lea

5m S of Matlock. From Wirksworth Market Place take B5023 towards Duffield. After 300yds turn R onto Summer Lane at mini r'about. Windward approx 500yds on R. **Visits by arrangement Mar to Sept for groups 10+. Adm incl refreshments.** *Donation to Framework Knitters Museum.* 1 acre of greenery, with pockets of colour. Wildlife friendly, furnished with many different habitats. Mature trees provide shady spots to sit and relax. The crinkle crankle Leylandii hedge and a lolly holly add a surprising touch of formality. An abundance of foliage and winding paths where you can easily lose yourself. Radio Derby's Gardening Guru said that the hostas were worthy of Chelsea. A quiet space, hidden away on the edge of a small town. Completely secluded. Home-made cakes, coffee, variety of herbal teas available.

🐕 🏠 ☕

56 26 WHEELDON AVENUE

Derby, DE22 1HN. Ian Griffiths, 01332 342204, idhgriffiths@gmail.com. *1m N of Derby. 1m from city centre & approached directly off Kedleston Rd or from A6 Duffield Rd via West Bank Ave. Limited on street parking.* **Visits by arrangement in June for groups 4+. Refreshments by prior arrangement and incl in adm price. Adm £5, chd free.** Tiny Victorian walled garden near to city centre. Lawn and herbaceous borders with newly expanded old rose collection, lupins, delphiniums and foxgloves. Small terrace with topiary, herb garden and lion fountain. Rose collection. Featured in English Home magazine, Derbyshire Life and on BBC TV. Garden on one level, lawn may be soft if wet.

♿ 🐕 ❀ ☕

57 WILD IN THE COUNTRY

Hawkhill Road, Eyam, Hope Valley, S32 5QQ. Mrs Gill Bagshawe, 07733 455876, gillbagshawe@aol.com. *In Eyam, follow signs to public car park. Located next to Eyam Museum & opp public car park on Hawkhill Rd.* Sat 29, Sun 30 July, Sat 26, Sun 27 Aug (11-4.30). Adm £2.50, chd free. **Visits also by arrangement July to Oct.** A rectangular plot devoted totally to growing flowers and foliage for

cutting. Sweet pea, rose, larkspur, cornflower, nigella, ammi. All the florist's favourites can be found here. There is a tea room, a village PH and several cafes in the village to enjoy refreshments.

♿ 🐕 ❀ ☕

58 26 WINDMILL RISE

Belper, DE56 1GQ. Kathy Fairweather. *From Belper Market Place take Chesterfield Rd towards Heage. Top of hill, 1st R Marsh Lane, 1st R Windmill Lane, 1st R Windmill Rise - limited parking only.* Sat 15, Sun 16 July (11.30-4.30); Thur 20 July (12-6.30). Adm £3.50, chd free. Light refreshments. Behind a deceptively ordinary looking façade, lies a surprise. Meander along extensive pathways lined with a tapestry of texture and light and shade with a lush and restful atmosphere. A plant lovers' organic garden divided into sections: woodland, Japanese, secret garden, cottage, edible, ponds and small stream. A large collection of rare and unusual plants and trees. Live background music during the weekend. Delicious home baking and light lunches available. Featured in Belper News.

❀ 🚗 ☕

59 WINDWARD

62 Summer Lane, Wirksworth, Matlock, DE4 4EB. Audrey & Andrew Winkler, 01629 822681, audrey.winkler@w3z.co.uk, www.grandmafrogsgarden.co.uk.

60 WOODEND COTTAGE

134 Main Street, Repton, DE65 6FB. Wendy & Stephen Longden, 01283 703259, wendylongden@btinternet.com. *6m S of Derby. From A38, S of Derby, follow signs to Willington, then Repton. In Repton straight on at r'about through village. Garden is 1m on R.* Sun 6 Aug (1.30-5.30). Adm £3, chd free. Home-made teas. **Opening with Repton NGS Village Gardens on Sun 16 July. Visits also by arrangement July & Aug for groups 10+.** Plant lover's garden with glorious views on a sloping 2½ acre site developed organically for yr-round interest. On lower levels herbaceous borders are arranged informally and connected via lawns, thyme bed, pond and pergolas. Mixed woodland and grassed labyrinth lead naturally into fruit, vegetable and herb potager with meadows beyond. Especially colourful in July and August. Easy and unusual perennials and grasses for sale. Why not visit St Wystan's Church Repton with its Saxon crypt, as part of your visit. Wheelchair access on lower levels only.

🐕 ❀ 🚗 ☕

DEVON

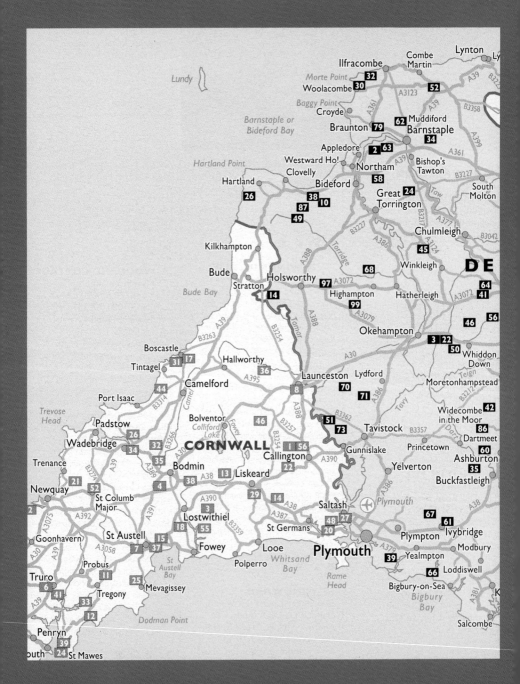

Lundy

Morte Point
Ilfracombe
Combe Martin
Lynton
Ly

Woolacombe **30** **32**
A3123
52

Baggy Point
Croyde
Braunton **79** **62** Muddiford
Barnstaple
34

Barnstaple or
Bideford Bay

Appledore
Westward Ho!
Clovelly
2 **63**
Northam
A361
A399

Hartland Point
Bideford
58
Bishop's Tawton
B3227

Hartland
26
Great Torrington **24**
South Molton

Kilkhampton
38 **10**
87
49
Chulmleigh
B3042

D E

Bude
Holsworthy
68
Winkleigh
45
A124

Bude Bay
Stratton
14
97 A3072
Highampton
99 A3079
Hatherleigh
A386
64
41

Boscastle
B3263
A39
B3254
Okehampton
3 **22**
46 **56**
50
Whiddon Down

Tintagel
31 **17**
Hallworthy
36
Launceston
Lydford
A30
70
71
Moretonhampstead

Camelford
A395
8
B3362
A386
Tavistock
B3357
Widecombe in the Moor **42**
86

Port Isaac
B3314
Bolventor
46
51
73
Dartmeet

Padstow
26
Colliford Lake
B3257
B3254
Gunnislake
Princetown
60
Ashburton

Wadebridge
32
34
1 **56**
Callington
A390
Yelverton
35

Trenance
A3274
A39
35
Bodmin
22
Buckfastleigh

Newquay
21
52
38 A38 **13** Liskeard
29
14 A38
Saltash
Plymouth
67
61
Ivybridge

2
St Columb Major
4
3
55
48 **27**
20
Plympton
Modbury

Goonhavern
15
Lostwithiel
18
St Germans
Looe
A379
39
Yealmpton
66
Loddiswell

Truro
7 **37**
Fowey
Polperro
Whitsand Bay
Plymouth
Bigbury-on-Sea

Probus
11
25
St Austell Bay
Rame Head
Bigbury Bay

6 **41**
33
Tregony
Mevagissey

12
Dodman Point
Salcombe

Penryn
39
24 St Mawes

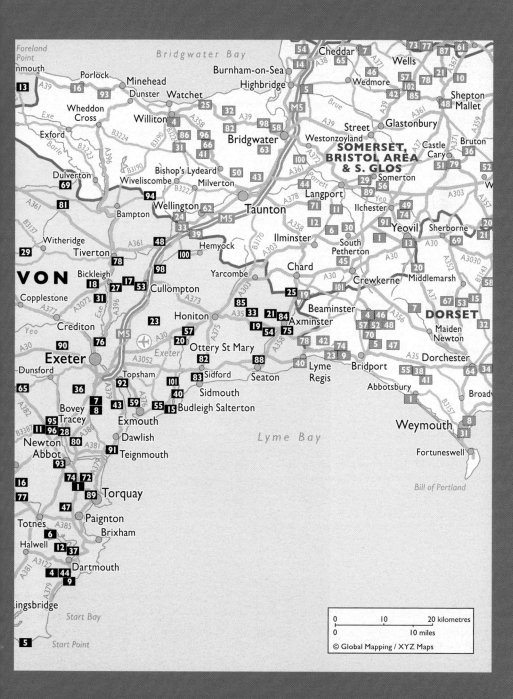

Volunteers

County Organisers
& Central Devon
Edward & Miranda Allhusen
01647 440296
Miranda@allhusen.co.uk

County Treasurer
Julia Tremlett
01392 832671
jandjtremlett@hotmail.com

Publicity
Brian Mackness
01626 356004
brianmackness@clara.co.uk

Cath Pettyfer
01837 89024
cathpettyfer@gmail.com

Booklet Co-ordinator
Edward Allhusen
01647 440296
edward@allhusen.co.uk

Assistant County Organisers

East Devon
Peter Wadeley 01297 631210
wadeley@btinternet.com

Exeter
Jenny Phillips 01392 254076
jennypips25@hotmail.co.uk

Exmoor
Juliet Moss 01398 341604
julietm@onetel.com

North Devon
Jo Hynes 01805 804265
hynesjo@gmail.com

North East Devon
Jill Hall 01884 38812
jill22hall@gmail.com

Plymouth
Maria Ashurst 01752 351396
maria.ashurst@sky.com

South Devon
Sally Vincent 01803 722227
salv@hotmail.co.uk

Torbay
Gill Treweek 01626 879313
gilltreweek@hotmail.co.uk

West Devon
Sara-Jane Cumming 01822 860281
sj@broadparkdesigns.co.uk

Devon is a county of great contrasts in geography and climate, and therefore also in gardening.

The rugged north coast has terraces clinging precariously to hillsides so steep that the faint-hearted would never contemplate making a garden there. But here, and on the rolling hills and deep valleys of Exmoor, despite a constant battle with the elements, NGS gardeners create remarkable results by choosing hardy plants that withstand the high winds and salty air.

In the south, in peaceful wooded estuaries and tucked into warm valleys, gardens grow bananas, palms and fruit usually associated with the Mediterranean.

Between these two terrains is a third: Dartmoor, 365 square miles of rugged moorland rising to 2000 feet, presents its own horticultural demands. Typically, here too are many NGS gardens.

In idyllic villages scattered throughout this very large county, in gardens large and small, in single manors and in village groups within thriving communities – gardeners pursue their passion.

Below: Sutton Mead, Moretonhampstead Gardens

OPENING DATES

All entries subject to change. For latest information check www.ngs.org.uk

Extended openings are shown at the beginning of the month.

Map locator numbers are shown to the right of each garden name.

January

High Garden (Every Tuesday to Friday from Tuesday 10th)	43

February

Snowdrop Festival

High Garden (Every Tuesday to Friday)	43

Friday 10th

Higher Cherubeer	45

Friday 17th

Higher Cherubeer	45

Saturday 18th

The Mount, Delamore	67

Sunday 19th

The Mount, Delamore	67

Sunday 26th

Higher Cherubeer	45

March

High Garden (Every Tuesday to Friday)	43

Sunday 5th

East Worlington House	29

Sunday 12th

East Worlington House	29

Sunday 19th

Summers Place	90

Saturday 25th

Haldon Grange	36

Sunday 26th

Gorwell House	34
Haldon Grange	36

April

High Garden (Every Tuesday to Friday)	43

Saturday 1st

Haldon Grange	36
The Haven	39

Sunday 2nd

Haldon Grange	36
The Haven	39
Heathercombe	42
Yonder Hill	101

Friday 7th

◆ Holbrook Garden	48

Saturday 8th

Haldon Grange	36
◆ Holbrook Garden	48
NEW Monkscroft	64

Sunday 9th

Haldon Grange	36
NEW Monkscroft	64
Wood Barton	100
Yonder Hill	101

Friday 14th

◆ Holbrook Garden	48

Saturday 15th

Haldon Grange	36
◆ Holbrook Garden	48

Sunday 16th

Haldon Grange	36
◆ Holbrook Garden	48
Kia-Ora Farm & Gardens	53
St Merryn	79
Yonder Hill	101

Monday 17th

Haldon Grange	36
Kia-Ora Farm & Gardens	53
Yonder Hill	101

Wednesday 19th

Haldon Grange	36
◆ Shapcott Barton Knowstone Estate	81

Saturday 22nd

Haldon Grange	36
Sidbury Manor	82

Sunday 23rd

Andrew's Corner	3
Haldon Grange	36
◆ Shapcott Barton Knowstone Estate	81
Sidbury Manor	82
Wood Barton	100
Yonder Hill	101

Friday 28th

◆ Holbrook Garden	48

Saturday 29th

Dicot	25
Haldon Grange	36
◆ Holbrook Garden	48
Sedgewell Coach House Gardens	80

Sunday 30th

Andrew's Corner	3
Dicot	25
Gorwell House	34
Haldon Grange	36
◆ Holbrook Garden	48
Kia-Ora Farm & Gardens	53
Mothecombe House	66
Sedgewell Coach House Gardens	80
Whitstone Bluebells	95
Yonder Hill	101

May

The Gate House (Every day from Saturday 20th)	32
High Garden (Every Tuesday to Friday)	43

Monday 1st

Andrew's Corner	3
Dicot	25
Haldon Grange	36
Kia-Ora Farm & Gardens	53
Yonder Hill	101

Saturday 6th

Haldon Grange	36
Sedgewell Coach House Gardens	80

Sunday 7th

Andrew's Corner	3
Haldon Grange	36
Higher Ash Farm	44
Sedgewell Coach House Gardens	80
Summers Place	90
Yonder Hill	101

Wednesday 10th

Haldon Grange	36

Saturday 13th

Haldon Grange	36
The Old Vicarage	69

Sunday 14th

Bickham House	8
Haldon Grange	36
Heathercombe	42
Higher Ash Farm	44
Kia-Ora Farm & Gardens	53
The Old Vicarage	69
St Merryn	79
Wick Farm Gardens	97
Yonder Hill	101

Wednesday 17th

Haldon Grange	36

Friday 19th

NEW Hawkern	40
◆ Holbrook Garden	48
Moretonhampstead Gardens	65

Saturday 20th

Haldon Grange	36
◆ Holbrook Garden	48
Moretonhampstead Gardens	65

Sunday 21st

Foamlea	30
Gorwell House	34
Haldon Grange	36
NEW Hawkern	40
Heathercombe	42
◆ Holbrook Garden	48
◆ Hotel Endsleigh	51
Moretonhampstead Gardens	65
Wick Farm Gardens	97
Yonder Hill	101

90th Anniversary Weekend

Saturday 27th

Bocombe Mill Cottage	10
NEW Dorweeke	27
NEW Greatcombe	35
Haldon Grange	36
Heathercombe	42
Lewis Cottage	56
Southcombe Gardens	86
Springfield House	88

Sunday 28th

Andrew's Corner	3
Bocombe Mill Cottage	10
The Bridge Mill	14
NEW Dorweeke	27
NEW Greatcombe	35
Haldon Grange	36
Heathercombe	42
Kia-Ora Farm & Gardens	53
Lewis Cottage	56
St Merryn	79
Southcombe Gardens	86

Springfield	87	Bulland Farm	16
Torview	93	Goren Farm	33
Wick Farm Gardens	97		
Yonder Hill	101	**Sunday 4th**	

Monday 29th

		Abbotskerswell Gardens	1
Andrew's Corner	3	Andrew's Corner	3
Bocombe Mill Cottage	10	Bovey Tracey Gardens	11
◆ Cadhay	20	Bulland Farm	16
🆕 Greatcombe	35	Burn Valley Butterleigh	
Haldon Grange	36	Gardens	17
Kia-Ora Farm &		Goren Farm	33
Gardens	53	Heathercombe	42
Lewis Cottage	56	Higher Cherubeer	45
Springfield	87	Little Ash Bungalow	57
Torview	93	The Lookout	59
Wick Farm Gardens	97	Southcombe Gardens	86
Yonder Hill	101	Yonder Hill	101

June

Friday 9th

Bickham House 8

**The Gate House
(Every day)** 32

Saturday 10th

Bocombe Mill Cottage	10
Cleave House	22
Dicot	25
◆ Fursdon	31
Goren Farm	33
◆ Winsford Walled	
Garden	99

**Goren Farm (Every
day from Saturday
3rd)** 33

**High Garden (Every
Tuesday to Friday)** 43

Friday 2nd

The Lookout 59

Sunday 11th

Bocombe Mill Cottage	10
Dicot	25
◆ Docton Mill	26
◆ Fursdon	31
Goren Farm	33
Hayne	41

Saturday 3rd

Abbotskerswell Gardens	1
Bovey Tracey Gardens	11

Hole Farm	49	Cottage	47
Kia-Ora Farm & Gardens	53	◆ Holbrook Garden	48
Portington	73	Kilmington (Shute Road)	
Southcombe Gardens	86	Gardens	54
◆ Winsford Walled		Portington	73
Garden	99	St Merryn	79
Yonder Hill	101	Sidmouth Gardens	83
		Southcombe Gardens	86
Friday 16th		Venn Cross Railway	
Bramble Torre	12	Gardens	94
◆ Cadhay	20	Yonder Hill	101
🆕 Hawkern	40		
◆ Holbrook Garden	48	**Friday 23rd**	
◆ Marwood Hill		Bickham House	8
Garden	62		
		Saturday 24th	
Saturday 17th		Ash Gardens	4
Bramble Torre	12	Cleave House	22
🆕 Dunley House	28	🆕 Clyst St Lawrence	
Goren Farm	33	Gardens	23
🆕 Higher Orchard		🆕 Greatcombe	35
Cottage	47	Harbour Lights	38
◆ Holbrook Garden	48	Lewis Cottage	56
Kilmington (Shute Road)		The Mill House	63
Gardens	54	Springfield House	88
Sidmouth Gardens	83	Teignmouth Gardens	91
Venn Cross Railway			
Gardens	94	**Sunday 25th**	
		Ash Gardens	4
Sunday 18th		Burn Valley Butterleigh	
Bramble Torre	12	Gardens	17
The Croft	24	🆕 Clyst St Lawrence	
🆕 Dunley House	28	Gardens	23
Goren Farm	33	Foamlea	30
Heathercombe	42	🆕 Greatcombe	35
🆕 Higher Orchard		Harbour Lights	38
		Heathercombe	42
		🆕 Kentisbury	
		Gardens	52
		Kia-Ora Farm &	
		Gardens	53
		Lewis Cottage	56
		The Mill House	63
		🆕 Pynes House	76
		Southcombe Gardens	86
		Teignmouth Gardens	91
		Yonder Hill	101

July

**The Gate House
(Every day)**	32
**Goren Farm (Every
day to Sunday 16th)**	33
**High Garden (Every
Tuesday to Friday)**	43
Saturday 1st	
Cleave Hill	21
The Priory	74

The Lookout

NEW St Andrew Street
South Gardens,
Tiverton 78
Willand Old Village
Gardens &
Allotments 98

Sunday 2nd
Cleave Hill 21
The Priory 74
NEW St Andrew Street
South Gardens,
Tiverton 78
Southcombe Gardens 86
Willand Old Village
Gardens &
Allotments 98
Yonder Hill 101

Saturday 8th
Cleave House 22
NEW The Olde
Cottage 70
NEW Park House 71

Sunday 9th
◆ Hotel Endsleigh 51
Kia-Ora Farm &
Gardens 53
NEW The Olde
Cottage 70
NEW Park House 71
NEW Riverford Field
Kitchen Garden 77
St Merryn 79
Yonder Hill 101

Friday 14th
◆ Holbrook Garden 48
Topsham Gardens 92

Saturday 15th
◆ Holbrook Garden 48
Springfield 87

Sunday 16th
Bickham House 8
The Croft 24
◆ Holbrook Garden 48
Hole Farm 49
Springfield 87
Topsham Gardens 92
Yonder Hill 101

Friday 21st
◆ Cadhay 20
Socks Orchard 84

Saturday 22nd
Budleigh Salterton
Gardens 15
Burnbridge Cottage 18
Cleave House 22
Hole's Meadow 50
Lewis Cottage 56

Socks Orchard 84
Venn Cross Railway
Gardens 94

Sunday 23rd
Budleigh Salterton
Gardens 15
Burnbridge Cottage 18
Hayne 41
Hole's Meadow 50
Kia-Ora Farm &
Gardens 53
Lewis Cottage 56
◆ Shapcott Barton
Knowstone Estate 81
Socks Orchard 84
Venn Cross Railway
Gardens 94
Yonder Hill 101

Wednesday 26th
◆ Shapcott Barton
Knowstone Estate 81

Saturday 29th
Dicot 25
NEW Greatcombe 35
Lower Spitchwick
Garden 60
Springfield House 88

Sunday 30th
Dicot 25
NEW Greatcombe 35
Hole's Meadow 50
Lower Spitchwick
Garden 60
Squirrels 89
Yonder Hill 101

August

The Gate House
(Every day) 32
High Garden (Every
Tuesday to Friday) 43
Saturday 5th
Brendon Gardens 13
Moretonhampstead
Gardens 65
NEW The Olde
Cottage 70
Squirrels 89

Sunday 6th
Brendon Gardens 13
Kia-Ora Farm &
Gardens 53
Moretonhampstead
Gardens 65
NEW The Olde
Cottage 70

Squirrels 89
Whitstone Farm 96
Yonder Hill 101

Saturday 12th
Ash Gardens 4
The Old Vicarage 69

Sunday 13th
Ash Gardens 4
Bickham House 8
The Old Vicarage 69
Yonder Hill 101

Saturday 19th
Brendon Gardens 13
Lewis Cottage 56
Sedgewell Coach
House Gardens 80
◆ Winsford Walled
Garden 99

Sunday 20th
Brendon Gardens 13
The Croft 24
Kia-Ora Farm &
Gardens 53
Lewis Cottage 56
Little Ash Bungalow 57
Sedgewell Coach
House Gardens 80
◆ Winsford Walled
Garden 99
Yonder Hill 101

Friday 25th
◆ Holbrook Garden 48

Saturday 26th
NEW Greatcombe 35
◆ Holbrook Garden 48
Sidmouth Gardens 83
Venn Cross Railway
Gardens 94

Sunday 27th
32 Allenstyle Drive 2
◆ Cadhay 20
NEW Greatcombe 35
◆ Holbrook Garden 48
Kia-Ora Farm &
Gardens 53
Sidmouth Gardens 83
Venn Cross Railway
Gardens 94
Yonder Hill 101

Monday 28th
◆ Cadhay 20
NEW Greatcombe 35
Kia-Ora Farm &
Gardens 53
Sidmouth Gardens 83
Yonder Hill 101

Donations
from the NGS
enable Perennial
to care for
horticulturalists

September

The Gate House
(Every day to
Sunday 10th) 32
High Garden (Every
Tuesday to Friday) 43
Friday 1st
Prospect House 75

Saturday 2nd
Prospect House 75

Sunday 3rd
32 Allenstyle Drive 2
Prospect House 75
NEW Riverford Field
Kitchen Garden 77
Yonder Hill 101

Saturday 9th
NEW Ash Park 5
Bickham House 8
◆ Fursdon 31
South Wood Farm 85

Sunday 10th
32 Allenstyle Drive 2
NEW Ash Park 5
Bickham House 8
◆ Fursdon 31
Kia-Ora Farm &
Gardens 53
South Wood Farm 85
Yonder Hill 101

Sunday 17th
32 Allenstyle Drive 2
Yonder Hill 101

Sunday 24th
32 Allenstyle Drive 2
Yonder Hill 101

October

High Garden (Every Tuesday to Friday) 43

Sunday 8th
Higher Ash Farm 44
Summers Place 90

Sunday 15th
Bickham Cottage 7

Sunday 22nd
Andrew's Corner 3

November

High Garden (Every Tuesday to Friday) 43

December

High Garden (Every Tuesday to Friday to Friday 15th) 43

February 2018

Friday 9th
Higher Cherubeer 45

Friday 16th
Higher Cherubeer 45

Sunday 25th
Higher Cherubeer 45

By Arrangement

32 Allenstyle Drive 2
Andrew's Corner 3
Avenue Cottage 6
Bickham Cottage 7
Bickham House 8
Bocombe Mill Cottage 10
Brendon Gardens 13
The Bridge Mill 14
Byes Reach, Sidmouth
  Gardens 83
Cleave Hill 21
The Croft 24
The Engine House,
  Venn Cross Railway
  Gardens 94

Foamlea 30
The Gate House 32
Goren Farm 33
Gorwell House 34
NEW Greatcombe 35
Haldon Grange 36
Hamblyn's Coombe 37
The Haven 39
NEW Hawkern 40
Hayne 41
Heathercombe 42
Higher Ash Farm 44
Higher Burnhaies, Burn
  Valley Butterleigh
  Gardens 17
Higher Cherubeer 45
Higher Cullaford 46
Higher Tippacott Farm,
  Brendon Gardens 13
Hole's Meadow 50
Lee Ford 55
Lewis Cottage 56
Little Ash Bungalow 57
Little Webbery 58
Lower Spitchwick
  Garden 60

The Mill House 63
Mothecombe House 66
Musselbrook Cottage 68
The Old Vicarage 69
Prospect House 75
St Merryn 79
Shutelake, Burn Valley
  Butterleigh Gardens 17
Socks Orchard 84
South Wood Farm 85
Southcombe Gardens 86
Springfield 87
Springfield House 88
Squirrels 89
Station House, Venn Cross
  Railway Gardens 94
Summers Place 90
Sutton Mead,
  Moretonhampstead
  Gardens 65
Venn Cross Railway
  Gardens 94
Whitstone Farm 96
Wick Farm Gardens 97
Wood Barton 100
Yonder Hill 101

Socks Orchard

THE GARDENS

GROUP OPENING

1 ABBOTSKERSWELL GARDENS

Abbotskerswell, TQ12 5PN. *2m SW of Newton Abbot town centre. A381 Newton Abbot/Totnes rd. Sharp L turn from NA, R from Totnes. Field parking at Fairfield. Maps available at all gardens and at Church House.* **Sat 3, Sun 4 June (1-5). Combined adm £6, chd free. Home-made teas at Church House. Teas available from 2pm. Maps and tickets from 1pm.** *Donation to Friends of St Marys Church.*

ABBOTSFORD
Mrs W Grierson.

ABBOTSKERSWELL ALLOTMENTS
Margaret Crompton.

1 ABBOTSWELL COTTAGES
Jane Taylor.

BRIAR COTTAGE
Peggy & David Munden.

FAIRFIELD
Brian Mackness.

2A MANOR CLOSE
Mrs Dorne Cornelius.

NEW 16 WILTON WAY
Katy & Chris Yates.

NEW 7 WILTON WAY
Mr & Mrs Cindy & Vernon Stunt.

10 WILTON WAY
Mrs Margaret Crompton.

NEW 18 WILTON WAY
Ced & Viv Bell.

For 2017, Abbotskerswell offers 3 new gardens, making 9 plus the village allotments. Ranging from very small to large they offer a wide range of planting styles and innovative landscaping. Cottage gardens, terracing, wild flower areas, specialist plants, vegetable production methods. We offer creative ideas for every type and size of garden. Visitors are welcome to picnic in the field or arboretum at Fairfield. Children will enjoy the miniature Shetland ponies, plus finding their way through winding paths among high grasses. See You Tube Abbotskerswell Gardens 2011 for a taster. Sales of plants, paintings, ceramics, garden produce, jams and chutneys and other creative crafts. Teas! Disabled access to 3 gardens.

✿ ☕

2 32 ALLENSTYLE DRIVE

Yelland, Barnstaple, EX31 3DZ. Steve & Dawn Morgan, 01271 861433, fourhungrycats@aol.com, www.devonsubtropicalgarden.co.uk. *5m W of Barnstaple. From Barnstaple take B3233 towards Instow. Through Bickington & Fremington. L at Yelland sign into Allenstyle Rd. 1st R into Allenstyle Dr. Light blue bungalow. From Bideford go past Instow on B3233.* **Every Sun 27 Aug to 24 Sept (11.30-5.30). Adm £4, chd free. Light refreshments. Visits also by arrangement Aug & Sept, a warm welcome awaits.** Small (50x100ft) garden in mild estuary location, which combines sub-tropical, cottage and prairie planting. Bananas, hedychiums (gingers), palms, colocasia, aroids, brugmansias and an exotic collection of passionflowers and much more. Lots of seating so you can take your time and enjoy scent, colour and high impact planting.

✿ ☕

3 ANDREW'S CORNER - ANDREWS CORNER

Belstone, EX20 1RD. Robin & Edwina Hill, 01837 840332, edwinarobinhill@outlook.com, www.andrewscorner.garden. *3m E of Okehampton. Signed to Belstone from A30. In village turn L, signed Skaigh. Follow NGS signs. Garden approx ½m on R. Visitors may be dropped off at house, parking in nearby field.* **Sun 23, Sun 30 Apr, Mon 1, Sun 7, Sun 28, Mon 29 May, Sun 4 June, Sun 22 Oct (2-5). Adm £4, chd free. Home-made teas. Visits also by arrangement Feb to Nov.** Well established, wildlife friendly, well labelled plantsman's garden in stunning high moorland setting. Variety of garden habitats incl woodland areas and pond; wide range of unusual trees, shrubs, herbaceous plants for yr-round effect with blue poppies, rhododendrons, bulbs and maples; spectacular autumn colour. Family friendly, with quiz sheet, fairy doors, playhouse, fruit, vegetables and chickens. Featured on BBC Radio Devon and in Devon Country Gardener magazine. Wheelchair access difficult when wet.

♿ 🐕 ✿ ☕ 🏠

GROUP OPENING

4 ASH GARDENS

Ash, Dartmouth, TQ6 0LR. *2m SW of Dartmouth. Leave A381 Totnes to Kingsbridge rd in Halwell taking A3122 for Dartmouth. Just before Sportsmans Arms turn R. At T junction turn R then 1st L. At Xrds turn R then parking 1st L.* **Sat 24, Sun 25 June, Sat 12, Sun 13 Aug (2-5). Combined adm £5, chd free. Tea.**

BAY TREE COTTAGE
Jenny Goffe.

HIGHER ASH FARM
Mr Michael Gribbin & Mrs Jennifer Barwell.
(See separate entry.)

2 delightful gardens in the tiny hamlet of Ash. The beautiful intimate little garden at Bay Tree Cottage sits in a quiet secluded valley with wonderful sunlit views across open farmland. The perfect curved lawn leads the eye to small rooms filled with surprise and clever planting. Ornamental trees punctuate the boundary and a tiny vegetable garden of raised beds overflows with produce. Higher Ash Farm has 2½ acres of established and developing garden situated around farmhouse and barn conversions. Large kitchen garden terraced into the hillside, orchard, pond, stream with bog planting and feature borders around the house offering seasonal and yr round interest.

🐕 ☕

5 NEW ASH PARK
East Prawle, Kingsbridge,
TQ7 2BX. **Chris & Cathryn
Vanderspar.** *Ash Park, East Prawle
South Devon. Take A379 Kingsbridge
to Dartmouth, at Frogmore after
PH R to East Prawle, after 1.1m L,
in 1.4m at Cousins Cross bear R
(middle of 3 roads). In village head
to Prawle Point.* **Sat 9, Sun 10
Sept (11-5). Adm £5, chd free.
Home-made teas.**
In a stunning location, with 180°
view of the sea, Ash Park nestles at
the foot of the escarpment, with
3½ acres of sub-tropical gardens,
paths to explore, woodland glades,
ponds and hidden seating areas. In
early Sept, cannas, hydrangeas, salvias
and dahlias should be at their best.
Limited access for wheelchairs.
🐕 ❀ ☕ 🏆

6 AVENUE COTTAGE
Ashprington, Totnes, TQ9 7UT.
**Mr Richard Pitts & Mr
David Sykes,** 01803 732769,
richard.pitts@btinternet.com,
www.avenuecottage.com. *3m SW
of Totnes. A381 Totnes to Kingsbridge
for 1m; L for Ashprington, into village
then L by PH. Garden ¼m on R
after Sharpham Estate sign.* **Visits
by arrangement Mar to Oct,
groups and individuals welcome.
Adm £4, chd free. Tea.**
11 acres of mature and young trees
and shrubs. Once part of an C18
landscape, the neglected garden has
been cleared and replanted over the
last 25 yrs. Good views of Sharpham
House and R Dart. Azaleas and
hydrangeas are a feature.
🐕 🏠 🏛 ☕

7 BICKHAM COTTAGE
Kenn, Exeter, EX6 7XL.
Steve Eyre, 01392 833964,
bickham@live.co.uk. *6m S of
Exeter. 1m off A38. Leave A38 at
Kennford Services, follow signs to
Kenn. 1st R in village, follow lane for
¾m to end of no through rd.* **Sun
15 Oct (2-5). Adm £4, chd free.
Home-made teas. Visits also by
arrangement Oct & Nov.**
Small cottage garden divided into
separate areas by old stone walls
and hedge banks. Front garden with
mainly South African bulbs and plants.

Lawn surrounded by borders with
agapanthus, eucomis, crocosmia,
diorama etc. Stream garden with
primulas. Pond with large Koi carp.
Glasshouses with National Collection
of Hardy Nerines, Nerine sarniensis
and cultivars, 3500 pots with in
excess of 450 varieties. Visitors are
also welcome to wander around
Bickham House gardens.
♿ ❀ 🚗 NPC ☕

8 BICKHAM HOUSE
Kenn, Exeter, EX6 7XL.
Julia Tremlett, 01392 832671,
jandjtremlett@hotmail.com. *6m
S of Exeter, 1m off A38. Leave A38
at Kennford Services, follow signs to
Kenn, 1st R in village, follow lane for
¾m to end of no through rd.* **Sun
14 May, Fri 9, Fri 23 June, Sun
16 July, Sun 13 Aug, Sat 9, Sun
10 Sept (2-5). Adm £5, chd free.
Home-made teas. Visits also by
arrangement Apr to Sept.**
7 acres with colour co-ordinated
borders, mature trees, lawns. Fern
garden and water garden. Formal
parterre with lily pond. 1 acre walled
garden with profusion of vegetables
and flowers. Palm tree avenue leading
to summerhouse. Spring garden with
cowslips, bluebells. Late summer
colour with dahlias, crocosmia,
agapanthus etc. Cactus and succulent
greenhouse. Lakeside walk. 9th &
10th September opening with Devon
Open Studios for Kerry Tremlett's
print maker's exhibition & sale.
♿ ❀ 🚗 ☕

**9 ♦ BLACKPOOL
GARDENS**
Dartmouth, TQ6 0RG. Sir
Geoffrey Newman, 01803 771801,
beach@blackpoolsands.co.uk,
www.blackpoolsands.co.uk. *3m
SW of Dartmouth. From Dartmouth
follow brown signs to Blackpool
Sands on A379. Entry tickets, parking,
toilets and refreshments available
at Blackpool Sands. Sorry, no dogs
permitted.* **For opening times and
information, please phone, email or
visit garden website.**
Carefully restored C19 subtropical
plantsman's garden with collection
of mature and newly planted tender
and unusual trees, shrubs and
carpet of spring flowers. Paths

and steps lead gradually uphill and
above the Captain's seat offering
fine coastal views. Recent plantings
follow the S hemisphere theme
with callistemons, pittosporums,
acacias and buddlejas. Open
1 Apr - 30 Sept (10-4) weather
permitting.

**10 BOCOMBE MILL
COTTAGE**
Bocombe, Parkham, Bideford,
EX39 5PH. Mr Chris Butler & Mr
David Burrows, 01237 451293,
www.bocombe.co.uk. *6m E of
Clovelly, 9m SW of Bideford. From
A39 just outside Horns Cross village,
turn to Foxdown. At Xrds follow
signs for parking.* **Sat 27, Sun 28,
Mon 29 May, Sat 10 June, Sun
11 June (12-5). Adm £4.50,
chd £1. Ploughmans lunches &
traditional home-made cakes
& cream teas. Visits also by
arrangement Mar to Sept for
groups of 10+.**
12 flower gardens and many
features that punctuate an
undulating, organic landscape of 5
acres. Streams, 3 bog gardens incl
the new upper bog garden, pools,
12 water features. White pergola.
Grotto and hermitage. Hillside
orchard. Soft fruit and kitchen
gardens. Garden kaleidoscope.
Wild meadow, a wildlife haven.
Circular walk around a mile - boots
suggested - garden plan incl 80+
specimen trees. Real hermit in
the hermitage with adjoining shell
grotto. Goats on hillside. Japanese
pavilion with buddha cascade.
❀ 🚗 ☕ 🏆

GROUP OPENING

**11 BOVEY TRACEY
GARDENS**
Bovey Tracey, TQ13 9NA. *6m N of
Newton Abbot. Gateway to Dartmoor.
Take A382 to Bovey Tracey. Car
parking at town car parks and on
some rds.* **Sat 3, Sun 4 June (1.30-
5.30). Combined adm £5, chd
free. Home-made teas at Gleam
Tor. Wine at Ashwell. Light
refreshments at Pineholm.**

ASHWELL
Tony & Jeanette Pearce.

NEW **THE BROOK**
Haytor Rd. Mrs Joy Dixon.

GLEAM TOR
Gillian & Colin Liddy.

GREEN HEDGES
Alan & Linda Jackson.

PINEHOLM
Lynda & Alan Pewsey.

2 REDWOODS
Mr & Mrs Tony Mooney.

11 ST PETER'S CLOSE
Pauline & Keith Gregory.

Bovey Tracey is a pretty cob and granite built town nestling in the foothills of Dartmoor beside R Bovey. Ashwell: steeply sloping Victorian walled garden, vineyard, colourful mixed borders, orchard with wild flowers, fruit and vegetables, distant views. The Brook: sweeping lawns, mature trees, colourful borders, vegetables and cordon fruit trees. Gleam Tor: far-reaching views in all directions. Long colourful herbaceous border, white garden, prairie planting and wild flower meadow. Green Hedges: mature garden with Dartmoor views. Well established colourful borders incl shrubs, bulbs, perennials, vegetables and soft fruit. Pineholm: sloping, terraced garden with orchard, woodland, stream and areas with exotic and native bogland plants, flowers and vegetables. Redwoods: mature trees, acid loving spring and summer shrubs. Moorland leat flows through unusual fernery. St Peter's Close: very colourful, sloping small garden with Dartmoor views. Most gardens allow dogs. Limited wheelchair access at some gardens.

12 BRAMBLE TORRE
Dittisham, nr Dartmouth, TQ6 0HZ. Paul & Sally Vincent, www.rainingsideways.com. ¾ m from Dittisham. Leave A3122 at Sportsman's Arms. Drop down into village, at Red Lion turn L to Cornworthy. Continue ¾ m Bramble Torre straight ahead. Fri 16, Sat 17, Sun 18 June (2-6). Adm £4.50, chd free. Cream teas.

Set in 20 acres of farmland, the 3-acre garden follows a rambling stream through a steep valley: lily pond, herbaceous borders, camellias, shrubs and roses dominated by huge embothrium glowing scarlet in late spring against a sometimes blue sky! A formal herb and vegetable garden runs alongside the stream while chickens scratch in an orchard of Ditsum plums and cider apples. Well behaved dogs on leads welcome. Limited wheelchair access, parts of garden very steep and uneven. Tea area with wheelchair access and excellent garden view.

GROUP OPENING

13 BRENDON GARDENS
Brendon, Lynton, EX35 6PU. 01598 741343, lalindevon@yahoo.co.uk. 1m S of A39 North Devon coast rd between Porlock and Lynton. Sat 5, Sun 6, Sat 19, Sun 20 Aug (12-5). Combined adm £4.50, chd free. Light lunches, homemade cakes & cream teas served at Higher Tippacott Farm. WC available. Visits also by arrangement July to Sept.

1 DEERCOMBE COTTAGES
Valerie & Stephen Exley.

DOONE COTTAGE
Carole & Jason Miller.

HIGHER TIPPACOTT FARM
Angela & Malcolm Percival, 01598 741343. Visits also by arrangement May to Sept.

Stunningly beautiful part of Exmoor. 2 gardens nestling in East Lyn river valley, 1 on heather moorland with views. Excellent walking alongside E Lyn river between Brendon and Rockford, dramatic coastal path nearby. 1 Deercombe Cottages: delightful small garden in steeply wooded valley, created using ditched stone to provide a variety of levels to display planting rich in contrasting foliage and variety of perennials. Doone Cottage: pretty garden surrounding

C17 grade 2 listed cottage at edge of river. Terraces containing variety of mature and newer planting designed for yr round colour and interest. Winding pathways provide stunning vistas over river. Kitchen garden. Higher Tippacott Farm: 950ft alt overlooking own pretty valley pasture with stream and pond. Sunny levels of interesting herbaceous planting, stone walls and old barns, all blending with its dramatic setting. Vegetable patch with distant sea views. Chickens. Bees in top-bar hive (hopefully). Organic. Plants, cards, books and bric-a-brac for sale.

14 THE BRIDGE MILL
Mill Rd, Bridgerule, Holsworthy, EX22 7EL. Rosie & Alan Beat, 01288 381341, rosie@thebridgemill.org.uk, www.thebridgemill.org.uk. In Bridgerule village on R Tamar between Bude and Holsworthy. Between chapel by river bridge and church at top of hill. The mill is at the bottom of the hill opp Short and Abbott, agricultural engineers. See above website for detailed directions. Sun 28 May (11-5). Adm £4, chd free. Home-made teas. Refreshments in garden with ducks or in the stable if wet! Plenty of dry seating. Visits also by arrangement May & June for groups of 15+.

One acre organic gardens set around mill house and restored water mill. Small cottage garden; herb garden with medicinal and dye plants; productive fruit and vegetable garden, and a wild woodland and water garden by the mill. The 16 acre smallholding will be open for lake and riverside walks through wildflower meadows. Friendly sheep, pigs and poultry. Exhibition of embroideries by Linda Chilton. The historic water mill was restored to working order in April 2012. The mill and smallholding are open for free educational visits throughout the year to school groups. Details on website. Wheelchair access to part of garden. WC with access for wheelchairs.

The National Garden Scheme is the largest single funder of the Queen's Nursing Institute

GROUP OPENING

15 BUDLEIGH SALTERTON GARDENS

Budleigh Salterton, EX9 6JY. *Off B3178 Exmouth Rd through Budleigh Salterton. Map issued with your ticket which can be purchased from any of the gardens.* **Sat 22, Sun 23 July (1-5). Combined adm £6, chd free. Home-made teas.**

THE SEA GARDENS 1,2,3,4,5A & 6 CLIFF TERRACE
Mrs Gilly Marshall-Lee.

4 WESTBOURNE TERRACE
Mr & Mrs Stewart.

The Sea Gardens lie on cliff top along Jurassic Coastal Path above beach looking towards mouth of R Otter and on to Lyme Bay. The gardens are planted to tolerate strong winds and sea spray in winter and hot dry conditions in summer. The Sea Gardens are on opp side of road from the houses, creating a quillet (strips of land together forming a larger plot). 4 Westbourne Terrace is a very well stocked, intriguing, enclosed garden with a windy path and surprises around every corner. wheelchair access to 80% of gardens.

&. ☕

16 BULLAND FARM

Ashburton, Newton Abbot, TQ13 7NG. S & L Middleton. *1m from A38. Exit A38 at Peartree Cross near Ashburton and follow signs directing towards Landscove. Turning R at top of hill, follow NGS signs From Totnes, NGS signs will direct you from A384.* **Sat 3, Sun 4 June (11-4). Adm £4, chd free. Home-made teas.**

Once an old cider orchard that had grown wild, over the last 6 years it has been transformed into a beautiful and productive garden. Set over 8 acres, it makes the most of wonderful views over rolling rural countryside. Designed with wildlife in mind it encompasses formal areas, prairie planting, boardwalk water garden, woodland trail, wildflower meadows and terraced vegetable garden. Steps and steep slopes although the central path of the garden is suitable for wheelchairs which allows great views over the countryside and garden.

&. 🐑 ✿ ☕

GROUP OPENING

17 BURN VALLEY BUTTERLEIGH GARDENS

Butterleigh, Cullompton, EX15 1PG. *Between Tiverton & Cullompton, Follow signs for Silverton from Butterleigh village. Take L fork 100yds after entrance to Pound Farm. Car park sign on L after 150yds.* **Sun 4, Sun 25 June (2-5.30). Combined adm £5, chd free. Home-made teas. Shutelake has indoor tea room if weather inclement.**

HIGHER BURNHAIES
Richard & Virginia Holmes, 01884 855748.
Visits also by arrangement Mar to Oct - located down narrow lanes.

SHUTELAKE
Jill & Nigel Hall, 01884 38812, jill22hall@gmail.com.
Visits also by arrangement Apr to Sept, cars/minibus only.

Two contrasting neighbouring gardens, Burnhaies was winner of the Western Morning News Best South West Garden 2016. 2½-acre site started in 1997. Situated in the beautiful Burn Valley, a plantsman's garden of herbaceous plantings with trees, shrubs, ponds and wildlife. Informal, country feel with Devon lane and wilderness walk. Vegetable garden. Uneven ground and steps. Live music. Cross a bridge over a stream to Shutelake, a garden terraced into a hillside. Several levels blend a Mediterranean feel with natural local landscape. Redesigned and planted herbaceous borders for this year, ponds, lake, sculptures, woodland walk. New knot garden in the making. Rockery area. An oasis of calm with plenty of places to sit and relax. Uneven ground and steps in both gardens, not good for unsteady walkers.

✿ ☕

18 BURNBRIDGE COTTAGE

Cadeleigh, Tiverton, EX16 8RY. Kate Leevers & Martin Callaghan. *From A3072 1½m from Bickleigh bridge, 6½m from Crediton, follow lane behind Blue Cross centre for ¾m. On R after stone bridge. From Cadeleigh village take lane opp PH. On L at bottom of hill.* **Sat 22, Sun 23 July (2-5). Adm £4, chd free. Home-made cakes and cream teas. Gluten free available.**

Mature trees and shrubs provide the backdrop for this informal, secluded 1¼ acre garden. Reclaimed from long neglect and developed for diversity of planting and wildlife. Late summer flowerbeds attract bees and butterflies. Other moods and habitats created by copse, hedges, pond, bog garden and stream. Mini arboretum and hillside wood can also be visited. Sloping grass & main garden accessible by wheelchairs if dry.

&. 🐑 ✿ ☕

19 ◆ BURROW FARM GARDENS

Dalwood, Axminster, EX13 7ET. Mary & John Benger, 01404 831285, enquiries@burrowfarmgardens.co.uk, www.burrowfarmgardens.co.uk. *3½m W of Axminster. From A35*

turn N at Taunton Xrds then follow brown signs. **For opening times and information, please phone, email or visit garden website.**
Beautiful 13 acre garden with unusual trees, shrubs and herbaceous plants. Traditional summerhouse looks towards lake and ancient oak woodland with rhododendrons and azaleas. Early spring interest and superb autumn colour. The more formal Millennium garden features a rill. Anniversary garden featuring late summer perennials and grasses. A photographer's dream. Open 1 April – 31 Oct (10am – 6pm). Adm £7. Café and gift shop. Various events incl spring and summer plant fair and open air theatre held at garden each year. Visit events page on Burrow Farm Gardens website for more details. Featured in Period Ideas Magazine.

20 ◆ CADHAY
Ottery St Mary, EX11 1QT. Rupert Thistlethwayte, 01404 813511, jayne@cadhay.org.uk, www.cadhay.org.uk. *1m NW of Ottery St Mary. On B3176 between Ottery St Mary and Fairmile and follow signs for Cadhay. From E exit A30 at Iron Bridge. From W exit A30 at Patteson's Cross and follow brown signs for Cadhay.* **For NGS: Mon 29 May, Fri 16 June, Fri 21 July, Sun 27 Aug, Mon 28 Aug (2-5.30). Adm £4, chd free. Our tea room serves a range of home-made cakes and cream teas. For other opening times and information, please phone, email or visit garden website.**
Tranquil 2-acre setting for Elizabethan manor house. 2 medieval fish ponds surrounded by rhododendrons, gunnera, hostas and flag iris. Roses, clematis, lilies and hellebores surround walled water garden. 120ft herbaceous border walk informally planted with cottage garden perennials and annuals. Walled kitchen gardens have been turned into allotments and old apple store is now tea room. Featured in Country Life Magazine. Gravel paths.

Higher Cherubeer

© Dianna Jazwinski

21 CLEAVE HILL
Membury, Axminster,
EX13 7AJ. Andy & Penny
Pritchard, 01404 881437,
penny@tonybenger.com. *4m NW
of Axminster. From Membury Village,
follow rd down valley. 1st R after Lea
Hill B&B, last house on drive, approx
1m.* **Sat 1, Sun 2 July (11-5).
Adm £4, chd free. Light lunches,
cream teas and cakes. Visits
also by arrangement, coach
parking 1m.**
Artistic garden in pretty village
situated on edge of Blackdown Hills.
Cottage style garden, planted to
provide all season structure, texture
and colour. Designed around pretty
thatched house and old stone
barns. Wonderful views, attractive
vegetable garden and orchard, wild
flower meadow.

22 CLEAVE HOUSE
Sticklepath, EX20 2NL.
Tim & Ruth Penrose,
www.bowdenhostas.com. *3½m
E of Okehampton. Follow brown
tourist signs for Bowden Hostas. From
Okehampton, Cleave House is on L,
covered with Virginia Creeper.* **Sat
10, Sat 24 June, Sat 8, Sat 22
July (10-4). Adm £4, chd free.
Cream teas. Donation to NCCPG.**
The National Collection of Hostas
(Halcyon and sports) is housed in a
beautifully mature garden of about
½ acre, alongside many interesting
trees, shrubs and other plants.
The evolving stumpery provides a
focal point for ferns and tree ferns.
Hostas, ferns, tree ferns, bamboos
and also agapanthus for sale with
expert advice available. Tim and
Ruth Penrose acquired Bowdens
in 2004 from Ruth's parents. Since
then they have been awarded
a total of 30 RHS Gold Medals.
Garden audio guide. Treasure slug
hunt and craft activities for children.
BBC TV coverage of Chelsea Flower
Show display with Belmond British
Pullman carriage. Featured in Devon
Life, Daily Telegraph, Guardian,
Okehampton Times. Partial
wheelchair access.

GROUP OPENING

23 NEW CLYST ST LAWRENCE GARDENS
Clyst St. Lawrence, Cullompton,
EX15 2NJ. *From Talaton/Cullompton
follow signs to Clyst Hydon then
NGS signs. From Broadclyst/Whimple
follow signs to Clyst St Lawrence then
NGS signs.* **Sat 24, Sun 25 June
(2-5). Combined adm £4, chd
free. Cream teas, home-made
teas at Scorlinch Farm.**

NEW LITTLE ORCHARD HOUSE
Joy & Robert Bagwell.

NEW SCORLINCH FARM
David & Hannah Foster.

Little Orchard House: Situated at
end of farm track approx ½ acre
garden with lovely views over
Devon countryside. Colourful mixed
herbaceous borders, roses, wild
flower garden, pond, vegetable plots.
Special apple tree from 50's cider
orchard, tree house and model farm.
Scorlinch Farm: C16 Devon long
house, recently refurbished. Garden is
work in progress, with pontoon and
decking area, herbaceous beds and
mixed raised bed. Gravel path. Guinea
fowl and chickens roam freely. Beside
the garden is a riverside and willow
walk, the willow being grown to help
run a biomass burner that heats the
farmhouse. Limited wheelchair access.

24 THE CROFT
Yarnscombe, Barnstaple,
EX31 3LW. Sam & Margaret Jewell,
01769 560535. *8m S of Barnstaple,
10m SE of Bideford, 12m W of
South Molton, 4m NE of Torrington.
From A377, turn W opp Chapelton
railway stn. Follow Yarnscombe signs,
after 3m. From B3232, ¼m N of
Huntshaw Cross TV mast, turn E
and follow Yarnscombe signs for 2m.
Parking in village hall car park.* **Sun
18 June, Sun 16 July, Sun 20 Aug
(2-6). Adm £4, chd free. Cream
teas. Visits also by arrangement
June to Aug, min 3 days notice
required. Donation to N Devon
Animal Ambulance.**

1-acre plantswoman's garden
featuring exotic Japanese garden
with tea house, koi carp pond and
cascading stream, tropical garden
with exotic shrubs and perennials,
herbaceous borders with unusual
plants and shrubs, bog garden with
collection of irises, astilbes and
moisture loving plants, duck pond.
Exotic borders, new beds around
duck pond and bog area, large
collection of rare and unusual plants.

25 DICOT
Chardstock, EX13 7DF. Mr & Mrs
F Clarkson, www.dicot.co.uk. *5m
N of Axminster. Axminster to Chard
A358 at Tytherleigh to Chardstock.
R at George Inn, L fork to Hook, R
to Burridge, 2nd house on L.* **Sat
29, Sun 30 Apr, Mon 1 May, Sat
10, Sun 11 June, Sat 29, Sun 30
July (2-5.30). Adm £4, chd free.
Cream teas.**
Secret garden hidden in East Devon
valley. 3 acres of unusual and exotic
plants - some rare. Rhododendrons,
azaleas and camellias in profusion.
Meandering stream, fish pool,
Japanese style garden and interesting
vegetable garden with fruit cage,
tunnel and greenhouses. Surprises
round every corner. Partial
wheelchair access.

26 ◆ DOCTON MILL
Lymebridge, Hartland,
EX39 6EA. Lana & John Borrett,
01237 441369,
docton.mill@btconnect.com,
www.doctonmill.co.uk. *8m W of
Clovelly. Follow brown tourist signs
on A39 nr Clovelly.* **For NGS: Sun
11 June (10-5). Adm £4.50, chd
free. Light refreshments. Cream
teas and light lunches available
all day. For other opening times
and information, please phone,
email or visit garden website.**
Situated in stunning valley location.
Garden surrounds original mill pond
and the microclimate created within
the wooded valley enables tender
species to flourish. Recent planting
of herbaceous, stream and summer
garden give variety through the
season. Not suitable for wheelchairs.

27 NEW DORWEEKE

Silverton, Exeter, EX5 4BZ. Helen & Paul Cooper. *From Exeter take the A396 towards Tiverton. Take R turn signed Butterleigh. Property approx 1½m up rd on R.* Sat 27, Sun 28 May (11-5.30). Adm £4, chd free. Light refreshments.
2 acre garden nestling in valley beside stream and surrounding thatched Devon longhouse. Developed over 45 years from original small holding. Many areas, incl koi, lily and natural ponds, bog area and vegetable garden. The natural planting includes mature trees and shrubs with many rhododendrons and azaleas to provide all yr round colour. A wildlife haven.

🐈 🚜 ✤ ☕

28 NEW DUNLEY HOUSE

Bovey Tracey, Newton Abbot, TQ13 9PW. Mr & Mrs F Gilbert. *2m E of Bovey Tracey on rd to Hennock. From A38 going W turn off slip rd R towards Chudleigh Knighton on B3344, in village follow yellow signs to Dunley House. From A38 eastwards turn off on Chudleigh K slip road L and follow signs.* Sat 17, Sun 18 June (2-5). Adm £4, chd free. Home-made teas.
9 acre garden set among mature oaks, sequoiadendrons and a huge liquidambar started from a wilderness in the mid eighties. Rhododendrons, camellias and over 40 species of magnolia. Arboretum, walled garden with borders and fruit and vegetables, rose garden and new enclosed garden with lily pond. Large pond renovated 2016 with new plantings. Woodland walk around perimeter of property.

🕭 🐈 🚜 ✤ ☕

29 EAST WORLINGTON HOUSE

East Worlington, Witheridge, Crediton, EX17 4TS. Mr & Mrs Barnabas Hurst-Bannister. *In centre of East Worlington, 2m W of Witheridge. From Witheridge Square R to East Worlington. After 1½m R at T-junction in Drayford, over bridge then L to Worlington. After ⅓m L at T-junction. Garden 200 yds on L. Parking nearby, disabled parking at house.* Sun 5, Sun 12 Mar (1.30-5). Adm £4, chd free. Cream teas in thatched parish hall next to house.
Thousands of crocuses. In 2 acre garden, set in lovely position with views down valley to Little Dart river, these spectacular crocuses have spread over many years through the garden and into the neighbouring churchyard. Cream teas in the parish hall (in aid of its modernisation fund) next door. Dogs on leads please.

🕭 🐈 ✤ ☕

The National Garden Scheme is committed to helping unpaid carers

---

30 FOAMLEA

Chapel Hill, Mortehoe, EX34 7DZ. Beth Smith, 01271 871182, bethmortepoint@fmail.co.uk. *¼m S of Mortehoe village. A361 N from Barnstaple. L onto B3343 to Mortehoe car park. No parking at or near garden. On foot L past church, down hill, then 200yds.* Sun 21 May, Sun 25 June (2-5). Adm £3.50, chd free. Home-made teas. Visits also by arrangement May to Sept for individuals and groups up to 35.
Coastal garden with uninterrupted view of Morte Point (NT), brim full of unusual and familiar plants from around the world. Rockery, colour rooms, mixed beds and borders all linked by slate steps and shillet paths. Several changed plantings including two new borders. Herbaceous and shrub Phlomis (Jerusalem sage) occur throughout. Featured on Alan Titchmarsh Love Your Garden, ITV, and in numerous publications. Garden on gradient, narrow paths. Sorry, no dogs.

✤ 🚗 NPC ☕

31 ◆ FURSDON

Cadbury, Thorverton, Exeter, EX5 5JS. David & Catriona Fursdon, 01392 860860, admin@fursdon.co.uk, www.fursdon.co.uk. *2m N of Thorverton. From Tiverton S on A396. Take A3072 at Bickleigh towards Crediton. L after 2½m. From Exeter N on A396. L to Thorverton and R in centre.* For NGS: Sat 10, Sun 11 June, Sat 9, Sun 10 Sept (2-5). Adm £4.50, chd free. Cream teas in Coach Hall from 2pm, also home-made cakes. Proceeds not for NGS. For other opening times and information, please phone, email or visit garden website.
Garden surrounds Fursdon House, home of the same family for 7 centuries. Hillside setting with extensive views S over parkland and beyond. Sheltered by house, hedges and cob walls, there are terraces of roses, herbs and perennials in mixed traditional and contemporary planting. Woodland walk, seasonal wild flowers and pond in meadow garden. Fursdon House open for guided tours on NGS days (separate entrance fee not for NGS). Parts of garden and estate featured on BBC Gardeners' World. Some steep slopes, grass and gravel paths.

🕭 🐈 🛏 ☕

32 THE GATE HOUSE

Lee, EX34 8LR. Mrs H Booker, 01271 862409. *3m W of Ilfracombe. Park in Lee village car park. Take lane alongside The Grampus PH. Garden approx 30 metres past inn buildings. Open most days but wise to check by phoning between 7pm & 9pm.* Daily Sat 20 May to Sun 10 Sept (10-3). Adm by donation. Visits also by arrangement May to Aug.
Described by many visitors as a peaceful paradise, this streamside garden incl collection of over 100 rodgersia (at their best end of June), interesting herbaceous areas, patio gardens with semi-hardy exotics, many unusual mature trees and shrubs and large organic vegetable garden. Level gravel paths.

🕭 🐈 ✤ NPC ☕

33 GOREN FARM

Broadhayes, Stockland,
Honiton, EX14 9EN.
Julian Pady, 07770 694646,
gorenfarm@hotmail.com,
www.goren.co.uk. *6m E of
Honiton, 6m W of Axminster. Go to
the Stockland television mast. 100
metres N signed from Ridge Cross.*
Evening openings Sat 3 June to
Sun 16 July (5-9). Sat 3, Sun 4,
Sat 10, Sun 11, Sat 17, Sun 18
June (10-5). Adm £3, chd free.
Teas and home-made cakes
with local produce from the
farm available. Cider, apple
Juice also available. Visits also
by arrangement June to Aug for
groups of 10+. Guided walk and
talk with teas can last 3 hrs.
Wander through 50 acres of natural
species rich wild flower meadows.
Dozens of varieties of wild flowers
and grasses. Orchids early June,
butterflies July. Stunning views of
Blackdown Hills. Georgian house
and walled gardens, guided walks
10.30 and 2.30 on open weekends,
and evenings. Picnic tables and BBQ
stations around the fields. Partial
wheelchair access to meadows.

点 🐐 ✿ ☕

34 GORWELL HOUSE

Goodleigh Rd, Barnstaple,
EX32 7JP. Dr J A Marston,
01271 323202,
artavianjohn@gmail.com,
www.gorwellhousegarden.co.uk.
*¾m E of Barnstaple centre on
Bratton Fleming rd. Drive entrance
between 2 lodges on L coming uphill
(Bear Street) from Barnstaple centre.*
Sun 26 Mar, Sun 30 Apr, Sun 21
May (2-6). Adm £4.50, chd free.
Cream teas by Goodleigh WI
Apr and May only. Visits also
by arrangement Mar to Sept,
groups of 10+ preferred.
Created mostly since 1979, this
4-acre garden overlooking the Taw
estuary has a benign microclimate
which allows many rare and tender
plants to grow and thrive, both
in the open and in walled garden.
Several strategically placed follies
complement the enclosures and
vistas within the garden. Opening in
March especially for the magnolias.
Featured in N Devon Journal, The
English Garden and Devon Life
magazines and on BBC Radio Devon.
Recently on web-based SW1TV
Summer Gardens. Mostly wheelchair
access but some steep slopes.

点 🐐 ✿ ☕

35 NEW ▶ GREATCOMBE

Holne, Newton Abbot, TQ13 7SP.
Sarah Richardson, 07725 314887,
sarah@greatcombe.com.
*Michelcombe, Holne, TQ13 7SP. 4m
NW Ashburton via Holne Bridge and
Holne Village. 4m NE Buckfastleigh via
Scorriton.* Sat 27, Sun 28, Mon 29
May, Sat 24, Sun 25 June, Sat 29,
Sun 30 July, Sat 26, Sun 27, Mon
28 Aug (1-5). Adm £3.50, chd

free. Home-made teas. Visits also
by arrangement Apr to Sept for
groups of 10+, teas on request.
Charming, tranquil garden nestled in
a valley on the southern slopes of
Dartmoor, intersected by a babbling
stream and featuring differing rooms
of planting schemes displaying
bright colours and textual foliage.
Gentle undulating paths and lawns
bordered by spring and summer
flowering shrubs, herbaceous
plants, ornamental grasses and
spectacular rambling roses. Artist's
Studio featuring brightly coloured
acrylic paintings, prints and cards all
available to purchase. Most areas are
accessible to wheelchairs.

点 🐐 ✿ ☕

36 HALDON GRANGE

Dunchideock, Exeter, EX6 7YE.
Ted Phythian, 01392 832349. *5m
SW of Exeter. From A30 through Ide
Village to Dunchideock 5m. Turn L
to Lord Haldon, Haldon Grange is
next L. From A38 (S) turn L on top
of Haldon Hill follow Dunchideock
signs, R at village centre to Lord
Haldon.* Sat 25, Sun 26 Mar, Sat
1, Sun 2, Sat 8, Sun 9, Sat 15,
Sun 16, Mon 17, Wed 19, Sat
22, Sun 23, Sat 29, Sun 30 Apr,
Mon 1, Sat 6, Sun 7, Wed 10,
Sat 13, Sun 14, Wed 17, Sat 20,
Sun 21, Sat 27, Sun 28, Mon 29
May (1-5). Adm £4.50, chd free.
Home-made teas. Visits also
by arrangement Mar to May
refreshments by arrangement
by phone or letter.
12 acre well established garden with
camellias, magnolias, azaleas, various
shrubs and rhododendrons; rare and
mature trees; small lake and ponds
with river and water cascades. 5 acre
arboretum planted 2011 with wide
range of trees, shrubs and a large
lilac circle. Additionally a wisteria
pergola with views over Exeter
and Woodbury. A Daily Telegraph
recommended garden. Wheelchair
access to main parts of garden.

点 ✿ ☕

37 HAMBLYN'S COOMBE

Dittisham, Dartmouth, TQ6 0HE.
Bridget McCrum, 01803 722228,
mccrum.sculpt@waitrose.com,
www.bridgetmccrum.com. *3m*

Abbotskerswell Gardens

N of Dartmouth. From A3122 L to Dittisham. In village R at Red Lion, The Level, then Rectory Lane, past River Farm to Hamblyn's Coombe. **Visits by arrangement, parking difficult for more than 20. Adm £5, chd free.**

7-acre garden with stunning views across the river to Greenway House and sloping steeply to R Dart at bottom of garden. Extensive planting of trees and shrubs with unusual design features accompanying Bridget McCrum's stone carvings and bronzes. Wild flower meadow and woods. Good rhododendrons and camellias, ferns and bamboos, acers and hydrangeas. Exceptional autumn colour. No wheelchair access.

HANGERIDGE FARMHOUSE
See Somerset, Bristol & South Gloucestershire

38 HARBOUR LIGHTS
Horns Cross, Bideford, EX39 5DW. Brian & Faith Butler. *7m W of Bideford, 3m E of Clovelly. On main A39 between Bideford and Clovelly, halfway between Hoops Inn and Bucks Cross.* **Sat 24, Sun 25 June (11-6). Adm £3.50, chd free. Home-made teas. Light lunches, home made cakes and cream teas, or perhaps a glass of wine.** ½ acre colourful garden with Lundy views. A garden of wit, humour, unusual ideas and surprises - including a volcano. Water features, shrubs, foliage area, grasses in an unusual setting, fernery, bonsai and polytunnel, time saving ideas. You will never have seen a garden like this! Superb conservatory for cream teas. Free leaflet. We like our visitors to leave with a smile! Child friendly. A 'must visit' garden. Intriguing artwork of various kinds.

HARCOMBE HOUSE
See Dorset

39 THE HAVEN
Wembury Road, Hollacombe, Wembury, South Hams, PL9 0DQ. Mrs S Norton & Mr J Norton, 01752 862149,

suenorton1@hotmail.co.uk. *20mins from Plymouth city centre. Use A379 Plymouth to Kingsbridge Rd. At Elburton r'about follow signs to Wembury. Parking on roadside. Bus stop nearby on Wembury Rd. Route 48 from Plymouth.* **Sat 1, Sun 2 Apr (12-5). Adm £3.50, chd free. Cream teas. Visits also by arrangement Apr to Sept.** ½-acre sloping plantsman's garden in the South Hams AONB. Tearoom and seating areas. 2 ponds. Substantial collection of large flowering Asiatic and hybrid tree magnolias. Large collection of camellias including camellia reticulata. Rare dwarf, weeping and slow growing conifers. Daphnes, early azaleas and rhododendrons, spring bulbs and hellebores. Magnolias, camellias. Wheelchair access to top part of garden.

40 NEW HAWKERN
Ladram Road, Otterton, Budleigh Salterton, EX9 7HT. Tony Mills, 01395 567304, clairemills2@hotmail.co.uk. *Once in Otterton, follow signs to Ladram Bay by turning into Bell St. At top of hill, just past unrestricted speed signs Hawkern is on L opp last lamp post.* **Fri 19 May (2-5); Sun 21 May, Fri 16 June (1.30-5). Adm £5, chd free. Home-made teas. Visits also by arrangement May to Sept for groups 15+.** The gardens, first planted in the 20s, are set in approx 3½ acres. Glorious panoramic views from Peak Hill round to Bicton and towards E Devon. 4 distinct planting areas with extensive mature trees, camellias, rhododendrons and a stump garden clothed in roses and underplanted with hostas and ferns together with a superb range of perennials in varied plantings.

41 HAYNE
Zeal Monachorum, Crediton, EX17 6DE. Tim & Milla Herniman, 01363 82515, www.haynedevon.co.uk. *Located ½m S of Zeal Monachorum. From Zeal Monachorum, keeping church on L, drive through village. Continue*

on this road for ⅓m, garden drive is 1st entrance on R. **Sun 11 June, Sun 23 July (2-6). Adm £4, chd free. Home-made teas. Visits also by arrangement May to Sept weekday evenings.**

Hayne has a magical walled garden brimming with mature trees, shrubs, roses and borders. Highlights incl beautiful tree peonies, mature wisteria in both purple and white and rambling wild roses in combination with a more modern Piet Oudolf style perennial planting which surrounds the recently renovated grade II* farm buildings ... magic, mystery and soul by the spadeful! Live jazz band. Evening by arrangement visits in the bewitching early evening light .... the magic starts to happen with a cocktail in hand! Disabled WC. Wheelchair access to walled garden through orchard.

42 HEATHERCOMBE
Manaton, Nr Bovey Tracey, TQ13 9XE. Claude & Margaret Pike Woodlands Trust, 01626 354404, gardens@pike.me.uk, www.heathercombe.com. *7m NW of Bovey Tracey. From Bovey Tracey take scenic B3387 to Haytor/ Widecombe. 1.7m past Haytor Rocks (before Widecombe hill) turn R to Hound Tor and Manaton. 1.4m past Hound Tor turn L at Heatree Cross to Heathercombe.* **Sun 2 Apr, Sun 14, Sun 21, Sat 27, Sun 28 May, Sun 4, Sun 18, Sun 25 June (1.30-5.30). Adm £5, chd free. Cream teas in pretty cottage garden or conservatory if wet. Visits also by arrangement Apr to Oct.** *Donation to Rowcroft Hospice.* Discover our secluded valley with streams tumbling through woods, ponds and lake (with new features): peaceful setting for 30 acres of spring/summer interest - daffodils, extensive bluebells complementing large displays of rhododendrons, pretty cottage gardens, woodland walks, many specimen trees, bog/ fern gardens, orchard and wild flower meadow, sculptures. Seats. 2m mainly level sandy paths. Featured on BBC Countryfile.

43 HIGH GARDEN

Chiverstone Lane, Kenton,
EX6 8NJ. Chris & Sharon Britton,
www.highgardennurserykenton.
wordpress.com. *5m S of Exeter on
A379 Dawlish Rd. Leaving Kenton
towards Exeter, L into Chiverstone
Lane, 50yds along lane. Entrance
clearly marked at High Garden
Nurseries. Phone for directions.*
**Every Tue to Fri 10 Jan to 15
Dec (9-5). Adm £3.50, chd free.
Light refreshments.** *Donation to
Hospiscare and FORCE cancer care
charities.*
Very interesting and wide ranging
planting of trees, shrubs, climbers
and perennials in relaxed but still
controlled 11 yr old garden. 70 metre
summer herbaceous border, colour-
themed beds, grass walkways with
surprises around each corner. Always
something to enjoy incl winter garden,
tropical jungle and seasonal planting.
Self-service tea room open March
to November. Garden attached to
plantsman's nursery, open at same
time. Slightly sloping site but the few
steps can be avoided.

44 HIGHER ASH FARM

Ash, Dartmouth, TQ6 0LR.
Mr Michael Gribbin & Mrs
Jennifer Barwell, 07595 507516,
matthew.perkins18@yahoo.co.uk,
www.higherashfarm.com. *Leave
A381 at Halwell for Dartmouth A3122.
Turn R before Sportsman's Arms to
Bugford. At T-junction go R then next L.
After 1½m at Xrds go R, Higher Ash
Farm entrance is 1st L.* **Sun 7, Sun 14
May (2-5); Sun 8 Oct (1.30-4.30).
Adm £5, chd free. Tea. Opening
with Ash Gardens on Sat 24,
Sun 25 June, Sat 12, Sun 13 Aug.
Visits also by arrangement Mar
to Oct for 1-15.**
Evolving garden, high up in South
Devon countryside. Sitting in 2½
acres there is a large kitchen garden
terraced into the hillside with
adjoining orchard underplanted
with a variety of daffodils. Vibrant
array of azaleas and rhododendrons
surround the barns and courtyard.
Farmhouse is surrounded by a mix
of herbaceous borders, shrubs and
lawns. Pond, stream, autumn interest.

45 HIGHER CHERUBEER

Dolton, Winkleigh, EX19 8PP.
Jo & Tom Hynes, 01805 804265,
hynesjo@gmail.com,
www.sites.google.com/site/
cherubeergardens/the-gardens.
*2m E of Dolton. From A3124 turn S
towards Stafford Moor Fisheries, take
1st R, garden 500m on L.* **Fri 10,
Fri 17, Sun 26 Feb (2-5); Sun 4
June (2.30-6). Adm £4, chd free.
Home-made teas. 2018: Fri 9,
Fri 16, Sun 25 Feb. Visits also
by arrangement Feb to Oct for
groups of 10+.**
1½-acre country garden with
gravelled courtyard, raised beds
and alpine house, lawns, large
herbaceous border, shady woodland
beds, large kitchen garden,
greenhouse, colourful collection of
basketry willows. Winter opening
for National Collection of cyclamen,
hellebores and over 300 snowdrop
varieties. Feature article in The
Cyclamen Society Journal. Main
areas wheelchair accessible. Steps
and gravel paths limit some areas.

46 HIGHER CULLAFORD

Spreyton, Crediton, EX17 5AX. Dr
& Mrs Kennerley, 01837 840974,
kenntoad@yahoo.com. *Approx
¾m from centre of Spreyton, 20m W
of Exeter, 10 E of Okehampton. From
A30 at Whiddon Down follow signs
to Spreyton. Yellow signs from A3124,
centre of village and Spreyton parish
church.* **Visits by arrangement
May to Oct. See website for
additional 'pop-up' openings.
Adm £3.50, chd free. Cream
teas.**
Traditional cottage style garden
developed over past 12yrs from
steep field and farmyard on
northern edge of Dartmoor
National Park. Mixed borders
of herbaceous plants, roses and
shrubs. 30ft pergola covered with
seagull rose and many varieties
of clematis. Wildlife pond. Newly
planted pleached hornbeam hedge.
Additional vegetable garden with
polytunnel and fruit cage and fruit
trees. Wheelchair access limited but
can drive in to garden on request.

47 NEW HIGHER ORCHARD COTTAGE

Aptor, Marldon, Paignton,
TQ3 1SQ. Mrs Jenny Saunders.
*1m SW of Marldon. A380 Torquay
to Paignton. At Churscombe Cross
r'about R for Marldon, L onto rd
to Berry Pomeroy, take 1st R into
Farthing Lane. Follow for 1m. Turn R
for Aptor at Garden Open sign.* **Sat
17, Sun 18 June (2-5). Adm £4,
chd free.**
Set in a secluded rural area, this
sloping 2 acre garden has abundant
colour themed herbaceous borders.
Large wildlife pond, productive
raised vegetable beds, grass path
walks through wild flower meadow
areas and lovely countryside views.

48 ◆ HOLBROOK GARDEN

Sampford Shrubs, Sampford
Peverell, EX16 7EN. Martin
Hughes-Jones & Susan Proud,
01884 821164,
www.holbrookgarden.com. *1m
NW from M5 J27. From M5 J27
follow signs to Tiverton Parkway. At
top of slip rd off A361 follow brown
sign to Holbrook Garden, 1m from
J27.* **For NGS: Fri 7, Sat 8 Apr;
Fri, Sat, Sun 14, 15, 16, 28, 29,
30 Apr, 19, 20, 21 May, 16, 17,
18 June, 14, 15, 16 July, 25, 26,
27 Aug (10-5). Adm £4, chd
free. Light refreshments. Self
serve tea and coffee, home-
made biscuits. For other opening
times and information, please
phone or visit garden website.**
2 acre garden, 35 yrs in the making.
S-facing with diverse habitats and
inspired by nature. Wet garden,
stone garden, pink garden and
woodland glades. Perfumes,
songbirds and nests are everywhere
in spring and early summer.
Anemones, tulips and fritillaries in
April; roses and geraniums in June;
crocosmia, salvias and rudbeckias
in summer. Productive vegetable
garden and polytunnel. Coach
parties by arrangement, please
phone or see holbrookgarden.com.
Donation to MSF UK (Medecin sans
Frontieres). Narrow paths restrict
access for wheelchairs and buggies.

49 HOLE FARM

Woolsery, Bideford, EX39 5RF.
Heather Alford. *11m SW of
Bideford. Follow directions for
Woolfardisworthy, signed from A39 at
Bucks Cross. From village follow NGS
signs from school for approx 2m.* **Sun
11 June, Sun 16 July (2-6). Adm
£4, chd free. Home-made teas
in converted barn.**
3 acres of exciting gardens with
established waterfall, ponds,
vegetable and bog garden. Terraces
and features incl round house have
all been created using natural stone
from original farm quarry. Peaceful
walks through Culm grassland and
water meadows border R Torridge
and host a range of wildlife. Home
to a herd of pedigree native Devon
cattle. Riverside walk not wheelchair
accessible.
&. ✿ ☕ ♥

50 HOLE'S MEADOW

Holes Meadow, South Zeal,
Okehampton, EX20 2JS. Fi & Paul
Reddaway, fireddaway@gmail.com,
https://herbsindartmoor.com.
*4½m from Okehampton on B3260,
4m from Whiddon Down. Signed
from main street when open. Half
way between the King's Arms and
Oxenham Arms and opp village hall.
A minute's fairly level walk along
private path.* **Sat 22, Sun 23, Sun
30 July (11-5). Adm £4, chd free.
Home-made teas. Visits also by
arrangement June & July.**
Situated within 2 acre medieval
burgage plot at the foot of
Dartmoor's Cawsand Beacon.
Featuring 2 Plant Heritage National
Plant Collections of around 100
forms each of both Monarda
(bergamot, bee balm) and Nepeta
(catmint). Complemented by
over 250 herbs, cutting flowers,
vegetables, orchard, ornamental and
coppicing trees.
✿ ✿ NPC ☕

51 ◆ HOTEL ENDSLEIGH

Milton Abbot, Tavistock, PL19 0PQ.
Olga Polizzi, 01822 870000,
mail@hotelendsleigh.com,
www.hotelendsleigh.com/garden.
*7m NW of Tavistock, midway between
Tavistock and Launceston. From
Tavistock, take B3362 to Launceston.*
*7m to Milton Abbot then 1st L, opp
school. From Launceston & A30,
B3362 to Tavistock. At Milton Abbot
turn R opp school.* **For NGS: Sun
21 May, Sun 9 July (11-4). Adm
£5, chd free. Light refreshments
at the hotel only which tends
to be busy so please pre-book
lunch/afternoon tea/dinner
beforehand. For other opening
times and information, please
phone, email or visit garden
website.**
200 year old Repton-designed
garden in 3 parts; formal gardens
around the house, picturesque dell
with pleasure dairy and rockery
and arboretum. Gardens were laid
out in 1814 and have been carefully
renovated over last 10yrs. Bordering
the R Tamar, it is a hidden oasis of
plants and views. Hotel was built
in 1810 by Sir Jeffry Wyattville for
the 6th Duchess of Bedford in the
romantic cottage Orne style. Plant
Nursery adjoins hotel's 108 acres.
Partial wheelchair access.
✿ 🚗 🛏 ☕

GROUP OPENING

52 NEW KENTISBURY GARDENS

Kentisbury, Barnstaple, EX31 4NT.
*From Barnstaple follow A39 to
Lynton. L at Kentisbury Ford, follow
B3229 for about 2m, Little Ley on L.
From S Molton follow A399, then L at
Easter Cross Close onto B3229 then
R.* **Sun 25 June (12-5). Combined
adm £5, chd free. Cream teas at
Beachborough Country House.
Cream teas and homemade
cakes provided by Kentisbury
WI.**

NEW BEACHBOROUGH COUNTRY HOUSE

Viviane Clout, 01271 882487,
viviane@beachboroughcountry
house.co.uk,
www.beachboroughcountry
house.co.uk.
🛏

NEW LITTLE LEY

Jerry & Jenny Burnett.

NEW SPRING COTTAGE

Nerys Cadvan-Jones.

Kentisbury is situated high in the
North Devon countryside a few
miles inland from the dramatic
coastline and bordering Exmoor
National Park. These 3 gardens
make good use of the landscape
and views, providing a variety
of planting and garden habitats.
Beachborough Country House is
a garden created from an artist's
perspective and home to hundreds
of roses. Interest incl herbaceous
borders, lawns, stream, pond and
large ornamental kitchen garden.
Little Ley is a large country garden
with pond, stream, mature trees and
shrubs, perennial flower and shrub
beds, plus wildlife areas. Productive
fruit and vegetable area. Early
spring interest and superb autumn
colour. Spring Cottage is a pretty
cottage garden with colourful flower
borders, shrubs, climbers and small
trees giving yr round interest. Devon
banks, a stream and stone walls
afford varying views and conditions
for planting and the growing
collection of hardy geraniums.
✿ ✿ ☕

---

53 KIA-ORA FARM & GARDENS

Knowle Lane, Cullompton,
EX15 1PZ. Mrs M B Disney,
www.kia-orafarm.co.uk. *On W
side of Cullompton and 6m SE of
Tiverton. M5 J28, through town centre
to r'about, 3rd exit R, top of Swallow
Way turn L into Knowle Lane, garden
beside Cullompton Rugby Club.* **Sun
16, Mon 17, Sun 30 Apr, Mon
1, Sun 14, Sun 28, Mon 29 May,
Suns 11, 25 June, 9, 23 July, 6,
20, 27 Aug, Mon 28 Aug, Sun 10
Sept (2-5.30). Adm £3, chd free.
Home-made teas. Teas and sales
not for NGS charities.**
Charming, peaceful 10 acre garden
with lawns, lakes and ponds. Water
features with swans, ducks and
other wildlife. Mature trees, shrubs,
rhododendrons, azaleas, heathers,
roses, herbaceous borders and
rockeries. Nursery avenue, novelty
crazy golf. Lots to see and enjoy.
&. 🚗 ☕

GROUP OPENING

54 KILMINGTON (SHUTE ROAD) GARDENS

Kilmington, Axminster, EX13 7ST. www.Kilmingtonvillage.com. 1½m W of Axminster. Signed off A35. **Sat 17, Sun 18 June (1.30-5). Combined adm £5, chd free. Home-made teas at Breach.**

BREACH
J A Chapman & B J Lewis.
SPINNEY TWO
Paul & Celia Dunsford.

Set in rural E Devon in AONB yet easily accessed from A35. 2 gardens ¼m apart. Spinney Two: ½ acre garden planted for yr-round colour, foliage and texture. Mature oaks and beech. Views. On gentle southerly slope. Spring bulbs, hellebores and shrubs incl azaleas, camellias, cornus, pieris, skimmias, viburnhams. Roses, acers, flowering trees, clematis and other climbers. Mixed borders and vegetable patch. Breach: set in over 3 acres with majestic woodland partially underplanted with rhododendrons and hydrangeas; shrubberies, areas of grass, colourful mixed border, vegetable garden, small orchard and ponds. Bog garden developed over last 5yrs using natural springs in garden.
🚻 🐄 ✿ ☕

55 LEE FORD

Knowle Village, Budleigh Salterton, EX9 7AJ. Mr & Mrs N Lindsay-Fynn, 01395 445894, crescent@leeford.co.uk, http://leeford.co.uk/. 3½m E of Exmouth. For SatNav use postcode EX9 6AL. **Visits by arrangement Apr to Sept, groups of 20+ discount, adm £5. Refreshments for groups of 10+, coffee/tea & cake, cream teas. Adm £6, chd free. Numbers and special dietary requests must be pre-booked.** Donation to Lindsay-Fynn Trust.
Extensive, formal and woodland garden, largely developed in 1950s, but recently much extended with mass displays of camellias, rhododendrons and azaleas, incl

many rare varieties. Traditional walled garden filled with fruit and vegetables, herb garden, bog garden, rose garden, hydrangea collection, greenhouses. Ornamental conservatory with collection of pot plants. Lee Ford has direct access to the Pedestrian route and National Cycle Network route 2 which follows the old railway line that linked Exmouth to Budleigh Salterton. Garden is ideal destination for cycle clubs or rambling groups. Formal gardens are lawn with gravel paths. Moderately steep slope to woodland garden on tarmac with gravel paths in woodland.
🚻 ☕ 🐾

56 LEWIS COTTAGE

Spreyton, nr Crediton, EX17 5AA. Mr & Mrs M Pell and Mr R Orton, 07773 785939, rworton@mac.com, www.lewiscottageplants.co.uk. 5m NE of Spreyton, 8m W of Crediton. From Hillerton Cross, keep Stone Cross to your R. Drive approx 1½m, Lewis Cottage on L, proceed across cattle grid down farm track. From Crediton follow A377 to Barnstaple for 1m turn L at NGS sign. **Sat 27, Sun 28, Mon 29 May, Sat 24, Sun 25 June, Sat 22, Sun 23 July, Sat 19, Sun 20 Aug (11-5). Adm £4.50, chd free. Home-made teas. Visits also by arrangement May to Sept for groups of 20 max.**
Located on SW-facing slope in rural Mid Devon, the 4 acre garden at Lewis Cottage has evolved primarily over the last 25 yrs, harnessing and working with the natural landscape. Using informal planting and natural formal structures to create a garden that reflects the souls of those who garden in it, it is an incredibly personal space that is a joy to share. Spring camassia cricket pitch, newly planted rose garden, large dew pond, woodland walks, bog garden, hornbeam rondel planted with late flowering narcissi, newly planted winter garden, hot & cool herbaceous borders, picking garden and outdoor poetry reading room. Featured on Radio Devon. Wheelchairs/motorised buggies not advised due to garden being on a slope (though many have successfully tried!).
🐾 ✿ ☕

57 LITTLE ASH BUNGALOW

Fenny Bridges, Honiton, EX14 3BL. Helen & Brian Brown, 01404 850941, helenlittleash@hotmail.com, www. facebook.com/littleashgarden. 3m W of Honiton. Leave A30 at Iron Bridge from Honiton 1m, Patteson's Cross from Exeter ½m and follow NGS signs. **Sun 4 June, Sun 20 Aug (12-5). Adm £4, chd free. Home-made teas. Visits also by arrangement June to Sept for groups of 10+.**
Country garden of 1½ acres, packed with different and unusual herbaceous perennials, trees, shrubs and bamboos. Designed for yr-round interest, wildlife and owners' pleasure. Inspirational naturalistic planting in voluptuous, colour coordinated mixed borders provides a backdrop to the view. Natural stream, pond and damp woodland area, mini wildlife meadows and raised gravel/ alpine garden. Grass paths.
🚻 🐄 ✿ 🚗 ☕

58 LITTLE WEBBERY

Webbery, Bideford, EX39 4PS. Mr & Mrs J A Yewdall, 01271 858206, jyewdall1@gmail.com. 2m E of Bideford. From Bideford (East the Water) along Alverdiscott Rd, or from Barnstaple to Torrington on B3232. Take rd to Bideford at Alverdiscott, pass through Stoney Cross. **Visits by arrangement May to Sept. Adm £4, chd free. Home-made teas.**
Approx 3 acres in valley setting with pond, lake, mature trees, 2 ha-has and large mature raised border. Large walled kitchen garden with yew and box hedging incl rose garden, lawns with shrubs and rose and clematis trellises. Vegetables and greenhouse and adj traditional cottage garden. Partial wheelchair access.
🚻 ☕

59 THE LOOKOUT

Sowden Lane, Lympstone,
EX8 5HE. Will & Jackie
Michelmore, www.lympstone.org/
businesses/lookout-landscapes/.
*9m SE of Exeter, 2m N of Exmouth
off A376. 12mins from M5. Follow
signs off A376 to Exmouth, next R
after marine camp.* **Fri 2 June (2-
5); Sun 4 June (2-6). Adm £4.50,
chd free. Cream teas. Coffees,
cakes & soft drinks available.**
No 2 in Alan Titchmarsh's top 10
'most challenging gardens' featured
in his Britain's Best Back Gardens
series, this wildlife-friendly 2 acres
sits with its toes in the Exe Estuary.
Lovingly created from a derelict site
to harmonise with its coastal location
and maximise on far reaching views.
Flotsam and jetsam sit amongst
naturalistic seaside planting to give that
washed up on the beach look. Giant
sandpit with buckets and spades for
children. Photographic display showing
how the site has evolved from 1920's
to present day. Love-Local pop up
shop featuring nautically inspired
West Country craft and gifts. Limited
wheelchair access to lower garden,
some gravel paths, steps and slopes.
Drop off area at gate. Good level
access to stalls and refreshments.

♿ ✿ ⛳

60 LOWER SPITCHWICK GARDEN

Poundsgate, TQ13 7NU.
Pauline Lee, 01364 631593,
paulineleeceramics@hotmail.com.
*4m NW of Ashburton. By Spitchwick
Common, nr New Bridge, Dartmoor.*
**Sat 29, Sun 30 July (1-5). Adm
£4, chd free. Light refreshments.
Visits also by arrangement June
to Sept.**
Beautiful valley alongside R Dart. East
Lower Lodge: atmospheric woodland
garden with imaginative planting in
natural setting. Contains jungle area
with bamboo teahouse, meandering
grass pathways, lawns, borders with
stream, potager and vegetable garden.
Artist/designer's gallery garden
showing plant inspired sculpture
placed in and amongst plantings to
create a symphony of forms, colour
and texture. Visitors can buy or
commission directly from the artist.

🐕 ✿ ⛳

Lewis Cottage

61 ♦ LUKESLAND

Harford, Ivybridge, PL21 0JF.
Mrs R Howell & Mr & Mrs
J Howell, 01752 691749,
lorna.lukesland@gmail.com,
www.lukesland.co.uk. *10m E of
Plymouth. Turn off A38 at Ivybridge.
1½m N on Harford rd, E side of
Erme valley.* **For opening times and
information, please phone, email or
visit garden website.**
24 acres of flowering shrubs,
wild flowers and rare trees with
pinetum in Dartmoor National
Park. Beautiful setting of small valley
around Addicombe Brook with
lakes, numerous waterfalls and pools.
Extensive and impressive collections
of camellias, rhododendrons, azaleas
and acers; also spectacular Magnolia
campbellii and huge Davidia
involucrata. Superb spring and
autumn colour. Children's trail. Open
Suns, Weds and BH (11-5) 26 March
- 11 June and 8 Oct - 12 November.
Adm £5, chd free. Featured in RHS
The Garden. Partial wheelchair
access incl tearoom and WC.

🐕 ✿ 🚗 ⛳

62 ♦ MARWOOD HILL GARDEN

Marwood, EX31 4EB. Dr J
A Snowdon, 01271 342528,
info@marwoodhillgarden.co.uk,
www.marwoodhillgarden.co.uk.
*4m N of Barnstaple. Signed from
A361 & B3230. Look out for brown
signs. See website for map. New
coach & car park.* **For NGS: Fri
16 June (10-4.30). Adm £6,
chd free. Light refreshments.
For other opening times and
information, please phone, email or
visit garden website.**
Marwood Hill is a very special
private garden covering an area of
20 acres with lakes and set in a valley
tucked away in N Devon. From early
spring snowdrops through to late
autumn there is always a colourful
surprise around every turn. National
Collections of astilbe, iris ensata and
tulbaghia, large collections of camellia,
rhododendron and magnolia. Winner
of MacLaren Cup at rhododendron
and camellia show RHS Rosemoor.
Partial wheelchair access.

♿ 🐕 ✿ 🚗 NPC ⛳

63 THE MILL HOUSE

Fremington, Barnstaple, EX31 3DQ. Martin & Judy Ash, 01271 344719, martin_s_ash@yahoo.co.uk. *3m W of Barnstaple. Off A39, take A3125 N. At 3rd r'about (Cedars) L on B3233. In Fremington L at top of Church Hill onto Higher Rd. All parking signed 100m away.* **Sat 24 June (1-5). Home-made teas. Sun 25 June (1-5). Light refreshments. Adm £4, chd free. Visits also by arrangement May to Sept any number less than 25.**
¾ acre garden, surrounding thatched mill house and bordered by Fremington water; the topography is the first wow factor here. Stepped ups and downs, ins and outs, surprises around every corner. There is so much on a small scale; bridges, borders, ponds, walkways, rockery, terracing, lawns, bog garden, quarry garden, wild garden, a small gallery, oh and a henge. Wandering minstrels!

64 NEW MONKSCROFT

Zeal Monachorum, Crediton, EX17 6DG. Mr & Mrs Ken and Jane Hogg. *Lane opp Church.* **Sat 8, Sun 9 Apr (11-5). Adm £3.50, chd free. Cream teas.**
Pretty, medium sized garden of oldest cottage in village. Packed with spring colours, primroses, primulas, daffodils, tulips, magnolias and camellias. Views to far hills. Also tranquil fishing lake with daffodils and wild flowers in beautiful setting, home to resident kingfisher. Steep walk to lake approx 20mins, or 5mins by car. Dogs on leads welcome. Parking and toilet at lake.
🐕 ✿ ☕ 🏆

GROUP OPENING

65 MORETONHAMPSTEAD GARDENS

Moretonhampstead, TQ13 8PW. *12m W of Exeter & N of Newton Abbot. On E slopes of Dartmoor National Park. Parking at both gardens.* **Fri 19, Sat 20, Sun 21 May, Sat 5, Sun 6 Aug (2-6).**

Combined adm £5, chd free. Home-made teas.

MARDON
Graham & Mary Wilson.

SUTTON MEAD
Edward & Miranda Allhusen, 01647 440296, miranda@allhusen.co.uk. **Visits also by arrangement Apr to Sept, coach possible but 100yd walk from main road.**

2 large gardens close to moorland town. One in a wooded valley, the other higher up with magnificent views of Dartmoor. Dogs on leads welcome. Plant sale, teas are a must. Both have mature orchards and yr round vegetable gardens. Substantial rhododendron, azalea and tree planting, croquet lawns, summer colour and woodland walks through hydrangeas and acers. Something for all the family. Mardon: 4 acres based on its original Edwardian design. Long herbaceous border, rose garden and formal granite terraces supporting 2 borders of agapanthus. Fernery beside stream-fed pond with its thatched boathouse. New arboretum with 60 specimen trees. Sutton Mead: Paths wander through tranquil woodland, unusual planting. Lawns surrounding granite-lined pond with seat at water's edge. Elsewhere dahlias, grasses, bog garden, rill-fed round pond, secluded seating and an unusual concrete greenhouse. Sedum roofed summerhouse. A garden of variety. Featured in Daily Telegraph and on Radio Devon. Limited wheelchair access.
🐕 ✿ 🚽 ☕ 🏆

66 MOTHECOMBE HOUSE

Holbeton, Plymouth, PL8 1LB. Mr & Mrs A Mildmay-White, amildmaywhite@gmail.com, www.flete.co.uk. *12m E of Plymouth. From A379 between Yealmpton and Modbury turn S for Holbeton. Continue 2m to Mothecombe.* **Sun 30 Apr (11-5). Adm £5, chd free. Cream teas. Visits also by arrangement, coach access limited by 11.25ft bridge.**

Queen Anne house (not open) with Lutyens additions and terraces set in private estate hamlet. Walled pleasure gardens, borders and Lutyens courtyard. Orchard with spring bulbs, unusual shrubs and trees, camellia walk. Autumn garden, streams, bog garden and pond. Bluebell woods leading to private beach. Yr-round interest. Sandy beach at bottom of garden, unusual shaped large liriodendron tulipifera. Featured in Country Life and new planting of bee friendly walled garden featured in Western Morning News. Gravel paths, one slight slope.
♿ 🐕 ✿ ☕ 🏆

67 THE MOUNT, DELAMORE

Cornwood, Ivybridge, PL21 9QP. Mr & Mrs Gavin Dollard. *Delamore Park PL21 9QP. Please park in car park for Delamore Park Offices not in village. From Ivybridge turn L at Xrds keep PH on L, follow wall on R to sharp R bend, turn R.* **Sat 18, Sun 19 Feb (10.30-3.30). Adm £4, chd free. Light refreshments.**
Welcome one of the first signs of spring by wandering through swathes of thousands of unusual varieties of snowdrops in this lovely wood. Closer to the village than to Delamore gardens (open only in May for the Sculpture and Art Exhibition) paths meander through a sea of these lovely plants, some of which are unique to Delamore and which were sold as posies to Covent Garden as late as 2002. Main house and garden open for sculpture exhibition every day in May. Possible wheelchair for part access but mainly rough paths/woodland tracks.
🐕 ✿ 🚽 ☕ 🏆

68 MUSSELBROOK COTTAGE

Sheepwash, EX21 5PE. Richard Coward, 01409 231677, coward.richard@sky.com. *1.4m N of Sheepwash. Leave Okehampton joining A386 going N. L onto A3072 in Hatherleigh. R on sharp bend in Highampton to Sheepwash. 1.6m after Sheepwash sign, turn L onto farm track signed Lake Farm.* **Visits by arrangement May to Oct day/eve to suit photographic**

groups (max 12 people/3 cars). Adm £4, chd free.
1 acre naturalistic/wildlife garden of all season interest. Many rare/unusual plants on sloping site. 8 ponds (koi, orfe, rudd, lilies). Stream, new Japanese garden, oriental features, Mediterranean gdn, wildflower meadow, clock golf, 1000s of bulbs. Many ericaceous plants and grasses. Good photographers' garden. Planting extremely labour intensive - ground is full of rocks. A mattock soon became my indispensable tool, even for planting bulbs. Featured in Devon Life.

69 THE OLD VICARAGE
West Anstey, South Molton, EX36 3PE. Tuck & Juliet Moss, 01398 341604, julietm@onetel.com. *9m E of South Molton. From South Molton go E on B3227 to Jubilee Inn. From Tiverton r'about take A396 7m to B3227 then L to Jubilee Inn. Follow NGS signs to garden.* **Sat 13, Sun 14 May, Sat 12, Sun 13 Aug (12-5). Adm £4.50, chd free. Cream teas. Visits also by arrangement May to Aug, coach turning and parking is available.**
Croquet lawn leads to multi-level garden overlooking 3 large ponds with winding paths, climbing roses and overviews. Brook with waterfall flows through garden past fascinating summerhouse built by owner. Benched deck overhangs first pond. Features rhododendrons, azaleas and primulas in spring and large collection of Japanese iris in July and wonderful hydrangeas in August. New wall fountain mounted on handsome, traditional dry-wall above house. Access by path through kitchen-garden. A number of smaller standing stones echoing local Devon tradition.

70 NEW THE OLDE COTTAGE
Dippertown, Lewdown, Okehampton, EX20 4PT. Emma Bending & Joe Baker. *8m E of Launceston signed off West Devon Drive. From Exeter follow A30 dual carriageway W, passing Okehampton. Turn off at Sourton, signed Tavistock.*

Bottom of slip road turn R and then immediately L, signed Lewdown. From Lewdown follow signs. **Sat 8, Sun 9 July, Sat 5, Sun 6 Aug (11-4). Adm £5, chd free. Teas and all home-made cakes, scones and biscuits.**
Attractive cottage garden set in the tiny hamlet of Dippertown. A range of mixed borders full of traditional cottage plants and fruit wind their way up steeply to the top of the garden where a wildlife pond sits, encouraging you stop and view the sweep of interesting trees and shrubs that lead to a more formal lawned area. Productive kitchen garden of stepped raised beds and soft fruit. Not good access for wheelchairs.

71 NEW PARK HOUSE
Liddaton, Coryton, Okehampton, EX20 4AB. Mr Roger Jennings. *9m outside Tavistock and near Brentor. From A386, turn R at Dartmoor Inn, follow signs for Brentor and Tavistock and look for yellow signs. From A30 dual carriageway get to Lewdown and follow signs from there.* **Sat 8, Sun 9 July (11-4). Adm £5, chd free. Home-made teas.**
Situated in the beautiful Lyd Valley this is an attractive 3 acre garden in two parts. Walk through banks of naturalistic, unusual and interesting planting combinations to a meadow with stunning views of Dartmoor and meandering mown paths leading to vibrant, traditional herbaceous borders, running water, a productive greenhouse and orchard. Not good wheelchair access.

72 ◆ PLANT WORLD
St Marychurch Road, Newton Abbot, TQ12 4SE. Ray Brown, 01803 872939, raybrown@plant-world-seeds.com, www.plant-world-gardens.co.uk. *2m SE of Newton Abbot. 1½m from Penn Inn turn-off on A380. Follow brown tourist signs at end of A380 dual carriageway from Exeter.* **For opening times and information, please phone, email or visit garden website.**
The 4 acres of landscape gardens with fabulous views have been called Devon's 'Little Outdoor Eden'. Representing each of the five

continents, they offer an extensive collection of rare and exotic plants from around the world. Superb mature cottage garden and Mediterranean garden will delight the visitor. Attractive new viewpoint café and shop. Open April 1st to the end of Sept (9.30-5.00). Wheelchair access to café and nursery only.

73 PORTINGTON
Lamerton, PL19 8QY. Mr & Mrs I A Dingle. *3m NW of Tavistock. From Tavistock take rd past hospital to Lamerton. Beyond Lamerton L at Carrs garage. 1st R (signed Horsebridge), next L then L again. From Launceston turn R at Carrs garage then as above.* **Sun 11, Sun 18 June (2-5). Adm £3, chd free. Home-made teas.** *Donation to Plymouth & District Deaf Children's Society 25%.*
Garden in peaceful rural setting with fine views over surrounding countryside. Mixed planting with shrubs and borders. Walk to small lake through woodland and fields, which have been designated a county wildlife site. Limited wheelchair access.

74 THE PRIORY
Priory Road, Abbotskerswell, Newton Abbot, TQ12 5PP. Priory Residents. *2m SW of Newton Abbot town centre. A381 Newton Abbot/ Totnes Rd. Sharp L turn from NA. R from Totnes. At mini r'about in village centre turn L into Priory Rd.* **Sat 1, Sun 2 July (1-5). Adm £5, chd free. Home-made teas.**
The Priory is a Grade II* listed building, originally a manor house extended in Victorian times as a home for an Augustinian order of nuns, now a retirement complex of 43 apartments and cottages. The grounds extend to approx 5 acres and incl numerous flower borders, a wild flower meadow, an area of woodland with some interesting specimen trees, cottage gardens and lovely views. Small Mediterranean garden and area of individually owned raised beds and greenhouses. Wheelchair access difficult when wet.

© Heather Edwards

Cleave Hill

Flower arranging and seed sowing demos throughout the day. The head gardener will be there to welcome visitors and answer any questions.

78 NEW ST ANDREW STREET SOUTH GARDENS, TIVERTON
EX16 6PL. Vanessa & Richard Pitman. *M5 junction 27. Central Tiverton. Close to museum. No parking in St Andrew St. Use Phoenix Lane multistory or Becks Square. Walk into Fore St, go past Boots. Turn L down St A St North, go over footbridge to St A St South. Gardens in 150 yds.* **Sat 1, Sun 2 July (10-4). Adm £4.50, chd free. Home-made teas at 62 The Old House St Andrew Street South. WC at No.59.**
Wander down historic St Andrew Street to find where a cluster of keen gardeners have joined together to share their surprise tucked away in the heart of old Tiverton. Cottage front gardens, secluded courtyards and the most unexpected back garden at 59 which goes right down to R Exe. Numbers 54, 56, 58, 59 and 62 are an urban treat with a variety of planting. Narrow gravel paths, varying levels and steps.

75 PROSPECT HOUSE
Lyme Road, Axminster, EX13 5BH. Peter Wadeley, 01297 631210, wadeley@btinternet.com. *½m uphill from centre of Axminster. Just before service station.* **Fri 1, Sat 2, Sun 3 Sept (1-5). Adm £4, chd free. Home-made teas. Visits also by arrangement June to Oct for groups of 6+.**
1 acre plantsman's garden hidden behind high stone walls with Axe Valley views. Well stocked borders with rare shrubs, many reckoned to be borderline tender. 200 varieties of salvia, and other late summer perennials incl rudbeckia, helenium, echinacea, helianthus, crocosmia and grasses creating a riot of colour. A gem, not to be missed. Featured in Garden Answers magazine and Gardeners' World.

76 NEW PYNES HOUSE
Upton Pyne, Exeter, EX5 5EF. Mr & Mrs Tilley and Mr & Mrs Chambers, www.pyneshouse.co.uk. *Take the A377 towards Crediton and turn R for Upton Pyne. After 400 yds, you will see two stone pillars next to Lodge. Follow the drive round to L and Pynes House is in front of you.* **Sun 25 June (1-5). Adm £4, chd free. Light refreshments.**

Gardens of Pynes House, a large country house, believed to have been the inspiration for Barton Park in Jane Austen's Sense and Sensibility. Large rose and lavender terrace with fountain and views across the Exe Valley, formal knot garden and parterre terrace. Historic woodland with ponds incl number of large specimen trees.

77 NEW RIVERFORD FIELD KITCHEN GARDEN
Wash Farm, Buckfastleigh, TQ11 0JU. Riverford Farm. *Take A384 between Totnes and Buckfastleigh. Take turning for Riverford Organic (not the Farm Shop) and follow yellow NGS signs.* **Sun 9 July, Sun 3 Sept (11-5.30). Adm £4, chd free. Tasty refreshments, hot and cold drinks available all day. Booking essential for the Field Kitchen Restaurant 01803 762000.**
Impressive 2 yr old large allotment style kitchen garden with an enormous 60mx9m polytunnel. Planted up with an interesting range of organic vegetables, herbs and flowers used to feed and beautify our two fantastic restaurants, the Field Kitchen here and the Duke of Cambridge, Islington, London. Come and be inspired to grow your own!

79 ST MERRYN
Higher Park Road, Braunton, EX33 2LG. Dr W & Mrs Ros Bradford, 01271 813805, ros@st-merryn.co.uk. *5m W of Barnstaple. On A361, R at 30mph sign, then at mini r'about, R into Lower Park Rd, then L into Seven Acre Lane, at top of lane R into Higher Park Rd. Pink house 200 yds on R.* **Suns 16 Apr, 14, 28 May, 18 June, 9 July (2-5.30). Adm £4, chd free. Cream teas. Visits also by arrangement Apr to Aug for small groups.**
Very sheltered, peaceful, gently sloping, S-facing, artist's garden, emphasis on shape, colour, scent and yr-round interest. A garden for pleasure with swimming pool. Thatched summerhouse leading down to herbaceous borders. Winding crazy paving paths, many seating areas. Shrubs, mature trees,

fish ponds, grassy knoll, gravel areas, hens. Many environmental features. Open gallery (arts & crafts).

ර් ⊬ ✿ ☕

80 SEDGEWELL COACH HOUSE GARDENS

Olchard, TQ12 3GU. Heather Jansch, www.heatherjansch.com. *4m N of Newton Abbot. 12m S of Exeter on A380, L for Olchard, straight ahead on private drive.* **Sat, Sun 29, 30 Apr, 6, 7 May, 19, 20 Aug (11-5). Adm £4.50, chd free.**
Heather Jansch, world-famous sculptor, brings innovative use of recycled materials to gardening. 14 acres incl stunning driftwood sculpture, fabulous views from thrilling woodland bluebell trail down to timeless stream-bordered water meadow walk, pools, herbaceous border, medicinal herb garden. Plentiful seating, come and picnic. Most sculpture is on level areas near the house. Limited disabled parking but there is a drop off point. Sorry no wheelchair accessible WC.

ර් ⊬ ♿ ☕

81 ♦ SHAPCOTT BARTON KNOWSTONE ESTATE

(East Knowstone Manor), East Knowstone, South Molton, EX36 4EE. Anita Allen, 01398 341664. *13m NW of Tiverton. J25 M5 take Tiverton exit. 6½m to r'about take exit South Molton 10m on A361. Turn R signed Knowstone. Leave A361 travel ¼m to Roachhill through hamlet turn L at Wiston Cross, entrance on L ¼m.* **For NGS: Wed 19, Sun 23 Apr, Sun 23, Wed 26 July (10.30-4.30). Adm £4, chd free. Light refreshments on Sundays when fine. For other opening times and information, please phone.** *Donation to Cats Protection.*
Large, ever developing garden of 200 acre estate around ancient historic manor house. Wildlife garden. Restored old fish ponds, stream and woodland rich in bird life. Unusual fruit orchard. Scented historic narcissi bulbs in Apr. Flowering burst July/Aug of National Plant Collections *Leucanthemum*

superbum (shasta daisies) and buddleja davidii. Many butterfly plants incl over 40 varieties of phlox. Kitchen garden and standard orchard. Fernery, over 100 cultivars of native and foreign hardy ferns. Ghost talks. Dowsing lessons. Very limited wheelchair access, steep slopes.

♿ 🚐 [NPC] 🏛 ☕

82 SIDBURY MANOR

Sidmouth, EX10 0QE. Sir John & Lady Cave, www.sidburymanor.co.uk. *1m NW of Sidbury. Sidbury village is on A375, S of Honiton, N of Sidmouth.* **Sat 22, Sun 23 Apr (2-5). Adm £5, chd free. Home-made teas.**
Built in 1870s this Victorian manor house built by owner's family and set within E Devon AONB comes complete with 20 acres of garden incl substantial walled gardens, extensive arboretum containing many fine trees and shrubs, a number of champion trees, and areas devoted to magnolias, rhododendrons and camellias. Partial wheelchair access.

ර් ⊬ ☕

GROUP OPENING

83 SIDMOUTH GARDENS

Rowan Bank 44 Woolbrook Park EX10 9DX, Byes Reach 26 Coulsdon Rd EX10 9JP, Sidmouth, EX10 9DX. *Sidmouth. From Exeter on A3052 10m. R at Woolbrook Rd. In ½m R at St Francis church. From Exeter on A3052 11m. R at Sidford T-lights. In ¾m turn L into Coulsdon Rd.* **Sat 17, Sun 18 June, Sat 26, Sun 27, Mon 28 Aug (2-5.30). Combined adm £4, chd free. Home-made teas. Gluten free available.**

BYES REACH
Lynette Talbot & Peter Endersby, 01395 578081, latalbot01@gmail.com. **Visits also by arrangement May to Sept for groups of 6-20.**

ROWAN BANK
Barbara Mence.

Situated on Jurassic Coast World Heritage Site, Sidmouth has fine beaches, beautiful gardens and magnificent coastal views. 2 contrasting gardens about 1m apart. Byes Reach: edible garden of ⅕ acre. Potager style, raised beds, espalier fruit trees on arched walkway, designed for those with mobility problems. Herbaceous borders, colour themed flower beds combining perennials, herbs, ferns and hostas. Pond, rockery, greenhouse and studio. Backing onto The Byes nature reserve and R Sid, offering an opportunity for a short walk from the garden gate. Rowan Bank is approx ¼ acre on a NW facing slope, generously planted with trees, shrubs, perennials and bulbs for yr-round interest. Steps lead to wide zigzag path rising gently to woodland edge of birch and rowan, with shady bench under Mexican pine. Seats at every corner and summerhouse looking towards wooded hills. Wheelchair access at Byes Reach, regret none at Rowan Bank.

ර් ⊬ ♿ ☕

84 SOCKS ORCHARD

Smallridge, Axminster, EX13 7JN. Michael & Hilary Pritchard, 01297 33693, michael.j.pritchard@btinternet.com. *2m from Axminster. From Axminster on A358 L at Weycroft Mill T-lights. Pass Ridgeway Hotel on L. Continue on lane for ½m. Park in field opp.* **Fri 21, Sat 22, Sun 23 July (1.30-5). Adm £4, chd free. Home-made teas. Visits also by arrangement Apr to Aug for small groups up to 25 with car sharing.**
1 acre plus plantaholic's garden designed for yr round structure and colour. Many specimen trees, large collection of herbaceous plants, over 200 roses, gravel and grass borders, small orchard, vegetable patch, small pond. Steep bank inset with shrubs underplanted with wild flowers (ongoing project). Chickens and bees. Limited wheelchair access.

ර් ⊬ ✿ ☕

85 SOUTH WOOD FARM

Cotleigh, Honiton,
EX14 9HU. Dr Clive Potter,
williamjamessmithson@gmail.com.
*3m NE of Honiton. From Honiton
head N on A30, take 1st R past
Otter Dairy layby. Follow for 1m. Go
straight over Xrds and take first L.
Entrance after 1m on R.* **Sat 9, Sun
10 Sept (2-5). Adm £5, chd free.
Home-made teas. Visits also by
arrangement June to Sept for
groups of 15+, guided tours of
garden.**
Large country garden surrounding
listed C17 Devon farmhouse set
deep in the Blackdown Hills. Incl
walled courtyard planted with
late summer herbaceous and yew
topiary, kitchen garden of raised
beds with step over pears, fruit
cages and trained fruit trees, sunken
dry stream bed walk and reflecting
pond, formal plum orchard, nuttery
and traditional Devon cobbled yard
with lean to glasshouse. Gravel
pathways, cobbles and steps.

🕭 🐕 🛊 🍵

GROUP OPENING

86 SOUTHCOMBE GARDENS

Dartmoor, Widecombe-in-the-
Moor, TQ13 7TU. 01364 621332,
amandasabin1@hotmail.com.
*6m W of Bovey Tracey. B3387
from Bovey Tracey after village
church take rd SW for 400yds then
sharp R signed Southcombe, after
200yds pass C17 farmhouse and
park on L.* **Sat 27, Sun 28 May,
Suns 4, 11, 18, 25 June, Sun 2
July (2-5). Combined adm £5,
chd free. Home-made teas at
Southcombe Barn. Southcombe
cakes are lavish, adventurous
and lovely. Visits also by
arrangement May & June (Mon -
Sat incl) for groups of 10+.**

SOUTHCOMBE BARN
Amanda Sabin & Stephen
Hobson.

SOUTHCOMBE HOUSE
Dr & Mrs J R Seale.

Village famous for its fair, Uncle Tom
Cobley and its C14 church - the

Cathedral of the Moor. Featured in
RHS The Garden. Southcombe Barn:
4 acres, trees and drifts of flowers,
abundantly wild and intensely
colourful. Beautiful all yr round and
busy with wildlife but this is its zenith
6 weeks of breathtaking glory. You
can spend hours in it. People do.
Southcombe House: 5 acres, SE-
facing garden, arboretum and orchid
rich restored wild flower meadow
with bulbs in spring and four orchid
species (early purple, southern
marsh, common spotted and greater
butterfly). On steep slope at 900ft
above sea level with fine views to
nearby tors. The teas are legendary.
People starting their own wild flower
meadows have used Southcombe
House seed-rich fresh-cut hay to
seed their newly cleared ground.
Yellow rattle is then usually abundant
in 1st year and orchids begin to
appear in the 4th year. With a bit of
a bumpy 100yds along the flat and
then 1 step wheelchair users can
access the tea lawn and look down
on some of the garden.

🐕 🚐 🍵

---

87 SPRINGFIELD

Woolsery, Bideford, EX39 5PZ. Ms
Asta Munro, 01237 431162. *Ignore
SatNav. 8m W of Bideford. 3m S of
Clovelly. Turn off A39 at Buck's Cross.
T-junction at school turn L past village
hall. L signed Putford. 1m L.* **Sun 28,
Mon 29 May, Sat 15, Sun 16
July (1-5.30). Adm £4, chd free.
Tea. Visits also by arrangement
May to Sept, 6+ preferred but
no one refused! Coach parties
welcome.**
2 acre S sloping rural plot with
views. Plantaholic's garden crammed
with shrubs, perennials inc 100+
hardy geraniums. Paved suntrap with
containers. Gravel area surrounded
with herbs, aromatic, silver and pastel
plants. Shade area. Small wildlife pond.
Meadow with meandering paths.
Kitchen garden fruit, vegetables, edible
flowers. Wildlife haven incl bats. Little
old fashioned 'sweetie shop' nursery.

🌼 🚐 🍵

88 SPRINGFIELD HOUSE

Seaton Road, Colyford,
EX24 6QW. Wendy Pountney,

01297 552481,
pountneys@talktalk.net. *Colyford.
Starting on A3052 coast rd, at
Colyford PO take Seaton Rd. House
500m on R. Ample parking in field.*
**Sat 27 May, Sat 24 June, Sat
29 July (11-5). Adm £4, chd
free. Cream teas. Visits also by
arrangement May to July for
groups, max 35.**
1 acre garden of mainly fairly new
planting. Numerous beds, majority
of plants from cuttings and seed
keeping cost to minimum, full of
colour. Also vegetable garden, fruit
cage and orchard with ducks and
chicken. Wonderful views over R
Axe and bird sanctuary, which is
well worth a visit, path leads from
the garden.

🐕 🌼 🍵

---

89 SQUIRRELS

98 Barton Road, Torquay,
TQ2 7NS. Graham & Carol
Starkie, 01803 329241,
calgra@talktalk.net. *5m S of
Newton Abbot. From Newton Abbot
take A380 to Torquay. After ASDA
store on L, turn L at T-lights up Old
Woods Hill. 1st L into Barton Rd.
Bungalow 200yds on L. Also could
turn by B&Q. Parking nearby.* **Sun
30 July, Sat 5, Sun 6 Aug (2-5).
Adm £4, chd free. Home-made
teas. Visits also by arrangement
15th July to 13th August.**
Plantsman's small town
environmental garden, landscaped
with small ponds and 7ft waterfall.
Interlinked through abutilons to
Japanese, Italianate, tropical areas.
Specialising in fruit incl peaches, figs,
kiwi. Tender plants incl bananas, tree
fern, brugmansia, lantanas, oleanders.
Mandevilla. Collections of fuchsia,
abutilons, bougainvilleas, topiary and
more. Enviromental and Superclass
Winners. 27 cleverly hidden rain
water storage containers. Advice
on free electric from solar panels
and solar hot water heating and
fruit pruning. 3 sculptures. Many
topiary birds, animals and balls. Huge
20ft Torbay palm. 9ft geranium.
15ft abutilons. New Moroccan
Area. Featured on BBC Gardeners'
World. Regret no wheelchair access.
Conservatory for shelter and seating.

🌼 🚐 🍵

90 SUMMERS PLACE

Little Bowlish, Whitestone, EX4 2HS. Mr & Mrs Stafford Charles, 01647 61786. *6m NW of Exeter. From M5, A30 Okehampton. After 7m R to Tedburn St Mary R at r'about past golf course 1st L after ½ m signed Whitestone straight ahead at Xrds follow signs. From Exeter on Whitestone rd 1m beyond Whitestone, follow sign from Heath Cross. From Crediton follow Whitestone rd through Fordton.* Sun 19 Mar, Sun 7 May, Sun 8 Oct (12-5). Adm £4.50, chd free. Light refreshments. Lunches 12-1.45, soup and sandwiches. Homemade teas 2.15-4.30. **Visits also by arrangement Mar to Nov 24 hrs notice required. Refreshments by arrangement.** Rambling rustic paths and steps (some steep) lead down a shaded woodland garden; unusual trees and shrubs (profusion of spring bulbs) to ornamental orchard (berries, fruit, hip, autumn colour) with follies, sculpture, stream and ponds. Conservation as important as horticulture (wild flowers). Intimate gardens round house. Craft artists and specialist nurseries attend. March attraction - willow sculptress with demos and sales table. Interesting animal sculpture, local artists/plant nurseries usually attend.

🐕 🚐 ☕

GROUP OPENING

91 TEIGNMOUTH GARDENS

Cliff Road, Teignmouth, TQ14 8TW. *1m from Teignmouth town centre. From Teignmouth take A379 towards Dawlish, at top of hill L into New Rd, take 3rd L into Ferndale Rd. Grosvenor Green Gdns and 16 Ferndale Rd at bottom of hill. For other gardens park in New Rd.* Sat 24, Sun 25 June (1-5). Combined adm £6, chd free. Home-made teas at High Tor.

BERRY COTTAGE
Maureen Fayle.

16 FERNDALE ROAD
Sue & Patrick Fischer.

GROSVENOR GREEN GARDENS
Michelle & Neal Fairley, www.grosvenorgreengardens.co.uk.

NEW 26 HAZELDOWN ROAD
Mrs Ann Sadler.

HIGH TOR
Gill Treweek.

NEW 65 TEIGNMOUTH ROAD
Mr Terry Rogers.

12 WOODLAND AVENUE
Liz Mogford.

2 new gardens join the popular Teignmouth gardens group in 2017. 26 Hazeldown Rd has an immaculate garden featuring clipped topiary and a large raised pond stocked with koi carp. At 65 Teignmouth Rd the lovely sea views are framed by plentiful flower beds planted with colourful and pollinator friendly plants. At 16 Ferndale Rd hard landscaping creates an imaginative backdrop for the numerous flower beds and small pond. At Grosvenor Green the stunning ⅓ acre plantsman's garden has a cottage garden feel. Naturalistic pond, large greenhouse and vegetable beds. 12 Woodland Ave is a beautifully planted secluded retreat with an abundance of flowers and vegetables, featuring some of the sculptor owners work (some for sale). At Berry Cottage the artist owner has developed a wildlife haven and will display some of her stunning artwork. High Tor has cottage garden style pollinator friendly planting with a productive greenhouse and amazing sea views. Mostly wheelchair access, limited at Berry Cottage, 16 Ferndale, 65 Teignmouth Road and 26 Hazeldown Road.

♿ ❀ ☕

GROUP OPENING

92 TOPSHAM GARDENS

Victoria Road, Topsham, Exeter, EX3 0EU. *Topsham is on E side of R Exe, between Exeter and Exmouth Regular train service running to Topsham. A map will be issued with your ticket purchased from any of the gardens. Victoria Rd is off High St.* Fri 14, Sun 16 July (11-5). Combined adm £5, chd free. Teas at Wixels.

NEW RED ROCK BUNGALOW
Elm Grove Road, Richard & Heather Carson.

19 VICTORIA ROAD
Ken & Margaret Barrett.

WIXELS
Mary & Chris Lambert.

Take a leisurely stroll through Topsham visiting 3 unique and beautiful gardens on the way. 19 Victoria Rd is a small tropical style walled garden with a wide variety of plants incl bamboo, tree ferns, bananas, palms and yuccas, a small pond and a larger one. Also a large conservatory with exotic plants. Red Rock Bungalow is an informal cottage garden surrounding the house with mixed borders, fruit trees, roses, raised beds for vegetables, 2 ponds and a greenhouse, backed by woodland. Wixels riverside garden is a very personal artist's creation from the unusual paving schemes, sculptures and semi-tropical plants to the long views up and down the River Exe, the large greenhouse and many inviting sitting places both sunny and sheltered. Wheelchair access at Red Rock, limited at 19 Victoria Road and not suitable for wheelchairs at Wixels.

🐕 ❀ ☕

Macmillan and the National Garden Scheme, partners for more than 30 years

93 TORVIEW

44 Highweek Village, Newton
Abbot, TQ12 1QQ. Ms Penny
Hammond. *On N of Newton Abbot
accessed via A38. From Plymouth:
A38 to Goodstone, A383 past Hele
Park, L onto Mile End Rd. From
Exeter: A38 to Drumbridges then
A382 past Forches X, R signed
Highweek. R at top of hill. Locally
take Highweek signs.* Sun 28, Mon
29 May (12-5). Adm £4, chd
free. Home-made teas.
Run by 2 semi-retired horticulturists:
formal Mediterranean front garden,
with wisteria-clad Georgian house,
small alpine house. Rear courtyard
with tree ferns, pots/troughs, lean-to
7m conservatory with tender plants
and climbers. Steps to 30x20m
walled garden - flowers, vegetables
and trained fruit. Shade tunnel of
woodlanders. Many rare/unusual
plants. Rear garden up 7 steps,
pebble areas in front garden.

GROUP OPENING

94 VENN CROSS RAILWAY GARDENS

Venn Cross, Waterrow, Taunton,
TA4 2BE. 01398 361392,
venncross@btinternet.com.
*Devon/Somerset border. 4m W of
Wiveliscombe, 6m E of Bampton
on B3227. Easy access. Ample
parking.* Sats, Suns 17, 18 June,
22, 23 July, 26, 27 Aug (2-5.30).
Combined adm £5, chd free.
Home-made teas. Selection of
gluten-free cakes also available.
Visits also by arrangement June
to Aug.

THE ENGINE HOUSE

Kevin & Samantha Anning,
01398 361392,
venncross@btinternet.com.
Visits also by arrangement
June to Aug.

STATION HOUSE

Pat & Bill Wilson, 01398 361665,
bill_wilson.daveneer@
btinternet.com.
Visits also by arrangement
June to Aug for groups of 10+.

Devon to Somerset and back
again – all in a matter of strides! 2
large adjoining and quite different
gardens occupying the site of a
former GWR railway station and
goods yard. A visit to these gardens
will interest railway enthusiasts
and gardeners alike. The Engine
House: 4 acres of yr-round interest
with the aim being to merge the
formal with the less formal and
the surrounding landscape. Approx
1 acre of orchid-rich wild flower
meadow and massed candelabra
primulas in early summer, sweeping
herbaceous borders bursting into
colour as summer progresses,
sculptures, railway relics, streams,
ponds (including koi), hornbeam
walkway, raised vegetable beds and
woodland paths. Station House:
2-acre sheltered garden in deep
cutting. Site of old station. Steep
banks featuring hostas and other
plants. Deep herbaceous beds
packed with flowers. Vegetable
beds. Tunnel (no entry permitted)
at end forming part of dell garden.
Access to top of tunnel with view
of garden. Woodland walk. Historic
railway interest (many photographs).
Wheelchair access to main areas.
Some gravel paths, gentle grass
slopes.

WAVERLEY
See Somerset, Bristol &
South Gloucestershire

GROUP OPENING

95 WHITSTONE BLUEBELLS

Bovey Tracey, Newton Abbot,
TQ13 9NA. 01626 832258,
katie@whitstonefarm.co.uk.
*Whitstone Lane. From A382 turn
towards hospital (sign opp golf
range), after ⅓m L at swinging sign
'Private road leading to Whitstone'.
Follow NGS signs.* Sun 30 Apr (2-
5). Combined adm £5, chd free.
Tea/coffee/home-made cakes
incl gluten free option.
Stunning spring gardens each with
its own character and far reaching
views over Dartmoor. Whitstone
House has clouds of bluebells

throughout woodland walk area
and at Whitstone Farm bluebells
intermingle among camellias, azaleas,
rhododendrons and magnolias.
Display of architectural metal
sculptures and ornaments. Enjoy the
views from Old Whitstone garden
to Haytor. Steps and gates divide
herbaceous borders and small, steep
wooded orchard with bluebells.

96 WHITSTONE FARM

Whitstone Lane, Bovey
Tracey, TQ13 9NA. Katie &
Alan Bunn, 01626 832258,
katie@whitstonefarm.co.uk.
*½m N of Bovey Tracey. From A382
turn towards hospital (sign opp golf
range), after ⅓m L at swinging sign
'Private road leading to Whitstone'.
Follow NGS signs.* Sun 6 Aug (2-5).
Adm £5, chd free. Home-made
cakes, gluten free option. Visits
also by arrangement May to
Sept for group and society
tours.
Nearly 4 acres of steep hillside
garden with stunning views of
Haytor and Dartmoor. Arboretum
planted 40 yrs ago, over 200
trees from all over the world incl
magnolias, camellias, acers, alders,
betula, davidias and sorbus. Major
plantings of rhododendron and
cornus. Late summer opening
for flowering eucryphias and
hydrangeas. National Collection
of Eucryphias. Beautiful yr-round
garden.

97 WICK FARM GARDENS

Cookbury, Holsworthy,
EX22 6NU. Martin & Jenny
Sexton, 01409 253760,
cookburywick@btinternet.com.
*3m E of Holsworthy. From
Holsworthy take Hatherleigh Rd
for 2m, L at Anvil Corner, ¼m then
R to Cookbury, garden 1½m on L.*
Sun 14, Sun 21, Sun 28, Mon 29
May (1.30-6). Adm £5, chd free.
Cream teas. Home-made cakes
and savoury refreshments. Visits
also by arrangement in May for
groups of 10+.
8 acre pleasure garden around
Victorian farmhouse arranged in

rooms with many attractive features. Fernery, ornamental pond, borders, sculptures, oriental garden with stone bell, lake with carp. Plants in long border to attract butterflies and bees. Crocosmia, croquet lawn, tropical oasis, stone henge with sacrificial stone, arboretum with over 300 trees, flowering cherries, rhododendrons and azaleas. Woodland bluebell walk 1m. Some gravel paths, motor wheelchair friendly. Woodland not suitable for wheelchairs.

& ⛟ ✿ � ☕ 🏆

GROUP OPENING

98 WILLAND OLD VILLAGE GARDENS & ALLOTMENTS

Willand Old Village, Cullompton, EX15 2RH. *From J27 or J28 of M5 follow signs B3181 to Willand. Turn at PO sign, gardens approx 200 yds, follow yellow signs. Parking in village. Allotments EX15 2RG, yellow signs off B3181.* **Sat 1, Sun 2 July (2-5.30). Combined adm £5, chd free. Home-made teas.**

4 BUTTERCUP ROAD
John & Sally Holmes.

8 BUTTERCUP ROAD
Julie De-Ath-Lancaster.

CHURCH LEA
Mrs D Anderson.

THE NEW HOUSE
Celia & Bryan Holmes.

OLD JAYCROFT FARM
D Keating & M Hollings.

NEW 6 RECTORY CLOSE
Cindy Wilkinson.

THE VILLAGE ALLOTMENTS
c/o Mrs S. Statham.

The 6 gardens, 56 allotments and award-winning composting scheme which make up the group opening offer a mix from small gardens in the recently-built housing estate to the larger ones at individual houses, the oldest of which is a 300 year old, Grade II listed farmhouse. All show what can be achieved in a limited space, whilst meeting various owners' needs, and providing yr round interest and colour. Each garden reflects differing interests and tastes. The allotment plots demonstrate a wide range of skills and production methods. We can promise visitors a full, interesting and varied afternoon. Church Lea featured in Amateur Gardening magazine. Gardens, village and church have good accessibility for wheelchair users with modest slopes and few changes of level. Allotments have partial access.

& ⛟ ✿ ☕

---

99 ◆ WINSFORD WALLED GARDEN

Halwill Junction, EX21 5XT. Dugald & Adel Stark, 01409 221477, dugald@dugaldstark.co.uk, www.winsfordwalledgarden.org.uk. *10m NW of Okehampton. On A3079 follow brown tourism signs from centre of Halwill Junction (1m). Straight on through Anglers Paradise and then follow yellow NGS signs.* **For NGS: Sat 10, Sun 11 June, Sat 19, Sun 20 Aug (10-5). Adm £5, chd free. Home-made teas. For other opening times and information, please phone, email or visit garden website.**

Historic walled gardens, redesigned and brimming with colourful, tall and lush planting. Large restored Victorian glasshouses and romantic ruins. Extensive mature bamboo grove. Giant pergola, fruit, vegetable and herb areas. Home of the painter, Dugald Stark. Studio open. Garden open May - Sept, Wed - Sun (10-5). Owner is wheelchair bound so access is good.

& ⛟ ✿ 🏆

---

100 WOOD BARTON

Kentisbeare, EX15 2AT. Mrs Rosemary Horton, 01884 266285. *8m SE of Tiverton, 3m E of Cullompton. 3m from M5 J28. A373 Cullompton to Honiton. 2m L to Bradfield/Willand, Horn Rd. After 1m at Xrds turn R. Farm drive ½m on L. Bull on sign.* **Sun 9, Sun 23 Apr (2.30-5.30). Adm £5, chd free. Home-made teas. Visits also by arrangement Mar to Oct entry** incl tea/biscuits. **Small buses only (max 30). Also Evening visits with wine & nibbles £10/ head.**

Established 2-acre arboretum with species trees on S-facing slope. Magnolias, 2 davidia, azaleas, camellias, rhododendrons, acers; several ponds and water feature. Autumn colour. New planting of woodland trees and bluebells opp house (this part not suitable for wheelchairs but dogs are welcome here). Sculptures and profiles in bronze resin. Renewed water garden.

& ✿ 🚗 ☕ 🏆

---

101 YONDER HILL

Shepherds Lane, Colaton Raleigh, Sidmouth, EX10 0LP. Judy McKay, Eddie Stevenson, Sharon Attrell, Bob Chambers, 07864 055532, judy@yonderhill.me.uk, www.yonderhill.org.uk. *4m N of Budleigh Salterton B3178 between Newton Poppleford and Colaton Raleigh. Take turning signed to Dotton and immed R into Shepherds lane, ¼m 1st R at top of hill opp public footpath.* **Suns 2, 9, 16, Mon 17, Suns 23, 30 Apr, Mon 1, Suns 7, 14, 21, 28, Mon 29 May, Suns 4, 11, 18, 25 June, Suns 2, 9, 16, 23, 30 July, Suns 6, 13, 20, 27, Mon 28 Aug, Suns 3, 10, 17, 24 Sept (1.30-4.30). Adm £3.50, chd £1.** Good selection of teas and coffee (make it yourself as you like it) and biscuits. **Visits also by arrangement Apr to Sept.**

Enjoy a warm welcome to 3½ acres planted with love. Blazing herbaceous borders buzzing with insects, cool woods alive with birdsong, rustling bamboos, delicious scents. Eucalyptus, grasses, conifer and fern collections. Rare plants, unusual planting, wildlife ponds, wild flower meadow, woodland tunnels, lots of benches. This garden will awaken your senses and soothe your soul. Garden attracts great variety of birds, insects and other wildlife. Limited wheelchair access, some slopes.

& ✿ 🚗 ☕ 🏆

DORSET

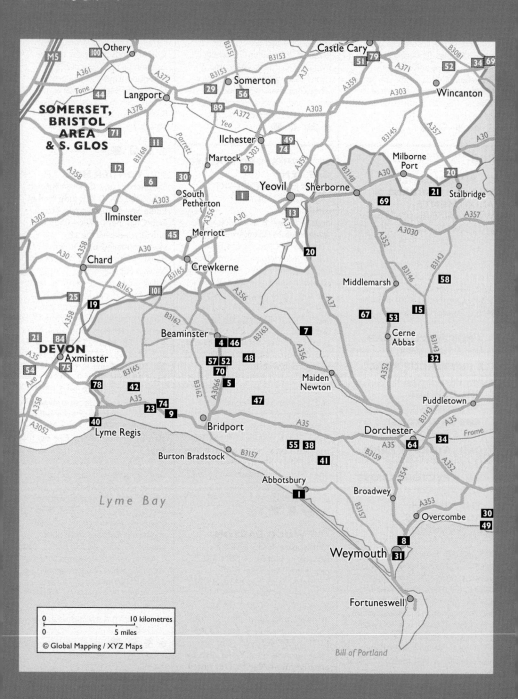

M5 · 100 Othery · A361 · Tone · 44 · Langport · A372 · A378 · B3153 · 29 · Somerton · 56 · 89 · Yeo · A372 · B3153 · Castle Cary · 51 · 79 · A371 · 52 · 34 · 69 · B3081 · A359 · Wincanton · A303 · A30

SOMERSET, BRISTOL AREA & S. GLOS · 71 · B3168 · 11 · Parrett · 12 · A358 · 6 · A303 · 30 · South Petherton · Martock · 91 · Ilchester · A303 · A37 · 49 · 74 · A359 · Yeovil · Sherborne · 1 · 13 · 69 · A352 · A3030 · B3148 · A30 · Milborne Port · 20 · 21 · Stalbridge · A357 · B3145 · A357

Ilminster · A303 · A358 · 45 · Merriott · A30 · Chard · B3165 · Crewkerne · A356 · A37 · 20 · Middlemarsh · B3146 · B3143 · 58 · 67 · 53 · 15 · Cerne Abbas · 32 · B3143

25 · 19 · A358 · B3162 · 101 · B3162 · Beaminster · 4 · 46 · 57 · 52 · 70 · 5 · B3163 · A3066 · 48 · A356 · 7 · A352 · Maiden Newton

21 · 84 · DEVON · Axminster · 75 · A35 · 54 · Axe · A338 · B3165 · 78 · 42 · A35 · 23 · 74 · 9 · B3162 · 40 · Lyme Regis · Bridport · A35 · 47 · Puddletown · B3143 · A35 · Frome · Dorchester · 64 · 34 · A352

A3052 · Burton Bradstock · B3157 · 55 · 38 · 41 · B3159 · A354 · A35 · A352

Abbotsbury · 1 · Broadwey · A353 · B3157 · Overcombe · 30 · 49

Lyme Bay · 8 · Weymouth · 31

Fortuneswell

0 —— 10 kilometres
0 —— 5 miles
© Global Mapping / XYZ Maps

Bill of Portland

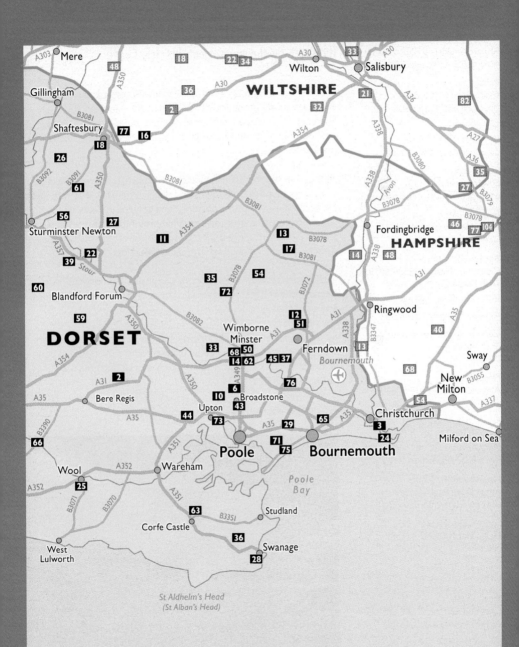

Volunteers

County Organiser
Alison Wright 01935 83652
wright.alison68@yahoo.com

County Treasurer
Richard Smedley 01202 528286
richard@carter-coley.co.uk

Publicity
Gillian Ford 01935 83645
gillianford33@btinternet.com

Social Media
Di Reeds 07973 241028
digardengate@hotmail.co.uk

Photographer
Edward Griffiths 01202 572288
eandj-griffiths@bhdorset.fsnet.co.uk

Booklet Editor
Judith Hussey 01258 474673
judithhussey@hotmail.com

Booklet Distributors
Charles Le Hardy 01258 860352
Trish Neale 01425 403565
trishneale1@yahoo.co.uk

Assistant County Organisers

Central East/Bournemouth
Trish Neale
(as above)

North Central
Alexandra Davies 01747 860351
alex@theparishhouse.co.uk

North East/Ferndown/
Christchurch
Mary Angus 01202 872789
mary@gladestock.co.uk

North West & Central
Annie Dove 01300 345450
anniedove1@btinternet.com

South Central/East
Helen Hardy 01929 471379
helliehardy@hotmail.co.uk

South Central/West
Di Reeds (as above)

South West
Christine Corson 01308 863923
christinekcorson@gmail.com

West Central
Alison Wright (as above)

Dorset is not on the way to anywhere. We have no cathedral and no motorways. The county has been inhabited forever and the constantly varying landscape is dotted with prehistoric earthworks and ancient monuments, bordered to the south by the magnificent Jurassic Coast.

Discover our cosy villages with their thatched cottages, churches and pubs. Small historic towns including Dorchester, Blandford, Sherborne, Shaftesbury and Weymouth are scattered throughout, with Bournemouth and Poole to the east being the main centres of population.

Amongst all this, we offer the visitor a wonderfully diverse collection of gardens, found in both towns and deep countryside. They are well planted and vary in size, topography and content. In between the larger ones are the tiniest, all beautifully presented by the generous garden owners who open for the NGS. Most of the county's loveliest gardens in their romantic settings also support us.

Each garden rewards the visitor with originality and brings joy, even on the rainiest day! They are never very far away from an excellent meal and comfortable bed.

So do come, discover and explore what the gardens of Dorset have to offer with the added bonus of that welcome cup of tea and that irresistible slice of cake, or a scone laden with clotted cream and strawberry jam!

Below: Knowle Cottage, Beaminster Gardens

25 Richmond Park Avenue

OPENING DATES

All entries subject to change. For latest information check **www.ngs.org.uk**

Extended openings are shown at the beginning of the month.

Map locator numbers are shown to the right of each garden name.

February

Snowdrop Festival

Saturday 25th
Edwardstowe   18
Manor Farm,
  Hampreston   45

Sunday 26th
Edwardstowe   18
Lawsbrook   39
Manor Farm,
  Hampreston   45

March

Saturday 4th
Kitemoor Cottage   35

Sunday 5th
Kitemoor Cottage   35

Sunday 12th
Frankham Farm   20

Sunday 19th
22 Holt Road   29
The Old Vicarage   61
Q   64

Sunday 26th
Herons Mead   25
Ivy House Garden   32
Q   64

April

Sunday 2nd
Q   64

Wednesday 5th
◆ Edmondsham House   17
The Old Vicarage   61

Friday 7th
The Old Vicarage   61

Sunday 9th
Q   64

Wednesday 12th
◆ Edmondsham House   17
The Old Vicarage   61

Saturday 15th
Chideock Manor   9
Old Smithy   60

Sunday 16th
Chideock Manor   9
Herons Mead   25
Ivy House Garden   32
The Old Rectory,
  Netherbury   57

Monday 17th
◆ Edmondsham House   17
Ivy House Garden   32

Tuesday 18th
The Old Rectory,
  Netherbury   57

Wednesday 19th
◆ Cranborne Manor
  Garden   13
◆ Edmondsham House   17
The Old Vicarage   61

Thursday 20th
Little Cliff   40

Friday 21st
The Old Vicarage   61

Saturday 22nd
Marren   49

Sunday 23rd
Broomhill   7
Frankham Farm   20
22 Holt Road   29
Kitemoor Cottage   35
Little Cliff   40
Marren   49
Q   64

Wednesday 26th
◆ Edmondsham House   17
The Old Vicarage   61

Thursday 27th
Staddlestones   72

Friday 28th
The Old Vicarage   61

Sunday 30th
Holworth Farmhouse   30
Ivy House Garden   32
Western Gardens   75
1692 Wimborne Road   76

May

Monday 1st
Holworth Farmhouse   30
Ivy House Garden   32

Saturday 6th
2 Spur Gate   71

Sunday 7th
Domineys Yard   15
Herons Mead   25
Mayfield   50
NEW The Old Rectory,
    Litton Cheney   55
Q   64
2 Spur Gate   71

Tuesday 9th
Braddocks   5

Wednesday 10th
NEW The Old Rectory,
    Litton Cheney   55

Thursday 11th
Staddlestones   72

Saturday 13th
Harcombe House   23

Sunday 14th
Harcombe House   23
The Old Rectory,
    Pulham   58
Old Smithy   60
1692 Wimborne Road   76
Wincombe Park   77
Wolverhollow   78

Monday 15th
Wolverhollow   78

Tuesday 16th
Deans Court   14
Harcombe House   23

Wednesday 17th
Wincombe Park   77

Saturday 20th
The Secret Garden   67
NEW Well Cottage   74

Sunday 21st
NEW Hanford School   22
22 Holt Road   29
Holworth Farmhouse   30
Mayfield   50
The Old Rectory,
    Netherbury   57
The Secret Garden   67
NEW Well Cottage   74

Tuesday 23rd
The Old Rectory,
    Netherbury   57

NEW Well Cottage   74

Thursday 25th
Anderson Manor   2
Mappercombe Manor   47

Friday 26th
Knitson Old
    Farmhouse   36

90th Anniversary Weekend

Saturday 27th
24 Carlton Road North 8
Edwardstowe   18
Knitson Old
    Farmhouse   36
Little Cliff   40

Sunday 28th
Annalal's Gallery   3
24 Carlton Road North 8
Edwardstowe   18
Knitson Old
    Farmhouse   36
Lawsbrook   39
The Manor House,
    Beaminster   46
Slape Manor   70
1692 Wimborne Road 76

Monday 29th
24 Carlton Road North 8
Knitson Old
    Farmhouse   36
The Manor House,
    Beaminster   46
Staddlestones   72

Wednesday 31st
Mayfield   50
Old Down House   54

June

Saturday 3rd
Marren   49

Sunday 4th
Frankham Farm   20
Marren   49

Tuesday 6th
Mappercombe Manor   47

Wednesday 7th
Donhead Hall   16
Mayfield   50
Old Down House   54

Thursday 8th
Anderson Manor   2
Little Cliff   40

Saturday 10th
Chideock Manor   9
The Old Rectory,
    Winterborne
    Stickland   59

Sunday 11th
Chideock Manor   9
Donhead Hall   16
Little Cliff   40
Manor Farm,
    Hampreston   45
Old Down House   54
The Old Rectory,
    Manston   56
The Old Rectory,
    Pulham   58
The Old Rectory,
    Winterborne
    Stickland   59
The Old Vicarage   61

Tuesday 13th
Braddocks   5

Wednesday 14th
The Old Rectory,
    Manston   56

Saturday 17th
Lytchett Minster
    Gardens   44
Puddledock Cottage   63

Sunday 18th
Beaminster Gardens   4
Holworth Farmhouse   30
Lytchett Minster
    Gardens   44
Mayfield   50
25 Richmond Park
    Avenue   65
Western Gardens   75

Tuesday 20th
◆ Littlebredy Walled
    Gardens   41

Wednesday 21st
Beaminster Gardens   4
Broomhill   7
◆ Sculpture by the
    Lakes   66

Saturday 24th
24 Carlton Road North 8
NEW The Hollow,
    Blandford Forum   27
The Manor House,
    Beaminster   46

Sunday 25th
Annalal's Gallery   3
24 Carlton Road North 8
Corfe Barn   10

Herons Mead   25
NEW The Hollow,
    Blandford Forum   27
22 Holt Road   29
The Manor House,
    Beaminster   46

Tuesday 27th
Deans Court   14
◆ Littlebredy Walled
    Gardens   41

Wednesday 28th
NEW The Hollow,
    Blandford Forum   27

Thursday 29th
Staddlestones   72

July

The Hollow, Swanage
(Every Wednesday)   28

Sunday 2nd
NEW The Old Rectory,
    Litton Cheney   55
25 Richmond Park
    Avenue   65

Wednesday 5th
NEW The Old Rectory,
    Litton Cheney   55
◆ Sculpture by the
    Lakes   66

Thursday 6th
Little Cliff   40

Saturday 8th
◆ Cranborne Manor
    Garden   13
Lower Abbotts Wootton
    Farm   42

Sunday 9th
Holworth Farmhouse   30
Little Cliff   40
Lower Abbotts Wootton
    Farm   42

Tuesday 11th
Braddocks   5

Sunday 16th
Broomhill   7
◆ Hilltop   26
22 Holt Road   29

Thursday 20th
The Secret Garden and
    Serles House   68

Saturday 22nd
Holy Trinity Primary
    School Garden   31
2 Spur Gate   71

The Hollow, Swanage

THE GARDENS

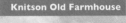

© Louise Jolley

Knitson Old Farmhouse

1 ◆ ABBOTSBURY GARDENS

Abbotsbury, Weymouth, DT3 4LA. Ilchester Estates, 01305 871387, www.abbotsburygardens.co.uk. *8m W of Weymouth. From B3157 Weymouth-Bridport, 200yds W of Abbotsbury village.* For opening times and information, please phone or visit garden website. 30 acres, started in 1760 and considerably extended in C19. Much recent replanting. The maritime micro-climate enables Mediterranean and southern hemisphere garden to grow rare and tender plants. National collection of Hoherias (flowering Aug in NZ garden). Woodland valley with ponds, stream and hillside walk to view the Jurassic Coast. Open all yr except Christmas week. Featured on Countrywise and Gardeners' World. Limited wheelchair access, some very steep paths and rolled gravel.

♿ 🐂 ✿ 🚐 [NPC] ☕

2 ANDERSON MANOR

Anderson, Blandford Forum, DT11 9HD. Jeremy & Rosemary Isaac, 01929 471320, r.isaac@talktalk.net, www.andersonmanor.co.uk. *3m E Bere Regis, 12m W Wimborne, 8m SW Blandford. Turn off A31 at Red Post Xrds to Anderson, follow rd around corner, entrance on R.* Thur 25 May, Thur 8 June (2-4.30). Adm £5, chd free. Cream teas. Visits also by arrangement Jan to Oct, min 10.
Approx 3 acres of mature topiary, roses, herbaceous borders surrounding Elizabethan/Jacobean manor house (Grade 1 listed, not open). Formal garden, gazebos, bowling green, walled garden, parterre and orchard. Yew and box hedges, pleached lime walk, old rose walk by R Winterborne and avenue of walnut trees. New rose garden added this year. C12 church open next to house. Separate car parking via Church Lane. All gardens accessible, some gravel, mainly grass.

♿ ✿ ☕

3 ANNALAL'S GALLERY

25 Millhams Street, Christchurch, BH23 1DN. Anna & Lal Sims, 01202 567585, anna.sims@ntlworld.com, www.annasims.co.uk. *Town centre. Park in Saxon Square PCP - exit to Millham St via alley at side of church.* Suns 28 May, 25 June, 23 July, 6 Aug (2-4). Adm £3, chd free. Visits also by arrangement May to Dec.
Enchanting 150 yr-old cottage, home of two Royal Academy artists. 32ft x 12½ft garden on 3 patio levels. Pencil gate leads to colourful scented Victorian walled garden. Sculptures and paintings hide among the flowers and shrubs. Unusual studio and garden room. Featured in Dorset Life magazine and Garden News. Not suitable for wheelchairs; not suitable for dogs.

GROUP OPENING

4 BEAMINSTER GARDENS

Beaminster, DT8 3BE. *6m N of Bridport, 6m S of Crewkerne on B3162. All gardens near town square or main car park (nearer parking only for disabled), all well signed from town square. Lots of yellow arrows/ balloons. Map issued with tickets.* Sun 18, Wed 21 June (2-5). Combined adm £5, chd free. Home-made teas in Beaminster Church from 3pm, long gradual stairway to main church door and lift for wheelchairs etc. West door open for wheelchair access.

NEW **KNOWLE COTTAGE** Mr John Norton.

NEW **PROSPECT COTTAGE** Shirley Samways.

SHADRACK HOUSE Mr & Mrs Hugh Lindsay.

SHORTS ORCHARD Mrs Sally Mallinson.

3 smallish town gardens, two with river running through, and one a much larger garden. All a total delight, masses of roses, unusual climbers, shrubs and swathes of perennials. Regret only minimal wheelchair access at Shorts Orchard, Shadrack House and Prospect Cottage.

🐂 ✿ ☕

5 BRADDOCKS

Oxbridge, Bridport, DT6 3TZ. Dr & Mrs Roger Newton, 01308 488441, rogernewton329@btinternet.com, www.braddocksgarden.co.uk. *3m N of Bridport. From Bridport, A3066 to Beaminster 3m, just before Melplash, L into Camesworth Lane signed Oxbridge. Single track rd, down steep hill. Garden signed.* Tue 9 May, Tue 13 June, Tue 11 July (2-5.30). Adm £4.50, chd free. Home-made teas. Visits also by arrangement Apr to Sept, groups of 10+ will be offered refreshments by arrangement.
3 acres of plant-packed sloping gardens, conceived, planted and looked after by owner. 'A feast of a garden at all times of the year'. Wild flower meadows and water. Herbaceous, underplanted shrubs and roses of all types and hues. Shady woodland garden and fine mature specimen trees. Featured in Dorset Life & House and Garden. Steep slopes and gravel paths make the garden unsuitable for wheelchairs.

✿ ☕

6 NEW 10 BROOKDALE CLOSE

Broadstone, BH18 9AA. Michael & Sylvia Cooper, 01202 693280. *Located just 100yds from centre of Broadstone, Brookdale Close is on Higher Blandford Rd, with additional parking in the next rd, Fairview Crescent.* **Sun 20 Aug (2-6), also open 22 Holt Road. Mon 21 Aug (2-6). Adm £3, chd free. Home-made teas. Visits also by arrangement in Aug, afternoon visits only.**

Described as a garden to lift your soul and the stuff of dreams, a rich kaleidoscope of colour, combining both tropical and cottage garden. Tree ferns, bananas, lilies, grasses and beautiful perennials with the unusual and unexpected planted among them, Centred round a wild life pond and tumbling waterfall, this 70 foot by 50 foot garden has been created in just 2 yrs. Limited wheelchair access.

7 BROOMHILL

Rampisham, Dorchester, DT2 0PU. Mr & Mrs D Parry, 01935 83266, carol.parry2@ btopenworld.com. *11m NW of Dorchester. From Dorchester A37 Yeovil, 4m L A356 to Crewkerne, 6m R to Rampisham. From Yeovil A37 Dorchester, 7m R Evershot. From Crewkerne A356, 1½m after Rampisham Garage L Rampisham. Follow signs.* **Sun 23 Apr, Wed 21 June, Sun 16 July, Sun 20 Aug (2-5). Adm £4.50, chd free. Home-made teas. Visits also by arrangement May to Aug for groups of 8+.**

Once a farmyard now a delightful, tranquil garden set in 1½ acres. Island beds and borders are planted with shrubs, roses, masses of unusual perennials and choice annuals to give vibrancy and colour into the autumn. Lawns and paths lead to a less formal area with a large wildlife pond, meadow, shaded areas, bog garden and late summer border. Featured in Gardens of Dorset. Gravel entrance, the rest is grass, some gentle slopes.

8 24 CARLTON ROAD NORTH

Weymouth, DT4 7PY. Anne & Rob Tracey. *8m S of Dorchester. A354 from Dorchester, R into Carlton Rd North. From Town Centre follow esplanade towards A354 Dorchester and L into C Rd N.* **Sat 27, Sun 28, Mon 29 May, Sat 24, Sun 25 June (2-5). Adm £3, chd free. Home-made teas.**

Long garden on several levels. Steps and narrow sloping paths lead to beds and borders filled with trees, shrubs and herbaceous plants incl many unusual varieties. A garden which continues to evolve and reflect an interest in texture, shape and colour. Wildlife is encouraged by the provision of homes. A small pond is the latest addition. Raised beds create a space for vegetable growing.

9 CHIDEOCK MANOR

Chideock, Bridport, DT6 6LF. Mr & Mrs Howard Coates, 07885 551795, deirdrecoates9@gmail.com. *2m W of Bridport on A35. In centre of village turn N at church. The Manor is ¼m along this rd on R.* **Sat 15, Sun 16 Apr, Sat 10, Sun 11 June (2-5). Adm £6, chd free. Home-made teas. Visits also by arrangement.**

6/7 acres of formal and informal gardens. Bog garden beside stream and series of ponds. Yew hedges and mature trees. Lime and crab apple walks, herbaceous borders, colourful rose and clematis arches, fernery and nuttery. Walled vegetable garden and orchard. Woodland and lakeside walks. Fine views. Partial wheelchair access.

10 CORFE BARN

Corfe Lodge Road, Broadstone, BH18 9NQ. Mr & Mrs John McDavid, 01202 694179. *1m W of Broadstone centre. From main r'about in Broadstone, W along Clarendon Rd ¾m, N into Roman Rd, after 50yds W into Corfe Lodge Rd.* **Sun 25 June (2-5). Adm £2.50, chd free. Home-made teas. Visits also by arrangement May to July, max 50.**

Very varied garden in pleasant semi-rural environment extending to about ⅔ acre. Mixture of usual and unusual trees, shrubs and flowers on 3 levels in and out of the barnyard. Wildlife friendly garden (so say Dorset Wildlife Trust). Positively the last opening. Last year was to be the Grand Finale but we are opening once more due to customer pressure!

11 COTTAGE ROW

School Lane, Tarrant Gunville, nr Blandford Forum, DT11 8JJ. Carolyn & Michael Pawson, 01258 830212, michaelpawson637@ btinternet.com. *6m NE of Blandford Forum. From Blandford take A354 towards Salisbury, L at Tarrant Hinton. After 1½m R in Tarrant Gunville into School Lane.* **Visits by arrangement Apr to Sept for groups of 6+. Roses/clematis at best June/July, cyclamen Sept. Adm £4, chd free. Home-made teas. Refreshments for groups discussed in advance.**

Maturing ½ acre partly walled garden. Formal and informal areas separated by yew hedges. Pergola, arbours, brick paths, tree house, kitchen garden and the sound of water; bees and butterflies abound in this tranquil spot. This sophisticated cottage garden reflects the owners' love of unusual plants, structure and an artist's eye for sympathetic colour also evident in new box plantings. Featured in Dorset Life.

Your visit helps Marie Curie work night and day in people's homes

12 COTTESMORE FARM

Newmans Lane, West Moors,
Ferndown, BH22 0LW. Paul &
Valerie Guppy, 01202 871939,
paulguppy@googlemail.com.
*1m N of West Moors. Off B3072
Bournemouth to Verwood rd. Car
parking in owner's field.* **Sun 30
July, Sun 6, Sun 13 Aug (2-5).
Adm £4, chd free. Home-made
teas. Visits also by arrangement
in Aug for groups of 10+,
afternoons only.**
Gardens of over an acre, created
from scratch over 17yrs. Wander
through a plantsman's tropical
paradise of giant gunneras,
bananas, towering bamboos and
over 100 palm trees, into a floral
extravaganza. Large borders and
sweeping island beds overflowing
with phlox, heliopsis, helenium and
much more combine to drown you
in scent and colour. Featured on
Radio Solent. Wheelchair access
to garden to avoid 2 lots of steps,
please ask on arrival to make use of
level route through main drive gate.
& ✿ ☕

13 ◆ CRANBORNE MANOR GARDEN

Cranborne, BH21 5PP. Viscount
Cranborne, 01725 517289,
info@cranborne.co.uk,
www.cranborne.co.uk. *10m N of
Wimborne on B3078. Enter garden
via Cranborne Garden Centre, on
L as you enter top of village of
Cranborne.* **For NGS: Wed 19
Apr, Sat 8 July (9.30-4). Adm £6,
chd £1. Light refreshments in
café, Cranborne Garden Centre
www.cranbornegardencentre.
co.uk. Breakfast, hot & cold
lunches, afternoon tea. For other
opening times and information,
please phone, email or visit garden
website.**
Beautiful and historic garden laid
out in C17 by John Tradescant and
enlarged into C20, featuring several
gardens surrounded by walls and
yew hedges: blue and white garden,
cottage style and mount gardens,
water and wild garden. Many
interesting plants, with fine trees and
avenues. Mostly wheelchair access.
& ✿ 🚗 ☕

14 DEANS COURT

Deans Court Lane, Wimborne
Minster, BH21 1EE. Sir William
Hanham, 01202 849314,
info@deanscourt.org,
www.deanscourt.org. *¼m SE of
Minster. Pedestrians: From Deans
Court Lane, continuation of High St,
over Xrds at Holmans shop (BH21
1EE). Cars: Follow yellow NGS signs
to entrance on A349, Poole Rd,
Wimborne (BH21 1QF).* **Tue 16
May, Tue 27 June (11-5). Adm
£4, chd free. Light refreshments
at Deans Court Café on Deans
Court Lane.** *Donation to Friends of
Victoria Hospital.*
13 acres of peaceful, partly wild
gardens in ancient setting with
mature specimen trees, Saxon fish
pond, herb garden and apiary beside
R Allen close to town centre. Apple
orchard with wild flowers. 1st Soil
Association accredited kitchen
garden within C18 serpentine walls.
Lunches and teas served in the
café, using estate produce (also for
sale). Tours of house £5 at 12 and
2pm, book upon arrival. Featured in
World of Interiors, You magazine,
The Garden Journal. For disabled
access, follow signs for parking
closer to the gardens. Some paths
have deeper gravel.
& 🐕 🚗 ☕

15 DOMINEYS YARD

Buckland Newton, Dorchester,
DT2 7BS. Mr & Mrs W
Gueterbock, 01300 345295,
cottages@domineys.com,
www.domineys.com;. *11m N of
Dorchester, 11m S of Sherborne. 2m
E A352 or take B3143. No through
road between church & Gaggle of
Geese (pub closed). Car Park 90yds
on R, enter 100yds on L.* **Sun 7
May (2-5.30). Adm £5, chd free.
Home-made teas. Visits also
by arrangement throughout yr,
refreshments by request.**
Welcome to our 31st year of
opening for the NGS and 56th year
here. Varied layout, which we continue
to change, in attractive setting
around thatched house and cottages.
Separate naturalised arboretum.
Superb soil, good micro climate. Plant
diversity to enjoy throughout the year.
Rare and well known trees, shrubs,

herbaceous, bulbs, annuals and pots,
fruit and vegetables. A place to revisit
all year. Plants will be on sale from
Picket Lane Nursery. Children very
welcome. Featured on Radio Solent,
in the Blackmore Vale Magazine
and Bournemouth and Dorset
Echo. Wheelchair access excludes
arboretum.
& ✿ 🚗 🚌 ☕

16 DONHEAD HALL

Donhead St. Mary, Shaftesbury,
SP7 9DS. Paul & Penny Brewer.
*4m E of Shaftesbury. A30 towards
Shaftesbury. In Ludwell turn R opp
brown sign sign to Tollard Royal.
Follow rd for ¾m and bear R at
T-junction. Donhead Hall 50 yds on
L on corner of Watery Lane, cream
gates.* **Evening opening Wed 7
June (6-8.30), wine. Sun 11 June
(3.30-6), home-made teas. Adm
£5, chd free.**
Walled garden overlooking deer
park. The house and garden are
built into the side of a hill with
uninterrupted views to Cranborne
Chase. Martin Lane Fox designed
the terracing and advised on the
landscaping of the gardens which
are on 4 different levels. Large
mixed borders and specimen trees,
kitchen garden with glasshouses.
Regret no wheelchair access
☕

17 ◆ EDMONDSHAM HOUSE

Edmondsham, Wimborne,
BH21 5RE. Mrs Julia Smith,
01725 517207. *9m NE of
Wimborne. 9m W of Ringwood.
Between Cranborne & Verwood.
Edmondsham off B3081. Wheelchair
access and disabled parking at
West front door.* **For NGS: Wed
5, Wed 12, Mon 17, Wed 19,
Wed 26 Apr (2-5). Every Wed
4 Oct to 25 Oct (2-5). Adm
£2.50, chd £0.50. Tea, coffee &
cake 3.30-4pm in Edmondsham
House, except on Monday 17th
April. For other opening times and
information, please phone.**
6 acres of mature gardens, grounds,
views, trees and shaped hedges
surrounding C16/C18 house, giving
much to explore incl C12 church
adjacent to garden. Large Victorian

walled garden is productive and managed organically (since 1984) using 'no dig' vegetable beds. Wide herbaceous borders planted for seasonal colour. Traditional potting shed and working areas. House also open on NGS days. Coaches welcome by appointment only. Some grass and gravel paths.

18 EDWARDSTOWE
50-52 Bimport, Shaftesbury, SP7 8BA. Mike & Louise Madgwick. *Park in town's main car park. Walk along Bimport (B3091) 500mts, Edwardstowe last house on L.* **Sat 25, Sun 26 Feb (11-3.30); Sat 27, Sun 28 May, Sat 19, Sun 20 Aug (11-5). Adm £3.50, chd free.** Evolving cottage garden with yr-round interest, set behind oldest house in Shaftesbury. Enormous magnolia tree greets visitors, courtyard opening to long lawns, divided by 2 colourful borders and self-sufficient vegetable garden. Chickens and bees complete the scene. Seasonal plant and produce sales. Snowdrop display 25/26 Feb.

19 ◆ FORDE ABBEY GARDENS
Forde Abbey, Chard, TA20 4LU. Mr & Mrs Julian Kennard, 01460 221290, info@fordeabbey.co.uk, www.fordeabbey.co.uk. *4m SE of Chard. Signed off A30 Chard-Crewkerne and A358 Chard-Axminster. Also from Broadwinsor B3164.* **For opening times and information, please phone, email or visit garden website.** 30 acres of fine shrubs, magnificent specimen trees, ponds, herbaceous borders, rockery, bog garden containing superb collection of Asiatic primulas, Ionic temple, working walled kitchen garden supplying the tearoom. Centenary fountain, England's highest powered fountain. Gardens open daily (10am-5.30pm, last adm 4.30pm). Please ask at reception for best wheelchair route. Wheelchairs available to borrow/hire: advance booking advised.

20 FRANKHAM FARM
Ryme Intrinseca, Sherborne, DT9 6JT. Susan Ross, www.Facebook.com/frankhamfarmgarden. *3m S of Yeovil. A37 Yeovil-Dorchester; turn E; ¼m; drive is on L.* **Suns 12 Mar, 23 Apr, 4 June, 15 Oct (11.30-5). Adm £5, chd free. Light refreshments. Home produced lunch - pulled pork or sausage in a roll, vegetarian soup. Home made teas.** 3½ acre garden, created since 1960 by the late Jo Earle for yr-round interest. This large and lovely garden is filled with a wide variety of well grown plants, roses, unusual labelled shrubs and trees from around the world. Productive vegetable garden. Climbers cover the walls. Spring bulbs through to autumn colour, particularly oaks. Sorry, no dogs.

21 FRITH HOUSE
Stalbridge, DT10 2SD. Mr & Mrs Patrick Sclater, 01963 250809, rosalynsclater@btinternet.com. *5m E of Sherborne. Between Milborne Port and Stalbridge. From A30 1m, follow sign to Stalbridge. From Stalbridge 2m and turn W by PO.* **Visits by arrangement Apr to July for groups of 10+ Mon-Fri only. Adm £5, chd free. Home-made teas.** Approached down long drive with fine views. 4 acres of garden around Edwardian house and self contained hamlet. Range of mature trees, lakes and flower borders. House terrace edged by rose border and featuring Lutyensesque wall fountain and game larder. Well stocked kitchen gardens.

22 NEW HANFORD SCHOOL
Child Okeford, Blandford Forum, DT11 8HN. Rory & Georgina Johnston. *From Blandford take A350 to Shaftesbury. Approx 2m after Stourpaine take L turn for Hanford. From Shaftesbury take A350 to Poole. After Iwerne Courtney take next R to Hanford.* **Sun 21 May (2-5). Adm £4.50, chd free. Home-made teas.** Perhaps the only school in England

with a working kitchen garden growing quantities of seasonal vegetables, fruit and flowers for the table. The rolling lawns host sports matches, gymnastics, dance and plays while ancient cedars look on. The stable clock chimes the hour and the chapel presides over it all. Teas in Great Hall (think Hogwarts). What a place to go to school or visit. Several steps/ramp to main house. No wheelchair access to WC.

23 HARCOMBE HOUSE
Pitmans Lane, Morcombelake, Bridport, DT6 6EB. Jan & Martin Dixon, 01297 489229, harcombe@hotmail.co.uk, http://jdmc49.wix.com/harcombe-house. *4m W of Bridport - ignore SatNav. A35 from Bridport: R to Whitchurch just past The Artwave Gallery. Immed R, bear L into Pitmans Lane. Approx 800m, park in paddock on L.* **Sat 13, Sun 14, Tue 16 May, Sat 12, Sun 13, Tue 15 Aug (11-5). Adm £4, chd free. Home-made teas. All cakes are home-made by Jan Dixon. Visits also by arrangement Apr to Sept, groups are welcome but lane is too narrow for coaches.** Landscaped into the hillside with wonderful views across Lyme Bay, the garden is laid out as a series of gravel paths and terraces connected by steps. Mature shrubs and perennials, many of which are unusual and visually stunning. The garden offers something for every season. A challenge to the less mobile visitor and unsuitable for wheelchairs and buggies. Fabulous views of the Char Valley, Charmouth and Lyme Regis, with beautiful view across Lyme Bay to Teignmouth and beyond.

Your visit to a garden will help more people be cared for by a Parkinson's nurse

24 NEW ◆ HENGISTBURY HEAD VISITOR CENTRE

Broadway, Southbourne, Bournemouth, BH6 4EN.
Bournemouth Borough Council, 01202 451618, hengistbury. head@bournemouth.gov.uk, www.visithengistburyhead.co.uk. *Near Christchurch on southern side of Christchurch Harbour. From B'mouth, take Southbourne Overcliff Drive, then Southbourne Coast Rd. Eventually, turn R onto Broadway. From Christchurch, cross R Stour on B3059. After r'about turn L onto Broadway.* **For opening times and information, please phone, email or visit garden website.**
The Visitor Centre garden was designed to inspire visitors to try things in their own seaside gardens. Features incl raised pond, wildflower meadow, woodland section, borders, raised bed, bug hotels and vegetable plot. Bird boxes with cameras, log pile and a gateway for hedgehogs. Plants incl wild flowers (to reflect the nature reserve) and a variety of garden plants. Visitors can also explore the Hengistbury Head Visitor Centre and its gift shop. Interactive exhibitions about the history, geology and wildlife of Hengistbury Head and regular art exhibitions. The Visitor Centre and garden (apart from the woodland section) are accessible to wheelchairs and mobility scooters.
&. ❀ 🚗 ☕ ❤

25 HERONS MEAD

East Burton Road, East Burton, Wool, BH20 6HF. Ron & Angela Millington, 01929 463872, ronamillington@btinternet.com. *6m W of Wareham on A352. Approaching Wool from Wareham, turn R just before level crossing into East Burton Rd. Herons Mead ¾m on L.* **Suns 26 Mar, 16 Apr, 7 May, 25 June, 17 Sept (2-5). Adm £3.50, chd free. Home-made teas. Visits also by arrangement Mar to Sept for groups of 10+.**
½ acre plantlover's garden full of interest from spring (bulbs, many hellebores, pulmonaria, fritillaries) through abundant summer perennials, old roses scrambling through trees and late seasonal

exuberant plants amongst swathes of tall grasses. Wildlife pond and plants to attract bees, butterflies, etc. Tiny woodland. Cacti. Featured on Radio Solent. Small wheelchairs can gain partial access - as far as the tea house!
&. 🐏 ❀ ☕

26 ◆ HILLTOP

Woodville, Stour Provost, Gillingham, SP8 5LY. Josse & Brian Emerson, 01747 838512, hilltopgardennursery@tiscali. co.uk, www.hilltopgarden.co.uk. *7m N of Sturminster Newton, 5m W of Shaftesbury. On B3092 turn E at Stour Provost Xrds, signed Woodville. After 1¼m thatched cottage on R. On A30, 4m W of Shaftesbury, turn S opp Kings Arms. 2nd turning on R signed Woodville, 100 yds on L.* **For NGS: Suns 16, 23, 30 July, 6, 13, 20 Aug (2-6). Adm £3, chd free. Home-made teas. For other opening times and information, please phone, email or visit garden website.**
Summer at Hilltop is a gorgeous riot of colour and scent, the old thatched cottage barely visible amongst the flowers. Unusual annuals and perennials grow alongside the traditional and familiar, boldly combining to make a spectacular display, which attracts an abundance of wildlife. Always something new, the unique, gothic garden loo a great success. Nursery.
🐏 ❀ 🚗 ☕ ❤

27 NEW THE HOLLOW, BLANDFORD FORUM

Tower Hill, Iwerne Minster, Blandford Forum, DT11 8NJ.
Sue Le Prevost, 01747 812173, sue.leprevost@hotmail.co.uk. *Between Blandford and Shaftesbury. Follow signs on A350 to Iwerne Minster. Turn off at Talbot Inn, continue straight to The Chalk, bear R along Watery Lane for parking in Parish Field on R. 5 min uphill walk to house.* **Sat 24, Sun 25, Wed 28 June (2-5). Adm £3, chd free. Cream teas. Home-made cakes and gluten-free available. Visits also by arrangement in July, garden groups welcome - 20 max encouraged.**

Hillside cottage garden built on chalk, about ⅓ acre with an interesting variety of plants in borders that line the numerous sloping pathways. Water features for wildlife and well placed seating areas to sit back and enjoy the views. Productive fruit and vegetable garden in converted paddock with raised beds and greenhouses. A high maintenance garden which is constantly evolving. Slopes, narrow gravel paths and steep steps so sadly not suitable for wheelchairs or limited mobility.
❀ 🚗 ☕

28 THE HOLLOW, SWANAGE

25 Newton Road, Swanage, BH19 2EA. Stuart & Suzanne Nutbeem, 01929 423662, gdnsuzanne@gmail.com. *½m S of Swanage town centre. From town follow signs to Durlston Country Park. At top of hill turn R at red postbox into Bon Accord Rd. 4th turn R into Newton Rd.* **Every Wed 5 July to 30 Aug (2-5.30). Adm £3, chd free. Visits also by arrangement July & Aug.**
Come and wander around a beautiful sunken garden on the site of an old stone quarry, a surprising find at the top of a hill above the seaside town of Swanage. Drystone terraces hold original plants and grasses with vast richness of colour & texture attracting butterflies and bees, changing from year to year showing the owners' passion for plants. Pieces of mediaeval London Bridge lurk in the walls. Exceptionally wide range of plants.
🐏

29 22 HOLT ROAD

Branksome, Poole, BH12 1JQ.
Alan & Sylvia Lloyd, 01202 387509, alan.lloyd22@ntlworld.com. *2½m W of Bournemouth Square, 3m E of Poole Civic Centre. From Alder Rd turn into Winston Ave, 3rd R into Guest Ave, 2nd R into Holt Rd, at end of cul de sac. Park in Holt Rd or in Guest Ave.* **Suns 19 Mar, 23 Apr, 21 May, 25 June, 16 July (2-5). Sun 20 Aug (2-5), also open 10 Brookdale Close. Adm £3.50, chd free. Home-made teas.**

Visits also by arrangement Mar to Sept for groups of 10+.

¾ acre walled garden for all seasons. Garden seating throughout the diverse planting areas, incl Mediterranean courtyard garden and wisteria pergola. Walk up slope beside rill and bog garden to raised bed vegetable garden. Return through shrubbery and rockery back to waterfall cascading into a pebble beach. Partial wheelchair access.

30 HOLWORTH FARMHOUSE

Holworth, Dorchester, DT2 8NH. Anthony & Philippa Bush, 01305 852242, bushinarcadia@yahoo.co.uk, www. inarcadia-gardendesign.co.uk. *7m E of Dorchester. 1m S of A352. Follow signs to Holworth. Through farmyard with duckpond on R. 1st L after 200yds of rough track. Ignore No Access signs.* Sun 30 Apr, Mon 1, Sun 21 May, Sun 18 June, Sun 9 July, Sun 6 Aug (2-5). Adm £4, chd free. Home-made teas. Visits also by arrangement May to Sept, teas or wine by arrangement.

This unusual garden is tucked away without being isolated and has an atmosphere of extraordinary peace and tranquility. At no point do visitors perceive any idea of the whole, but have to discover, by degrees and at every turn, its element of surprise, its variety of features and its appreciation of space. At all times you are invited to look back, to look round and up. Beautiful unspoilt views. Large vegetable garden. Ponds, fish, and water features.

31 HOLY TRINITY PRIMARY SCHOOL GARDEN

Cross Rd, Weymouth, DT4 9QX. Holy Trinity C E Primary School & Nursery, www. holytrinityenvironmentalgarden. blogspot.co.uk. *1m W of Weymouth centre. Take A354 from Weymouth Harbour junction by Asda. R at top of hill into Wyke Rd. 3rd L into Cross Rd. 200yds on R school car park.* Sat 22, Sun 23 July (1-5). Adm £4, chd free. Home-made teas.

An award winning wildlife garden, started in 2008 with the donation of a winning RHS Show Garden. Children's raised beds, large wildlife pond, WWII garden with Anderson shelter, tranquil Memory Corner, Dorset's largest living willow classroom, small orchard and bird garden. Lush Jurassic garden with many ferns and plants from the time of the dinosaurs completes the garden! Butterfly or dinosaur hunt for children. Featured in Dorset Life and Dorset Magazine. 1st prize in Dorset Wildlife Trust Wildlife Garden Competition (Schools section) twice since opening. Wheelchair access to most of garden and WC.

32 IVY HOUSE GARDEN

Piddletrenthide, DT2 7QF. Bridget Bowen, 01300 348255, bridgetpbowen@hotmail.com. *9m N of Dorchester. On B3143. In middle of Piddletrenthide village, opp PO/village stores near Piddle Inn.* Sun 26 Mar, Sun 16, Mon 17, Sun 30 Apr, Mon 1 May (2-5). Adm £4, chd free. Home-made teas. Visits also by arrangement Mar to May for groups of 10+.

Unusual and challenging ½ acre garden set on steep hillside with fine views. Wildlife friendly garden with mixed borders, ponds, propagating area, vegetable garden, fruit cage, greenhouses and polytunnel, chickens and bees, nearby allotment. Daffodils, tulips and hellebores in quantity for spring openings. Come prepared for steep terrain and a warm welcome! Run on organic lines with plants to attract birds, bees and other insects. Insect-friendly plants usually for sale. Honey and hive products usually available and, weather permitting, observation hive of honey bees in courtyard. Beekeeper present to answer queries. 3rd prize in large garden category of DWT Wildlife-friendly Garden awards and described as 'literally stunning in its sheer size, abundance and variety.'.

33 ◆ KINGSTON LACY

Wimborne Minster, BH21 4EA. National Trust, 01202 883402, kingstonlacy@nationaltrust.org. uk, www.nationaltrust.org.uk/ kingston-lacy. *2½ m W of Wimborne Minster. On Wimborne-Blandford rd B3082.* For opening times and information, please phone, email or visit garden website.

35 acres of formal garden, incorporating parterre and sunk garden planted with Edwardian schemes during spring and summer. 5 acre kitchen garden and allotments, Victorian fernery containing over 35 varieties. Rose garden, mixed herbaceous borders, vast formal lawns and Japanese garden restored to Henrietta Bankes' creation of 1910. 2 National Collections: Convallaria and Anemone nemorosa. Snowdrops, blossom, bluebells, autumn colour and Christmas light display. Deep gravel on some paths but lawns suitable for wheelchairs. Slope to visitor reception and South Lawn.

34 ◆ KINGSTON MAURWARD GARDENS AND ANIMAL PARK

Kingston Maurward, Dorchester, DT2 8PY. Kingston Maurward College, 01305 215003, events@kmc.ac.uk, www.morekmc.com. *1m E of Dorchester. Off A35. Follow brown Tourist Information signs.* For opening times and information, please phone, email or visit garden website.

35 acres of gardens laid out in the style popularised by Capability Brown. Generous terraces and gardens divided by hedges and stone balustrades. Stone features and interesting plants. Elizabethan walled garden laid out as demonstration. National Collections of penstemons and salvias. Open early Jan to mid Dec. Hours will vary in winter depending on conditions - check garden website or call before visiting. Partial wheelchair access only, gravel paths, steps and steep slopes. Map provided at entry, highlighting the most suitable routes.

35 KITEMOOR COTTAGE

Manswood, Wimborne,
BH21 5BQ. Alan & Diana Guy,
01258 840894, diana.kitemoor@
btinternet.com. *6m N of Wimborne.
From B3078 turn to Witchampton,
then from village centre follow signs
to Manswood.* **Sat 4, Sun 5 Mar
(12-4); Sun 23 Apr (2-5). Adm
£4, chd free. Homemade soup
and roll at lunchtime in March,
tea and cake in the afternoon.
Visits also by arrangement Mar
to June for groups of 15+.**
½ acre plantsperson's garden with
glorious countryside views. Diana
(formally of Welcome Thatch)
has created a new garden full of
treasures incl large collection of
hellebores. Planted for a long season
of interest. Pond, mini meadow,
naturalistic planting, cottage garden
borders. Fruit and vegetable gardens.
Many containers. Plants for sale,
exquisite Holmlea hybrid hellebores
for sale in March. Conservatory
available for refreshments in
inclement weather. Featured in
Dorset Life. Partial wheelchair
access. Narrow pathways and
different levels.

Corfe Barn

36 KNITSON OLD FARMHOUSE

Corfe Castle, Wareham, BH20 5JB.
Rachel Helfer, 01929 421681,
rjehelfer@gmail.com. *1m NW
of Swanage. 3m E of Corfe Castle.
Signed L off A351 to Knitson. Very
narrow rds for 1m. Ample parking in
yard or in adjacent field.* **Fri 26, Sat
27, Sun 28, Mon 29 May (2-8).
Adm £3.50, chd free. Cream
teas and delicious home-made
cakes from 2-5pm. After 5pm,
tea available or BYO bottle
of wine/drinks, savoury picnic
snacks for sale. Visits also by
arrangement Feb to Nov, max
30.**
Mature cottage garden with
exceptional views nestled at base
of chalk downland in dry coastal
conditions. Herbaceous borders,
rockeries, climbers and shrubs.
Evolved and designed over 50yrs for
yr-round colour and interest. Large
wildlife friendly kitchen garden for
self sufficiency. Rachel is delighted
to welcome visitors and discuss
gardening. We have used a lot of
local stone in the design and have
interesting old stones and stone
baths around the garden. Uneven,
sloping paths.

37 ◆ KNOLL GARDENS

Hampreston, Wimborne,
BH21 7ND. Mr Neil
Lucas, 01202 873931,
enquiries@knollgardens.co.uk,
www.knollgardens.co.uk. *2½m
W of Ferndown. ETB brown signs
from A31. Large car park.* **For
opening times and information,
please phone, email or visit garden
website.**
Evoking nature's profuse spontaneity,
meadow-style drifts merge almost
seamlessly from sunny perennial
meadows to prairie style plantings
and tough easy-care, green lawn
substitutes. Featuring plants from
Knoll's onsite nursery amidst mini-
arboretum of rare and unusual trees
and shrubs, discover an abundance
of practical planting ideas in this
inspirational environment. Specialist
nursery onsite. The garden is
also home to a registered charity,
the Knoll Gardens Foundation.

The Foundation researches and
promotes wildlife friendly gardening
and regularly hosts events in the
garden frequently with other wildlife
charities. A new stylish bee hotel is
a focal point in the Sunny Meadow.
Featured in numerous publications.
Some slopes. Various surfaces incl
gravel, paving, grass and bark.

38 LANGEBRIDE HOUSE

Long Bredy, DT2 9HU. Mrs J
Greener, 01308 482257. *8m W
of Dorchester. S off A35, midway
between Dorchester and Bridport.
Well signed. 1st gateway on L in
village.* **Visits by arrangement
Feb to July. Adm £4.50, chd
free. Teas at nearby Egg Cup
Tea Rooms, Vurlands Farm,
Coast Road, Swyre, DT2 9DB.
01308 897160..**
This old rectory garden has carpets
of anemones spreading out under
huge copper beech tree on lawn.
A lovely place to visit in spring and
early summer, with a large variety
of daffodils and early spring bulbs
amongst flowering shrubs, trees and
herbaceous borders with kitchen
garden. Some steep slopes.

39 LAWSBROOK

Brodham Way, Shillingstone,
DT11 0TE. Clive Nelson,
www.facebook.com/Lawsbrook.
*5m NW of Blandford. To Shillingstone
on A357. Turn up Gunn Lane (PO
box) - up lane (past Wessex Avenue
on L & Everetts Lane on R) then turn
R as rd bends to L. Lawsbrook 250m
on R.* **Sun 26 Feb (10-4); Sun 28
May (10-6); Sun 12 Nov (10-4).
Adm £3, chd free. Home-made
teas. Lunches (home-made) by
request on May opening, please
email/phone in advance.**
6 acres. Over 200 trees incl the
mature and unusual. Formal
borders, wild flower and wildlife
areas, vegetable garden. Relaxed
and friendly, lovely opportunity for
family walks in all areas incl wildlife,
stream, meadow. Children and
dogs welcome. Yr-round interest
incl extensive snowdrops (2 acres),
hellebores and bulbs in early spring
through full summer colour to

intense autumn hues. Large and unusual labelled tree collection. Garden activities for all the family. Gravel path at entrance, grass paths over whole garden.

 ♿ 🐕 ✿ ⛩ ☕

40 LITTLE CLIFF
Sidmouth Road, Lyme Regis, DT7 3EQ. Mrs Debbie Bell, 01297 444833, debbie@debbiebell.co.uk. *Edge of Lyme Regis. Turn off A35 onto B3165 to Lyme Regis. Through Uplyme to mini r'about by Travis Perkins. 3rd exit on R, up to fork and L down Sidmouth Rd following NGS arrows from mini r'about. Garden on R.* Thur 20, Sun 23 Apr, Sat 27 May, Thur 8, Sun 11 June, Thur 6, Sun 9 July (2-5). Adm £3.50, chd free. **Visits also by arrangement Apr to July, please arrange in advance.**
S-facing seaward, Little Cliff looks out over spectacular views of Lyme Bay. Spacious garden sloping down hillside through series of garden rooms where visual treats unfold. Vibrant herbaceous borders, with hot garden, white garden, bog garden all intermingled with mature specimen trees, shrubs and wall climbers. Steep slopes. Jungle walkway at bottom of garden, Indian influenced pavilion leading to white borders and vegetable garden. New hidden garden amongst the palms and rich colours of the hot garden. Featured in Country Homes and Interiors magazine and a finalist in The Daily Mail Garden of the Year competition.
✿

41 ♦ LITTLEBREDY WALLED GARDENS
Littlebredy, DT2 9HL. The Walled Garden Workshop, 01305 898055, secretary@wgw.org.uk, www.littlebredy.com. *8m W of Dorchester. 10m E of Bridport. 1½m S of A35. NGS days: park on village green then walk 300yd. For the less mobile (and on normal open days) use gardens car park.* For NGS: Tue 20, Tue 27 June (2-7). Adm £5, chd free. Cream teas. For other opening times and information, please phone, email or visit garden website.

1 acre walled garden on S-facing slopes of Bride River Valley. Herbaceous borders, riverside rose walk, lavender beds and potager vegetable and cut flower gardens. Original Victorian glasshouses, one under renovation. Gardens also open 2-5pm on Wed & Sun (see website for other days) from Easter Sunday to end Sept, weather permitting. Partial wheelchair access, some steep grass slopes. For disabled parking please follow signs to main entrance.
 ♿ 🐕 ✿ ☕

42 LOWER ABBOTTS WOOTTON FARM
Whitchurch Canonicorum, Bridport, DT6 6NL. Johnny & Clare Trenchard. *6m W of Bridport. Well signed from A35 at Morecombe Lake (2m) and Bottle Inn at Marshwood on B3165 (1.5m). Some disabled off-road parking.* Sat 8, Sun 9 July (2-5). Adm £4, chd free. Home-made teas.
The owner is a sculptor and the garden reflects her creative flair for form, shape and colour. New open gravel garden contrasts with the main garden consisting of lawns, borders and garden rooms which make a perfect setting for sculptures. The naturally edged pond provides a tranquil moment of calm, but beware of being led down the garden path by the running hares! Sculpture Garden. Partial wheelchair access.
🐕 ✿ ☕

43 [NEW] 44 LOWER BLANDFORD ROAD
Broadstone Poole, BH18 8NY. Mr Mike Clifford, 01202 904203, addicted2tropical44@icloud.co.uk. *Take Lower Blandford Rd leading up to Broadstone centre approaching from Derbys Corner r'about. Take 1st turning on R. (Fontmell Rd) then sharp L. Extra parking in Fontmell Rd.* Sat 5, Sun 6, Sat 26, Sun 27 Aug (1-5). Adm £3.50, chd free. Home-made teas. **Visits also by arrangement July to Sept for groups of 10+.**
Exotic front garden full of bananas, palms and lush tropical planting, leads you into the 35'x65' back garden filled with unusual and rare exotics. Paths

lead you through to an Abbotsbury inspired colonial summerhouse and water feature surrounded by tree ferns and shade loving plants. A true plantaholic's paradise!
✿ ☕

GROUP OPENING

44 LYTCHETT MINSTER GARDENS
Lytchett Minster, BH16 6JF. *3m W of Wimborne. From A35 Bakers Arms PH r'about (junction with A351), follow signs to Lytchett Minster B3067. Proceed through village to St Peters Finger Pub, then follow parking signs. Garden guide/adm at car park.* Sat 17, Sun 18 June (2-5). Combined adm £5.50, chd free. Home-made teas at The Old Bakehouse, 55 Dorchester Rd. Refreshments in aid of Dorset Air Ambulance.

57 DORCHESTER ROAD
Maureen & Stephen Kirkham.

FRIARS GREEN
Jane & Robin SeQueira.

HERON HOUSE
Geraldine & Phillip Stevens.

OLD BUTTON COTTAGE
Thelma & Paul Johns.

4 OLD FORGE CLOSE
Liz & Derek Allen.

10 ORCHARD CLOSE
Daphne Turner.

'The Gateway to the Purbecks', is W of Poole on the old Dorchester rd. Mixture of old and new houses, 2 churches, 2 PHs and an ancient pound. The 6 small to medium sized gardens offer variation in cottage style planting with many varieties of herbaceous perennials and hardy geraniums, some lush waterside planting, magnificent displays of climbing roses, small fruit and vegetable plots and many other interesting features. Dogs on leads in 3 gardens only. Flower festival in village. Although most of the gardens are accessible by wheelchairs, there are areas of gravel and steps in some.
 ♿ ✿ ⛩ ☕

45 MANOR FARM, HAMPRESTON

Wimborne, BH21 7LX. Guy & Anne Trehane. *2½ m E of Wimborne, 2½ m W of Ferndown. From Canford Bottom r'about on A31, take exit B3073 Ham Lane. ½ m turn R at Hampreston Xrds. House at bottom of village.* **Sat 25 Feb (10-1); Sun 26 Feb (1-4); Sun 11 June, Sun 30 July, Wed 2, Sun 13 Aug (1-5). Adm £4, chd free. Home-made teas. Soup also available at Feb openings.**
Traditional farmhouse garden designed and cared for by 3 generations of the Trehane family through over 100yrs of farming and gardening at Hampreston. Garden is noted for its herbaceous borders and rose beds within box and yew hedges. Mature shrubbery, water and bog garden. Open for hellebores and snowdrops in February. Dorset Hardy Plant Society sales at openings. Hellebores for sale in February.
& ✿ ☕

46 THE MANOR HOUSE, BEAMINSTER

North St, Beaminster, DT8 3DZ. Christine Wood. *200yds N of town square. Park in the square or public car park, 5 mins walk along North St from the Square. Limited disabled parking on site.* **Sun 28, Mon 29 May, Sat 24, Sun 25 June (11-5). Adm £5, chd free. Home-made teas in Coach House Garden 11am - 5pm or bring a picnic.**
Set in heart of Beaminster, 16½ acres of stunning parkland with mature specimen trees, lake and waterfall. Beautifully restored walled garden - 'Serendipity'. Designed and lovingly planted over last 9yrs. A peaceful garden with woodland walk and wild flower meadow. Featured in Dorset Life, Country Life & The English Garden magazine. Partial wheelchair access.
& 🐾 ✿ ☕

47 MAPPERCOMBE MANOR

Nettlecombe, Bridport, DT6 3SS. Annie Crutchley. *4m NE of Bridport. From A3066 turn E signed W Milton & Powerstock. After 3m leave Powerstock on your L, bear R at Marquis of Lorne PH, entrance drive 150yds ahead.* **Thur 25 May, Tue 6 June (12-5). Adm £4, chd free. Light refreshments.**
Monks' rest house with stew pond and dovecote. S-facing gardens on 4 levels with ancient monastic route. Approx 4 acres. Apart from stone work and mature trees, garden mostly replanted in last 25 yrs. Many old roses and a haven for bees and butterflies. Dogs on leads. Partial wheelchair access, gravel and stone paths, steps. 150 yd walk from car park, limited parking by house.
& 🐾 ✿ ☕

48 ♦ MAPPERTON GARDENS

Mapperton, Beaminster, DT8 3NR. The Earl & Countess of Sandwich, 01308 862645, office@mapperton.com, www.mapperton.com. *6m N of Bridport. Off A356/A3066. 2m SE of Beaminster off B3163.* **For opening times and information, please phone, email or visit garden website.**
Terraced valley gardens surrounding Tudor/Jacobean manor house. On upper levels, walled croquet lawn, orangery and Italianate formal garden with fountains, topiary and grottoes. Below, C17 summerhouse and fishponds. Lower garden with shrubs and rare trees, leading to woodland and spring gardens. Garden open 1 Mar to 31 Oct (except Sat) (11-5); Café open 2 Apr to 31 Oct (except Sat); House open 2 Apr to 31 Oct (except Fri and Sat). Partial wheelchair access (lawn and upper levels).
& ✿ 🚗 ☕

49 MARREN

Holworth, Dorchester, DT2 8NJ. Mr & Mrs Peter Cartwright, 01305 851503, wcartwright@tiscali.co.uk, www.wendycartwright.net. *SE of Dorchester. Don't use SatNav. Off A353 At Poxwell turn towards Ringstead. Straight ahead in NT Car Park at top of hill. Park before gate marked No Cars. Walk through gate, signed path, on R.* **Sat 22, Sun 23 Apr, Sat 3, Sun 4 June (2-5).**
Adm £4, chd free. Home-made teas. **Visits also by arrangement Apr to Sept, refreshments by arrangement for groups of 10+.**
4 acres. From NT car park down steep public footpath and 64 grass steps to woodland garden with tree sculptures. Views of Weymouth Bay and Portland. More formal Italianate garden around house with wonderful arbours. Mediterranean feel. Strong structural planting. Wildlife and seaside garden. Children's summerhouse, hornbeam house. Willow arbour to discover at the bottom. Fabulous sea views. Featured in Country Homes and Interiors. Stout footwear and strong knees recommended. Not suitable for wheelchairs but disabled access to house for tea by prior arrangement.
✿ 🅳 🛋 ☕

50 MAYFIELD

4 Walford Close, Wimborne Minster, BH21 1PH. Mr & Mrs Terry Wheeler, 01202 849838, terry.wheeler@tesco.net. *½ m N of Wimborne Town Centre. B3078 out of Wimborne, R into Burts Hill, 1st L into Walford Close.* **Sun 7, Sun 21 May (2-5). Wed 31 May, Wed 7 June (2-5), also open Old Down House. Sun 18 June (2-5). Adm £3.50, chd free. Home-made teas. Visits also by arrangement May & June for groups of 6+.**
Donation to The Friends of Victoria Hospital, Wimborne.
Town garden of approx ¼ acre. Front: formal hard landscaping planted with drought-resistant shrubs and perennials. Shaded area has wide variety of hostas. Back garden contrasts with a seductive series of garden rooms containing herbaceous perennial beds separated by winding grass paths and rustic arches. Pond, vegetable beds and greenhouses containing succulents and vines. Garden access is across a pea-shingle drive. If this is manageable, wheelchairs can access the back garden provided they are no wider than 65cms.
& 🐾 ✿ 🚗 ☕

52 THE MILL HOUSE

Crook Hill, Netherbury,
DT6 5LX. Michael & Giustina
Ryan, 01308 488267,
themillhouse@dsl.pipex.com.
*1m S of Beaminster. Turn R off
A3066 Beaminster to Bridport rd
signed Netherbury. Car park at
Xrds at bottom of hill.* **Visits by
arrangement Apr to Oct min
6, max 30. Adm £6, chd free.
Home-made teas.**
6½ acres of garden around R
Brit, incl mill stream and mill
pond. Extensive garden consisting
of formal walled, terraced and
vegetable gardens and bog garden.
Emphasis on spring bulbs, scented
flowers, hardy geraniums, lilies,
clematis and water irises. Wander
through the wild garden planted
with many rare and interesting
trees incl conifers, magnolias,
oak and fruit trees. Collection of
Magnolias flowering March to Sept.
Walled garden with water feature.
Collection of crab apples flowering
April to May and fruiting Aug to
Nov. Partial wheelchair access.
  🐕 ❀ 🚗 ☕

53 ◆ MINTERNE HOUSE

Minterne Magna, Dorchester,
DT2 7AU. The Hon Henry
& Mrs Digby, 01300 341370,
enquiries@minterne.co.uk,
www.minterne.co.uk. *2m N of
Cerne Abbas. On A352 Dorchester-
Sherborne rd.* **For opening times and
information, please phone, email or
visit garden website.**
As seen on BBC Gardeners'
World and voted one of the 10
prettiest gardens in England by The
Times. Famed for their display of
rhododendrons, azaleas, Japanese
cherries and magnolias in April/May.
Small lakes, streams and cascades
offer new vistas at each turn around
the 1m horseshoe shaped gardens
covering 23 acres. The season ends
with spectacular autumn colour.
Open mid Feb to 9 Nov (10-6).
Regret unsuitable for wheelchairs.
🐕 🚗 ☕

54 OLD DOWN HOUSE

Horton, Wimborne,
BH21 7HL. Dr & Mrs Colin
Davidson, 07765 404248,
pipdavidson59@gmail.com. *7½m N
of Wimborne. Horton Inn at junction of
B3078 with Horton Rd, pick up yellow
signs leading up through North Farm.
No garden access from Matterley
Drove. 5min walk to garden down
farm track.* **Wed 31 May, Wed 7
June (2-5), also open Mayfield.
Sun 11 June (2-5). Adm £3.50,
chd free. Home-made teas in
comfortable garden room if
weather inclement.**
Nestled down a farm track, this
¾ acre garden on chalk surrounds
C18 farmhouse. Stunning views
over Horton Tower and farmland.
Cottage garden planting with formal
elements, climbing roses clothe
pergola and house walls along
with stunning wisteria sinensis and
banksia rose. Part walled potager,
well stocked. Chickens. Not suitable
for wheelchairs.
❀ 🛏 ☕

55 NEW THE OLD RECTORY, LITTON CHENEY

Dorchester, DT2 9AH. Richard &
Emily Cave. *9m W of Dorchester.
1m S of A35, 6m E of Bridport. Small
village in the beautiful Bride Valley.
Park in village and follow signs.* **Sun
7, Wed 10 May, Sun 2, Wed 5
July (2-5). Adm £6, chd free.
Home-made teas.**
Steep paths lead to beguiling 4
acres of natural woodland with
many springs, streams, 2 pools one
a natural swimming pool planted
with native plants. Front garden
with pleached crabtree border,
topiary and soft planting incl tulips,
peonies, roses and verbascums.
Walled garden with informal
planting, kitchen garden, orchard
and 350 rose bushes for a cut
flower business. Formal front garden
designed by Arne Maynard. Featured
in Gardens Illustrated. Not suitable
for wheelchairs.
🐕 ☕

Western Gardens

56 THE OLD RECTORY, MANSTON

Manston, Sturminster Newton, DT10 1EX. Andrew & Judith Hussey, 01258 474673, judithhussey@hotmail.com. *6m S of Shaftesbury, 2½ m N of Sturminster Newton. From Shaftesbury, take B3091. On reaching Manston, past Plough Inn, L for Child Okeford on R-hand bend. Old Rectory last house on L.* Sun 11, Wed 14 June (2.30-5.30). Adm £5, chd free. Home-made teas. Visits also by arrangement May to Sept for groups of 4+.
Beautifully restored 5 acre garden. S-facing wall with 120ft herbaceous border edged by old brick path. Enclosed yew hedge flower garden. Wildflower meadow marked with mown paths and young plantation of mixed hardwoods. Well maintained walled Victorian kitchen garden. Knot garden now well established. Featured on BBC 2.
& ✿ 🚐 ☕

57 THE OLD RECTORY, NETHERBURY

Beaminster, DT6 5NB. Simon & Amanda Mehigan, www. oldrectorynetherbury.tumblr.com. *2m SW of Beaminster. Please park considerately in the village or the Mill House field near R Brit and walk up hill to garden. Disabled parking available at house.* Sun 16, Tue 18 Apr, Sun 21, Tue 23 May (11-5). Adm £5, chd free. Home-made teas. Refreshments from 11am.
5 acre garden developed by present owners over last 20 yrs. Formal areas with topiary near house, naturalistic planting elsewhere. Many bulbs including fritillaries, erythroniums, tulips and wood anemones. Extensive bog garden with pond and stream planted with candelabra primroses and other moisture lovers. Flowering trees: magnolias and cornus. Hornbeam walk. Decorative vegetable garden. Featured in Country Homes and Interiors & The English Garden.
🐕 ☕

58 THE OLD RECTORY, PULHAM

Dorchester, DT2 7EA. Mr & Mrs N Elliott, 01258 817595, gilly.elliott@hotmail.com. *13m N of Dorchester. 8m SE of Sherborne. On B3143 turn E at Xrds in Pulham. Signed Cannings Court.* Sun 14 May, Sun 11 June, Sun 6 Aug (2-5). Adm £6, chd free. Home-made teas. Visits also by arrangement May to Sept for groups, weekdays only.
4 acres formal and informal gardens surround C18 rectory, splendid views. Yew hedges, circular herbaceous borders with late summer colour. Exuberantly planted terrace, purple and white beds. Box parterres, mature trees, pond, fernery, ha-ha, pleached hornbeam circle. 10 acres woodland walks. Flourishing extended bog garden with islands; awash with primulas and irises in May. Dahlia garden in August. Interesting plants for sale. Featured on ITV and in Country Life, Dorset Life, Homes and Gardens, Country Homes and Interiors. Mostly wheelchair access.
& 🐄 ✿ 🚐 ☕

59 THE OLD RECTORY, WINTERBORNE STICKLAND

North Street, Winterborne Stickland, Blandford Forum, DT11 0NL. Kate & Gareth Penny. *5m SW of Blandford. From Blandford (Bryanston gates) follow signs on Fairmile Rd to Winterborne Stickland, 5m. On L past PH. From A354 take Whatcombe Lane through W Clenston to W Stickland. On R opp the green.* Sat 10, Sun 11 June (2-5). Adm £5, chd free. Home-made teas.
2 acre garden surrounding C17 house. 500 year old lime and superb ancient trees form the backdrop to a romantic unexpected and structured garden. Beech and yew hedges create terraced rooms on the sloping site for vegetable, rose and swimming pool gardens. Orchard with folly. Wood with hidden tree house. Formal around the house, drifting to less structured areas. Interesting garden sculptures. Slopes and steps.
☕

60 OLD SMITHY

Ibberton, DT11 0EN. Carol & Clive Carsley, 01258 817361, carolcarsley@btinternet.com. *9m NW of Blandford Forum. A357 Blandford to Sturminster Newton. After 6½ m L to Okeford Fitzpaine. Follow signs to Ibberton, 3m. Park at village hall. 5 min walk to garden. Mobility issues, park in drive opp Old Smithy.* Sat 15 Apr, Sun 14 May (2-5). Adm £4, chd free. Home-made teas in village hall. Visits also by arrangement Mar to Sept for groups of 10+.
Worth driving twisty narrow lanes to reach this rural 2½ acre streamside garden framing a thatched cottage. Back of beyond setting which inspired international best seller Mr Rosenblum's List. Succession of ponds. Mown paths. Spring bulbs in profusion, primula candelabras, aquilegia and hellebores. Sit beneath rustling trees. Views of Bulbarrow and church. Featured in Period Living, Dorset Life & Blackmore Vale Magazine.
🐄 ✿ ☕

61 THE OLD VICARAGE

East Orchard, Shaftesbury, SP7 0BA. Miss Tina Wright, 01747 811744, tina_lon@msn.com. *4½ m S of Shaftesbury, 3½ m N of Sturminster Newton. On B3091, on 90° bend, next to lay-by with phone box. Park in field opp, entrance as you turn corner towards Hartgrove & Fontmell Magna. Walk along verge, cross at 2nd open gate carefully checking for cars in the mirror.* Sun 19 Mar (1.30-4.30); Wed 5, Fri 7, Wed 12, Wed 19, Fri 21, Wed 26, Fri 28 Apr, Sun 11 June (2-5). Adm £4, chd free. Home-made teas. Teas will be inside if raining, with wood stove if cold. Visits also by arrangement Feb to Dec, any size group.
1.7 acre, award winning wildlife friendly garden. Swathes of crocus, primula and unusual snowdrops in spring. Many different daffodils and a tulip extravaganza with over 1000 tulip bulbs, then herbaceous borders and wild flowers. Sit by the bubbling stream or gaze at beautiful reflections in the swimming pond.

Dogs welcome and children can pond dip. Swing and tree platform overlooking Duncliffe woods. Teas indoors and various shelters around the garden if wet. Featured in numerous publications. Not suitable for wheelchairs if very wet.

 🐕 ✿ 🚻 ☕

62 NEW ♦ PRIEST'S HOUSE MUSEUM & GARDEN
23-27 High Street, Wimborne, BH21 1HR. Priest's House Museum Trust, 01202 882533, museum@priest-house.co.uk, www.priest-house.co.uk.
Wimborne town centre. Wimborne is just off A31. From W take B3078, from E take B3073 towards town centre. From Poole and Bournemouth enter town from S on A341. **For opening times and information, please phone, email or visit garden website.**
Discover a real gem tucked away in the centre of Wimborne. The walled garden, with its path leading from the back door to the mill stream, is 100 metres long. Colourful herbaceous borders and old varieties of apple and pear trees line the path further down. The garden is sheltered by brick walls which mark ancient property boundaries. Groups are asked to pre-book.

 🚻 ☕

63 PUDDLEDOCK COTTAGE
Scotland Heath, Norden, nr Corfe Castle, Wareham, BH20 5DY. Ray & Ann George, 01992 523947/01277 365398, rgeorge@mulberry-house.com.
Scotland Heath, Norden. From Wareham to Corfe Castle turn L at Norden Park and Ride, then L signed Slepe and Arne. Garden 500m on R. **Sat 17 June, Sat 5 Aug (12-4). Adm £4, chd free. Tea. Visits also by arrangement Apr to Sept for any size groups.** *Donation to Nationwide Christian Trust.*
Puddledock Cottage was originally a quarryman's cottage. Newly renovated, it now stands at the centre of a big lovingly created garden with streams and ponds edged with nectar rich plants that

attract a myriad of butterflies and bees. Shady walks snake though birch and willow, underplanted with rhododendrons and ferns. Views to Corfe Castle and Scotland Heath. Children's activities. Good wheelchair access.

 🐕 ✿ 🚻 ☕

64 Q
113 Bridport Road, Dorchester, DT1 2NH. Heather & Chris Robinson, 01305 263088, hmrobinson45@gmail.com. *Approx 300m W of Dorset County Hospital. From Top o' Town r'about head W towards Dorset County Hospital, Q 300 metres further on from Hospital on R.* **Suns 19, 26 Mar, 2, 9, 23 Apr, 7 May (2-5). Adm £3, chd free. Home-made teas. Visits also by arrangement Mar to July, min number 8, 40 max, 1wk notice preferred.**
Q is essentially all things to all men, a modern cottage town garden with many facets, jam packed with bulbs, shrubs, trees, climbers and bedding plants. Gazebo, statues, water, bonsai and topiary. Planting reflects the owners' many and varied interests including over 100 clematis, 1000+ spring bulbs purchased yearly. Q is a quirky garden, laid out in 'rooms' with each area displaying different gardening interest from Bonsai to water features. A variety of fruit and vegetables is also grown. Small number of paths available for wheelchair users.

 🚻 ☕

65 25 RICHMOND PARK AVENUE
Bournemouth, BH8 9DL. Barbara Hutchinson & Mike Roberts, 01202 531072, barbarahutchinson@tiscali.co.uk. *2½ m NE Bournemouth Town Centre. From T-lights at junction with Alma Rd and Richmond Park Rd, head N on B3063 Charminster Rd, 2nd turning on R into Richmond Park Ave.* **Sun 18 June (1-5), also open Western Gardens. Sun 2 July (1-5). Sun 23 July (1-5), also open 2 Spur Gate. Thur 3 Aug (1-5). Adm £3, chd free. Home-made teas. Visits also by arrangement in July for groups of 10+.**

Beautifully designed town garden with pergola leading to ivy canopy over raised decking. Cascading waterfall connects 2 wildlife ponds enhanced with domed acers. Circular lawn with colourful herbaceous border planted to attract bees and butterflies. Fragrant S-facing courtyard garden at front, sparkling with vibrant colour and Mediterranean planting including lilies, brugmansias and lemon tree. Featured in Dorset Country Gardener. Partial wheelchair access.

 ✿ 🚻 ☕

66 ♦ SCULPTURE BY THE LAKES
Pallington Lakes, Pallington, Dorchester, DT2 8QU. Mrs Monique Gudgeon, 07720 637808, sbtl@me.com, www.sculpturebythelakes.co.uk. *6m E of Dorchester. ½ m E of Tincleton, see beech hedge and security gates. From other direction ¾ m from Xrds. No children under 14. No dogs allowed.* **For NGS: Wed 21 June, Wed 5 July (11-5). Adm £7.50. Purbeck Ice cream available. For other opening times and information, please phone, email or visit garden website.**
Recently created modern garden with inspiration taken from all over the world. Described as a modern arcadia it follows traditions of the landscape movement, but for C21. Where sculpture has been placed, the planting palette has been kept simple, but dramatic, so that the work remains the star. Home to Monique and her husband, renowned British sculptor Simon Gudgeon, the sculpture park features over 30 of his most iconic pieces including Isis, which is also in London's Hyde Park and a dedicated gallery where some of his smaller pieces can be seen and purchased. Disabled access limited though possible to go round paths on mobility scooter or electric wheelchair if care taken.

 🚻 ☕

67 THE SECRET GARDEN

The Friary, Hilfield, Dorchester, DT2 7BE. The Society of St Francis, 01300 341345, hilfieldssf@franciscans.org.uk, www.hilfieldfriary.org.uk. *10m N of Dorchester, on A352 between Sherborne & Dorchester. 1st L after Minterne Magna, 1st turning on R signed The Friary. From Yeovil turn off A37 signed Batcombe, 3rd turning on L.* **Sat 20, Sun 21 May (2-5). Adm £5, chd free. Home-made teas. Visits also by arrangement May to Sept.** Ongoing reclamation of neglected woodland garden. New plantings from modern day plant hunters. Mature trees, bamboo, rhododendrons, azaleas, magnolias, camellias, other choice shrubs with stream on all sides crossed by bridges, and in spring a growing collection of loderi hybrids. New plantings from Crug Farm Plants. Stout shoes recommended for woodland garden. Friary grounds open where meadows, woods and livestock can be viewed. Friary Shop selling a variety of gifts.

🐕 🏛 🍵

68 THE SECRET GARDEN AND SERLES HOUSE

47 Victoria Road, Wimborne, BH21 1EN. Ian Willis. *Centre of Wimborne. On B3082 W of town, very near hospital, Westfield car park 300yds. Off-road parking close by.* **Thur 20, Sun 23, Sun 30 July (2-5). Thur 3 Aug (2-5), also open Staddlestones. Sun 6, Sun 20, Sun 27, Mon 28, Thur 31 Aug, Sat 2, Sun 3, Sun 10 Sept (2-5). Adm £3, chd free. Home-made teas.** *Donation to Wimborne Civic Society and NADFAS.* Alan Titchmarsh described this

amusingly creative garden as 'one of the best 10 private gardens in Britain'. The ingenious use of unusual plants complements the imaginative treasure trove of garden objects d'art. The enchanting house is also open. A feeling of a bygone age accompanies your tour as you step into a world of whimsical fantasy that is theatrical and unique. Oriental garden now open. Antiques and bric-a-brac on sale. Featured in Dorset Country Gardener, Stour & Avon magazine, Garden Answers. Wheelchair access to garden only. Narrow steps may prohibit wide wheelchairs.

⚧ 🐕 ✿ 🚗 🍵

69 ♦ SHERBORNE CASTLE

New Rd, Sherborne, DT9 5NR. Mr E Wingfield Digby, 01935 812072, www.sherbornecastle.com. *½ m E of Sherborne. On New Rd B3145. Follow brown signs from A30 & A352.* **For opening times and information, please phone or visit garden website.** 40+ acres. Grade I Capability Brown garden with magnificent vistas across surrounding landscape, incl lake and views to ruined castle. Herbaceous planting, notable trees, mixed ornamental planting and managed wilderness are linked together with lawn and pathways. Dry grounds walk. Partial wheelchair access, gravel paths, steep slopes, steps.

⚧ 🐕 🚗 🍵

70 SLAPE MANOR

Netherbury, DT6 5LH. Mr & Mrs Antony Hichens, 01308 488232, sczhichens@btinternet.com. *1m S of Beaminster. Turn W off A3066 to Netherbury. House ½ m S of*

Netherbury on back rd to Bridport signed Waytown. **Sun 28 May (2-5). Adm £4, chd free. Home-made teas. Visits also by arrangement for groups of 10+.** River valley garden with spacious lawns and primula fringed streams down to lake. Walk over the stream with magnificent hostas, gunneras and horizontal cryptomeria Japonica Elegans, and around the lake. Admire the mature wellingtonias, ancient wisterias, rhododendrons and planting around the house. Mostly flat with some sloping paths and steps.

⚧ 🐕 ✿ 🍵

71 2 SPUR GATE

24 Spur Hill Avenue, Parkstone, Poole, BH14 9PH. Mr & Mrs R J P Butler, 01202 732342, annebbutler@btinternet.com. *3m W of Bournemouth. At end of Wessex Way (A 338) take 3rd exit (Lindsay Rd). Continue to end. R at T-Lights. After next T-Lights, 2nd L into Kings Ave. Top of hill turn R into Spurhill Ave. Please park on rd.* **Sat 6, Sun 7 May, Sat 22 July (2-5). Sun 23 July (2-5), also open 25 Richmond Park Avenue. Adm £4, chd free. Home-made teas. Visits also by arrangement Apr to Oct for groups of 10 to 20.** Town garden designed around modern house on steep slope. Over 8yrs, this challenging site has been converted into a series of banks and terraces which progress from the formality of pool terraces to a gravel garden, Japanese area and woodland. The Teahouse offers a peaceful and sheltered destination from which to view the house set above its bank of Stipa grasses. New living roof. Regret no wheelchair access.

🍵

72 STADDLESTONES

14 Witchampton Mill, Witchampton, Wimborne, BH21 5DE. Mrs Annette Lockwood, 01258 841405. *5m N of Wimborne off B3078. Follow signs through village and park in sports field, 7 min walk to garden, limited disabled parking near garden.* **Thur 27 Apr, Thur 11, Mon 29 May, Thur 29 June (2-5). Thur 3 Aug (2-5), also open The Secret**

Chideock Manor

© Val Corbett

Garden and Serles House.
**Thur 7 Sept (2-5). Adm £4, chd
free. Cream teas. Visits also by
arrangement Apr to Sept for
groups of 10+.**
Cottage garden with colour themed
borders, pleached limes and hidden
gems, leading over chalk stream
to shady area which has some
unusual plants incl hardy orchids and
arisaemas. Plenty of areas just to
sit and enjoy the wildlife. Wire bird
sculptures by local artist. Featured
in Dorset Life. Wheelchair access to
first half of garden.
& ❀ ☕ ❤

**73 ◆ UPTON COUNTRY
PARK**
Upton, Poole, BH17 7BJ.
Borough of Poole, 01202 262753,
uptoncountrypark@poole.gov.uk,
www.uptoncountrypark.com. *3m
W of Poole town centre. On S side
of A35/A3049. Follow brown signs.*
**For opening times and information,
please phone, email or visit garden
website.**
Over 130 acres of award winning
parkland incl formal gardens, walled
garden, woodland and shoreline.
Maritime micro-climate offers a
wonderful collection of unusual
trees, vintage camellias and stunning
roses. Home to Upton House,
Grade II* listed Georgian mansion.
Regular special events. Plant centre,
art gallery and tea rooms. Free car
parking and entry to park. Open
8am - 6pm (winter) and 8am - 9pm
(summer). www.facebook.com/
uptoncountrypark.
& 🐐 ❀ 🚗 ☕ ❤

WATERDALE HOUSE
See Wiltshire

74 NEW WELL COTTAGE
Ryall, Bridport, DT6 6EJ. John &
Heather Coley. *Less than 1m N of
A35 from Morcombelake. From E:
R by farm shop in Morcombelake.
Garden 0.9m on R. From W: L entering
Morcombelake, immed R by village
hall and L on Pitmans Lane to T junc.
Turn R, Well Cott on L. Parking on site
and nearby.* **Sat 20, Sun 21, Tue 23
May, Sat 22, Sun 23, Tue 25 July
(11-5). Adm £4, chd free. Light
refreshments.**

1 acre garden brought back to
life over last 4½ yrs. There is now
much more light after some trees
were taken down and new areas
have been cultivated. The planting
is intended to be natural and the
emphasis is very much on colour.
A number of distinct areas, some
quite surprising but most still enjoy
wonderful views over Marshwood
Vale. Heather's textile art studio will
be open to view. Wheelchair access
possible but there are few hard
surface paths, slopes and steps.
🐐 ❤

75 WESTERN GARDENS
24A Western Ave, Branksome
Park, Poole, BH13 7AN. Mr Peter
Jackson. *3m W of Bournemouth.
From S end Wessex Way (A338) at
gyratory take The Avenue, 2nd exit.
At T-lights turn R into Western Rd
then at bottom of hill L. At church
turn R into Western Ave.* **Sun 30
Apr (2-5.30), also open 1692
Wimborne Road. Sun 18
June (2-5.30), also open 25
Richmond Park Avenue. Sun 30
July, Sun 3 Sept (2-5.30). Adm
£4, chd free. Home-made teas.**
'This secluded and magical 1-acre
garden captures the spirit of warmer
climes and begs for repeated visits'
(Gardening Which?). Created over
40 yrs it offers enormous variety
with rose, Mediterranean courtyard
and woodland gardens, herbaceous
borders and cherry tree and camellia
walk. Lush foliage and vibrant flowers
give yr-round colour and interest
enhanced by sculpture and topiary.
Home-made jams and chutneys for
sale. Wheelchair access to ¾ garden.
& 🐐 ❀ 🚗 ☕ ❤

**76 1692 WIMBORNE
ROAD**
Bear Cross, BH11 9AL. Sue
& Mike Cleall. *5m NW of
Bournemouth. On A341, 200yds E of
Bear Cross r'about.* **Sun 30 Apr (2-
5), also open Western Gardens.
Sun 14, Sun 28 May (2-5). Adm
£3.50, chd free. Home-made
teas.**
Suburban garden 120ft x 50ft.
Rhododendrons, acers and azaleas
are underplanted with woodland
plants for spring. Tulips add colour.

Man-made stream with waterfall
and water feature runs through
lawned area. Pond with statue.
Fountain attracts wildlife. Various
seating areas around garden and
tea in summerhouse is a pleasant
experience. Mostly flat areas.
& 🚗 ❤

77 WINCOMBE PARK
Shaftesbury, SP7 9AB. John &
Phoebe Fortescue. *2m N of
Shaftesbury. A350 Shaftesbury to
Warminster, past Wincombe Business
Park, 1st R signed Wincombe &
Donhead St Mary. ¾m on R.* **Sun
14, Wed 17 May (2-5). Adm
£5, chd free. Cream teas,
homemade cakes and biscuits,
tea, coffee, squash. Dairy and
gluten free available.**
Extensive mature garden with
sweeping panoramic views from
lawn over parkland to lake and
enchanting woods through which
you can wander amongst bluebells.
Garden is a riot of colour in spring
with azaleas, rhododendrons and
camellias in flower amongst shrubs
and unusual trees. Beautiful walled
kitchen garden. Partial wheelchair
access, slopes and gravel paths.
& 🐐 ❀ 🚗 ❤

78 WOLVERHOLLOW
Elsdons Lane, Monkton Wyld,
DT6 6DA. Mr & Mrs D Wiscombe,
01297 560610. *4m N of Lyme Regis.
4m NW of Charmouth. Monkton
Wyld is signed from A35 approx
4m NW of Charmouth off dual
carriageway. Wolverhollow next to
church.* **Sun 14, Mon 15 May, Sun
20, Mon 21 Aug (11.30-4.30).
Adm £4, chd free. Home-made
teas. Visits also by arrangement
May to Aug.**
Over 1 acre of informal mature
garden on different levels. Lawns
lead past borders and rockeries
down to a shady lower garden.
Numerous paths take you past a
variety of uncommon shrubs and
plants. A managed meadow has
an abundance of primulas growing
close to stream. A garden not to be
missed! Cabin in meadow area from
which vintage, retro and other lovely
things can be purchased.
🐐 ❀ ☕ ❤

ESSEX

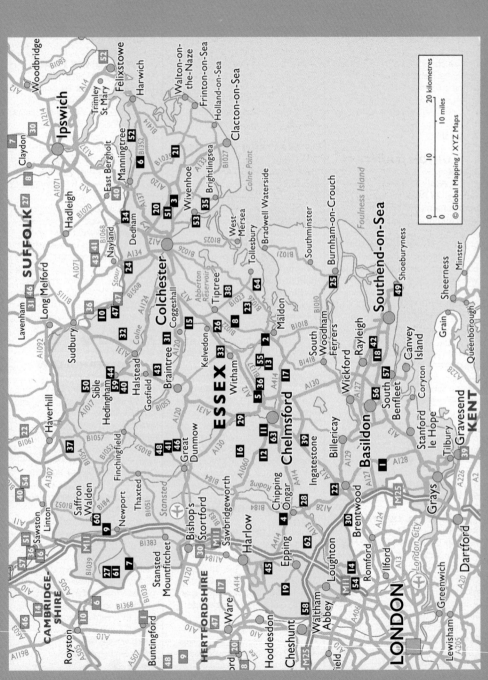

Close to London but with its own unique character, Essex is perhaps England's best kept secret - with a beautiful coastline, rolling countryside and exquisite villages. It is a little known fact that over seventy per cent of Essex is rural. There are wide horizons, ancient woodlands and hamlets pierced by flint church spires.

Please come and visit our Essex gardens and gain inspiration for your own keenly cultivated patch. It is full of surprises with glorious gardens spread across one amazing county. Essex is the home of 'Constable Country', and we have a range of attractive gardens in and around that delightful picturesque area. Indeed, from the four corners of Essex we offer lots to explore, from a garden featuring the smallest thatched cottage in England within its grounds, to grand country estates.

In 2017, we feature a new garden with a mile-long Labyrinth that is a perfect way to gain some moments of peace and tranquility. Essex is proud to have a collection of exciting and beautiful gardens for you to discover including our renowned tulip gardens, fragrant rose gardens and newly designed modern gardens. You will find gardens to suit all tastes. So why not take a few hours out of the hurly burly of life, unwind and wander around our county's picturesque gardens? Or plan a whole day out by making arrangements to visit a garden with a group. Remember, some of our gardens aren't just for plant enthusiasts but are perfect for the whole family to enjoy.

Visitors can be assured of a warm welcome at every open garden gate, whether hidden away down narrow country lanes, in attractive towns or along the estuaries of the east coast. Forget the clichés - rediscover Essex!

Volunteers

County Organiser
Susan Copeland
01799 550553
susan.copeland@ngs.org.uk

County Treasurer
Richard Steers
07392 426490
steers123@aol.com

Publicity & Booklet Co-ordinator
Doug Copeland
01799 550553
dougcopeland@btinternet.com

Publicity
David Cox
01245 222165
elwylodge@gmail.com

Assistant County Organisers
Tricia Brett
01255 870415
brett.milestones@hotmail.co.uk

Avril & Roger Cole-Jones
01245 225726
randacj@gmail.com

David Cox
(as above)

Linda & Frank Jewson
01992 714047
frank.jewson@btconnect.com

Groups and Talks
Linda Holdaway
01621 782137
lindaholdaway@btinternet.com

Talks
Neil Holdaway
01621 782137
mail@neilholdaway.com

Left: **Furzelea**

OPENING DATES

All entries subject to change. For latest information check **www.ngs.org.uk**

Extended openings are shown at the beginning of the month.

Map locator numbers are shown to the right of each garden name.

February

Snowdrop Festival

Wednesday 15th
Dragons   12

Saturday 18th
The Old Rectory   36

Sunday 19th
The Old Rectory   36

March

Saturday 4th
St Helens   46

Saturday 18th
◆ Beth Chatto Gardens   3

Sunday 19th
Wickets   61

April

Barnards Farm
(Every Thursday from
Thursday 20th)   1
Feeringbury Manor
(Every Thursday
and Friday from
Thursday 6th)   15

Sunday 16th
Tudor Roost   53

Monday 17th
Fairwinds   14
Tudor Roost   53

Friday 21st
NEW 30 Glenwood
Avenue   18

Sunday 23rd
NEW 30 Glenwood
Avenue   18

Peacocks   39

Wednesday 26th
Furzelea   17

Friday 28th
◆ Beeleigh Abbey
Gardens   2

Sunday 30th
Peppers Farm   40
Ulting Wick   55

May

Barnards Farm
(Every Thursday)   1
Feeringbury Manor
(Every Thursday
and Friday)   15

Monday 1st
Furzelea   17
Wickets   61

Friday 5th
Ulting Wick   55

Sunday 7th
◆ Green Island   20

Thursday 11th
Writtle University
College   63

Friday 12th
Ulting Wick   55

Sunday 14th
Elwy Lodge   13

Friday 19th
NEW Wycke Farm   64

Sunday 21st
NEW Wycke Farm   64

90th Anniversary Weekend

Sunday 28th
Chippins   6
Langley Village Gardens   27
Parsonage House   37
NEW 3 Pound Gate   41
Waltham Abbey
Group   58

Monday 29th
NEW Goosebury Hall   19
Rookwoods   44

Tuesday 30th
8 Dene Court   11

June

Barnards Farm
(Every Thursday)   1
Feeringbury Manor
(Every Thursday
and Friday)   15

Saturday 3rd
Boreham Gardens   5
Moverons   35
Tudor Roost   53

Sunday 4th
Boreham Gardens   5
Furzelea   17
8 Mill Lane   32
Moverons   35
Snares Hill Cottage   48
Tudor Roost   53

Tuesday 6th
8 Dene Court   11

Saturday 10th
NEW Woodhatch Farm   62

Sunday 11th
Clavering Gardens   7
Horkesley Hall   24
Miraflores   33
◆ Spencers   50
Washlands   59

Wednesday 14th
Long House Plants   30
Washlands   59

Thursday 15th
Little Waltham Hall   29

Friday 16th
8 Dene Court   11

Saturday 17th
Spring Cottage   51

Sunday 18th
◆ Daws Hall   10
Elwy Lodge   13
Keeway   25
NEW 3 Pound Gate   41
Rayleigh Gardens   42
Spring Cottage   51
Washlands   59

Wednesday 21st
Keeway   25

Friday 23rd
Ulting Wick   55

Saturday 24th
Barnards Farm   1

Sunday 25th
Barnards Farm   1
Blake Hall   4

---

37 Turpins Lane   54
37 Underhill Road   57

Tuesday 27th
8 Dene Court   11

July

Barnards Farm
(Every Thursday)   1
Feeringbury Manor
(Every Thursday
and Friday to
Friday 28th)   15

Saturday 1st
Tudor Roost   53

Sunday 2nd
Fudlers Hall   16
Little Myles   28
Tudor Roost   53
Wickets   61

Tuesday 4th
8 Dene Court   11

Saturday 8th
69 Rundells   45

Sunday 9th
Chippins   6
Wendens Ambo
Gardens   60

Tuesday 11th
8 Dene Court   11

Wednesday 12th
Long House Plants   30

Saturday 15th
14 Una Road   56
NEW Woodhatch Farm   62

Sunday 16th
Elwy Lodge   13
262 Hatch Road   22
14 Una Road   56

Friday 21st
8 Dene Court   11
Dragons   12

Sunday 23rd
Fudlers Hall   16
262 Hatch Road   22
NEW Havendell   23
37 Turpins Lane   54

Sunday 30th
60 Colchester Road   8
Rayleigh Gardens   42
South Shoebury Hall   49
37 Underhill Road   57

Wickets

THE GARDENS

1 BARNARDS FARM

Brentwood Road, West Horndon, Brentwood, CM13 3LX. Bernard & Sylvia Holmes & The Christabella Charitable Trust, 01277 811262, sylvia@barnardsfarm.eu, www.barnardsfarm.eu. *5m S of Brentwood. On A128 1½ m S of A127 Halfway House flyover. From Junction continue on A128 under the railway bridge. Garden on R just past bridge.* **Pre- booking is essential for our Musical Evening on Sat 24 June featuring the Dixie Mix Jazz Band, Rod Stewart's backing group on his 2014 UK tour. Booking via Barnards Farm website only. Bottles of wine available to purchase. Strawberries and cream are included. This is a 'Picnic' event so bring your own. Adm £25 chd £10. Gates open 5.00pm, concert starts 6.15pm & finishes at 9.00pm.** *Every Thur 20 Apr to 31 Aug (11-4). Adm £7.50, chd £2.50. Light refreshments. Evening opening Sat 24 June (5-9). Adm £25, chd £10. Wine. Sun 25 June, Sun 3 Sept (2-5). Adm £10, chd £3. Home-made teas. tea, coffee, cakes, soup and light lunches (Thurs), home-made cakes, tea, coffee (Suns) Strawberries & cream plus wine available, Sat 24 June.* **Visits** also **by arrangement May to Sept for groups of min 20** *Donation to St Francis Church.* So much to explore! Climb the Belvedere for the wider view and take the train for a woodland adventure. Spring bulbs and blossom, summer beds and borders, ponds, lakes and streams, walled vegetable plot. 'Japanese garden', sculptures grand and quirky enhance and delight... Barnards Miniature Railway rides (BMR) :Separate charges apply. Sunday extras: Bernard's Sculpture tour 2.30pm Veteran and vintage vehicle collection. 1920s Cycle shop. Collect loyalty points on Thur visits and earn a free Sun or Thur entry. Aviators welcome (PPO), see website for details.. Featured on

'Flog It'.. Wheelchair accessible WC Golf buggy tour available.
&. ✿ NPC ☕ 🍷

2 ◆ BEELEIGH ABBEY GARDENS

Abbey Turning, Beeleigh, Maldon, CM9 6LL. Christopher & Catherine Foyle, 07506 867122, www.visitmaldon.co.uk/beeleigh-abbey. *1m NW of Maldon. Leaving Maldon via London Road take 1st R after Cemetery into Abbey Turning.* For NGS: Fri 28 Apr (10.30-4.30). Adm £6, chd £2.50. Cream teas. Light Refreshments **For other opening times and information, please phone or visit garden website.** 3 acres of secluded gardens in rural historic setting. Mature trees surround variety of planting and water features, woodland walks underplanted with bulbs leading to tidal river, cottage garden, kitchen garden, orchard, wild flower meadow, rose garden, wisteria walk, magnolia trees, lawn with 85yd long herbaceous border. Scenic backdrop of remains of C12 abbey incorporated into private house (not open). Refreshments including Hot & Cold Drinks, Cakes and Rolls. Gravel paths, some gentle slopes and some steps. Large WC with ramp and handlebars.
&. ✿ ☕ 🍷

3 ◆ BETH CHATTO GARDENS

Elmstead Market, Colchester, CO7 7DB. Mrs Beth Chatto, 01206 822007, info@bethchatto.co.uk, www.bethchatto.co.uk. *¼m E of Elmstead Market. On A133 Colchester to Clacton Rd in village of Elmstead Market.* For NGS: Sat 18 Mar (9-5); Sun 1 Oct (10-5). Adm £6.95, chd free. Home-made teas. **For other opening times and information, please phone, email or visit garden website.** Internationally famous gardens, including dry, damp and woodland areas. The result of over 50 years of hard work and application of the huge body of plant knowledge possessed by Beth Chatto and her late husband Andrew. Visitors cannot fail to be affected by the peace

and beauty of the garden. We have a large Tearoom overlooking the Gravel Garden and nursery, offering homemade breakfasts, lunches and teas. It is also fully licensed. Large plant nursery. Adm £6.95, children under 16 and Carers free. March - Oct, £4 Nov - Feb. Featured in The Garden Magazine: Great Gardens Visits The Beth Chatto Gardens , The Guardian: Herbaceous Borders, The Beth Chatto Collections, Essex Life. Disabled WC & parking.
&. ✿ 🚗 ☕ 🍷

4 BLAKE HALL

Bobbingworth, CM5 0DG. Mr & Mrs H Capel Cure, www.blakehall.co.uk. *10m W of Chelmsford. Just off A414 between Four Wantz r'about in Ongar & Talbot r'about in North Weald. Signed on A414.* Sun 25 June (11-4). Adm £4, chd free. Home-made teas in C17 barn. 25 acres of mature gardens within the historic setting of Blake Hall (not open). Arboretum with broad variety of specimen trees. Spectacular rambling roses clamber up ancient trees. Traditional formal rose garden and herbaceous border. Sweeping lawns. Some gravel paths.
&. 🍷

GROUP OPENING

5 BOREHAM GARDENS

Boreham, Chelmsford, CM3 3EF. *4m NE Chelmsford. Take B1137 Boreham Village, turn into Church Rd at Lion Inn. Caynton Cottage is 50mtrs on L. Brookfield 400mtrs on R, Monalee is accessed from Brookfield.* Sat 3, Sun 4 June (1-5). Combined adm £6, chd free. Cream teas at Brookfield. Delicious home made cakes.

BROOKFIELD
Bob & Linda Taylor.

CAYNTON COTTAGE
Les & Lynn Mann, 01245 463490, lesmann15@gmail.com.
Visits also by arrangement June & July for groups up to 20. Tea/Coffee and home-made cake included in the admission fee.

Shrubs Farm

MONALEE
Andrew & Debora Overington.

Three stunning, inspirational and very different gardens in the lovely village of Boreham. At Brookfield, a rose covered wall backing a perennial border greets you, with a raised bed vegetable garden, perennial island beds and pond with shrub bank. A meadow, bright with buttercups, is bordered by many trees and a woodland walk, where the last rhododendrons and camellias may be seen. Roses abound and the Rambling Rector in the orchard is a delight. Since 2013 the new garden at Caynton Cottage has been designed and planted by the owners from a neglected and overgrown plot surrounding a C15 thatched cottage. It is now planted with an excellent selection of shrubs and perennials for maximum all year interest, with a small wildlife pond and dry stream. At Monalee, after the removal of several trees, the new light gained has allowed larger, colourful flower beds to flourish. Highlights are an oriental garden, raised pond, new cut flower bed, enclosed patio and summer house. Brookfield, wheelchair accessible, partial access to meadow. Caynton Cottage gravel paths throughout, Monalee narrow paths, not wheelchair friendly.

    ♿ ❀ ☕

6 CHIPPINS
Heath Road, Bradfield, CO11 2UZ. Kit & Ceri Leese, 01255 870730, ceriandkit1@btinternet.com. 3m E of Manningtree. Take A137 from Manningtree Station, turn L opp garage. Take first R towards Clacton. At Radio Mast turn L into Bradfield continue through village. Bungalow is opp primary school. **Sun 28 May, Sun 9 July (11-4.30). Adm £3.50, chd free. Home made teas. Delicious home made cakes also available!. Visits also by arrangement May to July groups very welcome - Kit is also an artist, and will happily show people around the studio!.** Artist's garden and plantaholics' paradise packed with interest. Springtime heralds irises, hostas and

alliums. Stream and wildlife pond brimming with bog plants. Summer hosts an explosion of colour with pots, hanging baskets. Wide borders feature hemerocallis, rambling roses, dahlias, salvias and exotics (front bed featuring, aeonium, unusual agaves, aloes and cacti) Studio open with press. Kit is a landscape artist and printmaker, pictures always on display. Afternoon tea with delicious homemade cakes is also available for small parties on specific days if booked in advance.

    ♿ ❀ 🚐 ☕

GROUP OPENING

7 CLAVERING GARDENS
Middle Street, Clavering, CB11 4QL. *7m N of Bishop's Stortford. On B1038. Turn W off B1383 at Newport. Parking at Fox & Hounds PH & in Middle St. Hawthorns ½m from village by windmills with parking. Limited parking in Pelham Rd nr Piercewebbs.* **Sun 11 June (11-5). Combined adm £6, chd free. Light refreshments at Chestnut Cottage. Light lunches and home-made teas.**

CHESTNUT COTTAGE
Carol & Mike Wilkinson.

NEW HAWTHORNS
Mr & Mrs Bob & Jane Woodhouse.

PIERCEWEBBS
Mrs J William-Powlett, jwp@william-powlett.net. **Visits also by arrangement Mar to Oct groups of 10-20 welcome.**

Popular village with many C16/17 timber-framed dwellings. Beautiful C14 church, village green with thatched cricket pavilion and pitch. Chestnut Cottage is 1 acre cottage garden with sweeping lawns and wide mixed borders, opposite Clavering Ford. Lots of pathways and seats to sit and contemplate, and stunning views over the medieval heart of the village. Come and see 'The Little House', (open), built in 1760 and reputedly the smallest thatched cottage in England. Hawthorns is approx ½ acre, designed for all year round colour and interest with mixture of herbaceous plants, shrubs for flowers and leaf colour and several small mature trees .Three sitting areas with acers in tubs and ericaceous containers. Large herbaceous border divides rear garden from shady orchard area. Roses and fuchsias add colour to shrub beds. Piercewebbs has formal old walled garden, shrubs, lawns, ha-ha, yew with topiary, stilt hedge, pond and trellised rose garden. Landscaped field walk. Extensive views over countryside. Jamie Oliver was brought up in Clavering where his parents still run The Cricketers PH. A footpath for keen walkers across fields gains access to Hawthorns from Chestnut Cottage. Local honey for sale. Some limited access at Chestnut Cottage due to slopes. Dogs on leads at Piercewebbs where wheelchair access is via gravel drive or shallow step.

    ♿ ❀ 🚐 ☕

8 60 COLCHESTER ROAD

Great Totham, nr Maldon,
CM9 8DG. Mrs Sue Jackman. *5m
NE of Maldon. On B1022 Maldon to
Colchester Rd at Totham North.* Sun
30 July (11-5). Adm £4, chd free.
Light refreshments.
A ¾ acre keen plantwoman's
garden with large colour-themed
borders, situated in both sun and
shade. Borders are planted for
a long season of interest with
many unusual species, particularly
perennials. Rock garden full of spring
and autumn bulbs and alpines. A rill
leading to watersteps, and circular
pool overlooked by a summerhouse.
Small vegetable garden.

9 CROSSWAYS

Rookery Lane, Wendens Ambo,
Saffron Walden, CB11 4JR.
Mrs Andrea Reynolds,
Familyreynolds@mac.com.
*3m from Saffron Walden, 1m from
Newport. Leave Newport on B1383
towards Cambridge over 1st r'about
then immed L- 250 yds on R
between main rd & level crossing.*
Visits by arrangement Mar
to Oct groups of 8+. Home-
made teas. Refreshments by
arrangement- teas, cakes, wine
etc.
Gently sloping garden, about
5 acres of informal 'family' garden
with mixed planting for year round
interest. Some wildlife areas and
wild flower area bordering part of
the garden. Large pond which is
haven for frogs! Interesting selection
of trees. Wheelchair access to most
of garden over short distance of
gravel.

10 ♦ DAWS HALL

Henny Road, Lamarsh, Bures,
CO8 5EX. Major & Mrs Iain
Grahame, 01787 269213,
info@majorbooks.co.uk,
www.dawshallnature.co.uk.
*3m from Sudbury. 2m from Bures
on Essex side of R Stour.* For NGS:
Sun 18 June (1-5). Adm £6,
chd free. Cream teas. For other
opening times and information,
please phone, email or visit garden
website.

Garden contains 8 acres rare
and unusual trees and shrubs, incl
400-yr-old cedar of Lebanon and
300-yr-old tulip tree, several species
of waterfowl incl breeding flock of
Red-breasted Geese. 25-acre nature
reserve with wildflower meadow,
river and ponds. Observation
beehive and honey for sale. For
guided tours for groups (min 8) in
aid of Daws Hall Trust, please tel,
teas by arrangement.

11 8 DENE COURT

Chignall Road, Chelmsford,
CM1 2JQ. Mrs Sheila Chapman,
01245 266156. *W of Chelmsford
(Parkway). Take A1060 Roxwell
Rd for 1m. Turn R at T-lights into
Chignall Rd. Dene Court 3rd exit on
R. Parking in Chignall Rd.* Tue 30
May, Tue 6, Fri 16, Tue 27 June,
Tue 4, Tue 11 July (2-5). Fri 21
July (2-5), also open Dragons.
Adm £3, chd free. Visits also by
arrangement June & July.
Beautifully maintained and designed
compact garden (250sq yds).
Owner is well-known RHS gold
medal-winning exhibitor (now
retired). Circular lawn, long pergola
and walls festooned with roses and
climbers. Large selection of unusual
clematis. Densely-planted colour
coordinated perennials add interest
from May to Sept in this immaculate
garden.

12 DRAGONS

Boyton Cross, Chelmsford,
CM1 4LS. Mrs Margot Grice,
01245 248651,
mandmdragons@tiscali.co.uk. *3m
W of Chelmsford. On A1060. ½m W
of The Hare PH.* Wed 15 Feb (12-
3). Fri 21 July (2-5), also open 8
Dene Court. Tue 15 Aug, Wed
20 Sept (2-5). Adm £4, chd free.
Home-made teas. Visits also by
arrangement Feb to Sept for
groups of 10+.
A plantswoman's ¾ acre garden,
planted to encourage wildlife.
Sumptuous colour-themed borders
with striking plant combinations,
featuring specimen plants, fernery,
clematis,and grasses. Meandering
paths lead to ponds, patio, scree

garden and small vegetable
garden. Two summerhouses, one
overlooking stream and farmland.

13 ELWY LODGE

West Bowers Rd, Woodham
Walter, CM9 6RZ. David &
Laura Cox, 01245 222165,
elwylodge@gmail.com. *Just outside
Woodham Walter village. From
Chelmsford, A414 to Danbury. L at
2nd mini r'about into Little Baddow
Rd. From Colchester, A12 to Hatfield
Peverel, L onto B1019. Follow NGS
signs.* Sun 14 May, Sun 18 June,
Sun 16 July (11-5). Adm £4.50,
chd free. Home-made teas.
Seasonal and Special home
made cakes not to be missed.
Visits also by arrangement May
to July.
On entering the drive, the hidden
secrets of this highly praised,
peaceful garden will surprise and
delight! Flowing lawns, herbaceous
borders, unusual plants, trees, wildlife
pond and a small meadow area.
Secluded chamomile-scented lower
garden with raised vegetable beds
and fruit trees leading to a delightful
summer house with amazing views
over the countryside towards
Blackwater Estuary. Enjoy! Sloping
uneven lawn in parts. Please check
wheelchair access with garden
owner before visiting.

14 FAIRWINDS

Chapel Lane, Chigwell
Row, IG7 6JJ. Sue & David
Coates, 07731 796467,
scoates@forest.org.uk. *2m SE of
Chigwell. Grange Hill Tube, turn R
at exit, 10 mins walk uphill. Car: Nr
M25 J26 & N Circular Waterworks
r'about. Follow signs for Chigwell.
Fork right for Manor/Lambourne
Rd. Park in Lodge Close Car Park.*
Mon 17 Apr (2-5). Adm £3, chd
free. Home-made teas. Free
refills of tea/coffee. Visits also
by arrangement Mar to Oct
refreshments by arrangement.
Groups of 10 to 20 only. Tours
if requested.
Gravelled front garden and three
differently styled back garden spaces
with something different every

year. Places for you to sit, relax and enjoy. Start with themed flower borders - planting influenced by Beth Chatto, Penelope Hobhouse and Christopher Lloyd. Move on to a woodland garden - shade planting and home to our hens. Beyond the rustic fence, lies the wildlife pond and vegetable plot. Happy hens. Happy insects in bee house, bug house, log piles and sampling the spring pollen. Newts in pond. There be dragons a plenty!! Gardeners World Magazine - photographs to support articles and setting for a number of their wildlife videos. Space for 2 disabled cars to park by the house. Wood chip paths in woodland area may require assistance.

  🚻 🐈 ☕️

15 FEERINGBURY MANOR
Coggeshall Road, Feering, Colchester, CO5 9RB. Mr & Mrs Giles Coode-Adams, 01376 561946, seca@btinternet.com, www.ngs.org.uk. *12m SW of Colchester. Between Feering & Coggeshall on Coggeshall Rd, 1m from Feering village.* Every Thur and Fri 6 Apr to 28 July (9-4). Every Thur and Fri 31 Aug to 6 Oct (9-4). Adm £5, chd free. Refreshments only by appointment. **Visits also by arrangement Feb to Oct. Conducted tours on request There is a charge for this.** *Donation to Feering Church.*
There is always plenty to see in this 10 acre garden with two ponds and river Blackwater. Jewelled lawn in early April then spectacular tulips and blossom lead on to a huge number of different and colourful plants, many unusual, culminating in a purple explosion of michaelmas daisies in Sept. Wonderful sculpture by Ben Coode-Adams. Featured in Country Life No wheelchair access to arboretum, no steep slope.

  🐈 🚗 ☕️

16 FUDLERS HALL
Fox Road, Mashbury, Chelmsford, CM1 4TJ. Mr & Mrs A J Meacock, 01245 231335. *7m NW of Chelmsford. Chelmsford take A1060,*

R into Chignal Rd. ½ m L to Chignal St James approx 5m, 2nd R into Fox Rd signed Gt Waltham. Fudlers 1m. FROM GT WALTHAM. Take Barrack Lane for 3m. Sun 2, Sun 23 July (2-6). Adm £5, chd free. Home-made teas. **Visits also by arrangement in July.**
An award winning, romantic 2 acre garden surrounding C17 farmhouse with lovely pastoral views, across the Chelmer Valley. Old walls divide garden into many rooms, each having a different character, featuring long herbaceous borders, ropes and pergolas festooned with rambling old fashioned roses. Enjoy the vibrant hot border in late summer. Yew hedged kitchen garden. Ample seating.

  ☕️

17 FURZELEA
Bicknacre Road, Danbury, CM3 4JR. Avril & Roger Cole-Jones, 01245 225726, randacj@gmail.com. *4m E of Chelmsford, 4m W of Maldon A414 to Danbury. At village centre turn S into Mayes Lane Take first R. Go past Cricketers PH, L on to Bicknacre Rd see NT carpark on L (Park in carpark) garden 50m further on R (3rd house on R).* Wed 26 Apr (2-6); Mon 1 May, Sun 4 June (11-5); Wed 13 Sept (2-6); Sun 17 Sept (11-5). Adm £4, chd free. Home-made teas. Renowned for the quality and variety of our home-made cakes. **Visits also by arrangement Apr to Sept groups 15+ (not Aug) refreshments available.**
A Victorian country house surrounded by a garden designed, created and maintained by the owners to provide maximum all year round interest. The colour coordinated borders and beds are enhanced with topiary, grasses, climbers and many unusual plants. Spring incl tulips and summer bursts into colour with roses and perennials continuing into autumn with vibrant showy dahlias and many other exotics. Opp Danbury Common (NT), short walk to Danbury Country Park and Lakes and short drive to RHS Hyde Hall. Featured in Landscape Magazine,

Rustica (France), Essex Life, and East Anglia Daily Times. Very limited wheelchair access, with some steps and gravel paths and drive.

  🌼 🚗 ☕️

18 NEW 30 GLENWOOD AVENUE
Leigh-On-Sea, SS9 5EB. Joan Squibb, 07543 031772, squibb44@gmail.com. *Follow A127 towards Southend . Past Rayleigh Weir . At Progress Rd T-lights turn L. At next T-lights turn L down Raleigh Road A1015. Past shops turn 2nd L into Glenwood Rd . Garden halfway down on R.* Fri 21, Sun 23 Apr, Fri 18, Sun 20 Aug (11-4). Adm £3.50, chd free. Tea, coffee and home made Cakes. **Visits also by arrangement Apr to Sept groups of 10-20.**
Nestled next to the busy A127, lies a beautifully transformed town garden in the English country garden style. Homemade raised beds . From a bland corridor of Cyprus trees and grass, arises an open garden. A vista of colour, inspiration and peaceful harmony. Visions of many colours, forms and scents. Hanging baskets blooming in the fruit trees and along the fences.

  ☕️

The National Garden Scheme and Perennial, helping gardeners when they are in need

19 NEW **GOOSEBURY HALL**
Epping Long Green, Epping Green, Epping, CM16 6QN. Mr Michael Chapman. *Enter Epping Green from the Epping direction. Turn 1st L into Carters Lane. Enter private drive at the end and continue 1m staying on the made up track.* Mon 29 May (12-5.30). Adm £3, chd free. Home-made teas.
3 acres of peaceful gardens in a wild, country setting with no formal borders. Plenty of places to sit and relax. The main feature is the Labyrinth of almost a mile. You are encouraged to quietly walk the grass path of the labyrinth through long grass and wild flowers. It is not an enclosed space such as is found in a maze and an explanation will be available on your visit. A labyrinth is an ancient pattern found in many cultures. Take time, sit quietly and reflect before beginning your walk. Children will enjoy the labyrinth. However, parents are asked to supervise them so all may enjoy the meditative aspects of the walk. No steps. Grass paths. Caution: deep water in pond.
&. ▣

20 ◆ **GREEN ISLAND**
Park Road, Ardleigh, CO7 7SP. Fiona Edmond, 01206 230455, fionaedmond7@aol.com, www.greenislandgardens.co.uk.
3m NE of Colchester. From Ardleigh village centre, take B1029 towards

Great Bromley. Park Rd is 2nd on R after level Xing. Garden is last on L. For NGS: Sun 7 May, Sun 15 Oct (10-5). Adm £6.50, chd £2. Light refreshments. For other opening times and information, please phone, email or visit garden website.
'A garden for all seasons'
A plantsman's paradise with 20 acres packed with rare and unusual plants. Carved within mature woodland are huge island beds, Japanese garden, terrace, gravel garden, seaside garden, water gardens and extensive woodland plantings. Also tearoom with home-made cakes and snacks and nursery offering plants all seen growing in the gardens. Bluebells and azaleas, acers and rhododendrons in May. Water gardens, island beds all summer. Stunning Autumn colour. Light lunches, home-made teas and cream teas served Flat and easy walking /pushing wheelchairs. Ramps at entrance and tearoom. Disabled parking and WC.
&. ✿ 🚗 🛏 ▣

21 **HANNAMS HALL**
Thorpe Road, Tendring, CO16 9AR. Mr & Mrs W Gibbon, 01255 830292, w.gibbon331@btinternet.com.
10m E of Colchester. From A120 take B1035 at Horsley Cross, through Tendring Village (approx 3m) pass Bicycle PH on R, after 1/3m over

small bridge 1st house L. Visits by arrangement Mar to Nov max 30. Adm £6.50, chd free. Tea. Wine and light refreshments also available for evening appointments..
C17 house (not open) set in 6 acres of formal and informal gardens and grounds with extensive views over open countryside. Herbaceous borders and shrubberies, many interesting trees incl flowering paulownias. Lawns and mown walks through wild grass and flower meadows, woodland walks, ponds and stream. Walled vegetable potager and orchard. Lovely autumn colour. Some gravel paths.
&. ✿ ▣

22 **262 HATCH ROAD**
Pilgrims Hatch, Brentwood, CM15 9QR. Mike & Liz Thomas.
2m N of Brentwood town centre. On A128 N toward Ongar turn R onto Doddinghurst Rd at mini-r'about (to Brentwood Centre) After the Centre turn next L into Hatch Rd. Garden 4th on R. Sun 16, Sun 23 July (11-4.30). Adm £4.50, chd free. Home-made teas.
A formal frontage with lavender. An eclectic rear garden of around an acre divided into 'rooms' with themed borders, several ponds, three green houses, fruit and vegetable plots and oriental garden. There is also a secret white garden, spring and summer wild flower meadows, Yin and Yang borders, a folly and an exotic area. There is plenty of seating to enjoy the views and a cup of tea.
&. ✿ ▣

23 NEW **HAVENDELL**
Beckingham Street, Tolleshunt Major, Maldon, CM9 8LJ. Malcolm & Val.
5m E of Maldon 3m W of Tiptree. From B1022 take Loamy Hill rd. At the Xrds L into Witham rd. Follow NGS signs. Sun 23 July (11-4.30). Adm £4, chd free. Home-made teas.
We have designed this garden around existing shrubs and trees over the last 6 years. Allow your mind to wander as you journey from one section to another. Sit and take in the atmosphere, in

3 Pound Gate

the many places the garden has to offer. Wildlife and nature walk hand in hand to create a peaceful atmosphere. WC available.

24 HORKESLEY HALL
Little Horkesley, Colchester, CO6 4DB. Mr & Mrs Johnny Eddis, 078085 99290, pollyeddis@hotmail.com, www.airbnb.co.uk/rooms/10354093. *6m N of Colchester City Centre. 2m W of A134. Drive through Little Horkesley Church car park & access is via low double black gates at the far end. 10 mins from A12, 20 from Sudbury & 1hr from Newmarket.* Sun 11 June (11-4.30). Adm £6, chd free. Home-made teas. **Visits also by arrangement Mar to Oct very flexible and warm welcome assured! Coffee, teas or light lunch available by arrangement.**
8 acres of romantic garden surrounding classical house (not open) in mature parkland setting. Stream feeds 2 lakes. Unusual, ancient & enormous trees. Largest ginkgo tree outside Kew. Walled garden, ornamental pears, acers, eucalyptus, blossom, spring bulbs, roses, hydrangeas. Formal terrace overlooking sweeping lawns to wild woodland. A timeless, family garden with recent and ongoing improvements. Wonderful natural setting, vast plane trees and stunning tree barks. Large Victorian glasshouse, walled garden, scented plants and established climbers including roses, clematis, wisteria, hydrangea. A charming enclosed swimming pool garden and long-established bay and yew. Plants sometimes for sale. Featured in The English Garden Magazine. Limited wheelchair access to some areas, gravel paths and slopes quite easy access to tea area with lovely views over lake and garden.

25 KEEWAY
Ferry Road, Creeksea, nr Burnham-on-Crouch, CM0 8PL. John & Sue Ketteley. *2m W of Burnham-on-Crouch. B1010 to Burnham on Crouch. At town sign*
take 1st R into Ferry Rd signed Creeksea & Burnham Golf Club & follow NGS signs. Sun 18, Wed 21 June (2-5). Adm £4, chd free. Home-made teas.
Large, mature country garden with stunning views over the R Crouch. Formal terraces surround the house with steps leading to sweeping lawns, mixed borders packed full of bulbs and early perennials, a formal rose and herb garden with interesting water feature. Further afield there are wilder areas, paddocks and lake. A productive greenhouse, vegetable and cutting gardens complete the picture.

26 KELVEDON HALL
Kelvedon, Colchester, CO5 9BN. Mr & Mrs Jack Inglis, 07973 795955, victoria.inglis@me.com. *Take Maldon Rd from Kelvedon High St. Go over bridge over Blackwater & A12 at T-junction turn R onto Kelvedon Rd. Take 1st L, single gravel road, oak tree on corner.* Visits by arrangement Apr to June min group of 20. Adm £5, chd free. Light refreshments in the Modern Pool House Walled Garden, weather permitting.
Varied 6 acre garden surrounding a pretty C18 Farmhouse. A blend of formal and informal spaces interspersed with modern sculpture. Pleached hornbeam and yew and box topiary provide structure. Courtyard walled garden juxtaposes a modern walled pool garden, both providing season long displays. Herbaceous borders offset an abundance of roses around the house. Lily covered ponds with a wet garden. Topiary, sculpture, tulips and roses. Featured in Country Homes and Interiors and Period Living. Wheelchair access not ideal as there is a lot of gravel.

GROUP OPENING

27 LANGLEY VILLAGE GARDENS
Langley Upper Green, Saffron Walden, CB11 4RY. *7m W of*
Saffron Walden 10m N of Bishops Stortford. At Newport take B1038. After 3m turn R at Clavering, signed Langley. Upper Green is 3m further on. Sheepcote Green will also be signed on day. Sun 28 May (11-5). Combined adm £7.50, chd free. Light refreshments at Village Hall on Langley Village Green. Light lunches & home-made teas.

APRIL COTTAGE
Mr & Mrs Harris.

THE CHESTNUTS
Jane & David Knight.

OLD BELL COTTAGE
Richard Vallance, 01799 550474, r.vallance1234@gmail.com. Visits also by arrangement in May.

WICKETS
Susan & Doug Copeland. (See separate entry)

April Cottage, at Sheepcote Green just 2m from Langley is a charming thatched cottage, with well established, very colourful garden packed with unusual plants; old fashioned roses, clematis, wildlife and ornamental ponds, lined damp garden, hosta collection. All to be discovered down winding paths. Ideas for different situations - plant list available. Old Bell Cottage has cottage garden with herbaceous beds well stocked with bulbs, alliums and delphiniums. Trees frame view across valley. Greenhouse, patio, sunken BBQ area. Raised vegetable beds and fruit cage. Natural pond. The Chestnuts is large garden with many mature trees. Planting beds designed and installed by Tristen Knight, RHS Young Designer 2012. Water feature with reclaimed sleeper jetty. New productive garden with oak walkways, sandstone paving and water feature. Meadow with mature trees. Tranquil place to linger and enjoy. Wickets has wide, mixed borders, roses, two landscaped meadows, lily pond, parterre and gravel garden. Langley is highest Essex village set in rolling countryside. Gravel drive at Wickets.

28 LITTLE MYLES

Ongar Road, Stondon Massey, Brentwood, CM15 0LD. Judy & Adrian Cowan, Littlemyles@gmail.com. 1½ m SE of Chipping Ongar. Off A128 at Stag PH, Marden Ash, towards Stondon Massey. Over bridge, 1st house on R after 'S' bend. 400yds Ongar side of Stondon Church. Sun 2 July (11-4). Adm £5, chd free. Home-made teas. Seating in Tea Room, also under trees and on main lawn.
A romantic, naturalistic garden full of hidden features, set in 3 acres. Full borders, meandering paths to Beach Garden, Perennial Prairie border, Exotic Jungle around elephant, monkeys and giraffe. Fountains, sculptures and tranquil benches. Hidden Asian garden, Slate garden, hornbeam pergola, ornamental vegetable patch and natural pond. Herb garden that inspired Little Myles herbal cosmetics. Crafts and handmade herbal cosmetics for sale. Explorers sheet and map for children. Gravel paths. No disabled WC available.
&. ✿ 🍵

29 LITTLE WALTHAM HALL

Little Waltham, Chelmsford, CM3 3LJ. Mr Rupert & Lady Vanessa Watson. On the corner of Brook Hill & Back Lane in Little Waltham. Entrance opp the gates to Little Waltham church. Please park carefully on the street. Thur 15 June (2-5). Adm £5, chd free. Home-made teas.
A four acre garden, with sweeping lawns bordered by mature shrubs, forms a fine setting for the C18 listed Hall. The walled garden, in which informal herbaceous planting complements structural formality, is of special interest. Good wheelchair access but paths are gravelled.
🍵

30 LONG HOUSE PLANTS

Church Road, Noak Hill, Romford, RM4 1LD. Tim Carter, 01708 371719, tim@longhouse-plants.co.uk, www.longhouse-plants.co.uk. 3½ m NW of J28 M25. J28 M25 take A1023 Brentwood. At 1st T-lights, turn L to South Weald after 0.8m turn L at T junction. After 1.6m turn L, over M25 after ½ m turn R into Church Rd, nursery opp church. Wed 14 June, Wed 12 July, Wed 16 Aug, Wed 13 Sept (11-4). Adm £5, chd £3. Home-made teas.
Visits also by arrangement Mon - Thur inclusive (not Bank Hol). Groups of 10+. Additional fee for conducted tours.
A beautiful garden - yes, but one with a purpose. Long House Plants has been producing home grown plants for more than 10 years - here is a chance to see where it all begins! With wide paths and plenty of seats carefully placed to enjoy the plants and views. It has been thoughtfully designed so that the collections of plants look great together through all seasons.
&. ✿ 🚗 🍵

31 ◆ MARKS HALL GARDENS & ARBORETUM

Coggeshall, CO6 1TG. Marks Hall Estate, 01376 563796, enquiries@markshall.org.uk, www.markshall.org.uk. 1½ m N of Coggeshall. Follow brown & white tourism signs from A120 Coggeshall bypass. For opening times and information, please phone, email or visit garden website.
Marks Hall Gardens and Arboretum features a tree collection from all the temperate areas of the world set in more than 200 acres of historic landscape providing interest and enjoyment throughout the year. Highlights include: the Millennium Walk designed for structure, colour and scent on the shortest days of the year; the largest planting in Europe of Wollemi pine and the inspired combination of traditional and contemporary planting in the C18 Walled Garden. Spring snowdrop and autumn colour displays are annual highlights. Hard paths lead to all key areas of interest. Wheelchairs or staff-driven buggy available for visitors with mobility issues (booking essential).
&. ✿ 🚗 🍵

32 8 MILL LANE

Pebmarsh, Halstead, CO9 2NW. Danny McGovern & Michael Roberts. Half way between Sudbury & Halstead. From Braintree A120 take A131. From Colchester A1124 at White Colne village green follow sign 'Pebmarsh 3m'. Sun 4 June (12-4). Adm £5, chd free. Home-made teas.
Our garden is a series of formal and informal 'rooms'. A mixture of herbaceous and shrub beds, with many beautiful trees, most of which we planted. Wildlife is very important in our garden and we keep areas in a natural (wild) state. This encourages a diverse variety of wild creatures which share the garden with us.
✿ 🍵

33 MIRAFLORES

5 Rowan Way, Witham, CM8 2LJ. Yvonne & Danny Owen, 07976 603863, danny@dannyowen.co.uk. Access to the garden through Front door of house, please follow yellow signs. Sun 11 June (2-5). Adm £3.50, chd free. Home-made teas. Visits also by arrangement in June min 10. max 20, £7 incl cream tea.
An award-winning, medium-sized garden described by one visitor as a "Little Bit of Heaven'. A blaze of colour with roses, clematis, pergola rose arch, triple fountain with box hedging and deep herbaceous borders. See our 'Folly',... and Secret Door, and our exuberant and cascading hanging baskets. Featured in Garden Answers and Essex Life. We have tranquil seating areas and homemade cakes to die for, and some being Gluten free.
✿ 🍵

34 MONKS COTTAGE

Monks Lane, Dedham nr Colchester, CO7 6DP. Nicola Baker, 01206 322210, nicola_baker@tiscali.co.uk. 6m NE of Colchester. Leave Dedham village with the church on L. Take 2nd main rd on R (Coles Oak Lane) Monks Lane is first rd on L. Visits by arrangement May to Aug small groups, daytime or evening visits welcome. Adm £3.50, chd

free. Light refreshments.
½ acre cottage garden on a sloping site in the heart of Constable country. A constantly evolving garden which features mature trees, pond, box-edged parterre beds, boggy area with strong foliage shapes, rill garden with cascade and small woodland garden. A gin-and-tonic balcony gives a high level vantage point over the garden and a raised terrace looks out over the surrounding countryside.

35 MOVERONS

Brightlingsea, CO7 0SB. Lesley & Payne Gunfield, 01206 305498, lesleyorrock@me.com, www.moverons.co.uk. *7m SE of Colchester. At old church turn R signed Moverons Farm. Follow lane & garden signs for approx 1m. Beware some SatNavs take you the wrong side of the river.* **Sat 3 Sun 4 June. An exhibition Framing the View: Connecting with the Landscape. Visitors can engage with an installation of art works around Moverons Farm and Gardens, created by artist, Julie Cuthbert. Sat 2 Sun 3 Sept. Payne Gunfield & Friends Exhibition of Sculpture in gardens & adjoining woodland.** Sat 3, Sun 4 June, Sat 2, Sun 3 Sept (10.30-5). Adm £5, chd free. Home-made teas. **Visits also by arrangement June to Sept for groups of 10+ only.** Beautiful tranquil 4 acre garden in touch with its surroundings and enjoying stunning estuary views. A wide variety of planting in mixed borders to suit different growing conditions and provide all year colour. Courtyard, reflection pool, large natural ponds, sculptures and barn for rainy day teas! Magnificent trees some over 300yrs old give this garden real presence.

36 THE OLD RECTORY

Church Road, Boreham, CM3 3EP. Sir Jeffery & Lady Bowman, 01245 467233, bowmansuzy@btinternet.com. *4m NE of Chelmsford. Take B1137 Boreham Village, turn into Church Rd at the Lion PH. ½m along on R opp church.* **Sat 18, Sun 19 Feb (12-3). Adm £5, chd free. Light refreshments. Hot soup & hot sausages in rolls (Feb). Visits also by arrangement Feb to July for groups of 10+. Soup and roll type lunch in winter. Teas or evening refreshments in summer.** 2½-acre garden surrounding C15 house (not open). Ponds, stream, with bridges and primulas, small wild flower meadow and wood with interesting trees and shrubs, herbaceous borders with emphasis on complementary colours. Vegetable garden. February opening for crocus, snowdrops and cyclamen. Possibly largest gunnera in Essex. Lovely views over Chelmer/Blackwater canal. Stream, ponds, woodland garden. Stunning wisteria in May. Herbaceous borders. Refreshments soup and roll type lunch in winter. Teas or evening refreshments in summer. Featured in Country Homes and Gardens. Wheelchair access, gravel drive but large part of garden accessible.

37 PARSONAGE HOUSE

Wiggens Green, Helions Bumpstead, Haverhill, CB9 7AD. The Hon & Mrs Nigel Turner. *3m S of Haverhill. From the Xrds in the village centre go up past the Church for approx 1m. Parking on R through a five bar gate into the orchard. Garden on L of the lane.* **Sun 28 May, Sun 10 Sept (2-5). Adm £4, chd free. Home-made teas. Apple juice from the orchard available on the day for sale.** C15 house (not open) surrounded by 3 acres of formal gardens with mixed borders, topiary, pond, potager and greenhouse. Further 3-acre wild flower meadow with orchids and rare trees and further 3 acre orchard of old East Anglian apple varieties in two small fields across the lane. Featured in The English Garden, Country Life, Gardens Illustrated, Hortus and to be featured in a book due to be published in September 2017 by Frances Lincoln called 'Secret Gardens of East Anglia' by Barbara Segall illustrated by Marcus Harpur. Gravel drive and small step into WC.

38 PATERNOSTER HOUSE

Barnhall Road, Tolleshunt Knights, Maldon, CM9 8HA. Julia & Michael Bradley, juliaabradley@gmail.com. *From A12 J24 (Kelvedon) Take B1023 to Tiptree through Tiptree on B1023 bottom of Factory Hill turn L to Tolleshunt Knights on Brook Rd S bend onto Barnhall Rd. Continue to 30mph sign house on R.* **Visits by arrangement Apr to July children welcome but MUST be supervised because of deep ponds. Adm £5, chd free. Home-made teas. Tea, coffee, orange juice & home made cakes..** Peaceful 5 acre garden rescued from a derelict state some 15 yrs ago. It has an enclosed flower garden, 2 meadows, orchards of apples, pears, stone fruit, mulberry trees and peaches. Ornamental kitchen garden with raised beds and extensive lawns with large shrubberies. Some rare and unusual shrubs (large collection of viburnums) and plants, young and mature trees. 3 beautiful ponds. Some vintage tractors and machinery. Chickens, mandarin ducks, guinea fowl (The Freds), golden pheasants and semi-permanent mallards. Gravel drive. Rough grass in meadows (parking), otherwise reasonably level.

The Queen's Nursing Institute founded the National Garden Scheme exactly 90 years ago

39 PEACOCKS

Main Road, Margaretting,
CM4 9HY. Phil Torr, 07802 472382,
phil.torr@btinternet.com.
*Margaretting Village Centre. From
village Xrds go 75yds in the direction
of Ingatestone, entrance gates will
be found on L set back 50 feet
from the road frontage.* Sun 23
Apr (1-4). Adm £5, chd free.
Home-made teas. **Visits also
by arrangement Mar to Sept
adm incl refreshments, smaller
groups welcome if flexible on
date.** *Donation to St Francis Hospice.*
5-acre garden surrounding
Regency house with mature native
and specimen trees. Restored
horticultural buildings. A series of
garden 'rooms' including 2 formal
walled gardens, long herbaceous/
mixed border. Vegetable garden.
Temple of Antheia sits on the banks
of a lilly lake. Large areas for wildlife
incl woodland walk and orchard.
Traditionally managed wildflower
meadow. Sunken dell, sculptures.
Display of old Margaretting
postcards. Artist studio, small art
exhibition. Garden sculpture. Wild
flower meadow in traditional
orchard. Most of garden wheelchair
accessible.

&. 🚗 NPC 🍵

40 PEPPERS FARM

Forry Green, Sible
Hedingham, CO9 3RP. Mrs
Pam Turtle, 01787 460221,
pam@peppersfarm.entadsl.com.
*1m SW of Sible Hedingham. From S
after Gosfield L for Southey Green.
L for Forry Green. From N for Sible
Hedingham R at Sugar Loaves,
Rectory Rd. L at White Horse until
Forry Green.* Sun 30 Apr (2-5).
Adm £4, chd free. Home-made
teas. **Visits also by arrangement
Mar to Sept.**
½ acre country garden set high
on quiet rural green with farmland
views. Hedges divide informal
borders featuring flowering
shrubs, fruit and specimen trees,
many grown from seed. Beautiful
alpine scree and sinks overlook
spring fed pond. In April, May
beautiful bluebells in Lowts Wood.
Stout shoes recommended. Free
standing Wisteria, and set in Essex

countryside. Featured in East
Anglian and Garden News. Partial
wheelchair access, large pond with
steep sides. Some gravel.

&. 🐕 ✿ 🍵 🌱

18 PETTITS BOULEVARD, RM1

See London

41 NEW 3 POUND GATE

Stebbing, Dunmow, CM6 3RH.
Wal & Jenny Hudgell. *3m E of
Great Dunmow. Leave Gt Dunmow
on B1256. Take first L to Stebbing.
At the War Memorial junction turn
L, down hill to High Street. Take 2nd
R past the School, signed to Garden
Fields.* Sun 28 May, Sun 18 June
(1-5). Adm £4, chd free.
Light refreshments.
Third of an acre plant lovers
garden. Reinvented 6 years ago and
an ongoing project. Herbaceous
borders packed with an eclectic
mix of perennials and shrubs for
all year round interest. Bluebells,
Iris, hemerocallis and hostas in
abundance. All punctuated by
numerous roses. There is a medium
size vegetable garden. The garden is
fully accessible to wheelchairs.

&. ✿ 🍵

GROUP OPENING

42 RAYLEIGH GARDENS

Rayleigh, SS6 9ND. *The group
gardens are walking distance from
each other and within ¾m from
Rayleigh station. From A127 take
A1245 towards Chelmsford. At
r'about turn towards Rayleigh on
A129, London Rd. At Travellers Joy
PH turn L (Downhall Rd) to access
2 gardens, the 3rd is off A129 on R.*
Sun 18 June, Sun 30 July (12-5).
Combined adm £5, chd free.
Light refreshments.

1 CHERRYDOWN

SS6 9ND. Richard & Gill
Thrussell, 01268 781057,
richardthrussell@lineone.net.
**Visits also by arrangement
June to Aug for groups of 6+**

35 LANGDON ROAD

SS6 9HY. Mrs Louise Reed.

36 LONDON ROAD

SS6 9JE. Jenny & Ron
Coutts, 01268 781329,
couttsier2@btinternet.com.
**Visits also by arrangement
July to Sept groups of 6+
welcome. Hot food can
be provided with prior
agreement. Adm to be agreed.**

Three diverse gardens to delight
and inspire. Cherrydown's colourful
garden bursts with over 350
different perennials. Bamboo and
shade planting opens out to a large
terrace, with lounging and dining
areas for viewing the raised borders.
A wisteria arch leads to fruit trees,
a pretty greenhouse, parterre herb
garden, agapanthus and alpines.
London Road has exotic hot planting,
succulents, gingers, brugmansia,
shrubs, perennials and Koi ponds to
the front. The rear lawned garden has
pergolas with climbers and baskets
which can be enjoyed from the
various seating areas. Langdon Road
is a delightful white garden with
over 100 amazing roses and unusual
perennials, all fitted into a compact
plot. Shady fernery, arches, pond
and a succession of fragrant blooms
surround the lawn providing interest
all summer long. Wheelchair access
to 36 London Rd.

&. ✿ 🍵

43 RAYNE HATCH FARM

Rayne Hatch, Stisted,
Braintree, CM77 8BY.
Dr Jill Chaloner, 01787 472396,
jill.chaloner@btinternet.com.
*1m NE Braintree. From Braintree
bypass take A131 towards Sudbury
passing through High Garrett &
Three Counties Crematorium on L
take R turn signed Stisted 2 then R
at T-junction 4th house on R.* Sun 3
Sept (10-4). Adm £6, chd free.
Light refreshments. **Visits also
by arrangement May to Sept for
groups of 15+.**
2½ acre garden surrounding grade
II listed Elizabethan farmhouse
lovingly created in past 14 yrs by
plantaholic owner with 4 ponds
providing a rich wildlife habitat.
Enjoy waterside paths, ornamental
bridge, well stocked herbaceous

borders, woodland walk, orchard and walled garden. Fragrant arbours and ample seating throughout aid contemplation and tranquility.

✿ ☕

44 ROOKWOODS

Yeldham Road, Sible Hedingham, CO9 3QG. Peter & Sandra Robinson, 07770 957111, sandy1989@btinternet.com. *8m NW of Halstead. Entering Sible Hedingham from the direction of Haverhill on A1017 take 1st R just after 30mph sign.* Mon 29 May (11.30-4.30). Adm £4, chd free. Cream teas. **Visits also by arrangement May to Sept, cream teas can be organised in advance.** Rookwoods is a tranquil garden. The herbaceous borders feature columns of tumbling roses, Pleached hornbeam rooms lead to a wild flower bed, buttercup meadow and ancient oak wood. There is no need to walk far, you can come and linger over tea, under a dreamy wisteria canopy, while enjoying the garden view. Gravel drive.

&. ✿ 🚗 ☕

Fudlers Hall

© Marcus Harpur

45 69 RUNDELLS

Harlow, CM18 7HD. Mr & Mrs K Naunton, 01279 303471, k_naunton@hotmail.com. *From M11 J7 A414 exit T-lights take L exit Southern Way, mini r'about 1st exit Trotters Rd leading into Commonside Rd, take 2nd L into Rundells.* Sat 8 July (2-5). Adm £2.50, chd free. Home-made teas. Home made cakes, tea, coffee and soft drinks. **Visits also by arrangement June to Sept please give plenty of notice, groups of 10+ can be accomodated (within reason).** As featured on Alan Tichmarsh's first 'Love Your Garden' series ('The Secret Garden') 69, Rundells is a very colourful, small town garden packed with a wide variety of shrubs, perennials, herbaceous and bedding plants in over 200 assorted containers. Hard landscaping on different levels incl's summer house, various seating areas and water features. Steep steps. Access to adjacent allotment open to view. Various small secluded seating areas.

A small fairy garden is planned for 2017 to add interest for younger visitors. The garden is next to a large allotment and this is open to view with lots of interesting features. Honey and other produce for sale (conditions permitting). Full size hot tub/jacuzzi.

✿ ☕

46 ST HELENS

High Street, Stebbing, CM6 3SE. Stephen & Joan Bazlinton, 01371 856495, revbaz@phonecoop.coop. *3m E of Great Dunmow. Leave Gt Dunmow on B1256. Take 1st L to Stebbing, at T-junction turn L into High St, garden 2nd on R.* Sat 4 Mar (12-3). Adm £4, chd free. Light refreshments. **Visits also by arrangement May to Sept.** *Donation to Dentaid.* A garden of contrasts due to moist and dry conditions, laid out on a gentle Essex slope from a former willow plantation. These contours give rise to changing vistas and unanticipated areas of seclusion framed with hedging and generous planting. Walkways and paths alongside natural springs and still waters. Partial wheelchair access.

&. ☕

47 SHRUBS FARM

Lamarsh, Bures, CO8 5EA. Mr & Mrs Robert Erith, 01787 227520, bob@shrubsfarm.co.uk, www.shrubsfarm.co.uk. *1¼m from Bures. On rd to Lamarsh, the drive is signed to Shrubs Farm.* **Visits by arrangement Apr to Oct groups min 6. No max Tours led by owner. Refreshments by arrangement served in barn. Adm £7, chd free. Home-made teas. Wine & canapes..** 2 acres with shrub borders, lawns, roses and trees. 50 acres parkland with wild flower paths and woodland trails. Over 70 species of oak. Superb 10m views over Stour valley. Ancient coppice and pollards incl largest goat (pussy) willow (*Salix caprea*) in England. Wollemi and Norfolk pines, and banana trees. Full size black rhinoceros. Display of Bronze Age burial urns. Large grass maze. Guided Tour to incl park and ancient woodland. Restored C18 Essex barn is available for refreshment by prior arrangement. Some ground may be boggy in wet weather.

&. 🐐 🚗 ☕

48 SNARES HILL COTTAGE

Duck End, Stebbing, CM6 3RY.
Pete & Liz Stabler, 01371 856565,
petestabler@gmail.com. *Between Dunmow & Bardfield. On B1057 from Great Dunmow to Great Bardfield, ½m after Bran End on L.* Sun 4 June, Sun 10 Sept (10.30-4). Adm £4, chd free. Home-made teas. **Visits also by arrangement.**

A 'quintessential English Garden' - Gardeners World. Our quirky 1½ acre garden has surprises round every corner and many interesting sculptures. A natural swimming pool is bordered by romantic flower beds, herb garden and Victorian folly. A bog garden borders woods and leads to silver birch copse, beach garden and 'Roman' temple. Natural Swimming Pond. Classic cars. Sculptures.

49 SOUTH SHOEBURY HALL

Church Road, Shoeburyness, SS3 9DN. Mr & Mrs M Dedman, 01702 299022, michael@shoeburyhall.co.uk. *4m E of Southend-on-Sea. Enter Southend on A127 to Eastern Ave A1159 signed Shoebury. R at r'about to join A13. Proceed S to Ness Rd. R into Church Rd. Garden on L 50 metres.* Sun 30 July (2-5). Adm £4, chd free. Light refreshments. **Visits also by arrangement Apr to Aug for groups of 10 + to a coach party.**

Delightful, 1-acre established walled garden surrounding Grade II listed house (not open) and bee house. New agapanthus and hydrangea beds. April is ablaze with 3000 tulips and fritillaria. July shows 200+ varieties of agapanthus. Unusual trees, shrubs, rose borders, with 50yr old plus geraniums, Mediterranean and Southern Hemisphere planting in dry garden. New planting for 2016 in large beds. C11 St Andrews Church open to visitors (by arrangement). Garden close to sea.

50 ◆ SPENCERS

Tilbury Road, Great Yeldham, CO9 4JG. Mr & Mrs Colin Bogie, 01787 238175, lynne@spencersgarden.net, www.spencersgarden.net. *Just N of Gt Yeldham on Tilbury Rd. In village centre, turn off A1017 at the 'Blasted Oak' (huge oak stump). Keep L, following stream (signed 'The Belchamps/Tilbury Juxta Clare'). Spencers is clearly signed on L after approx ½m.* For NGS: Sun 11 June, Sun 3 Sept (2-5). Adm £5, chd free. Home-made teas. **For other opening times and information, please phone, email or visit garden website.**

Romantic C18 walled garden laid out by Lady Anne Spencer, overflowing with blooms following Tom Stuart-Smith's renovation. Huge wisteria, armies of Lord Butler delphiniums ('Rab' lived at Spencers). Spectacular rose and herbaceous borders. Parkland with many specimen trees including Armada Oaks. Victorian woodland walk along River Colne.

51 SPRING COTTAGE

Chapel Lane, Elmstead Market, Colchester, CO7 7AG. Mr & Mrs Roger & Sharon Sciachettano. *3m from Colchester. Overlooking village green N of A133 through Elmstead Market. Parking limited adjacent to cottage, village car park nearby on S side of A133.* Sat 17, Sun 18 June (2-5). Adm £3.50, chd free. Home-made teas. Refreshments provided by the Elmstead in Bloom group. Tea/coffee & cake served on the village green in front of Spring Cottage.

From Acteas to Zauscherenias and Aressima to Zebra grass we hope our large variety of plants will please. Our award winning garden features a range of styles and habitats e.g. woodland dell, stumpery, Mediterranean area, perennial borders and pond. Our C17 thatched cottage and garden show case a number of plants found at the world famous Beth Chatto gardens ½m down the road.

52 STRANDLANDS

off Rectory Road, Wrabness, Manningtree, CO11 2TX. Jenny & David Edmunds, 01255 886260, strandlands@outlook.com. *1km along farm track from the corner of Rectory Rd. If using a SatNav, the post code will leave you at the corner of Rectory Road. Turn onto a farm track, signed to Woodcutters Cottage & Strandlands, & continue for 1km.* **Visits by arrangement May to July for groups of 10 to 25. Adm £5, chd free. Light refreshments. Tea, coffee & a slice of home made cake..**

Cottage surrounded by 4 acres of land bordering beautiful and unspoilt Stour Estuary. One acre of decorative garden: formal courtyard with yew, box and perovskia hedges, lily pond, summerhouse and greenhouse; 2 large island beds, secret 'moon garden', madly and vividly planted 'Madison' garden, 3 acres of wildlife meadows with groups of native trees, large wildlife pond, also riverside bird hide. View the Stour Estuary from our own bird hide. Grayson Perry's 'A House for Essex' can be seen just one field away from Strandlands. Mostly accessible and flat although parking area is gravelled.

53 TUDOR ROOST

18 Frere Way, Fingringhoe, Colchester, CO5 7BP. Chris & Linda Pegden, 01206 729831, pegdenc@gmail.com. *5m S of Colchester. In Fingringhoe by Whalebone PH follow sign to Ballast Quay, after ½m turn R into Brook Hall Rd, then 1st L into Frere Way.* Sun 16, Mon 17 Apr, Sat 3, Sun 4 June, Sat 1, Sun 2 July, Sat 12, Sun 13 Aug (2-5). Adm £3.50, chd free. Home-made teas. Large conservatory to sit in if inclement weather. **Visits also by arrangement Apr to Aug min 10 people, adm incl tea & cake £6-50.**

An unexpected hidden colourful ¼-acre garden. Well manicured grassy paths wind round island beds and ponds. Densely planted subtropical area with architectural and exotic plants - cannas, bananas, palms, agapanthus, agaves and tree ferns surround a colourful gazebo. Garden planted to provide yr-round colour and encourage wildlife. Many peaceful seating areas. Within 1m of Fingringhoe Wick Nature Reserve. Local PH that serves meals. PLEASE CONFIRM OPENING DATES ON NGS WEBSITE OR TELEPHONE. Featured in Look magazine, Mersea Courier, Essex County Standard, Mersea Life.

54 37 TURPINS LANE
Chigwell, Woodford Green, IG8 8AZ. Fabrice Aru & Martin Thurston, 0208 5050 739, martin.thurston@talktalk.net. *Between Woodford & Epping. Tube: Chigwell, 2m from North Circular Rd at Woodford, follow the signs for Chigwell (A113) through Woodford Bridge into Manor Rd & turn L, Bus 275.* Sun 25 June, Sun 23 July (11-6). Adm £3, chd free. **Visits also by arrangement May to Oct max 8.**
An unexpected hidden, magical, part-walled garden showing how much can be achieved in a small space. An oasis of calm with densely planted rich, lush foliage, tree ferns, hostas, topiary and an abundance of well maintained shrubs complemented by a small pond and 3 water features designed for yr round interest. Awarded 2nd place by Gardening News for Best Small Garden.

55 ULTING WICK
Crouchmans Farm Road, Maldon, CM9 6QX. Mr & Mrs B Burrough, 01245 380216, philippa.burrough@btinternet. com, www.ultingwickgarden.co.uk. *3m NW of Maldon. Take turning to Ulting off B1019 as you exit Hatfield Peverel. Garden on R after 2m.* Sun 30 Apr (11-5). Light refreshments. Fri 5, Fri 12 May, Fri 23 June, Sun 10, Fri 15 Sept (2-5). Home-made teas. Adm £5, chd free. Homemade soup using ingredients from the garden, filled rolls & home-made teas on 30 April. **Visits also by arrangement Mar to Oct groups of 15+. Other catering**

by arrangement. *Donation to All Saints Ulting Church.*
Listed black barns provide backdrop for vibrant and exuberant planting in 8 acres. Thousands of colourful tulips, flowing innovative spring planting, herbaceous borders, pond, mature weeping willows, kitchen garden, dramatic late summer beds with zingy, tender, exotic plant combinations. Drought tolerant perennial and mini annual wild flower meadows. Woodland. Many plants propagated in-house. Lots of unusual plants for sale. All Saints Church Ulting will be open in conjunction with the garden for talks on its history on Sun openings only. Beautiful dog walks along the R Chelmer from the garden. Featured in The English Garden (tulips), listed as one of the 50 'must see' Spring gardens by the Daily Telegraph, Country Living (late summer planting), Garden Answers, and 'Nest' (Belgium). Some gravel around the house but main areas of interest are accessible for wheelchairs.

With your support we can help raise awareness of Carers Trust and unpaid carers

56 14 UNA ROAD
Bowers Gifford, Basildon, SS13 2HU. Mr & Mrs John & Barbara Spooner. *4m E of Basildon on B1464 between Pitsea & Saddlers Farm r'about (A130/A13.) From Pitsea turn L into Pound Lane. From Southend (A127) X A130/A1245 junction. 1m turn L & follow NGS signs.* Sat 15, Sun 16 July (11-5). Adm £3.50, chd free. Wine.
A beautiful ½ acre garden featuring 2 ponds. Garden divided into 'rooms' each with an interesting view, drawing you on to the next room. Small vegetable patch with greenhouse plus a family of gnomes. Late winter garden opening including Christmas lights. Seasonal mulled wine, mince pies and refreshments on both evenings. WC available.

57 37 UNDERHILL ROAD
Benfleet, SS7 1EP. Mr Allan & Mrs Diane Downey, 01268 565291, allan.downey@yahoo.co.uk. *Approx 2m from Sadlers Farm r'about on A13. Towards Southend, take R turn at Tarpots Harvester continue to South Benfleet School turn L opp, in to Thundersley Park Rd, continue to Underhill Rd 500yds on R.* Sun 25 June, Sun 30 July (1-5). Adm £3.50, chd free. **Home-made teas. Visits also by arrangement June & July weekdays only, min 10.**
A ¼ acre garden offering a relaxing visit, featuring topiary shrubs and climbers incl campsis, clematis, honeysuckle and jasmine. Over 80 heucheras in beds with sedums, rudbeckias and hydrangeas. Lovely views from all areas. Undercover Bonsai area, many colourful baskets and containers. Several cast iron and stone sculptures. Patio area to enjoy refreshments.

58 WALTHAM ABBEY GROUP

Waltham Abbey, EN9 1LG. *8m W of Epping Town. M25, J26 to Waltham Abbey. At T-lights by McD turn R to r'about. Take 2nd exit to next r'about. Take 3rd exit (A112) to T-lights. L to Monkswood Av.* Sun 28 May, Sun 3 Sept (12-5.30). Combined adm £5, chd free. Home-made teas at Silver Birches, Quendon Drive. Bacon Sandwiches made to order and homemade cakes available.

62 EASTBROOK ROAD

Caroline Cassell, 07973 551196, cvcassell@gmail.com.
Open on Sun 28 May
Visits also by arrangement June to Aug vintage Afternoon Teas for groups of 3/4.

39 HALFHIDES

Chris Hamer.
Open on all dates

76 MONKSWOOD AVENUE

Cathy & Dan Gallagher.
Open on all dates

SILVER BIRCHES

Linda & Frank Jewson.
Open on all dates

Historic Waltham Abbey is near Epping Forest. The Abbey is purported to be last resting place of King Harold. Lee Valley Regional Park is nearby. Silver Birches boasts 3 lawns on 2 levels. This surprisingly secluded garden has many mixed borders packed with all year interest. Mature shrubs and trees create a short woodland walk. Crystal clear water flows through a shady area of the garden. At 39 Halfhides the garden has evolved over 45yrs. It features mixed shrubs and perennial borders on 2 levels. Waterfall linking two ponds leads to shade garden. Alpines thrive on scree and in troughs. Beautiful autumn colour. 76 Monkswood Ave is a plantswoman's garden . Mixed borders filled with specimen trees, shrubs and perennials incl asters, dahlias and late-flowering anemones. Wildlife pond. 62 Eastbrook Rd: No Parking in Eastbrook Rd. Off Honey Lane, walking distance from Halfhides and The Glade Way approx. 7 mins. This is a small cottage garden, traditional perennial planting, topiary and circular themed hard landscaping. Reclaimed chimney pots for sale as planters. 62 Eastbrook Rd not suitable for wheelchairs.

✿ ☕

59 WASHLANDS

Prayors Hill, Sible Hedingham, CO9 3LE. Tony & Sarah Frost, 01787 460732, tony@washlands.co.uk. *¼m NW of Sible Hedingham Church. At former Sugar Loaves PH on A1017 turn SW into Rectory Rd, R at former White Horse PH, pass St Peters Church on RH-side, ¼m NW on Prayors Hill.* Sun 11 June (2-5.30). Home-made teas. Evening opening Wed 14 June (6-8). Wine. Sun 18 June (2-5.30). Home-made teas. Adm £4, chd free. **Visits also by arrangement groups of 10+.**

Informal, tranquil garden approx 1 acre with good views over rolling countryside. Features incl a horse pond. Wide herbaceous, shrub and woodland borders incl roses and peonies. Many young and mature trees enhance the garden. Pond has steep banks. Woodland walk unsuitable for wheelchairs.

& 🐕 ✿ ☕

60 WENDENS AMBO GARDENS

Royston Road, Wendens Ambo, Saffron Walden, CB11 4JX. *Parking at village hall nr Church signed on day. All gardens are within walking distance. Map of gardens available on day.* Sun 9 July (11-4). Combined adm £5, chd free. Light refreshments at Loxley 10 - 5.

NEW **HIGH BANKS HOUSE**
Sarah Moynihan.

NEW **KELLERS**
Ms Susan Watson.

NEW **LOXLEY**
Robert Chappell.

Loxley is a young garden; both, front and rear, have been recently landscaped and planted and completed in late spring 2016. The garden itself features a good size Koi pond, surrounded by a lawn and flower beds which includes various ericaceous plants, bamboos, grasses, some rare plants as well as some traditional shrubs and flowers

South Shoebury Hall

all of which offers interest all year around. At High Banks House there are various raised and curved beds of summer planting, interspersed with a number of decks and terraces, seating areas and water feature. Mature trees around the boundaries and a secret garden at the end. Indoor pool house with predominantly glass wall reflecting flower beds. Kellers is an enclosed garden with terraced beds and circular lawn recently laid. A variety of hedges (yew, mixed native, rose, rosemary and ornamental grass) with mixed planting. Kellers is named after Helen Keller, the American humanitarian, who visited during the summer of 1930. Wendens Ambo is a meandering historic village with a busy B road through village. Please use car park. Beware. There is a lack of pavements in places so take great care if walking on the road. Audley very close to Audley End House. Steep drive at High Banks House leads to level path and lawn.

&. ☕

61 WICKETS
Langley Upper Green, CB11 4RY. Susan & Doug Copeland. *7m W of Saffron Walden, 10m N of Bishops Stortford. At Newport take B1038 After 3m turn R at Clavering, signed Langley. Upper Green is 3m further on. At cricket green turn R. House 200m on R.* Sun 19 Mar (11-4). Light refreshments at Village Hall opp. garden if weather is inclement. Mon 1 May, Sun 2 July (1-5). Home-made teas at Village Hall opp garden if weather is inclement. Adm £4.50, chd free. Home-made soup and rolls on 19 March. Opening with Langley Village Gardens on Sun 28 May. Peaceful country garden 'Far from the Madding Crowd'. Wide, informal mixed borders include narcissi, camassia, shrub roses and perennials. Two landscaped meadows and shepherd's hut with fine pastoral views. Large lily pond sheltered by silver birch. Griffin Glasshouse nearby. Curvilinear design links themed planting areas.

Espalier apples enclose parterre with standard weeping roses and lavender. Secluded gravel garden and views over rolling Essex countryside. Stout shoes or wellies recommended in March. Featured in Rustica magazine, Woman's Weekly Garden Supplement. Gravel drive.

&. ✿ ☕ ☕

62 NEW WOODHATCH FARM
Tawney Common, Theydon Mount, Epping, CM16 7PU. Mr Ray George, 01992 523947, rgeorge@mulberry-house.com. *3m from Epping, 4m from Chipping Ongar, Essex. At Tawney Common, Woodhatch Farm is close to The Mole Trap PH. There is a large pond in the front garden with a commemorative bench.* Sat 10 June, Sat 15 July, Sat 16 Sept (12-5). Adm £5, chd free. Cream teas in our Essex Barn. Tea, coffee, cakes and cream teas can be provided at an additional charge. Visits also by arrangement May to Oct. The owner is a keen plantswoman. The gardens have been developed over a 10 year period including borders planted with Spring bulbs, flowering shrubs and trees. The garden has several landscaped ponds and a lake stocked with fish. Ducks and Moorhens in abundance. An orchard features close to the house. There is a recently developed 5 acre wild flower meadow. The working livestock farm is a short walk away with sheep and shorthorn cattle, and farmer available to advise. We have a vegetable garden and a greenhouse and we supply a local hotel with fresh produce and organic meat from farm. Incredible views of the Essex countryside. Good flat well prepared paths throughout the gardens. Dogs welcome but must be kept on a lead. Ample parking & WC

&. 🐕 ☕ ☕

63 WRITTLE UNIVERSITY COLLEGE
Writtle, CM1 3RR. Writtle University College, 01245 424200 x 25758, Charlotte.Power@writtle.ac.uk, www.writtle.ac.uk. *4m W of Chelmsford. On A414, nr Writtle village, please approach the college from the direction of Writtle Village only as Chelmsford Marathon running through college grounds.* Thur 11 May (10-4). Adm £4, chd free. Light refreshments in The Garden Room (main campus) & The Lordship tea room (Lordship campus). Visits also by arrangement May to Oct. 15 acres; informal lawns with naturalised bulbs and wild flowers. Large tree collection, mixed shrubs, herbaceous borders. Landscaped gardens designed and built by students. Development of 13-acre parkland. Orchard meadow started. Landscaped glasshouses and wide range of seasonal bedding. Herbaceous perennial borders. Extended naturalised bulb areas on front campus lawns. Renovated Rockery Open Day is coordinated by Level 3 Horticultural Students who are on hand to assist visitors. Some gravel, however majority of areas accessible to all.

&. ✿ ☕ ☕

64 NEW WYCKE FARM
Pages Lane, Tolleshunt D'Arcy, Maldon, CM9 8AB. Nancy & Anthony Seabrook. *5m E of Maldon, 10m SW of Colchester. B1023 from Tolleshunt D'Arcy 1m towards Tollesbury. Turn R into Pages Lane. Follow for 1m to Wycke Farm.* Fri 19, Sun 21 May (11-5). Adm £4, chd free. Home-made teas. Large cottage style farmhouse garden situated in the peaceful Essex countryside with mature trees, mixed borders, vegetables, greenhouses and a small flock of sheep. Developed from a neglected state over 12 years ago with a fine view of the Blackwater Estuary. Some gravel and grass paths.

&. ☕ ☕

GLOUCESTERSHIRE

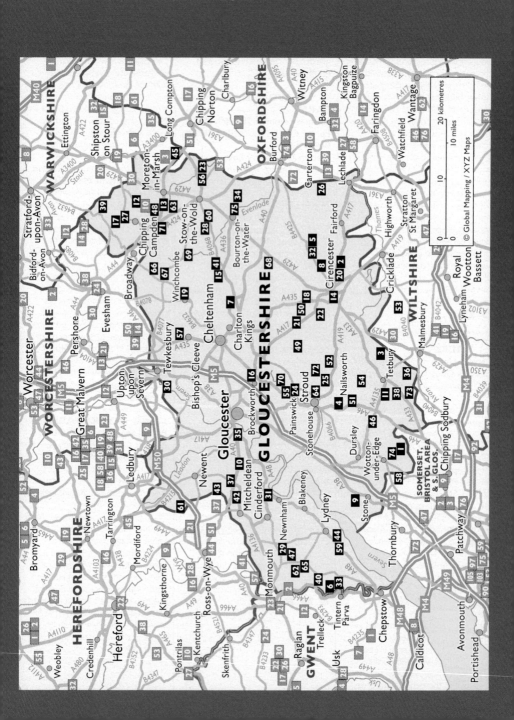

Gloucestershire is one of the most beautiful counties in England, spanning as it does a large part of the area known as the Cotswolds as well as the Forest of Dean and Wye and Severn Valleys.

The Cotswolds is an expanse of gently sloping green hills, wooded valleys and ancient, picturesque towns and villages; it is designated as an area of Outstanding Natural Beauty, and its quintessentially English charm attracts many visitors.

Like the county itself many of the gardens that open for the National Garden Scheme are simply quite outstanding. There are significant gardens which open for the public as well, such as Kiftsgate and Bourton House. There are also some large private gardens which only open for us, such as Highnam Court and Stowell Park.

There are however many more modest private gardens whose doors only open on the National Garden Scheme open day, such as Bowling Green Road in Cirencester with over 300 varieties of Hemerocallis. This tiny garden has now opened for over 35 years. The National collection of Rambling Roses is held at Moor Wood and that of Juglans and Pterocarya at Upton Wold.

Several very attractive Cotswold villages also open their gardens and a wonderful day can be had strolling from cottage to house marvelling at both the standard of the gardens and the beauty of the wonderful buildings, only to pause for the obligatory tea and cake!

Volunteers

County Organiser
Norman Jeffery
01793 762805
norman.jeffery@ngs.org.uk

County Treasurer
Pam Sissons
01242 573942
pamsissons1@gmail.com

Publicity
Vanessa Berridge
01242 609535
vanessa.berridge@sky.com

Booklet Coordinator
Nick Kane
07768 478668
nick@kanes.org

Assistant County Organisers
Sue Hunt
01453 521263
suehunt2@btinternet.com

Trish Jeffery
01793 762805
trishjeffery@aol.com

Valerie Kent
01993 823294

Shirley & Gordon Sills
01242 820606
shirley.sills@ngs.org.uk

Pat Willey
01285 762946
patwilley1@gmail.com

Gareth & Sarah Williams
01531 821654
dgwilliams84@hotmail.com

Left: Awkward Hill Cottage

OPENING DATES

All entries subject to change. For latest information check www.ngs.org.uk

Map locator numbers are shown to the right of each garden name.

January

Sunday 29th
Home Farm 37

February

Snowdrop Festival

Sunday 12th
Home Farm 37
Trench Hill 70

Sunday 19th
The Old Rectory,
Avening 54
Trench Hill 70

Saturday 25th
Lindors Country
House 40

Sunday 26th
Lindors Country
House 40

March

Sunday 12th
Home Farm 37

Sunday 19th
Trench Hill 70

Saturday 25th
Lindors Country
House 40

Sunday 26th
Lindors Country
House 40

April

Saturday 1st
South Lodge 65

Sunday 2nd
Beverston Castle 11

Sunday 9th
Home Farm 37

Monday 10th
◆ Kiftsgate Court 39

Sunday 16th
Trench Hill 70
Upton Wold 71

Monday 17th
Trench Hill 70

Tuesday 18th
Barnsley House 8

Sunday 23rd
Blockley Gardens 12

Tuesday 25th
Wortley House 74

Saturday 29th
South Lodge 65

Sunday 30th
Eastcombe, Bussage and
Brownshill Gardens 25
NEW 20 Forsdene
Walk 29
Home Farm 37
Meadow Cottage 47

May

Monday 1st
Eastcombe, Bussage and
Brownshill Gardens 25

Wednesday 3rd
South Lodge 65

Sunday 7th
Highnam Court 35
Ramblers 59
◆ Stanway Fountain &
Water Garden 67

Wednesday 10th
◆ Lydney Park Spring
Garden 44

Sunday 14th
◆ The Coach House
Garden 20
◆ Mill Dene Garden 48
Stowell Park 68

Wednesday 17th
NEW Downton House 24

Saturday 20th
Charingworth Court 19

Sunday 21st
Charingworth Court 19
◆ Matara Gardens of
Wellbeing 46

South Lodge 65

Wednesday 24th
Lower Farm House 43
South Lodge 65

90th Anniversary Weekend

Saturday 27th
Hookshouse Pottery 38
Lindors Country
House 40
Longhope Gardens 42

Sunday 28th
Barn House, Sandywell
Park 7
NEW Greenfields, Little
Rissington 34
Hookshouse Pottery 38
Lindors Country
House 40
Longhope Gardens 42
Pasture Farm 56

Monday 29th
Barn House, Sandywell
Park 7
Greenacres 32
Hookshouse Pottery 38
Lindors Country
House 40
Pasture Farm 56

Tuesday 30th
Hookshouse Pottery 38

Wednesday 31st
Greenacres 32
Hookshouse Pottery 38
Lower Farm House 43

June

Thursday 1st
Hookshouse Pottery 38

Friday 2nd
Hookshouse Pottery 38

Saturday 3rd
Hookshouse Pottery 38
◆ Misarden Park 49

Sunday 4th
Greenacres 32
Highnam Court 35
Hodges Barn 36
Hookshouse Pottery 38
The Manor 45

Monday 5th
Hodges Barn 36

Wednesday 7th
Eyford House 28
Rockcliffe House 60
Temple Guiting Manor 69
Trench Hill 70

Thursday 8th
Campden House 17
Ernest Wilson Memorial
Garden 27

Saturday 10th
Atcombe Court 4
Cotswold Farm 21
Longhope Gardens 42
Rose Cottage 61

Sunday 11th
Beverston Castle 11
Cotswold Farm 21
Longhope Gardens 42
Rose Cottage 61

Monday 12th
Berkeley Castle 9

Wednesday 14th
Trench Hill 70

Thursday 15th
Campden House 17
Ernest Wilson Memorial
Garden 27

Saturday 17th
Ashley & Culkerton
Gardens 3
Berrys Place Farm 10
Lindors Country
House 40

Sunday 18th
Ampney Brook House 2
Ashley & Culkerton
Gardens 3
Berrys Place Farm 10
◆ Cerney House
Gardens 18
Lindors Country
House 40
Stanton Village
Gardens 66
Stowell Park 68
Wells Cottage 72

Monday 19th
Brockworth Court 16

Tuesday 20th
Alderley Grange 1
Wortley House 74

Wednesday 21st
Berrys Place Farm 10
Trench Hill 70

Laurence House, Wyck Rissington Gardens

© Val Corbett

THE GARDENS

1 ALDERLEY GRANGE

Alderley, GL12 7QT. The Hon Mrs Acloque, 01453 842161, milly@acloque-alderley.co.uk. *2m S of Wotton-under-Edge. Turn NW off A46 Bath to Stroud rd at Dunkirk. L signed Hawkesbury Upton & Hillesley. In Hillesley follow sign to Alderley.* **Visits by arrangement May to July for small or large groups, max 40. Adm £6, chd free. Please phone 01453 842161 or milly@ acloque-alderley.co.uk. Tue 20 June (2-6). Combined adm with Wortley House £20, chd free. Pre-booking essential, please visit www.ngs.org.uk or phone 01483 211535 for information & booking. Home-made teas. For the joint opening with Wortley House, teas will be served at Wortley House.**

Originally designed by Alvilde Lees-Milne in the early 1960's, this quintessentially English garden boasts an abundance of old-fashioned roses and many aromatic and medicinal plants and herbs. Features include a pleached lime walk, fine trees and a Regency summerhouse. Some gravel paths.

&. 🐄 💷

2 AMPNEY BROOK HOUSE

School Lane, Ampney Crucis, Cirencester, GL7 5RT. Allan Hirst, 01285 851098, allan.hirst@clmail.co.uk. *From Cirencester go E on A417 toward Fairford. After passing the Crown of Crucis take 1st L and also immed L again onto School Lane and L again into the gated (open automatically) drive.* **Sun 18 June (11-4). Adm £5, chd free. Light refreshments. Visits also by arrangement Mar to Oct for groups of all sizes, we've had 1-55 so far. Light refreshments by mutual agreement prior to arrival.**

Striking Grade II Cotswold country house on 4.3 acres fronting Ampney Brook. The gardens are at the end of a 5yr project to create a haven for wildlife with fun and stimulating spaces yr-round. Incl woodland, kitchen garden, herbaceous borders, meadows, newly planted arbor. Ample areas and lawns for picnicking (encouraged). No wheelchair access to kitchen garden and greenhouse.

&. 🐄 🐕 ✻ 🚗 💷

GROUP OPENING

3 ASHLEY & CULKERTON GARDENS

Culkerton, Tetbury, GL8 8SS. *Between Tetbury and Cirencester off A433. From Tetbury A433. 2½m take R turn. Straight on at Xrds for parking and teas. From Cirencester, take Tetbury Rd A433 after 6½m turn L follow signs. From Malmesbury A429 L in Crudwell follow signs.* **Sat 17, Sun 18 June (2-5). Combined adm £5, chd free. Delicious home-made teas at Ox Barn, Culkerton.**

ASHLEY GRANGE
Mr & Mrs D Burke.

NEW **ASHLEY MANOR**

ASHLEY MANOR BARN
Michael & Liz Dallas.

DILLYCOT
Mr & Mrs M Oates.

NEW **THE GRANARY**
Mr & Mrs Trevor Jones.

THE LIME HOUSE
Mrs S Hoskins.

NEW **LINCHBANK**
Mr & Mrs S Tidman.

NEW **MANOR FARM BARN**
Mr & Mrs G Sanford.

NORTH FARM
Richard & Lyn White.

OX BARN
Jo & Johnny Nettleton.

Enjoy 2 quintessential Cotswold villages with 10 hidden gems, several open for the first time. From cottage gardens to larger more formal gardens with a great variety of plants and designs. You will find an abundance of old fashioned climbing and shrub roses, herbaceous and perennial borders and a great variety of high quality well-stocked and much loved gardens. Specimen trees, orchards and traditional vegetable gardens abound. Natural ponds, biodiverse garden, plantsman's garden and wonderful views. Beautiful small C12 St James church Ashley open both days. Plants at Ashley Manor Barn (GL8 8SX). Dillycot not accessible by wheelchair. Mostly level access at other gardens.

&. 🐄 ✻ 💷

---

4 ATCOMBE COURT

South Woodchester, GL5 5ER. John & Josephine Peach. *2m S of Stroud. Take turning off A46 signed S Woodchester, Frogmarsh Mill (do not use turning signed S Woodchester, The Ram).* **Sat 10 June (2-6). Adm £4, chd free. Home-made teas.**

12-acre grounds around C17 house (not open) with later Regency front. Delightful views over valley with lakes, mature trees and paddocks. Terraced herbaceous borders, lawns, extensive shrubberies, cutting garden mostly annuals. Long peony border. Woodland walk through beechwood. Partial wheelchair access.

✻ 💷

5 AWKWARD HILL COTTAGE

Awkward Hill, Bibury, GL7 5NH. Mrs Victoria Summerley, v.summerley@hotmail.com, www.awkwardhill.co.uk. *Bibury, Gloucestershire. No parking at the property, so best to park in village and walk past Arlington Row up Awkward Hill, or up Hawkers Hill from Catherine Wheel PH.* **Sun 2 July (2-6). Adm £3.50, chd free. Home-made teas. Evening opening Sun 27 Aug (6-8). Adm £5, chd free. Wine. Visits also by arrangement June to Sept for groups of 10-20, preferably on weekdays (when parking is easier).**

This country Cotswold garden is a work in progress. Since 2012, when the current owner bought the property, it has been redesigned to reflect the local landscape and encourage wildlife. Planting is both formal and informal contributing yr-round interest. Pond and waterfall. The owner, a journalist, is author of Secret Gardens of the Cotswolds and Great Gardens of London. Wonderful view over neighbouring meadow and woodland, 2 sunny terraces and plenty of places to sit and relax. Featured in press and on Radio Gloucestershire.

🐾 ☕

Ramblers

6 BARN HOUSE, CHEPSTOW

Brockweir Common, Chepstow, NP16 7PH. Mrs Kate Patel, 01291 680041, barnhousegarden@gmail.com, www.thegardenbarnhouse.com. *10m S of Monmouth & N of Chepstow, under 1 hr from Hereford, Cheltenham & Cardiff. From Chepstow A466 to Monmouth. 2m past Tintern Abbey R Brockweir Bridge then up Mill Hill ½m, 1st L at The Rock (cottage) continue uphill 1½m. BH on R. No large coaches.* **Sun 25 June (1-5.30). Combined adm with Greenfields £8, chd free. Home-made teas. Visits also by arrangement June to Sept, single visit Barn House (£4.50) or combined with Greenfields (£8). See www. thegardenbarnhouse.com.** Boldly and generously planted garden of an acre. Wealth of ornamental grasses plus long, late flowering perennials. Stunning mass plantings incl 70m miscanthus hedge. Imaginatively designed contrasting areas incl tranquil sunken terrace with lush Asian grasses, hot border of potted tender perennials, orchard and exuberantly planted vegetable garden screened by bamboos. Greenfields is a 10 min walk from Barn House. Visitors can enjoy a great day out in the Wye Valley and visit 2 spectacular gardens. See http:// thechattygardener.com/?p=2896. Featured on BBC Gardeners World and in Country Homes & Interiors.

❀ ☕

7 BARN HOUSE, SANDYWELL PARK

Whittington, Cheltenham, GL54 4HF. Shirley & Gordon Sills, 01242 820606, shirleyasills@gmail.com. *4m E of Cheltenham on A40. Between Andoversford and Whittington villages on A40.* **Sun 28, Mon 29 May, Sun 16 July, Sun 6 Aug (11-5). Adm £5, chd free. Home-made teas. Visits also by arrangement June & July for groups of 20+.** 2½-acre plantaholic's garden enclosed by the weathered walls of a former Victorian kitchen garden. Designed, created and maintained solely by the owners as a series of enclosures both formal and informal, sometimes quirky. Profusely and exuberantly planted for form, scent and colour and to attract wildlife. Herbaceous, climbers, shrubs, trees, lawns, hedges, structures, vistas, water features. See http:// thechattygardener.com/?tag=barn-house-sandywell-park. Featured in Cotswold Style magazine.

❀ ☕

8 BARNSLEY HOUSE

Barnsley, Cirencester, GL7 5EE. Calcot Health & Leisure Ltd, 01285 740000, reception@barnsleyhouse.com, www.barnsleyhouse.com. *4m NE of Cirencester. From Cirencester, take B4425 to Barnsley. House entrance on R as you enter village.* **Tue 18 Apr (10-4). Adm £5, chd free. Light refreshments.**

The beautiful garden at Barnsley House, created by Rosemary Verey, is one of England's finest and most famous gardens incl knot garden, potager garden and mixed borders in Rosemary Verey's successional planting style. The house also has an extensive kitchen garden which will be open with plants and vegetables available for purchase. Narrow paths mean restricted wheelchair access but happy to provide assistance.

♿ ❀ 🚌 🚗 ☕

9 BERKELEY CASTLE

Berkeley, GL13 9PJ. Mr & Mrs RJG Berkeley, www.berkeley-castle.com. *Half-way between Bristol & Gloucester, 10mins from J13 &14 of M5. Follow signs to Berkeley from A38 & B4066. Visitors' entrance is on L of Canonbury St, just before town centre.* **Mon 12 June (11-4). Adm £5, chd free. Delicious home-made cakes, savouries and locally sourced items available.** Unique historic garden of a keen plantsman, with far-reaching views across R Severn. Gardens contain many rare plants which thrive in the warm micro-climate against stone walls of mediaeval castle. Woodland, historic trees and stunning terraced borders. Butterfly house with free-flying tropical butterflies. Lunches, snacks and afternoon tea available in Yurt Restaurant. Gift shop and plant sales. Difficult for wheelchairs due to terraced nature of gardens.

❀ 🚗 ☕

© Val Corbett

Eastleach House

10 BERRYS PLACE FARM

Bulley Lane, Churcham,
Gloucester, GL2 8AS.
Anne Thomas, 07950 808022,
gary.j.thomas1953@gmail.com.
*6m W of Gloucester. A40 towards
Ross. Turning R into Bulley Lane at
Birdwood.* **Sat 17, Sun 18, Wed
21, Thur 22 June (11-5). Adm
£3.50, chd free. Home-made
teas, ploughmans lunches,
cream teas.**
Country garden, approx 1 acre,
surrounded by farmland and old
orchards. Lawns and large sweeping
mixed herbaceous borders with
over 100 roses. Formal kitchen
garden and beautiful rose arbour
leading to lake and summerhouse
with a variety of water lilies and
carp. All shared with peacocks and
ducks.

♿ ✿ ⛪ 🛌 ⛻

11 BEVERSTON CASTLE

Beverston, nr Tetbury, GL8 8TU.
Mrs A L Rook. *2m W of Tetbury. On
A4135 to Dursley between Tetbury
& Calcot Xrds.* **Sun 2 Apr, Sun 11
June (2-5.30). Adm £4, chd free.
Home-made teas.**
Overlooked by romantic C12-C17
castle ruin (not open), copiously-
planted paved terrace leads from
C18 house (not open) across moat
to sloping lawn with spring bulbs in
abundance, and full herbaceous and
shrub borders. Large walled kitchen
garden. Partial wheelchair access.

♿ 🐕 ✿ ⛻

GROUP OPENING

12 BLOCKLEY GARDENS

Blockley, GL56 9DB. *3m NW
of Moreton-in-Marsh. Just off the
Morton-in-Marsh to Evesham Rd
A44.* **Sun 23 Apr, Sun 25 June (2-
6). Combined adm £6, chd free.
Home-made teas at Mill Dene &
St George's Hall on April 23, at
St George's Hall & The Manor
House on June 25.**

CHURCH GATES
Mrs Brenda Salmon.
Open on Sun 23 Apr

LANDGATE
Mrs Hilary Sutton.
Open on all dates

THE MANOR HOUSE
George & Zoe Thompson.
Open on all dates

◆ MILL DENE GARDEN
Mrs B S Dare.
Open on all dates
(See separate entry)

NEW MILL GARDEN HOUSE
Andrew & Celia Goodrick-
Clarke.
Open on Sun 25 June

THE OLD CHEQUER
Mr & Mrs H Linley,
01386 700647,
g.f.linley1@btinternet.com.
Open on all dates
**Visits also by arrangement
Apr & May for groups of 10+.**

PORCH HOUSE
Mr & Mrs Johnson.
Open on Sun 23 Apr

◆ 'RODNEYS'
Mr Duncan & Mrs Amelia
Stewart.
Open on Sun 25 June

SNUGBOROUGH MILL
Rupert & Mandy Williams-Ellis,
01386 701310, rupert.williams-
ellis@talk21.com.
Open on Sun 25 June
🛌

WOODRUFF
Paul & Maggie Adams.
Open on all dates

This popular historic hillside village
has a great variety of high quality,
well-stocked gardens - large and
small, old and new. Blockley Brook,
an attractive stream which flows
right through the village, graces
some of the gardens; these incl
gardens of former water mills,
with millponds attached. From
some gardens there are wonderful
rural views. Shuttle coach service
provided. Children welcome but
close supervision required. Access
to some gardens quite steep and
allowances should be made.

✿ ⛪ ⛻

13 ◆ BOURTON HOUSE GARDEN

Bourton-on-the-Hill,
GL56 9AE. Mr & Mrs R
Quintus, 01386 700754,
info@bourtonhouse.com,
www.bourtonhouse.com. *2m W
of Moreton-in-Marsh. On A44.* **For
NGS: Sun 13 Aug (10-5). Adm
£7, chd free. Home-made teas
in Grade I listed C16 Tithe
Barn. Light refreshments as well
as home-made cakes. For other
opening times and information,
please phone, email or visit garden
website.**
Award winning 3 acre garden
featuring imaginative topiary, wide
herbaceous borders with many
rare, unusual and exotic plants,
water features, unique shade house
and many creatively planted pots.
Fabulous at any time of year but
magnificent in summer months.
Walk in 7 acre pasture with free
printed guide to specimen trees
available to garden visitors. 70%
access for wheelchairs.

♿ ⛪ ⛻

14 25 BOWLING GREEN ROAD

Cirencester, GL7 2HD.
Susan Beck, 01285 653778,
sjb@beck-hems.org.uk. *On NW
edge of Cirencester. Take A435 to
Spitalgate/Whiteway T-lights, turn into
The Whiteway (Chedworth turn), then
1st L into Bowling Green Rd.* **Sun
2 July (2-5); Mon 3 July (11-4);
Sun 9 July (2-5); Mon 10 July
(11-4); Sun 16 July (2-5); Mon**

17 July (11-4). Adm £3.50, chd free. **Visits also by arrangement June & July, max 35. Tea/coffee/ biscuits can be provided for small groups by arrangement.** Wander at will along winding walkways and billowing borders in a naturalistic mini jungle of heavenly hemerocallis, gorgeous grasses, curvaceous clematis, romantic roses and hopeful hostas to glimpse friendly frogs and a graceful giraffe, rated by visitors as a simply amazing hidden gem (and even as 'cool' by the young!). See http://thechattygardener. com/?p=2585. Featured in Sunshine Over Clover, Sarah Wint's book on her travels in her NGS Yellow Daisy Bus [published Sept 2016]. Also featured in Country Gardener, Glos Echo/Citizen and on Radio Gloucestershire. Sadly not suitable for wheelchair access.

🐄 ❀

15 NEW BROCKLEHURST
Hawling, Cheltenham, GL54 5TA. Mrs Anne Wood. *from A40 Cheltenham to Oxford at Andoversford turn onto A436 towards Stow-on-the-Wold and follow signed rd to Hawling.* **Sun 2, Sun 9 July (11-5). Combined adm with Littlefield Garden £8, chd free.** ¼ acre of romantic Cotswold garden surrounded by beautiful countryside with far reaching views. Traditional herbaceous borders with lawn leading down to a raised lily pond surrounded by scented planting incl roses, peonies and summerhouse. Hidden woodland wildlife garden with pond and productive cottage vegetable patch. Limited wheelchair access, some gravel paths.

🚶 🐄

16 BROCKWORTH COURT
Court Road, Brockworth, GL3 4QU. Tim & Bridget Wiltshire, 01452 862938, timwiltshire@hotmail.co.uk. *6m E of Gloucester. 6m W of Cheltenham. Adj St Georges Church on Court Rd. From A46 turn into Mill Lane, turn R, L, R at T junctions. From Ermin St, turn into Ermin Park, then R at r'about then L at next r'about.* **Mon**

19 June, Mon 24 July (2-5.30). Adm £5, chd free. Home-made teas in tithe barn. **Visits also by arrangement Apr to Sept, light refreshments by arrangement.** This intense yet informal tapestry style garden beautifully complements the period manor house which it surrounds. Organic,natural, with informal cottage-style planting areas that seamlessly blend together. Natural fish pond, with Monet bridge leading to small island with thatched Fiji house. Kitchen garden once cultivated by monks. Historic tithe barn. Views to Crickley and Coopers Hill. Adj Norman Church (open). Historic Tithe Barn, open for teas. Featured in Garden News magazine, Cotswold Life and The Citizen. Partial wheelchair access.

🚶 ❀ ☕ 🍷

17 CAMPDEN HOUSE
Chipping Campden, GL55 6UP. The Hon Philip & Mrs Smith. *Entrance on Chipping Campden to Weston Subedge Rd (Dyers Lane), approx ¼m SW of Campden, 1¼m drive. Do not use SatNav.* **Thur 8, Thur 15 June (2-6); Thur 24 Aug (2-5.30). Combined adm with Ernest Wilson Memorial Garden £6, chd free. Home-made teas.** 2 acres featuring mixed borders of plant and colour interest around house and C17 tithe barn (neither open). Set in fine parkland in hidden valley with lakes and ponds. Woodland garden and walks, vegetable garden. Gravel paths, steep slopes.

🚶 🐄 🍷

18 ◆ CERNEY HOUSE GARDENS
North Cerney, Cirencester, GL7 7BX. Mr N W Angus & Dr J Angus, 01285 831300, ladyangus@cerneygardens.com, www.cerneygardens.com. *4m NW of Cirencester. On A435 Cheltenham rd turn L opp Bathurst Arms, follow rd past church up hill, then go straight towards pillared gates on R (signed Cerney House).* **For NGS: Sun 18 June (10-5). Adm £5, chd free. Home-made teas. For other opening times and information,**

please phone, email or visit garden website. Romantic walled garden filled with old-fashioned roses and herbaceous borders. Working kitchen garden, scented garden, Bee garden and general borders. Snowdrops end Jan/Feb. The secret white garden escape. Spring bulbs in abundance all around the wooded grounds. Spectacular autumn colour. Bothy, pottery, walled garden, green and white garden, koi carp pond, woodland walks, knot garden, bee garden. Limited wheelchair access

🚶 🐄 ❀ 🚗 ☕ 🍷

19 CHARINGWORTH COURT
Broadway Road, Winchcombe, GL54 5JN. Susan & Richard Wakeford, 01242 603033, susanwakeford@gmail.com, www.charingworthcourtcotswolds garden.com. *8m NE of Cheltenham. 400 metres N of Winchcombe town centre car park in Bull Lane; walk down Chandos St, L onto Broadway Rd. Garden is on L or limited parking along Broadway Rd.* **Sat 20, Sun 21 May (11-5.30). Adm £5, chd free. Home-made teas from 2pm. Visits also by arrangement May to July for groups, day or eve.** Artistically and lovingly created 1½ acre garden surrounding restored Georgian/Tudor house (not open). Relaxed country style with Japanese influences, large pond and walled vegetable/flower garden, created over 20 years from a blank canvas. Mature copper beech trees, Cedar of Lebanon and Wellingtonia; and younger trees replacing an earlier excess of Cupressus leylandii. Garden will be the backdrop for the 6th Annual Charingworth Court garden sculpture selling exhibition curated by Jane Smoczynski of Winds of Change Gallery, Winchcombe. Featured in Daily Telegraph, Glos Echo, Cotswold Life & Country Homes and Interiors and on Radio Gloucestershire. Most paths are gravelled, several areas accessible without steps. Disabled Parking next to house.

🚶 🐄 ☕ 🍷

20 ◆ THE COACH HOUSE GARDEN

Ampney Crucis, Cirencester, GL7 5RY. Mr & Mrs Nicholas Tanner, 01285 850256, mel@thegenerousgardener.co.uk, www.thegenerousgardener.co.uk. *3m E of Cirencester. Turn into village from A417, immed before Crown of Crucis Inn. Over hump-back bridge, parking immed to R on cricket field (weather permitting) or signed nearby field.* **For NGS: Sun 14 May (2-5). Adm £5, chd free. Home-made teas. For other opening times and information, please phone, email or visit garden website.**
Approx 1½ acres, full of structure and design. Garden is divided into rooms incl rill garden, gravel garden, rose garden, herbaceous borders, green garden with pleached lime allee and potager. Created over last 28yrs by present owners and constantly evolving. Visitors welcome during April - July (groups of 10+), please see garden website. Rare Plant Sales (in aid of James Hopkins Trust) and Garden Lecture Days. Featured in Gardens Illustrated and Cotswold Life. Limited wheelchair access. Ramp available to enable access to main body of garden, steps to other areas.

CONDERTON MANOR

See Worcestershire

21 COTSWOLD FARM

Duntisbourne Abbots, Cirencester, GL7 7JS. Mrs Mark Birchall, 01285 821857, iona@cotswoldfarmgardens.org.uk, www.cotswoldfarmgardens.org.uk. *5m NW of Cirencester off old A417. From Cirencester L signed Duntisbourne Abbots Services, R and R underpass. Drive ahead. From Gloucester L signed Duntisbourne Abbots Services. Pass Services. Drive L.* **Sat 10, Sun 11 June (2-5). Adm £5, chd free. Cream Teas by WI. Visits also by arrangement all dates, no limit on numbers.** *Donation to A Rocha.*
Arts and Crafts garden in lovely position overlooking quiet valley on descending levels with terrace

designed by Norman Jewson in 1930s. Snowdrops named and naturalised, aconites in Feb. Winter garden. Bog garden best in May. White border overflowing with texture and scent. Shrubs, trees, shrub roses. Allotments in old walled garden, 8 native orchids, hundreds of wild flowers and Roman snails. Family day out. Croquet and toys on lawn. Picnics welcome. Featured in Gardens Illustrated, Cirencester Echo, Wilts & Glos Standard. Partial wheelchair access.

22 DAGLINGWORTH HOUSE

Daglingworth, nr Cirencester, GL7 7AG. David & Henrietta Howard, 01285 885626, ettajhoward@gmail.com. *3m N of Cirencester off A417/419. House with blue gate beside church in Daglingworth.* **Visits by arrangement May to Sept for groups between 4 & 25. Adm £6, chd free.**
Walled garden, water features, temple and grotto. Classical garden of 2 acres, views and vistas with humorous contemporary twist. Attractive planting, hedges, topiary shapes, herbaceous borders. Pergolas, woodland, pool, cascade and mirror canal. Lovely Cotswold village setting beside church - see www.ngs.org.uk for further details on garden. Partial wheelchair access.

23 DAYLESFORD HOUSE

Daylesford, GL56 0YG. Lord Bamford & Lady Bamford. *5m W of Chipping Norton. Off A436. Between Stow-on-the-Wold & Chipping Norton.* **Wed 28 June (1-5). Adm £6, chd free. Home-made teas.**
Magnificent C18 landscape grounds created 1790 for Warren Hastings, greatly restored and enhanced by present owners. Lakeside and woodland walks within natural wild flower meadows. Large walled garden planted formally, centred around orchid, peach and working glasshouses. Trellised rose garden. Collection of citrus within period orangery. Secret garden with pavilion and formal pools. Very large garden with substantial

distances to be walked. Partial wheelchair access.

24 NEW DOWNTON HOUSE

Gloucester St, Painswick, GL6 6QN. Ms Jane Kilpatrick. *Entry to garden via Hollyhock Lane only. Please note: no cars in Lane. Parking in Stamages Lane village car park below church or in Churchill Way (1st right off Gloucester Street – the B4073).* **Wed 17 May (1.30-5). Adm £5, chd free. Home-made teas.**
Enthusiast's walled ¼ acre garden in heart of historic Painswick. Planted for yr-round foliage colour and interest and packed with rare and unusual plants. Collection of tender plants in heated glasshouse.

GROUP OPENING

25 EASTCOMBE, BUSSAGE AND BROWNSHILL GARDENS

Eastcombe, GL6 7DS. *3m E of Stroud. 2m N of A419 Stroud to Cirencester rd on turning signed to Bisley & Eastcombe. Please park considerately in villages.* **Sun 30 Apr, Mon 1 May (2-6). Combined adm £6, chd free. Home-made teas at Eastcombe Village Hall. Cream teas/home-made cakes.** *Donation to Hope for Tomorrow; Myeloma UK; Stroud Valleys Project.*

CADSONBURY
Natalie & Glen Beswetherick.

THE CHALFONT
Mr & Mrs I Lambert.

HAWKLEY COTTAGE
Helen Westendorp.

12 HIDCOTE CLOSE
Mr & Mrs K Walker.

HIGHLANDS
Helen & Bob Watkinson.

1 THE LAURELS
Andrew & Ruth Fraser.

MARYFIELD AND MARYFIELD COTTAGE
Mrs M Brown.

NEW ◆ MONASTERY OF OUR LADY 8 ST BERNARD
Sisters Elizabeth-Mary & Mary Philippa.

REDWOOD
Rita Collins.

VATCH RISE
Peggy Abbott.

Medium and small gardens, set in picturesque hilltop location. Some approachable only by foot. (Exhibitions may be on view in Eastcombe village hall). Plants for sale at Eastcombe Village Hall and possibly in some gardens. Wheelchair access to some gardens. Please check at Eastcombe Village Hall.

---

26 EASTLEACH HOUSE
Eastleach Martin, Cirencester, GL7 3NW. Mrs David Richards, garden@eastleachhouse.com, www.eastleachhouse.com. *5m NE of Fairford, 6m S of Burford. Entrance opp church gates in Eastleach Martin. Lodge at gate, driveway is quite steep up to house.* **Visits by arrangement May to July for any size group. Adm £10, chd free. Refreshments at Victoria Inn, Eastleach, must book.**
Large traditional all-yr-round garden. Wooded hilltop position with long views S and W. New parkland, lime avenue and arboretum. Wild flower walk, wildlife pond, lawns, walled and rill gardens, with modern herbaceous borders, yew and box hedges, iris and paeony borders, lily ponds, formal herb garden and topiary. Rambling roses into trees. Featured in Secret Gardens of the Cotswolds by Victoria Sumerley. Limited wheelchair access.

27 ERNEST WILSON MEMORIAL GARDEN
Leysbourne, Chipping Campden, GL55 6DL. EWMG Trust. *High St, below church.* **Thur 8, Thur 15 June (2-6); Thur 24 Aug (2-5.30). Combined adm with Campden House £6, chd free.**

Gardens are at the heart of hospice care

The Ernest Wilson Memorial Garden was created in 1984 in memory of Ernest Wilson, the celebrated plant hunter who was born in Chipping Campden in 1876. This small tranquil walled garden in the centre of town features entirely plants, shrubs and trees introduced by Ernest Wilson.

28 EYFORD HOUSE
Upper Slaughter, Cheltenham, GL54 2JN. Mrs C Heber-Percy. *2½m from Stow on the Wold on B4068 Stow to Andoversford Rd.* **Wed 7, Wed 28 June (11-5). Adm £4, chd free. Home-made teas.**
1½-acre sloping N facing garden, ornamental shrubs and trees. Laid out originally by Graham Stuart Thomas, 1976. West garden and terrace, red border, walled kitchen garden, two lakes with pleasant walks and views, boots recommended! Holy well. Walled garden now open after reconstruction.

29 NEW 20 FORSDENE WALK
Coalway, Coleford, GL16 7JZ. Pamela Buckland, 01594 837179. *From Coleford take Lydney/Chepstow rd at T-lights. L after police station ½m up hill turn L at Xrds then 2nd R (Old Road) to end and turn L into Forsdene Walk.* **Sun 30 Apr (12-4); Sun 2 July (2-6). Combined adm with Meadow Cottage £5, chd free. Visits also by arrangement May to Sept for small groups.**
Corner plot garden redesigned by

new owner in 2016, full of interest in colour themed interlinking spaces, some on different levels. Filled with perennials, climbers, bamboos, grasses and ferns. Pergola and pots in abundance on gravelled areas. An evolving garden showing creative use of smaller spaces.

30 FORTHAMPTON COURT
Forthampton, Tewkesbury, GL19 4RD. John Yorke. *W of Tewkesbury. From Tewkesbury A438 to Ledbury. After 2m turn L to Forthampton. At Xrds go L towards Chaceley. Go 1m turn L at Xrds.* **Sun 2 July (12-4). Adm £4.50, chd free. Home-made teas.**
Charming and varied garden surrounding North Gloucestershire medieval manor house (not open) within sight of Tewkesbury Abbey. Incl borders, lawns, roses and magnificent Victorian vegetable garden.

31 THE GABLES
Riverside Lane, Broadoak, Newnham on Severn, GL14 1JE. Bryan & Christine Bamber, 01594 516323, bryanbamber@sky.com. *1m NE of Newnham on Severn. Park in White Hart PH overspill car park, to R of PH when facing river. Please follow signs to car park. Walk, turning R along rd towards Gloucester for approx 250yds. Access through marked gate.* **Sun 25 June, Sun 20 Aug (11-5). Adm £3.50, chd free. Home-made teas. Visits also by arrangement June to Aug for groups of 10+.**
Garden established 11 yrs ago from blank canvas. Large flat garden with formal lawns, colourful herbaceous borders, shrubberies and long border with mini stumpery. Incl wild flower meadow incorporating soft fruits and fruit trees, allotment-size productive vegetable plot, greenhouse and composting area. Disabled parking information available at entrance. All areas of garden visible for wheelchair users but with limited access.

32 GREENACRES

Hay Lane, Bibury, Cirencester, GL7 5LZ. Alan & Liz Franklin, www.greenacresgarden.uk. *½ m W of Bibury. From Cirencester, take B4425 to Bibury. Take L turn 50yds before entering Bibury signed Fosse Cross/Chedworth. House on R.* **Mon 29 May (11-6); Wed 31 May (2-6). Adm £4, chd free. Home-made teas. Evening opening Sun 4 June (6-9). Adm £6, chd free. Wine. All refreshments proceeds to Alzheimer's Society.**

1 acre level garden developed by present owners over 19yrs. Trees, shrubs, perennials and bulbs to create large informal borders providing variety with yr-round interest. Focus areas incl courtyard, pump, pipe (alpines), gazebo, wild/orchard, heather, coach house and vegetables/herbs with raised beds, polytunnel and greenhouses. Seating integrated in garden design. Wheelchair access to most of garden.

&. ♿ ☕

33 GREENFIELDS, BROCKWEIR COMMON

Brockweir, NP16 7NU. Jackie Healy, 07747 186302, greenfieldsgarden@icloud.com, www.greenfieldsgarden.com. *Located in the Wye valley - mid way between Chepstow and Monmouth. A446: from M'mouth: Thru Llandogo. L to Brockweir, (from Chepstow, thru Tintern. R to B'weir) over bridge, pass PH up hill, 1st L, follow lane to fork, take L at fork. 1st property on R. No coaches.* **Sun 25 June (1-5.30). Combined adm with Barn House, Chepstow £8, chd free. Home-made teas. Visits also by arrangement Apr to Aug, single visit Greenfields (£4.50) or combined with Barn House (£8.00). See greenfieldsgarden. com.**

1½ acre plant person's gem of a garden set in the beautiful Wye Valley. Many mature trees and numerous unusual plants and shrubs, all planted as discrete gardens within a garden. Greenfields is the passion and work of head gardener Jackie who has a long interest in the propagation of plants. See The Chatty Gardener

website(http://thechattygardener. com/?p=2774). Barn House is 10 mins from Greenfields. Enjoy a great day out in the Wye Valley and visit 2 spectacular gardens. Mostly wheelchair access.

&. ❀ ☕

34 NEW GREENFIELDS, LITTLE RISSINGTON

Cheltenham, GL54 2NA. Mrs Diana MacKenzie-Charrington. *Greenfields is on the Rissington Road between Bourton-on-the-Water and Little Rissington, opp the turn to Great Rissington (Leasow Lane). Satnav using postcode does not take you to house.* **Sun 28 May (2-6). Adm £5, chd free. Home-made teas.**

The honey coloured Georgian Cotswold stone house sits in 2 acres of garden, created by current owners over last 16 yrs. Lawns are edged with borders full of flowers and later flowering bulbs. A small pond and stream overlook fields. Bantams roam freely. Mature apple trees in wild garden, greenhouse in working vegetable garden. Sorry no dogs. Partial wheelchair access.

&. ☕

35 HIGHNAM COURT

Highnam, Gloucester, GL2 8DP. Mr & Mrs R J Head, www.HighnamCourt.co.uk. *2m W of Gloucester. On A40/A48 from Gloucester.* **Suns 7 May, 4 June, 2 July, 6 Aug, 3 Sept, 1 Oct (11-5). Adm £5, chd free. Light refreshments in Orangery. Tea, coffee from 11.00am. Sandwiches available until 1.30pm. Cream teas served from 1.30 to 5pm.**

40 acres of Victorian landscaped gardens surrounding magnificent Grade I house (not open), set out by artist Thomas Gambier Parry. Lakes, shrubberies and listed Pulhamite water gardens with grottos and fernery. Exciting ornamental lakes, and woodland areas. Extensive 1 acre rose garden and many features, incl numerous wood carvings. Some gravel paths and steps into refreshment area. Disabled WC outside.

&. 🐕🦽☕☕

36 HODGES BARN

Shipton Moyne, Tetbury, GL8 8PR. Mr & Mrs N Hornby. *3m S of Tetbury. On Malmesbury side of village.* **Sun 4, Mon 5 June (2-6). Adm £5, chd free.**

Very unusual C15 dovecote converted into family home. Cotswold stone walls host climbing and rambling roses, clematis, vines, hydrangeas and together with yew, rose and tapestry hedges create formality around house. Mixed shrub and herbaceous borders, shrub roses, water garden, woodland garden planted with cherries, magnolia and spring bulbs.

&. 🐕

37 HOME FARM

Newent Lane, Huntley, GL19 3HQ. Mrs T Freeman, 01452 830210, torill@ukgateway.net. *4m S of Newent. On B4216 ½ m off A40 in Huntley travelling towards Newent.* **Suns 29 Jan, 12 Feb (11-3); Suns 12 Mar, 9, 30 Apr (11-4). Adm £3, chd free. 2018: Suns 28 Jan, 11 Feb. Visits also by arrangement Jan to Apr.**

Set in elevated position with exceptional views. 1m walk through woods and fields to show carpets of spring flowers. Enclosed garden with fern border, sundial and heather bed. White and mixed shrub borders. Stout footwear advisable in winter.

🐕

38 HOOKSHOUSE POTTERY

Hookshouse Lane, Tetbury, GL8 8TZ. Lise & Christopher White, www.hookshousepottery.co.uk. *2½ m SW of Tetbury. Follow signs from A433 at Hare and Hounds Hotel, Westonbirt. Alternatively take A4135 out of Tetbury towards Dursley and follow signs after ½ m on L.* **Sat 27, Sun 28, Mon 29, Tue 30, Wed 31 May, Thur 1, Fri 2, Sat 3, Sun 4 June (11-6). Adm £4, chd free. Home-made teas.**

Garden offers a combination of dramatic open perspectives and intimate corners. Planting incl wide variety of perennials, with emphasis on colour interest throughout the seasons. Borders, shrubs, woodland glade, water garden containing treatment ponds (unfenced) and flowform cascades. Kitchen garden with raised beds, orchard. Sculptural features. Run on organic principles. Pottery showroom with hand thrown wood-fired pots incl frostproof garden pots. Art & Craft exhibition incl garden furniture and sculptures. Garden games and tree house. Mostly wheelchair accessible.

&. ⛨ ❀ ☕

39 ◆ KIFTSGATE COURT

Chipping Campden, GL55 6LN. Mr & Mrs J G Chambers, 01386 438777, info@kiftsgate.co.uk, www.kiftsgate.co.uk. *4m NE of Chipping Campden. Adj to Hidcote NT Garden. 3m NE of Chipping Campden.* **For NGS: Mon 10 Apr, Mon 14 Aug (2-6). Adm £8.50, chd £2.50. Home-made teas. For other opening times and information, please phone, email or visit garden website.**
Magnificent situation and views, many unusual plants and shrubs, tree peonies, hydrangeas, abutilons, species and old-fashioned roses incl largest rose in England, Rosa filipes Kiftsgate. Steep slopes and uneven surfaces.

&. ❀ 🚗 ☕

40 LINDORS COUNTRY HOUSE

The Fence, St. Briavels, Lydney, GL15 6RB. Christian Guild, 01594 530283, lindors@christianguild.co.uk, www.lindors.co.uk. *Lower Wye Valley. Monmouth 7m, Chepstow 9m, Coleford 4m. From Monmouth/ Chepstow use Wye Valley rd (A466). Turn at Bigswier Bridge towards St Briavels for ½ m. From St Briavels Castle head downhill towards River Wye. On L ½ m before bottom of hill.* **Sat 25, Sun 26 Feb, Sat 25, Sun 26 Mar, Sat 27, Sun 28, Mon 29 May, Sat 17, Sun 18 June, Sat 26, Sun 27, Mon 28 Aug (10-4). Adm £3.50, chd free. Refreshments available all day. Light meals 12–4pm, main meals 12–2pm.**
Reopening after extensive work. 9 acres of mature woodland gardens

with streams, ponds, formal gardens, wild flower meadows. Over 70 varieties of trees. Games on the lawns and garden tours. New for 2017: The green room. A quiet sunken retreat beside a stream designed entirely with shades of lush green. It also has green credentials, having been built using only reclaimed materials & plants. Putting green, bowls. Some gravel paths.

&. ⛨ 🚌 🚗 ☕

41 LITTLEFIELD GARDEN

Hawling, Cheltenham, GL54 5SZ. Mr & Mrs George Wilk. *From A40 Cheltenham to Oxford at Andoversford turn onto A436 towards Stow-On-The-Wold. Take 2nd signed rd to Hawling.* **Sun 2, Sun 9 July (11-5). Combined adm with Brocklehurst £8, chd free. Home-made teas.**
Surrounded by idyllic countryside with fine views over a small valley, site of the old Medieval village of Hawling, Littlefield Garden was originally designed by Jane Fearnley-Whittingstall. More recently the planting in the yew walk was created by Sherborne Gardens. Mixed borders, rose garden, lily pond, vegetable garden, lavender borders, wild flowers. Visitors can have tea and relax under the pergola. Featured in Cotswold Life, Homes & Gardens magazine and on BBC Radio Gloucestershire. Mostly wheelchair access. Gravel path and paved terraces.

&. ⛨ ❀ ☕

GROUP OPENING

42 LONGHOPE GARDENS

Longhope, GL17 0NA. 01452 830406, sally.j.gibson@btinternet.com. *10m W of Gloucester. 7m E of Ross on Wye. A40 take Longhope turn off to Church Rd. From A4136 follow Longhope signs and turn onto Church Rd. Parking available on Church Rd.* **Sat 27 May (12-5); Sun 28 May (2-6); Sat 10 June (12-5); Sun 11 June (2-6). Combined adm £5, chd free. Home-made teas. Visits also by arrangement May & June for groups of 10+.**

CHESSGROVE COTTAGE
Mr Peter Evans.

3 CHURCH ROAD
Rev Clive & Mrs Linda Edmonds.

SPRINGFIELD HOUSE
Sally & Martin Gibson.

WOODBINE COTTAGE
Mrs Lucille Roughley.

4 beautiful gardens set in the valley of Longhope. Each garden has its own style and delights for you to discover with sweeping views across the valley to May Hill and the Forest of Dean. 3 Church Road is a long garden divided into rooms with a large collection of hardy geraniums. Springfield House: a large enclosed garden with terraced lawns, a wide variety of shrubs and trees mingling with sweeping herbaceous. Woodbine Cottage: small, tranquil garden with traditional planting. Chessgrove Cottage: delightful garden, situated on the side of the valley, with spectacular views and access to 12 acres of surrounding woodland. Home-made cakes, refreshments and plant sales. Keep up to date with Longhope Gardens on our Facebook page. 3 Church Road and Springfield House featured in Amateur Gardening magazine.

&. ❀ ☕

43 LOWER FARM HOUSE

Cliffords Mesne, Newent, GL18 1JT. Gareth & Sarah Williams. *2m S of Newent. From Newent, follow signs to Cliffords Mesne and Birds of Prey Centre (1½m). Approx ½m beyond Centre, turn L at Xrds (before church).* **Wed 24, Wed 31 May (2-6). Adm £4, chd free. Cream teas.**
2 acre garden, incl woodland, stream and large natural lily pond with rockery and bog garden. Herbaceous borders, pergola walk, terrace with ornamental fishpond, kitchen and herb garden; collections of irises, hostas and paeonies. Many interesting and unusual trees and shrubs incl magnolias and cornus. Some gravel paths.

&. ⛨ ❀ ☕

44 ♦ LYDNEY PARK SPRING GARDEN

Lydney, GL15 6BU. The Viscount Bledisloe, 01594 842844/842922, www.lydneyparkestate.co.uk. ½ m SW of Lydney. On A48 Gloucester to Chepstow rd between Lydney & Aylburton. Drive is directly off A48. **For NGS: Wed 10 May (10-5). Adm £5, chd £0.50. Home-made teas & light lunches. For other opening times and information, please phone or visit garden website.**

Spring garden in 8 acre woodland valley with lakes, profusion of rhododendrons, azaleas and other flowering shrubs. Formal garden; magnolias and daffodils (April). Picnics in deer park which has fine trees. Important Roman Temple site and museum. Not suitable for wheelchairs due to rough pathway through garden and steps to WC.

🐕 ✿ 🍵

45 THE MANOR

Little Compton, Moreton-In-Marsh, GL56 0RZ. Mr R Sutton. Next to church in Little Compton. 1m from A44 and then 2m from A3400 follow signs to Little Compton and then pick up yellow ngs signs. **Sun 4 June, Sun 20 Aug (2-5). Adm £5.50, chd free. Home-made teas.**

C16 historic manor house (not open) and 4 acres of stunning gardens set in a beautiful location in village of Little Compton. Enjoy the many garden rooms, long herbaceous border, deer walk, Japanese garden, flower garden, arboretum and specimen trees. Garden staff on site, croquet and tennis courts available to play.

🐕 🍵

46 ♦ MATARA GARDENS OF WELLBEING

Kingscote, Tetbury, GL8 8YA. Matara, 01453 861050, info@matara.co.uk, www.matarawellbeing.com. 5½ m NW of Tetbury. Approx 20 mins from either J18 of M4 (12m) or J13 of M5 (8.5m). On A4135 between Tetbury and Dursley in Kingscote village. Entrance opp Hunter's Hall PH. **For NGS: Sun 21 May (1-5). Adm £5, chd £3. Home-made teas. You are welcome to bring your own picnics if you would like to picnic in the gardens. For other opening times and information, please phone, email or visit garden website.**

Trees of life - enjoy the tranquil beauty of Matara's Gardens of Wellbeing and its dedication to the symbolic, spiritual and cultural role of trees. What makes us special are our Chinese Scholar's garden, Japanese tea garden, Shinto woodlands, Celtic wishing tree, labyrinth, healing spiral, field of dreams and ornamental herb and flower gardens. Woodland walk, Chinese cloistered courtyard, barefoot trail, ponds, strolling walk, walled herb garden and vegetable garden. Featured in The Cotswolds' Finest Gardens by Tony Russell. Limited wheelchair access. Some steps and grass paths.

🚗 🛏 🍵

47 MEADOW COTTAGE

59 Coalway Road, Coalway, Coleford, GL16 7HL. Matt & Ella Beard, 01594 834672, ellabeard_1@hotmail.com. 1m SE of Coleford. From Coleford take Lydney & Chepstow Rd at T-lights in town. Turn L after police stn, signed Coalway & Parkend. Garden on L ½ m up hill opp layby. **Sun 30 Apr (12-4); Sun 2 July (2-6). Combined adm with 20 Forsdene Walk £5, chd free. Home-made teas. Visits also by arrangement May to July for max 20. Full afternoon tea can be provided for small groups, please contact for details.**

⅓-acre cottage garden with modern touches, from early spring. Gravelled entry, borders with shrubs, large-leaf plants, lavender in pots. Newly planted white border. Corner area with Japanese elements leading to paths which wind around colourful shrubs, climbers and perennial-filled borders. Small pond with waterfall. Vegetable/fruit garden in raised beds. Shade plants in pots. Many containers. Joint opening with Meadow Cottage's previous owner in her new garden at 20 Forsdene Walk.

✿ 🍵

48 ♦ MILL DENE GARDEN

School Lane, Blockley, Moreton-in-Marsh, GL56 9HU. Mrs B S Dare, 01386 700457, info@milldenegarden.co.uk, www.milldenegarden.co.uk. 3m NW of Moreton-in-Marsh. From A44 follow brown signs from Bourton-on-the-Hill to Blockley. Approx 1¼ m down hill turn L behind village gates. Limited parking. Coaches by appt. **For NGS: Sun 14 May (10.30-5). Adm £8, chd free. Light refreshments. Opening with Blockley Gardens on Sun 23 Apr, Sun 25 June. For other opening times and information, please phone, email or visit garden website.**

50 shades of green (!) at least in this 2½ acre garden hidden in the Cotswolds. Centrepiece is water mill dating from C10 (probably), with mill pond and stream. The owners have had fun creating a varied garden, from informal woodland full of bulbs, to rose walk, cricket lawn, then herb garden looking out over hills with church as backdrop. Talk on the garden given by owner for groups of 10+ (£25) Garden trail for children. Booklet re development of garden available £2.50. Featured on Love Your Garden & Countryfile and in Sunday Telegraph. Half of garden wheelchair accessible. Please ring for reserved parking/ramps. Garden in a valley but sides have slope or step alternatives.

♿ ✿ 🚗 🍵

49 ♦ MISARDEN PARK

Miserden, Stroud, GL6 7JA. Mr Nicholas Wills, 01285 821303, estate.office@miserdenestate.co.uk, www.misardenpark.co.uk. 6m NW of Cirencester Follow signs off A417 or B4070 from Stroud **For NGS: Sat 3 June (10-5). Adm £7.50, chd free. Home-made teas. For other opening times and information, please phone, email or visit garden website.**

This lovely, unspoilt garden, positioned high on the Wolds and commanding spectacular views was created in C17 and still retains a wonderful sense of timeless peace and tranquillity. Perhaps finest features in garden are double

92metre mixed border incl roses and clematis, in different colour sections. Much of original garden is found within ancient Cotswold stone walls Partial access for wheelchairs

50 MOOR WOOD

Woodmancote, GL7 7EB. Mr & Mrs Henry Robinson. *3½m NW of Cirencester. Turn L off A435 to Cheltenham at North Cerney, signed Woodmancote 1¼m; entrance in village on L beside lodge with white gates.* **Sun 25 June (2-6). Adm £5, chd free. Home-made teas.**
2 acres of shrub, orchard and wild flower gardens in beautiful isolated valley setting. Holder of National Collection of Rambler Roses. Not recommended for wheelchairs.

NPC

GROUP OPENING

51 NAILSWORTH GARDENS - OFF CHESTNUT HILL

Hanover Gardens, Chestnut Hill, Nailsworth, GL6 0RN. *Nailsworth is 4m S of Stroud on A46. At clock tower/weeping willow Xrds in Nailsworth follow signs. Parking at Prices Mill Surgery, Newmarket Rd.* **Sun 25 June (2-6). Combined adm £5, chd free. Home-made teas at Floris House. Tea, coffee, juices and home-made cakes.**

NEW **COPPERFIELD**
Mike & Gill Phillips.

DRIFTWOOD
Mrs M Ganner.

FLORIS HOUSE
Elly Austin.

Gardens within walking distant of town, 2 gardens clamber up the valley sides. All express owners' personalities in design, features and planting. Many steps.

GROUP OPENING

52 OAKRIDGE LYNCH OPEN GARDENS

Oakridge Lynch, Stroud, GL6 7NS. *2m S of Bisley, off Bisley to Eastcombe rd. From Bisley, turn L on leaving village. From Stroud, on A419, turn L to Chalford Hill, follow signs to Bisley. Turn R before entering Bisley.* **Sun 25 June (2-6). Combined adm £5, chd free. Home-made teas at Edgehill, The Broadway, Oakridge Lynch. Plant stall.**

NEW **THE COTTAGE**
Mr Mark Wright.

HILLSIDE
Mrs Elisabeth White.

HOPE COTTAGE
Gillian Wimperis.

OLD COTTAGE
Richard & Judy Mackie.

OLD POST OFFICE COTTAGE
Eileen Herbert.

NEW **WESLEY COTTAGE**
Dan & Anna Mead.

Beautiful hillside village of pretty cottages and stunning views. Selection of small to medium sized lovely gardens packed with interesting plants: herbaceous borders, roses, herbs, climbers, vines, fruit and vegetables. Limited wheelchair access at most gardens.

GROUP OPENING

53 NEW OAKWOOD FARM PLANT FAIR AND UPPER MINETY OPEN GARDENS

Upper Minety, Malmesbury, SN16 9PY. Mr & Mrs C Gallop, 01666 860286, katiegallop@btinternet.com. *7m SE of Cirencester. Follow signs from A429 (Cotswold Water Park) or alternatively from B4040 to Minety Church.* **Sun 25 June (11-5). Combined adm £5, chd free. Home-made teas.**
3 rarely seen gardens in Upper Minety, which takes its name from the wild mint plant found growing in and around the village, will be opening for the 1st time under the NGS. Offering inspiration from sweeping herbaceous borders, open meadows, productive fruit/ vegetable and formal gardens with St. Leonards Church floral arrangements. Specialist nurseries who know and care about plants alongside imaginative stalls offering accessories for your home and garden will be hosted at Oakwood Farm with teas on the farm lawn and where garden maps can be obtained. Ample parking, village walk. Some gravel, mostly grass. Disabled parking available. Coaches by prior arrangement only.

Lower Farm House

54 THE OLD RECTORY, AVENING

60 High Street, Avening, GL8 8NF.
Mrs Anthea Beszant. *3m W of
Tetbury. 2m N of Nailsworth. On
B4014 in High St close to Avening
Church. Opp Woodstock Lane, on
corner of Rectory Lane. Please park
carefully in High St.* **Sun 19 Feb
(11.30-4). Adm £3.50, chd free.
Tea.**
3-acre garden around C17
Cotswold Rectory (not open).
Walks through mature woodland.
Snowdrops. Paddock with stream
and Japanese bridge. Italianate
terrace, steep steps and banks.
Supported in places by ancient
megaliths transported here in the
1800s. Sculptures by Darren Yeadon.
Limited wheelchair access, gravel
paths, steep slopes and steps.

OVERBURY COURT

See Worcestershire

55 ♦ PAINSWICK ROCOCO GARDEN

Painswick, GL6 6TH.
Painswick Rococo Garden
Trust, 01452 813204,
info@rococogarden.org.uk,
www.rococogarden.org.uk. *½ m N
of Painswick. ½ m outside village on
B4073, follow brown tourism signs.*
**For opening times and information,
please phone, email or visit garden
website.**
Unique C18 garden from the
brief Rococo period, combining
contemporary buildings, vistas,
ponds, kitchen garden and winding
woodland walks. Anniversary maze,
on site restaurant, shop and plant
sales. Snowdrop display late winter.
Limited wheelchair access to garden
due to being in valley. Disabled
access to WC and restaurant.

56 PASTURE FARM

Upper Oddington, Moreton-
In-Marsh, GL56 0XG. Mr &
Mrs John LLoyd, 01451 830203,
ljmlloyd@yahoo.com. *Mid-
way between Upper and Lower
Oddington. Oddington lies about 3m
from Stow-on-the-Wold just off A436.*
Sun 28, Mon 29 May (11-6).

Adm £5, chd free. Home-made
teas. **Visits also by arrangement
June to Sept, coaches by
appointment only.**
Medium sized informal country
garden that has been developed
over 30yrs by current owners. All-yr
interest with mixed borders, topiary,
hedging both formal and informal,
orchard and wealth of garden trees.
In rural setting with very large spring
fed pond inhabited by collection
of ducks. Large plant stalls of
herbaceous, shrubs and vegetables
(proceeds to Kate's Home Nursing).
Public footpath across 2 small fields
arrives at C11 church, St Nicholas,
with doom paintings, set in ancient
woodlands. Truly worth a visit. See
Simon Jenkins' Book of Churches.

57 PEAR TREE COTTAGE

58 Malleson Road, Gotherington,
GL52 9EX. Mr & Mrs E
Manders-Trett, 01242 674592,
edandmary@talktalk.net. *4m N of
Cheltenham. From A435, travelling
N, turn R into Gotherington 1m
after end of Bishop's Cleeve bypass
at garage. Garden on L approx
100yds past Shutter Inn.* **Visits by
arrangement Apr to June for 30
max. Adm £4, chd free. Light
refreshments.**
Mainly informal country garden of
approx ½ acre with pond and gravel
garden, grasses and herbaceous
borders, trees and shrubs
surrounding lawns. Wild garden and
orchard lead to greenhouses, herb
and vegetable gardens. Spring bulbs,
early summer perennials and shrubs
particularly colourful.

**Springfield House,
Longhope Gardens**

58 PEMBERLEY LODGE

Churchend Lane, Old Charfield,
GL12 8LJ. Rob & Yvette
Andrewartha, 01454 260885,
yvette@gryfindor.info, www.
gryfindor.info/ourgarden.html.
*3m S of Wotton-under-Edge. From
M5 take J14 towards Wotton-
under-Edge. At r'about take 2nd
exit on to Churchend Lane. Garden
approx 600 metres on R.* **Visits
by arrangement, prior notice
required please, for groups of
10+. Home-made teas.**
Small private garden planted
to delight all yr round. Garden
wraps round house and has been
densely planted for interest and
low maintenance. Trees, shrubs,
perennials, grasses, water, gravel,
lawns and hard landscaping to give
an informal and peaceful feel. Roof
garden with a fantastic view to the
valley. The garden has to cope with
a pack of terriers! Roof garden not
wheelchair accessible.

59 RAMBLERS

Lower Common, Aylburton,
Lydney, GL15 6DS. Jane & Leslie
Hale, hale.les@outlook.com. *1½ m
W of Lydney. Off A48 Gloucester to
Chepstow Rd. From Lydney through
Aylburton, out of de-limit turn R
signed Aylburton Common, ¾ m along
lane.* **Sun 7 May (1.30-5.30). Adm
£4, chd free. Home-made teas.
Visits also by arrangement May
& June.**
Peaceful medium sized country
garden with informal cottage
planting, herbaceous borders and
small pond looking through hedge
windows onto wild flower meadow
and mature apple orchard. Some
shade loving plants and topiary.
Large productive vegetable garden.
Past winner of The English Garden
magazine's Britain's Best Gardener's
Garden competition.

60 ROCKCLIFFE HOUSE

Upper Slaughter, Cheltenham,
GL54 2JW. Mr & Mrs Simon
Keswick. *2m from Stow-on-the-Wold.
1½ m from Lower Swell on B4068
towards Cheltenham. Leave Stow on
the Wold on B4068 through Lower*

Swell. *Continue on B4068 for 1½m. Rockcliffe is well signed on R.* **Wed 7, Wed 28 June (11-5). Adm £5, chd free. Home-made teas. Donation to Kates Home Nursing.** Large traditional English garden of 8 acres incl pink garden, white and blue garden, herbaceous border, rose terrace, large walled kitchen garden and orchard. Greenhouses and pathway of topiary birds leading up through orchard to stone dovecot. Dramatic pond surrounded by 6 large cornus controversa variegata. Featured in several books and magazines. Sorry, no dogs. 2 wide stone steps through gate, otherwise good wheelchair access.

&. ❀ ☙

61 ROSE COTTAGE

Kempley, Nr Dymock, GL18 2BN. Naomi Cryer. *3m from Newent towards Dymock. From Newent on B4221 take turning just after PH, on R from Gloucester direction, signed Kempley. Follow rd for approx 3m.* **Sat 10, Sun 11 June (11-5). Adm £4, chd free. Home-made teas.** Approx 1 acre of flat garden, mostly herbaceous borders. Hot bed and long border leading to borrowed view, small parterre in orchard area, grass bed and pond. Small wild flower pasture, at its best in June. Rose garden, iris bed, hydrangea bed, vegetable and nursery beds and cutting garden. Home-made cakes, cards and plants for sale. Featured in Cotswold Life and Citizen Weekend. Although quite flat, wheelchair access mostly via lawn and grass which may make wheelchair use a little difficult especially in damp weather.

&. ❀ ☙

62 SCATTERFORD

Newland, Coleford, GL16 8NG. Sean Swallow, 01291 675483, nmklweare@tiscali.co.uk, www.seanswallow.com. *1m S of Newland and just N of Clearwell, opp junction to Coleford. From Monmouth take A466/Redbrook Rd to Redbrook. From Chepstow take B4228 turn off to Clearwell. From Coleford take Newland Street.* **Visits by arrangement May to Oct for horticultural and design groups**

of 10+. **Adm £5, chd free.** Well-crafted and maintained 2-acre garden between Wye valley and Forest of Dean. Formal pond, walled garden, sculpted terraces, courtyards, haha, hedges, orchards, hedgrows, natural pond and extensive borders. A contemporary design with serene atmosphere. Head Gardener: Kelly Weare. Designed by Sean Swallow and Askew Nelson Landscape Architects. Featured in Gardens Illustrated.

63 ◆ SEZINCOTE

Moreton-in-Marsh, GL56 9AW. Mrs D Peake, 01386 700444, enquiries@sezincote.com, www.sezincote.co.uk. *3m SW of Moreton-in-Marsh. From Moreton-in-Marsh turn W along A44 towards Evesham; after 1½m (just before Bourton-on-the-Hill) turn L, by stone lodge with white gate.* **For NGS: Sun 25 June (2-6). Adm £5, chd free. Home-made teas.** For other opening times and information, please phone, email or visit garden website. Exotic oriental water garden by Repton and Daniell with lake, pools and meandering stream, banked with massed perennials. Large semi-circular orangery, formal Indian garden, fountain, temple and unusual trees of vast size in lawn and wooded park setting. House in Indian manner designed by Samuel Pepys Cockerell. Garden on slope with gravel paths, so not all areas wheelchair accessible.

&. ☕ ☙

64 SLAD VALLEY HOUSE

203 Slad Road, Stroud, GL5 1RJ. Mr & Mrs Michael Grey. *Situated in Slad Valley 1m W of Stroud on rd to Slad. Follow B4070 along the valley through Slad towards Stroud. House is situated on R through gates up steep gravel drive. From Stroud drive 1m on B4070 towards Slad. Parking on Slad Road.* **Sat 15, Sun 16 July (2-4.30). Adm £3.50, chd free. Home-made teas.** Delightful informal steep terraced garden, with small woodland area, of approx 1 acre around C18 mill owner's manor house (not

open). Garden restoration work in progress in all areas. Numerous trees, 2 magnificent magnolias, shrubs, flowers and well stocked borders being developed. The garden is a chosen site for local art exhibitions. NB lots of steps and uneven paths, no handrails. Unsuitable for wheelchairs.

❀ ☕ ☙

Funds from NGS gardens help Macmillan support thousands of people every year

65 SOUTH LODGE

Church Road, Clearwell, Coleford, GL16 8LG. Andrew & Jane MacBean, 01594 837769, southlodgegarden@btinternet.com, www.southlodgegarden.co.uk. *2m S of Coleford. Off B4228. Follow signs to Clearwell. Garden on L of castle driveway. Please park on rd in front of church or in village. No parking on castle drive.* **Sat 1, Sat 29 Apr, Wed 3, Sun 21, Wed 24 May, Sat 24 June (1-5). Adm £4, chd free. Home-made teas. Visits also by arrangement Apr to June for groups of 15+.** Peaceful country garden in 2 acres with stunning views of surrounding countryside. High walls provide a backdrop for rambling roses, clematis, and honeysuckles. Organic garden with large variety of perennials, annuals, shrubs and specimen trees with yr-round colour. Vegetable garden, wildlife and formal ponds. Rustic pergola planted with English climbing roses and willow arbour in gravel garden. Rosy Hardy (from Hardys Cottage Garden Plants) award winning plantswoman and designer, winner of countless RHS medals incl 21 Chelsea Golds will be in the garden to talk about all aspects of perennials on Sat 1st April 1-5pm Gravel paths and steep grassy slopes.

&. ❀ ☕ ☙

GROUP OPENING

66 STANTON VILLAGE GARDENS

Stanton, nr Broadway, WR12 7NE.
3m S of Broadway. Off B4632, between Broadway (3m) & Winchcombe (6m). **Sun 18 June (2-6). Adm £6, chd free. Home-made teas in The Burland Hall in centre of village & in several open gardens. Ice cream trike in centre of village.** *Donation to local charities.*

Over 15 gardens open in this picturesque Cotswold village. Many houses border the street with long gardens hidden behind. Gardens vary from houses with colourful herbaceous borders, established trees, shrubs and vegetable gardens to tiny cottage gardens Some also have attractive, natural water features fed by the stream which runs through the village. Plant & book stall. Legendary home-made teas. Regret not all gardens suitable for wheelchair users.

&. 🐄 ✿ 🚗 🍴 ☕

67 ◆ STANWAY FOUNTAIN & WATER GARDEN

Stanway, Cheltenham, GL54 5PQ. The Earl of Wemyss & March, 01386 584528, stanwayhse@btconnect.com, www.stanwayfountain.co.uk. *9m NE of Cheltenham. 1m E of B4632 Cheltenham to Broadway rd or B4077 Toddington to Stow-to-the-Wold rd.* **For NGS: Sun 7 May, Sun 24 Sept (2-5). Adm £7, chd £4. Cream teas in Stanway Tea Room. For other opening times and information, please phone, email or visit garden website.**

20 acres of planted landscape in early C18 formal setting. The restored canal, upper pond and 165ft high fountain have re-created one of the most interesting Baroque water gardens in Britain. Striking C16 manor with gatehouse, tithe barn and church. Britain's highest fountain at 300ft, the world's highest gravity fountain which runs at 2.45 & 4.00pm for 30 mins each

time. Limited wheelchair access in garden, some flat areas, able to view fountain and some of garden. House is not wheelchair suitable.

&. 🐄 🚗 ☕ ☙

68 STOWELL PARK

Yanworth, Northleach, Cheltenham, GL54 3LE. The Lord & Lady Vestey, www.stowellpark.co.uk. *8m NE of Cirencester. Off Fosseway A429 2m SW of Northleach.* **Sun 14 May, Sun 18 June (2-5). Adm £6, chd free. Home-made teas.**

Magnificent lawned terraces with stunning views over Coln Valley. Fine collection of old-fashioned roses and herbaceous plants, with pleached lime approach to C14 house (not open). 2 large walled gardens containing vegetables, fruit, cut flowers and range of greenhouses. Long rose pergola and wide, plant filled borders divided into colour sections. New water features and hazel arch at bottom of garden. Open continuously for 50yrs. Plants for sale at May opening only.

✿ ☕ ☙

69 TEMPLE GUITING MANOR

Temple Guiting, Stow on the Wold, GL54 5RP. Mr & Mrs S Collins, www.templeguitingmanor.co.uk. *7m from Stow-on-the-Wold. From Stow-on-the-Wold take B4077 towards Tewkesbury. On descending hill bear L to village (signed) ½m. Garden in centre of village on R.* **Wed 7 June (10.30-4.30). Adm £6, chd free. Home-made teas at new village shop & tearoom.**

5 acres of formal contemporary gardens with kitchen garden, to a Grade I listed historic manor house (not open) in Windrush Valley. Designed by Jinny Blom, gold medal winner Chelsea Flower Show. Gravel pathways.

&. ✿ ☕ ☙

70 TRENCH HILL

Sheepscombe, GL6 6TZ. Celia & Dave Hargrave, 01452 814306, celia.hargrave@btconnect.com. *1½m E of Painswick. From Cheltenham A46 take 1st turn signed*

Sheepscombe and follow lane (about 1¼m) to bottom of hill then continue up hill towards Sheepscombe. Garden on L opp lane. **Suns 12, 19 Feb, 19 Mar (11-5); Sun 16, Mon 17 Apr (11-6); Weds 7, 14, 21 June, Sun 16 July (2-6); Suns 27 Aug, 10 Sept (11-6). Adm £4, chd free. Home-made teas. 2018: Suns 11, 18 Feb. Visits also by arrangement Feb to Sept, not suitable for large coaches, small coaches only, advise garden owner in advance.**

Approx 3 acres set in small woodland with panoramic views. Variety of herbaceous and mixed borders, rose garden, extensive vegetable plots, wild flower areas, plantings of spring bulbs with thousands of snowdrops and hellebores, woodland walk, 2 small ponds, waterfall and larger conservation pond. Interesting wooden sculptures, many within the garden. Run on organic principles. Wide variety of wooden sculptures in garden. Children's play area. Featured in Garden Answers & Country Homes and Interiors. Mostly wheelchair access but some steps and slopes.

&. ✿ 🚗 ☕ ☙

71 UPTON WOLD

Moreton-in-Marsh, GL56 9TR. Mr & Mrs I R S Bond, www.uptonwoldgarden.co.uk. *4½m W of Moreton-in-Marsh. On A44 1m past A424 junction at Troopers Lodge Garage, on R. Look out for marker posts.* **Sun 16 Apr (11-5). Adm £10, chd free. Home-made teas.**

Ever developing and changing garden, architecturally and imaginatively laid out around C17 house (not open) with commanding views. Yew hedges, herbaceous walk, some unusual plants and trees, vegetables, pond and woodland gardens, labyrinth. National Collections of Juglans and Pterocarya. 2 Star award from GGG.

✿ 🚗 NPC ☙

72 WELLS COTTAGE

Wells Road, Bisley, GL6 7AG. Mr & Mrs Michael Flint, 01452 770289, bisleyflints@bisleyflints.plus.com.

5m N E of Stroud. Gardens & car park well signed in Bisley village. Gardens on S edge of village at head of Toadsmoor Valley, N of A419. **Sun 18 June (2-6). Adm £3, chd free.** Just under 1 acre. Terraced on several levels with beautiful views over valley. Much informal planting of trees and shrubs to give colour and texture. Lawns and herbaceous borders. Collection of grasses. Formal pond area. Rambling roses on rope pergola. Vegetable garden with raised beds. No access to upper terraces for wheelchair users.

73 ◆ WESTONBIRT SCHOOL GARDENS
Tetbury, GL8 8QG. Holfords of Westonbirt Trust, 01666 881373, jbaker@holfordtrust.com, www.holfordtrust.com. *3m SW of Tetbury. Opp Westonbirt Arboretum, on A433. Enter via Holford wrought iron gates to Westonbirt House.* **For NGS: Sun 16 July (11-5). Adm £5, chd free. Tea, coffee & cake available to purchase in the Great Hall. For other opening times and information, please phone, email or visit garden website.**
28 acres. Former private garden of Robert Holford, founder of Westonbirt Arboretum. Formal Victorian gardens incl walled Italian garden now restored with early herbaceous borders and exotic border. Rustic walks, lake, statuary and grotto. Rare, exotic trees and shrubs. Beautiful views of Westonbirt House open with guided tours to see fascinating Victorian interior on designated days of the year. Tea, coffee and cake available to purchase on NGS and Open House and Garden Days. Afternoon tea with sandwiches and scones available for pre-booked private tours - groups of 10-60. Only some parts of garden accessible to wheelchairs. Ramps and lift allow access to house.

WHITCOMBE HOUSE
See Worcestershire

74 WORTLEY HOUSE
Wortley, Wotton-Under-Edge, GL12 7QP. Simon and Jessica Dickinson. *1m from Wotton-under-Edge. Full directions will be provided with ticket.* **Tue 25 Apr (2-5). Adm £12, chd free. Tue 20 June (3-6), combined adm with Alderley Grange £20, chd free. Pre-booking essential for both dates, please visit www.ngs.org.uk or phone 01483 211535 for information & booking. Home-made teas.**
This diverse garden of over 20 acres has been created through the last 30 yrs by current owners and incl walled garden, pleached lime avenues, nut walk, potager, ponds, Italian garden, shrubberies and wild flower meadows. Follies urns and statues have been strategically placed throughout to enhance extraordinary vistas, and the garden has been filled with plants, arbours, roses through trees and up walls and herbaceous borders. The stunning surrounding countryside is incorporated into the garden with views up the steep valley that are such a feature in this part of Gloucestershire. New tulips planted each year for spring display. Wheelchair access to most areas of the garden, golf buggy available as well.

The Manor

75 WYCK RISSINGTON GARDENS
Cheltenham, GL54 2PN. *Nr Stow-on-the-Wold & Bourton-on-the-Water. 1m from Fosse Way A429.* **Sun 10 Sept (1-5). Combined adm £7, chd free. Home-made teas in village hall.** *Donation to Friends of St Laurence.*

CHESTNUT COURT
Mrs Georgina Hampton.

COLLEGE FARM
Andrea & Hilary Ponti.

GREENFIELDS FARM
Andrew & Elizabeth Ransom.

LAURENCE HOUSE
Mr & Mrs Robert Montague.

MACES COTTAGE
Tim & Pippa Simon.

An unspoilt Cotswold village off the beaten track set round a village green and its pond. The gardens are within easy reach of convenient parking and of contrasting styles. You will find inspiration for autumn planting and can delight in the mellow hues of September. A popular group opening providing an enjoyable afternoon in a perfect Cotswold setting. Gardens included are at various stages of maturity. Laurence House (formerly the Stone House) has been developed with new features such as a wild life pond. College Farm is now back in the group, with a lovely new walled garden. Chestnut Court was completely re-made 6 years ago and is now maturing into a fascinating family garden. Greenfields has a mix of English roses, fruit trees, grasses and garden sculptures. Maces Cottage has fine borders and old fruit trees, and like Greenfields, has wonderful views over the Windrush Valley. Plants, garden produce, and subject to the season, honey for sale. The walk between gardens allows you to appreciate the historic buildings grouped around the village green and St Laurence's Church will be open to visitors. Wheelchair access available at all gardens and WC in village hall.

HAMPSHIRE

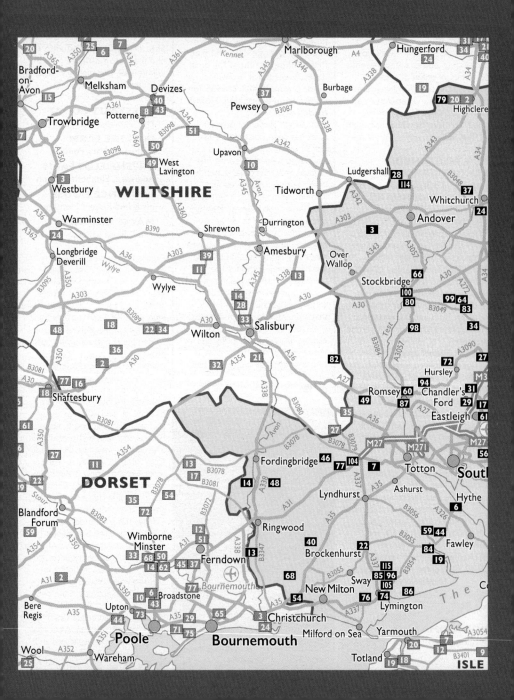

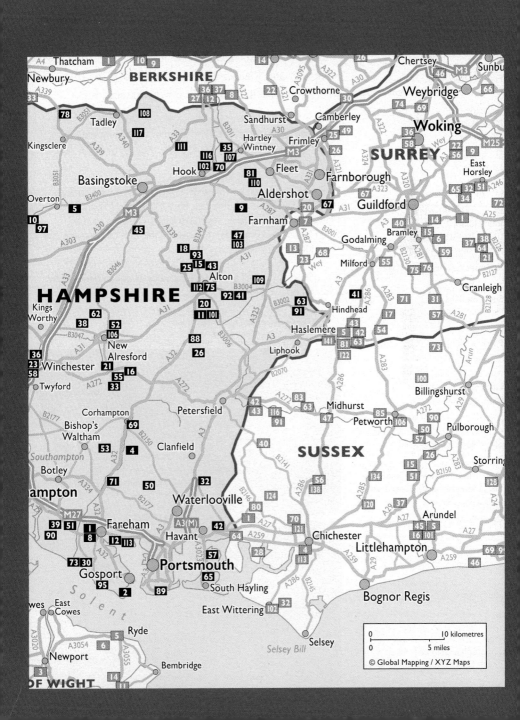

Volunteers

County Organiser
Mark Porter 01962 791054
markstephenporter@gmail.com

County Treasurer
Fred Fratter 01962 776243
fred@tanglefoot-house.demon.co.uk

Publicity
Mark Porter
(as above)

Social Media
Lorna Mann
07523 207713
lorna@meerkatmedia.net

Booklet Co-ordinator
John Huxford
01256 893518
john.huxford@btinternet.com

Assistant County Organisers

Central
Sue Cox 01962 732043
suealex13@gmail.com

Central West
Patricia Elkington 01962 776365
elkslc@btinternet.com

East
Linda Smith 01329 833253
linda.ngs@btinternet.com

North
Cynthia Oldale 01420 520438
c.k.oldale@btinternet.com

North East
Mary Trigwell-Jones 01420 83389
mary.trigwell-jones@outlook.com

North West
Carol Pratt 01264 710305
carolacap@yahoo.co.uk

South
Barbara Sykes 02380 254521
barandhugh@aol.com

South West
Elizabeth Walker 01590 677415
elizabethwalker13@gmail.com

West
Christopher Stanford
01425 652133
stanfordsnr@gmail.com

Hampshire is a large, diverse county. The landscape ranges from clay/gravel heath and woodland in the New Forest National Park in the south west, across famous trout rivers – the Test and Itchen – to chalk downland in the east, where you will find the South Downs National Park.

Our open gardens are spread right across the county, and offer a very diverse range of interest for both the keen gardener and the casual visitor.

We have a large number of gardens with rivers running through them, such as those in Longstock, Bere Mill, Dipley Mill and Weir House; gardens with large vegetable kitchen gardens such as Dean House and Bramdean House; and thirteen new gardens will open for the very first time.

You will be assured of a warm welcome by all our garden owners and we hope you enjoy your visits.

Below: Bridge Cottage, Amport & Monxton Gardens

OPENING DATES

All entries subject to change. For latest information check **www.ngs.org.uk** Extended openings are shown at the beginning of the month.

Map locator numbers are shown to the right of each garden name.

February

Snowdrop Festival

Sunday 19th
Bramdean House 16
🆕 ◆ Chawton House Library 20
The Down House 38
Little Court 64

Monday 20th
Little Court 64

Sunday 26th
Little Court 64

Monday 27th
Little Court 64

March

Sunday 26th
Bere Mill 10
Little Court 64

Wednesday 29th
Beechenwood Farm 9

Thursday 30th
2 Church Cottages 24

April

Beechenwood Farm (Every Wednesday) 9

Sunday 2nd
Durmast House 40

Sunday 9th
Bramdean House 16
Old Thatch & The Millennium Barn 81

Thursday 13th
2 Church Cottages 24

Friday 14th
Little Court 64
Paige Cottage 83

Sunday 16th
Pylewell Park 86
Terstan 100

Monday 17th
Little Court 64
Paige Cottage 83

Saturday 22nd
🆕 Ivanhoe 61

Sunday 23rd
🆕 Ivanhoe 61

Thursday 27th
2 Church Cottages 24

Friday 28th
Bluebell Wood 15

Saturday 29th
Bluebell Wood 15
The Island 60
Selborne 92
Walbury 103

Sunday 30th
The Cottage 29
The Island 60
Rotherfield Park 88
Selborne 92
◆ Spinners Garden 96
Tylney Hall Hotel 102
Walbury 103

May

Beechenwood Farm (Every Wednesday) 9

Monday 1st
Ashe Park 5
The Cottage 29
Little Court 64

Saturday 6th
🆕 Land of Nod 63

Sunday 7th
The Cottage 29
🆕 Land of Nod 63
Walhampton 105

Monday 8th
The Cottage 29

Thursday 11th
2 Church Cottages 24

Saturday 13th
Littlewood 65
2 Sampan Close 90

Sunday 14th
Brick Kiln Cottage 18
The House in the Wood 59
Littlewood 65
2 Sampan Close 90

Saturday 20th
21 Chestnut Road 22
Hollybrook 56
Selborne 92

Sunday 21st
Berry Cottage 11
21 Chestnut Road 22
Hinton Admiral 54
Hollybrook 56
Selborne 92

Wednesday 24th
Dean House 33

Thursday 25th
2 Church Cottages 24

90th Anniversary Weekend

Saturday 27th
Atheling Villas 6
Beechenwood Farm 9
Clover Farm 25
Hollybrook 56
Sandy Slopes 91

Sunday 28th
Amport & Monxton Gardens 3
Atheling Villas 6
Bisterne Manor 13
🆕 ◆ Chawton House Library 20
Hollybrook 56
Meon Orchard 71
🆕 Oaklands 77
Pylewell Park 86
Romsey Gardens 87
28 St Ronan's Avenue 89
Sandy Slopes 91
Waldrons 104
Weir House 106
West Silchester Hall 108

Monday 29th
Amport & Monxton Gardens 3
Atheling Villas 6
Romsey Gardens 87
Sandy Slopes 91
West Silchester Hall 108

June

Thursday 1st
30 Compton Way 27

Saturday 3rd
◆ Alverstoke Crescent Garden 2
30 Compton Way 27
Froyle Gardens 47
◆ Hinton Ampner 55

Sunday 4th
30 Compton Way 27
Dipley Mill 35
Froyle Gardens 47
🆕 Furzehill Farm 48
🆕 Manor House 69
🆕 Oaklands 77
Waldrons 104

Wednesday 7th
Appletree House 4
Beechenwood Farm 9

Thursday 8th
2 Church Cottages 24
Lake House 62

Saturday 10th
Bere Mill 10

Sunday 11th
Bere Mill 10
Berry Cottage 11
Bramdean House 16
Cranbury Park 31
🆕 Furzehill Farm 48
Lake House 62
🆕 Manor House 69
1 Maple Cottage 70
Old Thatch & The Millennium Barn 81
Shalden Park House 93
Tylney Hall Hotel 102

Wednesday 14th
Down Farm House 37
1 Maple Cottage 70

Thursday 15th
2 Church Cottages 24
1 Maple Cottage 70
Stockbridge Gardens 98

Saturday 17th
21 Chestnut Road 22
Moore Blatch 74

Sunday 18th
21 Chestnut Road 22
2 Church Cottages 24
Conholt Park 28
🆕 The Deane House 34

Dipley Mill	35
Emsworth Gardens	42
The Homestead	57
Longstock Park	66
Moore Blatch	74
Stockbridge Gardens	98
Wildhern Gardens	114

Wednesday 21st

Appletree House	4
Dean House	33
Wildhern Gardens	114

Thursday 22nd

Tanglefoot	99

Saturday 24th

NEW 61 Cottes Way	30
Down Farm House	37
East Worldham Gardens	41

Sunday 25th

19 Barnwood Road	8
Cheriton Cottage	21
Colemore House Gardens	26
NEW 61 Cottes Way	30
The Dower House	36
Durmast House	40
East Worldham Gardens	41
Fritham Lodge	46
Hambrooks Show Gardens	51
1 Maple Cottage	70
NEW The Old Rectory	79
Spring Pond	97
Tanglefoot	99
Terstan	100

Monday 26th

Colemore House Gardens	26
Spring Pond	97

Wednesday 28th

NEW The Old Rectory	79

Friday 30th

NEW 26 Lower Newport Road	67

Your visit
helps fund 389
Marie Curie
Nurses

July

Old Swan House (Every Tuesday) 80

Saturday 1st

NEW 26 Lower Newport Road	67

Sunday 2nd

Berry Cottage	11
Bleak Hill Nursery & Garden	14
Wicor Primary School Community Garden	113

Wednesday 5th

Dean House	33
NEW Wychwood	117

Thursday 6th

Ashe Park	5
Paige Cottage	83
Tanglefoot	99

Saturday 8th

Oak Tree Cottage	76

Sunday 9th

Ashe Park	5
Bramdean House	16
Oak Tree Cottage	76
Paige Cottage	83
Tanglefoot	99
West Silchester Hall	108
1 Wogsbarne Cottages	116

Monday 10th

1 Wogsbarne Cottages	116

Wednesday 12th

NEW Wychwood	117

Saturday 15th

21 Chestnut Road	22

Sunday 16th

Bleak Hill Nursery & Garden	14
21 Chestnut Road	22
Dean House	33
Dipley Mill	35
Michaelmas	73

Monday 17th

Michaelmas	73

Wednesday 19th

Appletree House	4

Thursday 20th

Tanglefoot	99

Saturday 22nd

8 Birdwood Grove	12

East Worldham Gardens	41

Sunday 23rd

Aviemore	7
Conholt Park	28
East Worldham Gardens	41
◆ The Hospital of St Cross	58
Tanglefoot	99
Terstan	100
White Gables	111

Tuesday 25th

◆ West Green House Gardens	107

Saturday 29th

Fairweather's Nursery	44
NEW Ivanhoe	61
Willows	115

Sunday 30th

Ashe Park	5
Bleak Hill Nursery & Garden	14
Fairweather's Nursery	44
Hill House	52
NEW Ivanhoe	61
Meon Orchard	71
Merdon Manor	72
Spindles	95
Willows	115

Monday 31st

Spindles	95

August

Wednesday 2nd

Dean House	33
Fairbank	43

Saturday 5th

Selborne	92
Willows	115

Sunday 6th

Dipley Mill	35
Selborne	92
West Silchester Hall	108
Willows	115

Monday 7th

Selborne	92

Tuesday 8th

Hill House	52

Thursday 10th

Hill House	52

Saturday 12th

Bucklers Spring	19

22 Mount Pleasant Road	75
42 Whitedown	112

Sunday 13th

Berry Cottage	11
Bramdean House	16
Bucklers Spring	19
Dean House	33
22 Mount Pleasant Road	75
42 Whitedown	112

Wednesday 16th

Wildhern Gardens	114

Saturday 19th

NEW Old Camps	78
Wheatley House	109

Sunday 20th

NEW Old Camps	78
Wheatley House	109

Saturday 26th

The Island	60

Sunday 27th

NEW ◆ Chawton House Library	20
Gilberts Nursery	49
The Island	60
Pilley Hill Cottage	85

Monday 28th

Hambledon House	50
Pilley Hill Cottage	85

September

Saturday 2nd

Willows	115

Sunday 3rd

Dipley Mill	35
The Down House	38
Meon Orchard	71
Willows	115

Saturday 9th

Pilley Hill Cottage	85

Sunday 10th

Bramdean House	16
Farleigh House	45
Pilley Hill Cottage	85
Terstan	100
Weir House	106

Thursday 14th

2 Church Cottages	24

Sunday 17th

Bere Mill	10
2 Church Cottages	24

October

Sunday 1st
Dipley Mill 35
Tylney Hall Hotel 102

Sunday 22nd
NEW ◆ Chawton House Library 20

Thursday 26th
Hambrooks Show Gardens 51

Bere Mill

© Nicola Stocken Tomkins

November

Thursday 23rd
Hambrooks Show Gardens 51

February 2018

Sunday 18th
Little Court 64

Monday 19th
Little Court 64

Sunday 25th
Little Court 64

Monday 26th
Little Court 64

By Arrangement

80 Abbey Road 1
Appletree House 4
Atheling Villas 6
Aviemore 7
19 Barnwood Road 8
Bere Mill 10
Berry Cottage 11
8 Birdwood Grove 12
Bleak Hill Nursery & Garden 14
Bramdean House 16
6 Breamore Close 17
Brick Kiln Cottage 18
21 Chestnut Road 22
12 Christchurch Road 23
Conholt Park 28
The Cottage 29
Crookley Pool 32
NEW The Deane House 34
The Dower House 36
The Down House 38
7 Downland Close 39
Durmast House 40
Fairbank 43
Fritham Lodge 46
Hambledon House 50
Hill House 52
Hill Top 53
The Homestead 57
The Island 60
Lake House 62
Little Court 64
NEW Manor House 69
Merdon Manor 72
Michaelmas 73
4 Mill Lane, Romsey Gardens 87
Ordnance House 82
Pilley Hill Cottage 85
Selborne 92
Spindles 95
Tanglefoot 99
Terstan 100
Weir House 106
West Silchester Hall 108
Wheatley House 109
Whispers 110
Willows 115

THE GARDENS

1 80 ABBEY ROAD

Fareham, PO15 5HW. Brian & Vivienne Garford, 01329 843939, vgarford@aol.com. *1m W of Fareham. From M27 J9 take A27 E to Fareham for approx 2m. At top of hill, turn L at lights into Highlands Rd. Turn 4th R into Blackbrook Rd. Abbey Rd is 4th L.* **Visits by arrangement Apr to Aug for groups of 25 max. Light refreshments.**

Unusual small garden with large collection of herbs and plants of botanical and historical interest, many for sale. Box hedging provides structure for relaxed planting. Interesting use of containers and ideas for small gardens. Two ponds and tiny meadow for wildlife. A garden trail for children. Living willow seat, summerhouse, and trained grapevine.

2 ◆ ALVERSTOKE CRESCENT GARDEN

Crescent Road, Gosport, PO12 2DH. Gosport Borough Council, www.alverstokecrescentgarden.co.uk. *1m S of Gosport. From A32 & Gosport follow signs for Stokes Bay. Continue alongside bay to small r'about, turn L into Anglesey Rd. Crescent Garden signed 50yds on R.* **For NGS: Sat 3 June (10-4). Adm by donation. Home-made teas. For other opening times and information, please visit garden website.**

Restored Regency ornamental garden, designed to enhance fine crescent (Thomas Ellis Owen 1828). Trees, walks and flowers lovingly maintained by community and council partnership. Garden's of considerable local historic interest highlighted by impressive restoration and creative planting. Adjacent to St Mark's churchyard, worth seeing together. Heritage, history and horticulture, a fascinating package. Plant sale and teas. Green Flag Award.

The Hospital Of St Cross

GROUP OPENING

3 AMPORT & MONXTON GARDENS

Amport and Monxton, SP11 8AY. *3m SW of Andover. Turn off the A303 signed East Cholderton from the E or Thruxton village from the W. Follow signs to Amport. Car parking in a field next to Amport village green. Please drive between the two villages.* **Sun 28, Mon 29 May (2-6). Combined adm £6, chd free. Cream teas at village hall, Monxton.**

AMPORT PARK MEWS
Amport Park Mews Ltd.

BRIDGE COTTAGE
Jenny Van de Pette.

FLEUR DE LYS
Ian & Jane Morrison.

SANDLEFORD HOUSE
Mr & Mrs Michael & Valerie Taylor.

WHITE GABLES
Mr & Mrs D Eaglesham.

Monxton and Amport are two pretty villages linked by Pill Hill Brook. Visitors have five gardens to enjoy. Bridge Cottage a 2 acre haven for wildlife, with the banks of the trout stream and lake planted informally with drifts of colour, a large vegetable garden, fruit cage, small mixed orchard and arboretum with specimen trees. Amport Park Mews has eleven borders arranged around a communal space surrounded by converted stable and carriage blocks in historic mews. Fleur de Lys garden is a series of rooms with glorious herbaceous borders, leading to a large orchard. Sandleford House has a locally built iron pergola walkway. The garden is entirely walled in brick and flint. White Gables a cottage style garden with a collection of trees, incl a young giant redwood, along with old roses and herbaceous plants. Amport has a lovely village green, come early and bring a picnic to enjoy the views of the thatched cottages, before the gardens open. No wheelchair access to White Gables.

&♿ ❀ 🚌 ☕

4 APPLETREE HOUSE

Station Road, Soberton, SO32 3QU. Mrs J Dover, 01489 877333, jennie.dover@yahoo.co.uk. *10m N of Fareham. A32 to Droxford, at Xrds turn onto B2150. Turn R under bridge into Station Rd, garden 1m. Parking in lay-by 300yds or on the road.* **Wed 7, Wed 21 June, Wed 19 July (12-4). Adm £3.50, chd free. Light refreshments. Visits also by arrangement May to July. Light lunches on request.**
Designed to look larger than its 40ft x 90ft, this garden has both a shady woodland style area and also sunny areas allowing a variety of planting. Winding paths lead to different views across the garden and of the meadows beyond. Lots of ideas for the smaller garden. Large collection of over 90 clematis, mainly viticella hybrids.

❀ ☕

5 ASHE PARK

nr Ashe, Overton, RG25 3AF. **Graham & Laura Hazell.** *2m E of Overton. Entrance on B3400, approx 500yds W of Deane.* **Mon 1 May (2-6). Home-made teas. Evening opening Thur 6 July (5.30-8.30). Light refreshments. Sun 9, Sun 30 July (2-6). Home-made teas. Adm £5, chd free.**
An extensive developing garden within the grounds of a Georgian country house and estate, now becoming more established with further initiatives in progress. Parkland and specimen trees, mature lime avenue, woodland and bluebell walks, wild flower areas, a large contemporary potager, and a series of land sculpted features. On Sun 30 July there will be a Jane Austen theme.

♿ 🐕 ❀ ☕

6 ATHELING VILLAS

16 Atheling Road, Hythe, Southampton, SO45 6BR. **Mary & Peter York,** 02380 849349, athelingvillas@gmail.com. *W side of Southampton Water. At M27 J2, take A326 for Hythe & Fawley. Cross all r'abouts until Dibden r'about. L to Hythe. After Shell garage take 2nd L & immed R.* **Sat 27, Sun 28,**

Mon 29 May (2-5). Adm £3, chd free. Home-made teas in the Old Laundry. Visits also by arrangement May & June for groups of 10+. *Donation to The Children's Society.*
Inspirational, imaginatively designed and comprehensively planted ⅓ acre Victorian villa garden, now in its 12th year of opening for the NGS. Explore meandering paths set amongst structural planting and delight in the flowering trees and shrubs (many rare), bulbs and herbaceous planting of this tranquil and welcoming garden. Several seating areas throughout garden. Features incl a self-guide leaflet, children's quiz, and a display of original art by owners in the Garden Room Gallery.

❀ 🚌 ☕

7 AVIEMORE

Chinham Road, Bartley, Southampton, SO40 2LF. **Sandy & Alex Robinson,** 02380 813651, hears2u@gmail.com. *3m N of Lyndhurst, 7m W of Southampton. From M27 J1 go towards Lyndhurst on A337. After ¾m turn L to Bartley & follow NGS signs.* **Sun 23 July (2-5). Adm £3.50, chd free. Visits also by arrangement Apr to Aug for groups of 10-50. Refreshments on request.**
A richly planted, small garden in north New Forest with lawns, gravel areas and a vegetable plot. Oak bridges criss-cross a small stream. Old alpine troughs and quirky artifacts add to its structure, texture and colour. We aim to please plant connoisseurs and show enthusiasts new plants and ideas for smaller gardens. Limited space dictates that each shrub, climber, perennial and grass must justify its place. No wheelchair access to some gravel and stream areas.

♿ ❀ 🚌 ☕

8 19 BARNWOOD ROAD

Fareham, PO15 5LA. **Jill & Michael Hill,** 01329 842156, Jillhillflowers@icloud.com. *1m W of Fareham. M27 J9, A27 towards Fareham. At top of Titchfield Hill, L at T-lights, 4th R Blackbrook Rd, 4th R Meadow Bank. Barnwood Rd is*

off Meadow Bank. Please consider neighbours when parking. **Sun 25 June (11-4). Adm £3.50, chd free. Home-made teas. Visits also by arrangement May to Aug for groups of 10-30.**
Step through the gate to an enchanting garden designed for peace with an abundance of floral colour and delightful features. Greek style courtyard leads to natural pond with bridge and bog garden, complemented by a thatched summerhouse and jetty, designed and built by owners. Secret pathways, hexagonal greenhouse and new mosaic seating area. Featured in Garden Answers and Period Ideas magazines.
✿ 🚌 ☕

9 BEECHENWOOD FARM
Hillside, Odiham, RG29 1JA. Mr & Mrs M Heber-Percy. *5m SE of Hook. Turn S into King St from Odiham High St. Turn L after cricket ground for Hillside. Take 2nd R after 1½m, modern house ½m.* **Every Wed 29 Mar to 7 June (2-5). Sat 27 May (2-5). Adm £4, chd free. Home-made teas.**
2 acre garden in many parts. Lawn meandering through woodland with drifts of spring bulbs. Rose pergola with steps, pots with spring bulbs and later aeoniums. Fritillary and cowslip meadow. Walled herb garden with pool and exuberant planting. Orchard incl white garden and hot border. Greenhouse and vegetable garden. Rock garden extending to grasses, ferns and bamboos. Shady walk to belvedere. 8 acre copse of native species with grassed rides. Assistance available with gravel drive, and some avoidable shallow steps.
& 🐄 ✿ ☕

10 BERE MILL
London Road, Whitchurch, RG28 7NH. Rupert & Elizabeth Nabarro, 01256 892210, rupertnab@gmail.com. *9m E of Andover, 12m N of Winchester. In centre of Whitchurch, take London Rd at r'about. Uphill 1m, turn R 50yds beyond The Gables on R. Drop-off point for disabled at garden.* **Sun 26 Mar, Sat 10, Sun 11 June, Sun 17**

Sept (1.30-5). Adm £5, chd free. Home-made teas. Visits also by arrangement Feb to Oct for groups of 15+. *Donation to Smile Train.*
On the Upper Test with water meadows and wooded valleys, this garden offers herbaceous borders, bog and Mediterranean plants as well as a replanted orchard and two small arboretums. Features incl early bulbs, species tulips, Japanese prunus, peonies, wisteria, irises, roses, and semi-tropical planting. At heart it aims to complement the natural beauty of the site, and to incorporate elements of oriental garden design and practice. The working mill was where Portals first made paper for the Bank of England in 1716. Unfenced and unguarded rivers and streams. Wheelchair access unless very wet.
& 🐄 ✿ 🚌 ☕

11 BERRY COTTAGE
Church Road, Upper Farringdon, nr Alton, GU34 3EG. Mrs P Watts, 01420 588318. *3m S of Alton off A32. Turn L at Xrds, 1st L into Church Rd. Follow road past Massey's Folly, 2nd house on R, opp church.* **Suns 21 May, 11 June, 2 July, 13 Aug (2-5.30). Adm £2.50, chd free. Home-made teas. Visits also by arrangement May to Sept for groups of 10+.**
Small organic cottage garden with yr-round interest, designed and maintained by owner, surrounding C16 house (not open). Spring bulbs, roses, clematis and herbaceous borders. The borders are colour themed and contain many unusual plants. Pond, bog garden and shrubbery. Close to Massey's Folly built by the Victorian rector incl 80ft tower with unique handmade floral bricks, C11 church and some of the oldest yew trees in the county.
& 🐄 ✿ 🚌 ☕

12 8 BIRDWOOD GROVE
Downend, Fareham, PO16 8AF. Jayne & Eddie McBride, 01329 280838, jayne.mcbride@ntlworld.com. *½m E of Fareham. M27 J11, L lane slip to Delme r'about, L on A27 to Portchester over 2 T-lights, completely*

around small r'about, Birdwood Grove 1st L. **Sat 22 July (1-5). Adm £3, chd free. Home-made teas. Visits also by arrangement July & Aug for groups of 2-25 max.**
The subtropics in Fareham! This small garden is influenced by the flora of Australia and New Zealand and incl many indigenous species and plants that are widely grown 'down under'. The 4 climate zones; arid, temperate, lush fertile and a shady fernery, are all densely planted to make the most of dramatic foliage, from huge bananas to towering cordylines. Fareham in Bloom gold award Small Plantsman's Back Garden and Best In Category for the 4th year running! Short gravel path not suitable for mobility scooters.
& 🐄 ✿ ☕

Donations from the National Garden Scheme help Parkinson's UK care for more people

13 BISTERNE MANOR
Bisterne, Ringwood, BH24 3BN. Mr & Mrs Hallam Mills. *2½m S of Ringwood on B3347 Christchurch Rd, 500yds past church on L. Entrance signed Stable Family Home Trust on L (blue sign), just past lodge. Disabled parking signed near the house.* **Sun 28 May (2-6). Adm £4.50, chd free. Cream teas.**
Glorious rhododendrons and azaleas form a backdrop for our C19 garden first opened in the 1930s for the fledgling NGS, now under restoration. The C16 manor house (not open) overlooks a grand parterre with box hedges and lavender. Rare tree specimens grace fine lawns and wild flower planting, leading to a boundary woodland walk with glimpses of surrounding pastures. There is a small kitchen garden. Wheelchair access to a level garden with wide gravel paths.
& 🐄 🚌 ☕

14 BLEAK HILL NURSERY & GARDEN

Braemoor, Bleak Hill, Harbridge, Ringwood, BH24 3PX.
Tracy & John Netherway & Judy Spratt, 01425 652983, jnetherway@btinternet.com.
2½m S of Fordingbridge. Turn off A338 at Ibsley. Go through Harbridge village to T-junction at top of hill, turn R for ¼m. **Sun 2, Sun 16, Sun 30 July (2-5.30). Adm £3.50, chd free. Home-made teas. Visits also by arrangement in July.**
Through the moongate and concealed from view are billowing borders contrasting against a seaside scene, with painted beach huts and a boat on the gravel. Herbaceous borders fill the garden with colour wrapping around a pond and small stream. Greenhouses with cacti and sarracenias. Vegetable patch and bantam chickens. Small adjacent nursery.
✿ 🚗 ☕

15 BLUEBELL WOOD

Stancombe Lane, Bavins, New Odiham Road, Alton, GU34 5SX.
Mrs Jennifer Ospici, www.bavins.co.uk. *On the corner of Stancombe Lane & the B3349 2½m N of Alton.* **Fri 28, Sat 29 Apr (11-4). Adm £5, chd free. Light refreshments.**

Unique 100 acre ancient bluebell woodland. If you are a keen walker you will have much to explore on the long meandering paths and rides dotted with secluded seats. Those who enjoy a more leisurely pace will experience the perfume of the carpet of blue, listen to the birdsong and watch the contrasting light through the trees nearer to the entrance of the woods. Refreshments will be served in an original rustic wooden building and incl soups using natural woodland ingredients.
🐐 ☕

16 BRAMDEAN HOUSE

Bramdean, Alresford, SO24 0JU. Mr & Mrs H Wakefield, 01962 771214, victoria@bramdeanhouse.com.
4m S of Alresford. In centre of village on A272. Entrance opp sign to the church. **Suns 19 Feb, 9 Apr, 11 June, 9 July, 13 Aug, 10 Sept (2-4). Adm £5, chd free. Home-made teas. Visits also by arrangement Feb to Sept for groups of 10+.**
Beautiful 5 acre garden famous for its mirror image herbaceous borders. Carpets of spring bulbs especially snowdrops. A large and unusual collection of plants and shrubs giving yr-round interest.

1 acre walled garden featuring prize-winning vegetables, fruit and flowers. Small arboretum. Trial of hardy Nerine cultivars in association with RHS. Features incl a wild flower meadow, boxwood castle, a large collection of old fashioned sweet peas. Home of the nation's tallest sunflower 'Giraffe'.
♿ ✿ 🚗 ☕

17 6 BREAMORE CLOSE

Boyatt Wood, Eastleigh, SO50 4QB. Mr & Mrs R Trenchard, 02380 611230, dawndavina6@yahoo.co.uk.
1m N of Eastleigh. M3 J12, follow signs to Eastleigh. Turn R at r'about into Woodside Ave, then 1st L into Broadlands Ave (park here). Breamore Close 3rd on L. **Visits by arrangement May to July for groups of 10+. Adm £3.50, chd free. Home-made teas.**
Delightful plant lover's garden with coloured foliage and unusual plants, giving a tapestry effect of texture and colour. Many hostas displayed in pots and in May a wonderful wisteria scrambles over a pergola. The garden is laid out in distinctive planting themes with seating areas to sit and contemplate. In July many clematis scramble through roses and there are many varieties of phlox. Small gravel areas.
♿ ✿ 🚗 ☕

18 BRICK KILN COTTAGE

The Avenue, Herriard, Nr Alton, RG25 2PR. Barbara Jeremiah, 01256 381301, barbara@klca.co.uk. *4m NE of Alton. A339 Basingstoke to Alton, 7m out of Basingstoke turn L along The Avenue, past Lasham Gliding Club on R, then past Back Lane on L & take next track on L, one field later.* **Sun 14 May (12-5). Adm £4, chd free. Home-made teas. Visits also by arrangement May & June.**
Bluebell woodland garden with 2 acres incl treehouse, pebble garden, billabong, stumpery, ferny hollow, shepherd's hut and a traditional cottage garden filled with herbs. The garden is maintained using eco-friendly methods as a haven

Fairbank

for wild animals, butterflies, birds and bees and English bluebells. Families welcome to this wild garden in a former brick works, with excellent cream teas, home-made cakes, sandwiches and pots of tea. Received a Hampshire & Isle of Wight Wildlife Trust Award for a wildlife friendly garden 2 yrs ago. Featured in Period Living (Mar 2016).

🐂 ✿ ☕

19 BUCKLERS SPRING

Bucklers Hard Road, Beaulieu, Brockenhurst, SO42 7XA. Adrienne Page & Adam Speker, www.bucklersspring.com. *M27 J2 (to avoid Lyndhurst traffic). Follow brown signs to Beaulieu & then 2m on to Bucklers Hard. Go to Master Builder Hotel (SO42 7XB), park in field leading off hotel car park.* **Sat 12, Sun 13 Aug (2-5.30). Adm £3.50, chd free. Home-made teas.**
Landscape designed garden of ½ acre; a view of the Beaulieu River, also reflected in winding streams of lavender enclosed within ornamental grass; colourful borders of summer perennials; crisp lawn enlivened with mounds of long grass; avenue of ornamental pear trees; border of clipped box; structural elements of pergola and raised deck; and gravel garden for cut flowers, herbs and outdoor cooking. The garden is adjacent to the beautiful historic village of Bucklers Hard, featuring a maritime museum, riverside walk, cycle tracks to Beaulieu and The Master Builder's Hotel. The National Motor Museum is 3m away. Partial wheelchair access owing to gravel paths and some steps.

♿ 🐂 ✿ Ⓓ ☕

Perennial, supporting horticulturalists since 1839

20 NEW ◆ CHAWTON HOUSE LIBRARY

Chawton, Alton, GU34 1SJ. Andrew Bentley, 01420 595903, andrew.bentley@chawtonhouse library.org, www.chawtonhouse.org. *2m S of Alton. Take the road opp Jane Austen's House museum towards St.Nicholas church. Property is at the end of this road on the L.* **For NGS: Suns 19 Feb, 28 May, 27 Aug, 22 Oct (11-5). Adm £4, chd free. Home-made teas. For other opening times and information, please phone, email or visit garden website.**
14 acre listed English landscape garden surrounding Grade II listed Elizabethan manor. Sweeping lawns, ha-ha, wilderness, terraces, fernery (in progress) and shrubbery walk. Walled Garden designed by Edward Knight now incl; rose garden, vegetable beds, orchard, cut flowers and 'Elizabeth Blackwell' garden, based on her book 'A Curious Herbal' of 1737-39. Parkland views. We have a tearoom in our old kitchen that offers a selection of teas, coffee, cold drinks and cakes. Due to slopes and gravel paths, we regret this garden is not suitable for wheelchairs.

🐂 ✿ 🚗 ☕

21 CHERITON COTTAGE

Cheriton, Alresford, SO24 0PR. Lord & Lady Amherst. *On B3046, N of A272, S of New Alresford. In centre of village. Disabled parking available, please telephone 07962 869105.* **Sun 25 June (11-5). Adm £5, chd free. Home-made teas.** *Donation to Inspire Foundation.*
This traditional 4 acre walled garden is a haven for butterflies and bees. Herbaceous borders host a variety of garden-worthy natives and old fashioned perennials, to form naturalistic planting schemes. The R Itchen meanders throughout the garden and on down into the wild area, with a surprise feature! Trees (dating back to late C18) and established shrubs give structure, while pasture land forms backdrop. Gravel driveway at front of house, all other areas are lawn and grass pathways.

♿ ✿ ☕

22 21 CHESTNUT ROAD

Brockenhurst, SO42 7RF. Iain & Mary Hayter, 01590 622009, maryiain.hayter@gmail.com, www.21-chestnut-rdgardens.co.uk. *New Forest, 4m S of Lyndhurst. At Brockenhurst turn R B3055 Grigg Lane. Limited parking, village car park nearby. Leave M27 J2, follow Heavy Lorry Route. Mainline station less than 10 mins walk.* **Sat 20 May (11-5); Sun 21 May (1-5); Sat 17 June (11-5); Sun 18 June (1-5); Sat 15 July (11-5); Sun 16 July (1-5). Adm £3.50, chd free. Home-made teas & gluten free options. Visits also by arrangement Apr to Aug for groups of 10+.**
Be enchanted by this third of an acre mature garden, brimming with ideas of how to use plants in different conditions, at the same time being wildlife friendly. There are formal, productive and relaxing areas, all aimed to inspire. Home-made refreshments can be enjoyed in various locations incl summerhouse and raised deck over pond. Children welcome to visit the fairies. No wheelchair access to narrow paths, gravel areas and to raised deck.

♿ 🐂 ✿ 🚗 ☕

23 12 CHRISTCHURCH ROAD

Winchester, SO23 9SR. Iain & Penny Patton, 01962 854272, pjspatton@yahoo.co.uk. *S side of city. Leave centre of Winchester by Southgate St, 1st R into St James Lane, 3rd L into Christchurch Rd.* **Visits by arrangement Feb to Oct for groups of 20 max. Home-made teas.**
Small town garden with strong design enhanced by exuberant and vertical planting. All yr interest incl winter flowering shrubs, bulbs and hellebores. Two water features incl slate edged rill and pergolas provide structure. Small front garden designed to be viewed from the house with bulbs, roses and herbaceous planting. See www.visitwinchester.com for B&B information. Partial wheelchair access due to small changes in levels.

♿ ✿ 🛏 ☕

24 2 CHURCH COTTAGES
Tufton, Whitchurch, RG28 7RF.
Jane & John Huxford. *N on A34 at Whitchurch exit, turn L off slip road, R at Xrds, house 2nd on R. From Whitchurch centre take Winchester Rd S. Before slip road bear R, turn R, turn R at Xrds, house 2nd on R.* **Thurs 30 Mar, 13, 27 Apr, 11, 25 May, 8, 15, Sun 18 June, Thur 14, Sun 17 Sept (2-5). Adm £4, chd free. Home-made teas.**
A stone's throw from the R Test, formerly an estate cowman's cottage, the front and back is a traditional cottage garden, but there is more! Through the gate in the hedge, you'll find a nursery, greenhouses, vegetables, cutting garden and small orchard. Passing sheep and chickens, a stroll through the fields leads to an area under development to form a spring walk with shade loving plants.

25 CLOVER FARM
Shalden Lane, Shalden, Alton, GU34 4DU. Mrs Sarah Floyd. *Approx 3m N of Alton in the village of Shalden. Take A339 out of Alton. After approx 2m turn R up lane. At top turn sharp R next to church sign.* **Sat 27 May (1.30-5). Adm £4, chd free. Teas will be served on the lawn.**
3 acre garden with views to die for! Herbaceous borders and sloping lawns down to reflection pond, wild flower meadow, lime avenue, rose and kitchen garden. Marcus Dancer will be selling his wonderful selection of clematis.

26 COLEMORE HOUSE GARDENS
Colemore, Alton, GU34 3RX. Mr & Mrs Simon de Zoete. *4m S of Alton (off A32). Approach from N on A32, turn L (Shell Lane), ¼ m S of East Tisted. Go under bridge, keep L until you see Colemore Church. Park on verge of church.* **Sun 25, Mon 26 June (2-6). Adm £5, chd free. Home-made teas.**
4 acres in lovely unspoilt countryside, featuring rooms containing many unusual plants and different aspects. A spectacular arched rose walk, water rill, mirror pond, herbaceous and shrub borders and a new woodland walk. Many admire the lawns, new grass gardens and thatched pavilion (built by students from the Prince's Trust). A small arboretum is being planted. Change and development is ongoing, and increasing the diversity of interesting plants is a prime motivation. We propagate and sell plants, many of which can be found in the garden. Some are unusual and not readily available elsewhere.

27 30 COMPTON WAY
Winchester, SO22 4HS. Susan Summers, www.summersgd.co.uk. *2m SW of Winchester. From M3 J11, follow A3090 Badger Farm Rd uphill. Turn L into Oliver's Battery Road South. Take 2nd L into Compton Way. House on R before Austin Ave. Follow directions for parking.* **Thur 1, Sat 3, Sun 4 June (2-5). Adm £4, chd free. Home-made teas.**
Contemporary garden owned by local garden designer on the outskirts of Winchester. Sunny hilltop ¼ acre plot. Themed borders of colourful mixed planting on chalky soil. Kitchen and herb gardens, and semi formal pond. For 2017 come and see our new fruit garden. There will be a wide selection of home grown vegetable plants, herbs and flowers for sale, many can be seen growing in the garden.

28 CONHOLT PARK
Hungerford Lane, Andover, SP11 9HA. Conholt Park Estate, 07917 796826, conholtgarden17@outlook.com. *7m N of Andover. Turn N off A342 at Weyhill Church, 5m N through Clanville. L at T-junction, Conholt ½ m on R, opp Chute Causeway. A343 to Hurstbourne Tarrant, turn R, go through Vernham Dean, L signed Conholt.* **Sun 18 June, Sun 23 July (11-5). Adm £6, chd free. Home-made teas. Visits also by arrangement June & July on weekdays only.**
10 acres surrounding Regency house (not open), with mature cedars and lawns. Rose, sensory and secret gardens. Private poppy garden (no dogs please). Glasshouses, two flower cartwheels, and orchard in the walled garden. Glasshouse rebuild complete. An Edwardian Ladies Walk. Large laurel maze with viewing platform. Visitors welcome to picnic. Deep gravel and steps, not suitable for wheelchairs.

Your visit helps the Queen's Nursing Institute to champion excellence in community nursing

29 THE COTTAGE
16 Lakewood Road, Chandler's Ford, SO53 1ES. Hugh & Barbara Sykes, 02380 254521, barandhugh@aol.com. *2m NW of Eastleigh. Leave M3 J12, follow signs to Chandler's Ford. At King Rufus on Winchester Rd, turn R into Merdon Ave, then 3rd road on L.* **Sun 30 Apr, Mon 1, Sun 7, Mon 8 May (2-6). Adm £3.50, chd free. Home-made teas. Visits also by arrangement Apr & May.**
¾ acre. Azaleas, bog garden, camellias, dogwoods, erythroniums, free-range bantams, geraniums, hostas, irises, jasmines, kitchen garden, landscaping began in 1950, maintained by owners, new planting, osmunda, ponds, quiz for children, rhododendrons, sun and shade, trilliums, unusual plants, viburnums, wildlife areas, eXuberant foliage, yr-round interest, zantedeschia. 'A lovely tranquil garden', Anne Swithinbank. Hampshire Wildlife Trust Wildlife Garden Award. Honey from our garden hives for sale.

COTTAGE IN THE TREES
See Wiltshire

30 NEW 61 COTTES WAY
Hill Head, Fareham, PO14 3NL. Norma Matthews & Alan Stamps. *4½ m S of Fareham. From Fareham follow signs to Stubbington, then Hill*

Head. Turn R into Bells Lane, L bend to Crofton Lane, R opp shops into Carisbrooke Ave, L into Cottes Way. **Sat 24, Sun 25 June (11-4). Adm £3, chd free. Home-made teas.** 33ft × 33ft garden, designed by owner in 2015, a fine example of a low maintenance, spacious and relaxing outdoor living room. Colourful with a wide variety of shrubs, perennials and climbers. Interesting art and metal work, water features and patterned natural stone patio. Many pots and containers incl chimney pots and champagne bottles create a blaze of colour. Small vegetable patch.

& 🐎 ✿ ☕

31 CRANBURY PARK

Otterbourne, nr Winchester, SO21 2HL. Mrs Chamberlayne-Macdonald. *3m NW of Eastleigh. Main entrance on old A33 at top of Otterbourne Hill. Entrances also in Hocombe Rd, Chandlers Ford & next to Otterbourne Church.* **Sun 11 June (2-6). Adm £5, chd free. Home-made teas.** *Donation to All Saints Church, North Baddesley.*
Extensive pleasure grounds laid out in late C18 and early C19 by Papworth; fountains, rose garden, specimen trees and pinetum, lakeside walk and fern walk. Family carriages and collection of prams will be on view, also photos of King George VI, Eisenhower and Montgomery reviewing Canadian troops at Cranbury before D-Day. All dogs on leads please. Disabled WC.

& 🐎 ✿ ☕

32 CROOKLEY POOL

Blendworth Lane, Horndean, PO8 0AB. Mr & Mrs Simon Privett, 02392 592662, jennyprivett@icloud.com. *5m S of Petersfield. 2m E of Waterlooville, off A3. From Horndean up Blendworth Lane between bakery & hairdresser. Entrance 200yds before church on L with white railings. Parking in field.* **Visits by arrangement Mar to Sept. Home-made teas on request. Adm £5, chd free.** Here the plants decide where to grow. Californian tree poppies elbow valerian aside to crowd

round the pool. Evening primroses obstruct the way to the door and the steps to wisteria shaded terraces. Hellebores bloom under the trees. Salvias, Pandorea jasminoides, Justicia, Pachystachys lutea and passion flowers riot quietly with tomatoes in the greenhouse. Not a garden for the neat or tidy minded, although this is a plantsman's garden full of unusual plants and a lot of tender perennials. Bantams stroll throughout. Watercolour paintings of flowers found in the garden will be on display and for sale.

& ✿ 🚗 ☕

33 DEAN HOUSE

Kilmeston Road, Kilmeston, Alresford, SO24 0NL. Mr P H R Gwyn, www.deanhousegardens.co.uk. *5m S of Alresford. Via village of Cheriton or off A272 signed at Cheriton Xrds. Follow signs for Kilmeston, through village & turn L at Dean House sign.* **Wed 24 May, Wed 21 June, Wed 5 July (10-4); Sun 16 July, Wed 2 Aug (12-4.30); Sun 13 Aug (10-4). Adm £6, chd free. Home-made cream teas & a wide selection of cakes in the Orangery.**
The 7 acres have been described as 'a well-kept secret hidden behind the elegant facade of its Georgian centrepiece'. Sweeping lawns, York stone paths, gravel pathways, many young and mature trees and hedges, mixed and herbaceous borders.

Rose garden, pond garden, working walled garden with glasshouses growing 125 different varieties of vegetables, which help to create a diverse and compact sliver of Eden. Over 1700 individually documented plant species and cultivars in our collection. 60 metre laburnum and wisteria tunnel. Gravel paths.

& ✿ 🚗 ☕

34 [NEW] THE DEANE HOUSE

Sparsholt, Winchester, SO21 2LR. Mr & Mrs Richard Morse, 01962 776425, chrissie@morse.eclipse.co.uk. *3½m NW of Winchester. Off A3049 Stockbridge Rd, onto Woodman Lane, signed Sparsholt. Turn L at 1st cottage on L, white with blue gables.* **Sun 18 June (2-6). Adm £5, chd free. Cream teas. Visits also by arrangement for groups of 10+.**
A flower arranger's heaven, set in about 3½ acres. These gardens, which roll out into the stunning Hampshire landscape, are at their scented best. Set high over Winchester, it is a surprise to hear the sound of a gentle chalk stream as a cascade of water flows near the house providing a refreshing respite from the heat of summer. A rose-draped walled garden, extensive herbaceous and shrub borders, grass beds all on different levels merge into natural wild flower areas and an orchard. A water sculpture, stained glass and croquet lawn add interest to this family garden.

& ✿ ☕

Fleur De Lys, Amport & Monxton Gardens

35 DIPLEY MILL

Dipley Road, Hartley Wintney, Hook, RG27 8JP. Miss Rose McMonigall, www.dipley-mill.co.uk. *2m NE of Hook. Turn E off B3349 at Mattingley (1½m N of Hook) signed Hartley Wintney, West Green & Dipley. Dipley Mill ½m on L just over bridge.* Suns 4, 18 June, 16 July, 6 Aug, 3 Sept, 1 Oct (2-5.30). Adm £6, chd free. Home-made teas.

A romantic adventure awaits as you wander by the meandering streams surrounding this Domesday Book listed mill! Explore many magical areas, such as the rust garden, the pill box grotto and the ornamental courtyard, or just escape into wild meadows. Alpacas. 'One of the most beautiful gardens in Hampshire' according to Alan Titchmarsh in his TV programme Love Your Garden. Featured on BBC TV and other press coverage as a result of a show garden at Hampton Court for Turismo De Galicia. Regret no dogs.

✤ ☒ ☕

36 THE DOWER HOUSE

Springvale Road, Headbourne Worthy, Winchester, SO23 7LD. Mrs Judith Lywood, 01962 882848, hannahlomax@ thedowerhousewinchester.co.uk, www.thedowerhousewinchester. co.uk. *2m N of Winchester. Entrance is directly opp watercress beds in Springvale Rd & near The Good Life Farm Shop. Parking at main entrance to house, following path to garden.* Sun 25 June (2.30-5.30). Adm £4.50, chd free. Home-made teas. Visits also by arrangement Mar to Sept for groups of 20-30.

The Dower House is set within 5½ acres of gardens with meandering paths allowing easy access around the grounds. There are plenty of places to sit, relax and enjoy the surroundings. Areas of interest incl a scented border, iris bed, geranium bed, shrubbery, a pond populated with fish and water lilies, bog garden, bluebell wood and secret courtyard garden.

&. ☒ ✤ ☕

37 DOWN FARM HOUSE

Whitchurch, RG28 7FB. Pat & Steve Jones. *1½m from the centre of Whitchurch. Please do not use SatNav. From the centre of Whitchurch take the Newbury road up the hill, over railway bridge & after approx 1m turn L.* Wed 14, Sat 24 June (1.30-5). Adm £4, chd free. Home-made teas.

Step back in time in this 2 acre garden, created from an old walled farmyard and the surrounding land. Many of the original features are used as hard landscaping, incl organic vegetables, succulents, alpine bed created from the old concrete capped well, informal and naturalistic planting, wooded area and orchard. The garden has been created slowly over the last 30 yrs. New wildlife pond for 2017. Wheelchair access by gravel drive onto lawn.

&. ☒ ✤ ☕

38 THE DOWN HOUSE

Itchen Abbas, SO21 1AX. Jackie & Mark Porter, 01962 791054, markstephenporter@gmail.com, www.thedownhouse.co.uk. *5m E of Winchester on B3047. 5th house on R after the Itchen Abbas village sign if coming on B3047 from Kings Worthy. 400yds on L after Plough PH if coming on B3047 from Alresford.* Sun 19 Feb (12-4); Sun 3 Sept (2-5.30). Adm £5, chd free. Home-made teas. Visits also by arrangement in Feb & Sept for groups of 20+.

3 acre garden laid out in rooms overlooking the Itchen Valley, adjoining the Pilgrim's Way, with walks to the river. In Feb come and see snowdrops, aconites and crocus, plus borders of coloured dogwood, willow stems and white birches. A garden of structure, pleached hornbeams, a rope-lined fountain garden, yew lined avenues and an ornamental potager. Following last year's popular late summer NGS wine event, we will once again be holding 'Vine to Wine' walks and talks at 2pm and 4pm on Sun 3 Sept, plus estate wine tasting.

&. ☒ ✤ ☒ ☕

39 7 DOWNLAND CLOSE

Locks Heath, nr Fareham, SO31 6WB. Roy & Carolyn Dorland, 07768 107779, roydorland@hotmail.co.uk. *3m W of Fareham. M27 J9 follow A27 on Southampton Rd to Park Gate. Past Kams Palace Restaurant, L into Locks Rd, 3rd R into Meadow Ave. 2nd L into Downland Close. Please park in Locks Rd (only 2 mins from garden).* Visits by arrangement May to July for groups of 15-25. Home-made teas.

Visit this prize-winning, beautiful, restful and inspirational 50ft x 45ft plantsman's garden, packed with ideas for the modest sized plot. Many varieties of hardy geraniums, hostas, heucheras, shrubs, ferns and other unusual perennials, weaving a tapestry of harmonious colour. Attractive water feature, plenty of seating areas and charming summerhouse. A garden to fall in love with!

✤ ☕

40 DURMAST HOUSE

Bennetts Lane, Burley, BH24 4AT. Mr & Mrs P E G Daubeney, 01425 402132, philip@daubeney.co.uk, www.durmasthouse.co.uk. *5m SE of Ringwood. Off Burley to Lyndhurst Rd, nr White Buck Hotel.* Sun 2 Apr, Sun 25 June (2-5). Adm £4, chd free. Cream teas. Visits also by arrangement Apr to July, incl talk on the history and planting of the garden for groups only. *Donation to Delhi Commonwealth Women's Assn Medical Clinic.*

Designed by Gertrude Jekyll, Durmast has contrasting hot and cool colour borders, formal rose garden edged with lavender and a long herbaceous border. Many old trees, Victorian rockery and orchard with beautiful spring bulbs. Rare azaleas; Fama, Princeps and Gloria Mundi from Ghent. Features incl new rose bowers with rare French roses; Eleanor Berkeley, Psyche and Reine Olga Wurtemberg. New Jekyll border with a blue, yellow and white scheme. BBC Solent Interview (July 2016). Many stone paths and some gravel paths.

&. ☒ ✤ ☒ ☒ ☕

GROUP OPENING

41 EAST WORLDHAM GARDENS

East Worldham, Alton, GU34 3AE. 01420 83389, mary.trigwell-jones@outlook.com, www.worldham.org. *2m SE of Alton on B3004. Gardens & car parking off B3004 signed in village. Tickets & maps available at each garden.* **Sat 24, Sun 25 June (2-5.30). Combined adm £5, chd free. Sat 22, Sun 23 July (2-5.30). Combined adm £4, chd free. Home-made teas.**

THE COTTAGE
Ken & Hazel Gosham.
Open on Sat 22, Sun 23 July

EAST WORLDHAM MANOR
Hermione Wood.
Open on Sat 24, Sun 25 June

SELBORNE
Brian & Mary Jones.
Open on all dates
(See separate entry)

East Worldham Gardens offers a combination of gardens with varied characters and styles on each of the two openings. East Worldham Manor is a large walled Victorian garden with restored greenhouses, orchard, vegetable area and rose garden and far-reaching views towards the Downs. Extensive borders feature hydrangeas, penstemons, roses, shrubs and climbing plants. Gravel paths wind through the garden. Selborne has extensive views across farmland from several viewpoints. Its 50 yr old orchard with dappled shade provides a pleasant place in which to take tea and stay awhile. Metal and stone sculptures, conservatory, and mixed borders, densely planted, featuring a range of hardy geraniums and other plants and shrubs. The Cottage has a small cottage-style garden that started in Nov 2014, full of roses, clematis and other climbing plants, conifers, acers and colourful herbaceous plants providing a wow factor for visitors. Shows what you can do in a small space! Garden quizzes, sandpit and bookstall at Selborne. C13 church

with some modern stained glass windows and Medieval monument of a lady. Home-made teas at East Worldham Manor & Selborne (June) and at Selborne & Three Horseshoes PH (July). Featured in Tindle Group of Newspapers. No wheelchair access at The Cottage.

&♿ 🐕 ✿ ☕ 🍷

GROUP OPENING

42 EMSWORTH GARDENS

Emsworth, PO10 7PR. *7m W of Chichester, 2m E of Havant. From Emsworth main r'about head N, under the railway bridge, under the flyover & the garden is immed on the LH-side up a slope. Parking at Horndean Recreation Ground (approx 5 min walk).* **Sun 18 June (2-5.30). Combined adm £5, chd free. Home-made teas at 23 New Brighton Road.**

MEADOWLARK, 4 ELDERFIELD CLOSE
Miss M Morelle.

23 NEW BRIGHTON ROAD
Lucy Watson & Mike Rogers.

Two gardens, one owned by Mother, 4 Elderfield Close and the other by Daughter, 23 New Brighton Road, in the delightful seaside village of Emsworth. In complete contrast to each other, but with similarity in places, they are both exuberantly planted and highlight the benefits of difficult gardening situations. One being extremely narrow and ending in full shade, the other developed into an age-challenged, friendly and maintainable garden. A plethora of planters and containers and unusual plants in both. Plant sale and old garden tool display at 23 New Brighton Road, along with a new feature for 2017, a shepherd's hut, built by one of the owners, and used as an art studio. From Horndean Recreation Ground visitors will have the opportunity to walk through the small but delightfully planted Memorial Garden situated in the corner.

🐕 ✿ ☕ 🍷

43 FAIRBANK

Old Odiham Road, Alton, GU34 4BU. Jane & Robin Lees, 01420 86665, j.lees558@btinternet.com. *1½m N of Alton. From S, past Sixth Form College, then 1½m beyond road junction on R. From N, turn L at Golden Pot & then 50yds turn R. Garden 1m on L before road junction.* **Wed 2 Aug (2-5). Adm £3.50, chd free. Home-made teas. Visits also by arrangement June to Sept for individuals or groups of 30 max.**

The planting in this large garden reflects our interest in trees, shrubs and fruit. A wide variety of herbaceous plants provide colour and are placed in sweeping mixed borders that carry the eye down the long garden to the orchard and beyond. Near the house, there are rose beds and herbaceous borders, as well as a small formal pond. There is a range of acers, ferns and unusual shrubs, with 60 different varieties of fruit, along with a large vegetable garden. Please be aware of uneven ground in some areas.

&♿ 🚗 ☕ 🍷

Beechenwood Farm

© Carole Drake

44 FAIRWEATHER'S NURSERY

Hilltop, Beaulieu, Brockenhurst, SO42 7YR. Patrick & Aline Fairweather, www.fairweathers.co.uk. *1½ m NE of Beaulieu village. Signed Hilltop Nursery on B3054 between Heath r'about (A326) & Beaulieu village.* **Sat 29, Sun 30 July (11-4). Adm £3, chd free. Cream teas at Aline Fairweather's garden.** Fairweather's hold a specialist collection of over 400 agapanthus grown in pots and display beds, incl plants being trialled for the RHS AGM. Features incl guided tours of the nursery at 11.30am and 2.30pm, demonstrations of how to get the best from agapanthus and companion planting. Agapanthus and a range of other traditional and new perennials for sale. Aline Fairweather's garden (adjacent to the nursery) will also be open, with mixed shrub and perennial borders containing many unusual plants. Also open Patrick's Patch at Fairweather's Garden Centre.

45 FARLEIGH HOUSE

Farleigh Wallop, Basingstoke, RG25 2HT. Viscount Lymington. *3m SE of Basingstoke. Off B3046 Basingstoke to Preston Candover road.* **Sun 10 Sept (2-5). Adm £5, chd free. Home-made teas.** Contemporary garden of great tranquillity designed by Georgia Langton, surrounded by wonderful views. 3 acre walled garden in 3 sections; ornamental potager, formal rose garden and wild rose garden. Greenhouse full of exotics, serpentine yew walk, contemplative pond garden and lake with planting for wildlife. The grounds cover approx 10 acres and will take about 1 hr to walk around.

46 FRITHAM LODGE

Fritham, SO43 7HH. Sir Chris & Lady Powell, 02380 812650, chris.powell@ddblondon.com. *6m N of Lyndhurst. 3m NW of M27 J1 (Cadnam). Follow signs to Fritham.* **Sun 25 June (2-4). Adm £4, chd free. Home-made teas. Visits** also by arrangement May to July.
Set in the heart of the New Forest in 18 acres with 1 acre old walled garden round Grade II listed C17 house (not open), originally one of Charles II hunting lodges. Parterre of old roses, potager with wide variety of vegetables, pergola, wisterias, herbaceous and blue and white mixed borders, tulips, and ponds. Features incl a walk across hay meadows to woodland and stream, with ponies, donkeys, sheep and rare breed hens.

GROUP OPENING

47 FROYLE GARDENS

Lower Froyle, Froyle, GU34 4LJ. Ernie & Brenda Milam. *5m NE of Alton. Access to Lower Froyle from A31 between Alton & Farnham at Bentley or access to Upper Froyle at Hen & Chickens PH also on A31. Maps given to all visitors.* **Sat 3, Sun 4 June (2-6). Combined adm £5, chd free. Home-made teas at Froyle Village Hall.**

BRAMLINS
Mrs Anne Blunt.

NEW 6 COLDREY COTTAGES
Mr & Mrs Roy Cranford.

DAY COTTAGE
Mr Nick Whines & Ms Corinna Furse, www.daycottage.co.uk.

FORDS COTTAGE
Mr & Mrs M Carr.

GLEBE COTTAGE
Barbara & Michael Starbuck.

OLD BREWERY HOUSE
Vivienne & John Sexton.

WALBURY
Ernie & Brenda Milam.
(See separate entry)

NEW WARREN COTTAGE
Mr & Mrs J Pickering.

You will certainly receive a warm welcome as eight Lower Froyle Gardens open their gates again this yr, enabling visitors to enjoy a wide variety of gardens. Again we have two new gardens, one previously open but now extended with new planting and a small immaculate colourful garden. The other gardens harmonise well with the surrounding landscape and most have spectacular views. The gardens themselves are diverse with rich planting often incorporating unusual plants. You will also see animals, greenhouses, vegetables and wild flower meadows as well as a gem of a courtyard garden. The teas served in the village hall are famous and always delicious. If that is not enough, visit St Mary's Church, Upper Froyle to see the large display of richly decorated C18 church vestments (separate donation). Featured in Farnham Life (2016). No wheelchair access to Glebe Cottage. Gravel drive at Bramlins, and gravel areas at Warren Cottage where there is disabled access on request.

48 NEW FURZEHILL FARM

FurzeHill, South Gorley, Fordingbridge, SP6 2PT. Richard & Sue Loader, www.furzehillfarm.garden. *In the New Forest between Ringwood & Fordingbridge. At Ibsley Church on A338 between Fordingbridge & Ringwood, follow yellow NGS signs for 2½ m.* **Sun 4, Sun 11 June (1-5). Adm £4.50. Home-made teas.** A 3 acre wildlife friendly garden in a New Forest smallholding setting. It has evolved over the last 20 yrs with a pretty cottage garden, vegetable plots, wildlife zones and a tiny oak wood coppice, all combining delightfully into a rambling mix that has a broad appeal whatever your gardening interests. Don't expect tidiness throughout, some areas are informal with nature allowed free rein. Walk through our wildflower meadow plots, see new plant varieties in patio containers, learn about innovative ways to grow garden produce and see interesting garden structures made from New Forest greenwood. Not suitable for wheelchairs due to inclines and loose surfaces.

Durmast House

© Leigh Clapp

49 GILBERTS NURSERY

Dandysford Lane, Sherfield English, nr Romsey, SO51 6DT. Nick & Helen Gilbert, www.gilbertsdahlias.co.uk. *Midway between Romsey & Whiteparish on A27, in Sherfield English Village. From Romsey 4th turn on L, just before small petrol station on R, visible from main road.* **Sun 27 Aug (10-4). Adm £3, chd free. Light refreshments.**

This may not be a garden but do come and be amazed by the sight of over 300 varieties of dahlias in our dedicated 1½ acre field. The blooms are in all colours, shapes and sizes and can be closely inspected from wheelchair friendly hard grass paths. An inspiration for all gardeners. 2016 four large gold medals awarded from county shows.

50 HAMBLEDON HOUSE

Hambledon, PO7 4RU. Capt & Mrs David Hart Dyke, 02392 632380, dianahartdyke@talktalk.net. *8m SW of Petersfield, 5m NW of Waterlooville. In village centre, driveway leading to house in East St. Do not go up Speltham Hill even if advised by SatNav.* **Mon 28 Aug (2-5). Adm £5, chd free. Home-made teas. Visits also by arrangement Apr to Oct. Teas by prior request.**

3 acre partly walled plantsman's garden for all seasons. Large borders filled with a wide variety of unusual shrubs and perennials with imaginative plant combinations culminating in a profusion of colour in late summer. Hidden, secluded areas reveal surprise views of garden and village rooftops. Planting a large central area, started in 2011, has given the garden an exciting new dimension. Partial wheelchair access as garden is on several levels.

51 HAMBROOKS SHOW GARDENS

135 Southampton Road, Titchfield, Fareham, PO14 4PR. Mr Mike Hodges. *On the old A27 opp B&Q.* **Sun 25 June (10-4). Evening openings Thur 26 Oct, Thur 23 Nov (6-8). Adm by donation. Light refreshments.**

16 individually designed showcase gardens ranging from the traditional to the contemporary, featuring outdoor kitchens, fireplaces, garden sofas, chandeliers, obelisks, ponds and streams. Our 3 special NGS events will be dressed for the season and lit after dark. We will also have live music, refreshments and entertainment. There is a covered walkway to protect you from the elements. Sun 25 June Summertime Fun, Thur 26 Oct Halloween Night and Thur 23 Nov Winter Garden Walk Into Christmas.

52 HILL HOUSE

Old Alresford, SO24 9DY. Mrs S Richardson, 01962 732720, hillhouseolda@yahoo.co.uk. *N of Alresford. From Alresford 1m along B3046 towards Basingstoke, then R by church.* **Sun 30 July, Tue 8, Thur 10 Aug (1.30-5). Adm £4, chd free. Home-made teas. Visits also by arrangement from mid July to mid Aug only.**

Traditional English 2 acre garden, established 1938, divided by yew hedge. Large croquet lawn framing the star of the garden, the huge multicoloured herbaceous border. Dahlia bed and butterfly attracting sunken garden in lavender shades. Prolific old fashioned kitchen garden with hens and bantams both fluffy and large. Small Dexter cows. Dried flowers.

53 HILL TOP

Damson Hill, Upper Swanmore, SO32 2QR. David Green, 01489 892653, tricia1960@btinternet.com. *1m NE of Swanmore. Junction of Swanmore Rd & Church Rd, up Hampton Hill, sharp L bend. After 300yds junction with Damson Hill, house on L. Disabled parking by house.* **Visits by arrangement May to Sept for groups of 20+. Adm £5, chd free.**

2 acres with extensive colourful borders and wide lawns, this garden has stunning views to the Isle of Wight. The glasshouses produce unusual fruit and vegetables from around the world. The outdoor vegetable plots bulge with well grown produce, much for sale in season. Potted specimen plants and interesting annuals.

54 HINTON ADMIRAL

Lyndhurst Road, Hinton, Christchurch, BH23 7DY. Sir George & Lady Meyrick. *4m NE of Christchurch. On N side of A35, ¾ m E of Cat & Fiddle PH.* **Sun 21 May (1-4.30). Adm £6, chd free.** *Donation to Julia's House Childrens Hospice.*

Magnificent 20 acre garden within a much larger estate, now being restored and developed. Mature plantings of deciduous azaleas and rhododendrons amidst a sea of bluebells. Wandering paths lead through rockeries and beside ponds, and a stream with many cascades. Orchids appear in the large lawns. The two walled gardens are devoted to herbs and wild flowers, and a very large greenhouse. The terrace and rock garden were designed by Harold Peto. Gravel paths and some steps.
&. 🐕

55 ◆ HINTON AMPNER

Alresford, SO24 0LA. National Trust, 01962 771305, hintonampner@nationaltrust. org.uk, www.nationaltrust.org.uk/ hinton-ampner. *3½ m S of Alresford. On A272 Petersfield to Winchester road, between Bramdean & Cheriton.* **For NGS: Sat 3 June (10-5). Adm £9.35, chd £4.50. Light lunches & afternoon tea in the tearoom. For other opening times and information, please phone, email or visit garden website.**

C20 garden created by Ralph Dutton covering 14 acres. Manicured lawns and topiary combine with unusual shrubs, climbers and herbaceous plants. Vibrant dahlias alternate in spring with tulips. Rose border incorporates over 45 old and new rose varieties. Dramatic foliage planting in the Dell; orchard with spring bulbs; magnolia and philadelphus walks; restored walled garden. Wheelchair access maps available from visitor reception.
&. ✿ 🚐 ☕

56 HOLLYBROOK

20a Chalk Hill, West End, Southampton, SO18 3BZ. Michael Hook & Janet Galpin. *3m E of Southampton. Exit M27 J7, take A27 to West End, at T-lights turn L into Chalk Hill. Two disabled spaces on drive, other parking on hill & side roads. Some parking at The Master Builder PH on A27, 2 mins from Chalk Hill.* **Sat 20, Sun 21, Sat 27, Sun 28 May (1-5). Adm £3, chd free. Home-made teas.**

Small 82ft × 39ft town garden started in 2008. Raised beds built using railway sleepers and imaginative use of other recycled and new materials to make interesting artistic garden pieces, to complement small herbaceous border, pergola and two ponds, one with a variety of fish. Structural planting incl bamboos, grasses and hostas. Small vegetable patch. Featured in Amateur Gardening magazine (Jan 2016).
&. ☕

57 THE HOMESTEAD

Northney Road, Hayling Island, PO11 0NF. Stan & Mary Pike, 02392 464888, jhomestead@aol.com, www.homesteadhayling.co.uk. *3m S of Havant. From A27 Havant & Hayling Island r'about, travel S over Langstone Bridge & turn immed L into Northney Rd. Car park entrance on R after Langstone Hotel.* **Sun 18 June (2-5.30). Adm £3.50, chd free. Home-made teas. Visits also by arrangement May to Sept for groups of 10+.**

1¼ acre garden surrounded by working farmland with views to Butser Hill and boats in Chichester Harbour. Trees, shrubs, colourful herbaceous borders and small walled garden with herbs, vegetables and trained fruit trees. Large pond and woodland walk with shade-loving plants. A quiet and peaceful atmosphere with plenty of seats to enjoy the vistas within the garden and beyond. Some gravel paths.
&. 🐕 ✿ 🚐 ☕

Farleigh House

58 ◆ THE HOSPITAL OF ST CROSS

St Cross Road, Winchester, SO23 9SD. The Hospital of St Cross & Almshouse of Noble Poverty, 01962 851375, porter@hospitalofstcross.co.uk, www.hospitalofstcross.co.uk. ½ m S of Winchester. From city centre take B3335 (Southgate St & St Cross Rd) S. Turn L immed before The Bell PH. If on foot follow riverside path S from Cathedral & College, approx 20 mins. **For NGS: Sun 23 July (2-5). Adm £4, chd free. Tea in the Hundred Men's Hall in the Outer Quadrangle. For other opening times and information, please phone, email or visit garden website.**

The Medieval Hospital of St Cross nestles in water meadows beside the R Itchen and is one of England's oldest almshouses. The tranquil, walled Master's Garden, created in the late C17 by Bishop Compton, now contains colourful herbaceous borders, old fashioned roses, interesting trees and a large fish pond. The Compton Garden has unusual plants of the type he imported when Bishop of London. There is wheelchair access, but please be aware surfaces are uneven in places.

& ❀ ☕ ♥

59 THE HOUSE IN THE WOOD

Beaulieu, SO42 7YN. Victoria Roberts. New Forest. 8m NE of Lymington. Leaving the entrance to Beaulieu Motor Museum on R (B3056), take next R signed Ipley Cross. Take 2nd gravel drive on RH-bend, approx ½ m. **Sun 14 May (2-5.30). Adm £5, chd free. Cream teas.**

Peaceful 12 acre woodland garden with continuing progress and improvement. New areas and streams have been developed and good acers planted among mature azaleas and rhododendrons. Used in the war to train the Special Operations Executive. A magical garden to get lost in and popular with birdwatchers.

🐕 🐐 🚗 ☕ ♥

60 THE ISLAND

Greatbridge, Romsey, SO51 0HP. Mr & Mrs Christopher Saunders-Davies, 01794 512100, ssd@littleroundtop.co.uk. 1m N of Romsey on A3057. Entrance alongside Greatbridge (1st bridge Xing the R Test), flanked by row of cottages on roadside. **Sat 29, Sun 30 Apr, Sat 26, Sun 27 Aug (2-5). Adm £5, chd free. Home-made teas. Visits also by arrangement Apr to Sept for groups of 15-20 (mornings only).**

6 acres either side of the R Test. Fine display of paeonies, wisteria and spring flowering trees. Main garden has herbaceous and annual borders, fruit trees, rose pergola, lavender walk and extensive lawns. An arboretum planted in the 1930s by Sir Harold Hillier contains trees and shrubs providing interest throughout the yr.

& ❀ ♥

61 🆕 IVANHOE

63 Bishopstoke Road, Bishopstoke, Eastleigh, SO50 6BF. Helen Fuller. 1m E of Eastleigh. M3 J12 take A335 to Eastleigh centre. At r'about take 2nd L to Bishopstoke Rd. 63 on L past playing field. Park in playing field car park or Toby Carvery along on R. Disabled parking at Tesco Express next door to 63. **Sat 22, Sun 23 Apr (2-5); Sat 29, Sun 30 July (2-6). Adm £3, chd free. Home-made teas.**

⅓ acre wildlife friendly woodland garden. Varied planting, with bright perennials in sunny areas, ferns and shade lovers under 8 mature sycamore trees, colourful climbers, masses of spring bulbs, flowering trees and shrubs, a lily pond with fish and a small vegetable garden. Pots of heucheras, ferns, acers and seasonal flowers cluster round doors to welcome visitors. Some flint and gravel paths.

& ❀ ☕ ♥

62 LAKE HOUSE

Northington, SO24 9TG. Lord Ashburton, 07795 364539, lukeroeder@hotmail.com. 4m N of Alresford. Off B3046. Follow English Heritage signs to The Grange, and then to Lake House **Thur 8, Sun 11 June (12-5). Adm £5, chd free. Home-made teas. Visits also by arrangement June to Oct for groups of 10+.**

2 large lakes in Candover Valley set off by mature woodland with waterfalls, abundant birdlife, long landscaped vistas and folly. 1½ acre walled garden with rose parterre, mixed borders, long herbaceous border, rose pergola leading to moon gate. Flowering pots, conservatory and greenhouses. Picnicking by lakes. Grass paths and slopes to some areas of the garden.

& 🐕 ❀ 🚗 ☕ ♥

63 🆕 LAND OF NOD

Grayshott Road, Headley Down, GU35 8SJ. Mrs Philippa Whitaker. 6m S of Farnham. Turn off the A3 towards Hindhead on the B3002. Drive through Grayshott leaving the church on your R, continue 2m & we are on the RH-side in Headley Down. **Sat 6, Sun 7 May (2-5.30). Adm £4, chd free. Home-made teas on the terrace, in front of the house.**

This 7 acre garden is situated within 100 acres of woodland. There is a Japanese garden in which you will find two ponds and colourful azaleas, acers and camellias. There are many different species of tree, incl wellingtonias and a monkey puzzle, some of which date back to the late 1800s. Accessible bridge over pond in Japanese garden. All dogs on leads please.

& 🐕 ❀ ☕ ♥

Your support helps Carers Trust to provide more help to unpaid carers

LANDFORD VILLAGE GARDENS
See Wiltshire

64 LITTLE COURT
Crawley, Winchester, SO21 2PU. Mrs A R Elkington, 01962 776365, elkslc@btinternet.com. *5m NW of Winchester. Between B3049 (Winchester - Stockbridge) & A272 (Winchester - Andover).* **Sun 19, Mon 20, Sun 26, Mon 27 Feb, Sun 26 Mar (2-5). Adm £3.50, chd free. Fri 14, Mon 17 Apr (2-5.30). Combined adm with Paige Cottage £6, chd free. Mon 1 May (2-5.30). Adm £4, chd free. Home-made teas in the village hall. 2018: Sun 18, Mon 19, Sun 25, Mon 26 Feb. Visits also by arrangement Feb to July with teas in the garden.**
In a small pretty village, a 3 acre walled and sheltered traditional country garden, which is spectacular from February. There are many naturalised bulbs, special snowdrops, and cowslips in the labyrinth. In summer the large beds of perennials are in harmonious colours, set off by a good lawn. It is fun for all ages with many places to sit and enjoy the views; for children there is a tree house and swings. Large kitchen garden and bantams. Comments from visitors in 2016 included 'glorious', 'many surprises', 'wonderful tranquillity'.
  ♿ ✿ ☕ ♨

65 LITTLEWOOD
West Lane, Hayling Island, PO11 0JW. Steven & Sheila Schrier. *3m S of Havant. From A27 Havant & Hayling Island junction, travel S for 2m, turn R into West Lane & continue 1m. House set back from road in a wood on the R.* **Sat 13, Sun 14 May (11-5). Adm £4, chd free. Home-made teas.**
2½ acre bluebell wood and spring flowering garden surrounded by fields and near sea, protected from sea winds by multi barrier hedge. Rhododendrons, azaleas, camellias and many other shrubs. Woodland walk to full size treehouse. Features incl pond, bog garden, house plants, summerhouse, conservatory and many places to sit outside and

under cover. Dogs on leads and picnickers welcome. Close to Hayling Billy Coastal Trail. Unload wheelchairs at top of shingle drive. Garden is level throughout.
  ♿ ☛ ✿ ☕

66 LONGSTOCK PARK
Leckford, Stockbridge, SO20 6EH. Leckford Estate Ltd, part of John Lewis Partnership, www.longstockpark.co.uk. *4m S of Andover. From Leckford village on A3057 towards Andover, cross the river bridge & take 1st turning to the L signed Longstock.* **Sun 18 June (2-5). Adm £6, chd £2. Light refreshments.**
Famous water garden with extensive collection of aquatic and bog plants set in 7 acres of woodland with rhododendrons and azaleas. A walk through the park leads to National Collections of *Buddleja* and *Clematis viticella*; arboretum and herbaceous border. Teas at Leckford Farm Shop, at Longstock Nurseries (last orders at 3.45pm). Assistance dogs only.
  ♿ ✿ ☕

67 NEW 26 LOWER NEWPORT ROAD
Aldershot, GU12 4QD. Mr & Mrs P Myles. *From the A331 coming off at the Aldershot junction, head towards Aldershot. Take the 1st R turn, opp the Fiat Showroom into North Lane & then 1st L into Lower Newport Rd.* **Fri 30 June, Sat 1 July (11-4). Adm £3, chd free. Light refreshments.**
A 'T' shaped small town garden full of ideas, split into four distinct sections; a semi-enclosed patio area with pots and water feature; a free-form lawn with a tree fern, perennials, bulbs and shrubs; secret garden with a 20ft x 6ft raised pond, exotic planting backdrop and African carvings; and a potager garden with a selection of vegetable, roses and plant storage. We also have 46 named varieties of hosta.
  ✿ ☕

68 ♦ MACPENNYS WOODLAND GARDEN & NURSERIES
Burley Road, Bransgore, Christchurch, BH23 8DB. Mr &

Mrs T M Lowndes, 01425 672348, office@macpennys.co.uk, www.macpennys.co.uk. *6m S of Ringwood, 5m NE of Christchurch. From Crown PH Xrds in Bransgore take Burley Rd, following sign for Thorney Hill & Burley. Entrance ¼m on R.* **For opening times and information, please phone, email or visit garden website.**
12 acres of nursery with 4 acre gravel pit converted into woodland garden planted with many unusual plants. Offering interest yr-round, but particularly in spring and autumn. Large nursery displaying for sale a wide selection of trees, shrubs, conifers, perennials, hedging plants, fruit trees and bushes. Tearoom offering home-made cakes, afternoon tea (pre-booking required), and light lunches using locally sourced produce wherever possible. Nursery closed Christmas through to the New Year. Partial wheelchair access.
  ♿ ☛ ✿ 🚗 ☕

69 NEW MANOR HOUSE
Church Lane, Exton, SO32 3NU. Tina Blackmore, 01489 877529, manorhouseexton@gmail.com, www.extonbedandbreakfast.com. *Off A32 just N of Corhampton. Pass The Shoe Inn on your L, go to the end of the road to a T-junction, turn R & Manor house is immed on the L, just below the church.* **Sun 4, Sun 11 June (2-5). Adm £4, chd free. Home-made teas. Visits also by arrangement Feb to Sept for groups of 10+.**
An enchanting 1 acre mature walled garden set in the Meon valley. Yew hedges and flint walls divide the garden into rooms. The white garden planted with hydrangeas and roses. A box parterre with fountain, woodland area, vegetable patch, wild pond and herbaceous borders packed with colourful cottage garden favourites; delphiniums, roses, geraniums and salvias.
  ♿ ✿ 🛏 ☕

70 1 MAPLE COTTAGE
Searles Lane, off London Road (A30), Hook, RG27 9EQ. John & Pat Beagley. *A30 Hartley Wintney side of Hook opp Hampshire Prestige*

Cars. Up Searles Lane (approx ¼m) parking close to rear of property. Follow yellow ribbons. **Sun 11, Wed 14, Thur 15, Sun 25 June (2-5). Adm £3.50, chd free. Home-made cakes, gluten free cakes & biscuits.**
½ acre garden evolved over 25 yrs, many ideas for smaller gardens. Shady, herbaceous and hot borders, wildlife pond with many hosta varieties, vegetable plots plus a wild area, and views over R Whitewater. Features incl a tree cave for children, and we feel we offer the most varied and quality plants for sale, from three experienced producers, incl a renowned local, retired nursery owner from Whispers. Featured on the front cover of local magazine, Hook Focus (June 2016). Some paved paths, mainly grassed areas.

71 MEON ORCHARD
Kingsmead, North of Wickham, PO17 5AU. Doug & Linda Smith, 01329 833253, meonorchard@btinternet.com. 5m N of Fareham. From Wickham take A32 N for 1½m. Turn L at Roebuck Inn. Garden in ½m. Park on verge or in field N of property. **Sun 28 May, Sun 30 July, Sun 3 Sept (2-6). Adm £5, chd free. Home-made teas.**
1½ acre garden designed and constructed by current owners. An exceptional range of rare, unusual and architectural plants inc National Collection of Eucalyptus. Dramatic foliage plants from around the world, see plants you have never seen before! Flowering shrubs in May/June; perennials in July; bananas, tree ferns, cannas, gingers, palms dominate in Sept; and streams and ponds, plus an extensive range of planters complete the display. Visitors are welcome to explore the 20 acre meadow and ½m of Meon River frontage attached to the garden. Extra big plant sale of the exotic and rare on Sun 3 Sept. Garden fully accessible by wheelchair, reserved parking.

72 MERDON MANOR
Merdon Castle Lane, Hursley, Winchester, SO21 2JJ. Mr & Mrs J C Smith, 01962 775215, vronk@fastmail.com. 5m SW of Winchester. From A3090 Winchester to Romsey road, turn R at Standon, onto Merdon Castle Lane. Proceed for 1¼m. Entrance on R between 2 curving brick walls. **Sun 30 July (2-6). Adm £4, chd free. Home-made teas. Visits also by arrangement May to Oct for groups of up to 50 max.**
5 acre country garden surrounded by panoramic views; pond with ducks, damsel flies, dragonflies and water lilies; large wisteria; roses; fruit-bearing lemon trees; extensive lawns; impressive yew hedges; small secret walled garden with fountains. Black Hebridean sheep (St. Kildas). Very tranquil and quiet. All areas are accessible but wheelchairs have to go down the drive to reach the sunken garden where azaleas rhododendrons and camelias grow.

73 MICHAELMAS
2 Old Street, Hill Head, Fareham, PO14 3HU. Ros & Jack Wilson, 01329 662593, jazzjack00@gmail.com. 4½m S of Fareham. From Fareham follow signs to Stubbington, then Hill Head. Turn R into Bells Lane. After 1m pass Osborne View PH on L, next R is Old St. **Sun 16, Mon 17 July (2-5). Adm £3.50, chd free. Home-made teas. Visits also by arrangement June to Aug for groups of 10-20.**
Very cheerful, colourful small garden with the wow factor. A variety of tall plants for a tall lady! Many are grown from seed or cuttings. Small vegetable garden, greenhouse, garden room, pot grown vegetables and flowers. Styled in the fashion of a country garden with a wide range of plants with the emphasis on perennials. As pictured in preface of The Gardens of England book. 1 min walk from beach, 5 mins walk from Titchfield Haven Nature Reserve.

The National Garden Scheme is Hospice UK's largest single funder

74 MOORE BLATCH
48 High Street, Lymington, SO41 9ZQ. Moore Blatch Solicitors. Top end of Lymington High St, on S side. Follow signs for Lymington town centre & use High St car parks. **Sat 17 June (9.30-1). Sun 18 June (2-5). Adm £3.50, chd free. Tea, coffee & cakes.**
Situated behind this elegant Georgian town house lies a surprising s-facing walled garden of 1 acre. From the raised terrace, enjoy the long vista across the croquet lawn to mature gardens beyond and then over to the Isle of Wight. Amusing and varied topiary underplanted with mixed herbaceous. Rose beds and vegetable plots should be in full swing. Attractions close by incl the Lymington Saturday Market and the lively waterfront at the bottom of the High St.

75 22 MOUNT PLEASANT ROAD
Alton, GU34 1NN. Phyllida McCormick. From A31 take A339 Alton. Follow signs for town centre, past Butts Green on L & garage on R. Next R is Mount Pleasant Rd. Car park on L. No 22 on R. Spaces on road for residents only please. **Sat 12, Sun 13 Aug (2-5). Combined adm with 42 Whitedown £5, chd free.**
A small garden, a few minutes' walk away from the town centre, yet quiet and peaceful. Three garden rooms are divided by arches and espalier fruit trees. There are perennials, roses and clematis, against a backdrop of mature shrubs and trees, with a covered path of clematis Viticella 'Mary Rose' in Aug which greets you at the gate.

© Leigh Clapp

Hambledon House

76 OAK TREE COTTAGE

Upper Common Road, Pennington, Lymington, SO41 8LD. Sue Kent. *2m NW of Lymington. From N off A337, turn into Sway Rd, 1½m to Wheel Inn. Turn L into Ramley Rd & follow signs. Leave M27 J2 & follow Heavy Lorry Route to avoid traffic in Lyndhurst.* **Sat 8, Sun 9 July (2-5.30). Adm £3.50, chd free. Home-made teas.**
This 1½ acre garden has a wealth of surprises, but with continuity. Using a limited palette of plants, with repetition of blue and silver, it flows from one secluded space to another. Designed with a gentle variation of levels and using many trees, contrasting foliage and flowers, one can become delightfully lost.

77 NEW OAKLANDS

Brook, Bramshaw, Nr Lyndhurst, SO43 7HD. Chris & Caroline Biggin. *Via M27 J1 signed Bramshaw & Brook, follow the B3078 for 1m to Brook. Then follow NGS signs.* **Sun 28 May, Sun 4 June (2-5). Combined adm with Waldrons £5, chd free. Home-made teas.**
Oaklands is in an elevated position overlooking paddocks and the forest, surrounded by a cottage style garden with mixed borders. Climbers, roses, wisteria and clematis abound, potted grasses and hostas jostle for space with planters on the patios. The vegetable garden, fruit cage and orchard provide produce yr-round. Walk around the orchard, paddock and large pond or sit and admire the view. Some paths have a step but adjacent lawns allow access to all areas.

78 NEW OLD CAMPS

Newbury Road, Headley, Thatcham, RG19 8LG. Mr & Mrs Adam & Heidi Vetere. *Old Camps can be found in Headley, situated off the A339, 1½m N of Kingsclere. Parking & access to the garden is through the neighbouring Plum Tree Farm which is located off Galley Lane. Limited disabled parking.* **Sat 19, Sun 20 Aug (10-5). Adm £5, chd free. Home-made teas.**
A breathtaking garden set over an acre, which benefits from panoramic views of Watership Down. Surprises await, ranging from traditional herbaceous borders through desert and prairie planting, an enchanted knot garden, formal potager to exuberant and exotic subtropical schemes, featuring bananas, cannas, hedychiums and much more. Partial wheelchair access. Non-disabled WC.

79 NEW THE OLD RECTORY

East Woodhay, Newbury, RG20 0AL. David & Victoria Wormsley. *6m SW of Newbury. Turn off A343 between Newbury & Highclere to Woolton Hill. Turn L to East End, continue ¾m beyond East End. Crossover at T-junction to parking in field. Garden opp St Martin's Church.* **Sun 25, Wed 28 June (2-5). Adm £5, chd free. Home-made teas.**
Classic English country garden of about 2 acres surrounding Regency Gothic former rectory (not open). Tranquil views over parkland, croquet lawn, large walled garden incl formal topiary, roses and unusual perennials, Mediterranean pool garden, wildflower meadow and fruit garden. Gravel drive and some steps.

80 OLD SWAN HOUSE

High Street, Stockbridge, SO20 6EU. Mr Henry Lawford. *9m W of Winchester. On A30, at junction of A3057 & B3049. Entrance in Recreation Ground Lane.* **Every Tue 4 July to 25 July (2-5). Adm £4, chd free. Soft drinks & biscuits included. Opening with Stockbridge Gardens on Thur 15, Sun 18 June.**
This garden offers a loggia hung with creepers, a mature fish pond with waterlilies, a long lawn under a 100 yr old hazel which faces mirror herbaceous borders, and an ancient brick and flint wall sheltering mixed planting and shrub roses. Euphorbias, rosemary and lavender abound. There is a square of grass garden in gravel, bounded by brick paths, a wildflower patch and a partly mature orchard.

Your visit helps fund 389 Marie Curie Nurses

GROUP OPENING

81 OLD THATCH & THE MILLENNIUM BARN

Sprats Hatch Lane, Winchfield, Hook, RG27 8DD. *3m W of Fleet. 1½m from Winchfield station, follow NGS signs. Parking in adjacent field if dry, or car park at Barley Mow Slipway. Garden ½m via lane or towpath.* **Sun 9 Apr, Sun 11 June (2-6). Combined adm £4, chd free. Home-made teas. Pimms if hot & mulled wine if cool.**

THE MILLENNIUM BARN

OLD THATCH

Jill Ede, www.old-thatch.co.uk.

Two gardens in one! A small secluded haven sits under the old oak tree next to the pond, surrounded by yr-round colour and seasonal fragrance from roses and honeysuckle. You can listen to birdsong, wind chimes and the trickling of a small waterfall whilst enjoying views of Old Thatch and the cottage garden beyond. Who could resist visiting Old Thatch, a chocolate box thatched cottage, featured on film and TV, an evolving smallholding with a 5 acre garden and woodland alongside the Basingstoke Canal (unfenced). A succession of spring bulbs, a profusion of wild flowers, perennials and homegrown annuals pollinated by our own bees and fertilised by the donkeys, who await your visit. Over 30 named clematis and rose cultivars. Sometimes lambs in April and donkey foals in summer. Children enjoy our garden quiz, adults enjoy tea and home-made cakes. Arrive by narrow boat! Trips on 'John Pinkerton' will stop at Old Thatch on NGS days www.basingstoke-canal. org.uk. Also Accessible Boating shuttle available from Barley Mow wharf approx every 30 mins. Featured in Period Living and Hampshire Life. Video clip on NGS website. Blue badge holders proceed to second entrance by red telephone box. Paved paths and grass slopes give access to the whole garden.

82 ORDNANCE HOUSE

West Dean, Salisbury, SP5 1JE. Terry & Vanessa Winters, 01794 341797, terry.winters@ordnancehouse.co.uk, www.ordnancehouse.co.uk. *8m W of Romsey, 8m E of Salisbury. From A36 Southampton to Salisbury road follow signs for West Dean via West Grimstead. From Romsey, follow signs via Awbridge, Lockerley & East Dean. From Stockbridge, follow signs from Broughton.* **Visits by arrangement May to July for groups of 10+. Adm £5, chd free.**

This is a garden that changes with the seasons. In late spring and summer, displays of purple and white alliums and foxgloves provide a striking colour palette. In high summer lavender and drifts of prairie plants dominate. A new programme of planting native wild flowers has also begun. Features a small orchard, vegetable garden, a variety of beds and borders plus seating areas to view the garden. In 2016 the garden was featured in many magazines incl Nest (Belgium), House Beautiful (UK), Countryside (UK) and Mon Jardin & ma maison (France).

83 PAIGE COTTAGE

Crawley, Winchester, SO21 2PR. Mr & Mrs T W Parker. *5m NW of Winchester. In the centre of the village, by the pond.* **Fri 14, Mon 17 Apr (2-5.30). Combined adm with Little Court £6, chd free. Thur 6, Sun 9 July (2-5.30). Combined adm with Tanglefoot £6, chd free. Home-made teas in the village hall.**

1 acre traditional English country garden surrounding a period thatched cottage (not open), with a two-level pond with waterfall, a small orchard with rare anemonies, and a small vegetable garden. Large variety of bulbs and wild flowers in spring, and herbaceous border and old varieties of climbing roses in summer. If you are lucky you may also see ducks from the adjacent village pond walking through.

84 ♦ PATRICK'S PATCH

Fairweather's Garden Centre, High Street, Beaulieu, SO42 7YB. Mr P Fairweather, 01590 612307, www.fairweathers.co.uk. *SE of New Forest at head of Beaulieu River. Leave M27 at J2 & follow signs for Beaulieu Motor Museum. Go up High St & park in Fairweather's on LH-side.* **For opening times and information, please phone or visit garden website.**

Model kitchen garden with a full range of vegetables, trained top and soft fruit and herbs. Salads in succession used as an educational project for all ages. Maintained by volunteers, primary school children and a part-time gardener. Open daily by donation from dawn to dusk.

85 PILLEY HILL COTTAGE

Pilley Hill, Pilley, Lymington, SO41 5QF. Steph & Sandy Glen, 01590 677844, stephglen@hotmail.co.uk. *New Forest. 2m N of Lymington off A337. To avoid traffic delays in Lyndhurst leave M27 at J2 & follow Heavy Lorry Route.* **Sun 27, Mon 28 Aug, Sat 9, Sun 10 Sept (2-5). Adm £3, chd free. Cream teas. Visits also by arrangement Aug & Sept for groups of 20+.**

Naturalistic, wildlife friendly garden of surprises around every corner. Enter through the creeper covered lych gate and the garden reveals itself to you little by little. Wild flowers rub shoulders with perennials among quaint objects and oak structures. Meander through the wild old orchard, through willow walks and oak archways, onto the shady pond garden. Enjoy a cream tea to complete your visit. Some slippery slopes. Visitors with wheelchairs have managed our garden, so please phone to discuss.

86 PYLEWELL PARK

South Baddesley, Lymington, SO41 5SJ. **Lord Teynham.** *Coast road 2m E of Lymington. From Lymington follow signs for Car Ferry to Isle of Wight, continue for 2m to South Baddesley.* **Sun 16 Apr, Sun 28 May (2-5). Adm £4, chd free. Home-made teas in The Old Mill.**

A large parkland garden laid out in 1890. Enjoy a walk along the extensive informal grass and moss paths, bordered by fine rhododendrons, magnolias, embothriums and cornus. Wild daffodils in bloom at Easter and bluebells in May. Large lakes are bordered by giant gunnera. Distant views of the Isle of Wight across the Solent. Lovely for families and dogs. Old glasshouses and other out buildings are not open to visitors. Wear suitable footwear for muddy areas.

GROUP OPENING

87 ROMSEY GARDENS

Town Centre, Romsey, SO51 8LD. *All gardens are within walking distance of each other & are clearly signed. Use Lortemore Place public car park (SO51 8LD), free on Sundays & BH.* **Sun 28, Mon 29 May (11-5). Combined adm £6, chd free. Home-made teas at King John's House.**

KING JOHN'S GARDEN
Friends of King John's Garden & Test Valley Borough, www.facebook.com/KingJohnsGarden/.

4 MILL LANE
Miss J Flindall, 01794 513926. **Visits also by arrangement Mar to Oct.**

THE NELSON COTTAGE
Margaret Prosser.

THE OLD THATCHED COTTAGE
Genevieve & Derek Langford.

Romsey is a small, unspoilt, historic market town with the majestic C12 Norman Abbey as a backdrop to 4 Mill Lane, a garden described by Joe Swift as 'the best solution for a long thin garden with a view'. King John's Garden, with its fascinating listed C13 house (not open), has all period plants that were available before 1700; it also has an award-winning Victorian garden with a courtyard where tea is served (no dogs, please). The Nelson Cottage was formally a PH; its ½ acre garden has a variety of perennial plants and shrubs, with a wild grass meadow bringing the countryside into the town. The Old Thatched Cottage (C15) has a small garden undergoing further development by new owners; it features a variety of shrubs, lawn, vegetable patch, fruit cordons, rockery and water feature. No wheelchair access at 4 Mill Lane.

88 ROTHERFIELD PARK

East Tisted, Alton, GU34 3QE. **Sir James & Lady Scott.** *4m S of Alton on A32. Please turn off your SatNav. Entry from A32 only.* **Sun 30 Apr (2-5). Adm £5, chd free. Home-made teas. Visitors may picnic in the park from 12 noon.**

Take some ancient ingredients: ice house, ha-ha, lime avenue; add a walled garden, fruit and vegetables, trees and hedges; set this 12 acre plot in an early C19 park (picnic here from noon) with views to coin clichés about. Mix in a bluebell wood and Kim Wilkie's modern take on an amphitheatre by the stable block. Top local growers selling plants, incl Marcus Dancer, Phoenix Perennial Plants and Seale Nurseries. Wheelchair access to walled garden.

19 Barnwood Road

© Nicola Stocken Tomkins

89 28 ST RONAN'S AVENUE

Southsea, Portsmouth, PO4 0QE. **Ian Craig & Liz Jones.** *St Ronan's Rd can be found off Albert Rd, Southsea. Follow signs from Albert Rd or Canoe Lake on seafront. Parking in Craneswater School.* **Sun 28 May (2-6). Adm £3.50, chd free. Home-made teas.**

Town garden 145ft x 25ft, 700 metres from the sea. A mixture of tender, exotic and dry loving plants along with more traditional incl king protea, bananas, ferns, agaves, echeverias, echium and puya. Wild flower area and wildlife pond. Two different dry gardens showing what can be grown in sandy soil. Recycled items have been used to create sculptures.

90 2 SAMPAN CLOSE

Warsash, Southampton, SO31 9BU. **Amanda & Robert Bailey.** *4½m W of Fareham. M27 J9 take A27 W, L at Park Gate into Brook Lane by Esso garage. Straight over 3 r'abouts, L at 4th r'about into Schooner Way. Sampan Close, 4th on R. Please park in Schooner Way.* **Sat 13, Sun 14 May (12-4). Adm £3, chd free. Home-made teas.**

Sited on former strawberry fields this compact garden 50ft x 27ft was designed by the owner, an enthusiastic horticulturalist, to give yr-round interest. Inspirational design ideas for tiny plots with perennials, grasses, old roses, trough planting and raised vegetable beds. A small brick rill edges a circle of lawn. A blue, lean-to glasshouse, against a brick garden wall is an attractive feature. Fareham in Bloom gold awards for Plantsman's Front Garden and Small Plantsman's Back Garden in 2016. Featured in Amateur Gardening (June 2016).

91 SANDY SLOPES

Honeysuckle Lane, Headley Down, Bordon, GU35 8EH. **Mr & Mrs R Thornton.** *6m S of Farnham. From A3 exit S side of Hindhead tunnel, proceed to Grayshott, then Headley Down via B3002. From Farnham proceed S, A325 to Bordon turn L onto B3002*

*via Lindford & Headley to Headley
Down.* **Sat 27, Sun 28, Mon 29 May
(2-5.30). Adm £3.50, chd free.
Home-made teas.**
A plantsman's garden with a
remarkable collection of mature
plants from China and other parts
of the world, many of these are rare
and exciting. Some are naturalised
and many are woodland shade lovers
such as trilliums, areseamas, primulas
and rare blue meconopsis, growing
beneath mature rhododendrons,
magnolias and rare trees. Rising
terraced ground with a stream and
wildlife pond. Some unusual plants
for sale. Steep slopes and steps,
unsuitable for pushchairs, wheelchairs
and visitors with walking difficulties.

92 SELBORNE

Caker Lane, East Worldham,
GU34 3AE. Brian & Mary Jones,
01420 83389,
mary.trigwell-jones@outlook.com,
www.worldham.org.uk. *2m SE of
Alton. On B3004 at Alton end of the
village of East Worldham opp The
Three Horseshoes PH. Please note:
'Selborne' is the name of the house
and it is not in the village of Selborne.
Parking signed.* **Sat 29, Sun 30 Apr
(2-5), also open Walbury. Sat
20, Sun 21 May, Sat 5, Sun 6,
Mon 7 Aug (2-5). Adm £3.50,
chd free. Home-made teas in
the orchard, with plenty of
seating. Opening with East
Worldham Gardens on Sat 24,
Sun 25 June, Sat 22, Sun 23 July.
Visits also by arrangement May
to Aug for individuals & groups.**
*Donation to East Worldham Church
Fabric Fund (Apr) & Tafara Mission
Zimbabwe (Aug).*
Described as a garden of surprises
this ½ acre mature garden with
views across farmland features
a 50 yr old orchard of named
varieties. Mixed, densely planted
borders contain hardy geraniums,
other herbaceous plants, shrubs
and climbers. Metal and stone
sculptures enhance the borders.
Relax and enjoy tea sitting in the
dappled shade of the orchard.
Summerhouses and conservatory
provide shelter. Book stall, garden
quizzes for children and a sandpit

for small children. Featured in Tindle
Group of Newspapers and on
Radio Solent. Wheelchair access,
please note some gravel paths.

93 SHALDEN PARK HOUSE

The Avenue, Shalden, Alton,
GU34 4DS. Mr & Mrs Michael
Campbell. *4½m NW of Alton.
B3349 from Alton or M3 J5 onto
B3349. Turn W at Golden Pot PH
marked Herriard, Lasham, Shalden.
Entrance ¼m on L. Disabled parking
on entry.* **Sun 11 June (2-5). Adm
£4, chd free. Home-made teas.**
Large 4 acre garden to stroll around
with beautiful views. Herbaceous
borders incl kitchen walk and
rose garden, all with large scale
planting and foliage interest. Pond,
arboretum, perfect kitchen garden
and garden statuary.

94 ♦ SIR HAROLD HILLIER GARDENS

Jermyns Lane, Ampfield, Romsey,
SO51 0QA. Hampshire County
Council, 01794 369317,
info@hants.gov.uk,
www.hilliergardens.org.uk. *2m NE
of Romsey. Follow brown tourist signs
off M3 J11, or off M27 J2, or A3057
Romsey to Andover. Disabled parking
available.* **For opening times and
information, please phone, email or
visit garden website.**
Established by the plantsman Sir
Harold Hillier, this 180 acre garden
holds a unique collection of 12,000
different hardy plants from across
the world. It incl the famous Winter
Garden, Magnolia Avenue, Centenary
Border, Himalayan Valley, Gurkha
Memorial Garden, Magnolia Avenue,
spring woodlands, Hydrangea Walk,
fabulous autumn colour, 14 National
Collections and over 400 champion
trees. The Centenary Border is
believed to be the longest double
mixed border in the country, a feast
from early summer to autumn.
Celebrated Winter Garden is one
of the largest in Europe. Electric
scooters are available for hire (please
pre-book). Disabled WC. Guide and
hearing dogs only.

95 SPINDLES

24 Wootton Road, Lee-on-
the-Solent, Portsmouth,
PO13 9HB. Peter & Angela
Arnold, 02393 115181,
angelliana62@gmail.com. *6m S
of Fareham. Exit A27, turn L onto
Gosport Rd A32. At r'about take 2nd
exit Newgate Lane B3385. Through
3 r'abouts, turn L into Marine Parade
B3333 onto Wootton Rd.* **Sun 30
July (2-5). Home-made teas.
Mon 31 July (2-5). Cream teas.
Adm £3, chd free. Visits also by
arrangement May to Aug for
groups of 6-30 (day & eve). Art
groups welcome.**
Small plantaholic's garden, 3 mins
from the beach, with creative
planting using every available space.
Traditional country garden meets
tropical splendour. Seating area and
conservatory to enjoy a home-made
tea, a warm welcome awaits you!

96 ♦ SPINNERS GARDEN

School Lane, Boldre, Lymington,
SO41 5QE. Andrew & Vicky
Roberts, 07545 432090,
info@spinnersgarden.co.uk,
www.spinnersgarden.co.uk.
*1½m N of Lymington. Follow the
brown signs off the A337 between
Lymington & Brockenhurst. Also
signed off the B3054 Beaulieu to
Lymington road. Map available on
website.* **For NGS: Sun 30 Apr (2-
5.30). Adm £5, chd free. Cream
teas. For other opening times and
information, please phone, email or
visit garden website.**
Peaceful woodland garden with
azaleas, rhododendrons, magnolias,
acers and other rare shrubs
underplanted with a wide variety
of choice woodland and ground
cover plants. The garden has been
extended over the last 5 yrs and
the views opened up over the
Lymington valley. More recently,
building work has been completed
on a new house in the grounds
designed to complement the garden.
Partial wheelchair access.

97 SPRING POND

Laverstoke, Whitchurch, RG28 7PD. Julian & Carolyn Sheffield, info@springpond garden.co.uk, www.springpondgarden.co.uk. *1m S of the B3400 in Laverstoke. 8m W of Basingstoke, 3m W of Overton. In Laverstoke turn L opp Bombay Sapphire brick building on B3400 to Micheldever Station. Spring Pond is 1m along road on the L.* **Sun 25, Mon 26 June (2-5). Adm £6, chd free. Home-made teas.**
Spring Pond is full of colour coordinated borders, with an abundance of roses and clematis, while hornbeam, yew and box hedges add structure to the garden. There is a pond with a wide variety of marginal plants, an arboretum full of ornamental trees, and a conservatory with Mediterranean and tropical plants. Hardy Garden Plants Nursery is 1m from Spring Pond.

&. 🐄 🚗 ☕

GROUP OPENING

98 STOCKBRIDGE GARDENS

Stockbridge, SO20 6EX. *9m W of Winchester. On A30, at junction of A3057 & B3049. Parking on High St. All gardens on High St & Winton Hill.* **Thur 15, Sun 18 June (2-5.30). Combined adm £7, chd free. Home-made teas on the lawn at St Peter's Church.** *Donation to St Peter's Church.*

LITTLE WYKE
Mrs Mary Matthews.

THE OLD RECTORY
Mr Robin Colenso.

OLD SWAN HOUSE
Mr Herry Lawford.
(See separate entry)

SHEPHERDS HOUSE
Kim & Frances Candler.

TROUT COTTAGE
Mrs Sally Milligan.

Stockbridge with its many listed houses, excellent shops and hostelries is on the famous R Test. Five gardens are open this yr offering a variety of styles and character. Tucked in behind the High St, Trout Cottage's small walled garden flowers for most of the yr. Little Wyke, next to the Town Hall, has a long mature town garden with mixed borders and fruit trees. The Old Rectory has a walled garden with formal pond, fountain, planting near the house, surrounded by woodland trees, shrubs and bog area. Old Swan House, at the east end of the High St, is a newly designed garden offering mature fish pond with waterlilies, long lawn facing mirror herbaceous borders, sheltering mixed planting and shrub roses, a gravel grass garden and orchard. Shepherds House is a s-facing, ¾ acre garden on rising ground with informal shrubberies, colourful borders, terraces, lawns, ponds, woodland glade and small orchard.

&. 🌼 ☕

---

99 TANGLEFOOT

Crawley, Winchester, SO21 2QB. Mr & Mrs F J Fratter, 01962 776243, fred@tanglefoot-house.demon.co.uk. *5m NW of Winchester. Between B3049 (Winchester - Stockbridge) & A272 (Winchester - Andover). Lane beside Crawley Court (Arqiva). Parking in adjacent mown field.* **Thur 22, Sun 25 June (2-5.30). Adm £4, chd free. Thur 6, Sun 9 July (2-5.30). Combined adm with Paige Cottage £6, chd free. Home-made teas in the village hall. Thur 20, Sun 23 July (2-5.30). Adm £4, chd free. Soft drinks & biscuits included 22, 25 June, 20, 23 July. Visits also by arrangement June & July.**
Designed and developed by owners since 1976, Tanglefoot's ½ acre garden is a blend of influences, from Monet-inspired rose arch and small wildlife pond to Victorian boundary wall with trained fruit trees. Highlights include a raised lily pond, small wildflower meadow, herbaceous bed (a riot of colour later in the summer), herb wheel, large productive kitchen garden and unusual flowering plants. In contrast to the garden, a 2 acre field is being converted into spring and summer wildflower meadows, with mostly native trees and shrubs; already it has delighted our visitors in summer 2015/2016. Watercolour flower paintings. Plants from the garden for sale.

&. 🌼 🚗 ☕ ☕

---

100 TERSTAN

Longstock, Stockbridge, SO20 6DW. Alexander & Penny Burnfield, penny.burnfield@andover.co.uk, www.pennyburnfield.wordpress. com. *½m N of Stockbridge. From Stockbridge (A30) turn N to Longstock at bridge. Garden ½m on R.* **Suns 16 Apr, 25 June, 23 July, 10 Sept (2-6). Adm £4, chd free. Home-made teas. Visits also by arrangement Apr to Sept with coach parking available.**
1 acre, intensively planted, with an artist's flair for colour and design. Relax on one of the many seats with views across the R Test to the Hampshire Downs and listen to gentle summer music. An exuberance of rare and unusual plants. Wheelchair access, but some gravel paths and steps.

&. 🌼 🚗 ☕

---

102 TYLNEY HALL HOTEL

Ridge Lane, Rotherwick, RG27 9AZ. Elite Hotels, 01256 764881, sales@tylneyhall.com, www.tylneyhall.co.uk. *3m NW of Hook. From M3 J5 via A287 & Newnham, M4 J11 via B3349 & Rotherwick.* **Sun 30 Apr, Sun 11 June, Sun 1 Oct (10-4). Adm £5, chd free. Light refreshments in the Chestnut Suite from 12pm.**
Large garden of 66 acres with extensive woodlands and fine vista being restored with new planting. Fine avenues of wellingtonias; rhododendrons and azaleas, Italian garden, lakes, large water and rock garden, dry stone walls originally designed with assistance of Gertrude Jekyll. New for 2017! On Sun 30 Apr there will be a selection of local produce suppliers joining us. Partial wheelchair access.

&. 🐄 🌼 🛏 ☕

103 WALBURY
Lower Froyle, Alton, GU34 4LJ.
Ernie & Brenda Milam. *5m NE of
Alton. Access to Lower Froyle from
A31 between Alton & Farnham
at Bentley. Parking available near
Walbury, at village hall.* **Sat 29, Sun
30 Apr (2-5). Adm £3, chd free.
Home-made teas. Also open
Selborne. Opening with Froyle
Gardens on Sat 3, Sun 4 June.**
⅓ acre garden divided into three
sections. Each section has a cottage
garden atmosphere with different
styles, packed with plants in colour
themed borders incl many unusual
plants. There are water features,
an alpine house and fern walk.
Wheelchair access to two sections
of the garden.
ᵭ 🐐 ✿ 💟

104 WALDRONS
Brook, Lyndhurst, SO43 7HE.
Major & Mrs J Robinson. *4m N of
Lyndhurst. On B3079 1m W from
M27 J1. 1st house L past Green
Dragon PH & directly opp Bell PH.*
**Sun 28 May, Sun 4 June (2-5).
Combined adm with Oaklands
£5, chd free. Home-made teas.**
A thick high hedge and a selection of
trees and shrubs surround our 1 acre
garden and C18 New Forest cottage
(not open). Raised beds and island
beds have been developed for shade
and sun loving plants, incl hostas, ferns,
alpines, unusual perennials, cottage
garden plants, flowering shrubs and
wild flowers. A small area of the
garden has raised vegetable beds,
three compost bins and greenhouse.
ᵭ 💟

105 WALHAMPTON
Beaulieu Road, Walhampton,
Lymington, SO41 5ZG.
Walhampton School Trust Ltd.
*1m E of Lymington. From Lymington
follow signs to Beaulieu (B3054) for
1m & turn R into main entrance at
1st school sign 200yds after top of
hill.* **Sun 7 May (2.30-5.30). Adm
£5, chd free. Home-made teas.**
Donation to St John's Church, Boldre.
Glorious walks through large C18
landscape garden surrounding
magnificent mansion (not open).
Visitors will discover three lakes,
serpentine canal, climbable prospect

mount, period former banana
house and orangery, fascinating shell
grotto, plantsman's glade and Italian
terrace by Peto (c1907), drives and
colonnade by Mawson (c1914).
Excedrae and sunken garden,
rockery, Roman arch, and fountain.
Seating, guided tours with garden
history. Gravel paths, some slopes.
ᵭ 💟

106 WEIR HOUSE
Abbotstone Road, Old Alresford,
SO24 9DG. Mr & Mrs G
Hollingbery, 01962 735549,
jhollingbery@me.com. *½m N of
Alresford. From New Alresford down
Broad St (B3046), past Globe PH,
take 1st L signed Abbotstone. Weir
House is 1st drive on L. Park in
signed field.* **Sun 28 May, Sun 10
Sept (2-5). Adm £5, chd free.
Home-made teas. Visits also by
arrangement for groups of 10+.
No refreshments available.**
Spectacular riverside garden with
sweeping lawn backed by old walls,
yew buttresses and mixed perennial
beds. Contemporary vegetable
garden at its height in Sept. Also incl
contemporary garden around pool
area, bog garden (at best in May) and
wilder walkways through wooded
areas. Children welcome. Wheelchair
access to most of the garden.
ᵭ 🐐 💟

**107 ◆ WEST GREEN
HOUSE GARDENS**
Thackhams Lane, Hartley
Wintney, RG27 8JB. Miss
Marylyn Abbott, 01252 844611,
enquiries@westgreenhouse.co.uk,
www.westgreenhouse.co.uk.
*3m NE of Hook. Turn off A30 at
Phoenix Green on to Thackhams
Lane. Continue 1¼m to the end of
Thackhams Lane. The entrance to
West Green House Gardens can be
found on the L corner.* **For NGS:
Evening opening Tue 25 July
(8-9.30). Adm £10, chd free.
Alcoholic & non alcoholic drinks
in The Lakefield Bar. Picnic
by the lake or undercover &
gardens will be illuminated at
9pm. For other opening times and
information, please phone, email or
visit garden website.**
Within its C18 walls the magnificent

Walled Garden is a tapestry
of exuberantly planted lavish
herbaceous borders, elaborate
potager and parterres. Outside
the walls an informal lake field is
studded with neoclassical follies,
chinoiserie bridges and cascades. A
grand water staircase and Italianate
fountain provide a dramatic focal
point. Special events throughout
the year, including Christmas Fair,
Winter Festival and Opera Season.
Wheelchair access, but some paths
are gravel and therefore not suitable
for large motorised wheelchairs.
ᵭ ✿ 🚗 💟

**108 WEST SILCHESTER
HALL**
Bramley Road, Silchester,
RG7 2LX. Mrs Jenny Jowett,
01189 700278,
www.jennyjowett.com. *8m N of
Basingstoke. 9m S of Reading, off
A340 (signed from centre of village).*
**Sun 28, Mon 29 May, Sun 9
July, Sun 6 Aug (2-5.30). Adm
£4, chd free. Home-made teas.
Visits also by arrangement May
to Sept for groups of 10+.**
This much loved 2 acre garden has
fascinating colour combinations
inspired by the artist owners',
with many spectacular herbaceous
borders filled with rare and unusual
plants flowering over a long period.
Many pots filled with half hardies, a
wild garden surrounding a natural
pond, banks of rhododendron, a
self supporting kitchen garden with
lovely views across a field of grazing
cattle. Large studio with exhibition
of the owners botanical, landscape
and portrait paintings, cards and
prints. Near Roman site. Wheelchair
access to large part of the garden,
gravel drive.
ᵭ 🐐 ✿ 🚗 💟

The National Garden
Scheme is the
largest single funder
of Macmillan

109 WHEATLEY HOUSE

Wheatley Lane, between Binsted & Kingsley, Bordon, GU35 9PA. Mr & Mrs Michael Adlington, 01420 23113, susannah@westcove.ie. *4m E of Alton, 5m SW of Farnham. Take A31 to Bentley, follow sign to Bordon. After 2m, R at Jolly Farmer PH towards Binsted, 1m L & follow signs to Wheatley.* **Sat 19, Sun 20 Aug (1.30-5.30). Adm £4.50, chd free. Home-made teas. Visits also by arrangement May to Oct for groups of 10+. Refreshments on request.**
Situated on a rural hilltop with panoramic views over Alice Holt Forest and the South Downs. The owner admits to being much more of an artist than a plantswoman, but has had great fun creating this 1½ acre garden full of interesting and unusual planting combinations. The sweeping, mixed borders and shrubs are spectacular with colour throughout the season, particularly in late summer. The black and white border, now with deep red accents, is proving very popular with visitors. Local craft stalls, paintings, and home-made teas in Old Barn. Wheelchair access with care on lawns, good views of garden and beyond from terrace.
  ♿ ❀ 🚗 ☕

110 WHISPERS

Chatter Alley, Dogmersfield, RG27 8SS. Mr & Mrs John Selfe, 01252 613568. *3m W of Fleet. Turn N to Dogmersfield off A287 Odiham to Farnham Rd. Turn L by Queen's Head PH.* **Visits by arrangement June to Aug for groups of 15+. Adm £5, chd free.**
Come and discover new plants in this 2 acre garden of manicured lawns surrounded by large borders of colourful shrubs, trees and long flowering perennials. Wild flower area, water storage system, greenhouse, kitchen garden and living sculptures. Spectacular waterfall cascades over large rock slabs and magically disappears below the terrace. A garden not to be missed. Gravel entrance.
  ♿ ❀ 🚗

111 WHITE GABLES

Breach Lane, Sherfield-on-Loddon, RG27 0EU. Terry & Brian Raisborough. *5m N of Basingstoke. From Basingstoke follow A33 to Reading for approx 5m. Breach Lane (unmade lane) immed on R before Sherfield-on-Loddon r'about. Parking in 2 free car parks in main village only. 150yds to garden.* **Sun 23 July (1-5). Adm £4, chd free. Home-made teas at Cydonia, next door.**
A plantaholic's paradise! Consisting of many sections, this garden provides a host of stimulating inspirations and ideas towards visitors own garden. Large collection of exotic plants, hostas, cacti and lots more, revealing the owners passion for plants. Meandering paths take the visitor through various themed areas on a journey through a yr-round garden containing life sized statues, various arches and areas of sheer enjoyment.
❀ ☕

112 42 WHITEDOWN

Alton, GU34 1LU. Ms Jo Carter. *In Alton, leave The Butts Green on your L, go past stone fountain & L into Borovere Gardens. Go down to T-junction then L into Whitedown, follow road round. 42 is on R. Park on road or at Butts Green.* **Sat 12, Sun 13 Aug (2-5). Combined adm with 22 Mount Pleasant Road £5, chd free. Home-made teas.**
A warm welcome awaits at this small town garden, it is a late summer feast for the eyes and showing what can be done within a small space. Garden designer Jo and her sculptor husband Richard have created from scratch an exuberant and varied collection of shapes, colours and textures, where traditional and exotic plants mingle with sculptures. In 2016 featured in Hampshire Life magazine and Amateur Gardenings 'Get the Look'.
❀ ☕

113 WICOR PRIMARY SCHOOL COMMUNITY GARDEN

Portchester, Fareham, PO16 9DL. Louise Moreton. *Halfway between Portsmouth & Fareham on A27. Turn S at Seagull PH r'about into Cornaway Lane, 1st R into Hatherley Drive. Entrance to school is almost opp.* **Sun 2 July (12-4). Adm £3.50, chd free. Home-made teas.**
Beautiful school gardens tended by pupils, staff and community gardeners. Wander along the Darwin's path to see the Jurassic garden, orchard, tropical bed, wildlife areas and allotment, plus one of the few camera obscuras in the south of England. The gardens are situated in historic Portchester with views of Portsdown Hill. The planting has been chosen to provide nectar and habitat for Wicor's rich wildlife. An opportunity to see Children's Art in the Garden. Wheelchair access to all areas, flat ground.
  ♿ 🐕 ❀ ☕

GROUP OPENING

114 WILDHERN GARDENS

Wildhern, Andover, SP11 0JE. *From Andover or Newbury A343. After Enham Alamein or Hurstbourne Tarrant turn at Xrd towards Penton Mewsey. Wildhern is ¾m on R. Parking at village hall.* **Sun 18, Wed 21 June (2-5.30). Combined adm £6, chd free. Wed 16 Aug (2-5.30). Combined adm £4, chd free. Cream teas & home-made cakes at Starlings.**

ELM TREE COTTAGE
Ian & Rosie Swayne.
Open on Sun 18, Wed 21 June

LITTLE ORCHARD
Mrs Sue McGregor.
Open on Sun 18, Wed 21 June

OAKWOOD
Jean Pittfield.
Open on all dates

STARLINGS
Annie Bullen & Roy Wardale.
Open on all dates

WILTON COTTAGE
Primrose Pitt.
Open on Sun 18, Wed 21 June

Five gardens within easy walking distance. Oakwood with mature borders is planted for yr-round interest and has a large pond framed by unusual plants. Elm Tree is a perfect cottage garden with formal elements incl manicured lawns, raised borders, path planting and many pots. Little Orchard is still a work in progress whose welcoming front garden bears fruit trees and mounded beds. The use of grasses is continued behind the house while an embryonic forest garden incl some uncommon edibles. The restoration of the ¾ acre garden at Starlings, begun 5 yrs ago, features a sunken gravel garden with nectar bearing plants, a small winter garden, a rose bearing pergola and enclosed vegetable beds. Wilton Cottage's pretty garden comprises herbaceous borders, shrubs, a rose pergola and trees incl walnut, fig and magnolia. Two gravel areas show off water features, roses and a mirror gate, young fruit trees, grasses and a reflective pool. No wheelchair access to Starlings, but can be viewed from decking. Gravel drives at Wilton Cottage, Elm Tree Cottage, and Little Orchard.

 ⅋ ☀ 🚗 ☕ ♿

115 WILLOWS

Pilley Hill, Boldre, Lymington, SO41 5QF. Elizabeth & Martin Walker, 01590 677415, elizabethwalker13@gmail.com, www.willowsgarden.co.uk. *New Forest. 2m N Lymington off A337. To avoid traffic in Lyndhust, leave M27 at J2 & follow Heavy Lorry Route. Disabled parking at gate.* Sat 29, Sun 30 July, Sat 5, Sun 6 Aug, Sat 2, Sun 3 Sept (2-5). Adm £3.50, chd free. Cream teas. Visits also by arrangement July & Aug for groups of 20+, incl talk, garden tour & cream teas.
Willows greets you with a wow! Late summer sizzle and vibrant exotics with a jungly mix of bananas, bamboos, gunnera and ferns around the tranquil pond and bog garden. Bold brilliant borders frame the front lawn. Rich red crocosmias, dahlias, zinnias, cannas and heleniums star in succession. Sunny hot upper borders of coleus, salvia, bedding dahlias with a backdrop of billowing grasses. Willows is holding a Dahlia Day on Sun 3 Sept, at 3pm Elizabeth will demonstrate how to take cuttings, plant and separate mature tubers. Also how to over winter plant dahlia tubers in the ground, dig up, and store if ground is unsuitable. Wheelchairs usually manage to access all of Willows garden.

 ♿ 🐕 ☀ 🚗 ☕ ♥

116 1 WOGSBARNE COTTAGES

Rotherwick, RG27 9BL. Miss S & Mr R Whistler. *2½ m N of Hook. M3 J5, M4 J11, A30 or A33 via B3349.* Sun 9, Mon 10 July (2-5). Adm £3, chd free. Home-made teas.
Small traditional cottage garden with a roses around the door look, much photographed for calendars, jigsaws and magazines, incl Hampshire Life (July 2016). Mixed flower beds and borders. Vegetables grown in abundance. Ornamental pond and alpine garden. Views over open countryside to be enjoyed whilst you take afternoon tea on the lawn. The garden has been open for the NGS for more than 30 yrs. Small vintage motorcycle display (weather permitting). Some gravel paths.

 ♿ ☀ ☕ ♥

117 NEW WYCHWOOD

Silchester Road, Little London, Tadley, RG26 5EP. Jenny Inwood. *Please do not park in The Plough car park. Access to Wychwood garden is by rear access. Follow the signs opp Beach's Crescent.* Wed 5, Wed 12 July (2-5). Adm £3.50, chd free. Light refreshments.
A joyful garden comprising a stunning water feature with statuary and countless containers brimming with annuals. A tranquil and peaceful atmosphere invites you to sit and enjoy the many seating areas, amidst shrubs, roses and trees. The garden offers gentle access to different levels and habitats, and extends into a natural wooded area with views over the fields beyond. Wheelchair access may be difficult on gravel path and through the woods.

 ♿ ☕ ♥

4 Mill Lane, Romsey Gardens

HEREFORDSHIRE

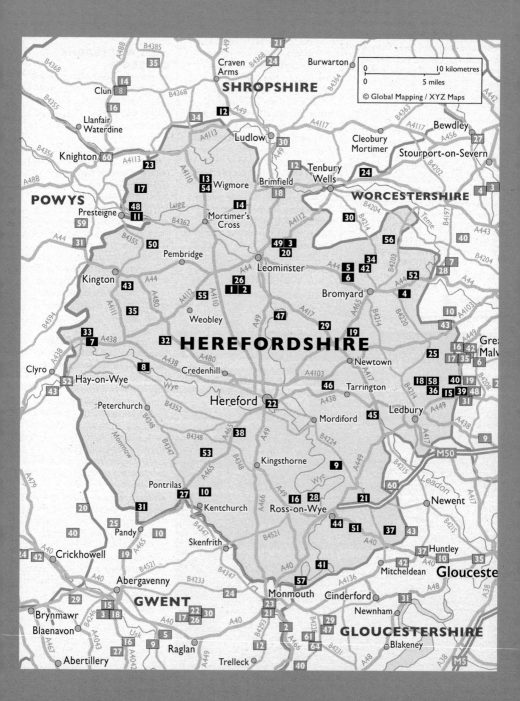

SHROPSHIRE

POWYS

WORCESTERSHIRE

HEREFORDSHIRE

GWENT

GLOUCESTERSHIRE

0   10 kilometres
0   5 miles
© Global Mapping / XYZ Maps

Craven Arms
Burwarton
Clun
Llanfair Waterdine
Ludlow
Cleobury Mortimer
Bewdley
Stourport-on-Severn
Knighton
Wigmore
Brimfield
Tenbury Wells
Mortimer's Cross
Presteigne
Pembridge
Leominster
Bromyard
Kington
Weobley
Newtown
Clyro
Hay-on-Wye
Credenhill
Tarrington
Ledbury
Peterchurch
Hereford
Mordiford
Kingsthorne
Pontrilas
Kentchurch
Ross-on-Wye
Newent
Pandy
Skenfrith
Crickhowell
Mitcheldean
Gloucester
Brynmawr
Huntley
Blaenavon
Abergavenny
Monmouth
Cinderford
Newnham
Abertillery
Raglan
Blakeney
Trelleck

Herefordshire is essentially an agricultural county, characterised by small market towns, black and white villages, fruit and hop orchards, meandering rivers, wonderful wildlife and spectacular, and often remote, countryside (a must for keen walkers).

As a major region in the Welsh Marches, Herefordshire has a long and diverse history, as indicated by the numerous prehistoric hill forts, medieval castles and ancient battle sites. Exploring the quiet country lanes can lead to many delightful surprises.

For garden enthusiasts the National Garden Scheme offers a range of charming and interesting gardens ranging from informal cottage plots to those of grand houses with parterres, terraces and parkland. Widely contrasting in design and plantings they offer inspiration and innovative ideas.

National collections of Asters and Siberian Iris can be found at The Picton Garden and Aulden Farm, respectively; and, for Galanthophiles, Ivycroft will not disappoint. The numerous specialist nurseries offer tempting collections of rare and unusual plants.

You can always be sure of a warm welcome at a National Garden Scheme open garden.

Volunteers

County Organiser
Rowena Gale
01568 615855
rowena.jimgale@btinternet.com

County Treasurer
Michael Robins
01531 632232
m.robins101@btinternet.com

Publicity
Sue Evans
01568 614501
s.evans.gp@btinternet.com

Booklet Coordinator
Chris Meakins
01544 370215
christine.meakins@btinternet.com

Booklet Distribution
Andrew Hallett
01981 570401
ar.hallett@gmail.com

Assistant County Organisers
David Hodgson
01531 640622
dhodgson363@btinternet.com

Sue Londesborough
01981 510148
slondesborough138@btinternet.com

Gill Mullin
01989 750593
gill@longorchard.plus.com

Penny Usher
01568 611688
pennyusher@btinternet.com

© Julia Stanley

Left: **Montpellier Cottage**

OPENING DATES

All entries subject to change. For latest information check www.ngs.org.uk

Extended openings are shown at the beginning of the month.

Map locator numbers are shown to the right of each garden name.

February

Snowdrop Festival

Ivy Croft (Every Thursday)	26
Sunday 12th	
The Old Corn Mill	37
Tuesday 21st	
Coddington Vineyard	18
Friday 24th	
Coddington Vineyard	18
Tuesday 28th	
Coddington Vineyard	18

March

Saturday 18th	
◆ Ralph Court Gardens	42
Sunday 19th	
◆ Ralph Court Gardens	42
Saturday 25th	
◆ The Bannut	4
Sunday 26th	
◆ The Bannut	4
The Old Corn Mill	37

April

Saturday 1st	
◆ Stockton Bury Gardens	49
Sunday 2nd	
Whitfield	53
Monday 3rd	
◆ Moors Meadow Gardens & Nursery	34

Sunday 9th	
Bury Court Farmhouse	13
Lower Hope	29
Sunday 16th	
Coddington Vineyard	18
The Old Corn Mill	37
Woofields Farm	58
Monday 17th	
Coddington Vineyard	18
The Old Corn Mill	37
Woofields Farm	58
Saturday 22nd	
◆ The Bannut	4
Sunday 23rd	
Aulden Farm	2
◆ The Bannut	4
◆ Brobury House Gardens	8
Ivy Croft	26
Sunday 30th	
Brilley Court	7
The Old Corn Mill	37
Perrycroft	39
◆ The Picton Garden	40
Whitfield	53
Woodview	57

May

Perrycroft (Every Thursday and Friday from Thursday 4th)	39
Windsor Cottage (Every Tuesday and Thursday from Tuesday 23rd)	55
Monday 1st	
NEW The Hurst	25
Friday 5th	
Rhodds Farm	43
Saturday 6th	
Rhodds Farm	43
Monday 8th	
◆ Bryan's Ground	11
◆ Moors Meadow Gardens & Nursery	34
Sunday 14th	
The Old Corn Mill	37
NEW Whitbourne Hall	52
Saturday 20th	
◆ Ralph Court Gardens	42
Sunday 21st	
Lower Hope	29
Montpelier Cottage	33
◆ Ralph Court Gardens	42

90th Anniversary Weekend

Saturday 27th	
◆ The Bannut	4
Stapleton Castle Court Garden	48
Sunday 28th	
Aulden Farm	2
◆ The Bannut	4
Ivy Croft	26
The Old Corn Mill	37
Sheepcote	45
Southbourne & Pine Lodge	47
Stapleton Castle Court Garden	48
Monday 29th	
Aulden Farm	2
Ivy Croft	26
The Old Corn Mill	37
Southbourne & Pine Lodge	47
Stapleton Castle Court Garden	48
Tuesday 30th	
Church Cottage	16
Wednesday 31st	
NEW Lower House Farm	30

June

Church Cottage (Every Tuesday and Wednesday)	16
Perrycroft (Every Thursday and Friday to Friday 23rd)	39
Windsor Cottage (Every Tuesday and Thursday)	55
Friday 2nd	
Rhodds Farm	43
Saturday 3rd	
Bredenbury, Mistletoe Lodge	5
Bredenbury, The Coppice	6
The Old Rectory	38
Rhodds Farm	43
Sunday 4th	
Bredenbury, Mistletoe Lodge	5
Bredenbury, The Coppice	6

◆ Caves Folly Nurseries	15
The Old Rectory	38
Monday 5th	
◆ Moors Meadow Gardens & Nursery	34
Saturday 10th	
Bredenbury, Mistletoe Lodge	5
Bredenbury, The Coppice	6
Sunday 11th	
Bredenbury, Mistletoe Lodge	5
Bredenbury, The Coppice	6
Brockhampton Cottage	9
The Brooks	10
Dovecote Barn	19
Grendon Court	21
Midland Farm	32
Old Colwall House	36
Monday 12th	
Newport House	35
Tuesday 13th	
Newport House	35
Wednesday 14th	
NEW Lower House Farm	30
Newport House	35
Thursday 15th	
Newport House	35
Friday 16th	
◆ Hereford Cathedral Gardens	22
Newport House	35
Saturday 17th	
Ross-on-Wye Community Garden	44
Wolferlow House	56
Sunday 18th	
Dovecote Barn	19
NEW The Hop House	24
Ross-on-Wye Community Garden	44
Shucknall Court	46
Saturday 24th	
◆ The Bannut	4
◆ Ralph Court Gardens	42
Sunday 25th	
◆ The Bannut	4
Cloister Garden	17
Kentchurch Gardens	27
Midland Farm	32
◆ Ralph Court Gardens	42

July

Church Cottage
(Every Tuesday and
Wednesday) 16

Windsor Cottage
(Every Tuesday
and Thursday) 55

Saturday 1st
Aulden Arts and
Gardens 1

Sunday 2nd
Aulden Arts and
Gardens 1

Monday 3rd
◆ Moors Meadow
Gardens & Nursery 34

Friday 7th
Rhodds Farm 43

Saturday 8th
Rhodds Farm 43

Sunday 9th
Lower Hope 29

Saturday 15th
Hill House Farm 23
◆ Ralph Court
Gardens 42

Sunday 16th
NEW Burnt House
Farm 12
Hill House Farm 23
Kentchurch Gardens 27
◆ Ralph Court Gardens 42
Woodview 57

Sunday 23rd
NEW Burnt House
Farm 12
Woodview 57

Saturday 29th
◆ The Bannut 4

Sunday 30th
◆ The Bannut 4

August

Church Cottage
(Every Tuesday
and Wednesday to
Wednesday 9th) 16

Windsor Cottage
(Every Tuesday
and Thursday to
Thursday 24th) 55

Friday 4th
Rhodds Farm 43

Saturday 5th
◆ The Picton Garden 40
Rhodds Farm 43

Sunday 6th
Aulden Farm 2
Ivy Croft 26

Monday 7th
◆ Moors Meadow
Gardens & Nursery 34

Sunday 13th
◆ The Picton Garden 40

Thursday 24th
◆ The Picton Garden 40

Saturday 26th
◆ The Bannut 4
◆ Middle Hunt House 31

Sunday 27th
◆ The Bannut 4
◆ Middle Hunt House 31
Southbourne &
Pine Lodge 47

Monday 28th
◆ The Picton Garden 40
Southbourne &
Pine Lodge 47

September

Perrycroft (Every
Thursday and Friday
from Thursday 7th) 39

Sunday 3rd
Midland Farm 32

Saturday 9th
Poole Cottage 41

Sunday 10th
◆ Brobury House
Gardens 8
The Brooks 10
The Old Rectory 38
Poole Cottage 41

Wednesday 13th
◆ The Picton Garden 40

Sunday 17th
Lower Hope 29
Wigmore Gardens 54

Sunday 24th
Dovecote Barn 19

Thursday 28th
◆ The Picton Garden 40

The Old Corn Mill

Saturday 30th
◆ The Bannut 4

October

Perrycroft (Every
Thursday and Friday to
Friday 13th) 39

Sunday 1st
◆ The Bannut 4
Perrycroft 39

Monday 9th
◆ The Picton Garden 40

Saturday 14th
◆ Ralph Court
Gardens 42

Sunday 15th
◆ Ralph Court
Gardens 42

Friday 20th
◆ The Picton Garden 40

February 2018

Ivy Croft
(Every Thursday) 26

By Arrangement

Aulden Farm 2
Bachefield House 3

THE GARDENS

GROUP OPENING

1 AULDEN ARTS AND GARDENS
Aulden, Leominster, HR6 0JT.
www.auldenfarm.co.uk/auldenarts.
4m SW of Leominster. From Leominster, take Ivington/Upper Hill rd, ¾ m after Ivington church turn R signed Aulden. From A4110 signed Ivington, take 2nd R signed Aulden. Sat 1, Sun 2 July (2-5). Combined adm £6. Home-made teas.

AULDEN FARM
Alun & Jill Whitehead.
(See separate entry)

HONEYLAKE COTTAGE
Jennie & Jack Hughes.

OAK HOUSE
Bob & Jane Langridge,
01568 720577,
oakcroft16@gmail.com.

Lost in the back lanes of Herefordshire, 3 gardens looking to celebrate the 90th Anniversary of the NGS. Our gardens vary from traditional to the more zany – as does our art! Come and see our work, explore the gardens, sit awhile and enjoy our yummy cakes! Aulden Farm art will be on display in our barn, alias our potting shed! - canvases inspired by walks, stitchery by Nature. We are drawn to that fertile ground where realism meets abstraction. Honeylake: Mature, peaceful garden designed to encourage wildlife with a pond and numerous nestboxes. Cottage flowers predominate, interspersed with fragrant English roses, lawns and a well-stocked traditional vegetable garden. The garden is an inspiration for art work using a variety of media, especially watercolour. Oak House: ⅔ acre of evolving garden with amazing views towards Upper Hill. Currently has good bones, but is fraying round the edges. Divided into several areas including borders, ponds, chickens and a working vegetable plot. Art is photography and textiles which will be displayed throughout the garden.

2 AULDEN FARM
Aulden, Leominster, HR6 0JT. Alun & Jill Whitehead, 01568 720129, web@auldenfarm.co.uk, www.auldenfarm.co.uk. *4m SW of Leominster. From Leominster take Ivington/Upper Hill rd, ¾ m after Ivington church turn R signed Aulden. From A4110 signed Ivington, take 2nd R signed Aulden.* Sun 23 Apr, Sun 28, Mon 29 May, Sun 6 Aug (2-5.30). Combined adm with Ivy Croft £7. Single garden adm £4. Home-made teas & ice cream. Opening with Aulden Arts and Gardens on Sat 1, Sun 2 July. Visits also by arrangement Apr to Sept groups or individuals.
Informal country garden surrounding old farmhouse, 3 acres planted with wildlife in mind. Emphasis on structure and form, with a hint of quirkiness, a garden to explore with eclectic planting. Irises thrive around a natural pond, shady beds and open borders, seats abound, feels mature but ever evolving. Our own ice cream and home-burnt cakes, Lemon Chisel a speciality! National Collection of Siberian Iris and plant nursery.

3 BACHEFIELD HOUSE
Kimbolton, HR6 0EP. Jim & Rowena Gale, 01568 615855, rowena.jimgale@btinternet.com. *3m E of Leominster. Take A4112 off A49 (signed Leysters), after 10yds 1st R (signed Stretford/Hamnish). 1st L to Grantsfield, over Xrds (signed Bache), continue for approx 1m, garden on R 200yds past rd to Gorsty Hill.* Visits by arrangement, individuals and groups up to 25, mid-May - June. Adm £4, chd free. Home-made teas.
Charming traditional cottage-style garden of 1 acre on gentle hill slope. Beds and borders bulge with beautiful blooms and foliage. Part-walled kitchen and cutting garden, gravel and herbaceous beds, rockery and pond. Good collections of roses, peonies, heritage pinks and irises. Summerhouse with fine views.

4 ♦ THE BANNUT
Bringsty, Bromyard, WR6 5TA. Gareth & Tamla Bowdler, 01885 483545, thebannut@yahoo.com, www.bannut.co.uk. *2½ m E of Bromyard. On A44 Worcester Rd, ½ m E of entrance to National Trust, Brockhampton.* For NGS: Sat, Sun 25, 26 Mar, 22, 23 Apr, 27, 28 May, 24, 25 June, 29, 30 July, 26, 27 Aug, 30 Sept, 1 Oct (11-4). Adm £4.50, chd free. Home-made teas. For other opening times and information, please phone, email or visit garden website.
Traditional 3 acre garden filled with a huge variety of indigenous and non-native species, planted in both formal and informal settings. The garden is designed to provide year round interest and we are showcasing the best of the season in our monthly NGS weekends. New garden features launching in 2017. Tea room serving sumptuous home-made cakes and refreshments. Children's activities and free refreshments for under 16s. Level garden accessible via a mix of gravelled and grassed pathways.

THE BARTON
See Worcestershire

BIRTSMORTON COURT
See Worcestershire

5 BREDENBURY, MISTLETOE LODGE
Wacton Lane, Bromyard, HR7 4TF. Jewels Williams Peplow & Mark Peplow, 01885 488029, jewelswilliams@hotmail.co.uk, www.jewelsporcelain.com. *A44 between Bromyard & Leominster. At Bredenbury turn onto Wacton Lane between Three Pines Garage & Barneby Inn. Garden 50yds on L. Drop off for disabled, other parking at Three Pines Garage.* Sat 3, Sun 4, Sat 10, Sun 11 June (11-5). Combined adm with Bredenbury, The Coppice £5, chd free. Single garden adm £3.

Stapleton Castle Court Garden

Home made teas, gluten free options available. **Visits also by arrangement in 5-9 June.**
Small but charming, secluded garden, centred around a natural pond with lush planting. 'A tranquil hidden gem.' Complimented by a mixed media art exhibition, 'Coast and Garden'. Home-made cakes, teas and coffee to enjoy in the garden. Suitable for wheelchairs with large wheels for graveled paths.
&. 💤

6 BREDENBURY, THE COPPICE
Wacton Lane, Bromyard, HR7 4TF. Peter & Wendy Kirk. *A44 between Bromyard & Leominster. At Bredenbury turn onto Wacton Lane between Three Pines Garage & Barneby Inn. Garden is 50 yards on L. Disabled drop off at garden. Parking at the Barneby Inn.* **Sat 3, Sun 4, Sat 10, Sun 11 June (11-5). Combined adm with Bredenbury, Mistletoe Lodge £5, chd free. Single garden adm £3. Homemade teas at Mistletoe Lodge.**
In collaboration with and in contrast to Mistletoe Lodge, next door, The Coppice garden is a mature garden with some recent changes by the present owners. The garden is a mixture of perennial borders with

mature Japanese acers, a fern garden, koi pond and a natural pond. In the front, a small coppice of white birch trees with woodland plants, and new rhododendron border. Suitable for wheelchairs with large wheels for some gravelled paths and grass.
&. ✿ 💤

BRIDGES STONE MILL
See Worcestershire

7 BRILLEY COURT
Whitney-on-Wye, HR3 6JF. Mr & Mrs David Bulmer, 01497 831467, rosebulmer@hotmail.com. *6m NE of Hay-on-Wye. 5m SW of Kington. 1½m off A438 Hereford to Brecon rd signed to Brilley.* **Sun 30 Apr (2-6). Adm £5, chd free. Home-made teas. Visits also by arrangement Apr to Oct for individuals and groups.**
Garden created 35 years ago, 7 acres in total, wild valley stream garden with special trees, ornamental walled kitchen garden, tulips and wild flower areas. Summer roses and herbaceous . Wonderful views to the Black Mountains. Regret no dogs (except guide dogs). Featured in Country Life and Country Living. Limited wheelchair access.
&. 🚗 💤

8 ◆ BROBURY HOUSE GARDENS
Brobury by Bredwardine, HR3 6BS. Keith & Pru Cartwright, 01981 500229, enquiries@broburyhouse.co.uk, www.broburyhouse.co.uk. *10m W of Hereford. S off A438 signed Bredwardine & Brobury. Garden 1m on L (before bridge).* **For NGS: Sun 23 Apr, Sun 10 Sept (11-4). Adm £5, chd £1. Home-made teas.** For other opening times and information, please phone, email or visit garden website.
9 acres of gardens, set on the banks of an exquisitely beautiful section of the R Wye, offer the visitor a delightful combination of Victorian terraces with mature specimen trees, inspiring water features, architectural planting and woodland areas. Redesign and development is ongoing. Bring a picnic, your paint brushes, binoculars and linger awhile. Wheelchair users, strong able-bodied assistant advisable.
&. 🐄 ✿ 🚗 🛏 💤

9 BROCKHAMPTON COTTAGE
Brockhampton, HR1 4TQ. Peter Clay. *8m SW of Hereford 5m N of Ross-on-Wye on B4224. In Brockhampton take rd signed to church, cont up hill for ½m, after set of farm buildings, driveway on L, over cattle grid. Car park 500yds from garden.* **Sun 11 June (1-4). Combined adm with Grendon Court £10, chd free. Single garden adm £6.**
Created from scratch in 1999 by the owner and Tom Stuart-Smith, this beautiful hilltop garden looks S and W over miles of unspoilt countryside. On one side a woodland garden and 5 acre wild flower meadow, on the other side a Perry pear orchard and in valley below: lake, stream and arboretum. The extensive borders are planted with drifts of perennials in the modern romantic style. Allow 1hr 30 mins. Picnic parties welcome by the lake . Visit Grendon Court (2 - 5.30) after your visit to us.
🐄 🚗 🇩 💤

10 THE BROOKS

Pontrilas, HR2 0BL.
Marion & Clive Stainton,
www.marionet.co.uk/the_brooks.
*12m SW of Hereford. From the A465
Hereford to Abergavenny rd, turn L
at Pontrilas onto B4347, take next
R, then immediate L signed Orcop &
Garway Hill. Garden 1¾m on L.* Sun
11 June, Sun 10 Sept (2-5). Adm
£4, chd free. Home-made teas.
This 2½-acre Golden Valley garden
incl part-walled enclosed vegetable
garden and greenhouse (wind/
solar-powered), orchard, ornamental,
perennial, shade and shrub borders,
wildlife pond, evolving arboretum
cum coppice, and meadows with
stunning views. Surrounding a stone
1684 farmhouse (not open), the
garden has mature elements, but
much has been created since 2006,
with future development plans.

❀ ☕

11 ◆ BRYAN'S GROUND

Letchmoor Lane, Stapleton,
Presteigne, LD8 2LP.
David Wheeler & Simon
Dorrell, 01544 260001,
simondorrell@gmail.com,
www.bryansground.co.uk. *12m
NW of Leominster. Between Kinsham
& Stapleton. At Mortimer's Cross take
B4362 signed Presteigne. At Combe,
follow signs. SATNAV is misleading.
Coaches: please pre-book.* For NGS:
Mon 8 May (2-5). Adm £6, chd
£2. Home-made teas. For other
opening times and information,
please phone, email or visit garden
website.
8-acre internationally renowned
contemporary reinterpretation of an
Arts and Crafts garden dating from
1912, conceived as series of rooms
with yew and box topiary, parterres,
colour-themed flower and shrub
borders, reflecting pools, potager,
Edwardian greenhouse, heritage
apple orchard, follies. Arboretum of
400 specimen trees and shrubs with
wildlife pool beside R Lugg. Home
of Hortus, garden journal. Featured
in RHS The Garden magazine. The
majority of the garden is accessible
by wheelchair, though there are
some steps adjoining the terrace.

♿ 🐑 🐄 ❀ 🚌 ☕

12 NEW BURNT HOUSE FARM

Ashford Carbonel, Ludlow,
SY8 4LD. Julie Alviti, 01584 711544,
juliealviti@hotmail.com. *3m SE
Ludlow. Turn L off A49 (Ludlow -
Leominster) at Xrds 0.25m past
B4361 signed Ashford Carbonel, over
2 bridges, over 1st Xrds, R at 2nd Xrds
signed Little Hereford, Tenbury. Large
white FM house on L in .75m.* Sun 16,
Sun 23 July (2-6). Adm £4, chd
free. Home-made teas. Visits also
by arrangement in July for groups
10+ booked in advance.
¾ acre farmhouse garden
developed over 35 years by
current owners. Lawn with mixed
borders, patio, pond and gazebo.
Garden rooms including vegetable
garden with raised beds, cut flower
garden, parterre and gravel garden.
Extensively planted stream and
pond, orchard, cottage garden with
traditional potting shed and vintage
tools. Unusual plants, 60+ clematis.
Many seating areas. Some deep
water. Indoor tearoom. Some steps.

♿ ❀ 🚌 ☕

13 BURY COURT FARMHOUSE

Ford Street, Wigmore, Leominster,
HR6 9UP. Margaret & Les Barclay,
01568 770618, l.barclay@zoho.com.
*10m from Leominster, 10m from
Knighton, 8m from Ludlow. On A4110
from Leominster, at Wigmore turn R
just after shop & garage. Follow signs to
parking and garden.* Sun 9 Apr (2-5).
Adm £4, chd free. Home-made
teas. Opening with Wigmore
Gardens on Sun 17 Sept. Visits
also by arrangement Feb to Oct
individual visitors and groups of
any size.
¾ acre garden, 'rescued' since
1997, surrounds the 1840's stone
farmhouse (not open). The courtyard
contains a pond, mixed borders, fruit
trees and shrubs, with steps up to
a terrace which leads to lawn and
vegetable plot. The main garden
(semi-walled) is on two levels with
mixed borders, greenhouse, pond,
mini-orchard with daffodils in spring,
and wildlife areas. Year-round colour.
Limited access only for wheelchairs
(gravelled access).

🐄 ❀ 🚌 ☕

14 BYECROFT

Welshman's Lane, Bircher,
Leominster, HR6 0BP. Sue &
Peter Russell, 01568 780559,
peterandsuerussell@btinternet.
com, www.byecroft.weebly.com.
*6m N of Leominster. From Leominster
take B4361. Turn L at T-junction
with B4362. ¼m beyond Bircher
village turn R at war memorial into
Welshman's Lane, signed Bircher
Common.* Visits by arrangement
Apr to Oct for groups of 10+.
Adm £4, chd free. Home-made
teas.
Developed almost from scratch
over 8 yrs, Byecroft is a compact
garden stuffed full of interesting
plants, many (incl all acers) grown
from seed. Herbaceous borders,
pergola with old roses, formal
pond, lots of pots, vegetable garden,
wild flower orchard, soft fruit area.
Sue and Peter are retired nursery
owners and hope to offer a good
sales table. Most areas accessible
with assistance. Some small steps.

❀ 🚌 ☕

15 ◆ CAVES FOLLY NURSERIES

Evendine Lane, Colwall,
WR13 6DX. Wil Leaper &
Bridget Evans, 01684 540631,
bridget@cavesfolly.com,
www.cavesfolly.com. *1¼m NE of
Ledbury. B4218. Between Malvern
& Ledbury. Evendine Lane, off
Colwall Green.* For NGS: Sun 4
June (2-5). Adm £3, chd free.
Home-made teas. For other
opening times and information,
please phone, email or visit garden
website.
Organic nursery and display gardens.
Specialist growers of cottage garden
plants herbs and alpines. All plants
are grown in peat free organic
compost. This is not a manicured
garden! It is full of drifts of colour
and wild flowers and a haven for
wildlife.

♿ 🐄 ❀ 🚌 🛏 ☕

16 CHURCH COTTAGE

Hentland, Ross-on-Wye,
HR9 6LP. Sue Emms & Pete
Weller, 01989 730222,
sue.emms@mac.com. *6m from
Ross-on-Wye. A49 from Ross. R turn*

to Hentland/Kynaston. At bottom of hill sharp R to St Dubricius Church. Narrow lane - please take care. Unsuitable for motor homes/ caravans. **Every Tue and Wed 30 May to 9 Aug (2-5). Adm £3, chd free. Home-made teas. Visits also by arrangement June to Aug groups welcome.**
Garden designer and plantswoman's ½-acre evolving garden packed with plants, many unusual varieties mixed with old favourites, providing interest over a long period. Wildlife pond, rose garden, potager, mixed borders, white terrace, gravel garden. Interesting plant combinations and design ideas to inspire.

✿ ☕

17 CLOISTER GARDEN

Pant Hall, Willey, Presteigne, LD8 2LY. Malcolm Temple & Karen Roberts, 01544 260066, karmal@live.co.uk, www.karenontheborders. wordpress.com. *3m N of Presteigne. Exactly 3m from Lugg Bridge at St Andrews Church in Presteigne. Follow rd from bridge, signed to Willey. Pass Stapleton Castle on R. Pant Hall on L on 3rd hill - blue house.* **Sun 25 June (2-5). Adm £4, chd free. Cream teas. Visits also by arrangement July & Aug small groups (5 to 10 people).**
Total 6 acres. ½ acre of lavender borders, rose bank, terraced lawns and shrubberies leading down to a bog garden. Over a brook to a birch grove, Wave Garden and up to orchard terraces. Beyond is a new 3 acre woodland, planted between avenues and a central meadow. Behind the house is a layout for the cloister, a swimming pond and wild field - level at the top ready for an Earthwork Art project. Artist designed garden.

✿ ☕

18 CODDINGTON VINEYARD

Coddington, HR8 1JJ. Sharon & Peter Maiden, 01531 641817, sgmaiden@yahoo.co.uk, www.coddingtonvineyard.co.uk. *4m NE of Ledbury. From Ledbury to Malvern A449, follow brown*

signs to Coddington Vineyard. **Tue 21, Fri 24, Tue 28 Feb (12-3). Adm £4.50, chd free. Home-made teas. Sun 16, Mon 17 Apr (12-4.30). Combined adm with Woofields Farm £8, chd free. Single garden adm £4.50. Afternoon teas and light lunches in barn. Visits also by arrangement Feb to Oct open for groups of 10 or more.**
5 acres incl 2-acre vineyard, listed farmhouse, threshing barn and cider mill. Garden with terraces, wild flower meadow, woodland with massed spring bulbs, large pond with wildlife, stream garden with masses of primula and hosta. Hellebores and snowdrops, hamamelis and parrotia. Azaleas followed by roses and perennials. Lots to see all year.

🏕 🐄 ✿ 🚌 🏛 ☕

19 DOVECOTE BARN

Stoke Lacy, Bromyard, HR7 4HJ. Gill Pinkerton & Adrian Yeeles. *4m S of Bromyard on A465. Turn into lane running alongside Stoke Lacy Church. Parking in 50 metres.* **Sun 11, Sun 18 June, Sun 24 Sept (2-5). Adm £4, chd free. Home-made teas at Stoke Lacy Church adjacent to Dovecote Barn.**
Nestling in the unspoilt Lodon Valley, a 2-acre, organic, wildlife-friendly garden designed in 2008. Featuring ornamental vegetable and fruit gardens, peaceful and romantic pond area, copse with specimen trees for spring and autumn colour, winter walk, wild flower meadow and dry garden. The C17 barn, framed by cottage garden planting, looks out over the garden to the Malvern Hills beyond. Gravel paths.

♿ ✿ ☕

20 GRANTSFIELD

nr Kimbolton, Leominster, HR6 0ET. Mrs R Polley, 01568 613338. *3m NE of Leominster. A49 N from Leominster, at A4112 turn R, then immed R (signed Hamnish), 1st L, then R at Xrds. Garden on R after ½m.* **Visits by arrangement Apr to Sept individuals and groups (max 10). Adm £3.50, chd free. Home-made teas.**
Large, informal country garden in contrasting styles surrounding old

stone farmhouse. Wide variety of unusual plants, mature specimen trees and shrubs, old roses, climbers, herbaceous borders, superb views. 1½-acre orchard and kitchen garden. Spring bulbs.

♿ ✿ ☕

21 GRENDON COURT

Upton Bishop, Ross on Wye, Herefordshire, HR9 7QP. Mark & Kate Edwards, 01971 339126, kate@grendoncourt.co.uk, www.icloud.com/ sharedalbum/#B0kGgZLKuGZ6oki. *3m NE of Ross-on-Wye. M50, J3 . Hereford B4224 Moody Cow PH, 1m open gate on R. From Ross. A40, B449, Xrds R Upton Bishop. 100yds on R by cream cottage.* **Sun 11 June (2-5.30). Combined adm with Brockhampton Cottage £10, chd free. Single garden adm £5. Home made teas. Visits also by arrangement June to Oct, lunch provided for groups up to 65.**
A contemporary garden designed by Tom Stuart-Smith. Planted on 2 levels, a clever collection of mass-planted perennials and grasses of different heights, textures and colour give all-yr interest. The upper walled garden with a sea of flowering grasses makes a highlight. Views of the new pond and valley walk. Visit Brockhampton Cottage (1-4) before you visit us (picnic in parking field). Please note that Grendon Court garden does not open until 2pm. Featured in Gardens Illustrated, Country Life, Country Gardens, Hereford Times. Wheelchair access possible.

♿ 🐄 🅳 ☕

The National
Garden Scheme
is Marie
Curie's largest
single funder

Midland Farm

sign to garden & parking. Good for SATNAV. **Sun 18 June (11-5). Adm £4, chd free. Home-made teas.** Recently created, this contemporary organic garden has large swathes and eclectic mixes of herbaceous plants and grasses giving an air of maturity. Alliums, Astrantias and interesting umbels meander through skeletal metal framework and patinated corrugated iron structures, referencing a past life. Atmospheric, serene. Aromatic gravel garden, swimming pond (unfenced). Stone paths. Panoramic Views.

✿ ⌂ ☕

25 NEW THE HURST

Bosbury Road, Cradley, Malvern, WR13 5LT. Mike Hames. *16m E of Hereford, 11m W of Worcester. 'The Hurst' is situated directly on the Bosbury Rd. The garden is to the rear. From the junction of A4103 & B4220, garden is 0.7m towards Bosbury on the L. On-road parking.* **Mon 1 May (12-5). Adm £3.50, chd free. Home-made teas.** A south-facing country garden of half an acre with strong cottage-garden influences and productive fruit and vegetable plots, backing onto a heritage orchard with a stream and extensive views to the western slopes of the Malvern Hills. The orchard is home to a small flock of Herdwick sheep. Colourful collection of spring bulbs. Mostly level but gently sloping gravel and grass track to lower area. Orchard not suitable for wheelchairs.

♿ ✿ ☕

26 IVY CROFT

Ivington Green, Leominster, HR6 0JN. Sue & Roger Norman, 01568 720344, ivycroft@homecall.co.uk, www.ivycroftgarden.co.uk. *3m SW of Leominster. From Leominster take Ryelands Rd to Ivington. Turn R at church, garden ¾m on R. From A4110 signed Ivington, garden 1¾m on L.* **Every Thur 2 Feb to 23 Feb (9-4). Adm £4, chd free. Home-made teas. Sun 23 Apr, Sun 28, Mon 29 May, Sun 6 Aug (2-5.30). Combined adm with Aulden Farm £7, chd free. Single garden adm £4. Home**

22 ◆ HEREFORD CATHEDRAL GARDENS

Hereford, HR1 2NG. Dean of Hereford Cathedral, 01432 374202, visits@herefordcathedral.org, www.herefordcathedral.org. *Centre of Hereford. Approach rds to the Cathedral are signed. Tours leave from information desk in the cathedral building or as directed.* For NGS: **Fri 16 June (10-4). Adm £5, chd free. Light refreshments in Cathedral's Cloister Café. For other opening times and information, please phone, email or visit garden website.** *Donation to Homeless Charity.*

Guided tours of historic award winning gardens which won 2 top awards in 'It's Your Neighbourhood 2012 &13'. The tour incl: courtyard garden; an atmospheric cloisters garden enclosed by C15 buildings; the Vicar's Choral garden; the Dean's garden; and 2 acre Bishop's garden with fine trees, vegetable and cutting garden, outdoor chapel for meditation in a floral setting, leading to the R Wye. Collection of plants with ecclesiastical connections in College Garden. Featured in Country Life Magazine. Partial wheelchair access.

♿ ⌂ ☕

HIGH VIEW
See Worcestershire

23 HILL HOUSE FARM

Knighton, LD7 1NA. Simon & Caroline Gourlay, 01547 528542, simongourlay@btinternet.com. *4m SE of Knighton. S of A4113 via Knighton (Llanshay Lane, 3m) or Bucknell (Reeves Lane, 3m).* **Sat 15, Sun 16 July (2-5.30). Adm £5, chd free. Cream teas. Visits also by arrangement May to Oct.** 5 acre south facing hillside garden developed over past 40 years with magnificent views over unspoilt countryside. Some herbaceous around the house with extensive lawns and mown paths surrounded by roses, shrubs and specimen trees leading to the half acre Oak Pool 200ft below house. Transport available from bottom of garden if required.

🐑 ⌂ ☕

24 NEW THE HOP HOUSE

Field Farm, Knighton-On-Teme, Tenbury Wells, WR15 8LT. Rob & Kim Hurst, www.thecottageherbery.co.uk. *Centre of Knighton-on-Teme Village. 5m E of Tenbury Wells on the A456 to Newnham Bridge follow sign L to Knighton-on-Teme approx 1m on L*

made teas. 2018: **Thur 1, Thur 8, Thur 15, Thur 22 Feb. Visits also by arrangement all year.** A maturing rural garden with areas of meadow, wood and orchard, blending with countryside and providing habitat for wildlife. The cottage is surrounded by borders, raised beds, trained pears and containers giving all year interest. Paths lead to the wider garden including herbaceous borders, vegetable garden framed with espalier apples and seasonal pond with willows, ferns and grasses. Snowdrops. Partial wheelchair access.

&♿ ❋ 🚌 ☕

GROUP OPENING

27 KENTCHURCH GARDENS
Pontrilas, HR2 0DB. *12m SW of Hereford. From Hereford A465 to Abergavanny, at Pontrilas turn L signed Kentchurch. After 2m fork L, after Bridge Inn. Drive opp church.* **Sun 25 June, Sun 16 July (11-5). Combined adm £5, chd free. Home-made teas.**

KENTCHURCH COURT
Mrs Jan Lucas-Scudamore,
01981 240228,
jan@kentchurchcourt.co.uk,
www.kentchurchcourt.co.uk.
🛏

UPPER LODGE
Jo Gregory.

Kentchurch Court is sited close to the Welsh border. The large stately home dates to C11 and has been in the Scudamore family for over 1000yrs. The deer-park surrounding the house dates back to the Knights Hospitallers of Dinmore and lies at the heart of an estate of over 5000 acres. Historical characters associated with the house incl Welsh hero Owain Glendower, whose daughter married Sir John Scudamore. The house was modernised by John Nash in 1795. First opened for NGS in 1927. Formal rose garden, traditional vegetable garden redesigned with colour, scent and easy access. Walled garden and herbaceous borders, rhododendrons and wild flower walk. Deer-park and ancient woodland. Extensive collection of mature trees and shrubs. Stream with habitat for spawning trout. Upper Lodge is a tranquil and well-established walled cottage garden situated at the centre of the main garden. Incl a wide variety of herbaceous plants, bulbs and shrubs ranging from traditional favourites to the rare and unusual. Most of the gardens can be accessed by wheelchairs.

&♿ ❋ 🚌 ☕

Upper Tan House

© Val Corbett

28 LAWLESS HILL

Sellack, Ross-on-Wye,
HR9 6QP. Keith Meehan &
Katalin Andras, 07595 678837,
Lawlesshill@gmail.com. *4m NW
of Ross-on-Wye. Western end of
M50. On A49 to Hereford, take
2nd R, signed Sellack. After 2m,
turn R by white house, to Sellack
church. At next church sign, turn L.
Garden halfway down lane, before
church.* Visits by arrangement
individuals and small groups
welcome. Adm £5, chd free.
Modernist Japanese-influenced
garden with dramatic views over R
Wye. Collection of 'rooms' sculpted
from the steep hillside using network
of natural stone walls and huge rocks.
Among exotic and unusual plantings,
natural ponds are held within
the terracing, forming waterfalls
between them. Due to steep steps
and stepping stones open by water,
the garden is unsuitable for the less
mobile and young children. Tea and
cake in the round house and magical
views overlooking waterfall and the
river valley.

LITTLE MALVERN COURT

See Worcestershire

29 LOWER HOPE

Lower Hope Estate, Ullingswick,
Hereford, HR1 3JF. Mr & Mrs
Clive Richards, 01432 820557,
cliverichards@crco.co.uk,
www.lowerhopefarms.co.uk. *5m S
of Bromyard. A465 N from Hereford,
after 6m turn L at Burley Gate onto
A417 towards Leominster. After
approx 2m turn R to Lower Hope.
After ½ m garden on L. Disabled
parking available.* Sun 9 Apr, Sun
21 May, Sun 9 July, Sun 17 Sept
(2-5). Adm £6, chd £1. Tea and
cakes. Visits also by arrangement
Apr to Sept for private parties
of 20+, only in week following
each NGS open day.
Outstanding 5-acre garden with
wonderful seasonal variations.
Impeccable lawns with herbaceous
borders, rose gardens, white garden,
Mediterranean, Italian and Japanese
gardens. Natural streams, man-made
waterfalls, bog gardens. Woodland
with azaleas and rhododendrons
with lime avenue to lake with wild
flowers and bulbs. Glasshouses
with exotic plants and breeding
butterflies. Prizewinning Hereford
cattle and Suffolk sheep. Featured in
Hereford Times and on local radio.

30 NEW LOWER HOUSE FARM

Vine Lane, Sutton, Tenbury
Wells, WR15 8RL. Mrs Anne
Durstan Smith, 01885 410233,
www.kyre-equestrian.co.uk. *3m
SE of Tenbury Wells; 8m NW of
Bromyard. From Tenbury take A4214
to Bromyard. After approx 3m turn
R into Vine Lane, then R fork to LH
Farm.* Wed 31 May, Wed 14 June
(2-6). Adm £3.50, chd free.
Home-made teas.
Award-winning country garden
surrounding C16 farm-house (not
open) on working farm. Herbaceous
borders, roses, box-parterre,
productive kitchen and cutting
garden, spring garden, ha-ha allowing
wonderful views. Wildlife pond
and children's activities in adjoining
field. Walkers can enjoy numerous
footpaths across the farm land.
Home to Kyre Equestrian Centre
with access to safe rides and riding
events.

31 ♦ MIDDLE HUNT HOUSE

Walterstone, Hereford,
HR2 0DY. Rupert & Antoinetta
Otten, 01873 860359,
rupertotten@gmail.com,
Gardenofthewind.co.uk. *4m W of
Pandy, 17m S of Hereford, 10m N of
Abergavenny. A465 to Pandy, West
towards Longtown, turn R at Clodock
Church, 1m on R. Disabled parking
available.* For NGS: Sat 26, Sun
27 Aug (2-5). Adm £5, chd free.
Home-made teas. For other
opening times and information,
please phone, email or visit garden
website.
A modern garden using swathes
of herbaceous plants and grasses,
surrounding stone built farmhouse
and barns with stunning views
of the Black Mountains. Special
features: rose border, hornbeam
alley, formal parterre with sensory
plants, fountain court with William
Pye water feature, architecturally
designed greenhouse complex,
vegetable gardens. Carved lettering
and sculpture throughout, garden
covering about 4 acres. Garden
seating throughout the site on
stone, wood and metal benches

Lower Hope

including some with carved lettering. The garden is also the home of part of the National Collection of Contemporary Memorial Art on loan from the Lettering and Commemorative arts Trust. Partial wheelchair access.

 ♿ 🐄 ✳ 🚗 ☕ ♨

Your visit has already helped 600 more people gain access to a Parkinson's nurse

32 MIDLAND FARM
Pig Street, Norton Wood, HR4 7BP. Sarah & Charles Smith, 01544 318575, sarah@midlandfarm.co.uk. *10m NW of Hereford. From Hereford take the A480 towards Kington. ½m after Norton Canon turn L towards Calver Hill. At bottom of the hill turn R into Pig St, garden ¼m on L.* Sun 11, Sun 25 June, Sun 3 Sept (12-4.30). Adm £4, chd free. Home-made teas. **Visits also by arrangement May to Sept.**
A new 1.2 acre cottage garden begun in 2008 . Designed as a series of rooms incl bee, spring and kitchen gardens; perennials a speciality. Featured in The Garden and Country Living.

✳ 🚐 ☕

33 MONTPELIER COTTAGE
Brilley, Whitney-on-Wye, Hereford, HR3 6HF. Dr Noel Kingsbury & Ms Jo Eliot, noel.k57@virgin.net, www.noelkingsbury.com. *Between Hay-on-Wye & Kington. From A438 ½m E of Rhydspence Inn, take rd signed Brilley, then 0.9m. From Kington, follow rd to Brilley, then 0.6m from Brilley Church.* Sun 21 May (2-5). Adm £5, chd free. Home-made teas.
Exuberant wild-style garden created

by well-known garden writer. Approx 1 acre of garden and trial beds where English cottage style meets German parks and American prairie. Wide range of perennials, plus ponds, vegetable garden and fruit. A further 3 acres incl hay meadow habitat and unusual wild flower-rich wet meadow. Children's playground.

🐄 ✳ 🚗 🚐 ☕

34 ♦ MOORS MEADOW GARDENS & NURSERY
Collington, Bromyard, HR7 4LZ. Ros Bissell, 01885 410318/07812 041179, moorsmeadow@hotmail.co.uk, www.moorsmeadow.co.uk. *4m N of Bromyard, on B4214. ½m up lane follow yellow arrows.* For NGS: Mon 3 Apr, 8 May, 5 June, 3 July, 7 Aug (11-5). Adm £6, chd £1. **For other opening times and information, please phone, email or visit garden website.**
Gaining international recognition for its phenomenal range of wildlife and rarely seen plant species, this inspirational 7-acre organic hillside garden is a 'must see'. Full of peace, secret corners and intriguing features and sculptures with fernery, grass garden, extensive shrubberies, herbaceous beds, meadow, dingle, pools and kitchen garden. Resident Artist Blacksmith. Huge range of unusual and rarely seen plants from around the world. Unique home-crafted sculptures. Britain's Best Gardeners Garden - bronze medal.

✳

35 NEWPORT HOUSE
Almeley, HR3 6LL. David & Jenny Watt, 07754 234903, david.gray510@btinternet.com. *5m S of Kington. 1m from Almeley Church, on rd to Kington. From Kington take A4111 to Hereford. After 4m turn L to Almeley, continue 2m, garden on L.* Mon 12, Tue 13, Wed 14, Thur 15, Fri 16 June (11-7). Adm £5, chd free. Home-made teas. **Visits also by arrangement May to Oct.**
20 acres of garden, woods and lake (with walks). Formal garden set on 3 terraces with large mixed borders framed by formal hedges, in front

of Georgian House (not open). 2½-acre walled organic garden in restoration since 2009.

♿ ☕

36 OLD COLWALL HOUSE
Old Colwall, Malvern, WR13 6HF. Mr & Mrs Roland Trafford-Roberts, 01684 540618, garden1889@aol.com. *3m NE of Ledbury. From Ledbury, turn L off A449 to Malvern towards Coddington. Signed from 2½m along lane. Signed from Colwall and Bosbury.* Sun 11 June (2-5). Adm £5, chd free. Home-made teas. **Visits also by arrangement groups of 10+ from mid April - mid October. Children very welcome.**
Early C18 garden on a site owned by the Church till Henry VIII. Walled lawns and terraces on various levels. The heart is the yew walk, a rare survival from the 1700s: 100 yds long, 30ft high, cloud clipped, and with a church aisle-like quality inside. Later centuries have brought a summer house, water garden, and rock gardens. Fine trees, incl enormous veteran yew; fine views. Steep in places.

🐄 ✳ ☕

37 THE OLD CORN MILL
Aston Crews, Ross-on-Wye, HR9 7LW. Mrs Jill Hunter, 01989 750059. *5m E of Ross-on-Wye. A40 Ross to Gloucester. Turn L at T-lights at Lea Xrds onto B4222 signed Newent, Garden ½m on L. Parking for disabled down drive. DO NOT USE THE ABOVE POSTCODE IN YOUR SATNAV - try HR9 7LA.* Sun 12 Feb, Sun 26 Mar, Sun 16, Mon 17, Sun 30 Apr, Sun 14, Sun 28, Mon 29 May (1-5). Adm £5, chd free, includes teas. **Visits also by arrangement Feb to Oct max 50+. Refreshments incl in adm.**
4 acres of woodland, meadows, ponds and streams. A tranquil and relaxed country garden of scents, sights and sounds. Interest all year with drifts of tulips, wild daffodils and common spotted orchids in spring. Good Autumn colour. Pop-up Art Exhibition in house. Featured in Country Homes and Interiors.

🐄 ✳ 🚗 ☕

38 THE OLD RECTORY

Thruxton, HR2 9AX. Mr & Mrs Andrew Hallett, 01981 570401, ar.hallett@gmail.com, www.thruxtonrectory.co.uk. *6m SW of Hereford. A465 to Allensmore. At Locks (Shell) garage take B4348 towards Hay-on-Wye. After 1½m turn L towards Abbey Dore & Cockyard. Car park 150yds on L.* **Sat 3, Sun 4 June, Sun 10 Sept (12-5.30). Adm £4, chd free. Home-made teas. Visits also by arrangement May to Sept.** With breathtaking views over Herefordshire countryside this four acre garden - two acres formal and two acres paddock with ornamental trees and shrubs, and heritage apples - has been created since 2007. Constantly changing plantsman's garden stocked with unusual perennials and roses, together with woodland borders, gazebo, vegetable parterre, glasshouse and natural pond. Many places to sit and relax. Most plants labelled. Chickens, Mr Reynard permitting. Mainly level with some gravel paths.

PEAR TREE COTTAGE

See Worcestershire

39 PERRYCROFT

Jubilee Drive, Upper Colwall, Malvern, WR13 6DN. Gillian & Mark Archer, 07858 393767, gillianarcher@live.co.uk, www.perrycroft.co.uk. *Between Malvern & Ledbury. On B4232 between British Camp & Wyche cutting. Park in Gardiners Quarry pay & display car park on Jubilee Drive, short walk to the garden. No parking at house except for disabled by prior arrangement.* **Sun 30 Apr (12-5). Combined adm with The Picton Garden £7.50, chd free. Single adm £5. Home-made teas. Every Thur and Fri 4 May to 23 June (1-5). Every Thur and Fri 7 Sept to 13 Oct (1-5). Tea. Sun 1 Oct (2-5). Adm £5, chd free. Home-made teas Suns only, self-service tea on Thursday and Friday. Visits also by arrangement Mar to Dec groups and individuals welcome**

by written arrangement excluding July & August. 10 acre garden and woodland on upper slopes of the Malvern Hills with magnificent views. Arts and Crafts house (not open), garden partly designed by CFA Voysey. Walled formal garden with mixed and herbaceous borders, yew and box hedges and topiary. Dry garden, natural wild flower meadows, ponds (unfenced), bog garden, woodland walks. Some steep and uneven paths. Featured in RHS The Garden magazine. This garden is not suitable for wheelchairs, due to steep and uneven grass and gravel paths, and steps.

40 ◆ THE PICTON GARDEN

Old Court Nurseries, Walwyn Road, Colwall, WR13 6QE. Mr & Mrs Paul Picton, 01684 540416, oldcourtnurseries@btinternet.com, www.autumnasters.co.uk. *3m W of Malvern. On B4218 (Walwyn Rd) N of Colwall Stone. Turn off A449 from Ledbury or Malvern onto the B4218 for Colwall.* **For NGS: Sun 30 Apr (12-5). Combined adm with Perrycroft £7.50, chd free. Single adm £3.50. Sat 5, Sun 13, Thur 24, Mon 28 Aug, Wed 13, Thur 28 Sept, Mon 9, Fri 20 Oct (11-5). Adm £3.50, chd free. Homemade teas at Perrycroft on Sun 30 April For other opening times and information, please phone, email or visit garden website.** 1½ acres W of Malvern Hills. Bulbs and a multitude of woodland plants in spring. Interesting perennials and shrubs in Aug. In late Sept and early Oct colourful borders display the National Plant Collection of Michaelmas daisies, backed by autumn colouring trees and shrubs. Many unusual plants to be seen, incl bamboos, more than 100 different ferns and acers. Features raised beds and silver garden. National Plant Collection of autumn-flowering asters and an extensive nursery that has been growing them since 1906. Featured in Amateur gardening. Wheelchair access gravel paths but

all fairly level, no steps.

41 POOLE COTTAGE

Coppett Hill, Goodrich, Goodrich, Ross on Wye, HR9 6JH. Jo Ward-Ellison & Roy Smith, 01600 890148, jo@ward-ellison.com, www.herefordshiregarden.wordpress.com. *5m from Ross on Wye, 7m from Monmouth. Above Goodrich Castle in Wye Valley AONB Goodrich signed from A40 or take B4234 from Ross. No parking close to garden. Park in village & follow signs. Shuttle service available up & down the hill or walk 10-15 minutes up from village.* **Sat 9, Sun 10 Sept (11-5). Adm £4, chd free. Home-made teas. Visits also by arrangement in Sept for individuals and groups of up to 15.** Home to designer Jo Ward-Ellison this 2 acre hillside garden is now 6 years old and maturing into the landscape. With a predominately naturalistic style, contemporary feel and many grasses and later flowering perennials 2017 is the 1st opportunity to visit in September. Features include grass hedges, a pond loved by wildlife, small orchard and kitchen garden with fabulous views.

42 ◆ RALPH COURT GARDENS

Edwyn Ralph, Bromyard, HR7 4LU. Mr & Mrs Morgan, 01885 483225, ralphcourtgardens@aol.com, www.ralphcourtgardens.co.uk. *From Bromyard follow the Tenbury rd for approx 1m. On entering the village of Edwyn Ralph take 1st turning on R towards the church.* **For NGS: Sat, Sun 18, 19 Mar, 20, 21 May, 24, 25 June, 15, 16 July, 14, 15 Oct (10-5). Adm £8, chd £5. Light refreshments. For other opening times and information, please phone, email or visit garden website.** 12 amazing gardens set in the grounds of a gothic rectory. A family orientated garden with a twist, incorporating an Italian Piazza, an African Jungle, Dragon Pool,

Alice in Wonderland and the elves in their conifer forest. These are just a few of the themes within this stunning garden. Licenced Tea room overlooks Malvern Hills. 120 seater Licenced Restaurant offering lunches, Sunday roasts, Afternoon tea and our homemade cakes. All areas ramped for wheelchair and pushchair access. Some grass areas, without help can be challenging during wet periods.

43 RHODDS FARM
Lyonshall, HR5 3LW. Richard & Cary Goode, 01544 340120, cary.goode@russianaeros.com, www.rhoddsfarm.co.uk. *1m E of Kington. From A44 take small turning S just E of Penrhos Farm, 1m E of Kington. Continue 1m, garden straight ahead.* **Fri 5, Sat 6 May, Fri 2, Sat 3 June, Fri 7, Sat 8 July, Fri 4, Sat 5 Aug (11-6). Adm £5, chd free. Tea and cake will be available for guests to help themselves in return for a donation.**
The garden began in 2005 and is still a work in progress. The site is challenging with steep banks rising to overhanging woodland but has wonderful views. Formal garden leads to new dovecote, mixed borders have interest throughout the year with the double herbaceous borders of hot colours being particularly good in summer. Woodland walks with wonderful bluebells in spring. See garden website for detailed description. Featured in English Garden & House and Garden.

44 ROSS-ON-WYE COMMUNITY GARDEN
Old Gloucester Rd, Ross-On-Wye, HR9 5PB. Haygrove Ltd. *The garden is situated halfway along Old Gloucester Rd and opp the former Walter Scott School.* **Sat 17, Sun 18 June (10-4). Adm £2.50, chd free.**
The Community Garden is a three and a half acre site in the centre of Ross. The project works mainly with adults with learning disabilities, mental health illnesses and those who are long term unemployed.

Produce and plants are for sale. Please note: Throughout 2017 and 2018 work will be undertaken to move away from a central focus on fruit and vegetables to four themed ornamental gardens. Half of the site is accessible for those using wheelchairs.

45 SHEEPCOTE
Putley, Ledbury, HR8 2RD. Tim & Julie Beaumont. *5m W of Ledbury off the A438 Hereford to Ledbury rd. Passenger drop off; parking 4 minute walk.* **Sun 28 May (1.30-6). Adm £5, chd free. Home-made teas.**
1/3 acre garden taken in hand from 2011 retaining many quality plants, shrubs and trees from earlier gardeners. Topiary holly, box, hawthorn, privet and yew formalise the varied plantings around the croquet lawn and gravel garden; beds with heathers, azaleas, lavender surrounded by herbaceous perennials and bulbs; pond in shade of ancient apple tree; kitchen garden with raised beds.

46 SHUCKNALL COURT
Hereford, HR1 4BH. Mr & Mrs Henry Moore, 01432 850230. *5m E of Hereford. On A4103, signed (southerly) Weston Beggard, 5m E of Hereford towards Worcester.* **Sun 18 June (11-6). Adm £5, chd free. Cream teas. Ploughman's lunches. Visits also by arrangement May & June.**
Tree paeonies in May. Large collection of species, old-fashioned and shrub roses. Mixed borders in old walled farmhouse garden. Wild garden, vegetables and fruit. Himalayan type roses growing into trees, from mid June. Partial wheelchair access.

SHUTTIFIELD COTTAGE
See Worcestershire

47 SOUTHBOURNE & PINE LODGE
Dinmore, Hereford, HR1 3JR. Lavinia Sole & Frank Ryding. *8m N of Hereford; 8m S of Leominster. From Hereford on A49, turn R at bottom of Dinmore Hill towards*

Bodenham, gardens 1m on L. From Leominster on A49, L onto A417 to Bodenham, follow NGS signs to garden. **Sun 28, Mon 29 May, Sun 27, Mon 28 Aug (11-4.30). Adm £5, chd free. Tea/coffee and homemade cakes.**
2 south facing adjacent gardens totalling 4½ acres opened as one with panoramic views over Bodenham Lakes to the Black Mountains and Malvern Hills. Southbourne: steep access to terraced lawns, herbaceous beds, shrubs and woodland garden. Pine Lodge: 2½ acres of wild woodland featuring most of Britain's native trees. Paths wind throughout the site. Rather spooky. Beware of Goblins!

Donations from the NGS enable Perennial to care for horticulturalists

48 STAPLETON CASTLE COURT GARDEN
Stapleton, Presteigne, LD8 2LS. Margaret & Trefor Griffiths. *2m N of Presteigne. From Presteigne cross Lugg Bridge at bottom of Broad St & continue to Stapleton. Do not turn towards Stapleton but follow signs to garden on R.* **Sat 27, Sun 28, Mon 29 May (2-5.30). Adm £4, chd free. Home-made teas.**
Situated on a gentle slope overlooked by the remains of Stapleton Castle. The garden, developed over the past 9 yrs by an enthusiastic plants-woman, benefits from considered and colour-themed borders. Guided tour of the castle 2.30 and 3.30 daily. Display of site history incl house ruins, mill pond, mill pit and disused turbine, etc. Your last chance to visit before the owners move next door. Wheelchairs not suitable for castle tour.

49 ◆ STOCKTON BURY GARDENS

Kimbolton, HR6 0HA. Raymond G Treasure, 07880 712649, twstocktonbury@outlook.com, www.stocktonbury.co.uk. *2m NE of Leominster. From Leominster to Ludlow on A49 turn R onto A4112. Gardens 300yds on R.* **For NGS: Sat 1 Apr (12-5). Adm £7, chd £3. Home-made teas in Tithe Barn** For other opening times and information, please phone, email or visit garden website.
Superb, sheltered 4 acre garden with colour and interest all yr. Extensive collection of plants, many rare and unusual set amongst medieval buildings. Features pigeon house, tithe barn, grotto, cider press, auricula theatre, pools, ruined chapel and rill, all surrounded by unspoilt countryside. Restaurant, serves coffee, light/ full lunches, homemade teas. All plants sold are grown on site. Stockton Bury has a small garden school - all classes to be found at www.stocktonbury.co.uk. We pride ourselves in offering great plant and gardening advice to our visitors. Over 5's £3. The garden is featured every fortnight in Amateur Gardening magazine in Tamsin Westhorpe's country gardener column. Partial wheelchair access.

  ♿ ❀ 🚗 ☕

50 UPPER TAN HOUSE

Stansbatch, Leominster, HR6 9LJ. James & Caroline Weymouth, 01544 260574, caroline. weymouth@btopenworld.com, www.uppertanhouse.com. *4m W of Pembridge. From A44 in Pembridge take turn signed Shobdon & Presteigne. After exactly 4m & at Stansbatch Nursery turn L down hill. Garden on L 100yds after chapel.* **Visits by arrangement June & July individuals and groups (16 max). Adm £5, chd free.**
S-facing garden sloping down to Stansbatch brook in idyllic spot. Deep herbaceous borders with informal and unusual planting, pond and bog garden, formal vegetable garden framed by yew hedges and espaliered pears. Reed beds, wild flower meadow with orchids. Diverse wildlife. Featured in Country Living, Garden News and Country Life.

  ❀ ☕

51 WESTON HALL

Weston-under-Penyard, Ross-on-Wye, HR9 7NS. Mr P & Miss L Aldrich-Blake, 01989 562597, aldrichblake@btinternet.com. *1m E of Ross-on-Wye. on A40 towards Gloucester.* **Visits by arrangement Apr to July groups only. Light refreshments by request at modest extra cost. Adm £4.50, chd free.**
6 acres surrounding Elizabethan house (not open). Large walled garden with herbaceous borders, vegetables and fruit, overlooked by Millennium folly. Lawns with both mature and recently planted trees, shrubs with many unusual varieties. Ornamental ponds and lake. 4 generations in the family, but still evolving year on year.

  ♿ ☕

52 NEW WHITBOURNE HALL

Whitbourne, Worcester, WR6 5SE. WHCL, www.whitbournehall.com. *6m E of Bromyard, 12m W of Worcester. From Bromyard: A44 towards Worcester, turn L into Whitbourne, L at old school (opp village hall), continue 1m, L at coach house. From Worcester: A44 towards Leominster, R to Whitbourne.* **Sun 14 May (12-4). Adm £5, chd free. Home-made teas.**
9 acres of garden with panoramic views surrounding a grade II* neo-Palladian country house built in 1862 on the Herefordshire border. Featuring an Italian parterre garden, Victorian walled garden, original glasshouses, orchard, border garden, rockery, tennis lawn and wilderness. Exhibition by resident artists.

  🐕 ☕

53 WHITFIELD

Wormbridge, HR2 9BA. Mr & Mrs Edward Clive, 01981 570202, tclive@whitfield-hereford.com, www.whitfield-hereford.com. *8m SW of Hereford. The entrance gates are off the A465 Hereford to Abergavenny rd, ½m N of Wormbridge.* **Sun 2, Sun 30** Apr (2-5). Adm £5, chd free. Home-made teas. **Visits also by arrangement Apr to Oct tour & refreshments available for 15+ groups at an extra charge.**
Parkland, wild flowers, ponds, walled garden, many flowering magnolias (species and hybrids), 1780 ginkgo tree, 1½m woodland walk with 1851 grove of coastal redwood trees. Picnic parties welcome. Dogs on leads welcome. Delicious teas. Partial access to wheelchair users, some gravel paths and steep slopes.

  ♿ 🐕 ❀ 🚗 ☕

GROUP OPENING

54 WIGMORE GARDENS

Wigmore, Leominster, HR6 9UP. *10m from Leominster, 10m from Knighton. On A4110 from Leominster, at Wigmore turn R just after shop & garage into Ford St. Follow signs to parking & gardens.* **Sun 17 Sept (2-5). Combined adm £7, chd free. Home made teas at Bury Court Farmhouse.**

BURY COURT FARMHOUSE
Margaret & Les Barclay.
(See separate entry)

2 BURY COURT PARK
Ivan & Cathy Jones.

The ancient village of Wigmore is known for its C12 castle, home to the Mortimer family and now a 'romantic ruin', and its medieval church. The two gardens are both within 100yds of the parking area. Bury Court Farmhouse has a ¾ acre garden, 'rescued' since 1997, surrounding an 1840's stone farmhouse (not open). The courtyard contains a pond, mixed borders, fruit trees and shrubs, with steps up to a terrace which leads to lawn and vegetable plots. The main garden (semi-walled) is on 2 levels with mixed borders greenhouse, pond, mini-orchard with daffodils in spring and wildlife area. The garden is designed for yr-round interest and colour. 2 Bury Court Park is a small garden with beautiful views. Herbaceous and evergreen shrub borders, pond, bog garden, gravelled areas, patio, pergola with climbers, raised beds with companion planting, greenhouse, arbour, paved seating and sun areas, lawns. Specimen trees, fruit area and watering system. Exhibition of paintings in pastel by Ivan Jones at 2 Bury Court Park.

✻ ☕ ▮

55 WINDSOR COTTAGE

Dilwyn, Hereford, HR4 8HJ. Jim & Brenda Collins, 01544 319011, jandb.windsor@gmail.com. *6m W of Leominster off A4112. Turn L off A4112 into Dilwyn. From centre of village, with PH on L, turn L. After 100y turn R. Cottage 400yds on L. Limited parking.* **Every Tue and Thur 23 May to 24 Aug (2-5.30). Adm £3.50, chd free. Home-made cakes, ground coffee and choice of teas, Gluten free available. Visits also by arrangement May to Aug for up to 20. Adm £6 incls home-made teas.**
½-acre wildlife friendly garden redesigned over the last 6yrs by present owners. Herbaceous borders, shrub bed, wildlife ponds, fruit and vegetables in raised beds. Extensive use of gravel beds. Wide selection of plants for all year

interest including peonies, irises, hostas and clematis. Exhibition of watercolour and oil paintings. Wildlife friendly garden. Plants chosen to encourage bees, birds, and butterflies. Featured in Amateur Gardening. Gravelled drive giving access to level, lawned garden.

♿ 🐕 ✻ ☕ ▮

56 WOLFERLOW HOUSE

Wolferlow, nr Upper Sapey, HR7 4QA. Stuart & Jill Smith, 01886 853311, hillheadfm@aol.com, www.holidaylettings.co.uk/ rentals/worcester/210892. *5m N of Bromyard. Off B4203 or B4214 between Upper Sapey & Stoke Bliss. Disabled parking at the house.* **Sat 17 June (10.30-5). Adm £4.50, chd free. Home-made teas.**
Visits also by arrangement June to Aug groups up to 20 or so.
Surrounded by farmland this former Victorian rectory is set within formal and informal gardens with planting to attract wildlife. Walks through the old orchard and ponds to sit by, space to relax and reflect taking in the views of borrowed landscape. Fruit, vegetable and cutting garden and wild flower meadow. Gravel paths.

♿ ✻ 🛏 ▮

57 WOODVIEW

Great Doward, Whitchurch, Ross-on-Wye, HR9 6DZ. Janet & Clive Townsend, 01600 890477, clive.townsend5@homecall.co.uk. *6m SW of Ross-on-Wye, 4m NE of Monmouth. A40 Ross/Mon At Whitchurch follow signs to Symonds Yat west, then to Doward Park campsite. Take forestry rd 1st L garden 2nd L - follow NGS signs.* **Sun 30 Apr, Sun 16, Sun 23 July (1-6). Adm £4, chd free. Home-made teas. Visits also by arrangement Apr to Sept please phone for details.**
Formal and informal gardens approx 4 acres in woodland setting. Herbaceous borders, hosta collection, mature trees, shrubs and seasonal bedding. Gently sloping lawns. Statuary and found sculpture, local limestone, rockwork and pools. Woodland garden, wild flower meadow and indigenous orchids. Collection of vintage tools and memorabilia. Croquet, clock golf and garden games.

♿ 🐕 ✻ ☕

58 WOOFIELDS FARM

Coddington, Ledbury, HR8 1JJ. Mrs Rosemary Simcock, 01531 640583. *3m N of Ledbury. From Ledbury to Malvern rd A449, follow brown signs to Coddington Vineyard.* **Sun 16, Mon 17 Apr (12-4.30). Combined adm with Coddington Vineyard £8, chd free. Single garden adm £4.50. Light lunches and afternoon teas at Coddington Vineyard. Visits also by arrangement Feb to Oct idividuals and groups.**
2-acre garden on working farm: an eclectic mixture of planting, colour all yr round. Variety in shape and texture. Spring bulbs and shrubs. Borders planted with roses, clematis, wide range of herbaceous plants, many alstromeria, gravel garden, ornamental pond. Natural pond recently re-landscaped and planted by Peter Dowle.

♿ ✻ ☕ ▮

Aulden Farm

HERTFORDSHIRE

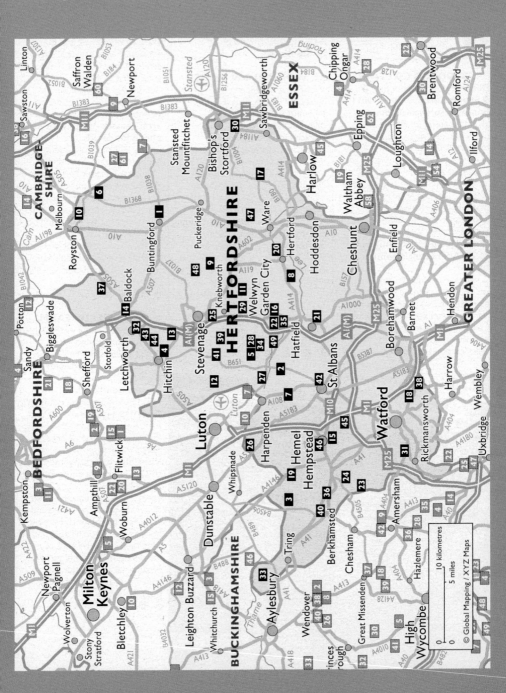

With its proximity to London, Hertfordshire became a breath of country air and a retreat for wealthy families wishing to escape the grime of the city – hence the count is peppered with large and small country estates, some of which open their garden gates for the NGS.

Hertfordshire was home for a long time to a flourishing fruit, vegetable and cut-flower trade, with produce sent up from nurseries and gardens to the London markets. There is a profusion of inviting rural areas with flower-filled country lanes and some of the best ancient woodlands carpeted with bluebells in late spring. Pretty villages sit in these rural pockets, with farmhouse and cottage gardens to visit.

Our towns, such as St Albans with its abbey, Baldock and Berkhamsted with their markets, and the garden cities of Welwyn and Letchworth all have interesting town gardens, both modern and traditional in their approach.

We have many gardens open 'by arrangement', and we are happy to arrange tours for large groups.

So next time you are heading through our county, don't just drive on – stop and visit one of our gardens to enjoy the warm welcome Hertfordshire has to offer.

Below: 120 Parkway

Volunteers

County Organiser
Julie Knight
01727 752375
julie.knight@ngs.org.uk

County Treasurer
Peter Barrett
01442 393508
peter.barrett@ngs.org.uk

Publicity
Kerrie Lloyd-Dawson
07736 442883
kerrield@yahoo.co.uk

Chris Roper
07793 739732
chris.roper79@gmail.com

Social Media
Edwina Robarts
07467 122397
edwina.robarts@gmail.com

Booklet Coordinator
Julie Loughlin
01438 871488
jloughlin11@gmail.com

New Gardens
Julie Wise
01438 821509
juliewise@f2s.com

Group Tours
Sarah Marsh
07813 083126
sarahkmarsh@hotmail.co.uk

Assistant County Organisers
Kate de Boinville
01438 869203
katedeboinville@btconnect.com

Christopher Melluish
01920 462500
c.melluish@btopenworld.com

Karen Smith
01462 673133
hertsgardeningangel@googlemail.com

OPENING DATES

All entries subject to change. For latest information check www.ngs.org.uk

Map locator numbers are shown to the right of each garden name.

February

Snowdrop Festival

Saturday 18th
Walkern Hall 48

Sunday 19th
Walkern Hall 48

Saturday 25th
Old Church Cottage 33

Sunday 26th
Old Church Cottage 33

April

Saturday 8th
◆ Hatfield House
West Garden 21
Walkern Hall 48

Sunday 9th
Walkern Hall 48

Sunday 23rd
Alswick Hall 1
◆ St Paul's Walden
Bury 41

Sunday 30th
Amwell Cottage 2

May

Sunday 7th
324 Norton Way
South 32
Patchwork 36

Friday 12th
42 Church Street 14

Sunday 14th
◆ Pembroke Farm 37
◆ St Paul's Walden
Bury 41

Sunday 21st
The Manor House,
Ayot St Lawrence 28

Friday 26th
The White Cottage 49

90th Anniversary Weekend

Sunday 28th
◆ Benington Lordship 9
NEW The Cherry Tree 13
Huntsmoor 24

Monday 29th
43 Mardley Hill 29
The White Cottage 49

June

Sunday 4th
◆ Ashridge House 3
NEW 35 Crofts Path 15
15 Gade Valley
Cottages 19
NEW Old Hall Farm
Cottage 34

Saturday 10th
Ayot Gardens 5

Sunday 11th
Ayot Gardens 5
◆ St Paul's Walden
Bury 41
Thundridge Hill House 47

Friday 16th
NEW 1 Elia Cottage 17
NEW The Millers
Cottage 30

Saturday 17th
The Lodge 26
120 Parkway 35

Sunday 18th
NEW Barley Gardens 6
NEW 1 Elia Cottage 17
The Lodge 26
NEW The Millers
Cottage 30
◆ Pembroke Farm 37
St Michael's Croft 40
Serge Hill Gardens 45

Friday 23rd
Hill House 22
Mackerye End House 27
Serendi 44

Sunday 25th
◆ Benington Lordship 9
Hill House 22
St Stephens Avenue
Gardens 42
Scudamore 43
Serendi 44

Friday 30th
Rustling End Cottage 39

July

Sunday 2nd
NEW Burloes Hall 10
◆ Home Farm Plants 23
Mackerye End House 27
Rustling End Cottage 39

Sunday 9th
9 Tannsfield Drive 46

Sunday 23rd
2 Barlings Road 7
8 Chapel Road 12
15 Gade Valley
Cottages 19

Saturday 29th
42 Falconer Road 18

Sunday 30th
35 Digswell Road 16
42 Falconer Road 18

August

Saturday 5th
42 Falconer Road 18

Sunday 6th
22a The Avenue 4
42 Falconer Road 18
9 Tannsfield Drive 46

Sunday 13th
Reveley Lodge 38

Friday 18th
8 Gosselin Road 20

Sunday 20th
8 Gosselin Road 20
Patchwork 36

Saturday 26th
NEW Beechleigh 8

Home Farm Plants

Monday 28th
NEW Beechleigh 8

September

Sunday 3rd
St Stephens Avenue
Gardens 42

Sunday 10th
Huntsmoor 24

Friday 15th
60 Bury Lane 11

Sunday 17th
60 Bury Lane 11

October

Sunday 22nd
35 Digswell Road 16

November

Saturday 4th
42 Falconer Road 18

By Arrangement

NEW 35 Crofts Path 15
35 Digswell Road 16
NEW 1 Elia Cottage 17
42 Falconer Road 18
Huntsmoor 24
NEW Morning Light 31
Patchwork 36
20 St Stephens Avenue,
St Stephens Avenue
Gardens 42
Scudamore 43
Serendi 44
9 Tannsfield Drive 46
Thundridge Hill House 47

THE GARDENS

1 ALSWICK HALL

Hare Street Road, Buntingford, SG9 0AA. Mike & Annie Johnson, www.alswickhall.co.uk. *1m from Buntingford on B1038. From the S take A10 to Buntingford, drive into town & take B1038 E towards Hare Street Village. Alswick Hall is 1m on R.* **Sun 23 Apr (12-4.30). Adm £5, chd free. Home-made teas. Teas & cake. Bar and Hog Roast.**
Listed Tudor House with 5 acres of landscaped gardens set in unspoiled farmland. Two well established natural ponds with rockeries. Herbaceous borders, shrubs, woodland walk and wild flower meadow with a fantastic selection of daffodils, tulips, camassias and crown imperial. Spring blossom, formal beds, orchard and glasshouses. Licensed Bar, Hog Roast, Teas, delicious home-made cakes, plant stall and various other trade stands. Featured in The English Garden Magazine and Hertfordshire Life. Good access for disabled with lawns and wood chip paths. Slight undulations.
& 🐕 ✿ 🚗 ☕

2 AMWELL COTTAGE

Amwell Lane, Wheathampstead, AL4 8EA. Colin & Kate Birss. *½m S of Wheathampstead. From St Helen's Church, Wheathampstead turn up Brewhouse Hill. At top L fork (Amwell Lane), 300yds down lane, park in field opp.* **Sun 30 Apr (2-5). Adm £4, chd free. Home-made teas.**
Informal garden of approx 2½ acres around C17 cottage. Large orchard of mature apples, plums and pear laid out with paths. Extensive lawns with borders, framed by tall yew hedges and old brick walls. A large variety of roses, stone seats with views, woodland pond, greenhouse, vegetable garden with raised beds and fire-pit area. Art in the Garden exhibition this year. Gravel drive.
& 🐕 ✿ Ⓓ ☕

3 ◆ ASHRIDGE HOUSE

Berkhamsted, HP4 1NS. Ashridge (Bonar Law Memorial) Trust, 01442 843491, events@ashridge.hult.edu, www.ashridgehouse.org.uk. *3m N of Berkhamsted. A4251, 1m S of Little Gaddesden.* For NGS: **Sun 4 June (2-6). Adm £4.50, chd £2.50. Light refreshments.**
For other opening times and information, please phone, email or visit garden website.
The gardens cover 190-acres forming part of the Grade II Registered Landscape of Ashridge Park. Based on designs by Humphry Repton in 1813 modified by Jeffry Wyatville. Small secluded gardens, as well as a large lawn area leading to avenues of trees. 2013 marked the 200th anniversary of Repton presenting Ashridge with the Red Book, detailing his designs for the estate.
& 🐕 🚗 ☕

4 22A THE AVENUE

Hitchin, SG4 9RL. Martin Woods, www.mwgardendesign.co.uk. *½m E of town centre. Opposite St Mary's Church head up Windmill Hill, continue to top, crossing Highbury Rd into Wymondley Rd. The Avenue is 1st turning on L.* **Sun 6 Aug (2-7). Adm £4, chd free. Light refreshments.**
Contemporary town garden combining clever design with knowledgeable plantsmanship. A patio area is bordered by a formal raised pond. Pots of unusual and interesting succulents, alpines, species pelargoniums and other tender plants line the steps which lead up to the lawn and garden beyond. Featured in The English Garden, House Beautiful and The Evening Standard. The garden is not wheelchair accessible.
☕

GROUP OPENING

5 AYOT GARDENS

Ayot St. Lawrence, Welwyn, AL6 9BT. *4m W of Welwyn, 20 mins J4 A1M. A1(M) J6 follow signs to Welwyn, Codicote (B656) then signs to Ayot St Lawrence (Shaws Corner NT). Parking in field, short walk to gardens. Disabled parking space adjacent to gardens.* **Sat 10 June (11-5). Home-made teas. Sun 11 June (2-5). Combined adm £6, chd free. Home made teas.**

2 RUINS COTTAGE

Joe & Heather Warwick.

WEST HOUSE

Alban & Susie Warwick.

Set in the centre of one of the most picturesque villages in Hertfordshire and surrounded by rolling countryside with a backdrop of the 11C ruined Church, are two quintessentially English country gardens. West House, part of The Old Rectory (not open), was landscaped 40 years ago and featured in Homes & Gardens 1987. Mature specimen trees, shrubs, herbaceous border, woodland and recently added old roses are a feature. 2 Ruins Cottages with entry through the adjacent ruined Church is an informal cottage garden with herbaceous border, fernery, ponds, rose garden, garden house, and tree deck with pastoral views towards the nearby Palladian Church where home-made teas are available all day. Coffees and lunches available at The Brocket Arms and BBQ in good weather. There are gravel paths in both gardens which may make access difficult.
& ✿ 🚗 ☕

The National Garden Scheme is the largest single funder of the Queen's Nursing Institute

GROUP OPENING

6 NEW BARLEY GARDENS

Smiths End Lane, Barley, Royston, SG8 8LL. Kristin Macdonald. *From M11, exit J10 (at Duxford) take A505 towards Royston. Follow A505 to intersection at Flint Cross, turn L for Barley (B1368). When in Barley, turn L onto Smiths End Lane. Sat Nav SG8 8LL.* Sun 18 June (12-5). Combined adm £6, chd free. Home-made teas at Dovehouse Shott. Gin and Tonics too!

NEW DOVEHOUSE SHOTT
Stephen & Justine Marsh.

NEW THE HOOPS
Georgie McMahon.

NEW SMITHS END BARN
Kristin & Sam Macdonald.

A group of 3 lovely family gardens all located along Smith's End Lane, a charming winding lane with spectacular far-reaching views over Hertfordshire. The three gardens share a variety of features, including lavender walks, luscious pink roses, deep herbaceous borders, small orchards, wildlife meadows, pond plantings and a courtyard garden. Wheelchair access is limited. Several steps to deal with but mostly manageable.

7 2 BARLINGS ROAD

Beesonend, Harpenden, AL5 2AN. Liz & Jim Machin. *1m S of Harpenden. Take A1081 S from Harpenden, after 1m turn R into Beesonend Lane, bear R into Burywick to T-junction. Turn R and follow signs.* Sun 23 July (2-5.30). Adm £3.50, chd free. Home-made teas.
A compact garden for all seasons. Borders and island beds packed with unusual perennials, climbers, shrubs and small trees. Small plant-filled formal pond. Colourful courtyard with unusual water feature Shady gold and silver corner. Some areas re-planted every year for extra interest.

❀ ☕

8 NEW BEECHLEIGH

Birch Green, Hertford, SG14 2LP. Jacky & Gary O'Leary, www.danielshea.co.uk/game-keepers-cottage-hertford. *From A1M follow signs to Hertford along A414. From Hertford on A414, take first L after Hertingfordbury roundabout and immediately right along Old Coach Road. House is mid way along Old Coach Road.* Evening opening Sat 26 Aug (5-8). Wine. Mon 28 Aug (12-5). Home-made teas. Adm £4.50, chd free.
Set in 2½ acres, the garden combines bold confident lines of contemporary planting with more traditional herbaceous borders. The house and outbuildings formed part of the historic Panshanger Estate with the new design incorporating reclaimed stone and red brick from the original buildings. Long beds of perennial grasses surround the 13m reflective pool, forming a focal point to the main house. Contemporary perennial grass borders. Wild flower meadow. Integrated fire pit and surrounding area. Artisan stalls, children's quiz. Some gravelled/stone areas.

♿ 🐾 ❀ Ⅾ ☕

9 ♦ BENINGTON LORDSHIP

Stevenage, SG2 7BS. Mr & Mrs R Bott, 01438 869668, garden@beningtonlordship.co.uk, www.beningtonlordship.co.uk. *4m E of Stevenage. In Benington Village, next to church. Signs off A602.* For NGS: Sun 28 May (12-4); Sun 25 June (12-5). Adm £5, chd free. Home-made teas in Benington parish hall, next door to garden entrance. For other opening times and information, please phone, email or visit garden website.
7-acre garden incl historic buildings, kitchen garden, lakes, roses. Spectacular herbaceous borders, unspoilt panoramic views. Wheelchair access is limited as garden is on a steep slope. Accessible WC available in parish hall only.

🚗 ☕

10 NEW BURLOES HALL

Royston, SG8 9NE. Lady Newman, www.burloeshallweddings.co.uk. *From M11/A505 turn L on Newmarket Road. 200yds 1st turning on L Burloes Hall.* Sun 2 July (12-5). Adm £5, chd free.
Home-made teas in marquee. Formal gardens with deep colourful mixed herbaceous borders. Bountiful Nepeta and white rose pergolas. Handsome beech trees and mature yew hedges with extensive lawns.

♿ 🐾 ❀ 🚗 Ⅾ ☕

11 60 BURY LANE

Datchworth, Knebworth, SG3 6SS. Delith & John Wringe. *5m S of Stevenage. Leave A1(M) at J6. Take B197 to Knebworth. Turn R at Woolmer Green signpost to Datchworth. Garden opposite Datchworth church.* Evening opening Fri 15 Sept (4-6.30). Wine. Sun 17 Sept (1-4.30). Home-made teas. Adm £4.50, chd free.
½ acre Edwardian house garden with lovely views of surrounding countryside. Windy, exposed situation demands innovative planting and a lively mix of perennials and grasses give a joyous display of texture and colour into the Autumn. Contrasting shady woodland brings some calm and respite. Hard working greenhouse area for propagation of unusual varieties. Pond and gravel garden.

♿ ❀ ☕

12 8 CHAPEL ROAD

Breachwood Green, Hitchin, SG4 8NU. Mr & Mrs Melvin Gore. *Midway between Hitchin, Harpenden & Luton, Breachwood Green is well signed. We are just 2 doors from Red Lion PH.* Sun 23 July (12-5). Adm £3, chd free. Home-made teas.
Standing in the heart of the village surrounding a C17 cottage is an informal garden having no lawns or straight level pathways with a good selection of perennials, shrubs and alpines. With one of the largest collections of vintage garden tools and machinery on display as featured in Garden News. Featured in Hertfordshire Life and Garden News.

13 THE CHERRY TREE

Stevenage Road, Little Wymondley, Hitchin, SG4 7HY. Patrick Woollard & Jane Woollard. ½ m West of J8 of the A1M. Follow sign to Little Wymondley; under railway bridge & house is R at central island flower bed opp Bucks Head PH. Parking in adjacent roads. **Sun 28 May (1-5). Adm £3.50, chd free. Light refreshments.**
The Cherry Tree is a small, secluded garden on several levels containing shrubs, trees and climbers, many of them perfumed. Much of the planting, including exotics, is in containers that are cycled in various positions throughout the seasons. A heated greenhouse and summerhouse maintain tender plants in winter. The garden has been designed to be a journey of discovery as you ascend.

14 42 CHURCH STREET

Baldock, SG7 5AF. Leila Shafarenko. Baldock town centre. 3m N of A1M J9 in the centre of Baldock. 2m S of A1M J10. At the end of High St turn R at r'about, soon L into Sun St, continue Church St. **Evening opening Fri 12 May (5-8). Adm £3.50, chd free. Wine.**
Secluded walled garden hidden behind a C16 house in the heart of Baldock's conservation area. Mature trees, incl a magnificent magnolia, wisteria-clad walls, wide herbaceous borders. Cottage-style planting featuring species peonies, and many varieties of thornless roses.

15 NEW 35 CROFTS PATH

Hemel Hempstead, HP3 8HB. Ms Jane Anthony, 01442 250108, jane@theartofgardens.co.uk. Leverstock Green. From the M1 travel along the dual carriageway over 1st 2 r'abouts. Turn L into Rant Meadow, just beyond the speed camera! Take, 3rd on R into St Michaels Ave, then R into Crofts Path. **Sun 4 June (1-4). Adm £3.50, chd free. Home-made teas and cakes, incl gluten free! Teas and coffee. Visits also by arrangement Mar to Oct.**
An oasis in suburbia! The garden has a mixture of shrubs, trees, grasses and perennials and a pond. I am a garden designer and have worked at ensuring there is as much interest and colour all year round. It has lots of roses: I have tried to use interesting plants not always seen in garden centres. My front garden faces south and is a jungle of figs and yucca among other things! Wheelchair access would be difficult. Garden has steps up into it and the threshold to cross at front and back doors.

16 35 DIGSWELL ROAD

Welwyn Garden City, AL8 7PB. Adrian & Clare de Baat, 01707 324074, adrian.debaat@ntlworld.com, www.adriansgarden.org. ½ m N of Welwyn Garden City centre. From the Campus r'about in city centre take N exit just past the Public Library into Digswell Rd. Over the White Bridge, 200yds on L. **Sun 30 July (2-5.30); Sun 22 Oct (1.30-4.30). Adm £4, chd free. Home-made teas. Visits also by arrangement July to Oct groups of up to 20 - adm £7, incl tea & cake.**
Town garden of around a third of an acre with naturalistic planting inspired by the Dutch garden designer, Piet Oudolf. The garden has perennial borders plus a small meadow packed with herbaceous plants and grasses. The contemporary planting gives way to the exotic, incl a succulent bed and under mature trees, a lush jungle garden incl bamboos, bananas, palms and tree ferns. Daisy Roots Nursery will be selling plants. The garden was featured in Garden News magazine. Grass paths and gentle slopes to all areas of the garden.

Alswick Hall

17 NEW 1 ELIA COTTAGE

Nether Street, Widford, Ware, SG12 8TH. Margaret & Hugh O'Reilly, 01279 843324, hughoreilly56@yahoo.co.uk. *B1004 from Ware, Wareside to Widford past Green Man PH into dip at Xrd take R Nether St. 8m W of Bishop's Stortford on B1004 through Much Hadham at Widford sign turn L. B180 from Stanstead Abbots.* **Evening opening Fri 16 June (6.30-9.30). Wine. Sun 18 June (2-6). Home-made teas. Adm £3.50, chd free. Visits also by arrangement Feb to Sept for groups up to 10. For snowdrops or spring opening please telephone.**

Approx third acre. Snowdrops and hellebores in spring. An informal jumble of roses and cottage garden flowers jostling with cow parsley, red campion and sweet rocket. Steep meandering paths on different levels lead to stream, pond and walkway of clematis and roses. Odd bits of art and statues peep at you from various vistas. Plenty of seats to sit and admire the nature that lives happily here. Due to the steep nature of the garden we are very sorry but there is no wheelchair access.

18 42 FALCONER ROAD

Bushey, Watford, WD23 3AD. Mrs Suzette Fuller, 077142 94170, suzettesdesign@btconnect.com. *M1 J5 follow signs for Bushey. From London A40 via Stanmore towards Watford. From Watford via Bushey Arches, through to Bushey High St, turn L into Falconer Rd, opp St James church.* **Sat 29, Sun 30 July, Sat 5, Sun 6 Aug (12-6). Evening opening Sat 4 Nov (4-8). Adm £3, chd free. Light refreshments. Visits also by arrangement in July.**

Enchanting magical unusual Victorian style space. Children so very welcome. Winter viewing for fairyland lighting, for all ages, bring a torch. Bird cages and chimneys a feature, plus a walk through conservatory with orchids.

19 15 GADE VALLEY COTTAGES

Dagnall Road, Great Gaddesden, Hemel Hempstead, HP1 3BW. Bryan Trueman. *3m N of Hemel Hempstead. Follow A4146 N from Hemel Hempstead. Past Water End. Go past turning for Great Gaddesden. Gade Valley Cottages on R. Park in village hall car park.* **Sun 4 June, Sun 23 July (1.30-5). Adm £3.50, chd free. Home-made teas.**

165ft × 30ft sloping rural garden. Patio, lawn, borders and pond. Paths lead through a woodland area emerging by wildlife pond and sunny border. A choice of seating offers sunny rural views or quiet shady contemplation with sounds of rustling bamboos and bubbling water. Featured in Garden News and local publications.

✿ ☕

> **The National Garden Scheme is committed to helping unpaid carers**

20 8 GOSSELIN ROAD

Bengeo, Hertford, SG14 3LG. Annie Godfrey & Steve Machin, www.daisyroots.com. *Take B158 from Hertford signed to Bengeo. Gosselin Rd 2nd R after White Lion PH (phone box on corner).* **Evening opening Fri 18 Aug (6-8.30). Wine. Sun 20 Aug (1-5). Adm £4, chd free.**

Owners of Daisy Roots nursery, garden acts as trial ground and show case for perennials and ornamental grasses grown there. Lawn replaced in 2010 by a wide gravel path,

flanked by deep borders packed with perennials and grasses. Sunken area surrounded by plants chosen for scent. Small front garden with lots of foliage interest.

✿ ☕

21 ◆ HATFIELD HOUSE WEST GARDEN

Hatfield, AL9 5HX. The Marquess of Salisbury, 01707 287010, visitors@hatfield-house.co.uk, www.hatfield-house.co.uk. *Pedestrian Entrance to Hatfield House is opposite Hatfield Railway Station, from here you can obtain directions to the gardens. Free parking is available, please use AL9 5HX with a sat nav.* **For NGS: Sat 8 Apr (11-5). Adm £6, chd free. For other opening times and information, please phone, email or visit garden website.**

Visitors can enjoy the spring bulbs in the lime walk, sundial garden and view the famous Old Palace garden, childhood home of Queen Elizabeth I. The adjoining woodland garden is at its best in spring with masses of naturalised daffodils and bluebells. Beautifully designed gifts, jewellery, toys and much more can be found in the Stable Yard shops. Visitors can also enjoy relaxing at the Coach House Restaurant which serves a variety of delicious foods throughout the day. There is a good route for wheelchairs around the West garden and a plan can be picked up at the garden kiosk.

♿ 🚗 ☕

22 HILL HOUSE

Water End Lane, Ayot St. Peter, Welwyn, AL6 9BB. Mr & Mrs Nic Savage. *1m S of Welwyn Village & J6 of A1(M), follow the B197 towards Stanborough for approx 1m. Turn R just past the Red Lion over the bridge onto Ayot Green, take L fork towards the Sawmills & follow signs. Disabled parking will be as close as possible, at top of meadow or on gravel drive.* **Evening opening Fri 23 June (6-9). Sun 25 June (2-5). Adm £4.50, chd free.**

Garden designers Nic and Geraldine Savage open their garden for the 2nd year. An acre of garden and 4 acres of meadow, with beautiful views. Features lawns, parterre, box hedging, mixed borders, mature shrubs and trees, terrace, pool and summer house, greenhouse, fruit cage and vegetable garden. Meadow with graceful grasses, wild flowers and ponds, plus beehives – from a distance – honey on sale. Wheelchair access to all areas.

  ♿ ☕ 🌿

23 ◆ HOME FARM PLANTS

Home Farm, Shantock Lane, Bovingdon, Hemel Hempstead, HP3 0NG. Mr Graham Austin, 07773 798068, enquiries@homefarmplants.com, www.homefarmplants.co.uk. *Approx 4m SW of Hemel Hempstead. From Bovingdon, take the B4505 towards Chesham, then turn L onto the Ley Hill Road. Turn L down Shantock Hall Lane. Follow to T-junction, turn R into Shantock Lane, then follow signs.* **For NGS: Sun 2 July (2-5). Adm £5, chd free. Light refreshments. For other opening times and information, please phone, email or visit garden website.**

Family run nursery set in lovely rural location. Specialising in Elatum Delphiniums growing over 60 named cultivars. The Delphiniums growing make a spectacular sight in mid summer. At 3pm a delphinium seed sowing demonstration by Nurseryman Graham Austin. Also seed from award winning Delphiniums for sale. As seen on BBC Gardeners World. PYO seasonal cut flowers grown on the nursery (weather dependent). Partial wheelchair access over grass.

  ♿ ✿ ☕ 🌿

24 HUNTSMOOR

Stoney Lane, Bovingdon, Hemel Hempstead, HP3 0DP. Mr & Mrs Brian & Jane Bradnock, 01442 832014, bradnock@btinternet.com. *Between Bovingdon & Hemel Hempstead. Do not follow SatNav directions along Stoney Lane. Huge pot holes and ruts in lane. Approach from Bushfield Rd.* **Sun 28 May, Sun 10 Sept (2-5). Adm £6, chd free. Home-made teas. Gluten free provided. Visits also by arrangement May to Sept for**

groups of 10+.

Rose garden, rhododendron border, arboretum, Koi pond, nature pond, shrub and herbaceous borders. Also has a 'cave', and lots of places to sit. Full access to garden including easy access to WC.

  ♿ ✿ 🚗 🌿

25 ◆ KNEBWORTH HOUSE GARDENS

Knebworth, SG1 2AX. The Hon Henry Lytton Cobbold, 01438 812661, info@knebworthhouse.com, www.knebworthhouse.com. *Nr Stevenage. Direct access from A1(M) J7 at Stevenage.* **For opening times and information, please phone, email or visit garden website.**

Knebworth's magnificent 28 acre gardens were laid out by Lutyens in 1910. Lutyens' garden rooms and pollarded lime walks, Gertrude Jekyll's herb garden, the restored maze, yew hedges, roses and herbaceous borders are key features of the formal gardens with peaceful woodland walks beyond. Gold garden, green garden, brick garden and walled kitchen garden. Delicious afternoon teas are served in the Garden Terrace Tea Room. Plants for sale in the Gift shop. RHS Partner Garden. Ideal for a gardening group visit, and garden tours can be arranged. Maze and Dinosaur trail for children, plus large Adventure Playground in the Park. Regularly featured in The Garden.

  ♿ ✿ 🚗 🌿

26 THE LODGE

Luton Road, Markyate, St Albans, AL3 8QA. Jan & John Paul. *2m N of M1 J9. Turn off A5 to Luton on B4540. The garden is between the villages of Markyate & Slip End.* **Sat 17, Sun 18 June (11-5). Adm £4.50, chd free. Light refreshments. Tea, coffee or squash and homemade cakes.** The garden, of nearly 3 acres, has evolved over 47yrs, partly through our own efforts and partly through nature growing plants wherever it chooses. The garden, mainly informal with a series of rooms, with small wooded area, a wild flower meadow and remains of an orchard full of common spotted orchids

and other lovely wild flowers all of which arrived by themselves. Come and see for yourself. Main entrance gravel. Garden mostly flat.

  ♿ ☕ 🌿

27 MACKERYE END HOUSE

Mackerye End, Harpenden, AL5 5DR. Mr & Mrs G Penn. *3m E of Harpenden. A1 J4 follow signs Wheathampstead, then turn R Marshalls Heath Lane. M1 J10 follow Lower Luton Road B653. Turn L Marshalls Heath Lane. Follow signs.* **Evening opening Fri 23 June (6-9). Light refreshments. Sun 2 July (12-5). Home-made teas. Adm £6, chd free.**

C16 (Grade 1 listed) Manor House (not open) set in 15 acres of formal gardens, parkland and woodland, front garden set in framework of formal yew hedges. Victorian walled garden with extensive box hedging and box maze, cutting garden, kitchen garden and lily pond. Courtyard garden with extensive yew and box borders. West garden enclosed by pergola walk of old English roses. All proceeds from the refreshments will be donated to the Isabel Hospice. Walled garden access by gravel paths.

  ♿ ✿ 🌿

28 THE MANOR HOUSE, AYOT ST LAWRENCE

Welwyn, AL6 9BP. Rob & Sara Lucas. *4m W of Welwyn. 20 mins J4 A1M. Take B653 Wheathampstead. Turn into Codicote Rd follow signs to Shaws Corner. Parking in field, short walk to garden. A disabled drop-off point is available at the end of the drive.* **Sun 21 May (11-5). Adm £5, chd free. Home-made teas.** 6-acre garden set in mature landscape around Elizabethan Manor House (not open). 1-acre walled garden incl glasshouses, fruit and vegetables, double herbaceous borders, rose and herb beds. Herbaceous perennial island beds, topiary specimens. Parterre and temple pond garden surround the house. Gates and water features by Arc Angel. Garden designed by Julie Toll. Home-made cakes and tea/coffee.

  🅳 🌿

29 43 MARDLEY HILL

Welwyn, AL6 0TT. Kerrie & Pete, www.agardenlessordinary.blogspot.co.uk. *5m N of Welwyn Garden City. On B197 between Welwyn & Woolmer Green, on crest of Mardley Hill by bus stop for Arriva 300/301.* Mon 29 May (1-5). Adm £4, chd free. Home-made teas.
An unexpected garden created by plantaholics and packed with unusual plants and inspiring combinations. Foliage in a wide range of colours and textures forms the backdrop to ever-changing flowers. Several seating areas offer different perspectives on the design and planting composition. From a small bridge see the man-made stream cascade to the pond. For sale: cakes, teas and home-grown plants.

✳ ☕

30 NEW THE MILLERS COTTAGE

Pig Lane, Bishop's Stortford, CM22 7PA. Mandy & Marcus Scarlett. *1m S of Bishop's Stortford. Leave Bishop's Stortford on the A1060 towards Hallingbury, after approx 1m turn R into Pig Lane. The Miller's Cottage is the first track on the L - after about 300yds. Car Parking available.* Evening opening Fri 16 June (6-9). Wine. Sun 18 June (10-5). Home-made teas. Adm £5, chd free.
Essentially a romantic cottage garden with hundreds of roses that - like Topsy - just growed. Now over three acres the garden embraces many different themes from the woodland brook side walk and a formal wedding pavilion, through formal parterre and kitchen gardens, an architectural pool garden to the wide vistas of the open fields. Most of all it is a garden in development with much still to do. Some steps but largely accessible by wheelchair.

♿ 🐕 🛇 🚐 ☕ ℗

31 NEW MORNING LIGHT

7 Armitage Close, Loudwater, Rickmansworth, WD3 4HL. Roger & Patt Trigg, 01923 774293, patt@triggmail.org.uk. *From M25 J18 take A404 towards Rickmansworth, after ¾m turn L into Loudwater Lane, follow bends, then turn R at T-junction and R again into Armitage Close.* Visits by arrangement Apr to Sept or evenings May to July, restricted parking (minibus OK). Adm £4, chd free. Light refreshments.
Compact, south-facing plantsman's garden, mainly hardy and tender perennials and shrubs in shady environment. Features include island beds, pond, chipped cedar paths and raised deck. Tall perennials can be viewed advantageously from the deck. Large conservatory (450 sq ft) stocked with sub-tropicals.

✳ ☕

32 324 NORTON WAY SOUTH

Letchworth Garden City, SG6 1TA. Roger & Jill Thomson. *Just off the A505, E of town centre. From the A1M leave at J9 (A505) to Letchworth. At 2nd r'about turn L to Hitchin, still on A505. At T-lights turn R into Norton Way South.* Sun 7 May (11-5). Adm £4, chd free. Home-made teas. Serving ploughman's lunches from 12 noon to 2pm then teas thereafter.
⅕ acre organic garden of a sympathetically extended Garden City house (1906). Features include an informal knot garden, a bespoke David Harber armillary sphere as focal point of a lawn surrounded by a rockery, scree garden, borders, summerhouse and pond with Koi carp. Mature trees, shrubs and seasonal planting in beds and containers, alpine troughs, sculptures, greenhouse and kitchen garden. Featured in Hertfordshire Life. Wheelchair access to most areas of the garden.

♿ ✳ ☕ ℗

33 OLD CHURCH COTTAGE

Chapel Lane, Long Marston, Tring, HP23 4QT. Dr John & Margaret Noakes. *A41 to Aylesbury take Tring exit. On outskirts of Tring take B488 towards Ivinghoe. At 1st r'about go on to Long Marston. Park at village hall, disabled parking & drop off only at house.* Sat 25, Sun 26 Feb (11.30-3). Adm £5, chd free. Light refreshments. Mulled wine and muffins incl in adm.
Small garden around a 400yr old thatched cottage adjoining a disused churchyard with ancient yews and Norman tower being the remnant of a Chapel of Ease. Many species and varieties of snowdrops together with cyclamen, crocuses, irises and other early spring bulbs. Garden is at the end of a very narrow country lane hence request to park at Village Hall. Ancient listed buildings in a conservation zone. Garden laid out with raised beds with many unusual snowdrops. Difficult for wheelchairs but we can help.

℗

34 NEW OLD HALL FARM COTTAGE

Hill Farm Lane, Ayot St Lawrence, Welwyn, AL6 9BW. Mr Michael Moynihan. *A1(M) J6 follow signs to Welwyn, Codicote (B656) then signs*

8 Gosselin Road

to Ayot St Lawrence (Shaws Corner NT). Parking in field, short walk to gardens. **Sun 4 June (11-5). Adm £5, chd free. Home-made teas.** Bordering glorious open countryside on the edge of the village this fine garden was lovingly created over the last two decades by Michael and his late wife, Joyce. The landscaped garden is immaculately maintained and features fine specimen trees, groomed lawns, arbours and topiary. Overflowing borders are filled with lush colourful planting. WC available. Parking in nearby field. Occasional low steps to negotiate.

🚷 ☕

35 120 PARKWAY
Welwyn Garden City, AL8 6HN. Peter Jenkins. *½m S from Welwyn Garden City town centre (or from John Lewis). From town centre take Parkway until dual carriageway merges; 120 is on R. From A1(M): J4, take A6129 N to r'about, turn R into Stanborough Rd & L into Parkway at next r'about; 120 is on L.* **Sat 17 June (2-5). Adm £3.50, chd free. Home-made teas, cakes, and Pimm's.** *Donation to Save the Children and Diabetes UK.*
An established garden, lovingly developed over 30 yrs, set against a backdrop of mature trees. The garden has a wide range of shrubs, perennials and small trees, incl some unusual and interesting varieties, providing year round interest. Other features incl rose beds, many attractive climbers, a wild area, small pond and rockery. Two small steps with ramps in access route to garden. Wheelchair access to most areas.

🚷 🐄 ✿ ☕

36 PATCHWORK
22 Hall Park Gate, Berkhamsted, HP4 2NJ. Jean & Peter Block, 01442 864731. *3m W of Hemel Hempstead. Entering E side of Berkhamsted on A4251, turn L 200yds after 40mph sign.* **Sun 7 May, Sun 20 Aug (2-5). Adm £4, chd free. Light refreshments.**
Visits also by arrangement Mar to Oct groups of 10 to 30.
¼ acre garden with lots of year-round colour, interest and perfume, particularly on opening days. Sloping

site containing rockeries, 2 small ponds, herbaceous border, island beds with bulbs in Spring and dahlias in Summer, roses, fuchsias, patio pots and tubs galore - all set against a background of trees and shrubs of varying colours. Seating and cover from the elements. Not suitable for wheelchairs, as side entrance is narrow, and there are many steps and levels.

🐄 ✿ ☕

37 ♦ PEMBROKE FARM
Slip End, Ashwell, Baldock, SG7 6SQ. Krysia Selwyn-Gotha, 01462 743100, www.pembrokefarmgarden.co.uk. *½m S of Ashwell. Turn off A505 (The Ashwell turn opp the Wallington & Rushden junction.) Go under railway bridge & past a cottage on R, after 200 yards enter the white farm gates on R. Car park close to garden entry.* **For NGS: Sun 14 May (12-5). Sun 18 June (12-5), also open Barley Gardens. Adm £4, chd free. Home-made teas in the courtyard. For other opening times and information, please phone or visit garden website.**
A country house garden with a wildlife walk and formal surprises. You are invited to meander through changing spaces creating a palimpsest of nature and structure.

🚷 🐄 ☕

38 REVELEY LODGE
88 Elstree Road, Bushey Heath, WD23 4GL. Bushey Museum Property Trust, www.reveleylodge.org. *3½m E of Watford & 1½m E of Bushey Village. From A41 take A411 signed Bushey & Harrow. At mini-r'about 2nd exit into Elstree Rd. Garden ½m on L. Disabled parking only onsite.* **Sun 13 Aug (2-6). Adm £4, chd free. Home-made teas.**
2½-acre garden surrounding a Victorian house bequeathed to Bushey Museum in 2003 and in process of re-planting and renovation. Featuring colourful annual, tender perennial and medicinal planting in beds surrounding a mulberry tree. Conservatory, lean-to greenhouse, vegetable garden and beehive. Analemmatic (human) sundial

constructed in stone believed unique to Hertfordshire. Partial wheelchair access.

🚷 🐄 ✿ ☕

39 RUSTLING END COTTAGE
Rustling End, Codicote, SG4 8TD. Julie & Tim Wise, www.rustlingend.com. *1m N of Codicote. From B656 turn L into '3 Houses Lane' then R to Rustling End. House 2nd on L.* **Evening opening Fri 30 June (6-8.30). Wine. Sun 2 July (2-5.30). Home-made teas. Adm £5, chd free.**
Meander through our wild flower meadow to a cottage garden with contemporary planting. Behind lumpy hedges explore a softly clipped box parterre, topiary, reflecting pool and abundant planting. Deep late flowering borders feature grasses and long lasting perennials. Our terrace hosts drought tolerant low maintenance simplistic planting. An abundant flowery vegetable garden provides produce for the summer. The garden also hosts many wild birds at our feeders. Hens in residence. Featured in The English Garden magazine.

✿ 🪑 ☕

40 ST MICHAEL'S CROFT
Woodcock Hill, Durrants Lane, Berkhamsted, HP4 3TR. Sue & Alan O'Neill, www.stmichaelscroft.co.uk. *1¼m W of Berkhamsted town centre. Leave A41 signed A416 Chesham. Follow sign to Berkhamsted, after 500 metres straight on to Shootersway. 1m on turn R into Durrants Lane. Garden 1st on L.* **Sun 18 June (1.30-5). Adm £4, chd free. Home-made teas.**
1 acre S-facing garden with variety of densely planted borders surrounded by mature trees. Rhododendrons, azaleas, hostas, ferns, alliums, palms and bananas. Water features and waterfall from lock gate. Pergolas with clematis and climbers, vegetable beds, 2 greenhouses. Playhouse. Working beehives. Seating and cover. Home made cakes and tea. Home produced honey and plants for sale. Easy access for wheelchairs.

🚷 🐄 ✿ ☕

41 ◆ ST PAUL'S WALDEN BURY

Whitwell, Hitchin, SG4 8BP.
Simon & Caroline Bowes Lyon,
stpaulswalden@gmail.com,
www.stpaulswaldenbury.co.uk.
5m S of Hitchin. On B651; ½m N of Whitwell village. From London leave A1(M) J6 for Welwyn (not Welwyn Garden City). Pick up signs to Codicote, then Whitwell. **For NGS: Sun 23 Apr, Sun 14 May, Sun 11 June (2-7). Adm £5, chd £1. Home-made teas.** For other opening times and information, please email or visit garden website.
Spectacular formal woodland garden, Grade 1 listed, laid out 1720. Long rides lined with clipped beech hedges lead to temples, statues, lake and a terraced theatre. Seasonal displays of snowdrops, daffodils, cowslips, irises, magnolias, rhododendrons, lilies. Wild flowers are encouraged. This was the childhood home of the late Queen Mother. Children welcome. 11th June, Open Garden combined with Open Farm Sunday with free tours of the farm. Wheelchair access to part of the garden. Steep grass slopes in places.
♿ ⛩ 🚐 ☕

GROUP OPENING

42 ST STEPHENS AVENUE GARDENS

St Albans, AL3 4AD. *1m S of St Albans City Centre. From A414 take A5183 Watling St. At double mini-r'bout by St Stephens Church/King Harry PH take B4630 Watford Rd. St Stephens Ave is 1st R.* **Sun 25 June, Sun 3 Sept (2-5.30). Combined adm £5, chd free. Home-made teas at No 20. Accessible WC, gluten free cake provided.**

20 ST STEPHENS AVENUE

Heather & Peter Osborne,
01727 856354, heather.
osborne20@btinternet.com.
Visits also by arrangement Apr to Oct for groups of 10+. Adm £3.50 garden only, or £6 incl drink and home made cake.

30 ST STEPHENS AVENUE

Carol & Roger Harlow.

Two gardens of similar size and the same aspect, developed in totally different ways. The plantswoman's garden at Number 20 has been designed to supply successional waves of coordinated colour. Varied habitats include cool shade, hot and dry, and lush pondside displays. Paths weave through the carefully maintained borders packed with unusual plants. Specimen trees and fences clothed with climbers contribute to the peaceful seclusion. Recent additions include a gravel bed of ornamental grasses and late summer perennials. Seating throughout the garden gives different views, a conservatory provides shelter. Number 30 has a southwest facing gravelled front garden that has a Mediterranean feel. Herbaceous plants, such as sea hollies and achilleas, thrive in the poor, dry soil. Clipped box, beech and hornbeam in the back garden provide a cool backdrop for the strong colours of the herbaceous planting. A gate beneath a beech arch frames the view to the park beyond. Plants for sale at June opening only. Compost making demonstrations at number 20.
❀ ☕ 🚗

43 SCUDAMORE

1 Baldock Road, Letchworth Garden City, SG6 3LB.
Michael & Sheryl Hann,
Mike_sheryl.hann@btinternet.com.
Opp Spring Rd, between Muddy Lane & Letchworth Lane. J9 A1. Follow directions to Letchworth. Turn L to Hitchin A505. After 1m House on L opp corner shop. Parking in Muddy Lane & Spring Rd. **Sun 25 June (11-5). Combined adm with Serendi £7.50, chd free. Home-made teas.** Visits also by arrangement June to Sept only for groups 10+. *Donation to Garden House Hospice.*
½ acre garden surrounding early C17 cottages that were converted and extended in 1920s to form current house (not open). Family

garden of mature trees, mixed herbaceous borders with shrubs, pond and stream, wet bed, wild garden and orchard/vegetable area. Many sculptures add interest to the garden.
♿ ⛩ 🚐 ❀ ☕

44 SERENDI

22 Hitchin Road, Letchworth Garden City, SG6 3LT. Valerie & Ian Aitken, 01462 635386,
valerie.aitken@ntlworld.com.
1m from city centre. A1(M) J9 signed Letchworth on A505. At 2nd r'about take first exit Hitchin A505. Straight over T-lights. Garden 1m on R. **Evening opening Fri 23 June (6-9). Adm £5, chd free. Wine. Sun 25 June (11-5). Combined adm with Scudamore £7.50, chd free. Home-made teas.** Visits also by arrangement June to Sept for groups of 10+.
Roses, shrubs and exuberant cottage style planting balanced by a quiet 'dribble' of large stones set in gravel with grasses and angel's fishing rod. A water rill and mirror area home to acers, hostas and fuchsias. A revamped bed for rose pillars and grasses lead onto greenhouse, rose arch and planted gravel area complementing the contemporary knot garden. A back yard of hostas with a momento wall. Garden of the week in 'Garden News'. Gravel entrance driveway and paths, plenty of lawns.
♿ ⛩ ❀ ☕

GROUP OPENING

45 SERGE HILL GARDENS

Serge Hill Lane, Bedmond,
Watford, WD5 0RT. *½m E of Bedmond. Go to Bedmond & take Serge Hill Lane, where you will be directed past the lodge & down the drive.* **Sun 18 June (2-5). Combined adm £8, chd free. Cream teas at Serge Hill.**

THE BARN

Sue & Tom Stuart-Smith.
Ⓓ

SERGE HILL

Kate Stuart-Smith.

Two very diverse gardens. At its entrance the Barn has an enclosed courtyard, with tanks of water, herbaceous perennials and shrubs tolerant of generally dry conditions. To the N there are views over the 5-acre wild flower meadow, and the West Garden is a series of different gardens overflowing with bulbs, herbaceous perennials and shrubs. Serge Hill is originally a Queen Anne House (not open), beautifully remodelled by Busby (architect of Brighton and Hove) in 1811. It has wonderful views over the ha-ha to the park; a walled vegetable garden with a large greenhouse, roses, shrubs and perennials leading to a long mixed border. At the front of the house there is an outside stage used for family plays, and a ship. Featured in RHS Garden magazine.

✿ ☕ 🍷

---

46 9 TANNSFIELD DRIVE
Hemel Hempstead,
HP2 5LG. Peter & Gaynor
Barrett, 01442 393508,
tterrabjp@ntlworld.com,
www.peteslittlepatch.co.uk. *Approx 1m NE of Hemel Hempstead town centre & 2m W of J8 on M1. From J8 cross r'about, A414 to Hemel Hempstead. Under ftbridge, cross r'about then 1st R across dual c'way to Leverstock Green Rd. Straight on to High St Green. L into Ellingham Rd then follow signs.* Sun 9 July, Sun 6 Aug (1.30-5). Adm £3, chd free. Home-made teas. **Visits also by arrangement June to Sept groups (min 4 adults max 10) are very welcome. Tea/coffee available by prior arrangement.**
This small, town garden is decorated with over 450 plants creating a welcoming oasis of calm. The owners regularly experiment with the garden planting scheme which ensures the look of the garden alters from year to year and occasionally month to month. Narrow paths divide, leading the visitor on a discovery of the garden's many features. The sound of water is ever-present. Water features, metal sculptures, wall art and mirrors run throughout the garden. As a time and cost saving experiment all

hanging baskets are planted with hardy perennials most of which are normally used for ground cover.

✿ ☕ 🍷

47 THUNDRIDGE HILL HOUSE
Cold Christmas Lane, Ware,
SG12 0UE. Christopher &
Susie Melluish, 01920 462500,
c.melluish@btopenworld.com.
2m NE of Ware. ¾m from The Sow & Pigs PH off the A10 down Cold Christmas Lane, crossing new bypass. Sun 11 June (2-5.30).
Adm £4.50, chd free. Cream teas. **Visits also by arrangement Apr to Sept for groups of ten or more.**
Well-established garden of approx 2½ acres; good variety of plants, shrubs and roses, attractive hedges. Visitors often ask for the unusual yellow-only bed. Several delightful places to sit. Wonderful views in and out of the garden especially down to the Rib Valley to Youngsbury, visited briefly by Lancelot 'Capability' Brown. 'A most popular garden to visit'. Featued in Hertfordshire Life.

♿ 🐕 ☕ 🍷

48 WALKERN HALL
Walkern, Stevenage, SG2 7JA.
Mrs Kate de Boinville. *4m E of Stevenage. Turn L at War Memorial as you leave Walkern, heading for Benington (immed after small bridge). Garden 1m up hill on R.* Sat 18, Sun 19 Feb (12-4.30); Sat 8, Sun 9 Apr (12-5). Adm £4.50, chd free. Home-made teas. Warming homemade soup.
Walkern Hall is essentially a winter woodland garden. Set in 8 acres, the carpet of snowdrops and aconites is a constant source of wonder in Jan/Feb. This medieval hunting park is known more for its established trees such as the tulip trees and a magnificent London plane tree which dominates the garden. Following on in March and April is a stunning display of daffodils and other spring bulbs. There is wheelchair access but quite a lot of gravel. No disabled WC.

♿ ✿ 🚗 ☕ 🍷

49 THE WHITE COTTAGE
Waterend Lane, Wheathampstead,
St. Albans, AL4 8EP. Sally Trendell,
07775 897713, 01582 8346,
sallytrendell@me.com. *2m E of Wheathampstead. Approx 10 mins from J5 A1M Take B653 to Wheathampstead. Soon after Crooked Chimney PH turn R into Waterend Lane, garden 300yds on L. Parking in field opp.* Evening opening Fri 26 May (5-9). Wine. Mon 29 May (12-6). Cream teas. Adm £5, chd free.
An idyllic and atmospheric setting. A riverside retreat of over an acre in rural position adjacent to a ford. The River Lea widens and forms the boundary to this wildlife haven which could be a setting for 'Wind in the Willows'. After three years Sally is still developing the cottage garden to reflect her eclectic style. Music recital Friday opening at 7pm. Picnickers welcome.

♿ 🐕 🛏 ☕ 🍷

42 Falconer Road

ISLE OF WIGHT

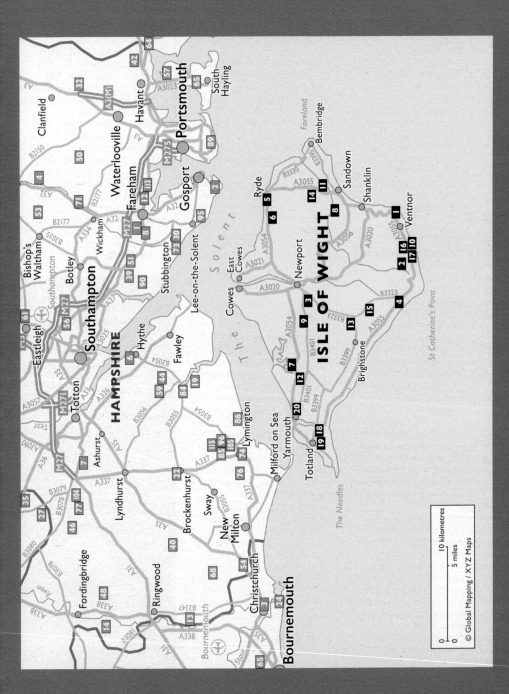

The island is a very special place to those who live and work here and to those who visit and keep returning. We have a range of natural features, from a dramatic coastline of cliffs and tiny coves to long sandy beaches.

Inland, the grasslands and rolling chalk downlands contrast with the shady forests and woodlands. Amongst all of this beauty nestle the picturesque villages and hamlets, many with gardens open for the NGS. Most of our towns are on the coast and many of the gardens have wonderful sea views.

The one thing that makes our gardens so special is our climate. The moderating influence of the sea keeps hard frosts at bay, and the range of plants that can be grown is therefore greatly extended.

Conservatory plants are planted outdoors and flourish. Pictures taken of many island gardens fool people into thinking that they are holiday snaps of the Mediterranean and the Canaries.

Our gardens are very varied and our small enthusiastic group of garden owners are proud of their gardens, whether they are small town gardens or large manor gardens, and they love to share them for the NGS.

Below: **Crab Cottage**

Volunteers

County Organiser
Jennie Fradgley
01983 730805
jenniemf805@yahoo.co.uk

County Treasurer
Jennie Fradgley
(as above)

Publicity
Jennie Fradgley
(as above)

Booklet Co-ordinator
Jennie Fradgley
(as above)

Assistant County Organisers
Mike Eastwood
01983 721060
mike@aristia.co.uk

Sally Parker
01983 612495
sallyparkeriow@btinternet.com

© Carole Drake

OPENING DATES

All entries subject to change. For latest information check www.ngs.org.uk

Map locator numbers are shown to the right of each garden name.

Visit a garden and support hospice care in your local community

May

Sunday 7th
Northcourt Manor Gardens — 13

Sunday 14th
Morton Manor — 11

Sunday 21st
Badminton — 3

June

Sunday 4th
Meadowsweet — 9
Thorley Manor — 20

Sunday 11th
♦ Nunwell House — 14

Sunday 18th
The Old Rectory — 15

Friday 23rd
Ashcliff — 1

Saturday 24th
Ashcliff — 1
NEW Carpe Diem — 6

Sunday 25th
NEW Carpe Diem — 6
NEW Miramar — 10
Pelham House — 16
The Shute — 17

July

Saturday 1st
Ashknowle House — 2
Sunny Patch — 18

Sunday 2nd
Ashknowle House — 2
Sunny Patch — 18

Saturday 8th
The Beeches — 4
Blenheim House — 5

Sunday 9th
Blenheim House — 5

Saturday 15th
NEW Lansdown — 8

August

Sunday 6th
NEW The Thatch — 19

Sunday 13th
Crab Cottage — 7

Sunday 20th
Morton Manor — 11

By Arrangement

Blenheim House — 5
Crab Cottage — 7
Morton Manor — 11
Ningwood Manor — 12
Northcourt Manor Gardens — 13
The Old Rectory — 15

THE GARDENS

1 ASHCLIFF

The Pitts, Bonchurch, nr Ventnor, PO38 1NT. Judi & Sid Lines. *From A3055 follow directions for Bonchurch. Follow signs for Bonchurch pond & park in village or continue, following signs for parking in Bonchurch Shute.* **Fri 23, Sat 24 June (11-4). Adm £3.50, chd free. Home-made teas.** The garden was started from a blank canvas 11 yrs ago and now contains many diverse areas of interest incl areas of sun and shade. Plantings are of interesting and unusual perennials, shrubs and trees over approx 1 acre blending into the natural landscape, part of which is a cliff.
🐕 ❀ ☕

2 ASHKNOWLE HOUSE

Ashknowle Lane, Whitwell, Ventnor, PO38 2PP. Mr & Mrs K Fradgley. *4m W of Ventnor. Take the Whitwell Rd from Ventnor or Godshill. Turn into unmade lane next to Old Rectory. Field parking. Disabled parking at house.* **Sat 1, Sun 2 July (12.30-4.30). Adm £4, chd free. Home-made teas.** A variety of features to explore in the grounds of this Victorian house. Woodland walks, wildlife and fish ponds. Many colourful beds and borders. The large well maintained kitchen garden is highly productive and boasts a wide range of fruit and vegetables grown in cages, tunnels, glasshouses and raised beds. Young productive orchard incl protected cropping of strawberries, peaches and apricots. Display and DVD of red squirrel antics.
🐕 ❀ ☕

3 BADMINTON

Clatterford Shute, Carisbrooke, Newport, PO30 1PD. Mr & Mrs G S Montrose. *1½m SW of Newport. Free parking in Carisbrooke Castle car park. Garden signed approx 200yds. Parking for disabled can be arranged, please phone 01983 526143, prior to opening.* **Sun 21 May (2-5). Adm £3.50, chd free. Home-made teas.** 1 acre garden on sheltered south and west facing site with good vistas. Planted for yr-round interest with many different shrubs, trees and perennials to give variety, structure and colour. Natural stream with bridges and waterfall. Pond being developed alongside kitchen garden.
🐕 ❀ ☕

4 THE BEECHES

Chale Street, Chale, Ventnor, PO38 2HE. Mr & Mrs Andrew & Anne Davidson. *Turn off A3055 at Chale onto B3399. Entrance between Old Rectory & bus stop, in gap in stone wall. On entry turn up the gravel drive towards our house which is two storey, tile hung.* **Sat 8 July (10-5). Adm £3, chd free. Light refreshments.** The garden is laid out mainly to shrubs and border plants designed for colour and texture. A haven of peace with extensive 270 degree views of the countryside incl the south west coast of the island down to The Needles and Dorset beyond. Features incl a wildflower meadow and a deep pond home to fish and wildlife (children to be supervised because of deep water). Come and see how the new wildflower meadow is settling in. The garden is not easy for wheelchairs due to gravel driveway and some steps, however can be accommodated with prior arrangement please phone 01983 551876.
♿ ❀ ☕

Meadowsweet

© Heather Edwards

5 BLENHEIM HOUSE
9 Spencer Road (use Market St entrance), Ryde, PO33 2NY. David Rosewarne & Magie Gray, 01983 614675, david65rosewarne@gmail.com. *Market St entrance behind Ryde Town Hall/Theatre.* Sat 8, Sun 9 July (11-4). Adm £3, chd free. Home-made teas. Visits also by arrangement May to Sept.
A garden developed over 12 yrs, exploring the decorative qualities and long term effects of pattern making, colour and texture. This terraced 116ft × 30ft sloping site is centred on a twisting red brick path that both reveals and hides interesting and contrasting areas of planting, creating intimate and secluded spaces that belie its town centre location.

6 NEW CARPE DIEM
75 Newnham Road, Binstead, Ryde, PO33 3TE. Tim & Tracy Welstead. *From the A3045 Newport to Ryde road, at Binstead Hill r'about, turn into Newnham Rd.* Sat 24, Sun 25 June (10.30-4). Adm £3.50, chd free. Tea.
This ¼ acre garden has evolved over 13 yrs. It is a garden that is ran on organic principles, for the benefit of both the gardeners and nature. It is divided into separate areas incl a vegetable plot, woodland areas, ponds, herb plantings, grass border and herbaceous borders. Insects and birds visit the garden in large numbers taking advantage of the plants chosen for their benefit.

7 CRAB COTTAGE
Mill Road, Shalfleet, PO30 4NE. Mr & Mrs Peter Scott, 07768 065756, mencia@btinternet.com. *4½m E of Yarmouth. At New Inn, Shalfleet, turn into Mill Rd. Continue 400yds. Please park in NT car park on L. Garden is further 200yds through NT gates on L, less than 5 mins walk.* Sun 13 Aug (11-5). Adm £4, chd free. Home-made teas & cakes. Visits also by arrangement May to Sept.
1¼ acres on gravelly soil. Part glorious views across croquet lawn over Newtown Creek and Solent leading to wild flower meadow, woodland walk and hidden waterlily pond. Part walled garden protected from westerlies, with mixed borders, leading to terraced sunken garden with ornamental pool and pavilion; planted with exotics, tender shrubs and herbaceous perennials. Gravel and uneven grass paths.

8 NEW LANSDOWN
Burnt House Lane, Alverstone, Sandown, PO36 0HB. Lynda & Larry Darby. *From the A3056, Arreton to Lake road. At Apse Heath r'about turn up Alverstone Rd. Follow road for about 1½m, Lansdown is on the R opp Youngwoods Way, by the bus stop.* Sat 15 July (1.30-4.30). Adm £4, chd £1. Light refreshments.
A garden within a 3 acre plot; s-facing, sloping, exposed, sandy soil with different areas of interest. A terrace, formal garden with pond, some vines, a fernery, large vegetable garden and our newest addition the souvenir garden set within the remains of an old glasshouse. The lower planted area has four island beds, two planted slopes and the wild pond with a small bog area. Some areas have been left cultivated for the benefit of wildlife. Two pet alpacas and a truly 180 degree view completes the scene. Sloping site with some steps, access to most of the garden without using steps.

9 MEADOWSWEET

5 Great Park Cottages, off Betty-Haunt Lane, Carisbrooke, PO30 4HR. Gunda Cross. *4m SW of Newport. From A3054 Newport/ Yarmouth road, turn L at Xrd Porchfield/Calbourne, over bridge into 1st lane on R. Parking along one side, on grass verge & past house.* **Sun 4 June (11.30-4.30). Adm £3.50, chd free. Home-made teas.** From windswept barren 2 acre cattle field to developing tranquil country garden. Natural, mainly native planting and wild flowers. Cottagey front garden, herb garden, orchard, fruit cage and large pond. The good life and a haven for wildlife! Flat level garden with grass paths.

⚃ ❄ ☕

10 NEW MIRAMAR

Woolverton Road, St. Lawrence, Ventnor, PO38 1XN. Richard & Avril Dickson. *2m W of Ventnor. Take A3055 past Botanical Gardens, ignore all 'road closed' signs. After St. Lawrence Parish Church take 1st L. Limited parking at Salem Manor, end of Salem Close (signed).* **Sun 25 June (11-5). Combined adm with Pelham House and The Shute £5, chd free. Home-made teas at St. Lawrence Village Hall.** Medium sized garden designed for yr-round interest, laid out on several levels with steps and slopes. Mostly mixed planting, with roses and clematis, a small wildlife pond, vegetable patch and cut flower bed. In contrast, at the front of the house is a gravelled area with grasses and sun-loving plants. Partial wheelchair access.

⚃ ☕

11 MORTON MANOR

Morton Manor Road, Brading, Sandown, PO36 0EP. Mr & Mrs G Godliman, 07768 605900, patricia.godliman@yahoo.co.uk, mortonmanorgardens.blogspot.co.uk. *Off A3055 5m S of Ryde, just out of Brading. At Yar Bridge T-lights turn into lower Adgestone Rd. Take next L into Morton Manor Rd.* **Sun 14 May, Sun 20 Aug (11-4). Adm £4, chd free. Light refreshments. Visits also by arrangement Apr to Sept.** A colourful garden of great plant variety. Mature trees incl many acers with a wide variety of leaf colour. Early in the season a display of rhododendrons, azaleas and camellias. Ponds, sweeping lawns, roses set on a sunny terrace and much more to see in this extensive garden surrounding a picturesque C16 manor house (not open). Gravel driveway.

⚃ 🐕 ❄ ☕

12 NINGWOOD MANOR

Station Road, Ningwood, Nr Newport, PO30 4NJ. Nicholas & Claire Oulton, 01983 761352, claireoulton@gmail.com. *Nr Shalfleet. From Newport, turn L opp the Horse & Groom PH. Ningwood Manor is 300-400yds on the L. Please use 2nd set of gates.* **Visits by arrangement June to Sept for individuals or large groups of 30 max. Adm £4, chd free. Light refreshments.** A 3 acre, landscape designed country garden divided into several rooms; a walled courtyard, croquet lawn, white garden and kitchen garden. They flow into each other, each with their own gentle colour schemes, the exception to this is the croquet lawn garden which is a riot of colour, mixing oranges, reds, yellows and pinks. Much new planting has taken place over the last few yrs. The owners have several new projects underway, so the garden is a work in progress. Features incl a vegetable garden with raised beds and a small summerhouse, part of which is alleged to be Georgian.

⚃ ☕

13 NORTHCOURT MANOR GARDENS

Main Road, Shorwell, PO30 3JG. Mr & Mrs J Harrison, 01983 740415, john@northcourt.info, www.northcourt.info. *4m SW of Newport. On entering Shorwell from Newport, entrance at bottom of hill on R. If entering from other directions head through village in direction of Newport. Garden on the L, on bend after passing the PO.* **Sun 7 May (12.30-5). Adm £5, chd free. Home-made teas. Visits also by arrangement. Teas or light lunch for groups.** 15 acre garden surrounding large C17 manor house (not open), incl walled kitchen garden, chalk stream, terraces, magnolias and camellias. Boardwalk along jungle garden. A large variety of plants enjoying the different microclimates. There are roses, primulas by the stream and hardy geraniums in profusion. Picturesque wooded valley around the stone manor house. Bathhouse and snail mount leading to terraces. 1 acre walled garden being restored. Last yr the house celebrated its 400th yr anniversary. Wheelchair access on main paths only, some paths are uneven and the terraces are hilly.

⚃ 🐕 ❄ 🛏 ☕

14 ◆ NUNWELL HOUSE

West Lane, Brading, PO36 0JQ. Mr & Mrs S Bonsey, 01983 407240, www.nunwellhouse.co.uk. *3m S of Ryde. Signed off A3055 into Coach Lane.* **For NGS: Sun 11 June (1-4.30). Adm £4, chd free. Home-made teas. For other opening**

Northcourt Manor Gardens

© Heather Edwards

times and information, please phone or visit garden website. 5 acres of beautifully set formal and shrub gardens, and old fashioned shrub roses prominent. Exceptional Solent views from the terraces. Small arboretum and walled garden with herbaceous borders. House (not open) developed over 5 centuries and full of architectural interest.

❀ 🚌 ☕

15 THE OLD RECTORY
Kingston Road, Kingston, PO38 2JZ. Derek & Louise Ness, louiseness@gmail.com, www.theoldrectorykingston.co.uk. *8m S of Newport. Entering Shorwell from Carisbrooke, take L turn at mini-r'about towards Chale (B3399). Follow road, house 2nd on L, after Kingston sign. Park in adjacent field.* **Sun 18 June (2-5). Adm £4, chd free. Home-made teas. Visits also by arrangement in June.** Constantly evolving romantic country garden surrounding the late Georgian Rectory (not open). Areas of interest incl the walled kitchen garden, orchard, formal and wildlife ponds, a wonderfully scented collection of old and English roses and two perennial wild flower meadows. Partial wheelchair access, some gravel and grass paths.

🐐 ❀ ☕

16 PELHAM HOUSE
Seven Sisters Road, St. Lawrence, Ventnor, PO38 1UY. Steve & Dee Jaggers. *1½m W of Ventnor. A3055 Undercliff Drive from Ventnor to Niton, ½m past botanical gardens, on R Seven Sisters Rd & village hall (free parking opp). Please ignore the 'road closed' signs we are unaffected by this.* **Sun 25 June (11-5). Combined adm with The Shute and Miramar £5, chd free. Home-made teas at St. Lawrence Village Hall.** Interesting 1 acre garden hidden away in the heart of the Undercliff. Stunning sea views and access into Pelham Woods. Planted for yr-round interest with trees, shrubs, perennials and unusual palms. Fish pond and sloping lawns lead to a swimming pool surrounded by exotic plants and tree ferns. Vegetable garden

with raised beds and greenhouse. Wheelchair access, although some steep slopes and steps.

♿ ❀ ☕

17 THE SHUTE
Seven Sisters Road, St. Lawrence, Ventnor, PO38 1UZ. Mr & Mrs C Russell. *Opp bottom of St. Lawrence Shute. Parking in Fishers or Twining Rd (2 mins walk) or in Undercliff Drive (10 mins uphill walk). Sorry, no parking in our shared drive.* **Sun 25 June (11-5). Combined adm with Miramar and Pelham House £5, chd free. Home-made teas at St. Lawrence Village Hall.** Approx ¾ acre, formerly part of a large Victorian garden. Views from the terrace across the lawn and white border to the sea. In the more sheltered area we mix fruit and vegetables with herbaceous borders. We usually open in August when the borders are ablaze with late summer colour. This year we are going to try to put more oomph into the early summer display. Come and see how we get on.

 ☕

18 SUNNY PATCH
Victoria Road, Freshwater, PO40 9PP. Mrs Eileen Pryer. *Halfway between Freshwater Village & Freshwater Bay. Down Afton Rd, L at garage up Stroud Rd. Keep L, just up from Parish Hall on same side. Parking in road outside house.* **Sat 1 July (10-4.30); Sun 2 July (9.30-4). Adm £3.50, chd free. Home-made teas.** A garden of an eccentric plantaholic and sculpture collector. This large and constantly evolving area has been created over 30 yrs to accommodate and reflect the owners passion. Seasonal interest is sustained and nurtured through an extensive and interesting collection of trees, shrubs, perennials and bulbs incl some rare specimens. Features incl a fairy wood, two ponds and a variety of seated areas from which to view the landscape. This garden is a celebration of fun, fantasy and life, so look closely to appreciate its diversity. There are no paved paths and yrs of mole activity has made the ground uneven.

❀ ☕

19 NEW THE THATCH
Bedbury Lane, Moon's Hill, Freshwater, PO40 9RN. Mrs Val Hudson. *Approx 1m from Freshwater Bay. From Freshwater Bay, drive up Bedbury Lane past Farringford. Take next L, Farringford Farm Rd, for parking at Farringford Farm. 5 mins walk to The Thatch at the bottom of Moon's Hill.* **Sun 6 Aug (11.30-4.30). Adm £3.50, chd free. Home-made teas.** Romantic 1 acre organic wildlife garden surrounds an C18 cottage (not open) in an AONB. Nectar rich bee borders with wild flowers, ornamental grasses, cottage garden plants, herbs, shrubs and roses, plus mature trees and young crabs and limes. Mown paths and informal lawns. A dragonfly pond, small orchard, hay meadow and wild hedgerows draw birds, insects and mammals. Gravel drive, uneven grass and steps.

❀ ☕

20 THORLEY MANOR
Thorley, Yarmouth, PO41 0SJ. Mr & Mrs Anthony Blest. *1m E of Yarmouth. From Bouldnor take Wilmingham Lane. House ½m on L.* **Sun 4 June (2-5). Adm £3.50, chd free. Home-made teas.** Delightful informal gardens of over 3 acres surrounding manor house (not open). Garden set out in a number of walled rooms incl herb garden, colourful perennial and self seeding borders, sweeping lawn and shrub borders, plus unusual island croquet lawn. Venue renowned for excellent home-made teas and the eccentric head gardener.

❀ ☕

Macmillan and the National Garden Scheme, partners for more than 30 years

KENT

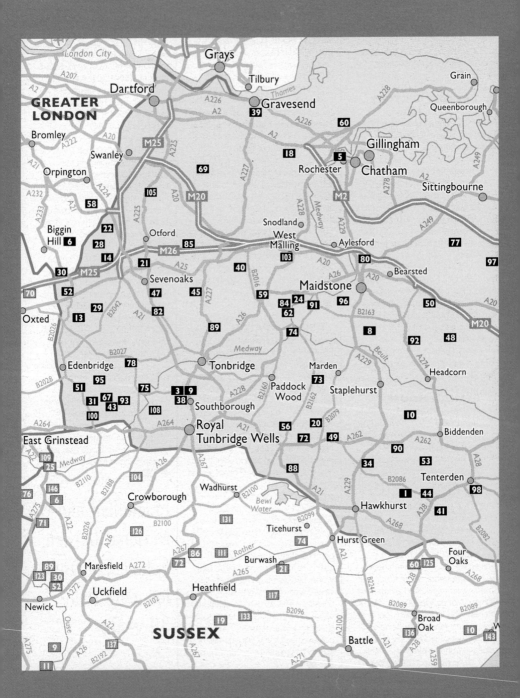

GREATER LONDON

Grays
Tilbury
Dartford
Gravesend **39**
60
Grain
Queenborough
Bromley
Swanley
Gillingham
Orpington
18
5 Rochester Chatham
Sittingbourne
69
58
105
Snodland
West Malling
Aylesford
77
Biggin Hill **6**
22
Otford
85
103
80
Bearsted
97
28
14
21
A25
40
30 M25
Sevenoaks
47
45
59
Maidstone
50
70
52
82
84 **24** **91**
96
48
Oxted
29
13
89
62
8
92
74
Edenbridge **78**
Tonbridge
Marden
Headcorn
95
73
Staplehurst
51
75
3 **9**
Paddock Wood
31 **67** **93**
38 Southborough
108
10
43
100
56 **20**
Biddenden
East Grinstead
109
Royal Tunbridge Wells
72 **49**
90
25
88
34 **53**
Tenterden
76
146
104
Wadhurst
98
6
Crowborough
1 **44**
Hawkhurst
71
126
131
Ticehurst
Hurst Green
41
89
86 **111**
Burwash
74
Maresfield
72
60 **125**
Four Oaks
123
30
21
52
Uckfield
Heathfield
117
Newick
19 **133**
Broad Oak
136
10
9
SUSSEX
Battle
143
137
11

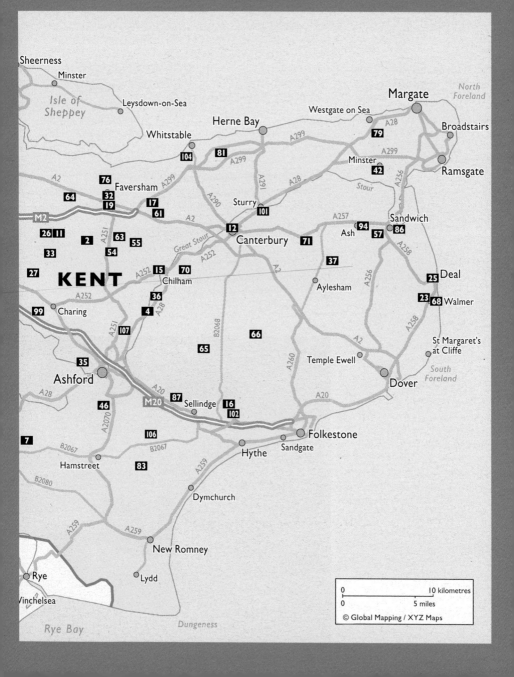

Sheerness
Minster
Isle of Sheppey
Leysdown-on-Sea
Whitstable
Herne Bay
Westgate on Sea
Margate
North Foreland
Broadstairs
79
Minster
42
Ramsgate
104
81
A299
A299
A256
76
Faversham
A299
64
32
17
Sturry
Stour
Sandwich
94
86
19
61
A2
101
Ash
57
M2
26 **11** **2**
63 **55**
12
Canterbury
A257
A258
33
54
Great Stour
A252
71
37
A256
Deal
27
KENT
A252
15
70
A252
A2
25
Charing
36
Chilham
Aylesham
23 **68** Walmer
99
A251
4
A28
A258
A252
St Margaret's at Cliffe
107
B2068
66
South Foreland
35
65
Temple Ewell
A260
A2
Ashford
A20
87 Sellindge
16
Dover
M20
102
46
A2070
A20
Folkestone
7
106
Hythe
Sandgate
B2067
83
B2067
Hamstreet
B2080
Dymchurch
A259
Rye
A259
New Romney
A259
Winchelsea
Lydd
Rye Bay
Dungeness

0   10 kilometres
0   5 miles
© Global Mapping / XYZ Maps

Volunteers

County Organiser
Jane Streatfeild 01342 850362
jane@hoath-house.freeserve.co.uk

County Treasurer
Andrew McClintock 01732 838605
mcclintockandrew@gmail.com

Publicity
Victoria Henderson
01892 870625
victoria_henderson@hotmail.com

Booklet Advertising
Marylyn Bacon 01797 270300
ngsbacon@ramsdenfarm.co.uk

Booklet Co-ordinator
Ingrid Morgan Hitchcock
01892 528341
ingrid@morganhitchcock.co.uk

Booklet Distribution
Diana Morrish 01892 723905
diana.morrish@hotmail.co.uk

Group Tours
Sue Robinson 01622 729568
suerobinson.timbers@gmail.com

Assistant County Organisers
Jacqueline Anthony 01892 518879
jacquelineanthony7@gmail.com

Marylyn Bacon (as above)

Clare Barham 01580 241386
clarebarham@holepark.com

Mary Bruce 01795 531124
mary.bruce@churchmans.co.uk

Bridget Langstaff 01634 842721
bridget.langstaff@btinternet.com

Virginia Latham 01303 862881
lathamvj@gmail.com

Caroline Loder-Symonds
01227 831203
caroline@dennehill.co.uk

Diana Morrish (as above)

Sue Robinson (as above)

Ros Scarlett 01689 851835
ros@scarlettonline.org.uk

Julia Stanton 01227 700421
familystanton@hotmail.com

Felicity Ward 01732 810525
hookwood1@yahoo.co.uk

Famously known as 'The Garden of England', Kent is a county full of natural beauty, special landscapes and historical interest.

Being England's oldest county, Kent unsurprisingly boasts an impressive collection of castles and historic sites, notably the spectacular Canterbury Cathedral, and the medieval Ightham Mote.

Twenty eight per cent of the county forms two Areas of Outstanding Natural Beauty: the Kent Downs and the High Weald. The landscapes of Kent are varied and breathtaking, and include haunting marshes, rolling downs, ancient woodlands and iconic white cliffs.

The gardens of Kent are well worth a visit too, ranging from the landscaped grounds of historic stately homes and castles, to romantic cottage gardens and interesting back gardens.

Never has a county been so close to London and yet feels so far away, so why not escape to the peace of a Kent garden? The variety of the gardens and the warmth of the garden owners will ensure a memorable and enjoyable day out.

Below: Thatched Cottage

© Leigh Clapp

OPENING DATES

All entries subject to change. For latest information check www.ngs.org.uk

Map locator numbers are shown to the right of each garden name.

February

Snowdrop Festival

Wednesday 1st
Spring Platt ... 92

Saturday 4th
Knowle Hill Farm ... 48
Spring Platt ... 92

Sunday 5th
Knowle Hill Farm ... 48
Spring Platt ... 92

Wednesday 8th
Spring Platt ... 92
Yew Tree Cottage ... 108

Sunday 12th
Copton Ash ... 19
◆ Goodnestone Park
Gardens ... 37

Sunday 19th
◆ Doddington Place ... 26
Mere House ... 59

Sunday 26th
Mere House ... 59
Yew Tree Cottage ... 108

March

Sunday 12th
Copton Ash ... 19
Yew Tree Cottage ... 108

Sunday 19th
◆ Mount Ephraim ... 61
Stonewall Park ... 93

Wednesday 22nd
Yew Tree Cottage ... 108

Sunday 26th
Copton Ash ... 19
◆ Godinton House &
Gardens ... 35
◆ Goodnestone Park
Gardens ... 37

◆ Great Comp Garden ... 40
Haven ... 42
Mere House ... 59

Wednesday 29th
◆ The Secret Gardens
of Sandwich at The
Salutation ... 86

April

Saturday 1st
◆ Ightham Mote ... 45

Sunday 2nd
Godmersham Park ... 36

Wednesday 5th
Yew Tree Cottage ... 108

Sunday 9th
Copton Ash ... 19
◆ Hole Park ... 44
Mere House ... 59

Friday 14th
Haven ... 42

Saturday 15th
Haven ... 42

Sunday 16th
Haven ... 42

Monday 17th
◆ Cobham Hall ... 18
Haven ... 42

Friday 21st
Oak Cottage ... 65

Saturday 22nd
Oak Cottage ... 65
Old Buckhurst ... 67
Watergate House ... 101

Sunday 23rd
Bilting House ... 4
34 Cross Road ... 23
Old Buckhurst ... 67
◆ Sissinghurst Castle
Garden ... 90
Yew Tree Cottage ... 108

Tuesday 25th
◆ Riverhill Himalayan
Gardens ... 82

Wednesday 26th
Great Maytham Hall ... 41

Saturday 29th
Old Buckhurst ... 67

Sunday 30th
Boldshaves ... 7
Copton Ash ... 19

Frith Old Farmhouse ... 33
Old Buckhurst ... 67
11 Raymer Road ... 80
43 The Ridings ... 81

May

Monday 1st
Copton Ash ... 19
Eagleswood ... 27

Wednesday 3rd
◆ Hole Park ... 44
Yew Tree Cottage ... 108

Saturday 6th
Little Gables ... 52

Sunday 7th
Calico House ... 11
◆ Doddington Place ... 26
Little Gables ... 52

Wednesday 10th
1 Brickwall Cottages ... 10

Thursday 11th
◆ Scotney Castle ... 88

Sunday 14th
NEW Balmoral Cottage ... 1
Copton Ash ... 19
◆ Godinton House &
Gardens ... 35
Old Buckhurst ... 67
Pheasant Farm ... 76
Stonewall Park ... 93
Torry Hill ... 97

Wednesday 17th
◆ Riverhill Himalayan
Gardens ... 82

Sunday 21st
Bilting House ... 4
Boughton Monchelsea
Place ... 8
1 Brickwall Cottages ... 10
NEW Elgin House ... 28
Ladham House ... 49
12 The Meadows ... 58
The Orangery ... 70
Orchard House, Spenny
Lane ... 73
Whitstable Gardens ... 104
Yew Tree Cottage ... 108

Wednesday 24th
Great Maytham Hall ... 41

90th Anniversary Weekend

Saturday 27th
Canterbury Cathedral
Gardens ... 12
Haven ... 42

Sunday 28th
Canterbury Cathedral
Gardens ... 12
The Coach House ... 17
Eagleswood ... 27
Falconhurst ... 31
Frith Old Farmhouse ... 33
◆ Goodnestone Park
Gardens ... 37
Haven ... 42
Old Bladbean Stud ... 66
Sandown ... 87

Monday 29th
The Coach House ... 17
Copton Ash ... 19
Haven ... 42
◆ Marle Place ... 56
Sandown ... 87

Wednesday 31st
1 Brickwall Cottages ... 10

June

Saturday 3rd
NEW Faversham
Gardens ... 32
Old Buckhurst ... 67
Rock Cottage ... 83
Wyckhurst ... 106

Sunday 4th
1 Brickwall Cottages ... 10
Haven ... 42
Rock Cottage ... 83
Smiths Hall ... 91
West Malling Early
Summer Gardens ... 103
Wyckhurst ... 106

Monday 5th
Haven ... 42

Wednesday 7th
◆ Doddington Place ... 26
Yew Tree Cottage ... 108

Saturday 10th
Churchfield ... 16
West Court Lodge ... 102
Wyckhurst ... 106

Sunday 11th
Chevening ... 14
Churchfield ... 16

Hole Park

Monday 24th
NEW Crowmarsh
House 24

Tuesday 25th
◆ Leeds Castle 50

Saturday 29th
Haven 42
The Orangery 70
Orchard End 72

Sunday 30th
Deal Gardens 25
Haven 42
The Orangery 70
Orchard End 72
Sandown 87

August

Sunday 6th
Knowle Hill Farm 48
Leydens 51
Old Bladbean Stud 66
Old Buckhurst 67
Orchard House,
Spenny Lane 73
NEW Sweetbriar 94

Wednesday 9th
Yew Tree Cottage 108

Saturday 12th
Eureka 30

Sunday 13th
The Courtyard 20
Eureka 30
Tram Hatch 99

Friday 18th
◆ Chilham Castle 15

Saturday 19th
◆ Chilham Castle 15
Yew Tree Cottage 108

Sunday 20th
Old Bladbean Stud 66

Wednesday 23rd
Great Maytham Hall 41

Saturday 26th
Eureka 30

Sunday 27th
NEW Crowmarsh
House 24
Eureka 30
Haven 42
Sandown 87

Monday 28th
NEW Crowmarsh House
24
Haven 42
Sandown 87

September

Sunday 3rd
Old Church House 68

Wednesday 6th
Yew Tree Cottage 108

Saturday 9th
Old Buckhurst 67
Rock Cottage 83

Sunday 10th
Boldshaves 7
Old Buckhurst 67
Rock Cottage 83
NEW Sweetbriar 94

Wednesday 13th
◆ Penshurst Place &
Gardens 75

Sunday 17th
The Courtyard 20
◆ Doddington Place 26

Tuesday 19th
◆ The Secret Gardens
of Sandwich at
The Salutation 86

Saturday 23rd
◆ Ightham Mote 45

Sunday 24th
◆ Mount Ephraim 61

Saturday 30th
Haven 42

October

Sunday 1st
◆ Goodnestone Park
Gardens 37
Haven 42
Nettlestead Place 62

Sunday 8th
◆ Hole Park 44
NEW Sweetbriar 94

Sunday 22nd
Mere House 59

Sunday 29th
◆ Great Comp Garden 40

February 2018

Saturday 3rd
Knowle Hill Farm 48
Spring Platt 92

Sunday 4th
Knowle Hill Farm 48

Spring Platt 92

Wednesday 7th
Spring Platt 92

Sunday 18th
Copton Ash 19
Mere House 59

Sunday 25th
Mere House 59

By Arrangement

THE GARDENS

1 BALMORAL COTTAGE

The Green, Benenden, Cranbrook, TN17 4DL. Charlotte Molesworth. *Few 100 yards down unmade track to W of St George's Church, Benenden.* **Sun 14 May (11-6). Adm £6, chd £2.50. Refreshments available at Hole Park (separate adm price).** An owner created and maintained garden now 33yrs mature. Varied, romantic and extensive topiary form the backbone for mixed borders. Vegetable garden, organically managed. Particular attention to the needs of nesting birds and small mammals lend this artistic plantswoman's garden a rare and unusual quality.

2 ◆ BELMONT

Belmont Park, Throwley, Faversham, ME13 0HH. Harris (Belmont) Charity, 01795 890202, administrator@belmont-house.org, www.belmont-house.org. *4½m SW of Faversham. A251 Faversham-Ashford. At Badlesmere, brown tourist signs to Belmont.* **For NGS: Sat 1, Sun 2 July (12-5). Adm £4, chd £2. Home-made teas. For other opening times and information, please phone, email or visit garden website.** Belmont House is surrounded by large formal lawns that are landscaped with fine specimen trees, a pinetum and a walled garden containing long borders, wisteria and large rose border. There is a second walled kitchen garden, restored in 2000 (to a design by Arabella Lennox Boyd), featuring lawns, hop arbours, pleached fruit, vegetables and flowers. During the season (April- Sept) the tea room is open on Wednesdays from 12pm for light lunches and afternoon teas. At the weekend tea and home-made cake available between 1-5pm. Out of season the tea room is open on a self service basis and welcomes visitors.

GROUP OPENING

3 BIDBOROUGH GARDENS

Bidborough, Tunbridge Wells, TN4 0XB. *3m N of Tunbridge Wells, between Tonbridge & Tunbridge Wells W off A26. Take B2176 Bidborough Ridge signed to Penshurst. Take 1st L into Darnley Drive, then 1st R into St Lawrence Ave.* **Sun 9 July (2-5). Combined adm £5, chd free. Home-made teas. Gluten and dairy free cake available.** *Donation to Hospice in the Weald.*

The Bidborough gardens (collect garden list from Boundes End) are in a small village at the heart of which are The Kentish Hare PH (book in advance), the church, village store and primary school. It is a thriving community with many clubs incl a very active Garden Association! In the surrounding countryside there are several local walks. The gardens are owner designed. Enjoy a variety of formal and informal features in front and main gardens, raised beds, a pebble bed, terraces and pergolas. There are specimen trees, interesting plants and plenty of places to sit and enjoy the peaceful surroundings. Partial wheelchair access, some steps to other gardens.

4 BILTING HOUSE

nr Ashford, TN25 4HA. Mr John Erle-Drax, 07764 580011, jdrax@marlboroughfineart.com. *5m NE of Ashford. A28, 9m S from Canterbury. Wye 1½m.* **Sun 23 Apr, Sun 21 May (2-6). Adm £5, chd free. Home-made teas. Visits also by arrangement Apr to July for groups 10+.**

6 acre garden with ha-ha set in beautiful part of Stour Valley. Wide variety of rhododendrons, azaleas and ornamental shrubs. Woodland walk with spring bulbs. Mature arboretum with recent planting of specimen trees. Rose garden and herbaceous borders. Conservatory.

5 BISHOPSCOURT

24 St Margaret's Street, Rochester, ME1 1TS. Mrs Bridget Langstaff. *Central Rochester, nr castle & cathedral. On St Margaret's St at junction with Vines Lane. Rochester train station 10 mins walk. Disabled parking only at garden but many car parks within 5-7 mins walk.* **Sat 17, Sun 18 June (1-5). Adm £3, chd free. Extensive range of delicious home-made cakes.** The residence of the Bishop of Rochester, this 1 acre historic walled garden is a peaceful oasis in the heart of Rochester with views of the castle from a raised lookout. Mature trees, lawns, yew hedges, rose garden, sculptures, fountain, wild flowers and mixed borders with perennials. Greenhouse and small vegetable garden. Parts of house incl C15 crypt chapel can also be visited. Most of garden is accessible by wheelchair. WC incl disabled.

6 THE BLACKSMITHS ARMS

Cudham Lane South, Cudham, Sevenoaks, TN14 7QB. Joyce Cole, 01959 572678, mail@theblacksmithsarms.co.uk. *Leave M25 at J4. At Hewitts r'about take 3rd exit onto A21. At Pratts Bottom r'about take 2nd exit onto A21. At r'about take 1st exit onto Cudham Lane North & follow for 4m.* **Daily Sat 1 July to Mon 31 July (12-5). Adm by donation. Visits also by arrangement July & Aug.** Exceptionally pretty and colourful summer garden set in the grounds of a C17 inn. Unusual varieties of summer bedding plants and annuals, mostly grown and cared for by the landlady. Decking and seating areas surrounded by spectacular hanging baskets and patio displays. Open lawn area with deep colour coordinated beds. We also are proud of our small natural area to attract and sustain wildlife. Partial wheelchair access inside PH.

7 BOLDSHAVES

Woodchurch, nr Ashford, TN26 3RA. Mr & Mrs Peregrine Massey, 01233 860302, masseypd@hotmail.co.uk, www.boldshaves.co.uk. *Between Woodchurch & High Halden off Redbrook St. From A28 towards Ashford turn R in High Halden at village green; 2nd R on to Redbrook St, then R down unmarked lane after ½m to brick entrance to Boldshaves at bottom of hill.* **Sun 30 Apr, Sun 10 Sept (2-6). Adm £5, chd free. Home-made teas in C18 Barn.** *Donation to Kent Minds.*

7 acre garden, partly terraced, S-facing, with wide range of ornamental trees and shrubs, walled garden, Italian garden, Diamond Jubilee garden, camellia dell, herbaceous borders (incl flame bed, red borders and new rainbow border), bluebell walks in April, woodland and ponds. **For details of other opening times see garden website www.boldshaves. co.uk.** Featured in Kent Life. Grass paths.

&. ❀ 🛏 ☕

8 BOUGHTON MONCHELSEA PLACE

Church Hill, Boughton Monchelsea, Maidstone, ME17 4BU. Mr & Mrs Dominic Kendrick, 01622 743120, www.boughtonplace.co.uk. *4m SE of Maidstone. From Maidstone follow A229 (Hastings Rd) S for 3½m to major T-lights at Linton Xrds, turn L onto B2163, house 1m on R; or take J8 off M20 & follow Leeds Castle signs to B2163, house 5½m on L.* **Sun 21 May, Sun 18 June (2-5.30). Adm £5, chd £1. Home-made teas.**

150 acre estate mainly park and woodland, spectacular views over own deer park and the Weald. Grade I manor house (not open). Courtyard herb garden, intimate walled gardens, box hedges, herbaceous borders, orchard. Planting is romantic rather than manicured. Terrace with panoramic views over deer park, bluebell woods, wisteria tunnel, David Austin roses, traditional greenhouse and kitchen garden. Do not miss St.

Leydens

© Leigh Clapp

Peter's Church next door. Fantastic selection of cakes supplied and served by ladies from St Peter's Church. **For other opening times and information please phone or see garden website** . Regret, no dogs.

❀ 🚗 ☕

9 BOUNDES END

2 St Lawrence Avenue, Bidborough, Tunbridge Wells, TN4 0XB. Carole & Mike Marks, 01892 542233, carole.marks@btinternet.com, www.boundesendgarden.co.uk. *Between Tonbridge & Tunbridge Wells off A26. Take B2176 Bidborough Ridge signed to Penshurst. Take 1st L into Darnley Drive, then 1st R into St Lawrence Ave.* **Wed 19 July (2-5). Adm £3, chd free. Home-made teas incl gluten and dairy free. Visits also by arrangement June to Aug, groups 20 max.** *Donation to Hospice in the Weald.*

Garden, designed by owners, on an unusually shaped ⅓ acre plot formed from 2 triangles of land. Front garden features raised beds, and the main garden divided into a formal area with terrace, pebble bed and 2 pergolas, an informal area in woodland setting with interesting features and specimen trees. Plenty of places to sit and enjoy the garden. Finalist in Kent Life Magazine -

Amateur Garden of the Year. Some uneven ground in lower garden.

&. 🐕 ❀ ☕

10 1 BRICKWALL COTTAGES

Frittenden, Cranbrook, TN17 2DH. Mrs Sue Martin, 01580 852425, sue.martin@talktalk.net, www.geumcollection.co.uk. *6m NW of Tenterden. E of A229 between Cranbrook & Staplehurst & W of A274 between Biddenden & Headcorn. Park in village & walk along footpath opp school.* **Wed 10, Sun 21, Wed 31 May, Sun 4 June (2-5). Adm £4.50, chd free. Home-made teas. Visits also by arrangement May & June, groups 30 max.**

Although less than ¼ acre, the garden gives the impression of being much larger as it is made up of several rooms all intensively planted with a wide range of hardy perennials, bulbs and shrubs, with over 100 geums which comprise the National Collection planted throughout the garden. Pergolas provide supports for climbing plants and there is a small formal pond. Some paths are narrow and wheelchairs may not be able to reach far end of garden.

&. 🐕 ❀ 🚗 NPC ☕

11 CALICO HOUSE

The Street, Newnham, Sittingbourne, ME9 0LN. Graham Lloyd-Brunt. *Garden located in middle of village on road that runs through Newnham from A2 to A20. Parking in field off Sharsted Hill.* **Sun 7 May (2-5). Cream teas. Sat 22 July (3-7.30). Wine. Adm £5, chd free.**

The garden at Calico House was made over the past decade using yew hedges and topiary dating from the 1920s. Terraced lawns and themed flower borders are set within a traditional English garden framework of hedges and walks. All borders are covered with tulips in May with contemporary plantings of tall herbaceous flowers in distinct cool, exotic and white palettes in July. Featured in House & Garden, Country Life and The English Garden.

GROUP OPENING

12 CANTERBURY CATHEDRAL GARDENS

Canterbury, CT1 2EP. 01227 762862, events@canterbury-cathedral.org, www.canterbury-cathedral.org. *Canterbury Cathedral Precincts.* **Enter precincts via main Christchurch gate**. *No access for cars, use park & ride or public car parks.* **Sat 27 May (11-5); Sun 28 May (2-5). Combined adm £5, chd free. Home-made teas on Green Court. Please note - on Sat, in addition to £5 adm, precinct charges apply.** On Sun there are no precinct charges.

ARCHDEACONRY
Archdeacon of Canterbury.

THE DEANERY
The Dean.

St Clere

© Leigh Clapp

---

15 THE PRECINCTS
Canon Papadapulos.

19 THE PRECINCTS
Canon Irvine.

22 THE PRECINCTS
Canon Clare Edwards.

A wonderful opportunity to visit and enjoy 5 Canonical gardens within the historic precincts of Canterbury Cathedral: The Deanery Garden with wonderful roses, wildflower planting and orchard, unusual medlar tree, vegetable garden and wild fowl enclosure; the Archdeaconry incl the ancient mulberry tree, contrasting traditional and modern planting and a Japanese influence; the three further Precinct gardens, varied in style, offer sweeping herbaceous banks, delightful enclosed spaces, and areas planted to attract and support birds, insects and wildlife. All the gardens now incl vegetable plots personal to each house. Step back in time and see the herb garden, which show the use of herbs for medicinal purposes in the Middle Ages. The walled Memorial Garden has wonderful wisteria, formal roses, mixed borders and the stone war memorial at its centre, and hidden Bastion Chapel in the city wall. Gardeners' plant stall and home-made refreshments. Dover Beekeepers Association, up close and personal opportunity with Birds of Prey and unique access to Bastion Chapel. Classic cars on Green Court. Wheelchair access to all gardens. Archdeaconry has separate entrance for people who require a flat entrance.

13 ◆ CHARTWELL

Mapleton Road, Westerham, TN16 1PS. National Trust, 01732 868381, chartwell@nationaltrust.org.uk, www.nationaltrust.org.uk/chartwell. *4m N of Edenbridge, 2m S of Westerham. Fork L off B2026 after 1½m.* **For NGS: Wed 14 June (10-4). Adm £6.75, chd free. Light refreshments.** For other opening times and

information, please phone, email or visit garden website.
Informal gardens on hillside with glorious views over Weald of Kent. Water garden and lakes together with red brick wall built by Sir Winston Churchill, former owner of Chartwell. Lady Churchill's rose garden. Avenue of golden roses runs down the centre of a must see productive kitchen garden. Hard paths to Lady Churchill's rose garden and the terrace. Some steep slopes and steps.
& ♞ ✿ ⛟ ☕

14 CHEVENING
Nr Sevenoaks, TN14 6HG.
The Board of Trustees of the Chevening Estate, www.cheveninghouse.com. *4m NW of Sevenoaks. Turn N off A25 at Sundridge T-lights on to B2211; at Chevening Xrds 1½m turn L.* **Sun 11 June (2-5). Adm £7, chd £1. Home-made teas.**
The pleasure grounds of the Earls Stanhope at Chevening House are today characterised by lawns and wooded walks around an ornamental lake. First laid out between 1690 and 1720 in the French formal style, in the 1770s a more informal English design was introduced. In early C19 lawns, parterres and a maze were established and many specimen trees planted to shade woodland walks. The garden is being gradually restored following a plan by Elizabeth Banks, developed by George Carter, which reflects all the main periods of its development. Group guided tours of parks and gardens can sometimes be arranged with the Estate Office when house is unoccupied. Gentle slopes, gravel paths throughout.
& ♞ ✿ ☕

15 ♦ CHILHAM CASTLE
Canterbury, CT4 8DB. Mr & Mrs Wheeler, 01227 733100, chilhamcastleinfo@gmail.com, www.chilham-castle.co.uk. *6m SW of Canterbury, 7m NE of Ashford, centre of Chilham Village. Follow NGS signs from A28 or A252 up to Chilham village square & through main gates of Chilham Castle.*

For NGS: Evening opening Fri 18 Aug (5-8). Light refreshments. Sat 19 Aug (2-5). Home-made teas. Adm £5, chd free. For other opening times and information, please phone, email or visit garden website.
The garden surrounds Jacobean house 1616 (not open). C17 terraces with herbaceous borders. Topiary frames the magnificent views with lake walk below. Extensive kitchen and cutting garden beyond spring bulb filled quiet garden. Established trees and ha-ha lead onto park. Check website for other events and attractions. Partial wheelchair access.
& ♞ ✿ ⛟ ☕

16 CHURCHFIELD
Pilgrims Way, Postling, Hythe, CT21 4EY. Mr & Mrs C Clark, 01303 863558, coulclark@hotmail.com. *2m NW of Hythe. From M20 J11 turn S onto A20. 1st L after ½m on bend take rd signed Lyminge. 1st L into Postling.* **Sat 10, Sun 11 June (12-5). Combined adm with West Court Lodge £6, chd free. Home-made teas. Visits also by arrangement May to Sept with West Court Lodge. Groups 35 max.**
At the base of the Downs, springs rising in this garden form the source of the East Stour. Two large ponds are home to wildfowl and fish and the banks have been planted with drifts of primula and large leaved herbaceous. The rest of the 5 acre garden is a Kent cobnut platt and vegetable garden, large grass areas and naturally planted borders. Postling Church open for visitors. Areas around water may be slippery. Children must be carefully supervised.
♞ ✿ ⛟ ☕

17 THE COACH HOUSE
Kemsdale Road, Hernhill, Faversham, ME13 9JP. Alison & Philip West, 07801 824867, alison.west@kemsdale.plus.com. *3m E of Faversham. At J7 of M2 take A299, signed Margate. After 600 metres take 1st exit signed Hernhill, take 1st L over dual carriageway to*

T-junction, turn R & follow yellow NGS signs. **Sun 28 May (11-6). Mon 29 May (11-6), also open Copton Ash. Adm £4, chd free. Cream teas. Visits also by arrangement May to Sept. Cream teas or coffee/tea and biscuits by prior arrangement.**
The ½ acre garden has views over surrounding fruit producing farmland. Sloping terraced site, and island beds with yr-round interest, a pond room, herbaceous borders containing bulbs, shrubs, and perennials, and a developing tropical bed. The different areas are connected by flowing curved paths. Unusual planting on light sandy soil where wildlife is encouraged. Gold Award from Kent Wildlife Trust - Wild about Gardens. Most of garden accessible to wheelchairs. Seating available in all areas.
& ♞ ✿ ☕

18 ♦ COBHAM HALL
Cobham, DA12 3BL. Mr D Standen (Bursar), 01474 823371, www.cobhamhall.com. *3m W of Rochester, 8m E of M25 J2. Ignore SatNav directions to Lodge Lane. Entrance drive is off Brewers Rd, 50 metres E from Cobham/Shorne A2 junction.* **For NGS: Mon 17 Apr, Sun 16 July (2-5). Adm £3, chd free. Home-made teas in the Gilt Hall. For other opening times and information, please phone or visit garden website.**
1584 brick mansion (open for tours) and parkland of historical importance, now a boarding and day school for girls. Some herbaceous borders, formal parterres, drifts of daffodils, C17 garden walls, yew hedges and lime avenue. Humphry Repton designed 50 hectares of park, most garden follies restored in 2009. Combined with tours to the Darnley Mausoleum. Film location for BBC's Bleak House series and films by MGM and Universal. ITV serial The Great Fire. CBBC filmed serial 1 & 2 of Hetty Feather. Gravel and slab paths through gardens. Land uneven, many slopes. Stairs and steps in Main Hall. Please call in advance to ensure assistance.
& ♞ ⛟ ☕

19 COPTON ASH
105 Ashford Road, Faversham, ME13 8XW. Drs Tim & Gillian Ingram, 01795 535919, coptonash@yahoo.co.uk, www.coptonash.plus.com. *½ m S of A2, Faversham. On A251 Faversham to Ashford rd. Opp E bound J6 with M2.* Sun 12 Feb (12-4); Sun 12, Sun 26 Mar, Sun 9 Apr (12-5). Sun 30 Apr (12-5), also open Frith Old Farmhouse. Mon 1 May (12-5), also open Eagleswood. Sun 14 May (12-5), also open Pheasant Farm. Mon 29 May (12-5), also open The Coach House. Adm £4, chd free. Home-made teas. Home-made soup (Feb only) 2018: Sun 18 Feb. Visits also by arrangement Feb to July.
Garden grown out of a love and fascination with plants. Contains very wide collection incl many rarities and newly introduced species raised from wild seed. Special interest in woodland flowers, snowdrops and hellebores with flowering trees and shrubs of spring. Refreshed Mediterranean plantings to adapt to a warming climate. Raised beds with choice alpines and bulbs. Small alpine nursery. Gravel drive, shallow step by house and some narrow grass paths.
&♿ ❀ 🚗 ☕

20 THE COURTYARD
Horsmonden, TN12 8BG. Mr & Mrs Iain Stewart, 01892 722769, georginacstewart@gmail.com. *From Horsmonden village, follow yellow NGS signs towards Goudhurst, leaving the Gun & Spitroast PH on R.* Sun 13 Aug, Sun 17 Sept (12-5). Adm £5, chd free. Cream teas. Visits also by arrangement June to Sept, groups 10+.
The Courtyard is a mid C19 Italianate garden, forming a substantial part of the Capel Manor estate built for the Austen family (relatives of the renowned Jane Austen) of Horsmonden. The Courtyard gardens cover several acres of formal gardens and woodland incl a stunning Mediterranean courtyard garden using tranquil coloured planting with a fountain at its centre. Amazing

tearoom situated in The Courtyard with plenty of seating and a delicious selection of cakes and scones. Most of the garden can be viewed easily by wheelchair but down towards, and within the formal woodland the paths are loose gravel.
&♿ 🚗 ☕

21 NEW 142 CRAMPTONS ROAD
Sevenoaks, TN14 5DZ. Mr Bennet Smith. *4m from M25 J5. 1½ m S of Sevenoaks, off Otford Road (A225) between Bat & Ball T-lights & Otford. Access to garden via side/rear passage. Limited parking in Cramptons Rd.* Sat 1, Sun 2 July (11-6). Adm £3, chd free. Light refreshments.
A very small and leafy plantsman's garden. An eclectic tapestry of plants chosen perhaps for their texture or elegance, their large leaves, red petioles or long season interest, or perhaps because they have an interesting habit or are rarely encountered. Schefflera, umbellifers, trochodendron, tetrapanax, pseudopanax and Aesculus wangii. Tiny front garden also recently developed. Featured in The English Garden.

22 CROMLIX
Otford Lane, Halstead, Sevenoaks, TN14 7EB. The Kitchener family, 01959 532282, geoffreykitchener@yahoo.com. *5m NW of Sevenoaks, 3m from M25 J4. Exit M25 at J4 for A211 A224. After ½ m, 1st exit at r'bout for Badgers Mount A224. At next r'bout 3rd exit to Shoreham Ln, past PH, turn L at Xrds to Otford Ln. Field access to garden 400yds on L.* Visits by arrangement June & July, groups 10+. Adm £5, chd free. Light refreshments. *Donation to West Kent Cruse Bereavement Care.*
13 acre grounds, of which 7 acres are a botanist's garden with some unusual plants. Colourful herbaceous borders, scented garden, croquet and tennis lawns contrast with informal wooded walks opening up varied vistas. Laid out in the 1960s with specimen trees incl Giant Redwood and further enhanced

since 2010; many bamboos. Wisteria covers tree tops and shaded areas accommodate c.400 ferns.
❀ ☕ ☕

23 34 CROSS ROAD
Walmer, CT14 9LB. Mr Peter Jacob & Mrs Margaret Wilson. *A258 Dover to Deal. In Upper Walmer turn L into Station Rd. Under railway bridge, Cross Rd is 2nd R. Do not approach from Ringwould as SatNav suggests.* Sun 23 Apr, Sun 18 June (11-5). Adm £3.50, chd free.
An exciting and lovely garden combining great artistic sensibility with an extensive and fascinating variety of plants. ⅓ acre plantsman's garden. Collection of daphnes, hardy geraniums, herbaceous beds, unusual trees, shrubs and alpines.
❀

24 NEW CROWMARSH HOUSE
Boormans Mews, Wateringbury, Maidstone, ME18 5DU. Mrs Yvonne Marks, 01622 434897, dandymarks@hotmail.co.uk. *4m SE of Maidstone. Located in private rd in centre of village nr A26 Xrds & opp free public village hall car park on B2015. Visitors should park here & follow yellow NGS signs.* Sun 23, Mon 24 July, Sun 27, Mon 28 Aug (11-5). Adm £3.50, chd free. Home-made teas. Visits also by arrangement June to Aug for groups 25 max.
Inspirational small courtyard Mediterranean style white garden created since 2004 and nestled in the heart of Wateringbury. Parterre with box topiary, lonicera nitida hedging and mind your own business paths. Fig and olive trees. Wisteria, roses, hibiscus and lavender. Raised beds with perennials. Water features, antique statuary and chimney pots. Seating to enjoy the garden. Please contact owner on arrival to enable access for wheelchairs.
&♿ ☕

GROUP OPENING

25 DEAL GARDENS
Deal, CT14 6EB. *A258 to Deal.
Signs from all town car parks,
maps & tickets at all gardens.*
**Sun 11 June, Sun 30 July
(10-5). Combined adm £5, chd
free.** Home-made teas at the
Vicarage and 3 Sandown Rd.

GLEANERS
Lyn Freeman & Barry Popple,
www.gleaners.co.uk.
Open on all dates
🛏

**THE LANDMARK
GARDEN**
Imogen Jenkins on behalf of the
DWCA, www.facebook.com/
thelandmarkgarden.
Open on all dates

NEW 30 PETER STREET
Barry & Carman Levrier.
Open on Sun 30 July

53 SANDOWN ROAD
Robin Green & Ralph Cade.
Open on all dates

NEW THE VICARAGE
Chris & Joy Spencer.
Open on all dates

88 WEST STREET
Lyn & Peter Buller.
Open on all dates

Riverhill Himalayan Gardens

© Leigh Clapp

Start tour from any town car
park (signs from here). 88 West
Street: Small cottage garden, full
of perennials, shrubs, clematis and
roses. Finalist Kent Life Amateur
Gardener Award. 53 Sandown Road:
Three rooms incl decked terrace
with pots, courtyard with water
feature and olive trees. Studio and
greenhouse. Landmark Community
Garden: Useful native plants, self
seeding, edible annuals, fruiting
perennials and useful foliage. 130
labelled plants. Gleaners: Down a
pretty alleyway a secret garden.
Colourful courtyard leading to a
vibrant cottage garden with summer
house. 30 Peter Street: Small N-
facing walled garden filled with
colourful annuals, perennials and
evergreens. The Vicarage: Secluded
family garden hidden behind brick
walls. Distinct areas provide space to
wander, sit, and play. Mixed borders,
shrubs and colourful pots, playhouse
and chickens; kitchen garden with
herbs, soft fruit and greenhouse.
Partial wheelchair access at 53
Sandown Rd and 88 West Street.
No access at Gleaners.
♿ ❊ ▣

**26 ◆ DODDINGTON
PLACE**
Church Lane, Doddington,
Sittingbourne, ME9 0BB. Mr & Mrs
Richard Oldfield, 01795 886101,
www.doddingtonplacegardens.
co.uk. *6m SE of Sittingbourne. From
A20 turn N opp Lenham or from
A2 turn S at Teynham or Ospringe
(Faversham), all 4m.* **For NGS: Sun
19 Feb (11-4); Sun 7 May, Wed
7 June, Sun 17 Sept (11-5). Adm
£6, chd £2.** For other opening
times and information, please
phone or visit garden website.
10 acre garden, landscaped with
wide views; trees and cloud clipped
yew hedges; woodland garden
with azaleas and rhododendrons;
Edwardian rock garden recently
renovated (not wheelchair
accessible); formal garden with
mixed borders. New gothic folly.
Snowdrops in February. Wheelchair
access possible to majority of
gardens except rock garden.
♿ 🐾 ❊ 🚐 ☕ ▣

Your visit helps Marie Curie work night and day in people's homes

27 EAGLESWOOD
Slade Road, Warren Street,
Lenham, ME17 2EG. Mike &
Edith Darvill, 01622 858702,
mike.darvill@btinternet.com.
*Going E on A20 nr Lenham, L into
Hubbards Hill for approx 1m then
2nd L into Slade Rd. Garden 150yds
on R. Coaches permitted.* **Mon 1
May (11-5). Sun 28 May (11-5),**
also open Frith Old Farmhouse.
**Adm £3.50, chd free. Light
refreshments.** Visits also by
arrangement Apr to Oct.
Donation to Demelza House Hospice.
2 acre plantsman's garden situated
high on N-Downs, developed
over the past 29yrs. Wide range of
trees and shrubs (many unusual),
herbaceous material and woodland
plants grown to give yr-round
interest, particularly in spring and for
autumn colour. Some gravel areas.
Grass paths may be slippery when
wet.
♿ ❊ 🚐 ☕ ▣

28 NEW ELGIN HOUSE
Main Road, Knockholt, Sevenoaks,
TN14 7LH. Mrs Avril Bromley. *Off
A21 between Sevenoaks/Orpington
at Pratts Bottom r'about road signed
Knockholt (Rushmore Hill) 3m on R,
follow yellow NGS signs. Main Road
is continuation of Rushmore Hill.* **Sun
21 May (12-5). Adm £5, chd
free. Home-made teas.**
Victorian family house surrounded
by a garden which has evolved over
the last 48yrs - rhododendrons,
azaleas, wisteria, camellias, magnolias,
mature trees, incl a magnificent
cedar tree, and spacious lawns. This
garden is on the top of the North
Downs.
❊ ▣

29 ♦ EMMETTS GARDEN

Ide Hill, Sevenoaks, TN14 6BA. National Trust, 01732 751507, emmetts@nationaltrust.org.uk, www.nationaltrust.org.uk/emmetts-garden. *5m SW of Sevenoaks. 1½m S of A25 on Sundridge-Ide Hill Rd. 1½m N of Ide Hill off B2042.* **For NGS: Wed 28 June (10-4). Adm £8.10, chd free. Light refreshments in the Old Stables. For other opening times and information, please phone, email or visit garden website.**
5 acre hillside garden, with the highest tree top in Kent, noted for its fine collection of rare trees and flowering shrubs. The garden is particularly fine in spring, while a rose garden, rock garden and extensive planting of acers for autumn colour extend the interest throughout the season. Hard paths to the Old Stables for light refreshments and WC. Some steep slopes. Volunteer driven buggy available for lifts up steepest hill.
  占 ☙ ❋ ⊟ ☕ ❤

30 EUREKA

Buckhurst Road, Westerham Hill, TN16 2HR. Gordon & Suzanne Wright. *Off A233, 1½m N of Westerham, 1m S from centre of Biggin Hill. 5m from J5 & J6 of M25. Parking at Westerham Heights Garden Centre at top of Westerham Hill on A233, 200yds from garden. Disabled parking at house.* **Sat 22, Sun 23 July, Sat 12, Sun 13, Sat 26, Sun 27 Aug (12-4). Adm £4.50, chd free. Home-made teas.**

Approx 1 acre garden with a blaze of colourful displays in perennial borders and the 8 cartwheel centre beds. Hundreds of annuals in over 150 tubs and troughs and 50 hanging baskets. Sculptures, garden art, chickens, lots of seating, and stairs to a viewing platform. Many quirky surprises at every turn, to appeal to adults and children alike. Garden art incl 12ft dragon, a horse's head carved out of a 200yr old yew tree stump and a 10ft dragonfly on a reed. Featured in Amateur Gardening magazine. Wheelchair access to most of the garden.
  占 ⊟ ☕ ❤

31 FALCONHURST

Cowden Pound Road, Markbeech, Edenbridge, TN8 5NR. Mr & Mrs Charles Talbot, 01342 850526, nicola@falconhurst.co.uk, www.falconhurst.co.uk. *3m SE of Edenbridge. B2026 at Queens Arms PH turn E to Markbeech. 2nd drive on R before Markbeech village.* **Sun 28 May, Fri 16, Fri 23 June, Sun 16, Fri 21 July (1.30-5). Adm £5, chd free. Home-made teas. Visits also by arrangement May to Sept. Groups 10 - 50 max. Refreshments available.**
4 acre garden with fabulous views devised and cared for by the same family for 160yrs. Deep mixed borders with old roses, peonies, shrubs and a wide variety of herbaceous and annual plants; ruin garden; walled garden; interesting mature trees and shrubs; kitchen garden; wildflower meadows with woodland and pond walks.

Woodland pigs; orchard chickens; lambs in the paddocks.
  占 ❋ ⊟ ☕ ❤

GROUP OPENING

32 NEW FAVERSHAM GARDENS

Faversham, ME13 8QN. *On edge of town, short distance from A2 & railway station. From M2 J6 take A251, L into A2, R into The Mall, cont along Forbes Road, then L before zebra crossing/into Athelstan Road. Combined tickets & maps from No 54.* **Sat 3 June (10-5). Combined adm £5, chd free.**

NEW 54 ATHELSTAN ROAD
Sarah Langton-Lockton.

NEW 19 NEWTON ROAD
Posy Gentles, www.posygentles.co.uk.

NEW 17 NORMAN ROAD
Mary & John Cousins.

3 distinctive walled gardens in historic Faversham. Start at 54 Athelstan Road. Newly planted on a neglected site, the garden mirrors the angular 1922 house. Ornamental vegetable beds take centre stage. Climbing roses, clematis, thalictrums, Regale lilies, sibirica irises and unusual shrubs thrive, sheltered by old walls. On to 17 Norman Road, an established town garden offering privacy and delight. A large apple tree gives dappled shade, wisteria and clematis clothe the walls, and magnolia overarches a large variegated weigela. Small ponds teem with wildlife. Vegetables and herbs are near the kitchen door; perennials interwoven with mature shrubs throughout. 19 Newton Road, a long, thin town garden, where the plant loving owner has used billowing roses, shrubs, climbers and perennials to blur boundaries. The judicious planting of trees, and curving paths, veil rather than conceal the garden as you move through it. Predominately soft colour scheme of creams, peaches and faded lilacs. Teas widely available in Faversham.

Orchard House, Spenny Lane

© Leigh Clapp

33 FRITH OLD FARMHOUSE

Frith Road, Otterden, Faversham, ME13 0DD. Drs Gillian & Peter Regan, 01795 890556, peter.regan@cantab.net. ½m off Lenham to Faversham rd. From A20 E of Lenham turn up Hubbards Hill, follow signs to Eastling. After 4m turn L into Frith Rd. From A2 in Faversham turn S towards Brogdale & cont, turning R 1½m beyond Eastling. Limited parking. **Sun 30 Apr, Sun 28 May, Sun 18 June (11-5). Adm £4, chd free. Home-made teas. Visits also by arrangement Apr to Sept, groups 50 max; please contact owners in advance.**

A riot of plants growing together as if in the wild, developed over 30yrs. No neat edges or formal beds, but a very wide range of unusual and interesting plants, together with trees and shrubs chosen for yr-round appeal. Special interest in bulbs and woodland plants. Visitor comments - 'a plethora of plants', 'inspirational', 'a hidden gem'. Featured in Kent Life and RHS The Garden.

✿ 🚐 ☕

34 GODDARDS GREEN

Angley Road, Cranbrook, TN17 3LR. John & Linde Wotton, 01580 715507, jpwotton@gmail.com, www.goddardsgreen.btck.co.uk. ½m SW of Cranbrook. On W of Angley Rd. (A229) at junction with High St, opp War Memorial. **Sun 2 July (12.30-4.30). Adm £5, chd free. Home-made teas. Visits also by arrangement May to Sept, coaches welcome. NB: no coach parking on site.**

Gardens of about 5 acres, surrounding beautiful 500yr old clothier's hall (not open), laid out in 1920s and redesigned over past 25yrs to combine traditional and modern planting schemes. Fountain and rill, water garden, fern garden, mixed borders, flowering shrubs, trees and exotics, birch grove, grass border, pond, kitchen garden, arboretum and mature orchard.

♿ 🐕 ✿ 🚐 ☕

35 ♦ GODINTON HOUSE & GARDENS

Godinton Lane, Ashford, TN23 3BP. The Godinton House Preservation Trust, 01233 643854, info@godintonhouse.co.uk, www.godintonhouse.co.uk. 1½m W of Ashford. M20 J9 to Ashford. Take A20 towards Charing & Lenham, then follow brown tourist signs. **For NGS: Sun 26 Mar, Sun 14 May, Fri 30 June (1-6). Adm £5, chd free. Home-made teas. For other opening times and information, please phone, email or visit garden website.**

12 acres complement the magnificent Jacobean house. Terraced lawns lead through herbaceous borders, rose garden and formal lily pond to intimate Italian garden and large walled garden with delphiniums, potager, cut flowers and iris border. March/April the wild garden is a mass of daffodils, fritillaries, other spring flowers. Large collection of Bearded Iris flowering late May. Delphinium Festival (23 June - 2 July). Garden sculpture show (22 July-13 Aug). Macmillan Coffee Morning (Sept). Garden workshop and courses throughout the yr. Partial wheelchair access to ground floor of house and most of gardens.

♿ ✿ ☕

36 GODMERSHAM PARK

Godmersham, CT4 7DT. Mrs Fiona Sunley, 01227 730293. 5m NE of Ashford. Off A28, midway between Canterbury & Ashford. **Sun 2 Apr, Sun 18 June (1-5). Adm £5, chd free. Home-made teas in The Mansion Orangery. Visits also by arrangement min 12, max 50.** Donation to Godmersham Church.

24 acres restored wilderness and formal gardens set around C18 mansion (not open). Topiary, rose garden, herbaceous borders, walled kitchen garden and recently restored Italian garden. Superb daffodils in spring and roses in June. Historical association with Jane Austen. Also visit the Heritage Centre. Deep gravel paths.

♿ 🐕 🚐 ☕

37 ♦ GOODNESTONE PARK GARDENS

Wingham, Canterbury, CT3 1PL. Francis Plumptre, 01304 840107, www.goodnestoneparkgardens. co.uk. 6m SE of Canterbury. Village lies S of B2046 from A2 to Wingham. Brown tourist signs off B2046. **For NGS: Sun 12 Feb, Sun 26 Mar (12-4); Sun 28 May (11-5); Sun 1 Oct (12-4). Adm £7, chd free. Delicious home-made cakes, cream teas and light lunches. For other opening times and information, please phone or visit garden website.**

One of Kent's outstanding gardens and the favourite of many visitors. 14 acres around C18 house (not open) and with views over cricket ground and parkland. Something special yr-round from snowdrops and spring bulbs to the famous walled garden with old fashioned roses and kitchen garden. Outstanding trees and woodland garden with cornus collection and hydrangeas later. 2 arboretums, contemporary gravel garden. Picnics welcome. Featured in The Lady magazine and Country Life.

♿ ✿ 🚐 ☕

38 NEW THE GRANGE

Franks Hollow Road, Bidborough, Tunbridge Wells, TN3 0UD. Lady Mills, 01892 525882. Between Penshurst & Southborough on B2176. Located 50 metres S of Kentish Hare PH at bottom of high street. **Fri 16 June (2-5). Adm £5, chd free. Home-made teas. Pre-booking essential, please phone for details and bookings**

2 acre formal garden surrounding Tudor house (not open). Traditional planting with box hedging and topiary. Herbaceous borders, pergolas, peonies and roses in sunken garden, vegetable garden with Victorian greenhouse and cold frames. Panoramic views.

 ☕

Old Buckhurst

© Leigh Clapp

GROUP OPENING

39 GRAVESEND GARDENS GROUP

Gravesend, DA12 1JZ. *Approx ½m from Gravesend town centre. From A2 take A227 towards Gravesend. At T-lights with Cross Lane turn R then L at next T-lights following yellow NGS signs. Park in Sandy Bank Rd or Leith Park Rd.* **Sat 15, Sun 16 July (12-5). Combined adm £4, chd free. Home-made teas.**

58A PARROCK ROAD
Mr Barry Bowen.

68 SOUTH HILL ROAD
Judith Hathrill.

Enjoy two lovely gardens, very different in character, close to Windmill Hill which has extensive views over the Thames estuary. 58A Parrock Road is a beautiful, well established town garden, approx 120ft × 40ft, nurtured by owner for 54yrs. There is a stream running down to a pond, luscious planting along the rocky banks, fascinating water features, mature trees and shrubs, magnificent display of hostas and succulents. 68 South Hill Road is an award winning wildlife garden, showing that wildlife friendly gardens need not be wild. Flowers, herbs and vegetables in the raised beds. Ferns, grasses, perennials and shrubs in the borders and fruit and vegetables grown in containers on the terrace. Tender vegetables thrive in the greenhouse, two ponds planted with native species and wild flowers. Jazz Trio at 58A Parrock Road.
✿ ☕

40 ◆ GREAT COMP GARDEN

Comp Lane, Platt, nr Borough Green, Sevenoaks, TN15 8QS. Great Comp Charitable Trust, 01732 885094, office@greatcompgarden.co.uk, www.greatcompgarden.co.uk. *7m E of Sevenoaks. 2m from Borough Green Station. Accessible from M20 & M26 motorways. A20 at Wrotham Heath, take Seven Mile Lane, B2016; at 1st Xrds turn R; garden on L*

½ m. For NGS: Sun 26 Mar, Sun 29 Oct (11-5). Adm £8, chd £3. Light refreshments at The Old Dairy Tearooms. For other opening times and information, please phone, email or visit garden website.

Skilfully designed 7 acre garden of exceptional beauty. Spacious setting of well maintained lawns and paths lead visitors through plantsman's collection of trees, shrubs, heathers and herbaceous plants. Early C17 house (not open). Magnolias, hellebores and snowflakes (leucojum), hamamellis and winter flowering heathers are a great feature in the spring. A great variety of perennials in summer incl salvias, dahlias and crocosmias. Tearoom open daily for morning coffee, home-made lunches and afternoon teas. Most of garden accessible to wheelchair users. Disabled WC.

♿ ✿ 🚐 ☕

41 GREAT MAYTHAM HALL

Maytham Road, Rolvenden, Tenterden, TN17 4NE. The Sunley Group. *3m from Tenterden. Maytham Rd off A28 at Rolvenden Church, ½ m from village on R. Designated parking for visitors.* Weds 26 Apr, 24 May, 28 June, 19 July, 23 Aug (1-4.30). Adm £6, chd free.

Lutyens designed gardens famous for having inspired Frances Hodgson Burnett to write The Secret Garden (pre Lutyens). Parkland, woodland with bluebells. Walled garden with herbaceous beds and rose pergola. Pond garden with mixed shrubbery and herbaceous borders. Interesting specimen trees. Large lawned area, rose terrace with far reaching views.

✿ 🚐

42 HAVEN

22 Station Road, Minster, Ramsgate, CT12 4BZ. Robin Roose-Beresford, 01843 822594, robin.roose@hotmail.co.uk. *Off A299 Ramsgate Rd, take Minster exit from Manston r'bout, straight rd, R fork at church is Station Rd.* Sun 26 Mar, Fri 14, Sat 15, Sun 16, Mon 17 Apr, Sat 27, Sun 28, Mon 29 May, Sun 4, Mon 5 June,

Sat 29, Sun 30 July, Sun 27, Mon 28 Aug, Sat 30 Sept, Sun 1 Oct (10-4). Adm £4, chd free. Visits also by arrangement Feb to Nov any day or time. 24hrs notice required.

Award winning 300ft garden, designed in the Glade style, similar to Forest gardening but more open and with use of exotic and unusual trees, shrubs and perennials, with wildlife in mind, devised and maintained by the owner, densely planted in a natural style with stepping stone paths. Two ponds (one for wildlife, one for fish with water lilies), gravel garden, rock garden, fernery, Japanese garden, cactus garden, hostas and many exotic, rare and unusual trees, shrubs and plants incl tree ferns and bamboos and yr-round colour. Greenhouse cactus garden (new for 2017). Mentioned in Thanet Extra (local free newspaper) and on Kent Radio.

🚐

43 HOATH HOUSE

Chiddingstone Hoath, Edenbridge, TN8 7DB. Mr & Mrs Richard Streatfeild, 01342 850362, jane@hoath-house.freeserve.co.uk. *4m SE of Edenbridge via B2026. At Queens Arms PH turn E to Markbeech. Approx 1m E of Markbeech.* Visits by arrangement Feb to Apr. Adm £5, chd free. Home-made teas.

Mediaeval/Tudor family house (not open) surrounded by mature and unusual young trees, gravel garden in former stable yard, knot garden, shaded garden, herbaceous borders, yew hedges. Massed daffodils, single snowdrops; drive edged with doubles from great grandmother's garden, growing collection of special snowdrops. Home-made teas/soup in this enchanting garden with stunning views over rural Kent. Wheelchair access to many snowdrop views via rough gravel drive.

♿ 🐴 🚐 ☕

44 ◆ HOLE PARK

Benenden Road, Rolvenden, Cranbrook, TN17 4JB. Mr & Mrs E G Barham, 01580 241344,

Your visit to a garden will help more people be cared for by a Parkinson's nurse

info@holepark.com, www.holepark.com. *4m SW of Tenterden. Midway between Rolvenden & Benenden on B2086. Follow brown tourist signs from Rolvenden.* For NGS: Sun 9 Apr, Wed 3 May, Wed 14 June, Sun 8 Oct (11-6). Adm £7, chd £1. Cream teas, home-made teas and light lunches served in The Coach House. For other opening times and information, please phone, email or visit garden website.

Hole Park is proud to stand amongst the group of gardens which first opened in 1927 soon after it was laid out by my great grandfather. Our 15 acre garden is surrounded by parkland with beautiful views and contains fine yew hedges, large lawns with specimen trees, walled gardens, pools and mixed borders combined with bulbs, rhododendrons and azaleas. Massed bluebells in woodland walk, standard wisterias, orchids in flower meadow and glorious autumn colours make this a garden for all seasons. Light lunches available on all openings. Winner, Visit Kent and Kent Life, Kentish Garden of the Year: The English Garden, Autumn colour feature. Good wheelchair access throughout but beware of steep inclines. Wheelchairs are available for free hire and may be reserved.

♿ ✿ 🚐 ☕

45 ◆ IGHTHAM MOTE

Ivy Hatch, Sevenoaks, TN15 0NT.
National Trust, 01732 810378,
ighthammote@nationaltrust.org.
uk, www.nationaltrust.org.uk. *6m
E of Sevenoaks. Off A25, 2½m S of
Ightham. Buses from train stations
Sevenoaks or Borough Green to Ivy
Hatch & Ightham Mote on weekdays.*
**For NGS: Sat 1 Apr, Sat 23
Sept (10-5). Adm £12, chd £6.
Light refreshments in The Mote
Café. For other opening times and
information, please phone, email or
visit garden website.**
14 acre garden and moated
medieval manor c1320, first opened
for NGS in 1927. North lake and
pleasure gardens, herbaceous
border, fernery and stumpery,
ornamental ponds and cascade
created in early C18. Orchard,
enclosed formal and cutting gardens
all contribute to the sense of
tranquility. Wheelchairs available
from visitor reception and shop.
Please ask for wheeled access guide
at visitor reception.

&. ❁ 🚗 🍵

46 NEW KINGSNORTH PRIMARY SCHOOL

Church Hill, Kingsnorth, Ashford,
TN23 3EF. Kingsnorth Church
of England Primary School,
www.kingsnorth.kent.sch.uk.
*Turn off at Ashford, J10 of M20.
Follow signs for Designer Outlet.
Turn L at 2nd r'about. Take 2nd exit
off next r'about then 1st L up hill.
School on L.* **Sun 25 June (12.30-
3.30). Adm by donation. Light
refreshments.**
This is a school Sacred Garden
which was renovated by the school
and community to celebrate the
150th yr of Kingsnorth Church
of England Primary School. The
garden was designed as a sacred
place for the children to explore,
pray and interact with nature, whilst
supporting the local wildlife. The
main features of the garden incl a
sculpted cross, storyteller's chair and
a prayer labyrinth. The school garden
is open as one of the attractions at
the Summer Fete. The garden was
Runner Up in the category of Kent's
Best Sacred School Garden and was
featured in Kent Life magazine. The

garden is on one level, but is slightly
sloped and gravelled.

&. 🍵 🌸

47 ◆ KNOLE

Knole, Sevenoaks, TN15 0RP.
Lord Sackville, 01732 462100,
knole@nationaltrust.org.uk,
www.nationaltrust.org.uk/knole.
*1½m SE of Sevenoaks. Leave M25
at J5 (A21). Park entrance S of
Sevenoaks town centre off A225
Tonbridge Rd (opp St Nicholas
Church). For SatNav use TN13 1HU.*
**For NGS: Tue 4, Tue 11 July
(11-3.30). Adm £9, chd £4.75.
For other opening times and
information, please phone, email or
visit garden website.**
Lord Sackville's private garden at
Knole is a magical space, featuring
sprawling lawns, a walled garden,
an untamed wilderness area and
a medieval orchard. Access is
through the beautiful Orangery, off
Green Court, where doors open
to reveal the secluded lawns of
the 26 acre garden and stunning
views of the house. Last entry at
3.30pm. Refreshments are available
in the Brewhouse Café. Bookshop
in Green Court. Gift shop and
plant sales in the Brewhouse Café.
Wheelchair access via the bookshop
into the Orangery. Some paths
may be difficult in poor weather.
Assistance dogs are allowed in the
garden.

&. 🚗 🍵

The National Garden Scheme and Perennial, helping gardeners when they are in need

48 KNOWLE HILL FARM

Ulcombe, Maidstone,
ME17 1ES. The Hon Andrew
& Mrs Cairns, 01622 850240,
elizabeth@knowlehillfarm.co.uk,
www.knowlehillfarmgarden.co.uk.
*7m SE of Maidstone. From M20 J8
follow A20 towards Lenham for 2m.
Turn R to Ulcombe. After 1½m, L at
Xrds, after ½m 2nd R into Windmill
Hill. Past Pepper Box PH, ½m 1st L
to Knowle Hill.* **Sat 4, Sun 5 Feb
(11-3). Light refreshments. Also
open Spring Platt. Sun 6 Aug (2-
6). Home-made teas. Adm £5,
chd free. 2018: Sat 3, Sun 4 Feb.
Visits also by arrangement Feb
to Sept, access for 25-30 seater
coaches.**
2 acre garden created over 30yrs
on S-facing slope of N Downs.
Spectacular views. Snowdrops and
hellebores, many tender plants, china
roses, agapanthus, verbenas, salvias
and grasses, flourish on light soil.
Topiary continues to evolve with
birds at last emerging. Lavender
ribbons hum with bees. Pool and
rill enclosed in small walled white
garden. New green garden is nearly
complete. Some steep slopes.

&. 🐐 ❁ 🚗 🍵

49 LADHAM HOUSE

Ladham Road, Goudhurst,
TN17 1DB. Mr Guy Johnson. *8m E
of Tunbridge Wells. On NE of village,
off A262. Through village towards
Cranbrook, turn L at The Goudhurst
Inn. 2nd R into Ladham Rd, main
gates approx 500yds on L.* **Sun 21
May (2-5). Adm £5, chd £1. Tea
(incl herbal), coffee, delicious
home-made cakes and biscuits
incl gluten free.**
A large garden with many interesting
plants, trees and shrubs, incl
rhododendrons, camellias, azaleas
and magnolias. A beautiful rose
garden, an arboretum, an Edwardian
sunken rockery, a woodland walk
leading to bluebell woods, ponds
and a vegetable garden. The garden
also has spectacular 60 metre twin
borders and a white pool garden
designed by Chelsea Flower Show
Gold Medal winner, Jo Thompson.

🍵

50 ◆ LEEDS CASTLE
Maidstone, ME17 1PL.
01622 765400,
www.leeds-castle.com. *Off J8 of M20.* **For NGS: Evening opening Tue 25 July (6.30-8.30). Adm £15, chd free. For other opening times and information, please phone or visit garden website.**
Visitors to the 'loveliest castle in the world' are often surprised and enchanted by the glorious gardens which surround this magnificent moated building. Natural woodland walks, the Culpeper Garden - a quintessential English cottage garden - and the Lady Baillie Garden - a Mediterranean style terraced garden overlooking the Great Water - are complemented by the beautiful surrounding parkland. There are several options for refreshments incl the Fairfax Restaurant serving hot and cold food, the Costa Cafe and the Maze Cafe. Fully wheelchair accessible with smooth paths through gardens, disabled WC and mobility bus.

51 LEYDENS
Hartfield Road, Edenbridge, TN8 5NH. Roger Platts, www.rogerplatts.com. *1m S of Edenbridge. On B2026 towards Hartfield (use Nursery entrance & car park).* **Sun 6 Aug (12-5). Adm £4.50, chd free. Home-made teas. Also open Old Buckhurst.**
Small private garden of garden designer, nursery owner and author who created NGS Garden at Chelsea in 2002, winning Gold and Best in Show, and in 2010 Gold and People's Choice for the M&G Garden and Gold in 2013. A wide range of shrubs and perennials incl late summer flowering perennial border adjoining wild flower hay meadow. Kitchen garden. Plants clearly labelled and fact sheet available.

52 LITTLE GABLES
Holcombe Close, Westerham, TN16 1HA. Mrs Elizabeth James. *Centre of Westerham. Off E side of London Rd A233, 200yds from The Green. Please park in public car park. No parking available at house.*

Sat 6, Sun 7 May (2-5). Adm £3, chd free. Sat 24, Sun 25 June (2-5). Adm £4, chd free. Home-made teas.
¾ acre plant lover's garden extensively planted with a wide range of trees, shrubs, perennials etc, incl many rare ones. Collection of climbing and bush roses. Large pond with fish, water lilies and bog garden. Fruit and vegetable garden. Large greenhouse.

53 [NEW] LITTLE MOCKBEGGAR
Mockbeggar Lane, Biddenden, Ashford, TN27 8ES. Derek & Sue East, 01580 291311, sueandderekeast@hotmail.co.uk. *Situated between Biddenden & Benenden. Opp Benenden Hospital, cont down Mockbeggar Lane for ½m until you see the egg sign.* **Sun 25, Wed 28 June (1-6). Adm £5, chd free. Cream teas. Visits also by arrangement in June.**
Little Mockbeggar is a charming cottage garden crammed with herbaceous borders, shrubs, roses and climbers, incl a wildlife pond and vegetable garden. A large wildlife meadow full of oxeye daisies and

many wild flowers of interest, with paths to meander through. No dogs please due to farm animals.

54 LORDS
Sheldwich, Faversham, ME13 0NJ. John Sell CBE & Barbara Rutter, 01795 536900, john@sellwade.co.uk. *On A251 4m S of Faversham & 3½m N of Challock Xrds. From A2 or M2 take A251 towards Ashford. ½m S of Sheldwich church find entrance lane on R adjacent to wood. (51.2654N 0.8803E).* **Sun 9 July (2-5). Adm £5, chd free. Home-made teas. Visits also by arrangement Apr to Aug, refreshments and adm by arrangement.**
C18 walled garden and greenhouse. A herb terrace overlooks a citrus standing. Flowery mead beneath medlar and quince trees. Across a grass tennis court a cherry orchard grazed by Jacob sheep. A shady fernery, lawns, ponds and wild area. Old specimen trees incl sweet chestnut, planes, copper beech, yew hedges and 120ft tulip tree. Daffodils, fritillaries, tulips in spring. Some gravel paths.

Mere House

55 LUTON HOUSE

Selling, ME13 9RQ. Sir John & Lady Swire, 07866 601230, w.stokes266@btinternet.com. *4m SE of Faversham. From A2 (M2) or A251 make for White Lion in Selling, entrance 30yds E on same side of rd.* **Visits by arrangement Mar to Oct, groups 10 to 20 max. Adm £5, chd free.**
6 acres. C19 landscaped garden with ornamental ponds, trees underplanted with azaleas, camellias, woodland plants, hellebores, spring bulbs, magnolias, cherries, daphnes, halesias, maples, Judas trees and cyclamen. Depending on the weather, those interested in camellias, early trees and bulbs may like to visit in late Mar/early April.

56 ◆ MARLE PLACE

Marle Place Road, Brenchley, TN12 7HS. Mrs Lindel Williams, 01892 722304, lindelwilliams@googlemail.com, www.marleplace.co.uk. *8m SE of Tonbridge. At Forstal Farm r'about N of Lamberhurst bypass on A21 take B2162 Horsmonden direction approx 3m. From Brenchley follow brown & white tourism signs 1½m.* **For NGS: Mon 29 May (11-5). Adm £8, chd £5. Light refreshments.**
For other opening times and information, please phone, email or visit garden website.
In March dancing daffodils. Victorian gazebo, plantsman's shrub borders, walled scented garden, Edwardian rockery, herbaceous borders, bog and kitchen gardens. Garden sculptures. Arboretum, woodland walks, mosaic terrace, artist's studio. Gallery with contemporary art. Autumn colour. Restored Victorian 40ft greenhouse with orchids. C17 listed house (not open) Guided tour at 2 pm. Cart-bay Café offering light lunches and scrumptious teas (closes at 4pm). Summer lunchtime menu and tea, coffee and cakes available all day, cream teas available from 3pm. All produce from the garden or locally sourced. Ramps in place for stepped areas. Access incl some sloping lawns and gravel paths. Wheelchair users enter free of charge.
& ❀ 🚗 ☕

57 MARSHBOROUGH FARMHOUSE

Farm Lane, Marshborough, Sandwich, CT13 0PJ. David & Sarah Ash, 01304 813679. *1½m W of Sandwich, ½m S of Ash. From Ash take R fork to Woodnesborough. After 1m Marshborough sign. L into Farm Lane at white thatched cottage, garden 100yds on L. Coaches must phone for access information.* **Visits by arrangement June to Aug (18 June - 29 June & 18 Aug - 31 Aug only). Groups 10+. Adm £5, chd free. Home-made teas.**
Interesting 2½ acre plantsman's garden, developed enthusiastically over 20yrs by the owners. Paths and lawns lead to many unusual shrubs, trees and perennials in island beds, borders, rockery and raised dry garden creating yr-round colour and interest. Tender pot plants, succulents in glass house, pond and water features. Over 70 varieties of Salvia both hardy and tender.
& 🚗 ☕

58 12 THE MEADOWS

Chelsfield, Orpington, BR6 6HS. Mr Roger & Mrs Jean Pemberton. *3m from J4 on M25. Exit M25 at J4. At r'about 1st exit for A224, next r'about 3rd exit - A224, ½m, take 2nd L, Warren Rd. Bear L into Windsor Drive. 1st L The Meadway, follow signs to garden.* **Sun 21 May (11-5.30). Adm £4, chd free. Home-made teas.**

Front garden Mediterranean style gravel with sun loving plants. Rear ¾ acre garden in 2 parts. Semi-formal area with two ponds, one Koi and one natural (lots of spring interest). Mature bamboos, acers, grasses etc and semi wooded area, children's path with 13ft high giraffe, Sumatran tigers and lots of points of interest. Designated children's area. Only children allowed access! Wheelchair access to all parts except small stepped area at very bottom of garden.
& 🐄 ❀ ☕

59 MERE HOUSE

Mereworth, ME18 5NB. Mr & Mrs Andrew Wells, www.mere-house.co.uk. *7m E of Tonbridge. From A26 turn N on to B2016 & then R into Mereworth village. 3½m S of M20/M26 junction, take A20, then B2016 to Mereworth.* **Suns 19, 26 Feb, 26 Mar, 9 Apr, 22 Oct (2-5). Adm £4.50, chd free. Home-made teas. 2018: Suns 18, 25 Feb.**
C18 landscape surrounding 6 acre garden, completely replanted since 1958, bounded to the south by lake created 1780. Increasing areas of snowdrops and daffodils in spring. Extensive lawns set off herbaceous borders, ornamental shrubs and trees with yr-round foliage contrast and striking autumn colour. Major tree planting since 1987 storm; woodland, park and lake walks can

Hookwood House, Shipbourne Gardens

© Leigh Clapp

be enjoyed beyond the garden. Garden featured in two page article in Kent Life

 ♿ 🐕 ✿ ☕

60 NEW THE MOUNT
Haven Street, Wainscott, Rochester, ME3 8BL. Susie Challen & Marc Beney, 01634 727434, challensusie@gmail.com. *3½ m N of Rochester. 7 mins from M2 J1. Take A289 towards Grain, at r'about turn R into Wainscott. Co-op ahead, turn R into Higham Rd. R into Islingham Farm Rd which turns sharply L. House is on L through white metal gate.* **Visits by arrangement May to July for groups 5 - 25 max. Adm £4, chd free. Home-made teas.**
Ongoing renovation of 1¾ acre plot, the garden is divided into three main areas by paths, hedging, walls and steps. Walled kitchen garden with espaliered fruit trees, climbing roses, vegetable beds and herbaceous border. Croquet lawn with yellow and white planting. Old grass tennis court area with assorted nut trees at one end. Mature specimen trees and lovely views of surrounding farmland. Gravel drive, uneven paths and steps.

☕

61 ◆ MOUNT EPHRAIM
Hernhill, Faversham, ME13 9TX. Mr & Mrs E S Dawes & Mr W Dawes, 01227 751496, info@mountephraim.co.uk, www.mountephraimgardens.co.uk. *3m E of Faversham. From end of M2, then A299 take slip rd 1st L to Hernhill, signed to gardens.* **For NGS: Sun 19 Mar, Thur 22 June, Sun 24 Sept (11-5). Adm £7, chd £2.50. Home-made cream teas, light refreshments, wine. For other opening times and information, please phone, email or visit garden website.**
Herbaceous border, topiary, daffodils and rhododendrons, rose terraces leading to small lake. Rock garden with pools, water garden, young arboretum. Rose garden with arches and pergola planted to celebrate the Millennium. Magnificent trees. Grass maze. Superb views over fruit farms to Swale estuary. Village craft centre. Partial wheelchair access; top part manageable, but steep slope. Disabled WC. Full access to tea room.

 ♿ 🐕 ✿ 🚌 ☕

62 NETTLESTEAD PLACE
Nettlestead, ME18 5HA. Mr & Mrs Roy Tucker, www.nettlesteadplace.co.uk. *6m W/SW of Maidstone. Turn S off A26 onto B2015 then 1m on L, next to Nettlestead Church.* **Sun 11 June, Sun 1 Oct (2-5). Adm £5, chd free. Home-made teas.**
C13 manor house in 10 acre plantsman's garden. Large formal rose garden. Large herbaceous garden of island beds with rose and clematis walkway leading to garden of China roses. Fine collection of trees and shrubs; sunken pond garden, terraces, bamboos, glen garden, acer lawn. Young pinetum adjacent to garden. Sculptures. Wonderful open country views. Gravel paths, partial access: sunken pond garden. New large steep bank and lower area in development.

 ♿ 🐕 ☕

63 6 NEWHOUSE FARM COTTAGES
Newhouse Lane, Sheldwich, Faversham, ME13 9QS. Ms Kylie O'Brien, 01795 590648, kylie.obrien@yahoo.co.uk. *Newhouse Lane is on L off A251, just before Sheldwich (from Faversham direction). House among small cluster of houses, opp big white house.* **Visits by arrangement July & Aug (mid-July onwards). Adm £3.50, chd free.**
½ acre country garden on the edge of Lees Court estate. Est 10yrs ago with classic drought resistant, prairie style and wildlife friendly plantings (gaura, stipas, salvias and artemesias). Terrace garden with yew topiary, wildlife pond and rugosa hedges give way to a cherry orchard surrounded by hollyhocks. Hen enthusiasts will enjoy the two flocks of rare brown and red Sussex hens. Within an Area of Outstanding Natural Beauty. Teas available at Macknade Fine Foods, Selling Road.

🐕 ✿ ☕

The Queen's Nursing Institute founded the National Garden Scheme exactly 90 years ago

64 NORTON COURT
Teynham, Sittingbourne, ME9 9JU. Tim & Sophia Steel, 07798 804544, sophia@nortoncourt.net. *Off A2 between Teynham & Faversham. L off A2 at Texaco garage into Norton Lane; next L into Provender Lane; L signed Church for car park.* **Mon 12, Tue 13 June (2-5). Adm £5, chd free. Home-made teas. Visits also by arrangement May to Sept, groups min 10, max 30.**
10 acre garden within parkland setting. Mature trees, topiary, wide lawns and clipped yew hedges. Orchard with mown paths through wild flowers. Walled garden with mixed borders and climbing roses. Pine tree walk. Formal box and lavender parterre. Tree house in the Sequoia. Church open, adjacent to garden. Flat ground except for 2 steps where ramp is provided.

 ♿ ☕

65 OAK COTTAGE
Elmsted, Ashford, TN25 5JT. Martin & Rachael Castle. *6m NW of Hythe. From Stone St (B2068) turn W opp the Stelling Minnis turning. Follow signs to Elmsted. Turn L at Elmsted village sign. Limited parking at house, further parking at Church (7mins walk).* **Fri 21, Sat 22 Apr, Fri 14, Sat 15 July (11-4). Adm £3.50, chd free. Cream teas.**
Get off the beaten track and discover this beautiful ½ acre cottage garden in the heart of the Kent countryside. This plantsman's garden is filled with unusual and interesting perennials, incl a wide range of salvias. There is a small specialist nursery packed with herbaceous perennials. For our April opening a large auricula collection will be showcased in a range of traditional theatres.

 ♿ ✿ ☕

66 OLD BLADBEAN STUD

Bladbean, Canterbury, CT4 6NA. Carol Bruce, www.oldbladbeanstud.co.uk. *6m S of Canterbury. From B2068, follow signs into Stelling Minnis, turn R onto Bossingham Rd, then follow yellow NGS signs through single track lanes.* **Suns 28 May, 11, 25 June, 9, 23 July, 6, 20 Aug (2-6). Adm £6, chd free. Home-made teas.**

5 interlinked gardens all designed and created from scratch by the garden owner on 3 acres of rough grassland between 2003 and 2011. Romantic walled rose garden with over 90 labelled old fashioned rose varieties, tranquil yellow and white garden, square garden with blended pastels borders and Victorian style greenhouse, 300ft long colour schemed symmetrical double borders. An experimental self sufficiency project comprises a wind turbine, rain water collection, solar panels and a ground source heat pump, an organic fruit and vegetable garden. The gardens are maintained entirely by the owner and were designed to be managed as an ornamental ecosystem with a large number of perennial species encouraged to set seed, and with staking, irrigation, mulching and chemical use kept an absolute minimum. Each garden has a different season of interest – please see the garden website for more information. To read a selection of published articles about the garden, visit www.oldbladbeanstud.co.uk/links-to-further-reading.

✽ ☕

67 OLD BUCKHURST

Markbeech, Edenbridge, TN8 5PH. Mr & Mrs J Gladstone. *4m SE of Edenbridge. B2026, at Queens Arms PH turn E to Markbeech. In approx 1½m, 1st house on R after leaving Markbeech. Parking in paddock if dry. Last entry 4.30pm.* **Sat 22, Sun 23, Sat 29, Sun 30 Apr (11-5). Sun 14 May (11-5), also open Stonewall Park. Sat 3 June, Sat 22, Sun 23 July (11-5). Sun 6 Aug (11-5), also open Leydens. Sat 9, Sun 10 Sept (11-5). Adm £4, chd free.**

1 acre partly walled cottage garden around C15 Grade II listed farmhouse with catslip roof (not open). Comments from Visitors' Book: 'perfect harmony of vistas, contrasts and proportions. Everything that makes an English garden the envy of the world'. 'The design and planting is sublime, a garden I doubt anyone could forget'. Stefan Buczacki in Garden News said - 'My favourite cottage garden is Old Buckhurst in Kent'. Mixed borders with roses, clematis, wisteria, poppies, iris, peonies, lavender, July/Aug a wide range of day lilies.

🐕 ✽

68 OLD CHURCH HOUSE

26a Church Street, Walmer, Deal, CT14 7RT. Christine & Mark Symons. *A258 Dover to Deal. In Upper Walmer turn on to Church St.* **Sun 2 July, Sun 3 Sept (1-5). Adm £4, chd free. Home-made teas.**

Delightful small garden packed with a wide variety of interesting plants. Gravelled front garden and several areas on different levels divided by pergola, paths and steps, each with their own character. Perennials, shrubs and trees, bamboos and palms, with pond area. Numerous Salvia and waving grasses in late summer.

✽ ☕

69 THE OLD RECTORY

Valley Road, Fawkham, Longfield, DA3 8LX. Karin & Christopher Proudfoot, 01474 707513, keproudfoot@firenet.uk.net. *1m S of Longfield. Midway between A2 & A20, on Valley Rd 1½m N of Fawkham Green, 0.3m S of Fawkham church, opp sign for Gay Dawn Farm/Corinthian Sports Club. Parking on drive only. Not suitable for coaches.* **Visits by arrangement in Feb for individuals and groups, 20 max. Also open by arrangement Feb 2018. Adm £4, chd free. Home-made teas.**

1½ acres with impressive display of long established naturalised snowdrops and winter aconites; over 70 named snowdrops added recently. Garden developed around the snowdrops over 30yrs, incl hellebores, pulmonarias and other early bulbs and flowers, with foliage perennials, shrubs and trees, also natural woodland. The first NGS Snowdrop Festival was launched at The Old Rectory last yr as part of Visit England's Year of the English Garden; George Plumptre and Lady Cobham, Chairman of Visit England, were photographed among the snowdrops for the press release. Gentle slope, gravel drive, some narrow paths.

♿ ✽ ☕

70 THE ORANGERY

Mystole, Chartham, Canterbury, CT4 7DB. Rex Stickland & Anne Prasse, 01227 738348, rex@mystole.fsnet.co.uk. *5m SW of Canterbury. Turn off A28 through Shalmsford Street. In 1½m at Xrds turn R downhill. Cont, ignoring rds on L & R. Ignore drive on L - Mystole House only. At sharp bend in 600yds turn L into private drive.* **Sun 21 May (1-6). Sat 29, Sun 30 July (1-5). Adm £4.50, chd free. Home-made teas. Visits also by arrangement Mar to Oct.**

1½ acre gardens around C18 orangery, now a house (not open). Front gardens, established well stocked herbaceous border and large walled garden with a wide variety of shrubs and mixed borders. Splendid views from terraces over ha-ha and paddocks to the lovely Chartham Downs. Water features and very interesting collection of modern sculptures set in natural surroundings. Ramps to garden.

♿ 🐕 🚌 ☕

71 NEW THE ORCHARD

Bramling, Canterbury, CT3 1NB. Mark Lane, 01227 207013, www.marklanedesigns.com. *5m E of East of Canterbury. Please call for further directions. Limited parking available.* **Visits by arrangement May to Sept for small groups of 4 max (slightly larger groups may be considered). Adm £4. Tea.**

The Orchard is the home to Mark Lane, the UK's first wheelchair-bound garden designer, published gardening writer and BBC TV presenter, and his civil partner Jasen. The acre garden incl: herb garden, blue and yellow border, white garden, grass borders with stepped granite water feature, roses and peonies, as well as a small orchard, lawn and the large colourful herbaceous borders. Featured on BBC Gardeners' World TV programme, BBC Gardeners' World magazine, The Guardian newspaper, Which? Gardening, RHS's The Garden. Full wheelchair access. Although complete circle of garden cannot be done, alternative routes to see all parts of the garden available.

&. ✿ ☕

72 ORCHARD END

Cock Lane, Spelmonden Road, Horsmonden, TN12 8EQ. Mr Hugh Nye, 01892 723118, hughnye@aol.com. *8m E of Tunbridge Wells. From A21 going S turn L at r'bout onto B2162 to Horsmonden. After 2m turn R onto Spelmonden Rd. After ½m turn R into Cock Lane. Garden on R.* **Sat 29, Sun 30 July (11-5). Adm £4, chd free. Home-made teas. Visits also by arrangement, groups 40 max.** *Donation to The Amyloidosis Foundation.*

Contemporary classical garden within a 4 acre site. Made over 15yrs by resident landscape designer. Divided into rooms with linking vistas. Incl hot borders, white garden, exotics, oak and glass summerhouse amongst magnolias. Dramatic changes in level. Formal pool with damp garden, ornamental vegetable potager. Wildlife orchards and woodland walks.

&. 🐐 ☕

73 ORCHARD HOUSE, SPENNY LANE

Claygate, Marden, Tonbridge, TN12 9PJ. Mr & Mrs Lerwill. 01892 730662 jeanette@lerwill.com. *Just off B2162 between Collier St & Horsmonden. Spenny Lane is adjacent to White Hart PH. Orchard House is 1st house on R about 400m from PH.* **Sun 21 May, Sun 6 Aug (11-4). Adm £4.50, chd free. Home-made teas.**
A relatively new garden created within the last 11yrs. Gravel garden with potted tender perennials, cottage garden and herbaceous borders. Potager with vegetables,

fruit and flowers for cutting. Bee friendly borders. Hornbeam avenue underplanted with camassia. Small nursery on site specialising in herbaceous perennials and ornamental grasses. Productive beehives and honey for sale. Selection of home-made cakes, cream scones, tea/coffee and cold drinks available. Featured in Kent Life. Access for wheelchairs, some pathways are gravel, grassed areas uneven in places.

&. 🐐 ✿ 🚗 ☕

74 PARSONAGE OASTS

Hampstead Lane, Yalding, ME18 6HG. Edward & Jennifer Raikes, 01622 814272, jmraikes@ parsonageoasts.plus.com. *6m SW of Maidstone. On B2162 between Yalding village & stn, turn off at Anchor PH over canal bridge, cont 150yds up lane. House & car park on L.* **Visits by arrangement Apr to July. Adm £4, chd free. Cream teas.**
Our garden has a lovely position on the bank of the R Medway. Typical Oast House (not open) often featured on calendars and picture books of Kent. 70yr old garden now looked after by grandchildren of its creator. ¾ acre garden with walls, daffodils, crown imperials, shrubs, clipped box and a spectacular magnolia. Small woodland on river bank. Featured in Period Living, Kent Life and English Garden magazines. Unfenced river bank. Gravel paths.

&. ☕

75 ♦ PENSHURST PLACE & GARDENS

Penshurst, TN11 8DG. Lord & Lady De L'Isle, 01892 870307, www.penshurstplace.com. *6m NW of Tunbridge Wells. SW of Tonbridge on B2176, signed from A26 N of Tunbridge Wells.* **For NGS: Wed 13 Sept (10.30-6). Adm £10.50. Cream teas. For other opening times and information, please phone or visit garden website.**
11 acres of garden dating back to C14. The garden is divided into a series of rooms by over a mile of yew hedge. Profusion of spring bulbs, formal rose garden and famous peony border. Woodland

trail and arboretum. Yr-round interest. Toy museum. Some paths not paved and uneven in places; own assistance will be required. 2 wheelchairs available for hire.

&. ✿ ☕

76 PHEASANT FARM

Church Road, Oare, Faversham, ME13 0QB. Jonathan & Lucie Neame, 01795 535366, neamelucie@gmail.com. *2m NW of Faversham. Enter Oare from Western Link Road. L at T-junction. R at Three Mariners PH into Church Road. Garden 450yds on R, beyond Pheasant Barn, before church. Parking on roadside & as directed.* **Sun 14 May (2-5), also open Copton Ash. Sun 11 June (2-5). Adm £4, chd free. Home-made teas. Visits also by arrangement Apr to June groups 10 - 30 max welcome.**
Redesigned in 2008, a walled garden surrounding C17 farmhouse with outstanding views over Oare marshes and creek. Main garden with shrubs and herbaceous plants. Infinity lawn overlooking Oare marshes and creek. Circular walk through orchard and adjoining churchyard. Two local public houses serving lunches. Wheelchair access in main garden only.

&. ☕

77 PLACKETTS HOLE

Bicknor, nr Sittingbourne, ME9 8BA. Allison & David Wainman. *5m S of Sittingbourne. W of B2163. Bicknor is signed from Hollingbourne Hill & from A249 at Stockbury Valley. Placketts Hole is midway between Bicknor & Deans Hill.* **Sun 11 June (2-6.30). Adm £5, chd free. Cream teas.**
Mature 3 acre garden in Kent Downland valley incl herbaceous borders, rose and formal herb garden, small, walled kitchen garden and informal pond intersected by walls, hedges and paths. Many unusual plants, trees and shrubs and small wildflower calcareous meadow. Most of garden accessible by wheelchair.

&. ✿ ☕

78　3 POST OFFICE COTTAGES

Chiddingstone Causeway, Tonbridge, TN11 8JP. Julie & Graham Jones-Ellis. *Approx 6m W of Tonbridge & approx 6m E of Edenbridge. On B2027 Clinton Lane into Chiddingstone Causeway same side as PO, garden is end of terrace cottage with hedge & small gravel driveway.* **Sun 25 June (12-5.30). Adm £3.50, chd free. Home-made teas.**
Small but charming cottage garden, with large selection of clematis and over 30 varieties of roses. Herbaceous borders filled with colour in May and June, with roses in their second flush in late August along with late flowering perennials. Several seating areas and small water features.
🐄 ✿ ☕

With your support we can help raise awareness of Carers Trust and unpaid carers

79　◆ QUEX GARDENS

Quex Park, Birchington, CT7 0BH. Powell-Cotton Museum, 01843 842168, enquiries@quexmuseum.org, www.quexpark.co.uk/museum/quex-gardens/. *3m W of Margate. Follow signs for Quex Park on approach from A299 then A28 towards Margate, turn R into B2048 Park Lane. Quex Park is on L.* **For NGS: Sun 9 July (10-5). Adm £4.50, chd £3.50. Light refreshments. For other opening times and information, please phone, email or visit garden website.**
10 acres of woodland and gardens with fine specimen trees unusual on Thanet, spring bulbs, wisteria, shrub borders, old figs and mulberries, herbaceous borders. Victorian walled garden with cucumber house, long glasshouses, cactus house, fruiting trees. Peacocks, dovecote, woodland walk, wildlife pond, children's maze, croquet lawn, picnic grove, lawns and fountains. Head Gardener will be available on NGS open days to give tours and answer questions. Mama Feelgood's Boutique Café serving morning coffee, lunch or afternoon tea. Quex Barn farmers market selling local produce and serving breakfasts to evening meals. Picnic sites available. Garden almost entirely flat with tarmac paths. Sunken garden has sloping lawns to the central pond.
♿ ✿ 🚗 ☕

80　11 RAYMER ROAD

Penenden Heath, Maidstone, ME14 2JQ. Mrs Barbara Badham. *1m from J6 M20. At M20, J6 at Running Horse r'about take Penenden Heath exit along Sandling Lane towards Bearsted. At T-lights turn into Downsview Rd & follow yellow NGS signs.* **Sun 30 Apr, Sun 2 July (11-4). Adm £3.50, chd free. Home-made teas.**
Inspirational small garden with lovely views of the Downs, divided into different areas and intensely planted for yr-round interest. Cottage garden border, oriental themed pond, secret woodland garden plus a selection of ferns and hostas arranged under the canopy of a strawberry tree. Organic fruit and vegetables in raised beds and containers, minarette fruit trees underplanted with wild flowers.
♿ ✿ ☕

81　43 THE RIDINGS

Chestfield, Whitstable, CT5 3QE. David & Sylvie Sayers, 01227 500775, sylviebuat-menard@hotmail.com. *Nr Whitstable. From M2 heading E cont onto A299. In 3m take A2990. From r'about on A2990 at Chestfield, turn onto Chestfield Rd, 5th turning on L onto Polo Way which leads into The Ridings.* **Sun 30 Apr (11-4). Adm £3.50, chd free. Light refreshments. Visits also by arrangement Apr to Sept for groups 8+. Coach 25 seater max.**
Delightful small garden brimming with interesting plants both in the front and behind the house. Many different areas. Dry gravel garden in front, raised beds with alpines and bulbs and borders with many unusual perennials and shrubs. The garden ornaments are always a source of interest for the visitors. The water feature will be of interest for those with a tiny garden as well as the smoky cauldron. There are many alpine troughs and raised beds as well as dry shade borders and mixed borders all in a fairly small space. Featured in article by Tim Ingram, (Google Buat-Menard).
🐄 ✿ 🚗 ☕

82　◆ RIVERHILL HIMALAYAN GARDENS

Riverhill, Sevenoaks, TN15 0RR. The Rogers Family, 01732 459777, sarah@riverhillgardens.co.uk, www.riverhillgardens.co.uk. *2m S of Sevenoaks on A225. Leave A21 at A225 & follow signs for Riverhill Himalayan Gardens.* **For NGS: Tue 25 Apr, Wed 17 May (10.30-5). Adm £8.25, chd £5.95. Light refreshments in the café (more details below). For other opening times and information, please phone, email or visit garden website.**
Beautiful hillside garden, privately owned by the Rogers family since 1840. Extensive views across the Weald of Kent. Spectacular rhododendrons, azaleas and fine specimen trees. Bluebell and natural woodland walks. Rose garden. Walled garden has extensive new planting, terracing and water feature. Children's adventure playground, den building trail, hedge maze and Yeti spotting. Café serving freshly ground coffee, speciality teas, light lunches, home-made cream teas, cakes, gluten free cakes and soya milk. Wheelchair access to Walled

Garden only. Good access to café, shop and tea terrace (no disabled WC).

♿ 🐕 ✿ 🚌 ☕

83 ROCK COTTAGE

New Church Road, Bilsington, Ashford, TN25 7LA. Bill & Penny Sisley. *6½m SE of Ashford. From M20, J10 take A2070 to Hastings. Join B2067 to Hamstreet, turn L on B2067 towards Bilsington, at White Horse PH turn R, onto New Church Rd. After 1m Rock Cottage is on L.* **Sat 3, Sun 4 June, Sat 9, Sun 10 Sept (10-5). Adm £5, chd free. Light refreshments.**

Tranquil 2 acre garden, created by the owners over the last 32yrs. A surprise around every corner with a series of garden rooms and a mixture of styles. Large collection of clematis, rambling roses. Wisteria walk, topiary garden, lime walk, wildflower meadow, living willow and native hedges, restored pond, fruit orchard. Dahlia beds. Specimen trees and shrubs, Mediterranean garden. Agaves. Partial wheelchair access.

♿ 🐕 ✿ 🚌 ☕

85 ST CLERE

Kemsing, Sevenoaks, TN15 6NL. Mr & Mrs Simon & Eliza Ecclestone, www.stclere.com. *6m NE of Sevenoaks. 1m E of Seal on A25, turn L signed Heaverham. In Heaverham turn R signed Wrotham. In 75yds straight ahead marked private rd; 1st L to house.* **Sun 18 June (2-5). Adm £5, chd £1. Home-made teas in Garden Room.**

4 acre garden, full of interest. Formal terraces surrounding C17 mansion (not open), with beautiful views of the Kent countryside. Herbaceous and shrub borders, productive kitchen and herb gardens, lawns and rare trees. Garden tours with Head Gardener at 2.30pm and 3.45pm (£1 per person). Some gravel paths and small steps.

☕

86 ◆ THE SECRET GARDENS OF SANDWICH AT THE SALUTATION

Knightrider Street, Sandwich, CT13 9EW. Mr & Mrs Dominic Parker, 01304 619919, enquiries@the-salutation.com, www.the-secretgardens.co.uk. *In the heart of Sandwich. Turn L at Bell Hotel & into Quayside car park. Entrance in far R corner of car park.* **For NGS: Wed 29 Mar, Thur 22 June, Tue 19 Sept (10-5). Adm £7, chd free. Home-made teas. For other opening times and information, please phone, email or visit garden website.**

3½ acres of ornamental and formal gardens designed by Sir Edwin Lutyens in 1911 surrounding Grade I listed house. Designated historic park and garden, lake. White, yellow, spring, woodland, rose, kitchen, vegetable and herbaceous gardens. Designed to provide yr-round changing colour. Unusual plants for sale. Gardens wheelchair friendly.

♿ 🐕 ✿ 🚌 🛏 ☕

The Secret Gardens of Sandwich at the Salutation

© Leigh Clapp

87 SANDOWN

Plain Road, Smeeth, nr Ashford, TN25 6QX. Malcolm & Pamela Woodcock. *4m SE of Ashford. Exit J10 onto A20, take 2nd L signed Smeeth, turn R Woolpack Hill, past garage on L, past next L, garden on L. From A20 in Sellindge at Church, turn R carry on 1m. Park in layby on hill.* **Sun 28, Mon 29 May, Sun 25 June, Sun 30 July, Sun 27, Mon 28 Aug (1-5). Adm £4, chd free. Cream teas.**

Our small compact Japanese style garden and Koi pond has visitor book comments such as: inspirational, just like Japan, a stunning hidden gem. There is a Japanese arbour, tea house/ veranda, waterfall and stream. Acers, bamboos, ilex crenata (Cloud Trees), ginkgo, fatsia japonica, akebia quinata, clerodendrum trichotomum, pinus mugos, wisterias, hostas and mind your own business for ground cover. WC available. Regret no small children owing to deep pond. Featured in local Parish magazines and mentioned on Radio Kent. Wheelchair access to top section of garden only.

✿ ☕

88 ◆ SCOTNEY CASTLE

Lamberhurst, TN3 8JN. National Trust, 01892 893820, scotneycastle@nationaltrust.org.uk, www.nationaltrust.org.uk/scotneycastle. *6m SE of Tunbridge Wells. On A21 London - Hastings, brown tourist signs. Bus: (Mon to Sat) Tunbridge Wells - Wadhurst, alight Lamberhurst Green.* **For NGS: Thur 11 May (10-5). Adm £14.30, chd £7.20. Light refreshments. For other opening times and information, please phone, email or visit garden website.**

The medieval moated Old Scotney Castle lies in a peaceful wooded valley. In C19 its owner Edward Hussey III set about building a new house, partially demolishing the Old Castle to create a romantic folly, the centrepiece of his picturesque landscape. From the terraces of the new house, sweeps of rhododendron and azaleas cascade down the slope in summer, mirrored in the moat. In the house three generations have made their mark, adding possessions and character to the homely Victorian mansion which enjoys far reaching views out across the estate. Wheelchairs available for loan.

♿ 🐕 ✿ 🚌 ☕

GROUP OPENING

89 SHIPBOURNE GARDENS
Shipbourne, TN11 9RJ. *Off A227 between Tonbridge & Borough Green. Gardens & car parking signed from Chaser PH. Combined group ticket & map available at both gardens and Village Hall.* Sat 17, Sun 18 June (11-5). Combined adm £5, chd free. Home-made teas in Village Hall.

HOOKWOOD HOUSE
Mr & Mrs Nicholas Ward.

PLANTATION HOUSE
Viv Packer.

Hookwood House is a charming country garden of 2 acres of formal features; old brick paths lead through small garden rooms enclosed by clipped native and yew hedges; mixed and herbaceous border, topiary, herb and vegetable gardens, nut plat, chickens, fruit orchard, cobbled Kentish ragstone yard and planted containers. Plantation House is an informal garden with serpentine beds of mixed shrubs and perennials, rhododendrons, roses, a grass border and a small wildlife pond. Organic vegetable garden with raised beds, soft fruit and chickens. Unusual specimen conifers and sculptures. Large terrace around the house with many tender plants. Teas in our pretty village hall on the village green which in June is a mass of wild flowers. If wet, only partial wheelchair access to both gardens.
&. ☕

90 ♦ SISSINGHURST CASTLE GARDEN
Sissinghurst, TN17 2AB. National Trust, 01580 710700, sissinghurst@nationaltrust.org.uk, www.nationaltrust.org.uk. *On A262 1m E of Sissinghurst. Bus: Arriva Maidstone-Hastings, alight Sissinghurst 1¼ m. Approx 30 mins walk from village.* For NGS: Sun 23 Apr (11-5.30). Light refreshments. NT admission prices will apply. Check website for details. For other opening times and information, please phone, email or visit garden website.
Garden created by Vita Sackville-West and Sir Harold Nicolson. Spring garden, herb garden, cottage garden, white garden, rose garden. Tudor building and tower, partly open to public. Moat. Vegetable garden and estate walks. Free welcome talks and estate walks leaflets. Café, restaurant and shop open from 10am-5.30pm daily, closed Christmas Eve and Christmas Day. Some areas unsuitable for wheelchair access due to narrow paths and steps.
&. ✿ 🏠 ☕

91 SMITHS HALL
Lower Road, West Farleigh, ME15 0PE. Mr S Norman, www.smithshall.com. *3m W of Maidstone. A26 towards Tonbridge, turn L into Teston Lane B2163. At T-junction turn R onto Lower Rd B2010. Opp Tickled Trout PH.* Sun 4 June, Sun 16 July (11-5). Adm £5, chd free. Home-made teas. *Donation to Heart of Kent Hospice.*
Delightful 3 acre gardens surrounding a beautiful 1719 Queen Anne House (not open). Lose yourself in numerous themed rooms: sunken water garden, iris beds, scented old fashioned rose walk, formal rose garden, intense wild flowers, peonies, deep herbaceous borders and specimen trees. Walk 9 acres of park and woodland with great variety of young native and American trees and fine views of the Medway valley. Cakes, quiche, jams and preserves available. Gravel paths.
&. 🐄 ✿ ☕

92 SPRING PLATT
Boyton Court Road, Sutton Valence, Maidstone, ME17 3BY. Mr & Mrs John Millen, 01622 843383, www.kentsnowdrops.com. *5m SE of Maidstone. From A274 nr Sutton Valence follow yellow NGS signs. Limited parking.* Wed 1 Feb (10-4). Sat 4, Sun 5 Feb (10-4), also open Knowle Hill Farm. Wed 8 Feb (10-4). Adm £4, chd free. Light refreshments. 2018: Sat 3, Sun 4, Wed 7 Feb. Visits also by arrangement in Feb 2017 & 2018 for groups 6+ only.
1 acre garden under continual development with panoramic views of the Weald. Over 600 varieties of snowdrop grown in tiered display beds with spring flowers in borders. An extensive collection of alpine plants in a large greenhouse. Vegetable garden and natural spring fed water feature. Home-made soup, home-made bread, tea/coffee and cake. Garden on a steep slope and many steps.
🐄 ✿ 🏠 ☕

93 STONEWALL PARK
Chiddingstone Hoath, nr Edenbridge, TN8 7DG. Mr & Mrs Fleming. *4m SE of Edenbridge. Via B2026. Halfway between Markbeech & Penshurst.* Sun 19 Mar (2-5). Sun 14 May (2-5), also open Old Buckhurst. Adm £5, chd free. Home-made teas in the conservatory. *Donation to Sarah Matheson Trust & St Mary's Church, Chiddingstone.*
Romantic woodland garden in historic setting featuring species rhododendrons, magnolias, azaleas, bluebells, a range of interesting trees and shrubs, sandstone outcrops, wandering paths and lakes. Historic parkland with cricket ground, sea of wild daffodils in March.
🐄 ✿ ☕

94 NEW SWEETBRIAR
69 Chequer Lane, Ash, nr Sandwich, CT3 2AX. Miss Louise Dowle & Mr Steven Edney, 01304 448476, lou.dowle@hotmail.co.uk. *8m from Canterbury, 3m from Sandwich. Turn off A257 into Chequer Lane, 100 meters from junction opp field.* Sun 6 Aug, Sun 10 Sept, Sun 8 Oct (11-5). Adm £3, chd free. Home-made teas. Visits also by arrangement July to Oct for groups min 10, max 20.
An average sized back garden transformed into an exotic jungle paradise, full of fabulous foliage and tempting tenders. A real plantsman's collection of many rare hardy and tender exotics to transport you into a lawn free tropical oasis. The

front garden is a traditional cottage kitchen garden combining flowers and vegetables with fruit and herbs. Newly installed meadow drive.

95 THATCHED COTTAGE
Hever Road, Hever, Edenbridge, TN8 7NH. Ivor & Wendy Macklin, 07970 156681, info@heverbedandbreakfast.co.uk. *200m from Hever Castle. 100m down hill from Henry VIII PH & St Peters Church.* Sat 24, Sun 25 June (1-5). Adm £5, chd free. Home-made teas.
Charming cottage garden with many roses, herbaceous and shrub borders. Herb garden, Tudor Well, natural pond with bridge and vegetable plot with small poly tunnel. Orchard leading onto meadow with wild flowers. Stunning views in AONB. Featured in Kent Life magazine and Winner Kent Life Garden Competition. Most of garden wheelchair accessible but some uneven surfaces.

96 TIMBERS
Dean Street, East Farleigh, nr Maidstone, ME15 0HS. Mrs Sue Robinson, 01622 729568, suerobinson.timbers@gmail.com, www.timbersgardenkent.co.uk. *2m S of Maidstone. From Maidstone take B2010 to East Farleigh. After Tesco's on R follow Dean St for ½m. Timbers on L behind 8ft beech hedge. Parking through gates. Access for 54 seater coaches.* Visits by arrangement Apr to July daytime and evening visits. Adm £5, chd free. Home-made teas. Light lunches by arrangement.
Beautiful 5 acre garden surrounding house designed with flower arranger's eye and colour a priority. Unusual perennials, annuals and shrubs. Tulips in spring. New partly walled garden, parterre, arbour, pergola, island beds, lawns and mature specimen trees plus 100yr old Kentish cobnut plat, wildflower meadows and woodland. Rock pool with waterfalls. Valley views. Plant List. Featured in Garden News Magazine. Most of garden is flat, some steep slopes to rear.

97 TORRY HILL
Frinsted/Milstead, Sittingbourne, ME9 0SP. Lady Kingsdown, 01795 830258, lady.kingsdown@btinternet.com. *5m S of Sittingbourne. From M20 J8 take A20 (Lenham). At r'about by Mercure Hotel turn L Hollingbourne (B2163). Turn R at Xrds at top of hill (Ringlestone Rd). Thereafter Frinsted-Doddington (not suitable for coaches), then Torry Hill/NGS signs. From M2 J5 take A249 towards Maidstone, then 1st L (Bredgar), Lagain (follow Bredgar signs), R at War Memorial, 1st L (Milstead), Torry Hill/NGS signs from Milstead. Please use entrance marked D (on red background) for disabled parking* Sun 14 May, Sun 11 June, Sun 16 July (2-5). Adm £4.50, chd free. Home-made teas. Visits also by arrangement May to July (Mon - Fri only). Groups 30 max. Adm £6.50 incl tea/coffee and biscuits. *Donation to St Dunstan's Church, Frinsted.*
8 acres; large lawns, specimen trees, flowering cherries, rhododendrons, azaleas and naturalised daffodils; walled gardens with lawns, shrubs, herbaceous borders, rose garden incl shrub roses, wild flower areas and vegetables. Extensive views to Medway and Thames estuaries. Some shallow steps. No wheelchair access to rose garden due to very uneven surface but can be viewed from pathway.

98 TOWNLAND
Sixfields, Tenterden, TN30 6EX. Alan & Lindy Bates, 01580 764505, alanandlindybates@yahoo.co.uk. *Just off Tenterden High St. Park in Bridewell Lane car park (Sunday free). From centre of Tenterden High St, walk down Jackson's Lane next to Webbs Ironmongers. Follow lane to end (400m). Phone for disabled parking.* Sun 11 June, Sun 16 July (2-5.30). Adm £5, chd free. Home-made teas. Visits also by arrangement June & July for groups 10+. *Donation to Pilgrims Hospice and ShelterBox.*
A 1 acre family garden in a unique position. Mixed borders, with a wide range of shrubs and flowers providing a riot of colour

throughout the year, flow into the more naturalistic planting which is adjacent to meadow areas and fruit trees. A gravel garden, rose arbour and intensive fruit and vegetable areas complete the experience. Small area redesigned this year due to encroaching development. Wide range of plants. Listed in Kent Life as one of the top 25 gardens to visit in Kent.

99 TRAM HATCH
Charing Heath, Ashford, TN27 0BN. Mrs P Scrivens, www.tramhatchgardens.co.uk. *10m NW of Ashford. A20 turn towards Charing Railway Stn on Pluckley Rd, over motorway then 1st R signed Barnfield to end, turn L carry on past Barnfield, Tram Hatch ahead.* Sat 17 June, Sun 9 July, Sun 13 Aug (12-5). Adm £5, chd free. Home-made teas.
Meander your way off the beaten track to a mature, extensive garden changing through the seasons. You will enjoy a garden laid out in rooms - what surprises are round the corner? Large selection of trees, vegetable, rose and gravel gardens, colourful containers. The R Stour and the Angel of the South enhance your visit. Please come and enjoy, then relax in our new garden room for tea. The garden is totally flat, apart from a very small area which can be viewed from the lane.

100 UPPER PRYORS
Butterwell Hill, Cowden, TN8 7HB. Mr & Mrs S G Smith. *4½m SE of Edenbridge. From B2026 Edenbridge-Hartfield, turn R at Cowden Xrds & take 1st drive on R.* Wed 21 June (12-6). Adm £5, chd free. Home-made teas.
10 acres of English country garden surrounding C16 house - a garden of many parts; colourful profusion, interesting planting arrangements, immaculate lawns, mature woodland, water and a terrace on which to appreciate the view, and tea!

Wyckhurst

© Leigh Clapp

101 WATERGATE HOUSE

King Street, Fordwich, Canterbury, CT2 0DB. Fiona Cadwallader, 01227 710470, fiona@cadwallader.co.uk, www.cadwallader.co.uk. *2m E of Canterbury. From Canterbury A257 direction, Sandwich, 1m L to Fordwich. 1m L on Moat Lane, direct to Watergate House bottom of High St. Follow parking instructions.* **Sat 22 Apr, Sat 17 June (2-6). Adm £4, chd free. Home-made teas. Visits also by arrangement Mar to Aug for groups 10+.** Magical walled garden by the R Stour: Defined areas of formal, spring, woodland, vegetable and secret garden reveal themselves in a naturally harmonious flow, each with its own colour combinations. Ancient walls provide the garden's basic structure, while a green oak pergola echoes a monastic cloister. The garden is mainly on one level with one raised walkway under pergola.

🅳 ☕

102 WEST COURT LODGE

Postling Court, The Street, Postling, nr Hythe, CT21 4EX. Mr & Mrs John Pattrick, 01303 863285, malliet@hotmail.co.uk. *2m NW of Hythe. From M20 J11 turn S onto A20. Immed 1st L. After ½m on bend take rd signed Lyminge. 1st L into Postling.* **Sat 10, Sun 11 June (12-5). Combined adm with Churchfield £6, chd free. Home-made teas in Village Hall or garden. Visits also by arrangement May to Sept combined with Churchfield. Groups 35 max.**

S-facing 1 acre walled garden at the foot of the N Downs, designed in 2 parts: main lawn with large sunny borders and a romantic woodland glade planted with shadow loving plants and spring bulbs, small wildlife pond. Lovely C11 church will be open next to the gardens.

🔥 🐐 ✿ 🚗 ☕

GROUP OPENING

103 WEST MALLING EARLY SUMMER GARDENS

West Malling, ME19 6LW. *On A20, nr J4 of M20. Park in West Malling for Town Hill Cottage & Went House where maps, directions to 1 & 2 New Barns Cottages & New Barns Oasts & combined tickets available.* **Sun 4 June (12-5). Combined adm £6, chd free. Home-made teas at New Barns Cottages.** *Donation to St Mary's Church, West Malling.*

NEW BARNS COTTAGES
Mr & Mrs Anthony Drake.

2 NEW BARNS OAST
Nick Robinson & Becky Robinson Hugill.

TOWN HILL COTTAGE
Mr & Mrs P Cosier.

WENT HOUSE
Alan & Mary Gibbins.

West Malling is an attractive small market town with some fine buildings. Enjoy four lovely gardens that are entirely different from each other and cannot be seen from the road. Went House is a Queen Anne house surrounded by a secret garden with a stream,

specimen trees, old roses, mixed borders, attractive large kitchen garden, Roman temple, fountain and parterre. Town Hill Cottage is a part walled garden with mature and interesting planting. New Barns Cottages have serpentine paths leading through woodland to roomed gardens: tea and cakes in the courtyard garden of the cottages. New Barns Oasts has bespoke landscape features and is a child friendly adults' garden. Town Hill Cottage garden and New Barns Cottages are difficult to access but the other gardens have wheelchair access.

🔥 🐐 ☕

GROUP OPENING

104 WHITSTABLE GARDENS

Whitstable, CT5 4LT. *Off A299, or A290. Drive down Borstal Hill, L by garage into Joy Lane to collect map of participating gardens. Parking available at Joy Lane Primary School.* **Sun 21 May (10-5). Combined adm £6, chd free. Home-made teas at Stream Walk Community Gardens.**

87 ALBERT STREET
Paul Carey & Phil Gomm.

6 ALEXANDRA ROAD
Andrew Mawson & Sarah Rees.

56 ARGYLE ROAD
Emma Burnham & Mel Green.

CAPLE HOUSE
Efua Thomas.

NEW 5 CLARE ROAD
Janet Maxwell & Philip Adam.

NEW THE GUINEA
Sheila Wyver.

19 JOY LANE
Francine Raymond, www.kitchen-garden-hens.co.uk.

NEW OCEAN COTTAGE
Katherine Pickering.

STREAM WALK FOOTPATH
Stream Walk Community Gardens.

34 VICTORIA STREET
Caroline Burgess.

Enjoy a day of eclectic gardens by the sea. 10 people are showing off their gardens, but others, marked with yellow balloons, are there to admire from the street. From fishermen's yards to formal gardens, residents of Whitstable are making the most of quirky plots, enjoying the mild climate and the range of plants we can grow. Drop in and admire wildlife (19 Joy Lane), edibles (Caple House), gravel gardens (The Guinea & Clare Rd), experimental gardens (6 Alexandra Rd), and those starting from scratch (56 Argyle Rd & 34 Victoria St). We're maximising our space, be it tiny (87 Albert St & Ocean Cottage), on a busy road or in deep shade. We garden on heavy Kent clay and are prone to northerly winds. Stream Walk is the heart of our gardening community, where residents can learn new skills & buy surplus produce - the ideal spot for those without outside space of their own. By opening, we're hoping to encourage those new to gardening with our ingenuity and style, rather than rolling acres. Combined adm £6 per adult or £10 for 2. Horticultural Society Plant Stall in front garden of 19 Joy Lane.

❀ ☕

---

105 ◆ THE WORLD GARDEN AT LULLINGSTONE CASTLE
Eynsford, DA4 0JA. Guy Hart Dyke, 01322 862114, www.lullingstonecastle.co.uk. *1m from Eynsford. Over Ford Bridge in Eynsford Village. Follow signs to Roman Villa. Keep Roman Villa immed on R then follow Private Rd to Gatehouse.* **For NGS: Sun 18 June (12-5). Adm £7, chd free. Light refreshments. For other opening times and information, please phone or visit garden website.** Interactive world map of plants laid out as a map of the world within a walled garden. The oceans are your pathways as you navigate the world in 1 acre. You can see Ayers Rock and walk alongside the Andes whilst reading tales of intrepid plant hunters. Discover the origins of some 6,000 different plants - you'll

be amazed where they come from! Plant Hunters Nursery and Lullingstone World Garden seeds for sale. Wheelchairs available upon request.

♿ ❀ 🚌 🏠 NPC ☕

---

106 WYCKHURST
Mill Road, Aldington, Ashford, TN25 7AJ. Mr & Mrs Chris Older, 01233 720395, cdo@rmfarms.co.uk. *4m SE of Ashford. From M20 J10 take A20 2m E to Aldington turning; turn R at Xrds & proceed 1½m to Aldington Village Hall. Turn R & immed L by Walnut Tree Inn down Forge Hill. After ¼m turn R into Mill Rd.* **Sat 3, Sun 4, Sat 10, Sun 11 June (12-6). Adm £5, chd free. Home-made teas on the Sun Terrace. Visits also by arrangement in June.** Delightful C16 Kent Cottage (not open) nestles in romantic seclusion at the end of a drive. This enchanting 1 acre garden is a mixture of small mixed herbaceous borders, roses and much unusual topiary incl a wild flower meadow. There is plenty of seating round the lawns to enjoy the garden and teas with extensive views of the Kent Countryside across to the Romney Marsh on towards the sea. There is a dell with a small water feature. And in the wildflower meadow is a shepherd's hut to enjoy after a stroll. Some gentle slopes which limit wheelchair access to some small areas.

♿ ❀ ☕

GROUP OPENING

107 WYE GARDENS
Harville Road, Wye, TN25 5EY. *3m NE of Ashford. From A28 take turning signed Wye. Bus: Ashford to Canterbury via Wye. Train: Wye. Next door to Spring Grove School.* **Sun 18 June (2-6). Combined adm £5, chd free. Home-made teas at Spring Grove Farmhouse.**

3 BRAMBLE CLOSE
Dr M Copland.

SPRING GROVE FARM HOUSE
Heather Van den Bergh.

Two gardens are open this year, both are situated on the North East edge of the village close to Wye station. A complete contrast to each other, they offer to gardeners and visitors of every level the opportunity to explore the Country garden. Spring Grove Farmhouse has been created from the original working farm replacing cow sheds and hardstanding area with a peaceful tranquil garden full of colour and interesting plants. A stream runs through the lawn area providing fabulous views of the Kent countryside. There will be afternoon teas available at Spring Grove thanks to the assistance of the ladies of Wye Church. At Bramble Lane you will enjoy the unique experience of a very wild garden, incl meadow, ponds and ditches as well as seeing the results of research carried out on the effect on wild life. A unique experience. Wye Gardens opening coincides with Stour Music Festival. Wheelchair access to Spring Grove Farm House only.

♿ ☕

---

108 YEW TREE COTTAGE
Penshurst, TN11 8AD. Mrs Pam Tuppen, 01892 870689. *4m SW of Tonbridge. From A26 Tonbridge to Tunbridge Wells, join B2176 Bidborough to Penshurst Rd. 2m W of Bidborough, 1m before Penshurst. Please phone for further directions. Unsuitable for coaches.* **Wed 8, Sun 26 Feb, Sun 12, Wed 22 Mar, Wed 5, Sun 23 Apr, Wed 3, Sun 21 May, Wed 7, Sun 25 June, Wed 5, Sun 23 July, Wed 9, Sat 19 Aug, Wed 6 Sept (12-5). Adm £3, chd free. Light refreshments.** Small, romantic cottage garden with steep hillside entrance. Lots of seats and secret corners, many unusual plants - hellebores, spring bulbs, old roses, many special perennials. Small pond; something to see in all seasons. Created and maintained by owner, a natural garden full of plants.

❀ ☕

LANCASHIRE
Merseyside, Greater Manchester

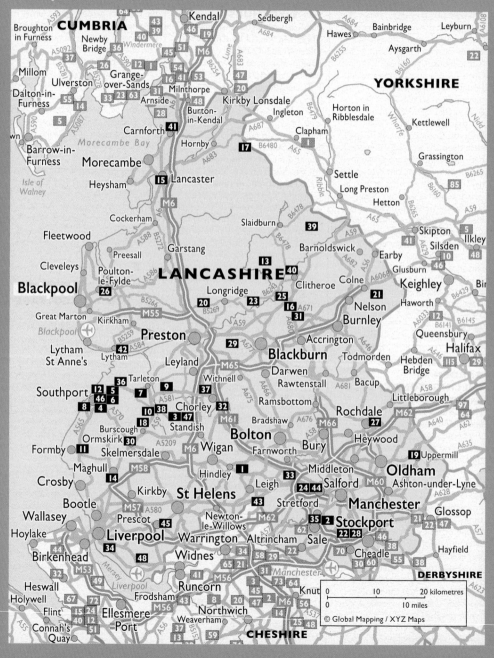

CUMBRIA

Broughton in Furness

Kendal

Sedbergh

Hawes

Bainbridge

Leyburn

Newby Bridge

Windermere

Aysgarth

YORKSHIRE

Millom

Ulverston

Grange-over-Sands

Milnthorpe

Kirkby Lonsdale

Horton in Ribblesdale

Kettlewell

Dalton-in-Furness

Arnside

Burton-in-Kendal

Ingleton

Clapham

Barrow-in-Furness

Carnforth

Hornby

Settle

Grassington

Isle of Walney

Morecambe Bay

Morecambe

Heysham

Lancaster

Long Preston

Hetton

Cockerham

Slaidburn

Skipton

Ilkley

Fleetwood

Garstang

Barnoldswick

Earby

Silsden

Preesall

LANCASHIRE

Longridge

Clitheroe

Colne

Glusburn

Keighley

Cleveleys

Poulton-le-Fylde

Nelson

Haworth

Blackpool

Burnley

Queensbury

Halifax

Great Marton

Kirkham

Accrington

Blackpool

Preston

Blackburn

Todmorden

Hebden Bridge

Lytham St Anne's

Lytham

Leyland

Darwen

Rawtenstall

Bacup

Littleborough

Southport

Tarleton

Chorley

Ramsbottom

Rochdale

Withnell

Burscough

Standish

Bradshaw

Heywood

Ormskirk

Bolton

Bury

Formby

Skelmersdale

Wigan

Farnworth

Uppermill

Maghull

Hindley

Leigh

Middleton

Oldham

Crosby

Kirkby

St Helens

Stretford

Salford

Ashton-under-Lyne

Bootle

Prescot

Newton-le-Willows

Manchester

Glossop

Wallasey

Liverpool

Warrington

Altrincham

Sale

Stockport

Hoylake

Widnes

Cheadle

Hayfield

Birkenhead

Runcorn

Manchester

Heswall

Frodsham

Knut

DERBYSHIRE

Holywell

Flint

Ellesmere Port

Northwich

Connah's Quay

Weaverham

CHESHIRE

0   10   20 kilometres
0   10 miles

© Global Mapping / XYZ Maps

You can always be sure of a really warm red-rose welcome when you visit any of Lancashire's beautiful gardens.

From the tiniest of cottage gardens to spectacular views of Pendle Hill – there is something to delight every taste in all parts of the county.

From Chorley Cakes to Eccles Cakes, from Lemon Drizzle to Victoria Sponge, we have delicacies to tempt every palate. Add a few choice plants to the mix and you can have a fantastic day out for under £10.

Volunteers

County Organiser
Margaret Fletcher
01704 567742
margaret.fletcher@ngs.org.uk

County Treasurer
Geoff Fletcher
01704 567742
geoffwfletcher@hotmail.co.uk

Publicity
Lynn Kelly
01704 563740
lynn-kelly@hotmail.co.uk

Christine Ruth
01517 274877
caruthchris@aol.com

Booklet Co-ordinator
Brenda Doldon
01704 834253
doldon@btinternet.com

Assistant County Organisers
Anne & Jim Britt
01614 458100
annebritt@btinternet.com

Peter & Sandra Curl
01704 893713
peter.curl@btinternet.com

Brenda Doldon
(as above)

Carole Ann & Stephen Powers
01254 824903
powers@carolepowers6.orangehome.
    co.uk

Eric & Sharon Rawcliffe
01253 883275
ericrawk@talktalk.net

© Fiona Lea

Left: 14 Saxon Road, Birkdale Village Gardens

OPENING DATES

All entries subject to change. For latest information check www.ngs.org.uk

Extended openings are shown at the beginning of the month.

Map locator numbers are shown to the right of each garden name.

February
Snowdrop Festival

Sunday 12th
Weeping Ash Garden   43

Sunday 19th
Weeping Ash Garden   43

Sunday 26th
Weeping Ash Garden   43

March

Sunday 5th
Weeping Ash Garden   43

April

Saturday 15th
Dale House Gardens   20

Sunday 16th
Dale House Gardens   20

May

The Secret Valley
(Every Sunday from Sunday 21st)   33

Warton Hall
(Every Day Saturday 6th to Sunday 14th)   42

Monday 1st
◆ The Ridges   32

Saturday 6th
Warton Hall   42

Sunday 7th
Didsbury Village
Gardens   22
Warton Hall   42
Weeping Ash Garden   43

Saturday 13th
Warton Hall   42

Sunday 14th
79 Crabtree Lane   18
Warton Hall   42

Sunday 21st
12 Bankfield Lane   6
NEW Heaton Gardens   28
Warton Gardens   41

90th Anniversary Weekend

Sunday 28th
Birkdale Gardens   8
Bretherton Gardens   9
◆ Clearbeck House   17
5 Crib Lane   19
NEW 12 The Croft   37
Waddow Lodge
Garden   40

Monday 29th
Bretherton Gardens   9
◆ Clearbeck House   17
5 Crib Lane   19

June

The Secret Valley
(Every Sunday)   33

Saturday 3rd
Mill Barn   29

Sunday 4th
◆ Browsholme Hall   13
Mill Barn   29

Saturday 10th
136 Buckingham Road   14
Mill Barn   29

Sunday 11th
136 Buckingham Road   14
Casa Lago   16
79 Crabtree Lane   18
Didsbury Village
Gardens   22
Mill Barn   29

Saturday 17th
NEW Alderbank   2
35 Ellesmere Road   24
NEW 11 Westminster
Road   44

Sunday 18th
NEW 8 Andertons Mill   3
Birkdale Gardens   8
Green Farm Cottage   26
Warton Gardens   41
NEW Woodstock Barn   47

Saturday 24th
Dale House Gardens   20
Dutton Hall   23
Great Mitton Hall   25
NEW Ormskirk Gardens   30

Sunday 25th
40 Acreswood Avenue   1
90 Brick Kiln Lane   10
NEW Bridge Inn
Community Farm   11
◆ Clearbeck House   17
Dale House Gardens   20
Dutton Hall   23
Great Mitton Hall   25
NEW Ormskirk Gardens   30
NEW 5 Thornton Close   38

Wednesday 28th
Dutton Hall   23

July

The Secret Valley
(Every Sunday)   33

Saturday 1st
Becconsall   7
Carr House Farm   15

Sunday 2nd
NEW 8 Balfour Road   4
Becconsall   7
Bretherton Gardens   9
Carr House Farm   15
◆ Clearbeck House   17
8 Park Head   31
NEW 91 Station Road   36
NEW 81 Windsor Road   46

Saturday 8th
NEW Woolton Village
Gardens   48

Sunday 9th
NEW 8 Andertons Mill   3
Birkdale Gardens   8
NEW Woodstock Barn   47

Saturday 15th
8 Bankfield Lane   5
12 Bankfield Lane   6

Sunday 16th
8 Bankfield Lane   5
12 Bankfield Lane   6
79 Crabtree Lane   18
Sefton Park Gardens   34
Waddow Lodge
Garden   40
Warton Gardens   41

Sunday 23rd
Southlands   35

August

The Secret Valley
(Every Sunday to
Sunday 13th)   33

Saturday 5th
The Growth Project   27

Saturday 12th
NEW Willowbrook Hospice
Gardens   45

Sunday 13th
NEW Willowbrook Hospice
Gardens   45

Sunday 27th
Bretherton Gardens   9

Monday 28th
◆ The Ridges   32

September

Sunday 10th
Weeping Ash Garden   43

By Arrangement

NEW 8 Andertons Mill   3
12 Bankfield Lane   6
NEW Bridge Inn
Community Farm   11
4 Brocklebank Road   12
Carr House Farm   15
Casa Lago   16
79 Crabtree Lane   18
Dale House Gardens   20
Dent Hall   21
71 Dunbar Crescent,
Birkdale Gardens   8
Green Farm Cottage   26
The Growth Project   27
22 Hartley Crescent,
Birkdale Gardens   8
Hazel Cottage,
Bretherton Gardens   9
72 Ludlow Drive,
Ormskirk Gardens   30
111 Main Street,
Warton Gardens   41
Mill Barn   29
Owl Barn, Bretherton
Gardens   9
14 Saxon Road,
Birkdale Gardens   8
The Secret Valley   33
Varley Farm   39
NEW 81 Windsor Road   46
NEW Woodstock Barn   47

THE GARDENS

79 Crabtree Lane

© Fiona Lea

1 40 ACRESWOOD AVENUE

Hindley Green, Wigan, WN2 4NJ. Angie Barker, www.angiebarker.co.uk. *4m E of Wigan. Take A577 from Wigan to Manchester, L at Victoria Hotel, at T-junction R & 1st L.* Sun 25 June (11-4). Adm £3.50, chd free. Light refreshments.

This small garden in the middle of a modern housing estate, has been created from scratch over the last 11 years. It uses planting to bring privacy to an overlooked space and has a mix of contemporary and cottage garden styles. It features a formal decked pond area, small wildlife pond and a small vegetable plot. In November 2015 a contemporary courtyard garden was added. Featured in Modern Gardens magazine.

2 NEW ALDERBANK

40c Edge Lane, Chorlton, Manchester, M21 9JW. Carolyn Shearman & Paul Harnett. *4m SE Manchester. On the L of Edge Lane heading towards Stretford from Chorlton. Alderfield Rd is on R just before Longford Park, Alderbank is on the corner.* Sat 17 June (12.30-5). Adm £3, chd free. Light refreshments.

A quirky Chorlton garden! Recycled materials. Wildlife friendly areas. Great variety of lush naturalistic cottage style planting. New wildlife friendly pond with bridge. Front garden with organic fruit, vegetables and herbs. Over 100 pots! Lots of roses, clematis, grasses, and some unusual plants. Secluded pergola with mosaics. Only 3 years in the making and still developing! Narrow, uneven paths and several steps so sorry not suitable for wheelchairs.

3 NEW 8 ANDERTONS MILL

Mawdesley, Ormskirk, L40 3TW. Mr & Mrs R Mercer, 01257 450636, margaret.mercer6@btinternet.com. *9m E of Ormskirk. M6 J27 A5209 over Parbold Hill, R Lancaster Lane/ Chorley Rd, L after Farmers Arms to Bentley Lane/Andertons Mill. Garden 500yds on R. From Burscough A59, A5209 towards Parbold, L Lancaster Lane.* Sun 18 June, Sun 9 July (12-5). Combined adm with Woodstock Barn £4.50, chd free. Home-made teas. Visits also by arrangement July to Sept for groups of 10 +.

This ½ acre cottage garden started in 2010, has many colourful borders of perennials, shrubs, and roses. A patio with raised beds, secluded potted plant area, large vegetable garden. Rose and clematis covered arches and many wrought iron features. An extensive bed of scented roses and a wonderful view of Harrock Hill. Wheelchair access to most areas across lawns.

& ✿ ☕ 🚽

4 NEW 8 BALFOUR ROAD

Southport, PR8 6LE. Mr & Mrs Stephenson, www.leadingahorticulture. wordpress.com. *1.4m SE of Southport. Off A570 Southport to Ormskirk rd. Turn L 1st rd up from football ground.* Sun 2 July (12-7). Combined adm with 81 Windsor Road £3.50, chd free. Home made soft drinks.

Walled garden given mainly to a plantswoman's collection of perennials and shrubs. Large Edwardian conservatory stocked with tropicals and an extensive cactus collection.

5 8 BANKFIELD LANE

Churchtown, Southport, PR9 7NJ. Alan & Gill Swift. *2½ m N of Southport. Turn R at T-lights on A565 in Churchtown, 1st L at r'about past Hesketh Arms PH & Botanic Gardens main entrance on L. Garden is 200yds on R.* Sat 15 July (11-5). Home-made teas. Sun 16 July (11-5). Combined adm with 12 Bankfield Lane £4, chd free. *Donation to NW Spinal Injuries Unit, Southport Hospital.*

Open aspect to rear of garden, double herbaceous borders, small vegetable garden, greenhouse, chickens coup, two raised patio areas. Front garden has trees, shrubs and roses. Restricted parking on Bankfield Lane. Parking available at rear of Botanic Gardens on Verulam Road. A short walk through Botanic Gardens to Bankfield Lane via main or side gate. Wheelchair access to most areas.

& ✿ ☕ 🚽

Glynwood House, Bretherton Gardens

6 12 BANKFIELD LANE
Churchtown, Southport,
PR9 7NJ. Alan & Eileen
Brannigan, 07570 799593,
abrannigan@sky.com. *2½m N of
Southport. Turn R at T-lights on A565
in Churchtown 1st L at r'about, then
past Hesketh Arms PH & Botanic
Gardens main entrance on L. Garden
is 220yds on R.* Sun 21 May (11-
5). Adm £3, chd free. Sat 15,
Sun 16 July (11-5). Combined
adm with 8 Bankfield Lane £4,
chd free. Home-made teas.
Visits also by arrangement
May to July for groups of 10 to
20. Adm incl refreshments for
group visits. *Donation to Freshfield
Animal Rescue and Liverpool Animal
Aid.*
This attractive walled garden has
been lovingly landscaped by current
owners over 30yrs and is continually
evolving. It has a well stocked
pond with waterfalls, a stone bed,
alpine troughs, mixed borders with
magnolias, and rhododendrons.
Open aspect to rear. Greenhouse
and patio areas. The front garden
has a stone bed and mixed borders.
Level paths but entrance gate
to rear garden too narrow for
wheelchairs.
✿

7 BECCONSALL
Hunters Lane, Tarleton Moss,
Tarleton, Preston, PR4 6JL. John &
Elizabeth Caunce. *11m S of Preston,
6m N of Southport. Situated off
A565. A59 to Tarleton, then A565 to
Southport. After 2m, turn R into Moss
Hey Lane. Follow signs to new car
park field. Disabled parking, follow
signs. (New parking arrangements
this year).* Sat 1, Sun 2 July (11-5).
Adm £3.50, chd free. Home-
made teas. Wine and beer.
An interesting 1 acre garden,
combining different areas of
lawn, rill, arboretum, herbaceous
border, wild flower area and raised
vegetable beds. Brass Band will be
playing each afternoon, weather
permitting. Featured in Lancashire
Life. Wheelchair access to most of
the garden.
♿ ✿

GROUP OPENING

8 BIRKDALE GARDENS
Birkdale, Southport, PR8 2AX.
*1m S of Southport. Off A565
Southport to Liverpool rd. 4th on L
after r'about, opp St James Church.
Maps available at each location.*
Sun 28 May, Sun 18 June, Sun
9 July (11-5). Combined adm
£5, chd free. Home-made teas
at Saxon Rd, & Quiet Garden.
Bacon sandwiches at 22 Hartley
Crescent. *Donation to Light for Life.*

23 ASHTON ROAD
John & Jennifer Mawdsley.
Open on Sun 28 May, Sun 18 June
NEW 33 CLOVELLY DRIVE
Mr & Mrs R Drummond.
Open on Sun 28 May, Sun 9 July
71 DUNBAR CRESCENT
Mrs Kimberley Gittins,
07779 181149,
kgo611@ymail.com.
Open on Sun 18 June, Sun 9 July
Visits also by arrangement
Apr to July, refreshments may
be incl for groups.
22 HARTLEY CRESCENT
Sandra & Keith Birks,
01704 567182,
sandie.b@talktalk.net.
Open on Sun 28 May, Sun 9 July
Visits also by arrangement
May to Aug groups of 10+.
NEW LINKS VIEW, 18
CLOVELLY DRIVE
Mr & Mrs D McGarry.
Open on Sun 28 May, Sun 9 July
10 MEADOW AVENUE
John & Jenny Smith.
Open on Sun 18 June, Sun 9 July
ST PETER'S CHURCH
QUIET GARDEN
St Peter's.
Open on Sun 28 May, Sun 18 June
14 SAXON ROAD
Margaret & Geoff Fletcher,
01704 567742,
margaret.fletcher@ngs.org.uk.
Open on all dates
Visits also by arrangement
May to July for groups of 10+.
66 SHAWS ROAD
Vivienne Rimmer.
Open on all dates

An established group of gardens
surrounding the NW in Bloom award
winning Victorian village of Birkdale,
some within easy walking distance,
others reached by a short car journey.
Some gardens opening on all 3
dates, others less. Gardens feature
a plantswoman's garden in cottage
garden style, a walled garden with
an array of tender plants amongst
informal island beds and a developing
family garden. An impressive example
of a Quiet Garden with labyrinth
and hut for peaceful contemplation.
A garden of different rooms with
inspirational fruit and vegetable plot,
a delightful L shaped garden with a
special secret garden. Returning after
major landscaping a quirky garden full
of surprises. Joining this year 2 gardens
full of colour and interest. Wheelchair
access to some gardens.

&. ✿ ☕ ▣

GROUP OPENING

9 BRETHERTON
GARDENS
South Road, Bretherton, Leyland,
PR26 9AD. *8m SW of Preston.
Between Southport & Preston, from
A59, take B5247 towards Chorley
for 1m. Gardens signed from South
Rd (B5247).* Sun 28, Mon 29 May,
Sun 2 July, Sun 27 Aug (12-5).
Combined adm £5, chd free.
Home-made teas at Bretherton
Congregational Church. Light
lunches (2 July only).

GLYNWOOD HOUSE
Terry & Sue Riding.

HAZEL COTTAGE
John & Kris Jolley, 01772 600896,
jolley@johnjolley.plus.com.
Visits also by arrangement.

OWL BARN
Richard & Barbara Farbon,
01772 600750,
farbons@btinternet.com.
Visits also by arrangement
May to Sept small groups up
to 12.

PEAR TREE COTTAGE
John & Gwenifer Jackson.

Four contrasting gardens spaced
across attractive village with

conservation area. Glynwood House
has ¾ acre mixed borders, pond
with drystone-wall water feature,
woodland walk, patio garden with
pergola and raised beds, all in a
peaceful location with spectacular
open aspects. Pear Tree Cottage
garden blends seamlessly into its
rural setting with informal displays of
ornamental and edible crops, water
and mature trees, against a backdrop
of open views to the West Pennine
Moors. Owl Barn has herbaceous
borders with cottage garden and
hardy plants, a productive kitchen
garden providing fruit, vegetables
and cut flowers, and two ponds
with fountains which complement
the C18 converted barn (not open).
Hazel Cottage garden has evolved
from a Victorian subsistence plot
to encompass a series of themed
spaces packed with plants to engage
the senses and the mind. Live
music at Glynwood. Home-made
preserves for sale at Pear Tree
Cottage. Location of BBC Radio
Lancashire's 'Lancashire Outdoors'
broadcast. Narrow or uneven paths
in some parts of all the gardens.

&. ✿ 🚗 ☕ ▣

Funds from
NGS gardens
help Macmillan
support
thousands of
people every
year

10 90 BRICK KILN LANE

Rufford, Ormskirk, L40 1SZ. Mrs
Jacky Soper. *From M6 J27, follow
signs for Parbold then Rufford. Turn
L onto the A59. Turn R at Hesketh
Arms PH. Turn 3rd L.* Sun 25 June
(12-5). Combined adm with 5
Thornton Close £3.50, chd free.
A small cottage garden, with a variety
of different garden rooms containing
shrubs, perennials, alpines, climbers,
cobbled courtyard and a small pond.
Wheelchair access limited: due to
narrow paths and large step down to
cobbled courtyard.
✻

11 NEW BRIDGE INN COMMUNITY FARM

Moss Side, Formby, Liverpool,
L37 0AF. Bridge Inn Community
Farm, 01704 830303,
bridgeinnfarm@talktalk.net,
www.bridgeinncommunityfarm.
co.uk. *7m S of Southport. Formby
by-pass A565, L onto Moss Side.*
Sun 25 June (10-4). Adm £3.50,
chd free. Light refreshments
in canteen. Visits also by
arrangement.
Bridge Inn Community Farm was
established in 2010 in response to a
community need. Our farm sits on
a beautiful four-acre small holding
with views looking out over the
countryside. We provide a quality
service of training in a real life
work environment and experience
in horticulture, conservation and
animal welfare.
🐑 🚗 ☕ 🍴

12 4 BROCKLEBANK ROAD

Southport, PR9 9LP. Alan
& Heather Sidebotham,
01704 543389,
alansidebotham@yahoo.co.uk.
*1¼ m N of Southport. Off A565
Southport to Preston Rd, opp North
entrance to Hesketh Park.* Visits
by arrangement May to Aug,
groups of 8+. Adm £3, chd free.
Home-made teas.

40 Acreswood Avenue

© Fiona Lea

A walled garden incorporating
a church folly. Landscaped with
reclaimed materials from historic
sites in the Southport area. There are
several water features, an extensive
herbaceous border and various areas
of differing planting, thus creating a
garden with much interest.
♿ 🚗 ☕ 🍴

13 ◆ BROWSHOLME HALL

Clitheroe Road, Cow Ark,
Clitheroe, BB7 3DE. Mr &
Mrs R Parker, 01254 827160,
cturner@browsholme.com,
www.browsholme.com. *5m NW
of Clitheroe. From Clitheroe, leave
on B6243 via Edisford Bridge, R to
Bashall Eaves. From Whalley turn
L to Great Mitton, then to Bashall
Eaves. From Longridge follow signs to
Trough of Bowland.* For NGS: Sun
4 June (10-5). Adm £3.50. Light
refreshments in the Tithe Barn
at Browsholme Hall (licensed).
For other opening times and
information, please phone, email or
visit garden website.
Historic garden and parkland in the
setting of a 500 year old grade 1
listed Hall (open). Evidence remains
of the C17 garden with magnificent
yew walk and 'wilderness'
undergoing restoration. The parkland
setting is in the style of Capability
Brown with C18 origins of lakes,
woodland views and a ha-ha;
while the immediate garden area
reflects the later Edwardian period.
Garden nursery stalls, guided walks,
demonstrations and tours of historic
house (separate charge). Gravel
paths and lawns. Car park 300 yds.
♿ 🐑 ✻ 🚗 ☕ 🍴

14 136 BUCKINGHAM ROAD

Maghull, L31 7DR. Debbie &
Mark Jackson. *7m N of Liverpool.
End M57/M58, A59 to Ormskirk
after ½m, 1st L after car superstore
onto Liverpool Rd South, cont' on
past Meadows PH, 3rd R into
Sandringham Rd, L into Buckingham
Rd.* Sat 10, Sun 11 June (12-5).
Adm £2.50, chd free.
Home-made teas.
A small suburban garden brimming
with roses, cottage garden plants,
containers and hanging baskets full

of colour. Wisteria covered pergola and small fishpond. The garden is planted to attract birds, butterflies and bees. Plenty of seating available and large selection of plants for sale.

& ✿ ☕

15 CARR HOUSE FARM

Carr House Lane, Lancaster, LA1 1SW. Robin & Helen Loxam, 01524 60646. *SW of Lancaster City. From A6 Lancaster city centre turn at hospital, past B&Q & 1st R, straight under railway bridge into farm.* **Sat 1, Sun 2 July (10-5). Adm £4, chd free. Home-made teas. Visits also by arrangement May to Aug for groups of 10+.** *Donation to Fairfield Flora & Fauna Association.*
A hidden gem in historic City of Lancaster. Farmhouse gardens incl Mediterranean, rustic and cottage flowers and trees intertwined beautifully with 2 ponds fed naturally by 'Lucy Brook' attracting all manner of wildlife. Apple, pear, plum, lemon and orange trees mix well within the scene. See rare breed cattle and enjoy nature walk in adjoining fields. Featured in Lancashire Life and Lancashire Magazine. Slope towards pond.

& 🐐 ✿ ☕

16 CASA LAGO

1 Woodlands Park, Whalley, BB7 9UG. Carole Ann & Stephen Powers, 01254 824903, powers@ carolepowers6.orangehome.co.uk. *2½m S of Clitheroe. From M6 J31, take A59 to Clitheroe. 9m take 2nd exit at r'about for Whalley. After 2m reach village & follow yellow signs. Parking in village car parks or nearby.* **Sun 11 June (1-5). Adm £4, chd free. Light refreshments. Visits also by arrangement May to Aug.**
Travel the globe through horticultural specimens with the rare and unusual, bonsai trees, koi ponds, succulent garden, oak pergolas, alpine displays, black limestone wall, hostas, decked elevated glass areas, Consistent visitor comments, paradise, breath taking, inspiring, absolutely fab u lous!

& ✿ ☕

17 ◆ CLEARBECK HOUSE

Mewith Lane, Higher Tatham via Lancaster, LA2 8PJ. Peter & Bronwen Osborne, 01524 261029, www.clearbeckgarden.org.uk. *13m NE of Lancaster. Signed from Wray (M6 J34, A683, B6480) & Low Bentham.* **For NGS: Sun 28, Mon 29 May, Sun 25 June, Sun 2 July (11-5). Adm £4, chd free. Light refreshments. For other opening times and information, please phone or visit garden website.**
'A surprise round every corner' is the most common response as visitors encounter fountains, streams, ponds, sculptures, boathouses and follies: Rapunzel's tower, temple, turf maze, giant fish made of CDs, walk-through pyramid. 2-acre wildlife lake attracts many species of insects and birds. Planting incl herbaceous borders, grasses, bog plants and many roses. Vegetable and fruit garden. Painting studio open. Children- friendly incl quiz. Artists and photographers welcome by arrangement. Wheelchair access - many grass paths, some sloped.

& 🐐 ✿ 🚗 ☕

18 79 CRABTREE LANE

Burscough, L40 0RW. Sandra & Peter Curl, 01704 893713, peter.curl@btinternet.com. *3m NE of Ormskirk. A59 Preston - Liverpool Rd. From N before bridge R into Redcat Lane signed for Martin Mere. From S over 2nd bridge L into Redcat Lane after ¾m L into Crabtree Lane.* **Sun 14 May, Sun 11 June, Sun 16 July (11-4). Adm £3.50, chd free. Home-made teas. Visits also by arrangement May to July short talk on how the garden developed.**
¾ acre all year round plants person's garden with many rare and unusual plants. Herbaceous borders and colour themed island beds leading to a pond and rockery, rose garden, spring area and autumn hot bed. Many stone features built with reclaimed materials. Shrubs and rhododendrons, Koi pond with waterfall, hosta and fern walk. Gravel garden with Mediterranean plants. Patio, surrounded by shrubs and raised alpine bed. Trees giving areas for shade loving plants. Featured in

Lancashire Life, Ormskirk Champion. Flat grass paths.

& ✿ 🚗 ☕

19 5 CRIB LANE

Dobcross, Oldham, OL3 5AF. Helen Campbell. *5m E of Oldham. From Dobcross village-head towards Delph on Platt Lane, Crib Lane opp Dobcross Band Club - go straight up the lane, limited parking for disabled visitors only opposite double green garage door.* **Sun 28, Mon 29 May (1.30-4.30). Adm £2, chd free. Home-made teas.**
A well loved and well used family garden which is challenging as on a high stony hillside and encompasses hens, a site for annual bonfires, some small wildlife ponds, vegetable garden, a poly tunnel and areas that are always being re thought and dug up and changed depending on time and aged bodies aches and pains! An art gallery in the garden is of additional interest with visiting artists. Plants for sale by the National Trust.

✿ ☕

37 NEW 12 THE CROFT

Euxton, Chorley, PR7 6LH. Mr & Mrs David & Jean Robinson. *3m NW of Chorley. A49 from Standish to Preston L at Bay Horse in Euxton. A49 Preston to Standish R into Runshaw Lane 4th Rd on L into Glencroft follow the Rd.* **Sun 28 May (11-5). Adm £3, chd free. Light refreshments.**
A small quirky garden with many interesting features. Amongst our collection of plants are Acers, Ferns, Auriculas. Interesting use of gravel leading to the hot tub. The summer house provides one of the many seating areas. Come along and meet Henry!

☕

Gardens are at the heart of hospice care

20 DALE HOUSE GARDENS

off Church Lane, Goosnargh, Preston, PR3 2BE. Caroline & Tom Luke, 01772 862464, tomlukebudgerigars@hotmail.com. *2½ m E of Broughton. M6 J32 signed Garstang Broughton, T-lights R at Whittingham Lane, 2½ m to Whittingham at PO turn L into Church Lane garden between nos 17 & 19.* **Sat 15, Sun 16 Apr, Sat 24, Sun 25 June (10-4). Adm £3.50, chd free. Home-made teas. Visits also by arrangement Mar to June.** *Donation to St Francis School, Goosnargh.*

½ acre tastefully landscaped gardens comprising of limestone rockeries, well stocked herbaceous borders, raised alpine beds, well stocked koi pond, lawn areas, greenhouse and polytunnel, patio areas, specialising in alpines rare shrubs and trees, large collection unusual bulbs. All year round interest. New features for 2017. Large indoor budgerigar aviary. 300+ budgies to view. Gravel path, lawn areas.

♿ ✻ 🚐 ☕

21 DENT HALL

Colne Road, Trawden, Colne, BB8 8NX. Mr Chris Whitaker-Webb & Miss Joanne Smith, 01282 861892, denthall@tiscali.co.uk. *Turn L at end of M65. Follow A6068 for 2m; just after 3rd r'about turn R down B6250. After 1½ m, in front of church, turn R, signed Carry Bridge. Keep R, follow road up hill, garden on R after 300yds.* **Visits by arrangement June to Sept for groups of 10+. Adm £5, chd free. Home-made teas.** *Donation to Widowed & Young and MIND.*

Nestled in the oldest part of Trawden villlage and rolling Lancashire countryside, this mature and evolving country garden surrounds a 400 year old grade II listed hall (not open); featuring a parterre, lawns, herbaceous borders, shrubbery, wildlife pond with bridge to seating area and a hidden summerhouse in a woodland area. Plentiful seating throughout. Some uneven paths and gradients.

✻ ☕

GROUP OPENING

22 DIDSBURY VILLAGE GARDENS

Tickets: Moor Cottage, Grange Lane, Manchester, M20 6RW. *5m S of Manchester. From M60 J5 follow signs to Northenden. Turn R at T-lights onto Barlow Moor Rd to Didsbury. From M56 follow A34 to Didsbury.* **Sun 7 May (12-5). Combined adm £5, chd free. Sun 11 June (12-5). Combined adm £6, chd free. Home-made teas at Moor Cottage & 68 Brooklawn Drive.**

68 BROOKLAWN DRIVE
Anne & Jim Britt.
Open on Sun 11 June

3 THE DRIVE
Peter Clare & Sarah Keedy.
Open on all dates

ESTHWAITE, 52 BARLOW MOOR ROAD
Margaret & Derek Crowther.
Open on all dates

GROVE COTTAGE, 8 GRENFELL ROAD
Mrs Susan Kaberry.
Open on Sun 11 June

MOOR COTTAGE
William Godfrey.
Open on all dates

2 PARKFIELD ROAD SOUTH
Conrad & Kate Jacobson, Mary Butterworth.
Open on Sun 11 June

38 WILLOUGHBY AVENUE
Simon Hickey.
Open on Sun 11 June

Didsbury is an attractive South Manchester suburb which retains its village atmosphere. There are interesting shops, cafes and restaurants, well worth a visit in themselves! This year we have 7 gardens. The gardens demonstrate a variety of beautiful spaces- one is a large family garden divided into several enchanting areas incl pretty courtyard and Jewel garden, another is an expertly planted shade garden with many rarities, whilst another

reflects the charm of the cottage garden ethos with rose covered pergola, old fashioned perennials and tranquil raised pool. Our smaller gardens show beautifully how suburban plots, with limited space, can be packed full of interesting features and a range of planting styles. Dogs allowed at some gardens. Wheelchair access to some gardens.

♿ 🐕 ✻ ☕

23 DUTTON HALL

Gallows Lane, Ribchester, PR3 3XX. Mr & Mrs A H Penny, www.duttonhall.co.uk. *2m NE of Ribchester. Signed from B6243 & B6245 also directions on website.* **Sat 24, Sun 25 June (1-5). Home-made teas. Evening opening Wed 28 June (6-8.30). Wine. Adm £5, chd free.**

Formal garden at front with backdrop of C17 house (not open). 2 acres at rear which incl large collection of old fashioned roses, water feature, meadow with orchids, analemmatic sundial and viewing platforms with extensive views over the Ribble Valley. Visitors requested to keep to mown paths in meadow areas. Also Orangery and Plant Heritage collection of Pemberton roses. Interesting collections of trees, shrubs and roses. Home-made teas provided by St John's Church. Plant Heritage Plant Stall. Disabled access difficult due to different levels and steps.

✻ NPC ☕

24 35 ELLESMERE ROAD

Eccles, Salford, Manchester, M30 9FE. Enid Noronha. *3m W of Salford, 4m W of Manchester. From M60 exit at M602 for Salford. Take A576 for Trafford Park & Eccles, stay on A576. Turn L onto Half Edge Lane, keep L to Monton on Half Edge Lane. Turn R onto Stafford Rd & L onto Ellesmere Rd.* **Sat 17 June (12.30-5). Combined adm with 11 Westminster Road £4, chd free. Home-made teas.**

Amidst the busy urban environment of Eccles in Salford, lies a hidden pocket of grand houses with wide roads, and these two havens of tranquillity. 35 Ellesmere Road is a peaceful country garden with deep herbaceous borders filled with shrubs, scented roses, and perennials. A climber covered pergola leads to a productive vegetable garden where raised beds and fruit trees add to the feeling of abundance.

& ☗ ✤ ☕

25 GREAT MITTON HALL

Mitton Road, Mitton, nr Clitheroe, BB7 9PQ. Jean & Ken Kay. *2m W of Whalley. Take Mitton Rd out of Whalley pass Mitton Hall on L, Aspinall Arms on R over bridge. Hall is on R.* Sat 24, Sun 25 June (1-5). Adm £4, chd free. Light refreshments. *Donation to Help for Heroes.*

Overlooked by C12 Allhallows Church, with stunning views to the river and Pendle Hill the terraced gardens with herbaceous borders, lawn, topiary and raised lily pond, sympathetically surround the medieval hall (not open). Chickens, fruit and vegetables, summer house and seating add to the overall experience. New for 2017 Owl tree sculptures

✤ ☕

26 GREEN FARM COTTAGE

42 Lower Green, Poulton-le-Fylde, FY6 7EJ. Eric & Sharon Rawcliffe, ericrawk@talktalk.net. *500yds from Poulton-le-Fylde Village. M55 J3 follow A585 Fleetwood. T- lights turn L. Next lights bear L A586. Poulton 2nd set of lights turn R Lower Green. Cottage on L.* Sun 18 June (10-5). Adm £3.50, chd free. Home-made teas. Visits also by arrangement June & July, groups of 15+.

½ acre well established formal cottage gardens. Feature koi pond, paths leading to different areas. Lots of climbers and rose beds. Packed with plants of all kinds. Many shrubs and trees. Well laid out lawns. Collections of unusual plants. A surprise round every corner. Said by visitors to be 'a real hidden jewel'.

🚗 ☕

27 THE GROWTH PROJECT

Kellett Street Allotments, Rochdale, OL16 2JU. Karen Hayday, k.hayday@hourglass.org.uk. *From A627M. R A58 L Entwistle Rd R Kellett St.* Sat 5 Aug (11.30-3.30). Adm £3, chd free. Home-made teas. Buffet lunch is available. Visits also by arrangement July to Sept for groups of 10+ Only available Wed and Thur. *Donation to The Growth Project (Rochdale & District Mind).*

With parking and guides to give horticultural advice and over an acre of organic unusual vegetable varieties, the Project incl wildlife pond, insect hotels, formal flower and wild flower borders and a potager. Visit the hand built straw house, stroll down the pergola walk and under the handcrafted arches. Afternoon tea is served in the Victorian style ornate 'Woodland Green' woodworking station. The Growth Project is a partnership between Hourglass and Rochdale and District mind. No disabled WC, ground can be uneven.

& ☗ ✤ 🚌 ☕

HAZELWOOD FARM

See Cumbria

GROUP OPENING

28 NEW HEATON GARDENS

Cannock Drive, Stockport, SK4 3JB. *5m S of Manchester. 1½m NW of J1 (Stockport) off M60. A5154 (Didsbury Rd). The rd takes a slight ascent and you need to turn in Lodge Court, then next L is Cannock Drive.* Sun 21 May (12-5). Combined adm £5, chd free. Home-made teas. Also sparkling wine and nibbles at Clifton Road.

    NEW 6 CANNOCK DRIVE
Andrea & Stefan Schumacher.

    NEW 33 CLIFTON ROAD
Dr Guy Makin.

    NEW 44 LEEGATE ROAD
Angie Taylor.

Heaton Moor is a leafy, attractive suburb. These three gardens are all hidden gems, opening together for the first time this year. The gardens demonstrate the huge variety of gardens to be found in one small area: the first, Cannock Drive, has a lawn that sweeps down to a beautiful small lake with central fountain, offering views over the surrounding area. This is a substantial garden with well- stocked, developing borders. In contrast, Clifton Road is a smaller corner plot which has recently been completely redesigned to provide a garden of two halves, one a pretty family garden , the other a decorative and productive potager with raised beds and espaliered fruit trees. And finally, Leegate Road, an airy, mature garden on different levels with beautiful herbaceous borders, rose arch and pond.

☗ ✤ ☕

29 MILL BARN

Goosefoot Close, Samlesbury, Preston, PR5 0SS. Chris Mortimer, 01254 853300, chris@millbarn.net, www.millbarn.net. *6m E of Preston. From M6 J31 2½m on A59/A677 Bl burn. Turn S. Nabs Head Lane, then Goosefoot Lane.* Sat 3, Sun 4, Sat 10, Sun 11 June (12.30-5). Adm £4, chd free. Cream teas. Visits also by arrangement May to July min group donation £40 or £4 per head.

The unique and quirky garden at Mill Barn is a delight: or rather a series of delights. Along the R Darwin, through the tiny secret grotto, past the suspension bridge and view of the fairytale tower, visitors can a stroll past folly, sculptures, lily pond, and lawns, enjoy the naturally planted flowerbeds, then enter the secret garden and through it the pathways of the wooded hillside beyond. A garden developed on the site of old mills gives a fascinating layout which evolves at many levels. Partial wheelchair access, visitors have not been disappointed in the past.

& ☗ ✤ 🚌 ☕

GROUP OPENING

30 NEW ORMSKIRK GARDENS

Ormskirk, L39 1LF. 13m N of Liverpool. From the end of M57 take A59 & follow signs for Ormskirk or from M58 J3 take A570 to Ormskirk. Sat 24, Sun 25 June (11-4). Combined adm £4.50, chd free. Home-made teas.

EDGE HILL UNIVERSITY
Edge Hill University.

72 LUDLOW DRIVE
Marian & Brian Jones, 01695 574628, 72ludlow@gmail.com. Visits also by arrangement June & July.

1 PINFOLD ROAD
Linda Murray.
Ⓓ

Ormskirk is an historic market town with an award winning University. The gardens are very diverse with something for everyone. 72 Ludlow Drive is a beautiful town garden overflowing with exuberant planting. Comprising a gravel garden, colourful herbaceous and shrub borders, raised shade and rose borders with many old and new roses and clematis. There is also an attractive raised pond and alpine troughs. 1 Pinfold Road was a small and difficult space behind a new build house which has been turned into a delightful garden composed of two separate linked rooms, filled with a diverse and colourful range of plants. The garden has a water feature and is framed by pleached hornbeams, a yew hedge and an architectural fence. Edge Hill has 160 acres of beautifully landscaped grounds with modern architecture. Features include 3 lakes, waterfalls, rock garden, allotment and wild flower meadows. Follow the Sculpture Trail and discover beautiful pieces integrated into the natural environment. The garden at 1 Pinfold contains some steps.
 ਠ ✿ ☕

31 8 PARK HEAD

Portfield Bar, Whalley, Clitheroe, BB7 9FB. Phil & Barbara Walton. 1m S of Whalley. Take exit from A59 onto A671 At 2nd T-lights follow A680 towards Accrington Parkhead is 1st L after these lights. Sun 2 July (1-5). Adm £3, chd free. Home-made teas.
Field to wildlife garden in 10yrs. Terrace with far reaching views. Exuberant perennial/shrub borders surround the house incl over 100 pots, whilst kitchen garden salads, fruit and vegetables squeeze among them! A dry river bed leads from the summer house to a natural pond and bog garden - newts, frogs and aquatic life abound. Grass pathways lead through wild flower meadows to a woodland stream.
 ਠ 🐄 ✿ ☕

32 ♦ THE RIDGES

Weavers Brow (cont. of Cowling Rd), Limbrick, Chorley, PR6 9EB. Mr & Mrs J M Barlow, 01257 279981, barbara@barlowridges.co.uk, www.bedbreakfast-gardenvisits.com. 2m SE of Chorley town centre. From M6 J.27, M61 J.8. Follow signs for Chorley A6 then signs for Cowling & Rivington. Passing Morrison's up Brooke St, mini r'about 2nd exit, Cowling Brow. Pass Spinners Arms on L garden on R. For NGS: Mon 1 May, Mon 28 Aug (11-5). Adm £4.50, chd free. Home-made teas. For other opening times and information, please phone, email or visit garden website.
3 acres, incl old walled orchard garden, cottage-style herbaceous borders, with perfumed rambling roses thru fruit the trees Arch leads to formal lawn, surrounded by natural woodland, shrub borders and trees with contrasting foliage. Woodland walks and dell. Natural looking stream, wildlife ponds. Walled water feature with Italian influence, and walled herb garden. Classical music played. Home made cakes, baked and served by ladies of St James Church, Chorley. Wheelchair access some gravel paths and woodland walks not accessible.
 ਠ 🐄 ✿ 🏠 ☕

33 THE SECRET VALLEY

The Reach, off Hopefold Drive, Worsley, Manchester, M28 3PN. Sally Berry, 07999 422731, info@thesecretvalley.com, www.thesecretvalley.com. 7½m from central Manchester. 1½m from J13 M60. Straight over r'about onto Walkden Rd, at 1st T-lights turn R onto A580, Take 1st L onto Old Clough Lane, turn L at T-junction onto A6. Park on A6 please. No parking on 'The Reach'. Every Sun 21 May to 13 Aug (11-5). Adm £5, chd free. Light refreshments. A selection of cakes, teas, coffee. Visits also by arrangement May to Sept please contact us for more info.
Large 2 acre water garden with ponds, streams, waterfalls, islands and lake. High variety of trees, plants and climbers. It is a haven for waterfowl and local wildlife (incl swans, ducks, geese, coots, moorhens, grebes, herons and kingfishers). Adjoining gardens and allotment are open on the first Sunday of the month. Waterfall, 1 acre lake, smaller ponds, streams, fountain, statues, wild swans and ducks, lots of seating and areas to relax. The entrance, central area are wheelchair friendly. However many paths are not and if its very wet then the wheelchair may struggle on grassy areas.
 ਠ ✿ 🚗 🏠 ☕

GROUP OPENING

34 SEFTON PARK GARDENS

Sefton Drive, Sefton Park, Liverpool, L8 3SD. 1m S of Liverpool city centre. From end of M62 take A5058 Queens Drive ring rd S through Allerton to Sefton Park. Parking roadside in Sefton Park. Sun 16 July (11-5). Combined adm £5, chd free. Home-made teas at Parkmount and The Allotments.

THE BLOOMIN' GREEN TRIANGLE
Mrs Helen Hebden.

THE COMMUNITY ORCHARD AND WILDLIFE GARDEN
The Society of Friends, www.tann.org.uk.

6 CROXTETH GROVE
Stuart Speeden.

FERN GROVE COMMUNITY GARDEN
Liverpool City Council.

NEW LAND
Family Refugee Support Project, www.familyrefugeesupportproject.org.uk.

PARKMOUNT
Jeremy Nicholls.

SEFTON PARK ALLOTMENTS
Sefton Park Allotments Society.

SEFTON VILLA
Patricia Williams, 0151 281 3687, seftonvilla@live.co.uk.

This fascinatingly varied group of Liverpool gardens is re-joined this year by The Bloomin' Green Triangle. Architecture group Assemble won the Turner Prize 2015 for their work with the four streets which make up the Triangle, along with their wild flower meadow. It was the guerrilla gardening of local residents which led to the area's regeneration. See what they have achieved in awkward and unusual spaces on their tour starting at the Ducie Street wild flower meadow at 3pm. See long colour themed borders and rare plants, both in the gardens and for sale, at Parkmount and Sefton Villa, plus the delightful small garden in Croxteth Grove. Vegetables and flowers abound in the ninety allotments, which include a children's and disabled plots, and at the Family Refugee Support Project, tended by gardeners from as far afield as Mongolia and Pakistan. There are two local gardening projects to see: Fern Grove Community garden has children's activities and a beekeeping demonstration at 2pm; and a Community Orchard is under development in the former Quaker Burial Ground in Arundel Avenue. Wheelchair access WC at Sefton Park Allotments

35 SOUTHLANDS
12 Sandy Lane, Stretford, M32 9DA. Maureen Sawyer & Duncan Watmough, www.southlands12.com. *3m S of Manchester. Sandy Lane (B5213) is situated off A5181 (A56) ¼m from M60 J7.* Sun 23 July (12-6). Adm £4, chd free. Home-made teas. Cake-away service (take a slice of your favourite cake home). Described by visitors as 'totally inspirational', this multi-award winning garden unfolds into a series of beautiful spaces including Mediterranean, Ornamental and Woodland gardens. Organic kitchen garden with large glasshouse containing vines and heritage tomatoes. Extensive herbaceous borders, hanging baskets and stunning container plantings throughout the garden, 2 ponds and water feature. Featured in Daily Mail 'Weekend' magazine and on ITV - Love your Garden.

36 NEW 91 STATION ROAD
Banks, Southport, PR9 8AY. Mr & Mrs P Edwards. *4m N of Southport. Take the A365 Southport to Preston rd. From Southport take 1st L by the car wash plant. From Preston take 3rd exit at Banks r'about then 1st L.* Sun 2 July (11-5). Adm £4, chd free. Home-made teas.

In a semi rural setting a charming garden of surprises featuring a courtyard with water feature and raised beds. Steps to the next level with secluded seating, winding paths with lush borders of cottage garden favourites and many roses. Another area features a pond with waterfall, a fruit bed and summer house. The garden is wildlife and bird friendly. Wheelchair access - different levels with some steps and narrow winding paths.

38 NEW 5 THORNTON CLOSE
Rufford, Ormskirk, L40 1UW. Mr & Mrs A Wright. *6m N of Ormskirk. From Ormskirk on A59 turn R in Rufford into Church Rd quick turn R and follow rd to Close.* Sun 25 June (12-5). Combined adm with 90 Brick Kiln Lane £3.50, chd free. Delightful small bungalow garden filled with colourful pots, Some unusual trees, shrubs and perennials. Alpine Troughs. It is hoped to give some basic information by means of a demonstration on how to propagate cuttings. Limited parking. Wheelchair Access [Some users may need assistance] Owner disabled Limited Blue Badge parking at bungalow.

Clearbeck House

39 VARLEY FARM

Anna Lane, Forest Becks, Bolton-by-Bowland, Clitheroe, BB7 4NZ. Mr & Mrs B Farmer, 07887 638436, varleyforestbecks@btinternet.com. *7m N of Clitheroe. A59 off at Sawley follow Settle 2nd L after Copy Nook onto Settle Rd turn L at rd sign on L. Follow lane 1m to a sharp R hand bend garden on L.* Visits by arrangement June to Aug for groups of 10+. Adm incl tea and Cake/biscuits. Adm £5, chd free. 1½-acre garden that's been developing from 2004. Varley Farm is 700ft above sea level with views across the Forest of Bowland and Pendle. Herbaceous lawned cottage garden, flagged herb garden and walled gravel garden, steps to orchard. Stream and pond area planted in 2009 still maturing with a grassed walk through natural meadow and wild flower meadow.

40 WADDOW LODGE GARDEN

Clitheroe Road, Waddington, Clitheroe, BB7 3HQ. Liz & Peter Foley, www.gardentalks.co.uk. *1½m N of Clitheroe. From M6 J31 take A59 (Preston-Skipton). A671 to Clitheroe then B6478. 1st house on L in village. Parking available on rd before entering village; blue badges in drive parking area on gravel.* Sun 28 May, Sun 16 July (1-5). Adm £4, chd free. Home-made teas. Inspirational 2 acre organic garden for all seasons surrounding Georgian house (not open) with views to Pendle and Bowland. An enthusiast's collection of many unusual plants with herbaceous borders, large island beds, shrubs, heathers, rhododendrons, small mature wooded area, old fashioned and hybrid roses. Extensive kitchen garden of vegetables and soft fruit, interesting heritage apple orchard, herbs, alpines and greenhouse, wildlife meadow and bog garden. Colourful containers. Featured in Lancashire Life. Some gravel/bark paths, otherwise level surfaces.
&. ❋ ☕

GROUP OPENING

41 WARTON GARDENS

Warton, LA5 9PJ. 01524 727 770, claire@lavenderandlime.co.uk. *1½m N of Carnforth. From M6 J35 take A601M NW for 1m, then N on A6 for 0.7m turn L signed Warton Old Rectory. Warton Village 1m down Borwick Lane. From Carnforth pass train station and follow signs Warton & Silverdale.* Sun 21 May, Sun 18 June, Sun 16 July (11-4.30). Combined adm £4, chd free. Home-made teas at 111 Main Street.

2 CHURCH HILL AVENUE

Mr & Mrs J Street.
Open on all dates

111 MAIN STREET

Mr & Mrs J Spendlove, 01524 727 770, claire@lavenderandlime.co.uk.
Open on all dates
Visits also by arrangement May to Aug gardening groups up to 20.
🛏

NEW 135 MAIN STREET

Mr Bendall.
Open on Sun 18 June, Sun 16 July

TUDOR HOUSE

Mr & Mrs T Singleton.
Open on Sun 21 May, Sun 18 June

The 4 gardens are spread across the village and offer a wide variety of planting and design ideas incl. ingenious use of limestone pavement, cottage charm, unusual herbaceous and more formal approaches. Visitors to the gardens will be able to park in the village or the public car park which is situated up Crag Rd in the centre of the village. Warton has 2 PHs and WCs. Warton is the birthplace of the medieval ancestors of George Washington, of which the family coat of arms can be seen in St Oswald's Church. The ruins of the Old Rectory (English Heritage) is the oldest surviving building in the village. Ascent of Warton Crag (AONB), provides panoramic views across Morecambe Bay to the Lakeland hills beyond. During the May opening, 3 local makers/designers will be displaying and selling garden related products. All gardens have steps and uneven surfaces unsuitable for wheelchair access.
❋ ☕

42 WARTON HALL

Lodge Lane, Lytham, Lytham St. Annes, FY8 5RP. Nicola and David Thompson, www.total-art.co.uk. *Lytham 10mins J3 exit M55 L for Kirkham, follow signs for Wrea Green, L towards Warton to the BAE T-lights, R, Lodge Lane on R after The Golf Academy & 2m before Lytham town centre* Sat 6, Sun 7 May (10-5). Daily Mon to Fri 8 May to 12 May (12-4). Sat 13, Sun 14 May (10-5). Adm £3, chd free. Light refreshments. Georgian Manor House set in 4 acre garden with Bluebell woodland walk. New additions to the gardens include Japanese style Water Garden and Dry Garden, courtyard and new pathways. The new 2017 Sculpture Trail, Yoga under the 400 year old Weeping Hornbeam tree (book online) and the Shop selling Art, plants and Garden gifts. The Tearoom will be serving light refreshment including homemade cakes. Art Classes in the newly refurbished Studio 'Gardens of Warton Hall' for updates on Facebook Wheelchair access to most of the garden
&. ❋ ☕

43 WEEPING ASH GARDEN

Bents Garden & Home, Warrington Road, Glazebury, WA3 5NS. John Bent, www.bents.co.uk. *15m W of Manchester. Located next to Bents Garden & Home, just off the East Lancs Rd A580 at Greyhound r'about near Leigh. Follow brown 'Garden Centre' signs.* Sun 12, Sun 19, Sun 26 Feb, Sun 5 Mar, Sun 7 May, Sun 10 Sept (12-4). Adm £3, chd free. Created by retired nurseryman and photographer John Bent, Weeping Ash is a garden of all-year interest with a beautiful display of early snowdrops. Broad sweeps of colour lend elegance to this stunning garden which is much larger than it initially seems with hidden paths and wooded areas creating a sense of natural growth. Weeping Ash Garden is located immed adjacent to Bents Garden & Home with its award winning Fresh Approach Restaurant and children's adventure play area. Partial wheelchair access and weather dependent.

44 NEW 11 WESTMINSTER ROAD

Eccles, Manchester, M30 9HF. Lynne Meakin. *3m W of Salford, 4m W of Manchester. First exit M602 Manchester direction 1st exit (r'dabout) 2nd T-lights turn L. After zebra crossing turn R, Victoria Rd 2nd R (Westminster Rd) no.11 on L.* **Sat 17 June (12.30-5). Combined adm with 35 Ellesmere Road £4. Wine. Homemade teas at Ellesmere Road.**

The garden at 11 Westminster Road has a pretty front garden with topiary chickens and is well stocked with perennials. mature trees, and box hedge. The garden is divided by a trellis and rose arch which separates the flower beds and lawn from the fruit growing area, and there are a large number of fuchsias grown in pots. A coach house to the rear of the garden is where will be wine and nibbles. The garden is on the flat except for a small area in the front garden, care will need to be taken in case the path is slippy.

45 NEW WILLOWBROOK HOSPICE GARDENS

Portico Lane, Eccleston Park, Prescot, L34 2QT. Willowbrook Hospice. *Portico Lane, Eccleston Park, Prescot L34 2QT. Leave M6 at exit 21A to M62. At J7 take A57 to Prescot/Liverpool. Continue on A57, turn R onto B5201 Willowbrook is on the R.* **Sat 12, Sun 13 Aug (11-4). Adm £3, chd free. Home-made teas.**

An oasis containing three distinctive National Japanese Garden Society built gardens; a "willowbrook" flower bed designed by RHS Wisley students, a community vegetable garden providing therapies and nourishment and an inner garden designed by Olivia Kirk, a Chelsea Flower Show Gold Medallist.

46 NEW 81 WINDSOR ROAD

Southport, PR9 9BX. Jeanette Grimley, 07739 789431, jghygienist@gmail.com. *From Southport on A570 turn L at Ash St T-lights after sharp bend turn L into Windsor Rd.* **Sun 2 July (12-7). Combined adm with 8 Balfour Road £3.50, chd free. Light refreshments. Visits also by arrangement June to Sept.**

This developing garden flows well with the house interior, making clever use of reclaimed materials to create an oasis of calm in a chaotic world! The borders are ever changing with the seasons and include a pretty mix of cottage plants, perennials and shrubs. The owners love of cooking is evident keeping hens, a varied range of herbs and edible planting, including a spectacular Fig tree.

47 NEW WOODSTOCK BARN

Andertons Mill, Mawdesley, Ormskirk, L40 3TW. Mr & Mrs J Bean, 01772 641033, johnpatbean@sky.com. *9m E of Ormskirk. M6 J27 A5209 over Parbold hill, R Lancaster Lane/ Chorley Rd, L after Farmers Arms to Bentley Lane/Andertons Mill. Garden 500 yds on L. From Burscough A59, A5209 towards Parbold, L Lancaster Lane.* **Sun 18 June, Sun 9 July (12-5). Combined adm with 8 Andertons Mill £4.50, chd free. Home-made teas. Some seating under cover available for upto 30 people. Visits also by arrangement July to Sept groups 10+.**

An established country garden of over ¾ acre with form, texture and a green tapestry all year round. Developed from a barren wilderness to one with wildlife, amidst tall trees, shrubs, mixed borders, pond, vegetable patch, woodland area and stream. There are several seating areas to enjoy the tranquil atmosphere of this relaxing garden. Limited wheelchair access - main pathway only if lawns are wet.

GROUP OPENING

48 NEW WOOLTON VILLAGE GARDENS

Woolton, Liverpool, L25 8QF. *7m S of Liverpool. Woolton Rd B5171 or Menlove Ave A562 follow signs for Woolton.* **Sat 8 July (12-5). Combined adm £4, chd free. Home-made teas. at 10 Acrefield Park, 16 Layton Close and Hospice.**

> NEW **10 ACREFIELD PARK**
> Lesley Gaskarth.
>
> NEW **16 LAYTON CLOSE**
> Bob & Carole Edisbury.
>
> NEW **LIVERPOOL MARIE CURIE HOSPICE**
> Hayley Hawkins.
>
> NEW **71 MANOR ROAD**
> John & Maureen Davies.

A group of 4 gardens surrounding the NW and Britain in Bloom award winning Woolton Village, all within a short walk or drive of each other. The contrasting gardens show what can be achieved in a suburban back garden. Gardens feature an impressive water fall with pond stocked with fish, well planted borders pots and tubs, a family garden with raised patio and decked area planted with roses, clematis and passion flowers, wildlife pond with hostas, ferns, trees and shrubs. A garden with a good sized vegetable plot, lots of mature plants, colourful beds and borders, raised pond with fish, well stocked with a lovely backdrop of trees, conifers and numerous Japanese Maples. Finally the Hospice Garden surrounding the octagonal Marie Curie building with well stocked herbaceous borders shrubberies and wonderful floral displays in large pots in the sheltered courtyards. Wheelchair access to some gardens.

LEICESTERSHIRE & RUTLAND

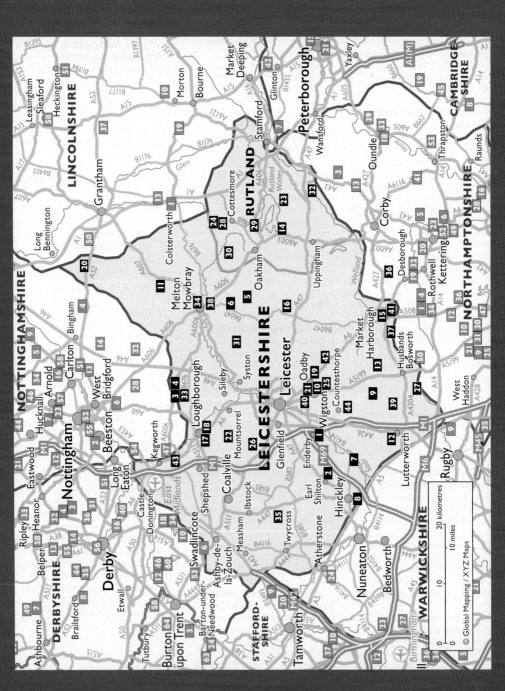

Leicestershire is very much in the centre of England, and has a diverse landscape and wide range of settlements.

Our open gardens are of corresponding variety. From compact Victorian terraces with inspirational planting, large country houses with broad vistas, an arboretum with four national champion trees, to an allotment with over 100 plots. Most gardens welcome groups, sell plants and offer tea and cake.

Confident in the knowledge that your donation goes to wonderful causes, you can look for inspiration for your own garden or plot, or simply take pleasure looking at beautiful gardens.

'Much in Little' is Rutland's motto. They say small is beautiful and never were truer words said.

Rutland is rural England at its best. Honey-coloured stone cottages make up pretty villages nestling amongst rolling hills; the passion for horticulture is everywhere you look, from stunning gardens to the hanging baskets and patio boxes showing off seasonal blooms in our two attractive market towns of Oakham and Uppingham.

There's so much to see in and around Rutland whatever the time of year, including many wonderful NGS gardens.

Below: Mountain Ash

Volunteers

Leicestershire

County Organiser
Colin Olle
01858 575791
colin.olle@ngs.org.uk

County Treasurer
Martin Shave
01455 556633
martinshave@kilworthaccountancy.co.uk

Publicity
Janet Currie
01509 212191
janet.currie@me.com

Assistant County Organisers
Mary Hayward
07545 817664
mary.hayward@ngs.org.uk

Verena Olle
01858 575791
colin.olle@ngs.org.uk

Pamela Shave
01858 575481
pamelashave@btconnect.com

David & Beryl Wyrko
01664 840385

Rutland

County Organiser
Rose Dejardin
01572 737788
rosedejardin@btopenworld.com

County Treasurer
David Wood
01572 737465
rdavidwood1@gmail.com

Publicity
Jane Alexander-Orr
01572 737368
janealexanderorr@hotmail.com

Assistant County Organiser
Jennifer Wood
01572 737465
rdavidwood1@gmail.com

Leicestershire & Rutland

Booklet Co-ordinator
Mary Hayward
07545 817664
mary.hayward@ngs.org.uk

OPENING DATES

All entries subject to change. For latest information check **www.ngs.org.uk**

Extended openings are shown at the beginning of the month.

Map locator numbers are shown to the right of each garden name.

February

Snowdrop Festival

Sunday 26th
6 Denis Road   8

March

Saturday 4th
Westview   42

Sunday 5th
Westview   42

Sunday 26th
Gunthorpe Hall   14

April

Long Close
(Every Wednesday to Sunday from Saturday 1st)   22

Sunday 9th
Parkside   31

Sunday 23rd
The Old Hall   28

Sunday 30th
Hedgehog Hall   16

May

Long Close
(Every Wednesday to Sunday)   22

Monday 1st
Hedgehog Hall   16
Long Close   22

Sunday 7th
Hammond Arboretum   15
Tresillian House   38

Sunday 14th
Burrough Gardens   5
Westbrooke House   41

Sunday 21st
Mill House   25
The Old Vicarage, Whissendine   30
♦ Whatton Gardens   43

Wednesday 24th
Thorpe Lubenham Hall   37

90th Anniversary Weekend

Sunday 28th
Newtown Linford Gardens   26
The Old Vicarage, Burley   29

Monday 29th
Long Close   22
Newtown Linford Gardens   26

June

Long Close
(Every Wednesday to Sunday)   22
Stoke Albany House
(Every Wednesday from Wednesday 7th)   36

Sunday 4th
12 Alexander Avenue   1
Manton Gardens   23

Saturday 17th
28 Gladstone Street   10
NEW 13 Highcroft Avenue   19

Sunday 18th
28 Gladstone Street   10
NEW 13 Highcroft Avenue   19

Sunday 25th
Hedgehog Hall   16
Market Overton Gardens   24
Walton Gardens   39

Wednesday 28th
NEW Greenfields   13
The Old Vicarage, Burley   29
Walton Gardens   39

July

Long Close (Every Wednesday to Sunday to Sunday 16th)   22
Stoke Albany House (Every Wednesday to Wednesday 26th)   36

Saturday 1st
NEW Shipmeadow   35

Sunday 2nd
NEW Shipmeadow   35
Tresillian House   38
Westbrooke House   41

Sunday 9th
Green Wicket Farm   12
Mill House   25

Wednesday 12th
Green Wicket Farm   12

Saturday 15th
28 Gladstone Street   10

Sunday 16th
28 Gladstone Street   10
NEW Honeytrees   20
Redhill Lodge   32

Sunday 23rd
Willoughby Gardens   44

Sunday 30th
119 Scalford Road   34

August

Sunday 13th
NEW The Firs   9
NEW Honeytrees   20

Sunday 27th
Tresillian House   38

September

Long Close (Every Wednesday to Sunday from Friday 1st)   22

Saturday 2nd
Goadby Marwood Hall   11

Sunday 3rd
Washbrook Allotments   40

Saturday 9th
Oak Tree House   27

Sunday 10th
NEW Honeytrees   20
Oak Tree House   27

October

Long Close (Every Wednesday to Sunday to Sunday 15th)   22

Sunday 22nd
Tresillian House   38

By Arrangement

Barracca   2
88 Brook Street   3
109 Brook Street   4
Crossfell House   6
Dairy Cottage   7
Farmway, Willoughby Gardens   44
Goadby Marwood Hall   11
Green Wicket Farm   12
134 Herrick Road   17
94 Herrick Road   18
NEW Honeytrees   20
Knighton Sensory   21
Long Close   22
Oak Tree House   27
The Old Vicarage, Burley   29
Parkside   31
Ridgewold Farm   33
119 Scalford Road   34
NEW Shipmeadow   35
Stoke Albany House   36
Tresillian House   38
Westbrooke House   41
Westview   42

Your visit helps fund 389 Marie Curie Nurses

THE GARDENS

1 12 ALEXANDER AVENUE

Enderby, Leicester, LE19 4NA. Mr & Mrs J Beeson. *4m S of Leicester. From M1 J21 take A5460 to Fosse Park, turn R on B4114. Turn R to Enderby at next r'about, straight on to church then follow yellow NGS signs.* **Sun 4 June (11-5). Adm £2.50, chd free. Home-made teas.**

Our small town garden has been carefully designed to make full use of the space available and to provide interest all yr-round. We have dispensed with the lawn giving us space to create different areas in the garden, incl a pond, and to accommodate a wide variety of plants chosen for colour and to attract wildlife. Our garden is an extension of the house, a place to potter, relax and enjoy. Tea served in a variety of interesting and unusual teapots! Some gravel areas.

Goadby Marwood Hall

2 BARRACCA

Ivydene Close, Earl Shilton, LE9 7NR. Mr & Mrs John & Sue Osborn, 01455 842609, susan.osborn1@btinternet.com, www.barraccagardens.co.uk. *10m W of Leicester. From A47 after entering Earl Shilton, Ivydene Close is 4th on L from Leicester side of A47.* **Visits by arrangement May to July for groups 10+. Smaller groups considered. Short notice bookings possible. Adm £7 incl refreshments.**

1 acre garden with lots of different areas, silver birch walk, wildlife pond with seating, apple tree garden, Mediterranean planted area and lawns surrounded with herbaceous plants and shrubs. Patio area with climbing roses and wisteria. There is also a utility garden with greenhouse, vegetables in beds, herbs and perennial flower beds, lawn and fruit cage. Part of the old gardens owned by the Cotton family who used to open approx 9 acres to the public in the 1920's. Adm incl tea/coffee and home-made cakes.

Additional catering (such as High Tea) considered on request. Partial wheelchair access.

3 88 BROOK STREET

Wymeswold, LE12 6TU. Adrian & Ita Cooke, 01509 880155, itacooke@btinternet.com. *4m NE of Loughborough. From A6006 Wymeswold turn S by church onto Stockwell, then E along Brook St. Roadside parking on Brook St.* **Visits by arrangement May & June (combined visits to incl 109 Brook Street possible).**

The ½ acre garden is set on a hillside, which provides lovely views across the village, and comprises 3 distinct areas: firstly, a cottage style garden; then a water garden with a stream and champagne pond; and finally at the top there is a vegetable plot, small orchard and wildflower meadow. The ponds are a breeding ground for great crested and common newts, frogs and toads.

4 109 BROOK STREET

Wymeswold, LE12 6TT. Maggie & Steve Johnson, 01509 880866, sameuk@tiscali.co.uk. *4m NE of Loughborough. From A6006 Wymeswold turn S onto Stockwell, then E along Brook St. Roadside parking along Brook St. Steep drive with limited disabled parking at house.* **Visits by arrangement May & June for groups 10+. Min 2 weeks notice please. (Combined visits to incl 88 Brook Street possible). Home-made teas.**

S-facing ¾ acre gently sloping garden with views to open country. Mature garden much improved. Patio with roses and clematis, wildlife and fish ponds, mixed borders, vegetable garden, orchard, hot garden and woodland garden. Something for everyone! Demonstration of rain water harvesting on limited budget. Superb home-made cakes served with beverages. Some gravel paths.

Long Close

meadows, culminating in spectacular countryside views, from our Shepherd's Hut and picnic area. We welcome you to bring your own picnic as well as the refreshments we provide. Access to patio and garden area, only partial access meadow. ♿ ☕

7 DAIRY COTTAGE
15 Sharnford Road, Sapcote, LE9 4JN. Mrs Norah Robinson-Smith, 01455 272398, nrobinsons@yahoo.co.uk. *9m SW of Leicester. Sharnford Rd joins Leicester Rd in Sapcote to B4114 Coventry Rd. Follow NGS signs at both ends.* **Visits by arrangement May to July for groups 10+. Adm £3, chd free. Home-made teas.**
From a walled garden with colourful mixed borders to a potager approached along a woodland path, this mature cottage garden combines extensive perennial planting with many unusual shrubs and specimen trees. More than 100 clematis and climbing roses are trained up pergolas, arches and into trees 50ft high – so don't forget to look up! ♿ ✿ ☕

8 6 DENIS ROAD
Burbage, LE10 2LR. Mr & Mrs D A Dawkins. *13m SW of Leicester. From M69 J1 take B4109 signed Hinckley. 1st L after 2nd r'about. Follow yellow signs.* **Sun 26 Feb (11-4). Adm £3, chd free. Home-made teas.**
Although a small garden, it hosts a large collection of many varieties of snowdrops. Mixed in with these are spring bulbs and hellebores. ✿ ☕

9 NEW THE FIRS
Main Street, Bruntingthorpe, LE17 5QF. Howard & Carmel Grant. *5m NE of Lutterworth. Exit J20 M1 to Lutterworth A426. Turn R to Gilmorton & Bruntingthorpe opp petrol station. From Leicester A5199 to Arnesby. Turn R & follow rd 2m to T-junction. Turn L to Bruntingthorpe.* **Sun 13 Aug (11-5). Adm £4, chd free. Home-made teas.**
A tranquil garden of 1½ acres with views over open countryside. The front garden features terraced borders and paving. The main rear

GROUP OPENING

5 BURROUGH GARDENS
Burrough on the Hill, Nr Melton Mowbray, LE14 2QZ. *Close to B6047. 10 mins from A606. 20 mins from Melton Mowbray.* **Sun 14 May (2-5). Combined adm £5, chd free. Light refreshments at Burrough Hall.**

BURROUGH HALL
Richard & Alice Cunningham.
BURROUGH HOUSE
Roger & Sam Weatherby.

2 large gardens, both with magnificent views over High Leicestershire. Burrough House, in the middle of the village, has an extensive garden surrounding a former stone farmhouse with stunning views over the surrounding countryside. The current owners are adding to the former established garden to create a series of vistas and spaces and maximise the views in and out of the garden with the use of clipped hedges and avenues. Burrough Hall, outside the village between Somerby and Burrough, was built in 1867 as a classic Leicestershire hunting lodge. The garden, framed by mature

trees and shrubs, was extensively redesigned by garden designer George Carter in 2007. This family garden, which continues to develop for the enjoyment of all generations, consists of extensive lawns, mixed borders, a vegetable garden and woodland walks. There will be a small collection of vintage and classic cars on display at Burrough Hall. ♿ ✿ ☕

6 CROSSFELL HOUSE
4d Nether End, Great Dalby, Melton Mowbray, LE14 2EY. Jane & Ian West, 01664 500585, janawest@gmail.com. *3m S of Melton Mowbray on B6047. On entering Great Dalby from Melton Mowbray remain on B6047. Crossfell House is on L approx 300 yards from village 30mph sign.* **Visits by arrangement May to July for groups 10-30 (smaller groups considered). Adm £6, chd £2. Home-made teas.**
A formal garden consisting of a terraced herbaceous border and rockery, flanked by a border of shrubs, two small areas of lawn and a sweeping path leading to a two acre meadow with wild grasses, flowers and a recently created wildlife pond. Paths crisscross the

garden has large areas of sweeping lawn and grass walkways around many flowing borders. There is a large variety of themed coloured planting, shrubs and trees. In amongst the borders can be found many unusual design features, artefacts and seating areas. Large sequoia tree at the front of the property was damaged by a bomber returning from a night training flight during the WW II. Short gravel drive, some paving, rest grass.

&. ✿

10 28 GLADSTONE STREET
Wigston Magna, LE18 1AE. Chris & Janet Huscroft. *4m S of Leicester. Off Wigston by-pass (A5199) follow signs off Mcdonalds r'about.* **Sat 17, Sun 18 June (11-5). Combined adm with 13 Highcroft Avenue £4, chd free. Sat 15, Sun 16 July (11-5). Adm £2.50, chd free. Home-made teas.**
Our small town garden is divided into rooms and bisected by a pond with a bridge. It is brimming with unusual hardy perennials, incl collections of ferns and hostas. David Austin roses chosen for their scent feature throughout, incl a 30' rose arch. An unusual shade house with rare plants, incl hardy orchids and arisaema's. Some replanting in 2015/2016. Come and see the difference! Frameworks Knitters Museum nearby - open Suns.

✿ ✿

11 GOADBY MARWOOD HALL
Goadby Marwood, LE14 4LN. Mr & Mrs Westropp, 01664 464202. *4m NW of Melton Mowbray. Between Waltham-on-the-Wolds & Eastwell, 8m S of Grantham. Plenty of parking space available.* **Sat 2 Sept (10-5). Adm £5, chd free. Home-made teas in Village Hall. Visits also by arrangement with refreshments on request.**
Redesigned in 2000 by the owner based on C18 plans. A chain of 5 lakes (covering 10 acres) and several ironstone walled gardens all interconnected. Lakeside woodland walk. Planting for yr-round interest. Landscaper trained under

plantswoman Rosemary Verey at Barnsley House. Beautiful C13 church open. Gravel paths and lawns.

&. 🐄 🏠 ☕ ✿

12 GREEN WICKET FARM
Ullesthorpe Road, Bitteswell, Lutterworth, LE17 4LR. Mrs Anna Smith, 01455 552646, greenfarmbitt@hotmail.com. *2m NW of Lutterworth J20 M1. From Lutterworth follow signs through Bitteswell towards Ullesthorpe. Garden situated behind Bitteswell Cricket Club. Field parking available subject to weather conditions.* **Sun 9, Wed 12 July (2-5). Adm £3.50, chd free. Home-made teas. Visits also by arrangement June to Sept for groups min 10, max 30.**
Created in 2008 on a working farm. Clay soil and very exposed but beginning to look established. Many unusual hardy plants along with a lot of old favourites have been used to provide a long season of colour and interest. Anemone nemorosa, Pacific coast iris, sedums and salvias are of particular interest. Formal ponds and water feature. Some gravel paths.

&. ✿ ☕ ✿

13 NEW GREENFIELDS
Saddington Road, Mowsley, Lutterworth, LE17 6NY. Janet Matthews. *10m S of Leicester. Mowsley is off the A5199 from Leicester. Follow yellow NGS arrows.* **Wed 28 June (11-5). Adm £2.50, chd free. Home-made teas.**
Greenfields as its name implies has an uninterrupted view of the rolling Laughton Hills, where cows graze. Climbing plants punctuate mixed boarders of shrubs and perennials. A small pond is home to goldfish and newts. Annual containers brighten up the patio area and if the weeding is ever finished a home-made chalet provides a quiet place to sit and relax.

☕ ✿

14 GUNTHORPE HALL
Gunthorpe, Oakham, LE15 8BE. Tim Haywood. *A6003 between Oakham & Uppingham; 1m from Oakham, up drive between lodges. Proceed over railway bridge to gardens, 600 yards ahead. Please*

follow the signs for parking. **Sun 26 Mar (2-5). Adm £4, chd free. Light refreshments.**
Large garden in a country setting with extensive views across the Rutland landscape with the carpets of daffodils and spring flowering shrubs being notable features. A great deal of recent re-design have transformed this garden with more recent works being undertaken on the kitchen garden and around the (former) stable yard.

&. 🐄 ✿ ✿

15 HAMMOND ARBORETUM
Burnmill Road, Market Harborough, LE16 7JG. The Robert Smyth Academy. *15m S of Leicester on A6. From High St, follow signs to The Robert Smyth Academy via Bowden Lane to Burnmill Rd. Park in 1st entrance on L.* **Sun 7 May (2-4.30). Adm £4, chd free. Home-made teas.**
A site of just under 2½ acres containing an unusual collection of trees and shrubs, many from Francis Hammond's original planting dating from 1913 to 1936 whilst headmaster of the school. Species from America, China and Japan with malus and philadelphus walks and a moat. Proud owners of 4 champion trees identified by national specialist. Guided walks and walk plans available. Some steep slopes.

&. 🐄 ✿ ☕ ✿

Donations from the National Garden Scheme help Parkinson's UK care for more people

16 HEDGEHOG HALL
Loddington Road, Tilton on the Hill, LE7 9DE. Janet & Andrew Rowe. *8m W of Oakham. 2m N of A47 on B6047 between Melton & Market Harborough. Follow yellow NGS signs in Tilton towards Loddington.* **Sun 30 Apr, Mon 1 May, Sun 25 June (11-4.30). Adm £3.50, chd free. Home-made teas.**
½ acre organically managed plant lover's garden. Steps leading to three stone walled terraced borders filled with shrubs, perennials, bulbs and a patio over looking the valley. Lavender walk, herb border, beautiful spring garden, colour themed herbaceous borders. Sheltered courtyard with collection of hostas and acers. Courtyard terrace planted for yr-round interest with topiary and perennials. Cakes for sale. Regret, no wheelchair access to terraced borders.
&. ❀ ☕ ☕

17 134 HERRICK ROAD
Loughborough, LE11 2BU. Janet Currie, 01509 212191, janet.currie@me.com, www.thesecateur.com. *1m SW of Loughborough centre. From M1 J23 take A512 Ashby Rd to L'boro. At r'about R onto A6004 Epinal Way. At Beacon Rd r'about L, Herrick Rd 1st on R.* **Visits by arrangement June to Sept, groups 10+ daytime or early evening. Adm £3, chd £1. Light refreshments.**
A small garden brimming with texture, colour and creative flair. Trees, shrubs and climbers give structure. A sitting area surrounded by lilies, raised staging for herbs and alpines. A lawn flanked with deeply curving and gracefully planted beds of perennials growing through willow structures made by Janet. A shaded area under the Bramley apple tree, raised vegetable beds and potting area. We're good at tea and cake, dietary requirements catered for. Just phone to discuss.
☕

18 94 HERRICK ROAD
Loughborough, LE11 2BT. Marion Smith, 01509 554927, marion_smith@ntlworld.com.

1m SW of Loughborough. From M1 J23 take A512 Ashby Rd to Loughborough. At r'about R onto A6004 Epinal Way. At Beacon Road r'about L, Herrick Road 1st on R. **Visits by arrangement June & July. Adm £3, chd £1. Tea.**
Traditional old-fashioned English medium sized garden at rear of Victorian house. Mainly perennial planting with interest in hardy geraniums and Heucheras. Small pond and three active beehives. Wormery, composting and green cone to use all household waste. This peaceful walled garden also has a Coach House. Ramp onto lawn, no steps otherwise.
&. ⛏ ❀ ☕

19 NEW 13 HIGHCROFT AVENUE
Oadby, Leicester, LE2 5UH. Sharon Maher & Mike Costall. *Just off A6, 5m S Leicester & 9m N Market Harborough. Follow NGS yellow arrows.* **Sat 17, Sun 18 June (11-5). Combined adm with 28 Gladstone Street £4, chd free. Home-made teas.**
Our garden is a work in progress, but we would now like to share it with you. It is approx 22 metres x 14 metres. We have a rose bed with lots of David Austin roses, a hot bed, a herbaceous border, a wildlife area, alpine bed, patio planters and a small wildlife pond. There's plenty of room on the patio to sit and enjoy the tea and cake too!
⛏ ☕

20 NEW HONEYTREES
85 Grantham Road, Bottesford, NG13 0EG. Julia Madgwick & Mike Ford, 01949 842120, Julia_madgwick@hotmail.com. *7m E of Bingham on A52. Turn into village, garden is on L on slip road behind hedge going out of village towards Grantham. Parking on grass opp property.* **Sun 16 July, Sun 13 Aug, Sun 10 Sept (10-5). Adm £3, chd free. Home-made teas. Visits also by arrangement June to Sept, small groups very welcome.**
The garden is on a S-facing slope which has evolved over the years into a tropical oasis. Tree ferns,

palms, cannas, gingers, bananas, paulownia, tetra panax, cacti, yuccas, hemerocallis, tibouchina, fuchsias etc plus greenhouses and a tropical dome. There are steps and some gravel but plenty to view and enjoy from a wheelchair.
&. ❀ ☕ ☕

21 KNIGHTON SENSORY
Knighton Park, Leicester, LE2 3YQ. Mike Chalk, 01162 104217, kpgc@hotmail.co.uk, www.knightonparkgardeningclub.com. *Off A563 (Outer Ring Rd) S of Leicester. From Palmerston Blvd, turn into South Kingsmead Rd then 1st L into Woodbank Rd. Park entrance at end of rd. Enter park, follow path to R, garden on R.* **Visits by arrangement June to Aug for groups 10 - 30. Adm £3, chd free. Home-made teas.**
This ¼ acre community garden stands in a secluded corner of Knighton Park away from the bustle of the city. It is a feast for all the senses incl shrubs, some traditional bedding, herbaceous borders, bog garden with bridge, dry riverbed with wild flowers and wildlife area, Separate area contains raised beds for edibles. Awarded outstanding by the It's Your Neighbourhood Scheme.
&. ⛏ ☕

22 LONG CLOSE
60 Main St, Woodhouse Eaves, LE12 8RZ. John Oakland, 01509 890376, www.longclose.org.uk. *4m S of Loughborough. Nr M1 J23. From A6, W in Quorn.* **Every Wed to Sun 1 Apr to 16 July. Mon 1, Mon 29 May. Every Wed to Sun 1 Sept to 15 Oct (10.30-4.30). Adm £4, chd 50p. Visits also by arrangement Apr to Oct, groups 15+.**
5 acres spring bulbs, rhododendrons, azaleas, camellias, magnolias, many rare shrubs, mature trees, lily ponds; terraced lawns, herbaceous borders, potager in walled kitchen garden, wildflower meadow walk. Winter, spring, summer and autumn colour, a garden for all seasons. 100yr old wild flower meadows open 3rd May to 16th July. Dogs on short lead.
⛏ ❀ ☕

GROUP OPENING

23 MANTON GARDENS

Oakham, LE15 8SR. *3m N of Uppingham. 3m S of Oakham. Manton is on S shore of Rutland Water ¼m off A6003. Please park carefully in village.* **Sun 4 June (12.30-5). Combined adm £5, chd free. Home-made teas in Village Hall (1.30 - 5.30).**

22 LYNDON ROAD
Chris & Val Carroll.

MANTON GRANGE
Anne & Mark Taylor.

MANTON LODGE FARM
Caroline Burnaby-Atkins, www.mantonlodge.co.uk.

3 ST MARY'S ROAD
Ruth Blinch.

SHAPINSAY
Tony & Jane Bews.

5 gardens in small village on S shore of Rutland Water. Manton Grange - 2½ acre garden with interesting trees, shrubs and herbaceous borders. Incl a rose garden, water features, a lime tree walk and clematis pergola. Shapinsay - ⅔ acre garden with mature trees framing views over the Chater Valley, incl a woodland walk, perennial borders, island shrub borders and a stream linking numerous ponds constructed in November 2011 by a local RHS gold medal garden designer. 22 Lyndon Rd - a beautiful combination of cottage garden and unusual plants in overflowing borders, hanging baskets and decorative pots. 3 St Mary's Road - a tiny garden where the use of every available space is maximised to create a series of areas within which to sit and enjoy beds, and numerous pots, packed with plants. Manton Lodge Farm - Stone country house (not open) nestled into hillside, with wonderful views from the steeply sloping gardens. Paths lead through borders of shrubs, roses and perennials. Featured in Rutland Pride magazine. Wheelchair access to Manton Grange and Shapinsay only.

♿ ✿ ☕

GROUP OPENING

24 MARKET OVERTON GARDENS

Market Overton, Oakham, LE15 7PP. *7m NE of Oakham. Turn R off Ashwell/Wymondham rd at Teigh.* **Sun 25 June (1.30-5). Combined adm £5, chd free. Home-made teas at the Cricket Pavilion.**

7 MAIN STREET
Ann Tibbert.

NEW **1 THISTLETON ROAD**
Martin Debenham.

35 THISTLETON ROAD
Richard Carruthers.

37 THISTLETON ROAD
Nick Buff.

47 THISTLETON ROAD
Jane Smeetem.

59 THISTLETON ROAD
Wg Cdr Andrew Stewart JP.

A village group opening of 6 gardens. At one end of the village, 59 Thistleton Road, is a 1.8 acre garden converted over the last 11yrs into a haven for wildlife with large pond, shrubbery, orchard, large colourful perennial beds and a short woodland walk. Further along Thistleton Rd, are 3 tiny, very individual gardens behind a row of pretty red brick terraced house all overlooking the cricket green. At the further end of the road is No.1 a small, enclosed garden with a lawn meandering through borders packed with ornamental shrubs, trees and herbaceous plants. Close by, 7 Main St is an illustration of how to develop a square patch of grass over 4yrs into an delightful garden divided into a series of areas richly planted to provide yr-round interest and featuring specimen trees, unusual shrubs and colourful planted pots and containers.

✿ ☕

25 MILL HOUSE

118 Welford Road, Wigston, LE18 3SN. Mr & Mrs P Measures. *4m S of Leicester. From Leicester to Wigston Magna follow A5199 Welford Rd S towards Kilby, up hill past Mercers Newsagents, 100yds on L.* **Sun 21 May, Sun 9 July (12-5). Adm £2.50, chd free. Home-made teas.**
Walled town garden with an extensive plant variety, many rare and unusual. A plant lovers garden, with interesting designs incorporated in the borders, rockery and scree. It is full of surprises with memorabilia and bygones a reminder of our past. Good variety of reasonably priced plants on sale both open days. Bargain plant sale 29/30 July (11-4).

✿ ☕

2 Church Farm Lane

GROUP OPENING

26 NEWTOWN LINFORD GARDENS

On Main Street & Ulverscroft Lane, Newtown Linford, Leicester, LE6 0AD. 6m NW Leicester. 2½ m from M1 J22. The gardens are on Main St (going N between Markfield Lane & Ulverscroft Lane) & in Ulverscroft Lane. It is 0.7m between gardens in Main St & Mountain Ash in Ulverscroft Lane. **Sun 28, Mon 29 May (11-5). Combined adm £5, chd free. Home-made teas at Mountain Ash.**

APPLETREE COTTAGE
Katherine Duffy Anthony.

BANK COTTAGE
Jan Croft.

MOUNTAIN ASH
Mike & Liz Newcombe.

WOODLANDS
Mary Husseini.

Newtown Linford is a historic village bordering Bradgate Park with the R Lin flowing through it and is part of the Charnwood Forest. Two of the gardens opening have river banks from where you can see brown trout and the occasional kingfisher. The gardens opening are each quite different. Appletree Cottage has a charming enclosed garden surrounding a C17 thatched cottage with interesting paths leading to lawns, borders, sun terrace and small lily pond. Bank Cottage has a typical cottage garden set on different levels that leads down to the river and provides yr-round colour but is prettiest in spring. The R Lin runs through Woodlands, a 1 acre garden where many varied shrubs and spring flowers grow round the mature trees. You can enjoy tea and cake at Mountain Ash, a 2 acre garden with many interesting features and with stunning views over the Charnwood countryside. There will also be plant sales and other stalls here. Come and enjoy your day with us! Plant sales and other stalls at Mountain Ash.

✿ ☙

27 OAK TREE HOUSE
North Road, South Kilworth, LE17 6DU. Pam & Martin Shave, 01858 575481, pamelashave@btconnect.com. 15m S of Leicester. From M1 J20, take A4304 towards Market Harborough. At North Kilworth turn R, signed South Kilworth. Garden on L after approx 1m. **Sat 9 Sept (1-5); Sun 10 Sept (11-5). Adm £3, chd free. Home-made teas. Visits also by arrangement 11 June - 2 July only**
⅔ acre garden. Beautiful country garden full of colour, formal design, softened by cottage style planting. Stone circle and sculpture. Large herbaceous borders, vegetable plots, pond, greenhouse, shady area, grass border. Extensive collections in pots, incl perennial violas. Trees chosen for attractive bark. Nearly 40 types of clematis and many more roses. Dramatic arched pergola. Photographs of the garden featured in The Harborough Mail.

& ✿ ⇔ ☙

28 THE OLD HALL
Main Street, Market Overton, LE15 7PL. Mr & Mrs Timothy Hart, 01572 767145, stefa@hambleton.co.uk. 6m N of Oakham. Beyond Cottesmore, 6m N of Oakham; 5m from A1 via Thistleton. 10m E from Melton Mowbray via Wymondham. **Sun 23 Apr (2-6). Adm £4.50, chd free. Home-made teas incl Hambleton Bakery cakes.**
Set on a southerly ridge overlooking Catmose Vale. Stone walls and yew hedges divide the garden into enclosed areas with herbaceous borders, shrubs, and young and mature trees. In 2006 the lower part of garden was planted with new shrubs to create a walk with mown paths. There are interesting plants flowering most of the time. Neil Hewertson has been involved in the gardens design since 1990s. Partial wheelchair access. Gravel and mown paths. Return to house is steep.

& ✿ ☙

29 THE OLD VICARAGE, BURLEY
Church Road, Burley, Nr Oakham, LE15 7SU. Jonathan & Sandra Blaza, 01572 770588, sandra.blaza@btinternet.com, www.theoldvicarageburley.com. 1m NE of Oakham. In Burley just off B668 between Oakham & Cottesmore. Church Rd is opp village green. **Sun 28 May (1.30-5). Home-made teas. Evening opening Wed 28 June (6-9). Light refreshments. Adm £4.50, chd free. Visits also by arrangement in June for groups 10+.**
Country garden, planted for yr round interest, incl a walled garden (with vine house) producing fruit, herbs, vegetables and cut flowers. Formal lawns and borders, lime walk, rose gardens and a rill with an avenue of standard wisteria. Wildlife garden with pond, 2 orchards and mixed woodland. Some gravel and steps between terraces.

& ⇥ ✿ ⇔ ☙

30 THE OLD VICARAGE, WHISSENDINE
2 Station Road, Whissendine, LE15 7HG. Prof Peter & Dr Sarah Furness, www.pathology.plus.com/Garden. Garden situated up hill from St Andrew's church in Whissendine. 1st gate on L in Station Rd. **Sun 21 May (2-5). Adm £4.50, chd free. Home-made teas in St Andrew's Church, Whissendine.**
⅔ acre packed with variety. Terrace with topiary, a formal fountain courtyard and raised beds backed by small gothic orangery burgeoning with tender plants. Herbaceous borders surround main lawn. Wisteria tunnel leads to new raised vegetable beds and large ornate greenhouse, four beehives, Gothic hen house plus ten rare breed hens. Hidden white walk, unusual plants and much, much more! Teas served in the Lady Chapel of the Church and outside if clement. Access to the church can be gained from the garden or from Main Street. Featured on BBC Radio Leicester and through the year on Ben Jackson programme. Featured

in Rutland Pride. Partial wheelchair access due to gravel paths, slopes and steps.

31 PARKSIDE
6 Park Hill, Gaddesby, LE7 4WH. Mr & Mrs D Wyrko, 01664 840385. *8m NE of Leicester. From A607 Rearsby bypass turn off for Gaddesby. L at Cheney Arms. Garden 400yds on R.* **Sun 9 Apr (11-5). Adm £3, chd free. Home-made teas. Visits also by arrangement Apr to June adm £6 incl tea and cake for groups 30 max.**
Woodland garden of approx 1¼ acres containing many spring flowers and bulbs. Vegetable garden with cordon fruit trees and soft fruit. Greenhouse, cold frame and pond with bog garden and other features. Informal mixed borders planted to encourage wildlife, to provide a family friendly environment and offering all yr-round interest.

32 REDHILL LODGE
Seaton Road, Barrowden, Oakham, LE15 8EN. Richard & Susan Moffitt, www.m360design.co.uk. *Redhill Lodge is 1m from village of Barrowden along Seaton Rd.* **Sun 16 July (12-5.30). Adm £5, chd free. Light refreshments.**
Still evolving bold contemporary design with formal lawns, grass amphitheatre and turf viewing mound, herbaceous borders and cutting garden. Praire style planting showing vibrant colour in late summer. Also natural swimming pond surrounded by Japanese style planting, bog garden and meadow area.

33 RIDGEWOLD FARM
Burton Lane, Wymeswold, LE12 6UN. Robert & Ann Waterfall, 01509 881689, robert.waterfall@yahoo.co.uk. *5m SE of Loughborough. Off Burton Lane between A6006 & B676. Ample car & coach parking.* **Visits by arrangement June & July for groups 10 - 50 max. Adm incl home-made teas. Adm £5.50.**

2½ acre rural garden in Leics Wolds. Conducted tours of garden and working farm, start on sweeping drive of specimen trees. Beech, laurel and saxon hedges divide different areas. Lawn, rill, water feature, summer house, shrubs, rose fence, clematis arch, wisteria, ivy tunnel, rose garden, herbaceous, orchard, vegetable patch and new pickery. Birch avenue with view of the village. Woodland walk. Wildlife pond.

34 119 SCALFORD ROAD
Melton Mowbray, LE13 1JZ. Richard & Hilary Lawrence, 01664 562821, randh1954@me.com. *½m N of Melton Mowbray. Take Scalford Rd from town centre past Cattle Market. Garden 100yds after 1st turning on L (The Crescent).* **Sun 30 July (11-5). Adm £2.50, chd free. Home-made teas incl gluten free. Visits also by arrangement June to Aug for groups 10 - 25 max.**
Larger than average town garden which has evolved over the last 27yrs. Mixed borders with traditional and exotic plants, enhanced by container planting particularly begonias. Vegetable parterre and greenhouse. Various seating areas for viewing different aspects of the garden. Water features incl ponds. Melton Times, RNIB media team, Fight for Sight media team. Partial wheelchair access. Gravelled drive, ramp provided up to lawn but paths not accessible.

Perennial,
supporting
horticulturalists
since 1839

35 NEW SHIPMEADOW
55 Main St, Barton in the Beans, Nr Nuneaton, CV13 0DJ. Viv McKee & Ian Woolley, 01455 291684, vivmckee@aol.com. *12m W of Leicester. From Barton towards Congerstone, follow NGS yellow arrows.* **Sat 1, Sun 2 July (10-8). Adm £4, chd free. Teas available in the studio. Visits also by arrangement Apr to Sept.**
The garden covers an acre plus with a wide variety of structures and planting. Although a garden in progress, it has a large natural pond and small coppice; a gravel garden developed to exhibit metal mermaid and Norfolk style beach hut; white formal garden; herb garden; wild garden and perennial and vegetable gardens. The studio/gallery, gazebo and patio offer places to rest.

36 STOKE ALBANY HOUSE
Desborough Road, Stoke Albany, Market Harborough, LE16 8PT. Mr & Mrs A M Vinton, 01858 535227, del.jones7@googlemail.com, www.stokealbanyhouse.co.uk. *4m E of Market Harborough. Via A427 to Corby, turn to Stoke Albany, R at the White Horse (B669) garden ½m on the L.* **Every Wed 7 June to 26 July (2-4.30). Adm £4.50, chd free. Visits also by arrangement for groups 10+ (Weds preferably).** *Donation to Marie Curie Cancer Care.*
4 acre country house garden; fine trees and shrubs with wide herbaceous borders and sweeping striped lawn. Good display of bulbs in spring, roses June and July. Walled grey garden; nepeta walk arched with roses, parterre with box and roses. Mediterranean garden. Heated greenhouse, potager with topiary, water feature garden and sculptures.

SULBY GARDENS
See Northamptonshire

37 THORPE LUBENHAM HALL

Farndon Road, Lubenham, LE16 9TR. Sir Bruce & Lady MacPhail. *2m W of Market Harborough. From Market Harborough take 3rd L off main rd, down Rushes Lane, past church on L, under old railway bridge & straight on up private drive.* **Wed 24 May (10.30-5). Adm £5, chd free. Adm incl cream tea.**

15 acres of formal and informal garden surrounded by parkland and arable. Many mature trees. Traditional herbaceous borders and various water features. Walled pool garden with raised beds. Ancient moat area along driveway. Gravel paths, some steep slopes and steps.

38 TRESILLIAN HOUSE

67 Dalby Road, Melton Mowbray, LE13 0BQ. Mrs Alison Blythe, 01664 481997, tresillianhouse@aol.com, www.tresillianhouse.com. *Situated on B6047 Dalby Rd (Melton to Gt Dalby) going S. Parking on site. NB: We are not actually in Great Dalby but in the south of Melton Mowbray.* **Sun 7 May, Sun 2 July, Sun 27 Aug, Sun 22 Oct (11-4.30). Adm £3, chd free. Visits also by arrangement Mar to Oct, groups no min, 30 max.**

¾ acre garden re-established by current owner since 2009. Beautiful blue cedar trees, excellent specimen tulip tree. Parts of garden original, others reinstated with variety of plants and bushes. Original bog garden and natural pond reinstated 2015. Koi pond added also in 2015. Vegetable plot. Cowslips and bulbs abound in Springtime. Quiet oasis. New cut flower bed planned for 2017. Ploughmans lunches, cream teas, home-made cakes and on cold days soup is also available. Featured several times in The Melton Times plus a feature in Gardening News. Slate paths, steep in places but manageable.

GROUP OPENING

39 WALTON GARDENS

Walton, LE17 5RG. *4m NE of Lutterworth. M1 J20, via Lutterworth follow signs for Kimcote & Walton, or from Leicester take A5199. After Shearsby turn R signed Bruntingthorpe. Follow signs.* **Sun 25, Wed 28 June (11-5). Combined adm £4, chd free. Home-made teas at Rylands Farmhouse.**

MULBERRY HOUSE
Mr Karl & Mrs Hazel Busch.

RAINBOW COTTAGE
Linda & Terry Allcott.

RYLANDS FARMHOUSE
Mark & Sonya Raybould.

SANDYLAND
Martin & Linda Goddard.

TOAD HALL
Sue Beardmore.

Small village set in beautiful S Leicestershire countryside with traditional country PH. The five gardens at Walton are in such contrasting sizes and styles that, together, they make the perfect garden visit. There is a walled garden with a unique water feature and a traditional garden with a small working pottery; an interesting garden with a stable and a serpentine hedge and also two delightful cottage gardens, one of which has an interesting green roof garden and the other usually combines planting with a bit of theatre to raise a smile. Some steps, wood chip and cobbled paths that would prove difficult for wheelchairs and for those with limited mobility.

59 Thistleton Road, Market Overton Gardens

ALLOTMENTS

40 WASHBROOK ALLOTMENTS
Welford Road, Leicester, LE2 6FP.
Sharon Maher. *Approx 2½m S of Leicester, 1½ m N of Wigston. Regret no onsite parking. Welford Rd difficult to park on. Please use nearby side rds & Pendlebury Drive (LE2 6GY).*
Sun 3 Sept (11-3). Adm £3, chd free. Home-made teas.
Our allotment gardens have been described as a hidden oasis off the main Welford Road. There are over 100 whole and half plots growing a wide variety of fruit and vegetables. We have a fledgling wildflower meadow, a composting toilet and a shop. Keep a look out for the remains of Anderson Shelters, and see how woodchip is put to good use. Circular route around the site is uneven in places but is suitable for wheelchairs.
♿ ✿ ☕

41 WESTBROOKE HOUSE
52 Scotland Road, Little Bowden, LE16 8AX. Bryan & Joanne Drew, 07872 316153, Jwsd1980@hotmail.co.uk.
½m S Market Harborough. From Northampton Rd follow NGS arrows.
Sun 14 May, Sun 2 July (11-5). Adm £5, chd free. Cream teas. Visits also by arrangement May to Aug.
Westbrooke House is a late Victorian property built in 1887. The gardens comprise 6 acres in total and are approached through a tree lined driveway of mature limes and wellingtonias. Key features are walled flower garden, walled kitchen garden, pond area, spring garden, lawns, woodland paths and a meadow with a wild flower area, ha-ha and Hornbeam avenue.
✿ 🅳 ☕

42 WESTVIEW
1 St Thomas's Road, Great Glen, LE8 9EH. Gill & John Hadland, 01162 592170, gill@hadland.wanadoo.co.uk. *7m S of Leicester. Take either r'about from A6 into village centre (War Memorial) then follow NGS signs.*

Please park in Oaks Rd. Sat 4, Sun 5 Mar (12-4). Adm £2.50, chd free. Home-made teas. Visits also by arrangement Feb to Oct for groups 20 max.
Organically managed small walled cottage style garden with yr-round interest. Interesting and unusual plants, many grown from seed. Formal box parterre herb garden, courtyard, herbaceous borders, small wildlife pond, greenhouse, beehives, vegetable and fruit area. Auricula display. Hand-made sculptures and artefacts made from recycled materials on display. Collection of Galanthus (snowdrops).
✿ ☕

43 ♦ WHATTON GARDENS
Long Whatton, Loughborough, LE12 5BG. Lord & Lady Crawshaw, 01509 842225, whattonhouse@gmail.com, www.whattonhouseandgardens.co.uk.
4m NE of Loughborough. On A6 between Hathern & Kegworth; 2½m SE of M1J24. For NGS: Sun 21 May (11-5). Adm £4, chd free. Home-made teas. For other opening times and information, please phone, email or visit garden website.
Often described by visitors as a hidden gem, this 15 acre C19 Country House garden is a relaxing experience for all the family. Listen to the birds, and enjoy walking through the many fine trees, spring bulbs and shrubs, large herbaceous border, traditional rose garden, ornamental ponds and lawns. Open daily (excl Sat) March to Oct. Available for group bookings. Gravel paths.
♿ 🐕 ✿ 🚌 ☕

GROUP OPENING

44 WILLOUGHBY GARDENS
Willoughby Waterleys, LE8 6UD.
9m S of Leicester. From A426 heading N turn R at Dunton Bassett lights. Follow signs to Willoughby. From Blaby follow signs to Countesthorpe. 2m S to Willoughby.

Sun 23 July (11-5). Combined adm £5, chd free. Home-made teas in Village Hall.

1 CHURCH FARM LANE
Kathleen & Peter Bowers.

2 CHURCH FARM LANE
Valerie & Peter Connelly.

FARMWAY
Eileen Spencer, 01162 478321, eileenfarmway9@msn.com.
Visits also by arrangement July & Aug, groups 25 max.

HIGH MEADOW
Phil & Eva Day.

JOHN'S WOOD
John & Jill Harris.

KAPALUA
Richard & Linda Love.

3 ORCHARD ROAD
Diane & Roger Brearley.

NEW WILLOUGHBY LODGE FARM
Liz & David Winterton.

Willoughby Waterleys lies in the South Leicestershire countryside. The Norman Church will be open, hosting a film of the local bird population filmed by a local resident. 8 gardens will be open. John's Wood is a 1½ acre nature reserve planted to encourage wildlife. 1 Church Farm Lane is a well stocked garden with lawn, trees and shrubs, roses, and climbers. 2 Church Farm Lane has been professionally designed with many interesting features. Farmway is a plant lovers garden with many unusual plants in colour themed borders. High Meadow has been evolving over 5yrs. Incl mixed planting and ornamental vegetable garden. Kapalua has interesting planting design incorporating open views of countryside. 3 Orchard Road is a small garden packed with interest. Willoughby Lodge Farm is a country garden incl a walled garden, pond area, summer house, mown grass paths and wildflower area and numerous native trees. Lawncare advice clinic 2-4pm. Willoughby embroidery on display in village hall. Wildlife film in the church.
✿ ☕

LINCOLNSHIRE

Lincolnshire is a county shaped by a rich tapestry of fascinating heritage, passionate people and intriguing traditions; a mix of city, coast and countryside.

The city of Lincoln is dominated by the iconic towers of Lincoln Cathedral. The eastern seaboard contains windswept golden sands and lonely nature reserves. The Lincolnshire Wolds is a nationally important landscape of rolling chalk hills and areas of sandstone and clay, which underlie this attractive landscape.

To the south is the historic, religious and architectural heritage of The Vales, with river walks, the fine Georgian buildings of Stamford and historic Burghley House. In the east the unqiue Fens landscape thrives on an endless network of waterways inhabited by an abundance of wildlife.

Beautiful gardens of all types, sizes and designs are cared for and shared by their welcoming owners. Often located in delightful villages, a visit to them will entail driving through quiet roads often bordered by verges of wild flowers.

Lincolnshire is rural England at its very best. Local heritage, beautiful countryside walks, aviation history and it is the home of the Red Arrows.

Left: Manor Farm

Volunteers

County Organisers
Helen Boothman
01652 628424
boothmanhelen@gmail.com

Sally Grant
01205 750486
sallygrant50@btinternet.com

County Treasurer
Helen Boothman
(as above)

Publicity
Margaret Mann
01476 585905
marg_mann2000@yahoo.com

Erica McGarrigle
01476 585909
ericamcg@hotmail.co.uk

Assistant County Organisers
Lynne Barnes
01529 497462
lynnebarnes14@googlemail.com

Tricia Elliot
01427 788517
triciaelliott921@btinternet.com

Stephanie Lee
01507 442151
marigoldlee@btinternet.com

Rita Morgan
01472 597529
rita.morgan1@sky.com

Sylvia Ravenhall
01507 526014
sylvan@btinternet.com

Jo Rouston
01673 858656
jo@rouston-gardens.co.uk

OPENING DATES

All entries subject to change. For latest information check **www.ngs.org.uk**

Map locator numbers are shown to the right of each garden name.

February
Snowdrop Festival

Saturday 25th
21 Chapel Street — 10

Sunday 26th
21 Chapel Street — 10

March

Saturday 25th
NEW The Manor House — 32

Sunday 26th
21 Chapel Street — 10

April

Sunday 2nd
Woodlands — 62

Saturday 8th
♦ Burghley House Private
South Gardens — 7

Sunday 9th
♦ Burghley House Private
South Gardens — 7
♦ Grimsthorpe Castle — 19

Friday 14th
♦ Easton Walled
Gardens — 13

Sunday 16th
Ashfield House — 2

Monday 17th
Firsby Manor — 15

Sunday 23rd
♦ Goltho House — 17
The Old Rectory — 42

Saturday 29th
Marigold Cottage — 33

Sunday 30th
Marigold Cottage — 33

May

Thursday 4th
♦ Brightwater Gardens — 6

Sunday 7th
Dunholme Lodge — 12
Nut Tree Farm — 39
Woodlands — 62

Sunday 14th
66 Spilsby Road — 53

Saturday 20th
2 Mill Cottage — 35

Sunday 21st
Holly House — 24
Mill Farm — 36
The Old Rectory — 42
The Old Vicarage — 43
Old White House — 44

90th Anniversary Weekend

Saturday 27th
Marigold Cottage — 33
NEW Oasis Garden -
Your Place — 40

Sunday 28th
Firsby Manor — 15
Manor House — 31
Marigold Cottage — 33

NEW Oasis Garden -
Your Place — 40
Pottertons Nursery — 48

Monday 29th
Manor Farm — 30

June

Saturday 3rd
NEW Inner Lodge — 28

Sunday 4th
Horncastle Gardens — 26
NEW Inner Lodge — 28
Pear Tree Cottage — 46
Woodlands — 62

Wednesday 7th
♦ Grimsthorpe Castle — 19

Sunday 11th
NEW Barrow Gardens — 5
Hackthorn Hall — 21

Sunday 18th
Aubourn Hall — 3
The Hawthorns — 23
NEW Pine Fields — 47
Shangrila — 51
West Syke — 58
Windrush — 61

Saturday 24th
Marigold Cottage — 33
Overbeck — 45
Thornham — 55

Sunday 25th
Marigold Cottage — 33
The Moat — 37

July

Sunday 2nd
Fenleigh — 14
NEW Gosberton Group
Gardens — 18
Shepherds Hey — 52
Woodlands — 62

Sunday 9th
Dunholme Lodge — 12

Wednesday 12th
68 Watts Lane — 57

Saturday 15th
NEW Inner Lodge — 28
NEW School House — 49

Sunday 16th
♦ Hall Farm — 22
NEW Inner Lodge — 28
The Old House — 41

Walnut Tree Cottage — 56

Saturday 22nd
Marigold Cottage — 33

Sunday 23rd
NEW Ballygarth — 4
Marigold Cottage — 33
The Stables — 54
Yew Tree Farm — 63

Sunday 30th
68 Watts Lane — 57

August

Sunday 6th
Ashcroft House — 1
♦ Gunby Hall & Gardens — 20
Sedgebrook Manor — 50
68 Watts Lane — 57
Woodlands — 62

Sunday 13th
Butterfly Hospice — 8
68 Watts Lane — 57
Willoughby Road
Allotments — 60

Saturday 19th
NEW Inner Lodge — 28

Sunday 20th
NEW Inner Lodge — 28
68 Watts Lane — 57

Thursday 24th
♦ Brightwater Gardens — 6

Saturday 26th
Marigold Cottage — 33

Sunday 27th
Manor House — 31
Marigold Cottage — 33
68 Watts Lane — 57

September

Sunday 3rd
Fotherby Gardens — 16
♦ Hall Farm — 22

Sunday 10th
45 Chapel Lane — 9
48 Westgate — 59

Saturday 16th
Inley Drove Farm — 27
NEW Mere House — 34

Sunday 17th
Inley Drove Farm — 27

Wednesday 20th
♦ Doddington Hall
Gardens — 11

Manor House

Your visit helps the Queen's Nursing Institute to champion excellence in community nursing

THE GARDENS

1 ASHCROFT HOUSE

45 Newton Way, Woolsthorpe by Colsterworth, Grantham, NG33 5NP. Lucienne Bennett. *7m from Grantham, 400 metres from Woolsthorpe Manor (NT). No parking in Newton Way. Plenty of parking along Woolsthorpe Rd or at Woolsthorpe Manor (if visiting property). 4 dedicated disabled parking spaces.* **Sun 6 Aug (12-5). Adm £3, chd free. Home-made teas. Gluten free cakes available.**
Back garden created in 2012 from part of a pony paddock on a filled in ironstone quarry. Sloping ground necessitated terracing and having natural springs running down one side, and boggy ground in deep shade at the bottom of the plot meant that this small garden needed careful planning.

15 Elmhirst Road, Horncastle Gardens

2 ASHFIELD HOUSE

Lincoln Road, Branston, Lincoln, LN4 1NS. John & Judi Tinsley, 07977 505682, john@tinsleyfarms.co.uk. *3m S of Lincoln on B1188. From Branston off B1188 Lincoln Rd on L. 1m from Branston Hall Hotel signed Ashfield Farms.* **Sun 16 Apr, Sun 29 Oct (12-4). Adm £3.50, chd free. Light refreshments. Visits also by arrangement.**
10 acre garden with sweeping lawns constructed around a planting of trees and shrubs. The main feature in the spring is the collection of some 110 flowering cherries of 40 different varieties along with massed plantings of spring flowering bulbs. We recently planted a magnolia collection in a newly constructed woodland garden. In the autumn the colours can be amazing. Fairly level garden. Grass paths.

3 AUBOURN HALL

Harmston Road, Aubourn, nr Lincoln, LN5 9DZ. Mr & Mrs Christopher Nevile, 01522 788224, paula@aubournhall.co.uk, www.aubournhall.co.uk. *7m SW of Lincoln. Signed off A607 at Harmston & off A46 at Thorpe on the Hill.* **Sun 18 June (2-5). Adm £4.50, chd free. Home-made teas. Visits also by arrangement in June.**
Approx 8 acres. Lawns, mature trees, shrubs, roses, mixed borders, rose garden, large prairie and topiary garden, spring bulbs, woodland walk and ponds. C11 church adjoining. Access to garden is fairly flat and smooth. Depending on weather some areas may be inaccessible to wheelchairs. Parking in field not on tarmac.

4 NEW ▶ BALLYGARTH

Post Office Lane, Whitton, Scunthorpe, DN15 9LF. Joanne & Adrian Davey, 07871 882339, joanne.davey1971@gmail.com. *From Scunthorpe on A1077 follow signs to West Halton. Through West Halton approx 3m to Whitton. Follow signs for parking at Village Hall.* **Sun 23 July (11-4). Adm £3, chd free. Home-made teas in Whitton Village Hall. Visits also by arrangement June to Aug.**
Set in the rural village of Whitton our end terraced house has approx ⅓ acre garden with large herbaceous and grass borders and two water features. Seating areas overlooking the garden, countryside and vegetable garden. Many home-made garden artifacts using recycled materials incl a small folly. Everything in wood, brick and metal has been made by us. Drop off for those with limited mobility but parking is at village hall.

&️ 🐕 🗟 ☕

**Burghley House
Private South Gardens**

GROUP OPENING

5 NEW ▶ BARROW GARDENS

Barrow on Humber, DN19 7DY. *Barrow on Humber is 3m S of Humber Bridge. From A15 follow B1206 towards Barrow upon Humber & Westcote Farm is immed L. NGS yellow signs will give directions to all gardens.* **Sun 11 June (11-5). Combined adm £6, chd free. Home-made teas at The Barn and 3 Westcote Farm House.**

NEW ▶ BANNER HOUSE
Paul & Kathryn Bartlett.

THE BARN
Lesley & Ian Pepperdine, 01469 533966.
Visits also by arrangement June & July.

3 WESTCOTE FARM HOUSE
Gary & Ali Baugh.

The Barn - An open space garden set in approx 1 acre with orchard, formal yew hedging, mature trees, topiary, herbaceous border and shrubbery. Expansion to the vegetable garden to incl new greenhouse in 2017. 3 Westcote Farm House - A garden designed to relax and enjoy the surrounding countryside. Yew hedges used to give a formal but contemporary feel, giving seclusion to each area. Large drifts of herbaceous planting. Roses, trees and shrubs are the backbone of the garden. Banner House - Many different areas featuring 2 summerhouses, a greenhouse, ornamental and wildlife pond. Lawned areas with cottage style borders. Small vegetable garden. Wheelchair and scooter access over lawn and most hard surfaces.

🐕 🗟 ☕

Your support helps Carers Trust to provide more help to unpaid carers

6 ◆ BRIGHTWATER GARDENS

The Garden House, Saxby, Market Rasen, LN8 2DQ. Chris Neave & Jonathan Cartwright, 01673 878820, info@brightwatergardens.co.uk, www.brightwatergardens.co.uk. *8m N of Lincoln; 2¼m E of A15. Turn off A15 signed Saxby.* **For NGS: Thur 4 May, Thur 24 Aug (11-4). Adm £5, chd free. Home-made teas. For other opening times and information, please phone, email or visit garden website.**
8 acre landscaped garden. Yew hedging and walls enclose magical garden rooms full of roses and herbaceous plants. Solar garden, long terrace, Dutch, pergola and obelisk gardens, lavender walk. Large natural damp garden. Dry garden, specimen trees overlooking a large reflective pond. Native woodland areas, prairie and wild lower meadow planted with massed bulbs. Adjacent St. Helen's Church attributed to Lancelot Capability Brown. RHS Partner Garden. Gravel paths, steep slopes.

&️ 🚌 ☕

7 ◆ BURGHLEY HOUSE PRIVATE SOUTH GARDENS

Stamford, PE9 3JY. Burghley House Preservation Trust, 01780 752451, burghley@burghley.co.uk, www.burghley.co.uk. *1m E of Stamford. From Stamford follow signs to Burghley via B1443.* **For NGS: Sat 8, Sun 9 Apr (11-4). Adm £4, chd free. Cream teas in The Orangery Restaurant. For other opening times and information, please phone, email or visit garden website.**
On 8th and 9th April the Private South Gardens at Burghley House will open for the NGS with spectacular spring bulbs in park like setting with magnificent trees and the opportunity to enjoy Capability Brown's famous lake and summerhouse. Entry to the Private South Gardens via Orangery. The Garden of Surprises, Sculpture Garden and House are open as normal. (Regular adm prices apply). Food Fair. Gravel paths.

&️ ❀ 🚌 ☕

Brightwater Gardens

© Lee Beel

8 BUTTERFLY HOSPICE

Rowan Way, Boston, PE21 9DH. Steve Doughty. *From Spilsby Rd, Hospital Ln, R into Linden Way then R again into Rowan Way.* **Sun 13 Aug (10-4). Combined adm with Willoughby Road Allotments £4, chd free. Cream teas.**

Set in 4 acres the gardens surrounding Butterfly Hospice are a mixture of traditional beds, orchard and large wildflower meadow. Willow arbours, pathways and disabled access greenhouse with raised beds are other parts of the peaceful and relaxing gardens which form part of the care provided to inpatients by the hospice.

9 45 CHAPEL LANE

North Scarle, Lincoln, LN6 9EX. Michael & Anna Peacock. *12m SW of Lincoln; 9m NW Newark. From A46 follow signs to Whisby & Eagle. On entering Eagle take 1st R, cont for approx 1m take 1st L. Cont to Xrds in centre of N Scarle. Turn R into Chapel Lane. Garden last on L.* **Sun 10 Sept (1.30-5). Adm £3, chd free. Home-made teas.**

A garden designed by the owners to give an all season, cottage style feel to a relatively modern edge of the village property. The ¾ acre garden was started from a blank canvas in 2011. Three offset circular lawns, connected by archways, are edged with bee friendly hardy perennials and annuals, lavenders, roses, shrubs and fruit trees. Gravel area with low rockery. Pretty gazebo. Some features made from recycled materials. Single cobble path may prove difficult to wheelchair users.

10 21 CHAPEL STREET

Hacconby, Bourne, PE10 0UL. Cliff & Joan Curtis and Sharon White, 01778 570314, cliffordcurtis@btinternet.com. *3m N of Bourne. A15, turn E at Xrds into Hacconby, L at village green.* **Sat 25, Sun 26 Feb, Sun 26 Mar (11-4). Adm £3, chd free. Home-made teas. Hot soup (Feb). Visits also by arrangement.**

A cottage garden behind a 300yr old cottage. Snowdrops, primroses, hellebores and many different spring flowering bulbs. Colour with bulbs and herbaceous plants through the yr, autumn with asters, dahlias, salvias and many of the autumn flowering yellow daises. Part gravel and part grass paths.

11 ◆ DODDINGTON HALL GARDENS

Doddington, Lincoln, LN6 4RU. Claire & James Birch, 01522 812510, info@doddingtonhall.com, www.doddingtonhall.com. *5m W of Lincoln. Signed clearly from A46 Lincoln bypass & A57, 3m.* **For NGS: Wed 20 Sept (11-4). Adm £7, chd £3.50. Home-made teas. For other opening times and information, please phone, email or visit garden website.**

5 acres of romantic walled and wild gardens. Naturalised spring bulbs and scented shrubs from Feb to May. Spectacular iris display late May/early June in box edged parterres of West Garden. Sumptuous herbaceous borders throughout summer, ancient chestnut trees, turf maze, Temple of the Winds. Fully productive, walled kitchen garden. Wheelchair access possible via gravel paths. Ramps also in use. Access map available from Gatehouse Shop.

12 DUNHOLME LODGE

Dunholme, Lincoln, LN2 3QA. Hugh & Lesley Wykes. *4m NE of Lincoln. Turn off A46 towards Welton at hand car wash garage. After ½m turn L up long concrete rd. Garden at top.* **Sun 7 May, Sun 9 July (11-5). Adm £3.50, chd free. Cream teas.**

3 acre garden. Spring bulb area, shrub borders, fern garden, topiary, large natural pond, wild flower area, orchard and vegetable garden. RAF Dunholme Lodge Museum and War Memorial in the grounds. Most areas wheelchair accessible but some loose stone and gravel.

13 ◆ EASTON WALLED GARDENS

Easton, NG33 5AP. Sir Fred & Lady Cholmeley, 01476 530063, info@eastonwalledgardens.co.uk, www.eastonwalledgardens.co.uk. *7m S of Grantham. 1m off A1. Follow village signposts via B6403.* **For NGS: Fri 14 Apr (11-4). Adm £7, chd £3. Light refreshments. For other opening times and information, please phone, email or visit garden website.**

12 acres of 400yr old forgotten gardens undergoing extensive renovation. Set in parkland with dramatic views. C16 garden with Victorian embellishments. Italianate terraces; yew tunnel; snowdrops and cut flower garden. David Austin roses, meadows and sweet pea collections. Cottage and vegetable gardens. Please wear sensible shoes suitable for country walking. Childrens' Trail. Regret no wheelchair access to lower gardens but tearoom, shop and upper gardens all accessible.

14 FENLEIGH

Inkerson Fen, Off Comon Road, Throckenholt, PE12 0QY. Jeff & Barbara Stalker. *2m from Gedney Hill. Turn R on to B1166 take next R into Common Rd following NGS signs approx 1m. From Parson Drove on B1166 turn L into Common Rd following NGS signs approx 3m.* **Sun 2 July (10-4). Adm £2.50, chd free. Light refreshments.**

Set in 4 acres incl 2 acre paddock. Quirky areas for easy maintenance. A fish pond dominates the garden surrounded with planting. Seating and two permanent gazebos if the weather is inclement. Patio with pots and raised beds, BBQ area containing ferns and acers. Small wooded area, poly tunnels and corners of the garden for wildlife. Large grass area for family fun and games.

15 FIRSBY MANOR

Firsby, Spilsby, PE23 5QJ. David & Gill Boldy, 01754 830386, gillboldy@gmail.com. *5m E of Spilsby. From Spilsby take B1195 to* Wainfleet all Saints. In Firsby, turn R into Fendyke Rd. Firsby Manor is 0.8m along lane on L. **Mon 17 Apr, Sun 28 May (1-4.30). Adm £3, chd free. Home-made teas. Visits also by arrangement Feb to Sept. Garden/photographic societies welcome.**

Firsby Manor, a garden of 3 acres surrounding a Georgian farmhouse has been developed over two decades to provide interest throughout the year, although it is at its most lovely in late spring and early summer. A visit in April offers a chance to see many different daffodil cultivars as the owners exhibit at the annual Lincolnshire Daffodil Society show each year. Featured in Lincolnshire Pride. Partial wheelchair access due to large areas of shingle and uneven ground. No WC access.

GROUP OPENING

16 FOTHERBY GARDENS

Peppin Lane, Fotherby, Louth, LN11 0UW. *2m N of Louth on A16 signed Fotherby. Please park on R verge opp allotments & walk to gardens. Free taxi service between Woodlands & Nut Tree Farm. No parking at gardens. Please do not park beyond designated area.* **Sun 3 Sept (11-5). Combined adm £5, chd free. Home-made teas at Woodlands.**

NUT TREE FARM
Tim & Judith Hunter.
(See separate entry)

SHEPHERDS HEY
Barbara Chester.
(See separate entry)

WOODLANDS
Ann & Bob Armstrong.
(See separate entry)

Start your visit at Shepherds Hey, a small garden packed with unusual and interesting perennials. Its open frontage gives a warm welcome, with a small pond, terraced border and steep bank side to a small stream. The rear garden, with colour themed borders, takes advantage of the panoramic views over open countryside. Recently featured in Lincolnshire Life. 350yds along Peppin Lane is Woodlands, a lovely mature woodland garden with many unusual plants set against a backdrop of an ever changing tapestry of greenery. A peaceful garden where wildlife can thrive and the front garden is a crevice area for alpine plants. There is a Plant Heritage collection of Codonopsis and the nursery, featured in RHS Plantfinder, gives visitors the opportunity to purchase plants seen in the garden. An award winning professional artist's studio/gallery is also open. The garden was featured in Lincolnshire Pride magazine. Complete your visit at Nut Tree Farm. The garden, est in 2007, is over an acre and enjoys stunning views of Lincolnshire Wolds. A sweeping herbaceous border frames the lawn and a double wall, planted with seasonal annuals, surrounds the house. From the raised terrace a rill runs to the large pond. As well as a raised brick edged vegetable garden, there is a prize winning flock of Hampshire Down sheep in fields surrounding part of garden. Locally made honey for sale.

17 ◆ GOLTHO HOUSE

Lincoln Road, Goltho, Wragby, Market Rasen, LN8 5NF. Mr & Mrs S Hollingworth, 01673 857768, bookings@golthogardens.com, www.golthogardens.com. *10m E of Lincoln. On A158, 1m before Wragby. Garden on L (not in Goltho Village).* **For NGS: Sun 23 Apr, Sun 24 Sept (10-4). Adm £5, chd free. Light refreshments. For other opening times and information, please phone, email or visit garden website.**

4½ acre garden started in 1998 but looking established with long grass walk flanked by abundantly planted herbaceous borders forming a focal point. Paths and walkway span out to other features incl nut walk, prairie border, wildflower meadow, rose garden and large pond area. Snowdrops, hellebores and shrubs for winter interest.

GROUP OPENING

18 NEW GOSBERTON GROUP GARDENS

Gosberton, Spalding, PE11 4NQ. *Entering Gosberton on A152, Westhorpe Rd is opp the Bell PH. Follow signs from school to locate gardens. Parking for all gardens at Gosberton House School (PE11 4EW).* **Sun 2 July (10.30-4). Combined adm £5, chd free. Light refreshments.**

NEW GOSBERTON HOUSE SCHOOL
Lee Gregory.

NEW MILLSTONE HOUSE
Mr John Chatterton.

NEW 4 SALEM STREET
Patricia Hogben.

The village of Gosberton welcomes visitors to Gosberton House Academy and 2 private houses to view their gardens. We hope that visitors will find interesting features during their tour and enjoy the 3 locations. Partial wheelchair access.

&. ✿ ☕

19 ◆ GRIMSTHORPE CASTLE

Grimsthorpe, Bourne, PE10 0LZ. Grimsthorpe & Drummond Castle Trust, 01778 591205, ray@grimsthorpe.co.uk, www.grimsthorpe.co.uk. *3m NW of Bourne. 8m E of A1 on A151 from Colsterworth junction. Main entrance indicated by brown tourist sign.* **For NGS: Sun 9 Apr, Wed 7 June (11-6). Adm £6, chd £2.50. Light refreshments. For other opening times and information, please phone, email or visit garden website.**
The Grade I listed gardens encompass nearly 65 acres and incl large formal lawns, fine topiary and formal hedges, ornamental and productive kitchen garden, large herbaceous borders, rose parterre and woodland walks with spring bulb displays. Visitors can explore the surrounding 3000 acre estate that encompasses a Capability

Brown landscape, in addition to the tranquil and relaxing gardens. Home-made lunches, afternoon tea and cakes. Gift shop, cycle hire and adventure playground, historic house, park trails. Gravel paths.

&. 🚗 ☕

20 ◆ GUNBY HALL & GARDENS

Spilsby, PE23 5SS. National Trust, 01754 890102, gunbyhall@nationaltrust.org.uk, www.nationaltrust.org.uk. *2½m NW of Burgh-le-Marsh. 7m W of Skegness. On A158. Signed off Gunby r'about.* **For NGS: Sun 6 Aug (11-5). Adm £6.25, chd £3.25. Light refreshments in Gunby tea-room. For other opening times and information, please phone, email or visit garden website.**
8 acres of formal and walled gardens. Old roses, herbaceous borders, herb garden and kitchen garden with fruit trees and vegetables. Greenhouses, carp pond and sweeping lawns. Tennyson's Haunt of Ancient Peace. House built by Sir William Massingberd in 1700. Wheelchair access in gardens and with Gunby's dedicated wheelchair on ground floor of house.

&. 🐎 ✿ 🛏 ☕

21 HACKTHORN HALL

Hackthorn, Lincoln, LN2 3PQ. Mr & Mrs William Cracroft-Eley, 01673 860423, office@hackthorn.com, www.hackthorn.com. *6m N of Lincoln. Follow signs to Hackthorn. Approx 1m off A15 N of Lincoln.* **Sun 11 June (1-5). Adm £3.50, chd free. Home-made teas at Hackthorn Hall Gardens. Visits also by arrangement for groups of 20+.**
Formal and woodland garden, productive and ornamental walled gardens surrounding Hackthorn Hall and church extending to approx 15 acres. Parts of the formal gardens designed by Bunny Guinness. The walled garden boasts a magnificent Black Hamburg vine, believed to be second in size to the vine at Hampton Court. Partial wheelchair access, gravel paths, grass drives.

&. 🐎 ✿ ☕

22 ◆ HALL FARM

Harpswell, Gainsborough, DN21 5UU. Pam & Mark Tatam, 01427 668412, pam.tatam@gmail.com, www.hall-farm.co.uk. *7m E of Gainsborough. On A631, 1½ m W of Caenby Corner.* **For NGS: Sun 16 July, Sun 3 Sept (1-5). Adm £4, chd free. Light refreshments. For other opening times and information, please phone, email or visit garden website.**
The 3 acre garden encompasses formal and informal areas, incl a parterre, a sunken garden, a courtyard with rill, a walled Mediterranean garden, double herbaceous borders for late summer, lawns, pond, giant chess set, and a flower and grass meadow. It is a short walk to the medieval moat, which surrounds an acre of wild semi woodland garden currently under development. Free seed collecting on Sun 3 Sept. Most of garden suitable for wheelchairs.

&. 🐎 ✿ 🚗 🛏 ☕

23 THE HAWTHORNS

Bicker Road, Donington, PE11 4XP. Colin & Janet Johnson, 01775 822808, colinj04@hotmail.com. *½m NW of Donington. Bicker Rd is directly off A52 opp Church Street. Parking available in Church Street or village centre car park.* **Sun 18 June (11-4). Adm £3.50, chd free. Home-made teas. Visits also by arrangement June to Aug for groups 12+.**
Traditional garden with extensive herbaceous borders, pond, large old English rose garden, vegetable and fruit areas with feature greenhouse. Cider orchard and area housing rare breed animals incl goats, pigs, sheep, cattle and chickens. Home produce available incl honey and goat's milk dairy products.

&. ☕

The National Garden Scheme is Hospice UK's largest single funder

24 HOLLY HOUSE

Fishtoft Drove, Frithville, Boston, PE22 7ES. Sally & David Grant, 01205 750486, sallygrant50@btinternet.com. *3m N of Boston. 1m S of Frithville. Unclassified rd. On W side of West Fen Drain. Marked on good maps.* **Sun 21 May (12-5). Adm £3.50, chd free. Home-made teas. Visits also by arrangement May to July for groups 10+. Adm £5 incl refreshments.**

Approx 1 acre informal mixed borders, steps leading down to pond with cascade and stream. Small woodland area. Quiet garden with water feature. Extra 2½ acres devoted to wildlife, especially bumble bees and butterflies. Featured in Lincolnshire Pride. Partial wheelchair access with some steep slopes and steps.

  ♿ 🐴 ✿ 🚐 ☕

25 HOPE HOUSE

15 Horsemarket, Caistor, LN7 6UP. Sue Neave, 07940 567079, hopehousegardens@aol.com, www.hopehousegardens.co.uk. *Off A46 Between Lincoln & Grimsby. Centre of town.* **Visits by arrangement May to Sept, groups welcome. Adm £3.50, chd free. Light refreshments.**

A country garden in an attractive historic town in the heart of the Lincolnshire Wolds. Small walled garden attached to an interesting Georgian house. Roses, perennials, shrubs, trees, fruit and a small raised vegetable area. Wildlife pond and formal water trough in the dining area. Yr-round colour and interest in a tranquil space created by its garden designer owner. Caistor Arts and Heritage Centre (opp) organise walks around the historic town and local areas of interest and provide information on the history of Caistor and the area. Cafe and Library. The garden featured as part of Alan Titchmarsh's TV programme - Love Your Garden.

🐴 ✿ 🛏 ☕

GROUP OPENING

26 HORNCASTLE GARDENS

Horncastle, LN9 5AS. *Take A158 from Lincoln. Just inside 40mph turn L into Accommodation Rd. Gardens signed from here. Roadside parking only. Please park sensibly.* **Sun 4 June (11-4.30). Combined adm £5, chd free. Home-made cakes incl gluten free at 15 Elmhirst Road.**

23 ACCOMMODATION ROAD

Mr & Mrs D Chapman.

40 ACCOMMODATION ROAD

Eddie & Marie Aldridge.

15 ELMHIRST ROAD

Sylvia Ravenhall, 01507 526014, sylvan@btinternet.com. **Visits also by arrangement in July daytime or evening visits, individuals or groups.**

30 ELMHIRST ROAD

Andy & Yvonne Mathieson.

The market town of Horncastle some 20m to the E of Lincoln on the A158 is often called The Gateway to the Wolds. These 4 very different gardens are within easy walking distance of each other. 23 Accommodation Rd is planted with a variety of perennials, iris, alpines, auriculas and fruit plus fishpond and seating. 40 Accommodation Rd is packed with perennials and climbers in a garden wrapped around three sides of a bungalow. 15 Elmhirst Rd is a long and narrow town garden, with winding gravel paths and shallow steps around secret corners. It is planted with perennials, shrubs, climbers, small trees and lawn. Many hostas are grown in pots and in the ground. There are plenty of seats. 30 Elmhirst Rd contains colourful planting, raised vegetable beds, small greenhouse and fruit. The quirky hand-made features raise a smile on most faces. Some gravel paths and shallow steps in all gardens, constricted turning area at 40 Accommodation Rd.

✿ ☕

Hall Farm

© Clive Nicholls

27 INLEY DROVE FARM

Inley Drove, Sutton St James, Spalding, PE12 0LX. Francis & Maisie Pryor, https://pryorfrancis. wordpress.com/. *Just off rd from Sutton St James to Sutton St Edmund. 2m S of Sutton St James. Look for yellow NGS signs on double bend.* Sat 16, Sun 17 Sept (11-5). Adm £4, chd free. Home-made teas.

Over 3 acres of Fenland garden and meadow plus 6½ acre wood developed over 20yrs. Garden planted for colour, scent and wildlife. Double mixed borders and less formal flower gardens all framed by hornbeam hedges. Unusual shrubs and trees, incl fine stand of Black Poplars, vegetable garden, woodland walks and orchard. Some gravel and a few steps but mostly flat grass.

28 NEW INNER LODGE

Somerby, Gainsborough, DN21 3HG. Paul & Karen Graves. *On A631 Gainsborough to Grimsby road. From Gainsborough, track on R at end of dual carriageway. Parking off long single track in small woodland glades.* Sat 3, Sun 4 June, Sat 15, Sun 16 July, Sat 19, Sun 20 Aug (11-5). Adm £3, chd free. Home-made teas and cold drinks.

Colourful cottage garden nestled in a woodland setting. We started our garden in 2013 and turned a muddy field into a lovely tranquil garden with herbaceous borders, small secret garden and vegetable garden. In 2016 we extended into the wasteland that in February is a carpet of snowdrops and was once part of the garden. Now an on going project. Approx 1 acre.

29 NEW LUDNEY HOUSE FARM

Ludney, Louth, LN11 7JU. Jayne Bullas, 07733 018710, jayne@theoldgatehouse.com. *Between Grainthorpe & Conisholme.* Visits by arrangement Apr to Sept for groups of 10 (smaller groups considered). Adm £6, chd free. Home-made teas and cakes..

A beautiful landscaped garden of several defined spaces containing formal and informal areas. There is an excellent mix of trees, shrubs, perennials and roses, also a long wild grass area which is home to the bee hives. In spring there is a nice selection of bulbs and spring flowers. There are plenty of seats positioned around to sit and enjoy a cuppa and piece of cake! Wheelchair access to most parts.

30 MANOR FARM

Horkstow Road, South Ferriby, Barton-upon-Humber, DN18 6HS. Geoff & Angela Wells. *3m from Barton-upon-Humber on A1077, turn L onto B1204, opp Village Hall.* Mon 29 May (11-5.30). Adm £4, chd free. Home-made teas.

A garden which is much praised by visitors. Set within approx 1 acre with mature shrubberies, herbaceous borders, gravel garden and pergola walk. There is also a rosebed, white garden and fernery. Many old trees with preservation orders. Wildlife pond set within a paddock. Featured in Lincolnshire Pride.

31 MANOR HOUSE

Manor Road, Hagworthingham, Spilsby, PE23 4LN. Gill Maxim & David O'Connor, 01507 588530, vcagillmaxim@aol.com. *5m E of Horncastle. S of A158 in Hagworthingham, turn into Bond Hayes Lane downhill, becomes Manor Rd. Please follow signs down gravel track to parking area.* Sun 28 May, Sun 27 Aug (2-5). Adm £3.50, chd free. Home-made teas. Visits also by arrangement May to Aug.

2 acre garden on S-facing slope, partly terraced and well protected by established trees and shrubs. Redeveloped over 15yrs with natural and formal ponds. Shrub roses, laburnum walk, hosta border, gravel bed and other areas mainly planted with hardy perennials, trees and shrubs.

32 NEW THE MANOR HOUSE

Manor House Street, Horncastle, LN9 5HF. Mr Michael & Dr Marilyn Hieatt. *Manor House Street runs off Market Square in middle of Horncastle, beside St Mary's Church. The Manor House is approx 100 metres from Market Square (on R).* Sat 25 Mar (12-4). Adm £3, chd free.

An informal spring garden and orchard bordered by the R Bain, hidden in the middle of Horncastle. The garden incl a short section of the 3rd or 4th Century wall that formed part of a Roman fort (Scheduled Ancient Monument) with the remnants of an adjacent medieval well.

33 MARIGOLD COTTAGE

Hotchin Road, Sutton-on-Sea, LN12 2NP. Stephanie Lee & John Raby, 01507 442151, marigoldlee@btinternet.com, www.marigoldcottage.webs.com. *16m N of Skegness on A52. 7m E of Alford on A1111. 3m S of Mablethorpe on A52. Turn off A52 on High St at Cornerhouse Cafe. Follow rd past playing field on R. Rd turns away from the dunes. House 2nd on L.* Sats & Suns 29, 30 Apr, 27, 28 May, 24, 25 June, 22, 23 July, 26, 27 Aug (2-5). Adm £3, chd free. Home-made teas. Visits also by arrangement Apr to Sept for groups 10+.

Slide open the Japanese gate to find secret paths, lanterns, a circular window in a curved wall, water lilies in pots and a gravel garden, vegetable garden and propagation area. Take the long drive to see the sea. Back in the garden, find a seat, enjoy the birds and bees. We face the challenges of heavy clay and salt ladened winds but look for unusual plants not the humdrum for these conditions. Most of garden accessible to wheelchairs along flat, paved paths.

34 NEW MERE HOUSE

Stow Road, Sturton by Stow, Lincoln, LN1 2BZ. Nigel & Alice Gray. *10m NW of Lincoln between Sturton & Stow. 1m from centre of Sturton village heading to Stow, house on L. NB: Postcode will not bring you far enough out of Sturton village.* **Sat 16 Sept (11-4). Adm £4, chd free. Tea.**

Approx 1½ acres of established garden planted for the first time in 1975, redesigned in 1996. Renovated over the last 3yrs to incl new beds with drift planting but still incl the formal parterre. There is also a new cutting garden, vegetable garden and orchard. Work in progress incl a new garden project, pleached hedge, and long herbaceous border.

🚗 ☕

35 2 MILL COTTAGE

Barkwith Road, South Willingham, Market Rasen, LN8 6NN. Mrs Jo Rouston. *5m E of Wragby. On A157 turn R at PH in East Barkwith then immed L to South Willingham. Cottage 1m on L. Please email or phone for more directions.* **Sat 20 May (12-5). Adm £3, chd free. Home-made teas.**

A garden of several defined spaces, packed with interesting features, unusual plants and well placed seating areas, created by garden designer Jo Rouston. Original engine shed, a working well, raised beds using local rock with small pond. Clipped box, alpines, roses, summerhouses and water feature. Box and lavender hedge to greenhouse and herb garden. Late season bed. Woven metal and turf tree seat. Partial wheelchair access. Gravel at far end of garden. Steps down to main greenhouse.

♿ ❄ ☕

36 MILL FARM

Caistor Road, Grasby, Caistor, DN38 6AQ. Mike & Helen Boothman, 01652 628424, boothmanhelen@gmail.com, www.millfarmgarden.co.uk. *3m NW of Caistor on A1084. Between Brigg & Caistor. From Cross Keys PH towards Caistor for approx 200yds.* **Sun 21 May (11-4). Adm £4, chd free. Home-made teas. Visits also by arrangement May to Aug, groups 10+.**

A chance to see the garden at a different time of the year. Over 3 acres of garden with many diverse areas. Formal frontage with shrubs and trees. The rear is a plantsman haven with a peony and rose garden, specimen trees, vegetable area, old windmill adapted into a fernery, alpine house and shade house with a variety of shade loving plants. Herbaceous beds with different grasses and hardy perennials. Small nursery on site with home grown plants available. Featured in Lincolnshire Pride. Mainly grass, but with some gravelled areas.

♿ 🐎 ❄ 🚗 ☕

37 THE MOAT

Newton, NG34 0ED. Mr & Mrs Mike Barnes, 01529 497462, lynnebarnes14@googlemail.com. *Off A52 10m E of Grantham. In Newton village, opp church. Please park sensibly in village.* **Sun 25 June (11-5). Adm £4, chd free. Tea. For evening visits wine and canapés. Visits also by arrangement May to Sept for groups 15+, evening visits welcome.**

Delightful 3 acre garden designed to blend into its country location. Beautiful herbaceous island beds planted with imagination to give yr-round colour. Small vegetable garden, orchard, pretty courtyard garden and formal box parterre, also a lovely natural pond which is a magnet for wildlife. This garden contains many unusual plants and trees. Garden featured in Lincolnshire Life. Garden on slope but accessible to wheelchair users.

♿ 🚗 ☕

38 NOVA LODGE

150 Horncastle Road, Roughton Moor, Woodhall Spa, LN10 6UX. Leo Boshier, 01526 354940, moxons555@btinternet.com. *On B1191. Approx 2m E of centre of Woodhall Spa on Horncastle Rd. Roadside parking.* **Visits by arrangement June & July for groups 10+. Adm £3, chd free. Home-made teas.**

⅔ acre traditional garden set within mature trees started 2009. Herbaceous borders and beds, rare and unusual perennials. Shrub beds with grasses and ferns, large collection of hostas and heucheras, area for vegetables, fruit and herbs. Summerhouse, greenhouses, lawns and ponds. Central arbour with climbing roses and clematis. Lightweight wheelchairs only; not suitable for motorised chairs.

♿ ❄ ☕

39 NUT TREE FARM

Peppin Lane, Fotherby, Louth, LN11 0UP. Tim & Judith Hunter. *2m N of Louth. Farm is at the end of Peppin Lane. The last ½m is along a farm track. Transport available for less mobile from Woodlands. Blue Badge holders can drive up by prior arrangement.* **Sun 7 May (11-5). Adm £4, chd free. Home-made teas at Woodlands. Combined adm with Woodlands Opening with Fotherby Gardens on Sun 3 Sept.**

A garden of over an acre established in 2007 with stunning views of the Lincolnshire Wolds. There is a sweeping herbaceous border framing the lawn. A double wall, planted with seasonal annuals, surrounds the house. A rill runs from the raised terrace to the large pond. There is also an attractive raised brick edged vegetable garden. Pedigree flock of prize winning Hampshire Down sheep in fields surrounding part of garden. Local Honey for sale. Some gravel paths.

♿ 🐎 ☕

40 NEW OASIS GARDEN - YOUR PLACE

Wellington Street, Grimsby, DN32 7JP. Grimsby Neighbourhood Church, www.yourplacegrimsby.com. *Enter Grimsby (M180) over flyover, along Cleethorpe Rd. Turn R into Victor Street, Turn L into Wellington Street. Your Place is on the R on junction of Wellington Street & Weelsby Street.* **Sat 27, Sun 28 May (10-3). Adm £3, chd free. Light refreshments.**

The multi award winning Oasis

Garden, Your Place, recently described by the RHS as the 'Most inspirational garden in the six counties of the East Midlands', is approximately 1½ acres and nestles in the heart of Great Grimsby's East Marsh Community. A working garden producing 15k plants per year, grown by local volunteers of all ages and abilities. Lawns, fruit, vegetable, perennial and annual beds.

&. ✿ ☕

41 THE OLD HOUSE

1 The Green, Welbourn, Lincoln, LN5 0NJ. Mr & Mrs David Close. *Turn off A607 into S end of village, on village green opp red phone box.* Sun 16 July (2-6). Combined adm with Walnut Tree Cottage £4, chd free. Home-made teas at Welbourn Village Hall, ice creams at The Old House.
The formal front garden of this listed Georgian house was redesigned by Guy Petheram. Gravel, paving and pebble mosaics provide hard landscaping around beds with box hedging, clipped Portuguese laurel, lavender and roses. Herbaceous border, white hydrangea bed, and small enclosed paved garden. Welbourn Blacksmiths shop and forge dating from 1864 and still in full working order open with Friends of Forge on hand to answer questions. Plant stall, artisan honey and products, metal sculpture, will have stands within the gardens. Some gravel.

&. 🐎 ✿ Ⓓ ☕

42 THE OLD RECTORY

Church Lane, East Keal, Spilsby, PE23 4AT. Mrs Ruth Ward, 01790 752477, rfjward@btinternet.com. *2m SW of Spilsby. Off A16. Turn into Church Lane by PO.* Sun 23 Apr, Sun 21 May (2-5). Adm £3.50, chd free. Home-made teas. Visits also by arrangement Feb to Oct refreshments on request.
Beautifully situated, with fine views, rambling cottage garden on different levels falling naturally into separate areas, with changing effects and atmosphere. Steps, paths and vistas to lead you on, seats well placed for appreciating special views or relaxing

and enjoying the peace. Dry border, vegetable garden, orchard, woodland walk, wildflower meadow. Yr-round interest. Welcoming to wildlife.

🚗 ☕

43 THE OLD VICARAGE

Low Road, Holbeach Hurn, PE12 8JN. Mrs Liz Dixon-Spain, 01406 424148, lizdixonspain@gmail.com. *2m NE of Holbeach. Turn off A17 N to Holbeach Hurn, past post box in middle of village, 1st R into Low Rd. Old Vicarage on R approx 400yds.* Sun 21 May (1-5). Combined adm with Old White House £5, chd free. Home-made teas at Old White House. Visits also by arrangement Mar to Oct.
2 acres of garden with 150yr old tulip, plane and beech trees: borders of shrubs, roses, herbaceous plants. Shrub roses and herb garden in old paddock area, surrounded by informal areas with pond and bog garden, wild flowers, grasses and bulbs. Small fruit and vegetable gardens. Kids love exploring winding paths through the wilder areas. Garden is managed environmentally. Gravel drive, some paths, mostly grass access.

🐎 ✿ 🚗 ☕

44 OLD WHITE HOUSE

Holbeach Hurn, PE12 8JP. Mr & Mrs A Worth. *2m N of Holbeach. Turn off A17 N to Holbeach Hurn, follow signs to village, cont through, turn R after Rose & Crown PH at Baileys Lane.* Sun 21 May (1-5). Combined adm with The Old Vicarage £5, chd free. Home-made teas.
1½ acres of mature garden, featuring herbaceous borders, roses, patterned garden, herb garden and walled kitchen garden. Large catalpa, tulip tree that flowers, ginko and other specimen trees. Flat surfaces, some steps, wheelchair access to all areas without using steps.

&. 🐎 ☕

45 OVERBECK

46 Main Street, Scothern, LN2 2UW. John & Joyce Good, 01673 862200, jandjgood@btinternet.com. *4m E*

of Lincoln. Scothern signed from A46 at Dunholme & A158 at Sudbrooke. Overbeck is at E end of Main St. Sat 24 June (11-5). Combined adm with Thornham £4, chd free. Light refreshments in Village Hall. Visits also by arrangement June & July, daytime and evenings.
Situated in an attractive village this approx ⅔ acre garden is a haven for wildlife. Long herbaceous borders and colour themed island beds with some unusual perennials. Hosta border, gravel bed with grasses, fernery, trees, numerous shrubs, small stumpery, climbers, a developing parterre and large prolific vegetable and fruit area.

&. ✿ 🚗 ☕

46 PEAR TREE COTTAGE

Butt Lane, Goulceby, Louth, LN11 9UP. Jill Mowbray & Miranda Manning Press, 01507 343201, chirpy@theraggedrobin.co.uk, www.theraggedrobin.co.uk. *6m N of Horncastle & 8m SW of Louth. 2m off A153 between Louth & Horncastle. 2m off Caistor High St (B1225). NB: This is a small rural village, please park considerately.* Sun 4 June (11-4). Adm £3, chd free. Home-made teas. Visits also by arrangement May to Aug for groups 15+.
Situated in the heart of the Wolds, the garden which surrounds the house on three sides, is an oasis of bright colour within the delightful village of Goulceby. The balance of perennials and annuals ensure a vibrant display throughout the seasons. Productive fruit and vegetable plots and greenhouses lie alongside the borders which only serves to add to the verdant atmosphere within the garden. Visit Workshop in the Wolds (www.workshopinthewolds.co.uk) at the bottom of Red Hill, between Goulceby and Donington-on-Bain. Joe has a wide range of indoor and outdoor furniture and gifts. Wheelchair access via front gate with access on grass paths only.

&. ✿ ☕

47 NEW PINE FIELDS

Wells Road, Healing, Grimsby, DN41 7QQ. Rita & Geoff Morgan. *3m W of Grimsby. From B1210 Stallingborough Rd turn into Wells Rd, Lane entrance ½m on L. From A18 take A1173, turn R into Wells Rd Lane entrance on R immed after white Healing sign.* **Sun 18 June (11-5). Adm £3.50, chd free. Tea.**

Large garden with herbaceous borders and beds interspersed with a mixture of trees and shrubs. Wildlife pond with water lilies and aquatic plants. Two pergolas in formal beds with box and yew hedging lead onto a winter garden and fruit orchard. A new formal parterre garden established 2016 is an ongoing project, the whole backed by a small woodland area.

🚲 🐕 ☕

48 POTTERTONS NURSERY

Moortown Road, Nettleton, Caistor, LN7 6HX. Rob & Jackie Potterton, www.pottertons.co.uk. *1m W of Nettleton. From A46 at Nettleton turn onto B1205 (Moortown). Nursery 1¼m, turn by edge of wood.* **Sun 28 May (10-4). Adm £3, chd free. Home-made teas.**

5 acre garden of alpine rockeries, stream and waterfall, raised beds, troughs, tufa bed, crevice garden, woodland beds, extensively planted with alpines, bulbs and woodland plants, which will be at their flowering peak. On the day we have invited Plant Hunters Fairs to the garden, with 8 specialist nurseries offering a range incl acers, shrubs, rare perennials, cottage garden plants and stoneware. There will be cream teas and light refreshments served in the garden with both covered and open air seating available. Access mostly on mixed grass surfaces.

🚲 🐕 ❀ ☕ ☕

49 NEW SCHOOL HOUSE

Market Rasen Road, Holton-le-Moor, Market Rasen, LN7 6AE. Chris & Rosemary Brown. *15m N of Lincoln. A46 towards Caistor,* take B1434 to Holton le Moor. School House on R next to village (Moot) hall. **Sat 15 July (12.30-5). Adm £5, chd free. Light refreshments. Adm incl tea/coffee and biscuits.**

An all around the house garden, ranging from shaded early area to summer and autumn flowering areas. Central gravel garden with alliums followed by agapanthus and supplemented with grasses. Designed and built by Chris Brown a now retired garden designer.

🐕 ❀ ☕

50 SEDGEBROOK MANOR

Church Lane, Sedgebrook, Grantham, NG32 2EU. Hon James & Lady Caroline Ogilvy. *2m W of Grantham on A52. In Sedgebrook village by church.* **Sun 6 Aug (1-5). Adm £4, chd free. Home-made teas.**

Yew and box topiary surround this charming Manor House (not open). Massed spring bulbs. Croquet lawn, herbaceous border and summer house. Bridge over small pond and two larger ponds. Ancient mulberry tree. Tennis court, vegetable patch, woodland area with chickens. Swimming pool in enclosed garden. Wheelchair access to most areas.

🚲 🐕 ❀ ☕

51 SHANGRILA

Little Hale Road, Great Hale, Sleaford, NG34 9LH. Marilyn Cooke & John Knight. *On B1394 between Heckington & Helpringham.* **Sun 18 June (11-5). Adm £4.50, chd free. Home-made teas.**

Approx 3 acre garden with sweeping lawns long herbaceous borders, colour themed island beds, hosta collection, lavender bed with seating area, topiary, acers, small raised vegetable area, 3 ponds and new exotic borders. Wheelchair access to all areas.

🚲 ❀ ☕

52 SHEPHERDS HEY

Peppin Lane, Fotherby, Louth, LN11 0UW. Barbara Chester. *2m N of Louth. Leave A16 to Fotherby. Peppin Lane is no-through rd running E from village centre. Please park on R verge opp allotments.* **Sun 2 July (11-5). Adm £4, chd free. Home-made teas at Woodlands. Combined adm with Woodlands. Opening with Fotherby Gardens on Sun 3 Sept.**

Small garden which has evolved since 2008. The front garden features a small wildlife pond, terraced borders, rose garden and cultivated steep banks to a stream. Visitors will walk over a newly constructed wooden walkway with trellis, over which trailing and climbing plants grow, to access the rear garden, which takes advantage of views over open countryside and has colour themed borders. Has featured in Lincolnshire Life. Wheelchair access to rear garden possible with care. Front garden can be viewed from road.

🚲 🐕 ☕

53 66 SPILSBY ROAD

Boston, PE21 9NS. Rosemary & Adrian Isaac. *From Boston town take A16 towards Spilsby. On L after Trinity Church. Parking on Spilsby Rd.* **Sun 14 May (11-4). Adm £3, chd free. Cream teas.**

1⅓ acre garden with mature trees, moat, tudor garden house, summer house and orangery, lawns and herbaceous borders. Children's Tudor garden house, gatehouse and courtyard. Wide paths.

🚲 🐕 ❀ ☕

54 THE STABLES

Ranby, Market Rasen, LN8 5LN. Russ & Chris Hibbins, 01507 343581, russhibbins@btinternet.com. *SW corner of Lincolnshire Wolds - between Horncastle & Market Rasen. On A158, halfway between Wragby & Horncastle, is Baumber. Here, turn N on B1225 (direction Caistor & Belmont tv mast) for 3m. Garden well signed. From N follow B1225 - Ranby is 3m N of Baumber.* **Sun 23 July (12.30-4.30). Adm £3.50, chd free. Home-made teas. Visits also by arrangement May to Sept, groups 10+ welcome.**

The garden approaches ½ acre and has been developed over last 15yrs as a place to sit, relax and look at a variety of trees, shrubs and plants

(some not so common), together
with statuary and sculptures. S-facing
and extremely fertile, well drained
soil helps most plants to quickly
become established. The many seats
around the garden are intended
for use! Some covered seating and
tables if needed. Wonderfully rural
setting, in a quiet hamlet, the garden
is not really visible from the road
and often surprises people who see
it for the first time. Features a much
admired foxglove gate. Featured in
local press. For wheelchair users
there is a slightly different entry to
the garden, along a flat gravel drive,
with no steps.

55 THORNHAM
Northing Lane, Scothern, Lincoln,
LN2 2WL. Janis Mason. *4m E of
Lincoln. Scothern is signed from A46
at Dunholme & A158 at Sudbrooke.
Thornham is a 150 metre walk
up Northing Lane, which is opp
Overbeck at E end of Main St.* **Sat
24 June (11-4). Combined adm
with Overbeck £4, chd free.
Light refreshments at Scothern
Village hall.**
Medium sized, densely planted,
naturalistic, perennial garden.
Many hardy plants, some unusual.
Plantaholic gardener aims to have
something in flower yr-round. Gravel
pathways lead through the flower
beds as there is no lawn.

The National
Garden Scheme
is the largest
single funder
of Macmillan

Firsby Manor

Woodlands

56 WALNUT TREE COTTAGE

6 Hall Lane, Welbourn, Lincoln, LN5 0NN. Malcolm & Nina McBeath. *Approx 11m S of Lincoln, 12m N of Grantham on A607. From Newark A17 then A607. On A607 from Lincoln turn R into Hall Lane by Welbourn Hall Nursing Home. From Leadenham take L turn after W Hall Nursing Home. Garden is 3rd gate on L. Parking at Village Hall (Beck Street).* **Sun 16 July (2-6). Combined adm with The Old House £4, chd free. Home-made teas at Welbourn Village Hall.**

A peaceful ½ acre garden full of interesting perennials planted in long, curved and colour themed borders. Winding paths surrounded by shrubs and climbing roses provide varied vistas and secluded seating areas. Many old varieties of roses feature throughout, with spectacular displays in June of Paul's Himalayan Musk and Climbing Cecil Brunner dominating two trees. Plants stall and Artisan honey and bee products for sale in this garden. Nearby, Welbourn Blacksmith's shop and forge, dating from 1864 and still in full working order (open 2pm until 4.30pm), with the fire lit and Friends of the Forge on hand to answer questions. Accessible gravel drive to front of house, with some steps and some narrow paths at the rear.

  ♿ 🐐 ✿ ☕ 🍴

57 68 WATTS LANE

Louth, LN11 9DG. Jenny & Rodger Grasham, 07977 318145, sallysing@hotmail.co.uk, www.facebook.com/thesecretgardenoflouth. *½m S of Louth town centre. Watts Lane off Newmarket (on B1200). Turn by pedestrian lights & Co-op. Some SatNavs unreliable. Try LN11 9DJ for Mount Pleasant Av, this leads on to Watts Lane.* **Wed 12, Sun 30 July, Sun 6, Sun 13, Sun 20, Sun 27 Aug (11-4). Adm £2.50, chd free. Home-made teas. Visits also by arrangement Aug & Sept, refreshments on request when booking.**

Blank canvas of ⅕ acre in early

90s. Developed into lush, colourful, exotic plant packed haven. A whole new world on entering from street. Exotic borders, raised island, long hot border, ponds, stumpery, developing prairie style border. Conservatory, grapevine. Intimate seating areas along garden's journey. Facebook page - The Secret Garden of Louth. Children, find where the frogs are hiding! Many butterflies and bees but how many different types? Feed the fish. Grass pathways, main garden area accessible. Wheelchairs not permitted on bridge over pond, both sides can be reached via pathways.

&. ✿ 🍵

58 WEST SYKE

38 Electric Station Road, Sleaford, NG34 7QJ. Ada Trethewey. *From A17, A15 & A153 take bypass exit at r'about to Sleaford Town centre. At HSBC & Lloyds Bank turn R into Westgate. Turn R, 38 at end of rd. Ample parking.* **Sun 18 June (12-5). Adm £3, chd free. Home-made teas.**
Over 1 acre, comprising bog gardens, rockeries, 3 large ponds, wildflower meadow, lawns and cottage garden planting. Rambling roses a feature. Designed for wildlife habitats; sustainable principles and a wealth of native species. Garden evolved over 30yrs. Lawned paths. WC wheelchair accessible.

&. ✿ 🍵

59 48 WESTGATE

Louth, LN11 9YD. Kenneth Harvey. *Approx 100 yrds before The Wheatsheaf PH, nr to Church.* **Sun 10 Sept (11-4). Adm £3.50, chd free. Home-made teas.**
Large town garden of about 1½ acres that crosses the R Ludd. Hidden away behind the high Georgian facades of Louth is a good example of a town garden of trees, herbaceous borders, two small ponds, a fern and white garden and formal vegetable parterre. Wonderful views of Louth church spire. The garden was originally planted in the late 1950s, but has been remodelled over the last 5yrs.

✿ 🍵

60 WILLOUGHBY ROAD ALLOTMENTS

Willoughby Road, Boston, PE21 9HN. Willoughby Road Allotments Association. *Entrance from Rowan Way.* **Sun 13 Aug (10-4). Combined adm with Butterfly Hospice £4, chd free. Light refreshments.**
Set in 5 acres the allotments comprise 60 plots growing fine vegetables, fruit, flowers and herbs. There is a small orchard and wildflower area and a community space adjacent. Grass paths run along the site. Several plots will be open to walk round. There will be a seed and plant stall.

✿ 🍵

61 WINDRUSH

Main Road, East Keal, Spilsby, PE23 4BB. Ian & Suzie MacDonald. *On A16, 4m S of Spilsby, opp A155 turning signed West Keal.* **Sun 18 June (11-4). Adm £4, chd free. Home-made teas.**
Country garden of approx 4 acres with herbaceous borders, shrub and climbing roses, clematis and grasses. Woodland walk and ponds, and vegetable garden. Meadow planted in 2013 with orchard of Lincolnshire apples. Newly planted gravel garden. Shallow steps and some uneven paths.

&. ✿ 🍵

62 WOODLANDS

Peppin Lane, Fotherby, Louth, LN11 0UW. Ann & Bob Armstrong, 01507 603586, annbobarmstrong@btinternet.com, www.woodlandsplants.co.uk. *2m N of Louth off A16 signed Fotherby. Please park on R verge opp allotments & walk approx 350 yds to garden. No parking at garden. Please do not drive beyond designated area.* **Sun 2 Apr (11-5). Adm £3, chd free. Sun 7 May (11-5). Adm £4, chd free. Combined adm with Nut Tree Farm. Sun 4 June (11-5). Adm £3, chd free. Sun 2 July (11-5). Adm £4, chd free. Combined adm with Shepherds Hey. Sun 6 Aug (11-5). Adm £3, chd free. Home-made teas. Opening with Fotherby Gardens on Sun 3 Sept. Visits also by**

arrangement Mar to Oct.
A lovely mature woodland garden where a multitude of unusual plants are the stars, many of which are available from the well stocked RHS listed nursery. This year the garden will feature a new Asiatic bed which is still being developed. Award winning professional artist's studio/gallery open to visitors. Specialist collection of Codonopsis for which Plant Heritage status has been granted. Garden News

🐄 ✿ NPC 🍵

63 YEW TREE FARM

Westhorpe Road, Gosberton, Spalding, PE11 4EP. Robert & Claire Bailey-Scott. *Nr Spalding. Enter the village of Gosberton. Turn into Westhorpe Rd, opp The Bell Inn, cont for approx 1½m. Property is 3rd on R after bridge.* **Sun 23 July (11-5). Adm £4, chd free. Home-made teas.**
A lovely country garden, 1½ acres. Large herbaceous and mixed borders surround the well kept lawns. Large wildlife pond with two bog gardens, woodland garden and shaded borders containing many unusual plants. A mulberry tree forms the centre piece of one lawn. Stunning annual flower meadow. Two magnificent yew trees, organic vegetable plot and orchard, under planted with a wildflower meadow. Gravel driveway, some gravel paths.

&. ✿ 🚗 🍵

The National Garden Scheme is Marie Curie's largest single funder

LONDON

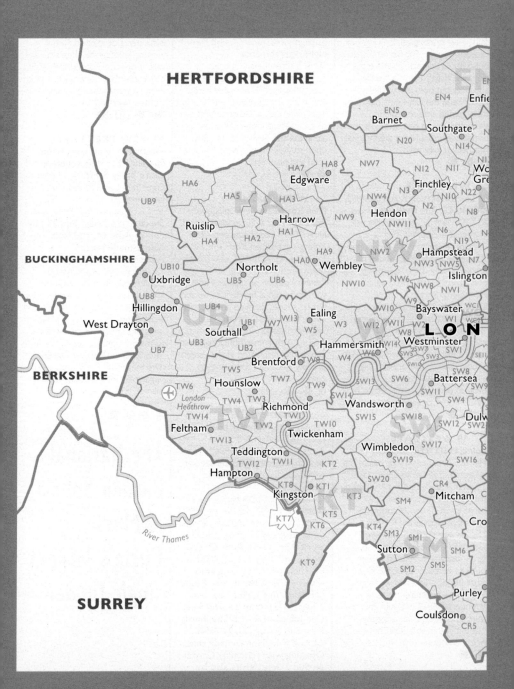

ESSEX

KENT

ENI EN3

ld

21

N9

Edmonton

Chingford

E4

NI8

Woodford
Green

IG8

od

en

Tottenham

N17

EI7

EI8

IG5

Walthamstow

N15

IG4

EII

E10

IG2

N16

E5

Ilford

IG3

EI2

IGI

E7

RM8

NI

EC1

E8

E9

EI5

Stratford

E2

E3

EI3

Barking

E6

IGII

RM9

Rainham

RM13

DON

EC2

EI

EI4

EI6

London
City

SE28

Thamesmead

SE1

DAI8

SE16

SE8

SEI0

SE7

SE2

DAI7

SEI7

SE18

DA8

SE15

SEI4

Greenwich

SE3

DA7

Bexleyheath

DAI

SE5

Peckham

SE4

SEI3

Lewisham

Eltham

DAI6

DA6

SE24

SE22

SE9

DA5

Bexley

ich

SE21

SE23

SEI2

SE6

DAI5

Sidcup

SE27

SE26

Chislehurst

DAI4

SE19

BRI

BR7

SE20

BR3

Bromley

BR5

R7

SE25

BR2

ydon

CR0

BR4

Orpington

Addington

BR6

CR2

BR2

R8

TNI4

Biggin Hill

TNI6

IG7

RM4

RM5

RMI

RM3

IG6

RM6

Romford

RM2

RM7

RMII

RMI2

Upminster

RMI4

RMI0

River Thames

0   5   10 kilometres
0   5 miles
© Global Mapping / XYZ Maps

Volunteers

County Organiser
Penny Snell
01932 864532
pennysnellflowers@btinternet.com

County Treasurer
Richard Raworth
07831 476088
raworthrichard@gmail.com

Publicity
Penny Snell (as above)

Booklet Co-ordinator
Sue Phipps
07771 767196
sue@suephipps.com

Booklet Distributor
Joey Clover
020 8870 8740
joeyclover@hotmail.com

Assistant County Organisers

Central London
Eveline Carn
07831 136069
evelinecbcarn@icloud.com

Clapham & surrounding area
Sue Phipps
(as above)

Croydon & outer South London
Ben & Peckham Carroll
0208 777 9012
b.j.carroll@btinternet.com

Dulwich & surrounding area
Clive Pankhurst
07941 536934
alternative.ramblings@gmail.com

E London
Teresa Farnham
07761 476651
farnhamz@yahoo.co.uk

Hackney
Philip Lightowlers
020 8533 0052
plighto@gmail.com

Hampstead
Joan Arnold
020 8444 8752
joan.arnold40@gmail.com

Hampstead Garden Suburb, Finchley & Barnet
Caroline Broome
020 8444 2329
carosgarden@virginmedia.com

Islington
Penelope Darby Brown
020 7226 6880
pendarbybrown@blueyonder.co.uk

Gill Evansky
020 7359 2484
gevansky@gmail.com

NW London
Susan Bennett & Earl Hyde
020 8883 8540
suebearlh@yahoo.co.uk

Outer NW London
James Duncan Mattoon
020 8830 7410
jamesmattoon@msn.com

SE London
Janine Wookey
07711 279636
j.wookey@btinternet.com

SW London
Joey Clover
(as above)

W London, Barnes & Chiswick
Jenny Raworth
020 8892 3713
jraworth@gmail.com

From the tiniest to the largest, London gardens offer exceptional diversity. Hidden behind historic houses in Spitalfields are exquisite tiny gardens, while on Kingston Hill there are 9 acres of landscaped Japanese gardens.

The oldest private garden in London boasts 5 acres, while the many other historic gardens within these pages are smaller – some so tiny there is only room for a few visitors at a time – but nonetheless full of innovation, colour and horticultural excellence.

London allotments have attracted television cameras to film their productive acres, where exotic Cape gooseberries, figs, prizewinning roses and even bees all thrive thanks to the skill and enthusiasm of city gardeners.

The traditional sit comfortably with the contemporary in London – offering a feast of elegant borders, pleached hedges, topiary, gravel gardens and the cooling sound of water – while to excite the adventurous there are gardens on barges and green roofs to explore.

The season stretches from April to October, so there is nearly always a garden to visit somewhere in London. Our gardens opening this year are the beating heart of the capital just waiting to be visited and enjoyed.

LONDON GARDENS LISTED BY POSTCODE

Inner London postcodes

E and EC London

Spitalfields Gardens E1
17 Greenstone Mews E11
37 Harold Road E11
Richard House Children's Hospice E16
87 St Johns Road E17
46 Cheyne Avenue E18
5 Brodie Road E4
16 Maida Way E4
Lower Clapton Gardens E5
42 Latimer Road E7
London Fields Gardens E8
Mapledene Gardens E8
17a Navarino Road E8
12 Bushberry Road E9
The Charterhouse EC1
The Inner and Middle Temple Gardens EC4

N & NW London

37 Alwyne Road N1
Angel Gardens N1
Arlington Square Gardens N1
Barnsbury Group N1
Canonbury House N1
4 Canonbury Place N1
De Beauvoir Gardens N1
Diespeker Wharf N1
41 Ecclesbourne Road N1
King Henry's Walk Garden N1
5 Northampton Park N1
20 St Mary's Grove N1
55 Dukes Avenue N10
48 Dukes Avenue N10
66 Muswell Avenue N10
Princes Avenue Gardens N10
5 St Regis Close N10
25 Springfield Avenue N10
33 Wood Vale N10
94 Brownlow Road N11
Golf Course Allotments N11
36 Avondale Avenue N12
5 Russell Road N13
2 Conway Road N14
53 Manor Road N16
15 Norcott Road N16
21 Gospatrick Road N17
77 Handsworth Road N17
159 Higham Road N17

94 Marsh Lane Allotments N17
36 Ashley Road N19
30 Mercers Road N19
66 Abbots Gardens N2
79 Church Lane N2
95 The Chine N21
91 Vicar's Moor Lane N21
1 Wades Grove N21
23 Imperial Road N22
Railway Cottages N22
31 Church Crescent N3
Gordon Road Allotments N3
31 Hendon Avenue N3
18 Park Crescent N3
32 Highbury Place N5
7 The Grove N6
North London Bowling Club, Fitzroy Park N6
3 The Park N6
Southwood Lodge N6
10 Woodside Avenue N6
9 Furlong Road N7
33 Huddleston Road N7
60 & 62 Hungerford Road N7
1a Hungerford Road N7
23 Penn Road N7
24b Penn Road N7
11 Park Avenue North N8
93a Priory Road N8
12 Warner Road N8
69 Gloucester Crescent NW1
70 Gloucester Crescent NW1
The Holme NW1
4 Park Village East (Tower Lodge Gardens) NW1
Royal College of Physicians' Medicinal Garden NW1
Hampstead Garden Suburb Gardens NW11
20 Exeter Road NW2
27 Menelik Road NW2
93 Tanfield Avenue NW2
58A Teignmouth Road NW2
208 Walm Lane, The Garden Flat NW2
Fenton House NW3
88 Frognal NW3
Marie Curie Hospice, Hampstead NW3
27 Nassington Road NW3
21 Thurlow Road NW3
Copthall Group NW7
Highwood Ash NW7
116 Hamilton Terrace NW8

S, SE and SW London

Garden Barge Square at Downings Roads Moorings SE1
The Garden Museum SE1
Lambeth Palace SE1
41 Southbrook Road SE12
Blackheath Gardens SE13

Choumert Square SE15
Lyndhurst Square Group SE15
85 Calton Avenue SE21
122 Court Lane SE21
22 Court Lane Gardens SE21
Dulwich Village Two Gardens SE21
1 Pond Cottages SE21
3 Pond Cottages SE21
9 The Gardens SE22
55 Jennings Road SE22
174 Peckham Rye SE22
4 Piermont Green SE22
45 Underhill Road SE22
86 Underhill Road SE22
Forest Hill Gardens Group SE23
5 Burbage Road SE24
2 Shardcroft Avenue SE24
South London Botanical Institute SE24
Stoney Hill House SE26
15a Sydenham Hill SE26
27 Thorpewood Avenue SE26
35 Camberwell Grove SE5
Camberwell Grove Gardens SE5
24 Grove Park SE5
74 Harfield Gardens SE5
Cadogan Place South Garden SW1
Eccleston Square SW1
4 Franconia Road SW14
97 Arthur Road SW19
123 South Park Road SW19
Eaton Square Garden SW1W
93 Palace Road SW2
Paddock Allotments & Leisure Gardens SW20
Chelsea Physic Garden SW3
51 The Chase SW4
2 Littlebury Road SW4
Royal Trinity Hospice SW4
35 Turret Grove SW4
The Hurlingham Club SW6

W London

57 St Quintin Avenue W10
Arundel & Ladbroke Gardens W11
12 Lansdowne Road W11
49 Loftus Road W12
Cleveland Square W2
Acacia House W3
Capel Manor College, Gunnersbury Park Campus W3
41 Mill Hill Road W3
65 Mill Hill Road W3
Zen Garden W3
Chiswick Mall Gardens W4
The Orchard W4
36 Park Road W4
56 Park Road W4
All Seasons W5

38 York Road W5
57 Prebend Gardens W6
27 St Peters Square W6
1 York Close W7
Edwardes Square W8
7 Upper Phillimore Gardens W8
57 Tonbridge House WC1H
40 Tonbridge House WC1H
14 Doughty Street WC1N
61 Doughty Street WC1N

Outer London postcodes

27 Elstree Hill BR1
153 Portland Road BR1
172 Ravensbourne Avenue BR2
174 Ravensbourne Avenue BR2
12 Overbrae BR3
209 Worsley Bridge Road BR3
109 Addington Road BR4
White Cottage BR5
2 Springhurst Close CR0
55 Warham Road CR2
Whitgift School CR2
Oak Farm EN2
West Lodge Park EN4
190 Barnet Road EN5
45 Great North Road EN5
26 Normandy Avenue EN5
31 Arlington Drive HA4
4 Manningtree Road HA4
12 Haywood Close HA5
470 Pinner Road HA5
25 Hallowell Road HA6
4 Ormonde Road HA6
Treetops HA6
254 Ashurst Drive IG6
20 Goldhaze Close IG8
Hurst House IG8
7 Woodbines Avenue KT1
9 Imber Park Road KT10
The Watergardens KT2
61 Wolsey Road KT8
18 Pettits Boulevard RM1
7 St George's Road TW1
Ormeley Lodge TW10
Petersham House TW10
Stokes House TW10
Hampton Hill Gardens TW12
Kew Green Gardens TW9
Marksbury Avenue Gardens TW9
Old Palace Lane Allotments TW9
Trumpeters House & Sarah's Garden TW9
L'escale WD6

OPENING DATES

All entries subject to change. For latest information check www.ngs.org.uk

February
Snowdrop Festival

Sunday 12th
7 The Grove, N6

Sunday 19th
7 The Grove, N6
33 Wood Vale, N10

April

Sunday 2nd
NEW 12 Overbrae, BR3
NEW 209 Worsley Bridge Road, BR3

Friday 7th
◆ Chelsea Physic Garden, SW3

Sunday 9th
Cadogan Place South Garden, SW1
7 The Grove, N6
Royal Trinity Hospice, SW4

Sunday 23rd
4 Canonbury Place, N1
51 The Chase, SW4
Edwardes Square, W8
17a Navarino Road, E8
20 St Mary's Grove, N1
South London Botanical Institute, SE24
7 Upper Phillimore Gardens, W8

Tuesday 25th
51 The Chase, SW4

Sunday 30th
Richard House Children's Hospice, E16
5 St Regis Close, N10

May

Monday 1st
NEW Hurst House, IG8
King Henry's Walk Garden, N1

Saturday 6th
The Hurlingham Club, SW6

Sunday 7th
The Orchard, W4
27 St Peters Square, W6

Sunday 14th
Arundel & Ladbroke Gardens, W11
Cleveland Square, W2
Eccleston Square, SW1
Highwood Ash, NW7
12 Lansdowne Road, W11
NEW Oak Farm, EN2
NEW 1 Pond Cottages, SE21
NEW 3 Pond Cottages, SE21
Princes Avenue Gardens, N10
Southwood Lodge, N6
45 Underhill Road, SE22
86 Underhill Road, SE22
The Watergardens, KT2
West Lodge Park, EN4

Sunday 21st
66 Abbots Gardens, N2
109 Addington Road, BR4
190 Barnet Road, EN5
Canonbury House, N1
Forest Hill Gardens Group, SE23
Garden Barge Square at Downings Roads Moorings, SE1
NEW 93a Priory Road, N8
Royal Trinity Hospice, SW4
Stoney Hill House, SE26
15a Sydenham Hill, SE26
Whitgift School, CR2
33 Wood Vale, N10

Wednesday 24th
Lambeth Palace, SE1

Friday 26th
Chiswick Mall Gardens, W4

90th Anniversary Weekend

Saturday 27th
NEW 27 Elstree Hill, BR1
Hampton Hill Gardens, TW12
4 Park Village East (Tower Lodge Gardens), NW1
1 York Close, W7

Sunday 28th
NEW Acacia House, W3
36 Ashley Road, N19
NEW 95 The Chine, N21
Chiswick Mall Gardens, W4
NEW 27 Elstree Hill, BR1
116 Hamilton Terrace, NW8
Hampton Hill Gardens, TW12
Kew Green Gardens, TW9
208 Walm Lane, The Garden Flat, NW2
1 York Close, W7

Monday 29th
36 Ashley Road, N19
17 Greenstone Mews, E11
123 South Park Road, SW19

June

Saturday 3rd
NEW Diespeker Wharf, N1
7 St George's Road, TW1
Zen Garden, W3

Sunday 4th
37 Alwyne Road, N1
31 Arlington Drive, HA4 7
Barnsbury Group, N1
NEW 85 Calton Avenue, SE21
35 Camberwell Grove, SE5
Choumert Square, SE15
48 Dukes Avenue, N10
NEW 55 Dukes Avenue, N10
41 Ecclesbourne Road, N1
NEW 4 Franconia Road, SW14
69 Gloucester Crescent, NW1
70 Gloucester Crescent, NW1
31 Hendon Avenue, N3

Kew Green Gardens, TW9
Lower Clapton Gardens, E5
27 Nassington Road, NW3
4 Ormonde Road, HA6
3 The Park, N6
11 Park Avenue North, N8
4 Park Village East (Tower Lodge Gardens), NW1
Royal College of Physicians' Medicinal Garden, NW1
Stokes House, TW10
91 Vicar's Moor Lane, N21
NEW 1 Wades Grove, N21
Zen Garden, W3

Tuesday 6th
The Charterhouse, EC1

Saturday 10th
Eaton Square Garden, SW1W
Spitalfields Gardens, E1

Sunday 11th
Arlington Square Gardens, N1
5 Brodie Road, E4
5 Burbage Road, SE24
Copthall Group, NW7
De Beauvoir Gardens, N1
NEW 21 Gospatrick Road, N17
7 The Grove, N6
NEW 25 Hallowell Road, HA6
77 Handsworth Road, N17
NEW 74 Harfield Gardens, SE5
NEW 12 Haywood Close, HA5
159 Higham Road, N17
Marksbury Avenue Gardens, TW9
174 Peckham Rye, SE22
Trumpeters House & Sarah's Garden, TW9
12 Warner Road, N8

Tuesday 13th
◆ Fenton House, NW3
The Inner and Middle Temple Gardens, EC4
49 Loftus Road, W12

Saturday 17th
41 Southbrook Road, SE12
Zen Garden, W3

Sunday 18th
NEW 36 Avondale Avenue, N12
97 Arthur Road, SW19
Dulwich Village Two Gardens, SE21
88 Frognal, NW3
9 Furlong Road, N7
32 Highbury Place, N5
60 & 62 Hungerford Road, N7
1a Hungerford Road, N7
L'escale, WD6
London Fields Gardens, E8
Lyndhurst Square Group, SE15
NEW North London Bowling Club, Fitzroy Park, N6
Ormeley Lodge, TW10
18 Park Crescent, N3
23 Penn Road, N7
24b Penn Road, N7
5 St Regis Close, N10
2 Shardcroft Avenue, SE24
41 Southbrook Road, SE12
58A Teignmouth Road, NW2
61 Wolsey Road, KT8
Zen Garden, W3

Saturday 24th
Capel Manor College, Gunnersbury Park Campus, W3
The Holme, NW1
5 Northampton Park, N1
Paddock Allotments & Leisure Gardens, SW20
18 Pettits Boulevard, RM1

Sunday 25th
109 Addington Road, BR4
NEW Blackheath Gardens, SE13
122 Court Lane, SE21
22 Court Lane Gardens, SE21

Hampstead Garden Suburb Gardens, NW11
The Holme, NW1
9 Imber Park Road, KT10
NEW Marie Curie Hospice, Hampstead, NW3
66 Muswell Avenue, N10
18 Pettits Boulevard, RM1
25 Springfield Avenue, N10
21 Thurlow Road, NW3
208 Walm Lane, The Garden Flat, NW2

July

Sunday 2nd
NEW Angel Gardens, N1
33 Huddleston Road, N7
NEW 16 Maida Way, E4
27 Menelik Road, NW2
30 Mercers Road, N19
93 Palace Road, SW2
36 Park Road, W4
Railway Cottages, N22
27 Thorpewood Avenue, SE26
57 Tonbridge House, WC1H
NEW 40 Tonbridge House, WC1H
White Cottage, BR5
7 Woodbines Avenue, KT1

Saturday 8th
18 Pettits Boulevard, RM1

Sunday 9th
20 Exeter Road, NW2
116 Hamilton Terrace, NW8
NEW Mapledene Gardens, E8
15 Norcott Road, N16
Old Palace Lane Allotments, TW9
2 Springhurst Close, CR0

Wednesday 12th
NEW 57 Prebend Gardens, W6

Friday 14th
41 Mill Hill Road, W3
65 Mill Hill Road, W3

Sunday 16th
12 Bushberry Road, E9

Camberwell Grove Gardens, SE5
61 Doughty Street, WC1N
14 Doughty Street, WC1N
17a Navarino Road, E8
18 Park Crescent, N3
NEW 57 Prebend Gardens, W6
172 Ravensbourne Avenue, BR2
174 Ravensbourne Avenue, BR2
57 St Quintin Avenue, W10

Wednesday 19th
9 The Gardens, SE22

Saturday 22nd
All Seasons, W5
42 Latimer Road, E7
38 York Road, W5

Sunday 23rd
All Seasons, W5
190 Barnet Road, EN5
31 Church Crescent, N3
55 Jennings Road, SE22
42 Latimer Road, E7
NEW 2 Littlebury Road, SW4
NEW 4 Manningtree Road, HA4
NEW 26 Normandy Avenue, EN5
Petersham House, TW10
5 St Regis Close, N10
Treetops, HA6
35 Turret Grove, SW4
55 Warham Road, CR2
38 York Road, W5

Sunday 30th
254 Ashurst Drive, IG6
79 Church Lane, N2
20 Goldhaze Close, IG8
37 Harold Road, E11
NEW 53 Manor Road, N16
56 Park Road, W4
4 Piermont Green, SE22
57 St Quintin Avenue, W10
93 Tanfield Avenue, NW2

August

Saturday 5th
The Holme, NW1

Sunday 6th
46 Cheyne Avenue, E18
69 Gloucester Crescent, NW1
70 Gloucester Crescent, NW1
45 Great North Road, EN5
The Holme, NW1
87 St Johns Road, E17
NEW 10 Woodside Avenue, N6

Sunday 13th
94 Brownlow Road, N11
41 Mill Hill Road, W3
65 Mill Hill Road, W3
153 Portland Road, BR1
5 Russell Road, N13
87 St Johns Road, E17
33 Wood Vale, N10

Sunday 20th
5 Brodie Road, E4
94 Marsh Lane Allotments, N17

September

Sunday 3rd
NEW 2 Conway Road, N14
Golf Course Allotments, N11
24 Grove Park, SE5
Royal Trinity Hospice, SW4

Saturday 9th
◆ The Garden Museum, SE1

Sunday 10th
Gordon Road Allotments, N3
NEW 2 Littlebury Road, SW4

Thursday 14th
93 Palace Road, SW2

Sunday 17th
NEW 470 Pinner Road, HA5

October

Sunday 1st
23 Imperial Road, N22

Sunday 8th
The Watergardens, KT2

Sunday 22nd
West Lodge Park, EN4

Also By Arrangement

THE GARDENS

1 66 ABBOTS GARDENS, N2

East Finchley, N2 0JH. Stephen & Ruth Kersley. *6 mins from rear exit along Causeway (ped) to East End Rd. 2nd L into Abbots Gardens. 143 stops at Abbots Gardens. 102, 263 & 234 on East End Rd.* **Sun 21 May (2-5.30). Adm £3.50, chd free. Home-made teas.**
Combining grass and glass - Stephen studied garden design at Capel Manor and Ruth is a glass artist. Designed for yr round interest, this garden creates a calming yet dramatic environment through plant form, colour, texture and asymmetrical geometry. Glass amphorae and feathers catch the eye among grasses, ornamental shrubs, perennials, vegetable plot and water features. Featured in Garden News and Garden Answers.

2 NEW ACACIA HOUSE, W3

Centre Avenue, Acton, London, W3 7JY. Lucy Maxwell. *Adjoining Acton Park. Centre Ave is off Uxbridge Rd directly opp Total Garage, KwikFit & Access SelfStorage. Far end of Centre Ave on R by park gate. Acton Central 4mins walk across park.* **207 & 266 bus at end of rd. Sun 28 May (3-6). Adm £5, chd free. Home-made teas.**
Hidden oasis in Acton. Once the home of Sean Connery, this densely planted walled cottage garden redesigned in 2015 now combines clipped box hedges, a wisteria covered pergola and a series of brick pathways leading you around the garden. Bordered by Acton Park on two sides.

> Your visit has already helped 600 more people gain access to a Parkinson's nurse

3 109 ADDINGTON ROAD, BR4

Coney Hall, West Wickham, BR4 9BG. Mrs Sheila Chivers. *A2022 Bromley to Croydon rd, between Glebe Way & Corkscrew Hill/Layhams Rd r'abouts. Please park on main rd.* **Sun 21 May, Sun 25 June (1.30-5.30). Adm £4, chd free. Home-made teas.**
An informal garden with winding paths lead you past hot sunny borders, cool shady areas with contrasting foliage plants, a bog garden and ponds with water lilies. There are shady seating areas surrounded by colourful borders, a summer house overlooking a woodland area. Hanging baskets and various containers adding extra colour and interest throughout the garden.

4 ALL SEASONS, W5

97 Grange Road, Ealing, W5 3PH. Dr Benjamin & Mrs Maria Royappa. *Tube: Ealing Broadway/ South Ealing/Ealing Common: 10-15 mins walk.* **Sat 22 July (1-6); Sun 23 July (12.30-6). Adm £3, chd free. Home-made teas.**
Garden designed, built and planted by owners, with new interesting planting, features incl ponds, pergolas, Japanese gardens, tropical house for orchids, exotics and aviaries. Several recycled features, composting and rain water harvesting, orchard, kiwi, grape vines, architectural and unusual plants incl ferns, bamboos, conifers and cacti. Partial wheelchair access.

5 37 ALWYNE ROAD, N1

London, N1 2HW. Mr & Mrs J Lambert. *Buses: 38, 56, 73, 341 on Essex Rd; 4, 19, 30, 43 on Upper St, alight at Town Hall; 271 on Canonbury Rd, A1. Tube: Highbury & Islington.* **Sun 4 June (2-5). Adm £4, chd free. Home-made teas. Also open 41 Ecclesbourne Road.** *Donation to The Friends of the Rose Bowl.*
The New River curves around

the garden, freeing it from the constraints of the usual London rectangle and allowing differing degrees of formality - roses along the river, topiary, a secluded spot where the life of the river is part of the charm. Visitors return to see what's new and to enjoy the spectacular array of very good home-made cakes. Plants for sale are chosen for all seasons. Shelter if it rains. Wheelchair access only with own assistant for 3 shallow entrance steps.

&. ✿ 💻

GROUP OPENING

6 NEW **ANGEL GARDENS, N1**

London, N1 8JQ. *Angel, Islington. Underground & Buses: 5 mins walk from Angel.* Sun 2 July (2-5.30). Combined adm £5, chd free. Home-made teas at 1 Devonia Road.

NEW **1 DEVONIA ROAD**
Fiona Cramb.

NEW **5 DEVONIA ROAD**
Dr R & Mrs M Clark-Majerus.

NEW **19 ST PETER'S STREET**
Adrian Gunning.

3 secluded town gardens linked by common themes: 5 Devonia Rd is a tiny formal town garden (8 × 5m) originally designed by George Carter. Small perennial borders recently added. Folly, fountain, ferns, grasses, climbers. 1 Devonia Rd is one of the widest gardens on the street as the house incl an original coach house through which the garden is accessed . Landscaped about 10yrs ago it is best described as traditional with modern accents. Box-edged borders filled with roses and a pergola with climbers surround a comfortable seating area. 19 St Peter's St is a charming secluded town garden, with roses, trees, shrubs, climbers, a patio with containers and a trompe l'oeil mural.

 💻

7 **31 ARLINGTON DRIVE, HA4**

Ruislip, HA4 7RJ. John & Yasuko O'Gorman. *Tube: Ruislip. Then bus H13 to Arlington Drive, or 15 mins walk up Bury St. Arlington Drive is opp Millar & Carter Steakhouse on Bury St.* Sun 4 June (2-5). Adm £3.50, chd free. Home-made teas.

80ft × 40ft NW facing garden, highly structured and loosely planted. To the front, wide borders and beds curve around an oval lawn. Climbing roses and clematis screen the rear section, which comprises rectangular beds and a small vegetable patch. Small trees, shrubs and perennials incl many varieties of acer, cornus, tree paeony, flowering cherry and hosta.

&. ✿ 💻

GROUP OPENING

8 **ARLINGTON SQUARE GARDENS, N1**

London, N1 7DP. www.arlingtonassociation.org.uk. *South Islington. Off New North Rd via Arlington Ave or Linton St. Buses: 21, 76, 141, 271.* Sun 11 June (1-5.30). Combined adm £7, chd free. Home-made teas at St James' Vicarage, 1A Arlington Square. Live music.

Diespeker Wharf

14 ARLINGTON AVENUE
Dominic Richards.

26 ARLINGTON AVENUE
Thomas Blaikie.

21 ARLINGTON SQUARE
Alison Rice.

25 ARLINGTON SQUARE
Michael Foley.

27 ARLINGTON SQUARE
Geoffrey Wheat & Rev Justin Gau.

28 ARLINGTON SQUARE
Mr & Mrs H Li.

NEW **30 ARLINGTON SQUARE**
James & Maria Hewson.

39 ARLINGTON SQUARE
Hazel Fletcher.

5 REES STREET
Gordon McArthur & Paul Thompson.

ST JAMES' VICARAGE, 1A ARLINGTON SQUARE
John & Maria Burniston.

Behind the early Victorian facades of Arlington Square are 10 town gardens that cover the full spectrum of gardening styles, from modern contemporary design to the traditional cottage garden. It is interesting to see how each garden has used the limited area available to create an inspiring and relaxing space. One new garden has joined the group which has been very much inspired by the diverse planting in Arlington Square and the owner is developing an increasing passion for rare and architectural plants. The other gardens in the group reflect the diverse tastes and interests of each garden owner who have got to know each other through the community gardening of Arlington Square. It is hard to believe you are minutes from the bustle of the City of London. Live music in the vicarage garden.

9 97 ARTHUR ROAD, SW19

Wimbledon, SW19 7DP. Tony & Bella Covill. *Wimbledon Park tube, then 200yds up hill on R.* **Sun 18 June (2-6). Adm £5, chd free. Light refreshments.**
⅓ acre garden of an Edwardian house. Garden established for more than 20yrs and constantly evolving with a large variety of plants and shrubs. It has grown up around several lawns with pond and fountains. Abundance of wildlife and a bird haven. A beautiful place with much colour, foliage and texture.
🚻 🐄 ☕ ▣

10 ARUNDEL & LADBROKE GARDENS, W11

Kensington Park Road, Notting Hill, W11 2LW. Arundel & Ladbroke Gardens Committee, 020 7460 8895, susan.lynn1@ntlworld.com, www.arundelladbrokegardens. co.uk. *Entrance on Kensington Park Rd, between Ladbroke & Arundel Gardens. Tube: Notting Hill Gate or Ladbroke Grove. Buses: 23, 52, 228, 452. Alight at stop for Portobello Market/Arundel Gardens.* **Sun 14 May (1.30-6). Adm £4, chd free. Home-made teas. Also open Cleveland Square. Visits also by arrangement Mar to Nov.**
This private communal garden retains its mid Victorian design and some typically Victorian shrubs. It has evolved into a woodland garden, with yr-round colour and interest, particularly in spring with rhododendrons, camellias, foreign exotics and spring bulbs, as seen in the large entrance bed planted as a woodland glade with silver birches set among grasses, spring flowering perennials and bulbs. Playground. Wheelchair access possible but 2 steps and gravel paths to negotiate.
🚻 🐄 ☕ ▣

11 36 ASHLEY ROAD, N19

London, N19 3AF. Alan Swann & Ahmed Farooqui, 020 7281 4586, swann.alan@googlemail.com. *Crouch Hill. Underground: Archway or Finsbury Park. Overground: Crouch Hill. Buses: 210 or 41 from Archway*
to Hornsey Rise. W7 from Finsbury Park to Heathville Road. Car: Free parking in Ashley Road at weekends. **Sun 28, Mon 29 May (2-6). Adm £3.50, chd free. Cream teas. Visits also by arrangement May to Aug.**
A lush town garden rich in textures, colour and forms. At its best in late spring as Japanese maple cultivars display great variety of shape and colour whilst ferns unfurl fresh, vibrant fronds over a tumbling stream and alpines and clematis burst into flower on the rockeries and pergola. The garden has a number of micro habitats incl ferneries, a bog garden, stream and pond plantings, rockeries, alpines and shade plantings. Young ferns and plants propagated from specimen plants in the garden for sale. Cream teas for sale. Indoor pop-up cafe with views over the garden when wet. Featured in the Ham & High.
🌼 ☕ ▣

12 254 ASHURST DRIVE, IG6

Barkingside, IG6 1EW. Maureen Keating. *2m S of Chigwell. Nearest tube: Barkingside on Central Line approx 8 mins walk. Bus: 150 stops outside Tesco's on Cranbrook Rd. 1st L Hatley Av into Ashhurst Drive.* **Sun 30 July (1-5). Adm £3. Tea.**
Bird friendly colour filled town garden with interesting nooks and crannies each telling a story. Contains 7 water features, 6 seating areas, waterfall, pond and stream, miniature railway, model village and vibrant planting all in 40 ft square area! Regret, garden unsuitable for children.
☕ ▣

13 NEW 36 AVONDALE AVENUE, N12

North Finchley, N12 8EN. Georgia Pairtrie. *5 mins from Woodside Park Tube on Northern Line High Barnet Branch. 5 mins from North Circular A406. 5 mins from M1 J2. Free roadside parking available all day.* **Sun 18 June (2-6). Adm £3.50, chd free. Home-made teas in the conservatory.**
A chance to see what can be achieved from scratch in just 5yrs.

The owner, an artist, has propagated many plants from seed, cuttings and division in the true spirit of a cottage garden. Plant lined path leads from front garden to back garden's upper terrace full of pots. Steps down to island beds linked by flower covered archways. Lawn links curved flowerbeds backed by mature trees.
✿ ☕ ▣

14 190 BARNET ROAD, EN5

Arkley, Barnet, EN5 3LF. Hilde & Lionel Wainstein, 020 8441 4041, hildewainstein@hotmail.co.uk. *1m S of A1, 2m N of High Barnet tube. Garden is located on corner of A411 Barnet Rd & Meadowbanks cul-de-sac. Nearest tube: High Barnet, then 107 bus, Glebe Lane stop. Plenty of unrestricted roadside parking.* **Sun 21 May, Sun 23 July (2-6). Adm £3.50, chd free. Home-made teas. Visits also by arrangement May to Sept.**
Garden designer's walled garden, approx 90ft × 36ft. Modern, asymmetric design thickly planted in flowing, natural drifts around trees, shrubs and central pond; changing array of interesting containers, recycled objects and sculptures. Copper trellis divides the space into contrasting areas. The garden continues to evolve as planted areas are expanded. We have now completely removed the lawn. Selection of home-made cakes worthy of Mary Berry! Wide range of interesting plants for sale, all propagated from the garden. Featured in Garden Answers Magazine. Single steps within garden.
🚻 ✿ ☕ ▣

Donations from the NGS enable Perennial to care for horticulturalists

10 Woodside Avenue

GROUP OPENING

15 **BARNSBURY GROUP, N1**

Islington, N1 1DB. *Barnsbury London N1. Tube: King's Cross, Caledonian Rd or Angel. Overground: Caledonian Rd & Barnsbury. Buses: 17, 91, 259 to Caledonian Rd.* **Sun 4 June (2-6). Combined adm £7, chd free.**

♦ **BARNSBURY WOOD**
London Borough of Islington, ecologycentre@islington.gov.uk.

1 BATTLEBRIDGE COURT
Mike Jackson, michaeljackson215@me.com. **Visits also by arrangement Mar to Sept, groups 10 max.**

44 HEMINGFORD ROAD
Peter Willis & Haremi Kudo.

NEW **57 HUNTINGTON STREET**
Julian Williams.

Walk through Islington's historic Georgian squares and terraces to these four contrasting spaces, all within walking distance of the vibrant development at King's Cross. Barnsbury Wood is London's smallest nature reserve and Islington's hidden secret, a tranquil oasis of wild flowers and massive trees just minutes from Caledonian Road. The three gardens have extensive collections of unusual plants; 57 Huntington St is a secluded garden room - an understorey of silver birch and hazel shades ferns, native perennials and grasses and a container pond. 44 Hemingford Road is a small, dense composition of trees (some unusual), shrubs, perennials and lawns – and a small pond. Battlebridge Court is a plantsman's small garden making optimum use of sun and shade beside the canal basin, together with four contrasting beds in front of the block of flats. All the gardens have evolved over many years, to incl plants to suit their particular growing conditions, and show what can be achieved while surmounting the difficulties of dry walls and shade.
✿ ☕

GROUP OPENING

16 NEW **BLACKHEATH GARDENS, SE13**
Lewisham, London, SE13 7EA. *Gardens sit between Lewisham & Blackheath stns. DLR: Buses 54, 89, 108, 122,178, 261, 321, 621.* **Sun 25 June (2-6). Combined adm £5, chd free. Home-made teas at Lee Rd and Michael's Close.**

28 GRANVILLE PARK
Joanna Herald, www.joannaherald.com.
D

49 LEE ROAD
Jane Glynn & Colin Kingsnorth.

NEW **1 MICHAEL'S CLOSE**
Jeffrey Warren.

Set among the hills of Blackheath are 3 gardens ranging from small to amazingly large, each with its own idiosyncratic style. Each to be lived in and enjoyed. A magnificent rambling rector rose blankets the tall hawthorn hedge backing on a small enclosed garden wrapped round three sides of a modern flat with densely planted borders defined by paths, steps and low retaining walls. A garden designer's 100ft x 35ft relaxing and softly contoured elegant family garden offers a wildlife friendly pool garden; herbaceous and shrub plantings and gravel garden. A sunken terrace with pots by the house provides a suntrap seating area. The third garden is a surprisingly spacious oasis of calm in the city. Benches are set beneath rambling roses overlooking generous formal lawns with flowerbeds. Winding paths through silver birches and grasses reveal a treehouse clad with roses and clematis. Serious vegetable growing. Plants at Granville Park and Michael's Close.
✿ ☕

17 5 BRODIE ROAD, E4

Chingford, London, E4 7HF. Mr & Mrs N Booth. *N E London. From Chingford train station take any bus to Chingford Green (Co-op), turn L at Prezzo restaurant, 2nd R (Scholars Rd), then 1st L to Brodie Road.* **Sun 11 June, Sun 20 Aug (2-5). Adm £3.50, chd free. Light refreshments.**
An unconventional suburban garden. Herbaceous borders, trellises, arches and secret arbour overflow with flowers loved by bees and butterflies. Masses of colour throughout spring and summer. New and unusual plantings every year to add interest and create new vistas. A visual feast for garden enthusiasts.

18 94 BROWNLOW ROAD, N11

Bounds Green, N11 2BS. Spencer Viner, www.northeleven.co.uk. *Close to N Circular. Tube: Bounds Green then 5 mins walk, direction N Circular. Corner of Elvendon Rd & Brownlow Rd.* **Sun 13 Aug (2-6). Adm £2.50, chd free. Light refreshments. Also open 5 Russell Road.**
A small courtyard for meditation. The conception of this garden by a designer transports the visitor to a different, foreign place of imagination and tranquillity, far away from the suburbs. Features incl reclaimed materials, trees, water, pergola, pleached limes, seating and a strong theme of pared back simplicity. Design and horticultural advice. Featured in Garden Design. A Book of Ideas - Marianne Majerus, Gardens Illustrated and Waitrose Magazine.

19 5 BURBAGE ROAD, SE24

Herne Hill, SE24 9HJ. Crawford & Rosemary Lindsay, 020 7274 5610, rl@rosemarylindsay.com, www.rosemarylindsay.com. *Nr junction with Half Moon Lane. Herne Hill & N Dulwich mainline stns, 5 mins walk. Buses: 3, 37, 40, 68, 196, 468.* **Sun 11 June (2-5). Adm £3.50, chd free. Home-made**

teas. **Visits also by arrangement Apr to July.**
The garden of a member of The Society of Botanical Artists. 150ft × 40ft with large and varied range of plants. Herb garden, herbaceous borders for sun and shade, climbing plants, pots, terraces, lawns. Gravel areas to reduce watering. Immaculate topiary. See our website for what the papers say. Included in The London Garden Book A-Z.

20 12 BUSHBERRY ROAD, E9

Hackney, E9 5SX. Molly St Hilaire. *Overground stn: Homerton, then 5 mins walk. Buses: 26, 30, 488, alight last stop in Cassland Rd.* **Sun 16 July (2-6). Adm £3, chd free. Home-made teas.**
Petite courtyard garden with water feature. Rambling roses, jasmine, vine and clematis cover the overarching pergola. Small but beautifully formed ... a pure joy to see.

21 CADOGAN PLACE SOUTH GARDEN, SW1

Sloane Street, Chelsea, SW1X 9PE. The Cadogan Estate, 07890 452992, Ric.Glenn@cadogan.co.uk. *Entrance to garden opp 97 Sloane St.* **Sun 9 Apr (10-4). Adm £3.50, chd free. Visits also by arrangement with head gardener tours by request.**
Many surprises and unusual trees and shrubs are hidden behind the railings of this large London square. The first square to be developed by architect Henry Holland for Lord Cadogan at the end of C18, it was then called the London Botanic Garden. Mulberry trees planted for silk production at end of C17. Cherry trees, magnolias and bulbs are outstanding in spring, when the fern garden is unfurling. Award winning Hans Sloane Garden exhibited at the Chelsea Flower Show. Pond. Spring walk on East side of garden. Feel free to bring a picnic to enjoy in the garden.

22 NEW 85 CALTON AVENUE, SE21

Dulwich, London, SE21 7DF. Frances Twinn. *From Dulwich Village turn into Calton Av past St Barnabas Church opp Alleyn's School playing fields. From East Dulwich (37 bus): East Dulwich Grove, turn into Townley Rd. Calton Av next R.* **Sun 4 June (2-5.30). Adm £3.50, chd free. Home-made teas. Also open 35 Camberwell Grove.**
A labour of love! Lovers of roses and peonies will be entranced by this immaculate garden that balances a spacious serpentine lawn with a choice of rooms off – offering a quiet spot for contemplation against elegant found masonry walls and corners perfect for tea. Bold blocks of planting fill the borders, persicarias is a favourite.

23 35 CAMBERWELL GROVE, SE5

London, SE5 8JA. Lynette Hemmant & Juri Gabriel, 020 7703 6186, juri@jurigabriel.com. *Backing onto St Giles Church, Camberwell Church St. From Camberwell Green go down Camberwell Church St. Turn R into Camberwell Grove.* **Sun 4 June (12-6.30). Adm £3.50, chd free. Light refreshments. Also open 85 Calton Avenue. Visits also by arrangement June & July, min charge £70. Groups 30 max.** *Donation to St Giles Church.*
Plant packed 120ft × 20ft garden with charming backdrop of St Giles Church. Evolved over 30yrs into a romantic country style garden brimming with colour and overflowing with pots. In June, spectacular roses stretch the full length of the garden, both on the artist's studio and festooning an old iron staircase. Artist's studio open. Lynette (who has earned her living by pen and brush throughout her life) has painted the garden obsessively for the past 20yrs; see her (lynettehemmant.com) and NGS websites.

Oak Farm

GROUP OPENING

24 CAMBERWELL GROVE GARDENS, SE5

Camberwell, SE5 8JE. *5 mins from Denmark Hill mainline & overgound stn. Buses: 12, 36, 68, 148, 171, 176, 185, 436. Entrance through garden rooms at rear.* **Sun 16 July (2-6). Combined adm £5, chd free. Home-made teas at 81 Camberwell Grove incl delicious home-made cakes.** *Donation to CJD Support Network.*

81 CAMBERWELL GROVE

Jane & Alex Maitland Hudson.

83 CAMBERWELL GROVE

Robert Hirschhorn & John Hall.

This year these neighbouring walled gardens behind C18 houses in this beautiful tree lined street are opening a month later than in previous years. At No.81 a Japanese maple a tall Trachycarpus Palm and a magnolia grandiflora shade York stone paving and borders filled with herbaceous perennials and shade loving ground cover. There is a pond and bog garden. Pots of all sizes line the steps to the kitchen door and the terrace outside the garden room and greenhouse. An exhibition by local sculptor, Jane Muir, will be a feature of our garden opening. No. 83 is a mature beautifully designed plant lovers' garden. Abundant unusual planting within a structure of box hedging provides varied and interesting areas of peace and privacy. As trees mature the nature of the garden is changing, and more shade tolerant perennials are being introduced. Contemporary garden room, gravel and York stone paths and seating areas, calming pool and lovely views of parish church.

25 CANONBURY HOUSE, N1

Canonbury Place, London, N1 2NQ. Mr & Mrs Gavin Ralston. *Junction of Canonbury Place & Alwyne Villas, next to Canonbury*

Tower. Tube & Overground: Highbury & Islington. Buses to Canonbury Sq. Entrance by side gate opp 1 Canonbury Place. **Sun 21 May (2-5.30). Adm £4, chd free. Home-made teas.**

Large secluded garden next to historic Canonbury Tower and 500yr old mulberry. Magnificent mature trees, woodland planting, clipped box lining lawn. Sheltered herbaceous border. Fountain and well stocked pond; hidden children's play area. Wheelchair entry via shallow ramp to patio area from which garden can be viewed.

26 4 CANONBURY PLACE, N1

London, N1 2NQ. Mr & Mrs Jeffrey Tobias. *Highbury & Islington Tube & Overground. Buses: 271 to Canonbury Square. Located in old part of Canonbury Place, off Alwyne Villas, in a cul de sac.* **Sun 23 Apr (2-5.30). Combined adm with 20 St Mary's Grove £5.50, chd free. Home-made teas.**

A paved, 100ft garden behind a 1780 house. Spectacular mature trees enclosed in a walled garden. Mostly pots and also interesting shrubs and climbers. Daffodlils, tulips and bluebells abound for this springtime opening. Artisan pastries and sourdough bread available.

27 CAPEL MANOR COLLEGE, GUNNERSBURY PARK CAMPUS, W3

The Walled Garden, Gunnersbury Park, Popes Lane, Ealing, London, W3 8LQ. Sarah Neophytou, www.capel.ac.uk/gunnersbury-park-centre.html. *Entering Popes Lane from the A406, park is on the L. Entrance to free car park is approx 200 metres on L, just past a pedestrian crossing.* **Sat 24 June (12-4.30). Adm £4, chd free.**

Sited within the Walled Garden in Gunnersbury Park, formerly owned by the Rothschild family, is one of the Capel Manor College campuses, specialising in teaching landbased industries such as Horticulture, Arboriculture, Animal Care and Floristry. Usually closed to the public, this garden is maintained entirely by horticulture students, one member of staff and a handful of student volunteers. There are a range of loosely themed borders, tropical, Mediterranean, herbaceous, and kitchen garden beds. At the top of the student practice area is a stumpery garden, built by students during 2013/2014. Tree ferns, a range of deciduous trees, woodland planting, give a magical feel while an imaginative use of dead wood and stumps contrast eerily with the planting. Paths through stumpery not suitable for wheelchair users but area can be viewed. Borders, and new garden have good access.

28 THE CHARTERHOUSE, EC1

Charterhouse Square, London, EC1M 6AN. The Governors of Sutton's Hospital, www.thecharterhouse.org. *Buses: 4, 55. Tube: Barbican. Turn L out of stn, L into Carthusian St & into square. Entrance around or through Charterhouse Square.* **Evening opening Tue 6 June (6-9). Adm £5, chd free. Wine. Evening to incl BBQ (additional charge).** Enclosed courtyard gardens within the grounds of historic Charterhouse, which dates back to 1347. English country garden style featuring roses, herbaceous borders, ancient mulberry trees and small pond. Various garden herbs found here are still used in the kitchen today. In addition, two other areas are being opened for the NGS. Pensioners Court, which is partly maintained by the private tenants and Master's Garden, the old burial ground which now consists of lawns, borders and wildlife garden planted to camouflage a war time air raid shelter. A private garden for the Brothers of Charterhouse, not usually open to the public. (Buildings not open).
&. ☕ ♥

29 51 THE CHASE, SW4

London, SW4 0NP. Mr Charles Rutheroford & Mr Rupert Tyler, www.charlesrutherfoord.net. *Off Clapham Common Northside. Tube: Clapham Common. Buses: 137, 452.* **Sun 23 Apr (12-5). Evening opening Tue 25 Apr (6-8). Adm £4, chd free. Light refreshments.** Member of the Society of Garden Designers, Charles has created the garden over 30yrs. In 2015 the main garden was remodelled, to much acclaim. Spectacular in spring, when 2000 tulips bloom among irises and tree peonies. Scented front garden. Rupert's geodetic dome shelters seedlings, succulents and subtropicals.
Ⅾ ☕ ♥

30 ◆ CHELSEA PHYSIC GARDEN, SW3

66 Royal Hospital Road, London, SW3 4HS. Chelsea Physic Garden Company, 020 7352 5646, www.chelseaphysicgarden.co.uk. *Tube: Sloane Square (10 mins). Bus: 170. Parking: Battersea Park (charged). Entrance in Swan Walk.* **For NGS: Fri 7 Apr (11-6). Adm £10.50, chd £6.95. Lunches and afternoon tea at Tangerine Dream Café. For other opening times and information, please phone or visit garden website.** Come and explore London's oldest botanic garden situated in the heart of Chelsea. With a unique living collection of around 5000 plants, this walled garden is a celebration of the importance of plants and their beauty. Highlights incl Europe's oldest pond rockery, the Garden of Edible and Useful Plants, the Garden of Medicinal Plants and the World Woodland Garden. Tours available. Wheelchair access is via 66 Royal Hospital Rd.
&. ✿ ♥

31 46 CHEYNE AVENUE, E18

South Woodford, Essex, E18 2DR. Helen Auty. *Nearest tube S Woodford. Short walk. From station take Clarendon Rd. Cross High Rd into Broadwalk, 3rd on L Bushey Ave. 1st R Cheyne Ave.* **Sun 6 Aug (12-5). Adm £4, chd free. Home-made teas.** On site of Lord Cheyne's original market garden, typical suburban garden with lawn and borders of shrubs, climbers and perennials - greenhouse and productive fruit and vegetable garden.
✿ ♥

The National Garden Scheme is the largest single funder of the Queen's Nursing Institute

32 NEW 95 THE CHINE, N21

London, N21 2EG. Mrs Asha Karunaratne. *6 mins walk from Grange Park Station. Buses W9 or 125 from Green Dragon Lane. Look out for NGS yellow arrows, The Chine is in 2 parts.* **Sun 28 May (2-5.30). Adm £3.50, chd free. Home-made teas.** Retirement encouraged owners to develop and share their horticultural passions. A long sunny raised border with shrubs, climbers and perennials provides scent and colour. A rose clad arbour creates central focus. Rhododendrons, acers and alliums shine in spring. Vegetables flourish, birds abound. Pleasant vistas and hidden gems offer visitors relaxation.
✿ ☕ ♥

GROUP OPENING

33 CHISWICK MALL GARDENS, W4

Chiswick, W6 9TN. *Car: Towards Hogarth r'about, A4 (W) turn Eyot Grds S. Tube: Stamford Brook or Turnham Green. Buses: 27, 190, 267 & 391 to Young's Corner. From Chiswick High Rd or Kings St S under A4 to river.* **Evening opening Fri 26 May (6-8.30). Combined adm £12.50, chd free. Wine at 16 Eyot Gardens. Sun 28 May (2-6). Combined adm £8, chd free. Tea at 16 Eyot Gardens.**

16 EYOT GARDENS
Dianne Farris.

FIELD HOUSE
Rupert King, www.fieldhousegarden.co.uk.

NEW LONGMEADOW
Charlotte Fraser.

ST PETERS WHARF
Barbara Brown.

SWAN HOUSE
Mr & Mrs George Nissen.

This peaceful riverside setting offers five unique gardens. Two walled gardens - one large and one small, artists' studio garden, exotic water garden and town house garden with extensive vegetable garden.
🐕 ✿ ♥

34 CHOUMERT SQUARE, SE15

Peckham, London, SE15 4RE. The Residents. *Off Choumert Grove. Trains from London Victoria, London Bridge, London Blackfriars, Clapham Junction to Peckham Rye; buses (12, 36, 37, 63, 78, 171, 312, 345). Free Car park (1 min) in Choumert Grove.* **Sun 4 June (1-6). Adm £4, chd free. Light refreshments. Also open 85 Calton Avenue.** *Donation to St Christopher's Hospice.*

About 46 mini gardens with maxi planting in Shangri-la situation that the media has described as a Floral Canyon, which leads to small communal secret garden. The day is primarily about gardens and sharing with others our residents' love of this little corner of the inner city; but it is also renowned for its demonstrable community spirit. Lots of stalls and live music. The popular open gardens will combine this year with our own take on a village fete with home produce stalls, arts, crafts and music. Light lunches, afternoon teas, Pimms and soft drinks. Featured in numerous articles in National and Local press, magazines, books and television gardening programmes incl BBC TV Gardeners' World. No steps within the Square just a tiny step to a raised paved space in the communal garden area.

&. ❀ ☕

35 31 CHURCH CRESCENT, N3

Finchley Church End, London, N3 1BE. Gerald & Margaret Levin. *7 mins walk from Finchley Central Underground (Northern Line, High Barnet branch). Buses nearby incl 82, 460, 125, 326, 143 and 382. No parking restrictions on Sun.* **Sun 23 July (2-6). Adm £3.50, chd free. Home-made teas.**

120ft x 30ft E-facing garden designed and built by us with no straight lines, three season interest and a wildlife pond as the focal point. A sunny terrace with tubs, three beds around the pond with interesting shrubs and perennials, and a more challenging shadier area with trees, shrubs and ferns. Removal of a large birch has given us many new planting opportunities.

National Garden Scheme support helps raise awareness of unpaid carers

Home-made jams and marmalade for sale. Stationary illustrated with photos of our garden flowers. Many plants in the garden are labelled. Featured in Ham and High. Partial wheelchair access. Two shallow steps from public footpath into garden, one within garden. Level access to refreshments in conservatory.

&. ☕

36 79 CHURCH LANE, N2

London, N2 0TH. Caro & David Broome. *Tube: E Finchley, then East End Rd for ¾m, R into Church Lane. Buses: 143 to Five Bells PH, 3 min walk; 263 to E Finchley Library, 5 min walk.* **Sun 30 July (2-6). Adm £3.50, chd free. Mouth watering selection of home-made cakes incl gluten free.**

Plantsman's garden full of humour and innovation. Contemporary front garden leads through to a plant filled enclave, opening out into the garden beyond. Borders bursting with shrubs, roses and unusual perennials, central curved rill with quirky water features. Rustic archway leads to secluded ferny glen, a secret hideaway and surprisingly exotic roof terrace. Always something new to see. Locally propagated perennials ideal for London clay soils. Ever popular raffle, children's treasure hunt. Home-made teas incl new recipes and old favourites. Garden News 'Over The Fence' columnist. Blogger for Thompson and Morgan. Winner of Best Small Back Garden - London Garden Society

❀ ☕

37 CLEVELAND SQUARE, W2

London, W2 6DD. The Residents Trust, 07941 468591, ethertons@btinternet.com, www.clevelandsquare.org. *Entrance on W side. 5 mins from Paddington,*

Queensway, Lancaster Gate, Royal Oak & Bayswater tube. 5 mins from many bus routes, eg 23, 27, 36, 94, 148. Metered parking on & nr Square. **Sun 14 May (2-6). Adm £4, chd free. Wine. Also open 12 Lansdowne Road. Visits also by arrangement Feb to June. Refreshments on request.**

A private gem hidden in a quiet London square, surrounded by grand Victorian stucco terraces. Perhaps you've seen it in a Woody Allen film or Inspector Morse. Everyone is welcome to enjoy it as a social space (esp with a drink from the pop-up cocktail bar), children love the play areas, and it has special appeal to horticulturists with its emphasis on design, biodiversity and succession planting. Feel free to bring a picnic. Play equipment for younger visitors. The garden has gravel paths but these are usable by wheelchairs.

&. ❀ 🚌 🅓 ☕

38 NEW 2 CONWAY ROAD, N14

Southgate, N14 7BA. Eileen Hulse. *Buses: 121 & W6 from Palmers Green or Southgate to Broomfield Park stop. Walk up Aldermans Hill R into Ulleswater Road 1st L into Conway Road.* **Sun 3 Sept (2-6). Adm £3.50, chd free. Home-made teas.**

A passion, nurtured from childhood, for growing unusual plants has culminated in two contrasting gardens. The original, calming with lawn, pond and greenhouse, compliments the adjoining, Mediterranean terraced rooms with pergolas clothed in exotic climbers, vegetable beds and cordon fruit. Tumbling goji, figs, datura and mimosa mingle creating a horticultural adventure. Those unsteady on their feet need to take care.

❀ ☕

GROUP OPENING

39 COPTHALL GROUP, NW7

Mill Hill, London, NW7 2NB. *Short bus ride (221) from Edgware tube or Mill Hill East. Free parking vouchers available if restrictions are in force.* **Sun 11 June (2-5.30). Combined adm £5, chd free. Home-made teas at 2 Copthall Drive.**

2 COPTHALL DRIVE
Janet Jomain.

13 COPTHALL GARDENS
Lise Marshfield.

Two small town gardens enthusiastically gardened by their plantaholic owners. 13 Copthall Gardens is a mature leafy garden in a quiet cul-de-sac. Emphasis on form and texture. Clipped shrubs, topiary, perennials and roses. Small pond. Portal to third dimension. Traditional Finnish swing seat. 2 Copthall Drive is a small E-facing town garden with more than 60 roses and many clematis, alliums, hydrangeas and a wildlife pond. A small but productive fruit and vegetable patch incl nectarines and kiwi fruit, with other exotic plants in the greenhouse. ✿ ☕ ♥

1 Michael's Close, Blackheath Gardens

Visit a garden and support hospice care in your local community

---

40 122 COURT LANE, SE21

Dulwich, SE21 7EA. Jean & Charles Cary-Elwes. *Buses P4, 12, 40, 176, 185 (to Dulwich Library) 37. Mainline; North Dulwich then 12 mins walk. Ample free parking.* **Sun 25 June (2-5.30). Adm £4, chd free. Home-made teas.**
Generously proportioned, mature garden with unusual and marginally tender shrubs which thrive in the hands of a keen propagator. Agapanthus, a signature plant followed by oleander, and a splendid clerodendron. Backing onto Dulwich Park it has a countryside feel - a true family garden with sandpit and hammock mingling with a hardworking greenhouse and a wormery, which will be demonstrated. Live jazz band, cakes and tea, children's trail, plant sales. Wheelchair access to terrace only but good view of garden. ♿ ✿ ☕ ♥

41 22 COURT LANE GARDENS, SE21

London, SE21 7DZ. Liz & Chris Campbell-Warner. *Buses: P4, 12, 40, 176, 185 (to Dulwich Library) 37. Mainline: North Dulwich rail station, ample street parking.* **Sun 25 June (2-5.30). Adm £4, chd free. Also open 122 Court Lane.**
The front garden features mature trees, shrubs, a lawn and woodland plants behind a topiary privet hedge. The rear backs onto Dulwich Park and is divided into three sections: two linked lawns surrounded by herbaceous perennials, trees and hedges and a vegetable garden with five raised beds and a summerhouse. ♿ 🐾 ✿

GROUP OPENING

42 DE BEAUVOIR GARDENS, N1

London, N1 4HU. *Highbury & Islington tube then 30 or 277 bus; Angel tube then 38, 56 or 73 bus; Bank tube then 21, 76 or 141 bus. 10 mins walk from Dalston Overground stations. Street parking available.* **Sun 11 June (11-3). Combined adm £7, chd free. Home-made teas at 158 Culford Road.**

158 CULFORD ROAD
Gillian Blachford.

NEW▶ 17 NORTHCHURCH ROAD
David & Elizabeth Ainger.

21 NORTHCHURCH TERRACE
Nancy Korman.

24 NORTHCHURCH TERRACE
Sue Pedder.

Four gardens to explore in De Beauvoir, a leafy enclave of Victorian villas near to Islington and Dalston. The area boasts some of Hackney's keenest gardeners and a thriving gardening club. New this yr is 17 Northchurch Rd, a classic courtyard garden filled with the sound of falling water. 24 Northchurch Terrace boasts 7 arches of Dublin Bay roses and shaped trees such as olive, pittosporum and feijoa. The walled garden at 21 Northchurch Terrace has a formal feel, with deep herbaceous borders, pond, fruit trees, pergola, patio pots and herb beds. 158 Culford Road is a long narrow garden with a romantic feel and a path winding through full borders with shrubs, small trees, perennials and many unusual plants. ☕

---

43 NEW▶ DIESPEKER WHARF, N1

38 Graham Street, London, N1 8JX. Pollard Thomas Edwards. *Beside Regents Canal, Angel, Islington. Underground & Buses: 5 mins from Angel.* **Sat 3 June (2-5.30). Adm £4, chd free. Home-made teas.**

An intriguing and unexpected garden in an historic industrial setting alongside the Regents Canal owned and converted by a firm of architects. The garden has become an enticing and unique space enjoyed both socially and for business. Interesting climbers clothe the high wall. Canalside beds incl aster monarch, verbena bonariensis, acanthus spinosis, astrantia major and euphorbia silver edge. The garden has won numerous awards from Islington in Bloom and London in Bloom.

44 14 DOUGHTY STREET, WC1N

London, WC1N 2PL. Gillian Darley & Michael Horowitz QC. *Off Guilford St or Theobalds Rd. Tube: Chancery Lane or Russell Sq. Buses: 19, 38, 55. Garden S of Guilford St on W side of Doughty St with brown LCC plaque to Sidney Smith on house.* **Sun 16 July (2-5.30). Adm £3.50, chd free. Light refreshments at 61 Doughty Street. Also open 61 Doughty Street.**
Small paved rear garden with a wilderness feel, surprisingly since the house opens directly off the street. Medlar tree, vine, plants jostling for space and pots, standing on boards over a redundant pond, add extra interest. Pleasing disorder best describes it.

45 61 DOUGHTY STREET, WC1N

London, WC1N 2JY. Bill Thomas & Teresa Borsuk. *Between Guilford St & Theobald's Rd. Tube: Chancery Lane or Russell Sq. Buses: 19, 38, 55.* **Sun 16 July (2-5.30). Adm £3.50, chd free. Light refreshments. Also open 14 Doughty Street.**
Demolition of offices left a space 40ft wide by 65ft deep at its longest. An acer, two magnolias, viburnum and silk tree flourish, with wisteria, passion flower, akebia (quinata and trifoliate), clematis, jasmine, honeysuckles, parthenocissus, holboelia. Hellebores, two tree peonies, actinidia kolomikta and schizophragma integrifolium. Two ponds and a rill. A space to relax and entertain.

47 48 DUKES AVENUE, N10

Muswell Hill, London, N10 2PU. Margo Buchanan. *Short walk from main Muswell Hill r'about. Tube: Highgate then bus 43 or 134 to Muswell Hill Broadway. W7 bus from Finsbury Park.* **Sun 4 June (2-6). Adm £3.50, chd free. Home-made teas. Also open 55 Dukes Avenue.**
Garden on 3 levels. DOWN to a secret, hidden retreat with ferns and shade tolerant flowering climbers. UP to a paved terrace with lawn and flowerbeds beyond. Specimen plants incl forest pansy and established acers. Planting in complementary colour combinations featuring unusual alliums and perennials, creating a relaxing environment for entertaining and contemplation. Home-made cakes and teas will be served. Gluten free cake available.

46 NEW 55 DUKES AVENUE, N10

Muswell Hill, N10 2PY. Jo de Banzie & Duncan Lampard. *W3 Bus (Alexandra Palace Garden Centre stop) or W7 Bus (Muswell Hill stop). Free on-street parking available on Dukes Av.* **Sun 4 June (2-6). Adm £3.50, chd free. Also open 48 Dukes Avenue.**
A photographer's small town garden uses curves and spheres to add shape and interest to a pretty, shady space. Gravel, paving, decking and a planting platform in an old apple tree create structure, whilst black bamboo, ferns and box provide the backdrop for a gentle palette of white and purple planting. The photographer's botanical photograms and prints will be on display in the house.

GROUP OPENING

48 DULWICH VILLAGE TWO GARDENS, SE21

London, SE21 7BJ. *Rail: N Dulwich or W Dulwich then 10 -15 mins walk. Tube: Brixton then P4 bus, alight Dulwich Picture Gallery stop. Street parking.* **Sun 18 June** (2-5). Combined adm £7, chd free. Home-made teas at 103 Dulwich Village. *Donation to Macmillan Cancer Care.*

103 DULWICH VILLAGE
Mr & Mrs N Annesley.

105 DULWICH VILLAGE
Mr & Mrs A Rutherford.

2 Georgian houses with large gardens, 3 mins walk from Dulwich Picture Gallery and Dulwich Park. 103 Dulwich Village is a country garden in London with a long herbaceous border, lawn, pond, roses and fruit and vegetable gardens. 105 Dulwich Village is a very pretty garden with many unusual plants, lots of old fashioned roses, fish pond and water garden. Amazing collection of plants for sale from both gardens. Teas and delicious home-made cakes.

49 EATON SQUARE GARDEN, SW1W

Eaton Square, London, SW1W 9BD. The Grosvenor Estate, www.grosvenorlondon.com. *Entry to garden via gate opp no. 42 Eaton Sq. Easy walk from Victoria Station or Sloane Sq. Many bus routes passing close to square incl C1, C2, 16, 38, 52 & 73.* **Sat 10 June (10-5). Adm £3, chd free. Light refreshments.**
Thomas Cubitt laid out the 6 formal gardens flanking either side of the Kings Road in 1826 in what was the main approach to Buckingham Palace. Eaton Square Gardens today combines well manicured lawns, shady pathways and mixed borders with quiet seating and contemporary sculptures. The fabulously preserved regency buildings form a fine backdrop, complimented by the square's mature London planes. This is a level access site with paths suitable for wheelchairs running the perimeter of the garden and a hard landscaped central area.

50 41 ECCLESBOURNE ROAD, N1

London, N1 3AF. Steve Bell & Sandie Macrae. *Tube: Highbury & Islington 12 mins walk or 271 bus to Ecclesbourne Rd. Angel tube 15 mins walk or bus 73, 38, 56, 341, 476 to Northchurch Rd. Cross Essex Rd, down Halliford Rd, R on Ecclesbourne Rd.* Sun 4 June (1.30-7). Adm £3.50, chd free. Home-made teas. Also open 37 Alwyne Road.

A delightful, interesting and surprising artists' minimalistic Mediterranean garden complemented by new contemporary architecture. This garden has a hoggin surface with trees and pots on two levels. Many edible plants incl a mature fig tree, young olive and almond trees and a prolific vine. There is a birch, a handkerchief tree, herbs, trailing clematis, roses, and unbelievably, a hand gilded bay.

51 ECCLESTON SQUARE, SW1

London, SW1V 1NP. Roger Phillips & the Residents, www.rogerstreesandshrubs.com. *Off Belgrave Rd nr Victoria Stn, parking allowed on Suns.* Sun 14 May (2-5). Adm £4, chd free. Home-made teas.

Planned by Cubitt in 1828, the 3 acre square is subdivided into mini gardens with camellias, iris, ferns and containers. Dramatic collection of tender climbing roses and 20 different forms of tree peonies. National Collection of ceanothus incl more than 70 species and cultivars. Notable important additions of tender plants being grown and tested. World collection of ceanothus, tea roses and tree peonies.

♿ ❄ [NPC] ☕

52 EDWARDES SQUARE, W8

South Edwardes Square, Kensington, London, W8 6HL. Edwardes Square Garden Committee. *Tube: Kensington High St & Earls Court. Buses: 9, 10, 27, 28, 31, 49 & 74 to Odeon Cinema.* *Entrance in South Edwardes Square.* Sun 23 Apr (11-4.30). Adm £5, chd free. Home-made teas.

One of London's prettiest secluded garden squares. 3½ acres laid out differently from other squares, with serpentine paths by Agostino Agliothe, Italian artist and decorator who lived at no.15 from 1814-1820, and a beautiful Grecian temple which is traditionally the home of the head gardener. Romantic rose tunnel winds through the middle of the garden. Good displays of bulbs and blossom. Tea and home-made cakes, Pimms if sunny. Childrens play area. WC. Good wheelchair access.

♿

53 NEW 27 ELSTREE HILL, BR1

Bromley, BR1 4JE. Carol Davidson. *Nearest station Ravensbourne. Turn off Warren Ave, parking in Elstree Hill (unmade road).* Evening opening Sat 27, Sun 28 May (6-8.30). Adm £6, chd free. Wine. Adm incl glass of wine and nibbles.

A small but beautifully designed modern garden in a difficult space.

Lovely detailing with interesting series of planting terraces formed by shuttered concrete inspired by The National Theatre and Frank Lloyd Wright with imaginative professional planting. Total area from small front space to side terrace and rear garden has been designed as one flowing area. Shed with living green roof.

☕

54 20 EXETER ROAD, NW2

London, NW2 4SP. Theo & Renee Laub. *Mapesbury. Nearest tube Kilburn few mins walk.* Sun 9 July (2-6). Adm £4, chd free. Home-made teas.

Garden designer's nearly new garden started from scratch 4yrs ago. Large by London standards, with many interesting features and unusual plants, sculpture and pots. No lawn, good collection of interesting plants - many perennials grown from seed. Water feature with living wall behind it, recently added!

❄

55 Duke's Avenue

55 ◆ FENTON HOUSE, NW3

Hampstead Grove, Hampstead, NW3 6SP. National Trust, www.nationaltrust.org.uk. *300yds from Hampstead tube. Entrances: Top of Holly Hill & Hampstead Grove.* **For NGS: Evening opening Tue 13 June (6.30-8.30). Adm £10, chd free. Pre-booking essential, please visit www.ngs.org.uk or phone 01483 211535 for information & booking. Wine.** For other opening times and information, please visit garden website.

Join the Gardener-in-Charge for a special evening tour. Andrew Darragh who brings over 10yrs experience from Kew to Fenton House will explore this timeless 1½ acre walled garden. Laid out over 3 levels, and featuring formal areas, a small sunken rose garden, a 300yr old orchard and kitchen garden, Andrew will present the garden and the changes he has made.

GROUP OPENING

56 FOREST HILL GARDENS GROUP, SE23

Forest Hill, London, SE23 3BP. *Off S Circular (A205) behind Horniman Museum & Gardens. Station: Forest Hill, 10 mins walk. Buses: 176, 185, 312, P4.* **Sun 21 May (1-6). Combined adm £7, chd free. Home-made teas.** *Donation to St Christopher's Hospice and Marsha Phoenix Trust.*

Macmillan and the National Garden Scheme, partners for more than 30 years

7 CANONBIE ROAD
June Wismayer.

THE COACH HOUSE, 3 THE HERMITAGE
Pat Rae.

HILLTOP, 28 HORNIMAN DRIVE
Frankie Locke.

27 HORNIMAN DRIVE
Rose Agnew, 020 8699 7710, roseandgraham@talktalk.net. **Visits also by arrangement Apr to Sept small groups welcome.**

53 RINGMORE RISE
Valerie Ward.

25 WESTWOOD PARK
Beth & Steph Falkingham-Blackwell.

Six very different gardens on the highest hill in SE London with spectacular views over London and the Downs. The gardens are within a short walk of each other, but a yellow ballooned 'taxi' service is on hand (donations) for those with mobility problems. Wander in a bee friendly organic flower and fruit haven with vintage summerhouse, gravelled terraces and billowing grasses. See an evolving plantswoman's garden, now with prairie planting in the sunny dry garden contrasting with a new watery fern garden. Also new for 2017: a small meadow, an ever changing story trail for children, and new chicken breeds in an eclectic country style garden. Delight in an artist's studio in an C18 courtyard filled with sculptures and plants and feed the resident robins! Enjoy an embroidery of a garden with vibrant colours and breathtaking views. Unwind with delicious cakes and listen to music from a talented duo amidst the drifting pastel hues of the tea lady's garden inspired by Beth Chatto – and Mary Berry! Great views everywhere. Plants for sale at 25 Westwood Park, 27 Horniman Drive and 7 Canonbie Rd.

57 [NEW] 4 FRANCONIA ROAD, SW14

Abbeville Village, Clapham, London, SW4 9ND. Paul Harris. *From Clapham Common tube, walk 600 metres S to Elms Rd (opp The Windmill hotel) walk along Elms Rd 400 metres to Abbeville Rd, then turn L. Franconia Rd is next on R after 100 metres.* **Sun 4 June (11-5). Adm £3.50, chd free. Light refreshments.**

A private residential garden with a SW aspect. Soil type heavy clay. The garden is a tranquil spot despite the close proximity of neighbours. Receiving sunshine throughout the day, the design offers a shady terrace as well as a sun terrace, separated by a sunken lawn. An exotic planting scheme helps one to escape, whilst being practical for the growing conditions in a London city heat climate. Floating pergola offering shade to the wildlife hotel and concealing the working area.

58 88 FROGNAL, NW3

Frognal, London, NW3 6XB. Mr & Mrs M Linell. *Tube: Hampstead on Northern Line then 7 mins walk. Buses: 46, 268, 13, 113, 82. Garden entrance at 12B Church Row, nr corner with Frognal.* **Sun 18 June (2-5.30). Adm £4, chd free. Home-made teas.**

½ acre garden hidden from view by historic high walls, designed on 2 levels with a terrace and large C19 conservatory near the house leading to lawns, all surrounded by herbaceous borders and ornamental trees, shrubs and climbers, many rare, planted and underplanted for yr round effect. Home propagated plants for sale. Bark chip sloping path gives wheelchair access to main lawn from entrance. Steps elsewhere in garden.

59 9 FURLONG ROAD, N7

Islington, London, N7 8LS. Nigel Watts & Tanuja Pandit. *Close to Highbury & Islington tube station. Tube & Overground: Highbury & Islington, 3 mins walk along Holloway Rd, 2nd L. Furlong Rd joins Holloway Rd & Liverpool Rd. Buses: 43, 271, 393.* Sun 18 June (2-6). Adm £3, chd free. Home-made teas.
Award winning small garden designed by Karen Fitzsimon which makes clever use of an awkwardly shaped plot. Curved lines are used to complement a modern extension. Raised beds contain a mix of tender and hardy plants to give an exotic feel and incl loquat, banana, palm, cycad and tree fern. Contrasting traditional front garden. Beehive. Featured in Small Family Gardens and Modern Family Gardens by Caroline Tilston.

60 GARDEN BARGE SQUARE AT DOWNINGS ROADS MOORINGS, SE1

31 Mill Street, London, SE1 2AX. Mr Nick Lacey. *5 mins walk from Tower Bridge Mill St off Jamaica Rd, between London Bridge & Bermondsey stns, Tower Hill also nearby. Buses: 47, 188, 381, RV1.* Sun 21 May (2-5). Adm £4, chd free. Tea. *Donation to RNLI.*
Series of 7 floating barge gardens connected by walkways and bridges. Gardens have an eclectic range of plants for yr-round seasonal interest. Marine environment: suitable shoes and care needed. Small children must be closely supervised.

61 ◆ THE GARDEN MUSEUM, SE1

Lambeth Palace Road, London, SE1 7LB. The Garden Museum, www.gardenmuseum.org.uk. *E side of Lambeth Bridge. Tube: Lambeth North, Vauxhall, Waterloo. Buses: 507 Red Arrow from Victoria or Waterloo mainline & tube stns, also 3, 77, 344.* For NGS: Sat 9 Sept (10.30-4). Adm £5, chd free. Light refreshments. For other opening times and information, please visit garden website.
Britain's only Museum of Gardens will re-open in spring 2017 after a £6.5 million refurbishment. The centre piece of a new extension will be a new garden designed by Dan Pearson as a contemporary re-interpretation of plant collectors' lust for plants, inspired by the life of John Tradescant, who is buried here. Please note that this will be a newly-planted emerging garden. The new extension incl a new cafe. The Museum curates three major exhibitions each year on the art and design of gardens, and has over fifty events in its public programme. The Museum is accessible for wheelchair users via ramps and access lift.
&

62 9 THE GARDENS, SE22

East Dulwich, London, SE22 9QD. Nigel Watts. *Off Peckham Rye, Dulwich side. Stations: Peckham Rye & Honor Oak, both on Overground. Buses: 12, 37, 63,197, 363. Free parking in square.* Evening opening Wed 19 July (6.30-8.30). Adm £20, chd free. Pre-booking essential, please visit www.ngs.org.uk or phone 01483 211535 for information & booking. Wine.
A plantsman's garden, constantly evolving, with jewel box colours, spectacular grasses and dramatic foliage, all designed to peak magnificently in high summer. A large collection of pots filled with shade loving woodland plants as well as sun loving, half hardy plants. All this contained within a formal framework measuring just 12m by 6m. Talks by owner. Featured in RHS The Garden magazine.

63 69 GLOUCESTER CRESCENT, NW1

Camden, London, NW1 7EG. Sandra Clapham, 020 7485 5764. *Between Regent's Park & Camden Town tube station. Tube: Camden Town 2 mins, Mornington Crescent 10 mins. Metered parking in Oval Rd.* Sun 4 June (2-5.30), also open Royal College of Physicians Medicinal Garden. Sun 6 Aug (2-5.30), also open The Holme. Combined adm with 70 Gloucester Crescent £5, chd free. Visits also by arrangement Apr to Oct.
Delightful little cottage front garden, opening with No.70, selling many of the plants you'll see there. It shows what can be done with a small front garden as a lovely alternative to a concrete parking space. Ursula Vaughan Williams lived here and the very old iceberg rose at the front, the yellow roses, the border of London pride and the crinum powellii rosea lily in a pot are all inherited from her. Many plants have been added since, incl a bed of tomatoes and a delicious 19yr old grape vine, trained up and along the balcony, that produced 8lbs of grape jelly in 2015!
✿

64 70 GLOUCESTER CRESCENT, NW1

London, NW1 7EG. Lucy Gent, 07531 828752 (texts only), gent.lucy@gmail.com. *Between Regent's Park & Camden Town tube station. Tube: Camden Town 2 mins, Mornington Crescent 10 mins. Metered parking in Oval Rd.* Sun 4 June (2-5.30), also open 4 Park Village East (Tower Lodge Gardens). Sun 6 Aug (2-5.30), also open The Holme. Combined adm with 69 Gloucester Crescent £5, chd free. Light refreshments at 4 Park Village East (4 June). Visits also by arrangement Apr to Oct, groups 30 max.
One of four fascinating gardens in NW1 opening on the same day. Here is an oasis in Camden's urban density, where resourceful planting outflanks challenges of space and shade. An August opening shows how wonderful the month can be in a town garden.
✿ 🚗 ☕

65 20 GOLDHAZE CLOSE, IG8

Woodford Green, IG8 7LE. Jenny Richmond. *Off A1009 Broadmead Rd, Orchard Estate Bus Stop for W14.* Sun 30 July (12.30-5). Adm £4, chd free. Home-made teas.
100ft L-shaped landscaped garden bursting with over 100 plants grown in different types of conditions. A huge 29 yr-old eucalyptus resembles

a mature oak with beautiful bark. Paths lined with plants such as a strawberry tree, roses, campsis, penstemons, crocosmia and vegetables (in pots grown from seed in a greenhouse) lead to a secret decked garden for relaxation.

✿ ☕

66 GOLF COURSE ALLOTMENTS, N11

Winton Avenue, London, N11 2AR. GCAA/Haringey, www.golfcourseallotments.co.uk. *Junction of Winton Av & Blake Rd. Tube: Bounds Green. Buses: 102, 184, 299 to Sunshine Garden Centre, Durnsford Rd. Through park to Bidwell Gdns. Straight on up Winton Ave. No cars on site.* **Sun 3 Sept (1-4.30). Adm £3.50, chd free. Light refreshments.**

Large, long established allotment with over 200 plots, some organic. Maintained by culturally diverse community growing wide variety of fruit, vegetables and flowers. Picturesque corners and quirky sheds - a visit feels like being in the countryside. Autumn Flower and Produce Show on Sun 3 Sep features prize winning horticultural and domestic exhibits and beehives. Tours of best plots. Fresh allotment produce, chutneys, jams, honey, cakes and light refreshments for sale. Wheelchair access to main paths only. Gravel and some uneven surfaces. WC incl disabled.

♿ 🐐 ✿ ☕

67 GORDON ROAD ALLOTMENTS, N3

Gordon Road, Finchley, London, N3 1EL. Judy Woollett, www. finchleyhorticulturalsociety.org. uk. *Finchley Central. 10 mins walk from Finchley Central tube. 326 bus. Parking in Gordon Rd & adjacent st. No parking on site.* **Sun 10 Sept (1.30-5.30). Adm £3.50, chd free. Home-made teas.**

Founded in 1940 to promote the interests of gardeners throughout Finchley with over 70 plots. Allotments comprise a mixture of traditional plots and raised beds for those with physical disabilities and for children from local schools. Also a thriving apiary with several

bee hives producing local honey for sale. Tours of best plots. Seasonal vegetables on sale incl perennial flowers. Wheelchair access on main paths only. Disabled WC.

♿ ✿ ☕

68 NEW 21 GOSPATRICK ROAD, N17

London, N17 7EH. Matthew Bradby. *In eastern half of Gospatrick Rd, near junction with Waltheof Ave. Bus 144, 217, 231 or 444 to Gospatrick Road (then cross The Roundway if travelling northbound), or bus 123 or 243 to Waltheof Ave.* **Sun 11 June (2-6). Adm £3.50, chd free. Home-made teas.**

Diverse S-facing 40 metre plot with lawn dominated by large weeping willow, underplanted with fan palms, bamboo, ferns and climbers. Fruit, herb and vegetable garden incl large banana plant, grapevine, olive tree, climbing roses, box hedging, greenhouse and goldfish pond. Patio with exotics in pots. Mainly organic and managed for nature, this is a very tranquil and welcoming garden. Home-made wine dependent on the success of the 2016 vintage.

🐐 ✿ ☕

69 45 GREAT NORTH ROAD, EN5

Barnet, EN5 1EJ. Ron & Miriam Raymond, 07880 500617, ron.raymond91@yahoo.co.uk. *1m S of Barnet High St, 1m N of Whetstone. Tube: Midway between High Barnet & Totteridge & Whetstone stns. Buses 34, 234, 263, 326, alight junction Great N Rd & Lyonsdown Rd. 45 Great North Rd is on the corner of Cherry Hill.* **Sun 6 Aug (2-6). Adm £2.50, chd free. Home-made teas. Visits also by arrangement July & Aug.**

45 Great North Road is designed to give a riot of colour during July. The 90ft × 90ft cottage style front garden is packed with interesting perennials. Tiered stands line the side entrance with over 64 pots displaying a variety of flowering and foliage plants. The rear garden incl nearly 100 tubs and hanging baskets. Small pond surrounded by tiered beds. Magnificent named tuberous begonias. Children's fun trail for 3-6yr

olds and adult garden quiz with prizes. Partial wheelchair access.

♿ 🐐 ✿ ☕

70 17 GREENSTONE MEWS, E11

Wanstead, London, E11 2RS. Mr & Mrs S Farnham. *Wanstead. Tube: Snaresbrook or Wanstead, 5 mins walk. Bus: 101, 308, W12, W14 to Wanstead High St. Greenstone Mews is accessed via Voluntary Place which is off Spratt Hall Road.* **Mon 29 May (12.30-5). Adm £5. Light refreshments.**

Coloured Slate paved garden (20ft × 17ft). Height provided by a mature strawberry tree. Sunken reused bath now a fishpond surrounded by climbers clothing fences underplanted with herbs, vegetables, shrubs and perennials grown from cuttings. Ideas aplenty for small space gardening. Home-made cakes, savoury snacks available. Books for sale. Regret, garden unsuitable for children. Wheelchair access through garage. Limited turning space.

♿ ✿ ☕

71 7 THE GROVE, N6

Highgate Village, London, N6 6JU. Mr Thomas Lyttelton, 07713 638161. *Between Highgate West Hill & Hampstead Lane. Tube: Archway or Highgate. Buses: 143, 210, 214 and 271.* **Sun 12 Feb (11-3). Adm £5, chd free. Light refreshments. Sun 19 Feb (11-3). Adm £5, chd free. Light refreshments. Also open 33 Wood Vale. Sun 9 Apr, Sun 11 June (2-5.30). Adm £4, chd free. Home-made teas. Visits also by arrangement Apr to Oct, refreshments on request.** *Donation to The Harington Scheme.*

½ acre garden designed for yr-round interest making a tapestry of greens and yellows. A wild garden with mature trees giving a woodland feel. Brilliant for hide and seek and young explorers. Water garden, 19 paths, vistas and views galore. Snowdrops in February. Exceptional camellias and magnolia in the spring. The garden has been open for the NGS for 60 consecutive yrs!

♿ 🚗 ☕

72 24 GROVE PARK, SE5
Camberwell, SE5 8LH. Clive Pankhurst, www.alternative-planting.blogspot.com. *Chadwick Rd end of Grove Park. Stns: Peckham Rye or Denmark Hill, both 10 mins walk. Easy bus from Oval (185) or Elephant and Castle (176, 40). Good street parking.* **Sun 3 Sept (2-5.30). Adm £3.50, chd free. Home-made teas.**
A jungle of lush big leafed plants, ponds and Southeast Asian influences. Towering paulownias, bananas, dahlias, tetrapanax and exotica transport you to the tropics. Huge hidden garden gives unexpected size. Lawn and lots of hidden corners give spaces to sit and enjoy. Renowned for delicious home-made cake. Featured on BBC Gardeners World, BBC Instant Gardener and in the Independent.

🐃 ✿ ☕ 💷

73 NEW 25 HALLOWELL ROAD, HA6
Northwood, HA6 1DT. Marietta Richardson. *5 mins walk from Northwood underground station. Parking available in Hallowell Road or nearby Chester Road.* **Sun 11 June (2-6). Adm £3.50, chd free. Home-made teas.**
A long narrow garden transformed into a beautiful tranquil space alive with the sound of bees and insects. The garden features deep herbaceous borders with all season interest. Roses, irises and geraniums are followed by a host of other perennials. The garden has a camomile lawn and productive fruit and vegetable plot. Yarn dyed with garden plants available to view. Tea and cakes available.

✿ ☕ 💷

74 116 HAMILTON TERRACE, NW8
London, NW8 9UT. Mr & Mrs I B Kathuria, 020 7625 6909, gkathuria@hotmail.co.uk. *Tube: Maida Vale (5 mins) or St Johns Wood (10 mins) Buses: 16, 98 to Maida Vale, 139, 189 to Abbey Rd. Free parking on Sundays.* **Evening opening Sun 28 May, Sun 9 July (4-8). Adm £5, chd free. Wine. Visits also by arrangement**

May to July. Donation to St. Mark's Church.
Lush front garden full of dramatic foliage, a water feature and tree ferns. Large back garden on different levels with Yorkshire stone paving, many large pots and containers, water feature and lawn. Wide variety of perennials and flowering shrubs, many unusual and subtropical plants, succulents, acers, ferns, climbers, roses, and prizewinning hostas. A great example of container gardening and plants of varied foliage and texture.

🚗 ☕

GROUP OPENING

75 HAMPSTEAD GARDEN SUBURB GARDENS, NW11
London, NW11 6YJ. *Golders Green. Car A1 & A406 Henley's Corner. Tube Golders Green, Bus H2, 82,102,460 to Temple Fortune. Tickets & map from 86 Willifield Way or 1 Asmuns Hill via Hampstead Way.* **Sun 25 June (12-5.30). Combined adm £8.50, chd free. Home-made teas at Fellowship House, Willifield Way.**

NEW 53 ADDISON WAY
Jeanette Jones.

4 ASMUNS HILL
Peter & Yvonne Oliver, 020 8455 8741, yvonne.oliver17@gmail.com. **Visits also by arrangement May to Aug groups 20 max. Adm incl tea & cake.**

48 ERSKINE HILL
Marjorie & David Harris, 020 8455 6507, marjorieharris@btinternet.com. **Visits also by arrangement May to Sept no min, max 20.**

NEW 94 HAMPSTEAD WAY
Patsy Larsen.

NEW 85 NORTHWAY
Susan Fischgrund.

94 OAKWOOD ROAD
Michael & Adrienne Franklin, 07836 541383, mikefrank@onetel.com. **Visits also by arrangement May & June, please phone or email.**

NEW WILLIFIELD WAY TF HILL ALLOTMENT
Ruth Beedle.

74 WILLIFIELD WAY
David Weinberg.

86 WILLIFIELD WAY
Diane Berger, 020 8455 0455, dianeberger@hotmail.co.uk. **Visits also by arrangement June to Sept for groups 10+.**

NEW 32 WORDSWORTH WALK
Chris Page.

A unique opportunity to explore one of the best known garden suburbs in England. Hampstead Garden Suburb is an oasis of 'sylvan restfulness' in the midst of a city. Surrounded by ancient woods and adjacent to Hampstead Heath, the Suburb is noted for its Arts and Crafts architecture. In the gardens behind the artisan cottages discover a riot of colour and array of planting schemes, seamlessly emerging from the borrowed woodland landscape beyond. Discover a hidden allotment site enclosed within the Suburb's signature hedges. Walk from the top of Erskine Hill, through Big Wood where Henry VIII hunted game, to two gardens in Oakwood Road. Many of the gardens can be accessed through a network of leafy twittens, or footpaths, that traverse the Suburb. Take afternoon tea by the village green. Children's Treasure Trail. Award winning gardens 86 Willifield Way, 48 Erskine Hill and 4 Asmuns Hill visited by Prince Edward, Earl of Wessex in his role as patron of the London Gardens Society. 74 Willifield Way, 32 Wordsworth Walk, 94 Oakwood Road are regular winners of Suburb in Bloom. Partial wheelchair access to several gardens.

♿ ✿ ☕

Your visit helps Marie Curie work night and day in people's homes

GROUP OPENING

76 HAMPTON HILL GARDENS, TW12
Hampton Hill, TW12 1DW. *3m from Twickenham. 4m from Kingston-upon-Thames. Between A312 (Uxbridge Rd) & A313 (Park Rd). Bus: 285 from Kingston stops on Uxbridge Rd, Windmill Rd Stop. Stn: Fulwell 15 mins walk.* Sat 27, Sun 28 May (2-5). Combined adm £5, chd free. Light refreshments at 30 St James's Road and 16 Links View Road.

18 CRANMER ROAD
Bernard Wigginton.

NEW 16 LINKS VIEW ROAD
Virginia Lewis.

30 ST JAMES'S ROAD
Jean Burman.

WAYSIDE
Mr Steve Croft.

4 gardens of diverse interest in an attractive West London suburb. With the backdrop of St James's Church spire, 18 Cranmer Rd is a colourful garden with herbaceous and exotic borders and a WW2 air raid shelter transformed as rockery and water garden with azaleas, helianthemums and foliage plants. The SE facing garden at 30 St James's Rd is subdivided into 5 rooms. Decking with seating leads to ponds surrounded by grasses and shrubs and an African themed thatched exterior sitting room. 25 St James's Rd is a large urban garden divided into several areas, the entire garden is planted to attract wildlife with 2 wildlife ponds, mixed herbaceous borders, water feature, urns and pots. 16 Links Rd is a new addition to the group this year and has many interesting features. Partial wheelchair access.
& 🐕 ☕

77 77 HANDSWORTH ROAD, N17
London, N17 6DB. Serge Charles. *Seven Sisters/Turnpike Lane 15 mins walk from either station or take W4 bus from T Lane, alight Broadwater Lodge stop. 230 bus first stop Philip Lane L into Handsworth Rd. Free parking.* Sun 11 June (2-6). Adm £2.50, chd free. Home-made teas at 159 Higham Road. Also open 159 Higham Road.
Narrow front garden is home to bamboos, roses and clematis which screen a secret knot garden of box. Container planted trees incl olive, mimosa and myrtle. Shady path, planted with a wide range of rare and unusual ferns and shade tolerant plants leads to a tiny back garden where the bamboos reach 25ft underplanted with tree ferns. Many other interesting plants and features inc sculptures.
❀ ☕

78 NEW 74 HARFIELD GARDENS, SE5
Grove Lane, Camberwell, SE5 8DB. Mrs Anne Jewitt. *Off Stories Road. Buses: 185, 176, 40 & 474. Nearest station is Denmark Hill.* Sun 11 June (2-5.30). Adm £3.50, chd free. Home-made teas. Also open 174 Peckham Rye.
Pergola with old roses provides the focal point in this small garden enclosed by high walls and fences disguised by climbers, making a peaceful green space. Shrubs incl a dark cut-leaf elder and viburnum plicatum and the formally edged lawn holds it together and adds an element of control.
☕

79 37 HAROLD ROAD, E11
Leytonstone, London, E11 4QX. Dr Matthew Jones Chesters. *Tube: Leytonstone exit L subway 5 mins walk. Overground: Leytonstone High Rd 5 mins walk. Buses: 257 & W14. Parking at station or limited on street.* Sun 30 July (1-5). Adm £3.50, chd free. Home-made teas.
50ft x 60ft pretty corner garden arranged around 7 fruit trees. Fragrant climbers, woodland plants and shade tolerant fruit along north wall. Fastigiate trees protect raised vegetable beds and herb rockery. Long lawn bordered by roses and perennials on one side; prairie plants on the other. Patio with raised pond, palms and rhubarb. Planting designed to produce fruit, fragrance and lovely memories. Plant list and garden plan available. Home-made cakes and preserves.
☕

80 NEW 12 HAYWOOD CLOSE, HA5
Pinner, HA5 3LQ. Brenda & Roy Jakes. *Approx ½ m from Pinner Met Line off Elm Park Rd. From Northwood, Stanmore, Harrow & Watford head towards Pinner Green & look for signs. Haywood Close is narrow; suggest parking in Elm Park Rd.* Sun 11 June (2-5). Adm £3.50, chd free. Home-made teas.
Suburban garden newly created by enthusiastic, plantaholic owners. Herbaceous perennial borders surround oval lawn. The garden contains over 50 varieties of roses and clematis, a covered rose walk, gazebo, sink garden, pleached hornbeam trees with box collars and a small vegetable and fruit garden. Seating areas to rest and relax. Many annuals and perennials grown by owner from seeds or cuttings. Most of garden wheelchair accessible.
& ❀ ☕

81 31 HENDON AVENUE, N3
Finchley, London, N3 1UJ. Sandra Tomaszewska. *Finchley Central. 15 mins walk from Finchley Central Tube. Buses: 326 & 143. Car: 5 mins from A1 via Hendon Ln. No parking restrictions on Sun.* Sun 4 June (2-6). Adm £4, chd free. Home-made teas.
An extensive garden with mature trees, shrubs and perennials divided into areas. Herbaceous beds in semi shade, a raised triangular bed with lavender, agapanthus and roses. Two arches, draped with grapevines, wisteria, kiwi and clematis, guide you into a tranquil, white garden and a wildlife pond, lead to tropical and Mediterranean beds with olive, bean and fig trees, palms, bamboos and cannas. Refreshments served from the pool house; relax by the pool in the tropical garden. Partial wheelchair access.
& ☕

82 159 HIGHAM ROAD, N17

Downhills Park, Tottenham, N17 6NX. Jess Kitley & Sally Gray. *Tube: Turnpike Lane then 15 mins walk/W4 alight Higham Rd or Seven Sisters then 41 bus alight Philip Lane, walk up through Downhills Park. Buses 341, 230,41,W4. Free parking on Higham Rd.* Sun 11 June (2-6). Adm £3.50, chd free. Home-made teas. Also open 77 Handsworth Road.

This 80ft x 30ft garden, incorporating sculptural elements amongst dense planting with shrubs, perennials and grasses demonstrating a unity of design and materials. Areas to sit, contemplate and enjoy as birds, bees and butterflies abound. A natural wildlife pond dug into clay harnesses natural springs, mitigating constant flooding. Backing on to woodland, big skies...and this is Tottenham!

83 32 HIGHBURY PLACE, N5

London, N5 1QP. Michael & Caroline Kuhn. *Highbury Fields. Highbury & Islington Tube; Overground & National Rail. Buses: 4, 19, 30, 43, 271, 393 to Highbury Corner. 3 mins walk up Highbury Place which is opp stn.* Sun 18 June (2-6). Adm £4, chd free. Home-made teas.

This 80ft long garden lies behind a C18 terrace house. An upper York stone terrace leads down to a larger terrace surrounded by overfilled beds of cottage garden style planting. Further steps lead to a lawn by a rill and an end terrace. A large willow tree dominates the garden which also has amerlanchiers and fruit trees as well as dwarf acers, a winter flowering cherry, lemon trees and a magnolia.

84 HIGHWOOD ASH, NW7

Highwood Hill, Mill Hill, NW7 4EX. Mr & Mrs R Gluckstein. *Totteridge & Whetstone on Northern line, then bus 251 stops outside - Rising Sun/Mill Hill stop. By car: A5109 from Apex Corner to Whetstone. Garden located opp The Rising Sun PH.* Sun 14 May (2-5.30). Adm £4.50, chd free. Tea.

Created over the last 50yrs, this 3¼ acre garden features rolling lawns, two large interconnecting ponds with koi, herbaceous and shrub borders and a modern gravel garden. A garden for all seasons with many interesting plants and sculptures. A country garden in London. Garden of the Week in Garden News. Partial access for wheelchairs, lowest parts too steep.

85 THE HOLME, NW1

Inner Circle, Regents Park, NW1 4NT. Lessee of The Crown Commission. *In centre of Regents Park on The Inner Circle. Within 15 mins walk from Great Portland St or Baker St Underground Stations, opp Regents Park Rose Garden Cafe.* Sat 24, Sun 25 June, Sat 5, Sun 6 Aug (2.30-5.30). Adm £5, chd free.

4 acre garden filled with interesting and unusual plants. Sweeping lakeside lawns intersected by islands of herbaceous beds. Extensive rock garden with waterfall, stream and pool. Formal flower garden with unusual annual and half hardy plants, sunken lawn, fountain pool and arbour. Gravel paths and some steps which gardeners will help wheelchair users to negotiate.

&

86 33 HUDDLESTON ROAD, N7

London, N7 0AD. Gilly Hatch & Tom Gretton. *5 mins from Tufnell Park Tube. Tube: Tufnell Park. Buses: 4, 134, 390 to Tufnell Park. Follow Tufnell Park Rd to 3rd rd on R.* Sun 2 July (2-6). Adm £3.50, chd free. Home-made teas. Also open 30 Mercers Road.

The rambunctious front garden weaves together perennials, grasses and ferns, while the back garden makes a big impression in a small space. After 40yrs, the lawn is now a wide curving path, a deep sunny bed on one side, mixing shrubs and perennials in an ever changing blaze of colour, on the other, a screen of varied greens and textures. This flowery passage leads to a secluded sitting area. Exhibition of paintings and hand-made prints by Gilly Hatch, with 10% of sales going to the NGS.

87 60 & 62 HUNGERFORD ROAD, N7

London, N7 9LP. John Gilbert, Lynne Berry & Frances Pine. *Between Camden Town & Holloway. Tube: Caledonian Rd, 6 mins walk. Buses: 29 & 253 to Hillmarton Rd stop in Camden Rd. Also 17, 91, 259, 393 to Hillmarton Rd. 10 to York Way.* Sun 18 June (2-6). Adm £5, chd free. Tea. Also open 1a Hungerford Road.

Joint opening of two contrasting gardens behind a Victorian terrace. No. 62 is a densely planted mature garden designed to maximise space for planting and create several different sitting areas, views and moods. Professional garden designer's own garden. No 60 is a family garden with a large lawn and a good range of shrubs, flowering perennials and trees. Together they form an inspiring oasis.

❄ ☕

88 1A HUNGERFORD ROAD, N7

London, N7 9LA. David Matzdorf, davidmatzdorf@blueyonder.co.uk, www.growingontheedge.net. *Between Camden Town & Holloway. Tube: Caledonian Rd. Buses: 17, 29, 91, 253, 259, 274, 390 & 393. Parking free on Sundays.* Sun 18 June (12-6). Adm £3, chd free. Also open 23 Penn Road. Visits also by arrangement Apr to Oct.

Unique eco house with walled, lush front garden in modern exotic style, densely planted with palms, acacia, bamboo, ginger lilies, bananas, ferns, yuccas, abutilons and unusual understorey plants. Floriferous and ambitious green roof resembling Mediterranean or Mexican hillside, planted with yuccas, dasylirions, agaves, aloes, flowering shrubs, euphorbias, grasses, alpines, sedums and aromatic herbs. Sole access to roof is via built in ladder. Garden and roof each 50ft x 18ft. Featured on Gardeners' World.

89 THE HURLINGHAM CLUB, SW6

Ranelagh Gardens, London, SW6 3PR. The Members of the Hurlingham Club, www.hurlinghamclub.org.uk. *Main gate at E end of Ranelagh Gardens. Tube: Putney Bridge (110yds). NB: No onsite parking. Meter parking on local streets & restricted parking on Sats (9-5).* Sat 6 May (10-5). Adm £5, chd free. Light refreshments in the Napier Servery in the East Wing.

Rare opportunity to visit this 42 acre jewel with many mature trees, 2 acre lake with water fowl, expansive lawns and a river walk. Capability Brown and Humphry Repton were involved with landscaping. The gardens are renowned for their roses, herbaceous and lakeside borders, shrubberies and stunning bedding displays. The riverbank is a haven for wildlife with native trees, shrubs and wild flowers. Garden Tours at 11am and 2pm - ticketed event, tickets available at entrance.

&. ☕

90 [NEW] HURST HOUSE, IG8

1 Broomhill Walk, Woodford Green, IG8 9HF. Nicola & Nicolas Munday, www.hursthousewoodford.com. *Overlooking southern tip of Woodford Green nr statue of Sir Winston Churchill. Private rd directly in front of house for drop off & pick up only. Parking in nearby rds.* Mon 1 May (2-5). Adm £5, chd free. Light refreshments.

Large, tranquil walled garden behind Queen Anne house. Well structured with York stone balustraded terrace leading to formal lawn and rose garden separated by an informal glade. Many of the trees and shrubs incl a weeping silver pear tree and handkerchief tree date back to 1954 to designs by Percy Cane (a well known Essex born designer). Temple portico at end of central axis. Weathered marble sculpture of Venus and Cupid in rose garden pond. A variety of areas for sitting and enjoying the different aspects of the garden. Featured in South Woodford Village Gazette - The

Importance of Hurst House. Garden accessed by gentle slopes and mainly level.

&. 🐄 ☕

91 9 IMBER PARK ROAD, KT10

Esher, KT10 8JB. Jane & John McNicholas. *½m from centre of Esher. From the A307, turn into Station Rd which becomes Ember Lane. Go past Esher train station on R. Take 3rd rd on R into Imber Park Rd.* Sun 25 June (1-5). Adm £3.50, chd free. Home-made teas.

An established cottage style garden, designed and maintained by the owners who are passionate about gardening and plants. The garden is S-facing, with well stocked, colourful herbaceous borders containing a wide variety of perennials, evergreen and deciduous shrubs, a winding lawn area and a small garden retreat.

 ✿ ☕

92 23 IMPERIAL ROAD, N22

London, N22 8DE. Kate Gadsby. *Off Bounds Green Rd between Bounds Green Tube & Wood Green Tube. 5 mins from Alexandra Palace mainline.* Sun 1 Oct (12.30-4.30). Adm £2.50, chd free. Home-made teas.

Tiny back garden overflowing with interesting and unusual plants where an inventive and inspiring approach to planting, has created a surprising number of perspectives. An early October opening to show how many varieties of aster can be fitted into a very small space. Semi covered deck allows enjoyment in sun and rain.

✿ ☕

93 THE INNER AND MIDDLE TEMPLE GARDENS, EC4

Crown Office Row, Inner Temple, London, EC4Y 7HL. The Honourable Societies of the Inner and Middle Temples, www.innertemple.org.uk/www. middletemple.org.uk. *London. Entrance: Main Garden Gate on Crown Office Row, access via Tudor*

Street gate or Middle Temple Lane gate. Tue 13 June (11.30-3). Adm £50. Pre-booking essential, please visit www.ngs.org.uk or phone 01483 211535 for information & booking. Light refreshments.

Inner Temple Garden is a haven of tranquillity and beauty with a sweeping lawns, unusual trees and charming woodland areas. The well known herbaceous border shows off inspiring plant combinations from early spring through to autumn. The award winning gardens of Middle Temple are comprised of a series of courtyards and one larger formal garden. Each courtyard has its own character and continues to offer peaceful respite from the bustle of central London as they have for centuries. **Adm incl conducted tour of the gardens by Head Gardeners. Light lunch in Middle Hall, one of the finest examples of an Elizabethan hall in the country.** Please advise in advance if wheelchair access is required.

&. ☕

94 55 JENNINGS ROAD, SE22

East Dulwich, London, SE22 9JU. Ms Antonia Schofield. *Train: North or East Dulwich 15 mins walk. Buses: 40, 185 & 176 along Lordship Lane, off alight Heber Rd stop.* Sun 23 July (2-6). Adm £3, chd free. Light refreshments.

A garden designer with a passion for plants, especially large leafed architectural ones, has used her small garden to experiment with unusual plants giving a tropical effect. The very sunny S-facing garden has been packed with giant plants to create a little tropical paradise. Favourite plants are tetrapanax, a real showstopper with leaves nearly a metre wide, Paulownia tomentosa coppiced to grow enormous foliage; hardy palm Trachycarpus fortunei and fig trees grown for their large scented leaves and their delicious fruit.

GROUP OPENING

95 KEW GREEN GARDENS, TW9

Kew, TW9 3AH. *NW side of Kew Green. Tube: Kew Gardens. Mainline stn: Kew Bridge. Buses: 65, 391. Entrance via riverside.* Sun 28 May (2-5). Combined adm £6, chd free. Evening opening Sun 4 June (6-8). Combined adm £8, chd free. Wine.

65 KEW GREEN
Giles & Angela Dixon.

67 KEW GREEN
Lynne & Patrick Lynch.

69 KEW GREEN
John & Virginia Godfrey.

71 KEW GREEN
Mr & Mrs Jan Pethick.

73 KEW GREEN
Sir Donald & Lady Elizabeth Insall.

Five long gardens behind a row of C18 houses on the Green, close to the Royal Botanic Gardens. These gardens feature the profusely planted and traditional borders of a mature English country garden, and contrast formal gardens, terraces and lawns, laid out around tall old trees, with wilder areas and woodland and wild flower planting. One has an unusual architect designed summerhouse, while another offers the surprise of a modern planting of espaliered miniature fruit trees.

🐾 ❀ ☕

96 KING HENRY'S WALK GARDEN, N1

11c King Henry's Walk, London, N1 4NX. Friends of King Henry's Walk Garden, www.khwgarden.org.uk. *Buses incl: 21, 30, 38, 56, 141, 277. Behind adventure playground on KHW, off Balls Pond Rd.* Mon 1 May (2-4.30). Adm £3.50, chd free. Home-made teas. *Donation to Friends of KHW Garden.*

Vibrant ornamental planting welcomes the visitor to this hidden oasis and leads you into a verdant community garden with secluded woodland area, beehives, wildlife pond, wall trained fruit trees, and plots used by local residents to grow their own fruit and vegetables. Disabled WC.

♿ ❀ ☕

97 LAMBETH PALACE, SE1

Lambeth Palace Road, London, SE1 7JU. The Church Commissioners, www.archbishopofcanterbury.org. *Entrance via Main Gatehouse facing Lambeth Bridge. Station: Waterloo. Tube: Westminster, Vauxhall all 10 mins walk. Buses: 3, C10, 77, 344, 507.* Evening opening Wed 24 May (5.30-8). Adm £5 chd free. Wine.

Lambeth Palace has one of the oldest and largest private gardens in London. It has been occupied by Archbishops of Canterbury since 1197. Formal courtyard boasts historic White Marseilles fig planted in 1556. Parkland style garden features mature trees, woodland and native planting, orchard and pond. There is a formal rose terrace, summer gravel border, scented chapel garden and active beehives. Tours will be available. Ramped path to rose terrace, disabled WC.

♿ 🐕 ❀ ☕

98 12 LANSDOWNE ROAD, W11

London, W11 3LW. The Lady Amabel Lindsay. *Tube: Holland Park. Buses: 12, 88, 94, 148, GL711, 715 to Holland Park, 4 mins walk up Lansdowne Rd.* Sun 14 May (2-6). Adm £5, chd free. Light refreshments. Also open Arundel & Ladbroke Gardens.

A country garden in the heart of London. An old mulberry tree, billowing borders, rambling Rosa banksiae, a greenhouse of climbing geraniums and a terrace filled with tender perennials. Partial wheelchair access.

♿ ☕

99 42 LATIMER ROAD, E7

Forest Gate, E7 0LQ. Janet Daniels. *8 mins walk from Forest Gate or Wanstead Park stn. From Forest Gate cross to Sebert Rd, then 3rd rd on L.* Sat 22, Sun 23 July (11-4.30). Adm £3.50, chd free. Saturday parking restrictions apply - free parking on Sunday. Home-made teas.

Passionate plant collector's garden in two separate areas. First (90ft × 15ft) has an abundance of baskets, climbers, shrubs, fruit trees and koi carp pond. Step down to large secret garden (70ft × 30ft) containing exuberant borders, wildlife pond with gunnera, walnut tree and Paulownia tree. Unusual and exotic plants and other quirky features. Wildlife friendly. Summerhouse full of collectables, dinky toys and collection of old wooden tools.

❀ 🚗 ☕

100 L'ESCALE, WD6

Barnet Lane, Elstree, Borehamwood, WD6 3QZ. Graham & Jacqueline Colover. *200 metres W of junction with Deacons Hill Rd on N side. Leave Stirling Corner r'about on A1 towards Elstree, next r'about 1st exit towards Elstree village. From Elstree/Borehamwood Station cross bridge 1st L Deacons Hill Road.* Sun 18 June (2-6). Adm £4, chd free. Cream teas.

Gentle hillside garden on clay soil, featuring live steam gauge 1 model railway, complete with station house, weaving through deep borders abundant with drifts of perennials and shrubs. Enter through densely planted terraces with steps leading down to railway garden, wild flower garden and wildlife ponds. Plantswoman's joy, the garden has developed over the last 2yrs as a celebration of life. Enjoy home-made teas on the main terrace overlooking the gardens and beyond. Children must be closely supervised at all times.

☕

101 NEW 2 LITTLEBURY ROAD, SW4

Clapham, SW4 6DN. Jack Wallington & Christopher Anderson, www.jackwallington.com. *2 mins from Clapham High Street station, 4 mins walk from Clapham North &*

Clapham Common. From main high st, head down Clapham Manor St, turn R down Voltaire Rd past leisure centre. Take 1st L on Littlebury Rd, house on R. **Sun 23 July (1-5), also open 35 Turret Grove. Sun 10 Sept (1-5). Adm £3.50, chd free. Home-made teas.**

Small garden, creatively packed with bright colours and interesting plants. Features a living wall of 50 fern species, a micro-pond, tropical plants and quirky indoor plants. In July colour comes from monad, clematis, acanthus, salvia and aliums. September opening sees Dahlias in triumphant, unmissable glory. Owned by a garden designer/ blogger who uses his garden as a trial ground for new ideas. Fern wall planned and constructed by us to house my collection of many rare and unusual fern species. Plants in every part of the house, from the front, through rooms and out to the garden. Cut flowers from Jack's allotment. Featured on series two of Monty Don's Big Dreams, Small Spaces on the BBC.

102 49 LOFTUS ROAD, W12
London, W12 7EH. Emma Plunket, emma@plunketgardens.com, www.plunketgardens.com. *Shepherds Bush or Shepherds Bush Market tube, train or bus to Uxbridge*

Rd. Free street parking. *Evening opening Tue 13 June (5.30-8). Adm £4, chd free. Wine.* **Visits also by arrangement May to Oct.**

Professional garden designer, Emma Plunket, opens her acclaimed walled garden. Richly planted, it is the ultimate hard working city garden with all year structure and colour; fruit, vegetables and herbs. Set against a backdrop of trees, it is unexpectedly open and peaceful. Garden plan, plant list and advice.

D ☕

GROUP OPENING

103 LONDON FIELDS GARDENS, E8
Hackney, London, E8 3LS. *On W side of London Fields park. Short walk from Haggerston stn, London Overground; or London Fields stn (from Liverpool St); or Bethnal Green tube & bus 106 or 254 towards Hackney; or Angel tube & bus 38, 56.* **Sun 18 June (2-6). Combined adm £6, chd free. Home-made teas at 84 Lavender Grove.**

84 LAVENDER GROVE
Anne Pauleau.

36 MALVERN ROAD
Kath Harris.

84 MIDDLETON ROAD
Penny Fowler.

Three gardens in London Fields, an area which takes its name from fields on the London side of the old village of Hackney. They are unexpected havens from the city's hustle and bustle, with an exciting range and variety of colours, scents and design. This year we have a courtyard garden, a scented cottage garden and a very unusual, long and secret garden where sculptures mingle with vegetation. Children's quiz. The beautiful, mysterious and fascinating garden in Middleton Road was featured in House of Hackney's advertising campaign last year.

🐾 ✿ ☕

GROUP OPENING

104 LOWER CLAPTON GARDENS, E5
Hackney, London, E5 0RL. *10 mins walk from Hackney Central or Hackney Downs stns. Buses 38, 55, 106, 253, 254 or 425, alight Lower Clapton Rd.* **Sun 4 June (2-6). Combined adm £5, chd free. Home-made teas at 16 Powerscroft Rd.**

8 ALMACK ROAD
Philip Lightowlers.

16 POWERSCROFT ROAD
Elizabeth Welch.

NEW 77 RUSHMORE ROAD
Penny Edwards.

Lower Clapton is an area of mid Victorian terraces sloping down to the R Lea. This group of gardens reflect their owner's tastes and interests. New this year is No. 77 Rushmore Rd which features a fruit and vegetable garden and wildlife pond. At No. 16 Powerscroft Rd we have a S-facing garden with a raised pond, space for meditation and mixed borders. No. 8 Almack Rd is a long thin garden with two different rooms, one incl a classic blue agave named Audrey.

✿ ☕

12 Haywood Close

GROUP OPENING

105 LYNDHURST SQUARE GROUP, SE15

Lyndhurst Square, London, SE15 5AR. Group Gardens. *Overground to Peckham Rye station; numerous bus routes.* **Sun 18 June (1.30-5). Combined adm £5, chd free. Home-made teas at 4 Lyndhurst Sq. Also open Dulwich Village Two Gardens.** *Donation to MIND.*

4 LYNDHURST SQUARE
Amelia Thorpe & Adam Russell.

5 LYNDHURST SQUARE
Martin Lawlor & Paul Ward.

6 LYNDHURST SQUARE
Iain Henderson & Amanda Grygelis.

7 LYNDHURST SQUARE
Pernille Ahlström & Barry Joseph.

4 very attractive gardens open in this small, elegant square of 1840s listed villas located in Peckham SE London. Each approx 90ft × 50ft has its own shape and style as the Square curves in a U shape. No. 4 is for a family, with a generous lawn, vegetables and herbs, and mature fruit trees adding lushness. At No. 5, the design combines Italianate and Gothic themes with roses, lavender, olives, euphorbia and ferns within yew and box parterres. Plants for sale here. No. 6 is an up to date family garden given drama with architectural plants. A wisteria pergola frames the vegetables bordered by espaliered apples. Check out the treehouse! Simplicity, Swedish style, is key at No. 7, with roses and raised beds, framed by yew hedges.

106 NEW 16 MAIDA WAY, E4

Chingford, E4 7JL. Mr & Mrs Francis. *1m from Chingford town centre off Kings Head Hill. Maida Way is a cul-de-sac off Maida Avenue that can be accessed via Kings Head Hill or Sewardstone Road.* **Sun 2 July (12-5). Adm £3.50, chd free.**

Light refreshments. Three distinct areas. Walled patio with raised beds of ferns, climbers, hostas and patio planters. Steps up to middle garden with a large koi pond, seating area, acers, shrubs, herbaceous plants, grasses and grapevine. Top garden reached via archway in a the bay hedge. Kitchen garden with raised beds of fruit trees and bushes, herbs and vegetables. Numerous retro artefacts creatively upcycled. Wheelchair access to patio area only.

107 NEW 4 MANNINGTREE ROAD, HA4

Ruislip, HA4 0ES. Costas Lambropoulos & Roberto Haddon. *Manningtree Road is just off Victoria Road, 10 mins walk from South Ruislip tube station.* **Sun 23 July (2-6). Adm £4, chd free.** Light refreshments. Compact garden with an exotic feel that combines hardy architectural plants with more tender ones. A feeling of a small oasis incl plants like Musa Basjoo, Ensette Montbelliardii, tree ferns, black bamboo etc. Potted mediterranean plants on the patio incl a fig tree and two olive trees. Home-made cakes and savoury pastries available.

108 NEW 53 MANOR ROAD, N16

Stoke Newington, N16 5BH. Jonathan Trustram. *Nr Stoke Newington station & Heathland Rd 106 bus stop.* **Sun 30 July (11-5). Adm £3.50, chd free. Home-made teas.**
Big garden for London, thickly enclosed by ivy, roses and jasmine, crowded with plants, many unusual: eryngiums, salvias, pelargoniums, eucomis, inulas, lilies, indigofera, azara etc. The myrtle, a site of pilgrimage for thousands of honey bees, at the end of July. Small sculptural rock garden. Tiny geological treasures. Soft fruit. Organic credentials finally lost in 30yrs war against slugs.

GROUP OPENING

109 NEW MAPLEDENE GARDENS, E8

Mapledene Road, Hackney, E8 3JW. *7 mins walk from 67, 149, 242, 243 (Middleton Rd stop), 10 mins from 30, 38 55 (Dalston Lane), 7 mins from Haggerston Overground. Also 10 mins walk through London Fields from Mare St buses.* **Sun 9 July (2-6). Combined adm £5, chd free. Home-made teas at 61 Mapledene Road.**

53 MAPLEDENE ROAD
Tigger Cullinan.

NEW 55 MAPLEDENE ROAD
Amanda & Tony Mott.

NEW 61 MAPLEDENE ROAD
Katja & Ned Staple.

These 3 strongly contrasting N-facing gardens with different design intentions and styles. 53 is an established plantaholic's garden, with jewel-like planting where clematis take pride of place. 55 is a garden with Moorish influenced terrace leading to a wildlife garden planted to attract birds, butterflies and bees while 61 is a newly planted family garden with large open lawn, wildflower meadow and delicate, ethereal planting.

110 NEW MARIE CURIE HOSPICE, HAMPSTEAD, NW3

Lyndhurst Gardens, London, NW3 5NS. Arlene Main. *Nearest tube: Belsize Park. Buses: 46, 268 & C11 all stop nr Hospice.* **Sun 25 June (2-5.30). Adm £3.50, chd free. Tea.**
This peaceful and secluded two part garden surrounds the Marie Curie Hospice, Hampstead. A garden tended to by dedicated volunteers makes for a wonderful space for patients to enjoy the shrubs and seasonal colourful flowers. The garden has seating areas for relaxation either in the shade or in

the sunshine with a great views of the garden, and in company with squirrels running through the trees.

GROUP OPENING

111 MARKSBURY AVENUE GARDENS, TW9

Richmond, TW9 4JE. *Approx 10 mins walk from Kew Gardens tube. Exit westbound platform to North Rd. Take 3rd L into Atwood Ave. Marksbury Ave is 3rd R. Buses 190, 419 or R68.* Sun 11 June (3-6). Combined adm £7, chd free. Home-made teas at 60 Marksbury Avenue.

26 MARKSBURY AVENUE
Sue Frisby.

NEW 34 MARKSBURY AVENUE
Annette Parshotam.

59 MARKSBURY AVENUE
Clarissa Fletcher.

NEW 60 MARKSBURY AVENUE
Gay Lyle.

61 MARKSBURY AVENUE
Siobhan McCammon.

Five neighbouring gardens reflecting the enthusiasm and knowledge of their owners. One features many New Zealand natives and a variety of fruit trees incl figs, apricots and vines. A trampoline is cleverly screened by black stemmed bamboo and copper beech. There is calming water and a camomile lawn. Another garden has evolved over 11yrs and features separate areas not all visible from the house. There is a continuing process of experimenting with plants. The group provides variety and charm for the visitors.

112 94 MARSH LANE ALLOTMENTS, N17

Marsh Lane, Tottenham, N17 0HY. Chris Achilleos. *Opp*

Northumberland Park stn, on the corner of Marsh Lane & Marigold Rd. Buses: W3, 318, 341, 476. Sun 20 Aug (2-6). Adm £5, chd free. Home-made teas.

An oasis in the city, a unique allotment exuding peace and tranquillity. An exuberant collection of decorative, edible and exotic plants. Gravel paths lined with potted tender specimens. Established herbaceous border, mini orchard of Mediterranean and native fruit trees. Central gazebo, wildlife pond, sculptures - something for everyone. Artwork and mosaics. Home-made cakes.

12 THE MEADOWS
See Kent

113 27 MENELIK ROAD, NW2

West Hampstead, NW2 3RJ. C Klemera, cklemera@hotmail.com. *E of Shoot up Hill, N of Mill Lane. From Kilburn tube, buses 16, 32, 189, 316, 332 to Mill Lane on Shoot up Hill, then walk Minster Rd to Menelik Rd at end. Or, from W Hampstead tube, C11 bus (direction Brent Cross) to Menelik Rd stop.* Sun 2 July (2-5.30). Adm £4, chd free. Home-made teas. **Visits also by arrangement June to Aug for groups 10+ with guided information by owner. Tea and cake available.**

A garden full of surprises and humour. A 30yr old Trachycarpus overlooks many exotic plants of strong shape, texture and colour. Discover a cloud pruned tree in the oriental corner from your seat in the tea house. Topiary pops up from the tapestry of flowers and the piazza is secluded by bay and banana trees, often in flower. Paths lead you between lush foliage to brush your senses! New additions annually.

114 30 MERCERS ROAD, N19

London, N19 4PJ. Ms Joanne Bernstein, www.joannebernstein-gardendesign.com. *Tufnell Park. Tube: Tufnell Park then 10 mins walk.*

Holloway Rd, then 5 min Bus 43, 271 to Manor Gardens stop. Sun 2 July (2-6). Adm £4, chd free. Home-made teas. Also open 33 Huddleston Road.

Created by the garden designer owner, strong geometry complements the contemporary architecture of the house extension, softened by billowing prairie style planting in the sunny area and shade tolerant shrubs and perennials in the woodland. There is openness and seclusion, light and shade, created by generous planting and simple hard landscaping. Featured on BBC Gardeners' World and several national and international gardening magazines.

115 41 MILL HILL ROAD, W3

London, W3 8JE. Marcia Hurst, 020 8992 2632 or 07989 581940, marcia.hurst@sudbury-house.co.uk. *Tube: Acton Town, turn R, Mill Hill Rd on R off Gunnersbury Lane.* **Evening opening Fri 14 July (7-9). Wine. Sun 13 Aug (2-6). Home-made teas. Combined adm with 65 Mill Hill Road £5, chd free. Visits also by arrangement June to Oct no min, max 20.**

120ft x 40ft garden. A surprisingly large and sunny garden, with lavender and hornbeam hedges, herbaceous planting and climbers, incl unusual and rare plants as the owner is a compulsive plantaholic. Good in July and August, with many salvias, clematis, dahlias and late flowering hardy and half hardy annuals. Lots of space to sit and enjoy the garden. A good selection of the plants growing in the garden are for sale in pots with planting and growing advice from the knowledgable owner. Featured twice in Weekend Mail magazine.

Your visit to a garden will help more people be cared for by a Parkinson's nurse

116 65 MILL HILL ROAD, W3

London, W3 8JF. Anna Dargavel, 07802 241965, annadargavel@mac.com. *Tube: Acton Town, turn R, Mill Hill Rd on R off Gunnersbury Lane.* **Evening opening Fri 14 July, Sun 13 Aug (7-9). Combined adm with 41 Mill Hill Road £6, chd free. Wine. Visits also by arrangement June to Aug, groups 12 max.**
Garden designer's own garden. A secluded and tranquil space, paved, with changes of level and borders. Sunny and shady areas, topiary, fruit trees and interesting planting combine to provide a wildlife haven. A pond and organic principles are used to promote a green environment and give a stylish walk to a studio at the end. Featured in Weekend Mail Magazine.

🐾 ✿ 🚗 ☕ 🍷

117 66 MUSWELL AVENUE, N10

London, N10 2EL. Kay Thomson & Nicholas Wood-Glover, 020 8883 6697, kaythomson378@gmail.com, www.66muswellavenue.weebly. com. *1st L into Muswell Ave from Alexandra Park Rd. Tube: Bounds Green or E Finchley then bus 102 or 299, alight Colney Hatch stop.* **Sun 25 June (2-6). Adm £3.50, chd free. Visits also by arrangement May to Oct.**
Four contrasting atmospheres: a small courtyard leads to terrace of mainly containerized Mediterranean planting incl oleander, jasmine, grapevine and herbs. Imaginatively planted lawn area leads through pergola to coastal echoes in suburbia with little pebble beaches, boat and pond. Dry stone wall beyond the patio with north Cornwall planting. Fish feeding -

The National Garden
Scheme and Perennial,
helping gardeners
when they are in need

4.30 pm. Photographed by Susi Koch of Metro Publications and Abigail Willis author of The London Garden Book A to Z.

&. ✿ ☕ 🍷

118 27 NASSINGTON ROAD, NW3

Hampstead, London, NW3 2TX. Lucy Scott-Moncrieff. *From Hampstead Heath rail stn & bus stops at South End Green, go up South Hill Pk, then Parliament Hill, R into Nassington Rd.* **Sun 4 June (2-6). Adm £5, chd free. Home-made teas.**
Double width town garden planted for colour and to support wildlife. Spectacular ancient wisteria, prolific roses; herbs and unusual fruit and vegetables in with the flowers. The main feature is a large eco pond, designed for swimming, with colourful planting in and out of the water. Pots and planters, arches, bowers, view of allotments and very peaceful location give a rural feel in the city. Pond dipping for newts and mini beasts all afternoon. Live music from the Secret Life Sax Quartet from 4:30 to 5:30pm. Cakes incl lemon drizzle made with lemons from the garden and gluten free cakes; teas incl rose hips from the garden but also real tea.

☕

119 17A NAVARINO ROAD, E8

Hackney, E8 1AD. Ben Nel & Darren Henderson. *Buses 30, 38, 242 or 277 alight Graham Rd. Short walk from Hackney Central or London Fields stns on Overground lines.* **Sun 23 Apr, Sun 16 July (2-5). Adm £3.50, chd free. Light refreshments.**
Established Italian and Japanese water garden. Features a square pond with Corinthian fountain, topiary yew border, lilies and Mediterranean trees. Leading to Japanese garden with pond, bridge and stream cutting the Soleirolia soleirolii landscape, with acer, cypress, ferns and bamboo, overlooked by a beautiful Japanese Tea House. Selection of teas and cakes.

☕

120 15 NORCOTT ROAD, N16

Stoke Newington, N16 7BJ. Amanda & John Welch. *Buses: 67, 73, 76, 106, 149, 243, 393, 476, 488. Clapton & Rectory Rd mainline stns. One way system: by car approach from Brooke Rd which crosses Norcott Rd, garden is in S half of Norcott Rd.* **Sun 9 July (2-6). Adm £3.50, chd free. Home-made teas.**
For the first time we are opening in July for a different look. This is a large (for London) walled garden. Developed by the present owners over the past 35yrs, it is a cottage style garden with a pond, ancient fruit trees and an abundance of herbaceous plants.

✿ ☕

121 NEW 26 NORMANDY AVENUE, EN5

Barnet, EN5 2JA. Derek Epstein & Jo Vargas. *Tube: High Barnet then 5 mins walk. Buses: 34, 184, 84, 107, 307, 263, 326, 234. Ample parking. Normandy Ave is opp QE Girls School with Old Court House on corner.* **Sun 23 July (2-6). Adm £3.50, chd free. Home-made teas.**
6yrs ago this garden was a jungle, over half inaccessible because of a solid mass of brambles. Two garden buildings with leaded-light windows dating from the 1920s, a woodland walk, goldfish pond and many ornaments, a host of plants and a vegetable patch. Like most gardens it is still evolving. Tea and cakes, plenty of seating and some of our sculpture and pottery will be on display.

☕

122 NEW NORTH LONDON BOWLING CLUB, FITZROY PARK, N6

Highgate, London, N6 6HT. Brigitte Ascher, www. northlondonbowlingclub.co.uk. *Car: use Merton Lane or Millfield Lane to reach club; On foot: walk from Highgate village down hill along Fitzroy Park.* **Sun 18 June (11-5). Adm £3.50, chd free. Cream teas.** *Donation to North London Bowling Club.*
The NLBC lies at the edge of

Hampstead Heath but has been hidden from the public eye for 125yrs. Follow the signs and you find yourself in another world - a garden of startling beauty surrounding a carefully tended bowling green. While the green has been looked after throughout the club's history, the garden has been regenerated over 8yrs by volunteer gardeners. A game of bowls may be in progress!

  ♿ 🐕 🚌 ☕ 💷

123 5 NORTHAMPTON PARK, N1

London, N1 2PP. Andrew Bernhardt & Anne Brogan. *Backing on to St Paul's Shrubbery, Islington. 5 mins walk from Canonbury stn, 10 mins from Highbury & Islington Tube (Victoria Line) Bus: 30, 277, 341, 476.* **Sat 24 June (2-6). Adm £4, chd free. Light refreshments.**
Early Victorian S-facing walled garden, (1840's) saved from neglect and developed over the last 22yrs. Arches, palms, box and yew hedging frame the cool North European blues, whites and greys moving to splashes of red/orange Mediterranean influence. The contrast of the cool garden shielded by a small park creates a sense of seclusion from its inner London setting. Strawberries and cream, Prosecco and teas available.

  ♿ 🐕 ☕

124 NEW OAK FARM, EN2

Cattlegate Road, Enfield, EN2 9DS. Genine & Martin Newport. *5 mins. from M25 J24 & J25. Follow yellow signs. Few mins walk from Crews Hill station. Opp Woldens Garden Centre. Entrance by Culver Nurseries.* **Sun 14 May (2-6). Adm £4.50, chd free. Home-made teas.**
From pig farm to pastoral idyll spanning 3 acres, reclaimed over 30yrs. Romantic woodland glade, burgeoning arboretum, relaxed planting around sloping lawns, stone ornaments. Walled garden leads to vegetable plot, greenhouse, chickens, small orchard. Martin built the house, Genine the gardens. Enjoy joint inspirational herculean labour of love.

  🌼 ☕ 💷

125 OLD PALACE LANE ALLOTMENTS, TW9

Old Palace Lane, Richmond, TW9 1PG. Old Palace Lane Allotment Group, www.kaleandhearty.wordpress.com. *Next to White Swan PH, through gate in wall. Mainline & tube: Richmond. Parking on meters in lane or round Richmond Green, or in Old Deer Park car park, entrance on A316 Twickenham Rd.* **Sun 9 July (2-5). Adm £3, chd free. Home-made teas.**
Hidden behind a door in an ancient wall, the Old Palace Lane Allotments in Richmond are like a secret garden. Each of the 33 plots has its own identity; some resemble cottage gardens with patchwork sheds where sun flowers and fennel mingle haphazardly with squash and zucchini, while others sport raised beds, regimented rows of runner beans and gleaming greenhouses. Produce stall, tea and cakes. Featured in Evening Standard, Amateur Gardening.

  🐕 ✿ ☕

126 THE ORCHARD, W4

40A Hazledene Road, Chiswick, London, W4 3JB. Vivien Cantor. *10 mins walk from Chiswick mainline & Gunnersbury tube. Off Fauconberg Rd. Close to junction of A4 & Sutton Court Rd.* **Sun 7 May (2-5.30). Adm £5, chd free. Home-made teas.**
Informal, romantic ¼ acre garden with mature flowering trees, shrubs and imaginative planting in flowing herbaceous borders. Climbers, fern planting and water features with ponds, a bridge and waterfall in this ever evolving garden.

  ✿ ☕

127 ORMELEY LODGE, TW10

Ham Gate Avenue, Richmond, TW10 5HB. Lady Annabel Goldsmith. *From Richmond Pk exit at Ham Gate into Ham Gate Ave, 1st house on R. From Richmond A307, after 1½m, past New Inn on R. At T-lights turn L into Ham Gate Ave.* **Sun 18 June (3-6). Adm £5, chd free. Tea.**

Large walled garden in delightful rural setting on Ham Common. Wide herbaceous borders and box hedges. Walk through to orchard with wild flowers. Vegetable garden, knot garden, aviary and chickens. Trellised tennis court with roses and climbers. A number of historic stone family dog memorials. Dogs not permitted.

  ♿ ✿ ☕ 💷

128 4 ORMONDE ROAD, HA6

Moor Park, Northwood, HA6 2EL. Hasruty & Yogesh Patel. *Approx 5m from J17 & 18, M25; 6½m from J5, M1. From Batchworth Lane take Wolsey Rd exit at mini r'about. Ormonde Rd is 2nd turning on L. Ample parking on Ormonde Rd & surrounding rds.* **Sun 4 June (2-6). Adm £4.50, chd free. Cream teas.**
Beautifully planted frontage entices visitors to large S-facing rear family garden. A calm oasis enclosed by mature trees. A rare variegated flowering tulip tree provides dappled shelter alongside magnolias incl yellow river, wieseneri and diverse acers. Lavender hues of phlox foam around generous beds surrounding the spacious raised patio.

  ♿ ✿ ☕

129 NEW 12 OVERBRAE, BR3

Beckenham, BR3 1SX. Mrs Alix Branch. *Off Worsley Bridge Road, nr Kent Cricket Ground. Nearest stations, Beckenham Junction, Lower Sydenham or Beckenham Hill. Each approx 1m.* **Sun 2 Apr (2-5). Combined adm with 209 Worsley Bridge Road £5, chd free. Home-made teas at 209 Worsley Bridge Road.**
Medium sized suburban garden. Herbaceous planting gradually being replaced with shrubs. Lots of tulips in pots. To the rear a woodland spring garden, under mature trees, planted with miniature daffodils, snowdrops, tulips and a good selection of hellebores. Some steep slopes require care.

  ✿ ☕ 💷

130 PADDOCK ALLOTMENTS & LEISURE GARDENS, SW20
51 Heath Drive, Raynes Park, SW20 9BE. Paddock Horticultural Society. *Bus:57, 131, 200 to Raynes Pk station then 10 min walk or bus 163. 152 to Bushey Rd 7 min walk; 413, 5 min walk from Cannon Hill Lane. Street parking.* **Sat 24 June (12-5). Adm £3.50, chd free. Light refreshments.**
An allotment site not to be missed, over 150 plots set in 5½ acres. Our tenants come from diverse communities growing a wide range of flowers, fruits and vegetables, some plots are purely organic others resemble English country gardens. Plants, jams and produce for sale. Display of arts and crafts by members of the Paddock Hobby Club. Ploughmans lunch available. Paved and grass paths, mainly level.
& ❀ ☕

131 93 PALACE ROAD, SW2
London, SW2 3LB. Charlotte & Matthew Vaight, 07968 288925, charlottespruce@tiscali.co.uk. *Stn: Tulse Hill. Buses: 2, 68, 322, 415, 432, 468.* **Sun 2 July (2-5). Adm £4, chd free. Home-made teas. Evening opening Thur 14 Sept (6-8). Adm £5, chd free. Wine. Visits also by arrangement. Garden groups welcome; refreshments by prior arrangement.**
After a few years off, this newly renovated garden is reopening for the NGS. The strong structural lines and pair of oval lawns are softened by overflowing textural evergreen and perennial borders. Two new sunny seating areas contrast the shady terrace, both offering great views of the garden, wildlife pond and sculptures. Fairy lighting in the evening.
☕

132 3 THE PARK, N6
off Southwood Lane, London, N6 4EU. Mr & Mrs G Schrager. *3 mins from Highgate tube, up Southwood Lane. The Park is 1st on R. Buses: 43, 134, 143, 263.* **Sun 4 June (2.30-5.30). Adm £3.50, chd free. Home-made teas.**

Established large garden with informal planting for colour, scent and bees. Pond with fish, frogs and tadpoles. Tree peonies, Crinodendron hookerianum and Paulownia. Plants, tea and home-made jam for sale. Children particularly welcome - a treasure hunt with prizes!
❀ ☕

133 11 PARK AVENUE NORTH, N8
Crouch End, London, N8 7RU. Mr Steven Buckley & Ms Liz Roberts. *Tube: Finsbury Park & Turnpike Lane, nearest bus stop W3, 144, W7.* **Sun 4 June (11.30-6). Adm £3.50, chd free. Home-made teas.**
An exotic 250ft T-shaped garden, threaded through what was once an Edwardian orchard. Dramatic, mainly spiky, foliage dominates, with the focus on palms, agaves, dasylirions, aeoniums, bananas, tree ferns, nolinas, cycads, bamboos, yuccas, cacti and hundreds of types of succulents. Aloes are a highlight. Rocks and terracotta pots lend a Mediterranean accent.
☕

134 18 PARK CRESCENT, N3
Finchley, N3 2NJ. Rosie Daniels, 020 8343 3270. *Tube: Finchley Central. Buses: 82 to Victoria Park, also 125, 460, 626, 683. Walk from Ballards Lane into Etchingham Pk Road, 2nd L Park Crescent.* **Sun 18 June, Sun 16 July (2-6). Adm £3.50, chd free. Home-made teas. Visits also by arrangement June & July, groups 8 max.**
Constantly evolving, charming small garden designed and densely planted by owner. Roses and clematis in June and salvias, rudbeckia, helenium and some new grasses in July. Small pond, tub water feature and bird haven. Stepped terrace with lots of pots. New glass installations and sculptures by owner. Hidden seating with view through garden. Secluded, peaceful, restorative. Children's treasure hunt. Extensive collection of clematis.
❀ ☕

135 36 PARK ROAD, W4
London, W4 3HH. Meyrick & Louise Chapman. *Adjacent to Chiswick House Gardens. Chiswick BR: 6 mins walk up Park Rd. District Line: Turnham Green 15 mins walk. Buses: E3 & 272 alight Chesterfield Rd then 4 mins walk. Free Street parking.* **Sun 2 July (2-6). Adm £4, chd free. Home-made teas.**
City garden with distinct structure and formality based on a series of rooms within hedging. Designed to create a flavour to each room; one hot, one cool and one dark using perennials, roses, hostas and ferns against a repeated background of yew, azalea and camellia. Green wall and reflective pool.
& ☕

136 56 PARK ROAD, W4
London, W4 3HH. Richard & Diane Treganowan. *Adjacent to Chiswick House. Chiswick BR: 6 mins walk up Park Rd. District Line: Turnham Green 15 mins walk. Buses: E3 & 272 alight Chesterfield Rd then 4 mins walk. Free street parking.* **Sun 30 July (2-6). Adm £4, chd free. Home-made teas.**
Distinctly and unexpectedly atmospheric, largely sub-tropically planted with rare and unusual hardy exotics and large leaved perennials. Planting chosen to be texturally diverse whilst retaining a strong complementary theme. Interesting collection of ferns and palms set amongst a mature stumpery. The garden was designed and planted by owners. Full plant list available.
& ❀ ☕

The Queen's Nursing Institute founded the National Garden Scheme exactly 90 years ago

137 4 PARK VILLAGE EAST (TOWER LODGE GARDENS), NW1
Regents Park, London, NW1 7PX. Eveline Carn, 07831 136069, evelinecbcarn@icloud.com. *Tube: Camden Town or Mornington Crescent 7 mins. Bus: C2 or 274 3 mins. Opp The York & Albany, just off junction of Parkway/Prince Albert Rd.* Evening opening Sat 27 May (5.30-8.30). Adm £6, chd free. Wine. Sun 4 June (2.30-6). Adm £5, chd free. Home-made teas. Also open 70 Gloucester Crescent. **Visits also by arrangement with refreshments or drinks and canapés, for groups 5+.**
Head here after Chelsea for drinks in the garden on Sat eve 27 May. Open again in June with three other local gardens. A large tranquil garden behind a John Nash house, screened by trees and descending over three terraces with stepped ponds to what was the Regents Canal. Emphasis on shape, texture and strong foliage set in good landscape architecture. A work in progress with areas of new planting. Tree hung swing.

138 174 PECKHAM RYE, SE22
East Dulwich, London, SE22 9QA. Mr & Mrs Ian Bland. *Stn: Peckham Rye. Buses: 12, 37, 63, 197, 363. Overlooks Peckham Rye Common from Dulwich side.* Sun 11 June (2.30-5.30). Adm £3.50, chd free. Home-made teas. Also open 74 Harfield Gardens. *Donation to St Christopher's Hospice.*
Visitors call our garden an oasis of calm in Peckham. Every year the garden evolves and matures. It is densely planted with a wide variety of contrasting foliage. Unusual plants with interesting colour and texture are combined with old favourites. It remains easy care and child friendly. Garden originally designed by Judith Sharpe. Home-made cakes are a must and the plant sale attracts enthusiasts. Easy wheelchair access via side alley into flat garden.

139 23 PENN ROAD, N7
London, N7 9RD. Pierre Delarue & Mark Atkinson. *Between Camden Town & Holloway. Buses: 29 & 253 to Hillmarton Rd or Camden Rd 'HMP Holloway' stop. Tube: Caledonian Road on Piccadilly line, 6 mins walk.* Sun 18 June (2-6). Combined adm with 24b Penn Road £4, chd free. Home-made teas. Also open 60 & 62 Hungerford Road. *Donation to Chicken Shed.*
75ft × 25ft walled garden, redesigned 7yrs ago after extension of Victorian house and renovation of unique garden studio. A plantsman's garden with yr-round interest mixing native and Mediterranean plants incl roses, ferns, tree ferns, camellias, palms, myrtle etc. Features a red bark Arbutus and a Californian Ironwood. Meadow like front garden planted between York stones and leafy side passage. Wide range of home-made cakes and buns available plus tea, coffee and cordial.

140 24B PENN ROAD, N7
London, N7 9RD. Eileen Robertson. *Between Camden Town & Holloway. Buses: 29 & 253 to Hillmarton Rd or Camden Rd 'HMP Holloway' stop. Tube: Caledonian Road on Piccadilly line, 6 mins walk.* Sun 18 June (2-6). Combined adm with 23 Penn Road £4, chd free. Also open 1a Hungerford Road.
45ft × 25ft walled garden with old fruit trees and a large selection of shrubs and perennials. Designed organically, it has become a pleasure garden, favouring borders over lawns.

141 PETERSHAM HOUSE, TW10
Petersham Road, Petersham, Richmond, TW10 7AA. Francesco & Gael Boglione, www.petershamnurseries.com. *Stn: Richmond, then 65 bus to Dysart PH. Entry to garden off Petersham Rd, through nursery. Parking very limited on Church Lane.* Sun 23 July (11-4). Adm £4, chd free. Home-made teas in the nursery.
Broad lawn with large topiary, generously planted double borders. Productive vegetable garden with chickens. Adjoins Petersham Nurseries with extensive plant sales, shop and café serving lunch, tea and cake.

142 18 PETTITS BOULEVARD, RM1
Rise Park, Romford, RM1 4PL. Peter & Lynn Nutley. *From M25 take A12 towards London, at Pettits Lane junction turn R, then R again into Pettits Boulevard.* Sat 24, Sun 25 June, Sat 8 July (1-5). Adm £3.50, chd free. Home-made teas.
A garden 80ft × 23ft on three levels with an ornamental pond, patio area with shrubs and perennials, many in pots. A large eucalyptus tree leads to a woodland themed area with many ferns and hostas. There are agricultural implements and garden ornaments giving a unique and quirky feel to the garden. There are also tranquil seating areas situated throughout. Agricultural implements on show.

143 4 PIERMONT GREEN, SE22
East Dulwich, London, SE22 0LP. Janine Wookey. *Triangle of green facing Peckham Rye at the Honor Oak end. Stns: Peckham Rye & Honor Oak. Buses: 63 & 363 (pass the door) & 12. No parking on Green but free parking on side streets nearby.* Sun 30 July (2-5.30). Adm £3.50, chd free. Home-made teas.
A makeover was sparked by the death of a beloved old apple tree resulting in a new look for this upside down L-shaped garden. Out with the vegetable patch and in with a gravel garden, blending gaura and dierama with grasses and crambe. A new brick edged lawn is laid with a flowery mound. A white border blooms in the newly freed apple tree space and the edible garden breathes free. Live music in the garden by Open Road.

144 NEW 470 PINNER ROAD, HA5

Pinner, HA5 5RR. Nitty Chamcheon. *N Harrow Station, L to T-lights, L at next T-lights, cross to be on Pinner Rd. L - 3rd house from T-lights. Parking: Pinner Rd & George V Av - yellow lines stop after 15 yds.* **Sun 17 Sept (2-6). Adm £4, chd free.**

Once (18yrs ago) a back yard with just a lawn in the first half and the second half a jungle with a very mature apple and pear tree; now a beautiful garden. A path passing through fruit and vegetable garden to the secret log cabin after a bridge over the pond with waterfall in front of a tree house in the pear tree. An attempt has been made to extend the season as far as possible.

145 NEW 1 POND COTTAGES, SE21

College Road, Dulwich, SE21 7LE. Helen Dolby. *Private rd opp Dulwich College. Entry to both No. 1 & No. 3 Pond Cottages via 1 Pond Cottages. Train: West Dulwich & Gypsy Hill. Bus: routes P4, P13 & No 3. Free parking available along College Road.* **Sun 14 May (2-5). Combined adm with 3 Pond Cottages £4, chd free. Home-made teas.**

A small garden where the cottage planting of a lush border in harmonious colours curves intimately around a secluded and romantic lawn area. This soft planting contrasts with crisp lines of rendered patio walls, structural planting and experimental combinations on the chalk deposits of old brickworks. Opened as part of Dulwich Artists Open House, incl paintings by owner Polly Bagnall (www.pollybagnall.co.uk), ceramics by Ali Tomlin (http://alitomlin.com). To be incl in the Dulwich Gardens Open for Charity, published by the Dulwich Society.

146 NEW 3 POND COTTAGES, SE21

College Road, Dulwich, SE21 7LE. Polly Bagnall. *private rd opp Dulwich College. Entry to both No. 1 & No. 3 Pond Cottages via 1 Pond Cottages.*

Train: West Dulwich & Gypsy Hill. Bus: routes P4, P13 & No 3. Free parking available along College Road. **Sun 14 May (2-5). Combined adm with 1 Pond Cottages £4, chd free. Home-made teas.**

This mature garden artfully blends a surprising range of planting genres, from the Spanish feel of a sun drenched patio with mature fig, olive and palm through a bright herbaceous border; lawn area enhanced by sculptured objects and mature shrubs and small trees, woodland planting beneath a mature cut leaf beech creating a cool shady seating area and raised beds providing room for vegetables. Opened as part of Dulwich Artists Open House, incl paintings by owner Polly Bagnall (www.pollybagnall.co.uk), ceramics by Ali Tomlin (http://alitomlin.com). Featured Dulwich Gardens Open for Charity publication, published by the Dulwich Society.

147 153 PORTLAND ROAD, BR1

Bromley, BR1 5AY. Lucia & Simon Parnell. *Off Burnt Ash Lane between Sundridge Park & Grove Park BR stns. From Burnt Ash Lane turn into New Street Hill, proceed up hill. Turn L into Portland Road, house is 2nd on R.* **Sun 13 Aug (2-5.30). Adm £4, chd free. Home-made teas.**

Award winning charming garden reopening this year. Enter via densely planted front garden, cont through to a beautifully structured garden with new planting alongside established shrubs. Central pathway framed by buxus leads through oak arbour to delightful pond area. Lawn with seating. arbutus, fatsia japonica, tree ferns, pergola with wisteria and seating complemented by new paving. Live music by Guitarist.

148 NEW 57 PREBEND GARDENS, W6

Stamford Brook, London, W6 0XT. Jennifer Taylor. *Tube: 2 min walk from Stamford Brook station. Buses: 27, 94, 190, 237, 267, 391, H91 all 3-4 mins walk. Drivers: approach from Bath Road. Street parking available.* **Evening opening Wed**

12 July (6-8). Wine. Sun 16 July (2-6). Home-made teas. Also open 57 St Quintin Avenue. Adm £4.50, chd free.

Colourful courtyard garden (55 × 25 ft). Professionally designed and planted 4yrs ago but constantly evolving as the owners seek perfection. Not yet achieved so advice and suggestions always welcome! Unusual varieties, changes of level, seating areas, lots of texture as well as colour. Alpine garden atop bike shed. Awarded 1st Prize - Kensington Gardeners Club.

GROUP OPENING

149 PRINCES AVENUE GARDENS, N10

Muswell Hill, N10 3LS. *Buses: 43 & 134 from Highgate tube; also W7, 102, 144, 234, 299. Princes Ave opp M&S in Muswell Hill Broadway, or John Baird PH in Fortis Green.* **Sun 14 May (2-6). Combined adm £4, chd free. Home-made teas.**

NEW **17 PRINCES AVENUE**
Patsy Bailey & John Rance.

28 PRINCES AVENUE
Ian & Viv Roberts.

In a beautiful Edwardian avenue in the heart of Muswell Hill Conservation Area, two very different gardens reflect the diverse life styles of their owners. The charming, immaculately maintained garden at No 17 is designed for relaxing and entertaining and is shaded by large surrounding trees - among which is a ginko. The garden features a superb hosta and fern display. No 28 is a well established traditional garden reflecting the charm typical of the era. Mature trees, shrubs, mixed borders and woodland garden creating an oasis of calm just off the bustling Broadway.

150 NEW 93A PRIORY ROAD, N8

Priory Road, Hornsey, N8 8LY.
Chris Kazamias & Fiona Barnes.
Nearest tube: Turnpike Lane then 144 bus to outside 93a or Finsbury Park then W3 to outside 93a. Bus stop called Hornsey Fire Station. W7 from Muswell Hill, alight Cranley Gdns, walk to Priory Rd. **Sun 21 May (2-5). Adm £3.50, chd free. Home-made teas.**
Serenity, simplicity, harmony of materials and planting create an atmosphere to enjoy all year. Water soothes the spirits, and attracts wildlife into a contemporary environment. Sensitive architectural design blends inside and outside seamlessly. A spacious studio sits beneath a majestic oak. Salvias soften a camomile lawn, beckoning you to relax.

GROUP OPENING

151 RAILWAY COTTAGES, N22

Dorset Road, Alexandra Palace, N22 7SL. *Tube: Wood Green, 10 mins walk. Overground: Alexandra Palace, 3 mins. Buses W3, 184. 3 mins. Free parking in local streets on Suns.* **Sun 2 July (2-5.30). Combined adm £4.50, chd free. Home-made teas at 2 Dorset Rd.**

2 DORSET ROAD
Jane Stevens,
janestevens_london
@yahoo.co.uk.
Visits also by arrangement July & Aug for groups 4+.

4 DORSET ROAD
Mark Longworth.

14 DORSET ROAD
Cathy Brogan.

NEW **16 DORSET ROAD**
Alan & Gill Kelson.

22 DORSET ROAD
Mike & Noreen Ainger.

24A DORSET ROAD
Eddie & Jane Wessman.

A row of historical railway cottages, tucked away from the bustle of Wood Green nr Alexandra Palace, takes the visitor back in time. No. 4 is a pretty secluded woodland garden, (accessed through the rear of No. 2), sets off sculptor owner's figurative and abstract work among acers, sambucus nigra, species shrubs and old fruit trees. Within the pretty surroundings sits the owner's working studio. Three front gardens at Nos. 14, 16, 22 and 24a, one nurtured by the grandson of the original railway worker occupant, show a variety of planting, incl aromatic shrubs, herbs, jasmine, flax, fig, fuchsia and vines. A modern raised bed vegetable garden adds further interest. The tranquil country style garden at No. 2 Dorset Rd flanks 3 sides of the house. Hawthorn topiary (by the original owner) and clipped box hedges contrast with climbing roses, clematis, honeysuckle, abutilon and cottage plants. Trees incl mulberry, quince, fig, apple and a mature willow creating an opportunity for an interesting shady corner. There is an emphasis on scented flowers that attract bees and butterflies and the traditional medicinal plants found in cottage gardens.

152 172 RAVENSBOURNE AVENUE, BR2

Bromley, BR2 0AY. John & Christine Parris. *Train: Shortlands & Ravensbourne. Parking in Ravensbourne Ave & adjacent rds.* **Sun 16 July (1.30-5.30). Combined adm with 174 Ravensbourne Avenue £6, chd free. Home-made teas.**
Rectangular terraced garden with a specious feel. Steps leading down to the lawn are lined with pots of giant lilies. There is an exotic feel with fantastic fuchsias, tall cannas in between taller palms. The arresting focal point in the garden is the large pond with multi coloured gigantic carp. No surprises to know that Christine does the flowers, John does the fish!

153 174 RAVENSBOURNE AVENUE, BR2

Bromley, BR2 0AY. Carmel & Patricia Zammit. *Train Stations: Shortlands & Ravensbourne. Parking in Ravensbourne Ave & adjacent rds.* **Sun 16 July (1.30-5.30). Combined adm with 172 Ravensbourne Avenue £6, chd free. Home-made teas.**
This vibrantly planted garden sits on two levels. At the top is a raised patio with colourful pots and a hosta theatre. Steps lead down to the lower area packed with colour, shape and form. It is divided by a wooden pergola swathed in clematis Polish spirit and rosa new dawn creating dramatic height and colour. A shaded area beyond the pergola is a perfect spot to sit quietly. Water feature, delicious home-made teas.

154 RICHARD HOUSE CHILDREN'S HOSPICE, E16

Richard House Drive, Beckton, E16 3RG. Richard House Children's Hospice, www.richardhouse.org.uk. *DLR to Royal Albert, follow footpath, cross Royal Albert Way, 1st L Stansfeld Way 2nd L Richard House Drive. Car: postcode for SatNav not reliable, enter Richard House Drive.* **Sun 30 Apr (2-5). Adm £3, chd free. Tea in Hospice dining hall.**
A series of individual areas around the hospice designed for children, young people, their families and others' enjoyment. Drought tolerant area with silver leaved plants (Save the Water) transferred from Chelsea Flower Show in 2001. Also one of a few sensory gardens in East London incl grassy mounds (Telly Tubby). Bulbs in spring. Shrubs and a mature fig tree. Small interesting woodland walk. Level grounds, with wheelchair accessible woodland path and other ramps as necessary.

155 ROYAL COLLEGE OF PHYSICIANS' MEDICINAL GARDEN, NW1

11 St Andrews Place, London, NW1 4LE. Royal College of Physicians of London, http://garden.rcplondon.ac.uk. *Tubes: Great Portland St & Regent's Park. Garden is one block N of station exits, on Outer Circle opp SE corner of Regent's Park.* **Sun 4 June (10-4). Adm £5, chd free. Light refreshments at the College. Also open 4 Park Village East (Tower Lodge Gardens).**
One of four beautiful and unusual gardens in NW1 opening on Sunday June 4th. 1100 different plants used in medicines around the world throughout history; plants named after physicians and plants which make modern medicines. Unique beds with the plants used medicinally in the College's Pharmacopoeia of 1618. See http://garden.rcplondon. ac.uk. Guided tours by physicians all day, explaining the uses of the plants, their histories and stories about them. Books about the plants in the medicinal garden will be on sale. The award winning College building will also be open for visitors. Wheelchair ramps at steps.

 ♿ 🚐 ☕

156 ROYAL TRINITY HOSPICE, SW4

30 Clapham Common North Side, London, SW4 0RN. Royal Trinity Hospice, www.royaltrinityhospice.org.uk. *Tube: Clapham Common. Buses: 35, 37, 345, 137 stop outside.* **Sun 9 Apr, Sun 21 May, Sun 3 Sept (10.30-4.30). Adm £3, chd free. Light refreshments.**
Royal Trinity's beautiful, award winning gardens play an important therapeutic role in the life and function of Royal Trinity Hospice. Over the years, many people have enjoyed our gardens and today they continue to be enjoyed by patients, families and visitors alike. Set over nearly 2 acres, they offer space for quiet contemplation, family fun and make a great backdrop for events. Picnics welcome. Ramps and pathways.

 ♿ 🐕 ✿ ☕

157 5 RUSSELL ROAD, N13

Bowes Park, N13 4RS. Angela Kreeger. *Close to N Circular Rd & Green Lanes. Tube: Bounds Green, 10 mins walk. Mainline: Bowes Park, 3 mins walk. Numerous bus routes. Off Whittington Rd.* **Sun 13 Aug (2-6). Adm £3, chd free. Home-made teas.**
A poem for the eyes. Billowing, overflowing, balanced by emerald lawn. Airy, dreamy planting in small woodland. Not manicured. Simple, unfussy with a contemporary feel, calm, quiet and peaceful. Large, late summer border full of colour. Golden in sunlight. Small bespoke greenhouse reminiscent of Dungeness and Hastings. Front garden vegetable bed. Truly delicious home-made cakes. Featured in Gardens Illustrated.

158 7 ST GEORGE'S ROAD, TW1

St Margarets, Twickenham, TW1 1QS. Richard & Jenny Raworth, 020 8892 3713, jraworth@gmail.com, www.raworthgarden.com. *1½m SW of Richmond. Off A316 between Twickenham Bridge & St Margarets r'about.* **Evening opening Sat 3 June (6-8). Adm £6, chd free. Wine. Visits also by arrangement May to July for groups 10+.**
Exuberant displays of Old English roses and vigorous climbers with unusual herbaceous perennials. Massed scented crambe cordifolia. Pond with bridge converted into child safe lush bog garden and waterfall. Large N-facing luxuriant conservatory with rare plants and climbers. Pelargoniums a speciality. Sunken garden and knot garden. Pergola covered with climbing roses and clematis. Water feature and fernery. Featured in Great Gardens of London Summerly/Majerus.

 ♿ ☕

159 87 ST JOHNS ROAD, E17

London, E17 4JH. Andrew Bliss. *15 mins walk from W'stow tube/ overground or 212/275 bus. Alight at St Johns Rd stop. 10 mins walk from Wood*

St overground. Very close to N Circular. **Sun 6, Sun 13 Aug (1-5). Adm £3.50, chd free. Home-made teas.**
My garden epitomises what can be achieved with imagination, design and colour consideration in a small typical terraced outdoor area. Its themes are diverse and incl a fernery, Jardin Majorelle, a water feature and 3 individual seating areas. All enhanced with circles, mirrors and over planting to create an atmosphere of tranquility within an urban environment.

 ☕

160 20 ST MARY'S GROVE, N1

London, N1 2NT. Mrs B Capel. *Canonbury, Islington. Highbury & Islington Tube & Overground. Buses: 4, 19, 30, 277 to St Paul's Rd. 271 to Canonbury Square.* **Sun 23 Apr (2-5.30). Combined adm with 4 Canonbury Place £5.50, chd free.**
Come and enjoy this delightful small paved garden with sweet smelling spring bulbs and shrubs - coronilla, viburnum, tree peony, choisia ternata, camellias, lilac. Look out for the variety of little potted favourites. Preserves for sale.

161 27 ST PETERS SQUARE, W6

London, W6 9NW. Oliver Leigh Wood. *Tube to Stamford Brook exit station & turn S down Goldhawk Rd. At T-lights cont ahead into British Grove. Entrance to garden at 50 British Grove 100 yds on L.* **Sun 7 May (2-6.30). Adm £4, chd free. Home-made teas.**
This long, secret space, is a plantsman's eclectic semi-tamed wilderness. Created over the last 9yrs it contains lots of camellias, magnolias and fruit trees. Much of the hard landscaping is from skips and the whole garden is full of other people's unconsidered trifles of fancy incl a folly and summer house.

 🐕 ✿ ☕

162 57 ST QUINTIN AVENUE, W10

London, W10 6NZ. Mr H Groffman, 020 8969 8292. *1m from Ladbroke Grove or White City tube. Buses: 7, 70, 220 all to North Pole*

Rd. Free parking on Sundays. Sun 16 July (2-6), also open 57 Prebend Gardens. Sun 30 July (2-6). Adm £4, chd free. Home-made teas. **Visits also by arrangement July & Aug, refreshments by advance arrangement.**
30ft x 40ft walled garden; wide selection of plant material incl evergreen and deciduous shrubs for foliage effects. Patio area mainly furnished with bedding material, colour themed. Focal points throughout. Refurbished with new plantings and special features. Garden theme this year is 90th birthday of the National Garden Scheme. Also celebrating 30yrs of opening for the NGS. Annual themed carpet bedding display complemented by patio colour scheme. Varied use of mirrors.
✿ ☕

163 5 ST REGIS CLOSE, N10
Alexandra Park Road, Muswell Hill, London, N10 2DE. Ms S Bennett & Mr E Hyde, 020 8883 8540, suebearlh@yahoo.co.uk. *Tube: Bounds Green then 102 or 299 bus, or E. Finchley take 102. Alight St Andrews Church. 134 or 43 bus stop at end of Alexandra Pk Rd, follow arrows.* Sun 30 Apr, Sun 18 June, Sun 23 July (2-6.30). Adm £4, chd free. Home-made teas. **Visits also by arrangement Apr to Oct for groups 10+. Home-made teas/light refreshments.**
Cornucopia of sensual delights. Artist's garden famous for architectural features and delicious cakes. New Oriental Tea House. Baroque temple, pagodas, Raku tiled mirrored wall conceals plant nursery. American Gothic shed overlooks Liberace Terrace and stairway to heaven. Maureen Lipman's favourite garden, combines colour, humour, trompe l'oeil with wildlife friendly ponds, waterfalls, weeping willow, lawns, abundant planting. A unique experience awaits! Open studio with ceramics and prints. Mega plant sale. Featured in The London Garden Book A-Z Wheelchair access to all parts of garden unless waterlogged.
♿ 🐕 ✿ 🚗 ☕

164 2 SHARDCROFT AVENUE, SE24
Herne Hill, London, SE24 0DT. Catriona Andrews. *Short walk from Herne Hill rail station & bus stops. Buses: 3, 68, 196, 201, 468 to Herne Hill. Closest tube Brixton. Parking in local streets.* Sun 18 June (2-6). Adm £4, chd free. Home-made teas.
A designer's garden with loose, naturalistic planting. Geometric terracing accommodates a natural slope, framing vistas from the house. Drought tolerant beds with cascading perennials and grasses, scented courtyard, formal wildlife pond, woodland glade with fire pit and green roofed shed provide wildlife habitats and a feast for the senses. Planted ecologically to benefit wildlife. Nesting boxes and log piles. http://www.gardenista.com/posts/lessons-learned-from-neglected-slope-to-charming-garden-in-south-london/.
✿ ☕

165 SOUTH LONDON BOTANICAL INSTITUTE, SE24
323 Norwood Road, London, SE24 9AQ. South London Botanical Institute, www.slbi.org.uk. *Mainline stn: Tulse Hill. Buses: 68, 196, 322 & 468 stop at junction of Norwood & Romola Rds.* Sun 23 Apr (2-5). Adm £3.50, chd free. Home-made teas. *Donation to South London Botanical Institute.*
London's smallest botanical garden, densely planted with 500 labelled species grown in a formal layout of themed borders. Wildflowers flourish beside medicinal herbs. Carnivorous, scented, native and woodland plants are featured, growing among rare trees and shrubs. Spring highlights incl mosses, unusual bulbs and flowering trees. The fascinating SLBI building is also open. Unusual plants for sale.
✿ ☕

166 123 SOUTH PARK ROAD, SW19
Wimbledon, London, SW19 8RX. Susan Adcock. *Mainline & tube: Wimbledon, 10 mins; S Wimbledon tube 5 mins. Buses: 57, 93, 131, 219 along High St. Entrance in Bridges Rd (next to church hall) off South Park Rd.* Mon 29 May (2-6). Adm £3, chd free. Light refreshments. Home-made cake and cordial.
This small L-shaped garden has a high deck amongst trees overlooking a woodland area, patio with pots, several small water containers, a fish pond, and a secluded courtyard with raised beds for flowers and herbs, as well as a discreet hot tub. Lots of ideas for giving a small space atmosphere and interest.
☕

Longmeadow

167 **41 SOUTHBROOK ROAD, SE12**
Lee, London, SE12 8LJ. Barbara & Marek Polanski, 020 8333 2176, polanski101@yahoo.co.uk. *Southbrook Rd is situated off S Circular, off Burnt Ash Rd. Train: Lee & Hither Green, both 10 mins walk. Bus: P273, 202.* **Sat 17, Sun 18 June (2-5.30). Adm £3.50, chd free. Home-made teas. Visits also by arrangement May to Aug (2-5.30).**
Developed over 14yrs, this large garden has a formal layout, with wide mixed herbaceous borders full of colour and interest, surrounded by mature trees, framing sunny lawns, a central box parterre and an Indian pergola. Ancient pear trees festooned in June with clouds of white kiftsgate and rambling rector roses. Discover fish and damselflies in 2 lily ponds. Many places to sit and relax. Enjoy refreshments in a small classical garden building with interior wall paintings, almost hidden by roses climbing way up into the trees. Orangery. Featured on Sky 1 TV series, Show Me Your Garden and in Garden Week, Bise and the Westcombe News. Side access available for standard wheelchairs, no steps.
♿ 🐴 ☕

168 **SOUTHWOOD LODGE, N6**
33 Kingsley Place, Highgate, N6 5EA. Mr & Mrs C Whittington, 020 8348 2785, suewhittington@hotmail.co.uk. *Tube: Highgate then 6 mins uphill walk along Southwood Lane. 4 min walk from Highgate Village along Southwood Lane. Buses: 143, 210, 214, 271.* **Sun 14 May (2-5.30). Adm £4, chd free. Home-made teas. Visits also by arrangement Apr to July, lunches (for 10+) or teas (any number) on request.**
Plantsman's garden hidden behind C18 house (not open). Great variety of unusual plants, many propagated for sale. Ponds, waterfall, frogs, toads, newts. Many topiary shapes formed from self sown yew trees. New sculpture carved from three trunks of a massive conifer which became unstable in a storm. Hard working

greenhouse! Only one open day this year so visits by appointment especially welcome. Featured in First Ladies of Gardening by Heidi Howcroft and Marianne Majerus. Toffee hunt for children. Secret Life Sax Quartet will perform in the garden from 2.30pm.
✿ 🚗 ☕

GROUP OPENING

169 **SPITALFIELDS GARDENS, E1**
London, E1 6QH. *Nr Spitalfields Market. 10 mins walk from Aldgate E Tube & 5 mins walk from Liverpool St stn. Overground: Shoreditch High St - 3 mins walk.* **Sat 10 June (10-4). Combined adm £15, chd free. Light refreshments at Town House, 5 Fournier St.**

26 ELDER STREET
The Future Laboratory

34 ELDER STREET

7 FOURNIER STREET
John Nicolson.

29 FOURNIER STREET
Juliette Larthe.

21 PRINCELET STREET
Marianne & Nicholas Morse.

37 SPITAL SQUARE
Society for the Protection of Ancient Buildings.

21 WILKES STREET
Rupert Wheeler.

A collection of hidden treasures behind some of the finest merchants and weavers houses in Spitalfields. Don't miss the informative courtyard of the Society for the Protection of Ancient Buildings (SPAB). The other nearby gardens incl two in Elder Street, one in Wilkes Street, one in Princelet Street, and two in Fournier Street. These gardens give the visitor an insight into the variety of ways people have adapted different spaces to complement these historic houses. Featured in Country Life and The London Magazine.
☕

170 **25 SPRINGFIELD AVENUE, N10**
Muswell Hill, N10 3SU. Nigel Ragg & Heather Hampson. *From main r'about at Muswell Hill (bus waiting zone) take steep rd towards Crouch End (named Muswell Hill). Springfield Av 1st L off hill.* **Sun 25 June (2-5.30). Adm £3.50, chd free. Home-made teas.**
We relandscaped our town garden in 2013, transforming it's plain incline to individual terraces. Each layer is unique, mixing an aura of spirituality with a country atmosphere. The mature trees of Alexander Palace lend the garden a spectacular backdrop and together with water features, pot and chimney planting, summerhouse and decking, make it unique. New for 2017 - the ungreying of the front garden. See how we are transforming the crazy paved front parking area into an environmentally friendly parking and garden space. Featured in Garden News magazine.
✿ ☕

171 **2 SPRINGHURST CLOSE, CR0**
Shirley Church Road, Croydon, CR0 5AT. Ben & Peckham Carroll. *2m S of Croydon. Off A2022 from Selsdon. Off A232 from Croydon. Close opp The Addington Golf Club. Tramline 3 to Addington Village. East Croydon Station.* **Sun 9 July (2-5.30). Adm £3.50, chd free. Cream teas.**
Newly established designer garden within ½ acre secluded woodland site. Now has terrace beds of specimen grasses, topiary, perennials, decorative trees and elegant water feature with extensive hosta collection. Planting is in a soft colour palette designed to attract bees with a new collection of black plants. Vegetable garden, bug hotel, fernery, woodland hydrangea walk add interest and variety. All cakes home-made. Extensive plant sale. Mainly level with grass paths but a few steps.
♿ ✿ 🅓 ☕

172 STOKES HOUSE, TW10

Ham Street, Ham, Richmond, TW10 7HR. Peter & Rachel Lipscomb, 020 8940 2403, rlipscomb@virginmedia.com. *2m S of Richmond off A307. ¼ m from A307. Trains & tube to Richmond & train to Kingston which link with 65 bus to Ham Common.* **Sun 4 June (2-5). Adm £4, chd free. Home-made teas. Visits also by arrangement Apr to Oct. Garden groups 10+ welcome.** Originally an orchard, this ½ acre walled country garden surrounding Georgian house (not open) is abundant with roses, clematis and perennials. There are mature trees incl ancient mulberries and wisteria. The yew hedging, pergola and box hedges allow for different planting schemes throughout the yr. Supervised children are welcome to play on the slide and swing. Herbaceous borders, brick garden, wild garden, large compost area and interesting trees. Many plants for sale. Teas, garden tour, history of house and area for group visits. Wheelchair access via double doors from street with 2 wide steps. Unfortunately no access for larger motorised chairs.

173 STONEY HILL HOUSE, SE26

Rock Hill, London, SE26 6SW. Cinzia & Adam Greaves. *Off Sydenham Hill. Train: Sydenham, Gipsy Hill or Sydenham Hill (closest) stations. Buses: To Crystal Palace, 202 or 363 along Sydenham Hill. House at end of cul-de-sac on L coming from Sydenham Hill.* **Sun 21 May (2-6). Adm £4, chd free. Home-made teas. Also open 15a Sydenham Hill.** Garden and woodland of approx 1 acre providing a secluded secret green oasis in the city. Paths meander through mature rhododendron, oak, yew and holly trees, offset by pieces of contemporary sculpture. The garden is on a slope and a number of viewpoints set at different heights provide varied perspectives. The planting in the top part of the

garden is fluid and flows seamlessly into the woodland. Delicious home-made cakes, generous mugs of tea (with free refills) and Fresalca, a wonderful saxophone quartet, will be playing for the afternoon. Shallow, wide brick steps at entrance to garden with grass slope alongside. Wheelchair access possible if these can be negotiated.

174 15A SYDENHAM HILL, SE26

Sydenham, London, SE26 6SH. Mrs Sue Marsh. *Nr Crystal Palace. At Crystal Palace end of Sydenham Hill, off mini r'bout on A212. Stn: Sydenham Hill 10 mins walk. Buses: to Crystal Palace & 363 along Sydenham Hill.* **Sun 21 May (2-5). Adm £3, chd free. Also open Stoney Hill House. Teas available at Stoney Hill House.** Beautifully located terraced hillside woodland garden (⅓ acre) with colourful mixed herbaceous borders, trellised roses, unusual trees and shrubs. Acer glade. Interesting collection of hollies and skimmias. Gravel garden with gazebo. Courtyard, pergola and fountain. A be-ferned stumpery corner and living willow hedge screening compost area. Cloud topiary and S-facing fence for climbers. Botanical print cards for sale.

175 93 TANFIELD AVENUE, NW2

Dudden Hill, London, NW2 7SB. Mr James Duncan Mattoon, 020 8830 7410. *Dudden Hill - Neasden. Nearest station: Neasden - Jubilee line then 10 mins walk; or various bus routes to Neasden Parade or Tanfield Av.* **Sun 30 July (2-6). Adm £4, chd free. Home-made teas. Visits also by arrangement May to Sept for groups 20 max.** Professional plantsman's petite hillside paradise! Arid/tropical deck with panoramic views of Wembley and Harrow, descends through Mediterranean screes and warm sunny slopes, to subtropical oasis packed with many rare and exotic plants e.g. Hedychium, Plumbago,

Punica, Tetrapanax. To rear, jungle shade terrace and secret summer house offer cool respite on sunny days. Previous garden was Tropical Kensal Rise (Doyle Gardens) featured on BBC2 Open Gardens and in Sunday Telegraph. This garden featured in Garden News magazine and Garden Answers magazine!

176 58A TEIGNMOUTH ROAD, NW2

Cricklewood, NW2 4DX. Drs Elayne & Jim Coakes, 020 8208 0082, elayne.coakes@btinternet.com, www.facebook.com/ gardening4bees. *Cricklewood (Willesden Green). Tube: Willesden Green or Kilburn 10 mins walk. Buses: 16, 32, 189, 226, 260, 266, 316, 332, 460. Teignmouth Rd just off Walm Lane.* **Sun 18 June (3-6.30). Adm £3.50, chd free. Home-made teas. Visits also by arrangement May to July, groups 15 max. Plenty of notice required.** Front and back gardens with eclectic planting schemes incl restrained palate coordinated beds, pergola with wisteria, climbing roses and 40+ clematis, 2 ponds, water features, acers, hardy, and unusual plants. Rainwater harvesting with integral watering system, native plants and organic treatment means a home for frogs, newts and bees. Under the terrace is a 3½ ton tank for the water harvesting system that feeds water to taps around the garden; Clematis and other climbing plants clothe the pergola and woodland walk as well as the fences. This is an energetic garden attracting wildlife and wild flowers. There are no lawns. Book available to read with press/magazine coverage and about the history of the garden. Some areas only accessible by stepping stones. Deep ponds.

177 27 THORPEWOOD AVENUE, SE26

Sydenham, London, SE26 4BU. Barbara & Gioni Nella. *½m from Forest Hill Stn. Just off the S Circular (A205) turning up Sydenham Hill nr Horniman Gdns or Dartmouth Rd from Forest Hill stn. Buses: 122, 176, 312 to Forest Hill library.* Sun 2 July (1.30-6). Adm £3.50, chd free. Home-made teas.

This ½ acre sloping garden blends a cool English woodland look with hotter Mediterranean styles and, with its bamboos and bananas, travels even further afield, all the way to the Antipodes. A particular joy lies in the garden's heart where woodland opens out to reveal a sunny glade packed with alpine delights. Barbara is a compulsive plants person - so come prepared to buy some interesting plants.

178 21 THURLOW ROAD, NW3

London, NW3 5PP. Jenny & Howard Ross. *Hampstead. Thurlow Rd is 5 mins walk from Hampstead tube down Rosslyn Hill. Also, equally nr are Belsize Park tube, Hampstead Heath Silverlink & 168, 268 and C11 buses.* Sun 25 June (2-5.30). Adm £4, chd free. Home-made teas.

Hidden beyond iron gates is a charming Victorian walled garden with a sunken area bordered by densely planted flowerbeds. The garden consists of herbaceous beds and plants incl lavenders, agapanthus, delphiniums, exceptional hydrangeas propagated from a Dorset garden and C19 roses, all in subtle muted tones. Clematis and hand crafted pergola with white wisteria. Home-made teas incl gluten free cakes.

179 57 TONBRIDGE HOUSE, WC1H

Tonbridge Street, London, WC1H 9PG. Sue Heiser. *S of Euston Road. Tube: King's Cross & St Pancras Stn & Russell Sq. Behind Camden Town Hall off Judd St. Turn into Bidborough St which becomes Tonbridge St. Side entrance to garden.* Sun 2 July (2-6). Combined adm with 40 Tonbridge House £5,

95 The Chine

chd free. Home-made teas.

Unexpected oasis off the Euston Road, overlooked on all sides by tall buildings. Mixed informal planting, with seating, rockery, pergola and shady areas. Mature magnolia, sycamore, holly and some long established shrubs and perennials incl ferns, hostas and heuchera. Small vegetable beds and herbs. Evolved over 35yrs on a low budget with plenty of help from friends. Wheelchair access from street and throughout garden.

180 NEW 40 TONBRIDGE HOUSE, WC1H

London, WC1H 9PJ. Anita & Paul Howard. *S of Euston Rd. Turn onto Judd Street from Euston Road, 1st L & follow rd round into Tonbridge Street. Entrance through courtyard garden.* Sun 2 July (2-6). Combined adm with 57 Tonbridge House £5, chd free. Light refreshments.

Walk through a lusciously planted courtyard into our secluded enclosed garden in Bloomsbury. It has a Mediterranean feel that echoes my family history in Portugal and in South Africa. The smell of lavender, jasmine and honeysuckle remind me of my childhood there. It's a gravel garden, with some flower beds and lots of plants in pots and also climbers.

181 TREETOPS, HA6

Sandy Lane, Northwood, HA6 3ES. Mrs Carole Kitchner. *Opp Northwood HQ. Tube: Northwood, 10 mins walk. Bus 8 stops at bottom of lane. Parking in lane.* Sun 23 July (2-6). Adm £4, chd free. Home-made teas.

Nestling in quiet lane in Northwood conservation area, sloping garden with long terrace and large pots. Rose covered pergola, water feature, small lawn, wide variety unusual shrubs incl magnolia grandiflora, paulownias, trochodendron. Peaking in high summer, heleniums, agapanthus, lobelias, eryngiums, crocosmias present a vibrant vision – well worth a visit! Mentioned in an article by Robin Lane Fox. Featured as Garden of the Week in Garden News (July 12th issue).

182 TRUMPETERS HOUSE & SARAH'S GARDEN, TW9

Richmond, TW9 1PD. Baroness Van Dedem. *Richmond riverside. 5 mins walk from Richmond Station via Richmond Green in Trumpeter's Yard. Parking on Richmond Green & Old Deer Park car park only.* Sun 11 June (2-5). Adm £5, chd free. Home-made teas.

The 2 acre garden is on the original site of Richmond Palace. Long lawns stretch from the house to banks of the River Thames. There are clipped yews, a box parterre and many unusual shrubs and trees, a rose garden and oval pond with carp. The ancient Tudor walls are covered with roses and climbers. Discover Sarah's secret garden behind the high walls. Wheelchair access on grass and gravel.

♿ ☕

183 35 TURRET GROVE, SW4

Clapham Old Town, SW4 0ES. Wayne Amiel, www.turretgrove.com. *Off Rectory Grove. 10 mins walk from Clapham Common Tube & Wandsworth Rd Mainline. Buses: 87, 137.* **Sun 23 July (10-5). Adm £4, chd free. Home-made teas. Also open 2 Littlebury Road.**

This garden shows what can be achieved in a small space (8m x 25m). The owners, who make no secret of disregarding the rule book, describe this visual feast of intoxicating colours as Clapham meets Jamaica. This is gardening at its most exuberant, where bananas, bamboos, gingers, tree ferns and fire bright plants flourish beside the traditional. Children welcome. See Wayne's Garden Blog for Press Coverage.

✳ ☕

184 45 UNDERHILL ROAD, SE22

London, SE22 0QZ. Nicola Bees. *Approx 200 metres from Lordship Lane. Train: Forest Hill 20 mins walk. Bus: Routes P13, P4, 63, 176, 185, 197, 363. Car: Off A205 nr junction with Lordship Lane. Free parking.* **Sun 14 May (2-6). Combined adm with 86 Underhill Road £6, chd free. Home-made teas.**

A restored Victorian garden of tamed disorder with a few modern twists. In spring naturalised bluebells mix with blowsy tulips, peonies and dogwood trees. A wildlife pond comes to life in the spring when frogs and newts appear in abundance. A corner summerhouse-come-shed provides a tranquil retreat at the bottom of the garden. Teas served in our conservatory tea room come rain or shine. Three deep steps into the garden. Gravel paths.

✳ ☕

185 86 UNDERHILL ROAD, SE22

East Dulwich, SE22 0QU. Claire & Rob Goldie. *Between Langton Rise & Melford Rd. Stn: Forest Hill. Buses: P13, 363, 63, 176, 185 & P4.* **Sun 14 May (2-6). Combined adm with 45 Underhill Road £6, chd free. Home-made teas.**

A generous family space bursting with colour. Mixed beds of medicinal, fragrant and edible planting. Secluded seating set among water barrels and bamboo. See if you can spot our friendly newts and then enjoy tea and cake in the spacious garden room built on tyres.

✳ ☕

186 7 UPPER PHILLIMORE GARDENS, W8

Kensington, London, W8 7HF. Mr & Mrs B Ritchie. *From Kensington High St turn into Phillimore Gdns or Campden Hill Rd; entrance at rear in Duchess of Bedford Walk.* **Sun 23 Apr (2.30-6.30). Adm £3.50, chd free. Light refreshments. Also open Edwardes Square.**

Well planned mature garden on different levels creating areas of varied character and mood. Pergola with Italian fountain and fishpond, lawn with border plants leading to the sunken garden with rockery. Also groundcover, mature trees (making a secluded haven in central London), flowering shrubs and a fine display of spring bulbs. Plenty of seating to relax and enjoy a cup of tea!

🐕 ✳ ☕

187 91 VICAR'S MOOR LANE, N21

Winchmore Hill, N21 1BL. Mr David & Dr Malkanthie Anthonisz. *Tube: Southgate then W9 to Winchmore Hill Green then short walk. Train: Winchmore Hill then short walk via Wades Hill.* **Sun 4 June (2-6). Adm £3.50, chd free. Home-made teas. Also open 1 Wades Grove.**

Established characterful garden. Paths wind through species acers, clematis, climbers shrubs, perennials planted for colour and form. Waterfall and stream flows under raised pergola, viewing platform to

home bred koi carp pond. Exotic elements, and art abound in this much loved evolving paradise. Summerhouse, terraces, sunken garden provide tranquil, comfortable places to sit and contemplate.

☕

188 NEW 1 WADES GROVE, N21

London, N21 1BH. C & K Madhvani. *Tube: Southgate then W9 to Winchmore Hill Green then short walk. Train: Winchmore Hill then short walk via Wades Hill.* **Sun 4 June (2-6). Adm £2.50, chd free. Light refreshments. Also open 91 Vicar's Moor Lane.**

Tiny secluded space in a charming peaceful cul-de-sac. Views divided by a selection of mature and young trees. Planting is loose and naturalistically maintained. Focusing on scented plants, edibles, ground and wall coverings and designed to encourage wildlife. Interesting use of recycled materials.

✳ ☕

189 208 WALM LANE, THE GARDEN FLAT, NW2

London, NW2 3BP. Miranda & Chris Mason, www.thegardennw2.co.uk. *Tube: Kilburn. Garden at junction of Exeter Rd & Walm Lane. Buses: 16, 32, 189, 226, 245, 260, 266, 316 to Cricklewood Broadway, then consult A-Z.* **Sun 28 May, Sun 25 June (2-6). Adm £3.50, chd free. Home-made teas.**

Tranquil oasis of green. Meandering lawn with island beds, curved and deeply planted borders of perennials, scented roses and flowering shrubs. An ornamental fishpond with fountain. Shaded mini woodland area of tall trees underplanted with rhododendrons, ferns, hostas and lily of the valley with winding path from oriental inspired summerhouse to secluded circular seating area. Live music and raffle prizes. Featured in Garden News - Garden of the Week and Garden Answers - Beautiful Gardens.

♿ 🐕 ☕

190 55 WARHAM ROAD, CR2

South Croydon, CR2 6LH. Shanthee Siva. *Off A23, S of central Croydon. Train: South or East Croydon, then buses 119, 405, 455. Free parking.* **Sun 23 July (2-6). Adm £3.50, chd free. Home-made teas.**

This is a plantswoman's much loved high summer season large garden with a broad, immaculate lawn framed by oversized flower packed borders with a variety of exotic perennials, punctuated by fruit trees and shrubs, all peaking at this time. Dahlias as big as plates! Bananas in profusion. Great plants for sale, many from garden cuttings. Home-made teas with a fusion of English and Sri Lankan snacks.

❀ ☕

191 12 WARNER ROAD, N8

London, N8 7HD. Linnette Ralph. *Nr Alexandra Palace, between Crouch End & Muswell Hill. Turning off Priory Rd. Tube to Finsbury Park then W3 bus to Hornsey Fire Station. Buses W7 & 144.* **Sun 11 June (2-5.30). Adm £3.50, chd free. Home-made teas.**

A garden divided into three distinct areas: secluded courtyard area, circular lawn surrounded by mixed planting and a kitchen garden with raised beds, potting shed and a second seating area. Established climbers clothe the tall fences promoting a feeling of seclusion and peace throughout the garden. Featured in The English Garden. Open this year in memory of my Dad, Bob, who died suddenly in 2016. Featured in The English Garden, The Ham & High and Groei & Bloei (Dutch magazine).

❀ ☕

192 THE WATERGARDENS, KT2

Warren Road, Kingston-upon-Thames, KT2 7LF. The Residents' Association. *1m E of Kingston. From Kingston take A308 (Kingston Hill) towards London; after approx ½m turn R into Warren Rd.* **Sun 14 May, Sun 8 Oct (2-4.30). Adm £5, chd free.**

Japanese landscaped garden originally part of Coombe Wood Nursery, planted by the Veitch family in the 1860s. Approx 9 acres with ponds, streams and waterfalls. Many rare trees which, in spring and autumn, provide stunning colour. For the tree lover this is a must see garden. Gardens attractive to wildlife.

193 WEST LODGE PARK, EN4

Cockfosters Road, Hadley Wood, EN4 0PY. Beales Hotels, 020 8216 3904, headoffice@bealeshotels.co.uk, http://www.bealeshotels.co.uk/westlodgepark/the-hotel/arboretum/. *1m S of Potters Bar. On A111. J24 from M25 signed Cockfosters.* **Sun 14 May (2-5); Sun 22 Oct (1-4). Adm £5, chd free. Light refreshments.**

Open for the NGS for over 30yrs, the 35 acre Beale Arboretum consists of over 800 varieties of trees and shrubs, incl National Collection of Hornbeam cultivars (Carpinus betulus) and National collection of Swamp Cypress (Taxodium). Network of paths through good selection of conifers, oaks, maples and mountain ash - all specimens labelled. Beehives and 2 ponds. Stunning collection within the M25. Guided tours available. Breakfasts, morning coffee/biscuits, restaurant lunches, light lunches, dinner all served in the hotel. Please see website.

♿ NPC 🛏 ☕

194 WHITE COTTAGE, BR5

Crockenhill Road, Kevington, BR5 4ER. John Fuller & Alida Burdett, 01689 875134, alidaburdett@aol.com. *Kevington. Crockenhill Rd is B258. Garden at junction with Waldens Rd.* **Sun 2 July (1-5). Adm £5, chd free. Home-made teas. Visits also by arrangement June to Sept.**

Traditional box, clipped hedging and reclaimed materials give structure to this informal garden surrounding a Victorian gardener's cottage. Colour themed beds contain grasses, perennials, shrubs and fruit trees. There is a small but

productive vegetable garden, a pond, rare chickens and bees. Wildlife promotion is a priority. Plenty of places to sit and enjoy the garden. Majority of garden accessible by wheelchair.

♿ 🐕 ❀ ☕

195 WHITGIFT SCHOOL, CR2

Haling Park, South Croydon, CR2 6YT. Sophie Tatzkow, www.whitgift.co.uk. *Train: South Croydon then 5 mins walk. Buses: 119, 197, 312, 466. School entrance on Nottingham Rd.* **Sun 21 May (1-5). Adm £4, chd free. Tea.**

Whitgift Gardens are a series of fascinating, well maintained gardens in a number of original styles within the extensive grounds of Whitgift, all of which help to provide a stimulating environment for students. Head Gardener, Sophie Tatzkow, is on a mission to make sure there isn't another school garden as excellent as this to be found in the UK. Wildlife and birds (wallabies, flamingos, peacocks in an enclosed area) are a feature of the School grounds. Most garden areas accessible by wheelchair. The Andrew Quadrangle can be accessed, but non accessible steps within the garden.

♿ ❀ ☕

196 61 WOLSEY ROAD, KT8

East Molesey, KT8 9EW. Jan & Ken Heath. *Less than 10 mins walk from Hampton Court Palace & station.* **Sun 18 June (2-6). Adm £4, chd free. Home-made teas.**

Romantic, secluded and peaceful garden of two halves designed and maintained by the owners. Part is shaded by two large copper beech trees with woodland planting. The second reached through a beech arch has cottage garden planting, pond and wooden obelisks covered with roses and sweet peas. Beautiful octagonal gazebo overlooks pond plus a new oak framed summerhouse designed and built by the owners. Extensive seating throughout the garden to sit quietly and enjoy your tea and cake, either in the cool shade of the gazebo under the copper beech trees, relaxing in the summerhouse or enjoying the full sunshine elsewhere in the garden. Most of garden wheelchair accessible.

197 33 WOOD VALE, N10

Highgate, N10 3DJ. Mona Abboud, 020 8883 4955, monaabboud@hotmail.com, www.monasgarden.co.uk. *Tube: Highgate, 10 mins walk. Buses: W3, W7 to top of Park Rd.* **Sun 19 Feb (11-3), also open 7 The Grove. Sun 21 May, Sun 13 Aug (2-5.30). Adm £3.50, chd free. Light refreshments. Soup (Feb), soft drinks/biscuits (May/Aug). Visits also by arrangement May to Aug, groups 20 max.**
This award winning garden is home to the Corokia National Collection along with a great number of other unusual Australasian, Mediterranean and exotic plants complemented by perennials and grasses which thrive thanks to 250 tons of topsoil, gravel and compost brought in by wheelbarrow. Emphasis on structure, texture, shapes and contrasting foliage, hence first time opening in Feb to showcase winter structure. Winner Best Back Garden - London Garden Society. Featured in Garden News and recently awarded NCCPG status for Corokia collection.

198 7 WOODBINES AVENUE, KT1

Kingston-upon-Thames, KT1 2AZ. Mr Tony Sharples & Mr Paul Cuthbert. *Take K2, K3, 71 or 281 bus. From Surbiton, bus stop outside Waitrose & exit bus Kingston University Stop. From Kingston, walk or get the bus from Eden Street (opp Heals).* **Sun 2 July (1-6). Adm £4, chd free. Light refreshments.**
We have created a winding path through our 70ft garden with trees, evergreen structure, perennial flowers and grasses. Deep borders create depth, variety, texture and interest around the garden. We like to create a garden party so feel welcome to stay as long as you like.

199 NEW 10 WOODSIDE AVENUE, N6

London, N6 4SS. Sheila & Anthony Rabin. *½ m from East Finchley underground station.* **Sun 6 Aug (2-6). Adm £3.50, chd free. Home-made teas.**
An attractive densely planted suburban garden created from scratch 3yrs ago. Large herbaceous perennial borders give colour from April to October. A good contrast with shade loving area and terraced patio with alpine planting.

200 NEW 209 WORSLEY BRIDGE ROAD, BR3

Beckenham, BR3 1RW. Mrs Lizzy Spencer. *100 metres from junction of Copers Cope Road & Worsley Bridge Road. 352 Bus route. Opp Kent County Cricket Ground.* **Sun 2 Apr (2-5). Combined adm with 12 Overbrae £5, chd free. Light refreshments.**
150ft suburban garden with a meandering path taking visitors from the pot-patio, through lawned area with mixed borders of roses, climbers, perennials shrubs and grasses, a paved shady area with a gargantuan bay tree and an ancient recumbent apple tree, up past more roses and mixed planting to a gravel area, and the upper pergola, covered in akebia, roses and clematis. Lovely spring flowering.

201 1 YORK CLOSE, W7

Hanwell, W7 3JB. Tony Hulme & Eddy Fergusson. *By road only, entrance to York Close via Church Rd. Nearest station Hanwell mainline. Buses E3, 195, 207.* **Sat 27 May (2-6). Adm £5, chd free. Sun 28 May (2-6). Adm £4, chd free.**
Tiny quirky, prize winning garden extensively planted with eclectic mix incl hosta collection, many unusual and tropical plants. Plantaholics paradise. Many surprises in this unique and very personal garden. Pimms on Saturday (incl in adm), Prosecco on Sunday for a donation!

202 38 YORK ROAD, W5

Ealing, W5 4SG. Nick & Elena Gough. *Northfields & South Ealing Tube - 5 mins. Buses: E3, 65. 5 mins. Free parking in local streets. Off Northfield Av & South Ealing Rd.* **Evening opening Sat 22 July (6.30-9). Adm £5.50, chd free. Wine. Sun 23 July (2-6). Adm £4.50, chd free. Tea.**
A hidden oasis full of surprises and built on several different levels. This walled corner garden was restored in under 10 months by its present owners, having been acquired in 2014. There are a number of beautiful and diverse areas within it, all of which add to its unique atmosphere, incl a woodland dell path, circular sun terrace, large pond with waterfalls and flower filled parterre. EalingToday.co.uk. Published article - Is this Ealing's Most Beautiful Garden? Judges Special Award for an Outstanding and Totally Delightful Garden.

203 ZEN GARDEN, W3

55 Carbery Avenue, Acton, London, W3 9AB. Three Wheels Shin Buddhist Temple, www.threewheels.org.uk. *Tube: Acton Town 5 mins walk, 200yds off A406.* **Sat 3, Sun 4, Sat 17, Sun 18 June (2-5). Adm £3, chd free. Home-made teas.**
Pure Japanese Zen garden (so no flowers) with 12 large and small rocks of various colours and textures set in islands of moss and surrounded by a sea of grey granite gravel raked in a stylised wave pattern. Garden surrounded by trees and bushes outside a cob wall. Oak framed wattle and daub shelter with Norfolk reed thatched roof. Japanese tea ceremony demonstration and talks by designer/creator of the garden. Buddha Room open to visitors. Featured in The Evening Standard online weekend gallery, The Time Out London things to do Absolute London.

NORFOLK

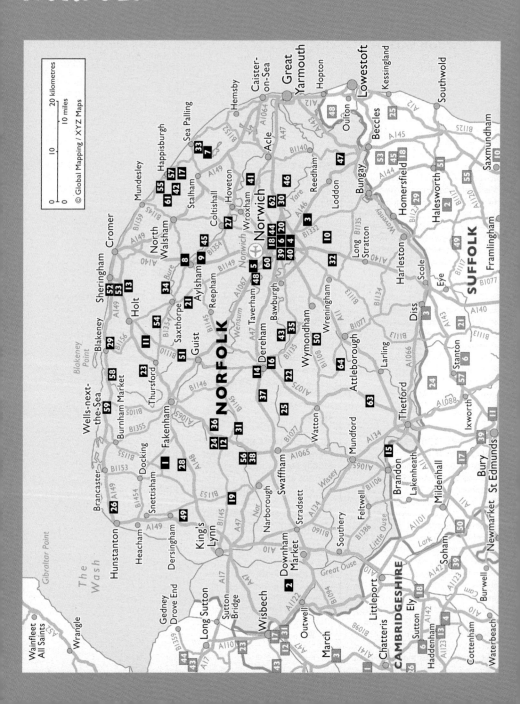

Norfolk is a lovely low-lying county, predominantly agricultural with a relatively small population.

Visitors come to Norfolk because they are attracted to the peaceful countryside, the medieval churches, the coastal area and the large network of rivers and waterways of the Broads. Norwich the capital is a fine city.

Our garden owners are a loyal group some of whom have been opening their garden gates for over 50 years, whilst others will be opening for the first time. Sizes vary enormously from those of the large estates and manor houses, to the smaller cottages, courtyards and town gardens. Located throughout the county, some styles are old and traditional, whilst others are modern or naturalistic.

So come and experience yourself what is affectionately known as 'Normal for Norfolk' and the great variety of beautiful gardens it has to offer.

Below: Sandringham Gardens

Volunteers

County Organisers
Fiona Black
01692 650247
fiona.black@ngs.org.uk

Julia Stafford Allen
01760 755334
julia.staffordallen@ngs.org.uk

County Treasurer
Neil Foster
01328 701288
neilfoster@lexhamestate.co.uk

Publicity
Graham Watts
01362 690065
graham.watts@ngs.org.uk

Social Media
Claire Reinhold
01485 576221
reinholdclaire@googlemail.com

Photographer
Simon Smith
01362 860530
helicoptersags@hotmail.com

Booklet Co-ordinator
Sally Bate
07881 907735
sally.bate@ngs.org.uk

Assistant County Organisers
Isabel Cator
01603 270748
isabel@markcator.co.uk

Jennifer Dyer
01263 761811
jennifer.dyer.16@outlook.com

Sue Guest
01362 858317
guest63@btinternet.com

Stephanie Powell
01328 730113
stephaniepowell@creake.com

Sue Roe 01603 455917
sue@cliveandsue.plus.com

OPENING DATES

All entries subject to change. For latest information check www.ngs.org.uk

Map locator numbers are shown to the right of each garden name.

February
Snowdrop Festival

Saturday 18th
Horstead House 27

Sunday 26th
Bagthorpe Hall 1
Chestnut Farm 13

March

Sunday 5th
Chestnut Farm 13
◆ Raveningham Hall 47

Sunday 26th
Gayton Hall 19

April

Sunday 2nd
16 Witton Lane 62

Sunday 9th
◆ Mannington Hall 34

Sunday 16th
Desert World Gardens 15
Wretham Lodge 63

Monday 17th
Desert World Gardens 15
Wretham Lodge 63

Saturday 22nd
◆ East Ruston Old
   Vicarage 17

Sunday 23rd
The Old House 41

Sunday 30th
NEW Lake House 30
Plovers Hill 46

May

Monday 1st
Lake House 30
Plovers Hill 46
Witton Hall 61

Sunday 7th
Bishop's House 6

Sunday 14th
Bolwick Hall 9
Holme Hale Hall 25

Thursday 18th
◆ Sheringham Park 53

Sunday 21st
Lexham Hall 31

Tuesday 23rd
◆ Stody Lodge 54

90th Anniversary Weekend

Saturday 27th
NEW Long Gores 33

Sunday 28th
NEW Bank House 2
NEW Long Gores 33
The Old Rectory,
   Brandon Parva 43
Warborough House 58

Monday 29th
Chestnut Farm 13

June

Sunday 4th
Kettle Hill 29

Thursday 8th
◆ Sheringham Park 53

Sunday 11th
High House Gardens 22

Wednesday 14th
High House Gardens 22

Friday 16th
NEW Sheringham Hall 52

Sunday 18th
Manor House Farm,
   Wellingham 36
Norwich Gardens 40

Thursday 22nd
◆ Mannington Hall 34

Sunday 25th
The Bear Shop 4

9 Bellomonte Crescent 5
Brinton Grange 11
The Grange, Heydon 21
NEW 27 St Edmunds
   Road 48
Walcott House 57

July

Sunday 2nd
Blickling Lodge 8
Desert World Gardens 15
NEW Holme-next-the-Sea 26

Sunday 9th
Chestnut Farm 13
Wells-Next-The-Sea
   Gardens 59
4 Wensum Crescent 60

Saturday 15th
Black Horse Cottage 7

Sunday 16th
Black Horse Cottage 7
68 Elm Grove Lane 18
Manor Farm, Coston 35
NEW Minns Farm Barns 38
Tudor Lodgings 56

Saturday 22nd
Dunbheagan 16

Sunday 23rd
Dunbheagan 16

Sunday 30th
Brick Kiln House 10
Dale Farm 14

August

Wednesday 2nd
Lexham Hall 31

Sunday 6th
38 Gorse Road 20
The Long Barn 32
NEW Mill Farm 37
North Lodge 39
33 Orchard Close 44
Warborough House 58

Sunday 13th
68 Elm Grove Lane 18
Holme Hale Hall 25
North Lodge 39
◆ Severals Grange 51

Sunday 20th
Oxnead Hall 45
Yeoman's Cottage 64

Saturday 26th
Suil Na Mara 55

Sunday 27th
Suil Na Mara 55

September

Sunday 3rd
Chapel Cottage 12
7 Holly Close 24
Sea Mere 50

Sunday 10th
High House Gardens 22
The Old Rectory,
   Ridlington 42

Wednesday 13th
High House Gardens 22

October

Sunday 1st
◆ Hindringham Hall 23

Saturday 7th
◆ East Ruston Old
   Vicarage 17

Sunday 22nd
NEW The Barn 3

By Arrangement

NEW Bank House 2
Bishop's House 6
Brick Kiln House 10
Chapel Cottage 12
Chestnut Farm 13
Dale Farm 14
Desert World Gardens 15
Dunbheagan 16
68 Elm Grove Lane 18
Holme Hale Hall 25
Lake House 30
NEW Mill Farm 37
Plovers Hill 46
Sea Mere 50
Suil Na Mara 55
Wretham Lodge 63
Yeoman's Cottage 64

With your support we can help raise awareness of Carers Trust and unpaid carers

THE GARDENS

1 BAGTHORPE HALL

Bagthorpe, Bircham, PE31 6QY.
Mr & Mrs D Morton,
01485 578528,
dgmorton@hotmail.com.
3½ m N of East Rudham, off A148.
King's Lynn to Fakenham. At East
Rudham L opp The Crown, 3½ m,
hamlet of Bagthorpe. Farm buildings
on L, wood on R, white gates set
back from rd, top of drive. **Sun 26
Feb (11-4). Adm £4, chd free.
Home-made teas. Home-made
soups made with vegetables
from the farm.**
Snowdrops carpeting a circular
woodland walk, returning through
the walled and main garden. Some
access for wheelchairs in the garden,
but not the woodland walk.
🐕 ❀ 🚗 🏛 ☕

2 NEW BANK HOUSE

Middle Drove, Marshland
St James, Wisbech, PE14 8JT.
Teresa Lovick & Andrew
Stephens, 01945 430599,
teresajoylovick@gmail.com.
A1122 at Outwell nr aquaduct, turn
onto Mullicourt Rd, sharp L onto
Angle Rd, R & R again onto Stow Rd.
5 min, turn L at sign onto Middle
Drove. Cross over bridge with T-lights.
**Sun 28 May (10-4). Adm £3.50,
chd free. Home-made teas.**
**Visits also by arrangement May
to July by arrangement only for
groups of 10 to 30.**
An exuberant and established
2 acre garden with a whole range
of growing conditions, from damp
shade to dry gravel: vegetable and
fruit areas, new grass garden, small
recently planted orchard, a bog
garden, formal lawn, mixed borders,
patios, terraces and variety of secret
spaces. Year-round interest but
especially a range of primulas, irises
and roses peaking from May to July.
Due to large amount of gravel paths
and changes of level, we regret this
garden has no wheelchair access.
🐕 ❀ ☕

3 NEW THE BARN

Spur Lane, Framingham Earl,
Norwich, NR14 7SA. Mr James
Colman. 3m SE of Norwich. From
A47 take A146 for 1½ m. Turn R at
Old Feathers signed Framingham
Pigot Business Centre. Follow the
signs to Poringland after 1m the
entrance is on L. **Sun 22 Oct (10-
3). Adm £5, chd free.**
The Arboretum at Framingham
currently some 14 hectares, lies
on the south slope of a 50 metre
hill from which there are extensive
views to the north east across some
ornamental ponds built in the C18,
and towards Great Yarmouth and
the sea. In the middle distance St
Andrew's church, Framingham Pigot
is framed.
☕

4 THE BEAR SHOP

Elm Hill, Norwich, NR3 1HN.
Robert Stone. Norwich City Centre.
From St Andrews, L to Princes St, then
L to Elm Hill. Garden at side of shop
through large wooden gate & along
alleyway. **Sun 25 June (11-4.30).
Adm £3, chd free. Home-made
teas.**
Considered to be based on a design
by Gertrude Jekyll, a small terraced
garden behind a C15 house in

the historic Cathedral Quarter of
Norwich. Enjoy the tranquillity of the
riverside. Wheel chair access is limited
to the upper level of the garden.
🐕 ☕

5 9 BELLOMONTE CRESCENT

Drayton, Norwich, NR8 6EJ.
Wendy & Chris Fitch. 5m N of
Norwich. Turn off A1067 at Drayton
Xds. Drive past front of Red Lion PH
towards church. Access through gate
back of churchyard or continue 1st
exit r'about to School Rd, 1st L turn
to Bellomonte Cres. **Sun 25 June
(11-5). Combined adm with 27
St Edmunds Road £6, chd free.
Home-made teas. and plant
sales at both gardens.**
On approx ¼ acre plot, the garden
has deep borders of traditional
shrubs and perennials mixed with
exotic mediterranean plants. A
large deck overlooks main lawn
with planted pergolas. Borrowed
landscape with views of Drayton
church gives interest and privacy.
Terraced upper garden with fruit
and vegetables and secluded
courtyard area. Home-made cakes
and plants for sale. No wheelchair
access to upper levels.
❀ ☕

Manor Farm

© Val Corbett

6 BISHOP'S HOUSE

Bishopgate, Norwich, NR3 1SB.
The Bishop of Norwich,
01603 614172, bishops.chaplain@
dioceseofnorwich.org, www.
dioceseofnorwich.org/gardens.
*City centre. Located in the city centre
near the Law Courts & The Adam &
Eve PH.* **Sun 7 May (1-5). Adm
£3, chd free. Home-made teas.**
Visits also by arrangement
4 acre walled garden dating back
to the C12. Extensive lawns with
specimen trees. Borders with many
rare and unusual shrubs. Spectacular
herbaceous borders flanked by
yew hedges. Rose beds, meadow
labyrinth, kitchen garden, woodland
walk and long border with hostas
and bamboo walk. Popular plant
sales. Gravel paths and some slopes.

& ❋ ☕

7 BLACK HORSE COTTAGE

The Green, Hickling, Norwich,
NR12 0YA. Yvonne Pugh. *3m E of
Stalham. Turn E off A149 at Catfield,
turn L onto Heath Road, 1½m to
centre of Hickling village. Next to The
Greyhound Inn (Good food!).* **Sat 15,
Sun 16 July (12-5). Adm £4, chd
free. Home-made teas.**
Thatched house with traditional barn
½m from Hickling Broad. Plantsman's
garden over 2 acres professionally
redesigned. Spacious borders
and islands with diverse range of
characterful planting. Particular
emphasis on achieving full year round
interest. Wide range of managed
mature specimen trees. Many
long two-way vistas. Wide mown
walkways through large meadow.
Various sitting opportunities!

& ❋ ☕

Gardens are at
the heart of
hospice care

8 BLICKLING LODGE

Blickling, Norwich, NR11 6PS.
Michael & Henrietta Lindsell. *½m
N of Aylsham. Leave Aylsham on old
Cromer rd towards Ingworth. Over
hump back bridge & house is on R.*
**Sun 2 July (2-5.30). Adm £4.50,
chd free.**
Georgian house (not open) set in
17 acres of parkland including cricket
pitch, mixed border, walled kitchen
garden, yew garden, woodland/water
garden and river walk.

& ❋ 🚗 ☕

9 BOLWICK HALL

Marsham, NR10 5PU. Mr & Mrs
G C Fisher. *8m N of Norwich off
A140. Heading N towards Aylsham,
at Marsham take 1st R after Plough
PH, signed 'By Road' then next R
onto private rd to front of Hall.* **Sun
14 May (1-5). Adm £5, chd free.
Home-made teas.**
Landscaped gardens and park
surrounding a late Georgian hall.
The original garden design is
attributed to Humphry Repton. The
current owners have rejuvenated
the borders, planted gravel and
formal gardens and clad the walls
of the house in old roses. Enjoy a
woodland walk around the lake as
well as as stroll through the working
vegetable and fruit garden with its
double herbaceous border. Please
ask at gate for wheelchair directions.

& ❋ ☕

10 BRICK KILN HOUSE

Priory Lane, Shotesham St
Mary, Norwich, NR15 1UJ. Jim
& Jenny Clarke, 01508 550232,
jennyclarke@uwclub.net. *6m S of
Norwich. Shotesham All Saints Church
may be approached from Poringland,
Stoke Holy Cross or Saxlingham
Nethergate. Priory Lane in 200m
from church on R on Saxlingham
Road.* **Sun 30 July (11-5). Adm
£5, chd free. Home-made teas.**
**Visits also by arrangement May
to Sept.**
2 acre garden with a mixture of
different types of planting and
sculpture. A large terrace, lawns and
herbaceous borders near the house.
A pergola with wisteria and clematis
through an intimate rose garden
surrounded by a 'topiaried 'yew

hedge. Mature trees and diverse
planting in a woodland garden with
a stream. Parking in field but easy
access to brick path.

& 🐄 ❋ ☕ 🌱

11 BRINTON GRANGE

Stody Road, Brinton, Melton
Constable, NR24 2QH. Richard &
Lesley Ellis. *Brinton, between Melton
Constable & Holt. From Norwich take
A1067 turn R at Guist on B1110.
From Holt take B1110 to Guist.
From Fakenham take B1354 towards
Briston turn L on B1110.* **Sun 25
June (11-4). Adm £5, chd free.
Home-made teas.**
Brinton Grange and The Coach
House are neighbouring properties
situated within this conservation
village with grounds totalling 6 acres
including mixed borders, a formal
parterre, water gardens, sculptures,
an orchard, walled vegetable garden,
wooded areas and wild flower
meadow. Lots of interest including
several specimen trees. Homemade
teas and cakes served in the garden.
Plants for sale. Wheelchair access
is limited but it is possible to reach
most of the garden. Access to
walled garden and meadow is more
difficult as gravel.

& 🐄 ❋ ☕

12 CHAPEL COTTAGE

Rougham, King's Lynn, PE32 2SE.
Sarah Butler, 01328 838347,
sarahbutler4@gmail.com. *15m
E from King's Lynn, 8m SW from
Fakenham. Rougham is situated on
B1145. Opp old school & next to
old methodist chapel. Parking in the
centre of the village.* **Sun 3 Sept
(11-5). Combined adm with
7 Holly Close £3, chd free.
Home-made teas Visits also by
arrangement**
A very naturalistic cottage garden
designed by owner who describes
herself as an 'ist', combining her
interest, study and work as a
landscape designer for biodiversity
and amateur naturalist, entomologist
and botanist. Divided into charming
peaceful areas that include a pond,
vegetables, shade, and herbs. Wild
flower lawns, and beehives. Plenty
of seating.

❋ ☕

13 CHESTNUT FARM

Church Road, West Beckham,
NR25 6NX. Mr & Mrs John
McNeil Wilson, 01263 822241,
judywilson100@gmail.com. 2½m
S of Sheringham. On A148 opp
Sheringham Park entrance. Take the rd
signed BY WAY TO WEST BECKHAM,
about ¾m to the village sign & you
have arrived. **Sun 26 Feb, Sun 5
Mar (11-4); Mon 29 May, Sun 9
July (11-5). Adm £5, chd free.
Light refreshments. Home-made
teas. Visits also by arrangement
Feb to July group sizes 5 - 50.
Conducted tours offered,
refreshments by request.**
Mature three acre garden with
bulbs, shrubs, trees and herbaceous
borders. A lifetime's collection
of plants, including many unusual
ones. In Spring over 90 different
varieties of Snowdrops, together
with seasonal flowering shrubs and
bulbs. Later the colourful borders
come into their own, including
the Handkerchief tree, Cornus
capitata and kousa and many other
flowering trees and shrubs. Featured
in Eastern Daily Press. Wheelchair
access tricky if wet.

  ♿ 🐄 ✿ 🚗 ☕ 🍷

14 DALE FARM

Sandy Lane, Dereham,
NR19 2EA. Graham & Sally
Watts, 01362 690065,
grahamwatts@dsl.pipex.com.
16m W of Norwich. 12m E of
Swaffham. From A47 take B1146
signed to Fakenham, turn R at
T-junction, ¼m turn L into Sandy Lane
(before pelican crossing). **Sun 30
July (11-5). Adm £4.50, chd free.
Home-made teas. Visits also by
arrangement June & July, groups
of 10+.**
2 acre plant lover's garden with a
large spring-fed pond. Over 900
plant species and varieties featured
in exuberantly planted borders
and waterside gardens. These incl a
collection of 90 species and varieties
of hydrangea. Vegetable plot, fruit
trees, naturalistic planting areas,
gravel garden and sculptures. Gravel
drive and some grass paths. Wide
range of plants for sale incl many
hydrangeas.

  🐄 ✿ 🚗 ☕ 🍷

The Grange

15 DESERT WORLD GARDENS

Thetford Road (B1107), Santon
Downham, IP27 0TU. Mr & Mrs
Barry Gayton, 01842 765861.
4m N of Thetford. On B1107
Brandon 2m. **Sun 16, Mon 17 Apr,
Sun 2 July (10-5). Adm £3.50,
chd free. Light refreshments.
Visits also by arrangement
Mar to Oct.**
1¼ acres plantsman's garden
created by Radio Cambridgeshire
gardener specializing in tropical
and arid plants. Hardy succulents
– sempervivums and plectranthus.
Bamboos, herbaceous, spring/
summer bulbs and over 70 varieties
of magnolias. View from roof garden.
Area of primula auriculas incl
theatre. Large collection of hardy
ferns. Glasshouses containing cacti/
succulent collection will be closed
on open day but viewing can be
made by appt. Featured on BBC
Radio Cambridgeshire and National
Gardeners' Question Time.

✿ 🚗 ☕ 🍷

16 DUNBHEAGAN

Dereham Road, Westfield,
NR19 1QF. Jean & John
Walton, 01362 696163,
jandjwalton@btinternet.com. 2m
S of Dereham. From Dereham take
A1075 towards Shipdham. L into
Westfield Rd at Vauxhall Garage.
At Xrds ahead into lane, becomes
Dereham Rd. **Sat 22, Sun 23 July
(12.30-5). Adm £4.50, chd free.
Home-made teas provided
by Marie Curie. Visits also by
arrangement June & July, groups
no minimum.**
Relax and enjoy walking among
extensive borders and island beds - a
riot of colour all Summer. Includes
unique 'heaven and hell' and a vibrant
hot border. Vast collection of rare,
unusual and more recognisable plants
in this ever changing plantsman's
garden. If you love flowers, you'll love
it here. We aim for the WOW factor.
New planting and ideas for 2017.
Sculptures by Toby Winterbourn.
Featured in Nick Bailey's new book
365 Days of Colour, Sarah Wint's
book Sunshine over Clover and
Garden Answers magazine. Covered
in local press. Gravel driveway.

  ♿ 🐄 ✿ 🚗 ☕ 🍷

East Ruston Old Vicarage

17 ♦ EAST RUSTON OLD VICARAGE

East Ruston, Norwich, NR12 9HN. Alan Gray & Graham Robeson, 01692 650432, erovoffice@btconnect.com, www.eastrustonoldvicarage.co.uk. *3m N of Stalham. Turn off A149 onto B1159 signed Bacton, Happisburgh. After 2m turn R 200yds N of East Ruston Church (ignore sign to East Ruston).* **For NGS: Sat 22 Apr, Sat 7 Oct (1-5.30). Adm £8.50, chd £1. Light refreshments.** For other opening times and information, please phone, email or visit garden website.

32-acre exotic coastal garden incl traditional borders, exotic garden, desert wash, sunk garden, topiary, water features, walled and Mediterranean gardens. Many rare and unusual plants, stunning plant combinations, wild flower meadows, old-fashioned cornfield, vegetable and cutting gardens.

  ♿ ✿ 🚗 ☕

18 68 ELM GROVE LANE

Norwich, NR3 3LF. Selwyn Taylor, 07939 230826, selwyntaylor@btconnect.com, www.selwyntaylorgarden.co.uk. *1¾ m N of Norwich city centre. Proceed from Norwich city centre to Magdalen St, to Magdalen Rd, bear L to St. Clements Hill turn L into Elmgrove Lane. No.68 is at bottom on R.* **Sun 16 July, Sun 13 Aug (11-4). Adm £4, chd free. Home-made teas. Selection of delicious homemade cakes, including gluten free. Visits also by arrangement June to Aug up to 15 people.**

This extended living/working space is the owner's endeavour to redefine a suburban garden and to provide inspiration when viewed from his studio window. Aesthetic values, initially took precedent over gardening know-how, but over 30 years a more balanced approach has resulted in an eclectic array of informal planting, rich in colour and form and full of surprises. Featured in Garden News, Amateur Gardening and Norfolk Magazine.

19 GAYTON HALL
Gayton, Kings Lynn, PE32 1PL.
Viscount & Viscountess Marsham.'
*6m E of King's Lynn. Gayton is
situated on B1145; R on B1153. R
down Back St 1st entrance on L.* Sun
26 Mar (1-5). Adm £5, chd free.
Home-made teas.
This rambling semi-wild 20 acre
water garden, has over 2m of
paths, and contains lawns, lakes,
streams, bridges and woodland.
In the traditional and waterside
borders are primulas, astilbes,
hostas, lysichiton and gunneras. A
variety of unusual trees many of
which are labelled, and shrubs have
been planted over the years. There
is an abundance of spring bulbs.
Wheelchair access to most areas,
paths are gravel and grass.

20 38 GORSE ROAD
Norwich, NR7 0AY. Mrs Ruth
Boden. *½m E of City Centre.
Proceed up Ketts Hill to Heartsease
r'about, straight across into
Plumstead Rd East, 1st turning on
R into Aerodrome Rd, 1st L Gorse
Rd, No 38 on R.* Sun 6 Aug (11-
4). Combined adm with 33
Orchard Close £4, chd free.
Home-made teas.
A plantsman's cottage style
garden, including mixed borders of
perennials (some unusual), shrubs,
roses and grasses. Woodland
area, small bog garden and white
garden. A curving gravel path,
between lawned area, leading to
summerhouse with a beach-themed
area. One small step into garden.

21 THE GRANGE, HEYDON
Heydon, Norwich, NR11 6RH. Mrs
T Bulwer-Long. *13m N of Norwich.
7m from Holt off B1149 signed
Heydon 2m, on entering village, 1st
drive on R, signed The Grange.* Sun
25 June (2-5.30). Adm £4, chd
free. Home-made teas.
Heydon Grange is a predominantly
C17 Dutch style Gabled Farmhouse
(not open) in mellow rose brick.
The Garden has been extenively
rejuvinated over the last 7 years and
is semi enclosed by ancient brick

walls and yew hedges with various
topiary that was planted cica 1920.
There are a mixture of herbaceous
borders and a wide selection of
shrub and climbing roses.

22 HIGH HOUSE GARDENS
Blackmoor Row, Shipdham,
Thetford, IP25 7PU. Mr & Mrs
F Nickerson. *6m SW of Dereham.
Take the airfield or Cranworth Rd off
A1075 in Shipdham. Blackmoor Row
is signed.* Sun 11, Wed 14 June,
Sun 10, Wed 13 Sept (2-5.30).
Adm £4, chd free. Home-made
teas.
3 acre plantsman's garden with
colour-themed herbaceous borders
with extensive range of perennials.
Box-edged rose and shrub borders.
Woodland garden, pond and bog
area. Newly planted orchard and
vegetable garden. Wildlife area.
Glasshouses. Gravel paths.

23 ♦ HINDRINGHAM HALL
Blacksmiths Lane, Hindringham,
NR21 0QA. Mr & Mrs
Charles Tucker, 01328 878226,
info@hindringhamhall.org,
www.hindringhamhall.org. *7m
from Holt/Fakenham/Wells. Turn off
A148 between Holt & Fakenham at
Crawfish PH. Drive into Hindringham
(2m). Turn L into Blacksmiths Lane.*
For NGS: Sun 1 Oct (10-4).
Adm £5, chd free. Home-made
teas. For other opening times and
information, please phone, email or
visit garden website.
Tudor Manor House surrounded
with complete C12 moat. Working
Walled Vegetable Garden, Victorian
Nut Walk, Medieval Fishponds,
Formal beds, Bog and Stream
gardens. The garden has something
of interest throughout the year
continuing well into autumn.
Described by most visitors as
'a natural english garden'. End of
year plant sale. Featured in The
Norfolk Magazine and on Mustard
TV. Suitable for wheelchairs able to
cope with gravel paths.

24 7 HOLLY CLOSE
Rougham, King's Lynn, PE32 2SJ.
Derek Barker. *15m E from King's
Lynn, 8m SW from Fakenham.
Rougham is situated on B1145.
Parking in the centre of the village.
Holly close is ¼m from the church.*
Sun 3 Sept (11-5). Combined
adm with Chapel Cottage £3,
chd free. Home-made teas at
Chapel Cottage.
The front garden demonstrates a
varied design of planting, with well
stocked borders filled with colour
and structure, to last throughout
the season. The rear garden is laid
out in potager style, with fruit trees,
flowers and vegetables encouraging
bees and wildlife, following an
organic theme. The garden shows
how much can be achieved in a
small plot providing late summer
colour.

25 HOLME HALE HALL
Holme Hale, nr Swaffham,
IP25 7ED. Mr & Mrs Simon
Broke, 01760 440328,
simon.broke@hotmail.co.uk. *6m
E of Swaffham, 8m W of Dereham,
5m N of Watton. 2m S of Necton
off A47 main rd. 1m E of Holme
Hale Village.* Sun 14 May, Sun
13 Aug (12-4). Adm £6, chd
free. Light refreshments in Tea
Rooms behind the Hall, close
to car park, available 12 til 4.
Visits also by arrangement
Apr to Sept coach parties very
welcome.
Noted for its spring display of tulips
and alliums, historic wisteria plus mid
and late summer flowering. Walled
kitchen garden and front garden
designed and planted in 2000 by
Chelsea winner Arne Maynard. The
garden incorporates herbaceous
borders, trained fruit, vegetables and
traditional greenhouse. The garden
was rejuvenated by Arne Maynard in
2016 and the results will be worth
seeing in 2017. Featured in Country
Life and The Gardens of Arne
Maynard. Wheelchair access available
to the Front Garden, Kitchen
Garden and tearoom.

GROUP OPENING

26 NEW HOLME-NEXT-THE-SEA

Norfolk, PE36 6LH. *The village of Holme-next-the-Sea is on the A149, 3m E of Hunstanton. Car parking in the centre of the village.* Sun 2 July (11-5). Combined adm £5, chd free. Light refreshments in the Village Hall.

NEW BERKELEY HOUSE
John & Janet Loversidge.

NEW THE STABLES
Sue Martin.

NEW SUNSET COTTAGE,
Marianne Charles.

NEW VINE COTTAGE
Mr and Mrs Malcolm Starr.

The pretty little village of Holme-next-the-Sea is located within the North Norfolk Heritage Coast and a designated Area of Outstanding Natural Beauty. Many of the houses are built using the local materials of clunch and carr stone which are often combined with brick, flint and cobbles resulting in the variety of individual patterns unique to this part of the county. Berkeley House opp church is a ½ acre garden which has been created over 20 years with neat herbaceous and shrub borders, and a Mediterranean style area with small water feature. The Stables is an informal cottage style garden of charm and character with plenty of colour and many roses. Sunset Cottage, a small cottage style garden, has borders which are packed with shrubs and perennials for year round interest, and is an example of what can be achieved by a plant lover who gardens with arthritis. Vine Cottage is a 1½ acre garden recently created and still under development, designed in symmetrical formality with contemporary block and soft planting of grasses and perennial flowers. Delicious refreshments will be served all day in the village hall. Disabled WC in the Church.

🐄 ✿ ☕

27 HORSTEAD HOUSE
Mill Road, Horstead, Norwich, NR12 7AU. Mr & Mrs Matthew Fleming. *6m NE of Norwich on North Walsham rd, B1150. Down Mill Rd opp the Recruiting Sargeant PH.* Sat 18 Feb (11-4). Adm £4, chd free. Home-made teas.
Millions of beautiful snowdrops carpet the woodland setting with winter flowering shrubs. A stunning feature are the dogwoods growing on a small island in R Bure, which flows through the garden. Small walled garden. Wheelchair access to main snowdrop area.

& 🐄 ☕

28 ♦ HOUGHTON HALL WALLED GARDEN
Bircham Road, New Houghton, King's Lynn, PE31 6UE. The Cholmondeley Gardens Trust, 01485 528569, info@houghtonhall.com, www.houghtonhall.com. *11m W of Fakenham. 13m E of King's Lynn. Signed from A148.* For opening times and information, please phone, email or visit garden website.
The award-winning, five-acre Walled Garden includes a spectacular double-sided herbaceous border, a rose parterre, a Mediterranean garden, and a kitchen garden with arches and espaliers of apples and pears. There are also glasshouses and antique statues and fountains. A special exhibition by British Sculptor and Turner Prize winner Richard Long will be held in 2017. Plants on sale. Gravel and grass paths. Electric buggies available for use in the walled garden.

& ✿ 🚗 ☕

29 KETTLE HILL
The Downs, Langham Road, Blakeney, NR25 7PN. Mrs Winch. *Turning to garden is off Langham Rd.* Sun 4 June (11-4.30). Adm £5, chd free. Home-made teas.
Kettle Hill has been quietly simmering but is now back on the boil! With a new fruit garden designed by Tamara Bridge, as well as re designed and re planted coastal and walled gardens. A formal parterre, long herbaceous borders, wild flower meadow and a secret garden. Stunning rose garden and grass paths through woods, a real treat for any garden lover. Excellent views across Morston to the sea, framed by lavender, roses and sky. Gravel drive way and lawns but hard paving near the house. Ramps are situated around the garden making all except the wood accessible for wheelchairs.

& 🐄 ✿ Ⓓ ☕

30 NEW LAKE HOUSE
Postwick Lane, Roman Drive, Brundall, NR13 5LU. Mrs Janet Muter, 01603 712933. *5m E of Norwich. On A47; take Brundall turn at r'about. Turn R into Postwick Lane at T-junction.* Sun 30 Apr, Mon 1 May (11-5). Combined adm with Plovers Hill £7, chd free. Home-made teas at Plovers Hill, Strumpshaw. Visits also by arrangement refreshments can be arranged.
In the centre of Brundall Gardens, a series of ponds descends through a wooded valley to the shore of a lake. Steep paths wind through a variety of shrubs and flowers in season, which attract many kinds of rare birds, dragonflies and mammals. Water features, great variety of bird life, dragonflies, pond life and forest trees.

🐄 ✿ 🚗 ☕

Funds from NGS gardens help Macmillan support thousands of people every year

31 LEXHAM HALL

nr Litcham, PE32 2QJ.
Mr & Mrs Neil Foster,
www.lexhamestate.co.uk. *2m
W of Litcham. 6m N of Swaffham
off B1145.* Sun 21 May, Wed 2
Aug (11-5). Adm £6, chd free.
Home-made teas.
Fine C17/18 Hall (not open).
Parkland with lake and river walks.
Formal garden with terraces, yew
hedges, roses and mixed borders.
Traditional kitchen garden with
crinkle crankle wall. A garden of
all year round interest. In May
rhododendrons, azaleas, camellias
and magnolias dominate the
3 acre woodland garden. Fine trees.
August sees the many walled garden
borders at their peak. Vegetables
and fruit trees, many espaliered.
A reed thatched summerhouse,
with 'Gothic' windows and door,
designs from which were found on
ruins of two other summerhouses.
A 15' wisteria clad 'Dome' is the
centrepiece in the walled garden
with trellis backed parallel borders.
Featured in Eastern Daily Press.

32 THE LONG BARN

Flordon Road, Newton Flotman,
Norwich, NR15 1QX. Mr & Mrs
Mark Bedini. *6m S of Norwich
along A140. Leave A140 in Newton
Flotman towards Flordon. Exit
Newton Flotman & approx
150 yards beyond 'passing place' on
L, turn L into drive. Note that SatNav
does not bring you to destination.*
Sun 6 Aug (11-5). Adm £5, chd
free. Home-made teas.
Herbaceous borders and woodland
garden mainly created in 2014
around sympathetic barn conversion
in parkland setting. Strong
Mediterranean influences around
outdoor pool, a walled group of
olive trees and courtyard feature.
Woodland walks and extensive
parkland views.

33 NEW LONG GORES

Hickling, Norwich, NR12 0BE.
Dominic Vlasto. *From Stalham/
Potter Heigham (A149 to Hickling
village follow yellow signs. Leave
village with church on R & take Sea*

*Palling Lane. Driveway to Long Gores
½m on R.* Sat 27, Sun 28 May
(10.30-4.30). Adm £5, chd free.
Home-made teas.
Set in undisturbed coastal pastures
between Hickling Broad and the sea,
semi-wild gardens surround cottages
on the edge of a wetland nature
reserve. Once home of ecologist
Marietta Pallis (1882-1963),
the gardens contain interesting
Mediterranean rarities collected
by her and two subsequent
generations of the same family. The
main feature in May/June is a large
collection of old bearded irises.
A 20-minute trail into part of the
reserve will be open for interested
naturalists, and for which waterproof
footwear will be essential. There
will be a small exhibition on the life
and work of Marietta Pallis. Sorry,
no dogs allowed. Not suitable for
wheelchairs.

34 ♦ MANNINGTON HALL

Mannington, Norwich,
NR11 7BB. The Lord & Lady
Walpole, 01263 584175,
admin@walpoleestate.co.uk,
www.manningtongardens.co.uk.
*18m NW of Norwich. 2m N of
Saxthorpe via B1149 towards Holt.
At Saxthorpe/Corpusty follow signs to
Mannington.* For NGS: Sun 9 Apr
(12-5). Evening opening Thur
22 June (6-9). Adm £6, chd free.
Light refreshments. For other
opening times and information,

please phone, email or visit garden
website.
20 acres feature shrubs, lake, trees
and roses. Heritage rose and period
gardens. Borders. Sensory garden.
Extensive countryside walks and
trails. Moated manor house and
Saxon church with C19 follies.
Wild flowers and birds. The Greedy
Goose tearooms offer home
made locally sourced food with
light lunches and home made teas.
Gravel paths, one steep slope.

35 MANOR FARM, COSTON

Coston Lane, Coston, Barnham
Broom, NR9 4DT. Mr & Mrs J O
Hambro. *10m W of Norwich. Off
B1108 Norwich - Watton Rd. Take
B1135 to Dereham at Kimberley.
After approx 300yds sharp L bend,
go straight over down Coston Lane,
house & garden on L.* Sun 16 July
(11-5). Adm £4.50, chd free.
Home-made teas.
Approx 3 acre country garden
set in larger estate. Several small
garden rooms with both formal
and informal planting. Walled
kitchen garden, white, grass and late
summer gardens, roses, herbaceous
and shrub borders. Wild flower
areas with new Pictorial Meadows
borders. Many interesting plants.
Dogs and picnics most welcome.
Featured in Country Life. Some
gravel paths and steps.

Holme Hale Hall

36 MANOR HOUSE FARM, WELLINGHAM

nr Fakenham, Kings Lynn, PE32 2TH. Robin & Elisabeth Ellis, 01328 838227, Libby.ellis@btconnect.com, www.manor-house-farm.co.uk. *7m W from Fakenham. 8m E from Swaffham, ½m off A1065 N of Weasenham. Garden is beside the church.* **Sun 18 June (11-5). Adm £6, chd free. Delicious home-made teas.**

Charming 4 acre country garden surrounds an attractive farmhouse: Formal quadrants with obelisks. 'Hot spot' of grasses and gravel. Small arboretum with unusual specimen trees. Pleached lime walk, vegetable parterre and rose tunnel. Unusual 'Taj' garden with old-fashioned roses, tree peonies, lilies and a pond. Good selection of herbaceous plants. Walled garden. Small herd of Formosan Sika deer. Featured in Country Life Magazine, Dutch Gardening Magazine. Norfolk Life and EDP. Wheelchair access some gravel and a few steps negotiable with assistance.

❀ 🚗 🛏 ☕

37 NEW MILL FARM

Swaffham Road, Wendling, Dereham, NR19 2LY. Dee & Peter Elleray, 07917 768476, deeelleray@hotmail.co.uk. *4m W of Dereham on Swaffham Rd. From Swaffham on A47, turn R at Longham/Wendling sign. From Norwich on A47, turn L at Longham/Wendling sign. Mill Farm is ¼m along on L.* **Sun 6 Aug (11-4). Adm £3.50, chd free. Light refreshments. Visits also by arrangement July & Aug small groups of 6 -12.**

One acre surrounding a detached Victorian house. The established garden is divided by hedges, fences and walls into six smaller gardens with mature borders, grasses, hydrangeas and clematis. Shaded areas including a secret space surrounded by tree ferns. Wildlife ponds. Vegetable garden containing soft fruit and small orchard. Courtyard with colourfully planted containers. There are a few steps, gravel and gates to negotiate, but wheelchair access is possible.

♿ ❀ ☕

38 NEW MINNS FARM BARNS

Castle Acre, King's Lynn, PE32 2AN. Geoff & Kate Hunnam. *Located in the centre of the village opposite the church.* **Sun 16 July (11-5). Combined adm with Tudor Lodgings £5, chd free. Light refreshments in The Barn at Tudor Lodgings.**

Just over an acre in size and developed over 16 years from a previous cattle yard and small paddock, the garden surrounds a stone and flint barn where wisteria and roses climb the walls. The courtyard is informal, allowing plants to seed and tumble in a controlled way. The flower beds in the former padddock are surrounded by box hedging, and the planting is exuberant with plenty of colour.

🐂 ☕

39 NORTH LODGE

51 Bowthorpe Road, Norwich, NR2 3TN. Bruce Bentley & Peter Wilson. *1½m W of Norwich City Centre. Turn into Bowthorpe Rd off Dereham Rd, garden 150 metres on L. By bus: 5, 21, 22, 23, 23A/B, 24 & 24A from City centre, Old Catton, Heartsease, Thorpe & most of W Norwich.* **Sun 6, Sun 13 Aug (11-5.30). Adm £4, chd free. Home-made teas.**

Town garden of almost ⅕ acre on difficult triangular plot surrounding Victorian Gothic Cemetery Lodge (not open). Strong structure and attention to internal vista with Gothic conservatory, formal ponds and water features, Oriental water garden, classical temple and 80ft deep well! Predominantly herbaceous planting. Self-guided walk around associated historic parkland cemetery also available. House extension won architectural award. Slide show of house and garden history. Featured in Norfolk Magazine. Wheelchair access possible but difficult. Sloping gravel drive followed by short, steep, narrow, brickweave ramp. WC not easily wheelchair accessible.

♿ ❀ ☕

GROUP OPENING

40 NORWICH GARDENS

Waverley Road, Norwich, NR4 6SG. *Three town gardens, all within easy walking distance. Along Waverley Rd which is parallel to Newmarket Rd, a few minutes from end of A11. Turn R at Eaton Rd T-lights or L if coming from the city centre. Waverley Rd is 1st turn on R.* **Sun 18 June (11-5). Combined adm £6, chd free. Home-made teas at 19 Branksome Road. Afternoon tea and cakes.**

19 BRANKSOME ROAD
Sue & Chris Pike.

15 WAVERLEY ROAD
Sue & Clive Lloyd.

17 WAVERLEY ROAD
Sue & John Tuckett.

Three gardens along the same road, all different. 15 Waverley Road is a long town garden that's pretending it is in the country and includes a miniature wild meadow and fruit trees. 17 Waverley Road has relaxed herbaceous planting around established shrubs and mature trees creating a woodland feel and Bamboos and Japanese Acers compliment rambling roses. 19 Branksome Road has varying shaped lawns and terraces that radiate from the house, to make the most of a corner plot. Interesting mixed planting, plus vegetables, fruit cage and greenhouse. Wheelchair access challenging but not impossible. There are a few steps and some gravel at 15 and 17 Waverley Road. Branksome Road is straightforward.

♿ ❀ ☕

41 THE OLD HOUSE

Ranworth, NR13 6HS. The Hon Mrs Jacquetta Cator. *9m NE of Norwich. Nr South Walsham, below historic Ranworth Church.* **Sun 23 Apr (11-4). Adm £5, chd free. Home-made teas.**

Attractive linked and walled gardens alongside beautiful, peaceful Ranworth inner broad. Bulbs, shrubs, potager and mown rides through arboretum where dogs may be walked on leads (dogs not allowed in garden itself). Spectacular views of the church and the broad. Some rough grass and gravel.

♿ ☕

42 THE OLD RECTORY, RIDLINGTON

Ridlington, nr North Walsham, NR28 9NZ. Peter & Fiona Black, 01692 650247, ridlingtonoldrectory@gmail.com, www.oldrectorynorthnorfolk. co.uk. *4m E of North Walsham 4m N of Stalham. Take B1159 Stalham to Bacton Rd, turn L at By Way to Foxhill sign, ½m to Xrds turn R, ½m to garden.* Sun 10 Sept (12-5). Adm £5, chd free. Barbecue 12-2. 2 acre gardens framing former Rectory, sheltered by walls and woods. Specimen trees and some topiary. Mixed borders of shrubs and perennials for year-round interest. Sermon Walk of Beech and line trees, leading to views across peaceful countryside. Raised vegetable beds. Greenhouse. Scavenger hunt for children Home made BBQ and Teas. Gravel drive and some paths might be difficult if wet.

♿ ❂ 🛏 ☕

43 THE OLD RECTORY, BRANDON PARVA

Stone Lane, Brandon Parva, NR9 4DL. Mr & Mrs S Guest. *9m W of Norwich. Leave Norwich on B1108 towards Watton, turn R at sign for Barnham Broom. L at T-junction, stay on rd approx 3m until L next turn to Yaxham. L at Xrds.* Sun 28 May (11-5). Adm £4.50, chd free. Home-made teas. 4 acre, mature garden with large collection (70) specimen trees, huge variety of shrubs and herbaceous plants combined to make beautiful mixed borders. The garden comprises several formal lawns and borders, woodland garden incl rhododendrons, pond garden, walled garden and pergolas covered in wisteria, roses and clematis which create long shady walkways. Croquet lawn open for visitors to play.

♿ 🐕 ❂ ☕

Manor House Farm

© Marianne Majerus

44 33 ORCHARD CLOSE

Norwich, NR7 9NZ. Mr Mike
& Mrs Jean Newstead. ½m E
of Norwich Centre. On outer ring
road. Off Heartsease Lane. By bus
23a 23b. Sun 6 Aug (11-4).
Combined adm with 38 Gorse
Road £4, chd free. Home-made
teas.
Small city garden with a central
pond and various colour themed
borders planted with dahlias, grasses
and perennials with lots of pleasant
features.

✿ ♥

45 OXNEAD HALL

Oxnead, Norwich, NR10 5HP.
Mr & Mrs David Aspinall. 3m from
Aylsham. From Norwich take A140
to Cromer. After Aylsham turn R to
Burgh-next-Aylsham. After Burgh take
R turn at next Xrds signed Brampton
& Buxton .After the Oxnead sign
take 1st L. Sun 20 Aug (11-5).
Adm £5, chd free. Home-made
teas.
The 14 acre gardens were laid
out by the Pastons between 1580
and 1660 and are largely intact.
The design consists of a series of
Italianate courtyards and terraces
which are embellished with statuary.
The gardens are undergoing
renovation with guidance from
George Carter and now incl a
parterre, viewing mound, water
garden, lake, herbaceous borders,
walled kitchen garden, and
woodland. There are slopes to most
parts of the garden, but some areas
cannot be accessed by wheelchair.

ᕕ ⌂ ♥

46 PLOVERS HILL

Buckenham Road,
Strumpshaw, NR13 4NL.
Jan Saunt, 01603 714587,
sauntjan@gmail.com. 9m E
of Norwich. Off A47 at Brundall
continuing through to Strumpshaw
village. Turn R 300yds past The
Huntsman, then take 1st R, at T
junction . Plovers Hill is 1st on R
up the hill. Sun 30 Apr, Mon 1
May (11-5). Combined adm
with Lake House £7, chd
free. Home-made teas. Single
garden adm £5. Visits also by
arrangement May to Sept.

1 acre garden of contrasts, small
C18 house (not open) with RIBA
award winning orangery. Formal
lawn hedged with yew and lesser
species, huge mulberry, gingko,
liquidambar and Japanese bitter
orange, herbaceous borders with
a range of varied plants and spring
bulbs. Kitchen garden with orchard
and soft fruits. Garden sculptures.
Water feature. Cast aluminium
silver birches. Featured in Let's Talk
Magazine. Wheelchair access to
main part of garden, some gentle
steps to teas.

ᕕ ➡ ✿ ⌂ ♥

47 ♦ RAVENINGHAM HALL

Raveningham, Norwich,
NR14 6NS. Sir Nicholas &
Lady Bacon, 01508 548480,
barbara@raveningham.com,
www.raveningham.com. 14m
SE of Norwich. 4m from Beccles
off B1136. For NGS: Sun 5
Mar (11-4). Adm £5, chd free.
Light refreshments. For other
opening times and information,
please phone, email or visit garden
website.
Traditional country house garden in
a glorious parkland setting. Restored
Victorian conservatory and walled
kitchen garden. Herbaceous
borders, newly planted stumpery.
An arboretum was established
after the 1987 gale and a lake to
mark the Millennium. There is also
a Time Garden inspired by Sir
Francis Bacon, a herb garden and
a rose garden. Sculpture by Susan
Bacon throughout the Garden.
February snowdrops are followed
by daffodils and narcissus and other
spring bulbs and flowering shrubs.
In May there are meadow flowers
and the herbaceous borders fill out.
The summer months showcase
the walled kitchen garden and the
agapanthus for which the garden is
known. There are gravelled paths
around the Garden which allow
wheelchair access. Access to the
Tea Room is through the courtyard
entrance.

ᕕ ➡ ✿ ⌂ ♥

48 NEW 27 ST EDMUNDS ROAD

Taverham, Norwich, NR8 6NY.
Alan Inness & Sue Collins. 6m N
of Norwich, just off the Fakenham
Road A1067. Coming from Norwich
on the A1067, drive through the
village of Drayton. Carry on up hill
to Taverham, turn L into Roeditch
Drive. The property will then be on
your R at T-junction. Sun 25 June
(11-5). Combined adm with 9
Bellomonte Crescent £5, chd
free. Home-made teas.
Half acre garden featuring part
woodland setting and view over the
Wensum valley via raised decking
area. The garden has undergone
substantial redevelopment over
the past seven years as it was
originally two separate gardens.
Redevelopment has included the
addition of vine covered pergola,
two summer houses, herbaceous
borders, small vegetable plot
with greenhouse. Plant sales. No
Wheelchair Access.

➡ ✿ ♥

49 ♦ SANDRINGHAM GARDENS

Sandringham, PE35 6EH.
Her Majesty The
Queen, 01485 545408,
visits@sandringhamestate.co.uk,
www.sandringhamestate.co.uk.
6m NW of King's Lynn. By gracious
permission, the House, Museum &
Gardens will be open. For opening
times and information, please
phone, email or visit garden
website.
60 acres of glorious gardens,
woodland and lakes, with rare plants
and trees. Colour and interest
throughout the year with sheets of
spring-flowering bulbs, avenues of
rhododendrons and azaleas, beds
of lavender and roses, and dazzling
autumn colour. Donations are given
from the Estate to various charities.
Open daily 1 April - 29 Oct, closed
Good Friday 14 April. House opens
daily Easter Sat 15 April to 29
Oct but closed from 22 - 28 July
inclusive. Gravel paths (not deep),
long distances - please tel or visit
website for our Accessibility Guide.

ᕕ ✿ ⌂ ♥

50 SEA MERE

Seamere Road, Hingham, Norwich, NR9 4LP. Judy Watson, 01953 850217, judywatson@seamere.com, www.seamere.com. *Off the B1108, 1m E of Hingham. From Norwich B1108, 2m after Kimberley railway crossing, turn L into Seamere Rd. Sea Mere drive is 2nd on L.* Sun 3 Sept (11-5). Adm £5, chd free. Home-made teas in Sea Mere Study Centre, adjacent to house. Tea/coffee and cake or wine and nibbles. **Visits also by arrangement Apr to Aug groups of 10+, guided tour with garden owner. Please mention the *Gardens to Visit* book when booking.**

The gardens border a 20 acre circular mere with spectacular views to the water over terraced lawns, gunnera and a new wetland garden. Mature trees, shrubs and perennials frame the view. The 5 acre garden includes an ornamental potager, formal oval garden with herbaceous borders, woodland garden, shrub roses in the orchard and a bamboo glade. The higher levels, near the house are wheelchair accessible. WC suitable for disabled use.

 ❧✿🚗☕💐

51 ◆ SEVERALS GRANGE

Holt Road, Wood Norton, NR20 5BL. Jane Lister, 01362 684206, hoecroft@hotmail.co.uk, www.hoecroft.co.uk. *8m S of Holt, 6m E of Fakenham. 2m N of Guist on L of B1110. Guist is situated 5m SE of Fakenham on A1067 Norwich rd.* For NGS: Sun 13 Aug (1-5). Adm £3.50, chd free. Home-made teas. For other opening times and information, please phone, email or visit garden website.

The gardens surrounding Severals Grange and the adjoining nursery Hoecroft Plants are a perfect example of how colour, shape and form can be created by the use of foliage plants, from large shrubs to small alpines. Movement and lightness are achieved by interspersing these plants with a wide range of ornamental grasses, which are at their best in late summer. Extensive range of ornamental grasses herbaceous plants and shrubs in various garden settings. Groups for guided tours by appt July - Sept.

 ♿❧✿🚗🛋️☕💐

52 NEW SHERINGHAM HALL

Sheringham Park, Upper Sheringham, Sheringham, NR26 8TB. *Directions issued with ticket* Evening opening Fri 16 June (6-8). Adm £20. Drinks PRE BOOKED TICKETS ONLY please contact jennifer.dyer.16@outlook.com or 01263 761811. Summer Evening Drinks. A unique opportunity to see this wonderful garden. Designed by Repton the park is open regularly, the hall and walled garden are private. Kitchen garden recreated by Arabella Lennox-Boyd with restored glasshouses and cold frames. Replanted orchards, hornbeam temple, new herbaceous borders, parterres and a white garden. Wild flower meadow between hot and cool borders in the east and restored Repton pleasure grounds in the west. Repton's walks have been reopened

 ☕

53 ◆ SHERINGHAM PARK

Wood Farm Visitors Centre, Upper Sheringham, NR26 8TL. National Trust, 01263 820550, sheringhampark@nationaltrust.org.uk, www.nationaltrust.org.uk/sheringham. *2m SW of Sheringham. Access for cars off A148 Cromer to Holt Rd, 5m W of Cromer, 6m E of Holt, signs in Sheringham town.* For NGS: Thur 18 May, Thur 8 June (10-5). No adm charges to Sheringham Park, car park charge £5.50 for non NT members. Light refreshments in Courtyard Cafe. For other opening times and information, please phone, email or visit garden website.

80 acres of species rhododendron, azalea and magnolia. Also numerous specimen trees incl handkerchief tree. Viewing towers, waymarked walks, sea and parkland views. No admission charge to Sheringham Park, car park charge payable by non NT members (Price for 2017 yet to be confirmed). Special walkway and WCs for disabled. 1½m route is accessible for wheelchairs, mobility scooters available to hire.

 ♿❧✿🚗☕💐

54 ◆ STODY LODGE

Melton Constable, NR24 2ER. Mr & Mrs Charles MacNicol, 01263 863994, enquiries@stodyestate.co.uk, www.stodylodgegardens.co.uk. *16m NW of Norwich, 3m S of Holt. Off B1354. Signed from Melton Constable on Holt Rd. For SatNav NR24 2ER. Gardens signed as you approach.* For NGS: Tue 23 May (1-5). Adm £6, chd free. Home-made teas For other opening times and information, please phone, email or visit garden website.

Spectacular gardens with one of the largest concentrations of rhododendrons and azaleas in East Anglia. Created in the 1920s, the gardens also feature magnolias, camellias, a variety of ornamental and specimen trees, late daffodils, tulips and bluebells. Expansive lawns and magnificent yew hedges. Woodland walks and 2 acre Water Gardens filled with over 2,000 vividly-coloured azalea mollis. Home-made teas provided by selected local and national charities. Access to most areas of the garden. Gravel paths to Azalea Water Gardens with some uneven ground.

 ♿❧✿🚗☕💐

Your visit helps fund 389 Marie Curie Nurses

55 SUIL NA MARA

North Walsham Road, Bacton, Norwich, NR12 0LG. Bill & Bev Kerr, 01692 652386, billkerr1@btinternet.com. *19m N of Norwich on N Norfolk coast. Take the N Walsham to Bacton rd. We are just past the Coastguard Station in Pollard St. From Mundesley & Walcott direction garden on R just as you enter Pollard St.* Sat 26, Sun 27 Aug (11-5). Adm £3.50, chd free. Light refreshments. **Visits also by arrangement June to Sept no min number.**

This ¼ acre exotic garden incorporates more than 250 plant varieties in an unusual mix of lush semi tropical planting meets Norfolk Coast-meets Industrial and rural decay. Set in a series of garden rooms the striking architectural plants mixed with beachcombed wood, rusty metal and unusual water features all provides plenty to look at and enjoy. Often described as a 'Tardis' of a garden! Featured in Amateur Garden, Eastern Daily Press Norfolk Magazine. Sorry all paths are gravelled and are difficult for wheelchair/mobility access.

56 TUDOR LODGINGS

Castle Acre, King's Lynn, PE32 2AN. Gus & Julia Stafford Allen. *4m N of Swaffham off A1065 Swaffham to Fakenham. Situated on L as you come into the village with parking in the field.* Sun 16 July (11-5). **Combined adm with Minns Farm Barns £5, chd free. Light refreshments in the Barn.** The C15 house (not open) and grounds incorporate part of the Norman earthworks, with beautiful views towards the R Nar. The 2 acre garden contains C18 dovecote, topiary, lawns and a knot garden. Recently planted block of ornamental grasses is surrounded by colourful borders. Productive fruit cage dominates the vegetable garden. A natural wild area includes a shepherds hut and informal pond. Wheelchair access is limited but is possible please ask for assistance beforehand. Disabled WC.

57 WALCOTT HOUSE

Walcott Green, Walcott, Norwich, NR12 0NU. Mr & Mrs Nick Collier. *3m N of Stalham. Off the Stalham to Walcott rd (B1159).* Sun 25 June (1.30-5). Adm £4, chd free. Light refreshments.

A young garden with emphasis on formal structure around the house and a traditional set of Norfolk farm buildings. These provide a series of connecting gardens which, through a south facing garden wall, lead to further gardens of clipped box, pleached hornbeam, fruit trees and roses. All set within recently planted woodland providing avenues and vistas. Small single steps to negotiate when moving between gardens in the yards.

58 WARBOROUGH HOUSE

2 Wells Road, Stiffkey, NR23 1QH. Mr & Mrs J Morgan. *13m N of Fakenham, 4m E of Wells-Next-The-Sea on A149 in the centre of village. Please DO NOT park in main rd as this causes congestion. Parking is available & signed at garden entrance. Coasthopper bus stop outside garden.* Sun 28 May, Sun 6 Aug (1-5.30). Adm £5, chd free. Home-made teas.

7 acre garden on a steep chalk slope, surrounding C19 house (not open) with views across the Stiffkey valley and to the coast. Woodland walks, formal terraces, shrub borders, lawns and walled garden create a garden of contrasts. Garden slopes steeply in parts. Paths are gravel, bark chip or grass. Disabled parking allows access to garden nearest the house and teas.

Bishop's House

© Val Corbett

GROUP OPENING

59 WELLS-NEXT-THE-SEA GARDENS
Wells-Next-The-Sea, NR23 1DP. *10m N of Fakenham. Bus stop at 'The Buttlands' follow NGS signs 1 min from stop.* **Sun 9 July (11-5). Combined adm £5, chd free. Home-made teas at Caprice.**

CAPRICE
Clubbs Lane. David & Joolz Saunders.

7 MARKET LANE
Off Burnt St. Hazel Ashley.

NORFOLK HOUSE
Burnt St. Katrina & Alan Jackson.

OSTRICH HOUSE
Burnt St. Mr Stuart Rangeley-Wilson & Ms Janey Burland.

POACHER COTTAGE
Burnt St. Roger & Barbara Oliver.

Wells-next-the-sea is a small, friendly coastal town on the glorious North Norfolk Coast: popular with families, walkers and bird watchers. The harbour has shops, cafes, fish and chips, while a mile along The Run lies Wells Beach, served by a narrow gauge railway. Of the five in the group four are smaller town gardens and one is somewhat larger: all demonstrate a variety of design and planting approaches incorporating herbaceous borders, 'cottage', shrub and fruit, with two of the gardens providing different 'rooms'. The route around the five gardens takes in the Parish Church of St Nicholas, the High Street with its beautiful once-shop windows and the tree lined Georgian green square, The Buttlands. Two gardens providing 'rooms'. One with new small alpine section. Details in The Quay local magazine, EDP and other newspapers. Wheelchair access at all gardens.
&. ☕ 🍷

60 4 WENSUM CRESCENT
Lower Hellesdon, Norwich, NR6 5DL. Mrs Moira Smith. *3m NW from City centre. From Norwich ring rd turn onto A1067, after 1m,* turn L at T-lights - Hospital Lane. After ½m turn R - Low Rd, take first L Wensum Valley Close, turn L - Wensum Crescent. **Sun 9 July (12-8). Adm £3, chd free. Home-made teas. Light alcoholic refreshments also available.**
Site was completely cleared May 2013 so a relatively new garden with some interesting and unusual plants including lots of evergreens, so it looks good all year round. Designed to create interesting views from around the garden with different patio and seating areas throughout. A bespoke garden room was built on site for lazy afternoons. Most areas accessible by wheelchair.
&. 🐐 ☕ 🍷

61 WITTON HALL
Old Hall Road, North Walsham, NR28 9UF. Sally Owles. *3½m from North Walsham. From North Walsham take Happisburgh Rd or Byway to Edingthorpe Rd off North Walsham bypass. Situated nr to Bacton Woods.* **Mon 1 May (12-4). Adm £3, chd free. Light refreshments.**
A natural woodland garden. Walk past the handkerchief tree and wander through carpets of English bluebells, rhododendrons and azaleas. Walk from the garden down the field to the church. Stunning views over farmland to the sea. Sensible footwear required as deer, rabbits and badgers inhabit this garden! Witton Park laid out by Humphrey Repton. Wheelchair access difficult if wet.
&. ❄ ☕ 🍷

62 16 WITTON LANE
Little Plumstead, NR13 5DL. Sally Ward & Richard Hobbs. *5m E of Norwich. Take A47 to Yarmouth, 1st exit after Postwick, turn L to Witton Green & Gt Plumstead, then 1st R into Witton Lane for 1½m. Garden on L.* **Sun 2 Apr (11-4). Adm £3, chd free.**
An 'Aladdin's Cave' for the alpine and woodland plant enthusiast. Tiny garden with wide range of rare and unusual plants will be of great interest with its species tulips, daffodils, scillas, dog's tooth violets, other bulbous plants and many trilliums and wood anemones. A garden for the plant specialist. National Collection of Muscari. Plants for sale and refreshments. Not suitable for wheelchair access due to narrow gravel paths.
❄ NPC 🍷

63 WRETHAM LODGE
East Wretham, IP24 1RL. Mr Gordon Alexander, 01953 498997. *6m NE of Thetford. A11 E from Thetford, L up A1075, L by village sign, R at Xrds then bear L.* **Sun 16, Mon 17 Apr (11-5). Adm £4, chd free. Visits also by arrangement Apr to Sept.**
In spring masses of species tulips, hellebores, fritillaries, daffodils and narcissi; bluebell walk. Walled garden, with fruit and interesting vegetable plots. Mixed borders and fine old trees. Double herbaceous borders. Wild flower meadows.
&. 🐐 ☕ 🍷

64 YEOMAN'S COTTAGE
Low Lane, Rockland All Saints, Attleborough, NR17 1TU. Karen Roseberry & Paul Rutter, 01953 483395, RocklandsYeomansCottage@gmail.com. *Approx 4m from Attleborough & A11. Take B1077 from Attleborough or Watton. At Xrds in Rocklands turn South onto The Street. Past village shop on R then garden is approx 200m on L. Parking is very easy along The Street.* **Sun 20 Aug (11-5). Adm £3.50, chd free. Home-made teas. Fruit Cup will be on offer if sunny and warm!. Visits also by arrangement May to Sept, groups of 10+.**
Artist and Plant-lover's cottage garden. Lots packed into 0.4 acre: 'Hot' border, 'Marshmallow' border, Exotic-ish lush bed, Shady woodland 'hop', 'Dry river bed' gravel garden, Pickery, Wildlife pond, Sculptures and 'Up-cycled' objects. Bees and butterflies abound. This is a garden where we party and entertain at any excuse so there are sitting areas aplenty! Mostly wheelchair accessible but Woodland 'hop' and pond are up a small bank. 'Dry river bed' is thick gravel but can be viewed from edge.
&. 🐐 ❄ ☕ 🍷

NORTH EAST

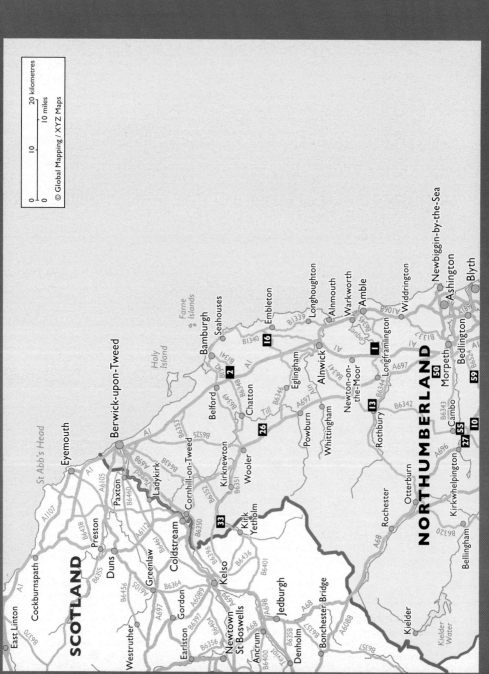

20 kilometres
10
0

10 miles
10
0

© Global Mapping / XYZ Maps

St Abb's Head

East Linton
Cockburnspath
Eyemouth
A1107
Preston
B6438
Duns
Westruther
B6355
Greenlaw
A6105
Gordon
Earlston
A697
Newtown
St Boswells
A68
Ancrum
A6088
Denholm
B6358
Jedburgh
Bonchester Bridge
B6357

SCOTLAND

Paxton
Ladykirk
B6460
A6112
A698
Coldstream
Kelso
A698
B6397
B6356
B6400
B6401
Tweed
A698

Berwick-upon-Tweed
A1
B6353
B6525
B6438
Cornhill-on-Tweed
B6350
B6396
Kirknewton
B6351
Wooler
Kirk
Yetholm
33

Holy
Island

Farne
Islands
Bamburgh
B3341
B3340
Seahouses
Embleton
16
B1339
B1340
Belford
B6349
B6348
Chatton
Till
26
Eglingham
A697
Powburn
Whittingham
13
Newton-on-
the-Moor
Longhoughton
Alnmouth
Warkworth
Amble
Alnwick
A1
B6341
Longframlington
A697
Rothbury
B6344
B6342
B6343
Cambo
Kirkwhelpington
A696
27 **55** **10**

Widdrington
A1068
Ashington
A189
Newbiggin-by-the-Sea
Blyth
Bedlington
B6345
A1
B1337
Morpeth
50
59

NORTHUMBERLAND

Otterburn
Rochester
A68
B6320
Kielder
Kielder
Water
Bellingham
B6357

2
1

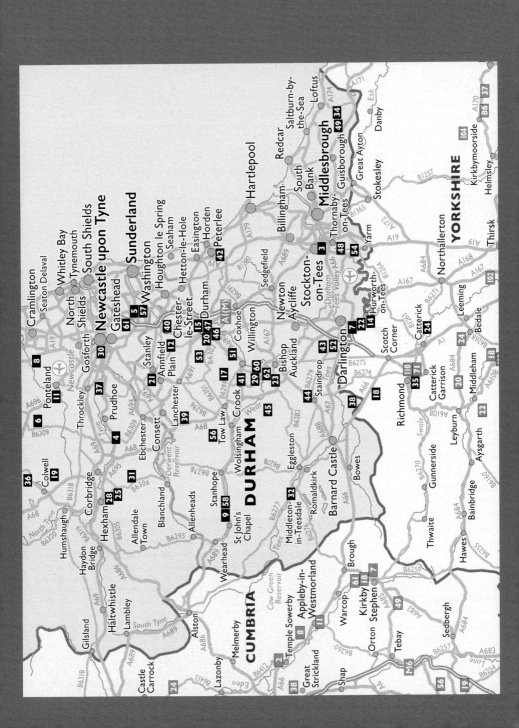

Volunteers

County Durham
County Organiser
Alison Morgan
01913 843842
alison.morgan@ngs.org.uk

County Treasurer
Sue Douglas
07712 461002
pasm.d@btinternet.com

Publicity
Peter Morgan
01913 843842
ngspublicity.durhamtees@gmail.com

Booklet Co-ordinator
Sheila Walke
07837 764057
sheila.walke@ngs.org.uk

Assistant County Organisers
Lynn Cameron 01915 863383
lynnanncameron@yahoo.co.uk

Gill Knights 01325 483210
gillianknights55@gmail.com

Gill Naisby 01325 381324
gillnaisby@gmail.com

Sue Walker
01325 481881
walker.sdl@gmail.com

Northumberland & Tyne and Wear
County Organiser
& Booklet Coordinator
Maureen Kesteven
01914 135937
kestevenmaureen@gmail.com

County Treasurer
David Oakley
07941 077594
david.oakley@ngs.org.uk

Publicity
Susie White
07941 077595
susie@susie-white.co.uk

Assistant County Organisers
Patricia Fleming 01668 217009
patriciaflemingwoop@gmail.com

Natasha McEwen 07917 754155
natashamcewengd@aol.co.uk

Liz Reid 01914 165981
lizreid52@ntlworld.com

Right: **Middle Grange**

County Durham: an unsung county.

At the heart of this once industrial land lies the medieval city of Durham. The city is a fascinating blend of ancient and modern, respecting the heritage and traditions of its forefathers whilst embracing changing lifestyles and culture.

This epitomises the county as a whole; old, industrial sites and coal mines have been sensitively cleared to restore the land to its original 'green' beauty.

Set amongst this varied and beautiful countryside are gardens which open their gates for the NGS.

So, stand amongst the rare and unusual plants at 14 Grays Terrace and be amazed by the spectacular view of Durham Cathedral, or visit the wonderful and imaginative hidden garden that has been created behind the working forge at Ravensworth.

Northumberland is a county rich in history with sturdy castles, stunning coastline and a wild landscape threaded with sheltered valleys.

Gardeners have learnt how to make the most of the land; terracing hillsides, enhancing the soil and often using the wonderful architecture as a backdrop, such as at Lilburn Tower.

Garden owners have managed to create gardens whatever the conditions. At Blagdon the solution has been to plant within an old quarry, and at Wallington to use a long narrow valley for shelter.

An eclectic range of gardens open for the NGS. Each reflects the style and character of their owners, with the extra attraction of home-made teas and plant sales.

© Susie White

OPENING DATES

All entries subject to change. For latest information check www.ngs.org.uk

Map locator numbers are shown to the right of each garden name.

February
Snowdrop Festival
Sunday 26th
Congburn Arboretum 12
◆ Crook Hall & Gardens 15

March
Sunday 5th
NEW Breckon Hill 9

April
Saturday 1st
Ravensford Farm 45

Sunday 2nd
Congburn Arboretum 12

Sunday 23rd
The Old Vicarage 38

Friday 28th
◆ Cragside 13

May
Sunday 14th
Harperley Hall Farm 21
Thornton Hall Gardens 52

Sunday 21st
Blagdon 8
Hillside Cottages 23

Saturday 27th
Adderstone House 2

90th Anniversary Weekend
Sunday 28th
Lilburn Tower 26

Monday 29th
NEW Woodbine House 60

June
Sunday 4th
Barnard Avenue Gardens
Nos 10 and 27 3
NEW 24 Bede Crescent 5
The Forge 18
Oliver Ford Garden 39
◆ Washington Old Hall 57

Saturday 10th
NEW Little Harle Gardens 27
NEW Southlands 48
NEW Ushaw College 53

Sunday 11th
Croft Hall 14
Parker Towers 41

Saturday 17th
Middleton-in-Teesdale 32

Sunday 18th
The Beacon 4
◆ Mindrum Garden 33

Saturday 24th
Fallodon Hall 16
NEW Middle Grange 31

Sunday 25th
Stanton Fence 50
NEW 3 Valley Close 54

July
Saturday 1st
Warrenfell 56
Woodlands 61

Sunday 2nd
Hidden Gardens of Croft Road 22
Warrenfell 56
◆ Whalton Manor Gardens 59

Thursday 6th
Woodlands 61

Saturday 8th
The Fold 17

Sunday 9th
Peerlee Gardens Safari 42
NEW Westgate Village Gardens 58

Thursday 13th
NEW Marie Curie Garden 30

Saturday 15th
◆ Raby Castle 44

Sunday 16th
Moorsholm Village 34
No. 2 Ferndene 37
St Margaret's Allotments 47

Sunday 23rd
NEW Kiplin Hall 24
Loughbrow House 28
NEW Stanghow Gardens 49
Woodside House 62

Sunday 30th
NEW Gardener's Cottage 19
NEW Lambshield 25
St Cuthbert's Hospice 46

August
Sunday 6th
Coldcotes Moor Farm 11
4 Stockley Grove 51

Saturday 12th
NEW Ushaw College 53

Sunday 13th
45 Blackwell 7

NEW Capheaton Hall 10
NEW Mr Yorke's Walled Garden 35

Sunday 20th
Adderstone House 2
Quarry End 43

September
Sunday 3rd
Bichfield Tower 6

Sunday 24th
Harperley Hall Farm 21

By Arrangement
Acton House 1
Adderstone House 2
The Beacon 4
NEW 24 Bede Crescent 5
NEW Breckon Hill 9
Coldcotes Moor Farm 11
The Fold 17
The Forge 18
14 Grays Terrace 20
Harperley Hall Farm 21
Hillside Cottages 23
Lilburn Tower 26
Loughbrow House 28
10 Low Row 29
NEW Middle Grange 31
Newonstead Cottage Garden 36
No. 2 Ferndene 37
25 Park Road South 40
Ravensford Farm 45
4 Stockley Grove 51
Thornton Hall Gardens 52
NEW Ushaw College 53
Warrenfell 56
Woodlands 61
Woodside House 62

Kiplin Hall

THE GARDENS

1 ACTON HOUSE
Felton, Morpeth, NE65 9NU.
Mr Alan & Mrs Eileen Ferguson,
Head Gardener 07779 860217.
jane@actonhouseuk.com. *N of
Morpeth. On old A1 N of Felton, take
turning to Acton, follow rd for ½ m
until fork and follow sign to Acton
House.* **Visits by arrangement
May to Aug for groups of 10+.
Adm £5, chd free.**
This stunning walled garden has
structure, colour and variety of
planting, with abundant herbaceous
perennials and different grasses.
Planted in the spring of 2011, it
has sections devoted to fruit and
vegetables, David Austin rose
borders, standard trees and climbers
spreading over the brick walls.
There are additional mixed borders,
a ha-ha, and developing woodland
planting, in total extending over
5 acres. Herbaceous perennial
plantings include species and
varieties favoured by butterflies and
bees.
&

2 ADDERSTONE HOUSE
Adderstone Mains, Belford,
NE70 7HS. John & Pauline
Clough, 01668 219171,
John.clough@me.com. *1m S of
Belford off A1. Best approached from
the N off A1 Adderstone Mains is
1m S of Belford, turn L off A1. From S,
0.7m N of Purdy Lodge on R but turn
dangerous, continue to Belford, turn &
approach from N. Ample parking.* **Sat
27 May, Sun 20 Aug (1-5). Adm
£5, chd free. Light refreshments
in the courtyard. Visits also by
arrangement Apr to Nov for
groups of 10+.**
A Victorian house, gardens, millpond
and grounds of 10½ acres.
Established and 'new projects' in
development with Sean Murray
(RHS Chelsea Challenge winner).
Walled garden with rose arbour,
mature shrubs; an orchard leads
to sunken garden; rose walk to
the formal garden, then on to the
mill pond,fruit/vegetable plots and
vineyard. Plant stall, teas and grape
juice from vineyard. A folly has
been added. Featured in Newcastle
Chronicle and Journal and Berwick
Advertiser.
❀ ☕ 🍷

GROUP OPENING

3 BARNARD AVENUE
GARDENS NOS 10 AND 27
Stockton-On-Tees, TS19 7AB. *10m
E of Darlington off A66. Heading E
or W from or towards Middlesbrough
take slip rd marked Hartburn &
Stockton W. L into Greens Lane,
follow yellow signs. Off Gainford Rd
& Oxbridge Rd W side of Stockton.
Park in Gainford Rd.* **Sun 4 June
(1.30-5.30). Combined adm £4,
chd free. Home-made teas at
Briarcroft (no 27).**

10 BARNARD AVENUE
Dennis & Jennifer Hodgson.

BRIARCROFT
27 Barnard Avenue.
Mr Glenn Sunman.
🔲

Enjoy a visit to two, small urban
gardens. No.10 is a mature secluded
garden with several seating areas.
Recently landscaped, it is divided
into 'rooms' and backed by mature
trees. There are two small ponds,
a water feature, a Judas tree which
is magnificent when in flower in
spring and, apart from hanging
baskets, no annuals. No.27 has
a wisteria covered pergola, wild
flower area, willow tunnel and
arbour, aerial hedge, kitchen garden
and herbaceous borders. We expect
to have our resident ukulele band
playing at different times during
the afternoon at no 27. Wheelchair
access; gravel paths in some areas.
& 🔲 ☕

---

4 THE BEACON
10 Crabtree Road, Stocksfield,
NE43 7NX. Derek & Patricia
Hodgson, 01661 842518,
patandderek@btinternet.com.
*12m W of Newcastle upon Tyne.
From A69 follow signs into village.
Station & cricket ground on L. Turn
R into Cadehill Rd then 1st R into
Crabtree Rd (cul de sac) Park on
Cadehill.* **Sun 18 June (2-6). Adm
£5, chd free. Home-made teas.
Visits also by arrangement
groups of 10+.**
This garden illustrates how to make
a cottage garden on a steep site
with loads of interest at different
levels. Planted with acers, roses
and a variety of cottage garden
and formal plants. Water runs
gently through it and there are
tranquil places to sit and talk or
just reflect. Stunning colour and
plant combinations. Wildlife friendly
- numerous birds, frogs,newts,
hedgehogs. Haven for butterflies
and bees. Featured in Tyndale Life
magazine. Steep, so not wheelchair
friendly but wheelchair users have
negotiated the drive and enjoyed
the view of the main garden.
❀ ☕

5 NEW 24 BEDE CRESCENT
Washington, NE38 7JA. Sheila
Brookes, 0191 417 9702,
sheilab24@hotmail.co.uk. *From
WOH, past Cenotaph, 600yds up
Village Lane past R C Church, &
Black Bush PH. Follow NGS sign
through cut to Town Centre, into
Bede Crescent, end house of 5,
facing grassed oval.* **Sun 4 June
(11-4). Adm £2, chd free. Light
refreshments at Washington
Old Hall. Also open Washington
Old Hall. Visits also by
arrangement June to Sept small
groups only. No refreshments,
but local PHs and cafes in
Village.**
A lesson in how to make a small
shady place colourful and interesting.
Small 'courtyard style' garden, with
central paved area, surrounded by
borders containing shrubs and box
balls for year round structure, and
packed with colourful Astilbes, lilies
and clematis for summer impact.
Small patio front garden, with gravel
border planted with box balls and
containerised shrubs. Access into
paved 'courtyard garden' via a side
gate, (which should accommodate
a small wheelchair, although not a
wide entrance).

6 BICHFIELD TOWER

Belsay, Newcastle Upon Tyne, NE20 0JP. Lesley & Stewart Manners, 075114 39606, lesleymanners@gmail.com, www.bitchfieldtower.co.uk. *Private rd off B6309, 4m N of Stamfordham and SW of Belsay village.* **Sun 3 Sept (1-4). Adm £5, chd free. Home-made teas in the carriage house garden and building.** 6 acre maturing garden, in its 2nd year of rejuvenation, set around a Medieval Pele Tower with an impressive stone water feature, large trout lake, mature woodland, wild meadow and 2 walled gardens. Featuring this year, two stunning iron flower covered windows providing spectacular views of the surrounding countryside. There are large herbaceous borders around the garden with extensive lawns. Historic building, tennis court, woodlands fairy walk for kids, sculpture walk throughout the grounds, croquet lawn and set, trout lake, pop-up shops of local businesses.

7 45 BLACKWELL

Darlington, DL3 8QT. Cath & Peter Proud. *SW Darlington, next to R.Tees. ½ way along Blackwell in Darlington, which links Bridge Rd (on A66 just past Blackwell Bridge) & Carmel Rd South. Alternatively, turn into Blackwell from Post Office on Carmel Rd South.* **Sun 13 Aug (1-5). Adm £4, chd free. Home-made teas. Teas, coffees and soft drinks and a selection of scones with home-made jams will be available.** No. 45 Blackwell rises from the R Tees up to a garden with many mature trees, wildlife meadow, pond with waterfall. Herb and Mediterranean garden, shady borders, lawns and colourful herbaceous borders. The Tees can be viewed from a rustic hut set in woodland high above the river. (Some neighbouring gardens may also open on the day). Refreshments and plants for sale. Well behaved dogs on leads welcome. Wheelchair access to patios and to lawn with assistance.

Mr Yorke's Walled Garden

8 BLAGDON

Seaton Burn, NE13 6DE. Viscount Ridley, www.blagdonestate.co.uk. *5m S of Morpeth on A1. 8m N of Newcastle on A1, N on B1318, L at r'about (Holiday Inn) & follow signs to Blagdon. Entrance to parking area signed.* **Sun 21 May (1-4.30). Adm £5, chd free. Home-made teas.** Unique 27 acre garden encompassing formal garden with Lutyens designed 'canal', Lutyens structures and walled kitchen garden. Valley with stream and various follies, quarry garden and woodland walks. Large numbers of ornamental trees and shrubs planted over many generations. National Collections of Acer, Alnus and Sorbus. Trailer rides around the estate (small additional charge) and stalls selling local produce. Partial wheelchair access.

🔥 🐴 ❀ NPC 🍵

9 NEW BRECKON HILL

Westgate, Bishop Auckland, DL13 1PD. Jennie & David Henderson, 01388 517735, lefontanil@gmail.com. *Approaching Westgate from Stanhope, on A689 you will come to Breckon Hill. It is accessed up a ½m tarmac rd to the R which will be clearly marked.* **Sun 5 Mar (10.30-3.30). Adm £4.50, chd free. Home-made teas. Gluten free to order. Visits also by arrangement Mar to July individual groups of up to 12 people, adm £4.50 to incl tea.** Breckon Hill is perched on the fellside at 1100ft above sea level, just outside the village of Westgate in Weardale, part of the North Pennines AONB. There are fabulous views of Weardale from our walled garden. South facing walled cottage garden, overlooking Weardale with 180 degree views. In February, the banks and beds of the driveway and walled area are bursting with snowdrops. Featured in the Weardale Gazette article on Westgate Open Gardens. Wheelchair users, please let us know if you plan to visit as we may have to remove a small gate.

🔥 🐴 ❀ 🍵

10 NEW CAPHEATON HALL

Capheaton, Newcastle Upon Tyne, NE19 2AB. William & Eliza Browne-Swinburne, www.capheatonhall.co.uk. *19m N of Newcastle off A696. From S turn L onto Silver Hill rd signed Capheaton. From N, past Wallington/Kirkharle junction, turn R.* **Sun 13 Aug (2-5). Adm £5, chd free. Home-made teas.** Set in parkland, Capheaton Hall has magnificent views over the Northumberland countryside. Formal ponds sit south of the house, which has an C18 conservatory, and a walk to a Georgian folly covered with climbing roses. The outstanding feature is the very productive walled garden with glasshouse, at its height in late summer, mixing colourful vegetables, espaliered fruit with annual and perennial flowering plants.

🐴 ❀ 🍵

11 COLDCOTES MOOR FARM

Ponteland, Newcastle Upon Tyne, NE20 0DF. Ron & Louise Bowey, 01661 822579, info@theboweys.co.uk. *Off A696 N of Ponteland. From S, leave Ponteland on A696 towards Jedburgh, after 1m take L turn marked 'Milbourne 2m'. After 400yds turn L into drive.* **Sun 6 Aug (1-5). Adm £5, chd free. Home-made teas. Visits also by arrangement July & Aug for groups of 10+ week commencing 31 July only.** The garden, landscaped grounds and woods cover around 15 acres. The wooded approach opens out to lawned areas surrounded by ornamental and woodland shrubs and trees. A courtyard garden leads to an ornamental walled garden, beyond which is an orchard, vegetable garden, flower garden and rose arbour. To the south the garden looks out over a lake and field walks, with woodland walk to the west. Small children's play area. Most areas can be accessed though sometimes by circuitous routes or an occasional step. WC access involves three steps.

🔥 🐴 ❀ 🍵

12 CONGBURN ARBORETUM

Edmondsley, Durham, DH7 6DY. Mr Alan Herbert, www.congburnnurseries.co.uk. *From B6532 at Edmondsley, follow yellow NGS signs.* **Sun 26 Feb, Sun 2 Apr (10-4). Adm £3, chd free.** Come and enjoy a woodland walk and find the snowdrops and hellebores in February or come in April to see the daffodils and narcissi. The arboretum is in the process of development and you will therefore see plenty of new planting amongst the already established trees. The site is on a hillside so please wear sturdy footwear. You can choose a longer or shorter route through the woods. The paths are steep and not suitable for wheelchairs.

❀ 🐴 🍵

13 ♦ CRAGSIDE

Rothbury, NE65 7PX. National Trust, 01669 620333, www.nationaltrust.org.uk/ cragside/things-to-see-and-do/ garden/. *13m SW of Alnwick. (B6341); 15m NW of Morpeth (A697).* **For NGS: Fri 28 Apr (10-5). Adm £18.80, chd £9.40. For other opening times and information, please phone or visit garden website.** The Formal Garden is in the 'High Victorian' style created by the 1st Lord and Lady Armstrong. Incl orchard house, carpet bedding, ferneries, Italian terrace and Rose borders. The largest sandstone Rock Garden in Europe with its tumbling cascades. Extensive grounds of over 1000 acres famous for rhododendrons in June, large lakes and magnificent conifer landscape. The House, mainly the design of Norman Shaw, with its very fine arts and crafts interiors is worth a separate visit. Limited wheelchair access to formal garden.

🔥 🐴 ❀ 🚐 🍵

14 CROFT HALL

Croft-on-Tees, DL2 2TB. Mr & Mrs Trevor Chaytor Norris. *3m S of Darlington. On A167 to Northallerton, 6m from Scotch Corner. Croft Hall is 1st house on R as you*

enter village from Scotch Corner. **Sun 11 June (2-5.30). Adm £5, chd free. Home-made teas.**
A lovely lavender walk leads to a Queen Anne-fronted house (not open) surrounded by a 5-acre garden, comprising a stunning herbaceous border, large fruit and vegetable plot, two ponds and wonderful topiary arched wall. Pretty rose garden and mature box Italianate parterre are beautifully set in this garden offering peaceful, tranquil views of open countryside. Wheelchair access, some gravel paths.
& ❀ ☕

15 ◆ CROOK HALL & GARDENS
Sidegate, Durham City, DH1 5SZ. Maggie Bell, 0191 384 8028, info@crookhallgardens.co.uk, www.crookhallgardens.co.uk. *Centre of Durham City. Crook Hall is short walk from Durham's Market Place. Follow the tourist info signs. Parking available at entrance.* **For NGS: Sun 26 Feb (11-3). Adm £7, chd £5. For other opening times and information, please phone, email or visit garden website.**
Described in Country Life as having 'history, romance and beauty'. Intriguing medieval manor house surrounded by 4 acres of fine gardens. Visitors can enjoy magnificent cathedral views from the 2 walled gardens. Other garden 'rooms' incl the silver and white garden. An orchard, moat pool, maze and Sleeping Giant give added interest! Refreshments in the Tea Room (main building) and the Café (entrance building). Wheelchair accessible and disabled WC.
& ❀ ♿ 🛏 ☕

16 FALLODON HALL
Alnwick, NE66 3HF. Mr & Mrs Mark Bridgeman, 01665 576252, luciabridgeman@gmail.com, www.bruntoncottages.co.uk. *5m N of Alnwick, 2m off A1. From the A1 turn R on B6347 signed Christon Bank & Seahouses, & turn into Fallodon gates after exactly 2m, at the Xrds. Follow drive for 1m.* **Sat 24 June (2-5). Adm £4.50, chd free.**

Home-made teas in stable yard.
Extensive, well established garden, including a 30 metre border, finishing beside a hot greenhouse and bog garden. The late C17 walls of the kitchen garden surround cutting and vegetable borders and the fruit greenhouse. The sunken garden from 1898 has been replanted by Natasha McEwen. Woodlands, pond and arboretum extend over 10 acres to explore. Renowned home-made teas in stable yard, and plant sale. 'Downton Abbey' was filmed at Fallodon during the final Christmas series. And Alexander Armstrong used the gardens as the setting for the videos for his latest album 'From a Different Shore'. Partial wheelchair access.
& 🛏 ❀ 🛏 ☕

17 THE FOLD
High Wooley, Stanley Crook, DL15 9AP. Mr & Mrs G Young, 01388 768412, gfamyounng@gmail.com. *3m N of Crook. Turn R at Xrds in Brancepeth, opp turn to Castle, drive 3m along the single track rd until you reach the junction on bend with the main rd. Entrance 100yards on L.* **Sat 8 July (1.30-4.30). Adm £4, chd free. Home-made teas. Visits also by arrangement Apr to Sept groups of 10+.**
Garden, approx ½ acre created over 20 years in an area that had been extensively mined. It stands at 700ft and enjoys splendid views over countryside. Herbaceous borders, alpine bed, island beds, ponds, numerous mature trees and small roof garden. Wide range of plants, mostly perennials, many grown from seed and cuttings. Emphasis on colour, harmony and texture to create all year interest. Art exhibition No disabled access as steep slopes and gravel paths.
❀ ♿ ☕

18 THE FORGE
Ravensworth, Richmond, DL11 7EU. Mr & Mrs Peter & Enid Wilson, 01325 718242, enid.wilson@btconnect.com. *7m N of Richmond. Travel 5½m W on A66 from Scotch Corner. Turn L to Ravensworth & follow*

NGS signs. **Sun 4 June (1-5.30). Adm £3, chd free. Cream teas. Homemade cakes. Visits also by arrangement May to Sept.**
The Blacksmith's Secret Garden - the garden is hidden from view behind The Forge House and Forge Cottage. It has small wildlife ponds with two natural stone features and a meadow. There are a number of unusual plants i.e. Dactylorhiza Fuchsia. Featured in Northern Echo, Teesdale Mercury, Amateur Gardener. Wheelchair access across gravel path.
& 🐐 ♿ ☕

Donations from the National Garden Scheme help Parkinson's UK care for more people

19 NEW GARDENER'S COTTAGE
Bingfield, Newcastle Upon Tyne, NE19 2LE. Andrew Davenport, www.gcplants.co.uk. *From N turn L off A68 signed Bingfield, after approx. 0.6m turn L at T junction, garden on R approx. 0.9m. From S turn R off A68 signed Bingfield, garden on R approx. 1.8m.* **Sun 30 July (11-4). Adm £3, chd free. Light refreshments.**
This compact (¼ acre) experimental garden provides an education in organic and sustainable gardening. Prolific vegetable, fruit, herb and floral gardens show the use of mulching, hen assisted composting and other ideas from the garden's inventive creator. Pollinator friendly wild flowers thrive amongst cultivated varieties in a range of attractive ornamental borders.
❀ ☕

20 14 GRAYS TERRACE
Redhills, Durham, DH1 4AU.
Mr Paul Beard, 0191 5972849,
pauljofraeard@yahoo.co.uk. *Just
off A167 on W side of Durham. ½ m
S of A167 / A691 r'about, turn L
into Redhills Lane. When road turns
R with no entry sign, Grays Terrace
is ahead. No.14 is at the very end.*
**Visits by arrangement Apr to
Aug. Adm by donation.**
A steeply sloping garden of about
⅔ acre with a superb view over
Durham Cathedral, Castle and
surroundings. Very informal garden;
no bedding and a significant
wild area. Planting is mixed with
interest throughout the year. Many
unusual and rare plants. Particularly
knowledgeable owner who is happy
to escort groups round the garden.
Not suitable for wheelchairs.

**21 HARPERLEY HALL
FARM**
Harperley, Stanley, DH9 9UB.
Gary McDermott,
01207 233318, enquiries@
harperleyhallfarmnurseries.co.uk,
www.harperleyhallfarmnurseries.
co.uk. *Leave A1 at J63. At r'about
take 2nd exit A693, continue for 5m.
After T-junction, turn R onto Shieldrow
Lane, then R onto Kyo Lane. At end
turn R onto Harperley Lane. Garden
500yds on L.* **Sun 14 May, Sun 24
Sept (10-4). Adm £3, chd free.
Home-made teas. Visits also
by arrangement Mar to Sept,
groups welcome daytime or
evenings.**
The garden is developing around
large ponds and is filled with
Primulas, including Primula 'Inverewe'
and P pulverulenta Bartleys
Hybrid,Meconopsis, including
M 'Lingholm', M quintuplinervia,
M cookei and the very rare
M punicea 'Sichuan Silk'. Also a
wide range of Hostas and Ferns.
We also grow an increasing range
of Orchids including Dactylorhiza
and Cypripedium. Many plants will
be sold at much reduced prices in
our end of season sale. The garden
is in a tranquil setting and a flock of
Rainbow and other Lorikeet fly at
liberty around the garden. Featured
in an article by Roy Lancaster in
RHS Garden magazine. The majority
of the garden and nursery can be
accessed by wheelchair users.

GROUP OPENING

**22 HIDDEN GARDENS OF
CROFT ROAD**
Darlington, DL2 2SD. *2m S
of Darlington on A167. ¾m S
from A167/A66 r'about between
Darlington & Croft.* **Sun 2 July
(1-5). Combined adm £5, chd
free. Home-made teas at Oxney
Flatts & Orchard Gardens.**
*Donation to Great North Air
Ambulance.*
4 very different and interesting
gardens, well named as 'Hidden
Gardens'. All are behind tall
hedges. Oxney Cottage is a very
pretty cottage garden with lawns,
herbaceous borders and roses,
colourful and varied unusual plants.
Nags Head Farm has a wonderful rill
running alongside a sloping garden
with a variety of plants leading to a
quiet, peaceful courtyard. There is
a large vegetable garden in which
stands a magnificent glass-house
with prolific vines and chilli plants.
A woodland walk enhances the
tranquility of this garden. Orchard
Gardens is a large interesting garden
of mixed planting, stump sculptures,
colourful themed beds, fruit trees
and different imaginative ornaments.
Oxney Flatts has well-stocked
herbaceous borders and a wild life
pond. Partial wheelchair access.

GROUP OPENING

23 HILLSIDE COTTAGES
Low Etherley, Bishop Auckland,
DL14 0EZ. Mary Smith, Eric
& Delia Ayres, 01388 832727,
mary@maryruth.plus.com. *Off the
B6282 in Low Etherley, nr Bishop
Auckland. To reach the gardens walk
down the track opp number 63
Low Etherley. Please park on main
rd. Limited disabled parking at the
cottages.* **Sun 21 May (1.30-5).
Combined adm £4, chd free.
Home-made teas. Visits also by
arrangement Feb to Oct.**

Newonstead Cottage Garden

1 HILLSIDE COTTAGE
Eric & Delia Ayres.

2 HILLSIDE COTTAGE
Mrs M Smith.

The gardens of these two C19 cottages offer contrasting styles. At Number 1, grass paths lead you through a layout of trees and shrubs including many interesting specimens. Number 2 is based on island beds and has a cottage garden feel with a variety of perennials among the trees and shrubs and also incl a wild area, vegetables and fruit. Both gardens have ponds and water features. This year we are opening to show off spring flowers and Rhododendrons. Featured in The Northern Echo and Bishop's Press. There are steps in both gardens.

🐂 ✳ ☙

24 NEW KIPLIN HALL
nr Scorton, Richmond, North Yorkshire, DL10 6AT. Kiplin Hall Trustees, www.kiplinhall.co.uk. *Between Richmond & Northallerton on B6271. Approx 5m east of A1. Due to its upgrade, we are unable to give precise directions from the A1 at time of going to print. Please consult maps or internet for up-to-the-minute directions.* **Sun 23 July (10-5). Adm £5.90, chd £3.20. Home-made teas. Home baking, cream teas & lunches using fresh garden produce. Hot/cold drinks, wine, beer.**
Fabulous lake views, gardens, woodland and parkland. These beautiful grounds, once in decline, are being restored to their former beauty in this lovely setting. Topiary surrounds the White and Rose Gardens. Perennial and Hot Borders, Knot and Sensory Gardens. Mayflies dance in the Bog Garden and the Walled Garden is once more productive. From snowdrops to glorious autumn colours, this garden is a joy! Featured in Dales Life Magazine, Saturday Telegraph, Northern Echo, Living North Magazine. and Yorkshire Post Wheelchair access, the gardens close to the house and Walled Garden are accessible. Coaches must be booked in advance.

♿ 🐂 ✳ 🚌 ☙

25 NEW LAMBSHIELD
Hexham, NE46 1SF. David Young. *2m S of Hexham. Take the B6306 from Hexham. After 1.6m turn R at chevron sign. Lambshield drive is 2nd on L after 0.6m.* **Sun 30 July (1.30-5). Adm £5, chd free. Home-made teas.**
2 acre country garden with strong structure and exciting plant combinations, begun in 2010 around a working farm. Distinct areas and styles with formal herbaceous, grasses, contemporary planting, cottage garden, pool and orchard. Cloud hedging, pleached trees, and topiary create a backdrop to colourful and exuberant planting. Modern sculpture. Oak building and fencing by local craftsmen. Level ground but gravel paths not suitable for wheelchairs.

✳ 🚐 ☙

26 LILBURN TOWER
Alnwick, NE66 4PQ. Mr & Mrs D Davidson, 01668 217291, davidson309@btinternet.com. *3m S of Wooler. On A697.* **Sun 28 May (2-5). Adm £5, chd free. Home-made teas. Visits also by arrangement May to Sept groups of 6+.**
10 acres of magnificent walled and formal gardens set above river; rose parterre, topiary, scented garden, Victorian conservatory, wild flower meadow. Extensive fruit and vegetable garden, large glasshouse with vines. 30 acres of woodland with walks. Giant lilies, meconopsis around pond garden. Rhododendrons and azaleas. Also ruins of Pele Tower, and C12 church. Featured in Berwick Advertiser; Northumberland Gazette. Partial wheelchair access.

♿ 🐂 ✳ 🚐 ☙

GROUP OPENING

27 NEW LITTLE HARLE GARDENS
Harle, Newcastle Upon Tyne, NE19 2PD. Kitty Anderson. *Entrance to Little Harle is 18m from Newcastle on the A696 Jedburgh rd. Past the airport, Ponteland and Belsay. 1m S of Kirkwhelpington*

Village. **Sat 10 June (1-5.30). Combined adm £5, chd free. Home-made teas.**
Extensive gardens around a C14 Pele Tower, protected by beautiful mature woodland. Well established rhododendrons and azaleas give vibrant colour in early summer. Shrub and herbaceous borders surround a 2 acre lawn. The terrace walk along the ha-ha offers views over Kirkharle Estate. Also 2½ acre Georgian walled garden with orchard, flower and vegetable beds. This garden is a secluded family home that is not open on a regular basis - this is a rare opportunity to view a private garden that is maintained almost entirely by those who live there. Close to Kirkharle Lake and Courtyard - birthplace of Lancelot 'Capability' Brown. Wheelchair access grounds area on one level with very few steps, paths are gravel and in order to view the gardens full access is over grassed area.

♿ ✳ ☙

28 LOUGHBROW HOUSE
Hexham, NE46 1RS. Mrs K A Clark, 01434 603351, patriciaclark351@btinternet.com. *1m S of Hexham on B6306. Dipton Mill Rd. Rd signed Blanchland, ¼m take R fork; then ¼m at fork, lodge gates & driveway at intersection.* **Sun 23 July (2-5). Adm £4, chd free. Home-made teas. Visits also by arrangement.**
A real country house garden with sweeping, colour themed herbaceous borders set around large lawns. Unique Lutyens inspired rill with grass topped bridges and climbing rose arches. Part walled kitchen garden and paved courtyard. Bog garden with pond. Developing new border and rose bed. Wild flower meadow with specimen trees. Woodland quarry garden with rhododendrons, azaleas, hostas and rare trees. Home-made jams and chutneys.

🐂 ✳ 🚐 🏠 ☙

29 10 LOW ROW

North Bitchburn, Crook, DL15 8AJ. Mrs Ann Pickering, 01388 766345, keightleyann@yahoo.co.uk. *3m NW of Bishop Auckland. From Bishop Auckland take A689 (N) to Howden-le-Wear. R up bank before petrol stn, 1st R in village at 30mph sign. Park in the village.* **Visits by arrangement Jan to Nov for individuals and groups of 20 max. Adm £3, chd free.** Unusual, original and truly organic, rambling garden: 90% grown from seeds and cuttings. Created without commercially bought plants or expense. Environmentally friendly. A haven for wildlife! Sloping garden with a myriad of paths and extensive views over the Wear Valley. Colour yr-round from snowdrops to autumn leaves. Knowledgeable garden owner who will make your visit one to remember. Open all yr except Tuesdays. Book by phone or e-mail. Refreshment offered in adjacent PH. Featured in The Guardian and on Television.

30 NEW MARIE CURIE GARDEN

Marie Curie Hospice, Marie Curie Drive, Newcastle Upon Tyne, NE4 6SS. Katie Searles, www.mariecurie.org.uk/help/hospice-care/hospices/newcastle/about. *The Hospice is in West Newcastle just off Elswick rd. It is at the bottom of a housing estate. The turning is between MA brothers & Dallas Carpets.* **Thur 13 July (2-4.30). Adm by donation. Cream teas. Refreshments served in our Garden Café.** The landscaped gardens of the purpose-built Marie Curie Hospice overlook the Tyne and Gateshead and offer a beautiful, tranquil place for patients and visitors to sit and chat. All rooms open onto a patio garden with gazebo and fountain. There are climbing roses, evergreens and herbaceous perennials. The garden is well maintained by volunteers. Come and see the work NGS funding helps make possible. A small fair in our Day Therapy Unit with a raffle, cake sale, tombola and plant sale. Refreshments

will be available. Possible screen showing Wimbledon matches. The Hospice and Gardens are wheelchair accessible.

> Your visit helps the Queen's Nursing Institute to champion excellence in community nursing

31 NEW MIDDLE GRANGE

Slaley, Hexham, NE47 0AA. Sir Michael & Lady Darrington, darringtondesign@hotmail.com. *5m S of Hexham. Approached from Riding Mill, entrance is on RHS approx 0.4m along. Approached from Hexham entrance is on L approx 0.3m along. Please leave cars at roadside & walk up drive.* **Sat 24 June (2-5.30). Adm £5, chd free. Tea and cakes available. Visits also by arrangement Apr to Aug well behaved children and dogs on leads welcome.** Hidden garden combining well executed design, traditional features and varied planting. Gravel garden, pond, large hexagonal pergola, lawn with borders, new rose garde and imposing 3 tier terrace topped by a seating area - all feature mature, colourful interesting planting of superb quality. Meadow area leads to a view across the countryside. Once farm land, this is now a secret herbaceous heaven! Featured in Northumbrian Magazine.

GROUP OPENING

32 MIDDLETON-IN-TEESDALE

Market Place, Middleton-In-Teesdale, Barnard Castle, DL12 0ST. *Middleton-in-Teesdale Open Gardens are all located in & near the village. Tickets & map with directions to each garden available from the Tourist Information Centre, in the centre of the village.* **Sat 17 June (11.30-4.30). Combined adm £4.50, chd free. Home-made teas in Masonic Hall. Gluten free scones available.** Middleton in Teesdale sits amongst the outstanding scenery of Upper Teesdale. It welcomes Pennine Way walkers, and is just 4m to the E of the famous High Force on the R Tees. 6 + gardens will be open in and around this delightfully picturesque village, covering a variety of sizes, designs and planting. The gardens, in and near the village, range in elevation from 1,200ft - 750ft above sea level, and present both alpine and cottage planting. Plants available for sale and teas offered in the Masonic Hall in the centre of the village. The Open Gardens event will be advertised in the Teesdale Mercury and Northern Echo. Wheelchair access to most gardens.

33 ♦ MINDRUM GARDEN

Mindrum, Northumberland, TD12 4QN. Mr & Mrs T Fairfax, 01890 850228, tpfairfax@gmail.com, www.mindrumestate.com. *6m SW of Coldstream, 9m NW of Wooler. Off B6352, 4m nth of Yetholm. 5m from Cornhill on Tweed. Disabled parking close to house.* **For NGS: Sun 18 June (2-5). Adm £5, chd free. Home-made teas. For other opening times and information, please phone, email or visit garden website.** 7 acres of romantic planting with old fashioned roses, violas, hardy perennials, lilies, herbs, scented shrubs, and intimate garden areas flanked by woodland and river walks.

45 Blackwell

Glasshouses with vines, jasmine. Large hillside limestone rock garden with water leading to a pond, delightful stream, woodland and wonderful views across Bowmont valley. Large plant sale, mostly home grown. Partial wheelchair access due to landscape. Wheelchair accessible WC available.

🐄 ✳ 🚍 🛏 ☕

GROUP OPENING

34 MOORSHOLM VILLAGE

Saltburn-By-The-Sea, TS12 3JF. www.moorsholminbloom.co.uk. *Moorsholm is 6m E of Guisborough on A171. Turn L at sign for Moorsholm. Village 1m from A171. Visitors proceed to centre of village where stewards will direct to car park. Guides & maps available.* **Sun 16 July (11-4). Combined adm £5, chd free. Home-made teas in the Church Hall and the Sports Pavilion. Cakes and scones, tea and coffee.**
A range of gardens to view including woodland gardens, cottage gardens large and small, and up to 16 allotments in a moorland setting. Farming and former ironstone

setting, 5m from the North Sea. 5 times winner of Northumbria in Bloom best village; winner in Britain in Bloom in 2014. The village boasts a range of heritage features and cultivated public areas, notably the 'Long Border' and wild flower areas. An interesting heritage walk takes in village allotment gardens, green lanes with wildlife habitats and conservation schemes. Victorian Churchyard, Church Hall and Quiet Garden won 'Best Grounds of a Religious Establishment' Northumbria in Bloom. Printed map and interpretation boards ensure visitors enjoy local features and natural history. Warm welcome from Moorsholm in Bloom volunteers who very much enjoy hosting the NGS Open Day. Depending on weather some of the green lanes could be unsuitable for wheelchairs, some open gardens have steps.

🚶 🐄 ✳ ☕

35 NEW MR YORKE'S WALLED GARDEN

Cravengate, Richmond, DL10 4RE. Mr & Mrs Dennis & Marcia McLuckie, 01748 825525, marcia@yorkshirecountryholidays. co.uk. *Third of the way down Cravengate, nr Richmond town centre On road out to Leyburn, 5 mins walk from Market Place up Finkle St, past Black Lion PH into Newbiggin (cobbled street). L at end of rd into Cravengate. Garden on R, 1/3 of way down. No parking at the garden.* **Sun 13 Aug (1-5.30). Adm £5, chd free. Light refreshments. Homemade cakes and scones.**
Charming C18 walled garden, redesigned with herbaceous border, ponds, mature trees, standard and climbing roses, vegetable garden, fruit trees, lawns and grassy paths. This is a garden in change, as the owners continue clearing it of rampant brambles, self-sets and weeds and designing and planting this one acre pleasant, tranquil town garden. Fabulous views of Richmond Castle and Culloden Tower. The garden is on a hill. Main grass paths accessible with a wheelchair, but they are quite steep.

🚶 🐄 ✳ 🛏 ☕

36 NEWONSTEAD COTTAGE GARDEN

Great Bavington, Newcastle Upon Tyne, NE19 2BJ. Philippa Hodkinson, 01830 540409, philippa.hodkinson@yahoo.co.uk. *NW of Newcastle upon Tyne. From A696 turn onto B6342 past Kirkharle Courtyard, then R to Great Bavington. From A68 turn onto B6342 approx halfway to A696, take L turn to Great Bavington. Follow yellow signs.* **Visits by arrangement June to Aug for groups of 10+. Adm £5, chd free.** Developing cottage garden on ½ acre site set in wild landscape. Dramatic backdrop of outcrop of whin sill. Stunning late season colour from hardy annuals and unusual perennials. Chickens wander amongst young trees set in the lawn. This is an artist's garden, which is run on green gardening principles. Wheelchair access - grass paths may be difficult after heavy rain.
&

37 NO. 2 FERNDENE

2 Holburn Lane Court, Holburn Lane, Ryton, NE40 3PN. Maureen Kesteven, 0191 413 5937, maureen@patrickkesteven.plus. com. *In Ryton Old Village, 8m W of Gateshead. Off B6317, on Holburn Lane in Old Ryton Village. Park in Co-op carpark on High St, cross rd and walk through Ferndene Park following yellow signs.* **Sun 16 July (1-4.30). Adm £5, chd free. Home-made teas. Pizzas from wood fired oven and prosecco. Visits also by arrangement Apr to July groups of 10+.**
¾ acre garden, developing since 2009, surrounded by trees. Informal areas of herbaceous perennials, more formal box bordered area, veg patch, sedum roof, wildlife pond, bog and fern gardens. Willow work. Early interest - hellebores, snowdrops, daffodils, bluebells and tulips. Summer interest from wide range of flowering perennials. 1½ acre mixed broadleaf wood. New central border and pond 'hide'. Pizzas (cooked in wood fired oven) and prosecco.
❀ ☕

38 THE OLD VICARAGE

Hutton Magna, Richmond, DL11 7HJ. Mr & Mrs D M Raw. *8m SE of Barnard Castle. 6m W of Scotch Corner on A66. Turn R, signed Hutton Magna. Continue to, and through, village. Garden 200yds past village on L, on corner of T-junction.* **Sun 23 Apr (2-5). Adm £4, chd free. Home-made teas.** S-facing garden, elevation 450ft. Plantings, since 1978, now maturing within original design contemporary to 1887 house (not open). Cut and topiary hedging, old orchard, rose and herbaceous borders featuring hellebores in profusion, with tulips and primulas. Large and interesting plant sale. Recent introduction of a loggery to encourage wildlife.
❀ ☕

Ravensford Farm

39 OLIVER FORD GARDEN

Longedge Lane, Rowley, Consett, DH8 9HG. Bob & Bev Tridgett, www.gardensanctuaries.co.uk. *5m NW of Lanchester. Signed from A68 in Rowley. From Lanchester take rd towards Sately. Garden will be signed as you pass Woodlea Manor.* **Sun 4 June (1-5). Adm £4, chd free. Home-made teas.**
A peaceful, contemplative 3 acre garden developed and planted by the owner and BBC Gardener of the Year as a space for quiet reflection. Arboretum specialising in bark, stream, wildlife pond and bog garden. Semi-shaded Japanese maple and dwarf rhododendron garden. Rock garden and scree bed. Insect nectar area, orchard and 1½ acre meadow. Annual wild flower area. Terrace and ornamental kitchen garden,. Has a number of sculptures around the garden. Unfortunately not suitable for wheelchairs.

40 25 PARK ROAD SOUTH

Chester le Street, DH3 3LS. Mrs A Middleton, 0191 388 3225. *4m N of Durham. Located at S end of A167 Chester-le-St bypass rd. Precise directions provided when booking visit.* **Visits by arrangement May to July. Adm £3, chd free. Light refreshments.**
Plantswoman's garden with all-yr round interest, colour, texture and foliage. Unusual perennials, grasses, shrubs and container planting. Cool courtyard garden using foliage only. Small front gravel garden. Plants for sale.

41 PARKER TOWERS

6 Garden Place, Church Hill, Crook, DL15 9DR. Clive Parker, www.facebook.com/parkersgarden270615?ref=hl. *Off Church Hill via access track. See entrance track opp St Cuthberts RC Church. On L after row of terraces on Church Hill if going up hill, before the barn & school.* **Sun 11 June (1-5). Adm £2.50, chd free. Home-made teas. Seating in the garden and in the conservatory.**
Mostly woodland garden sloping down to Crook Beck with terraces,

incl herbaceous borders, tall perennials, wild flower grassland, summer and spring flowering shrubs and a large collection of shade tolerant plants and bulbs. Includes rear 'potted' garden with alpine house. Most of the large feature trees are unusual and multi- featured e.g. bark, autumn colour and flowers. Has a large wooden greenhouse 10' x 6' in main garden, small summer house, water features and gazebo. House 175+ years old large terrace with unusual headstones/gargoyles on the eaves of Shakespeare and GB Shaw? Adjacent Church Hill Allotments 100m. Plant stall, cake stall and raffle on open day. The garden is very steep and not suitable for wheelchairs.

GROUP OPENING

42 PETERLEE GARDENS SAFARI

Shotton Hall Banqueting Suites, Old Shotton, Peterlee, SR8 2PH. Peterlee Town Council. *From S-bound carriageway of A19, turn L onto slip rd signed Peterlee. At mini r'about turn L & then take the 1st turn on R into the grounds of Shotton Hall Banqueting Suites.* **Sun 9 July (10-4). Combined adm £3, chd free. Home-made teas at Shotton Hall all day.**
Peterlee is opening about 8 of its prettiest gardens together with its well-managed allotments and the colourful grounds of Shotton Hall. While some of the gardens are of medium size, many are small, bijou spaces full of colour and interest. All have been ingeniously planted by imaginative owners. Because of the size of the town, visiting all the venues will take the form of a circular safari for which a vehicle will be needed. So, purchase a ticket and collect a map from Shotton Hall and start your journey wherever you wish on the well-signed route. Refreshments will be available throughout the day at Shotton Hall. Wheelchair access to most but not all gardens.

43 QUARRY END

Walworth, Darlington, DL2 2LY. Mr & Mrs Iain & Margaret Anderson. *Approx 5m W of Darlington on A68 or ½m E of Piercebridge on A67. Follow brown signs to Walworth Castle Hotel. Just up the hill from the Castle entrance, follow NGS yellow signs down private track.* **Sun 20 Aug (1.30-5). Adm £4, chd free. Home-made teas.**
Woodland garden, about ¾ acre in an ancient quarry setting. Redeveloped over 16 years the garden has an C18 ice house, a wide variety of trees, shrubs and perennials, a fernery and ornamental vegetable plot. Spectacular late summer display. Recent addition of a further 1 acre naturalised woodland in adjacent quarry is under development. Extensive views over South Durham. Very limited access to new woodland area especially if wet. Main garden includes some rough steps and gravel paths.

44 ◆ RABY CASTLE

Staindrop, Darlington, DL2 3AH. Lord Barnard, 01833 660202, admin@rabycastle.com, www.rabycastle.com. *12m NW of Darlington, 1m N of Staindrop. On A688, 8m NE of Barnard Castle.* **For NGS: Sat 15 July (11-5). Adm £7, chd £3. Light refreshments in the Raby Castle Stables Tearoom. For other opening times and information, please phone, email or visit garden website.**
This year Raby Castle is celebrating opening its gardens for the NGS since 1927. C18 walled gardens set within the grounds of Raby Castle. Designers such as Thomas White and James Paine have worked to establish the gardens, which now extend to 5 acres, displaying herbaceous borders, old yew hedges, formal rose gardens and informal heather and conifer gardens. Tearoom is located just outside the entrance gate to the Walled Gardens. Assistance will be needed for wheelchairs.

45 RAVENSFORD FARM
Hamsterley, DL13 3NH.
Jonathan & Caroline
Peacock, 01388 488305,
caroline@ravensfordfarm.co.uk.
*7m W of Bishop Auckland. From
A68 at Witton-le-Wear turn off W to
Hamsterley. Go through village & turn
L just before tennis courts at west
end.* **Sat 1 Apr (2-5). Adm £4,
chd free. Light refreshments.
Visits also by arrangement
please confirm numbers for
catering and parking in good
time.**
An April Fools day opening for this
large garden that has been with the
NGS for nearly two decades - but
has never before opened so early in
the year. Spring bulbs are a feature,
as are many unusual (labelled)
shrubs and trees. On NGS day we
sell plants and jams from the garden,
we serve home-made cakes for tea,
and Northumbrian pipers provide
the background music. Several
interesting items of garden statuary
andart. Featured in Garden News.
Some gravel, so assistance will be
needed for wheelchairs. Assistance
dogs only in the garden, but others
okay in the field.

  ♿ ✾ ☕ ♥

46 ST CUTHBERT'S HOSPICE
Park House Road, Durham,
DH1 3QF. Paul Marriott, CEO,
www.stcuthbertshospice.com.
*1m SW of Durham City on A167.
Turn into Park House Rd, the Hospice
is on the L after bowling green car
park. Parking available.* **Sun 30 July
(11-4). Adm £4, chd free. Hot &
cold drinks, homemade cakes.**
5 acres of mature gardens surround
this CQC outstanding-rated Hospice.
In development since 1988, the
gardens are cared for by volunteers.
Incl a Victorian-style greenhouse
and large vegetable, fruit and cut
flower area. Lawns surround smaller
scale specialist planting, and areas
for patients and visitors to relax.
Woodland area with short and long
walks, and an 'In Memory' garden
with stream. Plants and produce for
sale. We are active participants in
Northumbria in Bloom and Britain
in Bloom, with several awards in

recent years, including overall winner
in 2015 for the Care/ Residential /
Convalescent Homes / Day Centre
/ Hospices category. Almost all areas
are accessible for wheelchairs.

  ♿ ♥ ✾ 🚗 ☕ ♥

ALLOTMENTS

47 ST MARGARET'S ALLOTMENTS
Margery Lane, Durham, DH1 4QJ.
*From A1 take A690 to City Centre/
Crook. Straight ahead at T-lights
after 4th r'about. 10mins walk from
bus or rail station.* **Sun 16 July
(2-5). Combined adm £4, chd
free. Home-made teas in hall
adjacent to allotments.**
5 acres of 82 allotments against the
spectacular backdrop of Durham
Cathedral. This site has been cultivated
since the Middle Ages, and was saved
from development 25yrs ago, allowing
a number of enthusiastic gardeners
to develop plots which display a great
variety of fruit, vegetables and flowers.
Guided tours available. Many unusual
vegetables. Display of creative and fun
competitions for plot holders. The site
has some steep and narrow paths.

  ♥ ✾ ☕ ♥

48 NEW SOUTHLANDS
The Avenue, Eaglescliffe, Stockton-
On-Tees, TS16 9AS. Ian Waller.
*1½m from Yarm on A135. A66
junction signed A135 Stockton West/
Yarm. South towards Yarm for approx
1½ m past Preston Park. From
Yarm on A135 for 1½ m passing
Golf Course. The Avenue is opposite
junction to Railway Station.* **Sat 10
June (2-5.30). Adm £4, chd free.
Home-made teas, cakes and
scones.**
South facing High Victorian Gardens
created by Sir Samuel and Lady
Sadler. Elevated site with sloping
lawns, herbaceous borders, orchards
and woodland areas. A natural
stream runs through this 10 acre
garden with a miniature lake and
island. Established Rhododendrons
and Azaleas, specimen trees with
ginko, maples, beech, pines and
redwoods. Coaching house (serving
teas), Bothy, old Greenhouse and

fountain. Last opened in 1957 for
NGS. Steeply sloping site.

  ♥ ☕ ♥

GROUP OPENING

49 NEW STANGHOW GARDENS
Stanghow, Lingdale, Saltburn-
By-The-Sea, TS12 3JU. *Stanghow
Road, Stanghow. Stanghow is 5 km
E of Guisborough on A171. Turn L at
Lockwood Beck (signed Stanghow).
The Forge is at the crossroads,
Heather Holm below crossroads.* **Sun
23 July (12-4). Combined adm
£4, chd free. Home-made teas.
Refreshments at Heather Holm.**
These two quite different
gardens sit at 700 feet above sea
level on the edge of the North
Yorkshire Moors. Stanghow has
won numerous RHS Gold awards
for Best Small Village and was a
Champion among Champions in the
2013 Britain in Bloom competition.
Heatherholm has extensive topiary
which adds form and structure to
this ¼ acre garden. It is divided
into a series of rooms containing a
formal garden, lawns, shrubberies,
a raised pond, fruit trees, vegetable
garden and soft fruit area. There is
a summer house and greenhouse
and several comfortable seating
areas. Also herbaceous borders and
a wide array of shrubs, lilies, hostas,
clematis and unusual feature trees.
The Forge, on an exposed corner
plot, has an open aspect with views
of the North Yorkshire Moors and
sea. The owners inherited a largely
unkempt garden and have worked
hard to reclaim these overgrown
areas, replanting with a wide variety
of perennials, shrubs and vegetables.
Heather Holm has wheelchair
access to viewing deck only. The
Forge has limited wheelchair access.

  ♿ ✾ ☕ ♥

50 STANTON FENCE
Stanton, Morpeth, NE65 8PP. Sir
David & Lady Kelly. *5m NW of
Morpeth. Nr Stanton on the C144
between Pigdon & Netherwitton. OS
map ref NZ 13588.* **Sun 25 June
(1-5). Adm £5, chd free. Home-**

made teas. *Donation to St Giles Church Maintenance Fund.*
Contemporary 4.7 acre country garden designed by Chelsea Gold Medal winner, Arabella Lennox-Boyd, in keeping with its rural setting. A strong underlying design unites the different areas from formal parterre and courtyard garden to orchard, wild flower meadows and woodland. Romantically planted rose covered arbours and long clematis draped pergola walk. Nuttery, kitchen garden and greenhouse. Both Robert Iley, the garden builder, and the current gardener, will be available for questions. Delightful views. Featured in The Northumbrian. Wheelchair access for those chairs that can use mown paths as well as hard paving.

51 4 STOCKLEY GROVE
Brancepeth, DH7 8DU. Mr & Mrs Bainbridge, 079439 40708, fabb63@sky.com. *5m W of Durham City. Situated on the A690 between Durham & Crook. There is no parking available in Stockley Grove. From Durham direction turn L at village Xrds & park at castle at end of rd. Lifts to the garden will be available if required.* **Sun 6 Aug (1-5). Adm £4, chd free. Home-made teas. Visits also by arrangement May to Sept.**
A stunning ½ acre garden with inspirational planting to provide yr-round colour and interest. Landscaped with hidden grassy paths with many unusual trees, shrubs and plants incl wildlife pond, rockery area and water features. Rockery currently being extended. Winner of 'Beautiful Durham'.

52 THORNTON HALL GARDENS
Staindrop Road, Darlington, DL2 2NB. Michael & Sue Manners, 07713 508222, info@thorntonhallgardens.co.uk, www.thorntonhallgardens.co.uk. *On B6279 Staindrop Rd. 3m W of Darlington.* **Sun 14 May (1.30-5). Adm £6, chd £1. Home-made teas. Visits also by arrangement May to July.**

C16 Grade I listed hall (not open). 2 walled gardens with Elizabethan raised borders, separate vegetable garden. Plantsman's garden with emphasis on colour-themed borders, plant associations, form and foliage. Unusual perennials, interspersed with interesting trees and shrubs in mixed herbaceous borders. Large collection of tulips, auriculas, roses, clematis. Wildlife and ornamental ponds. For other opening times and information, please phone, email or visit garden website.

53 NEW USHAW COLLEGE
Woodland Road, Durham, DH7 9BJ. The Trustees of Ushaw College, 0191 3738502, meet@ushaw.org, www.ushaw.org. *3m W of Durham City. From A167 N of Neville's Cross turn on to minor road signed Bearpark & Ushaw College. The College entrance is signed to the R in 2½m.* **Sat 10 June, Sat 12 Aug (11-5). Adm £4, chd free. Home-made teas in the College. Visits also by arrangement Mar to Oct for 10+.**
Part of the 50 acre landscape within open countryside around Ushaw College, the gardens were originally laid out in 1840 in front of the Georgian house and feature a formal rhododendron garden with

herbaceous borders and rose beds. Extensive renovations to the garden have been under way for the last 3 years and continue, with some wild areas, a former pond, and extensive areas of woodland. Wheelchair access to concentric paths, but not to more overgrown areas.

54 NEW 3 VALLEY CLOSE
Yarm, TS15 9SE. Angela Johnson. *From A19, take A67 to Yarm. Approx 2m turn R at r'about along A1044. 0.3m L onto Kirk Rd, 0.3m continue to Valley Drive, 240yds L onto Valley Drive, 280 yds L onto Valley Close. No 3 on your R.* **Sun 25 June (12-5.30). Adm £4, chd free. Home-made teas. Hot and cold drinks, light refreshments, afternoon tea.**
Beautiful terraced garden which commences in a large landscaped patio area. The pathway then ascends, winding through the garden giving lovely views of different aspects and the herbaceous borders filled with a variety of perennials, annuals and shrubs. It provides year round interest but is at its best during spring and summer. Wheelchair access to patio only, but as the garden is on a steep slope the rest of the garden can be appreciated from the patio.

24 Bede Crescent

Lambshields

© Susie White

55 ◆ WALLINGTON

Cambo, NE61 4AR. National Trust, 01670 774389, simon. thompson@nationaltrust.org. uk, www.nationaltrust.org.uk/ wallington. *12m W of Morpeth 20m NW Newcastle. From N B6343; from S via A696 from Newcastle, 6m W of Belsay, B6342 to Cambo.* **For NGS Sun 9 July (10-5). Adm £11.80, chd £5.90. Light refreshments. For opening times and information, please phone, email or visit garden website.**

Magical walled, terraced garden with herbaceous and mixed borders. Packed with colour. Edwardian conservatory with unusual plants. 100 acres of woodland. Pleasure grounds, river and lakes. Set in a stunning landscape, with opportunities for walking. House dates from 1688. Wheelchair access limited to top terrace in Walled Garden but elsewhere possible with care and support.

& 🐎 ✿ 🚐 ☕

56 WARRENFELL

2 Filter Cottages, Tunstall Reservoir, Wolsingham, Bishop Auckland, DL13 3LX. Fran Toulson, 01388 528392, warrenfell@btinternet.com. *Weardale. W on A689 through Wolsingham Village centre. On edge of village take R turn by Wolsingham School, signed to Tunstall Reservoir. No through Road. Garden 2m on R below dam wall.* **Sat 1, Sun 2 July (10.30-4). Adm £3.50, chd free. Home-made teas. Visits also by arrangement Apr to Sept.**

Started in 2012 this garden sits at just over 650ft in approx ¼ acre. A beautiful location, the garden visit can be combined with a walk at the reservoir. The garden includes some more unusual plants in borders with shrubs, perennials, roses, peonies and in the alpine garden added in 2015 . Pergola and arbour. Kitchen garden with raised beds, espaliered apples and pears. Small wild flower area. Featured in the Northern Echo, Weardale Gazette and Garden News.

✿ ☕

57 ◆ WASHINGTON OLD HALL

The Avenue, Washington Village, NE38 7LE. National Trust, 0191 416 6879, www.nationaltrust. org.uk/washingtonoldhall. *7m SE of Newcastle upon Tyne. From A19 onto A1231, from A1 exit J64 onto A195 in both cases stay on the road until you pick up brown signs to Washington Old Hall.* **For NGS: Sun 4 June (11-4). Adm by donation. Light refreshments. Also open 24 Bede Crescent. For other opening times and information, please phone or visit garden website.**

The picturesque stone manor house and its gardens provide a tranquil oasis in an historic setting. It contains a formal Jacobean garden with box hedging borders around evergreens and perennials, vegetable garden, wild flower nut orchard with bee hives. Places to sit out and enjoy a picnic. Enjoy cakes, snacks and ice cream in the cafe. A private garden in the village will also open. Location map and entry tickets purchased at the NGS plant stall. Our café is located in the lower gardens, serving hot and cold drinks, cake, snacks and ice cream. Designated parking spaces, wheelchairs available onsite. Accessible WC located in lower gardens via outdoor lift. All formal paths accessible .

& ⚘ ✿ 🚗 ☕ ♿

GROUP OPENING

58 NEW WESTGATE VILLAGE GARDENS

County Durham, Bishop Auckland, DL13 1PD. 01388 517735, lefontanil@gmail.com. *Please come to the Village Hall on Front Street once you have reached the village on the A689. Collect gardens map and pay.* **Sun 9 July (11-4.30). Combined adm £4.50, chd free. Home-made teas at Village Hall on Front Street, Westgate. Also at Breckon Hill. Sandwiches and home made cakes, strawberry cream scones. Afternoon tea only at Breckon Hill.**
Westgate in Weardale is in the North Pennines AONB, little known to many but with wonderful views of the wild and lovely fells from at least two of our gardens, one of which sits 1115 ft above sea level, so we have special challenges to our growing! We have an award winning sweet pea grower; a lady who fills her garden with flowers to cut for bouquets; others with colourful baskets and tubs, ponds, summerhouses and more. PH in the village - Sunday roasts by booking only. Excellent playground by the river and beautiful riverside walk. Featured in the Weardale Gazette. Wheelchair access is rather limited owing to access and differing levels. Suggest contact with the organiser before visiting.

& ✿ 🛏 ☕

---

59 ◆ WHALTON MANOR GARDENS

Whalton, Morpeth, NE61 3UT. Mr & Mrs T R P S Norton, 01670 775205, gardens@whaltonmanor.co.uk, www.whaltonmanor.co.uk. *5m W of Morpeth. On the B6524, the house is at E end of the village & will be signed.* **For NGS: Sun 2 July (2-5). Adm £5, chd free. Home-made teas. For other opening times and information, please phone, email or visit garden website.**
The historic Whalton Manor, altered by Sir Edwin Lutyens in 1908, is surrounded by 3 acres of magnificent walled gardens, designed by Lutyens with the help of Gertrude Jekyll. The gardens have been developed by the Norton family since the 1920s and incl extensive herbaceous borders, 30yd peony border, rose garden, listed summerhouses, pergolas and walls, festooned with rambling roses and clematis. Partial wheelchair access, some stone steps.

& ✿ 🚗 🛏 ☕

---

60 NEW WOODBINE HOUSE

22 South View, Hunwick, Crook, DL15 0JW. Stewart Irwin & Colin Purvis. *On main road through the village opposite village green. B6286 off A689 Bishop Auckland - Crook or A690 Durham - Crook. On street parking, entrance to the rear of the property RHS of house.* **Mon 29 May (1-5). Adm £3.50, chd free. Home-made teas. All refreshments are home-made.**
The garden is approx a quarter of an acre, divided into two, one half used as a vegetable garden with large greenhouse. The other half of the garden is lawn with well stocked (and some unusual planting) herbaceous borders and small pond. Bees are kept in the vegetable garden, only one hive at present. The local PH (which is almost adjacent) organises a 'Snail Race', 'Nettle Eating' competition and other activities on the same day. Wheelchair access to refreshment area but paths in garden are not wide enough for wheelchairs.

& ✿ ☕

---

61 WOODLANDS

Peareth Hall Road, Gateshead, NE9 7NT. Liz Reid, 07719 875750, lizreid52@ntlworld.com. *3½m N Washington Galleries. 4m S Gateshead town centre. On B1288 turn opp Guide Post PH (NE9 7RR) onto Peareth Hall Rd. Continue for* ½m passing 2 bus stops on L. Third drive on L past Highbury Ave. **Sat 1, Thur 6 July (1.30-4.30). Adm £3, chd free. Home-made teas. Visits also by arrangement June to Aug groups of 10+.**
Mature garden on a site of approx one seventh acre- quirky, with tropical themed planting and Caribbean inspired bar. A fun garden with colour throughout the year, interesting plants, informal beds and borders, pond area and decks.

✿ ☕

---

62 WOODSIDE HOUSE

Witton Park, Bishop Auckland, DL14 0DU. Charles & Jean Crompton, 01388 609973, j.crompton@talktalk.net. *2m N of Bishop Auckland. From Bishop Auckland take A68 to Witton Park. In village DO NOT follow SatNav. Go down track next to St Pauls Church.* **Sun 23 July (2-5). Adm £5, chd free. Home-made teas. Visits also by arrangement Mar to Sept for groups of 10+. Coaches welcome.**
Stunning 3-acre, mature, undulating garden full of interesting trees, shrubs and plants. Superbly landscaped with island beds, flowing herbaceous borders, an old walled garden, rhododendron beds, fernery, 3 ponds and vegetable garden. Delightful garden full of interesting and unusual features: much to fire the imagination. Winner of Bishop Auckland in Bloom. Featured in Sunday Telegraph and Amateur Gardening. Partial wheelchair access.

& ✿ 🚗 ☕

Perennial, supporting horticulturalists since 1839

NORTHAMPTONSHIRE

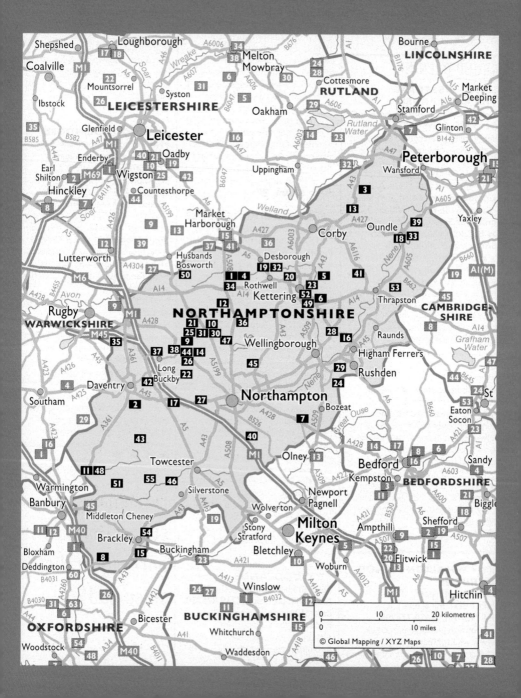

The county of Northamptonshire is famously known as the 'Rose of the Shires', but is also referred to as the 'Shire of Spires and Squires', and lies in the East Midlands area of the country bordered by eight other counties.

Take a gentle stroll around charming villages with thatch and stone cottages and welcoming inns. Wander around stately homes, discovering art treasures and glorious gardens open for the National Garden Scheme: Kelmarsh Hall, Lamport Hall, Holdenby House, Castle Ashby, Cottesbrooke Hall and Boughton House. In contrast visit some village groups, which include small imaginatively designed gardens.

Explore historic market towns such as Oundle and Brackley in search of fine footwear, antiques and curiosities. Or visit wildlife sanctuaries such as Sulby Gardens with 12 acres of interesting flora and fauna.

The serenity of our waterways will delight, and our winding country lanes and footpaths will guide you around a rural oasis, far from the pressures of modern living, where you can walk knee-deep in bluebells and snowdrops in spring at gardens such as Greywalls and Bosworth House, or view the late autumn colours of Boughton House.

Our first garden opens in February and the final opening occurs in November, giving a glimpse of gardens throughout the seasons.

Volunteers

County Organisers
David Abbott
01933 680363
d_j_abbott@btinternet.com

Gay Webster
01604 740203
gay.webster6@gmail.com

County Treasurer
Michael Heaton
01604 846032
ngs@mimomul.co.uk

Publicity
David Abbott
(as above)

Booklet Coordinators
David Abbott
(as above)

Michael Heaton
(as above)

Assistant County Organisers
Philippa Heumann
01327 860142
pmheumann@gmail.com

Geoff Sage
01788 510334
geoffsage256@btinternet.com

Left: Coton Manor Garden

OPENING DATES

All entries subject to change. For latest information check www.ngs.org.uk

Map locator numbers are shown to the right of each garden name.

February

Snowdrop Festival

Sunday 19th
Bosworth House 4

Sunday 26th
◆ Boughton House 5
67-69 High Street 28
Jericho 33

March

Sunday 5th
Greywalls 24

April

Saturday 8th
◆ The Old Rectory, Sudborough 41

Sunday 9th
Flore Gardens 17
◆ Kelmarsh Hall & Gardens 34

Sunday 16th
Briarwood 6
NEW The Old Vicarage 42

Sunday 23rd
Bosworth House 4
◆ Cottesbrooke Hall Gardens 10
◆ Deene Park 13

Thursday 27th
Sulby Gardens 50

Sunday 30th
Great Brington Gardens 22

May

Monday 1st
Titchmarsh House 53

Sunday 7th
Guilsborough Gardens 25

Sunday 21st
Charlton Gardens 8
Jericho 33
◆ Kelmarsh Hall & Gardens 34
Old Rectory, Quinton 40

Wednesday 24th
◆ Evenley Wood Garden 15

90th Anniversary Weekend

Monday 29th
Jericho 33
Titchmarsh House 53

June

Sunday 4th
NEW The Court House 11
Finedon Gardens 16
Preston Capes and Little Preston Gardens 43
NEW The Spring House 48

Saturday 10th
Titchmarsh House 53

Sunday 11th
Badby and Newnham Gardens 2
Kilsby Gardens 35
Slapton Gardens 46
Spratton Gardens 47

Saturday 17th
Flore Gardens 17

Sunday 18th
Flore Gardens 17
Foxtail Lilly 18
Harpole Gardens 27
Jericho 33
◆ The Old Rectory, Sudborough 41
Sulgrave Gardens 51
Turweston Gardens 54

Thursday 22nd
Sulby Gardens 50

Sunday 25th
Arthingworth Open Gardens 1
Finedon Gardens 16
Rosearie-de-la-Nymph 45
Weedon Lois & Weston Gardens 55

July

Sunday 2nd
◆ Castle Ashby Gardens 7
Rosearie-de-la-Nymph 45

Sunday 9th
◆ Holdenby House Gardens 30
Ravensthorpe Gardens 44

Sunday 23rd
Blatherwycke Estate 3
Long Buckby Gardens 37
Mill House 38
NEW Sunley Court 52

Sunday 30th
Froggery Cottage 19
NEW 136 High Street 29
Hostellarie 32

August

Saturday 5th
East Haddon Hall 14
◆ Haddonstone Show Gardens 26

Sunday 6th
East Haddon Hall 14
◆ Haddonstone Show Gardens 26
Hollowell Gardens 31
67 Stratfield Way 49

Sunday 13th
NEW Dale Farm 12
NEW The Green Patch 23

Thursday 24th
Sulby Gardens 50

September

Sunday 3rd
Old Rectory, Quinton 40

Sunday 10th
◆ Coton Manor Garden 9

Sunday 17th
NEW ◆ Lamport Hall 36

October

Thursday 12th
Sulby Gardens 50

Friday 13th
Sulby Gardens 50

Sunday 22nd
◆ Boughton House 5

November

Thursday 16th
Sulby Gardens 50

By Arrangement

Bosworth House 4
Briarwood 6
The Close, Harpole Gardens 27
Dripwell House, Guilsborough Gardens 25
Foxtail Lilly 18
Froggery Cottage 19
Glendon Hall 20
Gower House 21
Greywalls 24
67-69 High Street 28
Hostellarie 32
Jericho 33
19 Manor Close, Harpole Gardens 27
Mill House 38
The Old Bakery, Flore Gardens 17
The Old Black Horse 39
Pytchley House, Kilsby Gardens 35
Ravensthorpe Nursery, Ravensthorpe Gardens 44
Sulby Gardens 50
Titchmarsh House 53
NEW Wisteria House, Long Buckby Gardens 37

Your support helps Carers Trust to provide more help to unpaid carers

THE GARDENS

GROUP OPENING

1 ARTHINGWORTH OPEN GARDENS

Arthingworth, nr Market Harborough, LE16 8LA. *6m S of Market Harborough. From Market Harborough via A508, after 4m take L to Arthingworth. From Northampton, A508 turn R just after Kelmarsh.* **Sun 25 June (1.30-5.30). Combined adm £5, chd free. Home-made teas at Bosworth House & village hall.**

Arthingworth has been welcoming NGS visitors for more than 5 yrs. It is a village affair, with 8 to 9 gardens opening and 2 pop-up tearooms with home baked cakes. We now have some regulars who keep us on our toes and we love it. Come and enjoy the diversity, we aim to give visitors an afternoon of discovery. Our gardens have been chosen because they are all different in spirit, and tended by young and weathered gardeners. We have gardens with stunning views, traditional with herbaceous borders and vegetables, walled, and artisan. The village is looking forward to welcoming you. St Andrew's church Grade listed II* open. The village is next to the national cycle path. Wheelchair access to some gardens.

  ♿ ☕

GROUP OPENING

2 BADBY AND NEWNHAM GARDENS

Daventry, NN11 3AR. *3m S of Daventry. E side of A361. Maps provided for visitors.* **Sun 11 June (2-6). Combined adm £5, chd free. Home-made teas at Badby & Newnham Churches.**

THE BANKS
Newnham. Sue & Geoff Chester, www.suestyles.co.uk.

HILLTOP
Newnham. David & Mercy Messenger.

THE OLD HOUSE
Badby. Mr & Mrs Robert Cain.

SOUTHVIEW COTTAGE
Badby. Alan & Karen Brown.

TRIFIDIA
Badby. Colin & Shirley Cripps.

WREN COTTAGE
Newnham. Mr & Mrs Jim Dorkins.

6 gardens within 2 beautiful villages, with attractive old houses of golden coloured Hornton stone, set around their village greens. In Badby, there are 3 gardens of differing styles: a garden featuring spectacular views over Badby Wood; a newly developed elevated garden with views over the village; and a garden with pond, conservatory, glasshouses and vegetables, also featuring unusual plants that aim for yr-round interest. The 3 gardens in Newnham comprise: a 3 acre organic garden around a C17 thatched cottage with lawns, densely planted borders, vegetable and cutting garden, with feature trees and adjacent paddocks; a traditional C17 cottage garden with landscaped water feature and a large area set aside for growing vegetables; and a garden designer's garden to wander through, with pools, herbaceous borders, vegetables and herbs developed as rooms among mature trees. Both villages are hilly.

✿ ☕

3 BLATHERWYCKE ESTATE

Blatherwycke, Peterborough, PE8 6YW. Mr George. *Blatherwycke is signed off the A43 between Stamford & Corby. Follow road through village & the gardens entrance is immed next to the large river bridge.* **Sun 23 July (11-4). Adm £4, chd free. Home-made teas.**

Blatherwycke Hall demolished in the 1940s, its grounds and gardens lost until now! In April 2011 we started the renovation of the derelict 4 acre walled gardens. So far a large kitchen garden, wall trained fruit trees, extensive herbaceous borders, seasonal beds, parterre, pleaching orchard, and wild flower meadows have been built, planted and sown. Also a very large arboretum is being planted. Grass and gravel paths, some slopes and steps with ramps.

♿ 🐕 ✿ 🚗 ☕

Briarwood

Lawn Cottage, 36 East Street, Long Buckby Gardens

4 **BOSWORTH HOUSE**

Oxendon Road, Arthingworth, Nr Market Harborough, LE16 8LA. Mr & Mrs C E Irving-Swift, 01858 525202, irvingswift@btinternet.com. *From the phone box, when in Oxendon Rd, take the little lane with no name, 2nd to the R.* **Sun 19 Feb (12-4). Adm £3, chd free. Sun 23 Apr (2-6). Adm £4, chd free. Visits also by arrangement May to Aug for groups of 15+. Guided visit by Cecile Irving-Swift for 1½ hours £4, or with home-made cake £7.** Just under 3 acres, almost completely organic garden and paddock with fabulous panoramic views. Early in the season a pleasing display of snowdrops, wood anemones, fritillaries, daffodils, bluebells and tulips. The garden also incl herbaceous borders, orchard, cottage garden with greenhouse, vegetable garden, herbs and strawberries, and little spinney. There is a magnificent Wellingtonia. Partial wheelchair access.

 ♿ ☕

5 ◆ **BOUGHTON HOUSE**

Geddington, Kettering, NN14 1BJ. Duke of Buccleuch & Queensberry, KBE, 01536 515731, blht@boughtonhouse.co.uk, www.boughtonhouse.org.uk. *3m NE of Kettering. From A14, 2m along A43 Kettering to Stamford, turn R into Geddington, house entrance 1½m on R.* **For NGS: Sun 26 Feb, Sun 22 Oct (11-3). Adm £6, chd £3. Light refreshments in C18 Stable Block. For other opening times and information, please phone, email or visit garden website.** The Northamptonshire home of the Duke and Duchess of Buccleuch. The garden opening incl opportunities to see the historic walled kitchen garden and herbaceous border incl the newly created sensory and wildlife gardens. The wilderness woodland will open for visitors to view the spring flowers or the autumn colours. As a special treat the garden originally created by Sir David Scott (cousin of the Duke of Buccleuch) will also be open.

✿ ☕

6 BRIARWOOD

4 Poplars Farm Road,
Barton Seagrave, Kettering,
NN15 5AF. William & Elaine
Portch, 01536 522169,
briarwood.garden@yahoo.co.uk,
www.elainechristian-gardendesign.
co.uk. 1½m SE of Kettering Town
Centre. J10 off A14 turn onto Barton
Rd (A6) towards Wicksteed Park. R
into Warkton Lane, after 200 metres
R into Poplars Farm Rd. **Sun 16 Apr
(10-4). Adm £4.50, chd free.
Light refreshments. Visits also
by arrangement Apr to Sept.**
A garden in 2 parts with quirky
original sculptures and many faces.
Firstly a s-facing lawn and colourful
borders with spring bulbs, blossom
trees, summer colour, hedging,
palms, climbers, lily pond, and sunny
terrace. Secondly, a secret garden
with summerhouse, small orchard,
raised bed potager and water
feature. Crafts for sale and children's
quiz. Featured in Northamptonshire
Telegraph, Garden News.

&. ✿ ☕

7 ◆ CASTLE ASHBY GARDENS

Castle Ashby, Northampton,
NN7 1LQ. Earl Compton,
07771 871766,
www.castleashbygardens.co.uk. 6m
E of Northampton. 1½m N of A428,
turn off between Denton & Yardley
Hastings. Follow brown tourist signs
(SatNav will take you to the village,
look for brown signs). **For NGS:
Sun 2 July (10-5.30). Adm £5.50,
chd free. For other opening times
and information, please phone or
visit garden website.**
35 acres within a 10,000 acre estate
of both formal and informal gardens,
incl Italian gardens with orangery
and arboretum with lakes, all dating
back to the 1860s, as well as a
menagerie with various animals. Play
area, tearooms and gift shop. Gravel
paths within gardens.

&. 🐄 ✿ 🚌 ☕

GROUP OPENING

8 CHARLTON GARDENS

Banbury, OX17 3DR. 7m SE of
Banbury, 5m W of Brackley. From
B4100 turn off N at Aynho, or from
A422 turn off S at Farthinghoe.
Parking at village hall. **Sun 21 May
(2-5.30). Combined adm £6, chd
free. Tea at Walnut House.**

CHARLTON LODGE
Mr & Mrs Andrew Woods.

THE CROFT
Mr & Mrs R D Whitrow.

WALNUT HOUSE
Sir Paul & Lady Hayter.

Pretty stone village with a selection
of gardens large and small, incl
a cottage garden with colourful
planting, interesting corners and
lovely views; a large garden behind
C17 farmhouse (not open) with
colour themed borders, separate
small gardens; and a large terraced
garden with a 140ft long herbaceous
border and raised bed vegetable
patch, overlooking a lake.

&. 🐄 ✿ ☕

9 ◆ COTON MANOR GARDEN

Coton, Northampton,
NN6 8RQ. Mr & Mrs Ian
Pasley-Tyler, 01604 740219,
www.cotonmanor.co.uk. 10m N
of Northampton, 11m SE of Rugby.
From A428 & A5199 follow tourist
signs. **For NGS: Sun 10 Sept (12-
5.30). Adm £7, chd £2.50. Light
refreshments at Stableyard
Cafe. For other opening times and
information, please phone or visit
garden website.**
10 acre garden set in peaceful
countryside with old yew and holly
hedges and extensive herbaceous
borders, containing many unusual
plants. One of Britain's finest
throughout the season, the garden
is at its most magnificent in
September, and is an inspiration
as to what can be achieved in late
summer. Adjacent specialist nursery
with over 1000 plant varieties
propagated from the garden. Partial
wheelchair access as some paths are
narrow and the site is on a slope.

&. ✿ 🚌 ☕

10 ◆ COTTESBROOKE HALL GARDENS

Cottesbrooke, NN6 8PF.
Mr & Mrs A R Macdonald-
Buchanan, 01604 505808,
welcome@cottesbrooke.co.uk,
www.cottesbrooke.co.uk. 10m N
of Northampton. Signed from J1 on
A14. Off A5199 at Creaton, A508
at Brixworth. **For NGS: Sun 23
Apr (2-5.30). Adm £6, chd £4.
Tea, coffee & home-made cakes.
For other opening times and
information, please phone, email or
visit garden website.**
Award-winning gardens by Geoffrey
Jellicoe, Dame Sylvia Crowe, James
Alexander Sinclair and more
recently Arne Maynard. Formal
gardens and terraces surround
Queen Anne house with extensive
vistas onto the lake and C18
parkland containing many mature
trees. Wild and woodland gardens,
which are exceptional in spring,
a short distance from the formal
areas. Partial wheelchair access
as paths are grass, stone and
gravel. Access map identifies
best route.

&. 🚌 ☕

11 NEW THE COURT HOUSE

Mill Lane, Chipping Warden,
Banbury, OX17 1JZ. Mr & Mrs
Jonathan Ruck Keene. Chipping
Warden is a village on A361 approx
8m NE of Banbury. Both The Court
House & The Spring House are on
Mill Lane which leads S off A361.
**Sun 4 June (2-5.30). Combined
adm with The Spring House £5,
chd free. Tea.**
Large garden in the attractive
village of Chipping Warden on the
border of Northamptonshire and
Oxfordshire. The garden comprises
several areas each with distinctive
characteristics including herbaceous
borders, laburnum walk, terrace,
shrub garden and parterre.

☕

*The National Garden
Scheme is Hospice UK's
largest single funder*

12 [NEW] DALE FARM

Maidwell, Northampton, NN6 9JE. Mr & Mrs D Keir. *A508 from Northampton. In Maidwell take 1st L, opp the road to Draughton. After 1m take the R fork by a tree, to the house. Park only in field shown, not on the access road or verges.* **Sun 13 Aug (10-5). Adm £4, chd free. Home-made teas in the summerhouse.**
Dale Farm is a 2 acre garden, with formal hedging and trees. Flower borders near the house and secluded vegetable garden with cutting flowers. The garden has lovely views over the surrounding countryside, including the neighbouring stone barn.

13 ♦ DEENE PARK

Corby, NN17 3EW. The Trustees, 01780 450278, admin@deenepark.com, www.deenepark.com. *6m N of Corby. Off A43 between Stamford & Corby.* **For NGS: Sun 23 Apr (12-5). Adm £6, chd £3. Light refreshments in Old Kitchen Tea Room. For other opening times and information, please phone, email or visit garden website.**
Interesting garden set in beautiful parkland. Large parterre with topiary designed by David Hicks echoing the C16 decoration on the porch stonework, long mixed borders, old fashioned roses, Tudor courtyard and white garden. Lake and waterside walks with rare mature trees in natural garden. Wheelchair access available to main features of garden.

14 EAST HADDON HALL

Main Street, East Haddon, Northampton, NN6 8BU. Mr & Mrs John Beynon. *Located in the centre of the village, nr the church.* **Sat 5, Sun 6 Aug (11-5). Combined adm with Haddonstone Show Gardens £5, chd free. Home-made teas in Haddonstone Show Gardens.**
First opened for the NGS in 1928 and now restored by the present owners. 8 acres of parkland surrounding a Grade I listed Georgian house (not open) with extensive lawns, mature specimen trees and lovely views. More formal planting surrounds the house with many exuberantly planted containers.

15 ♦ EVENLEY WOOD GARDEN

Evenley, Brackley, NN13 5SH. Timothy Whiteley, 07776 307849, info@evenleywoodgarden.co.uk, www.evenleywoodgarden.co.uk. *¾ m S of Brackley. Turn off at Evenley r'about on A43 & follow signs within the village to the garden.* **For NGS: Wed 24 May (11-4). Adm £5, chd £1. Light refreshments in the pavilion. Picnics welcome. For other opening times and information, please phone, email or visit garden website.**
This 60 acre privately owned woodland garden contains a large and notable collection of trees, shrubs, bulbs, and more. Its unusual band of acid soil, in what is a predominantly alkaline area, allows the cultivation of plants which do not usually thrive in this location; including rhododendrons, camellias, and magnolias. Please take care as all paths are grass.

GROUP OPENING

16 FINEDON GARDENS

Finedon, NN9 5JN. *2m NE of Wellingborough. 6m SE Kettering. All gardens individually signed from A6 & A510 junction.* **Sun 4, Sun 25 June (2-6). Combined adm £3.50, chd free. Cream teas at 67-69 High Street.**

67-69 HIGH STREET
Mary & Stuart Hendry.
(See separate entry)

11 THRAPSTON ROAD
John & Gillian Ellson.

The gardens are very different with everything from vegetables to flowers on show. 67-69 High Street is an ever evolving ⅓ acre garden of a C17 cottage (not open) with mixed borders, many obelisks and containers. Planting for varied interest spring to autumn. 11 Thrapston Road is a ⅓ acre cottage garden with lawns and mixed borders, gravel and paved seating areas with planters and water features. Pergola, rose arches, summerhouse and treehouse. Mixed vegetable plot, and soft fruit and apple trees. Large selection of home raised plants for sale (all proceeds to the NGS).

GROUP OPENING

17 FLORE GARDENS

Flore, Northampton, NN7 4LQ. *7m W of Northampton on A45. 2m W of M1 J16. Free car park signed from A45 where garden map provided. Coaches, please phone 01327 341225 for advice related to parking.* **Sun 9 Apr (2-6); Sat 17, Sun 18 June (11-6). Combined adm £5, chd free. Home-made teas in Chapel School Room (Apr). Light lunches & teas in the Chapel School Room & teas in the Church (June).** *Donation to All Saints Church & United Reform Church, Flore.*

BEECH HILL
Dr R B White & Dr Valerie White.
Open on Sat 17, Sun 18 June

24 BLISS LANE
John & Sally Miller.
Open on all dates

[NEW] BUTTERCUP COTTAGE
Mrs Elizabeth Chignell.
Open on Sat 17, Sun 18 June

THE CROFT
John & Dorothy Boast.
Open on all dates

THE GARDEN HOUSE
Edward & Penny Aubrey-Fletcher.
Open on Sat 17, Sun 18 June

THE OLD BAKERY
John Amos & Karl Jones, 01327 349080, yeolbakery@aol.com, www.johnnieamos.co.uk.
Open on all dates
Visits also by arrangement for groups of 20-50.

PRIVATE GARDEN OF BLISS LANE NURSERY

Christine & Geoffrey Littlewood.
Open on all dates

ROCK SPRINGS

Tom Higginson & David Foster.
Open on all dates

RUSSELL HOUSE

Peter Pickering & Stephen George.
Open on all dates

17 THE GREEN

Mrs Wendy Amos.
Open on Sat 17, Sun 18 June

Flore gardens have been open since 1963 as part of the Flore Flower Festival, and the partnership with the NGS started in 1992. Flore is an attractive village with views over the Upper Nene Valley. We have a varied mix of gardens, developed by friendly and enthusiastic owners. Our gardens range from the traditional to the eccentric providing yr-round interest. There is a variety of garden structures, incl greenhouses, gazebos and summerhouses, with seating providing opportunities to rest while enjoying the gardens. In spring there are early flowering perennials, interesting trees, shrubs, and bulbs in pots and border drifts. There is planting for all situations from shade to full sun. June gardens open in association with Flore Flower Festival. The gardens incl formal and informal designs with lots of roses, clematis and many varieties of trees, shrubs, perennials, herbs, fruit and some

vegetables. This yr we incl a brand new garden designed and created in the last yr. Partial wheelchair access to most gardens, some assistance may be required.

 ♿ ✿ 🚗 ☕

---

18 FOXTAIL LILLY

41 South Road, Oundle, PE8 4BP.
Tracey Mathieson, 01832 274593,
tracey@foxtail-lilly.co.uk,
www.foxtail-lilly.co.uk. *I m from Oundle town centre. From A605 at Barnwell Xrds take Barnwell Rd, 1st R to South Rd.* **Sun 18 June (11-6).**
Adm £4, chd free. Home-made teas. **Visits also by arrangement May to Sept for groups of 60 max.**
A cottage garden where perennials and grasses are grouped creatively together amongst gravel paths, complementing one another to create a natural look. Some unusual plants and quirky oddities create a different and colourful informal garden. Lots of flowers for cutting, and a shop in the barn. New meadow pasture turned into new cutting garden. Featured in The Sunday Telegraph (Sept 2016).

🐕 ✿ 🚗 ☕

19 FROGGERY COTTAGE

85 Breakleys Road, Desborough, NN14 2PT. Mr John Lee, 01536 760002, johnlee@froggerycottage85.fsnet.co.uk. *6m N of Kettering. 5m S of Market Harborough. Signed off A6 & A14.*

Sun 30 July (11.30-5). Combined adm with Hostellarie £3, chd free. Light refreshments, lunches & gluten free cakes. Visits also by arrangement June to Sept for groups of 8+.
1 acre plantsman's garden full of rare and unusual plants. NCCPG Collection of 435 varieties of penstemons incl dwarfs and species. Mediterranean and water gardens with large herbaceous borders. Artifacts on display incl old ploughs and garden implements. Penstemon workshops throughout the day.

♿ 🐎 ✿ 🚗 NPC ☕

20 GLENDON HALL

Kettering, NN14 1QE.
Rosie Bose, 01536 711732,
rosiebose@googlemail.com. *1½m E of Rothwell. A6003 to Corby (A14 J7) W of Kettering, turn L onto Glendon Rd signed Rothwell, Desborough, Rushton. Entrance 1½m on L past turn for Rushton.* **Visits by arrangement for groups of 25 max. Adm £3, chd free.**
Mature specimen trees, topiary, box hedges, and herbaceous borders stocked with many unusual plants. Large walled kitchen gardens with glasshouse, and a shaded area well stocked with ferns. Some gravel and slopes, but wheelchair access via longer route.

♿ ✿ 🚗 ☕

21 GOWER HOUSE

Guilsborough, Northampton, NN6 8PY. Ann Moss, 01604 740140, cattimoss@aol.com. *Off High St by The Witch & Sow PH, through PH car park.* **Visits by arrangement May & June for combined visit with Dripwell House only. Light refreshments.**
Although Gower House garden is small, it is closely planted with specimen trees, shrubs, perennials, orchids, thyme lawn, wild flowers and alpines; some rare or unusual, with foliage colour being important. Several seating areas designed for elderly relatives incorporating recycled materials. Soft fruit and vegetable garden shared with Dripwell is an important part of our gardening.

☕

Russell House, Flore Gardens

GROUP OPENING

22 GREAT BRINGTON GARDENS

Northampton, NN7 4JJ. *7m NW of Northampton. Off A428 Rugby Rd. From Northampton, 1st L turn past main gates of Althorp. Free parking. Programmes & maps available at car park.* **Sun 30 Apr (11-5). Combined adm £5, chd free. Home-made teas & cakes in the Parish Church & morning coffee & lunches in the Reading Room.**

8 BEDFORD COTTAGES
Tony & Jayne Ryan.

BRINGTON LODGE
Mr & Mrs James Milne.

FOLLY HOUSE
Sarah & Joe Sacarello.

15 HAMILTON LANE
Mr & Mrs Robin Matthews.

ROSE COTTAGE
David Green & Elaine MacKenzie.

THE STABLES
Mrs A George.

SUNDERLAND HOUSE
Mrs Margaret Rubython.

NEW THE WICK
Ray & Sandy Crossan.

YEW TREE HOUSE
Mrs Joan Heaps.

Great Brington is proud of its nearly 25 yr association with the NGS and arguably one of the most successful one day scheme events in the county. This yr we offer 9 gardens open to view including one new garden which has never been accessible to the public. Our gardens provide superb quality and immense variety; many of the gardens continue to evolve each yr and most are designed, planted and maintained by their owners on a scale which is eminently practical and rewarding. Our particularly picturesque, predominately stone and thatch village is well worth a day out in its own right, and its configuration is perfect for the occasion; compact, self-contained, circular and virtually flat. On offer on the day, including our memorable gardens; a warm welcome, free car parking, programmes and maps, morning coffee, lunches and teas, plant stalls and a local history exhibition. Small coaches of groups up to 26 max welcome by prior arrangement only, please call 01604 770939.

✿ 🚐 ☕ 🅿

The National Garden Scheme is the largest single funder of Macmillan

23 NEW THE GREEN PATCH

Valley Walk, Kettering, NN16 0LU. Sue McKay. *Junction of Valley Walk & Margret Rd, signed from A4300 Stamford Rd.* **Sun 13 Aug (10-5). Adm £5, chd free. Home-made teas.**

The Green Patch is a 2½ acre, Green Flag award-winning community garden, situated on the edge of Kettering. We have hens, ducks, quails, beehives ponds, children's play area, orchard and so much more. We rely on our wonderful volunteers to make our friendly and magical garden the warm and welcoming place it is. Run by the environmental charity Groundwork Northamptonshire. Wheelchair access and disabled WC facilities.

& 🐄 ✿ 🚐 ☕

24 GREYWALLS

Farndish, NN29 7HJ. Mrs P M Anderson, 01933 353495, greywalls@dbshoes.co.uk. *2½m SE of Wellingborough. A609 from Wellingborough, B570 to Irchester, turn to Farndish by cenotaph. House adjacent to church.* **Sun 5 Mar (12-3). Adm £3.50, chd free. Light refreshments. Visits also by arrangement, coaches welcome.**

2 acre mature garden surrounding old vicarage (not open). Over 100 varieties of snowdrops, drifts of hardy cyclamen and hellebores. Alpine house and raised alpine beds. Water features and natural ponds with views over open countryside. Rare breed hens.

& ✿ 🚐 ☕

GROUP OPENING

25 GUILSBOROUGH GARDENS

High Street, Guilsborough, NN6 8RA. *10m NW of Northampton. 10m E of Rugby. Between A5199 & A428. J1 off A14. Car parking in field on Hollowell Rd out of Guilsborough. Information & maps from village hall, next to primary school.* **Sun 7 May (1-6). Combined adm £6, chd free. Home-made teas in the village hall.**

DRIPWELL HOUSE
Mr J W Langfield & Dr C Moss, 01604 740140, cattimoss@aol.com. **Visits also by arrangement May & June for combined visit with Gower House.**

FOUR ACRES
Mark & Gay Webster.

THE GATE HOUSE
Mike & Sarah Edwards.

GUILSBOROUGH HOUSE
Mr & Mrs John McCall.

OAK DENE
Mr & Mrs R A Darker.

THE OLD HOUSE
Richard & Libby Seaton Evans.

THE OLD VICARAGE
John & Christine Benbow.

Enjoy a warm welcome in this village with its very attractive rural setting of rolling hills and reservoirs. Seven varied village gardens, from a flower arranger's small garden surrounding a modern house, to large gardens with sweeping lawns, mature trees and beautiful views. There is plenty of room to sit and relax and picnics can be spread out in the car park field. Several of us are interested in growing fruit and vegetables, and a walled kitchen garden and a potager are an important part of our gardening. Plants both rare and unusual from our plantsmen's gardens are for sale, a true highlight here. Dripwell House has opened for the NGS since 1986, originally an individual garden and is a destination in its own right. There is thus a lot to see and visitors find that they need the whole afternoon. No wheelchair access at Dripwell and The Gate House. No dogs at Oak Dene.

🏃 🐄 ✳ 🚗 ☕

---

26 ◆ HADDONSTONE SHOW GARDENS

The Forge House, Church Lane, East Haddon, Northampton, NN6 8DB. Haddonstone Ltd, 01604 770711, info@haddonstone.co.uk, www.haddonstone.com. *7m NW of Northampton. Brown tourism signs from A428. Located in centre of village, nr church, & opp school.* **For NGS: Sat 5, Sun 6 Aug (11-5). Combined adm with East Haddon Hall £5, chd free. Home-made teas. For other opening times and information, please phone, email or visit garden website.**
See Haddonstone's classic garden ornaments in the beautiful setting of the walled manor gardens incl planters, fountains, statues, bird baths, sundials, balustrades and follies. The garden is on different levels with roses, clematis, climbers, herbaceous borders, ornamental flowers, topiary, specimen shrubs and trees. Latest additions incl designs from the Sir John Soane's Museum. The gardens incorporate planting, structures and ornaments used at the company's acclaimed Chelsea Flower Show exhibits. Wheelchair access to all key features of main garden.

🏃 ☕

GROUP OPENING

27 HARPOLE GARDENS

Harpole, NN7 4BX. *On A45 4m W of Northampton towards Weedon. Turn R at The Turnpike Hotel into Harpole. Village maps given to all visitors.* **Sun 18 June (1-6). Combined adm £5, chd free. Home-made teas at The Close.**

BRYTTEN-COLLIER HOUSE
James & Lucy Strickland.

THE CLOSE
Michael Orton-Jones, 01604 830332, michael@orton-jones.com. **Visits also by arrangement May to July for groups of 10+.**

14 HALL CLOSE
Marion & Charley Oliver.

19 MANOR CLOSE
Caroline & Andy Kemshed, 01604 830512, carolinekemshed@live.co.uk. **Visits also by arrangement in June, from Mon 19 June for one week only.**

MILLERS
Mrs M Still.

THE OLD DAIRY
David & Di Ballard.

We welcome everyone to join in the Harpole Gardens experience. Visit us and you will delight in varied gardens of all shapes, sizes and content. Harpole is an attractive village which is renowned for its annual Scarecrow Festival (2nd weekend of Sept). Amongst our various garden structures you will find a summerhouse, a treehouse, a vine-covered pergola and plenty of seating for the weary. We have herbaceous borders, luxuriant lawns, water features, and several ponds. You will see mixed borders with plants for both shade and sun, mature trees, herbs, vegetables and alpines. You'll be able to enjoy views over neighbouring farmland and perhaps best of all delicious home-made teas! Wheelchair access at Brytten-Collier House, The Close and The Old Dairy only.

🏃 ✳ ☕

---

28 67-69 HIGH STREET

Finedon, NN9 5JN. Mary & Stuart Hendry, 01933 680414, sh_archt@hotmail.com. *6m SE Kettering. Garden signed from A6 & A510 junction.* **Sun 26 Feb (11-3). Adm £3.50, chd free. Soup & roll. Opening with Finedon Gardens on Sun 4, Sun 25 June. Visits also by arrangement Feb to Sept.**
Constantly evolving ⅓ acre rear garden of C17 cottage (not open). Mixed borders, many obelisks and containers, kitchen garden and herb bed, and rope border. Spring garden with snowdrops and hellebores, summer and autumn borders all giving varied interest from Feb through to Oct. Home raised plants for sale. Well behaved dogs welcome. Look at the NGS website and twitter @NorthantsNGS for pop-up public openings in late May/June.

🐄 ✳ 🚗 ☕

---

29 NEW 136 HIGH STREET

Irchester, Wellingborough, NN29 7AB. Mr & Mrs Adrian Parker. *At end of High St, about ½ m before junction with A45.* **Sun 30 July (11-4). Adm £3, chd free. Home-made teas.**
½ acre garden with various different borders including those planted for shade, sun and bee friendly situations. Alpine houses, raised beds and planted stone sinks. Wildlife pond. Seasonally planted tubs.

✳ ☕

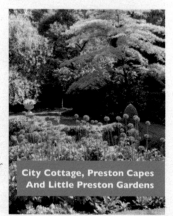

City Cottage, Preston Capes And Little Preston Gardens

30 ◆ HOLDENBY HOUSE GARDENS

Holdenby House, Holdenby, Northampton, NN6 8DJ. Mr & Mrs James Lowther, 01604 770074, office@holdenby.com, www.holdenby.com. *6m NW of Northampton. From A5199 or A428 between East Haddon & Spratton. Follow brown tourist signs.* For NGS: Sun 9 July (1-5). Adm £5, chd free. Cream teas. For other opening times and information, please phone, email or visit garden website.

Holdenby has an historic Grade I listed garden. The inner garden incl Rosemary Verey's renowned Elizabethan Garden and Rupert Golby's Pond Garden and long borders. There is also a delightful walled kitchen garden with original Victorian greenhouse. Away from the formal gardens the terraces of the original Elizabethan Garden are still visible, one of the best preserved examples of their kind. Victorian Tea Room. The estate includes gravel paths.

♧ 🐕 ☕ ❦

GROUP OPENING

31 HOLLOWELL GARDENS

Hollowell, NN6 8RR. *8m N of Northampton. ½m off A5199, turn off at Creaton. Roads are narrow &* twisting, so please use village hall car park which is clearly signed. *WC facilities available.* Sun 6 Aug (11-5). Combined adm £4, chd free. Light refreshments at the village hall.

HILLVIEW
Jan & Crawford Craig.

HOLLOWELL MANOR
Mr & Mrs N Wilson.

IVY COTTAGE
Rev John & Mrs Wendy Evans.

Three very different gardens in an attractive village on a steep hillside. Ivy Cottage is a haven for wildlife with relaxed planting, a stream, orchard and vegetable area. Hillview is a traditional country garden on three levels with a pond and box hedging from 1930s. Hollowell Manor garden has recently been redesigned and developed around a C17 manor house (not open). No wheelchair access at Hillview, partial access at remaining two gardens. Steep hills.

♧ ❦ ☕ ❦

---

32 HOSTELLARIE
78 Breakleys Road, Desborough, NN14 2PT. Stella Freeman, stelstan78@aol.com. *6m N of Kettering. 5m S of Market Harborough. From church & war memorial turn R into Dunkirk Ave,* then 3rd R. From cemetery L into Dunkirk Ave, then 4th L. Sun 30 July (11.30-5). Combined adm with Froggery Cottage £3, chd free. Light refreshments, lunches & gluten free cakes at Froggery Cottage. Visits also by arrangement June & July for groups of 10-25.

Over 180ft long town garden. Divided into rooms of different character; courtyard garden with a sculptural clematis providing shade, colour themed flower beds, ponds and water features, cottage gardens and gravel borders, clematis and roses, all linked by lawns and grass paths. The collection of hostas, over 50 different varieties, are taking up more space each year and are the pride of the garden.

❦ ☕

---

33 JERICHO
42 Market Place, Oundle, PE8 4AJ. Stephen & Pepita Aris, 01832 275416, stephenaris@btinternet.com. *East Jericho. From the Jericho cul-de-sac at the E end of the market place, go through facing red door, through passage, down yard to ticket desk & garden.* Sun 26 Feb, Sun 21, Mon 29 May, Sun 18 June (12-5). Adm £3.50, chd free. Tea. Visits also by arrangement Feb to July for groups of 10+. Refreshments on request.

Inspired by Vita Sackville-West 60 yrs ago, the 100 metre, s-facing, walled garden is divided into a series of secret spaces. The house is clothed in wisteria, clematis and roses. A plant-led garden with massive hornbeam hedge, clipped box and lavender. A hosta courtyard. Over 50 labelled species roses, a chamomile lawn, plus a hot border. Snowdrops, crocuses and hellebores in early spring. Wheelchair access is possible, but paths are quite narrow.

❦ ☕

---

34 ◆ KELMARSH HALL & GARDENS
Main Road, Kelmarsh, Northampton, NN6 9LY. The Kelmarsh Trust, 01604 686543, enquiries@kelmarsh.com, www.kelmarsh.com. *Kelmarsh is 5m*

Mill Hollow Barn, Sulgrave Gardens

S of Market Harborough & 11m N
of Northampton. From A14, exit J2 &
head N towards Market Harborough
on the A508. **For NGS: Sun 9 Apr,
Sun 21 May (11-5). Adm £6, chd
£3.50. Light lunches, cream teas
& cakes. For other opening times
and information, please phone,
email or visit garden website.**
Kelmarsh Hall is an elegant
Palladian house set in glorious
Northamptonshire countryside with
highly regarded gardens the work
of Nancy Lancaster, Norah Lindsay
and Geoffrey Jellicoe. Hidden gems
incl an orangery, sunken garden,
long border, rose gardens and at
the heart of it all, a historic walled
garden. Highlights throughout the
seasons incl fritillaries, tulips, roses
and dahlias. During 2017 Kelmarsh
is undertaking an exciting Heritage
Lottery Funded Project entitled
'Tunnelling Through The Past' which
will open up the 'below stairs' areas.
Featured in Saga magazine 'Doolally
for dahlias' (Sept 2016) and Good
Housekeeping 'Gardener's day out'
(Apr 2016). Blue badge disabled
parking is available close to the
Visitor Centre entrance. Paths
are loose gravel, wheelchair users
advised to bring a companion.
  🚲 ♿ ❀ 🚌 ☕

GROUP OPENING

35 KILSBY GARDENS
Kilsby Village, CV23 8XP. 5m SE
of Rugby. 6m N of Daventry on
A361. The road through village is
the B4038. **Sun 11 June (2-6).
Combined adm £5, chd free.
Home-made teas at Kilsby
Village Hall.**

BOLBERRY HOUSE
Mr & Mrs Richard Linnell.

GRAFTON HOUSE
Mr & Mrs Andy & Sally Tomkins.

PYTCHLEY GARDENS
Kathy Jenkins & Neighbours.

PYTCHLEY HOUSE
Mr & Mrs T F Clay,
01788 822373,
the.clays@tiscali.co.uk.
**Visits also by arrangement
June & July.**

RAINBOW'S END
Mr & Mrs J Madigan.

Kilsby is a stone and brick village
with historic interest, home of St
Faith's Church dating from the C12.
The village was the site of one of
the first skirmishes of the Civil War
in 1642, and also gave its name to
Stephenson's nearby lengthy rail
tunnel built in the 1830s. Four large,
and several attractive patio gardens
will be open this yr, all within easy
walking distance. Comments from
2016 said 'Kilsby is a particularly
friendly village', so please come and
see us. Partial wheelchair access to
most gardens. Narrow access to
Pytchley Gardens.
& ❀ ☕

36 NEW ♦ **LAMPORT HALL**
Northampton, NN6 9HD.
Lamport Hall Preservation Trust,
www.lamporthall.co.uk. If using
SatNav please use postcode NN6
9EZ. **For NGS: Sun 17 Sept (2-
5.30). Adm £6, chd free. Home-
made teas. For other opening
times and information, please visit
garden website.**
Home of the Isham family for over
400 yrs, the extensive herbaceous
borders complement the
Elizabethan bowling lawns, together
with topiary from the 1700s. In
September the 2 acre walled garden
is full of colour, with 250 rows of
perennials. Another highlight is the
famous Lamport Rockery, among
the earliest in England and home of
the world's oldest garden gnome.
In 2016 the gardens were featured
in the English Garden magazine and
Country Life. Gravel paths within
the gardens.
& 🚲 🚌 ☕

GROUP OPENING

**37 LONG BUCKBY
GARDENS**
Northampton, NN6 7RE. 8m NW
of Northampton, midway between
A428 & A5. Long Buckby is signed
from A428 & A5. 10 mins from J18
M1. Maps available at each garden
& in centre of village. **Sun 23 July**

(1-6). **Combined adm with Mill
House £5, chd free. Home-
made teas at Lawn Cottage.**

NEW **25 BERRYFIELD**
Mandy Morley & Jane Harrison.

3 COTTON END
Roland & Georgina Wells.

NEW **4 COTTON END**
Sue & Giles Baker.

NEW **THE GROTTO**
Andy & Chrissy Gamble.

7 HIGH STACK
Tiny & Sheila Burt.

**LAWN COTTAGE, 36
EAST STREET**
Michael & Denise Nichols.

10 LIME AVENUE
June Ford.

4 SKINYARD LANE
William & Susie Mitchell.

NEW **WISTERIA HOUSE**
David & Clare Croston,
07771 911892,
dad.croston@gmail.com.
**Visits also by arrangement
June to Sept for gardening
groups.**
🚐

WOODCOTE VILLA
Sue & Geoff Woodward.

Ten gardens in the historic villages
of Long Buckby and Long Buckby
Wharf, most within easy walking
distance of each other. Varying in
size and style, from courtyard and
canal side to cottage garden, some
are established and others evolving.
They incl water features, pergolas,
garden structures, chickens and
pigs, but the stars are definitely the
plants. Bursting with colour, visitors
will find old favourites and the
unusual, used in a variety of ways;
trees, shrubs, perennials, climbers,
annuals, fruit and vegetables. Our
award-winning local museum will
also be open. Of course there
will be teas and plants for sale
to complete the visit. Article in
Daventry Express (7 July 2016). Full
or partial wheelchair access to all
gardens, except 4 Skinyard Lane.
& 🚲 ❀ ☕

38 MILL HOUSE

Long Lane, East Haddon,
NN6 8DU. Ken & Gill Pawson,
01604 770103,
gillandken@pawsons.co.uk. *8m
NW of Northampton. Located at the
junction of Long Lane with the A428.*
**Sun 23 July (1-6). Combined
adm with Long Buckby Gardens
£5, chd free. Home-made teas
at Lawn Cottage. Opening with
Ravensthorpe Gardens on Sun 9
July. Visits also by arrangement
in July for groups of 40 max.**
Over 1 acre in open countryside.
Large fruit and vegetable plot with
some old and rare varieties. Owner
is Heritage Seed Library Guardian
and beekeeper. Orchard, wild flower
meadow, pergola, pond, grasses, hot
garden, borders and shady areas.
Foundations of East Haddon Windmill.
& 🐎 🚗 ☕

The National Garden Scheme is Marie Curie's largest single funder

39 THE OLD BLACK HORSE

Main Street, Tansor, Peterborough,
PE8 5HS. Mrs Pamela Metcalf,
01832 226302,
pamelametcalf@sky.com. *2m
N of Oundle off A605 towards
Peterborough, take L turn signed
Glapthorn & Cotterstock. Follow
signs to Tansor, turn R at Xrds signed
Main St. Parking on roadside.* **Visits
by arrangement Mar to July for
groups of 10-30. Adm £3.50,
chd free. Home-made teas.**
A cottage garden with mature trees,
lawns and mixed borders. Both
full sun and shady areas planted
to give a natural look. Spring bulbs,
daffodils, tulips, flowering shrubs and
herbaceous borders. Roses climb

and ramble over house, barn, arches,
trees and arbours. Productive
vegetable potager with greenhouse.
Wild meadow with views across
fields to Oundle.
& ❀ ☕

40 OLD RECTORY, QUINTON

Preston Deanery Road, Quinton,
Northampton, NN7 2ED.
Alan Kennedy & Emma Wise,
quintonoldrectory.com. *M1 J15,
1m from Wootton towards Salcey
Forest. House is next to the church.*
**Sun 21 May, Sun 3 Sept (11-5).
Adm £5, chd free. Teas & light
refreshments.**
A beautiful contemporary 3 acre
rectory garden designed by multi
award-winning designer, Anoushka
Feiler. Taking the Old Rectory's C18
history and its religious setting as a
key starting point, the main garden
at the back of the house has been
divided into six parts; a kitchen
garden, glasshouse and flower garden,
a woodland menagerie, a pleasure
garden, a park and an orchard.
Elements of C18 design such as
formal structures, parterres, topiary,
long walks, occasional seating areas
and traditional craft work have been
introduced, however with a distinctly
C21 twist through the inclusion of
living walls, modern materials and
features, new planting methods and
abstract installations. Wheelchair
access, but there are gravel paths.
& 🅳 ☕

41 ◆ THE OLD RECTORY, SUDBOROUGH

Kettering, NN14 3BX.
Mr & Mrs G Toller,
01832 734085, bookings@
theoldrectorygardens.co.uk,
www.theoldrectorygardens.co.uk.
*8m NE of Kettering. Exit 12 off
A14. Village just off A6116 between
Thrapston & Brigstock. Free private
parking in a small paddock adjacent
to the house.* **For NGS: Sat 8 Apr
(12-6); Sun 18 June (11-5). Adm
£7, chd free. Home-made teas &
cake. For other opening times and
information, please phone, email or
visit garden website.**
A charming 3 acre village garden
situated next to a church, including

extensive herbaceous borders, a
rose garden, gravel border and
highly regarded potager, designed
by Rosemary Verey. This is a garden
for all seasons with early spring
bulbs, a wide variety of old roses,
tree peonies, standard Lycianthes
Rantonnetii, a small lily pond and
charming woodland walk alongside
Harpers Brook. Set in a tranquil
conservation area with stunning
views and setting. Partial wheelchair
access as some gravel paths. Guide
dogs welcome.
& ❀ 🚗 ☕

42 NEW THE OLD VICARAGE

Daventry Road, Norton, Daventry,
NN11 2ND. Mr & Mrs Barry
& Andrea Coleman. *Norton is
about 2m E of Daventry, 11m W of
Northampton. From Daventry follow
signs to Norton for 1m. On A5 N
from Weedon follow road for 3m,
take L turn signed Norton. On A5 S
take R at Xrds signed Norton, 6m
from Kilsby. Garden is R of All Saints
Church.* **Sun 16 Apr (2-5). Adm
£4, chd free. Home-made teas
in village hall.**
Based upon a traditional but once
faded vicarage layout, the garden
aims to be lively and colourful
throughout the yr, using a few of the
original yews, pines and laurels as a
seasonal framework. The garden's
heritage incl a carpet of snowdrops
in winter, and irrepressible primroses
in spring. After yrs of taming and
shaping the garden, it now is quietly
developing a little touch of drama.
The interesting C14 church of All
Saints will be open to visitors.
🐎 ☕

GROUP OPENING

43 PRESTON CAPES AND LITTLE PRESTON GARDENS

Little Preston, Daventry,
NN11 3TF. *6m SW of Daventry.
13m NE of Banbury. 3m N of
Canons Ashby. Preston Capes and
Little Preston are ½m apart.* **Sun
4 June (12-5). Combined adm
£5, chd free. Home-made light
lunches & teas at Old West
Farm from 12-5.**

CITY COTTAGE
Mrs Gavin Cowen.

LADYCROFT
Mervyn & Sophia Maddison.

THE MANOR
Mr Graham Stanton.

NORTH FARM
Mr & Mrs Tim Coleridge.

OLD WEST FARM
Mr & Mrs Gerard Hoare.

A selection of five differing gardens in the beautiful unspoilt south Northamptonshire ironstone villages, most with a backdrop of fantastic views of the surrounding countryside. Gardens range from small contemporary, through to classical country style with old fashioned roses and borders. Features include attractive village with local sandstone houses and cottages, Norman church and wonderful views. Partial wheelchair access to some parts of the gardens.
♿ ❄ ☕

GROUP OPENING

44 RAVENSTHORPE GARDENS
Ravensthorpe, NN6 8ES. *7m NW of Northampton. Signed from A428. Mill House immed R as you turn off A428 down Long Lane, 1m from village. Wigley Cottage is in The Hollows off Bettycroft.* **Sun 9 July (1.30-5.30). Combined adm £5, chd free. Home-made teas at village hall.**

NEW **33 GUILSBOROUGH ROAD**
Mr & Mrs Tim & Deborah Hogben.

MILL HOUSE
Ken & Gill Pawson.
(See separate entry)

RAVENSTHORPE NURSERY
Mr & Mrs Richard Wiseman, 01604 770548, ravensthorpenursery @hotmail.com.
Visits also by arrangement May to Sept.

WIGLEY COTTAGE
Mr & Mrs Dennis Patrick.

Attractive village in Northamptonshire uplands near to Ravensthorpe reservoir and Top Ardles Wood Woodland Trust, which have bird watching and picnic opportunities. Established and developing gardens set in beautiful countryside displaying a wide range of plants, many of which are available from the Nursery. Offering inspirational planting, quiet contemplation, beautiful views, water features, gardens encouraging wildlife, fruit and vegetable garden owned by a Heritage Seed Library Guardian, and flower arranger's garden. Partial wheelchair access to Wigley Cottage.
♿ 🐄 ❄ ☕

45 ROSEARIE-DE-LA-NYMPH
55 The Grove, Moulton, Northampton, NN3 7UE. Peter Hughes, Mary Morris, Irene Kay, Steven Hughes & Jeremy Stanton. *N of Northampton town. Turn off A43 at small r'about to Overstone Rd. Follow NGS signs in village. The garden is on the Holcot Rd out of Moulton.* **Sun 25 June, Sun 2 July (11-5). Adm £4.50, chd free.** We have been developing this romantic garden for about 10 yrs and now have over 1800 roses, incl English, French and Italian varieties. Many unusual water features and

specimen trees. Roses, scramblers and ramblers climb into trees, over arbours and arches. We have tried to time our open days to cover the peak flowering period. Collection of 95 Japanese maples. Sorry, no refreshments available. Mostly flat, but there is a standard width doorway to negotiate.
♿ 🚌

GROUP OPENING

46 SLAPTON GARDENS
Slapton, Towcester, NN12 8PE. *A hamlet 4m W of Towcester. ¼m N of the Towcester to Wappenham road.* **Sun 11 June (2-5.30). Combined adm £5, chd free. Home-made teas at St Botolph's Church.**

BOXES FARM
James & Mary Miller.

BRADDEN COTTAGE
Mrs Philippa Heumann.

CORNER HOUSE
Mr & Mrs S Bell.

NEW **SOWBROOK HOUSE**
Mrs Caroline Coke.

Slapton is a very pretty Northamptonshire hamlet with only 30 houses of which 4 are opening their gardens. There is the lovely C12 St Botolph's Chuch with rare Medieval wall paintings. Partial wheelchair access. Narrow and gravel paths.
♿ ☕

Dale Farm

GROUP OPENING

47 SPRATTON GARDENS
Smith Street, Spratton, NN6 8HP. *6½m NNW of Northampton. On A5199 between Northampton & Welford. S from J1, A14. Car Park at Spratton Hall School with close access to gardens.* **Sun 11 June (11-5). Combined adm £6, chd free. Home-made teas.**

NEW THE COTTAGE
Mr & Mrs Andrew Elliott.

DALE HOUSE
Fiona & Chris Cox,
01604 846458,
fionacox19@aol.com.

FORGE COTTAGE
Daniel & Jo Bailey.

THE GRANARY
Margo Lerin.

11 HIGH STREET
Philip & Frances Roseblade.

STONE HOUSE
John Forbear.

WALTHAM COTTAGE
Norma & Allan Simons.

NEW I WILLOW CLOSE
Mr & Mrs Ken & Lorraine Bennett.

9A YEW TREE LANE
John Hunt.

As well as attractive cottage gardens alongside old Northampton stone houses, Spratton also has unusual gardens, including four showing good use of a small area; one dedicated to encouraging wildlife; a highly structured courtyard shrub garden; a newly renovated garden; mature gardens with fruit trees and herbaceous borders, one with a 300 yr old Holm Oak and miniature Shetland ponies looking on, surrounded by beautiful views of the agricultural landscape. There will be a 'Bug Hunt' for children. Tea, cakes and rolls will be available in the Norman St. Andrew's Church, Church Road with displays of the Pocket Park, a short walk away. The King's Head PH will be open, lunch reservations recommended.

48 NEW THE SPRING HOUSE
Mill Lane, Chipping Warden, Banbury, OX17 1JZ. Mr F Tuthill. *Chipping Warden is a village on A361 approx 8m NE of Banbury. Both The Court House & The Spring House are on Mill Lane which leads S off A361.* **Sun 4 June (2-5.30). Combined adm with The Court House £5, chd free. Tea at The Court House.**
Large garden of 3¾ acres with wonderful trees and bog garden. The garden, originally part of The Court House garden until The Spring House was built in the 1960s, was designed by the renowned landscape designer Kitty Lloyd Jones (responsible also for Greys Court, Achamore House on the Isle of Gigha and Upton House in Warwickshire).

49 67 STRATFIELD WAY
Kettering, NN15 6GS. Mrs Paula Mantle. *5 mins off A14 (J9) Kettering. Leave J9 & turn off r'about at Park Hotel & continue along the road, next L, straight over r'about, next R, follow signs.* **Sun 6 Aug (2-5). Adm £3, chd free.**
After an accident in 2010 that left me injured, my garden became my soulmate. This is a pretty garden with structure and softness, work is done at a recovering pace with bursts of energy. Colour alongside gentler combinations of delicate willowy flowers. From a 3 metre fatsia to dainty alpines, climbing hydrangea, dahlias, geraniums, crocosmia, fuscia, alliums, hosta, maples and show stopping campsis.
&

50 SULBY GARDENS
Sulby, Northampton, NN6 6EZ. Mrs Alison Lowe, 01858 880573, ecolowe@btinternet.com. *16m NW of Northampton, 2m NE of Welford off A5199. Past Wharf House Hotel, take 1st R signed Sulby. After R & L bends, turn R at sign for Sulby Hall Farm. Turn R at junction, garden is 1st L. Parking limited, no vans or buses please.* **Thur 27 Apr, Thur 22 June, Thur 24 Aug (2-5); Thur 12 Oct (1-4); Fri 13 Oct (11-4); Thur 16 Nov (1-4).**

Adm £4, chd free. Home-made teas. **Visits also by arrangement for groups of 10-50.**
Interesting and unusual property, on the Leicestershire border between Welford and Husbands Bosworth, covering 12 acres comprising working Victorian kitchen garden, orchard, and late C18 icehouse, plus species-rich nature reserve incl woodland, feeder stream to R Avon, a variety of ponds and established wild flower meadows. Open Day features incl April: snakeshead fritillaries, cowslips, bluebells. June: wild flower meadows at their peak. Aug: butterflies, dragonflies, aquatic plants. Oct: Apple Day, labelled display of apples, new season's Sulby Gardens Apple Juice, and apple-themed cakes. Nov: autumn colour. Regular plant sales. Interviewed by John Griff on Radio Northampton, and featured in The English Garden magazine (Oct 2016) NB: Children welcome but under strict supervision because of deep water.

GROUP OPENING

51 SULGRAVE GARDENS
Banbury, OX17 2RP. *8m NE of Banbury. Just off B4525 Banbury to Northampton road, 7m from J11 off M40. Car parking at church hall.* **Sun 18 June (2-6). Combined adm £6, chd free. Tea at Asby House, Manor Road.**

CHURCH COTTAGE
Hywel & Ingram Lloyd.

THE COTTAGE
George & Jo Ann Jenkins.

EAGLE HOUSE
Sue & Andrew Dixon.

THE HERB SOCIETY GARDEN AT SULGRAVE MANOR
The Herb Society.

MILL HOLLOW BARN
David & Judith Thompson.

RECTORY FARM
Charles & Joanna Smyth-Osbourne.

SULGRAVE ALLOTMENTS
Mrs Janet Smith.

◆ **SULGRAVE MANOR**
The Sulgrave Manor Trust,
01295 760205.

SUNNYMEAD
Bob & Jean Bates.

THREEWAYS
Alison & Digby Lewis.

THE WATERMILL
Mr & Mrs T Frost.

Sulgrave is a small historic village having recently celebrated its strong American connections in 2014 as part of the 150 yrs of the signing of the Treaty of Ghent. Ten gardens and allotments opening; Eagle House, a walled garden which has been recently extensively replanted and The Cottage, a compact garden on two levels with strong architectural features. Threeways, a small walled cottage garden with some vegetables grown in containers. Rectory Farm has lovely views, a rill and well, and planted arbours. The well-established Manor garden planted by Sir Reginald Blomfield in the 1920s and the adjoining National Herb Garden featuring the herbs that could have been taken to America with the Washington family and others that have been introduced from America. Church Cottage, ½ acre garden with mixed planting for colour, form and scent throughout the year. Mill Hollow Barn, a large garden with a 10 yr old arboretum with many rare and interesting trees. The Watermill, a contemporary garden designed by James Alexander Sinclair, set around a C16 watermill and mill pond. Sunnymead a mature garden with trees, shrubs and traditionally planted borders. The Allotments are a charming group of seven allotment gardens. An award-winning community owned and run village shop which will be open.

❀ ☕

---

52 NEW **SUNLEY COURT**
Pipers Hill Road, Kettering,
NN15 7RJ. Extracare Charitable Trust. *Turn into Pipers Hill Rd from London Rd, we are situated on the 2nd driveway on the LH-side.* **Sun 23 July (2-5). Adm £4, chd free. Home-made teas.**

A community garden situated within Sunley Court, maintained by residents and volunteers. We are proud to open our gardens for the first time after winning overall best scheme gardens award in 2016 as part of the ExtraCare Charitable Trust Garden Competition. The gardens are made up of raised beds, small individual plots, themed areas, heather garden, and lawned areas. Front garden has a seaside theme, and the rear garden a reminiscence area, featuring 1940s farming area. The gardens are fully accessible for wheelchairs throughout.

♿ ☕

53 TITCHMARSH HOUSE
Chapel Street, Titchmarsh,
NN14 3DA. Sir Ewan & Lady Harper, 01832 732439, ewh1939@outlook.com. *2m N of Thrapston. 6m S of Oundle. Exit A14 at junction signed A605, Titchmarsh signed as turning to E.* **Mon 1, Mon 29 May (2-6); Sat 10 June (12-5). Adm £4, chd free. Teas at community shop (May). BBQ lunch & teas at village fete (June). Visits also by arrangement Apr to June.**
4½ acres extended and laid out since 1972. Special collections of magnolias, spring bulbs, iris, peonies and roses with many rare trees and shrubs. Walled ornamental vegetable garden and ancient yew hedge. Some newly planted areas. Wheelchair access to most of the garden without using steps. No dogs.

♿ ☕

GROUP OPENING

54 TURWESTON GARDENS
Brackley, NN13 5JY. *2m E of Brackley. A43 from M40 J10. On Brackley bypass turn R on A422 towards Buckingham, ½m turn L signed Turweston.* **Sun 18 June (2-5.30). Combined adm £5, chd free. Tea at Turweston House.**

TURWESTON HOUSE
Mr & Mrs C Allen.

TURWESTON MILL
Mr Harry Leventis.

Charming unspoilt stone built village in a conservation area. Two quite large beautiful gardens. The Mill with bridges over the millstream and a spectacular waterfall, wildlife pond and newly designed kitchen garden. At Turweston House a 5 acre garden with borders, woodland and pond.

♿ ☕

GROUP OPENING

55 WEEDON LOIS & WESTON GARDENS
Weedon Lois, Towcester,
NN12 8PJ. *7m W of Towcester. 7m N of Brackley. In Weedon Lois; Old Barn is on High St, & Home Close, Kettle End & 4 Vicarage Rise are off High St. In Weston; Ridgeway Cottage is on High St & Gardener's Cottage is off High St, behind Weston Hall.* **Sun 25 June (2-5.30). Combined adm £5, chd free. Tea at Tove Valley Baptist Church, Weston.**

THE GARDENER'S COTTAGE
Mrs Sitwell.

HOME CLOSE
Clyde Burbidge.

LOIS WEEDON HOUSE
Lady Greenaway.

OLD BARN
Mr & Mrs John Gregory.

RIDGEWAY COTTAGE
Jonathan & Elizabeth Carpenter.

4 VICARAGE RISE
Ashley & Lindsey Cartwright.

Two adjacent villages in south Northamptonshire with a handsome Medieval church in Weedon Lois. The extension churchyard contains the graves of the poets Dame Edith Sitwell and her brother Sir Sacheveral Sitwell who lived in Weston Hall. There are four gardens in Weedon Lois comprising a large garden with terracing, large borders and outstanding views, a plantsman's garden, an award-winning garden and an informal cottage garden surrounding stone barn conversion. In Weston there are two charming cottage gardens, and teas being provided in the local church.

🐑 � ☕

NOTTINGHAMSHIRE

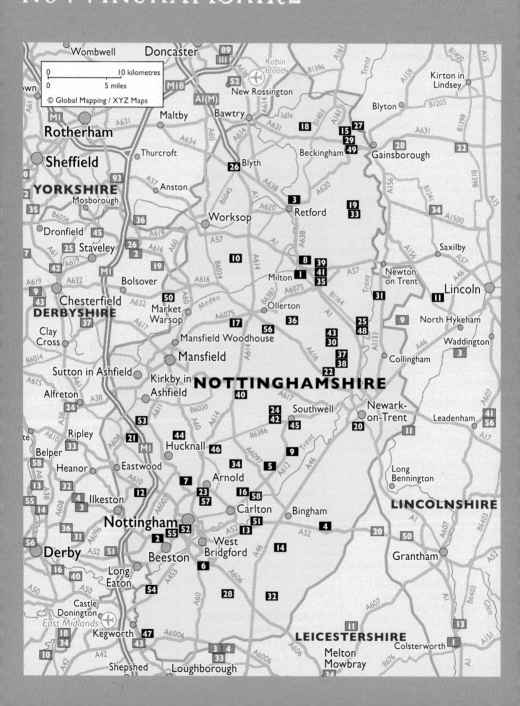

Nottinghamshire is best known as Robin Hood country. His legend persists and his haunt of Sherwood Forest, now a nature reserve, contains some of the oldest oaks in Europe. The Major Oak, thought to be 800 years old, still produces acorns.

Civil War battles raged throughout Nottinghamshire, and Newark's historic castle bears the scars. King Charles I surrendered to the Scots in nearby Southwell after a night at The Saracen's Head, which is still an inn today.

The Dukeries in the north of the county provide an unmatched landscape of lakes, parks and woods, so called because four dukes lived there, and their estates were contiguous. The dukes are gone, but their estates at Clumber, Thoresby and Welbeck continue to offer a pre-industrial haven in a thickly populated county.

Oaks in Sherwood, apples in Southwell (where the original Bramley tree still stands) and 100 kinds of rhubarb in the ducal kitchen garden at Clumber Park – they await your visit.

Volunteers

County Organiser
Georgina Denison
01636 821385
campden27@aol.com

County Treasurer
Nicola Cressey
01159 655132
nicola.cressey@gmail.com

Publicity
Steve & Paula Routledge
01636 636283 or 07811 399113
info@floralmedia.co.uk

Social Media
Malcolm Turner
01159 222831
malcolm.turner14@btinternet.com

Booklet Co-ordinator
Dave Darwent
01142 665881
dave.darwent@ngs.org.uk

Assistant County Organisers
Judy Geldart
01636 823832
judygeldart@gmail.com

Beverley Perks
01636 812181
perks.family@talk21.com

Mary Thomas
01509 672056
nursery@piecemealplants.co.uk

Andrew Young
01623 863327
andrew.young@ngs.org.uk

Left: The Chimes

OPENING DATES

All entries subject to change. For latest information check www.ngs.org.uk

Map locator numbers are shown to the right of each garden name.

February

Snowdrop Festival

Sunday 12th
The Beeches 1
Bolham Manor 3

Wednesday 15th
The Beeches 1

Sunday 26th
NEW Church Farm 8
Ellicar Gardens 18
Holmes Villa 27

March

Sunday 5th
◆ Hodsock Priory Gardens 26

April

Sunday 9th
Capability Barn 5

Sunday 16th
◆ Felley Priory 21

Sunday 30th
Sycamores House 53

May

Monday 1st
7 Colly Gate 12

Sunday 7th
The Old Vicarage 42

Sunday 14th
NEW Cherry Orchard 6
Cross Lodge 15
38 Main Street 34
◆ Norwell Nurseries 38

Sunday 21st
Beeston Gardens 2
NEW Cherry Orchard 6
Church House 9
Woodpeckers 58

90th Anniversary Weekend

Sunday 28th
5 Burton Lane 4
Papplewick Hall 44
Patchings Art Centre 46
Thrumpton Hall 54

Monday 29th
NEW The Echium Garden 17
Holmes Villa 27
NEW Ivy Bank Cottage 31

June

Sunday 4th
Floral Media 22
Home Farm House, 17 Main Street 28
Rose Cottage 52

Sunday 11th
Halam Gardens and Wildflower Meadow 24
Nursery House 40

Sunday 18th
Hopbine Farmhouse, Ossington 30
Ossington House 43

Sunday 25th
The Chimes 7
The Glade 23
Kinoulton Village Gardens 32
Norwell Gardens 37
Patchings Art Centre 46
6 Weston Close 57

Wednesday 28th
Norwell Gardens 37

July

Sunday 2nd
7 Colly Gate 12
The Manor 35
The National Holocaust Centre 36
Norwood Cottage 39
Oak Barn 41

Sunday 9th
The Coach House 11
NEW Cropwell Butler Village Gardens 14
Primrose Cottage 49

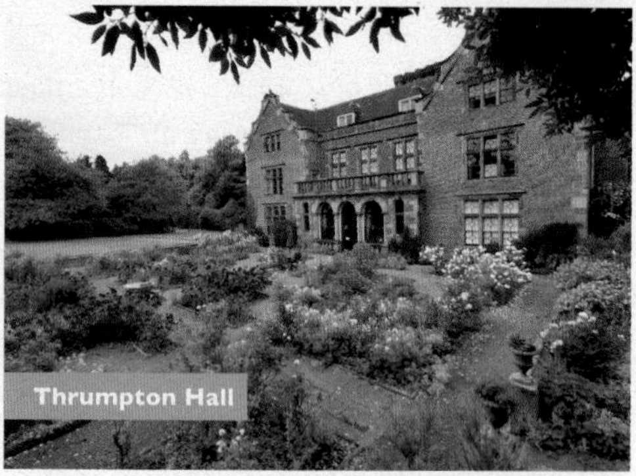

Thrumpton Hall

Rhubarb Farm 50
Wellow Village Gardens 56

Monday 10th
6 Weston Close 57

Saturday 15th
◆ Clumber Park Walled Kitchen Garden 10

Sunday 16th
Eton Avenue Growers Association 20
Lodge Mount 33
The National Holocaust Centre 36

Wednesday 19th
Riseholme, 125 Shelford Road 51

Sunday 23rd
The Elms 19
Park Farm 45

Sunday 30th
Cornerstones 13
NEW 5a High Street 25

August

Sunday 6th
The Chimes 7

Sunday 13th
The Old Vicarage 42

Sunday 20th
University Park Gardens 55

Monday 28th
5 Burton Lane 4

September

Sunday 3rd
Eton Avenue Growers Association 20

Sunday 10th
Oak Barn 41

Sunday 17th
Ellicar Gardens 18
Honeysuckle Cottage 29
Riseholme, 125 Shelford Road 51

October

Sunday 8th
◆ Norwell Nurseries 38

Sunday 15th
◆ Norwell Nurseries 38

By Arrangement

The Beeches 1
5 Burton Lane 4
Capability Barn 5
7 Colly Gate 12
Cornerstones 13
Dumbleside 16
Ellicar Gardens 18
The Elms 19
Holmes Villa 27
Home Farm House, 17 Main Street 28
Lodge Mount 33
The Manor 35
Oak Barn 41
The Old Vicarage 42
Park Farm 45
Piecemeal 47
The Poplars 48
Rhubarb Farm 50
Riseholme, 125 Shelford Road 51
Rose Cottage 52
Sycamores House 53
6 Weston Close 57
Woodpeckers 58

THE GARDENS

1 THE BEECHES

The Avenue, Milton, Newark,
NG22 0PW. Margaret & Jim
Swindin, 01777 870828, james91.
swindin@mypostoffice.co.uk. *1m
S A1 Markham Moor. Exit A1 at
Markham Moor, take Walesby sign
into village (1m). From Main St, L
up The Avenue.* Sun 12, Wed 15
Feb (11-4). Adm £3, chd free.
Home-made teas. **Visits also
by arrangement Feb to May,
tea/coffee, home-made cakes.
Groups min 4, max 50.**
1 acre garden full of colour and
interest to plant enthusiasts looking
for unusual and rare plants. Spring
gives some 250 named snowdrops
together with hellebores and early
daffodils. The lawn is awash with
crocus, fritillarias, anemones, narcissi
and cyclamen. Large vegetable
garden on raised beds. Lovely views
over open countryside. Newcastle
Mausoleum (adjacent) open.
Featured in Garden News and
Cottage Gardener booklet. Some
slopes and gravel paths.

& 🐴 ✿ 🚗 ☕

GROUP OPENING

2 BEESTON GARDENS

Audon Avenue, Beeston,
NG9 4AW. *J25 M1, A52 to
Nottinham. Turn R to Beeston B6006
at Nurseryman, follow signs. For
Audon Ave, up Wollaton Rd, through
Beeston to Tesco Xrds. Turn R, follow
rd to Christ Church. Audon Ave on L.
Maps available.* Sun 21 May (1.30-
5.30). Combined adm £4, chd
free. Home-made teas.

60 AUDON AVENUE
Anne & Rob Mason.

6 HOPE STREET
Elaine Liquorish.

Enjoy 2 contrasting gardens each with
their own appeal. 60 Audon Avenue
(The Bee Garden) – an interesting
wildlife oriented garden featuring
a range of areas, incl bee hives
(beekeeper present). Themed borders,
stumpery and dry shade planting,
pond, bug hotel, fruit and vegetable
beds and beach hut! 6 Hope Street
– a garden filled with a wide variety
of plants, incl alpines, hostas, ferns,
carnivorous plants, agapanthus, bulbs
and shrubs. Pond, troughs, pots and
a greenhouse with many subtropical
plants. Home-made crafts.

✿ ☕

3 BOLHAM MANOR

Bolham Way, Bolham, Retford,
DN22 9JG. Pam & Butch
Barnsdale. *1m from Retford. A620
Gainsborough Rd from Retford, turn L
onto Tiln Lane, signed 'A620 avoiding
low bridge'. At sharp R bend take rd
ahead to Tiln then L Bolham Way.* Sun
12 Feb (11-3). Adm £3.50, chd
free. Enjoy hot soup and a roll.
Enjoy this much loved 3 acre garden
carpeted with snowdrops, wander
amongst mature trees and dancing
ladies! Meander along the terraced
planting down to the ponds and
cave. Stroll past the herbaceous
borders, across the croquet lawn,
down mown paths into the old
orchard. Wheelchair access limited
to parts of garden.

& ✿ ☕

4 5 BURTON LANE

Whatton in the Vale, NG13 9EQ.
Ms Faulconbridge, 01949 850942,
jpfaulconbridge@hotmail.co.uk,
https://ayearinthegardenblog.
wordpress.com. *3m E of Bingham.
Follow signs to Whatton from A52
between Bingham & Elton. Garden
nr Church in old part of village. Follow
yellow NGS signs.* Sun 28 May, Mon
28 Aug (1.30-5). Adm £3.50, chd
free. Home-made teas. **Visits also
by arrangement May to Oct.**
Modern cottage garden which is
productive and highly decorative.
We garden organically and for
wildlife. The garden is full of colour
and scent from spring to autumn.
Several distinct areas, incl fruit and
vegetables. Large beds are filled
with over 500 varieties of plants
with paths through so you can
wander and get close. Also features
seating, gravel garden, pond, shade
planting and sedum roof. Historic
church, attractive village with walks.

Featured in Garden News - Garden
of the Week, Nottingham Evening
Post, Newark Advertiser.

✿ ☕

5 CAPABILITY BARN

Gonalston Lane, Hoveringham,
NG14 7JH. Malcolm &
Wendy Fisher, 01159 664322,
wendy.fisher111@btinternet.com,
www.capabilitybarn.co.uk. *8m
NE of Nottingham. A612 from
Nottingham through Lowdham. Take
1st R into Gonalston Lane. 1m on
L.* Sun 9 Apr (12.30-4.30). Adm
£3.50, chd free. Home-made
teas. **Visits also by arrangement
Apr to June adm £6 incl
refreshments.**
In early spring see brilliant displays
of daffodils, tulips and hyacinths.
Fritillarias star in the wildflower
meadow. May invites rhododendrons,
azaleas and wisteria flowers and
orchard apple blossom. Herbaceous
borders are filled with spring
beauties - erythroniums, anemones,
primulas and pulmonarias. Roses,
delphiniums, lupins, hostas,
vegetables/fruit will greet group
visitors later. Extensive collection of
dahlias and flowering begonias.

✿ 🚗 ☕

6 🆕 CHERRY ORCHARD

Old Road, Ruddington, Nottingham,
NG11 6NF. Bernadette & Paul
Harrison. *5m S of Nottingham. On
A52 ring road from A606 rbout, turn
L into Landmere Lane, then L into
Old Road. From Nottm on A60, after
crossing A52 ring road r'about, turn L
into Old Loughborough Road, L again,
then 1st R.* Sun 14, Sun 21 May
(12-3.30). Adm £3.50, chd free.
Home-made teas.
Cherry Orchard garden is just
under an acre, situated in a mature
English woodland setting. A central
lawned area is surrounded by some
fine trees and different beds, planted
to take advantage of shady, sunny,
dry and damp areas. It successfully
accommodates challenging soil
conditions and undulations. Planted
to provide interest throughout the
year and at its most resplendent in
Spring. Access to most of the garden
on brick and bark paths.

& ☕

7 THE CHIMES

37 Glenorchy Crescent, Heronridge, NG5 9LG. Stan & Ellen Maddock. *4m N of Nottingham. A611 towards Hucknall onto Bulwell Common. Turn R at Tesco Top Valley up to island. Turn L 100 yds. 1st L then 2nd L onto Glenorchy Crescent to bottom.* **Sun 25 June, Sun 6 Aug (12-5). Adm £3, chd free. Home-made teas.**
We would like to invite you to pass through our archway and into our own little oasis on the edge of a busy city. Come and share our well stocked although small garden, full of roses, peonies, lilies and much more. Visit us and be surprised. We look forward to seeing you.

8 NEW CHURCH FARM

Church Lane, West Drayton, Retford, DN22 8EB. Robert & Isobel Adam. *A1 exit Markham Moor. A638 Retford 500 yrds signed West Drayton. 1m, Church Lane, 1st R past church. Ample parking in farm yard.* **Sun 26 Feb (12-4): Adm £3, chd free. Light refreshments.**
The garden is essentially a spring garden and a little on the wild side. We have a small woodland area which is carpeted with many snowdrops, aconites and cyclamen which have seeded into the adjoining churchyard, with approx 180 named snowdrops growing in island beds. Limited amount of snowdrops and crocus for sale.

9 CHURCH HOUSE

Hoveringham, NG14 7JH. Alex & Sue Allan. *6m NE of Nottingham. Next to church hall in village.* **Sun 21 May (1-5). Adm £3, chd free.**
Small, charming walled cottage style garden with herbaceous borders, auricula theatre, Japanese area, stumpery and vegetable plot. Offering a delightful setting to relax in.

10 ◆ CLUMBER PARK WALLED KITCHEN GARDEN

Clumber Park, Worksop, S80 3AZ. National Trust, 01909 476592, clumberpark@nationaltrust.org.uk, www.nationaltrust.org.uk/clumber-park. *4m S of Worksop. From main car park or main entrance follow directions to Walled Kitchen Garden.* **For NGS: Sat 15 July (10-5). Adm £5.50, chd £2.80. Light refreshments. For other opening times and information, please phone, email or visit garden website.**
Beautiful 4 acre walled kitchen garden, growing unusual and old varieties of vegetables and fruits. Herbs and flower beds, incl the magnificent 400ft double herbaceous borders. 450ft glasshouse with grapevines. Museum of gardening tools. Soft fruit garden, rose garden. Garden has been awarded National Collection status for its collection of culinary rhubarbs (over 130 varieties) and regional (Nottinghamshire, Derbyshire, Lincolnshire, Leicestershire, Yorkshire) apples (72 varieties). Refreshments at Garden Tea House next to walled kitchen garden or at café in the park. Gravel paths and slopes.

11 THE COACH HOUSE

Fosse Road, Farndon, Newark, NG24 2SF. Sir Graeme & Lady Svava Davies. *On old A46 W of Farndon approx 250yrds on R past new overbridge turn off to Hawton. Entrance driveway marked Private Road.* **Sun 9 July (1-5). Adm £4, chd free. Home-made teas.**
The Coach House has two major garden areas set in approximately 0.9 acres. Both have several distinct sections and the planting throughout is designed to give color and interest through the seasons. There are many rare and unusual species among the mainly perennial plants, shrubs, grasses and trees. The planting in each area of the garden is fully detailed in a brochure for visitors.

12 7 COLLY GATE

Kimberley, Nottingham, NG16 2PJ. Doreen Fahey, 01159 192690, dfahey456@hotmail.com. *6m W of Nottingham. From M1 J26 take A610 towards Nottingham. L at next island (B600 to Kimberley) L at Sainsbury's mini island. L at top. Park here. Garden 500yds on R.* **Mon 1 May, Sun 2 July (1-5). Adm £3, chd free. Home-made teas. Visits also by arrangement May to Aug for groups 6+.**
Delightful garden created by a serious plant enthusiast and tucked away at the end of a short narrow lane in Swingate. It greets you with an impact of unexpected colour and delights you with the variety and sensitivity of the planting. A peaceful backwater in an urban setting. Full of ideas to inspire you for your own garden. Stained glass and mosaics. Some gravel paths.

Woodpeckers

13 CORNERSTONES
15 Lamcote Gardens, Radcliffe-on-Trent, Nottingham, NG12 2BS. Judith & Jeff Coombes, 01158 458055, judithcoombes@gmail.com, www.cornerstonesgarden.co.uk. *4m E of Nottingham. From A52 take Radcliffe exit at RSPCA junction, then 2nd L just before hairpin bend.* **Sun 30 July (1.30-5). Adm £3.50, chd free. Home-made teas. Visits also by arrangement July & Aug for groups 15+. Adm £7 incl refreshments and tour.**
Plant lovers' garden, approaching ½ acre. Flowing colour themed and specie borders, with rare, exotic and unusual plants, provide a wealth of colour and interest, whilst the unique fruit and vegetable garden generates an abundance of produce. Bananas, palms, fernery, fish pond, bog garden, lovely new summerhouse area and greenhouse. Enjoy tea and delicious home-made cake in a beautiful setting. Wheelchair access but some bark paths and unfenced ponds.

  👌 🐃 ✿ 🚗 ☕ 💷

GROUP OPENING

14 NEW CROPWELL BUTLER VILLAGE GARDENS
Cropwell Butler, NG12 3AA. *10m E of Nottingham. From Nottingham, keep on A52 E (towards Grantham) until R turn to village near Radcliffe on Trent. From A52/A46 r'about, follow signs to village. Maps with garden locations available in each garden.* **Sun 9 July (1-5). Combined adm £5, chd free. Home-made teas in Cropwell Bishop Village Hall.**

NEW LONG HOUSE
Mrs Elissa Anderson.

NEW THE MANOR
Mr & Mrs P Manning.

REDLAND HOUSE
Mrs Shelagh Barnes.

NEW VILLAGE HOUSE
Neil & Paddy Gledson.

The Long House offers visitors two gardens in one - a colourful typically English part contrasting with a secret Japanese style garden inspired by a Chelsea Gold Medal winner. The Manor House has a very large open garden, home to an eclectic tree collection mainly in woodland areas, as well as newly established flower beds. Deep gravel drive and paths. Redland House garden has been nurtured under a flower arranger's eye and incl colourful borders containing a variety of shrubs, trees and perennials, a woodland walk, new fernery and iris bed. Some gravel paths. An English garden may be found behind Village House with colour themed borders of shrubs and perennials, some supplemented by annuals, a terrace with vine covered pergola and a small vegetable area. Narrow access and steps.

  👌 ☕ 💷

15 CROSS LODGE
Beckingham Road, Walkeringham, DN10 4HZ. John & Betty Roberts. *A620 from Retford, A631 from Bawtry/Gainsborough, A161 to Walkeringham. Garden on A161. Parking at Village Hall approx 150 metres N of garden. For SatNav use DN10 4JF.* **Sun 14 May (1-5). Adm £3, chd free. Home-made teas in Walkeringham Village Hall.**
Ever changing 1¼ acre garden with successive displays of spring and summer flowers. Rhododendron walk in which there are over 50 varieties is at its best in May. Shrubs and perennial borders, rockeries, roses, conifers, old orchard and small woodland with large pond. New access from woodland to pond side path. Wheelchair access to all main features, except pond side paths.

  👌 ✿ ☕ 💷

16 DUMBLESIDE
17 Bridle Road, Burton Joyce, NG14 5FT. Mr P Bates, 01159 313725. *5m NE of Nottingham. Very narrow lane to walk up 100 yds - please park on Lambley Lane & walk if possible. Drop off if necessary for less mobile.* **Visits by arrangement Jan to Nov, talk and guided tours. Refreshments on request when booking (extra cost). Adm £4, chd free.**
Opening for groups/individual visits. Do come to see my beautiful garden of yr-round interest at almost any time, with perennials in extensive borders supplemented by dahlias, castor oil plants, cannas and many interesting and colourful annuals. Cyclamen will show under the trees and colchicum emerge in newly cut meadows. Primulas in wet areas are overshadowed with tree ferns and exotic foliage. Steep slopes towards stream therefore partial access only for wheelchairs.

  👌 🐃 ✿ 🚗 ☕ 💷

17 NEW THE ECHIUM GARDEN
Edwinstowe House, High Street, Edwinstowe, Newark, NG21 9PR. Linda & Ray Heywood, www.echiumworld.co.uk. *N of Newark on Trent, off A614. Edwinstowe House is located in centre of village. Please note: If you are using SatNav please use NG21 9QS.* **Mon 29 May (11-3). Adm £3, chd free. Light refreshments.**
The Echium Garden in Edwinstowe (The village of Robin Hood and Sherwood Forest) features the National Plant Collection of Echium incl the Giant Tree Echium growing to over 10ft tall. The garden is based in a modern office complex attached to a Georgian house used in more recent times as the headquarters for the National Coal Board. The herbaceous borders were redesigned in 2014 and the garden features a cascading pond. Silver medal winners for Echium World exhibit - Plants, Pollinators and People, RHS Hampton Court. BBC show coverage, BBC East Midlands Today, Radio Nottingham, Daily Telegraph, Gardening News, Gardeners World magazine - Tales from Titchmarsh.

  🐃 ✿ 🚗 NPC ☕ 💷

Your visit has already helped 600 more people gain access to a Parkinson's nurse

Dumbleside

18 ELLICAR GARDENS

Carr Road, Gringley-on-the-Hill, Doncaster, DN10 4SN. Will & Sarah Murch, 01777 817218, sarah@ellicargardens.co.uk, www.ellicargardens.co.uk. *Gringley-on-the-Hill. Approx 2m outside village of Gringley on the Hill. Turn onto Leys Lane, drive out of village, over canal, Ellicar Gardens on L on Carr Rd, opp cream house.* Sun 26 Feb (12-4). **Combined adm with Holmes Villa £4.50, chd 50p.** Sun 17 Sept (1-5). **Combined adm with Honeysuckle Cottage £5, chd 50p. Soup (Feb), Home-made teas (Sept). Visits also by arrangement Feb to Oct for groups 10+ during term times.**
This vibrant, naturalistic family garden is a haven for garden and wildlife enthusiasts and children. Sweeping borders with new perennials and grasses grow alongside wild flowers and specimen trees. Beautiful in winter and vibrant in summer, highlights incl a winter garden, hellebores, gravel garden, old roses, orchard and natural pool. Children love exploring the school garden and willow maze. New perennials and grasses, over 250 young specimen trees, wildlife garden, winter garden, natural pool, rare breed pets. Featured in The

English Garden, Waitrose Gardening Magazine Garten Traume, Garden Answers and Real Homes. Awarded Silver Gilt Award for Natural Pool UK Pool and Spa Awards, BBC TV Winner Cobra. Some uneven surfaces, grass and gravel paths.

19 THE ELMS

Main Street, North Leverton, DN22 0AR. Tim & Tracy Ward, 01427 881164, tracy@wardt2.fsnet.co.uk. *5m E of Retford, 6m SW of Gainsborough. From Retford take rd to Leverton for 5m, into North Leverton with Habblesthorpe.* Sun 23 July (2-5). **Adm £3, chd free. Home-made teas. Visits also by arrangement July to Sept.**
This garden is very different, creating an extension to the living space. Inspiration comes from Mediterranean countries, giving a holiday feel. Palms, bamboos and bananas, along with other exotics, create drama and yet make a statement true to many gardens, that of peace and calm. North Leverton Windmill may be open for visitors. Garden fully viewable, limited wheelchair access onto decked and tiled areas.

20 ETON AVENUE GROWERS ASSOCIATION

Hawton Road, Newark, NG24 4QA. Mrs Gillie Wilkinson, www.etonavenuegrowersassociation. wordpress.com. *1m from Farndon A46 turn off. Park on Hawton Rd, walk up alleyway between 77 & 79 Hawton Rd.* Sun 16 July, Sun 3 Sept (12-4). **Adm £3.50, chd free. Home-made teas.**
2½ acres taken over in Feb 2009 by a community group. Now a peaceful haven for long term unemployed. This enthusiastic group work hard, and choose which plants to grow to achieve a wildlife friendly spot. Dig for Victory allotment, ponds, tunnels, compost loos, flowers, fruit and vegetables - come and join us for something different and fun! Provides British cut flowers sold for many events.

21 ◆ FELLEY PRIORY

Underwood, NG16 5FJ. Ms Michelle Upchurch for the Brudenell Family, 01773 810230, michelle@felleypriory.co.uk, www.felleypriory.co.uk. *8m SW of Mansfield. Off A608 ½m W M1 J27.* For NGS: Sun 16 Apr (10-4). **Adm £5, chd free. Light refreshments.** For other opening times and information, please phone, email or visit garden website.
Garden for all seasons with yew hedges and topiary, snowdrops, hellebores, herbaceous borders and rose garden. There are pergolas, a white garden, small arboretum and borders filled with unusual trees, shrubs, plants and bulbs. The grass edged pond is planted with primulas, bamboo, iris, roses and eucomis. Bluebell woodland walk. Orchard with extremely rare daffodils.

22 FLORAL MEDIA

Norwell Road, Caunton, Newark, NG23 6AQ. Mr & Mrs Steve Routledge, 01636 636283, info@floralmedia.co.uk, www.floralmedia.co.uk. *Take Norwell Rd from Caunton. Approx ½m from Caunton on L.* Sun 4 June (10-4). **Adm £3.50, chd free.**

Home-made teas.
A beautifully well maintained country garden. Beds overflowing with a variety of roses, shrubs and flowers. A gravel/oriental garden, wildlife pond, vegetable, herb and fruit garden. New in 2015 a contemporary purple/white garden. This garden has many different rooms for you to indulge in! A local folk group called The Jolly Beggars will be playing music throughout the afternoon. Full wheelchair access incl disabled WC.

& ✿ ⛟ ☕

23 THE GLADE

2a Woodthorpe Avenue, Woodthorpe, Nottingham, NG5 4FD. Tony Hoffman. *3m N of Nottingham. A60 Mansfield Rd from Nottingham. After Sherwood shops turn R at T-lights by Woodthorpe Park into Woodthorpe Drive. 2nd L into Woodthorpe Av.* Sun 25 June (1-5). Combined adm with 6 Weston Close £5, chd free.

Exquisite medium sized garden developed over 8yrs on the site of a former Great Western Railway track with very free draining soil which allows Mediterranean plants to thrive. Feature plants incl tree ferns, 30ft high bamboos, fan palms, acers and other shrubs rarely seen. The railway arch, enclosed in trellis work, provides shade for a variety of ferns and hostas.

🐾 ✿ ☕

GROUP OPENING

24 HALAM GARDENS AND WILDFLOWER MEADOW

Nr Southwell, NG22 8AX. *Village gardens within walking distance. Hill's Farm wildflower meadow is a short drive of ½m towards Edingley village, turn R at brow of hill as signed.* Sun 11 June (12-5). Combined adm £5, chd free. Home-made teas at The Old Vicarage, Halam.

HILL FARM HOUSE
Victoria Starkey.
Open on Sat 10 June

HILL'S FARM
John & Margaret Hill.
Open on Sat 10 June

THE OLD VICARAGE
Mrs Beverley Perks.
Open on all dates
(See separate entry)

Unusual mixture of a long standing plant lover's NGS village garden, a new small attractive cottage garden and a 6 acre wildflower meadow - part of an organic farm where the cattle are fed the herb rich pasture which is cut in July - visitors can be assured of an inspiring discussion with a farmer; passionate about the benefits of this method of farming for the environment, his Shorthorn cattle and the meat produced.

& 🐄 ✿ ⛟ ☕

25 NEW 5A HIGH STREET

Sutton-on-Trent, Newark, NG23 6QA. Kathryn & Ian Saunders. *6m N of Newark. Leave A1 at Sutton on Trent, follow Sutton signs. L at Xrds. 1st R turn (approx 1m) onto Main Street. 2nd L onto High Street. Garden 50 yds on R. Park on road.* Sun 30 July (12-5). Adm £3, chd free. Tea.

This hidden plot started as a field 30yrs ago. All the trees and mature shrubs now form the backbone of a garden that has been re-invented in the last 5yrs. A series of ponds run through the garden with planting ranging from tropical to a more natural style. Woodland pathways pass through a Fernery with over 65 types of ferns. Herbaceous borders and further colour and interest.

✿ ☕

26 ♦ HODSOCK PRIORY GARDENS

Blyth, Worksop, S81 0TY. Sir Andrew & Lady Buchanan, 01909 591204, info@snowdrops.co.uk, www.snowdrops.co.uk. *North Nottinghamshire. 4m N of Worksop off B6045. M1 J30 or 31 & close to A1(M). Blyth-Worksop rd approx 2m from A1M. Well signed locally. Ample free parking.* For NGS: Sun 5 Mar (10-4). Adm £5, chd £1.

Light refreshments. For other opening times and information, please phone, email or visit garden website.
Visitors to the snowdrops in February can enjoy a leisurely walk through the surprisingly fragrant winter gardens and woods before having coffee, lunch or tea in our cafes. Aconites, irises, cornus, honeysuckles and hellebores on display. Free daily history talk by the campfire. Bacon sandwiches cooked in the wood. Wrap up warm and wear outdoors clothes and boots. See website for special offers, opening times and full details of our snowdrop events, talk and tours. Hodsock Snowdrops open daily from Sat 4th Feb to Sun 5th March (10-4). Shortbreaks available in our B&B. Some paths difficult for wheelchairs when wet.

& ✿ ⛟ 🛏 ☕

27 HOLMES VILLA

Holmes Lane, Walkeringham, Gainsborough, DN10 4JP. Peter & Sheila Clark, 01427 890233, clarkshaulage@aol.com. *4m NW of Gainsborough. A620 from Retford or A631 from Bawtry/Gainsborough & A161 to Walkeringham then towards Misterton. Follow NGS signs for 1m. Plenty of parking. Reserved disabled parking.* Sun 26 Feb (12-4). Combined adm with Ellicar Gardens £4.50, chd 50p. Mon 29 May (1-5). Adm £2.50, chd free. Home-made teas at Ellicar Gardens (Feb), Holmes Villa (May). Visits also by arrangement May to July.

1¾ acre plantsman's garden offering yr-round interest and inspiration starting with carpets of snowdrops, mini daffodils, hellebores and spring bulbs. Unusual collection of plants and shrubs for winter. Come and be surprised at the different fragrant and interesting plants in early spring. Places to sit and ponder, gazebos, arbours, wildlife pond, hosta garden, old tools on display and scarecrows. A flower arranger's artistic garden. Featured in Garden News and local press.

& ✿ ⛟ ☕

28 HOME FARM HOUSE, 17 MAIN STREET

Keyworth, Nottingham, NG12 5AA. Graham & Pippa Tinsley, 01159 377122, Graham_Tinsley@yahoo.co.uk, www.homefarmgarden.wordpress. com. *7m S of Nottingham. Follow signs for Keyworth from A60 or A606 & head for church. Garden about 50yds down Main St. Parking at village hall or on Bunny Lane.* **Sun 4 June (1-5). Combined adm with Rose Cottage £4, chd free. Home-made teas. Visits also by arrangement June & July.**
A large garden hidden behind old farmhouse in the village centre with views over open fields. Many trees incl cedars, limes, oaks and chestnuts which, with high beech and yew hedges, create hidden places to be explored. Old orchard, ponds, turf mound, rose garden, winter garden and old garden with herbaceous borders. Pergolas with wisteria, ornamental vine and roses. Interesting and unusual perennials for sale by Piecemeal Plants (www. piecemealplants.co.uk). Wheelchair access via gravel yard.

29 HONEYSUCKLE COTTAGE

Hunters Drive, Gringley on the Hill, Doncaster, DN10 4ZX. Miss J Towler. *Situated on R off Leys Lane in Gringley on the Hill.* **Sun 17 Sept (1-5). Combined adm with Ellicar Gardens £5, chd 50p. Home-made teas at Ellicar Gardens.**
Honeysuckle Cottage is a traditional terraced cottage garden with mixed borders and relaxed planting. An old Bramley Apple tree creates a focal point on the top terrace where elements of formality using clipped box help to create a tranquil atmosphere. Playful use of topiary (find Miss Piggy!) The productive garden has vegetables, a soft fruit section and small greenhouse.

30 HOPBINE FARMHOUSE, OSSINGTON

Hopbine Farmhouse, Main Street, Ossington, NG23 6LJ. Mr & Mrs Geldart. *From A1 N take exit marked Carlton, Sutton-on-Trent, Weston etc. At T-Junction turn L to Kneesall. Drive 2m to Ossington. In village turn R to Moorhouse & park in field.* **Sun 18 June (2-5). Combined adm with Ossington House £4, chd free. Home-made teas at The Hut, Ossington.**
A small but full garden with many interesting and unusual plants in a large herbaceous border facing SW. On the N side a hidden walled garden with a white wall of Clematis, R.Ghislaine Feligonde and Iceberg. Shrub and climbing roses incl a unique x - Mary Bracegirdle. Large hostas, herbs and an unusual Schizophragma Hydrangeoides creeping to the roof. A new island bed established this year. Ale House with original benches. Some narrow paths.

31 NEW IVY BANK COTTAGE

The Green, South Clifton, Newark, NG23 7AG. David & Ruth Hollands. *12m N of Newark. From S, exit A46 N of Newark onto A1133 towards Gainsborough. From N, exit A57 at Newton-on-Trent onto A1133 towards Newark.* **Mon 29 May (1-5). Adm £3, chd free. Home-made teas.**
A traditional cottage garden, with herbaceous borders, fruit trees incl a Nottinghamshire Medlar, vegetable plots, and many surprises, incl a stumpery, a troughery, dinosaur footprints and even fairies! Many original features: pigsties, double privy and a wash house. Children can search for animal models and explore inside the shepherd's hut. Seats around and a covered refreshment area.

GROUP OPENING

32 KINOULTON VILLAGE GARDENS

Nottingham, NG12 3EL. *8m SE of West Bridgford. Off A46 at junction with A606. Follow rd signs into village.* **Sun 25 June (1-5). Combined adm £5, chd free. Home-made teas in Kinoulton Village Hall.**

BISHOPS COTTAGE
Ann Hammond.

HALL FARM COTTAGE
Mrs Bel Grundy.

LINDY EDGE
Mrs Jan Osbond.

Bishops Cottage is a large, mature, cottage garden with mixed herbaceous borders with an emphasis on scent and colour coordination where possible. A wildlife pond and open views over the countryside. Plants for sale. Hall Farm Cottage is small but packed with plants and interest, and totally encircles the cottage. Archways smothered with fragrant jasmine, roses and clematis, potted lilies and exotic black/green aeoniums and stunning allium cristophii. Views over the Vale of Belvoir. Lindy Edge is an artisan garden created through imaginative planting and design with twists and turns providing surprises around every corner. Fruit and vegetables in raised beds. Plants and original art for sale.

33 LODGE MOUNT

Town Street, South Leverton, Retford, DN22 0BT. Mr A Wootton-Jones, 07427 400848, a.wj@live.co.uk. *4m E of Retford. Opp Bradley's Garage on Town Street.* **Sun 16 July (12-6). Adm £3, chd free. Home-made teas. Visits also by arrangement June to Sept.**
Originally a field, much of the ½ acre garden, although planned on paper for yrs, was landscaped within a few months during 2012 in order to fulfill an ambition following Helen Wootton-Jones' terminal diagnosis. Following organic principles, an orchard and large vegetable and fruit plots are complemented by an area of unusual perennial edibles, and helpful plants, with a view to self sufficiency. Clematis, roses, and climbers provide fragrance and a feeling of enclosure/peacefulness. Helen's aunt also had cancer and the garden was specifically designed to open for the NGS to raise money for cancer charities.

The Coach House

34 **38 MAIN STREET**
Woodborough, Nottingham, NG14 6EA. Martin Taylor & Deborah Bliss. *Turn off Mapperley Plains Rd at sign for Woodborough. Alternatively, follow signs to Woodborough off A6097 (Epperstone bypass). Property is between Park Av & Bank Hill.* Sun 14 May (1-5). Adm £3.50, chd free. Home-made teas. Varied ⅓ acre. Bamboo fenced Asian species area with traditional outdoor wood fired Ofuro bath, herbaceous border, raised rhododendron bed, vegetables, greenhouse, pond area and art studio and terrace.

35 **THE MANOR**
Church Street, East Markham, Newark, NG22 0SA. Ms Christine Aldred, 01777 872719, clownsca@yahoo.co.uk. *7m S of Retford. Take A1 Markham Moor r'about exit for A57 Lincoln. Turn at East Markham junction & follow signs for the church. Properties adjacent to the church.* Sun 2 July (1-5). Combined adm with Norwood Cottage £5, chd free. Light refreshments. Also open Oak Barn. **Visits also by arrangement Apr to Aug.**
An extensive, colour themed, scented garden on various levels. Set in lovely village next to C15 church. Planting for yr-round interest, complementing the property and incl pond with koi carp, sunken garden, herbaceous border and vegetable patch. Range of seating areas to pause and enjoy the beautiful views. Varied levels. Gravel paths.

36 **THE NATIONAL HOLOCAUST CENTRE**
Acre Edge Road, Laxton, Newark, NG22 0PA. Janet Mills, www.nationalholocaustcentre.net. *Take A614 from Nottingham. At Ollerton r'about take 4th exit A6075 signed Tuxford. On leaving Boughton turn sharp R signed Laxton. Disabled parking & WC.* Sun 2, Sun 16 July (10-4.30). Adm £3, chd free. Light refreshments.

The Memorial Garden is set in an acre of beautifully landscaped countryside and provides an important counterpoint to the museum. Over 1000 scented white roses have been planted, many of them dedicated by Holocaust survivors and their families. Each rose has an inscribed plaque helping visitors to understand that the victims are not just a catalogue of statistics but human beings, with names. Visitors are welcome to visit the Museum and exhibitions (separate charge). Refreshments incl sandwiches, home-made soup and cakes

GROUP OPENING

37 **NORWELL GARDENS**
Newark, NG23 6JX. *6m N of Newark. Halfway between Newark & Southwell. Off A1 at Cromwell turning, take Norwell Rd at bus shelter. Or off A616 take Caunton turn.* Sun 25 June (1-5). Evening opening Wed 28 June (6.30-9). Combined adm £4.50, chd free. Home-made teas in Village Hall (25 June) and Norwell Nurseries (28 June).

NEW **CEDAR HOUSE**
Mr Edward & Mrs Sheila Wright.

JUXTA MILL
Janet McFerran.

NORTHFIELD FARM
Mr & Mrs D Adamson.

NORWELL ALLOTMENT / PARISH GARDENS
Norwell Parish Council.

◆ **NORWELL NURSERIES**
Andrew & Helen Ward.
(See separate entry)
NPC

THE OLD FORGE
Adam & Hilary Ward.

THE OLD MILL HOUSE, NORWELL
Mr & Mrs M Burgess.

SOUTHVIEW COTTAGE
Margaret & Les Corbett.

This is the 21st yr that Norwell has opened a range of different, very appealing gardens all making superb use of the beautiful backdrop of a quintessentially English countryside village. It incl a garden and nursery of national renown and the rare opportunity to walk around vibrant allotments with a wealth of gardeners from seasoned competition growers to plots that are substitute house gardens, bursting with both flower colour and vegetables in great variety. To top it all there are a plethora of breathtaking village gardens showing the diversity that is achieved under the umbrella of a cottage garden description! The beautiful medieval church and its peaceful churchyard with grass labyrinth will be the setting for - 'Memories'. Flowers, images and structures will show how memories are captured and the enjoyment from pleasant ones revisited.

38 ◆ NORWELL NURSERIES

Woodhouse Road, Norwell, NG23 6JX. Andrew & Helen Ward, 01636 636337, wardha@aol.com, www.norwellnurseries.co.uk. *6m N of Newark halfway between Newark & Southwell. Off A1 at Cromwell turning, take rd to Norwell at bus stop. Or from A616 take Caunton turn.* **For NGS: Sun 14 May, Sun 8, Sun 15 Oct (2-5). Adm £2.50, chd free. Home-made teas. Opening with Norwell Gardens on Sun 25, Wed 28 June. For other opening times and information, please phone, email or visit garden website.**

Jewel box of over 2,500 different, beautiful and unusual plants sumptuously set out in a one acre plantsman's garden incl shady garden with orchids, woodland gems, cottage garden borders, alpine and scree areas. Pond with opulently planted margins. Extensive herbaceous borders and effervescent colour themed beds. Innovative Grassoretum (like an arboretum but for grasses). New borders every yr. Nationally renowned nursery open with over 1,000 different rare plants for sale. Autumn opening features UK's largest collection of hardy chrysanthemums for sale and the National Collection of Hardy Chrysanthemums. Feature articles in Landscape Magazine, Country Life and the highly prestigious Gardens to Visit book 2012-2017. Grass paths, no wheelchair access to woodland paths.

   🕭 ❀ 🚗 NPC 🍵

39 NORWOOD COTTAGE

Church Street, East Markham, Newark, NG22 0SA. Anne Beeby. *7m S of Retford. Take A1 Markham Moor r'about exit for A57 Lincoln. Turn at East Markham junction & follow signs for the church. Property adjacent the church.* **Sun 2 July (1-5). Combined adm with Oak Barn £5, chd free. Home-made teas at The Manor. Also open The Manor.**

Situated opp both the beautiful St John the Baptist church and The Manor House. Following my move 4yrs ago different areas of interest have been created incorporating roses, perennials, box hedging, acers and interesting foliage plants, trees and shrubs making for yr-round interest. Partial wheelchair access to parts of garden only. Steps leading to some areas.

   🕭 🐾 ❀ 🍵

40 NURSERY HOUSE

Top Street, Askham, Newark, NG22 0RP. Mr & Mrs D Bird. *Askham village. On R 1½m from A638. Flagpole in garden.* **Sun 11 June (2-6). Adm £3, chd free. Home-made teas at Canmore Lodge (next door).**

Secluded and very private garden of about ⅓ of an acre. A plantsman's garden of shrubs and herbaceous beds with every plant meticulously labelled and entered into catalogue. Waterfall and well stocked pond and a collection of 25 different hostas. Deep gravel at front.

   🕭 🐾 🍵

41 OAK BARN

Church Street, East Markham, Newark, NG22 0SA. Simon Bennett & Laura Holmes, 07812 146265, she_ra@hotmail.co.uk. *From A1 Markham Moor junction take A57 to Lincoln. Turn R at Xrds into E Markham. L onto High St & R onto Plantation Rd. Enter farm gates at T-Junction, garden located on L.* **Sun 2 July (1-5). Combined adm with The Manor £5, chd free. Also open Norwood Cottage. Sun 10 Sept (1-5). Adm £3, chd free. Home-made teas. Visits also by arrangement July to Oct, groups 30 max.**

This small rural garden started out as an empty plot back in 2009. Since then I have discovered a passion for exotic and subtropical plants. Over time it has evolved into a densely planted, jungle style, exotic oasis. From the lush green foliage of palms, tree ferns and bananas to the vibrant underplanting of dahlias, cannas, gingers and brugmansia, this garden explodes into life in the summer.

   ❀ 🚗 🍵

42 THE OLD VICARAGE

Halam Hill, Halam, NG22 8AX. Mrs Beverley Perks, 01636 812181, perks.family@talk21.com. *1m W of Southwell. Please park diagonally into beech hedge on verge with speed interactive sign or in village - a busy road so no parking on roadside.* **Sun 7 May, Sun 13 Aug (1-5). Adm £3.50, chd free. Home-made teas. Opening with Halam Gardens and Wildflower Meadow on Sun 11 June. Visits also by arrangement June to Aug for groups 20+.**

This beautifully designed organic, relaxing garden on S-facing hillside, offers history, texture and colour, all planted with an artistic eye. Swathes of snowdrops, followed by bounteous borders of unusual herbaceous plants, clematis, roses, shrubs and trees. Hidden nooks and crannies, wildlife ponds, swimming pool planting, kitchen garden, wildflower meadow with glorious views - soak up the peace and quiet. Beautiful C12 Church open only short walk down into the village or across field through attractively planted churchyard - rare C14 stained glass window. Gravel drive - undulating levels as on a hillside - plenty of cheerful help available.

   🐾 ❀ 🚗 🍵

43 OSSINGTON HOUSE

Moorhouse Road, Ossington, Newark, NG23 6LD. Georgina Denison. *10m N of Newark, 2m off A1. From A1 N take exit marked Carlton, Sutton-on-Trent, Weston etc. At T-junction turn L to Kneesall. Drive 2m to Ossington. In village turn R to Moorhouse & park in field next to Hopbine Farmhouse.* **Sun 18 June (2-5). Combined adm with Hopbine Farmhouse, Ossington £4, chd free. Home-made teas in The Hut, Ossington.**

Vicarage garden redesigned in 1960 and again in 2014. Chestnuts, lawns, formal beds, woodland walk, poolside planting. Orchard, kitchen garden. Terraces, yews, grasses. Ferns, herbaceous perennials, roses. Oaks, antipodean freaks, clematis. Disabled parking available in drive to Ossington House.

   🕭 ❀ 🚗 D 🍵

44 PAPPLEWICK HALL

Blidworth Waye, Papplewick, Nottinghamshire, NG15 8FE. J R Godwin-Austen Esq, www.papplewickhall.co.uk. 7m N of Nottingham. 300 yards out N end of Papplewick village, on B683 (follow signs to Papplewick from A60 & B6011). Free parking at Hall. Sun 28 May (2-5). Adm £3.50, chd free. Donation to St James' Church. This historic, mature, 8 acre garden, mostly shaded woodland, abounds with rhododendrons, hostas, ferns, and spring bulbs. Suitable for wheelchair users, but sections of the paths are gravel.

&

45 PARK FARM

Crink Lane, Southwell, NG25 0TJ. Ian & Vanessa Johnston, 01636 812195, v.johnston100@gmail.com. 1m SE of Southwell. From Southwell town centre go down Church St, turn R on Fiskerton Rd & 200yds up hill turn R into Crink Lane. Park Farm is on 2nd bend. Follow signs to car parking. Sun 23 July (1-5). Adm £3.50, chd free. Home-made teas. Visits also by arrangement May to July (guided tour 50ppp). Regret, no refreshments.

3 acre garden remarkable for its extensive variety of trees, shrubs and perennials, many rare or unusual. Long colourful herbaceous borders, roses, woodland garden, alpine/scree garden and a large wildlife pond. Spectacular views of the Minster across a wildflower meadow and ha-ha.

& ✿ ☕

46 PATCHINGS ART CENTRE

Oxton Road, Calverton, Nottingham, NG14 6NU. Chas & Pat Wood, www.patchingsartcentre.co.uk. N of Nottingham city take A614 towards Ollerton. Turn R on to B6386 towards Oxton. Patchings is on L before turning to Calverton. Brown tourist directional signs. Sun 28 May, Sun 25 June (10.30-1.30). Adm £3, chd free. Light refreshments at Patchings Cafe. Something very different, a woodland walk linked to art history. Colourful wild flowers and grasses dominate the grass path walk. The two dates selected show a range of species and colour within the rolling landscape of Patchings. The walk has been extended to incl the Impressionist section with the Monet Bridge and the lake area. There are four exhibition galleries, featuring paintings, jewellery and ceramics, card gallery and gift shop. Studio artists in residence. Grass paths, with some undulations and uphill sections accessible to wheelchairs with help. Please enquire for assistance.

🐐 �» ☕

47 PIECEMEAL

123 Main Street, Sutton Bonington, Loughborough, LE12 5PE. Mary Thomas, 01509 672056, nursery@piecemealplants.co.uk. 2m SE of Kegworth (M1 J24). 6m NW of Loughborough. Almost opp St Michael's Church & Sutton Bonington Hall. Visits by arrangement June to Aug for groups min 4, max 10. For 10+ please contact to discuss. Tea and biscuits available. Adm £2.75, chd free. Pots of pots! Tiny, sheltered walled garden housing very large collection of shrubs as well as various climbers, perennials and even a few trees, in around 400 containers as well as in small borders. Many unusual and not fully hardy. Focus on distinctive form, foliage shape and colour combination to provide interest from spring to autumn. Both garden and conservatory a jungle by midsummer! Featured in Garden News and BBC Gardeners World magazines.

✿ ☕

48 THE POPLARS

60 High Street, Sutton-on-Trent, Newark, NG23 6QA. Sue & Graham Goodwin-King, 01636 821240. 7m N of Newark. Leave A1 at Sutton/Carlton/Normanton-on-Trent junction. In Carlton turn L onto B1164. Turn R into Hemplands Lane then R into High St. 1st house on R. Limited parking. Visits by arrangement June to Sept for groups 10+. Adm £3, chd free. Home-made teas.

Mature ½ acre garden on the site of a Victorian flower nursery, now a series of well planted areas each with its own character. Exotics courtyard with late summer colour. Iron balcony overlooking pond and oriental style gravel garden. Jungle with castaway's shack. Black and white garden. Woodland area. Walled potager. Fernery and hidden courtyard, lawns, borders and charming sitting places. Some gravel paths and shallow steps, but most areas accessible.

🐐 ✿ ☕

49 PRIMROSE COTTAGE

Bar Road North, Beckingham, Doncaster, DN10 4NN. Terry & Brenda Wilson. 8m N of Retford. A631 to Beckingham r'about, enter village, L to village green, L to Bar Rd. Sun 9 July (1-5). Adm £3.50, chd free. Home-made teas at village Green Tea Room.

Old fashioned cottage garden. Walled herbaceous border, well stocked shrubbery, many old roses, kitchen garden, summerhouse and greenhouse. Secret fernery and courtyard, herb garden. Plant and other garden stalls on the village green.

✿ ☕

Donations from the NGS enable Perennial to care for horticulturalists

Sycamores House

(1-5). Combined adm with Home Farm House, 17 Main Street £4, chd free. Home-made teas. **Visits also by arrangement May to Aug for groups 10+.** Small cottage garden packed full with colourful informal planting. A pebble beach that replaces the lawn, mosaics, water features, and a brick well all add unique interest. There is a decked seating area and summerhouse. A wildlife stream, installed in 2013, meanders down to a pond and bog garden. A woodland area leads to herbs, fruit bushes and hens. Art studio will be open. Paintings and art cards designed by Julie and photos by Richard will be on sale.

50 RHUBARB FARM

Hardwick Street, Langwith, Mansfield, NG20 9DR. Community Interest Company, www.rhubarbfarm.co.uk. *On NW border of Nottinghamshire in village of Nether Langwith. From A632 in Langwith, by bridge (single file traffic) turn up steep Devonshire Drive. N.B. Turn off SatNav. Take 2nd L into Hardwick St. Rhubarb Farm at end. Parking to R of gates.* **Sun 9 July (10-4). Adm £2.50, chd free. Delicious cream teas and locally made cakes/biscuits. Visits also by arrangement June to Oct, min group size 15.**
52 varieties of fruit and vegetables organically grown not only for sale but for therapeutic benefit. This 2 acre social enterprise provides training and volunteering opportunities to 50 ex offenders, drug and alcohol misusers, and people with mental and physical ill health and disability. Timed tours at 10.30am, 12.30pm and 2.30pm. 3x 65ft polytunnels, outdoor classroom, willow domes and willow arches, 150 hens, sensory garden, watercress bed, outdoor pizza ovens, comfrey bed and comfrey fertiliser factory, composting toilet. Chance to meet and chat with volunteers who come to gain skills, confidence and training. Main path down site suitable for wheelchairs but bumpy. Not all of site accessible, or easy for wheelchairs. Composting toilet wheelchair accessible.

51 RISEHOLME, 125 SHELFORD ROAD

Radcliffe on Trent, NG12 1AZ. John & Elaine Walker, 01159 119867. *4m E of Nottingham. From A52 follow signs to Radcliffe. In village centre take turning for Shelford (by Co-op). Approx ¾ m on L.* **Evening opening Wed 19 July (6-9). Adm £4, chd free. Wine. Sun 17 Sept (2-5). Adm £3, chd free. Home-made teas. Visits also by arrangement May to Sept for groups 10+. Adm £3.50, refreshments extra.**
Imaginative and inspirational is how the garden has been described by many visitors. Colour and texture are important aspects of the planting using a huge variety of perennials, grasses, shrubs and trees. Fun jungle area, tender perennials particularly salvias thrive in raised beds and in gravel garden with stream. Unique garden mirrors and other interesting objects complement planting.

52 ROSE COTTAGE

81 Nottingham Road, Keyworth, Nottingham, NG12 5GS. Richard & Julie Fowkes, rosecottagedesign@yahoo.co.uk. *7m S of Nottingham. Follow signs for Keyworth from A606. Garden (white cottage) on R 100yds after Sainsburys. From A60, follow Keyworth signs & turn L at church, garden is 400yds on L.* **Sun 4 June**

53 SYCAMORES HOUSE

Salmon Lane, Annesley Woodhouse, Nottingham, NG17 9HB. Lynne & Barrie Jackson, 01623 750466, landbjackson@gmail.com, www.sycamoreshouse.weebly.com. *From M1 J27 follow Mansfield signs to Badger Box T-lights. Turn L. Gate on L just past 'No footway for 600 yds' sign.* **Sun 30 Apr (2-6). Adm £3, chd free. Home-made teas. Visits also by arrangement Apr to June for groups 10+ from mid April (adults only).**
A grassy field in 2005, this 1⅓ acre plantsman's garden now comprises a range of growing environments incl a large, productive, organic vegetable garden, polytunnel and orchard. Visitors will discover the secret pathways and quirky ideas along with the glass garden art. All plants are named to interest experienced gardeners with good ideas for the novice. More information available at https://www.facebook.com/Sycamores-House-Garden-225493997826406/. Children's trail for under 5s. Refreshments under cover. Garden suitable for wheelchair users . Couple of short steep slopes. Gravel paths nr house, grass further down. Ramp available for entrance steps.

54 THRUMPTON HALL

Thrumpton, NG11 0AX.
Miranda Seymour,
www.thrumptonhall.com. *7m
S of Nottingham. M1 J24 take
A453 towards Nottingham. Turn
L to Thrumpton village & cont to
Thrumpton Hall.* Sun 28 May (2-5).
Adm £5, chd free. Tea.
2 acres incl lawns, rare trees,
lakeside walks, flower borders, rose
garden and box bordered sunken
herb garden, all enclosed by C18 ha-
ha and encircling a Jacobean house.
Garden is surrounded by C18
landscaped park and is bordered
by a river. Rare opportunity to visit
Thrumpton Hall (separate ticket).
Jacobean mansion, unique carved
staircase, Great Saloon, State
Bedroom, Priest's Hole.
& 🐕 ✿ ☕ ▱

55 UNIVERSITY PARK GARDENS

Nottingham, NG7 2RD. University
of Nottingham, www.nottingham.
ac.uk/estates/grounds/. *Approx 4m
SW of Nottingham city centre & opp
Queens Medical Centre. NGS visitors:
Please purchase admission tickets
in the Millennium garden (in centre
of campus), signed from N & W
entrances to University Park & within
internal rd network.* Sun 20 Aug
(12.30-4). Adm £3, chd free.
Light refreshments at Lakeside
Arts Centre.
University Park has many beautiful
gardens incl the award winning
Millennium garden with its dazzling
flower garden, timed fountains and
turf maze. Also the huge Lenton Firs
rock garden, the dry garden and the
Jekyll garden. During summer, the
walled garden is alive with exotic
plantings. In total, 300 acres of
landscape and gardens. Picnic area,
cafe, walking tours, accessible minibus
to feature gardens within campus.
Plants for sale in Millennium garden.
Several awards for landscaping
inc Britain in Bloom Public Park
Award and Nottingham in Bloom
competition. Green Flag Award for
University Park for past 14yrs. Some
gravel paths and steep slopes.
& 🐕 ✿ 🚗 🏠 ☕

GROUP OPENING

56 WELLOW VILLAGE GARDENS

Potter Lane, Wellow, Newark,
NG22 0EB. *12m NW of Newark.
Wellow is on A616 between Ollerton
& Newark approx 1m from Ollerton.
Parking available around village green
& as indicated by car park signs.* Sun
9 July (10-5). Combined adm £5,
chd free. Home-made teas in
Wellow Memorial Hall. *Donation
to Wellow Memorial Hall.*

NEW **MAYFIELD**
Leslie & Brenda Acutt.

PARK HOUSE
Pam & Graham Axworthy.

4 POTTER LANE
Anne & Fred Allsop.

TITHE BARN
Andrew & Carrie Young.

Wellow, formerly Wellah, from the
number of wells, has a green and
a famous maypole. Not so well
known is the Wellow Dyke, which
surrounds the village and can still
be seen in some places. Now come
and see some Wellow gardens:
Mayfield. This eclectic garden is both
family and wildlife friendly. The wide
variety of plants is a smorgasbord
of pollen for insects and bees: Park
House. The rear is a lawned area
surrounded by mixed borders
containing roses, perennials and
shrubs plus a patio edged with box.
Mixed border separates the main
garden from the vegetable plot: 4
Potter Lane. Created over more
than 20 yrs, this series of gardens
has a section of the Wellow Dyke
at the top and has a well tended
vegetable garden. Shade garden
at side and colourful pleasure
garden in centre: Tithe Barn. The
approach to this garden between
yew hedges sets the tone to the
wide sweeps of lawn and generous
terrace. Herbaceous beds, roses and
rambling roses. Mature planting of
shrubs and weeping trees.
& ✿ ☕ ▱

57 6 WESTON CLOSE

Woodthorpe, Nottingham,
NG5 4FS. Diane & Steve
Harrington, 0115 9 857506,
mrsdiharrington@gmail.com. *3m
N of Nottingham. A60 Mansfield Rd.
Turn R at T-lights into Woodthorpe
Drive. 2nd L Grange Road. R into The
Crescent. R into Weston Close. Park
in The Crescent.* Sun 25 June (1-5).
Combined adm with The Glade
£5, chd free. Mon 10 July (1-5).
Adm £3, chd free. Home-made
teas. Visits also by arrangement
June to Aug for groups 10+.
Adm £5 incl refreshments.
Set on a substantial slope with
3 separate areas, dense planting
creates a full, varied yet relaxed
display incl many scented roses,
clematis and a collection of over
50 named mature hostas in the
impressive colourful rear garden.
Large plant sale packed with good
value home propagated plants.
Occasional craft stalls. Featured in
Garden Answers and Garden News.
✿ ☕ ▱

58 WOODPECKERS

35 Lambley Lane, Burton Joyce,
Nottingham, NG14 5BG. Lynn
& Mark Carr, 0115 9 313237,
info@woodpeckersdining.co.uk.
*6m N of Nottingham. In Burton
Joyce, turn off A612 (Nottingham
to Southwell rd) into Lambley Lane,
turn L onto private drive to access
gardens. Ample parking.* Sun 21
May (11-5). Adm £4, chd free.
Cream teas. Visits also by
arrangement Feb to Oct (ample
parking).
4 acres of mature woodland and
formal gardens with spectacular
views over the Trent Valley. 500
rhododendrons and azaleas. Scented
rose tunnel leading from the
main lawn to the wisteria arbour.
Balustrade terrace for teas. Glade
with 200yr old cedars overlooking
ponds, waterfalls and croquet
lawn. Bog garden and sunken area
below ha-ha, then onwards towards
ancient well. New glasshouse/
terrace. Gravel and grass paths,
steep slopes.
& 🐕 ✿ ☕ ▱

OXFORDSHIRE

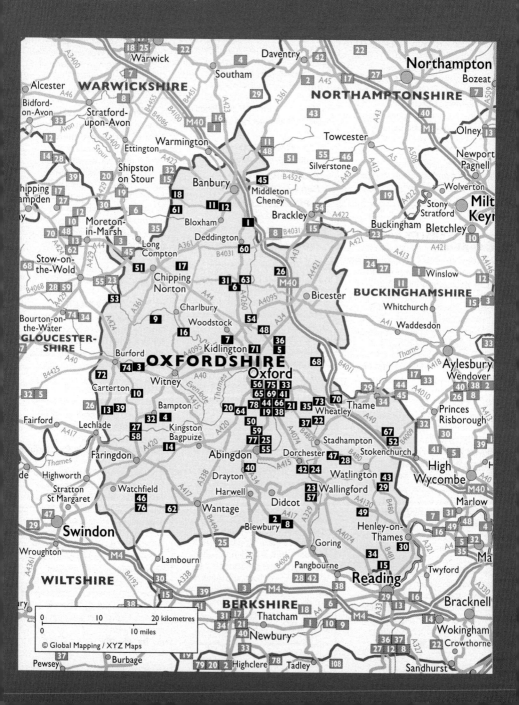

In Oxfordshire we tend to think of ourselves as one of the most landlocked counties, right in the centre of England and furthest from the sea.

We are surrounded by Warwickshire, Northamptonshire, Buckinghamshire, Berkshire, Wiltshire and Gloucestershire, and, like these counties, we benefit from that perfect British climate which helps us create some of the most beautiful and famous gardens in the world.

Many gardens open for Oxfordshire NGS between spring and late-autumn. Amongst these are the perfectly groomed college gardens of Oxford University, and the grounds of stately homes and palaces designed by a variety of the famous garden designers such as William Kent, Capability Brown and Harold Peto, Rosemary Verey, Tom Stuart-Smith and the Bannermans of more recent fame.

But we are also a popular tourist destination for our honey-coloured mellow Cotswold stone villages, and for the Thames which has its spring near Lechlade. More villages open as 'groups' for the NGS in Oxfordshire than in any other county, and offer tea, hospitality, advice and delight with their infinite variety of gardens.

All this enjoyment benefits the excellent causes that the NGS supports.

Volunteers

County Organisers
Marina Hamilton-Baillie
01367 710486
marina_hamilton_baillie@hotmail.com

David White
01295 812679
david.white@doctors.org.uk

County Treasurer
David White
(as above)

Publicity
Priscilla Frost
01608 810578
info@oxconf.co.uk

Social Media
Lara Cowan
lara.cowan@ngs.org.uk

Booklet Co-ordinator
Catherine Pinney
01491 612638

Assistant County Organisers
Lynn Baldwin
01608 642754
elynnbaldwin@gmail.com

Lara Cowan
(as above)

Petra Hoyer Millar
01869 338156
petra.hoyermillar@ngs.org.uk

John & Joan Pumfrey
01189 722848
joanpumfrey@lineone.net

Charles & Lyn Sanders
01865 739486
sandersc4@hotmail.com

© Andrew Lawson

Left: Broughton Castle

OPENING DATES

All entries subject to change. For latest information check **www.ngs.org.uk**

Map locator numbers are shown to the right of each garden name.

February

Snowdrop Festival

Sunday 12th
Stonehaven 64

Sunday 19th
Hollyhocks 36

March

Sunday 5th
Lime Close 40

Sunday 26th
Monks Head 48
Trinity College 65

April

Sunday 2nd
Buckland Lakes 14

Sunday 9th
Ashbrook House 2
Wadham College 69

Sunday 16th
◆ Waterperry
Gardens 70

Monday 17th
Kencot Gardens 39

Sunday 23rd
Church Farm Field 18
Hilltop Cottage 35
Magdalen College 41
Upper Green 68

Saturday 29th
50 Plantation Road 56

Sunday 30th
Adderbury Gardens 1
Broughton Grange 12
Hollyhocks 36
Monks Head 48
50 Plantation Road 56

May

Monday 1st
Hollyhocks 36
Monks Head 48
Sparsholt Manor 62

Saturday 6th
50 Plantation Road 56

Sunday 7th
50 Plantation Road 56

Sunday 14th
Meadow Cottage 43
Steeple Aston Gardens 63

Saturday 20th
◆ Blenheim Palace 7
Bolters Farm 9

Sunday 21st
Bolters Farm 9
Broughton Poggs &
Filkins Gardens 13
Charlbury Gardens 16
NEW Dobsons 23
The Grove 31
Headington Gardens 33
Midsummer House 46
NEW The Priory 57
Woolstone Mill House 76

90th Anniversary Weekend

Sunday 28th
Barton Abbey 6
Wolfson College 75

Monday 29th
Church Farm Field 18
Friars Court 27

June

Thursday 1st
Old Whitehill Barn 54

Sunday 4th
Cumnor Village
Gardens 20
Failford 25
Lime Close 40
NEW 116 Oxford Road 55
Wayside 71
Whitehill Farm 74

Thursday 8th
Old Whitehill Barn 54

Sunday 11th
Iffley Gardens 38
Manor House 42

Wednesday 14th
◆ Nuffield Place 49

Thursday 15th
Upper Chalford Farm 67

Saturday 17th
Field Cottage 26

Sunday 18th
Asthall Manor 3
Blewbury Gardens 8
Brize Norton Gardens 10
Corpus Christi College 19
Field Cottage 26
Middleton Cheney
Gardens 45

Tuesday 20th
◆ Greys Court 30

Wednesday 21st
Greenfield Farm 29

Saturday 24th
NEW Satin Lane
Allotments 60

Sunday 25th
Old Boars Hill Gardens 50
The Old Vicarage 52
The Old Vicarage,
Bledington 53
Sibford Gardens 61
Wheatley Gardens 73

Thursday 29th
Wootton Gardens 77

Placketts, Adderbury Gardens

THE GARDENS

GROUP OPENING

1 ADDERBURY GARDENS
Adderbury, OX17 3LS. *3m S of Banbury. Adderbury is on A4260. At The Green turn into village.* **Sun 30 Apr (2-5.30). Combined adm £5, chd free. Home-made teas at Church House (Library), High St.** *Donation to Katharine House Hospice.*

THE OLD VICARAGE
Christine & Peter Job.

PLACKETTS
Dr D White.

Attractive Ironstone village, with gardens ranging from quite small to very large. The Old Vicarage walled front garden, large rear garden stretching from ha-ha to small lake and flood meadows. Unusual plants and trees. Japanese maple plantation.

Placketts ⅕ acre walled garden with sheltered gravel courtyard, main garden exposed with views. Plethora of colourful plants throughout the yr with much colour in spring. Restricted access at Placketts. Dogs allowed at The Old Vicarage only.
&. ☕

2 ASHBROOK HOUSE
Blewbury, OX11 9QA. Mr & Mrs S A Barrett. *4m SE of Didcot. Turn off A417 in Blewbury into Westbrook St. 1st house on R. Follow yellow signs for parking in Boham's Rd.* **Sun 9 Apr, Sun 10 Sept (2-5.30). Adm £4, chd free. Home-made teas.** The garden where Kenneth Grahame read Wind in the Willows to local children and where he took inspiration for his description of the oak doors to Badger's House. Come and see, you may catch a glimpse of Toad and friends in this 3½ acre chalk and water garden in a beautiful spring line village. In spring the banks are a mass of daffodils and in late summer the borders are full of unusual plants.
&. 🐕 ☕

3 ASTHALL MANOR
Asthall, Burford, OX18 4HW. Rosanna Pearson, www.onformsculpture.co.uk/ asthall-manor. *3m E of Burford. Going from Witney to Burford on A40, turn R at r'about. Coming from Chipping Norton, come through Shipton-under-Wychwood & Swinbrook. The nearest bus stop (a 10 min walk) is on route 233.* **Sun 18 June (2-6). Adm £5, chd free. Light refreshments.** 6 acres of dramatic planting surround this C17 Cotswolds manor house (not open), once home to the Mitford family. The gardens, designed by I & J Bannerman in 1998, offer 'a beguiling mix of traditional and contemporary' as described by the Good Gardens Guide. Exuberant scented borders, sloping box parterres, wild flowers, a gypsy wagon, a turf sculpture and a hidden lake all contribute to the mix. Partial wheelchair access.
&. ✿ ☕

4 ASTON POTTERY

Aston, Bampton, OX18 2BT. Mr Stephen Baughan, www.astonpottery.co.uk. *On the B4449 between Bampton & Standlake. 4m S of Witney.* **Sun 27, Mon 28 Aug (12-5). Adm by donation. Light refreshments in the café.**

5 stunning borders flower from June until November, set around Aston Pottery's Gift Shop and Cafe. Featuring a 72 metre hornbeam walk with summerhouse and over 200 perennials, a 60 metre hot bank with kniphofia, alstroemeria, canna lilies, bananas and salvias, a double dahlia border with over 600 dahlias, agapanthus, asters and grasses, and a multi-layered traditional perennial border. Finally an 80 metre x 7 metre deep border full with over 5000 annuals and more than 180 types. Featured in the gardening section of The Telegraph.

AVON DASSETT GARDENS

See Warwickshire

5 NEW BANNISTERS

Middle Street, Islip, Kidlington, OX5 2SF. Wendy Price. *2m E of Kidlington & approx 5m N of Oxford. From A34, exit Bletchingdon & Islip. B4027 direction Islip, turn L into Middle St, beside Great Barn.* **Sun 3 Sept (2-5.30). Combined adm with Hollyhocks £5, chd free.**

Perennials and grasses, naturalistic planting contrasted with trained fruit trees and shrubs. A contemporary interpretation of an old garden. Gravel paths and some shallow steps.

6 BARTON ABBEY

Steeple Barton, OX25 4QS. Mr & Mrs P Fleming. *8m E of Chipping Norton. On B4030, ½ m from junction of A4260 & B4030.* **Sun 28 May (2-5). Adm £5, chd free. Home-made teas.**

15 acre garden with views from house (not open) across sweeping lawns and picturesque lake. Walled garden with herbaceous borders, separated by established yew hedges and espalier fruit, contrasts with more informal woodland garden paths with vistas of specimen trees and meadows.

Working glasshouses and fine display of fruit and vegetables.

7 ◆ BLENHEIM PALACE

Woodstock, OX20 1PX. His Grace the Duke of Marlborough, 01993 810530, operations@blenheimpalace.com, www.blenheimpalace.com. *8m N of Oxford. Bus: S3 Oxford-Chipping Norton, alight Woodstock.* **For NGS: Sat 20 May (10-6). Adm £4, chd £2. Light refreshments. For other opening times and information, please phone, email or visit garden website.**

Blenheim Gardens, originally laid out by Henry Wise, incl the formal Water Terraces and Italian Garden by Achille Duchêne, Rose Garden, Arboretum, and Cascade. The Secret Garden offers a stunning garden paradise in all seasons. Blenheim Lake, created by Capability Brown and spanned by Vanburgh's Grand Bridge, is the focal point of over 2,000 acres of landscaped parkland. The Pleasure Gardens complex incl the Herb and Lavender Garden and Butterfly House. Other activities incl the Marlborough Maze, adventure play area, giant chess and draughts. Some gravel paths, terrain can be uneven in places, incl some steep slopes. Dogs allowed in park only.

GROUP OPENING

8 BLEWBURY GARDENS

Blewbury, OX11 9QB. *4m SE of Didcot. On A417. Follow yellow signs for car parks.* **Sun 18 June (2-6). Combined adm £5, chd free.** Home-made teas at Blewbury Manor, all proceeds to the NGS.

BLEWBURY MANOR
Mr & Mrs M R Blythe.

BROOKS END
Jean & David Richards.

GREEN BUSHES
Phil Rogers.

HALL BARN
Malcolm & Deirdre Cochrane.

STOCKS
Norma & Richard Bird.

As celebrated by Rachel de Thame in Gardener's World, 5 gardens in charming downland village. Blewbury Manor with moat and 10 acre garden. Features incl; parterre, flower garden, herbaceous and mixed borders, pergola, vegetable, herb garden, stream planting, woodland, lake, sunken gravel garden, and courtyard. Brooks End a 1960s bungalow with colour themed beds, damp border, hidden garden, small orchard, shady border, greenhouse and vegetable garden. Green Bushes created by plant lover Rhon (dec'd 2007) around C15 cottage (not open); colour themed borders, ponds and poolside planting, ferns, pleached limes and roses. Hall Barn, 4 acres with traditional herbaceous borders, kitchen garden, croquet lawn, C16 dovecote, thatched cob wall and chalk stream. Stocks an early cruck-constructed thatched cottage, surrounded by densely planted lime tolerant herbaceous perennials offering tiers of colour yr-round. Plant stall in the car park by Edulis Plant Nursery. Wheelchair access to some gardens.

9 BOLTERS FARM

Chilson, Pudlicote Lane, Chipping Norton, OX7 3HU. Robert & Mandy Cooper, 07778 476517, art@amandacooper.co.uk. *Centre of Chilson village. On arrival in the hamlet of Chilson, heading N, we are the last in an old row of cottages on R with old white gates. Please drive past & park on the L in the lane.* **Sat 20 May (2-6). Tea. Sun 21 May (2-6). Tea. Also open Charlbury Gardens. Evening opening Sun 3 Sept (6-8). Wine. Adm £5, chd free. Gluten free options available. Visits also by arrangement Mar to Sept for groups of 20 max.** *Donation to Hands Up Foundation.*

A cherished old cottage garden restored over the last 10 yrs. Tumbly moss covered walls and sloping lawns down to a stream with natural planting and character. Wheelchairs have to negotiate sloping deep gravel!

GROUP OPENING

10 BRIZE NORTON GARDENS

Brize Norton, OX18 3LY.
www.bncommunity.org/ngs.
3m SW of Witney. Brize Norton Village, S of A40, between Witney & Burford. Parking at Elderbank Hall and various locations in village. Coaches welcome with plenty of parking nearby. **Sun 18 June (2-6). Combined adm £4.50, chd free. Home-made teas at Elderbank Village Hall.**

BARNSTABLE HOUSE
Mr & Mrs P Butcher,
www.ourgarden.org.uk.

CHURCH FARM HOUSE
Philip & Mary Holmes.

CLUMBER
Mr & Mrs S Hawkins.

3 DAUBIGNY MEAD
Mrs Denise Merriman.

GRANGE FARM
Mark & Lucy Artus.

MIJESHE
Mr & Mrs M Harper.

95 STATION ROAD
Mr & Mrs P A Timms.

STONE COTTAGE
Mr & Mrs K Humphris.

Doomsday village on the edge of the Cotswold's offering a number of gardens open for your enjoyment. You can see a wide variety of planting incl ornamental trees, herbaceous borders, ornamental grasses and traditional fruit and vegetable gardens. Features incl a Mediterranean style patio, courtyard garden, water features, plus gardens where you can just sit, relax and enjoy the day. Plants will be available for sale at individual gardens. A Flower Festival will take place in the Brize Norton St Britius Church. Partial wheelchair access to some gardens.

Waterperry Gardens

© Andrew Lawson

11 ◆ BROUGHTON CASTLE

Banbury, OX15 5EB. Lord Saye and Sele, 01295 276070, info@broughtoncastle.com, www.broughtoncastle.com. 2½m SW of Banbury. On Shipston-on-Stour road (B4035). **For NGS: Sun 23 July (2-5). Adm £5, chd free. Light refreshments. For other opening times and information, please phone, email or visit garden website.**
1 acre; shrubs, herbaceous borders, walled garden, roses, climbers seen against background of C14-C16 castle surrounded by moat in open parkland. House also open (additional charge).

♿ 🐄 🚗 ☕

12 BROUGHTON GRANGE

Wykham Lane, Broughton, Banbury, OX15 5DS. S Hester, www.broughtongrange.com. ¼m out of village. From Banbury take B4035 to Broughton. Turn L at Saye & Sele Arms PH up Wykham Lane (one way). Follow road out of village for ¼m. Entrance on R. **Sun 30 Apr, Sun 23 July, Sun 10 Sept (10-5). Adm £7, chd free. Home-made teas.**
An impressive 25 acres of gardens and light woodland in an attractive Oxfordshire setting. The centrepiece is a large terraced walled garden created by Tom Stuart-Smith in 2001. Vision has been used to blend the gardens into the countryside. Good early displays of bulbs followed by outstanding herbaceous planting in summer. Formal and informal areas combine to make this a special site incl newly laid arboretum with many ongoing projects.

✿ 🚗 🅓 ☕

GROUP OPENING

13 BROUGHTON POGGS & FILKINS GARDENS

Lechlade, GL7 3JH. www.filkins.org.uk. 3m N of Lechlade. 5m S of Burford. Just off A361 between Burford & Lechlade on the B4477. Map of the gardens available. **Sun 21 May (2-6).**

Combined adm £5.50, chd free. Home-made teas in Filkins Village Hall.

BROUGHTON HALL
Karen & Ian Jobling.

BROUGHTON POGGS MILL
Charlie & Avril Payne.

THE CORN BARN
Ms Alexis Thompson.

FIELD COTTAGE
Peter & Sheila Gray.

FILKINS ALLOTMENTS
Filkins Allotments.

FILKINS HALL
Filkins Hall Residents.

LITTLE PEACOCKS
Colvin & Moggridge.

PEACOCK FARMHOUSE
Pauline & Peter Care.

PIGEON COTTAGE
Lynne Savege.

PIP COTTAGE
G B Woodin.

THE TALLOT
Ms M Swann & Mr Don Stowell.

11 gardens and flourishing allotments in these beautiful and vibrant Cotswold stone twin villages. Scale and character vary from the grand landscape setting of Filkins Hall and the equally extensive but more intimate Broughton Hall, to the small but action packed Pigeon Cottage and The Tallot. Broughton Poggs Mill has a rushing mill stream with an exciting bridge; Pip Cottage combines topiary, box hedges and a fine rural view. In these and the other equally exciting gardens horticultural interest abounds. Features incl plant stall by professional local nursery, Swinford Museum of Cotswolds tools and artefacts, and Cotswold Woollen Weavers. Many gardens have gravel driveways, but most are suitable for wheelchair access. Most gardens welcome dogs on leads.

♿ 🐄 ✿ 🚗 ☕

14 BUCKLAND LAKES

Nr Faringdon, SN7 8QW. The Wellesley Family. 3m NE of Faringdon. Buckland is midway between Oxford (14m) & Swindon (15m), just off the A420. Faringdon 3m, Witney 8m. Follow the yellow NGS signs which will lead you to driveway & car park by St Mary's Church. **Sun 2 Apr (2-5). Adm £5, chd free. Home-made teas at Memorial Hall. Donation to RWMT (community bus).**
Descend down wooded path to two large secluded lakes with views over undulating historic parkland, designed by Georgian landscape architect Richard Woods. Picturesque mid C18 rustic icehouse, cascade with iron footbridge, thatched boathouse and round house, and renovated exedra. Many fine mature trees, drifts of spring bulbs and daffodils amongst shrubs. Norman church adjoins. Cotswold village. Children must be supervised due to large expanse of unfenced open water.

🐄 🚗 ☕

15 CHALKHOUSE GREEN FARM

Chalkhouse Green, Kidmore End, Reading, RG4 9AL. Mr & Mrs J Hall, 01189 723631, www.chgfarm.com. 2m N of Reading, 5m SW of Henley-on-Thames. Situated between A4074 & B481. From Kidmore End take Chalkhouse Green Rd. Follow NGS yellow signs. **Sun 2 July (2-6). Adm £3, chd free. Home-made teas. Visits also by arrangement Apr to Sept.**
1 acre garden and open traditional farmstead. Herbaceous borders, herb garden, shrubs, old fashioned roses, trees incl medlar, quince and mulberries, walled ornamental kitchen garden. New cherry orchard. Rare breed farm animals incl British White cattle, Suffolk Punch horses, donkeys, Berkshire pigs, chickens, ducks and turkeys. Plant and jam stall, donkey and pony rides, swimming in covered pool, trailer rides, farm trail, heavy horse and mule demonstrations, bee display. Partial wheelchair access.

♿ ✿ ☕

GROUP OPENING

16 CHARLBURY GARDENS

Charlbury, OX7 3PP. *6m SE of Chipping Norton. Large Cotswold village on B4022 Witney-Enstone Rd.* **Sun 21 May (2-5). Combined adm £5, chd free. Home-made teas in St Mary's Church. Also open Bolters Farm.**

GOTHIC HOUSE
Mr & Mrs Andrew Lawson.

THE PRIORY GARDEN
Dr D El Kabir & Colleagues.

2 varied gardens in the centre of this large Cotswold village, in the context of traditional stone houses. Gothic House with ⅓ acre walled garden designed with sculpture and colour in mind. New area of planted squares replaces lawn. False perspective, pleached lime walk, trellis, terracotta containers. The Priory Garden has 1 acre of formal terraced topiary gardens with Italianate features. Foliage colour schemes, shrubs, parterres with fragrant plants, old roses, water features, sculpture and inscriptions aim to produce a poetic, wistful atmosphere. Arboretum of over 3 acres borders the R Evenlode and incl wildlife garden and pond.

♿ ✿ ☕ ⛳

17 CHIVEL FARM

Heythrop, OX7 5TR. Mr & Mrs J D Sword, 01608 683227, rosalind.sword@btinternet.com. *4m E of Chipping Norton. Off A361 or A44.* **Visits by arrangement May to Sept, with adm dependent on group size. Light refreshments.**
Beautifully designed country garden with extensive views, designed for continuous interest that is always evolving. Colour schemed borders with many unusual trees, shrubs and herbaceous plants. Small formal white garden and a conservatory.

♿ ☕

18 CHURCH FARM FIELD

Church Lane, Epwell, Banbury, OX15 6LD. Mrs D V D Castle. *7½ m W of Banbury on N side of Epwell village.* **Sun 23 Apr, Mon 29 May, Mon 28 Aug, Sun 8 Oct (2-6). Adm £2, chd free. Home-made teas.**
Woods, arboretum with wild flowers (planting started 1992), over 90 different trees and shrubs in 4½ acres. Paths cut through trees for access to various parts. Lawn tennis court and croquet lawns. Light refreshments (weather permitting).

☕

19 CORPUS CHRISTI COLLEGE

Merton Street, Oxford, OX1 4JF. Domestic Bursar, www.ccc.ox.ac.uk. *Entrance from Merton St.* **Sun 18 June (2-6). Adm £2, chd free. Home-made teas in College Hall.**
David Leake, the College gardener since 1979, avoiding chemicals and sprays, has created a marvellous wild garden by blending a huge range of wild and cultivated flowers into a vivid, yet harmonious, landscape. In amongst beautiful buildings and with wonderful views of Christ Church meadows from the mound beside the ancient town wall, the Corpus garden is a real treasure. 2017 marks the 500th anniversary of the founding of the College. The garden incl one slope.

♿ 🐄 ☕

GROUP OPENING

20 CUMNOR VILLAGE GARDENS

Leys Road, Cumnor, Oxford, OX2 9QF. *4m W of central Oxford. From A420, exit for Cumnor & follow B4017 into the village. Parking on road & side roads, behind PO, or behind village hall in Leys Rd. Additional parking in Bertie & Norreys Rd.* **Sun 4 June (2-6). Combined adm £5, chd free. Home-made teas in United Reformed Church Hall, Leys Road.**

36 BERTIE ROAD
Esther & Neil Whiting.
🏴

10 LEYS ROAD
Penny & Nick Bingham.

41 LEYS ROAD
Philip & Jennie Powell.

STONEHAVEN
Dr Dianne & Prof Keith Gull.
(See separate entry)

1 THE WINNYARDS
Brenda & Roy Darnell.

Five gardens of varying styles in attractive village setting. 10 Leys Road, long narrow cottage garden with a wide variety of shrubs and trees with many interesting and unusual perennials. 41 Leys Road, ¾ acre plot including C16 cottage (not open) with flower and fruit garden, orchard, large vegetable garden, mature trees and wild flowers. 1 The Winnyards, a medium sized garden planted for yr-long interest, plus a water feature, pergola and open views across a meadow. 36 Bertie Road, a small professionally designed garden, structured layout of three rooms, pergola, raised vegetable bed, relaxed planting style with emphasis on form and texture. Stonehaven, front garden partially gravelled, side courtyard has pots, rear garden overlooks meadows. Unusual plants, many with black or bronze foliage, old apple trees, wildlife pond. Japanese influence. Wheelchair access to 1 The Winnyards and 36 Bertie Road. Partial access to Stonehaven due to pebbles. WC facilities in United Reformed Church Hall.

✿ ☕

The National Garden Scheme is the largest single funder of the Queen's Nursing Institute

© Andrew Lawson

Gothic House, Charlbury Gardens

21 103 DENE ROAD

Headington, Oxford, OX3 7EQ.
Mr & Mrs Steve & Mary
Woolliams, 01865 764153,
stevewoolliams@gmail.com. *S
Headington nr Nuffield. Dene Rd
accessed from The Slade from the
N, or from Hollow Way from the
S. Both access roads are B4495.
Garden on sharp bend.* **Visits by
arrangement Apr to Aug for
groups of 10 max, children very
welcome. Adm £3, chd free.
Home-made teas.**
A surprising eco-friendly garden
with borrowed view over the Lye
Valley Nature Reserve. Lawns, a wild
flower meadow, pond and large
kitchen garden are incl in a suburban
60ft x 120ft sloping garden. Fruit
trees, soft fruit and mixed borders
of shrubs, hardy perennials, grasses
and bulbs, designed for seasonal
colour. This garden has been noted
for its wealth of wildlife incl a
variety of birds and butterflies and
other insects, incl the rare Brown
Hairstreak butterfly and the rare
Currant Clearwing moth.

22 DENTON HOUSE

Denton, Oxford, OX44 9JF.
Mr & Mrs Luke, 01865 874440,
waveney@jandwluke.com. *In
a valley between Garsington &
Cuddesdon.* **Sun 30 July (1.30-6).
Adm £5, chd free. Home-made
teas. Visits also by arrangement
May to Oct for any group size
up to 30 max. Refreshments on
request.**
Large walled garden surrounds a
Georgian mansion (not open), with
shaded areas, walks, topiary and
many interesting mature trees. Large
lawns and herbaceous borders and

rose beds. The windows in the wall
were taken in 1864 from Brasenose
College Chapel and Library. Wild
garden and a further walled fruit
garden.

23 DOBSONS

Sotwell Street, Brightwell-cum-
Sotwell, Wallingford, OX10 0RH.
Anne Salisbury. *From Wallingford,
enter Brightwell-cum-Sotwell, go
through S bend. Dobsons is 50yds
on L. From Didcot, enter at 1st
sign to Brightwell-cum-Sotwell, go
through village, past the Red Lion PH,
Dobsons is on R.* **Sun 21 May (1-
5.30). Combined adm with The
Priory £5, chd free. Home-made
teas in cottage garden, 50yds
away.**
Dobsons (not open) has C16
origins; gardens are surrounded by
brick and flint walls that dated by
members of the Dobson family.
Pretty, old walled garden restored
over last 4 yrs with yr-round interest
with three distinct areas separated
by beech hedges; formal lawn
with herbaceous border, orchard
being regenerated with trees
underplanted with daffodils, and a
box knot garden. Mostly level with a
few shallow steps.

GROUP OPENING

24 DORCHESTER GARDENS

Dorchester-On-Thames,
Wallingford, OX10 7HZ. *Off
A4074 signed to Dorchester.
Parking at Bridge Meadow, at SE
end of Dorchester Bridge. Disabled
parking at 26 Manor Farm Road
(OX10 7HZ). Tickets available at*
26 Manor Farm Road (OX10 7HZ),
6 Monks Close (OX10 7JA), & 7
Rotten Row (OX10 7LJ). **Sat 8 July
(2-5). Combined adm £5, chd
free. Tea in Dorchester Abbey
Guesthouse.**

26 MANOR FARM ROAD
David & Judy Parker.

6 MONKS CLOSE
Leif & Petronella Rasmussen.

7 ROTTEN ROW
Michael & Veronica Evans.

Three contrasting gardens in
a historic village surround the
Medieval abbey, the scene of many
Midsomer Murders. 26 Manor Farm
Road was part of an old, neglected
garden which now has a formal
lawn and planting, vegetable garden
and greenhouse. From the yew
hedge down towards the R Thame
which often floods in winter is an
apple orchard underplanted with
spring bulbs. 6 Monks Close is idyllic
and surprising. A small spring-fed
stream and sloping lawn surrounded
by naturalistic planting runs down
to a monastic fish pond. Bridges
over this deep pond lead to the R
Thame with steep banks, children
should be accompanied. 7 Rotten
Row is Dorchester's lawnless garden,
a terrace with borders leads to a
lovely geometric garden supervised
by a statue of Hebe. Access is from
the allotments.

25 FAILFORD

118 Oxford Road, Abingdon,
OX14 2AG. Miss R Aylward. *118
is on the LH-side of Oxford Rd when
approaching from Abingdon town, or
on the RH-side when approaching
from the N. Entrance to this garden
is via 116 Oxford Rd.* **Sun 4 June
(11-4.30). Combined adm with
116 Oxford Road £3, chd free.
Home-made teas.**
This town garden won Abingdon
in Bloom best large back garden
competition. Both formal and
informal areas, an extension of the
home. Walkways through shaded
area, arches, kitchen garden, grasses,

roses, topiaries, acers, hostas, and heucheras. A wide variety of planting and features within an area 570 sq ft. Partial wheelchair access.

26 FIELD COTTAGE
Fritwell Road, Fewcott, Bicester, OX27 7NZ. Mrs Wendy Farha. *Follow public footpath sign, turning up drive past The Old Schoolhouse. Field Cottage is at the top of this drive & through the far gate on R.* **Sat 17, Sun 18 June (10.30-4). Adm £3.50, chd free. Light refreshments in wooden lodge on-site.**
1 acre organic garden with perennial borders and specimen bushes and trees. Eco-friendly techniques employed to encourage a variety of wildlife and birds. Green roof primarily of sedum to counter balance the emissions from the main house heating system. Wildlife pond and wild flower bund to compliment the eco-friendly ethos. A series of woodchip and garden paths surround the garden with large lawn area for viewing borders.

27 FRIARS COURT
Clanfield, OX18 2SU. Charles Willmer, www.friarscourt.com. *5m N of Faringdon. On A4095 Faringdon to Witney. ½ m S of Clanfield.* **Mon 29 May (2-6). Adm £4, chd free. Cream teas.**
3 acres of formal and informal gardens are within the remaining arms of a C16 moat, which partially surrounds the large C17 Cotswold stone farmhouse (not open). Three bridges span the water and beyond the moat is a woodland walk. A level path goes around the main gardens.

THE GRANARY
See Warwickshire

28 THE GRANGE
Berrick Road, Chalgrove, Oxford, OX44 7RQ. Mrs Vicky Farren, 01865 400883, vickyfarren@mac.com. *12m E of Oxford & 4m from Watlington off B480.* **Visits by arrangement June to Sept. Adm £5, chd free. Home-made teas.**

10 acre plot with an evolving garden incl herbaceous borders and a prairie with many grasses inspired by the Dutch style. Lake with bridges and an island, a brook running through the garden, wild flower meadow, a further pond, arboretum, old orchard and vegetable garden. There is deep water and bridges may be slippery when wet. Grass paths.

29 GREENFIELD FARM
Christmas Common, Nr Watlington, OX49 5HG. Andrew & Jane Ingram, 01491 612434, andrew@andrewbingram.com. *4m from J5 of M40, 7m from Henley. J5 M40, A40 towards Oxford for ½ m, turn L signed Christmas Common. ¾ m past Fox & Hounds PH, turn L at Tree Barn sign.* **Evening opening Wed 21 June (6-8). Adm £4, chd free. Visits also by arrangement May to Sept for groups of 8+.**
10 acre wild flower meadow surrounded by woodland, established 18 yrs ago under the Countryside Stewardship Scheme. Traditional Chiltern chalkland meadow in beautiful peaceful setting with 100 species of perennial wild flowers, grasses and 5 species of orchids. ½ m walk from parking area to meadow. Opportunity to return via typical Chiltern beechwood. A guided tour at 6pm, the tour will last approx 2hrs, and is 1½ m long.

30 ◆ GREYS COURT
Rotherfield Greys, Henley-on-Thames, RG9 4PG. National Trust, 01491 628529, www.nationaltrust.org.uk/greys-court. *2m W of Henley-on-Thames. From Nettlebed mini-r'about on A4130 take B481 & property is signed to the L after approx 3m.* **For NGS: Tue 20 June (10-5). Adm £4, chd £2. For other opening times and information, please phone or visit garden website.**
The tranquil gardens cover 9 acres and surround a Tudor house with many alterations, as well as a Donkey Wheel and Tower. They incl lawns, a maze and small arboretum. The highlights are the

series of enchanting walled gardens, a colourful patchwork of interest set amid Medieval walls. Meet the gardeners and volunteers who look after the gardens. Tea, coffee, lunches and afternoon teas served in The Cowshed. Partial wheelchair access. Loose gravel paths, slopes and some cobbles in garden.

31 THE GROVE
North Street, Middle Barton, Chipping Norton, OX7 7BZ. Ivor & Barbara Hill. *7m E Chipping Norton. On B4030, 2m from junction A4260 & B4030, opp Carpenters Arms PH. Parking in street.* **Sun 21 May (1.30-5). Adm £3, chd free. Home-made teas.**
Mature informal plantsman's ⅓ acre garden, planted for yr-round interest around C19 Cotswold stone cottage (not open). Numerous borders with wide variety of unusual shrubs, trees and hardy plants; several species weigela syringa viburnum and philadelphus. Pond area, well stocked greenhouse. Plant list and garden history available. Home-made preserves for sale. Wheelchair access to most of garden.

32 HAM COURT
Ham Court Farm, Weald, Bampton, OX18 2HG. Emma Bridgewater & Matthew Rice. *Drive through the village towards Clanfield. The drive is exactly opp Weald St.* **Sun 9 July (10-4). Adm £5, chd free. Tea.**
It is unusual to find a stone farmhouse in Oxfordshire with no garden at all. More unusually Ham Court was once the gate house of a major C14 castle. Emma Bridgewater and Matthew Rice have been making painfully slow progress in the project of putting this to rights. Beginning to dig a moat, planting thousands of trees, hiding thousands of tonnes of rubble and laying down the plans for their future garden. This is an opportunity to come and see work in progress, but at the very least give you a warm feeling that they, not you, have taken on such a ridiculous project.

GROUP OPENING

33 HEADINGTON GARDENS

Old Headington, OX3 9BT. *2m E from centre of Oxford. After T-lights in the centre of Headington heading towards Oxford take the 2nd turn on R into Osler Rd. Gardens at end of road in Old Headington, and across the London Rd in Kennett Rd.* **Sun 21 May (2-6). Combined adm £5, chd free. Home-made teas in the cafe at Ruskin College, next door to the vegetable garden.**

THE COACH HOUSE
David & Bryony Rowe.

10 KENNETT ROAD
Linda & David Clover,
01865 765881,
lindaclover@yahoo.co.uk.
Visits also by arrangement for groups of 8 max.

NEW MONCKTON COTTAGE
Julie Harrod & Peter
McCarter, 01865 751471,
petermccarter@msn.com.

40 OSLER ROAD
Nicholas & Pam Coote,
07804 932748,
pamjcoote@gmail.com.
Visits also by arrangement May to Aug.

RUSKIN COLLEGE
Ruskin College, http://
ruskincrinklecrankle.org/.

9 STOKE PLACE
Clive & Veronica Hurst.

WHITE LODGE
Denis & Catharine Macksmith
and Roger & Frances Little.

Situated above Oxford, Headington is an old village with high stone walls, narrow lanes and a Norman church. The 7 gardens offer wide variety. 40 Osler Road is a well-established garden with an Italian theme brimming with exotic planting. White Lodge provides a large park-like setting for a Regency property. The Coach House combines a formal setting with hedges, lawn and flowers and a courtyard with a water garden. 9 Stoke place has a traditional lawn and mixed border on one side and a formal garden on the other. The walled vegetable garden in the grounds of Ruskin College incorporates a Grade II listed Crinkle Crankle Wall with trained fruit trees. Two gardens are new this year. Monckton Cottage is a walled, woodland garden with a meadow area, intriguing topiary, and unusual plants. 10 Kennett Road is a well-planned small garden with lawns surrounded by borders, a pond and fernery, and a greenhouse. Partial wheelchair access to most gardens due to gravel paths and steps.

  ♿ �− ✿ ☕ 🍽

34 HEARNS HOUSE

Gallowstree Common, RG4 9DE.
John & Joan Pumfrey,
01189 722848,
joanpumfrey@lineone.net. *5m N of Reading, 5m W of Henley. From A4074 turn E at Cane End.*
Visits by arrangement with introductory talk by the owner. Adm £4, chd free. Home-made teas.
2 acre garden provides yr-round interest for artists and gardeners with pergolas, crinkle-crankle walls, sculptures and ponds. Inspirational indigenous and exotic planting is designed to suit dry shade under trees, and a hot bank. The nursery is full of wonderful plants propagated from the garden. An almost entirely paved walled garden has many self-seeding plants to give a pretty effect with low maintenance. Groups of gardeners and artists are welcome to enjoy/paint inspirational hard landscaping and planting. Grass lawn access generally, with occasional single steps at terrace.

  ♿ �− ✿ NPC ☕ 🍽

35 HILLTOP COTTAGE

Horton-cum-Studley, Oxford,
OX33 1AU. Professor Sarah
Randolph. *Centre of village on main road. Enter village, R up Horton Hill, Hilltop Cottage on L at the top. Two disabled spaces in lay-by opp, other parking at bottom of hill.*

Sun 23 Apr (2-5). Combined adm with Upper Green £5, chd free. Home-made teas at Studley Barn.
Plantaholic's large cottage garden, with productive vegetable plot, soft fruit and ornamentals. Beds incl herbaceous, shrubbery and prairie look. Small trees incl Acer griseum, Sorbus spp, silver-leaved shrubs. Colour in April with shrubs and a wide range of bulbs. Path with shallow steps.

  ♿ ☕

36 HOLLYHOCKS

North Street, Islip, Kidlington,
OX5 2SQ. Avril Hughes,
01865 377104,
ahollyhocks@btinternet.com.
3m NE of Kidlington. From A34, exit Bletchingdon & Islip. B4027 direction Islip, turn L into North St. **Sun 19 Feb (1.30-4.30). Adm £3, chd free. Home-made teas. Sun 30 Apr (2-5.30); Mon 1 May (1.30-5.30). Combined adm with Monks Head £5, chd free. Sun 3 Sept (2-5.30). Combined adm with Bannisters £5, chd free. Home-made teas. Visits also by arrangement Feb to Sept.**
Plantswoman's small Edwardian garden brimming with yr-round interest, especially planted to provide winter colour, scent and snowdrops. Divided into areas with bulbs, herbaceous borders, roses, clematis, shade and woodland planting especially Trillium, Podophyllum and Arisaema, late summer salvias and annuals give colour. There are several alpine troughs as well as lots of pots around the house. Some steps into the garden.

  ✿ ☕

37 HOME CLOSE

Southend, Garsington, OX44 9DH.
Ms M Waud & Dr P Giangrande,
01865 361394. *3m SE of Oxford. N of B480, opp Garsington Manor.*
Visits by arrangement Apr to Sept. Refreshments on request. Adm £4, chd free.
2 acre garden with listed house (not open) and listed granary. Unusual trees and shrubs planted for yr-round effect. Terraces, walls and

hedges divide the garden and the planting reflects a Mediterranean interest. Vegetable garden and orchard. I acre mixed tree plantation with fine views.

GROUP OPENING

38 IFFLEY GARDENS

Iffley, Oxford, OX4 4EF. *2m S of Oxford. Within Oxford's ring road, off A4158 Iffley road from Magdalen Bridge to Littlemore r'about to Iffley village. Map provided at each garden.* Sun 11 June (2-6). Combined adm £5, chd free. Home-made teas in the village hall.

17 ABBERBURY ROAD
Mrs Julie Steele.

25 ABBERBURY ROAD
Rob & Bridget Farrands.

NEW **29 ABBERBURY ROAD**
Sarah North & Andrew Rathmell.

86 CHURCH WAY
Helen Beinart & Alex Coren.

122 CHURCH WAY
Sir John & Lady Elliott.

6 FITZHERBERT CLOSE
Tom & Eunice Martin.

THE MALT HOUSE
Helen Potts.

THE THATCHED COTTAGE
Martin & Helen Foreman.

Secluded old village with renowned Norman church, featured on cover of Pevsner's Oxon Guide. Visit 8 gardens ranging in variety and style from the large Malt House garden and a thatched C17 cottage garden to a small professionally designed Japanese style garden, with maples and miniature pines. Varied planting throughout the gardens including herbaceous borders, shade loving plants, roses, fine specimen trees and plants in terracing. Features incl water features, formal gardens, vegetable gardens, small lake and Thames riverbank. Plant sale at The Malt House. Wheelchair access to some gardens only.
♿ ❋ ☕

GROUP OPENING

39 KENCOT GARDENS

Kencot, Lechlade, GL7 3QT. *5m NE of Lechlade. E of A361 between Burford & Lechlade. Village maps available.* Mon 17 Apr (2-6). Combined adm £4, chd free. Home-made teas in village hall.

THE ALLOTMENTS
Amelia Carter Trust.

BELHAM HAYES
Mr Joseph Jones.

HILLVIEW HOUSE
John & Andrea Moss.

IVY NOOK
Gill & Wally Cox.

THE MALTINGS
Mrs Jay Mathews.

MANOR FARM
Henry & Kate Fyson.

PINNOCKS
Joy & John Coxeter.

WELL HOUSE
Gill & Ian Morrison.

The Allotments: tended by 8 people, vegetables, flowers and fruit. Hillview House: 2 acre garden, lime tree drive, shrubs, borders, spring flowers ongoing planting of flower borders and vegetables. Ivy Nook: spring flowers, shrubs, rockery, small pond, waterfall, magnolia and fruit trees. The Maltings: small cottage garden, herb wheel, pots, and mature trees. Stone step background for climbing plants. Belham Hayes: mature cottage garden with mixed herbaceous borders, two old fruit trees. Emphasis on scent and colour

coordination. Small vegetable patch. Well House: ⅓ acre garden, mature trees, hedges, wildlife pond, waterfall, small bog area, bulbs giving early colour, mixed borders, rockeries. Pinnocks: mixed shrub and herbaceous borders, masses of spring bulbs and flowers, roadside border with daffodils, magnolia tree. Manor Farm: 2 acre walled garden with bulbs, wood anemones, fritillaria in mature orchards, old English fruit trees, pleached lime walk, 130 yr old yew ball, Black Hamburg vine. Pigs and chickens. Plant and craft sale in the car park. No wheelchair access to The Allotments.
♿ 🐔 ❋ 🚘 ☕

40 LIME CLOSE

35 Henleys Lane, Drayton, Abingdon, OX14 4HU. M C de Laubarede, mail@mclgardendesign.com. *2m S of Abingdon. Henleys Lane is off main road through Drayton.* Sun 5 Mar, Sun 4 June (2-5.30). Adm £5, chd free. Cream teas. Visits also by arrangement Feb to June for groups of 10+. *Donation to CLIC Sargent Care for Children.*
4 acre mature plantsman's garden with rare trees, shrubs, perennials and bulbs. Mixed borders, raised beds, pergola, unusual topiary and shade borders. Herb garden by Rosemary Verey. Listed C16 house (not open). Cottage garden by MCL Garden Design, focusing on colour combinations and an iris garden with 100 varieties of tall bearded irises. Winter bulbs. New arboretum with exotic trees planted in 2016.
♿ 🐔 ❋ 🚘 ☕

Lime Close

41 MAGDALEN COLLEGE

Oxford, OX1 4AU. Magdalen College, www.magd.ox.ac.uk. *Entrance in High St.* **Sun 23 Apr (1-6). Adm £5.50, chd £4.50. Light refreshments in the Old Kitchen.**

60 acres incl deer park, college lawns, numerous trees 150-200 yrs old; notable herbaceous and shrub plantings. Magdalen meadow where purple and white snake's head fritillaries can be found is surrounded by Addison's Walk, a tree lined circuit by the R Cherwell developed since the late C18. Ancient herd of 60 deer. Press bell at the lodge for porter to provide wheelchair access.

&. ☕

42 MANOR HOUSE

Manor Farm Road, Dorchester-on-Thames, OX10 7HZ. Simon & Margaret Broadbent. *8m SSE of Oxford. Off A4074, signed from village centre. Parking at Bridge Meadow (400 metres). Disabled parking at house.* **Sun 11 June (2-5). Adm £4, chd free. Home-made teas in Dorchester Abbey Guesthouse (90 metres).**

2 acre garden in beautiful setting around Georgian house (not open) and Medieval abbey. Spacious lawn leading to riverside copse of towering poplars, with fine views of Dorchester Abbey. Terrace with rose and vine covered pergola around lily pond. Colourful herbaceous borders, small orchard and vegetable garden. Gravel paths.

&. 🐕 ❀ ☕

43 MEADOW COTTAGE

Christmas Common, Watlington, OX49 5HR. Mrs Zelda Kent-Lemon, 01491 613779, zelda_kl@hotmail.com. *1m from Watlington. Coming from Oxford M40 to J6. Turn R & go to Watlington. Turn L up Hill Rd to top. Turn R after 50yds, turn L into field.* **Sun 14 May (12-5). Adm £5, chd free. Home-made teas. Visits also by arrangement Feb to Sept.**

1¾ acre garden adjoining ancient bluebell woods created by the owner from 1995 onwards, with many areas to explore. A

professionally designed vegetable garden, large composting areas, wild flower garden and pond, old and new fruit trees, many shrubs, much varied hedging and large areas of lawn. Shrubs, indigenous trees, copious hedges, C17 barn (not open). Tennis court and swimming pool. Wonderful snowdrops in Feb, and during the month of May visit the bluebell woodland and treehouse. Partial wheelchair access as gravel driveway and lawns.

&. 🐕 ❀ 🚗 ☕

44 MERTON COLLEGE OXFORD FELLOWS' GARDEN

Merton Street, Oxford, OX1 4JD. Merton College, 01865 276310. *Merton St runs parallel to High St.* **Sun 30 July (10-5). Adm £5.** Ancient mulberry, said to have associations with James I. Specimen trees, long mixed border, recently established herbaceous bed. View of Christ Church meadow.

&.

GROUP OPENING

45 MIDDLETON CHENEY GARDENS

Middleton Cheney, Banbury, OX17 2ST. *3m E of Banbury. From M40 J11 follow A422 signed Middleton Cheney. Map available at all gardens.* **Sun 18 June (1-6). Combined adm £5, chd free. Home-made teas at Peartree House.**

CROFT HOUSE
Richard & Sandy Walmsley.

NEW GLEBE BARN
John & Verena Childs.

PEARTREE HOUSE
Roger & Barbara Charlesworth.

NEW QUEEN'S COTTAGE
Elizabeth & Paul Franklin.

14 QUEEN STREET
Brian & Kathy Goodey.

SPRINGFIELD HOUSE
Lynn & Paul Taylor.

Large village with C13 church with renowned William Morris stained glass. 6 open gardens with a variety

of sizes, styles and maturity. Of the 3 smaller gardens, one contemporary garden contrasts formal features with colour-filled beds, borders and exotic plants. Another mature garden concentrates on formal structure, textures and shapes with many clipped shrubs. A garden that has evolved through family use features rooms and dense planting. The larger gardens incl a thatched barn conversion with a garden; everything you would expect from greenhouse to vegetables to chickens. Another continues with its renovation of a long lost garden where interesting finds continue along with restoring areas of orchard, beds and borders. A third has an air of mystery with hidden corners and an extensive water feature weaving its way throughout the garden.

&. ❀ ☕

46 MIDSUMMER HOUSE

Woolstone, Faringdon, SN7 7QL. Anthony & Penny Spink. *7m W & 7m S of Faringdon. Woolstone is a small village off B4507, below Uffington White Horse Hill.* **Sun 21 May (2-5). Combined adm with Woolstone Mill House £5, chd free.**

On moving to Midsummer House two years ago, new owners created the garden using herbaceous plants brought with them from their previous home at Mill House. Herbaceous border and espaliered Malus Everest. Opening with Mill House which is now owned by their son, renowned landscape architect Justin Spink.

47 MILL BARN

25 Mill Lane, Chalgrove, OX44 7SL. Pat Hougham, 01865 890020, pat@gmec.co.uk. *12m E of Oxford. Chalgrove is 4m from Watlington off B480. Mill Barn is in Mill Lane on the W of Chalgrove, 300yds S of Lamb PH. Parking in lane or gravel entrance yard.* **Visits by arrangement May to Sept. Adm £4, chd free. Cream teas.**

Mill Barn has an informal cottage garden with a variety of flowers, shrubs and fruit trees including medlar, mulberry and quince in sunny and shaded beds. Rose arches and a pergola lead to a vegetable plot surrounded by a cordon of fruit trees all set in a mill stream landscape. The nearby Manor House garden can be incl in the visit, combined adm £5, chd free

🚫 🐐 🌸 ☕

48 MONKS HEAD

Weston Road, Bletchingdon, OX5 3DH. Sue Bedwell, 01869 350155, bedwell615@btinternet.com. *Approx 4m N of Kidlington. From A34 take B4027 to Bletchingdon, turn R at Xrds into Weston Rd.* Sun 26 Mar (2-5.30). Adm £3, chd free. Sun 30 Apr, Mon 1 May (2-5.30). Combined adm with Hollyhocks £5, chd free. Home-made teas. Visits also by arrangement.

Plantaholics' garden for all year interest. Bulb frame and alpine area, greenhouse. Changes evolving all the time.

🌸 🚗 ☕

49 ◆ NUFFIELD PLACE

Huntercombe, Henley-on-Thames, RG9 5RX. National Trust, 01491 641224, emily. oneil@nationaltrust.org.uk, www. nationaltrust.org.uk/nuffield-place. *On the A4130 between Henley & Wallingford. There is a brown NT road sign opp Bradley Rd, off which Nuffield Place is situated.* For NGS: Wed 14 June (10-5). Adm £4, chd £2. For other opening times and information, please phone, email or visit garden website.

9¼ acres laid out during the Arts and Crafts period and just after WWI. This is a garden restoration in action where you can see mature specimen trees, yew hedges, a pergola, herbaceous borders, a rock garden and hidden pathways in various states of repair. A croquet lawn for a challenging game and a genuine wildlife rich meadow to meander through. Pathways around garden are gravel or Yorkstone. There are some small steps in the garden, but can be avoided by going over grass.

🐐 🌸 ☕

GROUP OPENING

50 OLD BOARS HILL GARDENS

Jarn Way, Boars Hill, Oxford, OX1 5JF. Charles & Lyn Sanders. *3m S of Oxford. From S ring road towards A34 at r'about follow signs to Wootton & Boars Hill. Up Hinksey Hill take R fork. 1m R into Berkley Rd to Old Boars Hill.* Sun 25 June (1-5.30). Combined adm £6, chd free. Home-made teas at Blackthorn & Uplands.

BLACKTHORN

Louise Edwards, 07803 136373, louise.b.edwards@me.com. Visits also by arrangement June & July for groups of 15+.

TANGLEWOOD
Wendy Becker.

UPLANDS
Charles & Lyn Sanders, 01865 739486, sandersc4@hotmail.com. Visits also by arrangement Apr to Oct.

YEW COTTAGE
John Hewitt.

Four delightful gardens in a semi rural conservation area with views over Oxford. Each garden has a different setting. Yew Cottage, a thatched cottage (not open) nestled into its new redesigned plot as well as the treat of seeing the owner's veteran cars. Blackthorn an 8 acre parkland garden with woodland walks, floral herbaceous borders and ponds. Uplands a southerly facing garden full of colour and an extensive range of plants for all seasons, and Tanglewood a splendid 2 acre garden with a wide variety of flowering plants in borders and beds, especially roses. Features incl a croquet lawn, an avenue of Robinia, a sculptural area made from fallen trees and drystone walling, a small stumpery area, a multilevel pond feature, a large vegetable garden and greenhouse.

🚫 🐐 🌸 🚗 ☕

National Garden Scheme support helps raise awareness of unpaid carers

51 OLD RECTORY

Salford, Chipping Norton, OX7 5YL. Mr & Mrs N M Chambers, 01608 643969. *Small village on A44, approx 3m W of Chipping Norton.* Visits by arrangement Feb to Sept for groups of 10 max. Adm £4, chd free.

1½ acres mainly enclosed by walls. Early spring garden with early flowering shrubs and many snowdrops. Some unusual plants in mixed borders, many old roses, small orchard and vegetable garden for yr-round interest. Bantams. Refreshments available at Salford Inn. Partial wheelchair access. No dogs.

🚫

52 THE OLD VICARAGE

Aston Rowant, Watlington, OX49 5ST. Julian & Rona Knight, 01844 351315, jknight652@aol.com. *Between Chinnor & Watlington, off B4009. From M40 J6, take B4009 towards Chinnor & Princes Risborough. After 1m, turn L signed Aston Rowant Village only.* Sun 25 June (2-5). Adm £4, chd free. Home-made teas in the local church. Visits also by arrangement June to Sept for groups of 10-30. Tea & home-made cake, or wine & snacks.

Romantic, 1¾ acre vicarage garden lovingly rejuvenated and enjoyed by the present family. Centered around a croquet lawn surrounded by beds brimming with shrubs and herbaceous plants, hot bed and roses. Lushly planted pond leading through a pergola overflowing with roses and clematis to a tranquil green garden. Small vegetable and cutting garden.

🚫 ☕

The Old Vicarage, Adderbury Gardens

53 THE OLD VICARAGE, BLEDINGTON

Main Road, Bledington, Chipping Norton, OX7 6UX. Sue & Tony Windsor, 01608 658525, tony.g.windsor@gmail.com. *6m SW of Chipping Norton. 4m SE of Stow-on-the-Wold. On the main street B4450 through Bledington. Not next to church.* **Sun 25 June (2-6). Adm £4, chd free. Home-made teas. Visits also by arrangement May to July. Wine & canapés for evening visits on request.**
1½ acre garden around a late Georgian vicarage (1843) not open. Borders and beds filled with hardy perennials, shrubs and trees. Informal rose garden with over 300 David Austin roses. Small pond and vegetable patch. Paddock with trees, shrubs and herbaceous border. Planted for yr-round interest. Gravel driveway and gently sloped garden.

54 OLD WHITEHILL BARN

Old Whitehill, Tackley, Kidlington, OX5 3AB. Gill & Paul Withers. *10m N of Oxford. 3m from Woodstock. Hamlet ¾m S of Tackley. Signed from A4260 & A4095.* **Evening opening Thur 1 June (6-8). Wine. Thur 8 June (2-5). Home-made teas. Adm £4, chd free.**

1 acre country garden on a sloping site around a stone barn conversion. Created by the owners from a farmyard and surrounding field over last 16 yrs. Sunny walled courtyard. Colour themed borders. Field of formal and informal areas, mature hedging, orchard, meadow grass and enclosed vegetable garden.

55 NEW 116 OXFORD ROAD

Abingdon, OX14 2AG. Mr & Mrs P Aylward. *116 Oxford Road is on the RH-side if coming from A34 N exit, or on the LH-side if approaching from Abingdon town centre.* **Sun 4 June (11-4.30). Combined adm with Failford £3, chd free. Home-made teas.**
This new town garden was cleared in 2013 and its creation started in 2014. The garden is wedge-shaped, 70ft wide near the house (not open), to 37ft wide at the bottom, and 80ft in length. The challenge was, it had to be interesting and look as though it had been there for years. It incorporates quirky features, raised beds, lawns, and herbaceous borders.

56 50 PLANTATION ROAD

Oxford, OX2 6JE. Philippa Scoones. *Central Oxford. N on Woodstock Rd take 2nd L. Coming into Oxford on Woodstock Rd turn*

R after Leckford Rd. No disabled parking nr house. **Sat 29, Sun 30 Apr, Sat 6, Sun 7 May (2-6). Adm £3.50, chd free. Home-made teas.**
Surprisingly spacious city garden designed in specific sections. N-facing front garden, side alley filled with shade loving climbers. S-facing, rear garden with hundreds of tulips in spring, unusual trees incl Mount Etna Broom, conservatory, terraced area and secluded water garden with water feature, woodland plants and alpines.

57 NEW THE PRIORY

Sotwell St, Brightwell-cum-Sotwell, Wallingford, OX10 0RH. Trish Scroggs. *From Wallingford, enter Brightwell-cum-Sotwell, go through S bend. The Priory is 100yds on L. From Didcot, enter at 1st sign to Brightwell-cum-Sotwell, go through village, past the Red Lion PH, The Priory is on the R.* **Sun 21 May (1-5.30). Combined adm with Dobsons £5, chd free. Home-made teas in cottage garden, 50yds away.**
The Priory is a beautiful listed Tudor, s-facing house (not open), with a small Italianate gravel garden leading to a larger pretty walled garden with herbaceous plants and rose beds. A plantswoman's garden with many interesting specimens.

58 RADCOT HOUSE

Radcot, OX18 2SX. Robin & Jeanne Stainer, www.radcothouse.com. *1¼m S of Clanfield. On A4095 between Witney & Faringdon, 300yds N of Radcot bridge.* **Sun 20 Aug, Sun 1 Oct (2-6). Adm £5, chd free.**
Approx 3 acres of dramatic yet harmonious planting in light and shade, formal pond, fruit and vegetable cages. Convenient seating at key points enables relaxed observation and reflection. Extensive use of grasses and unusual perennials and interesting sculptural surprises. Spectacular autumn display.

59 RIDGEWAY

Lincombe Lane, Boars Hill, Oxford, OX1 5DZ. John & Viccy Fleming, garden@octon.eu, www.facebook.com/RidgewayOpenGarden/. *Between Oxford & Abingdon. Off Foxcombe Rd & Fox Lane between A34 Hinksey Hill r'about & B4017 Wootton to Abingdon road. Nearly opp Fox PH.* **Visits by arrangement Mar to Oct. Home-made teas.**

Developed since 2004 to provide yr-round interest, this ¾ acre garden on sandy soil has some rare shrubs and plants. The intricate design incl 2 alpine beds, a fruit garden, a vegetable garden and multiple borders with varied planting. Paths are gravel and woodchip.

  ❀ ☕

ALLOTMENTS

60 NEW SATIN LANE ALLOTMENTS

Satin Lane (just off St. Thomas Street), Deddington, Banbury, OX15 0SY. Deddington Allotment Society. *6m S of Banbury. Satin Lane is small cul-de-sac off St. Thomas St in Deddington.* **Sat 24 June (2-5.30). Adm £5. Light refreshments.**

Delightfully located on the edge of the village, overlooking the fields and countryside, the Satin Lane allotments are a community treasure. Established in 1925, the land accommodates 47 beautiful individual plots. The site gently slopes down to the fields, and plot size and shapes vary substantially. A charismatic array of homespun fences have sprouted, adorned with climbing vegetable and flowers. Several of the plots have been worked over generations, where third generation allotmenteers are still diligently working them today. Many refreshments offered on the day will be made using produce grown on-site. Featured on The Oxonian Gardener Blog. Not suitable for wheelchair access due to uneven grass paths.

🐕 ☕

61 SIBFORD GARDENS

Sibford Gower, OX15 5RX. *7m W of Banbury. Nr the Warwickshire border, S of B4035, in centre of village nr Wykham Arms PH.* **Sun 25 June (2-6). Combined adm £6, chd free. Home-made teas at Sibford Gower Village Hall (opp the church).**

BUTTSLADE HOUSE

James & Sarah Garstin.

CARTER'S YARD

Sue & Malcolm Bannister, 01295 780365, sebannister@gmail.com. **Visits also by arrangement May to Sept for groups of 5+, guided by the owner.**

NEW HOME CLOSE

Graham & Carolyn White.

NEW LARKSPUR

Ivan & Veronique Tyrrell.

NEW STICKLEYS HOUSE

Stephen Gomersall.

In two charming small villages of Sibford Gower and Sibford Ferris, off the beaten track with thatched stone cottages, five contrasting gardens ranging from an early C20 Arts and Crafts house (not open) and garden, to varied cottage gardens bursting with bloom, interesting planting and some unusual plants. No wheelchair to Carter's Yard, partial at Buttslade House and Home Close.

❀ ☕

Asthall Manor

© Andrew Lawson

© Andrew Lawson

Broughton Grange

62 SPARSHOLT MANOR

Wantage, OX12 9PT. Sir Adrian & Lady Judith Swire. *3½ m W of Wantage. Off B4507 Ashbury Rd.* **Mon I May (2-6). Adm £4, chd free. Home-made teas in the village hall.**
Lakes and wildfowl; ancient boxwood, wilderness with walkways and summer borders. Wheelchair access to most of the garden.

GROUP OPENING

63 STEEPLE ASTON GARDENS

Steeple Aston, OX25 4SP. *14m N of Oxford, 9m S of Banbury. ½ m E of A4260.* **Sun 14 May (2-6). Combined adm £6, chd free. Home-made teas in village hall.**

CANTERBURY HOUSE
Peter & Harriet Higgins.

COMBE PYNE
Chris & Sally Cooper.

KRALINGEN
Mr & Mrs Roderick Nicholson.

THE LONGBYRE
Mr Vaughan Billings.

PRIMROSE GARDENS
Richard & Daphne Preston, 01869 340512, richard. preston5@btopenworld.com. **Visits also by arrangement Feb to Sept. Refreshments on request.**

Steeple Aston, often considered the most easterly of the Cotswold villages, is a beautiful stone built village with gardens that provide a huge range of interest. A stream meanders down the hill as the landscape changes from sand to clay. The 5 open gardens incl; small floriferous cottage gardens, large landscaped gardens, natural woodland areas, ponds and bog gardens, and themed borders. No wheelchair access at Primrose Gardens.

64 STONEHAVEN

6 High Street, Cumnor, Oxford, OX2 9PE. Dr Dianne & Prof Keith Gull. *4m from central Oxford. Exit to Cumnor from the A420. In centre of village opp PO. Parking at back of PO.* Sun 12 Feb (12.30-4). Adm £3, chd free. Opening with Cumnor Village Gardens on Sun 4 June. Front, side and rear garden of a thatched cottage (not open). Front is partially gravelled and side courtyard has pots. Rear garden overlooks meadows. Unusual plants, many with black or bronze foliage, planted in drifts, repeated throughout the garden. Old apple tree underplanted with ferns. Pond. Planting has mild Japanese influence; rounded, clipped shapes interspersed with verticals. Snowdrops in Feb. There are two PHs in the village; The Bear & Ragged Staff and The Vine. Gravel drive to access garden.

65 TRINITY COLLEGE

Broad Street, Oxford, OX1 3BH. Paul Lawrence, Head Gardener, www.trinity.ox.ac.uk. *Central Oxford. Entrance in Broad St.* Sun 26 Mar, Sun 30 July (1-5). Adm £2.50, chd free. Home-made teas in dining hall.
Historic main College Gardens with specimen trees incl aged forked catalpa, spring bulbs, fine long herbaceous border and handsome garden quad originally designed by Wren. President's Garden surrounded by high old stone walls, mixed borders of herbaceous, shrubs and statuary. Fellows' Garden: small walled terrace, herbaceous borders; water feature formed by Jacobean stone heraldic beasts. Award-winning lavender garden and walk-through rose arbour.

66 ◆ UNIVERSITY OF OXFORD BOTANIC GARDEN

Rose Lane, Oxford, OX1 4AZ. University of Oxford, 01865 286690, www.botanic-garden.ox.ac.uk. *1m E of Oxford city centre. Bottom of High St in central Oxford, on banks of the R Cherwell by Magdalen Bridge & opp Magdalen College Tower.* For opening times and information, please phone or visit garden website.
The Botanic Garden contains plants that originate from all over the world. It is one of the most biodiverse collections of plants per acre globally. These plants are grown in 7 glasshouses, water and rock gardens, large herbaceous border, walled garden and every available space. In total there are around 5,000 different plants to see. Features incl glasshouses, systematic beds, National Collection of hardy Euphorbia species, herbaceous border, the Merton borders, biodiversity hotspot collections, fruit and vegetable collection. Gravel paths.
🛇 [NPC]

67 UPPER CHALFORD FARM

between Sydenham & Postcombe, Chinnor, OX39 4NH. Mr & Mrs Paul Rooksby, 01844 351320, paulrooksby@talktalk.net. *4½m SE of Thame. M40 exit J6. A40 to Postcombe turn R to Chalford (L if on A40 from Oxford). After 1m L at 1st telegraph pole (halfway between Sydenham & Postcombe).* Evening openings Thur 15 June, Thur 13 July (4-7.30). Adm £5, chd free. Cream teas, wine or Pimms, & light snacks. Visits also by arrangement Apr to Sept for groups of up to 45 max. Refreshments on request.
Jacobean farmhouse garden surrounded by fields, old roses, shrubs and perennials. Unusual trees, an ancient black pine, and Caucasian wingnut tree. Hidden gardens with different plantings and peaceful places to sit. Spring fed ponds and stream with damp planted banks leading to reclaimed woodland with treehouse, bog garden and wild flower meadow. Features incl topiary, wildlife ponds, conservatory sundials and donkeys. Short gravel drive from car park. A closer drop-off point is possible.

68 UPPER GREEN

Brill Road, Horton cum Studley, Oxford, OX33 1BU. Susan & Peter Burge, 01865 351310, sue.burge@ndm.ox.ac.uk, www.uppergreengarden.co.uk. *6½m NE of Oxford. Enter village, turn R up Horton Hill. At T-junction turn L into Brill Rd. Upper Green 250yds on R, 2 gates before pillar box. Roadside parking.* Sun 23 Apr (2-5). Combined adm with Hilltop Cottage £5, chd free. Sun 23 July (2-5.30). Adm £4, chd free. Home-made teas at Studley Farmhouse on 23 Apr & at Upper Green on 23 July. Visits also by arrangement Feb to Oct for groups of up to 20 max. *Donation to The British Skin Foundation.*
Mature ½ acre garden with gravel area, mixed borders, potager, bog area and pond. Variety of snowdrops. Spring colour with marsh marigolds, hellebores, euphorbias, fritillaries and other bulbs. Perennials, ferns, grasses, and shrubs provide yr-round interest. Old apple trees support climbing roses. Plant lists for each bed. Metal sculptures by Sophie Thompson. Gravel drive limits wheelchair access.

69 WADHAM COLLEGE

Parks Road, Oxford, OX1 3PN. The Warden & Fellows. *Central Oxford. Wadham College gardens are accessed through the main entrance of the College on Parks Rd.* Sun 9 Apr, Sun 9 July (2-5). Adm £2, chd free.
5 acres, best known for trees, spring bulbs and mixed borders. In Fellows' main garden, fine ginkgo and *Magnolia acuminata*; bamboo plantation; in Back Quadrangle very large *Tilia tomentosa* 'Petiolaris'; in Mallam Court white scented garden est 1994; in Warden's garden an ancient tulip tree; in Fellows' private garden, Civil War embankment with period fruit tree cultivars, recently established shrubbery with unusual trees and ground cover amongst older plantings.
🛇

70 ◆ WATERPERRY GARDENS
Waterperry, Wheatley, OX33 1JZ. School of Economic Science, 01844 339226, office@waterperrygardens.co.uk, www.waterperrygardens.co.uk. *8m E of Oxford. For SatNav please use OX33 1LA.* **For NGS: Sun 16 Apr, Sun 17 Sept (10-5.30). Adm £7.50, chd free. Light refreshments in the teashop (10-5). For other opening times and information, please phone, email or visit garden website.**
Waterperry Gardens are an inspiration. 8 acres of landscaped gardens incl rose and formal knot garden, water lily canal, riverside walk and one of the country's finest purely herbaceous borders. There is also a plant centre, garden shop, teashop, art gallery, museum and Saxon church. National Collection of Kabschia and Silver Saxifrages. Fritillaries looking fantastic for Apr opening. Michaelmas Daisy weekends in Sept. Riverside Walk may be inaccessible to wheelchair users if very wet.
NPC

Upper Chalford Farm

71 WAYSIDE
82 Banbury Road, Kidlington, OX5 2BX. Margaret & Alistair Urquhart, 01865 460180, alistairurquhart@ntlworld.com. *5m N of Oxford. On R of A4260 travelling N through Kidlington.* **Sun 4 June (2-6). Adm £3, chd free. Tea. Visits also by arrangement May & June.**
¼ acre garden shaded by mature trees. Mixed border with some rare and unusual plants and shrubs. A climber clothed pergola leads past a dry gravel garden to the woodland garden with an extensive collection of hardy ferns. Conservatory and large fern house with a collection of unusual species of tree ferns and tender exotics. Featured in the Pteridologist and Oxford Times. Partial wheelchair access.

72 WESTWELL MANOR
Westwell, Nr Burford, OX18 4JT. Mr Thomas Gibson. *2m SW of Burford. From A40 Burford-Cheltenham, turn L ½m after Burford r'about signed Westwell. After 1½m at T-junction, turn R & Manor is 2nd house on L.* **Sun 2 July (2.30-6). Adm £5, chd free.** ***Donation to St Marys Church, Westwell.***
7 acres surrounding old Cotswold manor house (not open), with knot garden, potager, shrub roses, herbaceous borders, topiary, earth works, moonlight garden, auricula ladder, rills and water garden.

GROUP OPENING

73 WHEATLEY GARDENS
High Street, Wheatley, OX33 1XX. 01865 875022, echess@hotmail.co.uk. *5m E of Oxford. Leave A40 at Wheatley, turn into High St. Gardens at W end of High St, S side.* **Sun 25 June (2-6). Combined adm £4.50, chd free. Cream teas at The Manor House. Visits also by arrangement Apr to July.**

BREACH HOUSE GARDEN
Liz Parry.

NEW **CATCHMOLE COTTAGE**
Catherine Lane.

THE MANOR HOUSE
Mrs Elizabeth Hess.

Three adjoining gardens in the historic coaching village of Wheatley. Catchmole Cottage garden has been developed over 30 yrs to provide sanctuary for wildlife, birds, insects and slow-worms. Surrounded by ancient walls and high shrubs the garden is a frost pocket so is planted with hardy perennials, shrubs and ferns. Breach House Garden has an established main area with extensive shrubs and perennials, a more contemporary reflective space and a wild meadow with ponds. The Manor House is a 1½ acre garden surrounding an Elizabethan manor house (not open). Formal box walk, herb garden, cottage garden with rose arches and a shrubbery with old roses. A romantic oasis. All in all a lovely collection of gardens set in the heart of the busy village of Wheatley. Various musical events. Wheelchair accessible with assistance, although there are gravel paths, two shallow steps and grass.

74 WHITEHILL FARM
Widford, Burford, OX18 4DT. Mr & Mrs Paul Youngson, 01993 822894, anneyoungson@btinternet.com. *1m E of Burford. From A40 take road signed Widford. Turn R at the bottom of the hill. Ample car parking.* **Sun 4 June (2-6). Adm £3.50, chd free. Home-made teas. Visits also by arrangement May to Aug for groups of 10+ only.**
2 acres of hillside gardens and woodland with spectacular views overlooking Burford and Windrush valley. Informal plantsman's garden built up by the owners over twenty yrs. Herbaceous and shrub borders, ponds and bog area, old fashioned roses, ground cover, ornamental grasses, bamboos and hardy geraniums. Large cascade water feature, pretty tea patio and wonderful Cotswold views.

Visit a garden and support hospice care in your local community

75 WOLFSON COLLEGE

Oxford, OX2 6UD. President & Fellows of Wolfson College, www.wolfson.ox.ac.uk. ¾m N of Oxford city centre. Turn R off Banbury Rd to end of Linton Rd. **Sun 28 May (2-6). Adm £3, chd free. Home-made teas.**
A splendid modern garden of 9 acres by R Cherwell, developed in recent yrs with comprehensive plant collection tolerant of alkaline soils, grown in interesting and varied habitats around a framework of fine mature trees.

76 WOOLSTONE MILL HOUSE

Woolstone, Faringdon, SN7 7QL. Mr & Mrs Justin Spink. 7m W of Wantage. 7m S of Faringdon. Woolstone is a small village off B4507, below Uffington White Horse Hill. **Sun 21 May (2-5). Combined adm with Midsummer House £5, chd free. Home-made teas.**
Redesigned by new owner, garden designer Justin Spink in 2015, this 1½ acre garden has large mixed perennial beds, and small gravel, cutting, kitchen and bog gardens. Topiary, medlars and old fashioned roses. Treehouse with spectacular views to Uffington White Horse and White Horse Hill. C18 millhouse and barn (not open). Partial wheelchair access.

GROUP OPENING

77 WOOTTON GARDENS

Wootton, OX13 6DP. Wootton is 3m SW of Oxford. From the Oxford ring road S take the turning to Wootton. Parking for 142 Cumnor Rd at Bystander PH only, then walk 10 mins following the NGS signs. Parking for Fairfield garden is in the same road. **Thur 29 June (1-6). Combined adm £5, chd free. Tea.**

13 AMEY CRESCENT
Mr & Mrs Gleed.

60 BESSELSLEIGH ROAD
Mrs Freda East.

142 CUMNOR ROAD
Mr & Mrs Ersin & Kate Aydin.

NEW FAIRFIELD
Lyn & Nick Taylor.

22 SANDLEIGH ROAD
Mr & Mrs Peter & Jennie Debenham.

35 SANDLEIGH ROAD
Mrs Hilal Baylav Inkersole.

6 inspirational small gardens, 'all with very different ways of providing a personal joy. 13 Amey Cresent has a gravel garden with grasses and prairie plants. Small wildlife pond, alpine house and troughs. 60 Besselsleigh Road has 'The Deadwood Stage' with toadstools and a secret garden with many creatures to find. 142 Cumnor Road a sustainable wildlife garden with raised beds for vegetables, fences covered in espaliered fruit, and a small wildlife pond. Fairfield is a diverse garden of flowers and shrubs representing all seasons, with mature acer trees and mixed borders, full of interesting plants. 22 Sandleigh Road is a wildlife friendly garden packed with cottage garden favourites beside brick paths. A kitchen garden is complete with chickens and a beach hut! 35 Sandleigh Road is a mature garden, laid to lawn on two levels. Grown mostly from cuttings the garden is brimming with vibrant flowers, pond side planting and mature shrubs. Partial wheelchair access.

GROUP OPENING

78 NEW YARNELLS HILL & HURST RISE GARDENS

Yarnells Hill, Oxford, OX2 9BG. Mr & Mrs A Dawson. Take W road out of Oxford to Botley, pass under A34. Turn L into Westminster Way, Yarnells Hill 2nd on R, park at top of hill for Appleton Dene. For Hurst Rise Road continue R into Arnolds Way, 3rd road on R. **Sun 13 Aug (11-5). Combined adm £5, chd free.**

APPLETON DENE
Mr & Mrs A Dawson,
07701 000977,
annrobe@aol.com.
Visits also by arrangement June to Sept, please phone in advance.

NEW 68 HURST RISE ROAD
Stephen & Anne Wright.

86 HURST RISE ROAD
Ms P Guy & Mr L Harris.

Situated on the west side of Oxford three complementary gardens, off Cumnor Hill. Appleton Dene, a beautiful secluded garden set in a hidden valley bordered by woods and a field. The ¼ acre garden on a steeply sloping site surrounds a mature tulip tree. There is a skillfully incorporated level lawn area overlooked by deep borders incl a wide variety of plants for long seasonal interest. A small cut flower allotment ½m away (open 11-1). 86 Hurst Rise a small town garden brimming with herbaceous perennial plants, roses, clematis, shrubs and small trees. 68 Hurst Rise, w-facing town garden on clay, tiered to accommodate sloping site and divided into a series of rooms. Herbaceous borders and shrubs planted for yr-round interest, with a particular focus on roses. Featured in Garden News and Garden Answers 2016.

SHROPSHIRE

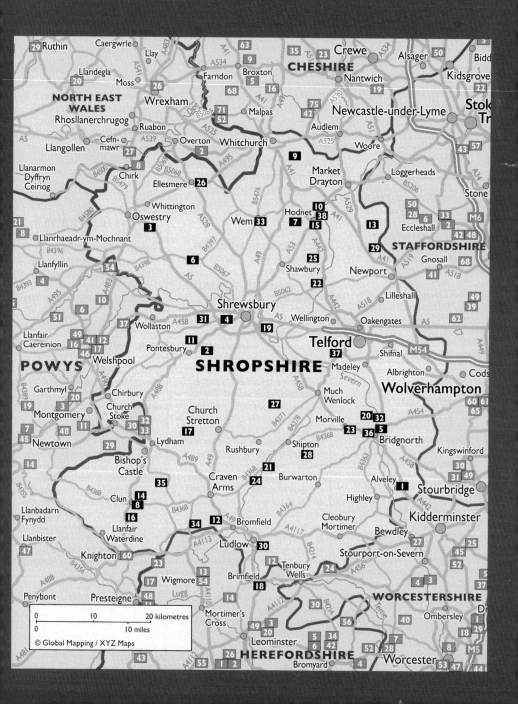

One of England's best kept secrets and one of the least populated areas in the country, Shropshire has a lot to offer visitors.

Our county has stunning gardens, majestic estates, interesting towns, history both modern and new (Shropshire was home to the ancient tribes of Mercia and also the birthplace of modern industry at Ironbridge), wonderful natural beauties such as the 'Blue Remembered Hills' that the poet A. E. Housman epitomised, and Shropshire is the self-proclaimed 'foodie' capital of Britain.

Above all, Shropshire's gardens are a must for the visitor. Generous garden owners and volunteers across the county have many open gardens, ranging from large estates to small, beautifully designed town gardens.

We hope 2017 will be another successful year where many garden openers welcome dogs and children and provide wonderful home-made teas and raise money for our very important charities.

Volunteers

County Organiser
Chris Neil
01743 821651
bill@billfneil.fsnet.co.uk

County Treasurer
Suzanne Stevens
01588 660314
harrystevens@btconnect.com

Publicity
Vicki Kirk
01743 821429
vlk@shrewsbury.org.uk

April Jones
apriladeumayne@gmail.com

Booklet Co-ordinator
Fiona Chancellor
01952 507675
fionachancellor@btinternet.com

Assistant County Organisers
Bill Neil
01743 821651
bill@billfneil.fsnet.co.uk

Penny Tryhorn
01746 783931
pennypottingshed@hotmail.co.uk

© Val Corbett

Left: Millichope Park

OPENING DATES

All entries subject to change. For latest information check www.ngs.org.uk

Extended openings are shown at the beginning of the month.

Map locator numbers are shown to the right of each garden name.

February

Snowdrop Festival

Sunday 19th
Millichope Park 21

April

Saturday 15th
48 Bramble Ridge 5

Monday 17th
Edge Villa 11

Friday 21st
8 Westgate Villas 36

Sunday 23rd
Sunningdale 33
8 Westgate Villas 36

Tuesday 25th
Brownhill House 6

May

Sunday 7th
Lyndale House 20
Millichope Park 21

Sunday 14th
Guilden Down
Cottage 14
Oteley 26

Friday 19th
Ruthall Manor 28

Saturday 20th
Ruthall Manor 28

Sunday 21st
Ancoireán 1
Bluebell Cottage 3
Mynd Hardy Plants 24

Wednesday 24th
Goldstone Hall
Gardens 13

90th Anniversary Weekend

Sunday 28th
The Citadel 7
Longner Hall 19
Upper Shelderton
House 34
Walcot Hall 35
♦ Wollerton Old Hall 38

Monday 29th
Upper Shelderton
House 34
Walcot Hall 35

Tuesday 30th
Brownhill House 6

Wednesday 31st
Goldstone Hall
Gardens 13

June

The Croft (Every Tuesday from Tuesday 6th) 9

Sunday 4th
The Croft 9
Stanley Hall 32
Windy Ridge 37

Wednesday 7th
Edge Villa 11

Friday 9th
Ruthall Manor 28

Saturday 10th
Ruthall Manor 28

Sunday 11th
Hodnet Hall Gardens 15
Morville Hall Gardens 23
Mynd Hardy Plants 24
Shoothill House 31

Wednesday 14th
Goldstone Hall
Gardens 13

Sunday 18th
Drayton Fields 10
Lyndale House 20

Saturday 24th
Secret Garden 30

Sunday 25th
Millichope Park 21

Tuesday 27th
Brownhill House 6

Wednesday 28th
Goldstone Hall
Gardens 13

July

The Croft (Every Tuesday) 9

Goldstone Hall Gardens (Every Wednesday from 12th to 26th) 13

Sunday 2nd
Bowbrook Allotment
Community 4
Holmcroft 18
Mynd Hardy Plants 24
Ruthall Manor 28

Monday 3rd
Ruthall Manor 28

Saturday 8th
NEW Clun Village 8

Sunday 9th
NEW Clun Village 8
Windy Ridge 37

Thursday 13th
NEW Oakgate Nursery
& Garden Centre 25

Friday 14th
NEW Oakgate Nursery
& Garden Centre 25

Sunday 16th
Sambrook Manor 29

Friday 28th
Ruthall Manor 28

Saturday 29th
Ruthall Manor 28

Sunday 30th
Mynd Hardy Plants 24

August

The Croft (Every Tuesday to Tuesday 22nd) 9

Goldstone Hall Gardens (Every Wednesday from 9th to 30th) 13

Sunday 13th
Sambrook Manor 29
Windy Ridge 37

Saturday 19th
NEW The Flower Garden
at Stokesay Court 12

Sunday 20th
Edge Villa 11
Mynd Hardy Plants 24

September

Sunday 3rd
Windy Ridge 37

Sunday 10th
Shoothill House 31

Wednesday 13th
Goldstone Hall
Gardens 13

Saturday 16th
Ruthall Manor 28

Sunday 17th
Ruthall Manor 28

Wednesday 20th
Goldstone Hall
Gardens 13

October

Sunday 15th
Millichope Park 21

By Arrangement

Ancoireán 1
Avocet 2
Bowbrook Allotment
Community 4
48 Bramble Ridge 5
Brownhill House 6
The Citadel 7
The Croft 9
Edge Villa 11
Goldstone Hall
Gardens 13
Guilden Down
Cottage 14
The Hollies 16
Holly Cottage 17
Moortown 22
Oteley 26
Preen Manor 27
Ruthall Manor 28
Sambrook Manor 29
Secret Garden 30
Shoothill House 31
Sunningdale 33
Upper Shelderton
House 34
Windy Ridge 37

THE GARDENS

1 ANCOIREÁN
24 Romsley View, Alveley,
WV15 6PJ. Judy & Peter Creed,
01746 780504, pdjc@me.com.
*6m S Bridgnorth off A442 Bridgnorth
to Kidderminster rd. N from
Kidderminster turn L just after Royal
Oak PH. S from Bridgnorth turn R
after Squirrel PH. Take 3rd turning
on R & follow NGS signs.* **Sun 21
May (1-5). Adm £4, chd free.
Home-made teas. Visits also by
arrangement May & June 20+.**
Natural garden layout on several
levels, developed over 30yrs, with a
large variety of herbaceous plants
and shrubs, water features, wooded
area with bog garden containing
numerous varieties of ferns and
hostas, and colourful alpine scree.
Features, wooded area, stumpery,
ornamental grass border and Spring
bulb collection, clematis collection,
acer and azalea beds. Selection of
plants, bird and insect boxes for
sale. Close to Severn Valley Railway
and Country Park and Dudmaston
Hall NT.

2 AVOCET
3 Main Road, Plealey,
Shrewsbury, SY5 0UZ. Malc &
Jude Mollart, 01743 791743,
malcandjude@btinternet.com.
*6m SW of Shrewsbury. From A5 take
A488 signed Bishops Castle, approx
½m past Lea Cross Tandoori turn L
signed Plealey. In ¾m turn L, garden
on R. SatNav unreliable!* **Visits by
arrangement May to July groups
of 10+. Adm £3.50, chd free.
Home-made teas.**
Cottage style garden with modern
twists owned by plantaholics and
shared with wildlife. Designed
around a series of garden
compartments and for year round
interest. Features incl a wildlife pool,
mixed borders, seaside garden,
gravel garden, trained fruit trees,
chickens and sculpture. Children are
welcome. Countryside views and
walks from the garden.

3 BLUEBELL COTTAGE
Aston, Oswestry, SY11 4JH.
Deborah Lewis. *1m E of Oswestry.
Between A483 & A5. Signed Mile
End Golf Course.* **Sun 21 May
(1.30-5). Adm £3.50, chd free.
Home-made teas.**
1½ acres of lawns, specimen trees,
ponds and various water features.
Elevated gazebo with views of
Breidden Hills. Timber framed rill.
Small bluebell wood and kitchen
garden. Several seating areas to
relax and enjoy the garden. Dove
cote and hen house, free ranging
chickens. Afternoon teas in aid of
Greyhound Rescue. Some gravel
paths, mostly level with good
wheelchair access if ground firm.

ALLOTMENTS

4 BOWBROOK ALLOTMENT COMMUNITY
Mytton Oak Road, Shrewsbury,
SY3 5BT. 01743 791743,
malcandjude@btinternet.com,
www.bowbrookallotments.co.uk.
*½m from Royal Shrewsbury Hospital.
From A5 Shrewsbury bypass take
B4386 following signs for hospital.
Allotments situated ½m along B4386.
(Mytton Oak Rd) on R.* **Sun 2 July
(2-6). Combined adm £3.50, chd
free. Light refreshments. Visits
also by arrangement July & Aug
groups of 10+.**
Recipient of RHS National
Certificate of Distinction, this 5 acre
site, comprising 93 plots, displays
wide ranging cultivation methods.
The site has featured on BBC
TV, local radio programmes and
in several magazines. Members
cultivate organically with nature in
mind using companion planting and
attracting natural predators. Green
spaces flourish throughout and
include Gardens of the 4 Seasons,
orchards, and many wildlife features
including wild flower meadows and
pond. Children are encouraged to
be part of the community and have
their own special places such as a
story telling willow dome, willow
tunnel, sensory garden and turf
spiral. See how the Contemplation
Garden and the Prairie Garden have
developed. Visitors can participate
in voting for Favourite Plot and
follow the interest trail. Children
are particularly welcome and can
enjoy their own quizzes. Wheelchair
access, flat wide grass paths allow
access to the main features of the
site and to the interest trail.

Ancoireán

5 48 BRAMBLE RIDGE

Bridgnorth, WV16 4SQ. Chris & Heather, 07572 706706, quendalebears1@btinternet.com. *From Bridgnorth N on B4373 signed Broseley. 1st on R Stanley Lane, 1st R Bramble Ridge. From Broseley S on B4373, nr Bridgnorth turn L into Stanley Lane, 1st R Bramble Ridge.* **Sat 15 Apr (10.30-6). Adm £4, chd free. Home-made teas. Visits also by arrangement Apr to Sept groups of 20+.**
Steep garden with many steps, part wild, part cultivated, terraced in places and overlooking the Severn valley with views to High Rock and Queens Parlour. Described by some as fascinating and full of interest; the garden incl shrubs, perennials, small vegetable plot, herbs, wildlife pond and summerhouse. Full of interesting plants. Roughly 88 steps from the front of the house to the very top of the garden.
✿ ☕

6 BROWNHILL HOUSE

Ruyton XI Towns, Shrewsbury, SY4 1LR. Roger & Yoland Brown, 01939 261121, brownhill@eleventowns.co.uk, www.eleventowns.co.uk. *9m NW of Shrewsbury on B4397. On the B4397 in the village of Ruyton XI Towns.* **Tue 25 Apr, Tue 30 May, Tue 27 June (1.30-5). Adm £4, chd free. Home-made teas. Visits also by arrangement May to July individuals or groups.**
"Has to be seen to be believed". A unique hillside garden (over 700 steps) bordering R Perry. Wide variety of styles and plants from formal terraces to woodland paths, plus large kitchen garden. Kit cars on show Considerable remodelling for 2017.
✿ 🛏 ☕

BRYNKINALT HALL

See North East Wales

7 THE CITADEL

Weston-under-Redcastle, SY4 5JY. Mr Beverley & Mrs Sylvia Griffiths, 01630 685204, griffiths@thecitadelweston.co.uk, www.thecitadelweston.co.uk. *12m N of Shrewsbury on A49. At Xrds*

turn for Hawkstone Park, through village of Weston-under-Redcastle, ¼m on R beyond village. **Sun 28 May (2-5). Adm £4.50, chd free. Home-made teas. Visits also by arrangement May & June groups of 10+.**
Imposing castellated house (not open) stands in 4 acres. Mature garden, with fine trees, rhododendrons, azaleas, acers and camellias. Herbaceous borders; walled potager and Victorian thatched summerhouse provide added interest. Paths meander around and over sandstone outcrop at centre.
♿ 🐕 🛏 ☕ 🍽

GROUP OPENING

8 NEW CLUN VILLAGE

Craven Arms, SY7 8JY. *Clun & Environs. Clun is situated on the B4368, 9m W of Craven Arms, 6m S of Bishop's Castle.* **Sat 8, Sun 9 July (1-5). Combined adm £5, chd free. Home-made teas in Hightown Community Room, Vicarage Road.**
Clun and the Clun Valley nestle in the Shropshire Hills Area of Outstanding Natural Beauty. A minimum of 8 gardens open, 6 are town gardens with a wide range of planting styles and innovative landscaping. Cottage gardens, terracing, wild flower areas, specialist plants, vegetable production areas. Two gardens are outside of Clun with beautiful vistas and space for large scale planting. Limited wheelchair access to some gardens, grass and gravel access in others.
♿ ✿ 🚗 ☕

Macmillan and the National Garden Scheme, partners for more than 30 years

9 THE CROFT

Ash Magna, Whitchurch, SY13 4DR. Peter & Shiela Martinson, 01948 663248, smartinson@ashbounty.co.uk. *2m S of Whitchurch. From Whitchurch bypass take A525 Newcastle (A530 Nantwich). 'Ash' signed at r'about. Village centre 2m. Please use Village Hall car park. Follow signs to garden.* **Sun 4 June (1-5). Every Tue 6 June to 22 Aug (1-5). Adm £3, chd free. Home-made teas. Visits also by arrangement May to Sept need at least a week's notice.**
As we enjoy all types of garden, we have incorporated many styles to create an interesting whole. The areas include herbaceous borders, banks of thyme, meandering paths, sunken hot spots, fruit terraces, bee and butterfly borders, shrubberies, woodland walks, poly-tunnel produce and a pond with a surprise. A little bit of everything, including contented chickens and four legged lawnmowers! Shortlisted in the 2016 Daily Mail Garden Competion.
🚗 ☕

10 DRAYTON FIELDS

Wollerton, Market Drayton, TF9 3LU. Mr & Mrs Roberts. *Northern edge of Wollerton Village, Drayton Rd. Garden is set back with white railings.* **Sun 18 June (1.30-5). Adm £4, chd free. Home-made teas.**
3½ acres of interesting trees, incl Wellingtonias, herbaceous borders, lawns, box hedging, lavender parterre, rose garden. Vegetable garden and greenhouse, small pond, flowers abound and combining into partly organised floral, scented chaos.
✿ ☕

11 EDGE VILLA

Edge, nr Yockleton, SY5 9PY. Mr & Mrs W F Neil, 01743 821651, bill@billfneil.fsnet.co.uk. *6m SW of Shrewsbury. From A5 take either A488 signed to Bishops Castle or B4386 to Montgomery for approx 6m then follow NGS signs.* **Mon 17 Apr (2-5). Home-made teas. Wed 7 June (9.30-1). Light**

refreshments. **Sun 20 Aug (2-5).** Home-made teas. Adm £4, chd free. **Visits also by arrangement Apr to Aug group 10+.**
Two acres nestling in South Shropshire hills. Self-sufficient vegetable plot. Chickens in orchard, foxes permitting. Large herbaceous borders. Dewpond surrounded by purple elder, irises, candelabra primulas and dieramas. Large selection of fragrant roses. Teas in sheltered courtyard. Wed 7 June is an am opening with plant sale. Wendy House and Teepee for children. Some gravel paths.

& ✿ 🚗 ☕

12 NEW THE FLOWER GARDEN AT STOKESAY COURT

Stokesay Court, Onibury, Craven Arms, SY7 9BD. Barney & Victoria Martin, www.flowergardenatstokesaycourt.co.uk. *In Onibury take the turning marked Clungunford. Drive through the gates marked 'Private Drive.' Follow the drive until you approach the house & bear L down to the marked car park.* **Sat 19 Aug (11-5). Adm £4, chd free. Home-made teas. in our bell tent.**
A magical 'secret' walled garden on the Stokesay Court Estate run as a commercial cutting garden and flower business. Wide variety of bulbs, annuals, perennials and shrubs all grown for cutting. Wild areas; soft fruit, lawns for playing and deckchairs for unwinding. Wheelchair access - no steps but no wheelchair paths.

& 🐕 ✿ ☕

13 GOLDSTONE HALL GARDENS

Goldstone, Market Drayton, TF9 2NA. Miss Victoria Cushing, 01630 661202, enquiries@goldstonehall.com, www.goldstonehall.com. *5m N of Newport on A41. Follow brown signs from Hinstock. From Shrewsbury A53, R for A41 Hinstock & follow brown signs.* **Wed 24, 31 May, Wed 14, 28 June (2-5). Every Wed 12 July to 26 July, 9 Aug to 30 Aug (2-5), Wed 13, 20 Sept (2-5). Adm £4.50, chd free. Home-made**

teas. **Visits also by arrangement May to Sept for groups of 10+.**
5 acres with highly productive beautiful kitchen garden. Unusual vegetables and fruits - Large Polytunnel with Alpine strawbs, Heritage toms and crammed with salad, chillies, celeriac. Roses in Walled Garden from May, Double herbaceous at its best July and August but Sedums and Roses stunning in September. Teas in Pavilion with cakes created by Award Winning Chef. Lawn aficionados will enjoy the Stripes. Good Food Guide listed restaurant AA Red Star Country House Hotel. Majority of garden can be accessed on gravel and lawns.

& ✿ 🚗 🛋 ☕

14 GUILDEN DOWN COTTAGE

Guilden Down, Clun, Craven Arms, SY7 8NZ. Mike Black & Sue Wilson, 01588 640124, sue.guilden@gmail.com. *In Clun Signs for YHA. Continue 1m up hill. Past cottages on L. At farm bear R through farm buildings. 100 yds at end of road .Garden on L.* **Sun 14 May (2-6). Adm £4.50, chd free. Home-made teas. Visits also by arrangement May to July refreshments on request.**
With spectacular views, this one

acre organic garden has been developed over the past 13 years to be in harmony with its surroundings. Divided into many rooms, there are vibrant herbaceous borders and terraces, rose trellises and a large vegetable plot. Our wild garden includes a natural pond, living willow structures, wild flower orchard, trees, shrubs and planted borders. Partial wheelchair access, front garden only.

& 🐕 ☕

15 HODNET HALL GARDENS

Hodnet, Market Drayton, TF9 3NN. Sir Algernon & The Hon Lady Heber-Percy, www.hodnethallgardens.org. *5½m SW of Market Drayton. 12m NE Shrewsbury. At junction of A53 & A442.* **Sun 11 June (12-5). Adm £7, chd £1. Light refreshments.**
60-acre landscaped garden with series of lakes and pools; magnificent forest trees, great variety of flowers, shrubs providing colour throughout season. Unique collection of big-game trophies in C17 tearooms. Kitchen garden. For details please see website and Facebook page. Maps are available to show access for our less mobile visitors.

& 🐕 🚗 NPC ☕

The Citadel

© Julia Stanley

16 THE HOLLIES

Rockhill, Clun, SY7 8LR. Pat & Terry Badham, 01588 640805, patbadham@btinternet.com. *10m W of Craven Arms. 8m S of Bishops Castle. From A49 Craven Arms take B4368 to Clun. Turn L onto A488 continue for 1½m. Bear R signed Treverward. After 50 yards turn R at Xrds, property is 1st on L.* **Visits by arrangement July to Sept groups of 10 -20. Adm £3.50, chd free. Refreshments in Clun..** A garden of approx 2 acres at 1000ft which was started in 2009. Features include a kitchen garden with raised beds and fruit cage. Large island beds and borders with perennials, shrubs and grasses, specimen trees. Wildlife dingle with stream. Wheelchair access is available to the majority of the garden over gravel and grass.
&. ❧

17 HOLLY COTTAGE

Prolley Moor, Wentnor, SY9 5EH. Julian French & Heather Williams, 01588 650610, heatherannw56@yahoo.co.uk. *7m NE of Bishop's Castle. From A489 take rd signed Wentnor. In Wentnor pass The Crown on R. Take next R signed Prolley Moor, then 1st L, signed Adstone. Holly Cottage is ½m on R.* **Visits by arrangement Apr to Aug any number. Adm £4, chd free. Light refreshments. Tea/coffee/soft drinks and biscuits/cakes..** Organic garden of 2½ acres set in beautiful countryside under the Long Mynd. Areas incl 1 acre of 13yr old native woodland, wild flower meadow with willow circle and allotment area. Nearer the house the flower garden is stocked with herbaceous plants, trees and shrubs with pond, trellis and improved layout in old orchard. New layout by pond. Refreshments available. Gravel and grass paths.
&. ☞ ❧ ❧

18 HOLMCROFT

Wyson Lane, Brimfield, nr Ludlow, SY8 4NW. Mr & Mrs Michael Dowding. *4m S of Ludlow & 6m N of Leominster. From Ludlow or Leominster leave the A49 at the Salway Arms PH, turn into lane signed Wyson only. From Tenbury Wells cross the A49 into Wyson Lane.* **Sun 2 July (2-5.30). Adm £4.50, chd free. Home-made teas.** C17 thatched cottage set in terraced gardens of ¾ acre. Quintessential English cottage garden planting.

Roses, which has been extended for this year to over 80, climbers, ramblers and rose bushes. Herbaceous borders, kitchen, gravel and woodland gardens all with spectacular views of surrounding countryside. Only the woodland walk is inaccessible for wheelchairs.
&. ❧ ☞ ❧

19 LONGNER HALL

Atcham, Shrewsbury, SY4 4TG. Mr & Mrs R L Burton. *4m SE of Shrewsbury. From M54 follow A5 to Shrewsbury, then B4380 to Atcham. From Atcham take Uffington rd, entrance ¼m on L.* **Sun 28 May (2-5). Adm £4, chd free. Home-made teas.** A long drive approach through parkland designed by Humphry Repton. Walks lined with golden yew through extensive lawns, with views over Severn Valley. Borders containing roses, herbaceous and shrubs, also ancient yew wood. Enclosed walled garden containing mixed planting, garden buildings, tower and game larder. Short woodland walk around old moat pond. 1-acre walled garden currently being restored now open to visitors. Woodland walk not suitable for wheelchairs.
&. ❧

20 LYNDALE HOUSE

Astley Abbotts, Bridgnorth, WV16 4SW. Bob & Mary Saunders. *2m out of Bridnorth off B4373. From High Town Bridgnorth take B4373 Broseley Rd for 1½m, then take lane signed Astley Abbotts & Colemore Green.* **Sun 7 May, Sun 18 June (2-5). Adm £4, chd free. Home-made teas.** Large 1½ acre garden which has evolved over 20yrs. Terrace with roses, alliums and iris surrounded by box hedging. Specimen trees planted in large lawn. Hundreds of tulips for spring colour. Clematis and allium walk to pool and waterfall. Vegetable garden and working greenhouses. Densely planted borders. Wealth of peonies, viburnums and acers. Stumpery with late spring bulbs. New scree bed in progress. Courtyard garden with topiary, pool with waterfall and 'pebble beach'.

The Hollies

Masses of blossom in spring. Birds in abundance. Please ask owner about wheelchair friendly access.

21 MILLICHOPE PARK
Munslow, Craven Arms, SY7 9HA. Mr & Mrs Frank Bury, www.boutsviolas.co.uk. *8m NE of Craven Arms. off B4368 Craven Arms to Bridgnorth Rd. Nr Munslow then follow yellow signs.* **Sun 19 Feb (2-5); Sun 7 May, Sun 25 June (1-6); Sun 15 Oct (2-5). Adm £5, chd free. Home-made teas.** Historic landscape gardens covering 14 acres with lakes, cascades dating from C18, woodland walks and wildflowers. Snowdrops in February, Bluebells and Violas in May, Roses and wild flower meadows in June and Autumn colour in October. Also open the Walled Garden at Millichope, an exciting restoration project bringing the walled gardens and C19 glasshouses back to life. opportunity to see the Bouts Viola collection. UK's largest collection of hardy, perennial, scented violas. Many varieties for sale during the May opening. Wildegoose nursery and the walled garden at Millichope will also be open. Partial wheelchair access, incl WC.

22 MOORTOWN
nr Wellington, TF6 6JE. Mr David Bromley, 01952 770205. *8m N of Telford. 5m N of Wellington. Take B5062 signed Moortown 1m between High Ercall & Crudgington.* **Visits by arrangement in June groups 10+. Adm £5, chd free.** Approx 1 acre plantsman's garden. Here may be found the old-fashioned, the unusual and even the oddities of plant life, in mixed borders of 'controlled' confusion. Has gardened for over 50 years and for 31 years for NGS.

GROUP OPENING

23 MORVILLE HALL GARDENS
Bridgnorth, WV16 5NB. *3m W of Bridgnorth. On A458 at junction*

with B4368. **Sun 11 June (2-5). Combined adm £6, chd free. Home-made teas in Morville Church.**

THE COTTAGE
Mrs J Bolton.

THE DOWER HOUSE
Dr Katherine Swift.

1 THE GATE HOUSE
Mr & Mrs Rowe.

2 THE GATE HOUSE
Mrs G Medland.

MORVILLE HALL
Mr & Mrs M Irving.

SOUTH PAVILION
Mr & Mrs B Jenkinson.

An interesting group of gardens that surround a beautiful Grade I listed mansion (not open). The Cottage has a pretty walled cottage garden with plenty of colour. The Dower House is a horticultural history lesson about Morville Hall which incl a turf maze, cloister garden, Elizabethan knot garden, C18 canal garden, Edwardian kitchen garden and more. It is the setting of Katherine Swift's bestselling book 'The Morville Hours', and the sequel 'The Morville Year'. 1 and 2 The Gate House are cottage-style gardens with colourful borders, formal areas, lawns and wooded glades. The 4-acre Morville Hall (NT) garden has a parterre, medieval stew pond, shrub borders and large lawns, all offering glorious views across the Mor Valley. South Pavilion features new thoughts and new designs in a small courtyard garden. Mostly level ground, but plenty of gravel to negotiate.

24 MYND HARDY PLANTS
Delbury Hall Estate, Mill Lane, Diddlebury, Craven Arms, SY7 9DH. Mr & Mrs Rallings, www.myndhardyplants.co.uk. *8m W of Craven Arms. 1m off B4368, Craven Arms to Bridgnorth, through village of Diddlebury, turn R at Mynd Hardy Plants sign.* **Sun 21 May, Sun 11 June, Sun 2, Sun 30 July, Sun 20 Aug (11-5). Adm £4, chd free. Home-made teas.**

Commercial nursery within old walled garden, offering and selling more than 800 varieties of herbaceous perennials. Collections include hemerocallis and penstemon and a growing range of late summer flowering plants. The garden is undergoing a major restoration programme. Gravel and grass paths.

25 NEW OAKGATE NURSERY & GARDEN CENTRE
Ellerdine Heath, nr Telford, TF6 6RL. Oakgate Garden Centre, www.oakgatenursery.co.uk. *Signed A53 between Shawbury & Hodnet. A442 Between Shawbirch & Hodnet.* **Thur 13, Fri 14 July (10-4). Adm £5, chd free. Tea. Coffee and slice of cake incl in adm.** The owners Philip and Valerie Newington moved to Shropshire 30yrs ago from Chobham, Surrey, when the complete site was a Pick Your Own Farm. Over the years the garden has been transformed to what it is today, a delightful haven of trees, shrubs, herbaceous and seasonal bedding. All dug by hand incl 2 ponds by Philip. The gardens are still maintained by the family who live on site but welcome visitors who enjoy the peaceful setting relaxing in our tearoom overlooking the pond. Limited wheelchair access.

26 OTELEY
Ellesmere, SY12 0PB. Mr R K Mainwaring, 01691 622514. *1m SE of Ellesmere. Entrance out of Ellesmere past Mere, opp Convent nr to A528/495 junction.* **Sun 14 May (2-5). Adm £4, chd free. Home-made teas. Visits also by arrangement for groups 10+.** 10 acres running down to The Mere. Walled kitchen garden, architectural features, many old interesting trees despite recent storms, rhododendrons, azaleas, wild woodland walk and views across Mere to Ellesmere. First opened in 1927 when NGS first started. Wheelchair access if dry.

27 PREEN MANOR

Church Preen, SY6 7LQ. Mrs Ann Trevor-Jones, 01694 771207. *6m W of Much Wenlock. From A 458 Shrewsbury to Bridgnorth road turn off at Harley follow signs to Kenley and Church Preen. From B4371 Much Wenlock to Church Stretton road go via Hughley to Church Preen.* **Visits by arrangement May to July for groups of 10+. Not evenings or weekends. Adm £6, chd free. Coffee/tea & biscuits £1..**

6-acre garden on site of Cluniac monastery and Norman Shaw mansion. Kitchen, chess, water and wild gardens. Fine trees in park; woodland walks. Developed for over 30yrs with changes always in progress.

❁ 🚗 ☕ ♿

QUEEN ANNE COTTAGE

See North East Wales

28 RUTHALL MANOR

Ditton Priors, Bridgnorth, WV16 6TN. Mr & Mrs G T Clarke, 01746 712608, clrk608@btinternet.com. *7m SW of Bridgnorth. Ruthall Rd signed nr garage in Ditton Priors. See yellow arrows.* **Fri 19, Sat 20 May, Fri 9, Sat 10 June, Sun 2, Mon 3, Fri 28, Sat 29 July, Sat 16, Sun 17 Sept (1-6). Adm £4, chd free. Home-made teas. Light meals by arrangement. Visits also by arrangement Apr to Oct refreshments on request.**

Offset by a mature collection of specimen trees, the garden is divided into intimate sections, carefully linked by winding paths. The front lawn flanked by striking borders, extends to a gravel, art garden and ha-ha. Clematis and roses scramble through an eclectic collection of wrought-iron work, unique pottery and secluded seating. A stunning horse pond features primulas, iris and bog plants. Jigsaws for sale Bring or buy. Collecting box some days if wet. Wheelchair access to most parts.

♿ 🐕 🚗 ☕ ♿

29 SAMBROOK MANOR

Sambrook, Newport, TF10 8AL. Mrs E Mitchell, 01952 550256, sambrookmanor@gmail.com. *Between Newport & Ternhill. 1m off A41 in the village of Sambrook.* **Sun 16 July, Sun 13 Aug (12.30-5). Adm £4, chd free. Home-made teas. Visits also by arrangement May to Aug for groups of 10+.**

The garden surrounds the early C18 manor house (not open) and contains a wide selection of herbaceous plants and roses. Features incl a waterfall down to a pond and various acers. A new development leading to the river along the edge of the garden is filled with a variety of shrubs and trees. Plants on sale from Barlow Nurseries.

♿ 🐕 🚗 🛏 ☕

30 SECRET GARDEN

21 Steventon Terrace, Steventon New Road, Ludlow, SY8 1JZ. Mr & Mrs Wood, 01584 876037, carolynwood2152@yahoo.co.uk. *Park & Ride if needed, stops outside garden.* **Sat 24 June (12.30-5.30). Adm £3.50, chd free. Home-made teas and cakes. Visits also by arrangement May to Sept refreshments if requested.**

½ acre of very secret S-facing garden, divided into different sections, roses, herbaceous borders, lawn and summer house. Developed over 30yrs by present owners. Terraced vegetable garden and greenhouses. ¼-acre project incl poly tunnel, vegetable plot, chickens, completed in 2011. Mediterranean style terrace garden. 3 times winners of Ludlow in Bloom.

🐕 ❁ 🚗 ☕

31 SHOOTHILL HOUSE

Ford, Shrewsbury, SY5 9NR. Colin & Jane Lloyd, 01743 850795, jane@lloydmasters.com. *5m W of Shrewsbury. From A458 turn L towards Shoothill (signed).* **Evening opening Sun 11 June (7-9). Adm £6.50, chd free. Wine. Sun 10 Sept (1.30-5). Adm £4.50, chd £1.50. Home-made teas. Visits also by arrangement May to Sept groups 10+.**

6-acre garden, incl small wood with swamp garden, wild flower meadows, tree house and several lawned areas surrounded by mixed borders. Large well maintained Victorian greenhouse in renovated walled kitchen garden. New areas of garden created in 2012. Mature wildlife pond surrounded by species trees and shrubs with extensive views over Welsh hills. Victorian manor house vintage tea stall walled garden. Wheelchair access is extremely difficult as the ground is uneven and there are also large areas of gravel.

🐕 ❁ 🛏 ☕ ♿

32 STANLEY HALL

Bridgnorth, WV16 4SP. Mr & Mrs M J Thompson. *½m N of Bridgnorth. Leave Bridgnorth by N gate B4373; turn R at Stanley Lane. Pass Golf Course Club House on L & turn L at Lodge.* **Sun 4 June (2-6). Adm £4, chd free. Home-made teas.**

Drive ½m with rhododendrons, fine trees and pools. Restored ice-house. Woodland walks. Also open Dower House (Mr & Mrs Colin Wells) 4 acre woodland and shrub garden with contemporary sculpture and walled vegetable garden. The Granary (Mr & Mrs Jack Major) Small trellis garden with flowers in hanging baskets and herbaceous borders and South Lodge (Mr Tim Warren) Cottage hillside garden.

♿ 🐕 ☕

33 SUNNINGDALE

9 Mill Street, Wem, SY4 5ED. Mrs Susan Griffiths, 01939 236733, sue.griffiths@btinternet.com. *Town centre Wem. Wem is on B5476. Parking in public car park Barnard St. The property is opposite the purple house below the church.* **Sun 23 Apr (11-4). Adm £3, chd free. Light refreshments. Visits also by arrangement Feb to Nov.**

A developing half acre town garden. Incorporating sculptural elements, koi pond with rockery waterfall, solar panelled greenhouse and borehole irrigation system. 8ft x 60ft Lawson Cypress trees, large borders filled with perennials, climbers and roses around a magnificent summer house used for serving home-made refreshments. Koi pond and natural stone waterfall rockery. Antique and modern sculpture. Sound break yew walkway. Large perennial borders. Although the garden is on the level, there are a number of steps especially around the pond area. Paths are in the main gravel, or uneven flags.

♿ ❀ ☕ ▣

34 UPPER SHELDERTON HOUSE

Shelderton, Clungunford, Craven Arms, SY7 0PE. Andrew Benton & Tricia McHaffie, 01547 540525. *Between Ludlow & Craven Arms. Heading from Shrewsbury to Ludlow on A49, take 1st R after Onibury railway crossing. Take 3rd R signed Shelderton. After approx 2½ m the house is on L. Garden will be signed.* **Sun 28, Mon 29 May (2-5). Adm £4.50, chd free. Home-made teas. Visits also by arrangement May, for groups of 10+.**

Set in a stunning tranquil position, our naturalistic and evolving 6½ acre garden was originally landscaped in 1962. Most of the trees, azaleas and rhododendrons were planted then. There is a wonderful new kitchen garden designed and planted by Jayne and Norman Grove. Ponds and woodland walk encourage wildlife. A large sweeping lawn leads in various directions revealing a multitude of colourful rhododendron and azaelea beds ponds a varied collection of trees and a very productive kitchen garden. There are plenty of tranquil seating areas from which to enjoy a moment in our garden.

🐎 ❀ ♿ 🚌 ☕ ▣

35 WALCOT HALL

Lydbury North, SY7 8AZ. Mr & Mrs C R W Parish, 01588 680570, secretary@walcothall.com, www.walcothall.com. *4m SE of Bishop's Castle. B4385 Craven Arms to Bishop's Castle, turn L by Powis Arms, in Lydbury North.* **Sun 28, Mon 29 May (1.30-5.30). Adm £4, chd free. Home-made teas.**

Arboretum planted by Lord Clive of India's son, Edward. Cascades of rhododendrons, azaleas amongst specimen trees and pools. Fine views of Sir William Chambers' Clock Towers, with lake and hills beyond. Walled kitchen garden; dovecote; meat safe; ice house

and mile-long lakes. Outstanding ballroom where excellent teas are served. Russian wooden church, grotto and fountain now complete and working; tin chapel. Relaxed borders and rare shrubs. Lakeside replanted, and water garden at western end re-established. The garden adjacent to the ballroom is accessible via a sloping garden, as is the walled garden and arboretum.

♿ 🐎 ❀ 🚌 🚗 ▣

36 8 WESTGATE VILLAS

Salop Street, Bridgnorth, WV16 4QX. Bill & Marilyn Hammerton. *From A458 Bridgnorth bypass, at Ludlow Rd r'about take rd into Bridgnorth signed town centre. At T-junction (parking at council offices here) turn R, garden is 100yds on L past Victoria Road.* **Evening opening Fri 21 Apr (7-9.30). Adm £5, chd free. Wine and Canapés. Sun 23 Apr (2-5.30). Adm £4, chd free. Tea and cake.**

Town garden having formal Victorian front garden with box hedging and water feature. Back garden has a shade border, patios with seating and potted plants, a lawn and small knot garden, together with a strong oriental influence incl Japanese style teahouse, Zen garden, Chinese style pebble path, moongate sculpture, prayer flags and basalt sett and gravel hard landscaping. Wine, canapes, music and garden lighting incl at evening opening. Partial wheelchair access.

♿ ☕

37 WINDY RIDGE

Church Lane, Little Wenlock, Telford, TF6 5BB. George & Fiona Chancellor, 01952 507675, fionachancellor@btinternet.com. *2m S of Wellington. Follow signs for Little Wenlock from N (J7, M54) or E (off A5223 at Horsehay). Parking signed. Do not rely on SatNav.* **Sun 4 June, Sun 9 July, Sun 13 Aug, Sun 3 Sept (12-5). Adm £5, chd free. Home-made teas. Visits also by arrangement June to Sept suitable for coaches.**

'Stunning' and 'inspirational' are how visitors frequently describe this multi-award-winning ⅔ acre village garden. The strong design and

exuberant colour-themed planting (over 1000 species, mostly labelled) offer a picture around every corner. The grass and perennial gravel garden has created a lot of interest and versions are now appearing in gardens all over the country! Some gravel paths but help available.

♿ ❀ 🚗 ☕ ▣

38 ♦ WOLLERTON OLD HALL

Wollerton, Market Drayton, TF9 3NA. Lesley & John Jenkins, 01630 685760, info@wollertonoldhallgarden.com, www.wollertonoldhallgarden.com. *4m SW of Market Drayton. On A53 between Hodnet & A53-A41 junction. Follow brown signs.* **For NGS: Sun 28 May (12-5). Adm £7, chd £1. Light refreshments. For other opening times and information, please phone, email or visit garden website.**

4 acre garden created around C16 house (not open). Formal structure creates variety of gardens each with own colour theme and character. Planting is mainly of perennials, the large range of which results in significant collections of salvias, clematis, crocosmias and roses. Ongoing lectures by Gardening Celebrities including Chris Beardshaw, Jules Hudson and Sir Roy Strong. Refreshments, food is freshly prepared in the Tea Room for each open day. Home-cooked, hot and cold lunches which have a reputation for excellent quality. Partial wheelchair access.

♿ ❀ 🚗 ☕ ▣

Your visit helps Marie Curie work night and day in people's homes

SOMERSET, BRISTOL AREA
& SOUTH GLOUCESTERSHIRE incl BATH

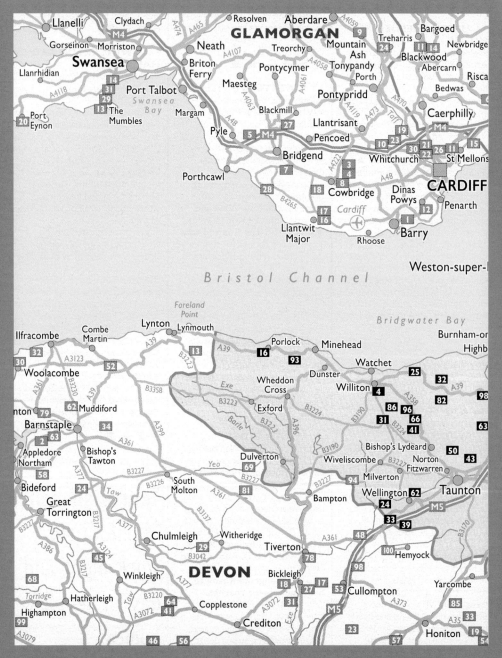

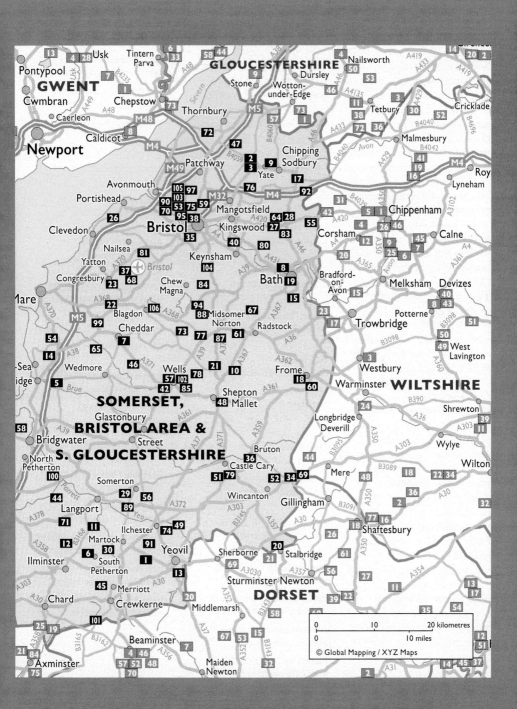

Somerset, Bristol, Bath and South Gloucestershire make up an NGS 'county' of captivating contrasts, with castles and countryside and wildlife and wetlands, from amazing cities to bustling market towns, coastal resorts and picturesque villages.

Bristol's stunning location and famous landmarks offer a wonderful backdrop to our creative and inspiring garden owners who have made tranquil havens and tropical back gardens in urban surroundings. The rolling estates of our National Trust properties offer the visitor an experience on a different scale.

Bath is a world heritage site for its Georgian architecture and renowned for its Roman Baths. Our garden visitors can enjoy the quintessentially English garden of Bath Priory Hotel with its billowing borders and croquet lawn, or explore the hidden gem behind the house at 25 Chaucer Road.

Somerset is a rural county of rolling hills such as the Mendips, the Quantocks and Exmoor National Park contrasted with the low-lying Somerset Levels. Famous for cheddar cheese, strawberries and cider; agriculture is a major occupation. It is home to Wells, the smallest cathedral city in England, and the lively county town of Taunton.
Visitors can explore more than 150 diverse gardens, mostly privately owned and not normally open to the public ranging from small urban plots to country estates.

Gardens on windswept hilltops, by the seaside, hidden in lush green countryside, in idyllic villages as well as communal town allotments are all to be visited, as well as historic gardens designed by Gertrude Jekyll, Margery Fish and Harold Peto.

Somerset Volunteers

County Organiser
Laura Howard 01460 282911
laura.howard@ngs.org.uk

County Treasurer
Sue Youell 01984 656741
braglands@hotmail.com

Publicity
Roger Peacock 01275 341584
barum@blueyonder.co.uk

Social Media
Bill Hodgson 07711 715311
somersetngs@outlook.com

Photographer
Sue Sayer 07773 181891
suesayer58@hotmail.com

Presentations
Dave & Prue Moon 01373 473381
davidmoon202@btinternet.com

Booklet Co-ordinator
Bill Hodgson (as above)

Booklet Distributor
Ash Warne 07548 889705
ashwarne@btinternet.com

Assistant County Organisers
Marsha Casely 07854 882616
marjac321@hotmail.com

Patricia Davies-Gilbert 01823 412187
pdaviesgilbert@btinternet.com

Alison Highnam 01258 821576
allies1@btinternet.com

Marion Jay 01823 431798
marion@garden84.net

Judith Stanford 01761 233045
judithstanford.ngs@hotmail.co.uk

Ash Warne (as above)

Bristol Area Volunteers

County Organiser
Su Mills 01454 615438
susanlmills@gmail.com

County Treasurer
Ken Payne 01275 333146
kg.payne@yahoo.co.uk

Publicity
Pat Davie 01275 790919
pattidavie@hotmail.com

Booklet Co-ordinator
Bill Hodgson 01823 431798
somersetngs@outlook.com

Booklet Distributor
Graham Guest 01275 472393
gandsguest@btinternet.com

Assistant County Organisers
Angela Conibere 01454 413828
aeconibere@hotmail.com

Pat Davie (as above)

Graham Guest (as above)

Tracey Halladay 01179 604780
thallada@icloud.com

Christine Healey 01454 612795
christine.healey@uwclub.net

Margaret Jones 01225 891229
ian@weircott.plus.com

Jeanette Parker 01454 299699
jeanette_parker@hotmail.co.uk

Jane Perkins 01454 414570
janekperkins@gmail.com

Irene Randow 01275 857208
irene.randow@sky.com

OPENING DATES

All entries subject to change. For latest information check www.ngs.org.uk

Map locator numbers are shown to the right of each garden name.

February

Snowdrop Festival

Saturday 4th
◆ Elworthy Cottage 31

Sunday 5th
◆ Elworthy Cottage 31
Rock House 72

Sunday 12th
Hanham Court 40
Rock House 72
◆ Sherborne Garden 77
Truffles 94

Monday 13th
◆ Sherborne Garden 77

Sunday 19th
◆ East Lambrook Manor Gardens 30
Nynehead Court 62
Truffles 94

Sunday 26th
Algars Manor 2
Algars Mill 3

March

Tuesday 7th
◆ Hestercombe Gardens 43

Sunday 26th
Rock House 72

April

Sunday 2nd
Fairfield 32
Rock House 72

Thursday 6th
◆ Elworthy Cottage 31

Friday 7th
Tormarton Court 92

Sunday 9th
Hangeridge Farmhouse 39
Rose Cottage 73

Thursday 13th
◆ Elworthy Cottage 31

Sunday 16th
Truffles 94

Monday 17th
◆ Elworthy Cottage 31
Truffles 94

Thursday 20th
◆ Elworthy Cottage 31

Saturday 22nd
◆ Barrington Court 6

Sunday 23rd
Watcombe 99

Thursday 27th
Bath Priory Hotel 8

Saturday 29th
Aller Farmhouse 4
◆ The Walled Gardens of Cannington 98

Sunday 30th
Aller Farmhouse 4
Bartley Cottage 7
NEW Sparrows 82
◆ The Walled Gardens of Cannington 98

May

Saturday 6th
Hillcrest 44

Sunday 7th
Algars Manor 2
Algars Mill 3
Hillcrest 44
◆ The Yeo Valley Organic Garden at Holt Farm 106

Wednesday 10th
◆ Kilver Court Gardens 48

Friday 12th
Little Yarford Farmhouse 50

Saturday 13th
Little Yarford Farmhouse 50

Sunday 14th
◆ Court House 25
Little Yarford Farmhouse 50
◆ Midney Gardens 56

◆ Milton Lodge 57
The Red Post House 71

Monday 15th
Little Yarford Farmhouse 50

Thursday 18th
Forest Lodge 34

Sunday 21st
◆ East Lambrook Manor Gardens 30
Hartwood House 41
Watcombe 99

Tuesday 23rd
NEW Lower Shalford Farm 52

Wednesday 24th
NEW Laughing Water 49

Thursday 25th
◆ Elworthy Cottage 31

90th Anniversary Weekend

Saturday 27th
1 Braggchurch 13
25 Chaucer Road 19
Marshfield Gardens 55
Orchard View 66

Sunday 28th
Abbey Farm 1
1 Braggchurch 13
25 Chaucer Road 19
Hanham Court 40
Hinton St George Gardens 45
Marshfield Gardens 55
St Monica Trust 75
◆ Tintinhull 91
Wayford Manor 101

Monday 29th
Abbey Farm 1
1 Braggchurch 13
◆ Elworthy Cottage 31
Hanham Court 40
Hinton St George Gardens 45

Tuesday 30th
Wellfield Barn 102

June

Thursday 1st
◆ Elworthy Cottage 31
NEW Lower Shalford Farm 52

Saturday 3rd
Babbs Farm 5

Sunday 4th
Babbs Farm 5
Bartley Cottage 7
Greystones 38
◆ Milton Lodge 57
16 Montroy Close 59

Tuesday 6th
◆ Hestercombe Gardens 43

Wednesday 7th
NEW Laughing Water 49

Thursday 8th
Watcombe 99

Saturday 10th
NEW Bowdens Farm 11
◆ East Lambrook Manor Gardens 30
Lower Cockhill Farmhouse 51
The Old Rectory, Doynton 64
NEW South Cary House 79
18 Woodgrove Road 105

Sunday 11th
9 Catherston Close 18
Church Farm House 21
Congresbury Gardens 23
1 Frobisher Road 35
Lower Cockhill Farmhouse 51
Lucombe House 53
NEW South Cary House 79
Stanton Court Nursing Home 84
Vellacott 96
Vine House 97

Monday 12th
Vellacott 96

Wednesday 14th
Church Farm House 21

Thursday 15th
◆ Special Plants 83

Friday 16th
9 Catherston Close 18
Tormarton Court 92

Saturday 17th
18 Woodgrove Road 105

Sunday 18th
9 Catherston Close 18
Model Farm 58
Penny Brohn UK 70
Stogumber Gardens 86
West Bristol Gardens 103

Wednesday 21st
Goblin Combe House 37
NEW Laughing Water 49
NEW Sparrows 82

Thursday 22nd
Forest Lodge 34

Saturday 24th
Lympsham Gardens 54
The Old Vicarage,
Weare 65

Sunday 25th
NEW Doynton House 27
Lympsham Gardens 54
The Old Vicarage,
Weare 65
NEW Swift House 90
◆ University of Bristol
Botanic Garden 95

Wednesday 28th
Goblin Combe House 37

July

Sunday 2nd
Hangeridge Farmhouse 39
◆ Milton Lodge 57
Nynehead Court 62
Vellacott 96

Monday 3rd
Vellacott 96

Tuesday 4th
Muriel Jones Field
Allotments 60

Wednesday 5th
9 Catherston Close 18
Hangeridge Farmhouse 39
NEW Laughing Water 49

Thursday 6th
◆ Elworthy Cottage 31

Saturday 8th
◆ Barrington Court 6

Sunday 9th
Brent Knoll Gardens 14
Gants Mill & Garden 36

Wednesday 12th
Park Cottage 68

Saturday 15th
Churchill Gardens 22

Sunday 16th
Churchill Gardens 22
◆ Court House 25
Honeyhurst Farm 46
Rugg Farm 74
Stowey Gardens 88

Wednesday 19th
Church Farm House 21

Thursday 20th
◆ Special Plants 83

Saturday 22nd
Park Cottage 68

Sunday 23rd
NEW Benter Gardens 10
Church Farm House 21
NEW Old Orchard 63
Sutton Hosey Manor 89

Wednesday 26th
◆ Ston Easton Park 87

Saturday 29th
◆ Cothay Manor &
Gardens 24

Sunday 30th
Camers 17
1 Frobisher Road 35

August

Sunday 6th
Hangeridge Farmhouse 39
◆ Jekka's Herbetum 47

Friday 11th
NEW Parish's House 67

Saturday 12th
NEW Parish's House 67

Thursday 17th
◆ Special Plants 83

Sunday 20th
Fernhill 33
NEW 65 Northmead
Road 61
Whitewood Lodge 104

Thursday 24th
Bath Priory Hotel 8
NEW 65 Northmead
Road 61

Sunday 27th
Babbs Farm 5

Monday 28th
Babbs Farm 5
◆ Elworthy Cottage 31

September

Wednesday 6th
◆ Kilver Court
Gardens 48

Saturday 9th
Broomclose 16

Pen Mill Farm 69

Sunday 10th
Beechwell House 9
Broomclose 16
Pen Mill Farm 69

Friday 15th
◆ Midney Gardens 56

Saturday 16th
◆ The Walled Gardens of
Cannington 98

Sunday 17th
◆ The Walled Gardens of
Cannington 98

Thursday 21st
◆ Special Plants 83

Saturday 30th
◆ Dyrham Park 28

October

Sunday 1st
◆ Dyrham Park 28

Thursday 19th
◆ Special Plants 83

February 2018

Sunday 11th
◆ Sherborne Garden 77

Monday 12th
◆ Sherborne Garden 77

Saturday 17th
◆ East Lambrook Manor
Gardens 30

By Arrangement

Aller Farmhouse 4
Babbs Farm 5
Ball Copse Hall, Brent
Knoll Gardens 14
Bartley Cottage 7
Bradon Farm 12
Brewery House 15
Broomclose 16
Camers 17
Cherry Bolberry Farm 20
Church Farm House 21
The Dairy 26
East End Farm 29
◆ Elworthy Cottage 31
Fernhill 33
Forest Lodge 34
Hangeridge Farmhouse 39
Hartwood House 41

4 Haytor Park, West
Bristol Gardens 103
Henley Mill 42
Hillcrest 44
Hinton St George
Gardens 45
Honeyhurst Farm 46
Hooper's Holding, Hinton
St George Gardens 45
Knoll Cottage, Stogumber
Gardens 86
NEW Laughing Water 49
Laurel Cottage, Churchill
Gardens 22
Little Yarford
Farmhouse 50
NEW Lower Shalford
Farm 52
Lucombe House 53
Nynehead Court 62
NEW Parish's House 67
Pen Mill Farm 69
Rock House 72
Rose Cottage 73
Rugg Farm 74
Serridge House 76
Sole Retreat 78
South Kelding 80
South Street Allotment,
Hinton St George
Gardens 45
Southfield Farm 81
NEW Sparrows 82
Sutton Hosey Manor 89
Tormarton Court 92
Troytes Farmstead 93
Vellacott 96
Watcombe 99
Waverley 100
Wellfield Barn 102
159 Westbury Lane, West
Bristol Gardens 103
Whitewood Lodge 104

*Your visit to a
garden will help
more people be
cared for by
a Parkinson's
nurse*

THE GARDENS

Orchard View

1 ABBEY FARM

Montacute, TA15 6UA. Elizabeth McFarlane. *4m from Yeovil. Follow A3088, take slip rd to Montacute, turn L at T-junction into village. Turn R between Church & King's Arms (no through rd).* Sun 28, Mon 29 May (11-4). Adm £5, chd free. Light refreshments.

2½ acres of mainly walled gardens on sloping site provide the setting for Cluniac Medieval Priory gatehouse. Interesting plants incl roses, shrubs, grasses, clematis. Herbaceous borders, white garden, gravel garden. Small arboretum. Pond for wildlife - frogs, newts, dragonflies. Fine mulberry, walnut and monkey puzzle trees. Seats for resting. Restored Grade 2 listed dovecote. Gravel area and one steep slope.

2 ALGARS MANOR

Station Rd, Iron Acton, BS37 9TB. Mrs B Naish. *9m N of Bristol, 3m W of Yate/Chipping Sodbury. Turn S off Iron Acton bypass B4059, past village green and past White Hart PH, 200yds, then over level crossing. No access from Frampton Cotterell via lane; ignore Sat Nav. Parking at Algars Manor.* Sun 26 Feb (2-5). Sun 7 May (2-5), home-made teas. Combined adm with Algars Mill £5, chd free. No teas available on 26th Feb.

2 acres of woodland garden beside River Frome, mill stream, native plants mixed with collections of 60 magnolias and 70 camellias, rhododendrons, azaleas, eucalyptus and other unusual trees and shrubs. Snowdrops and other early spring flowers. Partial wheelchair access only, gravel paths, some steep and uneven slopes.

3 ALGARS MILL

Frampton End Rd, Iron Acton, Bristol, BS37 9TD. Mr & Mrs John Wright. *9m N of Bristol, 3m W of Yate/Chipping Sodbury. (For directions see Algars Manor).* Sun 26 Feb (2-5). Sun 7 May (2-5), home-made teas. Combined adm with Algars Manor £5, chd free. No teas available on 26 Feb

2-acre woodland garden bisected by R Frome; spring bulbs, shrubs; very early spring feature (Feb-Mar) of wild Newent daffodils. 300-400yr-old mill house (not open) through which millrace still runs.

4 ALLER FARMHOUSE

Williton, nr Taunton, TA4 4LY. Mr & Mrs Richard Chandler, 01984 633702, sylvana.chandler@gmail.com. *7m E of Minehead, 1m S of Williton. From A358 Taunton turn L into Sampford Brett. Follow signs to Capton. Follow lane downhill to Aller Farm. Car park in field beyond house.* Sat 29, Sun 30 Apr (2-5.30). Adm £4, chd free. Cream teas. Visits also by arrangement Mar to Oct excl July and Aug for groups of 10-25. No coaches.

2-3 acres. Hot, dry, sunny, S-facing, surrounded by pink stone walls and sub-divided into 5 separate compartments by same. Cliff Garden is old 3-sided quarry. Old magnolias, figs and Judas tree; many unusual and/or tender plants incl Beschorneria yuccoides, echium vars, buddleia colvilei Kewensis, carpenteria, Eupatorium ligustrinum, Caesalpinia gilliesi, feijoa, kiwi fruit;. Partial direct wheelchair access; but top parts of garden accessible from upper (iron-bar) gate.

5 BABBS FARM

Westhill Lane, Bason Bridge, Highbridge, TA9 4RF. Sue & Richard O'Brien, 01278 793244. *1½m E of Highbridge, 1½m SSE of M5 exit 22. Turn into Westhill Lane off B3141 (Church Rd), 100yds S of where it joins B3139 (Wells-Highbridge rd).* Sat 3, Sun 4 June, Sun 27, Mon 28 Aug (2-5). Adm £4, chd free. Visits also by arrangement May to Sept.

¾ acre plantsman's garden in Somerset Levels, gradually created out of fields surrounding old farmhouse over last 20 yrs and still being developed. Trees, shrubs and herbaceous perennials planted with an eye for form and shape in big flowing borders. Various ponds (formal and informal), box garden, patio area and conservatory.

© Rowan Isaac

Hanham Court

6 ♦ BARRINGTON COURT
Barrington, Ilminster, TA19 0NQ.
National Trust, 01460 241938,
barringtoncourt@nationaltrust.
org.uk, www.nationaltrust.org.uk.
*5m NE of Ilminster. In Barrington
village on B3168. Follow brown NT
signs.* **For NGS: Sat 22 Apr, Sat 8
July (10.30-5). Adm £12.50, chd
£6.30. Cream teas at Strode
Dining & Tearoom, lunches also
served. For other opening times
and information, please phone,
email or visit garden website.**
Well known garden constructed
in 1920 by Col Arthur Lyle from
derelict farmland (C19 cattle stalls
still exist). Gertrude Jekyll suggested
planting schemes for the layout.
Paved paths with walled rose and
iris, white and lily gardens, large
kitchen garden. The kitchen garden
has been in continuous production
for over 90yrs. Some paths a little
uneven.
♿ ❀ 🚍 ☕

7 BARTLEY COTTAGE
Birch Hill, Cheddar, BS27 3JP. Mr &
Mrs S Cleverdon, 01934 740387,
cleverdonsteve@yahoo.co.uk.
*Cheddar town centre. Follow signs
for Cheddar Gorge. Follow yellow
signs. Parking on rd.* **Sun 30 Apr,
Sun 4 June (2-5). Adm £3, chd
free. Cream teas. Visits also by
arrangement.**

Small garden filled with over 100
very rare and unusual conifers
which will surprise our visitors
with differing colours, shapes and
textures. Large koi pond. Tranquil,
oriental style garden with large
outdoor bonsai, spring bulbs and
Japanese tea house. Spectacular
views of Cheddar Gorge. Cream
teas a speciality. Wood turning on
display. Featured in Mendip Times &
Somerset Country Gardener.
❀ ☕

8 BATH PRIORY HOTEL
Weston Rd, Bath, BA1 2XT.
Jane Moore, Head Gardener,
01225 331922,
info@thebathpriory.co.uk,
www.thebathpriory.co.uk. *Close to
centre of Bath. Metered parking in
Royal Victoria Park. No 4, 14, 39 and
37 buses from City centre.* **Thur 27
Apr, Thur 24 Aug (2-5). Adm
£3, chd free. Home-made teas.**
Discover 3 acres of mature walled
gardens. Quintessentially English,
the garden has billowing borders,
croquet lawn, wild flower meadow
and ancient specimen trees. Spring
is bright with tulips and flowering
cherries; autumn alive with colour.
Perennials and tender plants provide
summer highlights while the kitchen
garden supplies herbs, fruit and
vegetables to the restaurant. Gravel
paths and some steps.
♿ ❀ NPC 🛏 ☕

9 BEECHWELL HOUSE
51 Goose Green, Yate, BS37 5BL.
Tim Wilmot, www.beechwell.com.
*10m NE of Bristol. From Yate centre,
go N onto Church Ln. After ½m turn
L onto Greenways Rd then R onto
Church Ln. After 300yds take R fork,
garden 100yds on L.* **Sun 10 Sept
(1-5). Adm £3.50, chd free.
Home-made teas.**
Enclosed, level, subtropical garden
created over last 28 yrs and filled
with exotic planting, incl palms
(over 6 varieties), tree ferns, yuccas,
agaves and succulent bed, rare
shrubs, bamboos, bananas, and other
architectural planting. Wildlife pond
and koi pond. C16 40ft deep well.
Rare plant raffle every hour. Some
narrow pathways.
♿ ☕

GROUP OPENING

10 NEW BENTER GARDENS
Benter, Oakhill, Radstock, BA3 5BJ.
*Between the villages of Chilcompton
and Oakhill. On A37 between Bristol
and Shepton Mallet, turn off to the
gardens by village shop in Gurney
Slade. Follow lane for approx 1m,
turn R at signpost.* **Sun 23 July (10-
5). Combined adm £5, chd free.
Home-made teas at Fire Engine
House.**

NEW **COLLEGE BARN**
Alex Crossman & Jen Weaver.

NEW **FIRE ENGINE HOUSE**
Patrick & Nicola Crossman.

2 contrasting gardens in a beautiful,
rural setting. The garden at Fire
Engine House is mature and
established, with lawns, generous
borders and narrow, enticing paths;
through a garden door and tumble-
down bothy is a small orchard and
arboretum. College Barn garden
is 3 yrs old and draws upon the
surrounding meadows and woods
with hazel and hornbeam hedges,
swathes of perennials and prairie
planting with ornamental grasses.
An intimate walled garden is filled
with vegetables, herbs and flowers.
Amongst the planting is sculpture
and woodwork by Fiona Campbell
and Nick Weaver, whose designs
featured in one of the gold-winning
artisan gardens at Chelsea 2016.
Peace and tranquillity surrounds
Benter Gardens.
☕

11 NEW BOWDENS FARM
Hambridge, Langport, TA10 0BP.
Mary Lang. *10m E of Taunton. In
Curry Rivel turn off A378 by Shell
garage to Hambrige (B3168)
Continue for 1m, 50yds past
Hambridge village sign take 1st L
signed Bowdens Farm.* **Sat 10 June
(2-5). Adm £4, chd free. Home-
made teas.**
Peaceful garden with stunning views.
2 acres incl 6 yr old formal garden
with mixed herbaceous borders,
old fashioned roses, box, yew and

pergola smothered in climbers. Lily covered pond with drifts of wild orchid and flag iris, self seeded herb garden and pretty courtyard garden. Productive kitchen garden and seating on lawns amongst maturing trees. Mostly wheelchair access.

12 BRADON FARM

Isle Abbotts, Taunton, TA3 6RX. Mr & Mrs Thomas Jones, deborahjstanley@hotmail.com. *Take turning to Ilton off A358. Bradon Farm is 1½m out of Ilton on Bradon Lane.* **Visits by arrangement June to Aug for groups of 6 - 40. Adm £5, chd free. Home-made teas.**

Classic formal garden created in recent years, demonstrating the effective use of structure. Much to see incl parterre, knot garden, pleached lime walk, formal pond, herbaceous borders, orchard and wildflower planting.

13 1 BRAGGCHURCH

93 Hendford Hill, Yeovil, BA20 2RE. Veronica Sartin. *Walking distance of Yeovil centre. Approaching Yeovil on A30 from Quicksilver Mail PH r'about, garden 1st driveway on R down Hendford Hill, parking at Southwoods (next R down hill). Car park at bottom of Hendford Hill.* **Sat 27, Sun 28, Mon 29 May (2-6). Adm £5, chd free. Home-made teas. Entry to include tea/coffee and piece of cake - further refreshments by donation.**

Old garden of undulating lawns and mature trees evolving since May 2002 to semi-wild, nature-friendly, woodland garden with a few surprises within the new planting - refurbished tree house, dancing figures, Anderson shelter, pond, willow weaving, retreat with poetry, medlar tree enclosure, rhododendron hideaway and courtyard curios/mosaics. Partial wheelchair access, only main drive through garden to refreshment area.

GROUP OPENING

14 BRENT KNOLL GARDENS

Highbridge, TA9 4DF. *2m N of Highbridge. Off A38 & M5 J22. From M5 take A38 N (Cheddar etc) first L into Brent Knoll.* **Sun 9 July (12-5.30). Combined adm £7, chd free. Light refreshments & cream teas at Ball Copse Hall.**

BALL COPSE HALL
Mrs S Boss & Mr A J Hill, 01278 760301, susan.boss@gmail.com.
Visits also by arrangement Mar to Oct.

LABURNUM COTTAGE
Catherine Weber.

NEW **WOODBINE FARM**
Mrs Samantha Jackson.

The distinctive hill of Brent Knoll, an iron age hill fort, is well worth climbing 449ft for the 360° view of surrounding hills incl Glastonbury Tor and the Somerset Levels. Lovely C13 church renowned for its bench ends. Ball Copse Hall: S-facing Edwardian house (not open) on lower slopes of Knoll. Front garden maturing well with curving slopes and paths. Ha-ha, wild area and kitchen garden. Views to Quantock and Polden Hills. Kitchen garden enclosed by crinkle crankle wall. Flock of Soay sheep. Working beehive on show with honey for sale. Laburnum Cottage: ½-acre garden developed over 15 yrs with over 100 varieties of hemerocallis (day lilies) incl many unusual forms and spider types. Large, sweeping borders with mixed plantings of shrubs and herbaceous plants. Woodbine Farm: a quintessential English garden. Many very old, established climbers in old walled gardens and on house, incl roses, wisteria and clematis. Large herbaceous border. Cottage garden with hydrangeas, fruit and herbs. Paddock with huge lavender beds. Wheelchair access in all gardens, some restricted.

18 Woodgrove Road

15 BREWERY HOUSE

Southstoke, Bath, BA2 7DL. John & Ursula Brooke, 01225 833153, jbsouthstoke@gmail.com. *2½m S of Bath. A367 Radstock Rd from Bath. At top of dual carriageway turn L onto B3110. Straight on at double r'about. Next R into Southstoke.* **Visits by arrangement, please ring for parking arrangements and timings. Teas can be arranged on request. Adm £3.50, chd free.**
¾ acre garden in centre of village with splendid views to S over rolling countryside. Long established walled garden with fine, mature trees, shrubs and climbers. The mature planting gives a sense of mystery as one explores the contrast of colours, shapes and the unusual variety of species. Wheelchair access restricted to lower part of garden.
&. ✿ ☕

16 BROOMCLOSE

Porlock, Minehead, TA24 8NU. David & Nicky Ramsay, 01643 862078, davidjamesramsay@gmail.com. *Off A39 on Porlock Weir Rd, between Porlock and West Porlock. From Porlock take rd signed to Porlock Weir. Leave houses of Porlock behind, park in field immed on L of property. NB Some SatNavs direct wrongly from Porlock - beware!* **Sat 9, Sun 10 Sept (1-5). Adm £4, chd free. Home-made teas. Visits also by arrangement Apr to Oct.**
Large varied garden set around early 1900s Arts and Crafts house overlooking the sea. Original stone terraces, Mediterranean garden, long borders, copse, camellia walk, meadow with bee hives and vegetable garden. Maritime climate favours unusual sub-tropical trees, shrubs and herbaceous plants. Garden of the Week in Garden News.
✿ ☕

17 CAMERS

Old Sodbury, BS37 6RG. Mr & Mrs A G Denman, 01454 327929, jodenman@btinternet.com, www.camers.org. *2m E of Chipping Sodbury. Entrance in Chapel Lane off A432 at Dog Inn.* **Sun 30**

July (2-5). Adm £5, chd free. Home-made teas. **Visits also by arrangement Apr to Sept for groups of 20+.**
Elizabethan farmhouse (not open) set in 4 acres of constantly developing garden and woodland with spectacular views over Severn Vale. Garden full of surprises, formal and informal areas planted with very wide range of species to provide yr-round interest. Parterre, topiary, Japanese garden, bog and prairie areas, waterfalls, white and hot gardens, woodland walks. Some steep slopes.
&. 🐕 ✿ ☕

18 9 CATHERSTON CLOSE

Frome, BA11 4HR. Dave & Pru Moon. *15m S of Bath. Town centre W towards Shepton Mallet (A361). R at Sainsbury's r'about, follow lane for ½m. L into Critchill Rd. Over Xrds, 1st L Catherston Close.* **Sun 11, Fri 16, Sun 18 June, Wed 5 July (12-5). Adm £3.50, chd free.**
Small town garden which grew to ⅓ acre! Colour-themed shrub and herbaceous borders, pond, patios, pergolas and wild meadow areas lead to wonderful far reaching views. Productive vegetable and fruit garden with greenhouse. Exhibition of garden photography by the garden owner, from near and far, is displayed in the summerhouse. What a surprise around the corner in waiting! Gold winner in Frome-in-Bloom Competition. Featured in The Telegraph on Saturday, regional press and radio. Several shallow steps, gravel paths.
&. ✿

19 25 CHAUCER ROAD

Bath, BA2 4QX. Tina Payne. *From centre of Bath follow signs to Radstock (A367) along Wellsway to Bear Flat. At T-lights by The Bear PH take any road to L and these will take you to junction with Chaucer Road.* **Sat 27, Sun 28 May (1.30-5.30). Adm £3, chd free. Home-made teas.**
Compact town garden designed by present owners which has achieved Bath In Bloom gold and silver gilt awards. A courtyard of potted plants surrounded by attractive colour co-

ordinated herbaceous borders leads to the next levels which include small fish pond, resident tortoise and vegetable section. Garden is open to coincide with the Bear Flat Artists weekend.
✿ ☕

20 CHERRY BOLBERRY FARM

Furge Lane, Henstridge, BA8 0RN. Mrs Jenny Raymond, 01963 362177, cherrybolberryfarm@tiscali.co.uk. *6m E of Sherborne. In centre of Henstridge, R at small Xrds signed Furge Lane. Continue straight up lane, over 2 cattle grids, garden at top of lane on R.* **Visits by arrangement May & June for groups of 10+. Adm £5, chd free.**
40 yr-old award winning, owner designed and maintained 1 acre garden planted for yr-round interest with wildlife in mind. Colour themed island beds, shrub and herbaceous borders, unusual perennials and shrubs, old roses and an area of specimen trees. Lots of hidden areas, brilliant for hide and seek! Vegetable and flower cutting garden, greenhouses, nature ponds. Wonderful extensive views. Garden surrounded by our dairy farm which has been in the family for nearly 100 years. You will see Jersey cows, sheep, horses and hens!
&. 🐕 ✿ 🚗 🛏 ☕

Camers

© Mandy Bradshaw

21 CHURCH FARM HOUSE

Turners Court Lane, Binegar, nr Wells, BA3 4UA. Susan & Tony Griffin, 01749 841628, smgriffin@beanacrebarn.co.uk, www.beanacrebarn.co.uk. *5m NE of Wells. From Wells B3139 NE for 4½m, turn R signed Binegar, yellow NGS sign at Xrds. From A37 in Gurney Slade at George Inn follow sign to Binegar, past church, at Xrds NGS sign.* **Sun 11, Wed 14 June, Wed 19, Sun 23 July (11-4.30). Adm £4, chd free. Visits also by arrangement June & July, any number very welcome.**
Wrapped around an old farmhouse are 2 walled gardens planted in contemporary cottage style, roses and clematis on walls and unusual perennials in deep borders give interest all seasons. South garden has progressive colourist design. The ever expanding insect friendly planting in the gravel of the old farmyard creates an interesting display of form and colour often with self-seeded surprises! Featured in regional press and on radio. Gravel forecourt, 2 shallow steps.
♿ ✻ 🛌

GROUP OPENING

22 CHURCHILL GARDENS

Churchill, nr. Winscombe, BS25 5NB. *14m S of Bristol. Turn off A38 onto A368, towards WSM, at Churchill T-lights. All 3 gardens are in older part of village. Car parking signed.* **Sat 15, Sun 16 July (2-5). Combined adm £5, chd free. Home-made teas at Bay Tree House.**

BAY TREE HOUSE
Paul & Pam Millward.

CHURCH VIEW
John Simmons & Jill Maycock.

LAUREL COTTAGE
Colin Riddington & Alyson Holland, 01934 852093, c.riddington@btinternet.com. **Visits also by arrangement July & Aug for individuals or small groups Limited disabled parking available at Laurel Cottage.**

Bay Tree House: 2½ acres with partly walled vegetable and fruit garden, formal lawn with seasonally planted beds and rose garden. Victorian rockery, courtyard with camellias and fig tree, thatched summerhouse, tree house, laburnum arch, ponds, and mature Araucaria, Wellingtonia and beech trees. The layout is essentially unchanged from when the house was built, c1830. Church View: mature and overgrown 5 yrs ago, now incl fruit and vegetable beds and borders of shrubs and perennials. Wildflower area and shade garden are still emerging. Recent landscaping incl themed planting, pond, patio and, hopefully, a few exotics! Secluded Laurel Cottage garden has views to surrounding hills. A plantaholic's garden with all the right plants but not necessarily in the right order, developed to encourage wildlife incl birds, butterflies, bees and frogs. Features include pond, greenhouse, mature trees and shrubs, mixed borders, thriving fruit and vegetable plot (badger permitting!).
♿ 🐕 ✻ ☕

GROUP OPENING

23 CONGRESBURY GARDENS

Congresbury, Bristol, BS49 5JA. https://www.facebook.com/congresburygardensopen/. *Approx halfway between Bristol and Weston-super-Mare. 13m S of Bristol on A370 & B3133. Look for signs in the centre of village. Parking in Broad St, Ship & Castle PH and N of bridge.* **Sun 11 June (10.30-4). Combined adm £5, chd free. Home-made teas at Fernbank.**

CHURCH HOUSE
Mrs Lorraine Coles.

FERNBANK
Julia Thyer, http://:juliathyer.blogspot.co.uk.

LABURNUM COTTAGE
Mrs Mary Gilbert.

Visit 3 contrasting gardens within the Conservation area of what has been dubbed the 'kindest village' in Britain. Fernbank: enter an alternative universe in this quirky ⅓ acre garden with lots of surprises. Type your poetry in a hut, lounge on the lawn on a blanket, and enjoy sounds of trickling water and birdsong. While exploring the jungle in the conservatory, discover delicious home-made cakes then sigh with relief that you are not the one who has to water the many hundreds of pots on display. Church House: take inspiration from choice plants, bonsai and objets d'art expertly placed in a courtyard, and a front garden created from an area of concrete. I challenge you to resist a second viewing. Look round a special craft exhibition in the gallery. Laburnum Cottage: see how many trees one can grow in a small tranquil garden and still have room for a lawn, scented flower borders, patio and rose pergola. The most admired tree is a beautiful malus purchased from Lidl for £1.99. Sadly not suitable for wheelchairs.

24 ♦ COTHAY MANOR & GARDENS

Greenham, Wellington, TA21 0JR. Mrs Alastair Robb, 01823 672283, cothaymanor@btinternet.com, www.cothaymanor.co.uk. *5m SW of Wellington. 7m off M5 via A38, signed Greenham, follow brown signs for Cothay Manor & Gardens. See website for more detailed directions.* **For NGS: Sat 29 July (2-5). Adm £7.80. Cream teas. For other opening times and information, please phone, email or visit garden website.**
Few gardens are as evocatively romantic as Cothay. Laid out in 1920s and replanted in 1990s within the original framework, Cothay encompasses a rare blend of old and new. Plantsman's paradise set in 12 acres of magical gardens. Curiosity Shop, small nursery and tea room. Sorry no dogs or picnicing in gardens. House tours 11.45 and 2.15 (separate adm). Partial wheelchair access, gravel paths.
♿ ✻ 🚌 🛌 ☕

25 ◆ COURT HOUSE

East Quantoxhead, TA5 1EJ.
East Quantoxhead Estate (Hugh
Luttrell Esq), 01278 741271,
hugh_luttrell@yahoo.co.uk. *12m
W of Bridgwater. Off A39, house at
end of village past duck pond. Enter
by Frog Lane (Bridgwater/Kilve side
from A39). Car park 50p in aid of
church.* **For NGS: Sun 14 May,
Sun 16 July (2-5). Adm £5, chd
free. Cream teas. For other
opening times and information,
please phone or email.**
Lovely 5 acre garden, trees, shrubs
(many rare and tender), herbaceous
and 3 acre woodland garden with
spring interest and late summer
borders. Traditional kitchen garden
(chemical free). Views to sea and
Quantocks. Gravel, stone and some
mown grass paths.

26 THE DAIRY

Clevedon Road, Weston-in-
Gordano, Bristol, BS20 8PZ. Mrs
Christine Lewis, 01275 849214,
chris@dairy.me.uk. *Weston-in-
Gordano is on B3124 Portishead to
Clevedon rd. Find Parish Church on
main rd and take lane down side
of churchyard for 200m.* **Visits by
arrangement May to Sept. Adm
£5, chd free.**
The garden surrounds a barn
conversion and has been developed
from concrete milking yards and
derelict land. Once the site of
Weston in Gordano Manor House,
the ambience owes much to the use
of medieval stone which had lain
undiscovered in the land for over 2
centuries. 2017 should see several
changes. Come and share our plans
for the future. Changes of level,
with steps and gravel paths, make
wheelchair access difficult.

27 NEW DOYNTON HOUSE

Bury Lane, Doynton, Bristol,
BS30 5SR. Frances & Matthew
Lindsey-Clark. *5m S of M4 J18, 6m
N of Bath, 8m E of Bristol. Doynton is
NE of Wick (turn off A420 opp Bath
Rd) and SW of Dyrham (signed from
A46). Doynton House is at S end
of Doynton village, opp Culleysgate/
Horsepool Lane. Park in signed field.*
**Sun 25 June (2-6). Adm £4.50,
chd free. Home-made teas.**
A variety of garden areas separated
by old walls and hedges. Over the
last 5 yrs much work has been done
to rejuvenate parts, reinstate old
features and add new ones. Lawn
and borders, wall planting, parterre,
rill garden, walled vegetable garden,
cottage beds, pool garden, dry
garden, spring garden, peach house
and greenhouse. Paths are of hoggin,
stone and gravel. The grade of
the gravel makes it a hard push in
places but all areas are wheelchair
accessible.

28 ◆ DYRHAM PARK

Bath, SN14 8ER. National Trust,
01179 371331, dale.dennehy@
nationaltrust.org.uk, www.
nationaltrust.org.uk/dyrham-park.
*8m N of Bath, 12m E of Bristol. On
Bath to Stroud rd (A46), 2m S of
Tomarton interchange with M4, J18.
SatNav use SN14 8HY.* **For NGS:
Sat 30 Sept, Sun 1 Oct (10-4).
Adm £13, chd £6. For other
opening times and information,
please phone, email or visit garden
website.**
C17 mansion with formal gardens
on west side, lawns, herbaceous
borders, fine yew hedges, ponds and
cascade. Nichols orchard with perry
pear trees, wild flower meadow. On
E side of house is C17 orangery
traditionally used for citrus plants.
Garden tours, incl a look at the
historic pear orchard, at various
times during both days. Please
see NT website for times. Special
tours for NGS opening, ask at
Visitor Reception on the day. Steep
slopes in park, cobbles in courtyard.
Disabled WC.

29 EAST END FARM

Pitney, Langport, TA10 9AL. Mrs
A M Wray, 01458 250598. *2m E
of Langport. Please telephone for
directions.* **Visits by arrangement
in June. Adm £3.50, chd free.**
Approx ⅓ acre. Timeless small
garden of many old-fashioned roses
in beautiful herbaceous borders
set amongst ancient listed farm
buildings. Mostly wheelchair access.

30 ◆ EAST LAMBROOK MANOR GARDENS

Silver Street, East Lambrook,
TA13 5HH. Mike & Gail
Werkmeister, 01460 240328,
enquiries@eastlambrook.com,
www.eastlambrook.com. *2m N of
South Petherton. Follow brown tourist
signs from A303 South Petherton
r'about or B3165 Xrd with lights N
of Martock.* **For NGS: Sun 19 Feb,
Sun 21 May, Sat 10 June (10-5).
Adm £6, chd free. Tea. 2018: Sat
17 Feb. For other opening times
and information, please phone,
email or visit garden website.**

Muriel Jones Field Allotments

The quintessential English cottage garden created by C20 gardening legend Margery Fish. Plantsman's paradise with old-fashioned and contemporary plants grown in a relaxed and informal manner to create an extraordinary garden of great beauty and charm. With noted collections of snowdrops, hellebores and geraniums and the excellent specialist Margery Fish Plant Nursery. Moish Sokal watercolour exhibition June. Also open Feb and May to July Tues to Sun & BH Mons; Mar, Apr and Aug to Oct Tues to Sat and BH Mons; (10-5). Featured in Country Life. Main features not accessible to wheelchair users due to narrow paths and steps.

🐕 ✿ 🚗 ☕

31 ◆ ELWORTHY COTTAGE
Elworthy, Taunton, TA4 3PX. Mike & Jenny Spiller, 01984 656427, mike@elworthy-cottage.co.uk, www.elworthy-cottage.co.uk. *12m NW of Taunton. On B3188 between Wiveliscombe and Watchet.* **For NGS: Sat 4, Sun 5 Feb, Thur 6, Thur 13, Mon 17, Thur 20 Apr, Thur 25, Mon 29 May, Thur 1 June, Thur 6 July, Mon 28 Aug (11-5). Adm £3, chd free. Visits also by arrangement Apr to Sept and also in Feb for snowdrops. For other opening times and information, please phone, email or visit garden website.**
1 acre plantsman's garden in tranquil setting. Island beds, scented plants, clematis, unusual perennials and ornamental trees and shrubs to provide yr-round interest. In spring pulmonarias, hellebores and more than 300 varieties of snowdrops. Planted to encourage birds, bees and butterflies, lots of birdsong. Wild flower areas, decorative vegetable garden, living willow screen. Stone ex privy and pigsty feature. Adjoining nursery.

✿ 🚗

32 FAIRFIELD
Stogursey, Bridgwater, TA5 1PU. Lady Acland Hood Gass. *7m E of Williton. 11m W of Bridgwater. From A39 Bridgwater to Minehead rd turn*

N. Garden 1½ m W of Stogursey on Stringston rd. No coaches. **Sun 2 Apr (2-5). Adm £4, chd free. Home-made teas.**
Woodland garden with bulbs, shrubs and fine trees. Paved maze. Views of Quantocks and sea.

♿ ✿ ☕

33 FERNHILL
Whiteball, Wellington, TA21 0LU. Peter & Audrey Bowler, 01823 672423, muldoni@hotmail.co.uk, www.sampfordarundel.org.uk/fernhill/. *3m W of Wellington. At top of Whiteball hill on A38 going W just before dual carriageway, parking on site.* **Sun 20 Aug (2-5). Adm £3.50, chd free. Home-made teas. Visits also by arrangement July & Aug for groups of 10+.**
In approx 2 acres, a delightful garden to stir your senses, with a myriad of unusual plants and features. Intriguing almost hidden paths leading through English roses and banks of hydrangeas. Scenic views stretching up to the Blackdowns and its famous monument. Truly a Hide and Seek garden ..... for all ages. Well stocked herbaceous borders, octagonal pergola and water garden with slightly wild boggy area. Wheelchair access to terrace and other parts of garden from drive.

♿ 🐕 ✿ ☕

34 FOREST LODGE
Pen Selwood, BA9 8LL. Mr & Mrs James Nelson, 07974 701427, lucillanelson@gmail.com. *1½ m N of A303, 3m E of Wincanton. Leave A303 at B3081 (Wincanton to Gillingham rd), up hill to Pen Selwood, L towards church. ½ m, garden on L.* **Thur 18 May, Thur 22 June (2.30-4.30). Adm £5, chd free. Home-made teas. Visits also by arrangement Apr to Oct for groups of 5+.** *Donation to Heads Up Wells.*
3 acre mature garden with many camellias and rhododendrons in May. Lovely views towards Blackmore Vale. Part formal with pleached hornbeam allée and rill, part water garden with lake. Wonderful roses in June. Unusual spring flowering trees such as Davidia involucrata, many

beautiful cornus. Interesting garden sculpture. Wheelchairs access to front garden only however much of garden viewable from there.

♿ 🐕 ☕

35 1 FROBISHER ROAD
Ashton Gate, Bristol, BS3 2AU. Karen Thomas. *2m SW of city centre. Bristol City FC on R, next R Duckmoor Rd, 5th turning L before bollards.* **Sun 11 June, Sun 30 July (2-5). Adm £3, chd free. Home-made teas in conservatory.**
Compact city garden. Comments from visitors: 'Breathtaking the amount of plants you have, fantastic, a haven, magical, like in a wood, amazing so many different plants, it's a Tardis'. One 6 inch step in back garden.

♿ 🐕 ✿ ☕

36 GANTS MILL & GARDEN
Gants Mill Lane, Bruton, BA10 0DB. Elaine & Greg Beedle. *½ m SW of Bruton. From Bruton centre take Yeovil rd, A359, under railway bridge, 100yds uphill, fork R down Gants Mill Lane. Parking for wheelchair users.* **Sun 9 July (2-5). Adm £6, chd free. Home-made teas.**
¾ acre garden. Clematis, rose arches and pergolas, streams, ponds, waterfalls. Riverside walk to top weir, delphiniums, day lilies, 100+ dahlia varieties, vegetable, soft fruit and cutting flower garden. Garden is overlooked by the historic watermill, open on NGS day. Firm wide paths round the garden. Narrow entrance to mill not accessible to wheelchairs. WC.

♿ ☕

The National Garden Scheme and Perennial, helping gardeners when they are in need

Honeyhurst Farm

37 GOBLIN COMBE HOUSE

Plunder Street, Cleeve, Bristol, BS49 4PQ. Mrs H R Burn. *10m S of Bristol. A370, turn L onto Cleeve Hill Rd before Lord Nelson Inn; 300m L onto Plunder St, 1st drive on R. Parking just beyond Plunder St turning. On main bus route.* **Wed 21, Wed 28 June (2-5). Adm £4, chd free. Home-made teas.**
2 acre terraced garden with lovely views. Interesting collection of trees, mixed shrubs and herbaceous borders, surrounded by orchards, fields and woodlands. Home to the rare plant purple gromwell found on woodland edges with alkaline soils. Uneven and steep paths, very slippery when wet.
✿ ☕

38 GREYSTONES

Hollybush Lane, Bristol, BS9 1JB. Mr & Mrs P Townsend. *2m N of Bristol city centre, close to Durdham Down in Bristol, backing onto the Botanic Garden. A4018 Westbury Rd, L at White Tree r'about, L into Saville Rd, Hollybush Lane 2nd on R. Narrow lane, parking limited, recommended to park in Saville Rd.* **Sun 4 June (2-5). Adm £3.50, chd free. Home-made teas.**
Peaceful garden with places to sit and enjoy a quiet corner of Bristol. Interesting courtyard with raised beds and large variety of conifers and shrubs leads to secluded garden of contrasts - from sun drenched beds with olive tree and brightly coloured flowers to shady spots, with acers, hostas and a fern walk. Small apple orchard, espaliered pears and koi pond. Paved footpath provides level access to all areas.
♿ 🐕 ☕

39 HANGERIDGE FARMHOUSE

Wrangway, Wellington, TA21 9QG. Mrs J M Chave, 01823 662339, hangeridge@hotmail.co.uk. *2m S of Wellington. 1m off A38 bypass signed Wrangway. 1st L towards Wellington monument, over motorway bridge 1st R.* **Sun 9 Apr, Sun 2, Wed 5 July, Sun 6 Aug (2-5). Adm £3, chd free. Home-made teas. Visits also by arrangement**

Apr to Aug for groups of 10+.
Rural fields and mature trees surround this 1 acre informal garden offering views of the Blackdown and Quantock Hills. Magnificent hostas and heathers, colourful flower beds, cascading wisteria and roses and a trickling stream are features on offer. Relax with home-made refreshments on sunny or shaded seating admiring the views and birdsong.

 🚾 🐐 ☕

40 HANHAM COURT
Ferry Road, Hanham
Abbots, BS15 3NT.
Hanham Court Gardens,
www.hanhamcourtgardens.co.uk.
5m E of Bristol centre. Old Bristol Rd A431 from Bath, through Willsbridge (past Queen's Head), L at mini r'about, down Court Farm Rd for 1m. Drive entrance on sharp L bend between signs on Court Farm Rd.
Sun 12 Feb (11-4); Sun 28, Mon 29 May (12-5). Adm £5, chd free. Home-made teas.
Hanham Court Gardens develop this rich mix of bold formality, water, woodland, orchard, meadow and kitchen garden with emphasis on scent, structure and romance, set amid a remarkable cluster of manorial buildings between Bath and Bristol. Partial wheelchair access. Caution: dense gravel paths throughout and some steep landscape.

 🐐 ☕

41 HARTWOOD HOUSE
Crowcombe Heathfield, Taunton,
TA4 4BS. Cdr & Mrs David
Freemantle, 01984 667202,
hartwoodhouse@hotmail.com,
www.hartwoodhousebandb.co.uk.
Approx 10m from Taunton, 5m from Williton. Clearly signed from A358. Situated in quiet tree-lined lane known locally as the Avenue.
Sun 21 May (2-5). Adm £4, chd free. Cream teas. Visits also by arrangement Apr to Sept, teas only for groups of 10+.
2 acre garden surrounded by magnificent oak and beech trees. Wide range of specimen trees and flowering shrubs provide colour and scent all year. The formal garden

has a circular theme and colour coded borders. Vegetable and fruit garden laid out in potager style, further on, grassy paths lead into an ancient cider apple orchard being replanted with native trees. Garden mostly wheelchair accessible. Teas and toilet facilities easily accessed by wheelchair users.

 🚾 🐐 ♿ 🚌 🚐 ☕

The Queen's Nursing Institute founded the National Garden Scheme exactly 90 years ago

42 HENLEY MILL
Henley Lane, Wookey,
BA5 1AW. Peter & Sally
Gregson, 01749 676966,
millcottageplants@gmail.com,
www.millcottageplants.co.uk.
2m W of Wells, off A371 towards Cheddar. Turn L into Henley Lane, driveway 50yds on L through stone pillars to end of drive. **Visits by arrangement May to Oct, teas/home-made cake by arrangement. Adm £4.50, chd free.**
2½ acres beside R Axe. Scented garden with roses, hydrangea borders, shady folly garden and late summer borders with grasses and perennials. Zig-zag boardwalk at river level. Kitchen and cutting garden. Rare Japanese hydrangeas and new Chinese epimediums. We have been collecting the Benton bearded irises bred by Cedric Morris. Some may well be in flower in May/June. Garden is on one level but paths can get a bit muddy after heavy rain.

 🐐 ♿ 🚐 ☕

43 ♦ HESTERCOMBE GARDENS
Cheddon Fitzpaine, Taunton,
TA2 8LG. Hestercombe

Gardens Trust, 01823 413923,
info@hestercombe.com,
www.hestercombe.com. *4m N of Taunton, less than 6m from J25 of M5. Follow brown tourist signs rather than SatNav.* **For NGS: Tue 7 Mar, Tue 6 June (10-5). Adm £11.20, chd £5.60. For other opening times and information, please phone, email or visit garden website.**
Georgian landscape garden designed by Coplestone Warre Bampfylde, Victorian terrace and shrubbery and stunning Edwardian Lutyens/Jekyll partnership formal gardens. These together make up 50 acres of woodland walks, temples, terraces, pergolas, lakes and cascades. Hestercombe House is also now open comprising a contemporary art gallery, and a second-hand book shop. Special features: restored watermill and barn, lesser horseshoe bats, historic house and family garden trails. Gravel paths, steep slopes, steps. All abilities route marked. A Tramper mobility scooter is available - booking required.

 🚾 🐐 ♿ 🚐 ☕

44 HILLCREST
Curload, Stoke St. Gregory,
Taunton, TA3 6JA.
Charles & Charlotte
Sundquist, 01823 490852,
chazfix@gmail.com. *At top of Curload. From A358 turn L along A378, then branch L to North Curry and Stoke St. Gregory. L ½m after Willows & Wetlands centre. Hillcrest is 1st on R with parking directions.*
Sat 6, Sun 7 May (2-5). Adm £4, chd free. Home-made teas. Visits also by arrangement May & June (incl late afternoon/early evening).
The garden boasts stunning views of the Somerset Levels, Burrow Mump and Glastonbury Tor, but even on a hazy day this 5 acre garden offers plenty of interest. Woodland walks, varied borders, flowering meadow and several ponds; also kitchen garden, greenhouses, orchards and unique standing stone as focal point. Most of garden is level. Long gently sloping path through flower meadow to lower pond and wood.

 🚾 🐐 ♿ ☕

GROUP OPENING

45 HINTON ST GEORGE GARDENS

High Street, Crewkerne, TA17 8SE. 01460 76389, Klspencermills@gmail.com. *3m N of Crewkerne. N of A30 Crewkerne-Chard; S of A303 Ilminster Town Rd, at r'about signed Lopen & Merriott, then R to Hinton St George. Coaches must park on High St.* **Sun 28, Mon 29 May (2-5.30). Combined adm £6, chd free. Home-made teas at Hooper's Holding. Visits also by arrangement May to Aug, tea & cakes by prior arrangement.**

NEW ARKARINGA
Mr Derek Esp.

NEW 36 GREEN STREEET
Mr & Mrs Henry Brown.

HOOPER'S HOLDING
Ken & Lyn Spencer-Mills, 01460 76389, Klspencermills@gmail.com. **Visits also by arrangement May to Aug, tea and cakes by prior arrangement.**

THE OLIVE GARDEN
Pat Read.

NEW SOUTH ORCHARD
Mr & Mrs Wheeler.

SOUTH STREET ALLOTMENT
Mr John Studley, 07831 489391, johnstudley12@talktalk.net. **Visits also by arrangement Apr to Sept.**

Gardens varying in size and style in beautiful hamstone village. C15 church. Country seat of the Earls of Poullett for 600yrs until 1973. Arkaringa: Long, narrow sloping garden planned to avoid the rectangular and to provide contrast in colour, texture, shape and habit in the planting (both vertically and horizontally) yr-long. 36 Green St: Cottage garden restored after years of neglect. Newly planted 4 yrs ago with mixed herbaceous, shrubs and productive kitchen garden. Hooper's Holding: ⅓ acre garden in colour compartments. Rare plants, many exotics, garden mosaics and sculptures. The Olive Garden: a loving restoration of a site neglected for decades, maturing well. South Orchard: Garden is a work in progress, work began in 2014 and continues. Approx 1 acre divided between flowers, vegetables and soft fruit. Restoring some of the original features and adding new. The South Street Allotment is a miracle of productivity with ingenious methods of providing water and heating. Sale of art work by Karen Dupe at Hooper's Holding. Wheelchair access to Hooper's Holding only.

🐕 ✿ 🚌 ☕ 🍷

46 HONEYHURST FARM

Honeyhurst Lane, Rodney Stoke, Cheddar, BS27 3UJ. Don & Kathy Longhurst, 01749 870322, donlonghurst@btinternet.com, www.ciderbarrelcottage.co.uk. *4m E of Cheddar. From A371 between Wells and Cheddar, turn into Rodney Stoke signed Wedmore. Pass church on L and continue for almost 1m.* **Sun 16 July (2-5). Adm £3.50, chd free. Home-made teas. Cream teas. Visits also by arrangement Apr to Oct for groups of 10 to 40.**
⅔ acre part walled rural garden with babbling brook and 4 acre traditional cider orchard, with views. Specimen hollies, copper beech, paulownia, yew and poplar. Pergolas, arbour and numerous seats. Mixed informal shrub and perennial beds with many unusual plants. Many pots planted with shrubs, hardy and half-hardy perennials. Featured on Glastonbury FM. Level, grass and some shingle.

♿ 🐕 ✿ 🚌 🚐 🍷

47 ◆ JEKKA'S HERBETUM

Shellards Lane, Alveston, Bristol, BS35 3SY. Mrs Jekka McVicar, 01454 418878, sales@jekkasherbfarm.com, www.jekkasherbfarm.com. *7m N of M5 J16 or 6m S from J14 of M5. 1m off A38 signed Itchington. From M5 J16, A38 to Alveston, past church turn R at junction signed Itchington. M5 J14 on A38 turn L after T-lights to Itchington.* **For NGS: Sun 6 Aug (10-4). Adm £5, chd free. Home-made teas. For other opening times and information, please phone, email or visit garden website.**
Jekka's Herbetum is a living herb encyclopaedia displaying the largest collection of culinary herbs in the UK. A wonderful resource for plant identification for the gardener and a gastronomic experience for chefs and cooks. Wheelchair access possible however terrain is rough from car park to Herbetum.

♿ ✿ ☕ 🍷

48 ◆ KILVER COURT GARDENS

Kilver Street, Shepton Mallet, BA4 5NF. Roger & Monty Saul, 01749 340410, info@kilvercourt.com, www.kilvercourt.com. *Directly off A37 rd to Bath, opp cider factory in Shepton Mallet.* **For NGS: Wed 10 May, Wed 6 Sept (9.30-3.30). Adm £5, chd £2.50. Light refreshments in Sharpham Pantry Restaurant & Harlequin Café. For other opening times and information, please phone, email or visit garden website.**
Kilver Court Gardens in Somerset is the perfect day out for those looking to explore a little known treasure, created over 100 yrs ago as an oasis of tranquillity for a factory workforce. Today, the gardens, which have appeared on BBC Gardeners' World, are like stepping into another world - a peaceful oasis away from modernity. Featured in House & Garden, Homes & Garden, Gardens Illustrated, The English Garden, regional press and radio. Some slopes, rockery not accessible for wheelchairs but can be viewed. Disabled parking in lower car park.

♿ ✿ 🚌 ☕ 🍷

49 NEW LAUGHING WATER

Weir Lane, Yeovilton, Yeovil, BA22 8EU. Peter & Joyce Warne, 01935 841933, p.j.warne@btinternet.com. *2m from A303, 7m N of Yeovil. Leave A303 signed Ilchester, take B3151 dir RNAS Yeovilton, take Bineham Lane, signed Yeovilton village,*

Whitewood Lodge

Laughing Water last house on R at end of village. Park at weir just past house. Wed 24 May, Wed 7 June (11.30-4.30); Wed 21 June, Wed 5 July (1.30-6.30). Adm £3.50, chd free. Home-made teas. **Visits also by arrangement May to Aug for groups from 8-30, day or eve.**

½ acre+ garden hidden behind Grade II listed house (not open). A mature garden, remodelled since 2011, it reflects the owner's love of flowers and foliage with sweeping grass paths through mixed beds of shrubs, herbaceous perennials, annuals and bulbs. Floriferous from early spring through to autumn frosts. Large wildlife pond and ornamental water features. Picturesque weir (after which the house is named) on river 20 mtrs past house. Fleet Air Arm Memorial Church, with C13 Nave, in village worth a visit. Limited wheelchair access.

✿ ☕

50 **LITTLE YARFORD FARMHOUSE**

Kingston St Mary, Taunton, TA2 8AN. Brian Bradley, 01823 451350, yarford@ic24.net. *1½m W of Hestercombe, 3½m N of Taunton. From Taunton on Kingston St Mary rd. At 30mph sign turn L at Parsonage Lane. Continue 1¼m W, to Yarford sign. Continue 400yds. Turn R up concrete rd.* Fri 12 May (11-5). Light refreshments. Sat 13, Sun 14 May (2-5.30). Cream teas. Mon 15 May (11-5). Light refreshments. Adm £4.50, chd free. Weekdays incl, coffee, soup, bread & cheese. **Visits**

also by arrangement May to Oct day or eve.

This unusual garden embraces a C17 house (not open) overgrown with a tapestry of climbing plants. The 3 ponds exhibit a wide range of aquatic gems. Of special interest is the finest tree collection in Taunton Deane, 300+ rare and unusual cultivars, both broad leaf and conifer, all differing in form and colour; a tree for every place and occasion. Trees listed on NGS website. Guided tours of trees at 2 & 3.30. The 5 acres are a delight to both artist and plantsman. 'An inspirational, magical experience'. It is an exercise in landscaping and creating views both within the garden and without to the vale and the Quantock Hills. Mostly wheelchair access.

♿ 🐕 ✿ 🚌 ☕

51 **LOWER COCKHILL FARMHOUSE**

Cockhill, Castle Cary, BA7 7NZ. David Curtis & Biddy Peppin. *1m SW of Castle Cary. From Station Rd Castle Cary turn down Torbay Rd, at bend take rd signed North Barrow for 1m. From South St (B3152) take South Cary Lane and at bottom of hill turn L.* Sat 10, Sun 11 June (2-5.30). Combined adm with South Cary House £5, chd free. Cream teas at South Cary House.

Artist's small semi-walled garden in farm setting; courtyard, overflowing long borders planted for colour, contrasting shape and height, with self-seeding welcomed. Pyramidal yews, box-edging and espaliered fruit trees for structure. Climbing

roses, fan-trained cherry and pears. Narrow paths, no grass. Professional artists' studios open. Some narrow uneven paths in garden, one step up into studios;.

♿ ✿ ☕ 🍴

52 NEW **LOWER SHALFORD FARM**

Shalford Lane, Charlton Musgrove, Wincanton, BA9 8HE. Mrs Suki Posnett, 01963 34999, sukiaddington@btinternet.com. *Shalford Lane. 2m NE of Wincanton. Leave A303 at Wincanton go N on B3081. Turn R for Shalford Village ½m on L.* Tue 23 May, Thur 1 June (10-4.30). Adm £5, chd free. Light refreshments. **Visits also by arrangement Apr to Sept.**

Fairly large open garden with extensive lawns and wooded surroundings. Small winterbourne stream running through with several stone bridges. Walled rose/parterre garden, hedged herbaceous garden and several ornamental ponds. Work is in constant progress. Parts of the garden are suitable for wheelchair users.

☕

53 **LUCOMBE HOUSE**

12 Druid Stoke Ave, Stoke Bishop, Bristol, BS9 1DD. Malcolm Ravenscroft, 01179 682494, famrave@gmail.com. *4m NW of Bristol centre. On L at top of Druid Hill. Garden on R 200m from junction.* Sun 11 June (2-5.30). Adm £3.50, chd free. Home-made teas. **Visits also by arrangement May to Sept.**

Woodland area with over 30 mature trees planted in last 5 yrs underplanted with ferns, bluebells and white foxgloves. Front garden redesigned in 2016 to Art Deco design. Separate semi-formal area and untouched wild area under 250yr-old Lucombe oak now registered as third largest in Bristol. Landscape gardener will be on site and happy to answer questions. Rough paths in woodland area, 2 steps to patio.

♿ ✿ ☕

GROUP OPENING

54 LYMPSHAM GARDENS

Church Road, Lympsham, Weston-super-Mare, BS24 0DT. *5m S of Weston-super-Mare and 5m N of Burnham on Sea. 2m M5 J22. Entrance to both gardens from main gates of Manor at junction of Church Rd and Lympsham Rd.* **Sat 24, Sun 25 June (2-5). Combined adm £5, chd free. Home-made teas.**

CHURCH FARM
Andy & Rosemary Carr.

LYMPSHAM MANOR
James & Lisa Counsell.

At heart of stunning village of Lympsham is C15 church of St Christopher. The Manor, built as the rectory exactly 200 years ago, and C17 Church Farm are by the church and connected to each other by side gate. The Manor is a Gothic pinnacled, castellated rectory manor house with 2 octagonal towers (not open), set in 10 acres of formal and semi-formal garden, surrounded by paddocks and farmland. Main features are its carefully preserved, fully working Victorian kitchen garden and greenhouse, arboretum of trees from all parts of the world, large stocked fish pond and beautiful old rose garden. Old outside Victorian privy. Church Farm: ¾ acre informal country garden surrounding farmhouse. Well-stocked herbaceous border, shrub lined paths, raised vegetable beds and small courtyard herb garden.

  ♿ 🐴 ✿ ☕

GROUP OPENING

55 MARSHFIELD GARDENS

Marshfield, SN14 8LR. *7m NE of Bath. From Bath A46 to Cold Ashton r'about, turn R onto A420. From M4 J18 turn onto A46 and L at Cold Ashton r'about. From Chippenham A420 going W. Follow yellow signs into village.* **Sat 27, Sun 28 May (1-5). Combined adm £6, chd free. Light refreshments. Light lunches and teas from 12 noon 111 High St. All proceeds to Marshfield Almshouses.**

BRAMLEY COTTAGE
Mr & Mrs Glyn Watkins.

42 HIGH STREET
Mary & Simon Turner.

43 HIGH STREET
Linda & Denis Beazer.

111 HIGH STREET
Joy & Mervyn Pierce.

116 HIGH STREET
Mr Doug Bond.

3 OLD SCHOOL COURT
Mrs R Crew.

4 OLD SCHOOL COURT
Mrs Jenny Wilkinson.

WEIR COTTAGE
Ian & Margaret Jones.

YEELES HOUSE
Kay & Peter Little.

(Please note: This may be the last time Marshfield open on this scale). Interesting village with C13 Church, Almshouses, shops, pubs and a tea shop. 9 gardens of different sizes and styles coping with the extremes of Marshfield weather. We are usually 2 weeks behind Bath. 111 High St open at 12 noon for lunches and teas (proceeds to Marshfield Almshouses). Also Weir Cottage open 12 noon. 1pm - 5pm all gardens open. Plants for sale at 3 Old Sch. Court. 27th May guided walk by Cotswold Wardens around Marshfield. Boots recommended. No dogs. 28th May Guided walk in village with History Society. Both start 10.30am Market Place. 01225 891229 for info. No wheelchair access at 4 Old Sch. Court, Weir Cottage, 43 High St. Limited access in other gardens.

  ✿ ☕

---

56 ◆ MIDNEY GARDENS

Mill Lane, Midney, Somerton, TA11 7HR. David Chase & Alison Hoghton, 01458 274250, www.midneygardens.co.uk. *1m SE of Somerton. 100yds off B3151. From Podimore r'about on A303 take A372. After 1m R on B3151 towards Street. After 2m L on bend into Mill Lane.* **For NGS: Sun 14 May, Fri 15 Sept (11-5). Adm £5, chd free. Home-made teas. Cream teas also available. For other opening times and information, please phone or visit garden website.**

1.4 acre plantsman's garden, where unusual planting combinations, interesting use of colour, subtle themes and a natural flowing style create a garden full of variety and inspiring ideas. Increasingly known for it's wildlife friendly planting it includes a seaside garden, white garden, kitchen garden, woodland walk, wildlife pond and undercover world gardens. Nursery offers herbaceous perennials, alpines, herbs and grasses.

  ✿ ☕

---

57 ◆ MILTON LODGE

Old Bristol Road, Wells, BA5 3AQ. Simon Tudway Quilter, 01749 672168, www.miltonlodgegardens.co.uk. *½m N of Wells. From A39 Bristol-Wells, turn N up Old Bristol Rd; car park 1st gate on L signed.* **For NGS: Sun 14 May, Sun 4**

Tormarton Court

June, Sun 2 July (2-5). Adm £5, chd free. Home-made teas. Groupon vouchers not valid on NGS open days, all admission money donated to charity. Children under 14 free. For other opening times and information, please phone or visit garden website.

Mature Grade II, terraced garden conceived c1900. Sloping ground transformed into architectural terraces with profusion of plants, capitalising on views of Wells Cathedral and Vale of Avalon. 1960, garden lovingly restored to former glory, orchard replaced with raised collection of ornamental trees. Cross Old Bristol Rd to 7 acre woodland garden, the Combe, natural peaceful contrast to formal garden at Milton Lodge. First opened for NGS 1962. Also open Tues, Weds, Suns, BHs, Easter - 31 Oct (2-5). Featured in regional press and on radio. Unsuitable for wheelchairs or those with limited mobility due to slopes and differing levels.

58 MODEL FARM
Perry Green, Wembdon, Bridgwater, TA5 2BA. Mr & Mrs Dave & Roz Young, 01278 429953, daveandrozontour@hotmail.com, www.modelfarm.com. *4m from J23 of M5. Follow Brown signs from r'about on A39 2m W of Bridgwater.* Sun 18 June (2-5.30). Adm £4, chd free. Home-made teas.
4 acres of flat gardens to S of Victorian country house. Created from a field in last 7 yrs and still being developed. A dozen large mixed flower beds planted in cottage garden style with wildlife in mind. Wooded areas, lawns, wildflower meadows and wildlife pond. Plenty of seating throughout the gardens. Lawn games including croquet.

59 16 MONTROY CLOSE
Henleaze, Bristol, BS9 4RS. Sue & Rod Jones. *3½ m N of Bristol city centre. From Bristol, on B4056 continue past all Henleaze shops, R into Rockside Dr (opp Eastfield Inn). Up hill, across Xrds into The Crescent.*

Swift House

Montroy Close is 3rd turning on L. Sun 4 June (2-5.30). Adm £3.50, chd free. Home-made teas.
Large SW-facing town garden on corner plot. 20 ft stream, informal pond with pebble beach, pergola and seats. Lawn with curving flower beds incl ferns, shrubs, perennials, climbers, small rock garden with water feature, unusual partitioned greenhouse with alpine bench. 8 ft wide arch with climbers. Hanging baskets and many pots of fuchsias. Width of gateway: 79cm.

60 MURIEL JONES FIELD ALLOTMENTS
Birchill Lane, Feltham, Frome, BA11 5ND. *15m S of Bath. On Frome by-pass (take A361). At r'about exit B3092 signed Blatchbridge. Drive approx ½m towards Frome, turn R into Birchill Lane. Continue to allotments, parking on R.* Tue 4 July (11-5). Adm £4.50, chd free. Home-made teas.
Expect the unexpected! 98 pretty allotments on 5 acre site displaying a range of gardening styles from the traditional allotment to a more relaxed approach. A rural setting on the outskirts of Frome with views of Longleat Forest across the river and into the trees and Cley Hill

in the distance. Flowers, fruit and vegetables in abundance. Visitors are welcome to bring a picnic. Featured in Kitchen Garden Magazine, regional press and radio. Viewing area over allotments designated for wheelchair users. Accessible WC.

61 NEW 65 NORTHMEAD ROAD
Midsomer Norton, Radstock, BA3 2SH. Neil & Jose Ross. *A37 Wells to Bristol. Take A362 for 3m to Midsomer Norton. 100yds past Wickes/Tesco r'about, take footpath on R. Limited disabled parking at garden - turn R at next r'about, narrow drive immed on R.* Sun 20, Thur 24 Aug (2-5). Adm £4, chd free. Home-made teas.
Tucked down a long drive lies this hidden ¼ acre plantsman's haven. Colour-themed spaces are rich in eclectic perennials and foliage. Beautiful potager with greenhouse, hens, fruit and gravel garden. Pleached hornbeam tunnel leads to pond where wild corners peek into open countryside. Lush pots and climbers furnish the raised terrace with plentiful seating. Unusual plants for sale. Garden on slight slope, grassed and gravel areas.

62 NYNEHEAD COURT

Nynehead, Wellington, TA21 0BN. Nynehead Care Ltd, 01823 662481, nyneheadcare@aol.com, www.nyneheadcourt.co.uk. *Nynehead is a small village on the outskirts of wellington. M5 J26 B3187 towards Wellington. R on r'about marked Nynehead & Poole, follow lane for 1m, take Milverton turning at fork.* Sun 19 Feb, Sun 2 July (2-4.30). Adm £5, chd free. Home-made teas in the Orangery. **Visits also by arrangement Feb to Oct.**
Nynehead Court Gardens are on English Heritage's list of gardens of historic interest. Once the ancestral home of the Sanford family. Gardens laid out during the Victorian period, points of interest - pinetum, ice house, parterre and extended walks within parkland of old estate. A garden tour, approx 1 hr, will be conducted by Head Gardener, Justin Cole, at 2pm. Visitors can also explore freely using literature available. After 3pm, Justin will be on hand in the garden. Magnificent snowdrops to be seen at our Feb opening. Limited wheelchair access: cobbled yards, gentle slopes, chipped paths.
& ✿ ☕

63 NEW OLD ORCHARD

Goathurst, Bridgwater, TA5 2DF. Mr Peter Evered. *4m SW of Bridgwater or 2½m W of North Petherton. Close to church. Park in field at Northern end of village 500yds from garden.* Sun 23 July (11-5). Adm £3, chd free. Light refreshments in the village nearby.
¼ acre cottage style garden in centre of village. Planted to complement the cottage with over 100 clematis viticella interplanted with a wide range of shrubs, herbaceous perennials, annuals and bulbs. The planting gives all year colour and interest on all 4 sides of the cottage. Limited wheelchair access.
& ☕

64 THE OLD RECTORY, DOYNTON

18 Toghill Lane, Doynton, Bristol, BS30 5SY. Edwina & Clive Humby, www.doyntongardens.tumblr.com. *At heart of village of Doynton, between Bath and Bristol. Follow Toghill Lane up from The Holy Trinity Church about 500 metres, around cricket field to car park field. Signs to garden.* Sat 10 June (11-4). Adm £4, chd free. Home-made teas.
Doynton's Grade II-listed Georgian Rectory's walled garden and extended 15 acre estate. Renovated over 12 yrs, it sits within AONB. Garden has diversity of modern and traditional elements, fused to create an atmospheric series of garden rooms. It is both a landscaped and large kitchen garden, featuring a canal, vegetable plots, fruit cages and tree house. Partial wheelchair access, some narrow gates and uneven surfaces.
🐾 ✿ ☕

65 THE OLD VICARAGE, WEARE

Sparrow Hill Way, Weare, Axbridge, BS26 2LE. Trish & Jeremy Gibson, www.oldvicaragegardeners.com. *2.8m SW of Axbridge. Turn off A38 in Lower Weare, signed Wedmore, Weare. Turn L opp school into Sparrow Hill Way. Continue 0.3m. Garden on R on corner of Coombe Lane.* Sat 24, Sun 25 June (2-5.30). Adm £4, chd free. Home-made teas.
Behind tall hedges, discover how Victorian shrubberies and a hard tennis court have been transformed by relaxed, country style, planting. Around charming Georgian outbuildings lie terraces and courtyards, a stream garden and vegetable plot in 1½ acres of undulating lawns with mature trees and Mendip views. New this year - garden art show and sale in the barn. Partial wheelchair access. Some gravel/lawn paths and steep slopes. No disabled WC.
& ✿ ☕

66 ORCHARD VIEW

Flaxpool, Crowcombe, Taunton, TA4 4AW. Briar & Roger Norton-Harding. *On A358, 9m NW of Taunton. Approx 5m E of Williton. Garden is at bungalow to rear of Flaxpool Garage forecourt. Parking available at garage.* Sat 27 May (11-4.30). Adm £3, chd free. Light refreshments. Selection of beverages. Gluten and dairy free cake alternative.
Quaint medium sized cottage garden, lined with art pieces and containing diverse features. Attached to this beautiful garden is an artist's ceramics studio. A hidden gem of tranquility. Ceramic sculpture. Mainly gravel paths.
☕

67 NEW PARISH'S HOUSE

Hook Hill, Timsbury, Bath, BA2 0ND. Jackie Hamblen (Head Gardener), jackiehamblen@gmail.com. *On B3115. From Camerton/Tunley take Tiimsbury exit at mini r'about, follow rd sharp R. Garden is at eastern edge of village.* Fri 11, Sat 12 Aug (1-4). Adm £5, chd free. Light refreshments. **Visits also by arrangement Apr to Nov for groups of 10+ weekdays, conducted tours.**
Early C19 landscape park. Lawns, shrub and herbaceous borders, water feature, arboretum, walled kitchen garden and woodland walk. Wheelchair entry is through the back of the garden.
& 🐾 ✿ ☕

68 PARK COTTAGE

Wrington Hill, Wrington, Bristol, BS40 5PL. Mr & Mrs J Shepherd. *Halfway between Bristol & Weston S Mare. 10m S of Bristol on A370 turn L onto Cleeve Hill Rd before Lord Nelson PH; continue 1½ miles; car park in field on R approx 50m from garden on L.* Wed 12, Sat 22 July (11-5). Adm £4, chd free. Home-made teas provided by Wrington Pop-Up Vintage Cafe; proceeds to Weston Hospicecare.
Follow every path! Take a colourful journey through 1¼ acres of this established, herbaceous perennial garden. The potager, jungle, rainbow border, white garden and 90ft double herbaceous borders are some of the compartments in this

'Alice in Wonderland' garden divided by high hedges. Large Victorian-style greenhouse displays tender plants. Countryside views and plenty of seating. Sorry no dogs and no WC. Mostly good wheelchair access, some narrow bark chip paths. Narrow flagstone bridge with steps.

& ❀ ☕

69 PEN MILL FARM

Pen Selwood, Wincanton, BA9 8NF. Mr & Mrs Peter FitzGerald, 01747 840895, fitzgeraldatpen@aol.com, www.penmillcottage.co.uk. *1m from Stourhead, off A303 between Mere and Wincanton. Leave A303 on A3081 (Bruton exit). Turn off old A303 to Penselwood. 2nd L fork up narrow unsigned lane. R at grass triangle to Zeals down steep hill. Pen Mill Farm is on R.* Sat 9 Sept (2-5); Sun 10 Sept (12.30-5). Adm £4, chd free. Home-made teas. Ploughmans lunches available Sun. Visits also by arrangement Aug & Sept, groups of 10+ very welcome.
Romantic garden with acid-loving mature trees and shrubs in secluded valley on Dorset, Somerset and Wiltshire border where tributary of R Stour cascades into the lake. Late summer herbaceous borders with abundant colour and over 40 salvias. Enjoy the peace and quiet of this lovely setting - a very English garden. Plant stall incl unusual salvias. Flock of Castlemilk sheep. Featured in The English Garden, The Country Gardener, Garden Answers, Journal of Dorset Gardens Trust. Mostly wheelchair access. No dogs in garden but car park has shade and dogs can run in the fields.

& ❀ 🚐 ☕ ☕

70 PENNY BROHN UK

Chapel Pill Lane, Pill, North Somerset, BS20 0HH. Penny Brohn UK, 01275 370150, andrew.hufford@pennybrohn.org, www.pennybrohn.org.uk. *4m W of Bristol. Off A369 Clifton Suspension Bridge to M5 (J19 Gordano Services). Follow signs to Penny Brohn UK and to Pill/Ham Green (5 mins).* Sun 18 June (10-4). Adm £4, chd free. Light refreshments. Bed and

breakfast bookings available.
3½ acre tranquil garden surrounds Georgian mansion with many mature trees, wild flower meadow, flower garden, cedar summerhouse, fine views from historic gazebo overlooking R Avon, courtyard gardens with water features. Garden is maintained by volunteers and plays an active role in the Charity's Living Well with Cancer approach. Plants, teas, music and plenty of space to enjoy a picnic. Gift shop. Tours of centre to find out more about the work of Penny Brohn UK. Some gravel and grass paths.

& 🐎 ❀ 🚐 🛏 ☕

71 THE RED POST HOUSE

Fivehead, Taunton, TA3 6PX. The Rev Mervyn & Mrs Margaret Wilson. *3m E of Taunton. On the corner of A378 and Butcher's Hill, opp garage. From M5 J25, take A358 towards Langport, turn R at T-lights at top of hill onto A378. Garden is at Langport end of Fivehead.* Sun 14 May (2-5). Adm £3, chd free. Home-made teas.
⅓ acre walled garden with shrubs, borders, trees, circular potager. We combine beauty and utility. Further 1½ acres with various planting, orchard and vineyard. 40 apple and 20 pear, plus plums. Spectacular

Southfield Farm

apple blossom in May. Mown paths, longer grass, many roses. Views aligned on Ham Hill. Summerhouse with sedum roof, belvedere. Garden in its present form developed over last 12yrs. Paths are gravel and grass, belvedere is not wheelchair accessible.

& ❀ ☕

72 ROCK HOUSE

Elberton, BS35 4AQ. Mr & Mrs John Gunnery, 01454 413225. *10m N of Bristol. 3½m SW Thornbury. From Old Severn Bridge on M48 take B4461 to Alveston. In Elberton, take 1st turning L to Littleton-on-Severn and turn immed R.* Sun 5, Sun 12 Feb, Sun 26 Mar, Sun 2 Apr (11-4). Adm £3.50, chd free. Visits also by arrangement for small groups.
2 acre garden. Pretty woodland with snowdrops, hellebores and spring bulbs. Cottage garden plants, roses and many interesting varieties of trees. Limited wheelchair access.

❀

73 ROSE COTTAGE

Smithams Hill, East Harptree, Bristol, BS40 6BY. Bev & Jenny Cruse, 01761 221627, bandjcruse@gmail.com. *5m N of Wells, 15m S of Bristol. From B3114 turn into High St in EH. L at Clock Tower and immed R into Middle St, up hill for 1m. From B3134 take EH rd opp Castle of Comfort, continue 1½m. Car parking in field opp cottage.* Sun 9 Apr (2-5). Adm £4.50, chd free. Home-made teas. Visits also by arrangement in Apr.
1-acre hillside cottage garden with panoramic views over Chew Valley. Garden carpeted with primroses, spring bulbs and hellebores. Bordered by stream and established mixed hedges. New extended gravel garden. Scented arbour and plenty of seating areas to enjoy the views and teas, as well as the music of the Congresbury Brass Band. Wildlife area and pond in corner of car park field. Featured in regional press/radio. Limited wheelchair access, hillside setting.

🐎 ❀ 🚐 ☕ ☕

74 RUGG FARM

Church Street, Limington, nr Yeovil, BA22 8EQ. Morene Griggs, Peter Thomas & Christine Sullivan, 01935 840503, griggsandthomas@btinternet.com. *2m E of Ilchester. From A303 exit on A37 to Yeovil/ Ilchester. At 1st r'about L to Ilchester/Limington, 2nd R to Limington, continue 1½m.* Sun 16 July (11-5). Adm £4, chd free. Cream teas. Visits also by arrangement June & July, groups of 8+ welcome.

2 acre garden created since 2007 around former farmhouse and farm buildings. Diverse areas of interest. Ornamental, kitchen and cottage gardens, lawn and borders, courtyard container planting, orchard, wildlife meadows and pond, developing shrubberies, woodland plantings and walk (unsuitable for wheelchairs). Exuberant annuals and perennials throughout. Metalwork designs by Andy Stevenson Garden Sculptures. Compost Champion in residence. Some gravel paths.

& 🐕 ✿ 🍵

75 ST MONICA TRUST

Cote Lane, Westbury on Trym, Bristol, BS9 3UN. St Monica Trust. *A4018 towards Bristol from M5/ Cribbs Causeway, St Monica Trust is on R, just before start of Durdham Downs.* Sun 28 May (10.30-3). Adm £5, chd free. Light refreshments. Teas, cold drinks and cakes.

The gardens of the St Monica Trust retirement community are a mix of old established borders and new planting. The tree collection, documented in a tree guide, is extensive and impressive, with many unusual specimens. The scented garden is the centrepiece of the gardens and provides yr-round interest. The ponds and woodland wildlife areas benefit from being closed to traffic, and are home to a wide range of bird, mammal and insect species.

& 🐕 ✿ 🍵

76 SERRIDGE HOUSE

Henfield Rd, Coalpit Heath, BS36 2UY. Mrs J Manning, 01454 773188. *9m N of Bristol.*

On A432 at Coalpit Heath T-lights (opp church), turn into Henfield Rd. R at PH, ½m small Xrds, garden on corner with Ruffet Rd, park on Henfield Rd. Visits by arrangement July & Aug for groups of 12-70. Adm £5, chd free. Adm incl home made teas/ evening visits with a glass of wine.

2½ acre garden with mature trees, heather and conifer beds, island beds mostly of perennials, woodland area with pond. Colourful courtyard with old farm implements. Lake views and lakeside walks. Unique tree carvings. Mostly flat grass and concrete driveway. Wheelchair access to lake difficult.

& 🚗 🍵

77 ♦ SHERBORNE GARDEN

Litton, Radstock, BA3 4PP. Mrs Pamela Southwell, 01761 241220. *15m S of Bristol. 15m W of Bath, 7m N of Wells. On B3114 Chewton Mendip to Harptree rd, ½m past The Kings Arms.* For NGS: Sun 12, Mon 13 Feb (11-4). Adm £4, chd free. Light refreshments. 2018: Sun 11, Mon 12 Feb. For other opening times and information, please phone.

4½ acre gently sloping garden with small pinetum, holly wood and many unusual trees and shrubs. Cottage garden leading to privy. 3 ponds linked by wadi and rills with stone and wooden bridges. Snowdrops and hellibores. Hosta walk leading to pear and nut wood. Rondel and gravel gardens with grasses and phormiums. Collections of day lilies, rambling and rose species. Good labelling. Plenty of seats. Garden open for private visits and parties. Mendip Times and Chew Valley Gazette. Grass and gentle slopes.

& 🐕 🚗 🍵

78 SOLE RETREAT

Haydon Drove, Haydon, nr West Horrington, Wells, BA5 3EH. Jane Clisby, 01749 672648/07790 602906, janeclisby@aol.com, www.soleretreat.co.uk. *3m NE of Wells. From Wells take B3139 towards the Horringtons and keep on main road for 3m. L into Haydon*

Drove and Sole Retreat Reflexology, signed, garden 50yds on L. Visits by arrangement July & Aug for groups of 10+, please book teas in advance. Car sharing advised. Adm £4, chd free.

It is a challenge to garden at almost 1000ft on the Mendip Hills AONB but this has been described as 'stepping into a piece of paradise'. Laid out with tranquility and healing in mind, the garden is full of old garden favourites set in ⅓ acre. Within dry stone walls and raw face bedrock are 9 differing areas incl herbaceous borders, labyrinth, water feature, pool, vegetable plot and contemplation garden. Some gravel, narrow paths.

& 🐕 🏠 🍵

79 NEW SOUTH CARY HOUSE

South Street, Castle Cary, BA7 7ES. Sally Walford. *For South St, from Station Rd turn L then R onto B3152 into Castle Cary, turn R down high street, pass church on R onto South St.* Sat 10, Sun 11 June (2.30-5.30). Combined adm with Lower Cockhill Farmhouse £5, chd free. Cream teas.

Approx 1 acre of gardens in grounds of Grade II listed Georgian house. Newly constructed garden in development, semi walled garden with small woodnak walk with views of Lodge Hill, specimen trees, rose gardens, box-edging, colour border and pots and extensive lawns. Wheelchair access by arrangement.

& 🐕 🍵

80 SOUTH KELDING

Brewery Hill, Upton Cheyney, Bristol, BS30 6LY. Barry & Wendy Smale, 0117 9325145, wendy.smale@yahoo.com. *Halfway between Bristol and Bath off A431. Upton Cheyney lies ½m up Brewery Hill off A431 just outside Bitton. Detailed directions and parking arrangements given when appt made. Restricted access means pre-booking essential.* Visits by arrangement May to Sept, max 30. Adm £4, chd free.

7 acre hillside garden offering panoramic views from its upper levels, with herbaceous and shrub

beds, prairie-style scree beds, orchard, native copses and small arboretum grouped by continents. Large wildlife pond, boundary stream and wooded area featuring shade and moisture-loving plants. In view of slopes and uneven terrain this garden is unsuitable for disabled access.

81 SOUTHFIELD FARM
Farleigh Rd, Backwell, Bristol, BS48 3PE. Pamela & Alan Lewis, 01275 463807, Pamlewis9@hotmail.com. *6m S of Bristol. On A370, 500yds after George Inn towards WsM. Farm directly off main rd on R with parking. Large car park.* **Visits by arrangement in Feb, only 7, 8, 9 Feb (10.30-2.30), max 30. Adm £4, chd free. Light refreshments.**
2 acre owner-designed garden of rooms. Mixed shrub and herbaceous borders. Much winter colour and scent. Aconites, heathers, snowdrops, hellebores and more. Courtyards, terrace, orchard, vegetable and herb gardens. Paths through native meadow to woodland garden and large wildlife pond with bird hides. Indoor tearooms in old stable yard. Wheelchair access to most areas on grass paths. Some gravel and steps.

82 NEW SPARROWS
Over Stowey, Bridgwater, TA5 1HA. Mrs Annie Shoosmith, 01278 733595. *8m W of Bridgwater. Take A39 from Bridgwater to Minehead. After 8m at Cottage Inn, fork L to Over Stowey. Straight over 2 Xrds. Park in field on L before church. Walk west.* **Sun 30 Apr (2-5.30); Wed 21 June (2-6). Adm £5, chd free. Home-made teas. Visits also by arrangement Apr to June.**
Shaded cottage garden, full of interesting and unusual shrubs and plants. 3 very old copper beeches shade a collection of ferns and woodland plants, a path leads you to the middle lawn then to a pretty view of the foothills of the Quantocks. Sit and have a cup of tea in one of the many nooks

and crannies. Small vegetable and working area. Partial wheelchair access, phone in advance.

> With your support we can help raise awareness of Carers Trust and unpaid carers

83 ◆ SPECIAL PLANTS
Greenway Lane, Cold Ashton, SN14 8LA. Derry Watkins, 01225 891686, derry@specialplants.net, www.specialplants.net. *6m N of Bath. From Bath on A46, turn L into Greenways Lane just before r'about with A420.* **For NGS: Thur 15 June, Thur 20 July, Thur 17 Aug, Thur 21 Sept, Thur 19 Oct (11-5). Adm £5, chd free. Home-made teas.** For other opening times and information, please phone, email or visit garden website.
Architect-designed ¾ acre hillside garden with stunning views. Started autumn 1996. Exotic plants. Gravel gardens for borderline hardy plants. Black and white (purple and silver) garden. Vegetable garden and orchard. Hot border. Lemon and lime bank. Annual, biennial and tender plants for late summer colour. Spring fed ponds. Bog garden. Woodland walk. Allium alley. Free list of plants in garden. Wobbly bridge over previously hidden gorge. Featured on BBC Gardeners World and in RHS The Garden, Gardens Illustrated, Sunday Telegraph and The English Garden.

84 STANTON COURT NURSING HOME
Stanton Drew, BS39 4ER. www.stantoncourtnh.net. *5m S of Bristol. From Bristol on A37, R onto B3130 signed Chew Magna. Approx 1½m, L at old thatched toll house into Stanton Drew, 1st property on L.* **Sun 11 June (1-4). Adm £3.50, chd free. Light refreshments. Delicious light lunches and cream teas.**
2 acres of tranquil gardens around gracious Georgian House (grade II listed). Mature trees, extensive herbaceous borders with many interesting plants and spring bulbs. Large vegetable garden, fruit trees and soft fruit bushes. Gardener Judith Chubb Whittle keeps this lovely garden interesting in all seasons. Set in beautiful countryside. Stanton Drew's Ancient Stone Circle can be seen from the end of the garden - just a short walk from Stanton Court. Paved, level footpaths allow access to all parts of the garden.

85 ◆ STOBERRY GARDEN
Stoberry Park, Wells, BA5 3LD. Frances & Tim Young, 01749 672906, stay@stoberry-park.co.uk, www.stoberryhouse.co.uk. *½m N of Wells. From Bristol - Wells on A39, L into College Rd and immed L through Stoberry Park, signed.* **Open by arrangement 1 April to 30 Sept. Please confirm your visit is to support The National Garden Scheme when booking.** For other opening times and information, please phone, email or visit garden website.
With breathtaking views over Wells Cathedral, this 6 acre family garden planted sympathetically within its landscape provides a stunning combination of vistas accented with wildlife ponds, water features, sculpture, 1½ acre walled garden, gazebo, lime walk. Colour and interest in every season; spring bulbs, irises, salvias; wild flower circles, new meadow walk and fernery. Featured in regional press and on radio. Regret no wheelchair access.

GROUP OPENING

86 STOGUMBER GARDENS

Station Road, Stogumber, TA4 3TQ. 11m NW of Taunton. 3m W of A358. Signed to Stogumber, W of Crowcombe. Village maps given to all visitors. **Sun 18 June (2-6).** Combined adm £5, chd free. Home-made teas in village hall.

BRAGLANDS BARN
Simon & Sue Youell, www.braglandsbarn.com.

BROOK HOUSE
Jan & Jonathan Secker-Walker.

CRIDLANDS STEEP
Audrey Leitch.

HIGHER KINGSWOOD
Fran & Tom Vesey.

KNOLL COTTAGE
Elaine & John Leech, 01984 656689, john@Leech45.com, www.knoll-cottage.co.uk. **Visits also by arrangement May to Sept.**

MEADOWSWEET COTTAGE
Judy & Derek Illman.

POUND HOUSE
Barry & Jenny Hibbert.

7 delightful and very varied gardens in picturesque village at edge of Quantocks. 3 surprisingly large gardens in village centre, one semi-wild garden, and 3 very large gardens on outskirts of village, with many rare and unusual plants. Conditions range from waterlogged clay to well-drained sand. Walled garden, ponds, bog gardens, rockery, vegetable and fruit gardens, a collection of over 80 different roses, even a cider-apple orchard. Fine views of surrounding countryside. Dogs on leads allowed in 6 gardens. Wheelchair access to main features of all gardens.
& ⌑ ✿ ⌑ ☕ ♨

87 ◆ STON EASTON PARK

Ston Easton, Radstock, BA3 4DF. Ston Easton Ltd, 01761 241631, reception@stoneaston.co.uk, www.stoneaston.co.uk. *On A37 between Bath & Wells. Entrance to Park through high metal gates set back from main road, A37, in centre of village, opp bus shelter.* **For NGS: Wed 26 July (11-4).** Adm £4, chd free. Refreshments of tea/coffee and cake in hotel. Booking essential for lunch and/or full afternoon tea, please phone 01761 241631 to make reservation. For other opening times and information, please phone, email or visit garden website.
A hidden treasure in the heart of the Mendips, do come and see for yourself. Walk through the glorious parkland of the historic Repton landscape, along the quietly cascading R Norr. Productive walled Victorian kitchen garden, octagonal rose garden, stunning herbaceous border, fruit cage and orchard. July brings clematis, magnolias and early roses with the start of planting unusual vegetable seed, not forgetting the famous loofahs. Featured in Mendip Times, Country Gardener, regional press and radio. Deep gravel paths, steep slopes, shallow steps.
⌑ ✿ ⌑ ☕

STOURHEAD GARDEN
See Wiltshire

Weir Cottage, Marshfield Gardens

GROUP OPENING

88 STOWEY GARDENS

Stowey, Bishop Sutton, Bristol, BS39 5TL. *10m W of Bath. Stowey Village A368 between Bishop Sutton and Chelwood. From Chelwood r'about take Weston-s-Mare rd A368. At Stowey Xrds turn R to car park, 150 yards down lane, ample off road parking opp Dormers.* **Sun 16 July (2-6).** Combined adm £5, chd free. Home-made teas at Stowey Mead.

DORMERS
Mr & Mrs G Nicol.

NEW ◆ MANOR FARM
Richard Baines & Alison Fawcett.

STOWEY MEAD
Mr Victor Pritchard.

These gardens cover a broad spectrum of interest and styles which are developing year on year. Flower-packed beds, borders and pots, roses, topiary, hydrangeas, exotic garden, many unusual trees and shrubs, orchards, vegetables, ponds and specialist sweet peas. Manor Farm joins the group this year, a lovely, well-established garden of 1½ acres set within a 4 acre plot, with sweeping views over the adjoining valley. Abundant collection of mature trees and shrubs. Seating areas for enjoyment of some wonderful views from each garden. Something of interest for everyone. Plant sales at Dormers. Featured in Somerset Life, Mendip Times, Chew Valley Gazette, regional press and local radio. Wheelchair access restricted in places, many grassed areas in each garden. Limited strictly disabled parking at each garden which will be signed.
& ✿ ☕

89 SUTTON HOSEY MANOR

Long Sutton, TA10 9NA. Roger Bramble, 0207 3906700, rbramble@bdbltd.co.uk. *2m E of Langport, on A372. Gates N of A372 at E end of Long Sutton.* **Sun 23 July (2.30-6).** Adm £5, chd £2.

Home-made teas. **Visits also by arrangement Aug & Sept.**
3 acres, of which 2 walled. Lily canal through pleached limes leading to amelanchier walk past duck pond; rose and juniper walk from Italian terrace; judas tree avenue; ptelea walk. Ornamental potager. Driveside shrubbery. Music by Young Musicians Symphony Orchestra.

90 NEW SWIFT HOUSE
Stoke Bishop, Bristol, BS9 1BS.
Mark & Jane Glanville,
www.bristolgarden.weebly.com.
NW Bristol - 4m from city centre. 2m from M5 J18 Portway (A4). Turn into Sylvan Way. At lights take R onto Shirehampton Rd. After ¾m turn R into Sea Mills Lane. Lyndale Ave is 2nd rd on L - we're half way up. **Sun 25 June (2-5). Adm £3, chd free.**
We've designed our city garden to look beautiful, provide fruit and vegetables and to be a haven for wildlife. Plants are grown to provide food and shelter throughout the year, with the emphasis on flowers that are nectar rich. We also have the largest colony of swifts nesting in Bristol. Nest boxes with inbuilt cameras. Featured on BBC Springwatch & Autumnwatch and numerous newspapers featured our swift colony.

91 ◆ TINTINHULL
Tintinhull, Yeovil, BA22 8PZ.
National Trust, 01935 823289,
www.nationaltrust.org.uk/
tintinhull-garden. *5m NW of Yeovil. Tintinhull village. Signs on A303, W of Ilchester.* **For NGS: Sun 28 May (11-4). Adm £8, chd £4. Cream teas. For other opening times and information, please phone or visit garden website.**
Famous 2-acre garden in compartments developed 1900 to present day, partly influenced by Hidcote, many interesting plants. Wheelchair access with care to most of garden, uneven paths.

92 TORMARTON COURT
Church Road, Tormarton,
GL9 1HT. Noreen & Bruce

Finnamore, 01454 218236,
home@thefinnamores.com. *3m E of Chipping Sodbury, off A46 at J18 M4. Follow signs to Tormarton from A46 then follow signs for car parking.* **Fri 7 Apr, Fri 16 June (10-3.30). Adm £5, chd free. Home-made teas. Visits also by arrangement limited availability for groups of 12+, weekdays 10am-3pm, refreshments by prior arrangement.**
11 acres of formal and natural gardens in stunning Cotswold setting. Features incl roses, herbaceous, kitchen garden, Mediterranean garden, mound and natural pond. Extensive walled garden, spring glade and meadows with young and mature trees.

93 TROYTES FARMSTEAD
Tivington, Minehead, TA24 8SU. Mr Theodore Stone, 01643 704531,
mineheadcottages@gmail.com.
Take A39 from Minehead to Porlock. L at 1st Xrds for Wooton Courteney, garden ½m on R. **Visits by arrangement Apr to Sept. Adm by donation. Light refreshments by prior arrangement.**
Garden now 24yrs old. 2 acres originally neglected farmland has 2 small water courses incl ancient C12 sheep wash. Main feature some very fine trees well placed to view and photograph. Lawned areas, some slight slopes.

94 TRUFFLES
Church Lane, Bishop Sutton,
Bristol, BS39 5UP. Sally Monkhouse. *10m W of Bath. On A368 Bath to Weston-super-Mare rd. Take rd opp PO/stores uphill towards Top Sutton/Hinton Blewett. 1st R into Church Lane.* **Sun 12, Sun 19 Feb (11-3.30). Adm £2.50, chd free. Light refreshments. Sun 16, Mon 17 Apr (1-5). Adm £4, chd free. Home-made teas.**
In February: homemade soup and/or homemade teas. Easter Sunday 16 April - Easter Egg hunt.
2 acres, a surprising, relaxing large garden, views, new development of exciting large area re-sculpted

2016. Formal and wildlife planting linked with meandering paths, lots of sturdy seating. Magical wooded valley, stream, snowdrops. Wildlife pond, flower meadows, varied flower beds, some sculpture. Unique ¼ acre kitchen garden with several 21ft long × 4ft wide large waist high raised beds. Grass and gravel paths, partial wheelchair access. Sturdy seating throughout garden for resting en route.

95 ◆ UNIVERSITY OF BRISTOL BOTANIC GARDEN
Stoke Park Road, Stoke Bishop, Bristol, BS9 1JG.
University of Bristol Botanic Garden, 01173 314906,
botanic-gardens@bristol.ac.uk,
www.bristol.ac.uk/Botanic-Garden. *¼m W of Durdham Downs. Located in Stoke Bishop next to Durdham Downs 1m from city centre. After crossing the Downs to Stoke Hill, Stoke Park Rd is first on R.* **For NGS: Sun 25 June (10-4.30). Adm £4.50, chd free. Light refreshments. Hot and cold drinks, sandwiches, cakes and ice cream. For other opening times and information, please phone, email or visit garden website.** *Donation to University of Bristol Botanic Garden.*
Exciting contemporary botanic garden with organic flowing network of paths which lead visitors through collections of Mediterranean flora, rare native, useful plants (incl European and Chinese herbs) and those that illustrate plant evolution. Large floral displays illustrating pollination/flowering plant evolution. Glasshouses, home to giant Amazon waterlily, tropical fruit and medicine plants, orchids, cacti and unique sacred lotus collection. Open at other times by arrangement. Special tours of garden throughout day. Wheelchair and scooter available to borrow from Welcome Lodge. Wheelchair friendly route through garden available upon request, also accessible WC.

Gardens are at the heart of hospice care

96 VELLACOTT

Lawford, Crowcombe, TA4 4AL. Kevin & Pat Chittenden, 01984 618249, kevinchit@hotmail.co.uk. 9m NW of Taunton. Off A358, signed Lawford. For directions please phone. Sun 11, Mon 12 June, Sun 2, Mon 3 July (1-5). Adm £3, chd free. Home-made teas. Visits also by arrangement May to Sept, 30 max.

Large informal garden on S-facing slope with splendid views of the Quantock and Brendon Hills. Profusely planted with a wide selection of herbaceous perennials, shrubs and trees. Ponds, folly, potager and restored shepherd's hut. Places to sit and enjoy the surroundings.

✿ 🚗 🍵

VENN CROSS RAILWAY GARDENS

See Devon

97 VINE HOUSE

Henbury Road, Henbury, Bristol, BS10 7AD. Pippa Atkinson. 2m from M5 J17. From M5 J17 head to Bristol Centre. At 3rd r'about, R to Blaise. L at end of Crow Lane. 1st house on R. Sun 11 June (1.30-5). Adm £4, chd free. Light refreshments.

1½ acres of garden behind listed Georgian house. Mature trees, shrubs, herbaceous borders, rock stream and gunnera. Garden originally planted in 1940's for yr-round interest by the Hewer family, and features many unusual plants and trees. Limited wheelchair access. Some paths around upper area of garden.

⅙ 🐄 🍵

98 ◆ THE WALLED GARDENS OF CANNINGTON

Church Street, Cannington, TA5 2HA. Bridgwater College, 01278 655042, walledgardens@bridgwater.ac.uk, www.canningtonwalledgardens.co.uk. 3m NW of Bridgwater. On A39 Bridgwater-Minehead rd - at 1st r'about in Cannington 2nd exit, through village. War memorial, 1st L into Church Street then 1st L. For NGS: Sat 29, Sun 30 Apr, Sat 16, Sun 17 Sept (10-5). Adm £5, chd free. Light refreshments. For other opening times and information, please phone, email or visit garden website.

Within the grounds of a medieval Priory, the Gardens have undergone extensive redevelopment over the last few years. Classic and contemporary features incl National Collections of Deschampsia and Santolina, stunning blue garden, sub-tropical walk, hot herbaceous border with a large botanical glasshouse that includes an aquaponics system. Gravel paths. A motorised scooter can be borrowed free of charge (only one available).

⅙ 🐄 ✿ 🚗 NPC 🍵

99 WATCOMBE

92 Church Road, Winscombe, BS25 1BP. Peter & Ann Owen, 01934 842666, peter.o@which.net. 12m SW of Bristol, 3m N of Axbridge. From Axbridge, A371 to A38. R up hill, next L into Winscombe Hill. After approx.1m, pink house on L. From Bristol A38 S, pass Sidcot T-lights, next R into Winscombe Hill, then as above. Sun 23 Apr, Sun 21 May, Thur 8 June (2-5.30). Adm £3.50, chd free. Home-made cakes and cream teas, gluten-free available. Visits also by arrangement Apr to July, any size of group welcome.

¾-acre mature Edwardian garden with colour-themed, informally planted herbaceous borders. Strong framework separating several different areas of the garden; pergola with varied wisteria, unusual topiary, box hedging, lime walk, pleached hornbeams, cordon fruit trees, 2 small formal ponds and growing collection of approx 80 clematis. Many unusual trees and shrubs. Small vegetable plot. Featured in MendipTimes. Some steps but most areas accessible by wheelchair with minimal assistance.

⅙ 🐄 ✿ 🚗 🍵

100 WAVERLEY

Moorland, Bridgwater, TA7 0AT. Ash & Alison Warne, 01278 691058, ashwarne@btinternet.com. On Somerset Levels, with easy access 3m from J24, M5. Please phone for directions & parking advice. Visits by arrangement Apr to Aug for any numbers, from 1 - 25, day or eve. Phone to discuss catering arrangements for your visit. Adm £3.50, chd free. Home-made teas. Evening refreshments to meet your needs incl cheese & wine.. Started in 2010, this ⅓ acre garden is packed with informal arrangements of shrubs, trees and perennials. Flooded to a depth of 3ft for 3 weeks in Feb 2014, this garden demonstrates the resilience of nature in bouncing back after adversity. Over 75 roses and 20 clematis vie for space amongst 20 different young trees. Some 12 different species of bamboo thrive. Paths allow access to all areas. Gravel access drive. All paths are level, most paved, some wood chip/gravel.

⅙ ✿ 🍵

101 WAYFORD MANOR

Wayford, Crewkerne, TA18 8QG. 3m SW of Crewkerne. Turn N off B3165 at Clapton, signed Wayford or S off A30 Chard to Crewkerne rd, signed Wayford. Sun 28 May (2-5). Adm £5, chd £2.50. Home-made teas.

The mainly Elizabethan manor (not open) mentioned in C17 for its 'fair and pleasant' garden was redesigned by Harold Peto in 1902. Formal terraces with yew hedges and topiary have fine views over W Dorset. Steps down between spring-fed ponds past mature and new plantings of magnolia, rhododendron, maples, cornus and, in season, spring bulbs, cyclamen, giant echium. Primula candelabra, arum lily, gunnera around lower ponds.

102 WELLFIELD BARN

Walcombe Lane, Wells, BA5 3AG. Virginia Nasmyth, 01749 675129. *½ m N of Wells. From A39 Bristol to Wells rd turn R at 30 mph sign into Walcombe Lane. Entrance at 1st cottage on R, parking signed.* **Tue 30 May (11.30-4.30). Adm £4.50, chd free. Home-made teas. Visits also by arrangement June & July, max 29 seat coach on site.**
1½-acre garden, made by owners over past 20yrs from concrete farmyard. Ha-ha, wonderful views, pond, lawn, mixed borders, formal sunken garden, hydrangea bed, grass walks and interesting young and semi-mature trees. Structured design integrates house and garden with landscape. New areas under development. Special interest plants are the hardy geranium family. Moderate slopes in places, some gravel paths.

GROUP OPENING

103 WEST BRISTOL GARDENS

Bristol. *3m NW of Bristol city centre.* **Sun 18 June (1-5). Combined adm £6, chd free. Home-made teas at 159 Westbury Lane.**

CRETE HILL HOUSE GARDENS
Cote House Lane, BS9 3UW. John Burgess.

4 HAYTOR PARK
BS9 2LR. Mr & Mrs C J Prior, 07779 203626, p.l.prior@gmail.com. **Visits also by arrangement Apr to Aug for groups 10-30.**

159 WESTBURY LANE
BS9 2PY. Maureen Dickens, 01179 043008, 159jmd@gmail.com. **Visits also by arrangement Apr to Aug for groups 10-30.**

4 Haytor Park: Every year more to discover. Maybe another arch, sculpture or special plants in secret spaces. Take the dragon trail, how many can you find? Relax on hidden benches in a calm, leafy sanctuary, packed with interest at every level, a green roof and things to make you smile! 159 Westbury Lane: Lovely quiet garden, barely overlooked on edge of city. Planted to owners' design from scratch in cottage garden style. Full of interesting and many unusual plants bought from specialist nurseries. Primarily an early summer garden but being developed to show flowers all yr. Quirky touch with garden artifacts in many places. Many interesting visiting birds. Crete Hill House: C18 house, hidden corner of Bristol, mainly SW facing garden, 80'x40', with shaped lawn, heavily planted traditional mixed shrub, rose and herbaceous borders, pergola with climbers, small terrace with pond. Small semi-walled area on 2 levels with shady planting.

104 WHITEWOOD LODGE

Norton Lane, Whitchurch, Bristol, BS14 0BU. Guy & Selena Norfolk, 07753 322318, selena.gray@btopenworld.com. *S of Bristol off A37 Wells Rd. Leave Bristol on A37 Wells rd. Pass Whitchurch Village into green belt, R down Norton Lane for approx 1m, garden on R. Parking in field behind house.* **Sun 20 Aug (2-5). Adm £4, chd free. Home-made teas. Visits also by arrangement Mar to Nov for groups of 6-10 weekends or evenings.**
¾ acre garden developed over 30yrs from field. Pond, orchard, vegetable potager, mature trees and beds. Minimal use of chemicals in the garden, which aims to provide an ecologically friendly and sustainable environment. Many seats in different parts of garden from which to enjoy the wonderful views of Maes Knoll, an ancient hill fort. Partial wheelchair access, gravel paths and some steps.

105 18 WOODGROVE ROAD

Henbury, Bristol, BS10 7RE. Peter & Ruth Whitby. *4m N of Bristol. M5 J17, follow B4018, R at 3rd r'about signed Blaise Castle. R opp Blaise Castle car park - rd next to Avon riding centre.* **Sat 10, Sat 17 June (2-6). Adm £3.50, chd free. Home-made teas.**
Medium-sized garden divided into 3 sections. Traditional flower garden with Bonsai display and small wildlife pond. Cottage garden with greenhouse and plant sale area. Small orchard with dwarf fruit trees and small vegetable garden. Peter's art studio open for sale of watercolour and oil paintings, 10% to NGS. Gravel path from patio, or grass access for wheelchairs.

106 ◆ THE YEO VALLEY ORGANIC GARDEN AT HOLT FARM

Bath Road, Blagdon, BS40 7SQ. Mr & Mrs Tim Mead, 01761 461650, gardens@yeovalley.co.uk, www. theyeovalleyorganicgarden.co.uk. *12m S of Bristol. Off A368. Entrance is approx ½ m outside Blagdon towards Bath, on L, then follow garden signs past dairy.* **For NGS: Sun 7 May (2-5). Adm £5, chd free. Home-made teas. For other opening times and information, please phone, email or visit garden website.**
One of only a handful of ornamental gardens that is Soil Association accredited, 6.5 acres of contemporary planting, quirky sculptures, bulbs in their thousands, purple palace, glorious meadow and posh vegetable patch. Great views, green ideas. Events, workshops and exhibitions held throughout the year - see website for further details. Level access to the café, around garden some grass paths, some uneven bark and gravel paths. Accessibility map available at ticket office.

STAFFORDSHIRE
Birmingham & West Midlands

Northwich
CHESHIRE & WIRRAL
Winsford
Middlewich
Congleton
Macclesfield
Buxton
Baslow
Chesterfield
Bakewell
DERBYSHIRE
Rowsley
Clay Cross
Sandbach
Crewe
Alsager
Biddulph
Leek
Warslow
Matlock
Cromford
Nantwich
Kidsgrove
Newcastle-under-Lyme
Wirksworth
Amber
Audlem
Woore
Stoke-on-Trent
Longton
Cheadle
Waterhouses
Ashbourne
Belper
Market Drayton
Loggerheads
Stone
Brailsford
STAFFORDSHIRE
Weston
Uttoxeter
Sudbury
Etwall
Derby
Hodnet
Eccleshall
Gnosall
Stafford
Tutbury
Burton upon Trent
Swadlincote
Newport
Lilleshall
Penkridge
Rugeley
Barton-under-Needwood
Ashby-de-la-Zouch
SHROPSHIRE
Wellington
Oakengates
Cannock
Lichfield
Measham
Telford
Shifnal
Madeley
Codsall
Great Wyrley
Brownhills
Tamworth
Twycross
Ironbridge
Albrighton
Aldridge
Sutton Coldfield
Atherstone
Much Wenlock
Wolverhampton
Walsall
West Bromwich
Nuneaton
Morville
Bridgnorth
Dudley
Birmingham
Bedworth
Burwarton
Alveley
Stourbridge
Halesowen
Coventry
Highley
Solihull
Balsall Common
Dorridge
Kenilworth
Stourport-on-Severn
WARWICKSHIRE

0   10   20 kilometres
0   10 miles
© Global Mapping / XYZ Maps

Staffordshire, Birmingham and part of the West Midlands is a landlocked 'county', one of the furthest from the sea in England and Wales.

It is an NGS 'county' of surprising contrasts, from the 'Moorlands' in the North East, the 'Woodland Quarter' in the North West, the 'Staffordshire Potteries' and England's 'Second City' in the South East, with much of the rest of the land devoted to agriculture, both dairy and arable.

The garden owners enthusiastically embraced the NGS from the very beginning, with seven gardens opening in the inaugural year of 1927, and a further thirteen the following year.

The county is the home of the National Memorial Arboretum, the Cannock Chase Area of Outstanding Natural Beauty and part of the new National Forest.

There are many large country houses and gardens throughout the county with a long history of garden-making and with the input of many of the well known landscape architects.

Today, the majority of NGS gardens are privately owned and of modest size. However, a few of the large country house gardens still open their gates for NGS visitors.

Volunteers

County Organiser
John & Susan Weston
01785 850448
john.weston@ngs.org.uk

County Treasurer
Brian Bailey
01902 424867
brian.bailey@ngs.org.uk

Publicity
Graham & Judy White
01889 563930
graham&judy.white@ngs.org.uk

Booklet Co-ordinator
Peter Longstaff
01785 282582
peter.longstaff@ngs.org.uk

Assistant County Organisers
Jane Cerone
01827 873205
janecerone@btinternet.com

Ken & Joy Sutton
01889 590631
suttonjoy2@gmail.com

Sheila Thacker
01782 791244
metbowers@gmail.com

© Marianne Majerus

Left: **Grafton Cottage**

OPENING DATES

All entries subject to change. For latest information check www.ngs.org.uk

Map locator numbers are shown to the right of each garden name.

January

Wednesday 25th
◆ The Trentham Estate 57

March

Wednesday 8th
◆ The Trentham Estate 57

April

Sunday 2nd
23 St Johns Road 51
29 St John's Road 52

Sunday 9th
Millennium Garden 38

Sunday 23rd
Rowley House Farm 50

Sunday 30th
50 Pereira Road 47
Yew Tree Cottage 68

May

Wednesday 3rd
NEW Church Cottage 14

Thursday 4th
Yew Tree Cottage 68

Saturday 6th
Keeper's Cottage;
    Bluebell Wood 31

Sunday 7th
Keeper's Cottage;
    Bluebell Wood 31

Wednesday 10th
◆ Birmingham Botanical
    Gardens 7

Friday 19th
23 St Johns Road 51
29 St John's Road 52

Saturday 20th
41 Twentylands 58

Sunday 21st
The Beeches 4
Dorset House 18
Tanglewood Cottage 55

90th Anniversary Weekend

Sunday 28th
Hamilton House 27
89 Marsh Lane 36
The Mount, Great
    Bridgeford 42
The Old Dairy House 43
The Pintles 48
The Secret Garden 53

Monday 29th
Bridge House 10
The Old Dairy House 43

Tuesday 30th
◆ Middleton Hall 37

Wednesday 31st
◆ Middleton Hall 37

June

Thursday 1st
Yew Tree Cottage 68

Friday 2nd
Coley Cottage 15
The Secret Garden 53

Sunday 4th
The Garth 23
NEW 12 Waterdale 61
19 Waterdale 60

Thursday 8th
Yew Tree Cottage 68

Saturday 10th
◆ Biddulph Grange
    Garden 5

Sunday 11th
Ashcroft and Claremont 2
NEW 51 Featherstone
    Road 21
3 Marlows Cottages 35
91 Tower Road 56
NEW Wild Thyme
    Cottage 63
Wild Wood Lodge 64

Monday 12th
◆ Alton Towers Gardens 1
3 Marlows Cottages 35

Wednesday 14th
◆ The Trentham Estate 57

Saturday 17th
Hall Green Gardens 26

Sunday 18th
Coley Cottage 15
Hall Green Gardens 26
The Secret Garden 53

Wednesday 21st
Bankcroft Farm 3
NEW 5 East View
    Cottages 20

Saturday 24th
Colour Mill 16
The Old Vicarage 44

Sunday 25th
Brooklyn 11
NEW 5 East View
    Cottages 20
304 Ford Green Road 22
The Garth 23
The Mount, Coton,
    Gnosall 41
The Old Vicarage 44
Pereira Road Gardens 46
Priory Farm 49
23 St Johns Road 51
9 Station Road 54
NEW Vernon House 59
NEW 2 Woodland
    Crescent 65

Wednesday 28th
Bankcroft Farm 3

Friday 30th
Woodleighton Grove
    Gardens 66
Yarlet House 67

July

Sunday 2nd
NEW 344 Chester
    Road 13
Grafton Cottage 24
13 Lansdowne Road 32
NEW The Malthouse 33
NEW Marie Curie
    Hospice Garden 34
Millennium Garden 38
Mitton Manor 39
The Pintles 48
NEW 12 Waterdale 61
19 Waterdale 60

Thursday 6th
Yew Tree Cottage 68

Saturday 8th
◆ Castle Bromwich Hall
    Gardens 12
Woodleighton Grove
    Gardens 66

Sunday 9th
The Beeches 4
Birch Trees 6
Bournville Village 8
Woodleighton Grove
    Gardens 66

Friday 14th
22 Greenfield Road 25
23 St Johns Road 51

Sunday 16th
Grafton Cottage 24
22 Greenfield Road 25

Friday 21st
Grafton Cottage 24

Sunday 23rd
Dorset House 18
Moseley Corner,
    The Art of Gardens 40
Yew Tree Cottage 68

Sunday 30th
198 Eachelhurst Road 19
Grafton Cottage 24
The Mount, Great
    Bridgeford 42

August

Thursday 3rd
Colour Mill 16

Friday 4th
29 St John's Road 52

Sunday 6th
The Beeches 4
Grafton Cottage 24

Wednesday 9th
Coley Cottage 15
The Secret Garden 53

Sunday 13th
Wild Wood Lodge 64

Wednesday 16th
NEW Church Cottage 14

Sunday 20th
'John's Garden' at
    Ashwood Nurseries 30

Thursday 24th
The Wickets 62

Sunday 27th
Birch Trees 6
The Wickets 62

THE GARDENS

1 ◆ ALTON TOWERS GARDENS

Alton, Stoke on Trent, ST10 4DB. Alton Towers Resort, 01538 703344, www.altontowers.com. *6m N of Uttoxeter. From A50, follow 'brown signs' for Alton Towers. At the theme park access is via main Alton Towers theme park turnstiles. Complementary parking on the express car park* **For NGS: Mon 12 June (3-5.30). Adm £4.50, chd free. For other opening times and information, please phone or visit garden website.**
Alton Tower's magnificent early C19 gardens, designed by the flamboyant 15th Earl of Shrewsbury, feature pools, pagoda fountain, statues, mature trees, shrubs, rhododendrons and azaleas set in a steep sided valley with steep walks and viewing terraces. Access via main Alton towers theme park turnstiles. Complimentary car parking on the Express car park. One of the first gardens in Staffordshire to 'Open' for the NGS in 1932. Unfortunately the historic nature of the gardens makes them unsuitable for wheelchair users or those with limited mobility.
🚗

GROUP OPENING

2 ASHCROFT AND CLAREMONT

Eccleshall, ST21 6JP. *7m W of Stafford. J14 M6. At Eccleshall end of A5013 the garden is 100 metres before junction with A518. On street parking nearby. Note: Some Satnavs give wrong directions.* **Sun 11 June (2-5). Combined adm £4, chd free. Home-made teas at Ashcroft.**

ASHCROFT
Peter & Gillian Bertram.

26 CLAREMONT ROAD
Maria Edwards.

Two gardens as different as Monet's soft pastel colours are to Vincent's bright sunflowers. Ashcroft is a 1 acre wildlife-friendly garden, pond and covered courtyard. Rooms flow seamlessly around the Edwardian house. Herb bed, treillage, greenhouse with raised beds. Find the topiary peacock that struts in the gravel bed. In the woodland area Gollum lurks in the steps of the ruin. Claremont is a small town garden its design based on feng shui principles. Manicured lawns, herbaceous borders, shrubs, perennials and annuals. Constantly evolving with colour and new features, maintaining interest throughout the year. Come and be inspired! Maria is happy to explain the principles of feng shui in garden layout. Tickets, teas and plants available at Ashcroft. Wheelchair access at Ashcroft only.
♿ ❀ ☕

4 Dene Close

3 BANKCROFT FARM

Tatenhill, Burton-on-Trent,
DE13 9SA. Mrs Penelope Adkins.
*2m SW of Burton-on-Trent. Take
Tatenhill Rd off A38 Burton-
Branston flyover. 1m, 1st house on L
approaching village. Parking on farm.*
**Wed 21, Wed 28 June (2-5).
Adm £3, chd free.**
Lose yourself for an afternoon
in our 1½-acre organic country
garden. Arbour, gazebo and many
other seating areas to view ponds
and herbaceous borders, backed
with shrubs and trees with emphasis
on structure, foliage and colour.
Productive fruit and vegetable
gardens, wildlife areas and adjoining
12-acre native woodland walk.
Picnics welcome. Gravel paths.
&

4 THE BEECHES

Mill Street, Rocester, ST14 5JX.
Ken & Joy Sutton, 01889 590631,
suttonjoy2@gmail.com. *5m N of
Uttoxeter. On B5030 from Uttoxeter
turn R at 2nd r'about into village by
JCB factory. At Red Lion PH & mini
r'about take rd signed Mill Street.
Garden 250 yds on R. Parking at
JCB Academy Sunday's only.* **Sun 21
May, Sun 9 July, Sun 6 Aug, Sun
3 Sept (1.30-5). Adm £4, chd
free. Home-made teas. Visits**

also by arrangement May to
Sept min charge £80 if less than
20 people. Tea extra.
Stroll along the driveway containing
island beds planted with shrubs
and dazzling perennials, and enter
a stunning plant lover's garden of
approx ⅔ acre, enjoying views
of surrounding countryside. Box
garden, shrubs incl rhododendrons
and azaleas, vibrant colour-themed
herbaceous borders, scented roses,
clematis and climbing plants, fruit
trees, pools and late flowering
perennials, vegetable and soft fruit
garden, yr-round garden. New for
2017 small stumpery. Featured in
Garden News Magazine, Garden
Answers Magazine and local press.
Partial wheelchair access.
& ✿ 🚍 ☕ ▣

5 ◆ BIDDULPH GRANGE GARDEN

Grange Road, Biddulph, ST8 7SD.
National Trust, 01782 375 533,
biddulphgrange@nationaltrust.
org.uk, www.nationaltrust.org.uk.
*3½m SE of Congleton. 7m N of
Stoke-on-Trent off A527, Congleton
to Biddulph rd.* **For NGS: Sat 10
June (11-5). Adm £8.63, chd
£4.30. Self service tearoom on-
site. For other opening times and
information, please phone, email or**

visit garden website.
Amazing Victorian garden created
by Darwin contemporary and
correspondent James Bateman as
an extension of his beliefs, scientific
interests and collection of plants. Visit
the Italian terrace, Chinese inspired
garden, dahlia walk and the oldest
surviving golden larch in Britain
brought from China by the great plant
hunter Robert Fortune. Featured on
RHS Gardeners World Tatton Show.
✿ 🚍 ☕

6 BIRCH TREES

Copmere End, Eccleshall,
ST21 6HH. Susan & John
Weston, 01785 850448,
johnweston123@btinternet.com.
*1½m W of Eccleshall. On B5026,
turn at junction signed Copmere End.
After ½m straight across Xrds by
Star Inn.* **Sun 9 July, Sun 27, Mon
28 Aug (1.30-5). Adm £3.50, chd
free. Home-made teas. Visits
also by arrangement June to
Aug, groups of 10 - 30.**
Surprising ½ acre SW-facing sun
trap which takes advantage of
the 'borrowed landscape' of the
surrounding countryside. Take time
to explore the pathways between
the island beds which contain many
unusual herbaceous plants, grasses
and shrubs; also vegetable patch,
stump bed, alpine house, orchard
and water features.
& ✿ ☕

7 ◆ BIRMINGHAM BOTANICAL GARDENS

Westbourne Road, Edgbaston,
B15 3TR. Birmingham Botanical &
Horticultural Society,
0121 454 1860,
www.birminghambotanicalgardens.
org.uk. *1½m SW of the centre of
Birmingham. From J6 M6 take A38(M)
to city centre. Follow underpasses
signed Birmingham West to A456. At
Fiveways island turn L onto B4217
(Calthorpe Rd) signed Botanical
Gardens.* **For NGS: Wed 10 May
(10-6). Adm £7, chd free. Light
snacks & refreshments in Terrace
Pavilion tearoom. For other
opening times and information,
please phone or visit garden
website.**
Extensive botanical garden set in

Heath House

© Julia Stanley

a green urban environment with a comprehensive collection of plants from throughout the world growing in the glasshouses and outside. Four stunning glasshouses take you from tropical rainforest to arid desert. Fifteen acres of beautiful landscaped gardens. Roses, alpines, perennials, rare trees and shrubs. Playground, Children's Discovery Garden, Gallery, Gift Shop. Birmingham Botanical Gardens are open every day of the year except Christmas Day and Boxing Day.

♿ ✿ 🚗 ☕ ☕

GROUP OPENING

8 BOURNVILLE VILLAGE
Maple Road, Birmingham, B30 2AE. www.bvt.org.uk. *Follow brown signs to Cadbury World in Bournville. Route from Cadbury World to nearest garden signed - Selly Manor Museum, B30 2AE. On road parking & shoppers car park available.* **Sun 9 July (11-6). Combined adm £6, chd free. Home-made teas at various locations.**

NEW 19 GREEN MEADOW ROAD
Mr & Mrs Robert & Annette Booth.

39 HAWTHORNE ROAD
Mrs Harriet Martin.

NEW 82 HAY GREEN LANE
Mr Tony Walpole & Mrs Elsie Wheeler.

32 KNIGHTON ROAD
Mrs Anne Ellis & Mr Lawrence Newman.

SELLY MANOR MUSEUM
Ms Gillian Ellis,
www.sellymanormuseum.org.uk.

8 SYCAMORE ROAD
Mrs Sue Adams.

63 WITHERFORD WAY
Mr Nigel Wood, www.youtube.com/watch?v=vY8iFGVdBFo.

Bournville Village is showcasing: a Mediterranean inspired garden with seating, statuary and curios; an overgrown and now restored urban cottage garden; a wildlife friendly garden; a traditional Tudor garden and a George Cadbury-inspired garden. New for 2017: a north-facing ⅓ acre informal garden partially surrounded by mature woodland trees and a colourful front garden Bournville is famous for it's large gardens, outstanding open spaces and of course it's chocolate factory. A free information sheet/map/ walking trail will be available on the day. Gardens are spread across the 1,000 acre estate, with walks of up to 20 minutes between sites. For those visiting with a disability, full details of access are available on the NGS and Bournville Village Trust (BVT) websites: www.ngs.org.uk or www.bvt.org.uk. Visitors with particular concerns with regards to access are welcome to call BVT on 0300 333 6540 or email: CommunityAdmin@bvt.org.uk. Music and singing available across a number of sites. Please check on the day. Press release via BVT Press & PR at appropriate time before the day. Gardens featured Daily Telegraph gardening section Visitors with disabilities are advised to check before travelling.

♿ ✿ ☕

9 BREAKMILLS
Hames Lane, Newton Regis, Tamworth, B79 0NH. Mr Paul Horobin, 07966 531239. *Approx 5m N of Tamworth & 3m S of M42 J11. Signed from B5493, Hames Lane is a single track lane near the Queens Head PH. Disabled parking at the house, other visitors please follow parking signs or park in village centre.* **Visits by arrangement July & Aug for groups of 12+. Adm £3.50, chd free. Home-made teas.**

Just under 2 acres of low maintenance garden featuring small tropical area, island beds, shale area for grasses. Pond, man made stream, vegetable patch and mature trees. Originally a paddock area, trees planted some 15-20 yrs ago but garden really developed over the last 5yrs and still a work in progress. Lots of seating areas to enjoy both the fun aspects of our garden and the surrounding countryside. Larger grassed area may be difficult for wheelchairs on very wet days but access to long drive and eating area in all conditions.

♿ ☕

10 BRIDGE HOUSE
Dog Lane, Bodymoor Heath, B76 9JD. Mr & Mrs J Cerone, 01827 873205, janecerone@btinternet.com. *5m S of Tamworth. From A446 at Belfry Island take A4091 after 1m turn R onto Bodymoor Heath Lane & continue 1m into village, parking in field opp garden.* **Mon 29 May, Mon 28 Aug (2-5). Adm £4, chd free. Home-made teas. Visits also by arrangement May to Sept for groups 5-30.**

1 acre garden surrounding converted public house. Divided into smaller areas with a mix of shrub borders, azalea and fuchsia, herbaceous and bedding, orchard, kitchen garden with large greenhouse and wild flower meadow. Pergola walk, formal fish pool, pond, bog garden and lawns. Kingsbury Water Park and RSPB Middleton Lakes Reserve located within a mile.

♿ 🐕 ✿ ☕

11 BROOKLYN
Gratton Lane, Endon, Stoke-on-Trent, ST9 9AA. Janet & Steve Howell. *4m W of Leek. 6m from Stoke-on-Trent on A53 turn at Black Horse PH into centre of village, R into Gratton Lane 1st house on R. Parking signed in village.* **Sun 25 June (12-5). Adm £3.50, chd free. Cream teas.**

Cottage garden in heart of the old village of Endon. Pretty front garden overflowing with roses geraniums and astrantias. Pots house scented geraniums, annuals and houseleeks. Rear garden features shady area with hostas and ferns, small waterfall and pond. Steps to lawn surrounded by well stocked borders, summerhouse, seating areas with village and rural views. Enjoy tea and cake in the potting shed. Featured as garden of the week in Garden News Magazine.

 ✿ ☕

12 ◆ CASTLE BROMWICH HALL GARDENS

Chester Road, Castle Bromwich, Birmingham, B36 9BT. Castle Bromwich Hall & Gardens Trust, 0121 749 4100, admin@cbhgt.org.uk, www.castlebromwichhallgardens.org.uk. *4m East of Birmingham centre. 1m J5 M6 (exit N only).* **For NGS: Sat 8 July (12.30-4.30). Adm £4.50, chd £1. Cream teas. For other opening times and information, please phone, email or visit garden website.**

10 acres of restored C17/18 walled gardens attached to a Jacobean manor (now a hotel) just minutes from J5 of M6. Formal yew parterres, wilderness walks, summerhouses, holly maze, espaliered fruit and wild areas. Visitor Centre open for light refreshments in addition to cream teas on the lawn. Paths are either lawn or rough hoggin - sometimes on a slope. Most areas generally accessible, rough areas outside the walls difficult when wet.

& 🐂 ❀ 🚗 ☕

13 NEW 344 CHESTER ROAD

Boldmere, Sutton Coldfield, B73 5BU. Mr & Mrs David & Hilary Godbehere. *4m NW of Birmingham City Centre. Jct 6 M6, take Gravelly Hill Rd to 6 Ways, Summer Rd & then Gravelly Lane. Turn L onto Chester Rd, Boldmere, located between Lake House Rd & Sycamore Rd. Parking in nearby side rds.* **Sun 2 July (12-4.30). Adm £3.50, chd free. Home-made teas.**

Urban oasis with pond and waterfall, raised beds, multiple pathways threading through garden, unusual plants and tropical area. Refreshments and cakes. Wheelchair access possible but not easy.

❀ ☕

14 NEW CHURCH COTTAGE

Aston, Stone, ST15 0BJ. Andrew & Anne Worrall. *1m S of Stone. North side of St Saviour's Church, Aston. Go S 150 metres on A34 after junction with A51. Turn L at Aston Village Hall. 200 metres down lane into*

churchyard for parking. **Wed 3 May, Wed 16 Aug (12-4). Adm £3, chd free. Light refreshments.**

An acre of cottage garden with large pond, waterfall and stream. More than 60 trees, small orchard and wild flowers. Rhododendrons (May) and dahlias by award-winning grower Dave Bond (Aug). Views across the R Trent. Quiet seating. Bring a book! Wheelchair access to refreshments but only to a small part of the garden.

🐂 ☕

Funds from NGS gardens help Macmillan support thousands of people every year

15 COLEY COTTAGE

Coley Lane, Little Haywood, Stafford, ST18 0UU. Yvonne Branson, 01889 882715, yvonnebranson@outlook.com. *5m SE of Stafford. A51 from Rugeley or Weston signed Little Haywood. ½m from Seven Springs. A513 Coley Lane from Red Lion PH past Back Lane, 100yds on L opp red post box.* **Fri 2, Sun 18 June, Wed 9 Aug (11-4). Adm £2.50, chd free. Home-made teas in the garden. Also open The Secret Garden. Visits also by arrangement June to Aug pre bookings 10+.**

A plant lover's cottage garden, full of subtle colours and perfume, every inch packed with plants. Clematis and old roses covering arches, many hostas and agapanthus, a wildlife pool, all designed to attract birds and butterflies. This garden is now 9yrs old, trees, roses and herbaceous planting has become well established. Visited by radio Stoke. Featured in Gardeners News.

🐂 ❀ 🚗 ☕

16 COLOUR MILL

Winkhill, Leek, Staffs, ST13 7PR. Bob & Jackie Pakes, 01538 308680, jackie.pakes@icloud.com, www.colourmill.webplus.net. *7m E of Leek. Follow A523 from either Leek or Ashbourne, look for NGS signs on the side of the main rd which will direct you down to Colour Mill.* **Sat 24 June, Thur 3 Aug (1.30-5). Adm £3.50, chd free. Home-made teas. Visits also by arrangement June to Aug.**

¾ acre S-facing garden, created in the shadow of a former iron foundry, set beside the delightful R Hamps frequented by kingfisher and dipper. Informal planting in a variety of rooms surrounded by beautiful 7ft beech hedges. Large organic vegetable patch complete with greenhouse and polytunnel. Maturing trees provide shade for the interesting seating areas. Newly acquired willow area beside river. Featured in Staffordshire Life.

❀ 🛏 ☕

17 4 DENE CLOSE

Penkridge, ST19 5HL. David & Anne Smith, 01785 712580. *6m S of Stafford. On A449 from Stafford. At far end of Penkridge turn L into Boscomoor Lane, 2nd L into Filance Lane, 3rd R Dene Close. Please park with consideration in Filance Lane. Disabled parking only in Dene Close.* **Visits by arrangement June & July individuals and larger groups welcome. Coaches permitted. Adm £3, chd free. Home-made teas.**

A medium-sized garden of many surprises. Vibrant colour-themed herbaceous areas including a long 'rainbow border'. Many different grasses and bamboos creating texture and interest in the garden. Attractive display of many unusual hostas shown for great effect 'theatre style'. Shady area for ferns etc. Water feature. Summerhouse and quiet seating areas within the garden. Home made teas in aid of County Air Ambulance.

🚗 ☕

18 DORSET HOUSE

68 Station Street, Cheslyn Hay, WS6 7EE. Mary & David

Blundell, 01922 419437, david.blundell@talktalk.net. *2m SE of Cannock J11 M6 A462 towards Willenhall. L at island. At next island R into 1-way system (Low St), at T junction L into Station St. A5 Bridgetown L to island, L Coppice St. R into Station St.* Sun 21 May, Sun 23 July (11-5). Adm £3, chd free. Home-made teas. **Visits also by arrangement May to July groups of 10+.**

Step back in time with a visit to this inspirational ½ acre garden which incorporates country cottage planting at its very best. Unusual rhododendrons, acers, shrubs and perennials planted in mixed borders. Clematis-covered arches and hidden corners with water features including stream and wildlife pool all come together to create a haven of peace and tranquillity. Featured in local press.

  ♿ ✺ ☕

19 198 EACHELHURST ROAD

Walmley, Sutton Coldfield, B76 1EW. Jacqui & Jamie Whitmore. *5mins N of Birmingham. M6 J6, A38 Tyburn Rd to Lichfield, continue to T-lights at Lidl and continue on Tyburn Rd, at island take 2nd exit to destination rd.* Sun 30 July (12.30-4.30). Adm £3, chd free. Home-made teas.

A long garden approx 210ft × 30ft divided by arches and pathways. Plenty to explore incl wildlife pond, corner arbour, cottage garden and hanging baskets leading to formal garden with box-lined pathways, well, stocked borders, gazebo and chicken house then through to raised seating area, overlooking Pype Hayes golf course, with summer house and bar and Mediterranean plants.

✺ ☕

20 NEW 5 EAST VIEW COTTAGES

School Lane, Shuttington, nr Tamworth, B79 0DX. Cathy Lyon - Green, 01827 892244, cathyatcorrabhan@hotmail.com, www.ramblinginthegarden. wordpress.com. *2m NE of Tamworth. In Tamworth take*

Amington Rd or Ashby Rd (B5493) to Shuttington. From M42 J11 take B5493 signed Seckington & Tamworth. Disabled parking at house, other parking signed. Wed 21 June (11-4); Sun 25 June (1-6). Adm £3.50, chd free. Home-made teas. **Visits also by arrangement in July for groups of 5-25.**

Plantlover's garden, deceptive and full of surprises. Informally planted themed borders, cutting beds, woodland, woodland edge borders, shrub border, stream, water features, sitooterie, folly and many artefacts. Roses, clematis, hostas, perennials, foliage and annual fillers. Benches and seating areas to contemplate the garden and birdlife or enjoy homemade cake. Wheelchair access - some narrow paths and small steps.

✺ ☕

21 NEW 51 FEATHERSTONE ROAD

Birmingham, B14 6BA. Mr & Mrs Richard & Judy Green. *On the junction of Featherstone Rd & Livingstone Rd, ½m S of Kings Heath shopping centre just off A435 Alcester Rd. Street parking.* Sun 11 June (11-5). Adm £3, chd free. Light refreshments. Bread and cakes for sale.

A leafy suburban garden on a corner plot that has a large enclosed front garden and a small sheltered back garden. A wide variety of trees (esp. acer, cornus and magnolia), climbers (clematis, honeysuckle) perennials (peonies, hosta) and shrubs (camellia, pittosporum, weigela, roses) fill every part of the garden to create a tapestry of colour and texture. Garden won the Fine and Country Best UK Garden Award. There are tiny level changes between gravel paths and slabs; the rear garden is not easy for wheelchairs to negotiate through limited space.

♿ ☕

22 304 FORD GREEN ROAD

Norton Le Moors, Stoke-On-Trent, ST6 8LS. Janet Machin. *Leave A500 onto A5271 Tunstall/ Burslem follow signs for Ford Green Hall continue past the Hall garden approx 400yds on R. Parking at front & rear of St Mary's church/school.* Sun 25 June (12-5). Adm £3, chd free. Home-made teas.

A semi detached townhouse garden with my dream 13 year old large surprise attached. Many many areas of interest approx. ⅓ acre. Sorry ... Not suitable for wheelchair access.

✺ 🚗 ☕

Coley Cottage

© Julia Stanley

23 THE GARTH

2 Broc Hill Way, Milford, Stafford, ST17 0UB. Mr & Mrs David Wright, 01785 661182, anitawright1@yahoo.co.uk, www.anitawright.co.uk. 4½ m SE of Stafford. A513 Stafford to Rugeley rd; at Barley Mow turn R (S) to Brocton; L after ½ m. Sun 4, Sun 25 June (2-6). Adm £3, chd free. Cream teas. **Visits also by arrangement May to Sept.**

½ acre garden of many levels on Cannock Chase AONB. Acid soil loving plants. Series of small gardens, water features, raised beds. Rare trees, island beds of unusual shrubs and perennials, many varieties of hosta and ferns. Varied and colourful foliage, summerhouse, arbours and quiet seating to enjoy the garden. Ancient sandstone caves.

🐕 ❀ ☕

24 GRAFTON COTTAGE

Barton-under-Needwood, DE13 8AL. Margaret & Peter Hargreaves, 01283 713639, marpeter1@btinternet.com. 6m N of Lichfield. Leave A38 for Catholme S of Barton, follow sign to Barton Green, L at Royal Oak, ¼ m.

Sun 2, Sun 16 July (11.30-5). Adm £4, chd free. Home-made teas. Evening opening Fri 21 July (6.30-9). Adm £5, chd free. Wine. Sun 30 July, Sun 6 Aug (11.30-5). Adm £4, chd free. Home-made teas. **Visits also by arrangement June to Aug min adm £80 if less than 20 people.** Donation to Alzheimer's Research Trust.

A visitor from Dorset commented 'The best garden I've seen and I've seen a lot'. It is a great achievement in colour, form and inspiration to all. Admired over 24 years. Coloured themed borders with unusual herbaceous plants and perfume from old fashioned Roses, Sweet peas, violas, dianthus, phlox and lilies. Particular interests are viticella, clematis , salvia, penstemon, cottage garden annuals and use of foliage plants, pelargonium, parterre and babbling brook. This year will be our 25th year of opening for the NGS and we are having an anniversary evening with wine on Friday 21 July 6-30 till 9-00 adm £5. Waitrose garden (NGS supplement) Numerous press articles.

❀ 🚗 🚌 ☕

25 22 GREENFIELD ROAD

Stafford, ST17 0PU. Alison & Peter Jordan, 01785 660819, alison.jordan2@btinternet.com. 3m S of Stafford. Follow the A34 out of Stafford towards Cannock. 2nd L onto Overhill Rd. 1st R into Greenfield Rd. Evening opening Fri 14 July (6-9). Adm £4, chd free. Wine. Sun 16 July (2-5). Adm £2.50, chd free. Home-made teas. Evening opening 14 July, adm incl a glass of wine. **Visits also by arrangement Apr to July for groups up to 25.**

Suburban garden created in the last 5 years, working towards all year round interest. In spring interesting bulbs, in May stunning azaleas and rhododendrons, June onwards interesting perennials and grasses. A garden that shows being diagnosed with Parkinson's needn't stop you creating a peaceful place to sit, ponder and enjoy.

🐕 ❀ ☕

GROUP OPENING

26 HALL GREEN GARDENS

Hall Green, Birmingham, B28 8SQ. Off A34, 3m city centre, 6m from M42 J4. From City Centre start at Russell Rd B28 8SQ & and from M42 start at Boden Rd B28 9DL, Hall Green. Sat 17, Sun 18 June (1-5.30). Combined adm £5, chd free. Home-made teas at 111 Southam Rd & 120 Russell Road.

42 BODEN ROAD
Mrs Helen Lycett.

37 BURNASTON ROAD
Mrs Carolyn Wynne-Jones, 0121 608 2397, markwynne-jones@blueyonder.co.uk. Visits also by arrangement May to July 30 max

36 FERNDALE ROAD
Mrs E A Nicholson, 0121 777 4921. Visits also by arrangement Mar to Sept no min, 30 max

63 GREEN ROAD
Mr & Mrs A Wilkes.

Ashcroft

120 RUSSELL ROAD
Mr David Worthington,
0121 624 7906,
hildave@hotmail.com.
Visits also by arrangement Mar to July groups up to 30. Teas incl in adm.

NEW 111 SOUTHAM ROAD
Ms Val Townend & Mr Ian Bate.

19 STAPLEHURST ROAD
Mrs Sheena Terrace.

7 suburban gardens, each unique in style. A large restful garden with mature trees, 2 lawns, cottage style borders, seating areas and small vegetable area. A tranquil garden with curving borders containing different perennials, shade areas, soft fruit and vegetables. A florist's large suburban garden with many unusual plants giving year round interest, the garden is divided into distinct areas, large ornamental garden with ponds and waterfalls, fruit garden. An eccentric's north facing wildlife friendly garden. Plantsman's garden featuring formal raised pond and hosta collection with unusual perennials and container planting. Mature garden with well defined areas including ponds, white garden, rescue hens and a majestic cedar. A shady garden with mature trees, pond, cottage style borders. Steps, narrow side entry Staplehurst Rd, Boden Rd & Burnaston Rd patio viewing only, Russell Rd & Southam Rd door sill, Green Rd no wheelchair access.
♿ ✿ ⛾

---

27 HAMILTON HOUSE
Roman Grange, Roman Road, Little Aston Park, Sutton Coldfield, B74 3GA. Philip & Diana Berry, www.hamiltonhousegarden.co.uk. *3m N of Sutton Coldfield. Follow A454 (Walsall Rd) & enter Roman Rd, Little Aston Park. Roman Grange is 1st L after church but enter rd via pedestrian gate.* **Sun 28 May (2-5). Adm £5, chd free. Home made teas, coffee, cold drinks and cake.**
½ acre n-facing English woodland garden in tranquil setting, making

the most of challenging shade, providing haven for birds and other wildlife. Large pond with stone bridge, pergolas, water features, box garden with a variety of roses and herbs. Interesting collection of rhododendrons, clematis, hostas, ferns and old English roses. Join us for afternoon tea, listening to live music and admire the art of our garden. Featured on BBC 2 'The Great British Garden Revival', The Big TV Company Freeview Channel 8, The Birmingham Mail, The Journal, and The Sutton Coldfield Observer. The garden is being featured as 'Garden of the Week' in Garden News. Wheelchair access is possible but difficult in some areas with steps and narrow paths.
✿ ⛾

28 HEATH HOUSE
Offley Brook, Eccleshall, ST21 6HA. Dr D W Eyre-Walker, 01785 280318, neyrewalker@btinternet.com. *3m W of Eccleshall. From Eccleshall take B5026 towards Woore. At Sugnall turn L, after 1½m turn R immed by stone garden wall. After 1m straight across Xrds. Use Satnav, mobile phones do not work locally.* **Visits by arrangement Apr to Sept. Adm £5, chd free. Refreshments available for small numbers..**
1½ acre country garden of C18 miller's house in lovely valley setting, overlooking mill pool. Plantsman's garden containing many rare and unusual plants in borders, bog garden, woodland, alpine house, raised bed and shrubberies and incl slowly expanding collection of hardy terrestrial orchids. Vegetable garden now converted to wild flower meadow. Wheelchair access difficult with only partial access.
⛾

29 HIDDEN GEM
15 St Johns Road, Pleck, Walsall, WS2 9TJ. Maureen & Sid Allen, 07825 804670, maureenallen42@gmail.com. *2m W of Walsall. Off J10 M6. Head for Walsall on A454 Wolverhampton Rd. Turn R into Pleck Rd A4148 then 4th R into St Johns Rd.* **Visits by arrangement June & July groups**

of 10 to 30 (max). Adm £5, chd free. Home-made teas.
Situated between two busy motorway junctions. Come and visit our 'Hidden Gem.' What a surprise! A long narrow pretty garden, lovely foliage in June, pretty perennials, shrubs, trees, lush tropical plants from July onwards. Japanese area with stream. Shady walk with ferns, into pretty gravel garden lots of wildlife. Very relaxing atmosphere. WHAT A GEM!
♿ 🚗 ⛾

Your visit helps fund 389 Marie Curie Nurses

---

30 'JOHN'S GARDEN' AT ASHWOOD NURSERIES
Ashwood Lower Lane, Ashwood, nr Kingswinford, DY6 0AE. John Massey, www.ashwoodnurseries.com. *5m S of Wolverhampton. 1m past Wall Heath on A449 turn R to Ashwood along Doctor's Lane. At T-junction turn L. Park at Ashwood Nurseries.* **Sun 20 Aug (10-4). Adm £5, chd free.**
A stunning private garden adjacent to Ashwood Nurseries, it has a huge plant collection and many innovative design features in a beautiful canal-side setting. There are informal beds, woodland dells, a South African border, a rock garden, a fern stumpery and a wildlife meadow. Fine displays of grasses, herbaceous perennials and clematis together with a notable collection of hydrangeas. Tea Room, Garden Centre and Gift Shop at adjacent Ashwood Nurseries. Coaches are by appointment only. Disabled access difficult if very wet.
♿ 🚜 ✿ ☘ ⛾

31 KEEPER'S COTTAGE; BLUEBELL WOOD

24 Greensforge Lane, Stourton, Stourbridge, DY7 5BB. Peter & Jenny Brookes, 07974 454503, peter@brookesmedia.com. *2m NW of Stourbridge. At junction of A449 & A458 at Stourton, take Bridgnorth Rd (A458) westward, after ½m turn R into Greensforge Lane. Keeper's Cottage ½m on R.* Sat 6, Sun 7 May (11-3.30). Adm £4, chd free. Home-made teas. Visits also by arrangement in May. Visits will be restricted to the bluebell season and will have to be arranged around owners' work.

This stunning bluebell wood adorns the banks of a river deep in the South Staffordshire countryside, yet only a few miles from the conurbation. In May, the bluebells form a beautiful carpet, sweeping through the natural woodland and down to the river, the site of ancient nail making. It is a quintessentially English landscape which can only be glimpsed for a few short weeks of the year. Featured on BBC Radio WM and covered by the Express and Star and the Stourbridge News. The woods contain steep pathways, totally unsuitable for wheelchairs.

32 13 LANSDOWNE ROAD

Hurst Green, Halesowen, B62 9QT. Mr Peter Bridgens & Mr Michael King, 0121 421 7796. *7m W of Birmingham. A458 Hagley Rd out of Birmingham, towards Stourbridge. From M5 J2 take 1st exit A4123 towards Birmingham.* Sun 2 July (2.30-5.30). Adm £3.50, chd free. Home-made teas. Visits also by arrangement Apr to Sept groups of between 4 and 20.

A plantsman's suburban garden designed to ensure maximum use of space. The garden features rare and unusual plants, incl Meconopsis, Buddleia agathosma, Stewartia, Billadera, and Sinocallicanthus. Water features and area. The mixed borders are planted giving a long season of interest. Attention paid to plant association and colour themes. The garden presents a softly planted look and tropical feel. The entrance to the 'Secret' garden, and 36ft colour themed mixed border The use of exotic and architectural plants in a different way. The use of ornamentation within the garden.

Wild Thyme Cottage

33 NEW **THE MALTHOUSE**
82 High Street, Eccleshall,
ST21 6BZ. Mr & Mrs Warren
Griffiths. *7m NW of Stafford. J14
M6. A5013 to Eccleshall. High St.
(B5026) towards Loggerheads.
Garden adjacent to Holy Trinity
Church (Lychgate). On street parking
nearby.* Sun 2 July (2-5). Adm £3,
chd free. Home-made teas in
Parish Room located in adjacent
churchyard.
A long 'burgage' garden next to
impressive historic 12th C church
which will be open to visit. Colourful
patio area with short pathways to
lawn, flower and shrub borders. A
vegetable and fruit garden separate
this from orchard and small wooded
area, with views behind church
and across Town Meadow. Garden
not suitable for wheelchairs. Tea
proceeds to Holy Trinity Church.

34 NEW **MARIE CURIE
HOSPICE GARDEN**
Marsh Lane, Solihull, B91 2PQ.
Mrs Do Connolly, www.
mariecurie.org.uk/westmidlands.
*Close to J5 of M42 to the east of
Solihull Town Centre. Leave M42 at
J5 & travel toward Solihull on A41.
TakeL slip road towards Solihull to
join B4025 & after island take 1st
R onto Marsh Lane. Marie Curie
Hospice is on R.* Sun 2 July (11-4).
Adm £3.50, chd free. Light
refreshments.
The gardens include two large,
formally laid out patient's gardens
(including a ball fountain water
feature), indoor courtyards, a
vegetable plot, a long border
adjoining the car park gardens and
a beautiful wildlife and pond area
at the rear of the hospice. The
volunteer gardening team hope that
the gardens provide a peaceful and
comforting place for patients, their
visitors and staff.

MARLBROOK GARDENS
See Worcestershire

35 **3 MARLOWS
COTTAGES**
Little Hay Lane, Little Hay,
WS14 0QD. Phyllis Davies. *4m S*
*of Lichfield. Take A5127, Birmingham
Rd. Turn L at Park Lane (opp Tesco
Express) then R at T junction into
Little Hay Lane, ½m on L.* Sun 11,
Mon 12 June (11-4). Adm £3,
chd free. Home-made teas.
Long, narrow, gently sloping cottage
style garden with borders and beds
containing abundant herbaceous
perennials and shrubs leading to
vegetable patch.

36 **89 MARSH LANE**
Solihull, B91 2PE. Mrs Gail Wyldes.
*½m from Solihull town centre. A41
from M42 J5. Turn sharp L at first
T-lights. Garden on R. Parking 400
metres further along Marsh Lane at
Solihull Cricket Club by mini r'about.*
Sun 28 May (2-5). Adm £3.50,
chd free. Home-made teas.
Suburban Oasis. Trees, shrubs and
herbaceous planting for all year
interest with emphasis on leaf shape
and structure. Wildlife pond, bog
garden, water features, african style
gazebo, gravel gardens, shady places
and sunny seating areas. Patio with
pergola and raised beds. Hostas
and ferns abound. The garden is
continually evolving with new plants
and features. Wheelchair access -
small step from patio to the main
back garden and paths may be a
little narrow.

37 ♦ **MIDDLETON HALL**
Tamworth, B78 2AE.
Middleton Hall Trust,
www.middleton-hall.co.uk. *4m S of
Tamworth, 2m N J9 M42. On A4091
between The Belfry & Drayton
Manor.* For NGS: Tue 30, Wed
31 May (11-4). Adm £5, chd
free. Light refreshments in our
Courtyard Centre. For other
opening times and information,
please visit garden website.
Our formal gardens form part of the
42 estate of the Grade II* Middleton
Hall, the C17 home of naturalists
Sir Francis Willoughby and John Ray.
The formal gardens are made up
of two walled gardens a Glade and
an Orchard. The Walled gardens
contain a variety of herbaceous and
seasonal planting with specimen
plants that have a botanical and/
or historical significance to our site.
Bake 180 Coffee Shop will also be
open serving lunches and other
light refreshments, we also have a
sweet shop and cheese and ale shop.
Wheelchair access - walled garden
paths are paved, Glade and Orchard
paths are grass. No access to 1st
floor of the Hall and Nature Trail.

38 **MILLENNIUM GARDEN**
London Road, Lichfield,
WS14 9RB. Carol Cooper. *1m S
of Lichfield. Off A38 along A5206
towards Lichfield ¼m past A38
island towards Lichfield. Park in field
on L. Yellow signs on field gate.* Sun
9 Apr, Sun 2 July (1-5). Adm
£3.50, chd free.
2 acre garden with mixed spring
bulbs in the woodland garden and
host of golden daffodils fade slowly
into the summer borders in this
English country garden. Designed
with a naturalistic edge and with
the environment in mind. A relaxed
approach creates a garden of quiet
sanctuary with the millennium
bridge sitting comfortably, with its
surroundings of lush planting and
mature trees. Well stocked summer
borders give shots of colour to lift
the spirit and the air fills with the
scent of wisterias and climbing roses.
A stress free environment awaits
you at the Millennium Garden.

39 **MITTON MANOR**
Mitton, Penkridge, Stafford,
ST19 5QW. Mrs E A Gooch. *2m W
of Penkridge. Property is on Whiston
Rd. Parking in field before house.
No parking for coaches.* Sun 2 July
(11.30-4.30). Adm £5, chd free.
Cream teas.
This 7 acre country garden was
started in 2001 and has been
developed from an overgrown
wilderness. The garden surrounds
a Victorian manor (not open) and
contains rooms of different styles,
formal box/topiary, prairie planting
and natural woodland bordered by a
stream. Stunning vistas, water features
and sculpture. Live music. Many levels,
narrow and gravel paths. Wheelchair
users will need assistance.

GROUP OPENING

40 MOSELEY CORNER, THE ART OF GARDENS

Birmingham, B13 9PN. *3m S of city centre. From Moseley Xrds take St Mary's Row which becomes Wake Green Rd. After ½ m turn R into St Agnes Rd & L at the church, park here for all gardens.* Sun 23 July (1-5.30). Combined adm £4, chd free. Home-made teas at 56 St Agnes Road.

48 ST AGNES ROAD
Alan & Judith Wenban-Smith.

56 ST AGNES ROAD
Michael & Alison Cullen.

269 YARDLEY WOOD ROAD
Miss Marion Stoddart.

Two of the gardens are on St Agnes Road in Moseley. They demonstrate unique design, each expressing the garden owners' creative vision and endeavour. 56 St Agnes Road is immaculately maintained with curving borders around a formal lawn with delicate acers and contemporary sculpture. The tranquillity of this elegant garden is enhanced by a Victorian style fish pond with fountain and waterfall.
48 St Agnes Road has a courtyard leading to a pond with frogs, newts and water lilies. There are mature herbaceous borders with perennial and annual planting and poles for climbing roses and clematis, some unusual plants as well as fruit trees, currant bushes and vegetables. The third garden is a very short walk away on Yardley Wood Road. This is a beautifully designed three roomed garden with a terrace and large pergola, a lawned area with shrubs and herbaceous borders and a top garden which is very tranquil with a stream and pond, surrounded by interesting architectural plants.
☕ 💷

41 THE MOUNT, COTON, GNOSALL

Stafford, ST20 0EQ. Andrew & Celia Payne, 01785 822253,

ac.payne@waitrose.com. *8m W of Stafford. From Stafford take A518 W towards Newport/Telford. Go through Gnosall, over canal. Garden on edge of Gnosall Village on L of A518.* Sun 25 June (2-5). Adm £3.50, chd free. Home-made teas. Visits also by arrangement June & July for groups of 10+.
Richly planted wildlife friendly garden with large collection of unusual plants set in ¾ acre. Divided into areas, incl a wild flower meadow, cottage garden and vegetable plot, highlights consist of over 100 different hosta varieties, many colourful hardy geraniums, bamboos and a huge Kiftsgate rose. The plant stall will have over 40+ varieties of hosta for sale plus other interesting plants. Teas in aid of Macmillan Cancer Support.
❀ ☕ 💷

42 THE MOUNT, GREAT BRIDGEFORD

33 Newport Road, Great Bridgeford, Stafford, ST18 9PR. Adrian Hubble, 01785 282423, ilex66@btinternet.com. *2m NW of Stafford. From J14 M6 take A5013 to Great Bridgeford. Turn L on to B5405. Park at village hall on L, or with consideration in Jasmine Rd on R. Short walk along B5405 to last house on R.* Sun 28 May (1-5), also open The Pintles. Sun 30 July (1-5). Adm £3, chd free. Visits also by arrangement May to Sept groups of 20+.
The garden consists of distinct areas each with beds and borders with their own colour schemes planted with rare and choice plants spread over ⅓ acre. Raised beds, alpine garden, water feature and a Roman style feature. A garden of harmonies and contrasts guaranteed to provoke planting ideas. Refreshments will be available at 'The Pintles' on 28 May.
❀

43 THE OLD DAIRY HOUSE

Trentham Park, Stoke-on-Trent, ST4 8AE. Philip & Michelle Moore. *S edge of Stoke-on-Trent. Next to Trentham Gardens. Off Whitmore Rd. Please follow NGS signs or signs for Trentham Park Golf Club. Parking in*

church car park. Sun 28, Mon 29 May (1-5). Adm £3, chd free. Home-made teas.
Grade 2 listed house (not open) designed by Sir Charles Barry forms backdrop to this 2 acre garden in parkland setting. Shaded area for rhododendrons, azaleas plus expanding hosta and fern collection. Mature trees, 'cottage garden' and long borders. Narrow brick paths in vegetable plot. Large courtyard area for teas. Wheelchair access - some gravel paths but lawns are an option.
♿ ❀ ☕ 💷

44 THE OLD VICARAGE

Fulford, nr Stone, ST11 9QS. Mike & Cherry Dodson. *4m N of Stone. From Stone A520 (Leek). 1m R turn to Spot Acre & Fulford, turn L down Post Office Terrace, past village green/ PH towards church.* Sat 24, Sun 25 June (2-5). Adm £4, chd free. Home-made teas.
On edge of attractive village, 1½ acres of formal sloping garden around Victorian house. Sit on the back terrace or in the summerhouse and enjoy home-made cakes and tea amongst mature trees, relaxed herbaceous borders, roses and a small pond. Move onto the organic vegetable garden with raised beds, fruit cage and very big compost heaps! In complete contrast, walk around the natural setting of a two-acre reclaimed lake planted with native species designed to attract wildlife. Waterfall, jetty, fishing hut, acer and fern glade plus young arboretum provide more interest. Children will enjoy meeting the chickens and horses. Featured in Weekend Telegraph. Wheelchair access to most areas.
♿ 🐴 ☕ 💷

45 PAUL'S OASIS OF CALM

18 Kings Close, Kings Heath, Birmingham, B14 6TP. Mr Paul Doogan, 0121 444 6943, gardengreen18@hotmail.co.uk. *4m from city centre. 5m from the M42 J4. Take A345 to Kings Heath High St then B4122 Vicarage Rd. Turn L onto Kings Rd then R to Kings Close.* Visits by arrangement May to Aug groups up to 15. Adm

£2.50, chd free.
Garden cultivated from nothing into a little oasis. Measuring 18ft x 70ft. It's small but packed with interesting and unusual plants, water features and 7 seating areas. It's my piece of heaven. I have now been given permission by Birmingham City council to garden council land outside my house. Its 80 square meters so I have got more of an oasis for people to see. Featured in the Sunday Mirror and the back garden in Garden Answers.

🐕 🍵

GROUP OPENING

46 PEREIRA ROAD GARDENS

Harborne, Birmingham, B17 9JN. *Between Gillhurst Rd & Margaret Grove, ¼m from Hagley Rd or ½m from Harborne High St.* Sun 25 June (1.30-5). Combined adm £4, chd free. Home-made teas at Pereira Road allotments, accessed via driveway between 31 and 33 Pereira Road or through 55 Pereira Road. Drinks and homemade cakes plus jams and vegetables on sale.

14 PEREIRA ROAD
Mike Foster.

48 PEREIRA ROAD
Rosemary Klem & Julie Werrett.

50 PEREIRA ROAD
Peg Peil.
(See separate entry)

55 PEREIRA ROAD
Emma Davies & Martin Commander.

Group of 4 different urban gardens. No.14 a well established suburban garden with mixed herbaceous and shrub borders. Wildlife-friendly with 2 ponds and wild flower area. Ongoing alterations provide new areas of interest each year. No 48, new this year, has recently been relandscaped to create a terraced garden with steps linking a patio, herbaceous and shrub planting and a vegetable garden. No.50 is a plantaholic's paradise with over 1000 varieties,

many rare, incl fruits, vegetables, herbs, grasses and large bed of plants with African connections. Over 100 varieties on sale - see how they grow. No. 55 is a sloping garden, incl gravelled beds with mixed planting, grasses and small pond. All gardens have steps. In July, free admission to Harborne Nature Reserve and Pereira Road allotments incl.

🐕 ❄ 🍵

47 50 PEREIRA ROAD

Harborne, Birmingham, B17 9JN. Peg Peil. *Between Gillhurst Rd & Margaret Grove, ¼m from Hagley Rd or ½m from Harborne High St.* Sun 30 Apr (2-5). Adm £2.50, chd free. Opening with Pereira Road Gardens on Sun 25 June.
Plantaholic's garden with over 1000 varieties, many rare. Large bed of plants with African connections. Fruits, vegetables, herbs, grasses. Over 100 varieties available for sale. This garden slopes steeply and access to some areas may be difficult for less mobile visitors. Featured in Amateur Gardening

❄ 🍵

48 THE PINTLES

18 Newport Road, Great Bridgeford, Stafford, ST18 9PR. Peter & Leslie Longstaff, 01785 282582, peter.longstaff@ngs.org.uk. *J14 M6 take A5013 towards Eccleshall. In Great Bridgeford turn L onto B5405. Car park on L after ½m in Village Hall car park.* Sun 28 May (1-5), also open The Mount, Great Bridgeford. Sun 2 July (1-5). Adm £3, chd free. Home-made teas. **Visits also by arrangement May to July for groups of 10+.**
Located in the village of Great Bridgeford this traditional semi-detached house has a medium sized wildlife friendly garden designed to appeal to many interests. There are two greenhouses, over 400 cacti and succulents, orchids, vegetable and fruit plot, wildlife pond, weather station, and hidden woodland shady garden. Plenty of outside seating to enjoy the home made cakes and refreshments. Steps or small ramp into main garden.

🍵

Church Cottage

49 PRIORY FARM

Mitton Road, Bradley, Stafford, ST18 9ED. Debbie Farmer. *3½ m W Penkridge. At Texaco island on A449 in Penkridge take Bungham Lane. Continue for 2½ m past Swan & Whiston Hall to Mitton. Turn R to Bradley, continue 1m to Priory Farm on L.* Sun 25 June (10-4). Adm £4, chd free. Home-made teas. Delightful gardens and a warm welcome awaits you at Priory Farm. Stroll around the picturesque grounds and lake. Check out the wildlife. New projects for 2017. Scrumptious refreshments available. Delicious home made cakes. BBQ subject to availability. Entertainment. Featured in Express and Star. Limited wheelchair access.

✿ 🚗 ☕

50 ROWLEY HOUSE FARM

Croxton, Stafford, ST21 6PJ. Tony & Beryl Roe, 01630 620248. *4m W of Eccleshall. Between Eccleshall & Loggerheads on B5026. At Wetwood Xrds turn for Fairoak. Take 1st L turn & continue for ¾ m.* Sun 23 Apr (2-5). Adm £3.50, chd free. Home-made teas. **Visits also by arrangement June to Sept 50 max**
Quiet country garden, part reclaimed from farm rick-yard. Shrub roses in orchard, soft fruits, vegetables and water feature incl. Extensive views towards the Wrekin and Welsh hills from adjacent land at 570ft, with plantings of 130 varieties of 7 species of ilex, various corylus and specimen trees. Small water feature. Teas in aid of St. Paul's Church, Croxton. Wheelchair access - ground firm when dry.

♿ ✿ 🚗 ☕

51 23 ST JOHNS ROAD

Rowley Park, Stafford, ST17 9AS. Fiona Horwath, 01785 258923, fiona_horwath@yahoo.co.uk. *½ m S of Stafford Town Centre. From J13 M6, towards Stafford. After 2m turn L into St. John's Rd. Please park considerately.* Sun 2 Apr (2-5). Combined adm with 29 St John's Road £5, chd free. Home-made teas. Evening opening Fri 19 May (6.30-9). Combined adm with 29 St John's Road £6, chd free. Wine. Sun 25 June, Fri 14 July (2-5). Adm £4, chd free. **Visits also by arrangement Mar to Sept for groups of 10+.**
As you pass through the black and white gate you enter a part-walled plant lover's haven. There are bulbs and shady woodlanders in spring and a plethora of herbaceous plants and climbers.

🚗 ✿ 🚗 ☕

> Donations from the National Garden Scheme help Parkinson's UK care for more people

52 29 ST JOHN'S ROAD

Rowley Park, Stafford, ST17 9AP. Mrs Carol Shanahan, 07831 453130, shanahanfamily@hotmail.com. *1m from Stafford town centre, 2m from M6 J13. 2m on A449 to Stafford from M6 J13, turn L through the gates into St Johns Rd. From Stafford A449 towards Wolverhampton, 1st R after railway bridge. Private Park, please park considerately.* Sun 2 Apr (2-5). Combined adm with 23 St Johns Road £5, chd free. Home-made teas. Evening opening Fri 19 May (6.30-9). Combined adm with 23 St Johns Road £6, chd free. Wine. Fri 4 Aug (2-5). Adm £4, chd free. Home-made teas. **Visits also by arrangement Mar to Sept groups of 10+.**
Against a backdrop of mature Hornbeams there are 2 acres of informal garden made up of many complementary areas. View the wooded 'dingly dell', colourful terraces, abundant kitchen garden, bronze armillary, water features, circular lawns plus the roses and clematis that scramble through the trees. Don't miss the working area of the garden for the most upmarket compost bins – all made from decking. The majority of the garden is accessible by wheelchair and there are ramps at most of the steps.

♿ 🐴 🚗 ☕

53 THE SECRET GARDEN

3 Banktop Cottages, Little Haywood, ST18 0UL. Derek Higgott & David Aston. *5m SE of Stafford. A51 from Rugeley or Weston signed Little Haywood A513 Stafford Coley Lane, Back Lane R into Coley Grove. Entrance 50 metres on L.* Sun 28 May (11-4). Fri 2, Sun 18 June, Wed 9 Aug (11-4), also open Coley Cottage. Adm £3, chd free. Home-made teas. Wander past the other cottage gardens and through the evergreen arch and there before you a fantasy for the eyes and soul. Stunning garden approx ½ acre, created over the last 30yrs. Strong colour theme of trees and shrubs, underplanted with perennials, 1000 bulbs and laced with clematis; other features incl water, laburnum and rose tunnel and unique buildings. Is this the jewel in the crown? Raised gazebo with wonderful views over untouched meadows and Cannock Chase. Featured in Staffordshire Life. Wheelchair access - some slopes.

♿ ☕

54 9 STATION ROAD

Great Wyrley, Walsall, WS6 6LH. Mr & Mrs John Thurston. *Great Wyrley. J12 of M6 take A5 to Cannock, in 4m at bridge over M6 Toll take A34 to Walsall, take 1st turn R into Darges Lane. Turn R into Station Rd.* Sun 25 June (10.30-3). Adm £2.50, chd free. Tea. A small, wildlife friendly, plantsman's garden, measuring 80 x 30ft. Designed as a romantic, cottage style featuring herbaceous perennials, English shrub roses and climbers. Although planted in an informal style, the garden offers some formality in its overall design with the use of clipped box and bay trees. Winner of the House Beautiful magazine transformation of the year.

✿ ☕

55 TANGLEWOOD COTTAGE

Crossheads, Colwich, Stafford, ST18 0UG. Dennis & Helen Wood, 01889 882857, shuvitdog@hotmail.com. *5m SE of Stafford. A51 Rugeley/Weston R into Colwich. Church on L school on R, under bridge R into Crossheads Lane follow railway approx ¼ m (it does lead somewhere). Parking signed on grass opp brick kiln cottage.* **Sun 21 May (10.30-2.30). Adm £3, chd free. Home-made teas. Light lunches and home made cakes. Visits also by arrangement May to Aug for groups 15+. Catering requirements on request.**

A tranquil country cottage garden. koi carp pool, vegetables, fruit, chickens, aviary and an array of wonderful perennials. A garden of peace and tranquillity, different rooms with variety. Sit in the courtyard and enjoy Helen's home-made fayre. Year on year people spend many hours relaxing with us and don't forget Lucky the parrot - be warned he can be naughty! Art/ jewellery/crafts/book sales. Annual HPS Plant Fair in village hall Sun 21st May which is just around the corner. Tbc. Lots of gravel paths, people with walking sticks seem to manage quite well. Wheelchairs would have difficulty.

✿ ⊖ ☕

56 91 TOWER ROAD

Four Oaks, Sutton Coldfield, B75 5EQ. Heather & Gary Hawkins. *3m N Sutton Coldfield. From A5127 at Mere Green island, turn onto Mere Green Rd, L at St James Church, L again onto Tower Road.* **Sun 11 June (1.30-5.30). Adm £3, chd free. Home-made teas.**

163ft S-facing garden with sweeping borders and island beds planted with an eclectic mix of shrubs and perennials. A well stocked fishpond, imposing cast iron water feature and a hiding griffin enhance your journey around the garden. A vast array of home made cakes to tempt you during your visit. The ideal setting for sunbathing, children's hide and seek and lively garden parties. Amazing selection of home-made cream teas

to eat in the garden or take away. More than just an Open Garden, we like to think of it as a garden party!

🐕 ✿ ☕

57 ◆ THE TRENTHAM ESTATE

Stone Road, Stoke-on-Trent, ST4 8JG. Michael Walker, 01782 646646, enquiry@trentham.co.uk, www.trentham.co.uk. *M6 J15. Well signed on r'about, A34 with A5035.* **For NGS: Wed 25 Jan, Wed 8 Mar (1.30-3.30). Adm £8.70, chd free. Evening opening Wed 14 June, Thur 14 Sept (5.30-8). Adm £5.50, chd free. For other opening times and information, please phone, email or visit garden website.**

Trentham Gardens has undergone a major programme of restoration which has both revealed the historic landscape designed by Capability Brown and is replenishing this with vast new contemporary plantings of annuals, perennials, trees and shrubs. NGS Special Openings with Trenthams' Head of Garden and Estate, Michael Walker, and Garden Team Manager, Carol Adams, will provide a complimentary tour of the recently revealed areas around Browns mile long lake at 1.30pm

Wed 25 Jan and 8 March, and at 6pm 14 June and Sept.

♿ 🐕 ✿ ⊖ 🅳 🛏 ☕

58 41 TWENTYLANDS

Rolleston-on-Dove, Burton-on-Trent, DE13 9AJ. Maureen & Joe Martin, 01283 520208, joe.martin11@btinternet.com. *3m E of Tutbury. At r'about on Tutbury by-pass A511 take first exit, continue through Rolleston-on-Dove, past Scout HQ. Twentylands on R, opp the Jinny Inn. From A38 take turn off to Stretton continue to Rolleston.* **Sat 20 May, Sat 16 Sept (12-5). Adm £3, chd free. Home-made teas. Visits also by arrangement Apr to Sept 6 min 20 max. Teas.**

Small back garden. Every corner used and packed with plants. Herbaceous borders with fruit trees and shrubs. Herb corner, fernery, bog garden with many candelabra primula, in Spring, and other bog plants. Chinese garden with chess pavilion and bonsai, water features, small pond with lilys, wood carvings, greenhouses, Water harvesting and composting systems. Many plants raised from seed. Tutbury Castle, Blue Cross Horse Sanctuary and Jinny Nature Trail nearby. Wheelchair access to patio overlooking garden.

🐕 ✿ ☕

The Malthouse

59 NEW VERNON HOUSE

26, Vernon Road, Edgbaston, Birmingham, B16 9SH. Dr & Mrs Steve & Chris Smith. *2m W of Birmingham city centre. Take the A456 (Hagley Rd). If arriving from E (Birmingham) turn R in to Portland Rd, then 2nd R onto Vernon Rd. If arriving from W (M5) turn L in to Rotton Park Rd, then 2nd R (exit 3) onto Vernon Rd.* Sun 25 June (1-5). Adm £3.50, chd free. Light refreshments.

A large (over ⅓ acre) but secluded city garden framed by mature trees. There are extensive lawns and herbaceous borders with a wide range of planting creating several distinct areas. Decks, pergolas and patios offer a variety of places to sit and reflect. Featuring an ornamental koi pond, a wildlife pond with bog garden, a unique holly hedge and an original Victorian conservatory. Three small steps up to patio areas and a further 3 steps to access main garden.

60 19 WATERDALE

Compton, Wolverhampton, WV3 9DY. Anne & Brian Bailey, 01902 424867, m.bailey1234@btinternet.com, www.facebook.com/pages/Garden-of-Surprises/165745816926408.

1½m W of Wolverhampton city centre. From Wolverhampton Ring Rd take A454 towards Bridgnorth for 1m. Waterdale is on L off A454 Compton Rd West. Sun 4 June, Sun 2 July (12.30-5.30). Combined adm with 12 Waterdale £5, chd free. Home-made teas. Visits also by arrangement June to Aug for groups of 10-35.

A romantic garden of surprises, which gradually reveals itself on a journey through deep, lush planting, full of unusual plants. From the sunny, flower filled terrace, a ruined folly emerges from a luxuriant fernery and leads into an oriental garden, complete with tea house. Towering bamboos hide the way to the gothic summerhouse and mysterious shell grotto. Winner of Daily Mail National Garden Competition. Summerhouse and grotto featured in 'Amazing Spaces - Shed of the Year' TV programme. Featured in Express & Star and Daily Mail.

61 NEW 12 WATERDALE

Compton, Wolverhampton, WV3 9DY. Mr & Mrs Colin Bennett. *1½m W of Wolverhampton city centre. From Wolverhampton Ring Rd take A454 towards Bridgnorth for 1m. Waterdale is on the L off A454 Compton Rd West.* Sun 4 June, Sun 2 July (12.30-5.30). Combined adm with 19 Waterdale £5, chd free. Home-made teas at 19 Waterdale.

A riot of colour welcomes visitors to this quintessentially English garden. The wide central circular bed and side borders overflow with classic summer flowers, including the tall spires of delphiniums, lupins, irises, campanula, poppies and roses. Clematis tumble over the edge of the decked terrace, where visitors can sit among pots of begonias and geraniums to admire the view over the garden.

WESTACRES
See Worcestershire

62 THE WICKETS

47 Long Street, Wheaton Aston, ST19 9NF. Tony & Kate Bennett, 01785 840233, ajtonyb@talktalk.net. *8m W of Cannock, 10m N of Wolverhampton, 10m E of Telford. M6 J12 W towards Telford on A5; 3m R signed Stretton; 150yds L signed Wheaton Aston; 2m L; over canal, garden on R or at Bradford Arms on A5 follow signs.* Thur 24, Sun 27 Aug (1.30-5). Adm £3, chd free. Home-made teas. Visits also by arrangement June to Aug.

There's a delight around every corner and lots of quirky features in this most innovative garden. Its themed areas include a fernery, grasses bed, hidden gothic garden, succulent theatre, cottage garden beds and even a cricket match! It will certainly give you ideas for your own garden as you sit and enjoy our acclaimed tea and cake. Wheelchair access - two steps in garden.

63 NEW WILD THYME COTTAGE

Woodhouses, Barton Under Needwood, Burton-On-Trent, DE13 8BS. Ray & Michele Blundell. *B5016 Midway between villages of Barton & Yoxall. From A38 through Barton Village B5015 towards Yoxall. Or from A515 at Yoxall centre take Town Hill sign for Barton. Garden*

Hall Green Gardens

is 2m on L. Sun 11 June, Sun 10 Sept (11-5.30); Sun 29 Oct (10-4). Adm £3, chd free. Tea.
The garden surrounds a self built timber frame house now 20 years old and extends to ⅓ acre. There is a collection of over 120 Japanese Maples with other rare semi mature White bark Birch trees, shrubs and herbaceous perennials. Newly developed large beds of Ornamental grasses with taller perennials. Specialist growers of Zantedeschia (Arum Lily's). Plants sales. Garden featured on BBC Gardener's World. Partial wheelchair access on gravel and grass.

♿ ❋ ☕

64 WILD WOOD LODGE
Bushton Lane, Anslow, Burton-On-Trent, DE13 9QL.
Mr & Mrs Richard & Dorothy Ward, 01283 812100, poplarsfarm@breathe.com.
Bushton Lane is signed in centre of village. Wild Wood Lodge is ¼m down Bushton Lane. Sun 11 June, Sun 13 Aug (1.30-5). Adm £3.50, chd free. Home-made teas. **Visits also by arrangement May to Aug.**
Covering approx 2 acre it consists of a productive orchard with apples, pears and plums. A Soft Fruit Garden with Gooseberries, Red and Black Currants, Raspberries and a wide selection of vegetables on raised beds, colourful herbaceous borders, shrubs, ornamental trees, wild life pond and fishing lake. The Garden was overall winner in the Staffs. Agricultural Societies Farm Garden Competition. Level garden, wide paths.

♿ 🐔 🚐 ☕

65 NEW 2 WOODLAND CRESCENT
Finchfield, Wolverhampton, WV3 8AS. Mr & Mrs Parker, 01902 332392, alisonparker1960@hotmail.co.uk.
2m SW of Wolverhampton City centre. From Inner Ring Rd take A41 W to Tettenhall. At junction with A459 turn L onto Merridale Rd. Straight over Bradwell Xrds then R onto Trysull Rd. 3rd R onto Coppice Rd & 1st R onto Woodland Crescent.

Sun 25 June (11-5). Adm £3, chd free. Home-made teas.
Visits also by arrangement June & July. Groups of 10 to 25 welcome.
A semi-detached townhouse garden 120 x 25 ft, every inch packed with perennials, trees, shrubs, roses, hostas and clematis. Wildlife pond and nesting boxes to attract birds. Productive vegetable and fruit garden. Informal style but clipped box and topiary add some formality.

❋ ☕

GROUP OPENING

66 WOODLEIGHTON GROVE GARDENS
Woodleighton Grove, Uttoxeter, ST14 8BX. 01889 563930, graham&judy.white@ngs.org.uk.
SE of Uttoxeter. From Uttoxeter take B5017 (Marchington). Go over Town Bridge, 1st exit at r'about, then 3rd exit at r'about into Highwood Rd, After ¼m turn R. **Evening opening Fri 30 June (6-9). Combined adm £7, chd free.** Sat 8 July (11-5); Sun 9 July (1-5). Combined adm £4, chd free. **Visits also by arrangement June & July min 12 persons, adm £7 per head incl refreshments.**

APOLLONIA
Helen & David Loughton.

KARIBU
Graham & Judy White.

At the end of a quiet cul-de-sac in the Staffordshire market town of Uttoxeter, two next door neighbours will be delighted to welcome visitors to their intriguing and highly acclaimed gardens. Features include a Fruit Arch, Natural Stream, Summerhouses, Greenhouses, Alpine House on wheels, a new Bell Tower, a Folly, Gazebo, Stumpery, Dovecote, Arbour, Giant Insect Hotel and a Wormery. There are archways, bridges, steps, pagoda's and a boardwalk, all leading to tranquil resting places. As well as displaying many unusual and interesting plants, the gardens also discreetly house a number of artefacts, antiques,

collections and other items of interest. For the Open Evening on Fri 30 June the £7 adm incl wine and canapés, or tea, coffee or soft drink. For the Open Weekend 8/9 July, Home-made Teas are charged in addition to the £4 adm.

❋ 🚐 ☕

67 YARLET HOUSE
Yarlet, Stafford, ST18 9SD. Mr & Mrs Nikolas Tarling. *2m S of Stone. Take A34 from Stone towards Stafford, turn L into Yarlet School & L again into car park.* Fri 30 June (10-1). Adm £4, chd free. Home-made teas. *Donation to Staffordshire Wildlife Trust.*
4 acre garden with extensive lawns, walks, lengthy herbaceous borders and traditional Victorian box hedge. Water gardens with fountain and rare lilies. Sweeping views across Trent Valley to Sandon. Victorian School Chapel. 9 hole putting course. Boules pitch. Yarlet School Art Display. Gravel paths.

♿ 🐔 ❋ 🚐 ☕

68 YEW TREE COTTAGE
Podmores Corner, Long Lane, White Cross, Haughton, ST18 9JR. Clive & Ruth Plant, 01785 282516, pottyplantz@aol.com. *4m W of Stafford. Take A518 W Haughton, turn R Station Rd (signed Ranton) 1m, then turn R at Xrds ¼m on R.* Sun 30 Apr (2-5); Thur 4 May, Thur 1, Thur 8 June, Thur 6 July (11-5); Sun 23 July (2-5). Adm £3, chd free. Home-made teas.
Visits also by arrangement May to July.
Hardy Plant Society member's garden brimming with unusual plants. All-yr-round interest incl Meconopsis, Trillium, and Arisaema. National Collection Dierama. ½ acre incl gravel, borders, vegetables and plant sales area. Covered courtyard with oak-timbered vinery to take tea in if the weather is unkind, and seats in the garden for lingering on sunny days. Wheelchair access - level access, grass and paved paths, some narrow and some gravel.

♿ ❋ 🚐 NPC ☕

SUFFOLK

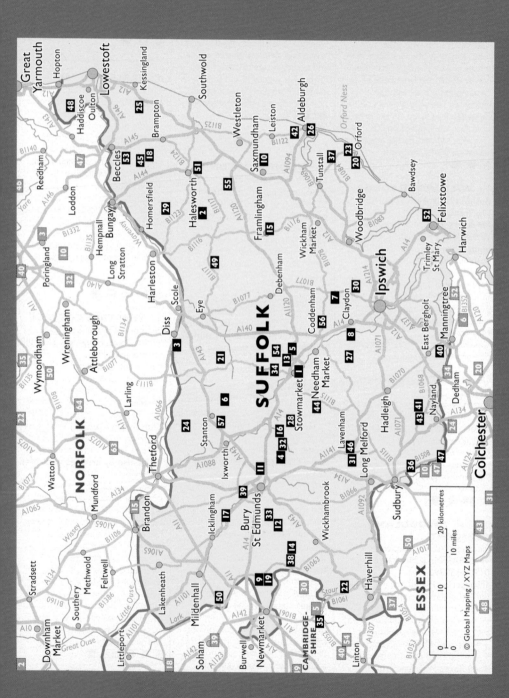

Suffolk has so much to offer – from charming coastal villages, ancient woodlands and picturesque valleys – there is a landscape to suit all tastes.

Keen walkers and cyclists will enjoy Suffolk's low-lying, gentle countryside, where fields of farm animals and crops reflect the county's agricultural roots.

Stretching north from Felixstowe, the county has miles of Heritage Coast set in an Area of Outstanding Natural Beauty. The Suffolk coast was the inspiration for composer Benjamin Britten's celebrated work, and it is easy to see why.

To the west and north of the county are The Brecks, a striking canvas of pine forest and open heathland, famous for its chalky and sandy soils – and one of the most important wildlife areas in Britain.

A variety of gardens to please everyone open for Suffolk NGS, so come along on an open day and enjoy the double benefit of a beautiful setting and supporting wonderful charities.

Volunteers

County Organiser
Jenny Reeve
01638 715289
j.reeve05@tiscali.co.uk

County Treasurer
David Reeve
01638 715289
dreeve43@gmail.com

Publicity
Jenny Reeve
(as above)

Booklet Co-ordinator
Adrian Simpson-James
01502 710555
adriansimpsonjames@gmail.com

Assistant County Organisers
Gilly Beddard
01394 450468
gbedd@btinternet.com

Frances Boscawen
01728 638768
francesboscawen@gmail.com

Michael Cole
01473 272920
michael.m.d.cole@btinternet.com

Yvonne Leonard
01638 712742
yj.leonard@btinternet.com

Marie-Anne Mackenzie
01728 831155
marieanne_mackenzie@yahoo.co.uk

Barbara Segall
01787 312046
barbara@bsegall.com

Peter Simpson
01787 249845
bergholt2002@btopenworld.com

Left: **9 Brookside**

OPENING DATES

All entries subject to change. For latest information check www.ngs.org.uk

Map locator numbers are shown to the right of each garden name.

February

Snowdrop Festival

Sunday 12th
Gable House 18

Sunday 19th
◆ Blakenham Woodland Garden 8

March

Sunday 26th
Woodwards 56

April

Sunday 2nd
Great Thurlow Hall 22
The Laburnums 29

Sunday 9th
2 High View 27
◆ The Place for Plants, East Bergholt Place Garden 40

Saturday 22nd
[NEW] Helyg 24

Sunday 23rd
The Beeches 6
Columbine Hall 13

Sunday 30th
◆ Blakenham Woodland Garden 8

May

Saturday 6th
The Old Rectory 35

Sunday 7th
The Old Rectory 35
◆ The Place for Plants, East Bergholt Place Garden 40
Woodwards 56

Saturday 13th
[NEW] Holm House 28

Sunday 14th
Bays Farm 5
Street Farm 50

Sunday 21st
Bay Tree House 4
◆ Fullers Mill Garden 17
The Priory 43
Rosedale 47
41 Westmorland Road 52

90th Anniversary Weekend

Sunday 28th
Appleacre 2
Lavenham Hall 31
Wenhaston Grange 51
Woodwards 56

Monday 29th
Abbot's Hall Walled Garden 1
Batteleys Cottage 3
Cattishall Farmhouse 11
Drinkstone Park 16

June

Saturday 3rd
◆ Wyken Hall 57

Sunday 4th
Gable House 18
Great Thurlow Hall 22
Wood Farm, Gipping 54
◆ Wyken Hall 57

Wednesday 7th
◆ Somerleyton Hall Gardens 48

Sunday 11th
Malting Farm 32
Old Rectory House 36
Orford Gardens 37
Ousden House 38
[NEW] Stradbroke Open Gardens 49

Saturday 17th
Larks' Hill 30

Sunday 18th
Drinkstone Park 16
Moat House 33
Wood Farm, Sibton 55

Sunday 25th
[NEW] Berghersh Place 7
[NEW] Helyg 24
Old Newton Gardens 34
[NEW] 5 Parklands Green 39
Priors Oak 42

Tuesday 27th
Woodwards 56

July

Saturday 1st
White House Farm 53

Sunday 2nd
Drinkstone Park 16
[NEW] Gedgrave Hall 20
[NEW] Green Lane House 23

Sunday 9th
Redisham Hall 45

Sunday 16th
Drinkstone Park 16

Sunday 23rd
Henstead Exotic Garden 25
Woodwards 56

August

Tuesday 1st
Woodwards 56

Saturday 5th
Gislingham Gardens 21

Sunday 6th
Gislingham Gardens 21
River Cottage 46
Rosedale 47

Sunday 13th
Cobbs Hall 12

Sunday 27th
Woodwards 56

September

Sunday 10th
[NEW] 11 Brookside 9
By the Crossways 10
[NEW] Garden House 19

Sunday 17th
[NEW] 1 Redbricks 44

Sunday 24th
Heron House 26

October

Sunday 8th
◆ The Place for Plants, East Bergholt Place Garden 40

By Arrangement

Batteleys Cottage 3
Bays Farm 5
By the Crossways 10
Cobbs Hall 12
Dip-on-the-Hill 14
28 Double Street 15
Drinkstone Park 16
Frythe Barn, Stradbroke Open Gardens 49
Henstead Exotic Garden 25
Heron House 26
Ivy Chimneys, Gislingham Gardens 21
Larks' Hill 30
Moat House 33
Polstead Mill 41
Priors Oak 42
The Priory 43
Redisham Hall 45
River Cottage 46
41 Westmorland Road 52
White House Farm 53
Wood Farm, Gipping 54
Woodwards 56

Holm House

THE GARDENS

1 ABBOT'S HALL WALLED GARDEN

Iliffe Way, Stowmarket, IP14 1DL. Museum of East Anglian Life, www.eastanglianlife.org.uk. *The Museum of East Anglian Life is adjacent to ASDA supermarket in Stowmarket. The Museum is signed from the main A14 trunk rd & B1115 to Great Finborough. For SatNav users please search for 'Iliffe Way'.* **Mon 29 May (10-4). Adm £2.50, chd free. Home-made teas.**
An oasis in the heart of Stowmarket this ½ acre walled Victorian kitchen garden has been restored and replanted since 2012. Showcasing many heritage vegetable varieties as well as trained fruit trees, herb bed, cut flower border, old roses and apple tunnel. It also boasts a renovated greenhouse, potting shed and conservatory. Good wheelchair access, gravel paths. A small car park is located in the grounds of Abbot's Hall for visitors with access needs only.
& 🐕 ✿ ☕

2 APPLEACRE

Bell Green, Cratfield, Halesworth, IP19 0DH. Mr & Mrs Tim & Naomi Shaw. *7m W of Halesworth. B1123 to Harleston. At Linstead Parva, turn L up Godfrey's Hill. After approx 1m turn R onto Mary's Lane & follow NGS signs. 50 metres W of the Poacher PH.* **Sun 28 May (11-5). Adm £3.50, chd free. Home-made teas.**
A country garden covering an acre that has evolved over forty years. A garden full of secrets waiting to be revealed, with open vistas over the Suffolk countryside. Explore a variety of large herbaceous borders, box topiary, mature trees, lily pond, greenhouse, lawns, vegetable garden and wildlife area. Partial wheelchair access, but caution needed in some areas.
& ✿ ☕

3 BATTELEYS COTTAGE

The Ling, Wortham, Diss, IP22 1ST. Mr & Mrs Andy & Linda Simpson, 07949 204820, lindaruth11@gmail.com. *3m W of Diss. Turn signed from A143 Diss/ Bury Rd at Wortham. By church turn R at T-junction. At top of hill turn L. Go down hill & round sharp L corner.* **Mon 29 May (1-5.30). Adm £4, chd free. Home-made teas.**
Visits also by arrangement May to Sept, refreshments available for groups on request.
A varied one acre garden planted for abundance in all seasons. Formality and informality, a mix of winding bark paths, light and shade, secluded spots to sit, new vistas at every turn. Fitting into its rural setting, it supports a wealth of bird life. There is a diversity of planting in densely planted borders as well as pots, sculptures, meadow, ponds, stream and vegetable areas to inspire you. Featured in Amateur Gardening and EDP Suffolk Magazines. Wheelchair access to most parts of the garden, gravel, grass and bark paths.
& ✿ 🚗 ☕

4 BAY TREE HOUSE

The Green, Rougham, Bury St. Edmunds, IP30 9JP. Mrs Claire Farthing. *Rougham Green. Come off A14 J45 & head for Rougham. At T-junction turn L follow road for approx 1½m, past Rougham Hall. Go round 90 degree bend to R. Disabled parking take 2nd L driveway. Follow signs for other parking.* **Sun 21 May (11-5). Adm £4.50, chd free. Home-made teas.**
Nearly 2 acres of garden. Decking with bench over looking a wildlife pond and small stream. Mature trees, 100ft long border, rose arbour, parterre garden. Green oak arches with wisteria and Italian pots. Lollipop hornbeams with curved yew hedging. Patio with wisteria draped pergola and cloud pruned tree. Lovely country views. Maybe a new sculpture. Wheelchair access the garden is mainly flat with only one small gravel path which can be avoided.
& 🐕 ✿ ☕

5 BAYS FARM

Forward Green, Earl Stonham, Stowmarket, IP14 5HU. Richard & Stephanie Challinor, 01449 711286, stephanie@baysfarmsuffolk.co.uk, www.baysfarmgardens.co.uk. *3½m E of Stowmarket. J50 A14, take A1120 direction Stowupland. Proceed through Stowupland on A1120 for 1m, at sharp L bend turn R signed Broad Green. 1st house on R.* **Sun 14 May (2-5.30). Adm £3.50, chd free. Home-made teas.**
Visits also by arrangement Mar to Oct refreshments will be available for groups whatever the size - please see website for details.
Bays Farm is an all year interest garden and will be opening for one day in 2017. Groups large or small are encouraged to call or email to visit at any time during the year when it suits them. Visitors will see for themselves how this true plantsman's garden changes from month to month in not only the formal flower beds but also the progress in the greenhouses, kitchen gardens and orchard. Formal gardens designed by Chelsea Gold Medal winner, Xa Tollemache of Helmingham Hall and recently redesigned moat. Featured in The Suffolk Magazine, The English Garden and Homes and Gardens. Gravel paths, uneven surfaces.
& 🐕 ✿ 🚗 🛏 ☕

6 THE BEECHES

Grove Road, Walsham-le-Willows, IP31 3AD. Dr A J Russell. *11m E of Bury St Edmunds. A143 to Diss. Turn R to Walsham-le-Willows. 1st Xrds in village turn R. Church on L. After 100yds turn L. Beeches on L.* **Sun 23 Apr (2-5). Adm £5, chd free. Home-made teas.** *Donation to St Marys Church, Walsham-le-Willows.*
150yr-old, 3-acre garden, which incl specimen trees, pond, stream, potager, memorial garden, lawns and a variety of beds. Stream area landscaped. Mediterranean bed and camellia bed. Gravel paths.
& 🐕 ☕

Silver Street Farmhouse

7 NEW **BERGHERSH PLACE**
Berghersh Drive, Witnesham,
Ipswich, IP6 9EZ. Mr & Mrs T C
Parkes. *Farm entrance on bend
of B1077 N of Witnesham village.
Approx 1m S of Ashbocking Xrds.
Concrete drive entrance on sharp
bend so please drive slowly. Turn in
between North Lodge & Berghersh
House.* **Sun 25 June (2-5.30).
Adm £3.50, chd free.
Home-made teas.**
Peaceful walled and hedged gardens
surround elegant Regency house
(not open) among fields above the
Fynn Valley. Circular walk from the
farm buildings, around house with
lawns and mature trees to a pretty
view of the valley. Mound, ponds,
bog area and orchard paddock.
Informal family garden with shrub
and perennial beds. Garden created
over last 20 years by current owner.
Parking for elderly and disabled
at end of farmyard close to family
garden. Most areas are accessible to
disabled visitors.
♿ 🐔 ☕

8 ◆ **BLAKENHAM
WOODLAND GARDEN**
Little Blakenham, Ipswich, IP8 4LZ.
M & M Blakenham, 07760 342131,
www.blakenhamwoodlandgarden.
org.uk. *4m NW of Ipswich. Follow
signs at Little Blakenham, 1m
off B1113 or go to Blakenham
Woodland Garden web-site.* **For
NGS: Sun 19 Feb (10-5); Sun
30 Apr (10-5.30). Adm £4, chd
£2. Tea, coffee, cakes & plant
sales are available on NGS days
only. For other opening times and
information, please phone or visit
garden website.**
Beautiful 6-acre woodland garden
with variety of rare trees and
shrubs, Chinese rocks and landscape
sculpture. Lovely in spring with
snowdrops, daffodils, camellias,
magnolias and bluebells followed by
roses in early summer. Woodland
Garden open from 1 March to 31
July. Donations to NGS on NGS
days. Partial wheelchair access.
♿ ❇ 🚗 ☕

9 NEW II BROOKSIDE

Moulton, Newmarket, CB8 8SG.
Elizabeth Goodrich & Peter
Mavroghenis. *Near the Packhorse
Bridge & PH. 3m due E of
Newmarket on B1085.* **Sun 10
Sept (2-6). Combined adm with
Garden House £5, chd free.
Home-made teas.**
1½ acres over 4 levels. Traditional
hedges, mature trees and roses
at the front while rear garden
landscaped in contemporary style.
Lower terrace with water feature
and fig trees. Terraced beds with
ornamental grasses, knot garden,
hosta courtyard. Metal retaining wall
to former paddock, many specimen
trees, apple espalier bordered
greenhouse with kitchen garden,
apples and vines.

10 BY THE CROSSWAYS

Kelsale, Saxmundham,
IP17 2PL. Mr & Mrs William
Kendall, 077678 24923,
miranda@bythecrossways.co.uk.
*2m NE of Saxmundham, just off
Clayhills Rd. ½m N of town centre,
turn R to Theberton on Clayhills Rd.
After 1½m, 1st L to Kelsale, then turn
L immed after white cottage.* **Sun 10
Sept (11-4). Adm £4, chd free.
Home-made teas. Visits also by
arrangement May to Sept for
groups of 10 during the week.**
3 acre wildlife garden designed as
a garden within an organic farm,
where wilderness areas lie next to
productive beds. Large semi-walled
vegetable and cutting garden, a
spectacular crinkle-crankle wall.
Extensive perennial planting, grasses
and wild areas. Set around the
owner's Edwardian family home
built by suffragist ancestor. The
garden is mostly flat, with paved
or gravel pathways around the
main house, a few low steps and
extensive grass paths and lawns.

II CATTISHALL FARMHOUSE

Cattishall, Great Barton,
Bury St. Edmunds, IP31 2QT.
Mrs J Mayer, 07738 936496,
joannamayer42@googlemail.com.
3m NE of Bury St Edmunds.

*Approach Great Barton from Bury
on A143 take 1st R turn to church.
If travelling towards Bury take last
L turn to church as you leave the
village. At church bear R and follow
lane to Farmhouse on R.* **Mon 29
May (1-5). Adm £4, chd free.
Home-made teas.**
Approx 2 acre farmhouse garden
enclosed by a flint wall and mature
beech hedge laid mainly to lawns
with both formal and informal
planting and large herbaceous
border. There is an abundance
of roses, small wildlife pond
and recently developed kitchen
garden incl a wild flower area and
fruit cages. Chickens, bees and a
boisterous Labrador also live here.
Generally flat with some gravel
paths. The occasional small step.

12 COBBS HALL

Great Saxham, IP29 5JN. Dick
& Sue Soper, 01284 850678,
soperdoc@gmail.com. *4½m W
of Bury St Edmunds. A14 exit to
Westley. R at Westley Xrds. L fork
at Lt.Saxham towards Chevington.
1.4m to R turn marked 'Gt Saxham'.
Mustard coloured house 300yds on
L.* **Sun 13 Aug (2-5.30). Adm £4,
chd free. Home-made teas. Visits
also by arrangement May to Aug
adm incl refreshments. Donation
to St Andrews Church, Gt Saxham.**
2 acres of lawns and colourful
herbaceous borders, ornamental
trees, large fish and lily pond.
Parterre, folly, walled kitchen garden,
fernery/stumpery, grass tennis court
and pretty courtyard. Cascade water
features. Generally flat with a few
gentle slopes and some gravel paths.

13 COLUMBINE HALL

Gipping Road, Stowupland,
Stowmarket, IP14 4AT. Hew
Stevenson & Leslie Geddes-
Brown, www.columbinehall.co.uk.
*1½m NE of Stowmarket. Turn N off
A1120 opp petrol station across
village green, then R at T-junction into
Gipping Rd. Garden on L just beyond
derestriction sign.* **Sun 23 Apr
(2-6). Adm £5, chd free.
Home-made teas.**
George Carter's formal garden

and herb garden surround moated
medieval manor (not open). Outside
the moat, vistas, stream, ponds and
bog garden, Mediterranean garden,
colour-themed vegetable garden,
orchards and parkland. Gardens
developed since 1994 with constant
work-in-progress, incl transformed
farm buildings and eyecatchers.
Disabled WC.

14 DIP-ON-THE-HILL

Ousden, Newmarket,
CB8 8TW. Dr & Mrs Geoffrey
Ingham, 01638 500329,
gki1000@cam.ac.uk. *5m E of
Newmarket; 7m W of Bury St
Edmunds. From Newmarket: 1m
from junction of B1063 & B1085.
From Bury St Edmunds follow signs
for Hargrave. Parking at village hall.*
**Visits by arrangement June to
Sept 20 max. Adm £4.50, chd
free. Home-made teas.**
Approx one acre in a dip on a
S-facing hill based on a wide range
of architectural/sculptural evergreen
trees, shrubs and groundcover:
pines; grove of Phillyrea latifolia;
'cloud pruned' hedges; palms; large
bamboo; ferns; range of kniphofia
and croscosmia. Visitors may wish to
make an appointment when visiting
gardens nearby. Featured in Country
Living and The English Garden.

15 28 DOUBLE STREET

Framlingham, IP13 9BN.
Mr & Mrs David Clark,
clarkdn@btinternet.com. *250yrds
from Market Hill (main square)
Framlingham opp Church. Leave
square from top L into Church
St. Double St is 100yds on R. Car
parking in main square & near to
Framlingham Castle.* **Visits by
arrangement groups of 10+.**
A town garden featuring roses
together with a wide range of
perennials and shrubs. Conservatory,
greenhouse, gazebo, summerhouse
and terrace full of containers all add
interest to the garden. Good views
of Framlingham's roofscape. Fine
shingle access drive with two ramps.

16 DRINKSTONE PARK

Park Road, Drinkstone, Bury St. Edmunds, IP30 9ST. Michael & Christine Lambert, 01359 272513, chris@drinkstonepark.co.uk, www.drinkstonepark.co.uk. *6m from Bury St Edmunds. E on A14 J46 turn L and the R for Drinkstone. W on A14 J46 turn R for Drinkstone. Turn into Park Rd. We are not in the village. Park Rd is parallel to the road that runs through the village.* **Mon 29 May, Sun 18 June, Sun 2, Sun 16 July (1-5.30). Adm £4, chd free. Home-made teas. Visits also by arrangement June to Aug refreshments on request to suit group.**

Three acre garden with wildlife pond formal Koi pond, herbaceous borders, orchard, woodland and wildlife area, large productive vegetable plot with poly tunnel and greenhouses. Some gravel paths.

 🚻 🚗 🏕 ☕

17 ◆ FULLERS MILL GARDEN

West Stow, IP28 6HD. Perennial, 01284 728888, fullersmillgarden@perennial.org.uk, www.fullersmillgarden.org.uk. *6m NW of Bury St Edmunds. Turn off A1101 Bury to Mildenhall Rd, signed West Stow Country Park, go past Country Park continue for ¼ m, garden entrance on R. Sign at entrance.* **For NGS: Sun 21 May (2-5). Adm £4, chd free. Home-made teas. For other opening times and information, please phone, email or visit garden website.**

An enchanting 7 acre garden on the banks of R Lark. A beautiful site of light, dappled woodland with a plantsman's paradise of rare and unusual shrubs, perennials and marginals planted with great natural charm. Euphorbias and lilies are a particular feature. A garden with interest in every season. In late Sept colchicums in flower incl outstanding white variety. Tea, coffee and soft drinks. Home-made cakes. Partial wheelchair access around garden.

 🚻 ❀ 🚗 ☕

18 GABLE HOUSE

Halesworth Road, Redisham, Beccles, NR34 8NE. John & Brenda Foster. *5m S of Beccles. A144 S from Bungay, L at St Lawrence School, 2m to Gable House. Or A12 Blythburgh, A145 to Beccles, Brampton Xrd L to Station Rd. 3m on is garden.* **Sun 12 Feb (11-4); Sun 4 June (11-5). Adm £4, chd free. Home-made teas. Warming soups available in February. Salad lunches in June.** *Donation to St Peter's Church, Redisham.*

This is our 40th anniversary year of opening our gardens for the NGS. We have a vast collection of snowdrops, cyclamen, hellebores etc for the Snowdrop Day in February. The summer borders include a wonderful display of many perennials including naturalised dieramas, aquilegias and roses. Greenhouses contain rare bulbs and tender plants. Featured in Suffolk magazine and East Anglian Daily Times.

 🚻 ❀ 🚗 ☕

19 [NEW] GARDEN HOUSE

5 Brookside, Moulton, CB8 8SG. Sue Maskelyne. *Near the Packhorse Bridge & PH. 3m due E of Newmarket on B1085.* **Sun 10 Sept (2-6). Combined adm with 11 Brookside £5, chd free. Home-made teas.**

Garden House is close to the Packhorse Bridge and faces the village green. Interesting ¾ acre plantsman's garden, roses, small woodland area, alpines and mixed borders. Small water feature, pergola: large number of clematis; Owner's late husband chaired the British Clematis Society; maintained by owner with the help of two long standing gardener friends.

 🚻 ☕

20 [NEW] GEDGRAVE HALL

Gedgrave, Orford, Woodbridge, IP12 2BX. Edward & Clare Greenwell. *In Orford, turn R, past Crown & Castle PH, past Castle, then 1st R, signed Gedgrave Rd. Gedgrave Hall is 1¼ m at the end of the rd on R after farm buildings.* **Sun 2 July (11-5). Combined adm with Green Lane House £6, chd free. Home-made teas.**

There was no garden at Gedgrave until 1977. Instead, there was a grass bank and a wartime Nissen hut. With no shelter the views were terrific, but so was the wind. We built brick walls and planted quite extensive yew hedges creating a number of 'rooms' in the garden. A mound was created in 2012. The soil is almost pure sand and dries out every year at some point in the summer. Typical English garden, yew hedges, walled garden, cutting garden, vegetable garden, newly planted rose garden. Mound designed by George Carter with views of sea and Orford. Wheelchair access, parking in adjoining field.

 🚻 ☕

GROUP OPENING

21 GISLINGHAM GARDENS

Mill Street, Gislingham, IP23 8JT. *4m W of Eye. Gislingham 2½ m W of A140. 9m N of Stowmarket, 8m S of Diss. Disabled parking at Ivy Chimneys.* **Sat 5, Sun 6 Aug (11-4.30). Combined adm £3.50, chd free. Light refreshments at Ivy Chimneys. Teas cakes and soft drinks.**

HAREBELLS
Jenny & Darrel Charles.

IVY CHIMNEYS
Iris & Alan Stanley, 01379 788737. **Visits also by arrangement Aug & Sept parties of 10 to 20 visitors.**

2 varied gardens in a picturesque village with a number of Suffolk timbered houses. Ivy Chimneys is planted for yr round interest with ornamental trees, some topiary, exotic borders and fishpond set in an area of Japanese style. Wisteria draped pergola supports a productive vine. Also a separate ornamental vegetable garden. New for 2014 fruit trees in the front garden. Harebells, 150 yards further down Mill Street from Ivy Chimneys, was a new build property in 2013 and the garden has since been developed from scratch. The garden has a feature round lawn edged by colour themed borders.

A walk through pergola leads to a productive area incl a greenhouse and raised vegetables beds, a wildlife pond and views over open countryside. Partial wheelchair access.

♿ ✹ ☕

22 GREAT THURLOW HALL

Great Thurlow, Haverhill, CB9 7LF. Mr George Vestey. *12m S of Bury St Edmunds, 4m N of Haverhill. Great Thurlow village on B1061 from Newmarket; 3½ m N of junction with A143 Haverhill/Bury St Edmunds rd.* **Sun 2 Apr, Sun 4 June (2-5). Adm £4, chd free. Home-made teas and cakes are available in the church.**

13 acres of beautiful gardens set around the R Stour, the banks of which are adorned with stunning displays of daffodil and narcissi together with blossoming trees in spring. Herbaceous borders, rose garden and extensive shrub borders come alive with colour from late spring onwards, there is also a large walled kitchen garden and arboretum. Plant Sale for the summer open day.

♿ 🐎 ☕

23 NEW GREEN LANE HOUSE

Castle Green, Orford, Woodbridge, IP12 2NF. Mr & Mrs Michael Flint. *SatNav IP12 2NG. Go past the Crown & Castle PH & Orford Castle, turn R into Gedgrave Rd. 200 yds along the rd on R there is a field gate. Parking is in field. The drive next to it leads to the garden.* **Sun 2 July (11-5). Combined adm with Gedgrave Hall £6, chd free. Home-made teas in Gedgrave Hall.**

A half-acre garden created in 1995 with views over Orfordness. A terrace with perennials and formal croquet lawn gives way to fruit trees in rough grass and large borders of shrubs including a good display of hostas. Colourful pots of summer annuals on terrace. Vegetable area and conservatory. The garden has superb views over Orford Castle and over the R Ore to Orfordness and out to sea. Cars conveying

wheelchair visitors can park at the top of the drive near the house.

♿ ☕

24 NEW HELYG

Thetford Road, Coney Weston, Bury St. Edmunds, IP31 1DN. Jackie & Briant Smith. *From Barningham Xrds/shop turn off the B1111 towards Coney Weston & Knettishall Country Park. Helyg will be found on the L behind some large willow trees after approx 1m.* **Sat 22 Apr, Sun 25 June (1-5). Adm £3.50, chd free. Cream teas.**

Just under half an acre of garden being developed for ease of maintenance and including several novel features. There is a woodland walk, raised flower and vegetable beds, small orchard, wildlife area and ponds, all planted with spring bulbs as well as a small rose garden, a lawned area and a large greenhouse. There is a composting toilet but this is not wheelchair accessible. Teas in aid of MIND. Most of the garden is wheelchair accessible with a variety of surfaces including concrete slab, gravel and wood-chip paths.

☕

25 HENSTEAD EXOTIC GARDEN

Church Road, Henstead, Beccles, NR34 7LD. Andrew Brogan, 01502 743006, andrew. hensteadexoticgarden@ hotmail.co.uk, www.hensteadexoticgarden.co.uk. *Equal distance between Beccles, Southwold & Lowestoft approx 5m. 1m from A12 turning after Wrentham (signed Henstead) very close to B1127.* **Sun 23 July (11-4). Adm £4, chd free. Home-made teas. Visits also by arrangement.**

2-acre exotic garden featuring 100 large palms, 20+ bananas and 200 bamboo plants. 2 streams, 20ft tiered walkway leading to Thai style wooden covered pavilion. Mediterranean and jungle plants around 3 large ponds with fish. Suffolk's most exotic garden. Newly extended this year. Featured in East Anglian Daily Times.

🐎 ✹ ☕

26 HERON HOUSE

Aldeburgh, IP15 5EP. Mr & Mrs Jonathan Hale, 01728 452200, jonathanrhhale@aol.com. *At the southeastern junction of Priors Hill Rd & Park Rd. Last house on Priors Hill Rd on R, at the junction where it rejoins Park Rd.* **Sun 24 Sept (2-5). Adm £5, chd free. Home-made teas. Visits also by arrangement.**

2 acres with views over coastline, river and marshes. Unusual trees, herbaceous beds, shrubs and ponds with waterfall in large rock garden, stream and bog garden. Interesting attempts to grow half hardy plants in the coastal micro-climate. Partial wheelchair access.

♿ 🐎 ☕

27 2 HIGH VIEW

Derrick Hill, Willisham, Ipswich, IP8 4SG. Mr & Mrs Hill. *6m NW of Ipswich. Just off Barking Rd between Bramford (B1113) & Barking (B1078). 500 metres from Offton Limeburners PH.* **Sun 9 Apr (10-4). Adm £3.50, chd free. Home-made teas.**

Garden divided into rooms on elevated ¾ acre site with views across valley towards Offton. Traditional cottage garden with herbaceous borders. Parterre with kitchen herb garden and spring bulbs. Raised vegetable plots, apple and pear archway, woodland nature area with primroses, cowslips, bluebells, anemones. Summerhouse with tropical plants and grasses. No wheelchair access. Only those with difficulties walking should park next to house.

✹ ☕

Perennial, supporting horticulturalists since 1839

28 [NEW] HOLM HOUSE

Garden House Lane, Drinkstone, Bury St. Edmunds, IP30 9FJ. Mrs Rebecca Shelley. *7m SE of Bury St Edmunds. Coming from the E exit A14 at J47 from the W J46. Follow signs to Drinkstone, then Drinkstone Green. Turn into Rattlesden Road & garden on L.* **Sat 13 May (10-5). Adm £5, chd free. Light refreshments.**

A beautifully-designed garden with six very different areas: lawn with mature trees and Holm Oaks; formal garden with topiary, box hedging and borders with year round interest; woodland walk with hellebores, camellias, rhododendrons and bulbs; flower garden with cutting beds; a large kitchen garden with impressive greenhouse; Mediterranean courtyard with old olive tree. Much of the garden is wheelchair accessible, but not the kitchen garden.

29 THE LABURNUMS

The Street, St James South Elmham, Halesworth, IP19 0HN. Mrs Jane Bastow. *6m W of Halesworth, 7m E of Harleston & 6m S of Bungay. Parking at nearby village hall. For disabled parking please phone to arrange.* **Sun 2 Apr (11-5). Adm £4.50, chd free. Home-made teas. Hot/Cold drinks, cakes and hot soup.**

1 acre garden is 20+ years old and is packed with annuals, perennials, flowering shrubs and trees and areas dedicated to wild flowers. The spring garden is awash with colour-snowdrops, aconites, hellebores, daffodils and much more. There are three ponds, a sunken garden and two glasshouses 2015 sees the new larger conservatory where the refreshments will be served surrounded by citrus plants etc. Plant stall with a variety of plants and bulbs. This garden has been featured in most of the local papers and in the past in the Garden News. Gravel drive. Partial wheelchair access to front garden. Steps to sunken garden. Concrete path in back garden.

30 LARKS' HILL

Clopton Road, Tuddenham St Martin, IP6 9BY. Mr John Lambert, 01473 785248, jrlambert@talktalk.net. *3m NE of Ipswich. From Ipswich take B1077, go through village, take the Clopton Rd.* **Sat 17 June (1.30-5). Adm £5, chd free. Home-made teas. Visits also by arrangement Apr to Aug groups of 15+.**

The gardens of eight acres comprise woodland, field and formal areas, and fall away from the house to the valley floor. A hill within a garden and in Suffolk at that! Hilly garden with a modern castle keep with an interesting and beautiful site overlooking the gentle Fynn valley and the village beyond. A garden worthy of supporting the House, its family members and its visitors. A fossil of a limb bone from a Pliosaur that lived at least sixty million years ago was found in the garden in 2013. The discovery was reported in the national press but its importance has been recognised world-wide. A booklet is available to purchase giving all the details.

31 LAVENHAM HALL

Hall Road, Lavenham, Sudbury, CO10 9QX. Mr & Mrs Anthony Faulkner, www.katedenton.com. *Next to Lavenham's iconic church & close to High St. From church turn off the main rd down the side of church (Potland Rd). Go down hill. Car Park on R after 100 metres.* **Sun 28 May (11-5). Adm £4, chd free. Home-made teas.**

5 acre garden built around the ruins of the original ecclesiastical buildings on the site and the village's 1 acre fishpond. The garden incl deep borders of herbaceous planting with sweeping vistas and provides the perfect setting for the sculptures which Kate makes in her studio at the Hall and exhibits both nationally and internationally. 40 garden sculptures on display. There is a gallery in the grounds which displays a similar number of indoor sculptures and working drawings. Teas in aid of St Nicholas Hospice Care, Bury St Edmunds. Wheelchair access - large number of gravel

paths and slopes within the garden.

32 MALTING FARM

Heath Road, Hessett, Bury St. Edmunds, IP30 9BJ. Mrs Klair Bauly. *In the village of Hessett. 5m E of Bury St Edmunds, A14 exit 46, at Beyton Green take Church Road up the side of the White Horse PH, at Hessett Green turn R into Heath Road. We are located opposite Hessett Green.* **Sun 11 June (2-6). Adm £3.50, chd free. Home-made teas.**

This new garden is now in its fifth year designed and maintained by the owner to sit with the surrounding landscape using formal and natural planting combined. A natural pond, aquatic and marginal planting, woodland walk, meadow with countryside views. 100ft border with repeat planting and sculptural forms. Wooded area with grass beds. Featuring the work of Kev Colbear, there is Sculpture situated beside the pond, a Gaudi inspired bridge and new sculpture planned for 2017. Fruit and vegetable garden in decorative oak cages and raised beds with a new water feature planned for 2017. The garden is designed to be a tranquil haven. Some gravel paths, woodland walk is unsuitable for wheelchairs.

33 MOAT HOUSE

Little Saxham, Bury St. Edmunds, IP29 5LE. Mr & Mrs Richard Mason, 01284 810941, rnm333@live.com. *2m SW of Bury St Edmunds. Leave A14 at J42 – through Westley Village, at Xrds R towards Barrow/Saxham 1.3m L (follow signs).* **Sun 18 June (1-5). Adm £4.50, chd free. Home-made teas. Visits also by arrangement May to July groups between min 20 max 50.**

Set in a 2 acre historic and partially moated site. This tranquil mature garden has been developed by the present owners over 20yrs. Bordered by mature trees the garden is in various sections incl a sunken garden, rose and clematis arbours, herbaceous borders with hydrangeas and alliums surrounded by box hedging, small arboretum,. Featured in Homes and Gardens, Suffolk magazine, Country Homes and Interiors, Garden News.

 ♿ ✿ 🚐 ☕

GROUP OPENING

34 OLD NEWTON GARDENS

Silver Street, Old Newton, Stowmarket, IP14 4HF. *2½m N of Stowmarket. From B1113 R at Shoulder of Mutton in Old Newton, parking 150yds on L at Village Hall IP14 4ED.* **Sun 25 June (1-5). Combined adm £4, chd free. Home-made teas at Silver Street Farmhouse.**

THE OLD VICARAGE
Mr & Mrs R M Brooks.

NEW SILVER STREET FARMHOUSE
Ms Cherry Sandford.

The Old Vicarage's small garden is for plant enthusiasts. It has been extensively developed since 2006. There are many interesting ornamental trees, shrubs and bulbs.

The informal beds are packed with herbaceous perennials. Clematis and roses scramble through trees and a pergola. Silver Street Farmhouse is a garden divided into different areas including: a studio garden with brick paths colourful flower beds with Clematis and Roses. Lawns surrounded with herbaceous borders, Box topiary and clipped Yew hedges, A vegetable garden with raised beds, a collection of unusual trees and shrubs. Not suitable for wheelchairs at the Old Vicarage: partially suitable at Silver Street Farmhouse.

✿ ☕

35 THE OLD RECTORY

Hall Lane, Brinkley, CB8 0SB. Mr & Mrs Mark Coley. *Hall Lane is a turning off Brinkley High St. At the end of Hall Lane, white gates on the R.* **Sat 6, Sun 7 May (1.30-5.30). Adm £3.50, chd free. Home-made teas in Brinkley Village Hall.**

Two acre garden started in 1973. Interesting trees planted to supplement beech, yew and chestnut already there. Mixed

Herbaceous borders. Tradtional Potager with box hedges planted in 1993. Small woodland area still being developed. Limited wheelchair access.

✿ ☕

36 OLD RECTORY HOUSE

Kedington Hill, Little Cornard, Sudbury, CO10 0PD. Jane & David Mann. *2½m outside Sudbury off B1508 Bures Rd. From Bures Rd follow signs to Little Cornard Parish Church. Garden is approx ½m up the lane on L. Parking opp.* **Sun 11 June (2-5). Adm £4, chd free. Home-made teas.**

Large country garden with established specimen trees and some interesting more recent plantings. Small woodland with ponds and stream. Cottage garden, roses, walled fruit and vegetable garden, greenhouse, parterre with tulips in late spring. Extensive bank with mixed planting including irises, grasses, herbaceous and shrubs. Surrounding meadows managed for native floral diversity. Wheelchair access - some slopes and uneven ground. Loose gravel in places.

♿ ✿ ☕

Green Lane House

GROUP OPENING

37 ORFORD GARDENS
High Street, Orford, Woodbridge, IP12 2NW. *8m from Woodbridge. Take the B1084 from Woodbridge & follow NGS signs to Orford. These will direct you to the Old Rectory. From the Old Rectory, follow signs down Rectory Road to Brundish Lodge.* **Sun 11 June (2-5). Combined adm £5, chd free. Home-made teas at Brundish Lodge.**

BRUNDISH LODGE
Mrs Elizabeth Spinney.
D

THE OLD RECTORY
Mr & Mrs Timothy Fargher.

Orford is a very attractive village with an historic castle and church. It also has excellent PHs and restaurants. Brundish Lodge is a garden of about one third of an acre and was completely redesigned, reconstructed and replanted in 2005. It is, therefore, quite a young garden and very much work in progress, It has beds which are a mixture of shrubs, herbaceous plants and grasses grouped around a central lawn. The Old Rectory garden is a 4-5 acre layout of mixed borders, shrubbery walks, fountain courtyard, C19 conservatory, vegetable garden largely as laid out by Lanning Roper in the late 1960's with modifications by Mark Rumary (1980), the vagaries of nature and the current owners.
&. ❦ 💷

Your visit helps the Queen's Nursing Institute to champion excellence in community nursing

---

38 OUSDEN HOUSE
Ousden, Newmarket, CB8 8TN. Mr & Mrs Alastair Robinson. *Newmarket 6m, Bury St Edmunds 8m. Ousden House stands at the west end of the village next to the Church.* **Sun 11 June (2-5.30). Adm £6, chd free. Home-made teas.** A large spectacular garden with fine views over the surrounding country. Herbaceous borders, rose garden, summerhouse lawn and borders, ornamental woodland, and lake. Additional special features include a long double crinkle-crankle yew hedge leading from the clock tower and a moat garden densely planted with flowering shrubs and moisture loving plants. Tea is served in the sheltered courtyard. Extensive garden on various levels not very suitable for wheelchairs.
❦ 💷

39 NEW 5 PARKLANDS GREEN
Fornham St Genevieve, Bury St. Edmunds, IP28 6UH. Mrs Jane Newton. *2m Northwest of Bury St Edmunds off B1106. Plenty of parking on the green.* **Sun 25 June (2-6). Adm £4, chd free. Home-made teas.**
1½ acres of gardens developed since the 1980s for all year interest. There are mature and unusual trees and shrubs and riotous herbaceous borders. Explore the maze of paths to find 4 informal ponds, a tree house, the sunken garden, greenhouses and woodland walks. Partial wheelchair access only.
🐕 ❦ 🚗 💷

40 ◆ THE PLACE FOR PLANTS, EAST BERGHOLT PLACE GARDEN
East Bergholt, CO7 6UP. Mr & Mrs Rupert Eley, 01206 299224, sales@placeforplants.co.uk, www.placeforplants.co.uk. *2m E of A12, 7m S of Ipswich. On B1070 towards Manningtree, 2m E of A12. Situated on the edge of East Bergholt.* **For NGS: Sun 9 Apr, Sun 7 May (2-5). Home-made teas. Sun 8 Oct (1-5). Adm £6, chd free. For other opening times and information, please phone, email or visit garden website.**

20-acre garden originally laid out at the turn of the last century by the present owner's great grandfather. Full of many fine trees and shrubs, many seldom seen in East Anglia. A fine collection of camellias, magnolias and rhododendrons, topiary, and the National Collection of deciduous Euonymus. Partial Wheelchair access in dry conditions - it is advisable to telephone before visiting.
&. ❦ NPC 💷

41 POLSTEAD MILL
Mill Lane, Polstead, Colchester, CO6 5AB. Mrs Lucinda Bartlett, 01206 265969, lucyofleisure@hotmail.com. *Between Stoke by Nayland & Polstead on the R Box. From Stoke by Nayland take rd to Polstead - Mill Lane is 1st on L & Polstead Mill is 1st house on R.* **Visits by arrangement May to Oct for groups of 10+. Adm £6.50. Home-made teas. A range of refreshments available from coffee and biscuits to full cream teas and even light lunches..**
The garden has been developed since 2002, it has formal and informal areas, a wild flower meadow and a large productive kitchen garden. The R Box runs through the garden and there is a mill pond, which gives opportunity for damp gardening, while much of the rest of the garden is arid and is planted to minimise the need for watering. Featured in Gardens Illustrated. Partial wheelchair access.
&. ❦ 💷

42 PRIORS OAK
Leiston Road, Aldeburgh, IP15 5QE. Mrs Trudie Willis, 01728 452580, trudie.willis@dinkum.free-online.co.uk, https://sites.google.com/site/priorsoakbutterflygarden. *1m N of Aldeburgh on B1122. Garden on L opp RSPB Reserve.* **Sun 25 June (2-6). Adm £5, chd free. Tea. Visits also by arrangement May to Sept.**
10-acre wildlife and butterfly garden. Ornamental salad and vegetable gardens with companion planting. Herbaceous borders, ferns and Mediterranean plants. Pond and wild

flower acid grassland with a small wood. Skirting the wood are 100 buddleia in excess of 30 varieties forming a perfumed tunnel. Very tranquil and fragrant garden with grass paths and yearly interest. Rich in animal and bird life. Specialist butterfly garden, as seen in SAGA magazine,and Horticulture in USA renovated railway carriages, tortoise breeding, donkeys, wildlife walks. Coaches or private visits by appointment only.

♿ ✿ ☕

43 THE PRIORY

Stoke by Nayland, Colchester, CO6 4RL. Mr & Mrs H F A Engleheart, 01206 262216. *5m SW of Hadleigh. Entrance on B1068 to Sudbury (NW of Stoke by Nayland).* **Sun 21 May (2-5). Adm £5, chd free. Home-made teas. Visits also by arrangement Apr to Sept groups of 10+, adm by arrangement.**

Interesting 9 acre garden with fine views over Constable countryside; lawns sloping down to small lakes and water garden; fine trees, rhododendrons and azaleas; walled garden; mixed borders and ornamental greenhouse. Wide variety of plants. Wheelchair access over most of garden, some steps.

♿ 🐕 ✿ 🚌 ☕

44 NEW I REDBRICKS

Worlds End Lane, Buxhall, Stowmarket, IP14 3ED. Mr Steve Pryke. *5m SW of Stowmarket. From A14 take exit 50 southbound to Stowmarket. Follow A1120, turn L into A1308, then R into B1115. Follow B1115 to Great Finborough then follow NGS signs.* **Sun 17 Sept (12-5). Adm £3.50, chd free. Home-made teas.**

A distinctive garden of one and half acres in a rural setting. Includes several large perennial beds planted in a naturalistic style, a mature seasonal pond, a newly developed bog garden, a recently established wildlife pond, semi-formal low maintenance drought tolerant north and south facing gardens, vegetable beds, greenhouse, summerhouse, and mixed orchard.

🐕 ✿ ☕

45 REDISHAM HALL

Redisham Rd, Redisham, nr Beccles, NR34 8LZ. The Palgrave Brown Family, 01502 575894, sarah.hammond7@hotmail.co.uk. *5m S of Beccles. From A145, turn W on to Ringsfield-Bungay rd. Beccles, Halesworth or Bungay, all within 5m.* **Sun 9 July (2-6). Adm £4.50, chd free. Home-made teas. Visits also by arrangement July to Sept groups 10 min.**

C18 Georgian house (not open). 5 acre garden set in 400 acres parkland and woods. Incl 2-acre walled kitchen garden (in full production) with peach house, vinery and glasshouses. Lawns, herbaceous borders, shrubberies, ponds and mature trees. Sorry No Dogs. We have been open for the NGS for over 50 yrs, during this time we have only been closed once due to an outbreak of foot and mouth. The garden has lots of gravel paths and there are lawned slopes. Wheelchair access is possible with assistance. Parking is on uneven parkland.

♿ ✿ ☕

46 RIVER COTTAGE

Lower Road, Lavenham, Sudbury, CO10 9QJ. Mr & Mrs Geoff Heald, 07747 827605, geoff@artmarketing.co.uk. *It is best to park your car in the Village Square & walk down Prentice Street which can be found by walking past The Angel & The Great House. Proceed to the bottom then turn R on Lower Rd.* **Sun 6 Aug (11-4). Adm £5, chd free. Home-made teas. A selection of home made cakes, teas and coffees. Visits also by arrangement Apr to Sept for Groups of 10 +.**

A tranquil plantsman's garden with a 400ft river frontage ending with a hydrangea walk with many newly planted hostas, dahlias, lilies,roses, clematis, ivies and grasses. The newly created woodland garden has many rare plants including Paris Arisaemas. Look out for a Spotty Dotty and a giant Amorphophallus. The new owners are always looking for new and unusual plants to delight visitors. There will be a wheelchair route clearly signed for use in dry weather.

✿ ☕

47 ROSEDALE

40 Colchester Road, Bures, CO8 5AE. Mr & Mrs Colin Lorking. *6m SE of Sudbury. From Colchester take B1508. After 10m garden on L as you enter the village, from Sudbury B1508 after 5m garden on R.* **Sun 21 May, Sun 6 Aug (12-5). Adm £3, chd free. Home-made teas.**

Approx one-third of an acre plantsman's garden developed over the last 24 years, containing many unusual plants, herbaceous borders and pond. For the May opening see a super collection of peonies and for the August opening a stunning collection of approx 60 Agapanthus in full flower.

✿ ☕

48 ◆ SOMERLEYTON HALL GARDENS

Somerleyton, NR32 5QQ. Lord Somerleyton, 01502 734901, www.somerleyton.co.uk. *5m NW of Lowestoft. From Norwich (30mins) - on the B1074, 7m SE of Great Yarmouth (A143). Coaches should follow signs to the rear west gate entrance.* **For NGS: Wed 7 June (10-5). Adm £6.95, chd £4.90. Light refreshments in Cafe. For other opening times and information, please phone or visit garden website.**

12½ acres of beautiful gardens contain a wide variety of magnificent specimen trees, shrubs, borders and plants providing colour and interest throughout the yr. Sweeping lawns and formal gardens combine with majestic statuary and original Victorian ornamentation. Highlights incl the Paxton glasshouses, pergola, walled garden and famous yew hedge maze. House and gardens remodelled in 1840s by Sir Morton Peto. House created in Anglo-Italian style with lavish architectural features and fine state rooms. All areas of the gardens are accessible, path surfaces are gravel and can be a little difficult after heavy rain. Wheelchairs available on request.

♿ ✿ 🚌 ☕

GROUP OPENING

49 NEW STRADBROKE OPEN GARDENS
Wilby Road, Stradbroke, Eye, IP21 5JP. *11m SE of Diss. Follow B1118 to Stradbroke. Bishops View is in the centre of the village on the junction of Wilby Rd & New St. Frythe Barn & Ivy Lodge are on B1118 towards Wilby.* **Sun 11 June (11-4). Combined adm £6, chd free. Home-made teas. Savoury, Gluten Free and Dairy Free options available at Frythe Barn. Cold Drinks at Ivy Lodge and Bishops View.**

NEW THE BISHOP'S VIEW
Ms Gillian Rennie-Dunkerley.

FRYTHE BARN
Don & Carol Darling, 01379 388098, caroldon01@gmail.com. **Visits also by arrangement May to July groups of 10 - 30.**

NEW IVY LODGE
Mrs Moyra Gibling.

This is the sixth year with the NGS for Frythe Barn. The two acre garden continues to develop with emphasis on wildlife friendly areas and planting. Main features are large grass beds, informal pond and stream, wild flower meadows and borders. The Bishop's View was originally The Old Rectory's walled vegetable area in the centre of the village, this garden continues to be renovated including the 100 feet long pond, wide herbaceous borders, many trees, rose pergola and sunken terrace. Ivy Lodge garden was started from scratch when the current owner and her late husband bought the house in 1998. Over the years it has evolved into a typical English country garden with overflowing herbaceous borders, old-fashioned shrub roses and a natural pond. Set at the back of paddocks and fruit trees this is a very tranquil corner of Suffolk. Illustrated articles about Frythe Barn in EADT and Suffolk magazine. Wheelchair access to main areas of all three gardens.

50 STREET FARM
North Street, Freckenham, IP28 8HY. David & Clodagh Dugdale. *3m W of Mildenhall. From Newmarket, follow signs to Snailwell, & Chippenham & then onto Freckenham.* **Sun 14 May (11-5). Adm £4, chd free. Light refreshments.**
Approx 1 acre of landscaped garden, with several mature trees. The garden includes a water cascade, pond with island and a number of bridges. Formal rose garden, rose pergola, herbaceous borders and hornbeam walk. Gravel paths with steps and slopes.

51 WENHASTON GRANGE
Wenhaston, Halesworth, IP19 9HJ. Mr & Mrs Bill Barlow. *Turn SW from A144 between Bramfield & Halesworth. Take the single track rd (signed Walpole 2) Wenhaston Grange is approx ½m, at the bottom of the hill on L.* **Sun 28 May (11-4). Adm £5, chd free. Home-made teas.**
Over 3 acres of varied gardens on a long established site which has been extensively landscaped and enhanced over the last 15 yrs. Long herbaceous borders, old established trees and a series of garden rooms created by beech hedges. Levels and sight lines have been carefully planned. The garden is on a number of levels, with steps so wheelchair access would be difficult.

52 41 WESTMORLAND ROAD
Felixstowe, IP11 9TJ. Mrs Diane Elmes, 01394 284647, dianeelmes@talktalk.net. *Enter Felixstowe on A154. At r'about take 1st exit then turn R into Beatrice Av. L to High Road East. Proceed to Clifflands Car Park. Follow signs No. 41 is on the corner of Wrens Park.* **Sun 21 May (11-5). Adm £4, chd free. Home-made teas. Cakes and savouries. Visits also by arrangement for groups up to 10.**
We moved into this house seven years ago, since when we have recovered the garden by taking down 21 leylandii trees and various other dead trees. It is now a perennial garden with interesting and eclectic features. All main areas wheelchair accessible.

53 WHITE HOUSE FARM
Ringsfield, Beccles, NR34 8JU. James & Jan Barlow, (gardener) 07780 901233, coppertops707@aol.com. *2m SW of Beccles. From Beccles take B1062 to Bungay, after 1¼ turn L signed Ringsfield. Continue for approx 1m. Parking opp church. Garden 300yds on L.* **Sat 1 July (10-4.30). Adm £4, chd free. Home-made teas. Cakes and savoury flans. Visits also by arrangement Apr to Sept, Tuesday - Friday, daytime or evening, not wk/ends.**
Tranquil park-type garden approx 30 acres, bordered by farmland and with fine views. Comprising formal areas, copses, natural pond, woodland walk, vegetable garden and orchard. Picnickers welcome. NB The pond and beck are unfenced. Partial wheelchair access to the areas around the house.

54 WOOD FARM, GIPPING
Back Lane, Gipping, Stowmarket, IP14 4RN. Mr & Mrs R Shelley, 07809 503019, els@maritimecargo.com. *From A14 take A1120 to Stowupland, Turn L opp Petrol Station, Turn R at T-junction, follow for approx 1m turn L at Allards Farm Shop, then imm R & follow for 1m along country lane. Wood Farm is on L.* **Sun 4 June (2-5.30). Adm £4, chd free. Home-made teas. Large Party Barn with Facilities. Visits also by arrangement May to July for groups of 10+.**
Wood Farm is an old farm with ponds, orchards and a magnificent 8 acre wild flower meadow (with mown paths) bordered with traditional hedging, trees and woodland. The large cottage garden was created in 2011 with a number of beds planted with flowers, vegetables and topiary. Wildlife is very much encouraged in all parts

5 Parklands Green

of the garden (particularly bees and butterflies). Partial wheelchair access.

♿ 🐕 ✳ ☕

55 WOOD FARM, SIBTON

Halesworth Road, Sibton, Saxmundham, IP17 2JL. Andrew & Amelia Singleton. *4m S of Halesworth. Turn off A12 at Yoxford onto A1120. Turn R after Sibton Nursery towards Halesworth. Take the 2nd drive on R after the White Horse PH.* **Sun 18 June (2-6). Adm £4, chd free. Home-made teas.**

Country garden surrounding old farmhouse, divided into colour themed areas, incl white garden, hot courtyard and blue and yellow border. Large (unfenced) ponds, vegetable garden, wild white flowering shrub area and mown walks. Garden designer owner. Previously featured in 'The English Garden','East Anglian Daily Times' and 'Gardening from Which'. Some gravel paths which are not suitable for wheelchairs.

♿ 🐕 ☕

56 WOODWARDS

Blacksmiths Lane, Coddenham, Ipswich, IP6 9TX. Marion & Richard Kenward, 01449 760639, richardwoodwards@btinternet.com. *7m N of Ipswich. From A14 turn onto A140, after ¼m take B1078 towards Wickham Market, Coddenham is on route. Coaches please use postcode IP6 9PS. Ample parking for coaches.* **Sun 26 Mar, Sun 7, Sun 28 May, Tue 27 June, Sun 23 July, Tue 1, Sun 27 Aug (10.30-5). Adm £2.50, chd free. Home-made teas. Visits also by arrangement Mar to Sept, groups 2-100+.**

Award winning S-facing gently sloping garden of 1½ acres, overlooking the rolling Suffolk countryside. Designed and maintained by owners for yr-round colour and interest, lots of island beds, well stocked with 1000s of bulbs, shrubs and perennials, vegetable plot, display of 100+ hanging baskets for spring and summer. Well kept lawns, with large mature trees. More than 25000 bulbs have been planted over the last 3yrs for our spring display.

♿ 🐕 ✳ 🚗 ☕

57 ♦ WYKEN HALL

Stanton, IP31 2DW. Sir Kenneth & Lady Carlisle, 01359 250262, www.wykenvineyards.co.uk. *9m NE of Bury St Edmunds. Along A143. Follow signs to Wyken Vineyards on A143 between Ixworth & Stanton.* **For NGS: Sat 3, Sun 4 June (10-6). Adm £4, chd free. Light refreshments in the restaurant and cafe. For other opening times and information, please phone or visit garden website.**

4-acres, with knot and herb garden, old-fashioned rose garden, kitchen and wild garden, nuttery, pond, gazebo and maze; herbaceous borders and old orchard. Woodland walk, vineyard. Restaurant and shop. Vineyard. Farmers' Market on Saturdays 9-1.

♿ ✳ ☕

SURREY

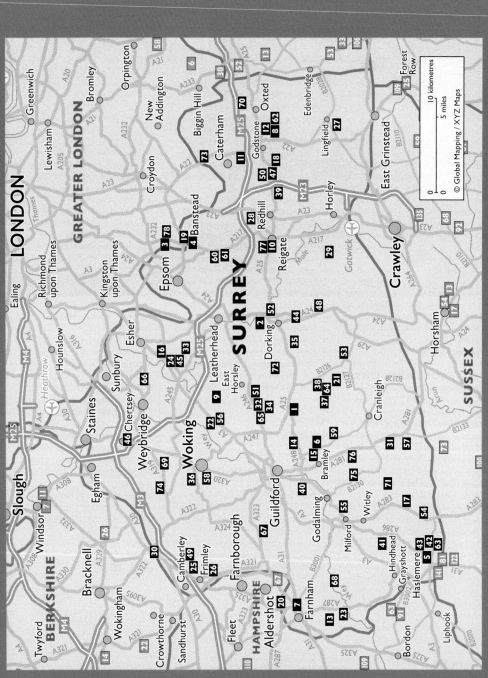

As a designated Area of Outstanding Natural Beauty, it's no surprise that Surrey has a wealth of gardens on offer.

With its historic market towns, lush meadows and scenic rivers, Surrey provides the ideal escape from the bustle of nearby London.

Set against the rolling chalk uplands of the unspoilt North Downs, the county prides itself on extensive country estates with historic houses and ancient manors. Visitors are inspired by the breathtaking panorama from Polesden Lacey, lakeside views at The Old Croft or timeless terraces at Albury Park.

Surrey is the heartland of the NGS at Hatchlands Park and the RHS at Wisley, both promoting a precious interest in horticulture. Surrey celebrates a landscape coaxed into wonderful vistas by great gardeners such as John Evelyn, Capability Brown and Gertrude Jekyll.

With many eclectic gardens to visit, there's certainly plenty to treasure in Surrey.

Volunteers

County Organiser
Maggie Boyd
01428 652283
maggie.boyd@ngs.org.uk

County Treasurer
David Boyd
01428 652283
david.boyd@ngs.org.uk

Publicity
Maggie Boyd
(as above)

Booklet Co-ordinator
Keith Lewis
01737 210707
kandelewis@ntlworld.com

Booklet Production & Group Tours
David Boyd
(as above)

Assistant County Organisers
Margaret Arnott
01372 842459
m.a.arnott@btinternet.com

Anne Barnes
01306 730196
spurfold@btinternet.com

Di Grose
01883 742983
di.grose@godstone.net

Annie Keighley
(as above)

Keith Lewis
(as above)

Caroline Shuldham
01932 596960
c.m.shuldham@btinternet.com

Shirley Stoneley
01737 244235
woodburycottage@gmail.com

Jean Thompson
01483 425633
norney.wood@btinternet.com

Left: Bardsey

OPENING DATES

All entries subject to change. For latest information check **www.ngs.org.uk**

Extended openings are shown at the beginning of the month.

Map locator numbers are shown to the right of each garden name.

January

Sunday 1st
Frimley Green Gardens 26

February Snowdrop Festival

Sunday 12th
◆ Gatton Park 28

March

◆ Vann (Every day from Sunday 26th to Friday 31st) 71

Sunday 5th
Timber Hill 69

Sunday 19th
Albury Park 1

Thursday 23rd
53 Commonfield Road 19

April

Sunday 9th
The Chalet 11
Coverwood Lakes 21

Sunday 16th
Caxton House 10
The Chalet 11

Monday 17th
Coverwood Lakes 21
Timber Hill 69

Thursday 20th
◆ Dunsborough Park 22

Sunday 23rd
Coverwood Lakes 21
41 Shelvers Way 60
NEW Springwood House 63

Thursday 27th
53 Commonfield Road 19

Sunday 30th
Chestnut Cottage 13
NEW Springwood House 63
57 Westhall Road 73

May

Chauffeur's Flat (Every day from Monday 22nd to Sunday 28th) 12

◆ Vann (Every day from Tuesday 2nd to Sunday 7th) 71

Monday 1st
Coverwood Lakes 21
Shieling 61
◆ Vann 71
Walton Poor House 72
57 Westhall Road 73

Saturday 6th
15 The Avenue 3

Sunday 7th
Coverwood Lakes 21
◆ Hatchlands Park 32
Stuartfield 66

Friday 12th
◆ Ramster 54

Saturday 13th
The Garth Pleasure Grounds 27
Hall Grove School 30

Sunday 14th
Coverwood Lakes 21
The Garth Pleasure Grounds 27
Malabar 42
NEW Roe Deer Farm 55
Walton Poor House 72
Wintershall Manor 76

Sunday 21st
Barnett Hill Country Hotel 6
Chilworth Manor 14
Knowle Grange 37
The Manor House 43
NEW The Therapy Garden 67
◆ Titsey Place Gardens 70

Thursday 25th
53 Commonfield Road 19

90th Anniversary Weekend

Saturday 27th
56 Copse Avenue 20
NEW Patchworking Garden Project 52

Sunday 28th
Chestnut Cottage 13
56 Copse Avenue 20
NEW Lower House 41
Monks Lantern 46
The Old Croft 48
Old Knowles 49
NEW Shamley Wood Estate 59

Monday 29th
15 The Avenue 3
NEW High Clandon Estate Vineyard 34
The Old Croft 48
Old Knowles 49
Shieling 61

June

Chauffeur's Flat (Every day from Monday 19th to Sunday 25th) 12

◆ Vann (Every day from Sunday 4th to Saturday 10th) 71

Sunday 4th
◆ Claremont Landscape Garden 16
53 Commonfield Road 19
◆ Winkworth Arboretum 75

Saturday 10th
Ghassan's Farm 29
Little Priory 39
7 Rose Lane 56

Sunday 11th
Ghassan's Farm 29
NEW Lark Rise 38
Little Priory 39

Friday 16th
Ashleigh Grange 2

Saturday 17th
◆ Dunsborough Park 22
Old Tunmore Farm 51

Sunday 18th
Ashleigh Grange 2
Banstead Community Junior School 4
◆ Loseley Park 40
The Old Rectory 50
Old Tunmore Farm 51
Saffron Gate 57
◆ Titsey Place Gardens 70

Wednesday 21st
Ashleigh Grange 2

Saturday 24th
The Coach House 17

Sunday 25th
NEW Bells Piece Leonard Cheshire Disability 7
2 Chinthurst Lodge 15
The Coach House 17
Fairmile Lea 24
Horsell Group Gardens 36
Moleshill House 45
Saffron Gate 57

Wednesday 28th
2 Chinthurst Lodge 15

July

Saturday 1st
Bardsey 5

Sunday 2nd
Bardsey 5
Pratsham Grange 53
NEW 116 St Johns Road 58

Saturday 8th
NEW The Bothy 8
Hall Place Farm 31
NEW Southlands Lodge 62
Woodbury Cottage 77
NEW Woodland 78

Sunday 9th
NEW The Bothy 8
NEW Southlands Lodge 62
Woodbury Cottage 77
NEW Woodland 78

Saturday 15th
NEW Patchworking Garden Project 52

Sunday 16th
Shieling 61

Saturday 22nd
Earleywood 23
The Old Croft 48

Sunday 23rd
Earleywood 23
Heathside 33
The Old Croft 48
Stuart Cottage 65
◆ Titsey Place Gardens 70

THE GARDENS

Banstead Community Junior School

1 ALBURY PARK
Albury, GU5 9BH. Trustees of Albury Estate. *5m SE of Guildford. From A25 take A248 towards Albury for ¼m, then up New Road, entrance to Albury Park immed on L.* **Sun 19 Mar, Sun 1 Oct (2-5). Adm £4.50, chd free. Home-made teas.**
14 acre pleasure grounds laid out in 1670s by John Evelyn for Henry Howard, later 6th Duke of Norfolk. ¼m terraces, fine collection of trees, lake and river. Gravel path and slight slope.

2 ASHLEIGH GRANGE
Off Chapel Lane, Westhumble, RH5 6AY. Clive & Angela Gilchrist, 01306 884613, ar.gilchrist@btinternet.com. *2m N of Dorking. From A24 at Boxhill/ Burford Bridge follow signs to Westhumble. Through village & L*

up drive by ruined chapel (1m from A24). **Evening opening Fri 16 June (6-8). Adm £6, chd free. Wine. Sun 18, Wed 21 June (2-5.30). Adm £4, chd free. Home-made teas. Visits also by arrangement May to July (sorry, no access for coaches).** *Donation to Barnardo's.*
Plant lover's chalk garden on 3½

acre sloping site in charming rural setting with delightful views. Many areas of interest incl rockery and water feature, raised ericaceous bed, prairie style bank, foliage plants, woodland walk, fernery and folly. Large mixed herbaceous and shrub borders planted for dry alkaline soil and widespread interest.

3 15 THE AVENUE

Cheam, Sutton, SM2 7QA. Jan & Nigel Brandon, 020 8643 8686. *1m SW of Sutton. By car; exit A217 onto Northey Av, 2nd R into The Avenue. By train; 10 mins walk from Cheam station. By bus; use 470.* **Evening opening Sat 6 May (6-9.30). Adm £7, chd £2. Wine. Mon 29 May (1-5). Adm £5, chd free. Home-made teas. Visits also by arrangement May to July for groups min 10, max 30.**

A contemporary garden designed by RHS Chelsea Gold Medal Winner, Marcus Barnett. Four levels divided into rooms by beech hedging and columns; formal entertaining area, lawn and wildflower meadow. Over 100 hostas hug the house. Silver birch, cloud pruned box, ferns, grasses, tall bearded irises, contemporary sculptures. Lit for evening opening. Contemporary sculpture. Featured on Alan Titchmarsh show and in The English Garden magazine. Partial wheelchair access, terraced with steps; sloping path provides view of whole garden but not all accessible.

&♿ ♿ ☕ ⚑

4 BANSTEAD COMMUNITY JUNIOR SCHOOL

The Horseshoe, Banstead, SM7 2BQ. Banstead Community Junior School, 01737 351788, jmarder@bcjs.org.uk. *3m S of Sutton heading S on A217 turn L at Banstead T-lights into Winkworth Rd. Turn R at mini r'about - Bolters Lane. 3rd turning on R - The Horseshoe. School car park is on L at 1st bend.* **Sun 18 June (1.30-4.30). Adm £3.50, chd free. Home-made teas. Visits also by arrangement in June (prior booking essential), groups 10 - 20 max welcome.**

The rear of our award winning school, opens up into a variety of gardening areas maintained by our Gardening Club. Please visit us and see our Greek Garden (it won silver gilt at Hampton Court Flower Show and donated by designer Tony Smith). Bottle greenhouse, raised vegetable beds, poly tunnel, wildlife area, living wall (planted in pallets), fruit bushes, outdoor classroom, multi sensory bed and more! Recycling is encouraged at school so lots of recycled items used throughout the school grounds incl water recycling.

&♿ ❀ ☕ ⚑

5 BARDSEY

11 Derby Road, Haslemere, GU27 1BS. Maggie & David Boyd, 01428 652283, maggie.boyd@live.co.uk, www.bardseygarden.co.uk. *¼m N of Haslemere station. Turn off B2131 (which links A287 to A286 through town) 400yds W of station into Weydown Rd, 3rd R into Derby Rd, garden 400yds on R.* **Sat 1, Sun 2, Sat 29, Sun 30 July (1-5). Adm £5, chd free. Home-made teas. Visits also by arrangement June & July for groups 10+.**

Unexpected 2 acre garden in the heart of Haslemere. Several distinct areas containing scent, colour, texture and movement. Stunning pictorial meadow within a parterre. Prairie planted border provides a modern twist. Large productive fruit and vegetable garden. Natural ponds and bog gardens. Several unusual sculptures. Bee hive and bug hotel. Ducks and chickens supply the eggs for cakes. Classic MGs on parade. Home-made produce stall. Featured in Surrey Life. First third of garden level, other two thirds sloping.

&♿ ♞ ♿ ☕ ⚑

6 BARNETT HILL COUNTRY HOTEL

Blackheath Lane, Wonersh, Guildford, GU5 0RF. Alexander Hotels, 01483 893361, barnett@sundialgroup.com. *Between Guildford & Cranleigh. From Guildford take A281 Shalford. At r'about 1st exit A248 Dorking. After 1m, just past 30mph & Wonersh signs go L into Blackheath Lane. Cont up narrow lane, turn R at top of hill.* **Sun 21 May (11.30-4.30). Adm £5, chd free. Home-made teas.**

A 26 acre, hill top estate known for its eclectic plantings and tranquil setting is filled with spring colour incl rhododendrons and azaleas. Paths wind down through different planted areas to the bluebell woods with views over the surrounding countryside. See the Wendy house and Edwardian greenhouses. Teas served on the terrace or in the Queen Anne style house. Huge plant sale. Good wheelchair access around upper gardens but some steps and steep pathways in places off main lawns.

&♿ ♞ ❀ ♿ 🛏 ☕

7 NEW BELLS PIECE LEONARD CHESHIRE DISABILITY

Hale Road, Lower Hale, Farnham, GU9 9RL. Davina Scott. *Approach Farnham town centre & 500 yds from the Hale r'about, Bells Piece is 1st turning on R, next to the Six Bells PH.* **Sun 25 June (10.30-4). Adm £5, chd free. Home-made teas, cream teas and child friendly snacks.**

Bells Piece offers an opportunity to visit a working nursery with polytunnels growing a variety of vegetables, fruit and plants. A sensory garden and pond surrounds the lawn area where cream teas will be served throughout the day. There is an on-site shop. Wear sensible footwear. Partial wheelchair access to Polytunnel area

&♿ ♞ ❀ ☕

8 NEW THE BOTHY

Tandridge Court, Tandridge Lane, Oxted, RH8 9NJ. Diane & John Hammond. *5 mins from J6 of M25, towards Oxted. From N, at r'about on A25 between A22 & Oxted go S into Tandridge Lane, after ¼m follow signs. From S, N up Tandridge Lane from Ray Lane, on exiting Tandridge Village follow signs.* **Evening opening Sat 8, Sun 9 July (5-9). Adm £5, chd £1. Wine. Also open Southlands Lodge.**

A hillside garden on 5 levels accessed by slopes and steps creating many moods and views. Explore this 1½ acre garden from wild, cultivated, floriferous, entertaining and relaxing areas, down to the kitchen garden and greenhouse. Continue to meander among specimen trees to a magical wooded walkway. Water features, garden artwork, chickens and more, all add interest to this garden of delights.

☕

9 BRIDGE END COTTAGE

Ockham Lane, Ockham, GU23 6NR. Clare & Peter Bevan, 01483 479963, c.fowler@ucl.ac.uk. *Nr RHS Gardens, Wisley. At Wisley r'about turn L onto B2039 to Ockham/ Horsley. After ½ m turn L into Ockham Lane. House ½ m on R. From Cobham go to Blackswan Xrds.* **Visits by arrangement May to July, groups 30 max. Adm £4.50, chd free. Home-made teas in the garden room.**
A 2 acre country garden with different areas of interest, incl perennial borders, mature trees, pond and streams, small herb parterre, fruit trees and a vegetable patch. An adjacent 2 acre field was sown with perennial wild flower seed in May 2013 and has flowered well in June ever since. Large perennial wildflower meadow. Partial wheelchair access.

10 CAXTON HOUSE

67 West Street, Reigate, RH2 9DA. Bob Bushby, 01737 243158, Bob.bushby@sky.com. *On A25 towards Dorking, approx ¼ m W of Reigate Parking on Rd or past Black Horse PH on Flanchford Rd.* **Sun 16 Apr (2-5). Adm £5, chd free. Cream teas. Visits also by arrangement Mar to Aug for groups 10+.**
Lovely large spring garden with Arboretum, 2 well stocked ponds, large collection of hellebores and spring flowers. Pots planted with colourful displays. Interesting plants. Small Gothic folly built by owner. Herbaceous borders with grasses, perennials, spring bulbs, and parterre. New bed with wild daffodils, and prairie style planting in summer. Antique dog cart completes the picture 7 Acres. Wheelchair access to most parts of the garden.

11 THE CHALET

Tupwood Lane, Caterham, CR3 6ET. Miss Lesley Manning & Mr David Gold. *½ m N of M25 J6. Exit J6 off M25 onto A22 to N. After ½ m take sharp 1st L, or follow signs from Caterham. Ample free parking. Disabled access via top gate.* **Sun 9, Sun 16 Apr (11-4.30). Adm £5, chd free. Home-made teas. Donation to St Catherine's Hospice.**
55 acres. Carpets of tens of thousands of daffodils; lakes, ornamental ponds, koi pond and waterfall. Ancient woodlands, grasslands and formal garden. Large planted terraces. Beautiful Victorian mansion (not open). Woodland and garden trail. On view, a limited edition Blue Train Bentley, a Phantom Rolls Royce and a helicopter plus the oldest FA Cup and other trophies. Partial wheelchair access, some steep slopes. 3 large unfenced ponds.

12 CHAUFFEUR'S FLAT

Tandridge Lane, Tandridge, RH8 9NJ. Mr & Mrs Richins, 01883 722661. *2m E of Godstone. 2m W of Oxted. Turn off A25 at r'about for Tandridge. Take drive on L past church. Follow arrows to circular courtyard.* **Daily Mon 22 May to Sun 28 May, Mon 19 June to Sun 25 June (10-5). Adm £5, chd free. Home-made teas (Sats & Suns only). Visits also by arrangement May & June. Donation to Sutton & Croydon MS Therapy Centre.**
Enter a 1½ acre tapestry of magical secret gardens with magnificent views. Touching the senses, all sure footed visitors may explore the many surprises on this constantly evolving exuberant escape from reality. Imaginative use of recycled materials creates an inspired variety of ideas, while wild and specimen plants reveal an ecological haven.

13 CHESTNUT COTTAGE

15 Jubilee Lane, Boundstone, Farnham, GU10 4SZ. Mr & Mrs David Wingent. *2½ m SW of Farnham. At A31 r'about take A325 - Petersfield, ½ m bear L. At r'about into School Hill, ½ m over staggered Xrds into Sandrock Hill Rd, 4th turn R after PH.* **Sun 30 Apr, Sun 28 May (2-5.30). Adm £4, chd free. Home-made teas.**
½ acre secret garden created

on different levels, with mature rhododendrons, azaleas, acers, herbaceous border all set in a sylvan setting. A particular feature of the garden is a pergola supporting a 24ft long wisteria. Attractive gazebo copied from the original National Trust's Hunting Lodge in Odiham. Visitors say wherever you sit there is a completely different vista. Plant expert John Negus will be in attendance.

14 CHILWORTH MANOR

Halfpenny Lane, Chilworth, Guildford, GU4 8NN. Mia & Graham Wrigley. *3½ m SE of Guildford. From centre of Chilworth village turn into Blacksmith Lane. 1st drive on R on Halfpenny Lane.* **Sun 21 May (11-5). Adm £6, chd free.**
Extensive grounds of lawns and mature trees surrounding C17/C18 manor house on C11 monastic site. Substantial C18 terraced walled garden developed by Sarah, Duchess of Marlborough, with herbaceous borders, topiary and fruit trees. Original monastic stewponds integrated with Japanese themed and woodland garden. Paddock home to alpacas. Plenty of space for visitors to explore and relax or participate in accompanied walks in this peaceful garden. Garden and tree walks at 12 noon, 1.30pm, 2.30pm and 4pm.

Your support helps Carers Trust to provide more help to unpaid carers

The Bothy

to Sept for groups 8+.
Garden designer's garden
comprising 1 acre walled garden and
additional courtyards, designed by
the owners and created since 2013.
Lawns divided into areas by trees
and borders filled with perennials,
shrubs and roses. A courtyard
rose garden, wildflower meadow,
white garden and kitchen garden
provide varied interest. A secluded
courtyard filled with garden pots
of exotic ferns and hostas. Mostly
accessible by wheelchair but paths
are grass so care needed if wet.
&. 🍵

18 COLDHARBOUR HOUSE
Coldharbour Lane, Bletchingley,
Redhill, RH1 4NA. Mr
Tony Elias, 01883 742685,
eliastony@hotmail.com.
*Coldharbour Lane off Rabies Heath
Rd ½m from A25 at Bletchingley &
0.9m from Tilburstow Hill Rd. Park in
field & walk down to house.* Sat 2,
Sun 3 Sept (1-5). Adm £5, chd
free. Home-made teas. Visits
also by arrangement Apr to Oct
for groups 10+.
This 1½ acre garden offers
breathtaking views to the South
Downs. Originally planted in the
1920's, it has since been adapted
and enhanced. Several mature trees
and shrubs incl a copper beech, a
Canadian maple, magnolias, azaleas,
rhododendrons, camellias, wisterias,
fuchsias, hibiscus, potentillas,
mahonias, a fig tree and a walnut
tree.
🍵

15 2 CHINTHURST LODGE
Wonersh Common, Wonersh,
Guildford, GU5 0PR. Mr & Mrs
M R Goodridge, 01483 535108,
michaelgoodridge@ymail.com. *4m
S of Guildford. From A281 at Shalford
turn E onto B2128 towards Wonersh.
Just after Waverley sign, before village,
garden on R.* Sun 25, Wed 28 June
(11-5.30). Adm £5, chd free.
Home-made teas. Visits also by
arrangement May to July for
groups 10+.
1 acre yr-round enthusiast's
atmospheric garden, divided into
rooms. Herbaceous borders,
dramatic white garden, specimen
trees and shrubs, gravel garden with
water feature, small kitchen garden,
fruit cage, 2 wells, ornamental ponds,
herb parterre and millennium
parterre garden, as featured in
Period Homes and Interiors (2015)
and Surrey Life (2016). Some gravel
paths, which can be avoided.
&. ❀ 🍵

16 ◆ CLAREMONT LANDSCAPE GARDEN
Portsmouth Road, Esher,
KT10 9JG. National
Trust, 01372 467806,
claremont@nationaltrust.org.uk,
www.nationaltrust.org.uk/

claremont. *1m SW of Esher. On E
side of A307 (no access from A3
bypass).* For NGS: Sun 4 June,
Sun 8 Oct (10-6). Adm £8.80,
chd £4.40. Light refreshments.
For other opening times and
information, please phone, email or
visit garden website.
One of the earliest surviving
English landscape gardens, begun by
Vanbrugh and Bridgeman before
1720 and extended and naturalised
by Kent and Capability Brown. Lake,
island with pavilion; grotto and
turf amphitheatre; viewpoints and
avenues. Free guided walk at 2pm
both NGS days with member of
the gardening team. Cafe serving
home-made cakes, light lunches
and afternoon teas. Access maps
available with recommended route.
&. ❀ 🍵

17 THE COACH HOUSE
The Green, Chiddingfold,
Godalming, GU8 4TU. Mr &
Mrs S Brooks, 01428 687767,
barbarabrooks@btinternet.com.
*7M S of Godalming. Eastern corner
of village green. Parking around
village green or along Pickhurst Rd.*
Sat 24, Sun 25 June (2-6). Adm
£4, chd free. Home-made teas.
Visits also by arrangement May

19 53 COMMONFIELD ROAD
Banstead, SM7 2JR. Jennifer
Russell. *From A217 turn into
Winkworth Rd, then 1st turning
on L after mini r'about. Parking on
rd, please do not block neighbours
drives.* Thur 23 Mar, Thur 27
Apr, Thur 25 May, Sun 4 June,
Thur 27 July, Thur 24 Aug, Sun
3, Thur 28 Sept (11-3). Adm £3,
chd free. Home-made teas Sun
4 June & Sun 3 Sept only.
A small colourful garden designed
and created by the present owner
in late 2012, to incorporate her

two passions, interesting plants and nature. Designed for yr-round interest, enter through a rose and clematis arch into a packed and interesting garden, small wildlife pond, bog garden, alpine bed, large rose arch, woodland with tree house and a screened working area. Small wheelchairs; lots of seating areas for less mobile.

ᐃ ❊ ☕

20 56 COPSE AVENUE

Farnham, GU9 9EA. Lyn & Jimmy James, 01252 323473, lynandjimmy@virginmedia.com. *Approx 1½m N of Farnham. At Shepherd & Flock r'about take A325 to Farnborough. At 2nd r'about take Weybourne exit. At T-lights turn L onto Upper Weybourne Lane. Turn R onto Oakland Avenue. At T-Junction turn L.* **Sat 27, Sun 28 May (12-5). Adm £4, chd free. Home-made teas. Visits also by arrangement May & June for groups 10+.**
A fascinating and unusual 1 acre garden in a residential area. The garden was originally landscaped in the late 1960s following the plans of a Chelsea Flower Show garden, but was subsequently allowed to become very overgrown. The present owners have restored many of the original features and are adding innovative areas of planting and interest. Accessible for wheelchairs but some steep steps and uneven paths.

ᐃ ❊ ☕

21 COVERWOOD LAKES

Peaslake Road, Ewhurst, GU6 7NT. The Metson Family, www.coverwoodlakes.co.uk. *7m SW of Dorking. From A25 follow signs for Peaslake; garden ½m beyond Peaslake on Ewhurst rd.* **Sun 9, Mon 17, Sun 23 Apr, Mon 1, Sun 7, Sun 14 May, Sun 15 Oct (11-5). Adm £5, chd free. Light refreshments.**
14 acre landscaped garden in stunning position high in the Surrey Hills with 4 lakes and bog garden. Extensive rhododendrons, azaleas and fine trees. 3½ acre lakeside arboretum. Marked trail through the 180 acre working farm with Hereford cows and calves, sheep

and horses, extensive views of the surrounding hills. Light refreshments, incl home produced beef burgers, gourmet coffee and home-made cakes.

ᐃ 🚌 ☕

22 ◆ DUNSBOROUGH PARK

Ripley, GU23 6AL. Baron & Baroness Sweerts de Landas Wyborgh, 01483 225366, office@sweerts.com, www.dunsboroughpark.com. *6m NE of Guildford. Entrance across Ripley Green via The Milkway past cricket green on R & playground on L, round corner to double brown wooden gates.* **For NGS: Thur 20 Apr (3-7); Sat 17 June, Sat 16 Sept (12-4). Adm £7, chd free.** Home-made teas. **For other opening times and information, please phone, email or visit garden website.**
6 acres of walled gardens redesigned by Penelope Hobhouse and Rupert Golby – a box hedged parterre showcasing spectacular tulip displays in April; different garden rooms; lush herbaceous borders with standard wisterias; 70ft Ginkgo hedge; Rose Walk; ancient mulberry tree; Italian Garden; potager; water garden and folly bridge. Enjoy Roses and Peonies in June and Dahlias in September. Festival of Tulips. NGS: Thurs 20 April 3-7pm. Not for NGS: Thurs 13, Sun 16 and Sat 22 Apr 12-4pm. Amazing tulip meadow display in April. Wild meadow with poppies and cornflowers in June. Dahlias in September. Produce for sale when available.

ᐃ ❊ 🚌 ☕

23 EARLEYWOOD

Hamlash Lane, Frensham, Farnham, GU10 3AT. Mrs Penny Drew. *3m S of Farnham just off A287. From A31 Farnham take A287 to Frensham. R 1st turn passed Edgeborough School. From A3, N on A287 to Frensham. Parking available, More House School Lower Car Park top of Hamlash Lane.* **Sat 22, Sun 23 July (11-5). Adm £5, chd free. Home-made teas.**
Award winning, ½ acre garden with

colourful shrubberies, unusual trees and mixed borders throughout. Wide variety of summer flowering shrubs, particularly hydrangeas, colour themed borders - vibrant reds and yellows and cool pinks and blues - also shady areas with groundcover and shade loving plants. Productive greenhouse. Gold award for Large Garden, Farnham Secret Gardens. Disabled drop off at front gate, short gravel drive then level lawns throughout.

ᐃ ❊ ☕

24 FAIRMILE LEA

Portsmouth Road, Cobham, KT11 1BG. Steven Kay. *2m NE of Cobham. On Cobham to Esher rd. Access by lane adjacent to Moleshill House & car park for Fairmile Common woods.* **Sun 25 June (2-5). Combined adm with Moleshill House £6, chd free. Home-made teas.**
Large Victorian sunken garden fringed by rose beds and lavender with a pond in the centre. An old acacia tree stands in the midst of the lawn. Interesting planting on a large mound camouflages an old underground air raid shelter. Caged vegetable garden. Formality adjacent to wilderness.

🐐 ☕

25 26 THE FAIRWAY

Camberley, GU15 1EF. Jacky Sheppard, 01276 683814, jb.s@btinternet.com. *1½m from M3 J4. Follow signs to Frimley Pk Hosp. At r'about take 3rd exit B311 Chobham Rd. Cont on B311 L at 2nd r'about. 1st L into Fairway.* **Visits by arrangement May to July for groups 4+. Adm £5, chd free. Light refreshments.**
Spring and summer is the ideal time to see the azaleas, rhododendrons and heathers that surround the house. Bulbs, primroses and winter hellibores give ground cover beneath the shrubs. Climbers and a variety of plants continue a theme to make way for summer flowering. A new water feature has been added, with other additions to the garden. Small area at back of garden not easily accessed by wheelchair.

ᐃ ❊ ☕

GROUP OPENING

26 FRIMLEY GREEN GARDENS

Frimley Green, GU16 6HE.
01252 668645 or 01252 838660,
angela.oconnell@icloud.com,
annie.keighley12@btinternet.com.
3m S of Camberley on B3411, from The Green turn into The Hatches. Short walk from village green.
Home-made teas. Wine on request. Visits by arrangement in June for groups 10+ for 2, 3 or all 4 gardens. Daytime or evening visits.

ELMCROFT

GU16 6NA. Geraldine Huggon.
Visits by arrangement in June for groups 10+ as part of Frimley Green village gardens.

OAKLEIGH

Angela O'Connell.
Visits by arrangement in June for groups 10+ as part of Frimley Green village gardens.

TABOR

Susan Filbin.
Visits by arrangement in June for groups 10+ as part of Frimley Green village gardens.

WILDWOOD

Annie Keighley.
Visits by arrangement in June for groups 10+ as part of Frimley Green village gardens.

Enjoy the personal touch at up to 4 very popular gardens in Frimley Green, together opening uniquely on a by arrangement basis for groups. Be inspired by immaculate designer chic in a very individual space at Tabor. Here you can admire a riot of hostas, colourful pots and soothing water features. At Elmcroft a huge *Buddleia alternifolia* forms a stunning backdrop for cottage classics in this propagator's paradise. Look for surprises at winding Oakleigh and delight at the vibrant and colourful borders. Enjoy Wildwood's quirky vegetable plot and stunning roses in a romantic cottage garden setting. Wildwood and Oakleigh have Surrey Wildlife Trust Gold Awards. Wildwood won Surrey Wildlife Trust Large Private Garden Award. Oakleigh, Wildwood and Tabor featured in Surrey Life. Partial wheelchair access due to some gravel paths and steps.

🚗 ☕

27 THE GARTH PLEASURE GROUNDS

Newchapel Road, Lingfield, RH7 6BJ. Mr Sherlock & Mrs Stanley, ab_post@yahoo.com, , www.oldworkhouse.webs.com.
From A22 take B2028 by Mormon Temple to Lingfield. The Garth is on L after 1½m, opp Barge Tiles. Parking: Barge Tiles and Gunpit Rd.
Sat 13, Sun 14 May (2-5.30). Adm £5, chd free. Visits also by arrangement May to Aug (please email 2 weeks in advance).
Mature 9 acre Pleasure Grounds created by Walter Godfrey in 1919 present an idyllic setting surrounding the former parish workhouse refurbished in Edwardian style. The formal gardens, enchanting nuttery, a spinney with many mature trees and a pond attract wildlife. Wonderful bluebells in spring. The woodland gardens and beautiful borders full of colour and fragrance for yr-round pleasure. Many areas of interest incl pond, woodland garden, formal gardens, spinney with large specimen plants incl 500yr old oak and many architectural features designed by Walter H Godfrey. Partial wheelchair access in woodland, iris and secret gardens.

🐕 ❀ 🚗 ☕

28 ◆ GATTON PARK

Rocky Lane, Merstham, RH2 0TW. Royal Alexandra & Albert School, 01737 649068, events@gatton-park.org.uk, www.gattonpark.com. *3m NE of Reigate. 5 mins from M25 J8 (A217) or from top of Reigate Hill, over M25 then follow sign to Merstham. Entrance off Rocky Lane accessible from Gatton Bottom or A23 Merstham.* **For NGS: Sun 12 Feb (11-4). Adm £4, chd free. Light refreshments at Gatton Hall. 2018: Sun 11 Feb.** **For other opening times and information,** please phone, email or visit garden website.
Gatton Park is the core 250 acres of the estate originally laid out by Capability Brown. Gatton also boasts a Japanese garden, rock and water garden and Victorian parterre nestled within the sweeping parkland. Stunning displays of snowdrops and aconites in February and March. Free activities for children. Tea, cake, soup and rolls available on the day. Partial wheelchair access.

♿ 🐕 ☕

29 GHASSAN'S FARM

Norwood Hill, Nr Horley, RH6 0HR. Mr Ghasan Al Nemar.
4m SW of Reigate Take A217 towards Horley; after 2m turn R down Irons Bottom Lane (just after Sidlow Bridge). 1st R Dean Oak Lane, then L at T-junction. Disabled drop off & parking **Sat 10, Sun 11 June (12-5). Adm £5, chd free. Home-made teas.**
The house where Lord Baden-Powell lived. 12 acre garden in lake setting around old farmhouse (not open). Walled garden, old fashioned roses, shrubs, herbaceous. Tudor courtyard and orchard. Bird and

butterfly garden. Kitchen garden with large greenhouses. Secret garden, parterre with box hedging Many areas of the garden are easily accessible for wheelchair users

& ✿ 🚗 ☕

30 HALL GROVE SCHOOL

London Road (A30), Bagshot, GU19 5HZ. Mr & Mrs A R Graham. *6m SW of Egham. M3 J3, follow A322 1m until sign for Sunningdale A30, 1m E of Bagshot, opp Long Acres garden centre, entrance at footbridge. Ample car park.* **Sat 13 May (2-5). Adm £5, chd free. Home-made teas.**
Formerly a small Georgian country estate, now a co-educational preparatory school. Grade II listed house (not open). Mature parkland with specimen trees. Historical features incl ice house, old walled garden under restoration, heated peach wall. Lake, woodland walks, rhododendrons and azaleas. Live music at 3pm.

& ✿ ☕

31 HALL PLACE FARM

Hall Place, Cranleigh, GU6 8LD. Mr & Mrs C Britton. *2m W of Cranleigh. From A281 take B2130 Dunsfold Rd; after ¾m turn L into Stovolds Hill at tight bend. After ½m take gravel track on L, signed 'Hall Place'. Follow signs to parking in field after 200yds.* **Sat 8 July (1.30-5.30). Adm £4, chd free. Home-made teas.**
Work in progress restoration of 2¼ acre gardens centred on 550yr old house. Elements of Victorian gardens created for Hall Place Estate in 1865 and parts created by present owners since 2010. A wide variety of character and planting; walled garden, wooded sunken dell, orchard, greenhouse, vegetable garden, walled cottage garden, formal courtyard with fountain, lawns with mixed borders and views. Wheelchair access to main parts of the garden.

& 🐕 ☕

32 ◆ HATCHLANDS PARK

East Clandon, Guildford, GU4 7RT. National Trust, 01483 222482, hatchlands@nationaltrust.org.uk, www.nationaltrust.org.uk. *4m E of Guildford. Follow brown signs to Hatchlands Park (NT).* **For NGS: Sun 7 May (10-5). Adm £7, chd £3.50. Light refreshments. For other opening times and information, please phone, email or visit garden website.**
Garden and park designed by Repton in 1800. Follow one of the park walks to the stunning bluebell wood in spring (2.5km/1.7m round walk over rough and sometimes muddy ground). In autumn enjoy the changing colours on the long walk. Partial wheelchair access to parkland, rough, undulating terrain, grass and gravel paths, dirt tracks, cobbled courtyard. Tramper booking essential.

& 🚜 ✿ 🚗 ☕

33 HEATHSIDE

10 Links Green Way, Cobham, KT11 2QH. Miss Margaret Arnott & Mr Terry Bartholomew, 01372 842459, m.a.arnott@btinternet.com. *1½m E of Cobham. Through Cobham A245, 4th L after Esso garage into Fairmile Lane. Straight on into Water Lane. Links Green Way 3rd turning on L. 5m from RHS Wisley.* **Sun 23 July (11-5). Adm £4, chd free. Home-made teas. Visits also by arrangement.**
⅓ acre terraced, plantsman's garden, designed for yr-round interest. A sumptuous collection of wonderful plants, all set off by harmonious landscaping. Urns and obelisks aid the display. Two ponds and four water features add tranquil sound. A contemporary parterre and various topiary shapes add formality. Stunning colour combinations excite. Many inspirational ideas.

✿ 🚗 ☕

34 NEW HIGH CLANDON ESTATE VINEYARD

High Clandon, East Clandon, Guildford, GU4 7RP. Mrs Sibylla Tindale, www.highclandon.co.uk. *A3 Wisley junction, L for Ockham/ Horsley for 2m to A246. R for Guildford for 2m, then 100yds past landmark Hatchlands NT, turn L into Blakes Lane straight up through gates High Clandon to vineyard entrance. Extensive parking in our woodland area.* **Mon 29 May (11-4). Adm £6, chd free. Home-made teas.**
Views, gardens, vineyard in the beautiful Surrey Hills AONB. 6 acres. Panoramic views to London, rolling gardens, water features, Japanese garden, wildflower meadow, trufflère, apiary, vineyard producing multi award, vintage only, English sparkling wine, High Clandon Cuvée. Sculptures in the Vineyard exhibition by noted artists of Surrey Hills. Percentage of sales for Cherry Trees charity. Atmospheric Glass Barn used for wine tastings and exhibitions. Sparkling wine tasting available at extra charge of £5. Featured in Surrey Life; We heard it on the Grapevine Vantage Magazine; English Sparkling Wine Surrey Mummy; England First Sparkling Wine Tour Uncorked Guide 2 Surrey; Magical Mystery Tour of Surrey Hills Vineyards.

& 🐕 ☕

35 HILL FARM

Logmore Lane, Westcott, Dorking, RH4 3JY. Helen Thomas. *1m W of Dorking. Parking on Westcott Heath just past Church. Entry to garden just opp.* **Sun 17 Sept (11.30-4.30). Adm £3.50, chd free. Home-made teas.**
1¾ acre recently redesigned garden set in the magnificent Surrey Hills landscape. The garden has a wealth of different natural habitats to encourage wildlife, and planting areas which come alive through the different seasons. A wildlife pond, woodland walk, a tapestry of heathers and glorious late summer grasses and perennials. A garden to be enjoyed by all. Everyone welcome. Pond dipping for children. Restoration details of lime kiln and history of the property available. Sloping garden, most areas are accessible to wheelchair users. Most paths are grass so care needed if very wet.

& 🐕 D ☕

GROUP OPENING

36 HORSELL GROUP GARDENS
Horsell, Woking, GU21 4XA. 1½ m W of Woking in Village of Horsell. Leave M25 at J11. Take A320 signed Woking then A3046 signed Chobham after approx 1m at r'about turn L signed Horsell, with parking on Village Green outside Cricketers PH. **Sun 25 June (11-5). Combined adm £5, chd free. Home-made teas.**

BIRCH COTTAGE
Celia & Mel Keenan.

3-4 BIRCH COTTAGES
Mr & Mrs Freeman.

HORSELL ALLOTMENTS
Horsell Allotments Association, www.horsellalots.wordpress.com.

2 gardens and an award winning allotment in the village of Horsell which is on the edge of the Common, famously mentioned in HG Wells's, War of the Worlds. 3-4 Birch Cottages is full of charm with an interesting courtyard with rill. Walk down this long garden through into a series of rooms with topiary and attractive planting and many specimen roses. Birch Cottage is a Grade II listed cottage with a box hedge style knot garden, a chinese slate courtyard with planted pots and hanging baskets, a canal water feature and an active white dove dovecote, surrounded with an abundance of planting. Horsell Allotments have over 100 individual plots growing a variety of unusual flowers and vegetables, many not seen in supermarkets, 2 working beehives with informative talks from their owners. Allotments are bumpy and 3-4 Birch Cottage are flat, Birch Cottage, has gravel and steps but wheelchair visitors can see main garden.
♿ ✿ ♺

37 KNOWLE GRANGE
Hound House Road, Shere, Guildford, GU5 9JH. Mr P R & Mrs M E Wood. 8m S of Guildford. From Shere (off A25), through village for ¾ m. After railway bridge, cont 1½ m past Hound House on R (stone dogs on gateposts). After 100yds turn R at Knowle Grange sign, go to end of lane. **Sun 21 May (11-4.30). Adm £6.50, chd free. Home-made teas.**

80 acre idyllic hilltop position. Extraordinary and exciting 7 acre gardens, created from scratch since 1990 by Marie-Elisabeth Wood, blend the free romantic style with the strong architectural frame of the classical tradition. Walk the rural 1 mile Bluebell Valley Unicursal Path of Life and discover its secret allegory. Featured on Austrian TV - Most Beautiful Gardens of Britain. Deep unfenced pools, high unfenced drops.
♺

38 [NEW] LARK RISE
Franksfield, Peaslake, Guildford, GU5 9SS. Sarah & Peter Copping. 8m SE of Guildford or 6.8m from Dorking along A25. From Peaslake Stores go N on Peaslake Lane; go around sharp L bend (rd now Pursers Lane) & take next R into Hoe Lane. Go steep uphill & turn R into Franksfield then R again. Signs to parking in field. **Sun 11 June (11-5). Adm £5, chd free. Home-made teas.**

A tranquil 1 acre garden created over many years to provide different areas of interest incl informal perennial borders set within formal yew hedging; wisteria clad pergola; a meadow surrounding a natural pond; productive vegetable plot with small greenhouse; spring garden with rhododendrons, ferns and spring flowers. Large compost area. Surprising variety of mature trees and unusual sculptures. Disable drop off arrangements possible. Gravel driveway, few steps but most of garden accessible via lawns.
♿ ♺

39 LITTLE PRIORY
Sandy Lane, South Nutfield, RH1 4EJ. Richard & Liz Ramsay. 1½ m E of Redhill. From Nutfield, on A25, turn into Mid St, following sign for South Nutfield. 1st R into Sandy Lane. Follow signs to parking on R, approx ½ m. Evening opening Sat 10 June (4-8). Adm £6.50, chd free. Wine. **Sun 11 June (11-5). Adm £5, chd free. Home-made teas. Light lunches also available.**

Explore this 5 acre country garden where old blends with new. Wander the modern flower garden; lose yourself in the old orchard meadow; discover cherries and kiwi fruit in the greenhouses of the Victorian kitchen garden; relax beside the large pond, and be inspired by the views. Partial wheelchair access.
♿ ✿ ♺

40 ♦ LOSELEY PARK
Guildford, GU3 1HS. Mr & Mrs M G More-Molyneux, 01483 304440/405112, pa@loseleypark.co.uk, www.loseleypark.co.uk. 4m SW of Guildford. For SatNav please use GU3 1HS Stakescorner Lane. **For NGS: Sun 18 June (11-5). Adm £5, chd £2.50. Light refreshments.** For other opening times and information, please phone, email or visit garden website.
Delightful 2½ acre walled garden. Award winning rose garden (over 1,000 bushes, mainly old fashioned varieties), extensive herb garden, fruit/flower garden, white garden with fountains, and spectacular organic vegetable garden. Magnificent vine walk, herbaceous borders, moat walk, ancient wisteria and mulberry trees. Refreshments available in our newly refurbished tea room.
♿ ✿ 🚙 ♺

41 [NEW] LOWER HOUSE
Bowlhead Green, Godalming, GU8 6NW. Mrs Georgina Harvey. Just over 1m off A3 from Thursley/Bowlhead Green junction. From A3 follow signs to Bowlhead Green. From A286 Brook turn N into Park Lane then 1st R into Beech Hill. At Xrds follow signpost to Lower House after 300yds stay R. Field parking. **Sun 28 May (11-5). Adm £6, chd free. Home-made teas.**

A large country garden for all the family to enjoy, providing vegetables, fruit, flowers and eggs. Lawns to play on and narrow paths to explore winding through plantings of mature trees, shrubs, perennials and bulbs. A topiary garden with a small pond and water feature, daffodils, azaleas, rhododendrons, roses, hydrangeas and autumn leaves add colour and shape throughout the yr. Home-made teas served in the Swimming Pool Barn/Orchard area. Alternative routes avoiding steps for wheelchairs users although some paths could be narrow.

 ♿ 🐕 ✿ ☕

42 MALABAR

Holdfast Lane, Haslemere, GU27 2EY. Beryl & Tony Bishop, 01428 661486, beryl.bishop@clara.co.uk. *Off B2136 Petworth Rd from Haslemere High St. Turn L in to Holdfast Lane, well before Lythe Hill Hotel. Parking in field opp. Please drop off disabled passengers before parking.* **Sun 14 May (12-5). Adm £5, chd free. Home-made teas. Visits also by arrangement May to Sept, groups 6+.**
2½ acre country garden bounded by mature oaks with climbing hydrangeas, clematis and roses. Undulating lawns bordered by imaginative colourful planting of unusual shrubs, rhododendrons, and azaleas. Bluebells, hellebores, primulas, lily of the valley and wood anemones throughout. Tranquil bark chipped level woodland walks with natural archways give a host of different vistas. How many Owls can you find? Paths are wide and firm.

 ♿ 🐕 ✿ ☕

43 THE MANOR HOUSE

Three Gates Lane, Haslemere, GU27 2ES. Mr & Mrs Gerard Ralfe. *1m NE of Haslemere. From Haslemere centre take A286 towards Milford. Turn R after Museum into Three Gates Lane. At T-Junction turn R into Holdfast Lane. Car park on R.* **Sun 21 May (12-5). Adm £5, chd free. Home-made teas.**
Described by Country Life as 'The hanging gardens of Haslemere', The Manor House gardens are in a valley of the Surrey Hills. One of Surrey's inaugural NGS gardens, fine views, 6 acres, water gardens.

 ☕

44 NEW ▶ MARLEY MEAD

Ridgeway Road, Dorking, RH4 3AJ. Mr William Flowitt. *Turn off Ridgeway Road on to Marley Rise, cont all the way to top to set of black double gates.* **Sat 29, Sun 30 July (11-5). Adm £5, chd free. Home-made teas.**
2 acre garden with ornamental ponds, koi and waterfall, a variety of plants and a large selection of mature and newly planted specimen trees. Ancient woodland walk, herbaceous boarder, wall garden, vegetable plot and greenhouses. Slopes and path to access garden, some of which are lawn.

 ♿ 🐕 ✿ ☕

45 MOLESHILL HOUSE

The Fairmile, Cobham, KT11 1BG. Penny Snell, pennysnellflowers@btinternet.com, , www.pennysnellflowers.co.uk. *2m NE of Cobham. On A307 Esher to Cobham Rd next to free car park by A3 bridge, at entrance to Waterford Close.* **Sun 25 June (2-5). Combined adm with Fairmile Lea £6, chd free. Home-made teas at Fairmile Lea. Visits also by arrangement May to Sept for groups 15+.**
Romantic garden. Short woodland path leads from dovecote to beehives. Informal planting contrasts with formal topiary box and garlanded cisterns. Colourful courtyard and pots, conservatory, fountains, bog garden. Pleached avenue, circular gravel garden replacing most of the lawn. Gypsy caravan garden, new green wall and stumpery. Chickens. Music at Moleshill House, teas at Fairmile Lea. Garden 5 mins from Claremont Landscape Garden, Painshill Park and Wisley, also adjacent excellent dog walking woods. Featured in English Garden magazine.

 ✿ 🚗 ☕

53 Commonfield Road

46 MONKS LANTERN

Ruxbury Road, Chertsey,
KT16 9NH. Mr & Mrs J
Granell, 01932 569578,
janicegranell@hotmail.com.
*1m NW from Chertsey. M25 J11,
signed A320/Woking. R'about 2nd
exit A320/Staines, straight over
next r'about. L onto Holloway Hill,
R Hardwick Lane. ½m, R over
motorway bridge, on Almners
then Ruxbury Rd.* **Sun 28 May
(1-5). Adm £4, chd free. Light
refreshments. Visits also by
arrangement May to Aug for
groups 10 - 15 max.**
A delightful garden with borders
arranged with colour in mind: silvers
and white, olive trees, nicotiana
and senecio blend together. Large
rockery and an informal pond. A
weeping silver birch leads to the
oranges and yellows of a tropical
bed, with large bottle brush, hardy
palms, and fatsia japonica. There is a
display of hostas, cytisus battandieri
and a selection of grasses in an
island bed. Aviary with small finches.
For wheelchair access, park on
gravel drive to front of house, side
access to garden, no steps, flat lawn.
ᕻ ✿ ☕

47 ODSTOCK

Castle Square, Bletchingley,
RH1 4LB. Averil & John Trott,
01883 743100. *3m W of Godstone.
Just off A25 in Bletchingley. At top
of village nr Red Lion PH.* **Visits by
arrangement May to Sept for
groups 10+. Light refreshments
by prior arrangement. Adm £5,
chd free.**
⅔ acre plantsman's garden
maintained by owners and
developed for yr-round interest.
Special interest in grasses,
climbers and dahlias. A no dig, low
maintenance vegetable garden.
Short gravel drive. Main lawn
suitable for wheelchairs but some
paths may be too narrow.
ᕻ ♿ ☕

48 THE OLD CROFT

South Holmwood, Dorking,
RH5 4NT. David &
Virginia Lardner-Burke,
www.lardner-burke.org.uk. *2m S
of Dorking. From Dorking A24 S for*
*2m, L to Leigh/Brockham into Mill
Rd. ½m on L, 2 free NT car parks
on Holmwood Com. Access 600yds
along woodland walk.* **Sun 28, Mon
29 May, Sat 22, Sun 23 July
(2-6). Adm £5, chd free. Home-
made teas.**
Beautiful 5 acre garden with many
diverse areas of natural beauty,
giving a sense of peace and
tranquillity. Stunning vistas incl lake,
bridge, pond fed by natural stream
running over rocky weirs, bog
gardens, roses, perennial borders,
elevated viewing hide, tropical
bamboo maze, curved pergola
of rambling roses, unique topiary
buttress hedge, many specimen
trees and shrubs. Visitors return
again and again. **For direct access
for disabled and elderly visitors
please phone 01306 888224.**
ᕻ 🐕 ☕

> The National
> Garden Scheme
> is the largest
> single funder
> of Macmillan

49 OLD KNOWLES

150 Upper Chobham Road,
Camberley, GU15 1ET. The Hobbs
Family. *2½m from M3 J4. Follow
signs to Frimley Pk Hosp. At r'about
take 3rd exit B311 Chobham Rd.
Cont on. Please park on Upper
Chobham Rd (B311) nr Prior Rd,
outside drive to Old Knowles.* **Sun
28, Mon 29 May (11-4). Adm £4,
chd free. Light refreshments.**
Take tea on the broad terrace
and enjoy a stunning panorama of
Douglas pines, bright azaleas, mature
rhododendrons and an oriental
surprise. Period sunken rose garden
and birch copse offer space to
wander or sit in shade. Children are
welcome to tumble on our family
friendly lawn. Care required near
poolside.
ᕻ ☕

50 THE OLD RECTORY

Sandy Lane, Brewer Street,
Bletchingley, RH1 4QW.
Mr & Mrs A Procter,
01883 743388 or 07515 394506,
trudie.y.procter@googlemail.com.
*Top of village nr Red Lion PH, turn
R into Little Common Lane then R
Cross Rd into Sandy Lane. Parking nr
house, disabled parking in courtyard.*
**Sun 18 June (11-4). Adm £5, chd
free. Home-made teas. Visits
also by arrangement Mar to
Sept, please phone/email for
bookings.**
Georgian Manor House (not open).
Quintessential Italianate topiary
garden, statuary, box parterres,
courtyard with columns, water
features, antique terracotta pots.
Much of the 4 acre garden is the
subject of ongoing reclamation. This
incl the ancient moat, woodland
with fine specimen trees, rill,
sunken and exotic garden under
construction. Featured in Town and
Country magazine. Gravel paths.
ᕻ 🐕 ✿ ☕

51 OLD TUNMORE FARM

Butlers Hill (off The Street), West
Horsley, Leatherhead, KT24 6AZ.
Mr & Mrs J Kopij. *5m E of Guildford.
Off A246, take The Street, W Horsley
at Bell & Colville Garage r'about.
1st L in 200m. From A3 (M25), E
Horsley B2309. R to E Lane, then
The Street. Pass PH & Ripley Lane:
Butlers Hill on R.* **Sat 17, Sun 18
June (2-5). Adm £4.50, chd free.
Home-made teas.**
Quintessential English cottage
and rose garden covering 3½
acres in idyllic setting with Grade
II farmhouse (c1420). There is a
circular walk taking in woodlands,
natural areas and the ancient village
pond with views over rolling Surrey
countryside. Around the house are
terraces teaming with old English

roses, various mixed borders, courtyards and cottage paths that delight at every turn. Partial wheelchair access. Garden set on hill with many steps and terraces.

&♥♨

52 NEW PATCHWORKING GARDEN PROJECT

Aviva Plc Sports Ground, Pixham Lane, Dorking, RH4 1QA. Patchworking Garden Project, www.patchworkinggardenproject. co.uk. ¼m N of Dorking, off A24. At Olympics 2012 cycling r'about on A24, turn R down Pixham Lane, garden is on L after 200 metres. **Sat 27 May, Sat 15 July (12-4). Adm £4, chd free. Home-made teas.** New volunteer run social horticultural project developed since autumn 2014. Large walled garden with outstanding views of Box Hill. Flower borders, raised vegetable beds, polytunnel, fruit cage, crafts workshed, bird hide, wildlife habitats and many other areas of interest. Wheelchair access to most parts of the garden.

&♨♣♨

53 PRATSHAM GRANGE

Tanhurst Lane, Holmbury St Mary, RH5 6LZ. Alan & Felicity Comber. 12m SE of Guildford, 8m SW of Dorking. From A25 take B2126. After 4m turn L into Tanhurst Lane. From A29 take B2126. Before Forest Green turn R on B2126 then 1st R to Tanhurst Lane. **Sun 2 July, Sun 20 Aug (1-5). Adm £5, chd free. Home-made teas.** 5 acre garden overlooked by Holmbury Hill and Leith Hill. Features incl 2 ponds joined by cascading stream, extensive scented rose and blue hydrangea beds. Also herbaceous borders, cutting flower garden, white and yellow beds. 3 new colourful beds planted for 2017. Some slopes and gravel paths. Deep ponds.

&♣♨

54 ◆ RAMSTER

Chiddingfold, Surrey, GU8 4SN. Mr & Mrs Paul Gunn, 01428 654167, office@ramsterhall.com, www.ramsterevents.com. On A283 1½m S of Chiddingfold, large iron gates

on R, entrance is signed from the road. **For NGS: Fri 12 May (10-5). Adm £7, chd free. Light refreshments. For other opening times and information, please phone, email or visit garden website.** A stunning, mature woodland garden set in over 20 acres, famous for its rhododendron and azalea collection and its carpets of bluebells in spring. Enjoy a peaceful wander down the woodland walk, explore the bog garden with its stepping stones, or relax in the tranquil enclosed tennis court garden. Tea house open every day while the garden is open, serving delicious cakes and sandwiches. Embroidery and textile art exhibition 10th - 26th March. The teahouse is wheelchair accessible, some paths in the garden are suitable for wheelchairs.

&♥♣♨♨

55 NEW ROE DEER FARM

Portsmouth Road, Godalming, GU7 2JT. Lucy & Justin Gurney. Godalming/Milford border next to Squire's Garden Centre (GU8 5HL). Please drive through Squire's garden centre car park towards the 'Pick your own'. Turn R & enter through back gate. No entrance from main road. **Sun 14 May (11-5). Adm £6, chd free. Home-made teas.** A diverse and varied 17 acre garden incl mature woodlands has been created over the past 10yrs by the present owners. Views through to the parkland setting can be seen from many of the formal and informal areas creating a garden full of interest throughout the seasons. Lawn terraces lead you to naturally planted woodland walks, a kitchen garden, bog garden, dingly-dell and a pirate ship! Families welcome and children invited to board the pirate ship and see the farm animals - pigs, ducks and chickens. Please be aware of open water features and swimming pool. Level access for wheelchairs and buggies. Some gravel paths and woodland paths may become difficult to traverse after rain.

&♨

56 7 ROSE LANE

Ripley, Woking, GU23 6NE. Mindi McLean, 01483 223200, info@broadwaybarn.com, www.broadwaybarn.com. Just off Ripley High St on Rose Lane, 3rd house on L next to shoe repair shop. **Sat 10 June (10-4). Adm £3.50, chd free. Home-made teas.** 7 Rose Lane is a small but perfectly formed village centre garden behind an historic listed cottage. It has 3 rooms - a traditional perennial flower garden laid to lawn; a vegetable and fruit garden with Agriframe orchard and a working garden with greenhouse, compost bins and shed. It is a perfect example of how to make the most of a cottage garden. Monthly Ripley Farmers Market held on 10 June (9-1).

♨♨

57 SAFFRON GATE

Tickners Heath, Alfold, Cranleigh, GU6 8HU. Mr & Mrs D Gibbison, 01483 200219, clematis@talk21.com. Between Alfold & Dunsfold. A281 between Guildford & Horsham approx 8m turn at Alfold crossways follow signs for Dunsfold. Do not turn at A281 T-lights for Dunsfold (wrong road). **Sun 18, Sun 25 June (11-4). Adm £4, chd free. Home-made teas. Visits also by arrangement Apr to July evening visits possible during summer months.** A garden created for our own plant collection, many rare plants. 2 new beds created after the loss of trees after a storm. Many different types of clematis, lots of which are summer flowering integrifolia, herbaceous and different species, grown in many different ways. The traditional herbaous borders will be starting to flower. Arbor with many varieties of climbers. A productive vegetable garden. Garden was subject of a lecture given at Great Dixter. Disabled drop off point.

&♥♣♨♨

58 NEW **116 ST JOHNS ROAD**
Woking, GU21 7PS. Mr & Mrs Tony Gilbert. *1½m from Woking town centre travelling towards St John's village. Take Goldsworth Road out of Woking into St. John's Road. Cottage is on L opp 2nd entrance to Winnington Way. Park in Winnington Way. Bus: 34 or 35.* **Sun 2 July (12-5). Adm £3, chd free. Home-made teas.**
Small and structurally interesting garden which over the last 20 yrs has been lovingly and haphazardly filled with a variety of plants. The garden is divided into rooms with a courtyard area, a small pond and a lawned area with herbaceous border. There is a greenhouse at the end of the garden and raised beds for growing vegetables.
🐕 ✿ ☕ ▼

59 NEW **SHAMLEY WOOD ESTATE**
Woodhill Lane, Shamley Green, Guildford, GU5 0SP. Mrs Claire Merriman, 07595 693132, claire@merriman.co.uk. *5m (15 mins) S of Guildford in village of Shamley Green. Entrance is approx ¼m up Woodhill Lane from centre of Shamley Green.* **Sun 28 May (11-4). Adm £5, chd free. Home-made teas incl gluten free options. Visits also by arrangement Feb to Sept. Tours given by owner for groups 10+ by prior arrangement.**
Open for the first time, this garden is worth visiting just for the setting! Sitting high on the North Downs, the garden enjoys beautiful views of the South Downs and is approached through a 10 acre deer park. Set within approximately 3 acres, there is a large pond and established rose garden. More recent additions incl a stream, fire pits, dry garden, heather and vegetable garden. Most of garden accessible by wheelchair. Large ground level WC but step up to access area.
♿ ☕ ▼

60 **41 SHELVERS WAY**
Tadworth, KT20 5QJ. Keith & Elizabeth Lewis, 01737 210707, kandelewis@ntlworld.com. *6m S of Sutton off A217. 1st turning on R*

after Burgh Heath T-lights heading S on A217. 400yds down Shelvers Way on L. **Sun 23 Apr, Sun 6 Aug (2-5.30). Adm £4, chd free. Home-made teas. Visits also by arrangement Apr to Aug for groups 10+.**
Visitors say 'one of the most colourful back gardens in Surrey'. In spring, a myriad of small bulbs with specialist daffodils and many pots of colourful tulips. Choice perennials follow, with rhododendrons and azaleas. Cobbles and shingle support grasses and self sown plants with a bubble fountain. Annuals, phlox and herbaceous plants ensure colour well into September. A garden for all seasons.
✿ 🚌 ☕ ▼

61 **SHIELING**
The Warren, Kingswood, Tadworth, KT20 6PQ. Drs Sarah & Robin Wilson, 01737 833370, sarahwilson@doctors.org.uk. *Kingswood Warren Estate. Off A217, gated entrance just before church on southbound side of dual carriageway after Tadworth r'about . ¾m walk from Station. Parking on The Warren or by church on A217.* **Mon 1, Mon 29 May (2-5). Home-made teas. Sun 16 July (11-4). Light refreshments. Adm £5, chd free. Visits also by arrangement May to July.**
1 acre garden restored to its original 1920s design. Formal front garden with island beds and shrub border. Unusual large rock garden and mixed borders with collection of beautiful slug free hostas and uncommon perennials. The rest is a woodland garden with acid loving plants and some old and interesting trees and shrubs. Plant list provided for visitors. Gravel drive and some narrow paths in back garden. Otherwise grass and paths easy for wheelchairs.
♿ 🐕 Ⓓ ☕ ▼

62 NEW **SOUTHLANDS LODGE**
Southlands Lane, Tandridge, Oxted, RH8 9PH. Colin David & John Barker. *3m from J6 of M25. From Tandridge Village head S down hill for ¼m to T-junction with Southlands*

Lane. Turn L along Southlands Lane, approx ¼m to Southlands Lodge entrance gate. **Sat 8, Sun 9 July (1.30-5.30). Adm £4, chd free. Tea. Also open The Bothy.**
A surprising garden, on the edge of a woodland, enjoying open views of adjacent fields. Formal and informal areas are scaled to compliment a late Georgian gatehouse. Mass planting offsets selected specimens, mostly chosen for their pollen and nectar that helps sustain the resident honey bees. An enclosed vegetable garden with greenhouse, a flock of Shetland sheep and chickens also feature. The garden contains a working apiary of 10 beehives. Tea, cakes and biscuits will be available to purchase, proceeds donated to charity (not NGS).
🐕 ☕ ▼

63 NEW **SPRINGWOOD HOUSE**
85 Petworth Road, Haslemere, GU27 3AX. Mr & Mrs Ian Bateson, 01428 645024, julie@springwood-house.co.uk. *1m E of Haslemere. Entrance to property is almost opp junction of Holdfast Lane with Petworth Road. Postcode for SatNav brings you approx 300yds W entrance.* **Sun 23, Sun 30 Apr (11-4). Adm £5, chd free. Home-made teas. Visits also by arrangement Apr to June, groups 10+.**
Wooded walkway with large amount of native bluebells when in season (end of April), and 24 small wooden bridges following spring-fed stream. 3 large ponds with further bridges set in parkland type garden, waterfalls connecting the ponds which contain fish and also three small islands. Two large fields with walkways round the perimeter, dogs welcome if on leads. Bridge walkway is narrow and bare earth, step of 2-3 inches at each bridge. At end of walk there is a steep path, return if necessary.
♿ 🐕 ☕ ▼

64 **SPURFOLD**
Radnor Road, Peaslake, Guildford, GU5 9SZ. Mr & Mrs A Barnes, 01306 730196, spurfold@btinternet.com. *8m*

SE of Guildford. A25 to Shere then through to Peaslake. Pass Village stores & L up Radnor Rd. **Visits by arrangement May to Aug, home-made teas (day), wine (eve). Group refreshments can be discussed. Adm £6, chd free.**
2½ acres, large herbaceous and shrub borders, formal pond with Cambodian Buddha head, sunken gravel garden with topiary box and water feature, terraces, beautiful lawns, mature rhododendrons and azaleas, woodland paths, and gazebos. Garden contains a collection of Indian elephants and other objets d'art. Topiary garden created 2010 and new formal lawn area created in 2012. Featured in Surrey Life and Period Living.

Wintershall Manor

© Leigh Clapp

65 STUART COTTAGE

Ripley Road, East Clandon, GU4 7SF. John & Gayle Leader, 01483 222689, gayle@stuartcottage.com, www.stuartcottage.com. *4m E of Guildford. Off A246 or from A3 through Ripley until r'about, turn L & cont through West Clandon until T-lights, then L onto A246. East Clandon 1st L.* **Sun 23 July (2-5). Adm £4, chd free. Home-made teas. Visits also by arrangement May to Sept for groups 15+ (no upper limit).**
This much visited ½ acre garden seems to please many, being planted to offer floral continuity through the seasons. In June, the romance of the rose walk combines with the sound of water, in July, flowerbeds are floriferous with soft coordinated colours and scented plants, in August, vibrant colours will lift the spirits and in September, tender perennials reach their zenith. Wheelchair access to all of garden.

66 STUARTFIELD

113 Silverdale Avenue, Walton-on-Thames, KT12 1EQ. Caroline Ingram MBE & Kevin Ingram. *1.3m S of Walton-on-Thames. From A3, A245 to Walton. R B365 Seven Hills Rd. At 2nd r'about A317 to Walton. L next r'about B365 Ashley Rd. Silverdale Av 2nd on L.* **Sun 7 May (11-5). Adm £4, chd free. Home-made teas.**
An inspiring garden that takes you to different parts of the world, whether through New Zealand tree ferns, Japanese acers, or a Moroccan inspired summerhouse. A mature garden with planting inspired by the tropics, as well as the challenges of shade. The garden was extensively redesigned by Joe Swift of Gardener's World fame. There is also a pond and many sculptural features to enjoy.

67 NEW THE THERAPY GARDEN

Manor Fruit Farm, Glaziers Lane, Normandy, Guildford, GU3 2DT. The Centre Manager, 01483 813846, info@thetherapygarden.org, www.thetherapygarden.org. *SW of Guildford. Take A323 travelling from Guildford towards Aldershot, turn L into Glaziers Lane in centre of Normandy village opp War Memorial. The Therapy Garden is 200yds on L.* **Sun 21 May (11-4). Adm £5, chd free. Light refreshments. Visits also by arrangement for groups or single visitors.**
The Therapy Garden is a horticulture and education charity that uses gardening to generate positive change for adults and teenagers living with learning difficulties and mental health challenges. Our gardens are designed for accessibility incl wheelchair friendly pathways, raised vegetable and flower beds, sensory areas and quiet spaces. The Therapy Garden is a registered charity that provides social and therapeutic horticulture to different groups in the local community. Light lunches, salads and sandwiches, teas, coffees and cakes all available. Paved pathways throughout the garden, many with substantial handrails.

68 TILFORD COTTAGE
Tilford Road, Tilford,
GU10 2BX. Mr & Mrs R Burn,
01252 795423 or 07712 142728,
rodneyburn@outlook.com,
www.tilfordcottagegarden.co.uk.
*3m SE of Farnham. From Farnham
station along Tilford Rd. Tilford
Cottage opp Tilford House.
Parking by village green.* **Visits
by arrangement Apr to Sept
for groups 6+. Refreshments
available on request. Adm £7,
chd free.**
Artist's garden designed to surprise,
delight and amuse. Formal planting,
herb and knot garden. Numerous
examples of topiary combine
beautifully with the wild flower river
walk. Japanese and water gardens,
hosta beds, rose, apple and willow
arches, treehouse and fairy grotto all
continue the playful quality especially
enjoyed by children. Dogs on lead
please. Holistic Healing centre. Art
Gallery. Partial wheelchair access.
Some gravel paths and steep slopes.

♿ 🐕 🐾 ✿ 🚗 ☕ 🍽

69 TIMBER HILL
Chertsey Road, Chobham,
GU24 8JF. Mr & Mrs Nick
Sealy, 01932 873875,
nicksealy@chobham.net,
www.timberhillgarden.co.uk. *4m
N of Woking. 2½ m E of Chobham
& ⅓ m E of Fairoaks aerodrome
on A319 (N side). 1¼ m W of
Ottershaw, J11 M25.* **Sun 5 Mar,
Mon 17 Apr, Sun 15 Oct (11-4).
Adm £5, chd free. Home-made
light lunches and teas. Visits
also by arrangement Feb & Mar
for crocuses and snowdrops;
June for roses. Check website
for pop-up openings.**
Beautifully kept 15 acre park like
garden and woodland with views
to N Downs. Fine oaks, liquidambar
and liriodendron. Early witch hazel
walk, a sea of snowdrops and
species crocus; beech, cherry, maples,
acers, over 200 camellias and
magnolias. Drifts of spring narcissi,
daffodils and stunning camassias,
tulips in borders; bluebells/azaleas
in May; early roses in June. Fine
autumn colour. A garden for all
seasons! Nature and wildlife trails
for children. Refreshments served in

beautiful old Surrey barn. Preferably
book for lunch or take pot luck! **For
alternative non NGS openings,
please phone or see garden
website** . Excellent help available for
disabled.

♿ 🐕 🐾 ✿ D ☕

70 ◆ TITSEY PLACE GARDENS
Titsey, Oxted, RH8 0SA. The
Trustees of the Titsey Foundation,
01273 407037, jamie.evans-
freke@struttandparker.com,
www.titsey.org. *3m N of Oxted.
A25 between Oxted & Westerham.
Follow brown signs to Titsey Estate
from A25 at Limpsfield or see
website directions.* **For NGS: Sun
21 May, Sun 18 June, Sun 23
July, Sun 20 Aug (1-5). Adm
£4.50, chd £1. For other opening
times and information, please
phone, email or visit garden
website.**
One of the largest surviving historic
estates in Surrey. Magnificent
ancestral home and gardens of the
Gresham family since 1534. Walled
kitchen garden restored early
1990s. Golden Jubilee rose garden.
Etruscan summer house adjoining
picturesque lakes and fountains. 15
acres of formal and informal gardens
in idyllic setting within the M25.
Tearooms with delicious home-
made teas served between 12:30-5
on open days. Last admissions to
gardens at 4pm, gardens close at
5pm. Dogs allowed in picnic area,
car park and woodland walks. Good
wheelchair access and disabled car
park alongside tearooms.

♿ ☕

71 ◆ VANN
Hambledon, GU8 4EF. Mrs
M Caroe, 01428 683413,
www.vanngarden.co.uk. *6m S of
Godalming. A283 to Wormley. Turn
L at Hambledon. On NGS days only,
follow yellow Vann signs for 2m.
Please park in field, not in road (or
see website instructions).* **For NGS:
Daily Sun 26 Mar to Fri 31 Mar
(10-6). Mon 1 May (2-6). Home-
made teas. Daily Tue 2 May to
Sun 7 May, Sun 4 June to Sat 10
June (10-6). Adm £6, chd free.
N.B. Home-made teas Mon 1**

May only. For other opening times
and information, please phone or
visit garden website.
5 acre English Heritage registered
garden surrounding Tudor and
William and Mary house (not open)
with Arts and Crafts additions by
W D Caröe incl a Bargate stone
pergola. At the front, brick paved
original cottage garden; to the rear,
¼ acre pond, yew walk with rill
and Gertrude Jekyll water garden.
Snowdrops and hellebores, spring
bulbs, spectacular Fritillaria in Feb/
March. Island beds, crinkle crankle
wall, orchard with wild flowers.
Vegetable garden. Centenary
Garden. Gertrude Jekyll water
garden. Deep water. Water garden
paths not suitable for wheelchairs,
but many others are. Please ring
prior to visit to request disabled
parking.

♿ ✿ 🚗 ☕

72 WALTON POOR HOUSE
Ranmore, RH5 6SX. Prue Calvert,
01483 282273 or 07889 650503,
wnscalvert@btinternet.com. *6m
NW of Dorking. From Dorking take
rd to Ranmore, cont for approx 4m,
after Xrds 1m on L. From A246 at
E Horsley go S into Greendene, 1st
L Crocknorth Rd, 1m on R.* **Mon 1
May (12-5). Home-made teas.
Sun 14 May, Sat 14, Sun 15 Oct
(12-5). Adm £3.50, chd free.
Visits also by arrangement Apr
to Oct for groups 10+.**
Tranquil, almost secretive, 4 acre
mostly wooded garden in North
Downs AONB, planted to show
contrast between colourful shrubs
and mature trees. Paths wind
through garden to pond, hideaway
dell and herb garden, planted to
show the use of aromatic plants
and shrubs. Specialist nursery with
wide variety of herbs, shrubs and
aromatic plants. Herb talks, recipe
leaflets and refreshments available
for groups by arrangement. Grass
paths.

♿ 🐕 🐾 ✿ 🚗 ☕

73 57 WESTHALL ROAD
Warlingham, CR6 9BG. Robert
& Wendy Baston. *3m N of M25.
M25, J6, A22 London, at Whyteleafe*

r'about, take 3rd R, under railway bridge, turn immed R into Westhall Rd. **Sun 30 Apr, Mon 1 May (2-5). Adm £3.50, chd free. Home-made teas.** *Donation to Warlingham Methodist Church.* Reward for the sure footed – many steep steps to 3 levels! Swathes of tulips and alliums. Mature kiwi and grape vines. Mixed borders. Raised vegetable beds. Box, bay, cork oak and yew topiaries. Amphitheatre of potted plants on lower steps. Stunning views of Caterham and Whyteleafe from top garden. Featured in Surrey Life.

🐂 ❀ ☕ 💷

74 WESTWAYS FARM

Gracious Pond Road, Chobham, GU24 8HH. Paul & Nicky Biddle, 01276 856163, nicolabiddle@rocketmail.com. *4m N of Woking. From Chobham Church proceed over r'about towards Sunningdale, 1st Xrds R into Red Lion Rd to junction with Mincing Lane.* **Visits by arrangement Apr to June for groups min 10, max 50. Home-made teas.** 6 acre garden surrounded by woodlands planted in 1930s with mature and some rare rhododendrons, azaleas, camellias and magnolias, underplanted with bluebells, lilies and dogwood; extensive lawns and sunken pond garden. Working stables and sandschool. Lovely Queen Anne House (not open) covered with listed *Magnolia grandiflora.* Victorian design glasshouse. New planting round garden room.

♿ 🐂 🚗 ☕ 💷

75 ◆ WINKWORTH ARBORETUM

Hascombe Road, Godalming, GU8 4AD. National Trust, 01483 208477, www.nationaltrust. org.uk/winkwortharboretum. *2m SE of Godalming on B2130. Car: nr Hascombe, 2m SE of Godalming on E side of B2130. Bus: 42/44 Guildford to Cranleigh (stops at Arboretum).* **For NGS: Sun 4 June, Sun 1 Oct (10-5.30). Adm £8.40, chd £4.20. Light refreshments. For other opening times and information, please phone or visit**

garden website.
This dramatic hillside Arboretum perfectly demonstrates what Dr Fox, the Arboretum's creator, described as 'using trees and shrubs to paint a picture'. Impressive displays of daffodils, bluebells and azaleas await in spring. Picnic by the lake in summer. Don't miss the stunning autumnal display created by maples, cherries and tupelos. Guided walk with member of the garden team. Some steep slopes.

♿ 🐂 🚗 ☕ 💷

The National Garden Scheme is Marie Curie's largest single funder

76 WINTERSHALL MANOR

Bramley, GU5 0LR. Mr & Mrs Peter Hutley & Mr & Mrs Nicholas Hutley. *3m S of Bramley Village. On A281 turn R, then next R. Wintershall Drive next on L. Bus: AV33 Guildford to Horsham, alight Palmers Cross, 1m.* **Sun 14 May (11-5). Adm £5, chd free. Home-made teas.** *Donation to St Anna's Children's Home, Ghana & GRACE.* 2 acre garden in first year of restoration and 200 acres of park and woodland. Bluebell walks in spring, wild daffodils, rhododendrons, specimen trees. Lakes and flight ponds; superb views. Chapel of St Mary, stations of Cross, Rosary Walk and St Francis Chapel. New courtyard garden in converted stables. Garden restoration to create large colourful but low maintenance garden full of hydrangeas. Hostas, variety of magnolias and shrubs. Ancient mulberry, redwood and fine Monkey Puzzle trees. New small trees. Wendy House and mud

kitchen for children. Hot and cold drinks, home-made cakes, cream teas.

♿ 🐂 🚗 ☕

77 WOODBURY COTTAGE

Colley Lane, Reigate, RH2 9JJ. Shirley & Bob Stoneley, 01737 244235. *1m W of Reigate. M25 J8, A217 (Reigate). Immed before level crossing turn R into Somers Rd, cont as Manor Rd. At end turn R into Coppice Lane & follow signs to car park. Do not come up Colley Lane from A25.* **Sat 8, Sun 9 July, Sat 2, Sun 3, Wed 6 Sept (1-5). Adm £4, chd free. Home-made teas. Visits also by arrangement June to Sept, groups 10+. Regret, no coaches.** Cottage garden just under ¼ acre. It is stepped on a slope, enhanced by its setting under Colley Hill and the North Downs. We grow a colourful diversity of plants incl perennials, annuals and tender ones. A particular feature throughout the garden is the use of groups of pots containing unusual and interesting plants. The garden is colour themed and is still rich and vibrant in September.

❀ 🚗 ☕

78 NEW WOODLAND

67 York Rd, Cheam, Sutton, SM2 6HN. Sean Hilton. *York Road runs parallel to Belmont Rise, main A217 from Sutton to Banstead. From A217 turn L (from N) or R (from S) at T-lights into Dorset Rd. York Rd is 1st L.* **Sat 8, Sun 9 July (11-5.30). Adm £3, chd free. Home-made teas.** Woodland is a suburban walled garden of approx ⅕ acre with a range of plants shrubs and young trees. Hard landscaping has created terraces, two lawns and four levels from the upward incline of the garden. Good selection of shrubs, perennials, hostas, bamboos and ferns. Central features of the garden are a pond with pergola, a weeping copper beech and a Victorian Plant House. Plant sales and refreshments in aid of Princess Alice Hospice. All but the top level accessible by wheelchair.

♿ ❀ ☕

SUSSEX

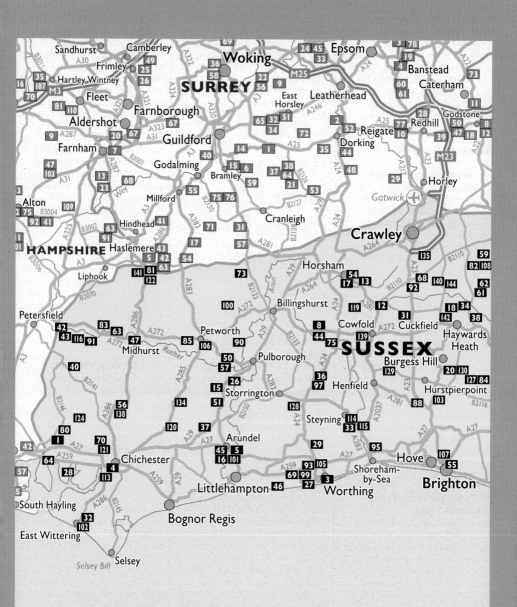

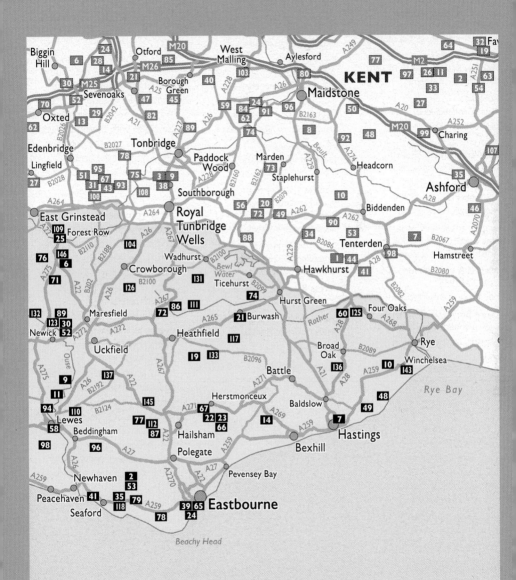

Biggin Hill
24
Otford
West Malling
32 Fav
64
19

6 **28**
85
Aylesford
77
M2
97 **26** **11** **2** **251**

14
M26
80
KENT
63

30 M25
21
Borough Green
40
A26
Maidstone
33 **54**

70 M25
47
A25
45
59
84 **24**
96
A20
27

52 Sevenoaks
82
91
B2163
50
A252
Charing

Oxted
29 B2042
A21
89
62
A26
74
8
M20
99
107

13
Tonbridge
Marden
92
48
35

Edenbridge
B2027
78
Paddock Wood
73
10
Ashford

Lingfield
51 **95**
75
3 **9**
Staplehurst
B2160
Headcorn
A28

27 B2028
31 **67**
38
B2161
56
10
Biddenden
46

100
43 **93**
108
Southborough
20
B2079
90
B2086
A2070

East Grinstead
A264
Royal Tunbridge Wells
88
34
53
Tenterden
7 B2067

109
Forest Row
A26
104
Wadhurst
Bewl Water
A229
1 **44**
198
Hamstreet

25
B2110
B2100
131
Hawkhurst
41
B2080

76 **146**
B2188
Crowborough
Ticehurst
74
B2099
60 **125**
Four Oaks
B2082

6
126
B2100
111
Hurst Green
Rother
136
A268
Rye

71
A22
72 **86**
A265
Burwash
21
60
Winchelsea

132 **89**
Maresfield
Heathfield
117
Broad Oak
B2089
10
143

123 **30**
A272
A267
19 **133**
B2096
Battle
136
A259
Rye Bay

Newick
52
Uckfield
137
A271
Baldslow
48

9
A26
B2192
145
Herstmonceux
269
49

11
A275
A22
67
Hailsham
14
7
Hastings

94 **110**
B2124
77 **112**
22 **23**
A259
Bexhill

58
Beddingham
87
66

98
96
A27
Polegate
Pevensey Bay

Newhaven
2
A2270
A27
Eastbourne

Peacehaven **41** **35** **79**
53
39 **65**
24

Seaford
118
78

Beachy Head

0   10 kilometres
0   5 miles
© Global Mapping / XYZ Maps

East & Mid Sussex Volunteers

County Organiser, Booklet & Advertising Co-ordinator
Irene Eltringham-Willson
01323 833770
irene.willson@btinternet.com

County Treasurer
Andrew Ratcliffe 01435 873310
anratcliffe@gmail.com

Publicity
Geoff Stonebanks 01323 899296
ngseastsussex@gmail.com

Twitter
Liz Warner 01273 586050
lizwarner69@outlook.com

Photographer
Liz Seeber 01323 639478
lizseeber@btinternet.com

Assistant County Organisers
Jane Baker 01273 842805
jane.baker47@btinternet.com

Michael & Linda Belton
01797 252984
belton.northiam@gmail.com

Lynne Brown 01273 556439
brown.lynne@ntlworld.com

Linda Field 01323 720179
lindafield3@gmail.com

Diane Gould 07773 289276
heron.brook@btinternet.com

Peggy Harvey 01424 532093
chantry@talktalk.net

Philippa Hopkins 01342 822090
piphop@btinternet.com

Aideen Jones 01323 899452
sweetpeasa52@gmail.com

Susan Laing 01444 892500
splaing@btinternet.com

Sarah Ratcliffe 01435 873310
sallyrat@btinternet.com

Geoff Stonebanks (as above)

Liz Seeber (as above)

Liz Warner (as above)

West Sussex Volunteers

County Organiser
Patty Christie 01730 813323
sussexwestngs@gmail.com

County Treasurer
Liz Collison 01903 719245
liz.collison@ngs.org.uk

Publicity
Adrian Skeates 07743 505392
as13cs@btinternet.com

Social Media
Claudia Pearce 07985 648216
claudiapearce17@gmail.com

Photographer
Judi Lion 07810 317057
judilion.ngs@gmail.com

Booklet Co-ordinators
Ian & Elizabeth Gregory
01903 892433
id.gregory@btinternet.com

Assistant County Organisers
Jane Allen 01428 683130
jane.allen01@me.com

Teresa Barttelot 01798 865690
tbarttelot@gmail.com

Sanda Belcher 01428 723259
sandambelcher@gmail.com

Jane Burton 01243 527822

Lesley Chamberlain 07950 105966
chamberlain_lesley@hotmail.com

Sue Foley 01243 814452
suefoley@mac.com

Jane Lywood 01403 820225
jmlywood@aol.com

Judi Lion (as above)

Carrie McArdle 01403 820272
carrie.mcardle@btinternet.com

Claudia Pearce (as above)

Fiona Phillips 01273 462285
fiona.h.phillips@btinternet.com

Susan Pinder 01403 820430
nasus.rednip@gmail.com

Caroline & Adrian Skeates
07743 505392
as13cs@btinternet.com

South & West of Chichester
Position Vacant
For details please contact
Patty Christie (as above)

Sussex is a vast county with two county teams, one covering East and Mid Sussex and the other covering West Sussex.

Over 80 miles from west to east, Sussex spans the southern side of the Weald from the exposed sandstone heights of Ashdown Forest, past the broad clay vales with their heavy yet fertile soils and the imposing chalk ridge of the South Downs National Park, to the equable if windy coastal strip.

Away from the chalk, Sussex is a county with a largely wooded landscape with imposing oaks, narrow hedged lanes and picturesque villages. The county offers much variety and our gardens reflect this. There is something for absolutely everyone and we feel sure that you will enjoy your garden visiting experience - from rolling acres of parkland, small courtyards, country and town gardens to school gardens and village trails. See the results of the owner's attempts to cope with the various conditions, discover new plants and talk with the owners about their successes.

Many of our gardens are open by arrangement, so do not be afraid to book a visit or organise a visit with your local gardening or U3A group.

Should you need advice, please e-mail ngseastsussex@gmail.com for anything relating to East and Mid Sussex or sussexwestngs@gmail.com for anything in West Sussex.

OPENING DATES

All entries subject to latest information check www.ngs.org.uk

Extended openings are shown at the beginning of the month.

Map locator numbers are shown to the right of each garden name.

Follers Manor

© Leigh Clapp

February

Snowdrop Festival

Sunday 5th
◆ West Dean Gardens 138

Sunday 12th
Manor of Dean 85

Saturday 25th
Westlands Court 139

Sunday 26th
The Old Vicarage 97

March

Sunday 5th
Manor of Dean 85

Sunday 12th
Aldsworth House 1

Tuesday 14th
Aldsworth House 1

Thursday 16th
Cissbury 29

Sunday 19th
The Old Vicarage 97

Thursday 23rd
Cissbury 29

Sunday 26th
◆ King John's Lodge 74

April

Saturday 1st
Lordington House 80

Sunday 2nd
Lordington House 80

Thursday 6th
Copyhold Hollow 34

Saturday 8th
Butlers Farmhouse 22

Sunday 9th
Butlers Farmhouse 22
Hammerwood House 63

Saturday 15th
Rymans 113

Sunday 16th
Hammerwood House 63
Palatine School Gardens 99
Penns in the Rocks 104
Rymans 113

Monday 17th
The Old Vicarage 97

Thursday 20th
Copyhold Hollow 34

Friday 21st
Weavers House 137

Saturday 22nd
Down Place 40
Sandhill Farm House 116
Winchelsea's Secret Gardens 143

Sunday 23rd
Down Place 40
Manor of Dean 85
Newtimber Place 88
Sandhill Farm House 116

Tuesday 25th
Bignor Park 15

Saturday 29th
Banks Farm 9
The Garden House 55

Sunday 30th
Banks Farm 9
The Garden House 55
◆ Highdown Gardens 69
Malt House 83
Offham House 94

May

Fittleworth House (Every Wednesday) 50

Monday 1st
Malt House 83

Tuesday 2nd
Copyhold Hollow 34

Saturday 6th
4 Birch Close 16
◆ King John's Lodge 74
Stone Cross House 126

Sunday 7th
Beedinglee 12
4 Birch Close 16
◆ Clinton Lodge 30
◆ King John's Lodge 74
Malt House 83
Stone Cross House 126

Saturday 13th
Cookscroft 32
Holly House 71

Sunday 14th
Champs Hill 26
Cookscroft 32
Gardeners' Cottage 56
Holly House 71
Peelers Retreat 101
Penns in the Rocks 104
Shalford House 122

Tuesday 16th
Bignor Park 15
Copyhold Hollow 34

Wednesday 17th
46 Westup Farm Cottages 140
Winterfield 144
NEW Wych Warren House 146

Thursday 18th
NEW ◆ Pleasure Grounds Of Petworth House And Park 106

Friday 19th
Caxton Manor 25
2 Quarry Cottages 109

Saturday 20th
96 Ashford Road 7
Blue Jays 17
Caxton Manor 25
2 Quarry Cottages 109

Sunday 21st
Bakers House 8
Blue Jays 17
Ham Cottage 62
Legsheath Farm 76
The Old Vicarage 97
Stonehealed Farm 127

Wednesday 24th
NEW 6 Elm Avenue 46

Thursday 25th
NEW 6 Elm Avenue 46

90th Anniversary Weekend

Saturday 27th
96 Ashford Road 7
◆ Borde Hill Garden 18
◆ Gardens & Grounds of Herstmonceux Castle 66
◆ The Priest House 108
Westlands Court 139

Sunday 28th
Sedgwick Park House 119
Stonehealed Farm 127
Upwaltham Barns 134
Westlands Court 139

Monday 29th
Great Lywood Farmhouse 61
Upwaltham Barns 134

Wednesday 31st
◆ Highdown Gardens 69
Sedgwick Park House 119

1 Rose Cottage

© Leigh Clapp

THE GARDENS

1 ALDSWORTH HOUSE

Emsworth Common Road, Aldsworth, PO10 8QT. Tom & Sarah Williams. *6m W of Chichester. From Havant follow signs to Stansted House until Emsworth Common Rd, stay on this road until Aldsworth. From Chichester B2178/B2146 follow road through Funtington to Aldsworth.* Sun 12, Tue 14 Mar, Sun 4, Wed 7 June (11-5). Adm £4, chd free. Light refreshments.

Sheets of crocus and daffodils under a 200 yr old plane tree herald spring. This six acre garden contains walled and gravel gardens, numerous mixed borders and two mini arboretums packed full of a wide variety of unusual trees, shrubs and perennials. Particular specialities are hellebores, peonies, roses, epimediums, hostas, magnolias, clematis and very old fruit trees. Children's quiz. Short film of the garden in the 1930s.

♿ ❇ 🚌 ☕

2 ◆ ALFRISTON CLERGY HOUSE

Alfriston, BN26 5TL. National Trust, 01323 871961, alfriston@nationaltrust.org.uk, www.nationaltrust.org.uk/alfriston. *4m NE of Seaford. Just E of B2108, in Alfriston village, adjoining The Tye & St Andrew's Church. Bus: RDH 125 from Lewes, Autopoint 126 from Eastbourne & Seaford.* For NGS: Tue 20 June (10.30-4.30). Adm £5.45, chd £2.75. For other opening times and information, please phone, email or visit garden website.

Enjoy the scent of roses; admire the vegetable garden and orchard in a tranquil setting with views across the R Cuckmere. Visit this C14 thatched Wealden hall house, the first building to be acquired by the NT in 1896. Our gardener will be available to talk to you about the garden. Partial wheelchair access.

♿ ❇

GROUP OPENING

3 AMBROSE PLACE BACK GARDENS

Richmond Road, Worthing, BN11 1PZ. *Worthing Town Centre. Entry points: Ambrose Villa, corner Portland Rd & Richmond Rd; No 10, opp Worthing Library.* Sun 25 June (11-5). Combined adm £6, chd free. Light refreshments available at some gardens. Please note all gardens closed 1-2pm.

1 AMBROSE PLACE

3 AMBROSE PLACE

4 AMBROSE PLACE
Graham & Terri Heald.

5 AMBROSE PLACE
Pat & Sue Owen.

6 AMBROSE PLACE
Sue Swanborough.

7 AMBROSE PLACE
Mark & Susan Frost.

8 AMBROSE PLACE
Steve & Claire Hughes.

9 AMBROSE PLACE
Anna Irvine.

10 AMBROSE PLACE
Marie Pringle.

11 AMBROSE PLACE
Steve & Carolyn Bailey.

12 AMBROSE PLACE
Peter May.

13 AMBROSE PLACE
Malcolm & Hilary Leeves.

14 AMBROSE PLACE
Andrew & Kristen Dryden.

AMBROSE VILLA
Mark & Christine Potter.

The highly acclaimed back gardens of Ambrose Place have been described as a 'horticultural phenomenon', and have a rich panoply of styles, plantings and layouts. Behind a classic Regency terrace, itself the architectural jewel of Worthing, the gardens draw inspiration from such exotic diversity as Morocco, Provence and the Alhambra to the more traditional sources of the English cottage and Victorian gardens. All within the typically limited space of a terrace (seriously restricted disabled access). A variety of imaginative water features add to the charm and attraction for all gardeners and prove that small can be beautiful. Do come and enjoy our special spaces, we have 14 gardens open this year. Featured on BBC Sussex Radio Dig-it programme, and in the Worthing Herald and West Sussex Gazette.

❇ ☕

4 NEW THE APULDRAM CENTRE

Appledram Lane South, Apuldram, Chichester, PO20 7PE. The Apuldram Centre, 01243 783370, info@apuldram.org, www.apuldram.org. *1m S of A27. Follow A259 Fishbourne & turn into Appledram Lane South.* Every Wed 7 June to 19 July (12-3). Adm £4, chd free. Light refreshments. Visits also by arrangement June & July for groups of 10+.

Award-winning Wildlife and Sensory Garden. Winding willow pathway sensitively planted with bee loving plants, all grown from seed, which leads to a tranquil pond and bog garden. Full of surprises, this garden encompasses many interesting features incl sculptures and other art works created by our adult trainees with learning difficulties. Teas, coffees, light lunches and home-made cakes served in the café until 4pm. Local produce incl our home-made apple juice, local honey, plants, bird boxes and bug boxes for sale in the shop. WC on-site. Wheelchair access throughout Sensory Garden. Restricted access to working greenhouses and vegetable plots.

♿ 🐕 ❇ ☕

Your visit has already helped 600 more people gain access to a Parkinson's nurse

5 ◆ ARUNDEL CASTLE & GARDENS - THE COLLECTOR EARL'S GARDEN

Arundel, BN18 9AB. Arundel Castle Trustees Ltd, 01903 882173, visits@arundelcastle.org, www.arundelcastle.org. *In the centre of Arundel, N of A27.* **For opening times and information, please phone, email or visit garden website.**
Ancient castle. Family home of the Duke of Norfolk. 40 acres of grounds and gardens. The Collector Earl's Garden with hot subtropical borders and wild flowers. English herbaceous borders. Stumpery. Wild flower garden, 2 restored Victorian glasshouses with exotic fruit and vegetables. Walled flower and organic kitchen gardens. C14 Fitzalan Chapel white garden.

6 ASHDOWN PARK HOTEL

Wych Cross, East Grinstead, RH18 5JR. Mr Kevin Sweet, 01342 824988, reservations@ashdownpark.co.uk, www.elitehotels.co.uk. *6m S of East Grinstead. Turn off A22 at Wych Cross T-lights.* **Sun 25 June (1-5). Adm £5, chd free. Light refreshments.**
186 acres of parkland, grounds and gardens surrounding Ashdown Park Hotel. Our Secret Garden is well worth a visit with many new plantings. Large number of deer roam the estate and can often be seen during the day. Enjoy and explore the woodland paths, quiet areas and views. Featured in Sussex Life and local press. Some gravel paths and uneven ground with steps.

7 96 ASHFORD ROAD

Hastings, TN34 2HZ. Lynda & Andrew Hayler. *From A21 (Sedlescombe Rd N) towards Hastings take 1st exit on r'about A2101, then 3rd on L.* **Sat 20, Sat 27 May (1-5). Adm £3, chd free.**
Small (100ft × 52ft) Japanese inspired front and back garden. Full of interesting planting, with many acers, azaleas and bamboos. Over 100 different hostas, many miniature. Lower garden with greenhouse and raised beds. Also an attractive Japanese Tea House. Featured in The Telegraph (June 2016).

8 BAKERS HOUSE

Bakers Lane, Shipley, RH13 8GJ. Mr & Mrs Mark Burrell, 01403 741215, margot@dragons.me.uk. *5m S of Horsham. Take A24 to Worthing, then A272 W, 2nd turn to Dragon's Green. L at George & Dragon PH, Bakers Lane then 300yds on L.* **Sun 21 May, Sun 18 June (2-5.30). Adm £5, chd free. Home-made teas. Visits also by arrangement May & June.**
There is so much to see in this large parkland garden incl great oaks, lake, laburnum tunnel, rose walks with old fashioned roses, scented knot garden, woodland hosta walk, bog gardens and a big kitchen garden with potager. Partial wheelchair access, garden has gravel paths.

9 BANKS FARM

Boast Lane, Barcombe, Lewes, BN8 5DY. Nick & Lucy Addyman. *From Barcombe Cross follow signs to Spithurst & Newick. 1st road on R into Boast Lane towards the Anchor PH. At sharp bend carry on into Banks Farm.* **Sat 29, Sun 30 Apr (11-4). Adm £4, chd free. Home-made teas.**
9 acre garden set in rural countryside, extensive lawns and shrub beds merge with the more naturalistic woodland garden set around the lake. An orchard, vegetable garden, ponds and a wide variety of plant species add to an interesting and very tranquil garden.

10 BEAUCHAMPS

Float Lane, Udimore, Rye, TN31 6BY. Matty & Richard Holmes. *3m W of Rye. 3m E of Broad Oak Xrds. Turn S off B2089 down Float Lane ½m.* **Sun 2 July (2-5). Adm £4.50, chd free. Home-made teas.**
We are opening our lovely garden a month later than usual this year, so that visitors can enjoy its different delights in midsummer, and its wide range of unusual herbaceous plants, shrubs and trees, including Cornus controversa Variegata and lochroma tubulosa. Small woodland area, kitchen garden and orchard. Fine countryside views across the Brede Valley. Many home propagated plants for sale. Full wheelchair access, except after any recent rainfall.

Aldsworth House
© Judi Lion

11 THE BEECHES

Church Road, Barcombe, Lewes, BN8 5TS. Sandy Coppen, 01273 401339, sand@passionforplants.net. *From Lewes, A26 towards Uckfield for 3m, turn L signed Barcombe. Follow road for 1½m, turn L signed Hamsey & Church. Follow road for approx ¾m & parking is in church car park on LH-side.* Sun 23, Sun 30 July (2-5). Adm £5, chd free. Home-made teas. **Visits also by arrangement June to Aug for groups of 12 max. Teas, & wine for early eve visits.**

C18 walled garden with cut flowers, vegetables, salads and fruit. Separate orchard and rose garden. Herbaceous borders and hot border. There are two ponds, one with a willow house. Extensive lawns and an C18 barn. Some of the ground is a little bumpy but everything is accessible without steps.

&. ✿ 🛏 ☕

© Leigh Clapp

The Homegrown Flower Company

12 BEEDINGLEE

Brighton Road, Lower Beeding, Horsham, RH13 6NQ. Mrs Jo Longley, 01403 891251, joslongley@gmail.com. *4m SE of Horsham on A281 to Cowfold. Approx ½m N of South Lodge Hotel on A281 from Cowfold to Horsham. The entrance is almost opp a red post box on a stalk.* Sun 7 May (1-5). Adm £5, chd free. Home-made teas. **Visits also by arrangement May to Oct for groups of 25 max.**

Originally part of the Leonardslee

Estate, the 1987 hurricane brought down much of the Victorian/Edwardian planting. The present 6 acre garden has evolved since then with many interesting and unusual trees and shrubs, and a longer flowering season. Still an informal garden, there are hidden paths, a secret garden, lawns and a wild flower garden.

🐄 ✿ ☕

13 4 BEN'S ACRE

Horsham, RH13 6LW. Pauline Clark, 01403 266912, brian.clark8850@yahoo.co.uk. *N of Horsham. From A281 via Cowfold, after Hilliers Garden Centre, take 2nd R by Tesco, St Leonards Rd, then into Comptons Lane. 5th R Heron Way after mini-r'about, 2nd L Glebe Cres, 1st L Ben's Acre.* Sat 1 July, Sat 26 Aug (1-5). Adm £4, chd free. Home-made teas. **Visits also by arrangement late June to early Sept, for groups of 15-35. Refreshments on request.**

A keen Hardy Plant Society member's garden (100ft × 45ft), said to have the wow effect, with surprises and delights for the visitor. On the edge of St Leonards Forest and riverside walk, steps and terraces take you to borders planted to capacity with an interesting potpourri of colour, texture and form. Featuring arbours, summerhouse, ponds with waterfall, topiary and pots of succulents. Many seats around the garden to rest on while having one of our delicious teas. Come, enjoy and take home some ideas for your garden. Featured in Sussex Life and winner of BBC Sussex & Surrey Dig It 2016 Gardening Competition (back gardens category).

🐄 ✿ 🚗 ☕

GROUP OPENING

14 BEXHILL GARDENS

Bexhill. *Bexhill & Little Common. Proceed to Little Common r'about on A259, then see individual addresses below. Follow NGS signs or SatNav & yellow balloons will be displayed outside each garden. Tickets & maps available at each garden.* Sun 4

June (1.30-5). Combined adm £4, chd free.

GARDEN FLAT 1, ELM TREE HOUSE

5 Hastings Road, TN40 2HJ. Linda Exley.

GREEN HEDGES

Birchington Close, TN39 3TF. Sara & Paul Barker.

26 WINSTON DRIVE

TN39 3RP. Ron & Clare Brazier.

An attractive Edwardian residential seaside town famous for its De la Warr Pavilion Arts Centre that also has a cafe overlooking the sea. Gardens incl: Elm Tree House a pretty cottage style garden with interesting mixed planting, pergola and wildlife ponds. Green Hedges has an extensive mix of planting incl tropical plants, wildlife pond and greenhouse (no parking please in Birchington Close). 26 Winston Drive has been established over the past 10 yrs with 275 different plants. Wheelchair access to some gardens.

&. ✿ ☕

15 BIGNOR PARK

Pulborough, RH20 1HG. The Mersey Family, www.bignorpark.co.uk. *5m S of Petworth & Pulborough. Well signed from B2138. Nearest villages Sutton, Bignor & West Burton. Approach from the E, directions & map available on website.* Tue 25 Apr, Tue 16 May, Sun 25 June (2-5). Adm £5, chd free. Home-made teas.

11 acres of peaceful garden to explore with magnificent views of the South Downs. Interesting trees, shrubs, wild flower areas, with swathes of daffodils in spring. The walled flower garden has been replanted with herbaceous borders. Temple, Greek loggia, Zen pond and unusual sculptures. Former home of romantic poet Charlotte Smith, whose sonnets were inspired by Bignor Park. Spectacular Cedars of Lebanon and rare Holm Oak. Wheelchair access to shrubbery and croquet lawn, gravel paths in rest of garden and steps in stables quadrangle.

&. 🐄 ✿ ☕

16 4 BIRCH CLOSE

Arundel, BN18 9HN. Elizabeth & Mike Gammon, 01903 882722, e.gammon@talktalk.net. *1m S of Arundel. From A27 & A284 r'about at W end of Arundel take Ford Rd. After ½m turn R into Maxwell Rd & follow signs.* Sat 6, Sun 7 May (2-5). Adm £3.50, chd free. Home-made teas. **Visits also by arrangement in May for groups of 10+.**

⅓ acre of woodland garden on edge of Arundel. Wide range of mature trees and shrubs with many hardy perennials. Emphasis on extensive selection of spring flowers and clematis with over 100 incl 12 montana. All in a tranquil setting with secluded corners, meandering paths and plenty of seating. Partial wheelchair access to approx half of garden.

&. ✿ ☕

17 BLUE JAYS

Chesworth Close, Horsham, RH13 5AL. Stella & Mike Schofield, 01403 251065. *5 mins walk SE of St Mary's Church Horsham. From A281 (East St) L down Denne Rd, L to Chesworth Lane, R to Chesworth Close. Garden at end of close. 4 disabled spaces, other parking in local streets & Denne Rd car park (free on Suns).* Sat 20, Sun 21 May, Sun 18 June (12.30-5). Adm £3.50, chd free. Home-made teas. **Visits also by arrangement Apr to July for groups of 8+. Refreshments on request.** *Donation to The Badger Trust.*

Wooded 1 acre garden with rhododendrons, camellias and azaleas. Candelabra primulas and ferns edge the R Arun. Primroses and spring bulbs border woodland path and stream. Cordylines, gunneras, flower beds, a pond, a fountain and new formal rose garden set in open lawns. Arch leads to a vegetable plot and orchard bounded by the river. Large WW2 pill box in the orchard; visits inside with short talk are available. Wheelchair access to most areas.

&. 🐎 ✿ ☕

18 ◆ BORDE HILL GARDEN

Borde Hill Lane, Haywards Heath, RH16 1XP. Borde Hill Garden Ltd, 01444 450326, info@bordehill.co.uk, www.bordehill.co.uk. *1½m N of Haywards Heath. 20 mins N of Brighton, or S of Gatwick on A23 taking exit 10a via Balcombe.* For NGS: Sat 27 May (10-6); Mon 2 Oct (10-5). Adm £8.20, chd £5.50. For other opening times and information, please phone, email or visit garden website.

One of the original 1927 gardens, now celebrating 90 yrs association with the NGS. To mark this occasion there will be a special opening on Sat 27 May. Rare plants and stunning landscapes make Borde Hill Garden the perfect day out for horticulture enthusiasts, families and those who love beautiful countryside. Enjoy tranquil outdoor 'rooms', incl Rose and Italian gardens, champion trees, woodland walks, playground, picnic areas, home-cooked food and events throughout the open season. Wheelchair access to formal garden (17 acres). Dogs welcome on leads.

&. 🐎 ✿ 🚌 ☕

19 BRIGHTLING DOWN FARM

Observatory Road, Dallington, TN21 9LN. Mr & Mrs P Stephens, 07770 807060 / 01424 838888, valstephens@icloud.com. *1m from Woods Corner. At Swan PH at Woods Corner, take road opp signed Brightling. Take 1st L, signed Burwash. Almost immed turn into 1st driveway on L.* Visits by arrangement May to Oct for groups of 10-30. Adm £8, chd free. Home-made teas.

The garden has several different areas incl a Zen garden, water garden, walled vegetable garden with two large greenhouses, herb garden and herbaceous borders. The garden makes clever use of grasses and is set amongst woodland with stunning countryside views. A woodland walk is being developed. Winner of the Society of Garden Designers award. Most areas can be accessed with the use of temporary ramps.

&. Ⓓ ☕

GROUP OPENING

20 BURGESS HILL NGS GARDENS

Burgess Hill. *10m N of Brighton. Tickets & maps from any garden.* Sun 23, Mon 24 July (1-5). Combined adm £5, chd free. Home-made teas at 14 Barnside Avenue.

14 BARNSIDE AVENUE
RH15 0JU. Brian & Sue Knight.

NEW PEPPERS
RH15 8AL. Sussex Oak Charity.

9 SYCAMORE DRIVE
RH15 0GG. Peter Machin & Martin Savage.

30 SYCAMORE DRIVE
RH15 0GH. John Smith & Kieran O'Regan.
(See separate entry)

59 SYCAMORE DRIVE
RH15 0GG. Steve & Debby Gill.

This diverse group of five gardens is a mixture of established and small new gardens. Three of the group are a great example of what can be achieved over a 8 yr period from a blank canvas in a new development (Sycamore Drive) while close by is 14 Barnside Avenue, a wisteria clad house (pruning advice given) with a family lawn and borders. Peppers, 54 Leylands Road is a garden full of colour that is being restored by volunteers. Many useful ideas for people living in new build properties with small gardens and heavy clay soil. Plants for sale at Peppers, 54 Leylands Road for Sussex Oak Charity. Partial wheelchair access to some gardens.

&. 🐎 ✿ ☕

Donations from the NGS enable Perennial to care for horticulturalists

GROUP OPENING

21 BURWASH GARDENS

Burwash, TN19 7EN. *Burwash is on the A265, 3m E of junction with A21 at Hurst Green; 6m W of Heathfield. Ample parking at Swan Meadow sports field, Ham Lane, Burwash. Follow signs from High St. Tickets & detailed map at entry points: Bowzell, Church House, Longstaffes & Mandalay. Sat 1 July (2-5). Combined adm £6, chd free. Home-made teas in Swan Meadow Sports Pavilion, Ham Lane adjacent to parking area.*

BOWZELL
Shirley Viney.

CHURCH HOUSE
Rosemary & Graham Sendall.

FARLEY HOUSE
Ian & Nancy Craston.

LIME COTTAGE
Shelagh Bedford-Turner.

LINDEN COTTAGE
Philip & Anne Cutler.

LONGSTAFFES
Dorothy & Paul Bysouth.

MANDALAY
David & Vivienne Wright.
D

NEW MOUNT HOUSE
Richard & Lynda Maude-Roxby.

Burwash is a small village beautifully situated in the High Weald AONB. Gardens are situated on or close to the High St, a conservation area with numerous listed buildings dating back to the C16. The eight gardens (all bar one of which are behind listed properties) vary in size, design and planting, and are within a 550yds level walk of each other. The village has two PHs both serving food, and tea rooms that also serve lunches. The C11 parish church is worth visiting and has beautiful views over the Dudwell Valley; Rudyard Kipling's former home at Bateman's (NT) is just ½m away. Being mainly terraced properties wheelchair access to rear gardens is restricted. Access possible in four gardens.
& ✿ ☕

22 BUTLERS FARMHOUSE

Butlers Lane, Herstmonceux, BN27 1QH. Irene Eltringham-Willson, 01323 833770, irene.willson@btinternet.com, www.butlersfarmhouse.co.uk. *3m E of Hailsham. Take A271 from Hailsham, go through village of Herstmonceux, turn R signed Church Rd then approx 1m turn R. Do not use SatNav! Sat 8, Sun 9 Apr (2-5). Adm £3.50, chd free. Sat 12, Sun 13 Aug (2-5). Adm £6, chd free. Home-made teas. Jazz in the garden in Aug.* **Visits also by arrangement Mar to Oct with refreshments provided.**

Lovely rural setting for 1 acre garden surrounding C16 farmhouse with views of South Downs. Pretty in spring with primroses and hellebores. Mainly herbaceous with rainbow border, small pond, Cornish inspired beach corners. Restored to former glory, as shown in old photographs, but with a few quirky twists such as a poison garden, secret jungle garden and some naturalistic areas. Relax and listen to live jazz in the garden in Aug. Featured in an American documentary 'A World of Gardens' about the NGS. Most of garden accessible by wheelchair.
& ✿ ☕ ☕

23 NEW CAMBERLOT HALL

Camberlot Road, Lower Dicker, Hailsham, BN27 1QH. Nicky Kinghorn. *500yds S of A22 at Lower Dicker, 4½m N of A27 Drusillas r'about. From A27 Drusillas r'about through Berwick Station to Upper Dicker & L into Camberlot Rd after Plough PH, we are 1m on the L. From the A22 we are 500yds down Camberlot Rd on the R. Sat 5, Sun 6 Aug (2-5). Home-made teas. Evening opening Fri 25 Aug (5-8). Wine. Adm £4, chd free.*

A 3 acre country garden with a lovely view across fields and hills to the South Downs. Created from scratch over the last 5 yrs with all design, planting and maintenance by the owner. Lavender lined carriage driveway, naturalistic border, vegetable garden, shady garden, mini annual meadow, newly planted 30 metre white border and exotic garden. Wildflower meadow in

development. Gravel drive and some uneven ground.
& ☕

24 51 CARLISLE ROAD

Eastbourne, BN21 4JR. Mr & Mrs N Fraser-Gausden. *200yds inland from seafront (Wish Tower), close to Congress Theatre. Sat 10, Sun 11 June (11-4). Combined adm with Littleholme £4, chd free. Home-made teas.*

Walled, s-facing garden (82ft x 80ft) with mixed beds intersected by stone paths and incl small pool. Profuse and diverse planting. Wide selection of shrubs, old roses, herbaceous plants and perennials mingle with specimen trees and climbers. Constantly revised planting to maintain the magical and secluded atmosphere.
✿ ☕

25 CAXTON MANOR

Wall Hill, Forest Row, RH18 5EG. Adele & Jules Speelman. *1m N of Forest Row, 2m S of East Grinstead. From A22 take turning to Ashurstwood, entrance on L after ⅓m, or 1m on R from N. Fri 19, Sat 20 May (2-5). Adm £5, chd free. Home-made teas. Donation to St Catherine's Hospice, Crawley.*

Delightful 5 acre Japanese inspired gardens planted with mature rhododendrons, azaleas and acers surrounding large pond with boathouse, massive rockery and waterfall, beneath the home of the late Sir Archibald McIndoe (house not open). Japanese tea house and Japanese style courtyard. Featured in the Sussex Life (June 2016). **Also open 2 Quarry Cottages (separate admission)**.
✿ ☕ ☕

26 CHAMPS HILL

Waltham Park Road, Coldwaltham, Pulborough, RH20 1LY. Mr & Mrs David Bowerman, 01798 831205, mary@thebct.org.uk. *3m S of Pulborough. On A29 turn R to Fittleworth into Waltham Park Rd, garden 400 metres on R. Sun 14 May, Sun 13 Aug (2-5). Adm £5, chd free. Tea.* **Visits also by arrangement Apr to Aug for groups of 10+.**

Celebrating the 40th yr of opening,

Champs Hill has been developed around three disused sand quarries since 1960. The woodlands are full of beautiful rhododendrons and azaleas, but the most striking feature is the collection of heathers, over 300 cultivars. The garden also has some interesting sculptures, and stupendous views.

27 CHANNEL VIEW
52 Brook Barn Way, Goring-by-Sea, Worthing, BN12 4DW. Jennie & Trevor Rollings, 01903 242431, tjrollings@gmail.com. *1m W of Worthing nr seafront. Turn S off A259 into Parklands Ave, L at T-junction into Alinora Cres. Brook Barn Way is immed on L.* Sat 1, Sun 2 July (2-5). Adm £4.50, chd free. Home-made teas. Visits also by arrangement May to Sept for groups of 10-25 only.
A seaside Tudor cottage garden blending traditional and subtropical plants. Dense planting, secret rooms and intriguing sight-lines, with brick paths radiating from a wildlife pond. Shady viewpoints, sunny patios, insect friendly flowers and unusual structures supporting over a hundred roses, clematis and other climbers. Many unusual home grown plants for sale. Featured in Worthing Herald, Worthing Journal and Goring Guide 2016. Partial wheelchair access.

28 CHIDMERE GARDENS
Chidham Lane, Chidham, Chichester, PO18 8TD. Jackie & David Russell, www.chidmerefarm.com. *6m W of Chichester on A259. Turn into Chidham Lane, continue until a RH-bend, followed by a 2nd RH-bend. Chidmere Gardens is on the L immed after the large village pond.* Thur 15 June, Thur 7 Sept (2-5). Adm £5, chd free. Home-made teas. Wisteria clad C15 house (not open) surrounded by yew and hornbeam hedges situated next to Chidmere pond; a natural wildlife preserve approx 5 acres. Garden incl formal rose garden, well stocked herbaceous borders and 8 acres of orchards with wide selection of

heritage and modern varieties of apples, pears and plums incl 200 yr old varieties of Blenheim Orange and Bramley Seedling. Partial wheelchair access.

29 CISSBURY
Nepcote Lane, Findon, Worthing, BN14 0SR. Geoffrey & Etta Wyatt, 01903 899638, events@cissbury.com, www.cissbury.com. *5m N of Worthing in the hamlet of Nepcote, Findon. From A24 S follow signs to Worthing. Only turn L at the sign for Nepcote. After about 100 metres at the sharp LH-corner, turn R into Cissbury's driveway.* Thur 16, Thur 23 Mar (10-4). Adm £4, chd free. Home-made teas. Visits also by arrangement in Mar.
Set in its own parkland and grounds in the SDNP with views towards Cissbury Ring and the sea. Spectacular drifts of daffodils and snowdrops. Cedar trees and a holm oak hedge line the drive; by the pond is a metasequoia glyptostroboides. Walled kitchen garden with plots let out to Findon Gardening Club. Original L-shaped greenhouse featuring cork screw winding gear, still in partial working order. Wheelchair

access is available from the car park, around the house and walled garden.

30 ◆ CLINTON LODGE
Fletching, Uckfield, TN22 3ST. Lady Collum, 01825 722952, garden@clintonlodge.com, www.clintonlodgegardens.co.uk. *4m NW of Uckfield. Clinton Lodge is situated in Fletching High St, N of Rose & Crown PH. Off road parking provided. It is important visitors do not park in street. Parking available from 1pm.* For NGS: Sun 7 May, Mon 12, Mon 26 June, Mon 31 July (2-5.30). Adm £6, chd free. Home-made teas. For other opening times and information, please phone, email or visit garden website. *Donation to local charities.*
6 acre formal and romantic garden overlooking parkland with old roses, William Pye water feature, double white and blue herbaceous borders, yew hedges, pleached lime walks, copy of C17 scented herb garden, Medieval style potager, vine and rose allée, wild flower garden. Canal garden, small knot garden, shady glade and orchard. Caroline and Georgian house (not open).

Hoopers Farm, Mayfield Gardens

© Leigh Clapp

31 COLWOOD HOUSE

Cuckfield Lane, Warninglid,
RH17 5SP. Mr & Mrs Patrick
Brenan, 01444 461831,
rbrenan@me.com. *6m W of
Haywards Heath, 6m SE of Horsham.
Entrance on B2115 (Cuckfield
Lane). From E, N & S, turn W off A23
towards Warninglid for ¾ m. From
W come through Warninglid village.*
**Visits by arrangement Mar to
Oct for groups of 8+.** *Donation to
Seaforth Hall.*
12 acres of garden with mature and
specimen trees from the late 1800s,
lawns and woodland edge. Formal
parterre, rose and herb gardens.
100ft terrace and herbaceous
border overlooking flower rimmed
croquet lawn. Cut turf labyrinth and
forsythia tunnel. Water features,
statues and gazebos. Pets' cemetery.
Giant chessboard. Lake with island
and temple. The garden has gravel
paths and some slopes.

32 COOKSCROFT

Bookers Lane, Earnley, Chichester,
PO20 7JG. Mr & Mrs J Williams,
01243 513671, williams.
cookscroft330@btinternet.com,
www.cookscroft.co.uk. *6m S of
Chichester. At end of Birdham Straight
A286 from Chichester, take L fork
to E Wittering B2198. 1m on before
sharp bend, turn L into Bookers Lane,
2nd house on L. Parking available.*
**Evening opening Sat 13 May
(5-9). Wine. Sun 14 May (1-5).
Cream teas. Adm £5, chd free.**
**Visits also by arrangement May
to Sept, groups welcome, ample
parking.**
This is a garden for all seasons
which delights the visitor. Started in
1988, it features cottage, woodland
and Japanese style gardens, water
features and borders of perennials
with a particular emphasis on
southern hemisphere plants.
Unusual plants for the plantsman
to enjoy, many grown from seed.
Extensive open borders with
correas, corokias, leptospermum,
prostatheras and trees from 'down
under'. The garden has grass paths
and unfenced ponds.

33 NEW 43 COOMBE DROVE

Bramber, Steyning, BN44 3PW.
Lynne Broome, 01903 814170,
lynne-david-b@freedom255.com.
*From Bramber Castle r'about, take
Clays Hill signed Steyning, turn 2nd L
into Maudlin Lane, after 100 metres,
turn R into Coombe Drove. Garden at
top of road.* **Visits by arrangement
in March & June for groups of
10+. If your group is smaller, ask if
you can join another group. Adm
£4, chd free. Home-made teas.**
⅓ acre garden situated on lower
slope of the South Downs. Very
wide variety of plants, many unusual.
Portland stone terracing, with a
small but steep woodland path
with many snowdrops, hellebores,
aconites and cyclamen in spring.
In summer the garden bursts into
colour with a white bed, hot bed,
an array of containers and hanging
baskets and a beautiful pergola
covered in roses and clematis. Due
to steep slope and steps, wheelchair
access only to lower lawn.

34 COPYHOLD HOLLOW

Copyhold Lane, Borde Hill,
Haywards Heath, RH16 1XU.
Frances Druce, 01444 413265,
ngs@copyholdhollow.co.uk,
www.copyholdhollow.co.uk. *2m
N of Haywards Heath. Follow signs
for Borde Hill Gardens. With Borde
Hill Gardens on L over brow of hill,
take 1st R signed Ardingly. Garden
½ m. If the drive is full, please park
in the lane.* **Thur 6, Thur 20 Apr,
Tue 2, Tue 16 May, Thur 1, Tue
6 June, Thur 27 July, Thur 10
Aug (12-4). Adm £4, chd free.
Home-made teas. Visits also
by arrangement Apr to Aug for
groups of 4+.**
A different NGS experience,
come and find Frances scaling the
vertiginous slopes of her quarry
garden! A challenge to both visitor
and gardener. Cottage garden
surrounding C16 house (not open)
with spring fed pond, primulas,
stumpery, dizzy crow's nest viewing
platform. Garden blending into
woodland. Not a manicured garden.
Warning - some love it, others hate it!

35 CUPANI GARDEN

8 Sandgate Close, Seaford,
BN25 3LL. Dr D Jones & Ms
A Jones OBE, 01323 899452,
sweetpeasa52@gmail.com,
www.cupanigarden.com. *From
A259 follow signs to Alfriston, E of
Seaford. Turn R into Hillside Ave, L
into Hastings Ave, R into Deal Close
& R into Sandgate Close. Bus route
12A from Brighton & Eastbourne
to Hillside Ave. A walk down narrow
pathway (twitten) & garden on L.* **Fri
30 June, Tue 4, Fri 21 July (12-
5). Adm £3.50, chd free. Light
refreshments. Opening with
Seaford Gardens on Fri 14 July.
Visits also by arrangement June
& July. Adm incl refreshments.
Combined visit with Driftwood
for larger groups.**
Cupani Garden is a green and
tranquil haven with a delightful
mix of trees, shrubs and perennial
borders in different themed
beds. Courtyard garden, gazebo,
summerhouse, water feature, sweet
pea obelisks, huge range of plants
in all seasons. Plenty of places to
sit and enjoy, either in the shade or
under cover. Delicious afternoon tea
and a good range of lunches, phone
in advance if any special dietary
needs (always vegetarian options).
Plants, jams, books and china for
sale. Great venue for group outings
or celebrations. Mostly flat but with
a small number of steps into the
courtyard. Paths to the WC are
narrow, so not suitable for wide
based wheelchairs.

36 DACHS

Spear Hill, Ashington, RH20 3BA.
Bruce Wallace, 01903 892466,
wallacebuk@aol.com. *Approx
6m N of Worthing. From A24 at
Ashington onto B2133 Billingshurst
Rd, R into Spear Hill. We are the 1st
house, garden runs along Billingshurst
Rd.* **Sun 13, Sun 20 Aug (2.30-
5.30). Adm £4.50, chd free.
Home-made teas. Visits also by
arrangement Apr to Sept for
day or eve visits.**
A waterlogged field turned into a
beautiful garden of about 2 acres
incl white garden, bog area and
stream. Several other themed

beds with perennials of different textures and colours. Large number of dahlias. Free gifts for children to encourage them to grow things. Large number of plants for sale at economical prices. Featured in Sussex Life.

🚶 🐕 ❀ 🚗 ☕ 🍷

37 DALE PARK HOUSE
Madehurst, Arundel, BN18 0NP. Robert & Jane Green, 01243 814260, robertgreen@farming.co.uk. *4m W of Arundel. Take A27 E from Chichester or W from Arundel, then A29 (London) for 2m, turn L to Madehurst & follow red arrows. Sun 11 June (2-5). Adm £4.50, chd free. Home-made teas.* **Visits also by arrangement May to Aug for any size group.**
Set in parkland within the SDNP, enjoying magnificent views to the sea. Come and relax in the large walled garden which features an impressive 200ft herbaceous border. There is also a sunken gravel garden, mixed borders, a small rose garden, dreamy rose and clematis arches, interesting collection of hostas, foliage plants and shrubs, an orchard and kitchen garden.

❀ 🚗 ☕

38 NEW 47 DENMANS LANE
Lindfield, Haywards Heath, RH16 2JN. Sue & Jim Stockwell, 01444 459363, jamesastockwell@aol.com, www.lindfield-gardens.co.uk/47denmans-lane. *Approx 1½m NE of Haywards Heath town centre. From Haywards Heath railway station follow B2028 signed Lindfield & Ardingly for 1m. At T-lights turn L into Hickmans Lane, then after 100 metres take 1st R into Denmans Lane. Visits by arrangement Mar to Oct for groups of 10-40. Adm incl tea, coffee & biscuits or home-made cakes. Adm £8, chd free.*
A beautiful and tranquil 1 acre garden created by the owners, Sue and Jim Stockwell, over the past 20 yrs. The garden is divided into different areas planted for interest throughout the yr. Spring bulbs and woodland flowers from Feb to May followed by azaleas, rhododendrons,

alliums, roses, and herbaceous perennials. The garden also incl ponds, vegetable and fruit gardens. NB: Deep water. Most of the garden accessible by wheelchair, but some areas involve steep slopes.

🚶 ❀ 🚗 ☕ 🍷

39 DITTONS END
Southfields Road, Eastbourne, BN21 1BZ. Mrs Frances Hodkinson, 01323 647163. *Town centre, ⅓m from train station. Off A259 in Southfields Rd. House directly opp Dittons Rd. 3 doors from NGS open garden Hardwycke. Sun 18 June, Sun 20 Aug (11-5). Combined adm with Hardwycke £5, chd free. Home-made teas at Hardwycke.* **Visits also by arrangement May to Sept.**
Lovely well maintained, small town garden. At the back, a very pretty garden (35ft x 20ft) with small lawn area, patio surrounded by a selection of pots and packed borders with lots of colour. In the front a compact lawn with colourful borders (25ft x 18ft). No steps.

🚶 🐕 ❀ 🛏 ☕

40 DOWN PLACE
South Harting, Petersfield, GU31 5PN. Mr & Mrs D M Thistleton-Smith, 01730 825374, selina@downplace.co.uk. *1m SE of South Harting. B2141 to Chichester, turn L down unmarked lane below top of hill. Sat 22, Sun 23 Apr, Sat 17, Sun 18 June (2-6). Adm £4, chd free. Home-made teas.* **Visits also by arrangement Apr to July for groups of 15+. Donation to Friends of Harting Church.**
7 acre hillside, chalk garden on the north side of the South Downs with fine views of surrounding countryside. Extensive herbaceous, shrub and rose borders on different levels merging into natural wild flower meadow renowned for its collection of native orchids. Fully stocked vegetable garden and greenhouses. Spring flowers and blossom. Substantial top terrace and borders accessible to wheelchairs.

🚶 ❀ ☕

41 DRIFTWOOD
4 Marine Drive, Bishopstone, Seaford, BN25 2RS. Geoff Stonebanks & Mark Glassman, 01323 899296, geoffstonebanks@gmail.com, www.driftwoodbysea.co.uk. *A259 between Seaford & Newhaven. Turn L into Marine Drive from Bishopstone Rd, 2nd on R. Please park carefully in road, but not on bend beyond house. Tue 20 June, Tue 11, Tue 25 July, Sun 6 Aug (11-5). Adm £4, chd free.* **Visits also by arrangement June & July for groups of 4-20, incl personal guided tour. Combined with Cupani Garden for larger groups.**
Monty Don said on BBC 2 Gardeners' World feature in Sept 2016 'It's a small garden by the sea with inspired planting and design'. The Sunday Telegraph said 'Geoff's enthusiasm is catching, and he and his amazing garden deserve every visitor that makes their way up his enchanting garden path'. This characterful and exuberant seaside garden is 112ft x 40ft. This is a real must see garden say many TripAdvisor visitors. Large selection of home-made cakes and savoury items available, all served on vintage china, on trays in the garden. In 2016, Driftwood was a finalist, runner-up in Gardeners' World, Garden of The Year (Small Space). Featured in Period Homes & Interiors (July) and was a local news item on BBC South East Today (Sept). Steep drive, narrow paths and many levels with steps, but help readily available on-site or call ahead before visit.

🐕 ❀ 🍷

The National Garden Scheme is the largest single funder of the Queen's Nursing Institute

42 NEW DURFORD ABBEY BARN

Petersfield, GU31 5AU. Mr & Mrs Lund, tinwhistles@hotmail.com.
3m from Petersfield. Situated on the S side of A272 between Petersfield & Rogate, 1m from the junction with B2072. Visits by arrangement on Sat 24, Sun 25 June (1-5.30). Pre-booking essential due to limited parking. Adm £4, chd free. Delicious home-made teas.
With lovely views across open countryside to the South Downs, this 1 acre garden is set around a converted barn in the National Park. It has distinct levels and areas incl cottage garden with roses and herbaceous borders, a natural pond, shady vine covered pergola, productive vegetable terrace, lawns and shrubberies, prairie border, and seating placed to soak up the views. Partial wheelchair access as some areas have quite steep grass slopes to negotiate.

43 DURFORD MILL HOUSE

West Harting, Petersfield, GU31 5AZ. Mrs Sue Jones, 01730 821125,
sdurford@btinternet.com. *3m E of Petersfield. Turn off A272 between Petersfield & Rogate, signed Durford Mill & the Hartings. From Chichester into South Harting past village shop, 1st L to West Harting.* Sat 3, Sun 4 June (2-5.30). Adm £4, chd free. Home-made teas. Visits also by arrangement.
Come and relax in our peaceful mill garden with its meandering stream and quiet places to sit. Wander along the paths and over the bridges among the flowers, shrubs and beautiful trees. Finishing up with delicious home-made cakes and tea. Wheelchair access to main garden and tea area.

44 DURRANCE MANOR

Smithers Hill Lane, Shipley, RH13 8PE. Gordon & Joan Lindsay, 01403 741577, galindsay@gmail.com. *7m SW of Horsham. A24 to A272 (S from Horsham, N from Worthing), turn W towards Billingshurst. Approx 1¾m, 2nd L Smithers Hill Lane signed to Countryman PH. Garden 2nd on L.* Mon 28 Aug (2-6). Adm £5, chd free. Home-made teas. Visits also by arrangement Apr to Oct.
This 2 acre garden surrounding a Medieval hall house (not open) with Horsham stone roof, enjoys uninterrupted views over a ha-ha of the South Downs and Chanctonbury Ring. There are Japanese inspired gardens, a large pond, wild flower meadow and orchard, colourful long borders, hosta walk, and vegetable garden. A Monet style bridge over a pond with waterlilies should be in place in 2017.

45 NEW EAST LODGE

Tortington Lane, Arundel, BN18 0UX. Carol & Patrick Hill. *1m W of Arundel on the A27 opp the White Swan Hotel, turn into Tortington Lane. Parking in field as signed just past East Lodge.* Sat 10 June (11-5). Adm £4, chd free. Home-made teas.
This ⅓ acre garden is a hidden oasis full of cottage plants, acers and maples, with a pond and a small vegetable garden, and several secluded seating areas all surrounded by mature trees. Sadly, not suitable for wheelchair users.

46 NEW 6 ELM AVENUE

East Preston, Littlehampton, BN16 1HJ. Helen & Derek Harnden, 07870 324654, derek@shiningmylight.plus.com. *Over railway crossing from A259, turn L into North Lane. Continue straight onto Golden Ave. Elm Ave crosses Golden Ave, turn R for No 6.* Wed 24, Thur 25 May, Sat 16, Sun 17 Sept (11-5). Adm £4.50, chd free. Light refreshments. Visits also by arrangement May to Sept for groups of 10+. If your group is smaller, ask if you can join another group.
S-facing garden 154ft × 49ft, in its second yr. A stunning Purbeck stone wall with moon gate bisects the garden, creating two distinct halves. Within these, there are several sections incl contemporary fish pond with stainless steel waterfall, circular lawns surrounded by herbaceous borders with a variety of grasses and trees for yr-round interest. Japanese area, vegetables, fruit cages and much more. Our terrace overlooks the garden, and refreshments will be served from here, including our special coffee, for that extra little treat. Right side of the house has direct access to the garden on flat paving.

47 54 ELMLEIGH

Midhurst, GU29 9HA. Wendy Liddle, 07796 562275, wendyliddle@btconnect.com. *¼m W of Midhurst off A272. Wheelchair users please use designated parking spaces at top of drive, phone on arrival for assistance.* Sats & Suns 3, 4, 17, 18 June, 1, 2, 15, 16 July (10-5). Adm £3.50, chd free. Home-made teas. Visits also by arrangement May to Sept. Coaches please drop off visitors, then park in Midhurst Coach Park.
Come and walk around this beautiful, award-winning garden on the edge of Midhurst. Planted with majestic Scots pines, shrubs, perennials and annuals, packed with interest, a tapestry of unusual plants giving all season colour. Many raised beds and numerous statues. A child-friendly garden. New wildlife pond, bog garden and stumpery.

48 FAIRLIGHT END

Pett Road, Pett, Hastings, TN35 4HB. Chris & Robin Hutt, 07774 863750, chrishutt@btopenworld.com, www.fairlightend.co.uk. *4m E of Hastings. From Hastings take A259 to Rye. At White Hart Beefeater turn R into Friars Hill. Descend into Pett village. Park in village hall car park, opp house.* Sat 24, Sun 25 June (11-5). Adm £5, chd free. Home-made teas & Pimms.
Visits also by arrangement May to Sept for groups of 10+. *Donation to Pett Village Hall.*
Gardens Illustrated, June 2016,

said 'The 18th century house is at the highest point in the garden with views down the slope over abundant borders and velvety lawns that are punctuated by clusters of specimen trees and shrubs. Beyond and below are the wild flower meadows and the ponds with a backdrop of the gloriously unspoilt Wealden landscape'. As seen on ITV's 'Love your Garden' with Alan Titchmarsh, 2017. Steep paths, gravelled areas, unfenced ponds.

♿ ☕ ▯ ☕ ⚘

49 FAIRLIGHT HALL
Martineau Lane, Hastings, TN35 5DR. Mr & Mrs David Kowitz, www.fairlighthall.co.uk. *2m E of Hastings. A259 from Hastings towards Dover & Rye, 2m turn R into Martineau Lane.* **Thur 3 Aug (10-4). Adm £6, chd free. Sat 16, Sun 17 Sept (10-4). Adm £8, chd free. Light refreshments.**
A recently restored stunning garden in East Sussex. The formal gardens extend over 9 acres and surround the Victorian Gothic mansion. Features semitropical woodland avenues, a huge contemporary walled garden with amphitheatre and two 110 metre perennial borders above and below ha-ha with far reaching views across Rye Bay. Sept opening will incorporate a large Plant Fair. Most of the garden can be viewed by wheelchair, please inform us when you arrive, so we can direct you to a disabled parking place.

♿ ⚘ ☕

50 FITTLEWORTH HOUSE
Bedham Lane, Fittleworth, Pulborough, RH20 1JH. Edward & Isabel Braham, 01798 865074, marksaunders66.com@gmail.com, www.marksaunders66.com. *2m E, SE of Petworth. Midway between Petworth & Pulborough on the A283 in Fittleworth, turn into lane by sharp bend signed Bedham. Garden is 50yds along on the L.* **Every Wed 3 May to 26 July (2-5). Adm £5, chd free. Wed 9, Wed 16 Aug (2-5). Adm by donation. Home-made teas. Visits also by arrangement Apr to Aug for groups of 5+.**

3 acre tranquil country garden featuring working walled kitchen garden with long herbaceous borders and a wide range of fruit and vegetables. Large glasshouse and old potting shed, mixed flower borders, rose beds, rhododendrons and lawns. Magnificent 112ft tall cedar overlooks wisteria covered Grade II listed Georgian house (not open). Wildlife pond, wild garden, long grass areas and spring bulbs. The two Aug openings by donation will focus on families with invisible disabilities such as Autism and Tourettes. Picnics welcome. Please contact us for further information. The garden sits on a gentle slope but is accessible for wheelchairs and buggies. Non-disabled WC.

♿ ⚘ ☕ 🚌 ☕

51 FIVE OAKS COTTAGE
Petworth, RH20 1HD. Jean & Steve Jackman, 07939 272443, jeanjackman@hotmail.com. *5m S of Pulborough. SatNav does not work! To ensure best route, please ring or email & printed directions will be provided.* **Visits by arrangement in July for groups of 5-35, from 9.30am-8.30pm. Happy to do tea & cake or wine & nibbles. Adm £5, chd free.**
An acre of delicate jungle surrounding an Arts and Crafts style cottage, owned by artists and founders of The Floral Fringe Fair. Stunning views of the South Downs from an unconventional garden, which is designed to encourage maximum wildlife. Knapweed meadow on clay attracting clouds of butterflies in July, two small ponds and lots of seating. Exhibition of paintings.

☕

52 FLETCHING SECRET GARDENS
High Street, Fletching, Uckfield, TN22 3SS. *4m NW of Uckfield. Parking signed to Church Farm, Church St, TN22 3SP. Tickets at each garden.* **Sat 8 July (12-5). Combined adm £4, chd free. Home-made teas at 4 Corner Cottages.**

4 CORNER COTTAGES
Mrs Jackie Pateman.

STONES
Belinda & David Croft.

In the heart of the picturesque village of Fletching and near the historic church are two small, welcoming cottage style gardens, each with their own character. 4 Corner Cottages where home-made teas will be served, has a small restful garden, tucked behind the High St, with a pond, water feature, small white border and more. Stunning views across farmland to Sheffield Park. Close by, the garden at Stones is packed with interest in a relatively small space. Colourful hanging baskets and pots, vegetable plot, fruiting kiwi climber, cardoon bed and mistletoe. The edge of the garden is wild to provide habitat for birds and wildlife. Castle for children to climb into under supervision. Linger in the tranquility of these gardens and ask the owners about their plants and gardens. Partial wheelchair access to some parts of the gardens.

♿ ☕

Durford Mill House

© Judi Lion

Clinton Lodge

53 FOLLERS MANOR

White Way, Alfriston, BN26 5TT.
Geoff & Anne Shaw,
anne.shaw1@hotmail.com,
www.follersmanor.co.uk. ½m S of
Alfriston. From Alfriston uphill towards
Seaford. Park on L in paddock before
garden. Garden next door to the old
Alfriston Youth Hostel immed before
road narrows. **Sat 24, Sun 25
June (12-5). Adm £5, chd free.
Home-made teas.**
Contemporary garden designed
by Ian Kitson attached to C17
listed historic farmhouse. Entrance
courtyard, sunken garden,
herbaceous displays, wildlife pond,
wild flower meadows, woodland
area and beautiful views of the
South Downs. Winner of Sussex
Heritage Trust Award and three
awards from the Society of Garden
Designers; Best Medium Residential
Garden, Hard Landscaping and, most
prestigious, the Judges Award. New
for 2017, a newly designed area of
the garden by original designer Ian
Kitson. We have no idea what he will
come up with so all very exciting
judging by his previous efforts. In
2016 featured in Mon Jardin & Ma
Maison in June (French), Nest Jardins
in Spring (Belgium), and Nest Tuinen
in Spring (Dutch).
✿ ▨ 🛏 ☕

54 FOXGLOVE COTTAGE

29 Orchard Road, Horsham,
RH13 5NF. Peter & Terri Lefevre,
01403 256002,
teresalefevre@outlook.com.
Horsham Station. Over bridge signed

Crawley, 1st r'about 4th exit, 1st L
Station Rd signed Brighton, 1st L
Depot Rd, 3rd R Orchard Rd. From
A281 Clarance Rd B2180 to 5th R
Depot Rd. Street parking. **Sun 25
June, Sun 9 July (1-5). Adm £4,
chd free. Cream teas. Visits also
by arrangement June & July for
groups of 10+.**
Unusual 150ft x 50ft plantaholic's
garden with a plethora of planted
containers, quirky vintage finds
and gardenalia. Gravel and bark
paths are interspersed by planting
areas encompassing sun drenched
and shady borders, with plenty
of seating dotted about. A beach
inspired summerhouse and decking
are flanked by a water feature; the
end of the garden is dedicated to
propagation, cut flowers and fruit
growing.
✿ ☕ 🐾

55 THE GARDEN HOUSE

5 Warleigh Road, Brighton,
BN1 4NT. Bridgette Saunders &
Graham Lee,
07729 037182, contact@
gardenhousebrighton.co.uk,
www.gardenhousebrighton.co.uk.
1½m N of Brighton Pier. The Garden
House can be found 1½m N of
seafront, 1st L off Ditching Rd, past
T-lights. Street paid parking available.
**Sat 29, Sun 30 Apr (11.30-
4.30). Adm £3.50, chd free.
Home-made teas. Visits also by
arrangement Mar to Sept for
groups of 10+.**
Tucked away in the heart of the
city this really is a secret garden, in
Victorian times a market garden.
The garden is organic and gives
interest all yr, supporting cut flowers,
vegetables, fruit, old climbing roses
and a pond. Many of the plants
have been propagated by the
garden owner, and the garden has
unique features using many recycled
materials. Garden produce and
plants for sale.
✿ ☕

56 GARDENERS' COTTAGE

West Dean, Chichester,
PO18 0RX. Jim Buckland & Sarah
Wain. 6m N of Chichester. Off A286
follow signs to West Dean Gardens

& park in car park. Follow signs to
cottage. **Sun 14 May (11-5). Adm
£3.50, chd free. Cream teas.**
The home garden of the husband
and wife Head Gardener team
at the neighbouring West Dean
Gardens. Small, serene and
secluded theatrical retreat with
strong emphasis on texture, foliage
and good structure created by
trees, topiary, labyrinthine paths,
and interesting spaces. Separate
courtyard garden with pond and
extensive pot grown succulent,
hosta and fern collections. Delicious
range of home-made cakes, good
tea and coffee.

57 THE GRANGE

Hesworth Lane, Fittleworth,
Pulborough, RH20 1EW. Mr & Mrs
W Caldwell. 3m W of Pulborough.
From Pulborough or Petworth on
reaching Fittleworth turn S onto
B2138, then W at Swan PH. From
the S, turn L off A29 onto B2138 at
Bury Gate, then L again at Swan PH.
Please do not use SatNav. **Sat 22,
Sun 23 July, Sun 3 Sept (2-5).
Adm £4.50, chd free. Home-
made teas.**
3 acre garden gently sloping to the
R Rother surrounding pretty C18
house (not open). Formal areas
enclosed by yew hedges comprising
colour themed beds, potager,
small orchard and herbaceous
borders containing a wide variety
of interesting plants. The garden has
gravel paths.
♿ 🐕 ✿ ☕

58 6 GRANGE ROAD

Lewes, BN7 1TR. Bridget
Millmore. Gate between 2 &
3 Grange Rd. 350 metres W of
Southover Grange Gardens & the
historic cobbled Keere St. **Sun 25
June (2-5.30). Adm £4, chd free.
Home-made teas.**
Hidden historic town garden
established in the 1930s by the
Martin sisters and developed since
the 1980s by the late Paul Millmore.
Accessed via steps to a narrow
cobbled passageway which opens
out to reveal a truly secret garden.
½ acre in size, laid out formally
with brick paviour paths, perennial

borders, pond, mature trees and topiary. A magical space in the midst of bustling urban life.

59 GRAVETYE MANOR

West Hoathly, RH19 4LJ. Jeremy & Elizabeth Hosking, 01342 810567, info@gravetyemanor.co.uk, www.gravetyemanor.co.uk. *From M23, J10 East Grinstead, A264 Dukes Head, B2028 Turner's Hill. After Turner's Hill take L fork for Sharpthorne, then take first L into Vowels Lane.* Sat 1 July (2-5). Adm £20, chd free. Pre-booking essential, please visit www.ngs. org.uk or phone 01483 211535 for information & booking. Adm incl tea & home-made cake.
The gardens at Gravetye Manor can be considered amongst the most influential in English gardening history. The manor was the home of revolutionary gardener, William Robinson, from 1884-1935. Thanks to the backing of new owners a major restoration project has now been underway for 6 yrs, overseen by head gardener Tom Coward, formerly of Great Dixter. Parts of the garden are accessible via ramps.

60 ◆ GREAT DIXTER HOUSE, GARDENS & NURSERIES

Northiam, TN31 6PH. Great Dixter Charitable Trust, 01797 253107, office@greatdixter.co.uk, www.greatdixter.co.uk. *8m N of Rye. ½m W of Northiam off A28, follow brown signs.* For opening times and information, please phone, email or visit garden website.
Designed by Edwin Lutyens and Nathaniel Lloyd. Christopher Lloyd officiated over these gardens for 50 yrs creating one of the most experimental and constantly changing gardens of our time, a tradition now being carried on by Fergus Garrett. Clipped topiary, wild flower meadows, pot displays and the famous Long Border and Exotic Garden.

61 GREAT LYWOOD FARMHOUSE

Lindfield Road, Ardingly, RH17 6SW. Richard & Susan Laing, 01444 892500, splaing@btinternet.com. *2½m N of Haywards Heath. Between Lindfield & Ardingly on B2028. From Lindfield, after ¾m turn L (W) down signed paved track. 1st house on R, car park beyond house.* Mon 29 May, Fri 2, Sun 4 June (2-6). Adm £5, chd free. Home-made teas. Visits also by arrangement in June for groups of 10+, no coaches.
Approx 1½ acre garden surrounding C17 Sussex farmhouse (not open). The extensive but accessible and gentle terracing provides immediate views of many different aspects of the garden and distant views towards the South Downs. There are garden seats on every level making this a garden in which to rest and enjoy the countryside. Wheelchair access possible, some slopes and short grass.

62 HAM COTTAGE

Hammingden Lane, Highbrook, Ardingly, RH17 6SR. Peter & Andrea Browne, 01444 892746, aegbrowne@btinternet.com. *5m N of Haywards Heath. On B2028 1m S of Ardingly turn into Burstow Hill Lane. Signed to Highbrook, then follow NGS signs.* Sun 21 May, Sun 6 Aug (2-5). Adm £5, chd free. Home-made teas. Visits also by arrangement Apr to Sept.
8 acre garden created from agricultural land during the last 20 yrs by the present owners. The garden is now well established with yr-round colour bursting from the many borders, large bog garden and winter garden. A gentle stream flows down over waterfalls into a bluebell carpeted wood. Above the arboretum there is an amphitheatre within an old sandstone quarry.

63 HAMMERWOOD HOUSE

Iping, Midhurst, GU29 0PF. Mr & Mrs M Lakin. *3m W of Midhurst. Take A272 from Midhurst, approx 2m outside Midhurst turn R for Iping. From A3 leave for Liphook, follow B2070, turn L for Milland & Iping.* Sun 9, Sun 16 Apr (1.30-5). Adm £5, chd free. Home-made teas. *Donation to Iping Church.*
Large s-facing garden with lots of mature shrubs incl camellias, rhododendrons and azaleas. An arboretum with a variety of flowering and fruit trees. The old yew and beech hedges give a certain amount of formality to this traditional English garden. Tea on the terrace is a must with the most beautiful view of the South Downs. For the more energetic there is a woodland walk. Partial wheelchair access as garden is set on a slope.

64 HARBOURSIDE

Prinsted Lane, Prinsted, Emsworth, PO10 8HS. Ann Moss, 01243 370048, ann.moss8@btinternet.com. *6m E of Chichester. Turn off A27 Tesco r'about onto A259 W, after 2nd r'about take 2nd turning on L. Chinese takeaway on corner, follow road until forced to turn R at Scout Hut. House next door with boat in front garden.* Visits by arrangement for groups of 12-24. Various refreshment options available, please call and ask.
Award-winning coastal garden takes you on a journey through garden styles from around the world. Visit France, Holland, Spain, New Zealand and Japan. View and enjoy tree ferns, topiary, shady area, secret woodland parlor, potager, containers, unusual shrubs, silver birch walk and herbaceous borders for yr-round interest. Wide variety of plants, music, seating, art and crafts. Wheelchair access to most of the garden, after 10ft of gravel at the garden entrance.

65 HARDWYCKE

Southfields Road, Eastbourne, BN21 1BZ. Lois Machin, 01323 729391, loisandpeter@yahoo.co.uk. *Centre of Eastbourne, Upperton. A259 towards Eastbourne, Southfields Rd on R just before junction with A2270 (Upperton Rd). Limited parking, public car park (pay) in Southfields Rd.* Sun 18 June, Sun 20 Aug (11-5). Combined adm with Dittons End £5, chd free. Home-made teas. **Visits also by arrangement Apr to Aug for groups of 10-25. Refreshments on request.** Delightful s-facing town garden mainly of chalky soil, with many usual and unusual plants. Separate vegetable garden with restored 1920s summerhouse. Wide selection of shrubs incl fifty types of clematis. L-shaped garden that has two spaces 70ft × 50ft and 18ft × 50ft. Wheelchair access with care, two slight steps to rear garden area

  ♿ 🐕 ❋ ☕ 🍵

National Garden Scheme support helps raise awareness of unpaid carers

66 ◆ GARDENS & GROUNDS OF HERSTMONCEUX CASTLE

Herstmonceux, Hailsham, BN27 1RN. Bader International Study Centre, Queen's University (Canada), 01323 833816, c_harber@bisc.queensu.ac.uk, www.herstmonceux-castle.com. *Located between Herstmonceux & Pevensey on the Wartling Rd. From Herstmonceux take A271 to Bexhill, 2nd R signed Castle. Do not use SatNav.* For NGS: Sat 27 May (10-6). Adm £6, chd £3. Cream teas & light lunches in Chestnuts Tearoom. **For other opening times and information, please phone, email or visit garden website.**

Herstmonceux is renowned for its magnificent moated castle set in beautiful parkland and superb Elizabethan walled gardens, leading to delightful discoveries such as our rhododendron, rose and herb gardens and onto our woodland trails. Take a slow stroll past the lily covered lakes to the 1930s folly and admire the sheer magnificence of the castle. The Gardens & Grounds first opened for the NGS in 1927. Featured in The Telegraph (June 2016). Partial wheelchair access to formal gardens.

  ♿ 🐄 ❋ 🚌 ☕ 🍵

GROUP OPENING

67 HERSTMONCEUX PARISH TRAIL

Hailsham, BN27 4JF. *4m NE of Hailsham. 5m S of Heathfield or Herstmonceux. Herstmonceux Parish Trail can start at Cowbeech House in the centre of Cowbeech village, opp the Merrie Harriers PH or at any other garden listed. Map of the trail will be provided.* Sun 2 July (12-5). Combined adm £5, chd free. Light refreshments in the café at Lime Cross Nursery (closes at 4.30pm).

2 ACRES
Di Tate.

THE ALLOTMENTS, STUNTS GREEN
George Taylor.

COWBEECH HOUSE
Mr Anthony Hepburn.

1 ELM COTTAGES
Audrey Jarrett.

MONTANA
Paul & Caroline Lucas.

Five gardens will open as part of the Herstmonceux Parish Trail this yr. Cowbeech House has an exciting range of water features in the garden that dates back to 1731. 2 Acres is on the same site as Lime Cross Nursery who are making their café and WC available to trail visitors. 2 Acres has mature trees and a large pond with fish. A short short ½m stroll or drive into Windmill Hill brings you to 1 Elm

Cottages, a stunning cottage garden packed full of edible and flowering plants you cannot afford to miss; particularly impressive as this space was transformed from wasteland into the garden that it is today. The Allotments comprise of 54 allotments growing a huge variety of traditional and unusual crops. Montana is a romantic garden with beautiful planting.

❋ ☕

68 ◆ HIGH BEECHES WOODLAND AND WATER GARDEN

High Beeches Lane, Handcross, Haywards Heath, RH17 6HQ. High Beeches Gardens Conservation Trust, 01444 400589, gardens@highbeeches.com, www.highbeeches.com. *5m NW of Cuckfield. On B2110, 1m E of A23 at Handcross.* For NGS: Sun 11 June, Sun 24 Sept (1-5). Adm £7.50, chd free. Cream teas in the High Beeches Tea Room. **For other opening times and information, please phone, email or visit garden website.** 25 acres of enchanting landscaped woodland and water gardens with spring daffodils, bluebells and azalea walks, many rare and beautiful plants, an ancient wild flower meadow and glorious autumn colours. Picnic area. National Collection of Stewartias.

🚌 NPC ☕

69 ◆ HIGHDOWN GARDENS

33 Highdown Rise, Littlehampton Road, Goring-by-Sea, Worthing, BN12 6FB. Worthing Borough Council, 01903 501054, highdown. gardens@adur-worthing.gov.uk, www.highdowngardens.co.uk. *3m W of Worthing. Off A259 approx 1m from Goring-by-Sea Train Station.* For NGS: Sun 30 Apr, Wed 31 May (10-6). Adm by donation. **For other opening times and information, please phone, email or visit garden website.** Famous garden created by Sir Frederick Stern situated on downland countryside in a chalk pit. The garden contains a wide

collection of plants; many were raised from seed brought from China by great collectors like Wilson, Farrer and Kingdon-Ward. In 2016, winner of Gold Award South East in Bloom Heritage Section, Green Flag Award, and TripAdvisor Certificate of Excellence. Partial wheelchair access to hillside garden with mainly grass paths.

 NPC

Jacaranda

© Judi Lion

70 4 HILLSIDE COTTAGES

Downs Road, West Stoke, Chichester, PO18 9BL. Heather & Chris Lock, 01243 574802, chlock@btinternet.com. *3m NW of Chichester. From A286 at Lavant, head W for 1½ m, nr Kingley Vale.* Sun 23 July (2-5). Adm £3.50, chd free. Home-made teas.

Visits also by arrangement June to Aug.
Garden 120ft x 27ft in a rural setting, densely planted with mixed borders and shrubs. Large collection of roses, mainly New English shrub roses; walls, fences and arches covered with mid and late season clematis; baskets overflowing with fuchsias. A profusion of colour and scent in a well maintained small garden.

71 HOLLY HOUSE

Beaconsfield Road, Chelwood Gate, Haywards Heath, RH17 7LF. Mrs Deirdre Birchell, 01825 740484, db@hollyhousebnb.co.uk, www.hollyhousebnb.co.uk. *7m E of Haywards Heath. From Nutley village on A22 turn off at Hathi Restaurant signed Chelwood Gate 2m. Chelwood Gate Village Hall on R, Holly House is opp the village hall.* Sat 13, Sun 14 May, Sat 15, Sun 16 July, Sat 19, Sun 20 Aug (2-5). Adm £4.50, chd free. Home-made teas.

Visits also by arrangement May to Aug.
An acre of English garden providing views and cameos of plants and trees round every corner with many different areas giving constant interest. A fish pond and a wildlife pond beside a grassy area with many shrubs and flower beds. Among the trees and winding paths

there is a cottage garden which is a profusion of colour and peace. Exhibition of paintings and cards by owner. Garden accessible by wheelchair in good weather, but it is not easy.

72 THE HOMEGROWN FLOWER COMPANY

The Old Forge, Butchers Cross, Five Ashes, Mayfield, TN20 6JN. Zelie Billins, www.thehomegrownflowercompany.co.uk. *¼ m NE of Five Ashes. From Five Ashes village proceed N on A267 towards Mayfield. Turn L on Skippers Hill for parking on lane.* Wed 21 June, Wed 19 July, Wed 16 Aug (1-5). Adm £4, chd free. Home-made teas.
A well stocked garden in a beautiful setting with views over the High Weald AONB. Ornamental garden surrounding self-built oak framed house incl decorative cut flower beds, a topiary and grasses border, greenhouse and small vegetable plot with raised beds. Large working cut flower plot in field (some uneven ground and slopes) supplying an abundance of flowers and foliages for floristry business. Cut flowers for sale.

73 JACARANDA

Chalk Road, Ifold, RH14 0UE. Brian & Barbara McNulty, 01403 751532, bmcn0409@icloud.com. *1m S of Loxwood. From A272/A281 take B2133 (Loxwood). ½ m S of Loxwood take Plaistow Rd, then 3rd R into Chalk Rd. Follow signs for parking & garden. Wheelchair users can park in driveway.* Sun 3 Sept (2-5). Adm £4, chd free. Home-made teas.
Visits also by arrangement Apr to Oct for groups of 20 max.

A ¼ acre garden created from a bare plot by the current owners. Curving borders contain perennials, roses, climbers, bulbs and many interesting trees and shrubs. An old walnut tree provides a shady home for a Hosta Theatre. The kitchen garden has a large raised bed, a greenhouse, a herb garden in pots, and a potting bench and compost area. A delightfully tranquil plant lover's garden. Featured in Sussex Life (Sept 2016).

74 ◆ KING JOHN'S LODGE

Sheepstreet Lane, Etchingham, TN19 7AZ. Jill Cunningham, 01580 819220, harry@kingjohnsnursery.co.uk, www.kingjohnsnursery.co.uk. *2m W of Hurst Green. A265 Burwash to Etchingham. Turn L before Etchingham Church into Church Lane which leads into Sheepstreet Lane after ½ m. Turn L after 1m.* For NGS: Sun 26 Mar, Sat 6, Sun 7 May, Sat 24, Sun 25 June, Sun 10 Sept (11-5). Adm £5, chd free. Home-made teas & lunches in the tearoom of King John's Nursery. **For other opening times and information, please phone, email or visit garden website.**
4 acre romantic garden for all seasons surrounding an historic listed house (not open). Formal garden with water features, rose walk and wild garden and pond. Rustic bridge to shaded ivy garden, large herbaceous borders, old shrub roses and secret garden. Further 4 acres of meadows, fine trees and grazing sheep. Nursery and shop. Garden is mainly flat. Stepped areas can usually be accessed from other areas. No disabled WC.

75 KNEPP CASTLE

West Grinstead, Horsham, RH13 8LJ. Sir Charles & Lady Burrell. *8m S of Horsham. Turning to Shipley off the A272. ½ m to entrance on L. Follow driveway through the parkland.* Sun 17 Sept (11-5). Adm £5, chd free. Home-made teas.

Recently designed and replanted garden surrounding Knepp Castle (not open). Main garden dominated by three old Cedar of Lebanon, clipped yew, box and a ha-ha overlooking the spectacular lake and Repton Park, with free roaming deer, cattle and Exmoor ponies. Sympathetic planting to reflect the landscape, 2 acre walled garden containing vegetables, fruit, flowers, herbs and a pool.

76 LEGSHEATH FARM

Legsheath Lane, nr Forest Row, RH19 4JN. Mr & Mrs M Neal, legsheath@btinternet.com. *4m S of East Grinstead. 2m W of Forest Row, 1m S of Weirwood Reservoir.* Sun 21 May (2-4.30). Adm £5, chd free. Home-made teas. **Visits also by arrangement Apr to Sept for groups of 15+.** *Donation to Holy Trinity Church, Forest Row.*

Panoramic views over Weirwood Reservoir. Exciting 10 acre garden with woodland walks, water gardens and formal borders. Of particular interest, clumps of wild orchids, fine davidia, acers, eucryphia and rhododendrons. Mass planting of different species of meconopsis on the way to ponds.

77 LIMEKILN FARM

Chalvington Road, Chalvington, Hailsham, BN27 3TA. Dr J Hester & Mr M Royle. *10m N of Eastbourne. Nr Hailsham. Turn S off A22 at Golden Cross & follow the Chalvington Rd for 1m. The entrance has white gates on the LH-side. Disabled parking space close to the house, other parking 100 metres further along road.* Sat 19, Sun 20 Aug (2-5). Adm £5, chd free. Home-made teas in the Oast House.

The garden was designed in the 1930s when the house was owned by Charles Stewart Taylor, MP for Eastbourne. It has not changed in basic layout since then. The planting aims to reflect the age of the C17 property and original garden design. The house and garden are mentioned in Virginia Woolf's diaries of 1929, depicting a dilapidated charm that still exists today. Flint walls enclose the main lawn, herbaceous borders and rose garden. There is a vegetable garden, informal pond, secret garden, mature and newly planted specimen trees and late flowering annuals and dahlias.

78 NEW LITTLEHOLME

20 Michel Dene Road, East Dean, Eastbourne, BN20 0JN. Tina Woodley-Roberts. *The village of East Dean can be found between Eastbourne & Seaford off the A259. Michel Dene Rd is off the A259 & Littleholme can be found 400yds on the RH-side.* Sat 10, Sun 11 June (11-4). Combined adm with 51 Carlisle Road £4, chd free. Home-made teas.

A newly developed garden designed in a country-contemporary style, designed and planted by the owner. A 120ft x 40ft s-facing garden on chalk, with mixed planting of various perennials and shrubs featuring a small wildflower meadow and feature thyme lawn. Hard landscaping has been used to compliment the levels of the garden.

79 THE LONG HOUSE

The Lane, Westdean, Nr Seaford, BN25 4AL. Robin & Rosie Lloyd, 01323 870432, rosiemlloyd@gmail.com, www.thelonghousegarden.co.uk. *3m E of Seaford, 6m W of Eastbourne. From A27 follow signs to Alfriston then Litlington, Westdean 1m on L. From A259 at Exceat, L on Litlington Rd, ¼ m on R. Free parking in the village.* Thur 6 July (2-5). Adm £5, chd free. Home-made teas. **Visits also by arrangement May to July for groups of 10+.**

The Long House's 1 acre garden is in the idyllic South Downs hamlet of Westdean. Lavenders, hollyhocks, roses, wild flower meadow, long perennial border, water folly, pond. American visitors wrote: 'My heavens! We couldn't stop talking about your garden, and in fact still haven't. Spectacular, beautiful, romantic, peaceful. Highlight of our trip.' They liked the cakes too! Situated on The South Downs Way in the SDNP. Gravel forecourt at entrance, some slopes and steps.

80 LORDINGTON HOUSE

Lordington, Chichester, PO18 9DX. Mr & Mrs John Hamilton, 01243 375862. *7m W of Chichester. On W side of B2146, ½ m S of Walderton, 6m S of South Harting. Enter through white railings.* Sat 1, Sun 2 Apr, Sat 22, Sun 23 July (1.30-4.30). Adm £4.50, chd free. Home-made teas. **Visits also by arrangement June & July, regret no coaches.**

Early C17 house (not open) and walled gardens in SDNP. Clipped yew and box, lawns, borders and fine views. Vegetables, fruit and poultry in old kitchen garden. Carpet of daffodils in spring. Nearly 100 roses planted since 2008. Various trees both mature and young. Lime avenue planted in 1973 to replace elms. Overlooks farmland, Ems Valley and wooded slopes of South Downs, all in AONB. Gravel paths, some uneven paving and slopes.

81 LOWDER MILL

Bell Vale Lane, Fernhurst, Haslemere, GU27 3DJ. Anne & John Denning, 01428 644822, anne@denningconsultancy.co.uk, www.lowdermill.com. *1½ m S of Haslemere. Follow A286 out of Midhurst towards Haslemere, through Fernhurst & take 2nd R after Kingsley Green into Bell Vale Lane. Lowder Mill is approx ½ m on R.* Sat 3 June (11-5.30); Sun 4 June (10.30-5.30). Adm £4.50, chd £2. A wide range of home-made cakes served overlooking the lake.

C17 mill house and former mill

Beauchamps

set in 3 acre garden. The garden has been restored with the help of Bunny Guinness. Interesting assortment of container planting, forming a stunning courtyard between house and mill. Streams, waterfalls, innovative and quirky container planting around the potting shed and restored greenhouse. Raised vegetable garden. Rare breed chickens and ducks, as well as resident kingfishers. Extensive plant stall, mainly home propagated. Choir singing on Sun. Featured in Country Life, Country Living, Sussex Life and the Secret Gardens of England.

82 LUCTONS
North Lane, West Hoathly, East Grinstead, RH19 4PP. Drs Hans & Ingrid Sethi, 01342 810085, ingrid@sethis.co.uk. *4m SW of East Grinstead, 6m E of Crawley. Off minor road between Turners Hill & Forest Row. Nr Church, Cat Inn & Priest House. Car parks in village.* Sat 1 July (1-5), also open The Priest House. Tue 4 July (1-5). Adm £5, chd free. Home-made teas. **Visits also by arrangement May to Sept for groups of 10-30.**
A 2 acre garden in Gertrude Jekyll style, with small box parterre, lawns, yew topiary, shrubberies, pond, much loved mixed borders, large fruit and vegetable garden. Many culinary, medicinal and other herbs, chickens, vine, peach and

greenhouses, and wild flower orchard with meadow flowers and spotted orchids in June.

83 MALT HOUSE
Chithurst Lane, Rogate, Petersfield, GU31 5EZ. Mr & Mrs G Ferguson, 01730 821433, g.ferguson34@btinternet.com. *3m W of Midhurst. On A272 turn N signed Chithurst for 1½m, narrow lane; or off A3 at Liphook to old A3 (B2070) for 2m, L to Milland following signs to Chithurst for 1½m. Narrow lanes not suitable for coaches.* Sun 30 Apr, Mon 1, Sun 7 May (2-6). Adm £5, chd free. Home-made teas. **Visits also by arrangement Apr to Oct.**
6 acre garden situated on the South Downs; flowering shrubs incl exceptional rhododendrons and azaleas, leading to 50 acres of arboretum and lovely woodland walks, plus many rare plants and trees. Partial wheelchair access only.

84 MALTHOUSE FARM
Streat Lane, Streat, Hassocks, BN6 8SA. Richard & Helen Keys, 01273 890356, helen.k.keys@btinternet.com. *2m SE of Burgess Hill. From r'about between B2113 & B2112 take Folders Lane & Middleton Common Lane E; after 1m, R into Streat Lane, garden is ½m on R. Ample parking on grass verge.* Sun 20, Wed 23 Aug (2-5.30). Adm £5, chd free.

Home-made teas. **Visits also by arrangement Apr to Sept for groups of 10+.**
Rural 5 acre garden with stunning views to South Downs. Garden divided into separate rooms, box parterre and borders with glass sculpture, herbaceous and shrub borders, mixed border for seasonal colour, and kitchen garden. Orchard leading to partitioned areas with grass walks, snail mound, birch maze and willow tunnel. Wildlife farm pond with planted surround. Featured in Period Living, Sussex Life and Architectural Digest. Wheelchair access possible although some steps. Caution if wet as much access is across grass.

85 MANOR OF DEAN
Tillington, Petworth, GU28 9AP. Mr & Mrs James Mitford, 07887 992349, emma@mitford.uk.com. *3m W of Petworth. From Petworth towards Midhurst on A272, go through Tillington & turn R on to Dean Lane following NGS signs. From Midhurst on A272 towards Petworth past Halfway Bridge, turn L following NGS signs.* Sun 12 Feb (2-4); Sun 5 Mar, Sun 23 Apr, Sun 6 Aug (2-5). Adm £4, chd free. Home-made teas. **Visits also by arrangement Feb to Sept for groups of 15+, regret no coaches.**
Traditional English garden, approx 3 acres with herbaceous borders, a variety of early flowering bulbs, snowdrops, spring bulbs, grass walks and grass steps. Walled kitchen garden with fruit, vegetables and cutting flowers. Lawns, rose garden and informal areas with views of the South Downs. Garden under a long-term programme of improvements. Come along to one of our themed open days: Rhubarb Sunday (23 Apr), and Dahlia Sunday (6 Aug) when you can see how they are grown, buy some to take home and enjoy the productive walled garden. Come early to avoid disappointment. Garden on many levels with old steps and paths.

GROUP OPENING

86 MAYFIELD GARDENS

Mayfield, TN20 6AB. *10m S of Tunbridge Wells. Turn off A267 into Mayfield. Parking is available in the village & field parking at Hoopers Farm. A detailed map will be available at each of the gardens.* Sat 10, Sun 11 June (1-5). Combined adm £6, chd free. Home-made teas at Hoopers Farm.

HOOPERS FARM
Andrew & Sarah Ratcliffe.

MEADOW COTTAGE
Adrian & Mo Hope.

MULBERRY
M Vernon.

NEW OAKCROFT
Ms Jennifer Smith.

SOUTH STREET PLOTS
Val Buddle.

Mayfield is a beautiful Wealden village with tearooms, an old PH and many interesting historical connections. The gardens to visit are all within walking distance of the village centre. They vary in size and style, including colour themed, courtyard and cottage garden planting, wildlife meadows and fruit and vegetable plots. There are far reaching, panoramic views over the beautiful High Weald. Partial wheelchair access to some gardens; see leaflet for details.

🐕 ❄ ☕ 🍴

The Old Vicarage
© Judi Lion

87 ◆ MICHELHAM PRIORY

Upper Dicker, Hailsham, BN27 3QS. Sussex Archaeological Society, 01323 844224, www.sussexpast.co.uk. *3m W of Hailsham. A22 N from Eastbourne, exit L to Arlington Rd W. 1⅙m turn R, Priory on R after approx 300yds.* **For opening times and information, please phone or visit garden website.**
The stunning 7 acre gardens at Michelham Priory (open to the public) are enclosed by England's longest water-filled moat, which teams with wildlife and indigenous waterlilies. Cloister and Physic gardens weave together features of medieval gardening. Over 40 yrs of developments have created a variety of features incl herbaceous borders, orchard, kitchen garden and tree lined Moat Walk.

♿ ❄ 🚗

88 NEWTIMBER PLACE

Newtimber, BN6 9BU. Mr & Mrs Andrew Clay, 01273 833104, andy@newtimberholidaycottages.co.uk, www.newtimberplace.co.uk. *7m N of Brighton. From A23 take A281 towards Henfield. Turn R at small Xrds signed Newtimber in approx ½m. Go down Church Lane, garden is at end of lane on L.* Sun 23 Apr (2-5.30). Adm £5, chd free. Home-made teas.
Beautiful C17 moated house (not open). Gardens and woods full of bulbs and wild flowers in spring. Herbaceous border and lawns. Moat flanked by water plants. Mature trees, wild garden, ducks, chickens and fish. Wheelchair access across lawn to some of garden, tearoom and WC.

♿ 🐕 ❄ 🛏 ☕

89 NORTH HALL

North Hall Lane, Sheffield Green, Uckfield, TN22 3SA. Celia & Les Everard, 01825 791103, indigodogs@yahoo.co.uk. *1½m NW of Fletching village. 6m N of Uckfield. From A272 turn N at Piltdown or N Chailey. From A275 turn E at Sheffield Green into North Hall Lane.* Sat 24, Sun 25 June (2-5.30). Adm £4, chd free. Home-made teas. **Visits also by arrangement mid April to May for groups 10-20. June to mid July for groups 10-40.**
This quintessential cottage garden surrounding a C16 house (not open) is planted to please the senses. Roses tumble, clematis scramble and the dense and varied planting needs little support, a palette of soft colours and heady scent. Themed island beds and a moated terrace add to the many other cottage garden features. Wildlife and self-seeding encouraged. Home grown plants and scrumptious teas.

🐄 ❄ 🚗 ☕

90 NORTH SPRINGS

Bedham, nr Fittleworth, RH20 1JP. Mr & Mrs R Haythornthwaite. *Between Fittleworth & Wisborough Green. From Wisborough Green take A272 towards Petworth. Turn L into Fittleworth Rd signed Coldharbour & proceed 1½m. From Fittleworth take Bedham Lane off A283 & proceed for approx 3m NE. Limited parking.* Sun 4 June (1-6). Adm £4.50, chd free. Home-made teas.
Hillside garden with beautiful views surrounded by mixed woodland. Focus on structure with a wide range of mature trees and shrubs. Stream, pond and bog area. Abundance of roses, clematis, hostas, rhododendrons and azaleas.

☕

91 NYEWOOD HOUSE

Nyewood, Rogate, GU31 5JL. Mr & Mrs C J Wright, 01730 821563, s.warren.wright@gmail.com. *4m E of Petersfield. From A272 at Rogate take South Harting Rd for 1½m. Turn L at pylon towards South Downs Manor. Nyewood House 2nd on R over cattle grid.* **Visits by arrangement May to July for groups of 20+. Home-made & cream teas or wine & nibbles.**
Victorian country house garden with stunning uninterrupted views of the South Downs. 3 acres comprising formal gardens with rose walk and arbours, pleached hornbeam, colour themed herbaceous borders, shrub borders, lily pond and fully stocked kitchen garden with greenhouse. Wooded

area featuring spring flowers followed by wild orchids and wild flowers. Gravel drive.

♿ 🐕 ❀ ☕

92 ◆ NYMANS

Handcross, RH17 6EB. National Trust, 01444 405250, nymans@nationaltrust.org.uk, www.nationaltrust.org.uk/nymans. *4m S of Crawley. On B2114 at Handcross signed off M23/A23 London-Brighton road. Metrobus 271 & 273 stop nearby.* For NGS: Sun 24 Sept (10-5). Adm £12, chd £6.50. Light refreshments. **For other opening times and information, please phone, email or visit garden website.**

One of the National Trust's premier gardens, Nymans was a country retreat for the creative Messel family, and has views stretching out across the Sussex Weald. Today it's still a place to recharge the batteries where you can glimpse hidden corners through stone archways, walk along tree lined avenues and be surrounded by lush green countryside. Some level pathways. See full access statement on the Nymans website.

♿ ❀ 🚐 ☕

93 OAK GROVE COLLEGE GROUNDS

The Boulevard, Worthing, BN13 1JX. Oak Grove College. Ms C Elderfield, 01903 708870, oakgrovecollege.org.uk. *1m W of Worthing. When driving W on A2032 dual carriageway, turn into Oak Grove College car park immed on L before r'about (The Boulevard turn off).* Sun 25 June (11-5). Adm £4, chd free. Light refreshments. **Visits also by arrangement Mar to July.**

An inspiring example of how special needs children have transformed their school grounds into a green oasis. Extensive and unusual planting, polytunnels, vegetable growing area, herb garden, sculptures and mosaics. Small reclaimed woodland, camera obscura, outdoor performance and cooking areas.

♿ 🐕 ❀ ☕

94 OFFHAM HOUSE

The Street, Offham, Lewes, BN7 3QE. Mr S Goodman and Mr & Mrs P Carminger. *2m N of Lewes on A275. Offham House is on the main road (A275) through Offham between the filling station & the Blacksmiths Arms.* Sun 30 Apr, Sun 4 June (1-5). Adm £5, chd free. Tea & home-made cake.

Romantic garden with fountains, flowering trees, arboretum, double herbaceous border, long peony bed. 1676 Queen Anne house (not open) with well knapped flint facade. Herb garden and walled kitchen garden with glasshouses, coldframes, chickens, guinea fowl, sheep and friendly pig.

🐕 ❀ ☕

95 OLD ERRINGHAM COTTAGE

Steyning Road, Shoreham-By-Sea, BN43 5FD. Fiona & Martin Phillips, 01273 462285, fiona.h.phillips@btinternet.com. *2m N of Shoreham by Sea. From A27 Shoreham flyover take A283 towards Steyning. Take 2nd R into private lane. Follow sharp LH-bend at top, house on L.* **Visits by arrangement mid May to early July for groups of 10+. If your group is smaller, ask if you can join another group.** Adm £5, chd free. Home-made teas.

Plantsman's garden set high on the South Downs with panoramic views overlooking the Adur valley. 1⅓ acres with flower meadow, stream bed and ponds, formal and informal planting areas with over 600 varieties of plants. Very productive fruit and vegetable garden with glasshouses. Many plants grown from seed and coastal climate gives success with tender plants. Part of house dates from 1480 (not open).

☕

96 OLD VICARAGE

The Street, Firle, Lewes, BN8 6NR. Mr & Mrs Charlie Bridge. *Off A27 5m E of Lewes. Signed from main road.* Sat 17 June (1-4). Adm £5, chd free. Cream teas.

Garden originally designed by Lanning Roper in the 1960s. 4 acre garden with lots of different rooms,

set around a Regency vicarage (not open) with wonderful Downland views. Features a walled garden with vegetable parterre and flower borders, wild flower meadow, pond, pleached limes and over 100 roses. Partial wheelchair access as some areas may be difficult.

♿ 🐕 ☕

Visit a garden and support hospice care in your local community

97 THE OLD VICARAGE

The Street, Washington, RH20 4AS. Sir Peter & Lady Walters, 07766 761926, meryl.walters@me.com. *2½m E of Storrington, 4m W of Steyning. From Washington r'about on A24 take A283 to Steyning. 500yds R to Washington. Pass Frankland Arms, R to St Mary's Church.* Sun 26 Feb (11-3.30); Sun 19 Mar (10.30-4); Mon 17 Apr, Sun 21 May, Sun 18 June, Sun 20 Aug (10.30-4.30); Sun 15 Oct (10.30-3). Adm £5, chd free. Home-made teas. Gluten free cakes & biscuits available. **Visits also by arrangement Apr to Oct for groups of 10+.**

Gardens of 3½ acres set around 1832 Regency house (not open). The front, formally laid out with topiary, wide lawn, mixed border, and contemporary water sculpture. The rear, features new and mature trees from C19, herbaceous borders, water garden and stunning uninterrupted views of the North Downs. Also Japanese garden with waterfall and pond, a large copse, stream and treehouse. Architectural stumpery new for 2017 and 2000 tulips have been planted for spring. Listed as one of the top 25 gardens in Sussex in Sussex Life. Mentioned in The Daily Telegraph and featured in Period Living and Sussex Style. Wheelchair access to the front garden, but the rear garden is on a slope.

♿ 🐕 ❀ ☕

GROUP OPENING

98 OUSE VALLEY TO THE COAST TRAIL

Visitors can start at any of the 4 gardens listed. Sat 22, Sun 23 July (1-5). Combined adm £5, chd free. Home-made teas.

NEW 12 AINSWORTH AVENUE

BN2 7BG. Jane Curtis.

CATTLEGATE

BN7 3PE. Caroline Courtauld.

144 RODMELL AVENUE

BN2 8PJ. Sue & Ray Warner, 01273 305137, suwarner@xeonflux.com. Visits also by arrangement July & Aug for groups of 2-20.

NEW SKYSCAPE

BN2 7BG. Lorna & John Davies.

Four uniquely different Sussex gardens flowing from the Ouse Valley down to the coast! Cattlegate in Swanborough has a small garden surrounding a white modernist house, with a spectacular view as painted by the artist Eric Ravilious, and stunning views of the South Downs. It is full of architectural interest and thoughtful planting. Down on the coast there is 144 Rodmell Avenue in Saltdean, a fun jungle garden, 65ft x 36ft, but appearing larger with winding paths meandering through lush jungle and insect friendly planting, listen out for the parrots squawking in the trees! Finally, new for 2017, Skyscape at 46 Ainsworth Avenue in Ovingdean, a 250ft s-facing rear garden on a sloping site with fantastic views of South Downs and sea. Also 12 Ainsworth Avenue, a small coastal garden begun in 2014 and still developing. Pergola, arches and arbor strategically positioned to provide privacy and a choice of places to sit with different aspects, even a glimpse of the sea. No wheelchair access at 144 Rodmell Avenue and partial access at other gardens.

♿ 🍵

99 PALATINE SCHOOL GARDENS

Palatine Road, Worthing, BN12 6JP. Mrs N Hawkins, www.palatineschool.org. *Turn S off A2032 at r'about onto The Boulevard signed Goring. Take R at next r'about into Palatine Rd. School approx 100yds on R.* Sun 16 Apr (2-5). Adm £4, chd free. Cream teas.

This is a many roomed mature garden with varied planting. Constructed by teachers, volunteers and children with special needs, it never ceases to surprise visitors. Wildlife corner, large and small ponds, themed gardens and children's outdoor art features, along with rockeries, living willow, labyrinth, mosaics and interesting tree collection.

♿ 🐄 ✳ 🍵

100 PARSONAGE FARM

Kirdford, RH14 0NH. David & Victoria Thomas. *5m NE of Petworth. From centre of Kirdford (before church) turn R through village towards Balls Cross, past Foresters PH on R. Entrance on L, just past R turn to Plaistow. For SatNav use RH14 0NG.* Fri 23 June, Sun 10 Sept (2-6). Adm £6, chd free. Home-made teas.

Major garden in beautiful setting developed over 20 yrs with fruit theme and many unusual plants. Formally laid out on grand scale with long vistas; C18 walled garden with borders in apricot, orange, scarlet and crimson; topiary walk; pleached lime allée; tulip tree avenue; rose borders; large vegetable garden with trained fruit; turf amphitheatre; lake; informal autumn shrubbery and jungle walk.

♿ 🍵

101 PEELERS RETREAT

70 Ford Road, Arundel, BN18 9EX. Tony & Lizzie Gilks, 01903 884981, timespan70@tiscali.co.uk, www.peelersretreat.co.uk. *1m S of Arundel. At Chichester r'about take exit to Ford & Bognor Regis onto Ford Rd. We are situated close to Maxwell Rd, Arundel.* Sun 14 May, Fri 23 June, Fri 21 July, Sun 13 Aug, Sun 10 Sept (2-5). Adm £3.50, chd free. Home-made teas. Visits also by arrangement May to Sept for groups of 2-30.

This beautiful garden has been designed to create a paradise in which to entertain and relax in. A concentrated effort has been made by two talented owners to incorporate eye-catching woodland sculptures including 'Joey the war horse' and 'Wee Brodie' our stag who peers out through lush planting whilst our bugs are well catered for in their No 10 Downing Street bug box. Exhibition of historical artefacts. Restricted wheelchair access due to our narrow side entrance, regret no motorised wheelchairs.

🐄 ♿ 🍵 🍵

102 33 PEERLEY ROAD

East Wittering, PO20 8PD. Paul & Trudi Harrison, 01243 673215, stixandme@aol.com. *7m S of Chichester. From A286 take B2198 to Bracklesham. Turn R into Stocks Lane, L at Royal British Legion into Legion Way. Follow road round to Peerley Rd. No 33 is halfway along.* Sun 16 July (12-4). Adm £3.50, chd free. Visits also by arrangement May to Oct for groups of up to 20 max.

Small seaside garden 65ft x 32ft, 110yds from the sea. Packed full of ideas and interesting plants using every inch of space to create rooms and places for adults and children to play. A must for any suburban gardener. Specialising in unusual plants that grow well in seaside conditions with advice on coastal gardening.

✳

103 PEMBURY HOUSE

Ditchling Road (New Road), Clayton, Hassocks, BN6 9PH. Nick & Jane Baker, 01273 842805, jane.baker47@btinternet.com, www.pemburyhouse.co.uk. *6m N of Brighton, off A23. On B2112, 110yds from A273. Parking for groups at house. Please car share. Overflow parking at village green, BN6 9PJ; then enter by Cinder Track & back gate. Good public transport service.* Visits by arrangement Feb & Mar for groups of 10-30. Individuals can be added to groups. Adm incl home-made teas. Adm £9.

Depending on the vagaries of the season, hellebores and snowdrops are at their best in Feb. It is a country garden, tidy but not manicured. There is always work in progress on new areas. Winding paths give a choice of walks through 2 acres of owner maintained garden, which is in, and enjoys views of the SDNP. Wellies, macs and winter woolies advised. Featured in Sky 1 TV garden series, Japanese TV, Gardeners World and numerous UK and European magazines.

🐕 ☕

104 PENNS IN THE ROCKS

Groombridge, Tunbridge Wells, TN3 9PA. Mr & Mrs Hugh Gibson, www.pennsintherocks.co.uk. *7m SW of Tunbridge Wells. On B2188 Groombridge to Crowborough road, just S of Xrd to Withyham. For SatNav use TN6 1UX which takes you to the white drive gates, through which the visitor should enter the property.* Sun 16 Apr, Sun 14 May (2-6). Adm £6, chd free. Home-made teas.

Large garden with spectacular outcrop of rocks, lake, C18 temple and woods. Daffodils, bluebells, azaleas, magnolias and tulips. Old walled garden with herbaceous borders, roses and shrubs. Part C18 house (not open). Walls recently restored by Richard and Columba Strachey. Restricted wheelchair access. No disabled WC. Dogs on lead in park only.

♿ 🐕 ✿ ☕

105 6 PLANTATION RISE

Worthing, BN13 2AH. Nigel & Trixie Hall, 01903 262206, trixiehall@btinternet.com. *2m from seafront on outskirts of Worthing. A24 meets A27 at Offington r'about. Turn into Offington Lane, 1st R into The Plantation, 1st R again into Plantation Rise.* Visits by arrangement Mar to Sept for groups of 4-20, incl home-made teas. Adm £5, chd free.

Our garden is 70ft x 80ft with pond, summerhouse, folly, flower decked pergolas over patios, 9 silver birches, plus evergreen shrubs, azaleas, rhododendrons and acers. Heathers

in spring, and a profusion of roses, clematis and perennials in Aug, all to ensure yr-round colour and interest. We are also in the Worthing Eco programme in Sept. The garden has some steps. WC available on request.

♿ 🚗 ☕ ☕

106 NEW ◆ PLEASURE GROUNDS OF PETWORTH HOUSE AND PARK

Petworth, GU28 0HX. National Trust, www.nationaltrust.org.uk. *Park at Sylvia Beaufoy Car Park (GU28 0HX) on the A272 W of Petworth, before the junction with A285. Meet just inside the Cricket Lodge gates in the wall opp. Other parking & facilities at Petworth Main Town Car Park (GU28 0AP).* For NGS: Thur 18 May (10.30-12.30). Adm £6, chd free. Two hour guided tour starts at 10.30am. Pre-booking essential due to limited numbers, please phone 01730 813323 or email sussexwestngs@gmail.com. For other opening times and information, please visit garden website.

A gentle perambulation with level surfaces round the Pleasure Grounds of Petworth House and Park. A magnificent 40 acre spring garden; see rhododendrons, camelias, bluebells and daffodils. The park and garden were originally designed by Lancelot 'Capability' Brown and incl a rotunda and a Doric temple, with stunning views of the South Downs and Petworth Park. Tour led by Gerald Gresham-Cooke, HeartSmart trained and assisted by Graham Ferguson of Malt House, a very knowledgeable local garden owner. NB: No entry to Petworth House and facilities. Please check website to see if dogs are allowed.

☕

Macmillan and the National Garden Scheme, partners for more than 30 years

GROUP OPENING

107 PRESTON PARK GARDENS

Preston Park Avenue, Brighton, BN1 6HG. *Preston Park is 1½ m N of Brighton centre on the A23. Entry points: 31 Preston Park Ave, BN1 6HG (Preston Park Ave runs E of the park) & 32 Clermont Terrace, BN1 6SJ (Clermont Terrace is 2 mins W, off Cumberland Rd).* Fri 9, Sat 10 June (11-5). Combined adm £5, chd free. Light refreshments & home-made cakes at 32 Claremont Terrace & 31 Preston Park Avenue.

24 CLERMONT TERRACE
Sue Shepherd.

32 CLERMONT TERRACE
Sue Fletcher.

PRESTON MANOR WALLED GARDEN
George Harris.

30 PRESTON PARK AVENUE
Anastasia Broome.

31 PRESTON PARK AVENUE
Lindy Craig-Hall.

Four urban gardens with the same challenges of chalk soil, varying slopes and levels, all tackled in individual ways. 30 Preston Park Avenue has had a large amount of hard landscaping creating areas from formal to a wild area. 31 Preston Park Avenue, created 11 yrs ago, incorporating natural and cultivated planting with new pink steps. 32 Clermont Terrace, sympathetically landscaped for this romantic and lovely garden with fascinating echos of its past history. 24 Clermont Terrace, approached from within the house, the garden has impact and draws you upward into its exotic secrets. These gardens lie either side of the beautiful Preston Manor walled garden where the head gardener and volunteers will show you around and explain the history. We also highly recommend visiting the Rockery, which is opposite Preston Park.

✿ ☕

108 ◆ THE PRIEST HOUSE

North Lane, West Hoathly, RH19 4PP. Sussex Archaeological Society, 01342 810479, priest@sussexpast.co.uk, www.sussexpast.co.uk. *4m SW of East Grinstead. Turn E to West Hoathly, 1m S of Turners Hill at Selsfield Common junction on B2028. 2m S turn R into North Lane, garden ¼m.* For NGS: Sat 27 May (10.30-5.30). Sat 1 July (10.30-5.30), also open Luctons. Adm £2, chd free. For other opening times and information, please phone, email or visit garden website.

C15 timber framed farmhouse with cottage garden on acid clay. Large collection of culinary and medicinal herbs in a small formal garden and mixed with perennials and shrubs in exuberant borders. Long established yew topiary, box hedges and espalier apple trees provide structural elements. Traditional fernery and stumpery, recently enlarged with a small secluded shrubbery and gravel garden. Adm to Priest House Museum £1 for NGS visitors.

🐃 ✿

109 2 QUARRY COTTAGES

Wall Hill Road, Ashurst Wood, East Grinstead, RH19 3TQ. Mrs Hazel Anne Archibald. *1m S of East Grinstead. From N turn L off A22 from East Grinstead, garden adjoining John Pears Memorial Ground. From S turn R off A22 from Forest Row, garden on R at top of hill.* Fri 19, Sat 20 May (2-5). Adm £3.50, chd free. Home-made teas.

Peaceful little garden that has evolved over 40 yrs in the present ownership. A natural sandstone outcrop hangs over an ornamental pond; mixed borders of perennials and shrubs with specimen trees. Many seating areas tucked into corners. Highly productive vegetable plot. Terrace round house revamped in 2013. Florist and gift shop in barn. Featured in Garden Answers (Apr 2016). Also open Caxton Manor (separate admission).

🐃 ✿ 🍵

110 RINGMER PARK

Ringmer, Lewes, BN8 5RW. Deborah & Michael Bedford, www.ringmerpark.com. *On A26 Lewes to Uckfield road. 1½m NE of Lewes, 5m S of Uckfield.* Sun 17 Sept (2-5). Adm £5, chd free.

The garden at Ringmer Park has been developed over the last 30 yrs as the owner's interpretation of a classic English country house garden. It extends over nearly 8 acres and comprises 13 carefully differentiated individual gardens and borders which are presented to optimise the setting of the house (not open) close to the South Downs.

♿ 🐃 🐕 🚗 🍵

111 NEW ROLFS FARM

Witherenden Road, Mayfield, TN20 6RP. Kate Langdon. *2m E of Mayfield (approx 5 mins). On Witherenden Rd, we are ½m from Mayfield end of road. Do not follow SatNav to postcode. Long, narrow, uneven driveway downhill through woods.* Wed 14, Wed 21 June (10-3). Adm £4, chd free. Home-made teas.

Very different from the usual NGS garden! Large wildlife friendly garden (no boundary fences to encourage visiting wildlife), with wildflower meadows, hazel trees, and clipped box hedging. Large orchard next to the garden. Tom Stuart-Smith designed modern meadow garden. Two ponds, small vegetable garden, and informal, naturalistic planting throughout. Uneven grass paths, sensible shoes please. Sorry, no wheelchair access as steep uneven driveway, and many steps in garden.

🍵

112 1 ROSE COTTAGE

Chalvington Road, Golden Cross, Nr Hailsham, BN27 3SS. Chris & Jackie Burgess, 01825 872753, www.rosecottagegarden.co.uk. *Approx 11m N of Eastbourne, just off A22, turn into Chalvington Rd immed S of Golden Cross PH.* Mon 26 June (11-5). Combined adm with 2 Woodside £5.50, chd free. Home-made teas. Visits also by arrangement June to Aug for groups of 10+.

A cottage garden with densely planted borders. Roses, honeysuckles and clematis, plus a wide range of perennials viewed as you walk along meandering paths, some ending with secluded seating. Colour themed borders planted for yr-round interest. Fruit cage, polytunnel and several raised vegetable beds add interest. Plants propagated by owners will be on sale. Pots of tea and home-made cakes served on pretty china, with delightful tablecloths. No wheelchair access.

✿ 🍵

113 RYMANS

Apuldram, Chichester, PO20 7EG. Mrs Michael Gayford, 01243 783147, suzanna.gayford@btinternet.com. *1m S of Chichester. Take Witterings Rd, at 1½m SW turn R signed Dell Quay. Turn 1st R, garden ½m on L.* Sat 15, Sun 16 Apr, Sat 17, Sun 18 June, Sat 16, Sun 17 Sept (2-5). Adm £5, chd free. Home-made teas. Visits also by arrangement Apr to Sept for groups of 10+.

Walled and other gardens surrounding lovely C15 stone house (not open); bulbs, flowering shrubs, roses, ponds, and potager. Many unusual and rare trees and shrubs. In late spring the wisterias are spectacular. The heady scent of hybrid musk roses fills the walled garden in June. In late summer the garden is ablaze with dahlias, sedums, late roses, sages and Japanese anemones. Featured in Country Life (Aug 2016). No wheelchair access.

🐃 ✿ 🚗

114 SAFFRONS

Holland Road, Steyning, BN44 3GJ. Tim Melton & Bernardean Carey, 01903 810082, tim.melton@btinternet.com. *6m NE of Worthing. Exit r'about on A283 at S end of Steyning bypass into Clays Hill Rd. 1st R into Goring Rd, 4th L into Holland Rd. Park in Goring Rd & Holland Rd.* Sun 23, Wed 26 July (2-5.30). Adm £4.50, chd free. Home-made teas. Visits also by arrangement in July for groups of 10+.

A stylish garden of textural contrasts and rich colour. The herbaceous beds are filled with agapanthus, spiky eryngium and fragrant lilies, alliums and salvias. A broad lawn is surrounded by borders with Japanese maples, rhododendrons, hydrangeas and specimen trees interspersed with ferns and grasses. Fruit cage, vegetable beds and fruit trees. Wheelchair access difficult in very wet conditions.

♿ 🐕 ✽ ☕

115 ◆ ST MARY'S HOUSE GARDENS

Bramber, BN44 3WE. Peter Thorogood & Roger Linton, 01903 816205, info@stmarysbramber.co.uk, www.stmarysbramber.co.uk. *1m E of Steyning. 10m NW of Brighton in Bramber village off A283.* **For NGS: Fri 23, Sat 24 June (2-5.30). Adm £5.50, chd free. Home-made teas. For other opening times and information, please phone, email or visit garden website.**

5 acres incl formal topiary, large prehistoric *Ginkgo biloba*, and magnificent *Magnolia grandiflora* around enchanting timber-framed Medieval house (not open for NGS). Victorian 'Secret Gardens' incl splendid 140ft fruit wall with pineapple pits, Rural Museum, Terracotta Garden, Jubilee Rose Garden, King's Garden and circular Poetry Garden. Woodland walk and Landscape Water Garden. In the heart of the SDNP. St Mary's is featured in This England Annual 2016. Level paths throughout.

♿ ✽ 🚌 ☕

116 SANDHILL FARM HOUSE

Nyewood Road, Rogate, Petersfield, GU31 5HU. Rosemary Alexander, 07551 777873, r.a.alexander@talk21.com, www.rosemaryalexander.co.uk. *4m SE of Petersfield. From A272 Xrds in Rogate take road S signed Nyewood & Harting. Follow road for approx 1m over small bridge. Sandhill Farm House on R, over cattle grid.* **Sat 22, Sun 23 Apr, Sat 17, Sun 18 June, Sat 16, Sun 17 Sept (2-5). Adm £4.50, chd free. Home-made teas. Visits also by arrangement Mar to Oct for groups of 10+. Gardening Club bookings welcome.**

Front and rear gardens broken up into garden rooms incl small kitchen garden. Front garden incl small woodland area planted with early spring flowering shrubs, ferns and bulbs; topiary and white garden, large leaf border and terraced area. Rear garden has mirror borders, small decorative vegetable garden, red border, and grasses border. Home of author and principal of The English Gardening School. The garden has gravel paths and a few steps not easily negotiated in a wheelchair.

♿ ✽ D ☕

117 ◆ SARAH RAVEN'S CUTTING GARDEN

Perch Hill Farm, Willingford Lane, Robertsbridge, Brightling, TN32 5HP. Sarah Raven, 01424 838000, school@thecuttinggarden.com, www.sarahraven.com. *7m SW of Hurst Green. From Burwash turn off A265 by church & memorial, follow road for 3m. From Woods Corner take road opp Swan Inn, take 1st L, go uphill & take 1st L again. Parking is in a field (uneven ground possible).* **For NGS: Thur 31 Aug (9.30-4). Adm £5, chd free. Tea, coffee & cake served all day. Lunch available from 12.15. For other opening times and information, please phone, email or visit garden website.**

Sarah's inspirational, productive 2 acre working garden with different garden rooms incl large cut flower garden, vegetable and fruit garden, salads and herbs area, plus two ornamental gardens. We have some steps and gravel paths so wheelchair access is difficult in these areas.

☕

GROUP OPENING

118 SEAFORD GARDENS

Seaford. *Start at any garden. All will be signed from the A259 & maps are available at each garden for the trail. 12a bus route goes to Seaford. 3 gardens are close together but this is not a walking trail.* **Sun 25 June, Fri 14 July (12-5). Combined adm £5, chd free. Light refreshments.**

NEW **2 BARONS CLOSE**
BN25 2TY. Diane Hicks.
Open on Sun 25 June

34 CHYNGTON ROAD
BN25 4HP. Dr Maggie Wearmouth & Richard Morland.
Open on all dates

CUPANI GARDEN
Dr D Jones & Ms A Jones OBE.
Open on Fri 14 July
(See separate entry)

ELIZABETH COTTAGE
22 Sherwood Road, BN25 3EH. Sue Wright.
Open on Sun 25 June

HIGH TREES
83 Firle Road, BN25 2JA. Tony & Sue Luckin.
Open on Sun 25 June

LAVENDER COTTAGE
69 Steyne Road, BN25 1QH. Christina & Steve Machan.
Open on all dates

4 SUNNINGDALE CLOSE
BN25 4PF. Mick & Debbie Hibberd, 01323 899385, 4sunnyclose@gmail.com.
Open on all dates
Visits also by arrangement June to Aug for groups of 10+.

Seven unique gardens opening for Seaford Gardens group; six on 25 June and four on 14 July. High Trees is a beautiful garden with interesting plants, ferns and grasses, plus a woodland garden. Lavender Cottage is a flinted walled garden with a coastal and kitchen garden, terraced bank, and views of Seaford Head from the balcony. 34 Chyngton Road is divided into garden rooms with pastels, hot beds, a small meadow, Japanese inspired courtyard and a prairie. 2 Barons Close or Granny's Garden, new this year, is full of colour with roses providing the structure and a huge variety of other plants. Elizabeth Cottage is small and delightful with cottage plants, vegetables, mature ginko and silver birch. 4 Sunningdale Close has beautifully planted front and back gardens with a rich mix of perennial planting. Cupani Garden is a green and tranquil haven with a delightful mix of planting. Level wheelchair access to part of the garden at 34 Chyngton Road and Lavender Cottage. Some gardens allow dogs on leads but not all.

119 SEDGWICK PARK HOUSE

Sedgwick Park, Horsham, RH13 6QQ. John & Clare Davison, 01403 734930, clare@sedgwickpark.com, www.sedgwickpark.co.uk. *1m S of Horsham off A281. A281 towards Cowfold, Hillier Garden Center on R, then 1st R into Sedgwick Lane. At end of lane enter N gates of Sedgwick Park or W gate via Broadwater Lane, from Copsale or Southwater off A24. Sun 28 May (1-5); Wed 31 May (2-6.30). Adm £5, chd free. Home-made teas.* **Visits also by arrangement May to Sept for tours of house & gardens.** Parkland, meadows and woodland. Formal gardens by Harold Peto featuring 20 interlinking ponds, impressive water garden known as The White Sea. Large Horsham stone terraces and lawns look out onto clipped yew hedging and specimen trees. Well stocked herbaceous borders, set in the grounds of Grade II listed Ernest George Mansion. One of the finest views of the South Downs, Chanctonbury Ring and Lancing Chapel. Turf labyrinth and organic vegetable garden with chickens. Featured in All About Horsham, and a 2016 new book Paradise Found: Gardens of Enchantment by Clive Nichols. Garden has uneven paving, slippery when wet; unfenced ponds and swimming pool.

120 SELHURST PARK

Selhurst Park, Halnaker, Chichester, PO18 0LZ. Richard & Sarah Green. *8m S of Petworth. 4m N of Chichester on A285. Sun 18 June (2-5). Adm £4, chd free.*

Home-made teas. Come and explore the varied gardens surrounding a beautiful Georgian flint house (not open) approached by a Chestnut avenue. The flint walled garden has a mature 160ft herbaceous border with unusual planting along with rose, hellebore and hydrangea beds. Pool garden with exotic palms and grasses divided from a formal knot and herb garden by Espalier apples. Kitchen and walled fruit garden. Wheelchair access to walled garden, partial access to other areas.

121 SENNICOTTS

West Broyle, Chichester, PO18 9AJ. Mr & Mrs James Rank, www.sennicotts.com. *2m NW of Chichester. White gates diagonally opp & W of the junction between Salthill Rd & the B2178. Mon 19, Tue 20, Wed 21 June (9.30-4). Adm £4, chd free. Home-made teas in the walled garden.* Historic gardens set around a Regency villa (not open) with views across mature Sussex parkland to the South Downs. Working walled kitchen and cutting garden. Lots of space for children and a warm welcome for all.

122 SHALFORD HOUSE

Square Drive, Kingsley Green, GU27 3LW. Sir Vernon & Lady Ellis. *2m S of Haslemere. Just S of border with Surrey on A286. Square Drive is at brow of hill to the E. Turn L after approx ¼m & follow road to R at bottom of hill. Sun 14 May, Sun 9 July, Sun 3 Sept (2-5.30). Adm £5, chd free. Home-made teas.* Highly regarded 10 acre garden designed and created from scratch over last 24 yrs. Beautiful hilly setting with streams, ponds, waterfall, sunken garden, good late borders, azaleas and walled kitchen garden. Wild flower meadow with orchids, prairie style plantation and stumpery merging into further 7 acre woodland. Additional 30 acre arboretum with beech, rhododendrons, bluebells, ponds and specimen trees.

123 ◆ SHEFFIELD PARK AND GARDEN

Uckfield, TN22 3QX. National Trust, 01825 790231, sheffieldpark@nationaltrust.org.uk, www.nationaltrust.org.uk. *10m S of East Grinstead. 5m NW of Uckfield; E of A275. For NGS: Wed 21 June (10-5). Adm £10.10, chd £5. Light refreshments in Coach House Tearoom. For other opening times and information, please phone, email or visit garden website.* Magnificent 120 acres (40 hectares) landscaped garden laid out in C18 by Capability Brown and Humphry Repton. Further development in early yrs of this century by its owner Arthur G Soames. Centrepiece is original lakes with many rare trees and shrubs. Beautiful at all times of the yr, but noted for its spring and autumn colours. National Collection of Ghent azaleas. Natural play trail for families on South Park. Large number of Champion Trees, 87 in total. Garden largely accessible for wheelchairs, please call for information.

124 NEW SHEPHERDS COTTAGE

Milberry Lane, Stoughton, Chichester, PO18 9JJ. Jackie & Alan Sherling. *9½m NW Chichester. Off B2146, next village after Walderton. Cottage is near telephone box & beside St Mary's Church. No parking in lane beside house. Tue 20, Thur 22 June (11-4.30). Adm £5, chd free. Donation to St Mary's Church, Stoughton.* A compact terraced garden using the borrowed landscape of Kingly Vale in the South Downs. The s-facing flint stone cottage (not open) is surrounded by a Purbeck stone terrace, magnificent planting schemes, steps down to a small orchard, under-planted with chalk-loving meadow, lawns, yew hedges, ilex balls and drifts of wind grass provide structure and yr-round interest. Design ideas for a small garden. There is ample seating throughout the garden to enjoy the views. Garden books for sale.

Lunches and teas at the Hare & Hound PH, a 5 min walk away. Not suitable for wheelchairs or people with mobility issues.

✿ ⧅

125 SOUTH GRANGE
Quickbourne Lane, Northiam, Rye, TN31 6QY. Linda & Michael Belton, 01797 252984, belton.northiam@gmail.com. *Between A268 & A28, approx ½m E of Northiam. From Northiam centre follow Beales Lane into Quickbourne Lane, or Quickbourne Lane leaves A286 approx ½m S of A28 & A286 junction. Disabled parking at front of house.* Wed 12 July, Sat 23, Sun 24 Sept (2-5). Adm £4, chd free. Home-made teas. Sandwiches made to order at Sept openings only. **Visits also by arrangement Apr to Oct for groups of 20 max.**
Hardy Plant Society members' garden for all yr interest combining grasses, herbaceous perennials, with a late Sept date to showcase our aster collection. Also shrubs, trees, raised beds, wildlife pond, and vegetable plot. Orchard incl meadow flowers, fruit cage with willow windbreak, rose arbour and polytunnel. Woodland is left wild. House roof runoff diverted to pond and bulk storage. We try to maintain varied habitats for most of the creatures that we share the garden with, hoping that this variety will keep the garden in good heart. Home propagated plants for sale.

126 STONE CROSS HOUSE
Alice Bright Lane, Crowborough, TN6 3SH. Mr & Mrs D A Tate. *1½m S of Crowborough Cross. At Crowborough T-lights (A26) turn S into High St & shortly R onto Croft Rd. Over 3 mini-r'abouts to Alice Bright Lane. Garden on L at next Xrds.* Sat 6, Sun 7 May (2-5). Adm £5, chd free. Home-made teas.
Beautiful 9 acre country property with gardens containing a delightful array of azaleas, acers, rhododendrons and camellias, interplanted with an abundance of spring bulbs. The very pretty cottage

Brightling Down Farm

garden has interesting examples of topiary and unusual plants. Jacob sheep graze the surrounding pastures. Mainly flat and no steps. Gravel drive.

♿ 🐴 ☕

127 STONEHEALED FARM
Streat Lane, Streat, BN6 8SA. Lance & Fiona Smith, 01273 891145, afionasmith@hotmail.com. *2m SE of Burgess Hill. From Ditchling B2116, 1m E of Westmeston, turn L (N) signed Streat, 2m on R immed after railway bridge.* Sun 21, Sun 28 May (2-5.30). Adm £5, chd free. Home-made teas. **Visits also by arrangement Apr to Sept for groups of 10+.** *Donation to St Peter & St James Hospice.*
From pony paddock to tranquil garden in 20 yrs. A viewing platform in an ancient oak overlooks garden, fields and the Downs. Meander from cool shade to sunny borders, over a pond with its serpentine bridge, through to a raised vegetable garden. Planted with unusual trees, shrubs, climbers and seasonal perennials, plus a plethora of pots, collections of succulents, salvia and pelargonium. Delicious home-made teas served under cover. Some gravel paths and steps not suitable for wheelchairs.

♿ ✿ 🚗 ☕

128 NEW SULLINGTON OLD RECTORY
Sullington Lane, Storrington, Pulborough, RH20 4AE. Oliver & Mala Haarmann. Mark Dixon, Head Gardener, 07795 568343, mark@sullingtonoldrectory.com. *Traveling S on A24 take 3rd exit on Washington r'about. Proceed to Xrds on A283 for Sullington Lane & Water Lane. Take L onto Sullington Lane & garden located at the top.* Visits by arrangement in July for groups of 10+, incl tour with Head Gardener. If group is smaller, ask if you can join another group. Adm £5, chd free. Home-made teas.
With a backdrop of stunning views of the South Downs, the naturalistic style of this country garden sits well into the surrounding landscape. Many areas to enjoy incl potager, orchard, herb garden, pleached lime walk, perennial borders and moist meadow. With a strong framework of established trees and shrubs, new plantings and areas under development. Wheelchair access to most areas.

♿ 🐴 ✿ 🚗 ☕

129 ◆ **SUSSEX PRAIRIES**
Morlands Farm, Wheatsheaf Road
(B2116), Henfield, BN5 9AT. Paul
& Pauline McBride, 01273 495902,
morlandsfarm@btinternet.com,
www.sussexprairies.co.uk. *2m NE
of Henfield on B2116 Wheatsheaf
Rd (also known as Albourne Rd).
Follow Brown Tourist signs indicating
Sussex Prairie Garden.* For NGS:
Mon 28 Aug (11-5). Adm £7,
chd free. Home-made teas.
For other opening times and
information, please phone, email or
visit garden website.
Exciting prairie garden of approx
8 acres planted in the naturalistic
style using 50,000 plants and over
1500 different varieties. A colourful
garden featuring a huge variety
of unusual ornamental grasses.
Expect layers of colour, texture and
architectural splendour. Surrounded
by mature oak trees with views
of Chanctonbury Ring and Devil's
Dyke on the South Downs.
Permanent sculpture collection and
exhibited sculpture throughout the
season. Rare breed sheep and pigs.
Woodchip paths in borders not
accessible, but plenty of flat garden
for both wheelchairs and mobility
scooters. Disabled WC.
♿ 🐄 ✿ 🚗 ☕

130 **30 SYCAMORE DRIVE**
RH15 0GH. John Smith &
Kieran O'Regan, 01444 871888,
jsarastroo@aol.com,
www.kjsycamoredrive.co.uk. *8m
N of Brighton. Sycamore Drive is off
Folders Lane (B2113) in Burgess Hill
at Ditchling Common end.* Evening
openings Sat 9, Sun 10 Sept (7-
9.30). Adm £6. Wine. Opening
with Burgess Hill NGS Gardens
on Sun 23, Mon 24 July. Visits
also by arrangement May to
Sept for 10 max. Home-made
teas.
See this garden transform at night
into a candlelit calm oasis with
summerhouse, gravel garden and
grasses. Have a glass of wine and
canapés as you enjoy this magical
space. Adm includes wine & canapés,
no concessions. Licenced bar
available. Ticket only event, please
phone or email for information and
booking. Regret no children. A small

pond has been added, along with
some ferns in a shady area. Featured
in the Saturday Daily Mail, Sussex
Living, Amateur Gardener and on
ITV Good Morning Britain.
🐄 ☕

131 **TIDEBROOK MANOR**
Tidebrook, Wadhurst, TN5 6PD.
Edward Flint, Head Gardener.
*Between Wadhurst & Mayfield. From
Wadhurst take B2100 towards Mark
Cross, L at Best Beech PH, downhill
200 metres past church on R, then
a drive on L.* Wed 7 June, Wed 6
Sept (10-4). Adm £5, chd free.
4 acre garden developed over
the last decade with outstanding
views of the Sussex countryside. In
the Arts and Crafts tradition, the
garden features large mixed borders,
intimate courtyards, meadows,
hydrangea walk, kitchen garden with
raised beds, a willow plat and a wild
woodland of particular interest in
the spring. A lively and stimulating
garden throughout the yr. There will
be tours with Edward Flint, Head
Gardener at 1pm (£2.50 additional
charge), and plants for sale.
Refreshments available in nearby
Mayfield. No wheelchair access to
woodland area.
♿ ✿

132 **TOWN PLACE**
Ketches Lane, Freshfield, Sheffield
Park, RH17 7NR. Anthony &
Maggie McGrath, 01825 790221,
mcgrathsussex@hotmail.com,
*5m E of Haywards Heath. From
A275 turn W at Sheffield Green into
Ketches Lane for Lindfield. 1¾ m on
L.* Thur 15, Sun 25 June, Sun 2,
Sun 9 July (2-6). Adm £6, chd
free. Cream teas. Visits also by
arrangement June & July for
groups of 20+.
A stunning 3 acre garden with a
growing international reputation
for the quality of its design, planting
and gardening. Set round a C17
Sussex farmhouse (not open),
the garden has over 600 roses,
herbaceous borders, herb garden,
topiary inspired by the sculptures of
Henry Moore, ornamental grasses,
an ancient hollow oak, potager, and
a unique 'ruined' Priory Church and
Cloisters, in hornbeam. Featured in

Sussex Living (June 2016).
♿ ✿ 🚗 ☕

133 **TURNERS HOUSE**
Turners Green, Heathfield,
TN21 9RB. Christopher
Miscampbell & Julia Padbury,
01435 831191,
chrisandjoolz@gmail.com. *4m E
of Heathfield. S off B2096 at Middle
Lane, 3 Cups Corner signed Rushlake
Green, Hailsham, for ⅓ m. Look for
big clock face on L. Park on green, not
roads.* Visits by arrangement mid
June to mid Aug for individuals
& groups with advanced notice.
Home-made teas on request.
Adm £4, chd free.
Yummy cakes in nice garden. Lots
of plants, nooks, crannies and seats.
We cannot run a big open day
because of limited parking, but we
are not scary, you do not need
to be fluent in botanical latin, and
you are welcome to wander at
leisure. So do come and share our
pleasure in our garden. Some notice
preferred, please. Partial wheelchair
access following wet weather. Grass,
old brick paths, stepping stones, and
some gravel. Non-disabled WC on
request.
♿ ☕

134 **UPWALTHAM BARNS**
Upwaltham, GU28 0LX. Roger &
Sue Kearsey. *6m S of Petworth. 6m
N of Chichester on A285.* Sun 28,
Mon 29 May (1.30-5.30). Adm
£4.50, chd free. Home-made
teas. *Donation to St Mary's Church.*
Unique farm setting transformed
into a garden of many rooms.
Entrance is a tapestry of perennial
planting to set off C17 flint barns.
At the rear is a walled, terraced
garden redeveloped and planted
with an abundance of unusual plants.
Extensive vegetable garden. Beautiful
inner courtyard and sitting area.
Roam at leisure, relax and enjoy
in all seasons. Features incl lovely
views of the South Downs and a
C12 Shepherds Church (open to
visitors). The grounds have some
gravel paths.
♿ 🐄 ✿ ☕

135 NEW THE WALLED GARDEN AT TILGATE PARK

Tilgate Drive, Tilgate, Crawley, RH10 5PQ. Crawley Borough Council. *SE Crawley. Leave M23 at J11. From r'about follow A23 Brighton Rd for short distance. Turn R at sign to Tilgate Park. Disabled parking at entrance of the walled garden, other car park 150 metres away. Coach parking by arrangement.* Evening openings Wed 19, Thur 20 July (6.30-9). Adm £8, chd free. Adm incl a glass of wine & canapés. Prepaid event only, please call 01293 521168, payment by card only. Leave contact details if no reply.

Enjoy an evening event in a walled garden set in a 200 acre estate. Explore gardens from informal to wild and get lost in the maze, all within the larger walled garden. The experienced and knowledgeable Head Gardener, Nick Hagon, will give an introductory talk at 7pm, with tree trails to follow in the surrounding park. A garden gem, a special space, under the auspices of Crawley Borough Council. Accompanied children under 16 free. No concessions. Light refreshments and drinks may be purchased. Wheelchair access within the walled garden.

♿ ❄ ☕

GROUP OPENING

136 NEW WATERWORKS & FRIENDS

Broad Oak & Brede. *Waterworks Cots Brede, off A28 by church & opp Red Lion PH, ¾m at end of lane. Woodlands & Sculdown on B2089 Chitcombe Rd, W off A28 at Broad Oak Xrds. Start at any garden, a map will be provided.* Sat 3 June (10.30-4). Combined adm £5, chd free. Light refreshments at Sculdown.

NEW SCULDOWN
TN31 6EX. Mrs Christine Buckland.

NEW 4 WATERWORKS COTTAGES
TN31 6HG. Mrs Kristina Clode, www.kristinaclodegardendesign.co.uk.
♿

NEW WOODLANDS
TN31 6EU. Mr George Terry.
♿

An opportunity to visit 3 unique gardens and discover the Brede Steam Giants 35ft Edwardian water pumps and Grade II listed pump house located behind 4 Waterworks Cottages. Garden designer Kristina Clode created her wildlife friendly garden at 4 Waterworks Cottages over the last 7 yrs. Delightful perennial wildflower meadow, pond, wisteria covered pergola and mixed borders packed full of unusual specimens with yr-round interest and colour. Woodlands is an intensely colourful back garden in 3 sections, also designed by Kristina Clode. Mixed borders, lawn and pleached hornbeam hedge, leading to a formal quartered box edged garden with filigree gazebo, spiral topiary and vibrant planting. Framed view to the perennial wildflower meadow beyond. Sculdown's garden is dominated by a very large wildlife pond formed as a result of iron-ore mining over 100 yrs ago. The stunning traditional cottage provides a superb backdrop for several colourful herbaceous borders and poplar trees. Plants for sale at 4 Waterworks Cottages. At Brede Steam Giants WC available, regret no disabled facilities and assistance dogs only (free entry, donations encouraged). Wheelchair access at Sculdown (please park in the flat area at the top of the field) and in the front garden of Waterworks Cottages only.

♿ 🐕 ❄ ☕

137 WEAVERS HOUSE

Knowle Lane, Halland, Lewes, BN8 6PR. Mrs Miranda Gibb. *3m S of Uckfield. From Uckfield A22, turn R before Halland, 1st house on R. From Lewes go N on A26, through Ringmer village onto Broyle, continue 3¼m. Turn L onto Knowle Lane & continue ¾m. House on L.* Fri 21 Apr (2-5.30). Adm £4, chd free. Home-made teas.

Sloping south and west facing garden, stocked with fragrant flowers, shrubs and trees. There is an attractive rill along the base of a sloping bank of seasonal snowdrops, daffodils and primroses. From the garden two sets of steep steps take you to the ancient bluebell wood with seasonal ponds and mature broad leaf trees. The woodland is approximately 3½ acres and is covered in swathes of English bluebells in April and early May. There is a developing bog garden and choice of walks around wood. Wellies recommended.
☕

Upwaltham Barns

© Judi Lion

138 ◆ WEST DEAN GARDENS
West Dean, Nr Chichester, PO18 0RX. Edward James Foundation, 01243 818221, www.westdean.org.uk/gardens. *5m N of Chichester. On A286 midway between Chichester & Midhurst.* **For NGS: Sun 5 Feb (9-4). Adm £5.50, chd free. Light refreshments in the cafe. For other opening times and information, please phone or visit garden website.**
35 acre historic garden in downland setting. This yr we are participating in the Snowdrop Festival. Over 500,000 bulbs have been planted in recent yrs throughout the gardens; every yr the display is more impressive. 300ft Harold Peto pergola, 2½ acre walled garden with fruit collection, specimen trees, 13 Victorian glasshouses, large working kitchen garden and an extensive plant collection. Circuit walk (2¼ m) climbs through parkland to 45 acre St Roche's Arboretum. Most areas of the walled garden and grounds are accessible.

139 WESTLANDS COURT
Cowfold Road, West Grinstead, Horsham, RH13 8LZ. Mrs Jane Gates, 07774 980819, jane.er.gates@gmail.com. *Off the A272 between Buck Barn Services & Cowfold. From A24 Buck Barn, A272 E towards Haywards Heath for 2m, take 3rd L drive after Maplehurst Rd. Or from M23, A272 W through Cowfold towards Billingshurst for 1¼ m, drive 1st R after Burnthouse Lane.* **Sat 25 Feb (11-4). Light refreshments. Sat 27, Sun 28 May (11-5). Home-made teas. Adm £5, chd free. Visits also by arrangement Feb to Sept for groups of 10-30.**
Owned by a garden designer, the garden is 1 acre with 2 acres of meadow with unusual mature trees and a lake. Laid out in organically shaped beds the planting is mainly prairie style with grasses, structural plants, shrubs and herbaceous plants. In early spring masses of snowdrops and hellebores bring welcome interest followed by narcissus Thalia, naturalised narcissus, tulips and alliums.

Westlands Court
© Judi Lion

140 46 WESTUP FARM COTTAGES
Balcombe, RH17 6JJ. Chris Cornwell, 01444 811891, chris.westup@btinternet.com. *3m N of Cuckfield on B2036 or J10A off M23 into B2036. Turn into concealed lane off B2036 by Balcombe Primary School down long lane. Parking signed. Walk to garden.* **Wed 17 May, Sat 17 June (12-5). Combined adm with Winterfield £4, chd free. Home-made teas at Winterfield. Visits also by arrangement Apr to Sept for groups of 4+.**
Hidden in the countryside of the High Weald, this cottage garden contains unique and traditional features, linked by intimate paths through lush and subtle planting. The garden is packed with vegetables, unusual shrubs and herbaceous planting. Maximum use is made of the greenhouses. Rural charm in an AONB, with a feast of plants and an owner very keen on plants.

141 WHITEHANGER
Marley Lane, Haslemere, GU27 3PY. David & Lynn Paynter, 07774 010901, l.paynter@btopenworld.com. *3m S of Haslemere. Take the A286 Midhurst road from Haslemere & after approx 2m turn R into Marley Lane (opp Hatch Lane). After 1m turn into drive shared with Rosemary Park Nursing Home.* **Visits by arrangement June to Aug for groups of 10+. Refreshments incl tea & cake (day), wine (eve).**
Set in 6 acres on the edge of the SDNP surrounded by NT woodland, this rural garden was started in 2012 when a new Huf house was built on a derelict site. Now there are lawned areas with beds of perennials, a serenity pool with Koi carp, a wild flower meadow, a Japanese garden, a sculpture garden and a woodland walk.

142 NEW 5 WHITEMANS CLOSE
Cuckfield, Haywards Heath, RH17 5DE. Shirley Carman-Martin, 01444 473520, shirleycarmanmartin@gmail.com. *1m N of Cuckfield. B2036 signed Balcombe on L 20yds before de-restriction signs. Some public transport. Parking on road. Car sharing appreciated.* **Visits by arrangement June & July for individuals & groups of 12 max. Adm £8. Adm incl home-made teas.**
A garden visit for plant lovers. This relatively small cottage garden is packed full of exciting and unusual plants. The enthusiastic Hardy Plant Society member will take the group around the garden whilst talking about the most interesting and noteworthy plants. There will be time to explore the garden after tea, coffee and cake.

Your visit helps Marie Curie work night and day in people's homes

GROUP OPENING

143 WINCHELSEA'S SECRET GARDENS

Winchelsea, TN36 4EJ. *2m W of Rye, 8m E of Hastings. Purchase ticket for all gardens at first garden visited; a map will be provided showing gardens & location of teas.* Sat 22 Apr, Sat 17 June, Sat 29 July (1-5.30). Combined adm £6, chd free. Home-made teas.

ALARDS
Vicky Jessup.
Open on Sat 17 June

ALARDS PLAT
Richard & Cynthia Feast.
Open on Sat 29 July

THE ARMOURY
Mr & Mrs A Jasper.
Open on Sat 22 Apr, Sat 17 June

BACKFIELDS END
Sandra & Peter Mackenzie Smith.
Open on Sat 29 July

CLEVELAND HOUSE
Mr & Mrs J Jempson.
Open on Sat 22 Apr, Sat 17 June

CLEVELAND PLACE
Sally & Graham Rhodda.
Open on Sat 22 Apr, Sat 29 July

NEW LOOKOUT COTTAGE
Mary & Roger Tidyman.
Open on Sat 29 July

MAGAZINE HOUSE
Susan & Stuart Stradling.
Open on Sat 17 June

THE ORCHARDS
Brenda & Ralph Courtenay.
Open on Sat 29 July

PERITEAU HOUSE
Dr & Mrs Lawrence Youlten.
Open on Sat 22 Apr, Sat 17 June

RYE VIEW
Howard Norton & David Page.
Open on Sat 22 Apr, Sat 29 July

SOUTH MARITEAU
Robert & Sheila Holland.
Open on Sat 17 June

2 STRAND PLAT
Mr & Mrs Anthony & Gillian Tugman.
Open on Sat 17 June

THE WELL HOUSE
Alice Kenyon.
Open on Sat 22 Apr

Many styles, large and small, secret walled gardens, spring bulbs, herbaceous borders and more in the beautiful setting of the Cinque Port town of Winchelsea. Summer opening this year will be in two separate groups; seven gardens in June and six different gardens in July. Also six spring gardens in April. Explore the town with its magnificent church and famous medieval merchants' cellars. Town information at winchelsea.com and winchelseachurch.co.uk. Enquiries to david@ryeview.net, 01797 226524. If you are bringing a coach, please let us know. Guided tours of cellars, all dates at 11am, see winchelseacellars.com, booking essential 07596 182874. Wheelchair access to four of the gardens at each opening; see map for details.

  ♿ ❀ �
------

144 WINTERFIELD

Oldlands Avenue, Balcombe, RH17 6LP. Sue & Sarah Howe, 01444 811380, sarahjhowe_uk@yahoo.co.uk. *Just N of Balcombe station, R into Newlands, follow road uphill. Garden on R once road has become Oldlands Ave.* Wed 17 May, Sat 17 June (12-5). Combined adm with 46 Westup Farm Cottages £4, chd free. Home-made teas. Visits also by arrangement Apr to Sept for groups of 4+.
Plantsman's garden incl herbaceous and shrub borders, pond, wild flowers, gravelled areas, alpine troughs, secret garden, summerhouse and as many trees and shrubs as can be crammed into ⅓ acre. Newly renovated areas. Enthusiastic owners keen to tell you about the garden. Partial wheelchair access.

  ♿ 🐕 🚗 🚰

145 2 WOODSIDE

Lewes Road, Laughton, Lewes, BN8 6BL. Dick & Kathy Boland, 01323 811507, kathy.boland01@btinternet.com. *Approx 6m E of Lewes on B2124. In Laughton village 300yds E of Roebuck PH.* Mon 26 June (11-5). Combined adm with 1 Rose Cottage £5.50, chd free. Tea at 1 Rose Cottage. Visits also by arrangement June & July for groups of up to 25 max.
The garden was designed for summer living by its retired owners. The garden of approx ⅓ acre comprises a herb garden, a rockery and pond with fish, lawn and herbaceous borders, a small stream and wildlife pond, fruit trees, rose garden and vegetables in raised beds. A shaded area is being developed in a less formal setting among trees, planted with shade loving plants.

  🐕 ❀ 🚰

146 NEW WYCH WARREN HOUSE

Wych Warren, Forest Row, RH18 5LF. Colin King & Mary Franck. *1m S of Forest Row. Proceed on A22, track turning on L, 100 metres past 45mph warning triangle sign. Or 1m N of Wych Cross T-lights track turning on R. Go 400 metres across golf course till the end.* Wed 17 May (2-5.30). Home-made teas. Evening opening Wed 12 July (5-9). Wine. Adm £4, chd free.
6 acre garden in Ashdown Forest, AONB, much of it mixed woodland. Perimeter walk around property (not open). Delightful and tranquil setting with various aspects of interest, as works in progress incl a large pond, bog garden, Mediterranean and exotic garden and mixed herbaceous borders. Fine specimen trees and shrubs, rhododendrons and azaleas, lovely stonework. Much to please the eye! From the terrace beautiful views and refreshments available. Partial wheelchair access by tarmac track to the kitchen side gate.

  ♿ 🐕 ❀ 🚰

WARWICKSHIRE

For Birmingham & West Midlands see Staffordshire

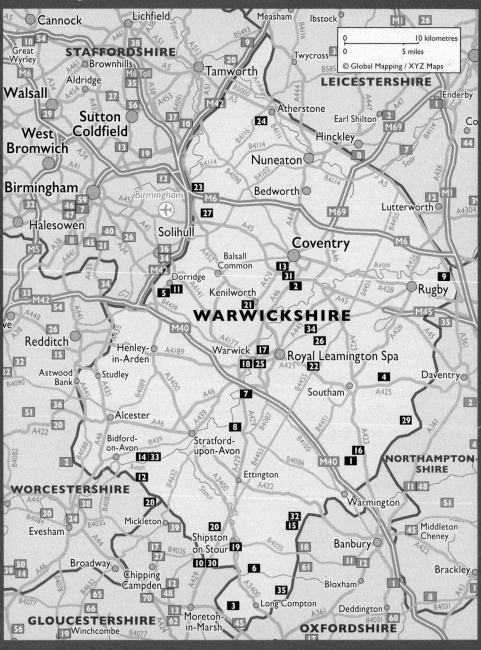

This county – say it 'Worrick-sher' – is a landlocked county, with a small capital town, a fashionable spa and plenty of quintessentially English villages.

There are also many welcoming Tudor beam and pretty stone 'foodie' pubs, and many varieties of plants and trees, depending on the soil type, all year round. Undulating countryside takes you from the edge of the Cotswolds in the south to the Evesham Vale in the west, up to the hillside of Atherstone in the north and on to Rugby and the farming land of the east. The gardens of Warwickshire are as varied as its landscape; gardens of every shape and size welcome visitors in aid of the National Garden Scheme.

Today, Warwickshire has a new theme for a new century – Tourism. Inspired by our old poacher William Shakespeare at Stratford-upon-Avon, the Bard's fans flock to Warwickshire from all over the world to delight in theatre, history and castles. But Warwickshire's gardens are also well worth a visit, being wonderfully varied in size and style, and all lovingly-looked after by very generous owners.

So next time you are visiting Warwickshire be sure to bring your Garden Visitor's Handbook with you, and enjoy the wonderful gardens our county has to offer!

Volunteers

County Organisers
Julia Sewell
01295 680234
sewelljulia@btinternet.com

Brenda Boardman
07769 913686
brenboardman@me.com

County Treasurer
Eleni Tovey
02476 419049
elenitovey@aol.com

Publicity
Lily Farrah
01789 204858
lily.farrah@ngs.org.uk

Social Media
Sal Renwick
01564 770215
sal.renwick@blueyonder.co.uk

Booklet Co-ordinator
Hugh Thomas
01926 423063
hugh@charityview.co.uk

Assistant County Organisers
Elspeth Napier
01608 666278
elspethmjn@gmail.com

David Ruffell
01926 316456
de.ruffell@btinternet.com

Liz Watson
01926 512307
liz.watson@talktalk.net

Left: Grump Cottage, Ilmington Gardens

OPENING DATES

All entries subject to change. For latest information check **www.ngs.org.uk**

Extended openings are shown at the beginning of the month.

Map locator numbers are shown to the right of each garden name.

February

Snowdrop Festival

Saturday 18th
Elm Close   14

Sunday 19th
Court House   10
◆ Hill Close Gardens   18

April

◆ Bridge Nursery
(Every Saturday and Sunday from Saturday 15th, plus Monday 17th)   4

Sunday 9th
Stretton-on-Fosse
   Gardens   30

Sunday 16th
Broadacre   5

May

◆ Bridge Nursery
(Every Saturday and Sunday, plus Monday 1st and Monday 29th)   4

Monday 1st
Earlsdon Gardens   13

Sunday 7th
Packington Hall   27

Sunday 14th
Merevale Hall   24

90th Anniversary Weekend

Sunday 28th
Barton House   3
The Granary   16
Pebworth Gardens   28

Monday 29th
The Granary   16
NEW Mallory Court
   Hotel   22
Pebworth Gardens   28

June

◆ Bridge Nursery
(Every Saturday and Sunday)   4

Saturday 3rd
Tysoe Gardens   32

Sunday 4th
Tysoe Gardens   32

Saturday 10th
Weston under
   Wetherley Gardens   34

Sunday 11th
Dorsington Gardens   12
Maxstoke Castle   23
Styvechale Gardens   31
Weston under
   Wetherley Gardens   34

Sunday 18th
Honington Village
   Gardens   19
Kenilworth Gardens   21
Whichford & Ascott
   Gardens   35

Thursday 22nd
◆ Charlecote Park   8

July

Saturday 24th
Ilmington Gardens   20
Welford-on-Avon &
   District Gardens   33

Sunday 25th
NEW Dorridge
   Gardens   11
Ilmington Gardens   20
Welford-on-Avon &
   District Gardens   33

July

◆ Bridge Nursery
(Every Saturday and Sunday)   4

Sunday 2nd
Avon Dassett Gardens   1
5 Carter Drive   7

Saturday 22nd
Garden Cottage &
   Walled Kitchen
   Garden   15
NEW Guy's Cliffe
   Walled Garden   17

Sunday 23rd
◆ Avondale Nursery   2
Garden Cottage &
   Walled Kitchen
   Garden   15
Stretton-on-Fosse
   Gardens   30

August

◆ Bridge Nursery
(Every Saturday and Sunday, plus Monday 28th)   4

Thursday 17th
◆ Charlecote Park   8

Sunday 20th
◆ Avondale Nursery   2

Sunday 27th
The Granary   16

Monday 28th
The Granary   16

September

◆ Bridge Nursery
(Every Saturday and Sunday to Sunday 24th)   4

Saturday 2nd
◆ Hill Close Gardens   18

Saturday 9th
Burmington Grange   6

Sunday 10th
Burmington Grange   6

By Arrangement

10 Avon Carrow, Avon
   Dassett Gardens   1
Barton House   3
Broadacre   5
NEW Clifton Hall Farm   9
Court House   10
16 Delaware Road,
   Styvechale Gardens   31
Elm Close   14
Fieldgate, Kenilworth
   Gardens   21
The Granary   16
2 The Hiron, Styvechale
   Gardens   31
Ilmington Manor,
   Ilmington Gardens   20
The Motte   26
Priors Marston Manor   29

Priors Marston Manor

Your visit to a garden will help more people be cared for by a Parkinson's nurse

Packington Hall

THE GARDENS

GROUP OPENING

1 AVON DASSETT GARDENS

Southam, CV47 2AE. *7m N of Banbury. From M40 J12 turn L & L again B4100. 2nd L into village. Park in village & at cemetery car park at the top of the hill.* **Sun 2 July (1-5). Combined adm £5, chd free. Home-made teas at The Limes.**

10 AVON CARROW

Anna Prosser, annaatthecarrow@btopenworld.com.

Visits also by arrangement Apr to Oct (excl Sun 2 July) for groups of 5+.

11 AVON CARROW

Mick & Avis Forbes.

THE COACH HOUSE

Diana & Peter Biddlestone.

THE EAST WING, AVON CARROW

Christine Fisher & Terry Gladwin.

HILL TOP FARM

Mrs N & Mr D Hicks.

THE LIMES

John & Diane Anderson.

OLD MILL COTTAGE

Mike & Jill Lewis.

THE OLD RECTORY

Lily Hope-Frost.

POPPY COTTAGE

Bob & Audrey Butler.

THE THATCHES

Trevor & Michele Gill.

Pretty Hornton stone village sheltering in the lee of the Burton Dassett hills, well wooded with parkland setting and The Old Rectory mentioned in Domesday Book. Wide variety of gardens incl kitchen gardens, gravel and tropical gardens. Range of plants incl alpines, herbaceous, perennials, roses, climbers and shrubs. Features incl book sale, plant sales, tombola and historic church open. Wheelchair access to most gardens.

  🚪 🐐 ✳ 🚌 ☕

2 ◆ AVONDALE NURSERY

at Russell's Nursery, Mill Hill, Baginton, CV8 3AG. Mr Brian Ellis, 02476 673662, enquiries@avondalenursery.co.uk, www.avondalenursery.co.uk. *3m S of Coventry. At junction of A45 & A46* *take slip road to Baginton, 1st L to Mill Hill, opp Old Mill Inn.* **For NGS: Sun 23 July, Sun 20 Aug (11-4). Adm £3, chd free. For other opening times and information, please phone, email or visit garden website.**

Vast array of flowers and ornamental grasses, incl National Collections of *Anemone nemorosa*, *Sanguisorba* and *Aster novae-angliae*. Choc-a-bloc with plants, our Library Garden is a well labelled reference book illustrating the unusual, exciting and even some long-lost treasures. Adjacent nursery is a plantaholic's delight! Big collections of *Helenium*, *Crocosmia*, *Sanguisorba* and ornamental grasses, and the garden will be looking at its best in July and August!

  🚪 🐐 ✳ 🚌 [NPC] ☕

3 BARTON HOUSE

Barton-on-the-Heath, GL56 0PJ. Mr & Mrs I H B Cathie, 01608 674303, hamish.cathie@ thebartonfarms.com. *2m W of Long Compton. 2m W off A3400 Stratford-upon-Avon to Oxford road; 1¼m N off A44 Chipping Norton to Moreton-in-Marsh road.* **Sun 28 May (2-6). Adm £5, chd free. Visits also by arrangement spring to autumn, for groups of 25+.**

6½ acres with mature trees, azaleas, species and hybrid rhododendrons, magnolias, moutan tree peonies. National collections of *Arbutus* and *Catalpa*. Japanese garden, rose garden, secret garden and many rare and exotic plants. Victorian kitchen garden. Exotic garden with palms, cypresses and olive trees established 2002. Taste wine from the vineyard, planted in 2000. Manor house by Inigo Jones (not open). Some gravel paths and steps. Can be slippery but generally wheelchair friendly. Dogs strictly on short leads only.

  👌 🐄 ✿ 🚐 NPC 🍵

4 ◆ BRIDGE NURSERY

Tomlow Road, Napton, Southam, CV47 8HX. Christine Dakin & Philip Martino, 01926 812737, chris.dakin25@yahoo.com, www.bridge-nursery.co.uk. *3m E of Southam. Brown tourist sign at Napton Xrds on A425 Southam to Daventry road.* **For NGS: Every Sat and Sun 15 Apr to 24 Sept (10-4). Mon 17 Apr, Mon 1, Mon 29 May, Mon 28 Aug (10-4). Adm £3, chd free. Light refreshments. For other opening times and information, please phone, email or visit garden website.**

Clay soil? Don't despair. Here is a garden full of an exciting range of plants which thrive in hostile conditions. Grass paths lead you round borders filled with many unusual plants. Features incl a pond and a bamboo grove complete with panda! A peaceful haven for wildlife and visitors. Visits also by arrangement, groups welcome, all proceeds to the NGS.

  👌 🐄 ✿ 🚐 🍵

5 BROADACRE

Grange Road, Dorridge, Solihull, B93 8QA. John Woolman, 07818 082885, jw234567@gmail.com, www.broadacregarden.org. *Approx 3m SE of Solihull. On B4101 opp Railway PH. Plenty of parking available.* **Sun 16 Apr (2-6). Adm £5, chd free. Home-made teas. Visits also by arrangement for any group size.**

Broadacre is a semi-wild garden, managed organically. Attractively landscaped with pools, lawns and trees, beehives, and adjoining stream and wild flower meadows. Bring stout footwear to follow the nature trail. Dorridge Cricket Club is on-site (the bar will be open). Lovely venue for a picnic. Dogs and children are welcome. Excellent country PH, The Railway at the bottom of the drive.

  👌 🐄 ✿ 🚐 🍵

BROUGHTON GRANGE

See Oxfordshire

6 BURMINGTON GRANGE

Cherington, Shipston on Stour, CV36 5HZ. Mr & Mrs Patrick Ramsay. *2m E of Shipston-on-Stour. Take Oxford Rd (A3400) from Shipston-on-Stour, after 2m turn L to Burmington, go through village & continue for 1m, turn L to Willington & Barcheston, on sharp L bend turn R over cattle grid.* **Sat 9, Sun 10 Sept (2-6). Adm £5, chd free. Home-made teas.**

Interesting plantsman's garden extending to about 1½ acres, set in the rolling hills of the North Cotswolds with wonderful views over unspoilt countryside. The garden is well developed considering it was planted 13 yrs ago. Small vegetable garden, beautiful sunken rose garden with herbaceous and shrub borders. Orchard and tree walk with unusual trees.

  🍵

7 5 CARTER DRIVE

Barford, Warwick, CV35 8ET. Mary & David Stenning. *8m NE of Stratford. From J16 on M40 take A429 Wellesbourne. Turn L signed Barford. At mini-r'about turn L into*

Church St, turn L into Kytes Lane (Barford village shop), turn 2nd L into Carter Drive. **Sun 2 July (12-4). Adm £3, chd free. Teas, coffee, or wine.**

Welcome to our jewelled haven, meandering down to the banks of the Avon where bright perennials bloom. We look forward to you visiting our unique garden soon! Small gravel area.

  👌 ✿ 🍵

8 ◆ CHARLECOTE PARK

Wellesbourne, Warwick, CV35 9ER. National Trust, 01789 470277, www.nationaltrust. org.uk/charlecote-park. *5m E of Stratford-upon-Avon, 6m S of Warwick, 1m W of Wellesbourne. J15 of M40 take A429 towards Cirencester, then signs for Charlecote Park. From Stratford-upon-Avon B4086 towards Wellesbourne, then signs for Charlecote Park.* **For NGS: Evening openings Thur 22 June, Thur 17 Aug (6-8). Adm £10, chd free. Drinks & canapés. Private tour of gardens lead by the Park & Garden Manager. Pre-booking essential, please phone to book (25 places for each opening). For other opening times and information, please phone or visit garden website.**

Charlecote Park has been home to the Lucy family for more than 800 yrs. The gardens incl a formal parterre, woodland walk, herbaceous border and wider parkland which is a Capability Brown landscape offering picturesque views across the R Avon. A herd of fallow deer has been in the park since Tudor times. Charlecote Park was one of the first gardens to open in support of NGS back in 1927. House not open. Gravel paths around the grounds.

  👌 🍵

9 NEW CLIFTON HALL FARM

Lilbourne Road, Clifton-upon-Dunsmore, CV23 0BB. Bob & Jenny Spencer, 07717 650837. *2m E of Rugby. From Clifton Church take Lilbourne Rd out of village. 1st farm on R, just past village sign.* **Visits by arrangement. Adm £5, chd free. Home-made teas.**

A feast of flowers down on the farm. A garden blossoming with emerald lawns and billowing borders. Silvery foliage, pond, waving grasses and 'pop' plants from hostas to alstromerias, bananas, tree ferns, it is all here! Farmer Bob's tractor display and a cuppa with Jenny will round off your visit. Two hour farm walks for groups available at no extra cost. A few gravel areas.

   🚗 🐕 ♿ ☕

10 COURT HOUSE

Stretton on Fosse, GL56 9SD. Christopher White, 01608 663811, mum@star.co.uk. *Off A429 between Moreton-in-Marsh & Shipston-on-Stour.* **Sun 19 Feb (11-2.30). Adm £5, chd free. Opening with Stretton-on-Fosse Gardens on Sun 9 Apr, Sun 23 July. Visits also by arrangement Feb to Sept.**
4 acre garden with yr-round interest and colour. Extensive and varied spring bulbs, and garden of winter interest. Herbaceous borders, spring beds, fernery, recently redesigned and restored walled kitchen garden. Rose garden, pond area and paddocks established with wild flowers. Featured in Cotswold Life. Wheelchair access is not impossible, but difficult with a gravel drive.

🚗

6 DINGLE END

See Worcestershire

Guy's Cliffe Walled Garden

GROUP OPENING

11 NEW DORRIDGE GARDENS

Blue Lake Road, Dorridge, Solihull, B93 8BH. *E of M40 & S of M42. Approx 4m S of Solihull. No parking in Temple Rd, but unlimited parking in Avenue Rd or Blue Lake Rd.* **Sun 25 June (1.30-5.30). Combined adm £5.50, chd free. Home-made teas at Carnlea House, 37 Temple Rd.**

NEW 44 AVENUE ROAD
Mr & Mrs M B Bullett.

75 BLUE LAKE ROAD
Sal & Peter Renwick.

NEW CARNLEA HOUSE
Miss Maureen Hill.

A unique chance to enjoy three beautiful gardens in Dorridge, with varied character and style. At 44 Avenue Road, you'll find a lovely informal cottage style garden, created by the owners over the last 30 yrs with a profusion of plants, shrubs and trees. There is also a stunning vintage car collection to admire! The rear garden gate also gives access to Carnlea in Temple Road, this s-facing garden, featuring island beds, a pergola clad with roses, acers, shrubs and perennials, has been totally redesigned over a number of yrs by its enthusiast plantswoman owner. Varied seating areas provide different perspectives of the garden. 75 Blue Lake Road is a lovely ½ acre garden, laid out with lawns, hedges, topiary and deep herbaceous borders, bursting with perennials. Paths lead to secret corners and sitting areas, incl a gazebo by a large pond, a wonderful spot to sit quietly and look for wildlife, incl newts, water boatmen and the occasional toad! Wheelchair access at 44 Avenue Road only. Sloping ground and steps at other gardens.

   🚗 🐕 ❀ ☕

GROUP OPENING

12 DORSINGTON GARDENS

Dorsington, CV37 8AR. *6m SW of Stratford-upon-Avon. On B439 from Stratford turn L to Welford-on-Avon, then R to Dorsington. Disabled parking available, please follow signs.* **Sun 11 June (12-5). Combined adm £6, chd free. Home-made teas in the village (signed on the day).**

CRABTREE FARM HOUSE
Nigel & Jane Davies.

2 DORSINGTON MANOR
Mr & Mrs C James.

10 DORSINGTON MANOR
Mr & Mrs Mansford.

1 GLEBE COTTAGES
Mr & Mrs A Brough.

NEW MEADOW HOUSE
Margaret Lindsay.

THE OLD RECTORY
Mr & Mrs Nigel Phillips.

NEW WELFORD PASTURES COTTAGE
Annie & John Daly.

Dorsington is a tranquil hamlet mentioned in the Domesday book, with a conservation area at its heart. You can visit a varied selection of gardens, ranging from extensive mature gardens to small cottage gardens. Each garden has the distinctive touch of their individual owners, so enjoy the abundant herbaceous borders, mature trees, neatly kept lawns, fruit and vegetable gardens, but do not forget to visit our lovely marquee for a splendid home-made tea. Additional village gardens will open on the day.

   ♿ 🐕 ❀ ☕

The National Garden Scheme and Perennial, helping gardeners when they are in need

GROUP OPENING

13 EARLSDON GARDENS

Coventry, CV5 6FS. *Turn towards Coventry at A45 & A429 T-lights. Take 3rd L into Beechwood Ave, continue ½ m to St Barbara's Church at Xrds with Rochester Rd. Maps & tickets at St Barbara's Church Hall.* **Mon 1 May (11-4). Combined adm £3.50, chd free. Light refreshments at St Barbara's Church Hall.**

43 ARMORIAL ROAD
Gary & Jane Flanagan.

3 BATES ROAD
Victor Keene MBE.

40 HARTINGTON CRESCENT
Viv & George Buss.

114 HARTINGTON CRESCENT
Liz Campbell & Denis Crowley.

40 RANULF CROFT
Mr & Mrs Spencer & Sue Swain.

54 SALISBURY AVENUE
Pam Moffit.

2 SHAFTESBURY ROAD
Ann Thomson & Bruce Walker.

23 SPENCER AVENUE
Susan & Keith Darwood.

NEW **27 SPENCER AVENUE**
Helene Devane.

NEW **84 SPENCER AVENUE**
Mr & Mrs Chris & Ruth Winters.

8 Alderman Way, Weston Under Wetherley Gardens

Varied selection of town gardens from small to more formal with interest for all tastes incl a mature garden with deep borders bursting with spring colour; a large garden with extensive lawns and an array of rhododendrons, azaleas and large mature trees; densely planted town garden with sheltered patio area and wilder woodland; and a surprisingly large garden offering interest to all ages! There is also a pretty garden set on several levels with hidden aspect; a large peaceful garden with water features and vegetable plot; a large mature garden in peaceful surroundings; and a plantaholic's garden with a large variety of plants, clematis and small trees.

14 ELM CLOSE

Welford on Avon, CV37 8PT. Eric & Glenis Dyer, 01789 750793, glenisdyer@gmail.com. *5m SW of Stratford, off B4390. Elm Close is between Welford Garage & The Bell Inn.* **Sat 18, Feb (1.30-3.30). Adm £3, chd free. Opening with Welford-on-Avon & District Gardens on Sat 24, Sun 25 June. Visits also by arrangement Feb to Sept for groups of 10-50. Adm £3 per head or min £30. Refreshments by prior request only.**

Drifts of snowdrops, aconites, erythroniums and hellebores in spring are followed by species peonies, sumptuous tree peonies, herbaceous peonies and delphiniums. Colourful Japanese maples, daphnes and cornus are underplanted with hostas, heucheras, and brunneras. Then agapanthus, salvias and hydrangeas extend the seasons, with hundreds of clematis providing yr-round colour. Gravel front drive slightly sloping. Garden mainly flat.

15 GARDEN COTTAGE & WALLED KITCHEN GARDEN

Shipston Road, Upper Tysoe, Warwick, CV35 0TR. Sue & Mike Sanderson. *W of A422, NW of Banbury (9m). E of A3400 & Shipston on Stour (4m). N of A435 & Brailes (3m). Parking opp entrance to garden.* **Sat 22, Sun 23 July (2-6). Adm £4, chd free. Home-made teas. Opening with Tysoe Gardens on Sat 3, Sun 4 June.**

Started in 2009 from an overgrown field covered in brambles and ivy clad fruit trees, the owners are developing this one acre plot into a modern walled kitchen garden. The garden contains a willow fedge, living roof and unusual vegetables grown following organic methods. There are many plants grown from cuttings and heritage seeds, fruit and vegetables, four greenhouses and many seating areas.

16 THE GRANARY

Fenny Compton Wharf, Fenny Compton, Southam, CV47 2FE. Lucy & Mike Davies, 01295 770033, bookings@the-granary.co.uk, www.the-granary.co.uk. *7m S of Southam. On A423 Southam to Banbury road. 200yds S of turning to Fenny Compton, turn R into service road signed Fenny Compton Wharf. Follow NGS signs.* **Sun 28, Mon 29 May, Sun 27, Mon 28 Aug (11-4.30). Adm £5, chd free. Light lunches & home-made teas. Visits also by arrangement Apr to Sept for groups of 15-35.**

Attractive 1 acre canal-side garden with views of the Oxford canal and Dassett Hills. Recent additions incl herbaceous beds, water feature, a cutting garden and herb garden. Beyond is a kitchen plot comprising a vegetable area (grown on organic principles), a polytunnel for propagation and salad crops, fruit cage and orchard. There is also a copse of native British trees in the 3 acre paddock. Refreshments incl teas with home-made cakes, light lunches, quiches and produce from the garden incl jams and preserves. Gravel paths with steps down to the herb garden and up to the vegetable area.

17 NEW GUY'S CLIFFE WALLED GARDEN

Coventry Road, Guy's Cliffe, Warwick, CV34 5FJ. Sarah Ridgeway, www.guyscliffe walledgarden.org.uk. *Behind Hintons Nursery in Guy's Cliffe, Warwick (use Hintons car park). Guy's Cliffe is on the A429, between North Warwick & Leek Wootton.* **Sat 22 July (10-3.30). Adm £2.50, chd free. Home-made teas.** A Grade II listed garden of special historic interest, having been the kitchen garden for Guy's Cliffe House. The garden dates back to the mid-1700s. Restoration work started 3 yrs ago; using plans from the early C19, the garden layout has already been reinstated and the beds, once more, planted with fruit, flowers and vegetables incl many heritage varieties. Glasshouses awaiting restoration. Original C18 walls. Exhibition of artefacts discovered during restoration.

&. 🐐 ☕

18 ◆ HILL CLOSE GARDENS

Bread and Meat Close, Warwick, CV34 6HF. Hill Close Gardens Trust, 01926 493339, centremanager@hcgt.org.uk, www.hillclosegardens.com. *Town centre. Follow signs to the racecourse. Entry from Friars St onto Bread & Meat Close. Car park by entrance next to racecourse. 2 hrs free parking. Disabled parking outside the gates.* **For NGS: Sun 19 Feb (11-4); Sat 2 Sept (11-5). Adm £4, chd £1. Light refreshments in Visitor Centre. For other opening times and information, please phone, email or visit garden website.** Restored Grade II* Victorian leisure gardens comprising 16 individual hedged gardens, 8 brick summerhouses. Herbaceous borders, heritage apple and pear trees, C19 daffodils, over 100 varieties of snowdrops, many varieties of asters and chrysanthemums. Heritage vegetables. Plant Heritage border, auricula theatre, and Victorian style glasshouse. Children's garden. Wheelchair available, please book in advance by phone. Access route indicated on plan of the gardens.

&. ✱ � NPC ☕

GROUP OPENING

19 HONINGTON VILLAGE GARDENS

Shipston-on-Stour, CV36 5AA. *1½m N of Shipston-on-Stour. Take A3400 towards Stratford-upon-Avon then turn R signed Honington.* **Sun 18 June (2-5.30). Combined adm £6, chd free. Home-made teas.**

HONINGTON GLEBE
Mr & Mrs J C Orchard.

HONINGTON HALL
B H E Wiggin.

THE MALTHOUSE
Mr & Mrs R Hunt.

THE OLD COTTAGE
Liz Davenport.

THE OLD HOUSE
Mr & Mrs I F Beaumont.

ORCHARD HOUSE
Mr & Mrs Monnington.

SHOEMAKERS COTTAGE
Christopher & Anne Jordan.

C17 village, recorded in Domesday, entered by old toll gate. Ornamental stone bridge over the R Stour and interesting church with C13 tower and late C17 nave after Wren. Seven super gardens. 2 acre plantsman's garden consisting of rooms planted informally with yr-round interest in contrasting foliage and texture, lily pool and parterre. Extensive lawns and fine mature trees with river and garden monuments. Secluded walled cottage garden with roses, and a structured cottage garden formally laid out with box hedging and small fountain. Small, developing garden created by the owners with informal mixed beds and borders. Wheelchair access to most gardens.

&. 🐐 ✱ 🚗 ☕

GROUP OPENING

20 ILMINGTON GARDENS

Ilmington, CV36 4LA. 01608 682230. *8m S of Stratford-upon-Avon. 8m N of Moreton in Marsh. 4m NW of Shipston-on-Stour off A3400. 3m NE of Chipping Campden.* **Sat 24, Sun 25 June** (2-6). Combined adm £7, chd free. Cream teas in the Ilmington Community Shop, Upper Green (Sat) & at the village hall (Sun). *Donation to Warwickshire & Northamptonshire Air Ambulance.*

THE BEVINGTONS
Mr & Mrs N Tustain.

CHERRY ORCHARD
Mr Angus Chambers.

CRAB MILL
Mr & Mrs D Brown.

FROG ORCHARD
Mr & Mrs Jeremy Snowden.

GRUMP COTTAGE
Mr & Mrs Martin Underwood.

ILMINGTON MANOR
Mr Martin Taylor, 01608 682230, mtilmington@btinternet.com. **Visits also by arrangement.**

PARK FARM HOUSE
Mike & Lesley Lane.

NEW PEAR TREE COTTAGE
Susan Carr.

RAVENSCROFT
Mr & Mrs Clasper.

NEW STUDIO COTTAGE
Sarah Hobson.

Ilmington is an ancient hillside Cotswold village 2m from the Fosse Way with two good PHs and splendid teas at the village hall. Buy your ticket at Ilmington Manor (next to the Red Lion PH); wander the 3 acre gardens with fish pond. Then walk to the upper green behind the village hall to tiny Grump Cottage's small stone terraced suntrap. Up Grump Street to Crab Mill's hillside gardens, then up to Ravenscroft's large sculpture filled sloping vistas commanding the hilltop. Walk to nearby Frog Lane, view cottage gardens at Park Farm House, Cherry Orchard, Frog Orchard, Pear Tree Cottage and Studio Cottage. Then to the Bevingtons huge cottage garden at the bottom of Vallenders Lane near the church and manor ponds. The Ilmington Morris Men performing round the village on Sun 25 June only.

☕

GROUP OPENING

21 KENILWORTH GARDENS

Kenilworth, CV8 1BT. *Fieldgate Lane off A452. Tickets & maps available at all gardens. Parking available at Abbey Fields. Street parking on Fieldgate Lane (limited), Malthouse Lane & Beehive Hill.* **Sun 18 June (1-5). Combined adm £5.50, chd free. Home-made teas at St Nicholas Parochial Hall.**

BEEHIVE HILL ALLOTMENTS
Madeleine Sexton.

FIELDGATE
Liz & Bob Watson, 01926 512307, liz.watson@talktalk.net. **Visits also by arrangement Apr to Aug for groups of 5-30.**

14C FIELDGATE LANE
Mrs Sandra Aulton.

NEW 1 FIELDGATE LAWN
Sandra Clough.

7 FIELDGATE LAWN
Mr Simon Cockell.

25 MALTHOUSE LANE
David & Linda Pettifor.

ST NICHOLAS PAROCHIAL HALL
St Nicholas Church.

Kenilworth was historically a very important town in Warwickshire. It has one of England's best castle ruins and plenty of PHs and good restaurants. This yr we welcome a new garden at 1 Fieldgate Lawn to the group making seven gardens in all, providing great variety. There are small and large gardens, with shrubs, herbaceous borders, ponds, formal lawns and more intimate, wildlife friendly areas, plus plenty of vegetables at the allotments. Many of the gardens have won Gold in the Kenilworth in Bloom garden competition. Partial wheelchair access to most of the gardens.

&. 🐐 ❀ 🚗 ☕ ⬛

22 NEW MALLORY COURT HOTEL

Harbury Lane, Leamington Spa, CV33 9BQ. Mrs Sarah Baker, General Manager, 01926 330214, www.mallory.co.uk. *3½m S of Leamington Spa, just off the B4087, between Whitnash & Bishop's Tachbrook.* **Mon 29 May (2-6). Adm £5, chd free. Home-made teas on the Brasserie Terrace.** Mallory Court is a breathtakingly beautiful country house hotel set in 10 acres of gardens that incl sweeping lawns, a croquet lawn, rose gardens, herbaceous borders and beds of seasonal flower displays. A range of herbs, vegetables and soft fruits are grown yr-round in the hotel's kitchen gardens for use in the restaurant. The gardens, which had become overgrown, are currently undergoing significant rejuvenation to return them to their former glory.

🚌 🛏 ☕

THE MANOR
See Gloucestershire

23 MAXSTOKE CASTLE

Coleshill, B46 2RD. Mr & Mrs M C Fetherston-Dilke. *2½m E of Coleshill. E of Birmingham, on B4114. Take R turn down Castle Lane, Castle Drive 1¼m on R.* **Sun 11 June (11-5). Adm £7.50, chd £5. Home-made teas.** Approx 5 acres of garden and grounds with herbaceous, shrubs and trees in the immediate surroundings of this C14 moated castle. No wheelchair access to house.

&. ❀ ☕

74 MEADOW ROAD
See Worcestershire

24 MEREVALE HALL

Atherstone, CV9 2HG. Sir William 'Matthew' & Lady Paige Dugdale. *¾m SW of Atherstone. Entrance is 300yds SE of r'about on A5 at Merevale Lane, between 2 single storey gate houses. Garden 1m up drive. SatNav: Merevale Rd, Atherstone.* **Sun 14 May (2-5). Adm £7, chd free. Light refreshments.**

Good mixture of formal and wilderness over 29 acres, incl a parterre by Nesfield, stumpery, bog garden and walled garden. In May it is a riot of colour with bluebells, azaleas and rhododendrons.

🐐 ☕

25 ◆ THE MILL GARDEN

55 Mill Street, Warwick, CV34 4HB. Julia (née Measures) Russell & David Russell, www.visitwarwick.co.uk/placeofinterest/the-mill-garden. *Off A425 beside old castle gate, at the bottom of Mill St. Disabled parking & drop off only, use nearby St Nicholas car park.* **For opening times and information, please visit garden website.** This garden lies in a magical setting on the banks of the R Avon beneath the walls of Warwick Castle. Winding paths lead round every corner to dramatic views of the castle and ruined Medieval bridge. This informal cottage garden is a profusion of plants, shrubs and trees. Beautiful all year. In 2016 the garden won first prize in the Warwick in Bloom competition for the best garden open to the public. Open daily 1st April to 31st October (9-6). Partial wheelchair access. Not suitable for electric wheelchairs or large pushchairs.

&. ❀

MORTON HALL
See Worcestershire

26 THE MOTTE

School Lane, Hunningham, Leamington Spa, CV33 9DS. Margaret & Peter Green, 01926 632903, pjg@trillium.fsnet.co.uk. *5m E of Leamington Spa. 1m NW off B4455 (Fosse Way) at Hunningham Hill Xrds.* **Visits by arrangement May to Aug for groups of up to 20 max. Tea, coffee and home-made cake on request. Adm £3.50, chd free.** Plant lover's garden of about ⅓ acre, well stocked with unusual trees, shrubs and herbaceous plants. Set in the quiet village of Hunningham with views over the R Leam and surrounding countryside. The garden has been developed over the last 14 yrs and incl woodland, exotic and herbaceous borders, raised alpine bed, troughs, pots and wildlife pond. Plant-filled conservatory. Access to front and upper rear garden.

 ⌖ 🐄 ☕

27 PACKINGTON HALL
Meriden, nr Coventry, CV7 7HF. Lord & Lady Aylesford. *Midway between Coventry & Birmingham on A45. Entrance 400yds from Stonebridge Island towards Coventry. For SatNav please use CV7 7HE.* **Sun 7 May (2.30-5). Adm £5.50, chd free. Home-made teas.** Packington is the setting for an elegant Capability Brown landscape. Designed from 1750 in 100 acres of parkland which sweeps down to a lake incl 1762 Japanese bridge. Delicious WI teas on the terrace or in The Pompeiian Room if wet. Wheelchair access to gardens, but all areas are grass, so difficult in wet conditions.

 ⌖ ☕

GROUP OPENING

28 PEBWORTH GARDENS
Stratford-upon-Avon, CV37 8XZ. *9m SW of Stratford-upon-Avon. On B439 at Bidford turn S towards Honeybourne, after 3m turn L at Xrds signed Pebworth.* **Sun 28, Mon 29 May (12-6). Combined adm £7, chd free. Home-made teas at Pebworth Village Hall.**

BANK HOUSE
Clive & Caroline Warren.

NEW EDGEFIELD, 4 ORCHARD CLOSE
Mr & Mrs G Grainger.

I ELM CLOSE
Mr & Mrs G Keyte.

FELLY LODGE
Maz & Barrie Clatworthy.

IVYBANK
Mr & Mrs R Davis.
NPC

JASMINE COTTAGE
Ted & Veronica Watson.

THE KNOLL
Mr & Mrs K Wood.

MAPLE BARN
Mr & Mrs Richard & Wendi Weller.

MEON COTTAGE
David & Sally Donnison.

PETTIFER HOUSE
Mr & Mrs Michael Veal.

4 WESLEY GARDENS
Anne & Mike Johnson.

Pebworth received a Gold Medal in Britain in Bloom Heart of England competition 2016. The gardens in Pebworth are topped by St Peter's Church (open), which came 4th in Worcestershire Best Kept Churchyard 2015, and has a large ring of ten bells which is unusual for a small rural church. This is a delightful village with old thatched cottages, and properties of various ages. There are a variety of garden styles to be seen from cottage gardens to modern, walled and terraced gardens. This yr we have 11 gardens opening, with yummy tea and cakes provided by the Pebworth WI. No wheelchair access to several of the gardens.

 ⌖ ✿ ♿ ☕

The Queen's Nursing Institute founded the National Garden Scheme exactly 90 years ago

29 PRIORS MARSTON MANOR
The Green, Priors Marston, CV47 7RH. Dr & Mrs Mark Cecil, 07934 440949, whewitt15@yahoo.co.uk. *8m SW of Daventry. Off A361 between Daventry & Banbury at Charwelton. Follow sign to Priors Marston approx 2m. Arrive at T-junction with war* memorial on R. Manor on L. Minibus & small coach parking. **Visits by arrangement June to Sept Mon-Thur only (excl BH). Home-made teas for group bookings only. Adm £5, chd free.** Arrive in Priors Marston village and explore the manor gardens. Greatly enhanced by present owners to relate back to a Georgian manor garden and pleasure grounds. Wonderful walled kitchen garden provides seasonal produce and cut flowers for the house. Herbaceous flower beds and a sunken terrace with water feature by William Pye. Lawns lead down to the lake around which you can walk amongst the trees and wildlife, with stunning views up to the house and garden aviary. Sculpture on display. Partial wheelchair access.

 ⌖ ☕

GROUP OPENING

30 STRETTON-ON-FOSSE GARDENS
Stretton on Fosse, GL56 9SD. *Off A429 between Moreton-in-Marsh & Shipston-on-Stour. Two gardens in the centre of the village. Court House is next to the church, Old Beams a few doors away.* **Sun 9 Apr, Sun 23 July (2-5.30). Combined adm £6, chd free. Home-made teas at Court House.**

COURT HOUSE
Christopher White.
(See separate entry)

OLD BEAMS
Mrs Hilary Fossey.

Court House is a continually evolving, 4 acre garden with yr-round interest and colour. Extensive and varied spring bulbs. Herbaceous borders, fernery, recently redesigned and restored walled kitchen garden. Rose garden, newly planted winter garden, pond area and paddocks which are gradually being established with wild flowers. Old Beams is a walled cottage garden on a slope with traditional cottage garden plants, small lawn, rockery, fruit cage and vegetable garden.

 ✿ ☕

GROUP OPENING

31 STYVECHALE GARDENS

Baginton Road, Coventry, CV3 6FP.
The gardens are located on the s-side of Coventry close to A45. Tickets & map available on the day from West Orchard United Reformed Church, The Chesils, CV3 6FP. Advance tickets available from suepountney@ btinternet.com. **Sun 11 June (11-5). Combined adm £4, chd free. Light refreshments.** *Donation to Coventry Myton Hospice.*

11 BAGINTON ROAD
Ken & Pauline Bond.

164 BAGINTON ROAD
Fran & Jeff Gaught.

59 THE CHESILS
John Marron & Richard Bantock.

16 DELAWARE ROAD
Val & Roy Howells,
02476 419485,
valshouse@hotmail.co.uk.
Visits also by arrangement May to Sept with other Styvechale gardens.

2 THE HIRON
Sue & Graham Pountney,
02476 502044,
suepountney@btinternet.com.
Visits also by arrangement May to Aug with other Styvechale gardens.

177 LEAMINGTON ROAD
Barry & Ann Suddens.

8 THE SPINNEY
Professor Michael & Eleni Tovey.

A collection of lovely, mature, suburban gardens, each one different in style and size. Come and enjoy the imaginatively planted herbaceous borders, spectacular roses, water features, fruit and vegetable patches, cottage garden planting and shady areas, something for everyone and plenty of ideas for you to take home. Relax in the gardens and enjoy the warm, friendly welcome you will receive from us all. There will be refreshments available and plants for sale in some of the gardens. Other gardens will be open on the day.

A vehicle will be required to visit 8 The Spinney, but a garden well worth the trip; an easy 10 min drive from the ticket office.

🐂 ✿ 🚗 ☕ 🍷

GROUP OPENING

32 TYSOE GARDENS

Middle and Upper Tysoe, Warwick, CV35 0SE. *W of A422, N of Banbury (9m). E of A3400 & Shipston-on-Stour (4m). N of A4035 & Brailes (3m). Parking on the recreation ground CV35 0SE. Entrance tickets & maps at the village hall. Free bus.* **Sat 3, Sun 4 June (2-6). Combined adm £6, chd free. Home-made teas in Tysoe Village Hall & cold drinks at Garden Cottage.**

CHURCH FARM HOUSE
Sylvia & Charles Davies.

DINSDALE HOUSE
Julia & David Sewell.

GARDEN COTTAGE & WALLED KITCHEN GARDEN
Sue & Mike Sanderson.
(See separate entry)

IVYDALE
Sam & Malcolm Littlewood.

7 JEFFS CLOSE
Emma & Tom Moffatt.

KERNEL COTTAGE
Christine Duke.

LAUREL HOUSE
Damaris & Michael Appleton.

THE OLD BUTCHER'S HOUSE
Sue & Gerald Hart.

THE OLD POLICE HOUSE
Bridget & Digby Norton.

SMARTSWELL COTTAGE
Jan & Colin Lumley.

NEW **THE WILLOWS**
Alan & Ethel Birkbeck.

Tysoe, an original old Hornton stone village divided into three parts, sits at the bottom of the north-eastern edge of the Cotswold Hills near the site of the Battle of Edgehill. The eleven gardens making up this group in Middle Tysoe are diverse

in character of house, planting, size and style. Opening last year for the first time we were amazed at the number of NGS supporters who visited our gardens. Over 25 people either baked or served delicious home-made cakes and teas. The bakers will be baking again very soon! A truly village affair. The 'Shipston Link' bus will be available for free transport around the village. Vintage and classic cars will be exhibiting near the village hall. Please come and see our gardens including the Old Police House and the Old Butcher's House, the willow fedge and living roof in a modern walled garden, several cottage gardens and (new) the picturesque thatched cottage with its newly planted garden. A warm welcome awaits. Partial wheelchair access.

♿ ✿ 🚗 ☕ 🍷

GROUP OPENING

33 WELFORD-ON-AVON & DISTRICT GARDENS

Welford-on-Avon, CV37 8PT.
5m SW of Stratford-upon-Avon. Off B4390. **Sat 24, Sun 25 June (2-6). Combined adm £5, chd free. Home-made teas in the village hall.**

ASH COTTAGE
Mr & Mrs Peter & Sue Hook.

BOX ACRE
Phil Irons.

ELM CLOSE
Eric & Glenis Dyer.
(See separate entry)

NEW **THE OLD RECTORY**
Frank Kennedy.

6 QUINEYS LEYS
Mr & Mrs Gordon & Penny Whitehead.

SOUTHLAWNS
Dr & Mrs Guy & Amanda Kitteringham.

In addition to its superb position on the river, with serene swans, dabbling ducks and resident herons, Welford-on-Avon has a beautiful church, an excellent family butcher's shop, a very convenient general store and a selection of PHs serving great food. Just down the road is a highly popular farm shop where seasonal fruit and vegetables are much in demand. With its great variety of house styles, including an abundance of beautiful cottages with thatched roofs and chocolate-box charisma, Welford also has an army of keen gardeners. The gardens open for the NGS range from small to large, from established to newly designed and planted, to those with wild areas, sculptures and croquet lawns. Fruit and vegetable areas are also integral to these gardens for all seasons.

✿ ☕

GROUP OPENING

34 WESTON UNDER WETHERLEY GARDENS
Rugby Road, Weston Under Wetherley, Leamington Spa, CV33 9BY. *3m NE of Leamington Spa on B4453. Park at village hall & near church. Disabled parking at some gardens. All gardens well signed & a guide to gardens available at car parks.* **Sat 10, Sun 11 June (12.30-5.30). Combined adm £5, chd free. Home-made teas at the village hall, Sabin Drive.**

4 ALDERMAN WAY
Mr Paddy Taylor.

7 ALDERMAN WAY
Jane Jones.

8 ALDERMAN WAY
Tracy & Bill Byrne.

10 ALDERMAN WAY
Alastair Rodda.

23 ALDERMAN WAY
Lynne Williams.

GLEBE COTTAGE
Stephen Evans.

NEW LITTLE HAVEN
Carolyn Davis.

THE OLD FORGE
Sarah & Peter Haine.

NEW RANCH HOUSE
Mr & Mrs Duncan Brown.

5 RUGBY ROAD
Bren Boardman, www.brenboardman.com.

13 RUGBY ROAD
Jean Smith.

Originating as the 'West stone of the hundred of Knightlow SE of Wetherley Wood', the village's early residents made a living from the land, and agriculture is still strong in the area. Hence, many gardens have been shaped over centuries, though current owners have put their distinctive mark on them. Newer properties will equally be enjoyed, with their formal, informal and highly inventive gardens. In all, eleven gardens will be open offering a wide variety of features. Enjoy the newly created oasis at Little Haven, a wildflower meadow at The Ranch House, several cottage-style gardens, maturing wildlife habitats at The Old Forge, and some strikingly contrasting gems for visitors exploring the newer homes in Alderman Way. All of this accompanied by stunning views of the surrounding countryside, craft stalls and refreshments at the village hall. Plants for sale at some gardens. You also have the opportunity to visit our historic C12 Church of St Michael. Most properties have wheelchair access with parking nearby.

&. 🐐 ✿ 🚗 ☕

GROUP OPENING

35 WHICHFORD & ASCOTT GARDENS
Whichford & Ascott, Shipston-on-Stour, CV36 5PP. *6m SE of Shipston-on-Stour. Taking the A3400, the turning to Whichford & Ascott is equidistant between Chipping Norton & Shipston-on-Stour. From Banbury & villages to the NE, take the Hook Norton & Whichford road from Bloxham. Free car parking opp the church, & some in Ascott.* **Sun 18 June (2-5.30). Combined adm £6, chd free. Home-made teas at Knights Place.**

ASCOTT LODGE
Charlotte Copley.

NEW BELMONT HOUSE
Robert & Yoko Ward.

KNIGHT'S PLACE
Mr & Mrs Derek Atkins.

THE OLD RECTORY
Peter & Caroline O'Kane.

PLUM TREE COTTAGE
Janet Knight.

WHICHFORD HILL HOUSE
Mr & Mrs John Melvin.

THE WHICHFORD POTTERY
Jim & Dominique Keeling, www.whichfordpottery.com.

This group of gardens reflects a range of several garden types and sizes. The two villages are in an AONB. They nestle within a dramatic landscape of hills, pasture and woodland, which is used to picturesque effect by the garden owners. Fine lawns, mature shrub planting and much interest to plantsmen provide a peaceful visit to a series of beautiful gardens. Many incorporate the inventive use of natural springs, forming ponds, pools and other water features. Classic cottage gardens contrast with larger and more classical gardens which adopt variations on the traditional English garden of herbaceous borders, climbing roses, yew hedges and walled enclosures. Other amenities are the C12 church, the internationally renowned pottery, and a PH serving meals. Featured in The Daily Telegraph (2016). Always covered by the Stratford Herald, the Cotswold Journal and the Banbury Guardian. Partial wheelchair access as some gardens are on sloping sites.

&. 🐐 ✿ 🛏 ☕

The East Wing, Avon Carrow, Avon Dassett Gardens

WILTSHIRE

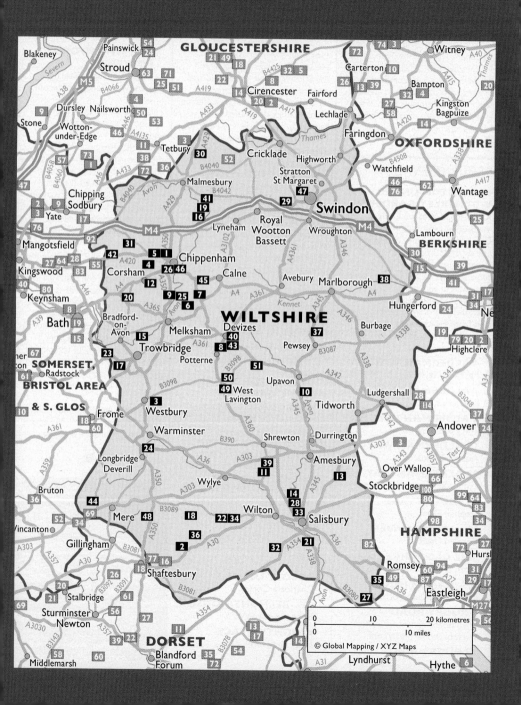

Wiltshire, a predominantly rural county, covers 1,346 square miles and has a rich diversity of landscapes, including downland, wooded river valleys and Salisbury Plain.

Chalk lies under two-thirds of the county, with limestone to the north, which includes part of the Cotswolds Area of Outstanding Natural Beauty. The county's gardens reflect its rich history and wide variety of environments.

Gardens opening for the National Garden Scheme include the celebrated landscape garden of Stourhead and other National Trust properties, large privately owned gems such as Broadleas, Biddestone Manor and Mawarden Court, and more modest properties that are lovingly maintained by the owners, such as Sweet Briar Cottage and Duck Pond Barn.

The season opens with the snowdrops at Lacock Abbey and continues with fine spring gardens like Fonthill House, Corsham Court and Allington Grange.

A wide selection of gardens, large and small, are at their peak in the summer. There are also town gardens, a new village opening at Landford, allotments, a lavender garden and a Chinese garden at Beggars Knoll. There is something to delight the senses from February to October.

Volunteers

County Organisers
Sean & Kena Magee
01666 880009
spbmagee@googlemail.com

County Treasurers
Sean & Kena Magee
(as above)

**Publicity
& Booklet Co-ordinator**
Tricia Duncan
01672 810443
tricia@windward.biz

Social Media
Marian Jones
01249 657400
marian.jones@ngs.org.uk

Assistant County Organiser
Suzie Breakwell
01985 850297
suzievb@me.com

Sarah Coate
01722 782365
sarah.coate@woodfordvalley.net

Jo Hankey
01722 742472
rbhankey@gmail.com

Shirley Heywood
01985 844486
shirleyheywood@btinternet.com

Diana Robertson
01672 810515
diana@broomsgrovelodge.co.uk

Left: 5 Whitehorn Drive,
Landford Village Gardens

OPENING DATES

All entries subject to change. For latest information check www.ngs.org.uk

Map locator numbers are shown to the right of each garden name.

February

Snowdrop Festival

Saturday 25th
◆ Lacock Abbey
  Gardens   25

March

Sunday 19th
Fonthill House   18

Sunday 26th
Allington Grange   1

April

Sunday 9th
◆ Corsham Court   12

Saturday 22nd
Job's Mill   24

Sunday 23rd
Cottage in the Trees   13
◆ Iford Manor   23
Oare House   37
◆ Stourhead Garden   44

May

Sunday 7th
Little Durnford Manor   28
◆ Waterdale House   48

Sunday 14th
◆ Corsham Court   12

Wednesday 17th
Bowden Park   6
Hazelbury Manor
  Gardens   20

Sunday 21st
Broadleas House
  Gardens   8
Cantax House   9

◆ Twigs Community
  Garden   47

Friday 26th
Windmill Cottage   50

90th Anniversary Weekend

Sunday 28th
Allington Grange   1
Biddestone Manor   4
Cottage in the Trees   13
Hyde's House   22

Monday 29th
Allington Grange   1

June

Saturday 3rd
Job's Mill   24

Sunday 4th
Ark Farm   2

Tuesday 6th
◆ The Courts Garden   15

Thursday 8th
Windmill Cottage   50

Friday 9th
Windmill Cottage   50

Saturday 10th
West Lavington Manor   49

Sunday 11th
Chisenbury Priory   10
Cottage in the Trees   13
Dauntsey Gardens   16
Hazelbury Manor
  Gardens   20

Friday 16th
NEW Pear Cottage   40
NEW 1 Southview   43

Saturday 17th
Great Somerford
  Gardens   19

Sunday 18th
Bolehyde Manor   5
Great Somerford
  Gardens   19
NEW Manor Farm   30
North Cottage   36

Tuesday 20th
NEW New Forest Lavender   35

Thursday 22nd
Windmill Cottage   50

Friday 23rd
Windmill Cottage   50

Sunday 25th
Broadleas House
  Gardens   8
Oare House   37
The Old Mill   38
NEW The Old Rectory   39
Ridleys Cheer   42

July

Sunday 2nd
Duck Pond Barn   17
North Cottage   36

Thursday 6th
The Manor House,
  Castle Combe   31

Saturday 8th
NEW Landford Village
  Gardens   27

Sunday 9th
NEW Landford Village
  Gardens   27
Mitre Cottage   34
84 Studley Lane   45

Thursday 13th
Windmill Cottage   50

Friday 14th
Windmill Cottage   50

Sunday 16th
Broadleas House
  Gardens   8
◆ Lydiard Park Walled
  Garden   29

Wednesday 19th
Manor House,
  Stratford Tony   32

Sunday 23rd
Horatio's Garden   21
Mawarden Court   33
Sweet Briar Cottage   46
◆ Twigs Community
  Garden   47

Tuesday 25th
NEW New Forest Lavender   35

Sunday 30th
130 Ladyfield Road
  and Allotments   26

August

Wednesday 9th
The Old Mill   38

Sunday 27th
NEW Wudston House   51

September

Sunday 3rd
Broadleas House
  Gardens   8
Cottage in the Trees   13

Wednesday 6th
Manor House,
  Stratford Tony   32

Wednesday 13th
Hazelbury Manor
  Gardens   20

October

Saturday 7th
Ridleys Cheer   42

February 2018

Saturday 24th
◆ Lacock Abbey
  Gardens   25

By Arrangement

Allington Grange   1
Beggars Knoll
  Chinese Garden   3
Bolehyde Manor   5
Cantax House   9
Chisenbury Priory   10
Cockspur Thorns   11
Cottage in the Trees   13
The Court House   14
Duck Pond Barn   17
The Garden Cottage,
  Dauntsey Gardens   16
Manor House,
  Stratford Tony   32
North Cottage   36
NEW Pear Cottage   40
The Pound House   41
NEW 1 Southview   43
84 Studley Lane   45
Sweet Briar Cottage   46
West Lavington Manor   49
Windmill Cottage   50

THE GARDENS

1 ALLINGTON GRANGE

Allington, Chippenham,
SN14 6LW. Mrs Rhyddian Roper,
01249 447436,
rhyddianroper@hotmail.co.uk,
www.allingtongrange.com. *2m W
of Chippenham. Take A420 W from
Chippenham. 1st R signed Allington
Village, entrance 1m up lane on L.*
**Sun 26 Mar (2-4.30); Sun 28,
Mon 29 May (2-5). Adm £4, chd
free. Home-made teas. Visits
also by arrangement Feb to
June for groups.**
Informal country garden of approx
1½ acres, around C17 farmhouse
(not open) with yr-round interest
and a diverse range of plants.
Snowdrops followed by hellebores
and many early spring bulbs. Mixed
and herbaceous borders, colour
themed; white garden with water
fountain. Pergola lined with clematis
and roses. Walled potager. Small
orchard with chickens. Wildlife pond
with natural planting. Featured in the
English Garden and Wiltshire Life
magazines. Mainly level with ramp
into potager. Dogs on leads. For
March opening, please check NGS
website or telephone if very wet.

2 ARK FARM

Old Wardour, Tisbury, Salisbury,
SP3 6RP. Mrs Miranda Thomas.
*Old Wardour is 2m from Tisbury.
Drive down High Street and on, past
station, take 1st R. Follow signs to Old
Wardour Castle.* **Sun 4 June (2-5).
Adm £4, chd free. Home-made
teas.**
Informal hidden gardens in beautiful
setting with small wooded area,
pond, water plants, lakeside walk,
views of Old Wardour castle.
This is a very difficult garden for
wheelchairs. Not advised!

3 BEGGARS KNOLL CHINESE GARDEN

Newtown, Westbury, BA13 3ED.
Colin Little & Penny Stirling,
01373 823383,
silkendalliance@talktalk.net. *1m
SE of Westbury. Turn off B3098 at
White Horse Pottery, up hill towards
the White Horse for ¾ m. Parking at
end of drive for 10-12 cars.* **Visits by
arrangement June & July, group
max 24, but smaller numbers
and individuals are welcome.
Visits incl guided tour. Adm
£5.50, chd free. Tea and home-
made cake £3.50. We already
have quite a reputation for the
homemade cakes - especially the
walnut and coffee cake.**

This inspirational 1-acre garden,
divided up into a series of Chinese
rooms, is filled with colourful
plantings set against a backdrop
of Chinese pavilions, gateways,
statues and dragons. Intricate
Chinese mosaic pavements wind
around ponds and rocks. Rare
Chinese shrubs, mature trees and
flower filled borders form a haven
of serenity. Large potager houses
chickens. Spectacular views too!

4 BIDDESTONE MANOR

Chippenham Lane, Biddestone,
SN14 7DJ. Rosie Harris, Head
Gardener. *5m W of Chippenham.
On A4 between Chippenham &
Corsham turn N. From A420, 5m W
of Chippenham, turn S. Use car park.*
**Sun 28 May (3-7). Adm £5, chd
free. Bring a picnic or cheese
and wine served.**
A longer opening to enjoy the
peaceful acres of wide lawns, lakes
and ponds, arboretum, wild flowers,
kitchen garden, cutting garden and
fruit garden. Wheelchair access to
most parts, a few steps, help always
available.

5 BOLEHYDE MANOR

Allington, SN14 6LW. The Earl &
Countess Cairns, 01249 443056,
amandamcairns@gmail.com. *1½ m
W of Chippenham. On Bristol Rd
(A420). Turn N at Allington Xrds. ½ m
on R. Parking in field.* **Sun 18 June
(2.30-5.30). Adm £5, chd free.
Home-made teas. Visits also
by arrangement May & June,
groups on weekdays preferred.**
Series of gardens around C16
manor house (not open), enclosed
by walls and topiary. Formal
framework densely planted with
many interesting shrubs and
climbers, especially roses. Mixed
borders. Blue walk of alliums
and agapanthus. Inner courtyard
with troughs full of tender plants.
Collection of tender pelargoniums.
Vegetable/fruit garden and
greenhouse.

Beggars Knoll Chinese Garden

© Carole Drake

6 BOWDEN PARK

Lacock, Chippenham, SN15 2PP. Bowden Park Estate. *10 mins from Chippenham. Entrance via Top Lodge at top of Bowden Hill, between A342 at Sandy Lane and A350 in Lacock.* **Wed 17 May (11-4). Adm £5, chd free. Light refreshments.** 22 acre private garden within surrounding parkland. Pleasure garden, water garden, working kitchen garden with formal lawns and grotto. Rhododendrons and azaleas in flower.

7 ◆ BOWOOD WOODLAND GARDENS

Calne, SN11 9PG. The Marquis of Lansdowne, 01249 812102, reception@bowood.org, www.bowood.org. *3½ m SE of Chippenham. Located off J17 M4 nr Bath & Chippenham. Entrance off A342 between Sandy Lane & Derry Hill Villages. Follow brown signs.* **For opening times and information, please phone, email or visit garden website.**
This 60 acre woodland garden of azaleas, magnolias, rhododendrons and bluebells is one of the most exciting of its type in the country. From the individual flowers to the breathtaking sweep of colour formed by hundreds of shrubs, this is a garden not to be missed. The Woodland Gardens are located 2m from Bowood House and Garden. Open from April to June. Please visit garden website for the exact seasonal opening dates.

8 BROADLEAS HOUSE GARDENS

Devizes, SN10 5JQ. Mr & Mrs Cardiff. *1m S of Devizes. From Hartmoor Rd turn L into Broadleas Park, follow rd for 350 metres then turn R into estate. Please note, there is no access from A360 Potterne Rd.* **Sun 21 May, Sun 25 June, Sun 16 July, Sun 3 Sept (2-5.30). Adm £5, chd free. Home-made teas.**
6 acre garden of hedges, herbaceous borders, rose arches, bee garden and orchard stuffed with good plants. It is overlooked by the house

and arranged above the small valley garden which is crowded with magnolias and rhododendrons, cornus and hydrangeas.

9 CANTAX HOUSE

Lacock, SN15 2JZ. Andrew & Deborah van der Beek, dvdb@deborahvanderbeek.com, www.deborahvanderbeek.com. *3m S of Chippenham. Off A350 between Chippenham & Melksham. Please use signed public car park if possible (except disabled). Entrance to garden in Cantax Hill.* **Sun 21 May (2-6). Adm £5, chd free. Cream teas. Visits also by arrangement Apr to Oct, 10+ preferred.** *Donation to Amnesty International.*
Queen Anne former vicarage (not open). Medium-sized garden of colour, pattern and scent straddling the Bide Brook. Designed and maintained by sculptor owner for 28yrs; both common and unusual plants incl wild flower sports; hornbeam spire, yew castle and other topiary; old orchard wildflower garden; sculpture by owner and friends. In lovely old village featured in many films. House front featured in Cranford, BBC Emma and Harry Potter (Slughorn's house).

10 CHISENBURY PRIORY

East Chisenbury, SN9 6AQ. Mr & Mrs John Manser, Peterjohnmanser@yahoo.com. *3m SW of Pewsey. Turn E from A345 at Enford then N to E Chisenbury, main gates 1m on R.* **Sun 11 June (2-6). Adm £5, chd free. Home-made teas. Visits also by arrangement May to July.**
Medieval Priory with Queen Anne face and early C17 rear (not open) in middle of 5 acre garden on chalk. Mature garden with fine trees within clump and flint walls, herbaceous borders, shrubs, roses. Moisture loving plants along mill leat, carp pond, orchard and wild garden, many unusual plants. Front borders redesigned in 2009 by Tom Stuart-Smith.

11 COCKSPUR THORNS

Berwick St James, Salisbury, SP3 4TS. Stephen & Ailsa Bush, 01722 790445, stephenjdbush@gmail.com. *8m NW of Salisbury. 1m S of A303, on B3083 at S end of village of Berwick St James.* **Visits by arrangement May to Aug for groups of 10+, weekdays preferred. Adm £4.50, chd free. Home-made teas.**
2¼ acre garden, completely redesigned 16yrs ago and developments since, featuring roses (particularly colourful in June), herbaceous border, shrubbery, small walled kitchen garden, secret pond garden, mature and new unusual small trees, fruit trees and areas of wild flowers. Beech, yew and thuja hedgings planted to divide the garden. Small number of vines planted during winter of 2015.

12 ◆ CORSHAM COURT

Corsham, SN13 0BZ. Lord Methuen, 01249 701610, staterooms@corsham-court.co.uk, www.corsham-court.co.uk. *4m W of Chippenham. Signed off A4 at Corsham.* **For NGS: Sun 9 Apr, Sun 14 May (2-5). Adm £5, chd £2.50. For other opening times and information, please phone, email or visit garden website.**
Park and gardens laid out by Capability Brown and Repton. Large lawns with fine specimens of ornamental trees surround the Elizabethan mansion. C18 bath house hidden in the grounds. Spring bulbs, beautiful lily pond with Indian bean trees, young arboretum and stunning collection of magnolias. Wheelchair (not motorised) access to house, gravel paths in garden.

13 COTTAGE IN THE TREES

Tidworth Rd, Boscombe Village, nr Salisbury, SP4 0AD. Karen & Richard Robertson, 01980 610921, robertson909@btinternet.com. *7m N of Salisbury. Turn L of A338 just before Social Club. Continue past church, turn R after bridge to Queen Manor, cottage 150yds on R.* **Suns 23 Apr, 28 May, 11 June, 3**

Sept (1.30-5). Adm £3, chd free. Home-made teas. **Visits also by arrangement Mar to Sept for groups of 10+.**
Enchanting ½ acre cottage garden, immaculately planted with water feature, raised vegetable beds, small wildlife pond and gravel garden. Spring bulbs, hellebores and pulmonarias give a welcome start to the season, with pots and baskets, roses and clematis. Mixed borders of herbaceous plants, dahlias, grasses and shrubs giving all-yr interest.
🐾 🐄 ❀ ⛟ ⛾

14 THE COURT HOUSE
Lower Woodford, SP4 6NQ. Mr & Mrs J G Studholme, 01722 782237, joestudholme@icloud.com. *6m S of Amesbury. Driving S on Woodford Valley rd (parallel to A360 & A345) The Court House is 2nd house on L after Lower Woodford village sign.* **Visits by arrangement Apr to Sept, best months for visits June & July. No min number, max 30 for groups. Adm £5, chd free.**
4½ acre garden on banks of R Avon. Herbaceous borders, waterside planting, yew hedges, rambler roses and wild flowers. Unusual trees. Ancient site of Bishop's Palace when Salisbury Cathedral was at Old Sarum. Tree house. Garden developed by present owners over past 26 years. Featured in Wiltshire Garden Trust Journal. Most of the garden is flat, with access over lawns and mown grass paths.
♿ 🐄 ⛟

15 ◆ THE COURTS GARDEN
Holt, Trowbridge, BA14 6RR. National Trust, 01225 782875, courtsgarden@nationaltrust.org.uk, www.nationaltrust.org.uk/courts-garden/. *2m E of Bradford-on-Avon. S of B3107 to Melksham. In Holt follow NT signs, park at village hall and at overflow car park when signed.* **For NGS: Tue 6 June (11-5.30). Adm £7.40, chd £3.70. Light refreshments. Hot & cold lunches in The Rose Garden tea-room. For other opening times and information, please phone, email or visit garden website.**
Beautifully kept but eclectic garden. Yew hedges divide garden compartments with colour themed borders and organically shaped topiary. Water garden with 2 pools, temple, conservatory and small kitchen garden split by an apple allée, all surrounded by 3½ acres of arboretum with specimen trees. Wheelchair access map available.
♿ ❀ 🚗 ⛾

GROUP OPENING

16 DAUNTSEY GARDENS
Church Lane, Dauntsey, Chippenham, SN15 4HW. *5m SE of Malmesbury. Approach via Dauntsey Rd from Gt Somerford, 1¼m from Volunteer Inn Great Somerford.* **Sun 11 June (1-5). Combined adm £6, chd free.**

THE COACH HOUSE
Col & Mrs J Seddon-Brown.

DAUNTSEY PARK
Mr & Mrs Giovanni Amati, 01249 721777, enquiries@dauntseyparkhouse.co.uk.
🚐

THE GARDEN COTTAGE
Miss Ann Sturgis, ann@dauntseypark.co.uk. **Visits also by arrangement June & July.**

IDOVER HOUSE
Mr & Mrs Christopher Jerram.

THE OLD POND HOUSE
Mr & Mrs Stephen Love.

This group of 5 gardens, centred around the historic Dauntsey Park Estate, ranges from the Classical C18 country house setting of Dauntsey Park, with spacious lawns, old trees and views over the R Avon, to mature country house gardens and traditional walled gardens. Enjoy the formal rose garden in pink and white, old fashioned borders and duck ponds at Idover House, and the quiet seclusion of The Coach House with its thyme terrace and gazebos, climbing roses and clematis. Here, mop-headed pruned crataegus prunifolia line the drive. The Garden Cottage has a traditional walled kitchen garden with organic vegetables, apple orchard, woodland walk and yew topiary. Meanwhile the 2 acres at The Old Pond House are both clipped and unclipped! Large pond with lilies and fat carp, and look out for the giraffe and turtle.
♿ ❀ ⛾

17 DUCK POND BARN
Church Lane, Wingfield, Trowbridge, BA14 9LW. Janet & Marc Berlin, 01225 777764, janet@berlinfamily.co.uk. *On B3109 from Frome to Bradford on Avon, turn R opp Poplars PH into Church Lane. Duck Pond Barn is at end of lane. Big field for parking.* **Sun 2 July (2-5). Adm £4, chd free. Home-made teas. Visits also by arrangement Apr to Sept.**
Garden of 1.6 acres with large duck pond, flower garden, orchard, vegetable garden, spinney and wild area of grass and trees. Large dry stone wall topped with flower beds. Set in farmland and mainly flat. Coach parties please ring in advance for catering purposes.
♿ 🚗 ⛾

18 FONTHILL HOUSE
Tisbury, SP3 5SA. The Lord Margadale of Islay, www.fonthill.co.uk/gardens. *13m W of Salisbury. Via B3089 in Fonthill Bishop. 3m N of Tisbury.* **Sun 19 Mar (12-5). Adm £6, chd free. Light refreshments. Sandwiches and cakes, all proceeds to NGS.**
Large woodland garden. Daffodils, rhododendrons, azaleas, shrubs, bulbs; magnificent views; formal gardens. The gardens have been extensively redeveloped under the direction of Tania Compton and Marie-Louise Agius. The formal gardens are being continuously improved with new designs, exciting trees, shrubs and plants. Partial wheelchair access.
♿ 🐄 ⛾

With your support we can help raise awareness of Carers Trust and unpaid carers

GROUP OPENING

19 GREAT SOMERFORD GARDENS

Great Somerford, Chippenham, SN15 5JB. Doreen Jevons. *4m SE of Malmesbury. 4m N of M4 between J16 & J17. 2m S of B4042 Malmesbury to Royal Wootton Basset. 3m E of A4209 Cirencester to Chippenham rd. Cross river bridge in Great Somerford. Park opp The Mount, additional parking on Dauntsey Road opp allotments and West St opp Manor House.* **Sat 17, Sun 18 June (1.30-5.30). Combined adm £5, chd free. Home-made teas at The Mount. Ice creams.**

GREAT SOMERFORD'S FREE GARDENS & ALLOTMENTS

In trust to Great Somerford Parish Council.
Open on all dates

MANOR HOUSE

Mr & Mrs Davies.
Open on all dates

THE MOUNT

Mr & Mrs McGrath.
Open on all dates

THE OLD POLICE HOUSE

Steve & Diane Hunt.
Open on all dates

SOMERFORD HOUSE

Dr & Mrs Hyde.
Open on Sat 17 June

Great Somerford is a medium-sized village, with a lovely walk by R Avon. Maintained by very active gardeners, there are 3 well-established large gardens and a charming smaller one and Gt Somerford's Free Gardens and Allotments. Partial wheelchair access.

  ♿ 🐃 ✿ ☕

20 HAZELBURY MANOR GARDENS

Wadswick, Box, SN13 8HX. Mr L Lacroix. *5m SW of Chippenham, 5m NE of Bath. From A4 at Box, A365 to Melksham, at Five Ways junction L onto B3109 toward Corsham, 1st L at top of hill, drive immed on R.* **Wed 17 May (11-3). Sun 11 June (2-5.30), home-made teas. Wed 13 Sept (11-3). Adm £5, chd free. Teas Sun only.**

8 Acres of Grade II landscaped organic gardens around C15 fortified manor (not open). Edwardian garden with yew hedges and topiary, beech stilt hedges, laburnum tunnel and pleached lime avenue. Large variety of plants, shrubs fill 5000 sq metres of planting, many herbal and native species. Productive vegetable

gardens, orchards and a circle of megaliths. Wild flower drive from butterfly rich common.

✿ 🚍 ☕

21 HORATIO'S GARDEN

Duke of Cornwall Spinal Treatment Centre, Salisbury Hospital NHS Foundation Trust, Odstock Road, Salisbury, SP2 8BJ. Horatio's Garden Charity, www.horatiosgarden.org.uk. *1m from centre of Salisbury. Please park in car park 8 or 10.* **Sun 23 July (2-5). Adm £5, chd free. Tea, served in Horatio's Garden mugs made by Emma Bridgewater, and delicious cakes made by Horatio's Garden volunteers.** *Donation to Horatio's Garden.*

Award winning hospital garden which opened in Sept 2012 and was designed by Cleve West for patients with spinal cord injury at the Duke of Cornwall Spinal Treatment Centre. Built from donations given in memory of Horatio Chapple who was a volunteer at the centre in his school holidays. Low limestone walls, which represent the form of the spine, divide densely planted beds and double as seating. Everything in the garden has been designed to benefit patients during their long stays in hospital. Garden is run by Head Gardener and team of volunteers. At 3pm there will be a talk about therapeutic gardens by Charity Chair Dr Olivia Chapple & Head Gardener. 3 Society of Garden Designers Awards 2015 and Bali Award 2014. Cleve West has 8 RHS gold medals, incl Best in Show at Chelsea Flower Show in 2011 and 2012. Beneficiary Charity of the NGS 2016, supporting the third Horatio's Garden at Stoke Mandeville Spinal Injury Centre. Fully accessible to wheelchairs.

♿ ✿ 🚍 🅓 ☕ ☕

22 HYDE'S HOUSE

Dinton, SP3 5HH. Mr George Cruddas. *9m W of Salisbury. Off B3089 nr Dinton Church on St Mary's Rd.* **Sun 28 May (2-5). Adm £5.50, chd free. Home-made teas at Thatched Old School Room with outside tea tables.**

3 acres of wild and formal garden

Allington Grange

in beautiful situation with series of hedged garden rooms. Numerous shrubs, flowers and borders, all allowing tolerated wild flowers and preferred weeds, while others creep in. Large walled kitchen garden, herb garden and C13 dovecote (open). Charming C16/18 Grade I listed house (not open), with lovely courtyard. Every year varies. Free walks around park and lake. Steps, slopes and gravel paths.

23 ◆ IFORD MANOR

Lower Westwood, Bradford-on-Avon, BA15 2BA. Mrs Cartwright-Hignett, 01225 863146, info@ifordmanor.co.uk, www.ifordmanor.co.uk. *7m S of Bath. Off A36, brown tourist sign to Iford 1m. Or from Bradford-on-Avon or Trowbridge via Lower Westwood Village (brown signs).* **For NGS: Sun 23 Apr (2-5). Adm £5.50, chd free. Cream teas. Tea room also serves home-made cakes, ice cream, fresh coffee and selection of specialist teas. For other opening times and information, please phone, email or visit garden website.**

Very romantic award-winning, Grade I listed Italianate garden famous for its tranquil beauty. Home to Edwardian architect and designer Harold Peto 1899-1933. Garden is characterised by steps, terraces, sculpture and magnificent rural views. (House not open). 2016 is yr 4 of a 5 yr historic replant of Great Terrace and rose garden. Housekeeper's cream teas and home-made cakes at weekends. Light refreshments in Loggia at other times. World famous Summer Arts festival June to Aug, www.ifordarts.org.uk. Please see website for wheelchair access details.

24 JOB'S MILL

Five Ash Lane, Crockerton, Warminster, BA12 8BB. Lady Silvy McQuiston. *1½m S of Warminster. Down lane E of A350, S off A36 r'about.* **Sat 22 Apr (2-5); Sat 3 June (2-6). Adm £4, chd free. Home-made teas.**
Delightful 5 acre garden through

which R Wylye flows. Laid out on many levels surrounding an old converted water mill. Water garden, herbaceous border, vegetable garden, orchard, riverside and woodland walks and secret garden. Grass terraces designed by Russell Page. Bulbs and Erythronium in the spring and perhaps the tallest growing wisteria?

25 ◆ LACOCK ABBEY GARDENS

High Street, Lacock, Chippenham, SN15 2LG. National Trust, 01249 730459, lacockabbey@nationaltrust.org.uk, www.nationaltrust.org.uk/lacock. *3m S of Chippenham. Off A350. Follow NT signs. Use public car park (parking fee).* **For NGS: Sat 25 Feb (10.30-5.30). Adm £6, chd £3. Light refreshments in village, there are several PHs and tea rooms. 2018: Sat 24 Feb. For other opening times and information, please phone, email or visit garden website.**
Woodland garden with carpets of aconites, snowdrops, crocuses and daffodils. Botanic garden with greenhouse, medieval cloisters and magnificent trees. Mostly level site, some gravel paths.

26 130 LADYFIELD ROAD AND ALLOTMENTS

Ladyfield Road, Chippenham, SN14 0AP. Philip & Pat Canter and Chippenham Town Council. *1m SW of Chippenham. Between A4 Bath and A420 Bristol rds. Signed off B4528 Hungerdown Lane which runs between A4 & A420.* **Sun 30 July (1.30-5.30). Adm £3.50, chd free.**
Very pretty small garden with more than 40 clematis, climbing roses and small fish pond. Curved neat edges packed with colourful herbaceous plants and small trees. 2 patio areas with lush lawn, pagoda and garden arbour. Also Hungerdown Allotments, 15 allotments owned by Chippenham Town Council. Wheelchair access to garden and to allotments on main drive only.

GROUP OPENING

27 NEW LANDFORD VILLAGE GARDENS

Landford, Salisbury, SP5 2AX. *Landford is off A36 between Salisbury and Southampton. From S leave M27 at J2 onto A36. From S/N A36 turn into Landford and through village. At Xrds take Forest Rd. Parking on L.* **Sat 8, Sun 9 July (2-5). Combined adm £5, chd free. Home-made teas at Bentley, Whitehorn Drive.**

NEW BENTLEY
Jacky Lumby.

NEW COVE COTTAGE
Mrs Gina Dearden.

NEW FOREST COTTAGE
Norah Dunn.

NEW THE GATEHOUSE
Mrs Jackie Beatham.

NEW 5 WHITEHORN DRIVE
Jackie & Barry Candler.

Landford is a small village set in the northern New Forest, famous for the beauty of its beech and oak trees and freeroaming livestock. The 5 gardens range in size, planting conditions and setting. 3 are in the village, adjacent to Nomansland with its green grazed by New Forest ponies. The Gatehouse has formal herbaceous borders with exuberant planting and colour schemes in mixed herbaceous borders, looking out over paddocks to the forest. Bentley is a small garden, a green oasis containing a wide range of plants and raised vegetable borders. 5 Whitehorn Drive is a small garden with lush colour and surprises in planting. A short distance away in the forest itself are Forest Cottage, a naturalistic garden with hidden delights around each corner, incl field of wild orchids, and next door Cove Cottage, a mature garden showing a digital screening of the wildlife found in both gardens yr round, which may be of special interest to children.

28 LITTLE DURNFORD MANOR

Little Durnford, Salisbury, SP4 6AH. The Earl & Countess of Chichester. *3m N of Salisbury. Just N beyond Stratford-sub-Castle. Remain to E of R Avon at road junction at Stratford Bridge and continue towards Salterton for ½ m heading N. Entrance on L just past Little Durnford sign.* Sun 7 May (2-5). Adm £4, chd free. Home-made teas in cricket pavilion.

Extensive lawns with cedars, walled gardens, fruit trees, large vegetable garden, small knot and herb gardens. Terraces, borders, sunken garden, water garden, lake with islands, river walks, labyrinth walk. Little Durnford Manor is a substantial grade II listed, C18 private country residence (not open) built of an attractive mix of Chilmark stone and flint. Camels, alpacas, llama, pigs, pygmy goats, donkeys and sheep are all grazing next to the gardens. Gravel paths, some narrow. Steep slope and some steps.

&. 🐄 🌼 🚌 ☕ ☕

29 ♦ LYDIARD PARK WALLED GARDEN

Lydiard Tregoze, Swindon, SN5 3PA. Swindon Borough Council, 01793 466664, lydiardpark@swindon.gov.uk, www.lydiardpark.org.uk. *3m W Swindon, 1m from J16 M4. Follow brown signs from W Swindon. Light refreshments in Coach House Tea Rooms.* For NGS: Sun 16 July (11-5). Adm £3, chd £2. Light refreshments. For other opening times and information, please phone, email or visit garden website.

Beautiful ornamental C18 walled garden. Trimmed shrubs alternating with individually planted flowers and bulbs incl rare daffodils and tulips, sweet peas, annuals and wall-trained fruit trees. Unique features incl well and sundial. Wide level paths, no steps.

&. 🌼 🚌 [NPC] ☕

30 NEW MANOR FARM

Crudwell, Malmesbury, SN16 9ER. Mr & Mrs J Blanch. *4m N of Malmesbury on A429. Heading N on A429 in Crudwell, turn R signed to Eastcourt. Farm entrance is on L 200m after end of speed limit sign.* Sun 18 June (2-6). Adm £5, chd free. Home-made teas.

Set within Cotswold stone walls and with a backdrop of Crudwell church lies a half acre garden with a further 5 acres of mini parkland ideal for a Sunday afternoon stroll. The garden is divided by box and yew hedges to create different areas both formal and informal. Herbaceous borders, old fashioned roses, catmint are grown among fountains and extensive lawns.

&. 🐄 🌼 ☕

31 THE MANOR HOUSE, CASTLE COMBE

Castle Combe, Chippenham, SN14 7HR. The Manor House, Castle Combe, 01249 782206, enquiries@manorhouse.co.uk, www.exclusive.co.uk. *15 mins from J17 of M4. Follow signs for Castle Combe race circuit, continue past circuit, follow rd round to R, take 3rd L into village. Hotel immediately R after hump back bridge.* Thur 6 July (11-4). Adm £5, chd free. Light refreshments. Tea and cake incl in entry fee.

200 yr old Italian garden design with kitchen garden supplying our Michelin starred restaurant. Mature wild flower orchard with bee hives and livestock area with rare breed pigs and various birds and fowl. The garden also boasts intricate rock gardens, mature Japanese magnolias, stunning walks and over 2000 years of fascinating history linked to the estate and village of Castle Combe. Garden is in grounds of C14, 5 star Manor House Hotel and is also a fantastic wildlife area, abundant in flora and fauna. Regret no wheelchair access.

🐄 🛏 ☕

32 MANOR HOUSE, STRATFORD TONY

Stratford Tony, Salisbury, SP5 4AT. Mr & Mrs Hugh Cookson, 01722 718496, lucindacookson@stratfordtony.co.uk, www.stratfordtony.co.uk. *4m SW of Salisbury. Take minor rd W off A354 at Coombe Bissett. Garden on S after 1m. Or take minor rd off A3094 from Wilton signed Stratford Tony and racecourse.* Wed 19 July, Wed 6 Sept (2-5). Adm £5, chd free. Home-made teas. Visits also by arrangement Apr to Oct for garden groups, refreshments by arrangement.

Varied 4 acre garden with all yr interest. Formal and informal areas. Small lake fed from R Ebble, waterside planting, herbaceous borders with colour from spring to late autumn. Pergola-covered vegetable garden, formal parterre garden, orchard, shrubberies, roses, specimen trees, winter colour and structure, many original contemporary features and places to sit and enjoy the downland views. Some gravel.

&. 🌼 🚗 🚌 ☕

33 MAWARDEN COURT

Stratford Road, Stratford Sub Castle, SP1 3LL. Alastair & Natasha McBain. *2m WNW Salisbury. A345 from Salisbury, L at T-lights, opp St Lawrence Church.* Sun 23 July (2-5). Adm £5, chd free. Home-made teas in pool pavilion. *Donation to Friends of St Lawrence.*

Mixed herbaceous and rose garden set around C17 house (not open). Pergola walk down through white beam avenue to R Avon and pond pontoon with walk through poplar wood and along river.

&. 🌼 ☕

34 MITRE COTTAGE

Snow Hill, Dinton, SP3 5HN. Mrs Beck. *9m W of Salisbury. From B3089 turn up Snowhill by shop. From Wylye bear L at fork by church.* Sun 9 July (2-6). Adm £3.50, chd free.

'Mitre cottage exemplifies what can be achieved In ¾ of an acre without looking contrived or over designed. Well chosen and often unusual plants are balanced at this time of the year by effusive plantings of old fashioned roses and perennials. Set on a slight hillside, paths lead enticingly from one area to another.' Daily Telegraph July 2016.

&. 🐄

35 NEW NEW FOREST LAVENDER

Giles Lane, Landford, Salisbury, SP5 2BG. Mr Michael Hayward, www.newforestlavender.com. *11m from Southampton, 11m from Salisbury on A36. From Salisbury: Village landmark on A36 Royal Jaipur Indian restaurant approx 1m turn L. From Southampton landmark The Shoe Inn approx 1m turn R.* **Tue 20 June (12-8); Tue 25 July (10-6). Adm £4, chd free. NGS days: cream teas, cakes and light lunches.**

Small lavender field with adjacent cottage and annual garden. Mostly grass pathways in garden area. Cottage plants, lavender, herbs and roses. Tearoom, nursery and gift shop open Wed - Sun (10-4). Featured in local press. Wheelchair access from car park to tea room and plant sales area. Remainder of access level grassed area. Disabled WC

&

36 NORTH COTTAGE

Tisbury Row, Tisbury, SP3 6RZ. Jacqueline & Robert Baker, 01747 870019, baker_jaci@yahoo.co.uk. *12m W of Salisbury. From A30 turn N through Ansty, L at T-junction, towards Tisbury. From Tisbury take Ansty road. Car park entrance nr junction signed Tisbury Row.* **Sun 18 June, Sun 2 July (11.30-5). Adm £3, chd free. Home-made light lunches and teas. Visits also by arrangement June & July for groups of 10+.**

On leaving car park, walk past vegetables and through wild flowers to reach house and gardens. Although small there is much variety to find. Garden is divided, much to explore as each part differs in style and feel. From the intimacy of the garden go out to see the orchard, find the ponds, walk the coppice wood and see the rest of the smallholding. It will be a memorable visit. Ceramics and handicrafts all made by garden owners, many made from their own sheep's wool.

37 OARE HOUSE

Rudge Lane, Oare, nr Pewsey, SN8 4JQ. Sir Henry Keswick. *2m N of Pewsey. On Marlborough Rd (A345).* **Sun 23 Apr, Sun 25 June (2-6). Adm £5.50, chd free. Cream teas. Donation to The Order of St John.**

1740s mansion house later extended by Clough Williams Ellis in 1920s (not open). The formal gardens originally created around the house have been developed over the years to create a wonderful garden full of many unusual plants. Current owner is very passionate and has developed a fine collection of rarities. Garden is undergoing a renaissance but still maintains split compartments each with its own individual charm; traditional walled garden with fine herbaceous borders, vegetable areas, trained fruit, roses and grand mixed borders surrounding formal lawns. The Magnolia garden is wonderful in spring with some trees dating from 1920s, together with strong bulb plantings. Large arboretum and woodland with many unusual and champion trees. In spring and summer there is always something of interest, with the glorious Pewsey Vale as a backdrop. Partial wheelchair access.

&

38 THE OLD MILL

Ramsbury, SN8 2PN. Annabel & James Dallas. *8m NE of Marlborough. From Marlborough head to Ramsbury. At The Bell PH follow sign to Hungerford. Garden behind yew hedge on R 100yds beyond The Bell.* **Sun 25 June, Wed 9 Aug (2-6). Adm £5, chd free. Home-made teas.**

Water running through a multitude of channels no longer drives the mill but provides a backdrop for whimsical garden of pollarded limes and naturalistic planting. Paths meander by streams and over small bridges. Vistas give dramatic views of downs beyond. Potager style kitchen garden and separate cutting garden provide a more formal contrast to the relaxed style elsewhere. Limited wheelchair access as gravel paths and bridges.

39 NEW THE OLD RECTORY

Church Street, Winterbourne Stoke, Salisbury, SP3 4SW. Mr & Mrs J Dutton. *10m NW of Salisbury. 3m W of Stonehenge. Follow Church Street (turning on S side of A303 opp Bell PH & garage) over small bridge. Entrance gates on L just after yellow salt bin.* **Sun 25 June (2-5). Adm £5, chd free. Home-made teas.**

3 acre garden in idyllic setting surrounding Georgian rectory with lovely views. Mirrored herbaceous perennial borders with abundant colour Apr-Oct blend with backdrop of mature and specimen trees and contrast with wildflower areas. 120ft west-facing wall with climbing roses & clematis; parterre with 100+ roses; orchard; ornate trellis and cottage garden planting around pool; croquet lawn, pergola.

40 NEW PEAR COTTAGE

28 Pans Lane, Devizes, SN10 5AF. Mary & Paul Morgan, 01380 722582, mary.morgan.amor@gmail.com. *From Devizes Mkt Pl go S (Long St). At r'about go L (Southbroom) & R at r'about - Pans Ln. Park in road or roads nearby.* **Fri 16 June (2-5). Combined adm with 1 Southview £6, chd free. Visits also by arrangement May to Sept for individuals or groups, max 10.**

A 'jewel of a small garden' choc full of interest all yr. Spiral paths and low hedges, with alpines, hellebores, perennials, peonies in the front. Vibrant exotic patio at the back, steps up to quirky topiary, roses, grasses, clematis, herbs, fruit. Timber greenhouse. Beyond is a tranquil wild garden with trees, perennials, alliums, willow arbour and pond with toads, newts, frogs and dragonflies. Many places in Devizes for lunches and teas. 10 minutes level walk, plenty of parking in town. Wheelchair access to front garden and rear patio only.

PEN MILL FARM

See Somerset, Bristol & South Gloucestershire

41 THE POUND HOUSE

Little Somerford, Chippenham, SN15 5JW. Mr & Mrs Michael Baines, 01666 823212, squeezebaines@yahoo.com. *2m E of Malmesbury on B4024. In village turn S, leave church on R. Car park on R before railway bridge.* **Visits by arrangement June to Aug, all welcome, admission incl teas. Adm £6, chd free. Home-made teas.**

Large well planted garden surrounding former rectory attached to C17 house. Mature trees, hedges and spacious lawns. Well stocked herbaceous borders, roses, shrubs, pergola, parterre, swimming pool garden, water, ducks, chickens, alpacas and horses. Raised vegetable garden and lots of places to sit. A very beautiful English garden!

🚭 🚗 🛏 ☕

42 RIDLEYS CHEER

Mountain Bower, N Wraxall, Chippenham, SN14 7AJ. Mr & Mrs A J Young, www.ridleyscheer.co.uk. *9m WNW of Chippenham. At The Shoe, on A420 8m W of Chippenham, turn N (signed Grittleton) then take 2nd L & 1st R.* **Sun 25 June (2-5). Adm £5, chd free, home-made teas. Sat 7 Oct (2-5). Adm £3, chd free.**

Largely informal garden; mixed borders, lawns, extensive collection of shrubs and trees incl acers, magnolias, liriodendrons, tree peonies, deutzias, daphnes, oaks, beech, birch and hollies. Some 130 rose varieties; old-fashioned and modern shrub roses, and magnificent tree ramblers. Potager, miniature box garden, arboretum, 3 acre wild flower meadow, plus new ½ acre flower meadow. Dew pond. The main features of the garden in late June are the old-fashioned shrub roses and tree ramblers, the mixed borders and wildflower meadows. Early shrub roses and Banksian roses in full bloom as well as Abutilon vitifolium and tulip trees. Oxeye daisies in the wild flower meadows. In autumn, extensive carpets of cyclamen hederifolium and glorious autumn colours. Wheelchair access from car park in meadow.

🚭 ❀ ☕

43 NEW 1 SOUTHVIEW

Wick Lane, Devizes, SN10 5DR. Teresa Garraud, 01380 722936, tl.garraud@hotmail.co.uk. *From Devizes Mkt Pl go S (Long St). At r'about go L (Southbroom) & R at r'about - Pans Lane, continue over bridge turn R at r'about (Wick Ln). Gdn on R. Park in road or roads nearby.* **Fri 16 June (2-5). Combined adm with Pear Cottage £6, chd free. Visits also by arrangement May to Sept for individuals or groups, max 10.**

An atmospheric small town garden that leads you through many different, fascinating areas as it seems to go on and on. A plantswoman's garden with mature topiary and trees including acers and a Cercis canadensis setting off colourful shrub/herbaceous borders and a multitude of large pots on the patios featuring unusual herbaceous plants, giving delightful contrasts in colour and texture. Many places in Devizes for lunches & teas. 10 minutes level walk, plenty of parking in town.

SPECIAL PLANTS

See Somerset, Bristol & South Gloucestershire

44 ◆ STOURHEAD GARDEN

Stourton, Warminster, BA12 6QD. National Trust, 01747 841152, www.nationaltrust.org.uk/ stourhead. *3m NW of Mere on B3092. Follow NT signs, the property is very well signed from all main roads incl A303.* **For NGS: Sun 23 Apr (9-6). Adm £17.60, chd £8.80. Admission incl house and garden. For other opening times and information, please phone or visit garden website.**

One of the earliest and greatest landscape gardens in the world, creation of banker Henry Hoare in 1740s on his return from the Grand Tour, inspired by paintings of Claude and Poussin. Planted with rare trees, rhododendrons and azaleas over last 250yrs. Wheelchair access, buggy available.

🚭 ❀ 🚗 🛏 ☕

45 84 STUDLEY LANE

Studley, Calne, SN11 9NH. Stephen Cox, 01249 812968, stephencox. gardentrust@gmail.com, stephencoxgarden.simplesite.com. *Studley Lane: just off A4 between Chippenham & Calne. At A4 Studley. Turn opp Derry Hill & Bowood. 1st house in lane. Purple fence/gates. Park in field.* **Sun 9 July (2-6). Adm £3, chd free. Tea & biscuits. Visits also by arrangement May to Sept for groups, max 20. Student groups for art & nature studies also welcome. Study placements.**

Created from field a garden of rooms: Orchard, vegetables, conifers, dianthus, roses, fuchsias; grasses, exotics, coastal, heathers, herbarium, alpines, begonias, cottage, specimen trees. All divided by lawns, paths, arches. Fish pond, fountains, waterfall, wetland, beach. Stone statues, 30 plaques of garden wisdom. Relax in 18 seating areas. Stephen is a tenant of the Bowood Estate (the entrance to Bowood House & Gardens is less than 200 metres away). Private conducted tours are also available. Educational literature for visitors.

❀ ☕

46 SWEET BRIAR COTTAGE

19 Gladstone Road, Chippenham, SN15 3BW. Paul & Joy Gough, 01249 656005, paulgough@btopenworld.com. *Chippenham town centre. In town centre, turn off A4 Ave La Fleche into Gladstone Rd. Park in Borough Parade car parks. Garden just above car park opp Angel Hotel.* **Sun 23 July (1-5). Adm £4, chd free. Home-made teas. Visits also by arrangement June & July.**

Town centre oasis of nearly 1 acre of wildlife friendly planted beds, still wowing our visitors. Low Box edged borders full of succession flowering plants has the garden buzzing throughout the year. Large collection of roses, ornamental and fruit trees. Garden can be accessed by slate paths. 2 small ponds, 4ft beds, gravel beds, crisp edged lawns. Large patio and seating throughout. BBC West Finalist Best Private Garden. Featured on BBC Wiltshire Radio.

❀ ☕

47 ◆ TWIGS COMMUNITY GARDEN

Manor Garden Centre, Cheney Manor, Swindon, SN2 2QJ. TWIGS, 01793 523294, twigs.reception@gmail.com, www. twigscommunitygardens.org.uk. *From Gt Western Way, under Bruce St Bridges onto Rodbourne Rd. 1st L at r'about, Cheney Manor Industrial Est. Through estate, 2nd exit at r'about. Opp Pitch & Putt. Signs on R to Manor Garden Centre.* **For NGS: Sun 21 May, Sun 23 July (1-5). Adm £3, chd free. Home-made teas. Excellent hot and cold lunches available at Olive Tree café within Manor Garden centre adj to Twigs. For other opening times and information, please phone, email or visit garden website.** Delightful 2 acre community garden, created and maintained by volunteers. Features incl 7 individual display gardens, ornamental pond, plant nursery, Iron Age round house, artwork, fitness trail, separate kitchen garden site, Swindon beekeepers and the haven, overflowing with wild flowers. Featured in Garden Answers & Wiltshire Life magazine and on Great British Gardens website. In Top 100 Attractions in South West England. Most areas wheelchair accessible. Disabled WC.

♿ 🐕 ❀ 🚗 ☕ 🍽

48 ◆ WATERDALE HOUSE

East Knoyle, SP3 6BL. Mr & Mrs Julian Seymour, 01747 830262. *8m S of Warminster. N of East Knoyle, garden signed from A350. Do not use SatNav.* **For NGS: Sun 7 May (2-6). Adm £5, chd free. Home-made teas. For other opening times and information, please phone.** 4 acre mature woodland garden with rhododendrons, azaleas, camellias, maples, magnolias, ornamental water, bog garden, herbaceous borders. Bluebell walk. Shrub border created by storm damage, mixed with agapanthus and half hardy salvias. Sensible footwear is essential due to difficult surfaces, parts of the garden are very wet. Limited wheelchair access.

♿ 🐕 ☕ 🍽

49 WEST LAVINGTON MANOR

1 Church Street, West Lavington, SN10 4LA. Andrew Doman, andrewdoman01@gmail.com. *6m S of Devizes, on A360. House opp White St, where parking available.* **Sat 10 June (11-6). Adm £10, chd free. Home-made teas provided by West Lavington Youth Club. Visits also by arrangement for groups of 10+ any weekday.** *Donation to West Lavington Youth Club.* 5 acre walled garden first established in C17 by John Danvers who brought Italianate gardens to the UK. Herbaceous border, redeveloped Japanese garden, new rose garden, orchard and arboretum with some outstanding specimen trees all centred around a trout stream and duck pond. New White Birch grove and walk along southern bank of the stream.

🐕 ❀ 🚗 Ⓓ ☕ 🍽

50 WINDMILL COTTAGE

Kings Road, Market Lavington, SN10 4QB. Rupert & Gill Wade, 01380 813527. *5m S of Devizes. Turn E off A360 1m N of West Lavington, 2m S of Potterne. At top of hill turn L into Kings Rd, L into Windmill Lane after 200yds. Limited parking on site, ample parking nearby.* **Fri 26 May, Thur 8, Fri 9, Thur 22, Fri 23 June, Thur 13, Fri 14 July (2-5). Adm £4, chd free. Home-made teas. Visits also by arrangement May to July for groups of 4+.** 1 acre cottage style, wildlife friendly garden on greensand. Mixed beds and borders with long season of interest. Roses on pagoda, vegetable patch for kitchen and exhibition at local shows, greenhouse. Whole garden virtually pesticide free for last 19yrs. Small bog garden by wildlife pond. Secret glade with prairie. New for 2017 - grandchildren's little wood and annual flower meadow in July.

🐕 ❀ 🚗 ☕

51 NEW WUDSTON HOUSE

High Street, Wedhampton, Devizes, SN10 3QE. David Morrison. *Wedhampton lies on N side of A342 approx 4m E of Devizes. House half way up High Street. Parking signed.* **Sun 27 Aug (2-5). Adm £10, chd free. Pre-booking essential, please visit www.ngs.org.uk or phone 01483 211535 for information & booking. Home made teas incl in admission charge.** The garden of Wudston House was started in 2010 following completion of the house. It consists, inter alia, of formal gardens round the house, a perennial meadow, pinetum and an arboretum. Nick Macer and James Hitchmough (who pioneered flower meadows at the 2012 Olympic Park) have been extensively involved in aspects of the garden, which is still developing. Partial wheelchair access.

☕

Chisenbury Priory

© Val Corbett

WORCESTERSHIRE

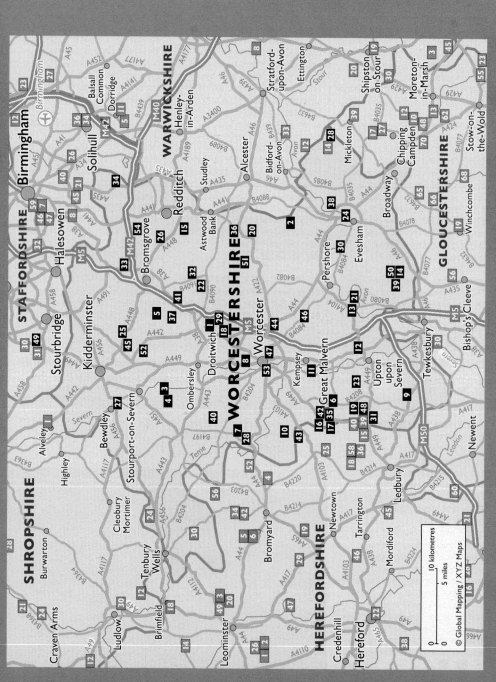

Worcestershire has something to suit every taste, and the same applies to its gardens.

From the magnificent Malvern Hills, the inspiration for Edward Elgar, to the fruit orchards of Evesham which produce wonderful blossom trails in the spring, and from the historic city of Worcester, with its 11th century cathedral and links to the Civil War, to the numerous villages and hamlets that are scattered throughout the county, there is so much to enjoy in this historic county.

Worcestershire is blessed with gardens created by celebrated gardeners such as Capability Brown to ordinary amateur gardeners, and the county can boast properties with grounds of over one hundred acres to small back gardens of less than half an acre, but all have something special to offer.

Visitors to Worcestershire's NGS gardens will find some with wonderful arrays of plants, trees and vegetables, while others show the owners' creativity or sense of fun. There are gardens with significant historical interest and some with magnificent views. We also have a number of budding artists involved with the Scheme, and a few display their works of art on garden open days.

Worcestershire's garden owners guarantee visitors beautiful gardens, some real surprises and a warm welcome.

Volunteers

County Organiser
David Morgan
01214 453595
meandi@btinternet.com

County Treasurer
Cliff Woodward
01746 769239

Publicity
Pamela Thompson
01886 888295
peartree.pam@gmail.com

Booklet Advertising & Co-ordinator
Alan Nokes
01214 455520
alan.nokes@ngs.org.uk

Assistant County Organisers
Brian Bradford
07816 867137
brianbradford101@outlook.com

Lynn Glaze
01386 751924
lynnglaze@cmail.co.uk

Below: Round Hill Garden, Marlbrook Gardens

OPENING DATES

All entries subject to change. For latest information check **www.ngs.org.uk**

Map locator numbers are shown to the right of each garden name.

February

Snowdrop Festival

Saturday 4th
◆ Whitlenge Gardens 52

Sunday 5th
◆ Whitlenge Gardens 52

March

◆ Little Malvern Court (Every Friday to Friday 24th) 31

Sunday 5th
NEW Brockamin 11

April

Sunday 9th
Bridges Stone Mill 10
White Cottage & Nursery 51

Friday 14th
◆ Spetchley Park Gardens 44

Sunday 16th
24 Alexander Avenue 1
Bylane 12

Monday 17th
White Cottage & Nursery 51

Saturday 22nd
Morton Hall 36
The Walled Garden 47

Wednesday 26th
The Walled Garden 47

Saturday 29th
Shuttifield Cottage 43

May

Monday 1st
◆ Little Malvern Court 31

Saturday 6th
Hewell Grange 26
New House Farm, Elmbridge 37
Shuttifield Cottage 43

Sunday 7th
Hewell Grange 26
New House Farm, Elmbridge 37

Saturday 20th
Shuttifield Cottage 43
◆ Whitlenge Gardens 52

Sunday 21st
◆ Harrells Hardy Plants Nursery Garden 24
Model Farm 35
◆ Whitlenge Gardens 52

Thursday 25th
5 Beckett Drive 8

90th Anniversary Weekend

Saturday 27th
Eckington Gardens 21
Shuttifield Cottage 43
68 Windsor Avenue 53

Sunday 28th
1 Church Cottage 13
Eckington Gardens 21

Hiraeth 29
Marlbrook Gardens 33
White Cottage & Nursery 51
68 Windsor Avenue 53

Monday 29th
1 Church Cottage 13
Eckington Gardens 21
Rothbury 42
White Cottage & Nursery 51

June

Saturday 3rd
The Barton 7
Whitcombe House 50

Sunday 4th
Ashley 2
The Barton 7
Bylane 12
◆ Harrells Hardy Plants Nursery Garden 24
Pear Tree Cottage 40

Monday 5th
◆ Harrells Hardy Plants Nursery Garden 24

Saturday 10th
◆ Hanbury Hall & Gardens 22

1 Church Cottage

The Lodge

THE GARDENS

1 24 ALEXANDER AVENUE

Droitwich Spa, WR9 8NH. Malley & David Terry, 01905 774907, terrydroit@aol.com. *1m S of Droitwich. Droitwich Spa towards Worcester A38. Or from M5 J6 to Droitwich Town centre.* Sun 16 Apr, Sun 23 July (2-5.30). Adm £3.50, chd free. Visits also by arrangement Apr to Sept.
Beautifully designed giving feeling of space and tranquillity. 100+ clematis varieties interlacing high hedges. Borders with rare plants and shrubs. Sweeping curves of lawns and paths to woodland area with shade-loving plants. Drought-tolerant plants in S-facing gravel front garden. Alpine filled troughs. April spring bulbs, July clematis. Partial wheelchair access.
&. ✿ ♿

2 ASHLEY

Low Road, Church Lench, Evesham, WR11 4UH. Roy & Betty Bowron, 01386 871347, bettybowz@gmail.com. *6m N of Evesham. In centre of Church Lench take Low Rd N at junction with Main Street. Ashley is 4th property on R.* Sun 4 June (2-6). Adm £3.50, chd free. Home-made teas.
Visits also by arrangement Apr to Aug groups up to 12.
Sloping garden with steps down to lawn, garden pond with plants and fish. Mixed flower beds, greenhouse and vegetable garden. Large pergola with climbing roses, and shaded section with semi-exotic plants which incl tree ferns, other ferns, banana plants, etc. Plants on the large patio incl sago palms, bird of paradise (strelitzia), Hawaiian Palm, agaves and various other plants.
🐄 ❧

GROUP OPENING

3 ASTLEY COUNTRY GARDENS

Group Co-ordinator Roger Russell, Astley, Stourport-on-Severn, DY13 0SG. *3m SW of Stourport-on-Severn. Register at Village Hall to receive map. Situated off B4196 - accessed via Ridleys Cross in centre of Astley (DY13 0RE). Car parking available at each venue.* Sat 24, Sun 25 June (1-6). Combined adm £6, chd free. Cream teas at Astley Towne House and Longmore Hill Farmhouse.

ASTLEY TOWNE HOUSE
Tim & Lesley Smith.
(See separate entry)

LITTLE LARFORD
Lin & Derek Walker.

LITTLE YARHAMPTON
Skene & Petrena Walley.

LONGMORE HILL FARMHOUSE
Roger & Christine Russell.

THE WHITE HOUSE
Tony & Linda Tidmarsh.

THE WHITE HOUSE
John & Joanna Daniels.

NEW **WOOD FARM**
Mr & Mrs W Yarnold.

A wonderful range of 7 country gardens of great variety, in picturesque, peaceful and colourful settings. These incl the garden of a Grade II listed half timbered house with sub tropical planting, stumpery with tree ferns and woodland temple, underground grotto and water features; classical style garden with a variety of features celebrating events in the owner's family; ½ acre garden with mixed borders, 'wheel' herbery and large paddock with specimen trees overlooking the Severn Valley; a Grade II listed C16 farmhouse garden with mixed borders, small feature courtyard leading to a part-walled terrace and lily pond; thatched cottage surrounded by mixed borders, bedding displays and woodland; spacious garden with beautiful views and a lake in a secluded valley with an arboretum; farmhouse garden with stream and bog garden, mixed borders and pathways through shrubs and woodland.
🐄 ✿ ❧ ☕

4 ASTLEY TOWNE HOUSE

Astley, DY13 0RH. Tim & Lesley Smith, www.astleytownehousesubtropical garden.co.uk. *3m W of Stourport-on-Severn. On B4196 Worcester to Bewdley Road.* Sun 30 July (12.30-5); Sun 27, Mon 28 Aug, Sun 10 Sept (1-5). Adm £4, chd free. Home-made teas. Opening with Astley Country Gardens on Sat 24, Sun 25 June.
2½ acres garden of a Grade II listed timber building (not open) incl sub-tropical planting. Stumpery garden with tree ferns and woodland temple. Mediterranean garden, tree house, revolving summerhouse and underground grotto with shell mosaics and water features. A recent addition is 'Mr McGregor's' vegetable garden. Featured in Gardener's World and many garden publications. Partial wheelchair access.
&. 🐄 ☕

5 NEW BADGE COURT

Purshull Green Lane, Elmbridge, Droitwich, WR9 0NJ. Stuart & Diana Glendenning. *5m N of Droitwich Spa. 2½m from J5 M5. Turn off A38 at Wychbold down side of the Swan Inn. Turn R into Berry Lane. Take next L into Cooksey Green Lane. Turn R into Purshull Green Lane. Garden is on R.* Sat 22 July (1.30-6). Adm £5, chd free. Home-made teas.
Tudor house (not open) set in over 2 acres of garden which includes a large pool, aquaponic fish tanks, topiary garden, rockery, orchard (with 16 varieties of apple trees) formal lawns and borders, large vegetable garden with soft fruits, aviary, greenhouses and terrace where teas are served. Also within the curtilage is the Garden House with cottage garden.
☕

6 BARNARD'S GREEN HOUSE

Hastings Pool, Poolbrook Road, Malvern, WR14 3NQ. Mrs Sue Nicholls, 01684 574446. *1m E of Malvern. At junction of B4211 & B4208.* Visits by arrangement Feb to Sept any number welcome. Adm £4, chd free. Light refreshments.
With a magnificent backdrop of the

Conderton Manor

Malvern Hills, this 1½ acre old-fashioned garden is a plantsman's paradise. The main feature is a magnificent cedar. 3 herbaceous and 2 shrub borders, rose garden, red and white and yellow borders, an evergreen and hydrangea bed, 2 rockeries, pond, sculptures and vegetable garden. Good garden colour throughout the year. Was the home of Charles Hastings - founder of the British Medical Association (1794-1866). Featured in Garden News. Dogs on leads.

7 THE BARTON

Berrow Green, Martley, WR6 6PL. David & Vanessa Piggott, 01886 822148, v.piggott@btinternet.com. *1m S of Martley. On B4197 between Martley & A44 at Knightwick, corner of lane to Broadheath. Parking & lunches (12.30 to 2.30) at Admiral Rodney PH opp.* Sat 3, Sun 4 June (1-5). Adm £4, chd free. Home-made teas. **Visits also by arrangement in June groups of between 10 & 20.**

This ½ acre cottagey garden full of colour and texture contains unusual shrubs and billowing herbaceous planting. Paths wind through colour-themed gardens, gravel and grass beds. Roses, clematis and unusual climbers decorate pergolas and trellises. Terracotta-decorated walls enclose a vegetable plot and new tender bed. Visitors comments 'Best private garden I've seen.' ' So unusual and beautiful.'. Book sale. Featured in Garden News.

8 5 BECKETT DRIVE

Northwick, Worcester, WR3 7BZ. Jacki & Pete Ager, 01905 451108, agers@outlook.com. *1½m N of Worcester city centre. Cul-de-sac off A449 Ombersley Rd directly opp Grantham's Autocare, 1m S of Claines r'about on A449.* Thur 25 May, Sat 1, Sun 2 July (2-5). Adm £3, chd free. Home-made teas. Evening opening Tue 1 Aug (6-9). Adm £4, chd free. Wine. **Visits also by arrangement May to Aug groups or societies between 10 & 30 visitors**

An extraordinary town garden on the northern edge of Worcester packed with different plants and year-round interest guaranteed to give visitors ideas and inspiration for their own gardens. Over the past 13 years visitors have enjoyed the unique and surprising features of this garden which has many planting schemes for a variety of situations. Plants at bargain prices and delicious home-made teas. Featured in Worcester News.

9 BIRTSMORTON COURT

Birtsmorton, nr Malvern, WR13 6JS. Mr & Mrs N G K Dawes. *7m E of Ledbury. Off A438 Ledbury/Tewkesbury rd.* Sun 11 June (1.30-7.30). Adm £6, chd free. Home-made teas.

10 acre garden surrounding beautiful medieval moated manor house (not open). White garden, built and planted in 1997 surrounded on all sides by old topiary. Potager, vegetable garden and working greenhouses, all beautifully maintained. Rare double working moat and waterways including Westminster Pool laid down in Henry VII`s reign to mark the consecration of the knave of Westminster Abbey. Ancient yew tree under which Cardinal Wolsey reputedly slept in the legend of the Shadow of the Ragged Stone. No dogs.

10 BRIDGES STONE MILL

Alfrick Pound, WR6 5HR. Sir Michael & Lady Perry. *6m NW of Malvern. A4103 from Worcester to Bransford r'about, then Suckley Rd for 3m to Alfrick Pound.* **Sun 9 Apr (2-5.30). Adm £5, chd free. Home-made teas.**

Once a cherry orchard adjoining the mainly C19 flour mill, this is now a 2½-acre all-year-round garden laid out with trees, shrubs, mixed beds and borders. The garden is bounded by a stretch of Leigh Brook (an SSSI), from which the mill's own weir feeds a mill leat and small lake. A newly completed traditional Japanese garden and an ornamental vegetable 'potager' complete the scene. Wheelchair access by car to courtyard.

&. ❀ ☕

11 NEW BROCKAMIN

Old Hills, Callow End, Worcester, WR2 4TQ. Margaret Stone, 01905 830370, stone.brockamin@btinternet.com. *5m S of Worcester. ½m S of Callow End on the B4424, on an unfenced bend, turn R into the car-park signed Old Hills. Walk towards the houses keeping R.* **Sun 5 Mar, Sun 11 June, Sun 1 Oct (11-4). Adm £3, chd free. Home-made teas. Visits also by arrangement Feb to Oct for groups of 10+**

An informal 1½ acre garden adjacent to common land. Mixed borders contain a wide variety of hardy perennials, including Plant Heritage National Collections of Symphyotrichum (Aster) novae-angliae and some Hardy Geraniums. Flowering starts with spring bulbs, including a collection of snowdrops. There is a seasonal pond and kitchen garden. An access path reaches a large part of the garden.

&. ❀ 🚌 NPC ☕

12 BYLANE

Worcester Road, Earls Croome, WR8 9DA. Shirley & Fred Bloxsome, 01684 592489, shirleymay70@hotmail.co.uk. *1m N of Upton on Severn turning. On main A38 directly past Earls Croome Garden Centre, signed Bridle Way. Directly behind Earls Croome Garden Centre, turn down bridle way to park.* **Sun 16 Apr, Sun 4 June, Sun 3 Sept (1-5). Adm £3, chd free. Home-made teas. Visits also by arrangement Apr to Sept please give one months notice. Adm £5 to include tea.**

Herbaceous garden, paddock with wildlife pond, vegetable garden, and chickens, wood with mature trees and bluebells. Approximatley 2 acres in all. Private parties welcome. Plenty of seating areas and shelter if needed, very quiet and secluded.

🐂 ❀ ☕

13 1 CHURCH COTTAGE

Church Road, Defford, Worcester, WR8 9BJ. John Taylor & Ann Sheppard, 01386 750863, ann98sheppard@btinternet.com. *3m SW of Pershore. A4104 Pershore to Upton rd, turn into Harpley Rd, Defford, black & white cottage at side of church. Parking in village hall car park.* **Sun 28, Mon 29 May, Sun 27, Mon 28 Aug (11-5). Adm £3, chd free. Home-made teas. Visits also by arrangement May to Sept groups of 10 - 30.**

True countryman's ⅓ -acre garden. Interesting layout. Japanese - style feature with 'dragons den'. Specimen trees; water features; perennial garden, vegetable garden; poultry and cider making. New small stream side bog garden under construction. Wheelchair access to most areas.

&. 🐂 ❀ ☕

14 CONDERTON MANOR

Conderton, nr Tewkesbury, GL20 7PR. Mr & Mrs W Carr, 01386 725389, carrs@conderton.com. *5½ m NE of Tewkesbury. From M5 - A46 to Beckford - L for Overbury/Conderton. From Tewkesbury B4079 to Bredon - then follow signs to Overbury. Conderton from B4077 follow A46 directions from Teddington r'about.* **Visits by arrangement Mar to Nov individuals and groups welcome. 30 max. Adm £6, chd free. Light refreshments. Coffee and biscuits in the morning. Tea and biscuits/cakes in the afternoon Wine and snacks in the evening.**

7-acre garden, recently replanted in a contemporary style with magnificent views of Cotswolds. Flowering cherries and bulbs in spring. Formal terrace with clipped box parterre; huge rose and clematis arches, mixed borders of roses and herbaceous plants, bog bank and quarry garden. Many unusual trees and shrubs make this a garden to visit at all seasons. Visitors are particularly encouraged to come in spring and autumn. This is a garden/small arboretum of particular interest for tree lovers. The views towards the Cotswolds are spectacular and it provides a peaceful walk of about an hour. Some gravel paths and steps - no disabled WC.

&. 🚌 ☕

15 THE COTTAGE, 3 CRUMPFIELDS LANE

Webheath, Redditch, B97 5PN. Victor Johnson, pjohnson889@btinternet.com. *From A448 through Redditch take slip rds signed to Headless Cross, at r'about take 3rd exit then follow NGS signs.* **Sat 15 July (10.30-4); Sun 16 July (11-4). Adm £5, chd free. Home-made teas. Tea/coffee, cakes and soft drinks. Visits also by arrangement in July for groups from 2 to 20.**

Recently established 1½ - acre garden landscaped to provide 5 rooms on 4 levels stepped into a hillside. From the 2nd level are stunning views over Vale of Evesham. 2 water features, (1 in a cave) and places to sit and enjoy the wildlife. Wonderland can be found in meadow area of wild flowers. Partial wheelchair access to levels 2 and 3 are accessible with able body escort (help available).

&. ❀ ☕

16 COWLEIGH LODGE

16 Cowleigh Bank, Malvern, WR14 1QP. Jane & Mic Schuster, 01684 439054, dalyan@hotmail.co.uk. *7m SW from Worcester, on the slopes of the Malvern Hills. From Worcester or Ledbury follow the A449 to Link Top. Take North Malvern Rd (behind Holy Trinity church), follow yellow signs. From Hereford take B4219 after Storridge church, follow yellow signs.* **Sun 25 June, Sun 6 Aug (11-5).**

Adm £4, chd free. Home-made teas. **Visits also by arrangement June to Aug min 10, max 30.**
Just under an acre, the garden is on the slopes of the Malvern Hills and has been described by one visitor as 'quirky'! Formal rose garden, grass beds, bamboo walk, colour themed beds, nature path leading to a pond. Large vegetable plot and orchard with 'Michaels Mount' viewing platform overlooking the Severn Valley. Explore the poly tunnel and then relax with a cuppa and slice of homemade cake. This is the third year of opening of a developing and expanding garden - visitors from previous years will be able to see the difference! Lots of added interest with staddle stones, troughs, signs and other interesting artefacts. Slopes and steps throughout the garden. WC and refreshments.

🐕 ❀ ☕ 💷

17 24 CROFT BANK
Malvern, WR14 4DU. Andy & Cathy Adams, 01684 899405, andrewadams2005@yahoo.co.uk. *From Worcester on A449 to Gt Malvern. R onto B4232 signed Bromyard & West Malvern. Continue approx 1½ m. Turn R at Elim College Conference centre onto Croft Bank. No 24 is on R.* Sun 25 June (12-5). Adm £3.50, chd free. Home-made teas and cakes available. **Visits also by arrangement June to Aug open for groups and individuals (max 30).**
The garden enjoys wonderful far reaching south and westerly views from high on the Malvern Hills. This half acre garden has undergone extensive landscaping and rebuilding and now contains flower borders for all seasons, trained fruit trees, vegetable beds, some specimen trees and small woodland area. Garden Studio has a display of paintings and cards inspired by the garden. Sloping areas and woodland walk not suitable for wheelchairs.

♿ ☕

18 DAVID'S GARDEN
Badgers Way, Ash Lane, Martin Hussingtree, Worcester, WR3 8TB. Sarah & David Beauchamp, 01905 340104, davidsnurseries0@tiscali.co.uk. *Parking at David's Nurseries, Martin Hussingtree and follow yellow signs from car park.* Sun 25 June, Sun 2, Sun 16 July (11-4). Adm £4.50, chd free. Home-made teas. **Visits also by arrangement June to Sept.**
After retiring from running the Garden Centre, David and Sarah followed their passion for plants dividing their garden into areas each with its own unique style and planting incl secluded fairy garden, romantic folly garden, beach garden and wildlife pond, herbaceous borders, vegetable garden, Potager and greenhouses with a collection of Streptocarpus. Japanese inspired garden and prairie are new additions. This 1½ acre garden has been created from scratch over the last 2 years. Most areas of the garden are wheelchair friendly.

♿ 🐕 ❀ 🚐 ☕

19 THE DELL HOUSE
2 Green Lane, Malvern Wells, WR14 4HU. Kevin & Elizabeth Rolph, 01684 564448, stay@thedellhouse.co.uk, www.thedellhouse.co.uk. *2m S of Great Malvern. Behind former church on corner of Wells Rd & Green Lane just north of petrol station on A449 Wells Rd.* **Visits by arrangement Apr to Nov £4, child free. Groups up to 20 max. Combined adm with 223 Wells Road (200 yds) £7. Light refreshments.**
Two acre wooded hillside garden of the 1820s Dell House, a former rectory now a B&B. In the latter stages of recovery by new owners.

Peaceful and natural, the garden contains many magnificent specimen trees including a Wellingtonia Redwood. Informal in style with spectacular tree carvings, meandering bark paths, historic garden buildings, garden railway and a paved terrace with distant views. The garden contains several tree carvings by Steve Elsby, and a variety of other sculptures by various artists. Wheelchair access limited. Parking is on gravel. Sloping bark paths, some quite steep.

🐕 🏠 ☕

20 6 DINGLE END
Inkberrow, Worcester, WR7 4EY. Mr & Mrs Glenn & Gabriel Allison, 01386 792039. *12m E of Worcester. A422 from Worcester. At the 30 sign in Inkberrow turn R down Appletree Lane then 1st L up Pepper St. Dingle End is 4th on R of Pepper St. Limited parking in Dingle End but street parking on Pepper St.* **Visits by arrangement Apr to Oct groups min 6, max 26. Adm £3, chd free. Home-made teas.**
Over 1 acre garden with formal area close to the house opening into a flat area featuring a large pond, stream and weir with apple orchard and woodland area. Large vegetable garden incl an interesting variety of fruits. Garden designed for wildlife. Ducks, giant redwood tree. Refreshments for pre arranged groups can be tailored by arrangement e.g. soup and sandwiches, tea and cakes etc. Wheelchair access - slopes alongside every terrace.

♿ 🐕 ☕

Bridges Stone Mill

Funds from NGS gardens help Macmillan support thousands of people every year

21 ECKINGTON GARDENS

Brook House, Manor Rd, Eckington, WR10 3BH. Group Coordinator Lynn Glaze, 01386 751924, lynnglaze@cmail.co.uk. *4 gardens - 1 in Manor Rd, 2 in or close to New Rd/Nafford Rd, 3rd 1m out on Nafford Rd. A4104 Pershore to Upton & Defford, L turn B4080 to Eckington. In centre, by war memorial turn R for Brook House & L for other gardens.* **Sat 27, Sun 28, Mon 29 May (11-5). Combined adm £6, chd free. Home-made teas at Brook House on Saturday & Monday; at Nafford House on Sunday. Visits also by arrangement May to Sept could be all or some of the gardens depending on dates/availability. Price will reflect availability.**

BROOK HOUSE
George & Lynn Glaze.

HILLTOP
Richard & Margaret Bateman.

MANTOFT
Mr & Mrs M J Tupper.

NAFFORD HOUSE
Janet & John Wheatley.

4 very diverse gardens; cottage garden and koi fish pond; formal walled garden; hilltop garden with' windows' in formal hedging and natural wooded garden sloping down to the riverside. Set in/close to lovely village of Eckington with riverside parking and picnic site. Brook House - acre of cottage style planting with koi carp pond and new summer house/patio area. Mantoft - formal walled garden with fish pond, topiary and dew pond, with ducks and geese. Hedges and stone paths, gazebo overlooking garden and new dovecote. Hilltop - 1 acre with sunken garden/pond, rose garden, herbaceous borders and formal hedging with 'windows' and views over extensive countryside. Nafford House - 2 acre mature natural garden/wood with slopes to R Avon, formal gardens around the house and magnificent wisteria. Some wheelchair access issues at all gardens esp. Nafford House - see NGS website for details.

&. ✿ ☕

22 ♦ HANBURY HALL & GARDENS

School Road, Hanbury, Droitwich, WR9 7EA. National Trust, 01527 821214, hanburyhall@ nationaltrust.org.uk, www.nationaltrust.org.uk/ hanburyhall. *4m E of Droitwich. From M5 exit 5 follow A38 to Droitwich; from Droitwich 4m along B4090.* **For NGS: Sat 10, Sun 11 June (10-5). Adm £8, chd £4 (garden & park only). Light refreshments in the Tea-room. For other opening times and information, please phone, email or visit garden website.**
The early eighteenth century gardens and park at Hanbury Hall are a rare example of the work of Royal Designer, George London. The pre-eminent Gardener of his time, his creations provided soothing, order in a chaotic world and initiated the later English Landscape Movement. Servants Hall Tea-Room - hot lunches, tea and cake. Stableyard Cafe for take away snacks and drinks. Chambers Tea-Room for afternoon teas. Featured on and in

Antiques Roadshow BBC1, Inside Out Malvern Gazette Worcester Life Gardens Through Time (TV and book) The Landscapes of Lancelot 'Capability' Brown, Sarah Rutherford (book) Property Website Social Media. Buggy available to bring visitors from the car park to the front of the property and wheelchairs are available to borrow from the Hall.

&. ✿ 🚗 ☕

23 HANLEY SWAN NGS GARDENS

Hanley Swan, Worcester, WR8 0DJ. Group Co-ordinator Brian Skeys, 01684 311297, brimfields@icloud.com. *5m E of Malvern, 3m NW of Upton upon Severn, 9m S of Worcester & M5. From Worcester/Callow End take B4424 to Hanley Castle then turn R. From Upton upon Severn B4211 to Hanley Castle turn L. From Malvern/ Ledbury from A449 take B4209. Signed from village Xrds.* **Sat 10, Sun 11 June (1-5). Combined adm £5, chd free. Cream teas at 19 Winnington Gardens. Visits also by arrangement June to Sept for groups of 10-30. Number of gardens depends on availability which price will reflect.**

CHASEWOOD
Mrs Sydney Harrison, 01684 310527, Sydneyharrison@btinternet. com.
🛏

MEADOW BANK
Mrs Lesley Stroud & Mr Dave Horrobin, 01684 310917, Dave@meadowbankhs. freeserve.co.uk.
🛏

THE PADDOCKS
Mr & Mrs N Fowler.

19 WINNINGTON GARDENS
Brian & Irene Skeys.

NEW 20 WINNINGTON GARDENS
Mr & Mrs Pete & Tina Sauntson.

5 gardens different in style in Hanley Swan. Chasewood has lavender and old fashioned roses. A gravel garden with an Iris and Thyme walk. A collection of Bonsai and Coach Built Prams. Meadow Bank is a modern interpretation of a cottage garden, with a hot border, Dahlias grown for show and collections of Iris and Auriculas. The Paddocks is a wildlife garden with ponds, a tadpole nursery, mixed borders, and a collection of cacti and succulents. Developed since 2011 when their son 'gave them back the football pitch', and a curved patio was built, 20 Winnington Gardens has an octagonal greenhouse, two water features and other decorative details constructed by the owners surrounded by a manicured lawn, colourful beds and planters to provide year round colour. 19 Winnington Gardens is a garden of rooms. Mixed borders enclosed with climbing roses, a small oriental garden, trained fruit trees, raised herb bed with a special standard gooseberry bush and greenhouses. Entrance tickets from Chasewood. Gardens access too narrow for wheelchairs and mobility scooters.

✿ ☕

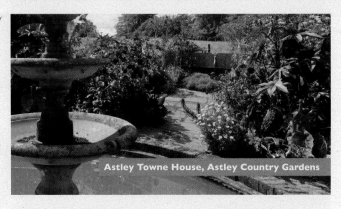

Astley Towne House, Astley Country Gardens

24 ◆ HARRELLS HARDY PLANTS NURSERY GARDEN

Rudge Road, Evesham, WR11 4JR. Liz Nicklin & Kate Phillips, 01386 443077, mail@harrellshardyplants.co.uk, www.harrellshardyplants.co.uk. *¼m from centre of Evesham. From A4184 turn into Queens Rd R at end, then L, Rudge Rd. 150 yds on R down lane. SatNav WR11 4LA.* **For NGS: Sun 21 May, Sun 4 June (2-5); Mon 5 June (10-12); Sun 9 July (2-5); Mon 10 July (10-12); Sun 23 July (2-5). Adm £4, chd free. Tea. Coffee and home-made cakes. For other opening times and information, please phone, email or visit garden website.**

This garden is naturalistic in style and informally planted with a glorious array of hardy perennials, grasses and a large range of

hemerocallis. The sloping 1-acre site consists of beds and borders accessed by bark paths, with several seating areas giving views over the garden. 'Harrell's Hardy Plants is an absolute gem! The garden is absolutely breathtaking- the web site gives you a hint, you really do need to visit to appreciate the wonderful planting scheme, and learn the story behind the garden'. 'Harrell's -A Hidden Plant Paradise' The Chatty Gardener. The top part of the garden is flat with gravel paths but the bulk of the garden is sloping with bark paths.

✿ 🚗 ☕

25 ◆ HARVINGTON HALL

Harvington, Kidderminster, DY10 4LR. The Roman Catholic Archdiocese of Birmingham, 01562 777846, harvingtonhall@btconnect.com, www.harvingtonhall.com. *3m SE of Kidderminster. ½m E of A450 Birmingham to Worcester Rd & approx ½m N of A448 from Kidderminster to Bromsgrove.* **For NGS: Sat 1, Sun 2 July (11.30-5). Adm £3.50, chd £1.50. Light refreshments at Harvington Hall. For other opening times and information, please phone, email or visit garden website.**

Romantic Elizabethan moated manor house with charming gardens and a small Elizabethan-style herb garden, all tended by volunteers. Tours of the Hall, which contain secret hiding places and rare wall paintings, are also available. Visitor Centre, Tea Room serves light

lunches, homemade cakes, hot and cold beverages, shop and WC. Wheelchair access to gardens, ground floor of Malt House.

♿ ✿ 🚗 ☕ 🌸

26 HEWELL GRANGE

Hewell Lane, Tardebigge, Redditch, B97 6QS. HMP Hewell. *2m NW of Redditch. HMP Hewell is situated on B4096. For SatNav use B97 6QQ. Follow signs to Grange Resettlement Unit. Visitors must book in advance via email (address above). This is a prison with booking and security procedures to be followed.* **Sat 6, Sun 7 May (10-4). Adm by donation. Home-made teas. Suggested donation £5. Visitors must be pre booked by email to roy.jones01@hmps.gsi.gov.uk before arrival No booking will result in no entry.**

C18 landscape park and lake by Lancelot Brown, modified c1812 by Humphery Repton. Rhododendrons and azaleas, lake and Repton bridge, formal garden, water tower, rock garden and mature woodland. Not a flower garden. Visitors will be escorted in small groups. Tour may be over 60 mins and visitors must be able to walk for this length of time. Uneven surfaces so sensible walking footwear is essential. Lakeside walk and bluebell walk a chance to see a historic garden not normally open to the public. Please Note - All visits have to have been booked prior to date for security reasons. There is no wheelchair access to the Gardens.

✿ ☕

Little Larford, Astley Country Gardens

© Suzanne Shacklock

27 NEW ▶ **47 HIGH STREET**
Bewdley, DY12 2DJ. Simon &
Penny Smith, 07850 089988,
simon@rhwork.co.uk. *In centre of
Bewdley. No parking at premises -
public parking in either Dog Lane or
Gardners Meadow car parks within
500 yards of the property.* **Evening
opening Wed 21 June, Wed 19
July, Wed 16 Aug (6-9). Adm
£3.50, chd free. Wine. Adm
incl one free glass of locally
produced beer or wine (or a soft
drink if preferred) and a range
of olives & snacks. Visits also
by arrangement May to Sept
visitors are welcome by prior
arrangement individually or in
groups up to 20.**
This small garden is to the rear of a
listed town house, only 120 ft long.
The owners have tried to use every
inch of space to create outside
living space and maximum summer
long interest. Intensively planted
mixed borders link the house,
with its hosta bed, wall mounted
planters and hot garden specimens,
to a contemporary designed upper
terrace with summerhouse, pizza
oven and copper lined rills. Attached
at the rear of the garden is one of
only a handful of air raid shelters still
in existence in the area.

28 HIGH VIEW
Martley, WR6 6PW. Mike &
Carole Dunnett, 01886 821559,

mike.dunnett@btinternet.com,
www.highviewgarden.co.uk. *1m
S of Martley. On B4197 between
Martley & A44 at Knightwick.* **Visits
by arrangement June to Aug
groups of 10+. Adm £5, chd
free. Home-made teas.**
An intriguing mature 2½ acre
garden. Many trees shrubs
herbaceous plants and sculptures.
Visitors have described it as
magical, inspirational, a horticultural
treasure. Views over the Teme
valley. Be prepared for steps and
slopes. Extend your stay by visiting
the kitchen garden at the Talbot
Hotel Knightwick (see below
and our website). The Talbot are
offering visitors to High View the
opportunity of a guided tour of
their interesting kitchen garden. Ask
for details.

29 HIRAETH
30 Showell Road, Droitwich,
WR9 8UY. Sue & John Fletcher,
07752 717243 or 01905 778390,
sueandjohn99@yahoo.com. *1m S
of Droitwich. On The Ridings estate.
Turn off A38 r'about into Addyes Way,
2nd R into Showell Rd, 500yds on
R. Follow the yellow signs!* **Sun 28
May (2-5.30); Wed 28 June (2-
5); Sun 23 July (2-5.30); Wed 2
Aug (2-5). Adm £3.50, chd free.
Home-made teas. Visits also by
arrangement June to Sept for
groups of 10-30.**

Third acre gardens, front, rear
contain many plant species, cottage,
herbaceous, hostas, ferns, 300yr
old Olive Tree, pool, waterfall, oak
sculptures, metal animals etc inc
giraffes, elephant, birds. An oasis of
colours in a garden not to be missed
described by visitor as 'A haven on
the way to Heaven'. Excellent tea,
coffee, cold drinks, home-made
cakes and scones served with china
cups, saucers, plates, tea-pots and
coffee-pots - silver service! Partial
wheelchair access.
✿ ☕ 🍴

30 HOLLAND HOUSE
Main Street, Cropthorne,
WR10 3NB. Holland House
Charitable Trust, 01386 860330,
reservations@hollandhouse.org,
www.hollandhouse.org. *5m W of
Evesham. The village of Cropthorne
is situated between Pershore &
Evesham.* **Sun 25 June, Sun 16
July (10.30-4). Adm £4, chd free.
Cream teas.**
Formal gardens laid out by Lutyens
in 1904 with rose garden; thatched
house dating back to C16 (not
open). Lovely riverside setting with
roses in June. Sunken garden, with
steps at each angle and a central
sundial. Large vegetable garden.
Holland House kitchens will be open
to serve cream teas/afternoon tea.
✿ 🛏 ☕ 🍴

31 ◆ LITTLE MALVERN COURT

Little Malvern, WR14 4JN. Mrs T M Berington, 01684 892988, littlemalverncourt@hotmail.com, www.littlemalverncourt.co.uk. 3m S of Malvern. On A4104 S of junction with A449. For NGS: Every Fri 3 Mar to 24 Apr (2-5). Adm £5, chd free. Mon 1 May (2-5). Adm £7, chd free. Home-made teas. No refreshments in March. For other opening times and information, please phone, email or visit garden website.

10 acres attached to former Benedictine Priory, magnificent views over Severn valley. Garden rooms and terrace around house designed and planted in early 1980s; chain of lakes; wide variety of spring bulbs, flowering trees and shrubs. Notable collection of old-fashioned roses. Topiary hedge and fine trees. The May Bank Holiday - Flower Festival in the Priory Church. Partial wheelchair access.

&. ✿ ☕

32 NEW THE LODGE

off Holmes Lane, Dodderhill Common, Hanbury, Bromsgrove, B60 4AU. Mark & Lesley Jackson. 1m N of Hanbury Village. 3½m E from M5 J5, on A38 at the Hanbury Turn Xrds, take A4091 S towards Hanbury. After 2½m turn L into Holmes Lane, then IMMEDIATE L again into dirt track. Car Park (Worcs Woodland Trust) on L. Sat 15, Sun 16 July (11-4). Adm £3, chd free. Home-made teas.

A one and half acre garden attached to a part C16 black and white house (not open) with 3 lawned areas, pond with water features, new traditional greenhouse, various beds plus stunning views from Dodderhill Common over the North Worcestershire countryside.

✿ ☕

GROUP OPENING

33 MARLBROOK GARDENS

Braces Lane, Marlbrook, Bromsgrove, B60 1DY. Group Co-ordinator Alan Nokes, 0121 445 5520, alyn.nokes@btinternet.com.

2m N of Bromsgrove. 1m N of M42 J1, follow B4096 signed Rednal, turn L at Xrds into Braces Lane. 1m S of M5 J4, follow A38 signed Bromsgrove, turn L at T-lights into Braces Lane. Parking available. Sun 28 May, Sun 20 Aug (1.30-5.30). Combined adm £5, chd free. Home made teas in both gardens. Visits also by arrangement May to Aug for groups of 10+ Viewing for one or both gardens.

OAK TREE HOUSE

Di & Dave Morgan, 0121 445 3595, meandi@btinternet.com. Visits also by arrangement May to Aug groups of 10+.

ROUND HILL GARDEN

Lynn & Alan Nokes, 0121 445 5520, alyn.nokes@btinternet.com, www.roundhillgarden.weebly.com. Visits also by arrangement June to Aug groups of 10+.

Two unique and stunning gardens, each have opened individually in their own right. Experience the contrasting styles, Round Hill Garden a traditional garden with a twist into the exotic and unusual. Rear garden divided into four distinct areas, Mediterranean, Patio/pond, Lawn with borders and islands and vegetable garden with raised beds and greenhouses. Oak Tree House a plantswoman's cottage garden with views over open fields. Past the twisted rail, through the arch leads to a garden packed full of shrubs and herbaceous planting with grass paths weaving in and out. Both gardens overflowing with plants for sun and shade, also ponds, water features, patios, artifacts and sculptures. Recognised for excellence, with many articles over the years published in national papers/gardening magazines. Continually evolving, many repeat visitors enjoy sharing with us their new discoveries. Art displays at both gardens by garden owners. Garden Quiz for children. Both gardens ideal for art groups. Featured in Garden News.

✿ 🚗 ☕

34 74 MEADOW ROAD

Wythall, B47 6EQ. Joe Manchester, 01564 829589, joe@cogentscreenprint.co.uk. 4m E of Alvechurch. 2m N from J3 M42. On A435 at Becketts Farm r'about take rd signed Earlswood/Solihull. Approx 250 metres turn L into School Drive, then L into Meadow Rd. Visits by arrangement May to Aug. Adm £3, chd free.

Has been described one of the most unusual urban garden dedicated to woodland, shade-loving plants. 'Expect the unexpected' in a few tropical and foreign species. Meander through the garden under the majestic pine, eucalyptus and silver birch. Sit and enjoy the peaceful surroundings and see how many different ferns and hostas you can find.

✿ 🚗 ☕

35 MODEL FARM

Montpelier Road, West Malvern, WR14 4BP. Deirdre & Phil Drake. W side of Malvern Hills. B4232 at Elim Pentecostal HQ (Stately stone building). Turn down Croft Bank 200yds & park. Walk L down Montpelier Rd to Model Farm. Sun 21 May (1.30-5.30). Adm £5.50, chd free. Home-made teas, cream teas and home made cakes.

Stunning 2-acre tranquil garden in the Malvern Hills. Victorian tudor-style house (not open) surrounded by well-stocked borders, patio and courtyard. Picturesque contours of garden complemented by natural stream, ponds, mixed borders, orchard, bog garden, meadow. Ancient oaks, specimen trees, acers, panoramic views to Hay Bluff. Steep in some areas. Wonderful spring bulbs, wisteria and clematis. Further development of high level circular folly for 2017. New spectacular viewpoint from fallen ancient oak site (not for the faint hearted)! Some of the main features of the garden afford assisted wheelchair access incl the 'welcome bed', the new 60ft border, courtyard, orchard, etc.

✿ 🚗 ☕

36 MORTON HALL

Morton Hall Lane, Holberrow Green, Redditch, B96 6SJ. Mrs A Olivieri, 01386 791820, morton.garden@mhcom.co.uk, www.mortonhallgardens.co.uk. *In the centre of Holberrow Green, at a wooden bench around a tree, turn up Morton Hall Lane. Follow the NGS signs to the gate opposite Morton Hall Farm.* Sat 22 Apr, Sat 17 June (10-3.30). Adm £7, chd free. **Visits also by arrangement Apr to Sept (groups of 10+) see website for availability and booking conditions.**
One of Worcestershire's best kept secrets. Perched atop an escarpment with breath taking views, hidden behind a tall hedge, lies a unique garden of outstanding beauty. A garden for all seasons, it features one of the country's largest fritillary spring meadows, sumptuous herbaceous summer borders, a striking potager, a majestic woodland rockery and an elegant Japanese Stroll Garden with tea house. For by arrangement visits only; refreshments tea/coffee and savoury snack for morning appointments, tea/coffee and cake for afternoon visits. Unable to cater for special dietary requirements. Featured in Country Life.

🚐 ☕ 🍽

37 NEW HOUSE FARM, ELMBRIDGE

Elmbridge Lane, Elmbridge, WR9 0DA. Charles & Carlo Caddick, 01299 851249, Carlocaddick@hotmail.com. *2½m N of Droitwich Spa. A442 from Droitwich to Cutnall Green. Take lane opp Chequers PH. Go 1m to T-junction. L towards Elmbridge Green/Elmbridge (past church & hall). At T-junction go R into Elmbridge Lane, garden on L.* Sat 6, Sun 7 May, Sat 2, Sun 3 Sept (2-4.30). Adm £4, chd free. **Visits also by arrangement May to Sept.**
This charming one acre garden surrounding an early C19 farm house (not open) has a wealth of rare trees and shrubs under planted with unusual bulbs and herbaceous plants. Special features are the topiary and perry wheel, potager

ornamental vegetable garden, natural pond, dry garden, rose garden, and small courtyard retreat. Exotics for sun and shade. Plants for sale.

🐏 ✿ 🚐 ☕

Donations from the National Garden Scheme help Parkinson's UK care for more people

GROUP OPENING

38 OFFENHAM GARDENS

Main Street, Offenham, WR11 8QD. *Approaching Offenham on B4510 from Evesham, L into village signed Offenham & ferry ¾m. Follow road round into village. Park in Village Hall car park opp Church. Walk to gardens from car park.* Sat 5, Sun 6 Aug (11-5). **Combined adm £4, chd free. Home-made teas.**

DECHMONT
Angela & Paul Gash.

LANGDALE
Sheila & Adrian James,
www.adrianjames.org.uk.

WILLOWAY
Stephen & Linda Pitts.

Offenham is a picturesque village in the heart of the Vale of Evesham, with thatched cottages and traditional maypole. Three gardens of diverse interests from woodland and wildlife to topiary, herbaceous and exotic. Langdale is a plant lovers garden designed for all year round interest. Surrounding a formal rill

are relaxed borders in a variety of styles leading down to a productive vegetable garden and experimental naturalistic planting of mainly southern Africa plants. Willoway, an oasis of sound and colour, is initially hidden by the traditional front garden. A corridor of Hostas leads the visitor to the patio, a lush carpet of lawn, and then, via the bamboo curtain, to the oriental area. A streptocarpus collection contains varieties from Eastern Europe and Japan. With a mature walnut tree Dechmont features box topiary, patio areas, year round interest from conifers, shrubs and acers, colour from bulbs, perennials, annuals, clematis and roses set within curved borders.

✿ ☕

39 OVERBURY COURT

Overbury, Tewkesbury, GL20 7NP. Mr & Mrs Bruce Bossom, 01386 725111 (office), gardens@overburyestate.co.uk. *5m NE of Tewkesbury. Village signed off A46. Turn off village rd beside the church. Park by gates & walk up drive.* **Visits by arrangement Mar to Oct for groups of 10+ No refreshments available on site. Adm £4.50, chd free.**
Georgian house 1740 (not open); landscape garden of same date with stream and pools; daffodil bank and grotto. Plane trees, yew hedges; shrubs; cut flowers; coloured foliage; gold and silver; shrub rose borders. Norman church adjoins garden. Close to Whitcombe and Conderton Manor. Some slopes, while all the garden can be viewed, parts are not accessible to wheelchairs.

♿ 🐏 🚐

40 PEAR TREE COTTAGE

Witton Hill, Wichenford, Worcester, WR6 6YX. Pamela & Alistair Thompson, 01886 888295, peartree.pam@gmail.com, www.peartreecottage.me. *13m NW of Worcester & 2m NE of Martley. From Martley, take B4197. Turn R into Horn Lane then take 2nd L signed Witton Hill. Keep L & Pear Tree Cottage is on R at top of hill.* Sun 4 June (12-6). Sun 27 Aug

(2-10). Home-made teas. Adm
£5, chd free. Wine served after
6pm on Sun 27 Aug. **Visits also
by arrangement all visitors very
welcome but please telephone
first!.**
A Grade II listed black and white
cottage (not open) with SW-facing
gardens and far reaching views
across orchards to Abberley clock
tower. The gardens extend to
approx ¾ acre and comprise of
gently sloping lawns with mixed
and woodland borders, shade
and plenty of strategically placed
seating. The garden exudes a quirky
and humorous character with the
odd surprise! 'Garden by Twilight'
evenings are very popular. Trees,
shrubs and sculptures are softly uplit
and the garden is filled with candles
and nightlights (weather permitting!)
Visitors are invited to listen to the
owls and watch the bats whilst
enjoying a glass of wine. Featured
in The English Garden Magazine,
Worcester News, Worcestershire
Life and on BBC Hereford &
Worcester. Partial wheelchair access.
& ☕

41 ◆ RIVERSIDE GARDENS
AT WEBBS
Wychbold, Droitwich, WR9 0DG.
Webbs of Wychbold, 01527 860000,
www.webbsdirect.co.uk. 2m N of
Droitwich Spa. 1m N of M5 J5 on
A38. Follow tourism signs from M5.
For opening times and information,
please phone or visit garden
website.

2½ acres. Themed gardens incl
Colour spectrum, tropical and dry
garden, Rose garden, vegetable
garden area, seaside garden,
bamboozelum, Contemplation and
self sufficient Garden. New Wave
gardens opened 2004, is home to
our new hobbit house and includes
natural seasonal interest with grasses
and perennials. This area is also home
to beehives which produce honey
for our own food hall. The New
Wave Garden was slightly changed
over 2014 to become more of a
natural wildlife area. There are willow
wigwams made for children to play
in. This area now incl a bird hide
and new in 2016 the Hobbit house.
Open all yr except Christmas, Boxing
Day and Easter Sun. Our New Wave
Gardens area has grass paths which
are underlaid with mesh so people
with heavy duty wheelchairs can be
taken around.
& ✿ 🚗 ☕

42 ROTHBURY
5 St Peters Road, North
Malvern, WR14 1QS. John
Bryson, Philippa Lowe & David,
p.a.lowe140@btinternet.com. 7m
W of M5 J7 (Worcester). Turn off
A449 Worcester to Ledbury Rd at
B4503, signed Leigh Sinton. Almost
immed take the middle rd (Hornyold
Rd). St Peter's Rd is ¼m uphill, 2nd
R. Mon 29 May (8.30-5); Sat
24 June, Sat 22, Sun 23 July
(11.30-5). Adm £3, chd free.
Light refreshments. Continental
breakfast on 29 May between

8.30 & 11am. Fresh coffee, pots
of tea, filled rolls, homemade
cakes & cream teas available
at all openings. **Visits also by
arrangement June & July for
groups of 10+.**
Set on slopes of Malvern Hills,
⅓ acre plant-lovers' garden
surrounding Arts and Crafts house
(not open), created by owners
since 1999. Herbaceous borders,
rockery with thyme walk, wildlife
pond, vegetable patch, small
orchard, containers. A series of
hand-excavated terraces accessed
by sloping paths and steps. Views
to Lickey Hills and Worcester
and of the Malverns. Seats. Partial
wheelchair access. One very low
step at entry, one standard step to
main lawn and one to WC. Decking
slope to top lawn.
& ✿ ☕

43 SHUTTIFIELD
COTTAGE
Birchwood, Storridge,
WR13 5HA. Mr & Mrs
David Judge, 01886 884243,
judge.shutti@btinternet.com. 8m
W of Worcester. Turn R off A4103
opp Storridge Church to Birchwood.
After 1¼m L down steep tarmac
drive. Please park on roadside at the
top of the drive but drive down if
walking is difficult (150 yards). Sat
29 Apr, Sat 6, 20, 27 May, Sat
8 July, Sat 5, 26 Aug (1.30-5).
Adm £5, chd free. Home-made
teas. **Visits also by arrangement
Apr to Sept.**
Superb position and views.
Unexpected 3-acre plantsman's
garden, extensive herbaceous
borders, primula and stump
bed, many unusual trees, shrubs,
perennials, colour-themed for all-yr
interest. Walks in 20-acre wood with
ponds, natural wild area. Anemones,
bluebells, rhododendrons and
azaleas are a particular spring
feature. Large old rose garden
with many spectacular climbers.
Good garden colour throughout
the yr. Small deer park, vegetable
garden. Wildlife ponds, wild flowers
and walks in 20 acres of ancient
woodland. Some sloping lawns and
steep paths in wooded area.
✿ ☕

The Tynings

44 ◆ SPETCHLEY PARK GARDENS

Spetchley, Worcester, WR5 1RS. Mr John Berkeley, 01905 345106, enquiries@spetchleygardens.co.uk, www.spetchleygardens.co.uk. *2m E of Worcester. On A44, follow brown signs.* **For NGS: Fri 14 Apr, Sun 2 July (11-6). Adm £7, chd £2.50. Light refreshments. For other opening times and information, please phone, email or visit garden website.**

Surrounded by glorious countryside lays one of Britain's best-kept secrets. Spetchley is a garden for all tastes containing one of the biggest private collections of plant varieties outside the major botanical gardens. Spetchley is not a formal paradise of neatly manicured lawns or beds but rather a wondrous display of plants, shrubs and trees woven into a garden of many rooms and vistas. Plant sales, gift shop and Tea Room. Annual Specialist Plant Fair held on 23 April. Gravel paths.

&. ✿ 🚗 ☕

45 ◆ STONE HOUSE COTTAGE GARDENS

Church Lane, Stone, DY10 4BG. James & Louisa Arbuthnott, 07817 921146, www.shcn.co.uk. *2m SE of Kidderminster. Via A448 towards Bromsgrove, next to church, turn up drive.* **For opening times and information, please phone or visit garden website.**

A beautiful and romantic walled garden adorned with unusual brick follies. This acclaimed garden is exuberantly planted and holds one of the largest collections of rare plants in the country. It acts as a shop window for the adjoining nursery. Open Wed to Sat late March to early Sept 10-5. Partial wheelchair access.

&. ✿ 🚗

46 THE TYNINGS

Church Lane, Stoulton, Worcester, WR7 4RE. John & Leslie Bryant, 01905 840189, johnlesbryant@btinternet.com. *5m S of Worcester; 3m N of Pershore. On the B4084 (formerly A44) between M5 J7 & Pershore. The Tynings lies beyond the church at the extreme end of Church Lane. Ample parking.* **Visits by arrangement June to Sept. Adm £4, chd free. Light refreshments.**

Acclaimed plantsman's ½-acre garden, generously planted with a large selection of rare trees and shrubs. Features incl specialist collection of lilies, many unusual climbers and rare ferns. The colour continues into late summer with dahlia, berberis, euonymus and tree colour. Surprises around every corner. You will not be disappointed. Lovely views of adjacent Norman Church and surrounding countryside. Plants labelled and plant lists available.

&. ✿ 🚗 ☕

47 THE WALLED GARDEN

6 Rose Terrace, off Fort Royal Hill, Worcester, WR5 1BU. William & Julia Scott. *Close to the City centre. ½m from Cathedral. Via Fort Royal Hill, off London Rd (A44). Park on 1st section of Rose Terrace & walk the last 20yds down track.* **Sat 22, Wed 26 Apr (1-5). Adm £3.50, chd free. Light refreshments.**

This C19 Walled Kitchen Garden, reawakened in 1995 is a peaceful oasis near the centre of Worcester. A tapestry of culinary and medicinal herbs, fruit of all sorts including medlar, mulberry and quince, vegetables and flowers are all grown organically. History is at the centre of the rescue and evolution of this enclosed garden. Featured in Kitchen Garden magazine.

✿ ☕

48 NEW 223 WELLS ROAD

Malvern, WR14 4HF. Brian & Elaine Hitchens, 01684 897716, brianhitchens281@btinternet.com. *2½m S of Great Malvern. On A449 - shared drive with 225 Wells Road.* **Visits by arrangement Apr to Nov adm £4, child free. Groups up to 20 max. Combined adm with Dell House (200 yds) £7. Light refreshments.**

½ acre garden developed over the last five years on the eastern slope of the Malvern Hills. The front is closely planted with shade loving plants such as hostas together with camellias, magnolias rhododendrons and foliage plants such as tree ferns, palms, etc. The rear comprises lawns, mixed border's and small formal pool complex. It has scarce and tender shrubs and herbaceous perennials. Unsuitable for wheelchairs.

 ☕

49 WESTACRES

Wolverhampton Road, Prestwood, Stourbridge, DY7 5AN. Mrs Joyce Williams, 01384 877496. *3m W of Stourbridge. A449 in between Wall Heath (2m) & Kidderminster (6m). Ample parking Prestwood Nurseries (next door).* **Sat 22, Sun 23 July (11-4). Adm £4, chd free. Home-made teas. Visits also by arrangement June to Aug min 15, max 30.**

¾-acre plant collector's garden with unusual plants and many different varieties of acers, hostas, shrubs. Woodland walk, large koi pool. Covered tea area with home-made cakes. Come and see for yourselves, you won't be disappointed. Described by a visitor in the visitors book as 'A garden which we all wished we could have, at least once in our lifetime'. Garden is flat. Disabled parking.

&. 🐄 ✿ ☕ ☕

50 WHITCOMBE HOUSE

Overbury, Tewkesbury, GL20 7NZ. Faith & Anthony Hallett, 01386 725206, faith.hallett1@gmail.com. *9m S of Evesham, 5m NE Tewkesbury. Leave A46 at Beckford to Overbury (2m). Or B4080 from Tewkesbury through Bredon/Kemerton (5m). Or small lane signed Overbury at r'about junction A46, A435 & B4077. Approx 5m from J9 M5.* **Sat 3 June (2-5). Adm £4, chd free. Home-made teas. Visits also by arrangement Apr to Sept and evening visits (with wine) also possible.**

An alluring acre for every season in a Cotswold stone walled idyll. Spring promise yields to vibrant blues and white, pastel shades and flowering shrubs. Acers, roses, campanula and then the hot borders of fiery oranges, red and yellows. The babbling stream banked by hosta, astilbe, primula, hebe, helenium with yet more roses provide late summer colour. Everywhere are seats for joy and reflection. Featured in Cotswold Life. For easiest wheelchair access please contact us in advance for details.

 ♿ 🐎 ✿ 🚗 ☕

51 WHITE COTTAGE & NURSERY

Earls Common Road, Stock Green, Inkberrow, B96 6SZ. Mr & Mrs S M Bates, 01386 792414, smandjbates@aol.com, whitecottage.garden. *2m W of Inkberrow, 2m E of Upton Snodsbury. A422 Worcester to Alcester, turn at sign for Stock Green by Red Hart PH, 1½m to T-junction, turn L 500 yds on the L.* **Sun 9, Mon 17 Apr, Sun 28, Mon 29 May, Sun 11, Sun 25 June, Sun 16 July, Sun 10 Sept (11-4.30). Adm £3.50, chd free. Home-made teas. Visits also by arrangement Apr to Oct groups and individuals welcome. Nursery open on request.**

2 acre garden with large herbaceous and shrub borders, island beds, stream and bog area. Spring meadow with 100's of snakes head fritillaries. Formal area with lily pond and circular rose garden. Alpine rockery and new fern area. Large collection of interesting trees incl Nyssa Sylvatica, Parrotia persica, and Acer 'October Glory' for magnificent Autumn colour and many others. Gravel drive to the gate but it is manageable for wheelchair users.

 ♿ ✿ 🚗 ☕

52 ◆ WHITLENGE GARDENS

Whitlenge Lane, Hartlebury, DY10 4HD. Mr & Mrs K J Southall, 01299 250720, keith. southall@creativelandscapes. co.uk, www.whitlenge.co.uk. *5m S of Kidderminster, on A442. A449 Kidderminster to Worcester L at T-lights, A442 signed Droitwich, over island, ¼m, 1st R into Whitlenge Lane. Follow brown signs.* **For NGS: Sat 4, Sun 5 Feb, Sat 20, Sun 21 May, Sat 15, Sun 16 July (10-5). Adm £4, chd free. Light refreshments in the adacent Tea rooms. For other opening times and information, please phone, email or visit garden website.**

3 acre show garden of professional designer with over 800 varieties of trees, shrubs etc. Twisted pillar pergola, Moongate, waterfalls, ponds and streams. Mystic features of the Green Man, 'Sword in the Stone' and cave fernery. Walk the turf labyrinth and take refreshments in The Garden 'Design Studio' tearoom. 2½ metre high reclaim brick and solid oak Moongate with 4 cascading waterfalls, deck walk through giant Gunnera leaves, Camomile paths through herb gardens, 400 sq metre grass labyrinth, play and pet corner. Locally sourced home-made food in tearoom, plant nursery. Garden was showcased on Alan Titchmarsh's 'Love your Garden'.

 ♿ ✿ 🚗 ☕

53 68 WINDSOR AVENUE

St Johns, Worcester, WR2 5NB. Roger & Barbara Parker. *W area of Worcester, W side of R Severn. Off the A44 to Bromyard. Into Comer Rd, 3rd L Into Laugherne Rd, 3rd L into Windsor Ave, at bottom in Cul-de-sac. Limited parking, please park courteously on road sides, car share if possible.* **Sat 27, Sun 28 May (11-4). Adm £4.50, chd free. Tea, cake and soft drinks also available.**

Almost one acre garden divided into three areas, situated behind a 1930's semi detached house in a cul-de-sac. Visitors are amazed and often comment on size of garden. and the tranquility! The garden includes bog gardens, flower beds, 'oriental' area, vegetable patch, five greenhouses and a Koi pond plus three other ponds each in very different styles. We also have chickens and Ornamental Pheasants. Gravel paths are everywhere.

 ✿ ☕

GROUP OPENING

54 WITHYBED GREEN

Alvechurch, B48 7PP. *3m N of Redditch, 11m SW of Birmingham. 6mins from J2 of M42. From Alvechurch centre take Tanyard Lane or Bear Hill. Follow NGS signs along Snake Lane & Withybed Lane. Rail Alvechurch Stn then a 10 minute walk up the canal towpath.* **Sun 25 June (1-6). Combined adm £5,** chd free. Home-made teas at 'The New Smithy' next to the Crown PH.

NEW THE BUNGALOW
Robert Radbourne.

FAIRVIEW
Bryan & Angela Haycocks.

NEW 5 FORWARD COTTAGES
Mary Green.

2 FRONT COTTAGES
Clive & Ann Southern.

3 FRONT COTTAGES
Sarah & Steve Beddoe.

4 FRONT COTTAGES
Leon Southern.

6 FRONT COTTAGES
Mr & Mrs Horne.

THE MOUSEHOLE
Lucy Hastie.

6 REAR COTTAGES
John Adams & Amelda Brown.

SELVAS COTTAGE
Mr & Mrs J L Plewes.

10 varied gardens (two new this year) opening biennially. Withybed Green is a secret hamlet to the W of Alvechurch set between semi-wooded hillsides and the Birmingham Worcester Canal. The gardens include a rose garden, ancient woodland, allotments, small terrace cottage gardens and a stream-side walk. Withybed Green is compact and in a charming environment and you can easily walk round all ten gardens. Refreshments will be hosted by the New Smithy. The houses and cottages mostly date from C19, built for farm workers, nail makers, canal and railway builders. Withybed has its own canal-side PH, The Crown. All but one garden accept dogs on leads. Only 3 gardens are suitable for wheelchair access.

 🐎 ✿ ☕

Gardens are at the heart of hospice care

YORKSHIRE

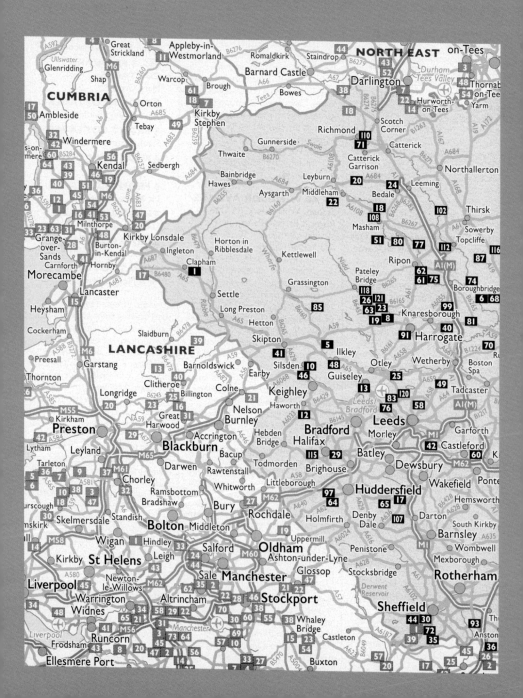

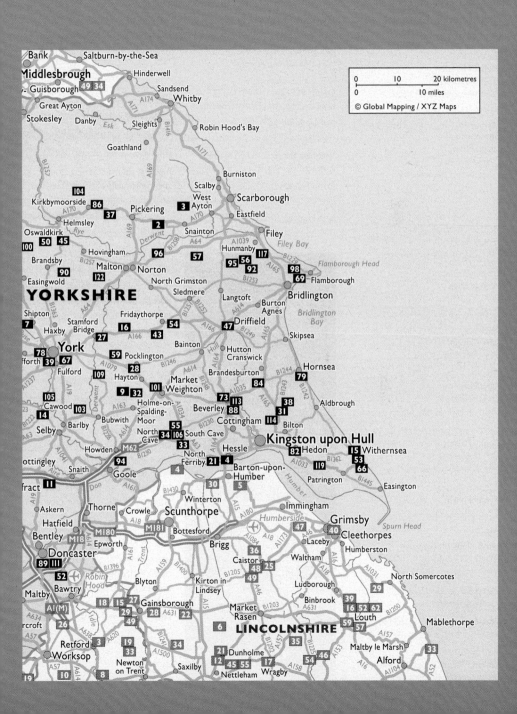

Volunteers

County Organisers

East Yorks
Helen Marsden
01430 860222
jerryhelen@btinternet.com

North Yorks – Cleveland,
Hambleton, Richmond, Rydale &
Scarborough
Hugh Norton
01653 628604
hughnorton0@gmail.com

South & West Yorks & North
Yorks -
Craven, Harrogate, Selby & York
Bridget Marshall BEM
01423 330474
biddymarshall@btinternet.com

County Treasurer
Angela Pugh
01423 330456
amjopugh@clannet.co.uk

Publicity
Jane Cooper 01484 604232
jane.cooper@ngs.org.uk

Booklet Advertising
John Plant
01347 888125
plantjohnsgarden@btinternet.com

By Arrangement Visits
Penny Phillips
01937 834970
hornington@btinternet.com

Clubs & Societies
Penny Phillips (as above)

Assistant County Organisers

East Yorks
Ian & Linda McGowan
01482 896492
adnil_magoo@yahoo.com

Hazel Rowe 01430 861439
hrowe@uwclub.net

Natalie Verow 01759 368444
natalieverow@aol.com

North Yorks
Gillian Mellor 01723 891636
gill.mellor@btconnect.com

Josephine Marks 01845 501626
carlton331@btinternet.com

Judi Smith 01765 688565
lowsutton@hotmail.co.uk

West & South Yorks
Deborah Bigley 01423 330727
debsandbobbigley@btinternet.com

Felicity Bowring 01729 823551
diss@austwick.org

Veronica Brook 01423 340875
veronicabowring@me.com

Rosie Hamlin 01302 535135
rosiehamlin@aol.com

Jane Hudson 01924 840980
janehudson42@btinternet.com

© Ann Curtis

Yorkshire, England's largest county, stretches from the Pennines in the west to the rugged coast and sandy beaches of the east: a rural landscape of moors, dales, vales and rolling wolds.

Nestling on riverbanks lie many historic market towns, and in the deep valleys of the west and south others retain their 19th century industrial heritage of coal, steel and textiles.

The wealth generated by these industries supported the many great estates, houses and gardens throughout the county. From Hull in the east, a complex network of canals weaves its way across the county, connecting cities to the sea and beyond.

The Victorian spa town of Harrogate with the RHS garden at Harlow Carr, or the historic city of York with a minster encircled by Roman walls, are both ideal centres from which to explore the gardens and cultural heritage of the county.

We look forward to welcoming you to our private gardens - you will find that most of them open not only on a specific day, but also 'by arrangement' for groups and individuals - we can help you to get in touch.

Left: **Rivelin Cottage**

OPENING DATES

All entries subject to change. For latest information check www.ngs.org.uk

Extended openings are shown at the beginning of the month.

Map locator numbers are shown to the right of each garden name.

February
Snowdrop Festival

Sunday 19th
Devonshire Mill   28

Wednesday 22nd
Austwick Hall   1

Sunday 26th
Bridge Farm House   11
Sutton Gardens   108

April

Sunday 2nd
Goldsborough Hall   40

Sunday 9th
Ellerker House   32

Thursday 13th
Hotham Hall   55

Thursday 20th
Hotham Hall   55

Saturday 22nd
Low Westwood
  Garden   64

Sunday 23rd
The Circles Garden   17

Sunday 30th
Highfield Cottage   47

May

Friday 5th
◆ Himalayan Garden &
  Sculpture Park   51

Sunday 7th
The Red House   89
◆ RHS Garden
  Harlow Carr   91

Tamarind   111

Wednesday 10th
Beacon Hill House   5
Pilmoor Cottages   87

Sunday 14th
Highfield Cottage   47
Hillbark   49
Low Hall   63
◆ Stillingfleet Lodge   105
Warley House
  Garden   115
Woodlands Cottage   118

Wednesday 17th
◆ Parcevall Hall
  Gardens   85
Warley House
  Garden   115

Sunday 21st
Barnville   2
◆ Jackson's Wold   57
The Ridings   92
NEW Scape Lodge   97

Friday 26th
◆ Shandy Hall
  Gardens   100

90th Anniversary Weekend

Sunday 28th
Beacon Garth   4
Creskeld Hall   25
115 Millhouses Lane   72
Nutkins   79
Rewela Cottage   90
NEW Rosemary
  Cottage   94

Wednesday 31st
5 Hill Top   48

June

◆ Dove Cottage
Nursery Garden
(Every Friday from
Friday 2nd)   29

Saturday 3rd
Hunmanby Grange   56
Old Sleningford Hall   80
Shiptonthorpe
  Gardens   101

Sunday 4th
Brookfield   12
Clifton Castle   18
The Court   21
Ellerker Manor   33

16 Hallam Grange
  Croft   44
5 Hill Top   48
Hunmanby Grange   56
23 Molescroft Road   73
Old Sleningford Hall   80
The Orchard   83
Shiptonthorpe
  Gardens   101
◆ The Yorkshire
  Arboretum   122

Wednesday 7th
Sleightholmedale
  Lodge   104

Friday 9th
Fawley House   34

Saturday 10th
Fawley House   34

Sunday 11th
NEW Bramble Croft   10
Bridge Farm House   11
High Hall   46
Linden Lodge   59
Marston Grange   70
Penny Piece Cottages   86

Tuesday 13th
Skipwith Hall   103

Wednesday 14th
Pilmoor Cottages   87

Saturday 17th
Holmfield   54

Sunday 18th
Dowthorpe Hall & Horse
  Pasture Cottage   31
NEW Glaramara   38
Holmfield   54
◆ Jackson's Wold   57
The Manor House   67

Saturday 24th
Omega   82
Sion Hill Hall   102

Sunday 25th
Birstwith Hall   8
Fernleigh   35
2 Hollin Close   52
Manor Farm   66
Millgate House   71
Omega   82
Rivelin Cottage   93
Sion Hill Hall   102
Swale Cottage   110
Yorke House   121

Friday 30th
◆ Shandy Hall
  Gardens   100

July

◆ Dove Cottage
Nursery Garden
(Every Friday)   29

Saturday 1st
NEW Crakehall   24

Sunday 2nd
Beechcroft Farmhouse   6
NEW Crakehall   24
Havoc Hall   45
Hillbark   49
Millgate House   71
NEW Myton Grange   74
◆ Norton Conyers   77
The Ridings   92
Wyedale   119

Saturday 8th
Cawood Gardens   14

Sunday 9th
Basin Howe Farm   3
Cawood Gardens   14
Dacre Banks &
  Summerbridge
  Gardens   26
Queensgate & Kitchen
  Lane Allotments   88
NEW 1 School Lane   98
Sutton upon Derwent
  School   109
Two Walled Gardens of
  Beverley   113

Saturday 15th
Sue Proctor Plants
  Nursery Garden   107

Sunday 16th
3 Church Walk   16
Cow Close Cottage   23
Daneswell House   27
54 Hollym Road   53
The Nursery   78
Sue Proctor Plants
  Nursery Garden   107
Sutton Gardens   108

Wednesday 19th
The Grange   41
The Nursery   78

Saturday 22nd
Stonefield Cottage   106

Sunday 23rd
Goldsborough Hall   40
High Hall   46
Little Eden   60
Sleightholmedale
  Lodge   104
Stonefield Cottage   106

RHS Garden Harlow Carr

THE GARDENS

1 AUSTWICK HALL

Town Head Lane, Austwick, Settle, LA2 8BS. James E Culley & Michael Pearson, 015242 51794, austwickhall@austwick.org, www.austwickhall.co.uk. *5m W of Settle. Leave the A65 to Austwick. Pass the PO on R, Gamecock Inn on L. Take first L onto Town Head Lane. Parking on Town Head Lane.* **Wed 22 Feb (12-4). Adm £4, chd free. Light refreshments. 2018: Wed 21 Feb.**

Set in the dramatic limestone scenery of the Dales the garden nestles into a steeply wooded hillside. Extensive drifts of common single and double snowdrops are an impressive sight with examples of over 50 other varieties. Sculptures along the trail add further interest. Woodland paths may be slippery in wet weather so sensible footwear is recommended.

2 BARNVILLE

Wilton, Pickering, YO18 7LE. Bill & Liz Craven, lizcraven40@gmail.com. *4m E of Pickering. On main A170, travelling from Pickering towards Scarborough, enter village of Wilton. Turn R. House on L in 200yrds.* **Sun 21 May, Sun 6 Aug (12-5). Adm £3.50, chd free. Home-made teas. Members of Wilton Village Hall provide and serve home-baked cakes and cream teas in the garden. Visits also by arrangement May to Oct for groups of 10+, adm £5.50 incl light refreshments.**

Over an acre of hidden gardens on the edge of the North York Moors. Unusual plants make a garden for all seasons: Winter is coloured by cyclamen, snowdrop, hellebore and witchhazel. Spring, magnolia and azalea shelter naturalised bulbs, trillium and erythronium. Summer's cool green foliage highlights allium, agapanthus and foxtail lilies. Autumn brings a blaze of coloured foliage, berries and late flowers. Featured in The Sunday Telegraph Garden

Special: picked as one of the top 10 gardens to visit for families, nature lovers and plant collectors. Lower garden unsuitable for wheelchairs in wet, but level stone paths in upper gardens. Access to sunken garden via steps - can be viewed from above.

3 BASIN HOWE FARM

Cockmoor Road, Sawdon, Scarborough, YO13 9EG. Mr & Mrs Richard & Heather Mullin, 01723 850180, info@basinhowefarm.co.uk, www.basinhowefarm.co.uk. *Turn off A170 between Scarborough & Pickering at Brompton by Sawdon follow sign to Sawdon. Basin Howe Farm 1½m above Sawdon village on the L.* **Sun 9 July (12-5). Adm £5, chd free. Home-made teas. Visits also by arrangement May to Aug (not Sats) Groups and couples welcome too.**

These gardens have a lovely atmosphere. 3 acres of garden with box parterre with seasonal planting and koi pond, herbaceous borders, wildlife pond and elevated viewing deck with Pod summer house and a number of sculptures. Orchard and woodland, ferns, lawns and shrubs. Paved seating areas but gravel paths. Basin Howe is high above the Wolds and has a Bronze Age Burial Mound. Maintained by owners. Winners of Gold in the Scarborough in Bloom Muck and Magic Competition and Gold winners in Yorkshire in Bloom. Wheelchair Access is possible to most areas but a helper is required. Access is via gravel paths and grass.

4 BEACON GARTH

Redcliff Road, Hessle, Hull, HU13 0HA. Ivor & June Innes, 01482 646140, ivorinnes@mac.com. *4½m W of Hull. Follow signs for Hessle Foreshore. Parking available in foreshore car park followed by a short walk up Cliff Rd. Enter the garden through the double gates on Redcliff Rd.* **Sun 28 May (12-5.30). Adm £4.50, chd free. Home-made teas. Visits also by arrangement Mar to Oct.**

Edwardian, Arts and Crafts House (mentioned in Pevsner's Guide to Hull) and S-facing garden set in 3½ acres, in an elevated position overlooking the Humber. Stunning sunken rock garden with bulbs and specimen trees, hostas and ferns. Mature trees, large lawns and herbaceous borders. Gravel paths, haha, box hedges and topiary. Child friendly; children's play area. Teas served in main hallway of house. Partial wheelchair access.

Your visit helps fund 389 Marie Curie Nurses

5 BEACON HILL HOUSE

Langbar, Ilkley, LS29 0EU. Mr & Mrs H Boyle, 01943 607544, josephine@humphreyboyle.co.uk. *4m NW of Ilkley. 1¼m SE of A59 at Bolton Bridge.* **Wed 10 May (1.30-5). Adm £4.50, chd free. Home-made teas. Visits also by arrangement Apr to July max 25.** *Donation to Riding for the Disabled.*

Delightful but steep walks, with long distance views, take you up through the woodland which shelters this seven acre garden. Although nearly 1000ft above sea level and adjacent to a grouse moor, many unusual trees and shrubs grow here. Spring is the showiest time for this garden with its Magnolias and Rhododendrons. Small kitchen garden and orchard, pond, some original Victorian features. No wheelchair access.

6 BEECHCROFT FARMHOUSE

Aldwark, nr Alne, York, YO61 1UB.
Alison Pollock. *14m NW of York,
17m E of Harrogate, 7m SW of
Easingwold. Follow signs for Aldwark
Manor hotel & golf course for village.
Approach from A1(M) and W is via
Aldwark Toll Bridge (40p toll for cars).*
Sun 2 July (1-5). Adm £3.50, chd
free. Home-made teas.
Country garden surrounding
Georgian farmhouse (not open).
All yr interest starts with rare
snowdrops, hellebores and borders
for winter colour. Winding paths lead
through series of smaller gardens
with different planting themes.
Cottage borders with old roses,
tulips, clematis. Hidden areas with
seating give a secluded feel. Gravel
courtyard with small formal pool, late
and unusual perennials and grasses.
Featured in The English Garden.

7 ♦ BENINGBROUGH HALL, GALLERY & GARDENS

Beningbrough, York, YO30 1DD.
National Trust, 01904 472027,
beningbrough@nationaltrust.
org.uk, www.nationaltrust.org.
uk/beningbrough. *8m N of York.
Easily accessed from A19 or over toll
bridge & country roads from A59.*
For opening times and information,
please phone, email or visit garden
website.
In the garden surrounding the
magnificent Baroque Hall, the formal
Edwardian style mixed borders
contrast with sweeping lawns. There
is a restored walled garden and
play area where children can let off
steam. With plenty of garden seats,
you can take your time, relax and
enjoy the picture-postcard views of
the parkland. New for 2017 the Ha
ha walk will be a glorious display of
300,000 spring flowering bulbs.

8 BIRSTWITH HALL

High Birstwith, Harrogate,
HG3 2JW. Sir James & Lady
Aykroyd, 01423 770250,
ladya@birstwithhall.co.uk.
*5m NW of Harrogate. Between
Hampsthwaite & Birstwith villages,
close to A59 Harrogate/Skipton Rd.*
Sun 25 June (2-5). Adm £4, chd
free. Home-made teas. **Visits
also by arrangement groups and
small coaches welcome.**
Large 4 acre garden nestling in
secluded Yorkshire dale with formal
garden and ornamental orchard,
extensive lawns, picturesque stream,
large pond and Victorian greenhouse.

9 BOUNDARY COTTAGE

Seaton Ross, York, YO42 4NF. Roger
Brook, www.nodiggardener.co.uk.
*5m SW of Pocklington. From A64 York
take Hull exit and immed. B1228,
Approx 10m to Seaton Ross. From
M62 Howden N on B1228. From
A1079 follow Seaton Ross.* Sun 10
Sept (12-4.30). Adm £5, chd
free. Light refreshments. In
conservatory.
Lecturer and creator of Bolton
Percy churchyard garden, Roger
Brook's own no-dig garden. 1500
different plant varieties, many rare,
provide colour all year round.
The acre garden has numerous
and varied intimate features,
visually connected in sweeping
views. Horticulturally unorthodox,
especially the fruit and vegetables,
the overall effect is dramatic.
The garden holds the National
Collection of Dicentra. Very friendly
rheas in the field next door! Artist in
the garden. Access to all parts of the
garden. Some pushing required on
fescue lawns. WC access up a step.

10 [NEW] BRAMBLE CROFT

Howden Road, Silsden, Keighley,
BD20 0JB. Debbi Wilson. *Next to
Springbank Nursing Home, please
park in Howden Rd.* Sun 11 June,
Sun 3 Sept (11-4). Adm £3, chd
free. Light refreshments.
Bramble's small hidden hillside
artist's garden full of colour, texture
and newly developed borders
includes perennials, ferns, climbers,
grasses, topiary and sculptures,
lies on the edge of Silsden village.
Wildlife encouraged with pond, bird
and insect boxes. Original paintings
are on show and for sale in the new
tranquil garden room. Terrace and
outdoor covered dining patio.

The Jungle Garden

11 BRIDGE FARM HOUSE

Long Lane, Great Heck, Selby, DN14 0BE. Barbara & Richard Ferrari, 01977 661277, barbaraferrari@mypostoffice. co.uk. *6m S of Selby, 3m E M62 J34. At M62 J34 take A19 to Selby, at r'about turn E to Snaith on A645. R at T-lights, L at T-junction onto Main St, past Church, to T-junction, cross to car park.* Sun 26 Feb, Sun 11 June (12-4.30). Adm £4, chd free. Home-made teas in church (opp). **Visits also by arrangement Feb and June.**
2 acre garden divided by hedges into separate areas planted with unusual and interesting plants. All yr interest starts with rare snowdrops, hellebores and winter shrubs. Long double mixed borders; bog, with orchids; gravel garden, with grasses and pond; interesting trees. hens; compost heaps and wildlife areas. Wheelchair access easiest by front gate, please ask.

12 BROOKFIELD

Jew Lane, Oxenhope, Keighley, BD22 9HS. Mrs R L Belsey, 01535 643070. *5m SW of Keighley. From Keighley take A629 (Halifax). Fork R A6033 towards Haworth & Oxenhope, turn L at Xrds into village. Turn R (Jew Lane) at bottom of hill.* Sun 4 June (1.30-5). Adm £4, chd free. Home-made teas. **Visits also by arrangement May to end July max 30 visitors. Refreshments available on request.**
1 acre, intimate garden, incl large pond with an island, mallards and wild geese also greylags. Many varieties of primula, candelabra and florindae; azaleas and rhododendrons. Unusual trees and shrubs, screes, greenhouses and conservatory. Series of island beds. 'Round and Round the Garden' children's quiz. Partial wheelchair access - steep slope and steps.

13 BUTTERFIELD HEIGHTS

4 Park Crescent, Guiseley, Leeds, LS20 8EL. Vicky Harris, 078521 63733, vickyharris1951@gmail.com. *11m NW of Leeds. From Guiseley A65 (Otley-Leeds) A6038 towards Shipley (Bradford Rd). Park Crescent ½m on L. Park on Bradford Rd.* Wed 9 Aug (11-5). Adm £3.50, chd free. Home-made teas. **Visits also by arrangement in Aug for groups of 15+.**
Garden completely restored over 20 years but retaining and enhancing the original 1930's landscaping. Mixed planting of unusual shrubs, perennials and mature trees now undergoing further transitions as the owners try to reduce their garden workload. Statuesque planting creates a riot of colour while topiary features and tall perennials add to the character of the garden at the height of summer. Tree carving and Fairy Post Office (with gifts). Featured in Amateur Gardening and Yorkshire Post. Garden on three levels with some steep steps and gravel paths.

GROUP OPENING

14 CAWOOD GARDENS

Cawood, nr Selby, YO8 3UG. *On B1223 5m N of Selby & 7m SE of Tadcaster. Between York & A1 on B1222. Village maps available at all gardens.* Sat 8, Sun 9 July (12-5). Combined adm £6, chd free. Home-made teas at 9 Anson Grove & 21 Great Close. **Visits also by arrangement June & July.**

9 ANSON GROVE
Tony & Brenda Finnigan.

21 GREAT CLOSE
David & Judy Jones.

THE PIGEONCOTE
Maria Parks & Angela Darlington.

These three contrasting gardens in an attractive historic village are linked by a pretty riverside walk to the C11 church and Memorial garden and across the Castle Garth to the remains of Cawood Castle. 9 Anson Grove is a small garden with tranquil pools and secluded sitting places. Narrow winding paths and raised areas give views over oriental-style pagoda, bridge and Zen garden. 21 Great Close is a flower arranger's garden, designed and built by the owners. Interesting trees and shrubs combine with herbaceous borders incl many grasses. Two ponds are joined by a stream, winding paths take you to the vegetable garden and summerhouse, then back to the colourful terrace for views across the garden and countryside beyond. The small walled garden, Pigeoncote at 2 Wistowgate is surrounded by historic C17 buildings. A balanced design of formal box hedging, cottage garden planting and creative use of grasses. Angled brick pathways lead to shaded seating areas with all day sunny views. Crafts and paintings on sale at 9 Anson Grove. Wheelchair access limited at 9 Anson Grove and 21 Great Close.

15 14 CHELLSWAY

Chellsway, Withernsea, HU19 2EN. Neil & Caroline Ziemski. *15m E of Hull Enter Withernsea on A1033, turn L onto B1362, 2nd L onto Carrs Meadow, L onto Beaconsfield R onto Chellsway.* Sun 6 Aug (12-6). Adm £2.50, chd free. Home-made teas and cakes.
Jungle garden with grass and gravel paths surrounded by hardy and tender plants. Collection of bamboo, bananas, gingers, palms, succulents and other exotic plants, combine to create a tropical effect rarely seen on the Yorkshire coast. An authentic jungle hut and various seating areas allow the visitor to see different aspects of the garden. Small pond and rockery.

Perennial, supporting horticulturalists since 1839

16 3 CHURCH WALK

Bugthorpe, York, YO41 1QL.
Barrie Creaser & David
Fielding, 01759 368152,
barriecreaser@gmail.com.
*Stamford Bridge to Bridlington rd,
after 4m you will see the yellow
direction arrows, for Bugthorpe, park
in the village outside the church.*
Sun 16 July (10-4). Adm £3.50,
chd free. Also open Daneswell
House, Stamford Bridge YO41
1AD. Refreshments available
in both gardens. Visits also by
arrangement June & July for
15 max.
A garden created from scratch
16 years ago, surprisingly mature,
with mixed borders and trees,
water feature and pond. Raised
vegetable garden and greenhouse.
The lawn leads onto a paddock with
views of open countryside, lots of
seating to sit and enjoy the different
vistas. Wheelchair access: garden
accessible, but gravel in courtyard.
Please contact owners prior to
arrival to ensure access to garden
by car.

☕

17 THE CIRCLES GARDEN

8 Stocksmoor Road, Midgley, nr
Wakefield, WF4 4JQ. Joan Gaunt.
*Equidistant from Huddersfield,
Wakefield & Barnsley, W of M1 Turn
off A637 in Midgley at the Black
Bull PH (sharp bend) onto B6117
(Stocksmoor Rd). Please park on L
adjacent to houses.* Sun 23 Apr
(1.30-5). Adm £3.50, chd free.
Home-made teas.
An organic and self-sustaining
plantswoman's ½ acre garden on
gently sloping site overlooking fields,
woods and nature reserve opposite.
Designed and maintained by owner.
Interesting herbaceous, bulb and
shrub plantings linked by grass and
gravel paths, a woodland area with
mature trees, spring and summer
meadows, fernery, greenhouse, fruit
trees, viewing terrace with pots.
Also, around 100 hellebores grown
from my seed. South African plants,
hollies, small bulbs are particular
interests.

✿ ☕

18 CLIFTON CASTLE

Ripon, HG4 4AB. Lord & Lady
Downshire. *2m N of Masham. On
rd to Newton-le-Willows & Richmond.
Gates on L next to red telephone
box.* Sun 4 June (2-5). Adm £4,
chd free. Home-made teas.
Fine views, river walks, wooded
pleasure grounds with bridges
and follies. Cascades, wild flower
meadow and C19 walled kitchen
garden. Gravel paths and steep
slopes to river.

&. 🐕 ✿ ☕

19 COLD COTES

Cold Cotes Road, Kettlesing,
Harrogate, HG3 2LW.
Susan Bailey, 01423 770937,
info@coldcotes.com,
www.coldcotes.com. *7m W of
Harrogate off A59. From Skipton
turn L after Menwith Hill. From
Harrogate turn R for Menwith Hill/
Cold Cotes. Coldcotes has a brown
ACCOMMODATION sign from both
directions.* Sun 17 Sept (1-5).
Adm £3.50, chd free. Cream
teas. Prior booking available
for lunches/afternoon teas for
groups of 10+. Fully licensed.
Visits also by arrangement
May to Sept for groups of 10+
afternoons from 1pm. Adm incl
cream tea £5.99.
This large peaceful garden with
expansive views under new
ownership is at ease in its rural
setting. Year round interest moves
through a series of discrete gardens
incl formal areas around the house,
sweeping herbaceous borders
inspired by designer Piet Oudolf
peaking in late summer, pond
with bridge. Woodland garden
underplanted with masses of bulbs
and perennials for spring to autumn
interest. Limited garden access for
wheelchairs, disabled WC. Ramp to
tea room and WC.

&. ✿ 🚗 🚌 ☕

20 ◆ CONSTABLE BURTON HALL GARDENS

Constable Burton, Leyburn,
DL8 5LJ. Mr D'Arcy
Wyvill, 01677 450428,
gardens@constableburton.com,
www.constableburton.com. *3m E
of Leyburn. Constable Burton Village.*
*On A684, 6m W of A1, between the
towns of Bedale & Leyburn.* For
opening times and information,
please phone, email or visit garden
website.
Large romantic garden with
terraced woodland walks. Garden
trails, shrubs, roses and water
garden. Display of daffodils and
over 6,500 tulips planted annually
amongst extensive borders. Fine
John Carr house (not open) set
in splendour of Wensleydale
countryside. Constable Burton Hall
Gardens plays host to a magnificent
Tulip Festival, on the first May Bank
Holiday weekend. Sponsored by
Chelsea award winning nursery
Bloms Bulbs, over 6,500 traditional
and new variant tulips are planted
throughout the gardens.

&. 🐕 🚗

21 THE COURT

Humber Road, North
Ferriby, HU14 3DW. Guy
& Liz Slater, 01482 633609,
liz@guyslater.karoo.co.uk. *7m W
of Hull. Travelling E on A63 to Hull,
follow sign for N Ferriby. Through
village to Xrds with war memorial,
turn R & follow rd to T-junction with
Humber Rd. Turn L & immed R into
cul-de-sac, last house on L.* Sun 4
June (1-5). Adm £3.50, chd free.
Home-made teas. Visits also
by arrangement Feb to Aug,
groups of 10+.
Romantic and restful, with hidden
seating areas offering different vistas.
Roses and clematis scrambling up
walls and trees. Two summerhouses,
small pond and waterfall with
secluded arbours and historical
items. A long tunnel of wisteria,
clematis and laburnum leads to a
little path with Betula jacquemontii,
small stumpery, and grown up
swing. Two small areas have been
re-designed owing to the loss of
2 large trees last winter near the
larger summerhouse. Featured on
BBC Radio Humberside.

&. 🐕 ✿ ☕

22 COVERHAM ABBEY

Middleham, Leyburn, DL8 4RL.
Mr & Mrs Nigel Corner. *A6108
to Middleham then Coverdale rd out
of Middleham following signs to 'The*

Forbidden Corner', past pond on R. Drive at bottom of steep bank on L before church. Sun 17 Sept (11-4). Adm £3.50, chd free. Light refreshments.
Stunning gardens set in the heart of tranquil Coverdale. Within the grounds of C13 premonstratensian Abbey ruins, a large intricate knot garden, mixed borders, parterre and yew rondel with rose arches. Some areas being developed. Wild flower meadow.

❀ ☕

23 COW CLOSE COTTAGE
Stripe Lane, Hartwith, Harrogate, HG3 3EY. William Moore & John Wilson, 01423 779813, cowclose1@btinternet.com. *8m NW of Harrogate. From A61(Harrogate-Ripon) at Ripley take B6165 to Pateley Bridge. 1m beyond Burnt Yates turn R signed Hartwith onto Stripe Lane. Parking available.* Sun 16 July (10.30-4.30). Adm £4, chd free. Cream teas. Visits also by arrangement June to Aug min 8 for group visits. Teas by prior arrangement.
⅔-acre recently redeveloped country garden on sloping site with stream and far reaching views. Large borders with drifts of interesting, well-chosen, later flowering summer perennials and some grasses contrasting with woodland shade and streamside plantings. Gravel path leading to vegetable area. Terrace and seating with views of the garden. Orchard and ha-ha with steps leading to meadow.

  ☕ ❀ ☕

24 NEW CRAKEHALL HALL
Crakehall, Bedale, DL8 1HH. Mr Russell Jarvis. *3m NW of Bedale. From A1 North or South, take the A684 Bedale exit & follow the road towards Leyburn.* Sat 1, Sun 2 July (2-5.30). Adm £5, chd free. Home-made teas.
Restored Walled Gardens behind C18 house (not open) overlooking village green. Borders planted in rhythmic colour, clipped yew, espaliered apples, thyme walk and herb knot, white garden. Vistas and seating. Warm terrace under the house with roses. Lavender alley.

Woodland seeded with Martagon Lilies. Wheelchair access to walled garden only.

  ☕

25 CRESKELD HALL
Arthington, Leeds, LS21 1NT. J & C Stoddart-Scott. *5m E of Otley. On A659 between Pool & Harewood.* Sun 28 May (12-5). Adm £4, chd free. Home-made teas.
Historic picturesque 3½ acre Wharfedale garden with beech avenue, mature rhododendrons and azaleas. Gravel path from terrace leads to attractive water garden with canals set amongst woodland plantings. Walled kitchen garden and flower garden. Specialist nurseries.

  ❀ ☕

GROUP OPENING

26 DACRE BANKS & SUMMERBRIDGE GARDENS
Nidderdale, HG3 4EW. 01423 780456, pat@yorkehouse.co.uk, www.yorkehouse.co.uk. *4m SE Pateley Bridge, 10m NW Harrogate, 10m N Otley, on B6451 and B6165. Parking at each garden. Maps available to show garden locations.* Sun 9 July (12-5). Combined adm £8, chd free. Cream teas at Yorke House, Low Hall and Woodlands Cottage. Visits also by arrangement June & July for groups of 12+.

LOW HALL
Mrs P A Holliday.
(See separate entry)

RIVERSIDE HOUSE
Joy Stanton.

WOODLANDS COTTAGE
Mr & Mrs Stark.
(See separate entry)

YORKE HOUSE
Tony & Pat Hutchinson.
(See separate entry)

Dacre Banks and Summerbridge Gardens are situated in the beautiful countryside of Nidderdale and designed to take advantage of the

scenic Dales landscape. The gardens are linked by an attractive walk along the valley and each may be accessed individually by car. Low Hall has a romantic walled garden set on different levels around the historic C17 family home (not open) with herbaceous borders, shrubs, climbing roses and tranquil water garden. Riverside House is a mysterious waterside garden on many levels, supporting shade-loving plants and incorporates a Victorian folly, fernery, courtyard and naturalistic riverside plantings. Woodlands Cottage is a garden of many rooms, with exquisite formal and informal plantings,which together with an attractive wild flower meadow harmonise with the boulder-strewn woodland. Yorke House has extensive colour-themed borders, fabulous waterside plantings of candelabra primula and a secluded millennium garden full of fragrant plants and rambling roses. Visitors welcome to use orchard picnic area at Yorke House. Featured on BBC Radio York and Harrogate Advertiser. Partial wheelchair access at some gardens.

🐕 ❀ 🚗 ☕

Your visit helps the Queen's Nursing Institute to champion excellence in community nursing

27 DANESWELL HOUSE

35 Main Street, Stamford Bridge, YO41 1AD. Brian & Pauline Clayton, 01759 371446, Pauline-clayton44@outlook.com. *7m E of York. On A166 at the E end of the village. Garden on your L as you leave the village towards Bridlington.* Sun 16 July (10-4). Adm £4, chd free. Cream teas at Daneswell House. Also open 3 Church Walk, Bugthorpe YO41 1QL. Visits also by arrangement July & Aug for groups of 10+.

A ¾ acre secluded garden that sweeps down to the R Derwent. It has tiered terraces, ponds, water feature, shrubs, borders. The garden attracts abundant wildlife. Teas are served at the top of the garden. This is a sloping garden down to river, however access is possible with care.

&. 🚗 ☕

28 DEVONSHIRE MILL

Canal Lane, Pocklington, York, YO42 1NN. Sue & Chris Bond, 01759 302147, chris.bond.dm@btinternet.com, www.devonshiremill.co.uk. *1m S of Pocklington. Canal Lane, off A1079 at The Wellington Oak PH.* Sun 19 Feb (11-5). Adm £4, chd free. Home-made teas.
2018: Sun 18 Feb.
Drifts of double snowdrops, hellebores and ferns surround the historic grade II listed water mill. Explore the two acre garden with mill stream, orchards, woodland, herbaceous borders, hen run and greenhouses. The old mill pond is now a vegetable garden with raised beds and a polytunnel. Over the past twenty years the owners have developed the garden on organic principles to encourage wildlife.

🐄 🛏 ☕

29 ♦ DOVE COTTAGE NURSERY GARDEN

Shibden Hall Road, nr Halifax, HX3 9XA. Kim & Stephen Rogers, 01422 203553, info@dovecottagenursery.co.uk, www.dovecottagenursery.co.uk. *1m E Halifax. From Halifax take A58 turn L signed Claremount, cont over bridge, cont ½ m. J26 M62- A58 Halifax. Drive 4m. L turn at Paw Prints pet store down Tanhouse Hill, cont ½ m.* Every Fri 2 June to 29 Sept (10-5). Adm £3.50, chd free. Tea. For other opening times and information, please phone, email or visit garden website.
Hedges and green oak gates enclose ⅓ acre sloping garden, generously planted by nursery owners over 20yrs. A beautiful mix of late summer perennials and grasses. Winding paths and plenty of seats incl a romantic tulip arbour. Plants for sale in nursery. Wildlife friendly. 'Considered good example of cottage garden' (Carole Klein thought so!). Featured in the RHS The Garden magazine. Appearing on Gardeners World during 2017.

✿ 🚗 ☕

30 34 DOVER ROAD

Hunters Bar, Sheffield, S11 8RH. Marian Simpson, 079575 36248, marian@mjsimpson.plus.com. *1½ m SW of city centre. From A61 (ring rd) A625 Moore St/Ecclesall Rd for approx 1m. Dover Rd on R.* Visits by arrangement May to Aug for groups of 10+. Home-made teas. Wide range of home made drinks and cakes..
Colourful, small town garden packed with interest and drama, combining formality with exotic exuberance. Attractive alpine area replacing old driveway, many interesting containers and well-stocked borders. Conservatory, seating areas and lawns complement unusual plants and planting combinations. Featured in Daily Mail, Yorkshire Post, ITV (Alan Titchmarsh 'Love Your Garden'), Sheffield Telegraph, BBC Radio Sheffield.

🐄 ✿ ☕

31 DOWTHORPE HALL & HORSE PASTURE COTTAGE

Skirlaugh, Hull, HU11 5AE. Mr & Mrs J Holtby, 01964 562235, john.holtby@farming.co.uk, www.dowthorpehall.com. *6m N of Hull, 8m E of Beverley. From Hull A165 towards Bridlington. Through Ganstead & Coniston. 1m S of Skirlaugh on R, (long drive white railings & sign at drive end).* Sun 18 June (11-5). Adm £5, chd free. Visits also by arrangement Apr to June a fork lunch or supper is available by arrangement.
Dowthorpe Hall: 3½ acres, large herbaceous borders, lawns, shady area, pond with bridge, scree garden, hardy garden, orchards and vegetable potager. Horse Pasture Cottage: small cottage garden, herbaceous border and woodland water feature. The sundial border with 100's of pink and blue Hyacinths in spring, roses and catmint in summer, forms a central feature linking to other borders. Gravel, lawns, no steps.

&. 🐄 🛏 ☕

32 ELLERKER HOUSE

Everingham, York, YO42 4JA. Mrs R Los & Mr M Wright, www.ellerkerhouse.weebly.com. *15m SE of York. 5½ m from Pocklington. Just out of the village heading towards Harswell.* Sun 9 Apr (10-5). Adm £5, chd free. Home-made teas. Savouries served over lunch time.
5 acres of garden on sandy soil. Lots of spring bulbs and plants. Many unusual mature trees in a parkland setting, formal lawns, woodland walkway and stumpery around lake. 11 acres of bluebell woods to stroll around. Traditional oak and thatched breeze hut. Several seating areas around the garden. Rose archway, colour themed herbaceous borders planted with many unusual plants for all year colour. RARE PLANT FAIR (Many different stalls selling a variety of unusual plants).

&. ✿ 🚗 ☕

33 ELLERKER MANOR

Cave Lane, Ellerker, Brough, HU15 2DX. Philip & Sally Bean, 01430 423035, Pmegabean@aol.com. *From the S Cave exit on the A63 turn towards West End S Cave and the lorry sign to Ellerker. At T-junction, turn L. Garden on L after Ellerker Village sign.* Sun 4 June (11-5). Adm £4, chd free. Home-made teas. Visits also by arrangement.

A village garden belonging to the previous owners of Saltmarshe Hall. The garden has good trees and shrubs, borders packed with herbaceous plants and bulbs. Climbers grow on trellis. The pretty potager has vegetables and flowers. A less structured part of the garden has ponds and wild flower area. Gravel driveway, and wheelchairs would need to be pushed across grass, but most of the garden can be seen.

&. ✿ ☕ 💐

34 FAWLEY HOUSE
7 Nordham, North Cave, Brough, HU15 2LT. Mr & Mrs T Martin, 01430 422266, louisem200@hotmail.co.uk, www.nordhamcottages.co.uk. 15m W of Hull. L at J38 on M62. L at '30' & signs: Wetlands & Polo. At LH bend, R into Nordham. Fawley is on RHS. Carpark further ahead. From Beverley, B1230 to N Cave. R at church into Nordham. Car park ahead. Fri 9, Sat 10 June (1.30-5.30). Adm

£4, chd free. Home-made teas. 2018: Sun 18 Feb. **Visits also by arrangement May & June for groups of 10+, adm £8 to incl home-made tea.**
Tiered, 2½ acre garden with lawns, mature trees, formal hedging and gravel pathways. Lavender beds, mixed shrub/herbaceous borders, and hot double herbaceous borders. Apple espaliers, pears, soft fruit, produce and herb gardens. Terrace with pergola and vines. Sunken garden with white border. Woodland with naturalistic planting and spring bulbs. Quaker well, stream and spring area with 3 bridges, ferns and hellebores near mill stream. Beautiful snowdrops and aconites early in year. Art Exhibition: Art in the Garden by East Riding Artists. Treasure Hunt for children. Self catering accommodation at Nordham Cottages see website. Partial wheelchair access to top of garden and terrace on pea gravel.

&. ✿ 🛏 ☕ 💐

35 FERNLEIGH
9 Meadowhead Avenue, Meadowhead, Sheffield, S8 7RT. Mr & Mrs C Littlewood, 01142 747234, littlewoodchristine@gmail.com. 4m S of Sheffield city centre. From Sheffield city centre. A61, A6102, B6054 r'about, exit B6054. 1st R Greenhill Ave, 2nd R. From M1 J33, A630 to A6102, then as above. Sun 25 June, Sun 30 July, Sun 27 Aug (11-5). Adm £3, chd free. Home-made teas. **Visits also by arrangement Apr to Sept for groups of 10 to 30.**
Plantswoman's ⅓ acre cottage style garden. Large variety of unusual plants set in differently planted sections to provide all-yr interest. Seating areas to view different aspects of garden. Auricula theatre, patio, gazebo and greenhouse. Miniature log cabin with living roof and cobbled area with unusual plants in pots. Sempervivum, alpine displays and wildlife 'hotel'. Wide selection of home grown plants for sale. Animal search for children. Featured in Sheffield Telegraph & Star.

✿ ☕ 💐

Sutton Grange

ALLOTMENTS

36 FIRVALE ALLOTMENT GARDEN
Winney Hill, Harthill, nr Worksop, S26 7YN. Don & Dot Witton, 01909 771366, donshardyeuphorbias@ btopenworld.com, www.euphorbias.co.uk. 12m SE of Sheffield, 6m W of Worksop. M1 J31 A57 to Worksop. Turn R to Harthill. Allotments at S end of village, 26 Casson Drive at N end on Northlands Estate. **Visits by arrangement Apr to July. Adm £3, chd free.** Home-made teas at 26 Casson Drive Harthill (S26 7WA).
Large allotment containing 13 island beds displaying 500+ herbaceous perennials incl the National Collection of hardy Euphorbias with over 100 varieties flowering between March and October. Organic vegetable garden. Refreshments, WC, plant sales at 26 Casson Drive – small garden with mixed borders, shade and seaside garden.

✿ 🚌 NPC ☕ 💐

37 FRIARS HILL

Sinnington, YO62 6SL. Mr & Mrs C J Baldwin, 01751 432179, friars.hill@abelgratis.co.uk. *4m W of Pickering. On A170.* **Visits by arrangement Mar to July, for groups of 10+. Adm £4, chd free.** Plantswoman's 1¾ acre garden containing over 2500 varieties of perennials and bulbs, with yr-round colour. Early interest with hellebores, bulbs and woodland plants. Herbaceous beds. Hostas, delphiniums, old roses and stone troughs. Excellent Autumn colour.

38 NEW GLARAMARA

Lambwath Lane, New Ellerby, Hull, HU11 5BT. Pam & Giles Hufford. *From Hull, leave A165 just before Skirlaugh, turn R onto Mulberry Lane. After 1½m, turn L on to Lambwath Lane. Glaramara is 200yds on L.* **Sun 18 June (10.30-4). Adm £3, chd free. Home-made teas.** Wildlife haven on the highest point of the Holderness Plain. Steps leading to patio, lawn with borders and small pond. Archway to henhouse and willow windbreaks surrounded by too many trees and plants to list. Twisting pathways to the sleep house and secret garden. Small wooded area with gate leading to greenhouse, apiary, mixed fruit and vegetable plots with specimen trees.

39 ◆ GODDARDS HOUSE & GARDENS

Tadcaster Road, York, YO2 1GG. The National Trust, 01904 771930, goddards@nationaltrust.org.uk, www.nationaltrust.org.uk/goddards. *27 Tadcaster Rd. 2m from York centre on A64, next to Swallow Chase Hotel.* **For opening times and information, please phone, email or visit garden website.** 1920s garden designed by George Dillistone, herbaceous borders, yew hedges, terraces with aromatic plants, rock garden and ponds.

40 GOLDSBOROUGH HALL

Church Street, Goldsborough, HG5 8NR. Mr & Mrs M Oglesby, 01423 867321, info@goldsboroughhall.com, www.goldsboroughhall.com. *2m SE of Knaresborough. 3m W of A1M. Off A59 (York-Harrogate) carpark 300yds past PH on R.* **Sun 2 Apr (12-4); Sun 23 July (12-5). Adm £5, chd free. Home-made teas, light lunches, sandwiches and cakes.** *Donation to St Mary's Church, Goldsborough.* Previously opened for NGS from 1928-30 and now beautifully restored by present owners (re-opened in 2010). 12-acre garden and formal landscaped grounds in parkland setting and Grade II*, C17 house, former residence of the late HRH Princess Mary, daughter of George V and Queen Mary. Gertrude Jekyll inspired replanted 120ft double herbaceous borders and rose garden. Quarter-mile Lime Tree Walk planted by royalty in the 1920s and a flower border featuring 'Yorkshire Princess' rose, named after Princess Mary. Various magazine articles and local radio. Gravel paths and some steep slopes.

41 THE GRANGE

Carla Beck Lane, Carleton in Craven, Skipton, BD23 3BU. Mr & Mrs R N Wooler, 07740 639135, margaret.wooler@hotmail.com. *1½m SW of Skipton Turn off A56 (Skipton-Clitheroe) into Carleton. Keep L at Swan PH, continue to end of village then turn R into Carla Beck Lane* **Wed 19 July, Wed 16 Aug (12-4.30). Adm £5, chd free. Cream teas. Visits also by arrangement, July & Aug, groups of 30+.** *Donation to Sue Ryder Care Manorlands Hospice.* Over 4 acres set in the grounds of Victorian house (not open) with mature trees and panoramic views towards The Gateway to the Dales. The garden has been restored by the owners over the last 2 decades with many areas of interest being added to the original footprint. Bountiful herbaceous borders with many unusual species, rose walk,

parterre, mini-meadows and water features Large greenhouse and raised vegetable beds. Oak seating placed throughout the garden invites quiet contemplation, a place to 'lift the spirit' Gravel paths and steps

42 GRASMERE

48 Royds Lane, Rothwell, LS26 0BH. Terry & Tina Cook. *5m S of Leeds, 6½m N of Wakefield. M62 J30 follow A642 towards Leeds. Turn L after 200yds (Royds School) Pennington Lane follow rd for 1m. Car parking at school opp or in rd nr Squash Club.* **Sun 30 July (1-5). Adm £3.50, chd free. Home-made teas.** Amongst old orchard trees is hidden a restful family suburban garden of ⅓ acre. Wildlife relaxes by many nesting boxes, ponds, wild flower area, log piles for hedgehogs and flowers to attract butterflies. Secluded summerhouse enclosed by colourful tapestry hedge and architectural planting. Pergola walkway leads to hidden vegetable garden.

43 GREENWICK FARM

Huggate, York, YO42 1YR. Fran & Owen Pearson, 01377 288122, greenwickfarm@hotmail.com. *2m W of Huggate. From York on A166, turn R 1m after Garrowby Hill, at brown sign for picnic area & scenic route. White wind turbine on drive.* **Sun 20 Aug (1-5). Adm £4, chd free. Home-made teas. Tea tables in conservatory & outside. Visits also by arrangement July to Sept refreshments to be agreed upon when visit is arranged.** 1 acre woodland garden created 7 yrs ago from disused area of the farm. Set in a large dell with many mature trees . Paths up the hillside through borders lead to terrace planted with Hydrangeas, many seating areas with spectacular views across wooded valley and the Wolds, small stumpery and new hot border. Herbaceous/shrub borders. Described by guests as a graceful and very tranquil garden. Access for wheelchairs difficult, but good view of garden from hard standing outside house/tea area.

44 16 HALLAM GRANGE CROFT

Fulwood, Sheffield, S10 4BP. Tricia & Alistair Fraser, 0114 230 6508, tricia.fraser@talktalk.net. *Approx 4m SW of Sheffield city centre. Follow A57 (Glossop). 1½m after University turn L at Crosspool shops just beyond Tesco. After 1m turn L at top of hill & follow signs.* Sun 4 June (12.30-4.30). Adm £3.50, chd free. Hot and cold drinks and a selection of cakes, mostly home-made, available. Visits also by arrangement May to July min entry charge for 10 people applies.

Developed over 20 years, a plantswoman's SE-facing sloping wildlife-friendly garden. Backed by mature trees with established perennial and shrub planting incl many unusual hardy geraniums, geums and erodiums. Shady areas, pond, summerhouse and greenhouse. Raised bed, rockery and decking area feature alpines and sun-loving perennials. Plants propagated by the owners on sale. Featured in Sheffield Telegraph and Sheffield Star.

45 HAVOC HALL

York Rd, Oswaldkirk, York, YO62 5XY. David & Maggie Lis, 01439 788846, maggielis@me.com, www.havochall.co.uk. *21m N of York. On B1363, 1st house on R as you enter Oswaldkirk from S & last house on L as you leave village from N.* Sun 2 July (1-5). Adm £5, chd free. Home-made teas.

Started in 2009, comprising 8 areas incl knot, herbaceous, mixed shrub and flower gardens, courtyard, vegetable area and orchard, woodland walk and large lawned area with hornbeam trees and hedging. To the S is a 2-acre wild flower meadow and small lake. Extensive collection of roses, herbaceous perennials and grasses. See website for other opening times. Some steps but these can be avoided.

46 HIGH HALL

St Stephen's Road, Steeton, Keighley, BD20 6SB. Roger & Christine Lambert, 01535 657060, c.miskin@btinternet.com. *3m W of Keighley. Enter Steeton from A629. Turn R at lights & R after 100yds & down St Stephens Rd. No parking at house except disabled. Follow signs for parking in village.* Sun 11 June, Sun 23 July (11-5). Adm £4, chd free. Home-made teas.

Visits also by arrangement June & July.

2 acre well-hidden Arts and Crafts garden and historic house (not open) adjacent to St Stephen's Church. Formal walled garden with pond, belvedere, pergola, dovecote, summerhouse and ancient yew, herbaceous planting in formal beds connected by gravel paths. Walled kitchen garden with vegetable beds and fruit trees. Natural woodland area, bog garden, and small croquet lawn. Historical notes available. Exhibition of Alexander Keighley photographs and pottery display by Barbara Miskin. Child-friendly activities. Wheelchair access some steps and gravelled paths may make access difficult in places.

47 HIGHFIELD COTTAGE

North Street, Driffield, YO25 6AS. Debbie Simpson. *30m E of York, 29m E of M62. Exit at A614/A166 r'about onto York Rd into Driffield. Carry straight until you reach the park with the Rose & Crown PH opp. Highfield Cottage is the white detached house next to PH.* Sun 30 Apr, Sun 14 May (11-3). Adm £3.50, chd free. Cream teas.

A ¾ acre suburban garden bordered by mature trees and stream. Structure is provided by numerous yew and box topiary, a pergola and sculptures all created and maintained by the owner. Lawns with island beds, mixed shrubs, fruit trees and herbaceous borders ensure year round interest. A natural and evolving garden, described as 'magical' by NGS visitors.

48 5 HILL TOP

Westwood Drive, Ilkley, LS29 9RS. Lyn & Phil Short. *½m S of Ilkley town centre, steep uphill. Turn S at town centre T-lights up Brook St, cross The Grove taking Wells Rd up to the Moors and follow NGS signs.* Wed 31 May, Sun 4 June (11-4.30). Adm £3.50, chd free. Home-made teas.

Delightful ⅔ acre steep garden on edge of Ilkley Moor. Sheltered woodland underplanted with naturalistic, flowing tapestry of foliage, shade-loving flowers, shrubs and ferns amongst large moss covered boulders. Many Japanese maples. Natural stream, bridges, meandering gravel paths and steps lend magic to 'Dingley Dell'. Lawns, large rockery and summerhouse with stunning views.

49 HILLBARK

Church Lane, Bardsey, Leeds, LS17 9DH. Tim Gittins & Malcolm Simm, www.hillbark.co.uk. *4m SW of Wetherby. Turn W off A58 into Church Lane, garden on L before church.* Sun 14 May, Sun 2 July (11-4.30). Adm £4, chd free. Home-made teas.

Award-winning 1-acre country garden with 3 S-facing levels, hidden corners and surprise views. Formal topiary, relaxed perennial planting. Dramatic specimen yew. Ornamental ponds, summerhouse overlooking gravel, rock and stream gardens, large natural pond with ducks. Marginal planting incl bamboo. Woodland area. Large rambling roses. Unusual ceramics.

Your support helps Carers Trust to provide more help to unpaid carers

York Gate

© Carole Drake

50 HILLSIDE

West End, Ampleforth, York, YO62 4DY. Sue Shepherd & Jon Borgia, 01439 788993. *West End of Ampleforth village, 4m S of Helmsley. From A19, follow brown sign to Byland Abbey & continue to Ampleforth. From A170 take B1257 to Malton, after 1m turn R to Ampleforth. Roadside parking only. Please be considerate.* Sun 10 Sept (1-5). Adm £4, chd free. Home-made teas. **Visits also by arrangement June to Sept groups of 10 or more.**

Half acre garden on a south facing slope. The design is evolving, based on informal planting and a wildlife friendly approach. Woodland and meadow areas. 2 ponds and drainage ditch with bog garden. Lawn rising up to summer house and deck with fine views of the Coxwold - Gilling Gap. Fruit trees and kitchen garden. All year round interest with an emphasis on autumn colour.

✿ 🏠 ☕

51 ◆ HIMALAYAN GARDEN & SCULPTURE PARK

Hutts Lane, Grewelthorpe, Ripon, HG4 3DA. Mr & Mrs Peter Roberts, 01765 658009
info@himalayangarden.com
www.himalayangarden.com. *5m NW of Ripon. From N: A1(M) J51 A684 (Bedale) then B6268 (Masham). From S: A1M J50 (Ripon) then A6108 (Masham) after North Stainley turn L (Mickley & Grewelthorpe). Follow garden signs.* For NGS: Fri 5 May (10-4). Adm £7.50, chd free. Light refreshments. Chd under 12 free. For other opening times and information, please phone, email or visit garden website.

A stunning hidden gem 20 acre woodland garden. Home to an extensive collection of rare Rhododendrons, Azaleas and Himalayan plants, set amongst plantings of showy hybrids. A rich tapestry of spring colour with streams meandering through valleys, teaming with arrays of plants and sculptures, leading down to peaceful lakes. Tearoom and Garden Nursery. Group tours and talks available. Limited Wheelchair Access.

🐐 ✿ 🚌 ☕

52 2 HOLLIN CLOSE

Rossington, nr Doncaster, DN11 0XX. Mr & Mrs Hann. *5m S of Doncaster. From J3 on M18 take A6182 signed Airport. At T-lights, A638 signed Bawtry turn R (Littleworth Lane) 5m N of Bawtry after T-lights signed Airport take next L (Littleworth Lane). Hollin Close is 2nd R.* Sun 25 June (11-5). Adm £3, chd free. Home-made teas. ⅓ acre terraced garden designed and maintained by owners with four themes on three levels. Cottage style herbaceous planting surrounds a circular lawn alongside a tranquil oriental garden. Steps lead to the greenhouse and Mediterranean gravel garden with sun-loving plants for bees and butterflies. Below lies a wildlife friendly small woodland glade with bug hotel, stumpery, fruit and ferns. 3 times winner of Doncaster in Bloom Best Private Residents Garden.

✿ ☕

53 54 HOLLYM ROAD

Withernsea, HU19 2PJ. Mr Matthew Pottage. *23m E of Hull, 16m S of Hornsea. Enter Withernsea from A1033 onto Hollym Rd. From Hornsea, B1242 through town onto Hollym Rd.* Sun 16 July (11-5). Adm £3, chd free. Cream teas. Gluten free cake available. Beautifully displayed garden brimming with colourful herbaceous perennials, roses, and masses of foliage plants including hostas and ferns. Unusual exotics feature here too, with many plants of New Zealand origin, all mixed into a magical setting with a pond, topiary hedge, meadow, cactus and succulent collection. Family home of Matthew Pottage, Curator of RHS Wisley. Excellent plantsman's display of plants and extensive plant sales. Featured on Look North as a 'must visit' garden in East Yorkshire. Unsuitable for wheelchairs after very wet weather as most of the garden is accessed via the lawn.

♿ 🐐 ✿ ☕

54 HOLMFIELD

Fridaythorpe, YO25 9RZ. Susan & Robert Nichols, 01377 236627, susan.nichols@which.net. *9m W of Driffield. From York A166 through Fridaythorpe. 1m turn R signed Holmfield. 1st house on lane.* Sat 17, Sun 18 June (12-5). Adm £4, chd free. Home-made teas. **Visits also by arrangement May to July, groups of 10+.**

Informal 2 acre country garden on gentle S-facing slope. Developed from a field over last 27yrs. Large mixed borders, bespoke octagonal gazebo, family friendly garden with 'Hobbit House', sunken trampoline, large lawn, tennis court, hidden paths for hide and seek. Productive fruit cage, vegetable and cut flower area. Collection of Phlomis. Display of wire sculptures. Bee friendly planting. Some gravel areas, sloping lawns.

     ♿ ❀ ☕

55 HOTHAM HALL

Hotham, YO43 4UA. Stephen & Carolyn Martin, 01430 422054, carolynandstephenmartin@btinternet.com. *15m W of Hull. J38 of M62 turn towards North Cave Wetlands, & at sharp corner go straight on to Hotham. Turn R & R again through Hall gates.* Thur 13, Thur 20 Apr (11-3). Adm £5.50, chd £3. Light refreshments. Refreshments incl in adm. **Visits also by arrangement Mar to June tea, coffee and cake or scones incl in adm.**

C18 Grade II house (not open), stable block and clock tower in mature parkland setting with established gardens. Bridge over lake to island walk/arboretum. Garden with Victorian pond and mixed borders. Many spring flowering bulbs. Child ticket gives access to children's play area, games, treasure hunt with Easter egg prize, Easter craft and incl picnic basket. Adult ticket also incl refreshments. Pea gravel pathways.

     ♿ 🐾 ☕

56 HUNMANBY GRANGE

Wold Newton, Driffield, YO25 3HS. Tom & Gill Mellor. *12½m SE of Scarborough. Hunmanby Grange home of Wold Top Brewery, between Wold Newton & Hunmanby on rd from Burton Fleming to Fordon.* Sat 3, Sun 4 June (11-5). Adm £5, chd free. Light refreshments in Wold Top Brewery bar area. Field and Forage will also be catering in courtyard.

3 acre garden created over the last 34 yrs from exposed open field, on top of Yorkshire Wolds nr coast. Hedges and fences now provide shelter from wind, making series of gardens with yr-round interest and seasonal highlights. In the courtyard, the water feature from The Welcome to Yorkshire Chelsea Garden - The Brewers Yard. The Wold Top Brewery will be open with catering from Field and Forage. Wold Top Brewery open with garden. There is plenty of space in the woodland with mown paths for children to play and explore. Steps can be avoided by using grass paths and lawns. Pond garden not completely accessible to wheelchairs but can be viewed from gateway.

     ♿ 🐾 ❀ 🚗 ☕

57 ◆ JACKSON'S WOLD

Sherburn, Malton, YO17 8QJ. Mr & Mrs Richard Cundall, 07966 531995, sarahcundall1@gmail.com, www.jacksonswoldgarden.com. *11m E of Malton, 10m SW of Scarborough. Signs only from A64. A64 Eastbound to Scarborough. R at T-lights in Sherburn take the Weaverthorpe rd after 100 metres R fork to Helperthorpe & Luttons. 1m to top of hill, turn L at garden sign.* For NGS: Sun 21 May, Sun 18 June (1-5). Adm £3, chd free. Home-made teas. **For other opening times and information, please phone, email or visit garden website.**

2 acre garden with stunning views of the Vale of Pickering. Walled garden with mixed borders, numerous old shrub roses underplanted with unusual perennials. Woodland paths lead to further shrub and perennial borders. Lime avenue with wild flower meadow. Traditional vegetable garden with roses, flowers and framed by a Victorian greenhouse. Adjoining nursery. Tours by appointment.

     ♿ ❀ 🚗 ☕

58 THE JUNGLE GARDEN

76 Gledhow Wood Avenue, Roundhay, Leeds, LS8 1NX. Nick & Gill Wilson, 0113 266 5196, nick.wilson@thejunglegarden.uk. *4m NE of Leeds. A58 from Leeds for 3½m to Oakwood. Turn L onto Gledhow Lane & follow NGS signs.* Sun 30 July (11-5). Adm £3, chd free. **Visits also by arrangement July to Sept for groups of 10 to 30.**

Multi level garden with jungle style planting and accents of hot tropical colour. Boardwalks and bark paths. Crown lifted trees create overhead canopy. Walk under mad, huge Gunnera leaves. 2 ponds, walkway over lower pond and raised deck with seating overlooks upper pond. Elevated 'Jungle Lodge' and aerial walkway with views over the garden. Tea room at Tropical World at Roundhay Park (1m). Featured on and in TV- Monty Don's Big Dreams Small Spaces, BBC Great British Garden Revival. Amateur Gardening and Yorkshire Ridings magazines.

     ❀

KIPLIN HALL

See North East

59 LINDEN LODGE

Newbridge Lane, nr Wilberfoss, York, YO41 5RB. Robert Scott & Jarrod Marsden, 07900 003538, rdsjsm@gmail.com. *10m E of York. Do not enter the village of Wilberfoss from the A1079, take the turning signed Bolton village.* Sun 11 June (1-5). Adm £4, chd free. Cream teas in the Bothy. **Visits also by arrangement 15 - 22 July for 20+**

6 acres in all. 1 acre garden owner designed and constructed since 2000. Gravel paths edged with brick or lavender, many borders with unusual mixed herbaceous perennials, shrubs and feature trees. A wildlife pond, summer house, kitchen garden, glasshouse. Orchard and woodland area. Formal garden with pond and water feature. 5 acres of developing meadow, trees, pathways, hens and Shetland sheep. Plant sales. Featured in 100 Inspirational Gardens of England, The Yorkshire Post, Kitchen Garden, Amateur Gardening and Yorkshire Life. Gravel paths and shallow steps.

     ♿ 🐾 ❀ 🚗 ☕

60 LITTLE EDEN

Lancaster Street, Castleford, WF10 2NP. Melvyn & Linda Moran, 01977 514275, melvynmoran609@btinternet.com. *2½m NW of M62 J32. A639 (Castleford) 1st r'about 2nd exit B6136. At hill top turn L at T-lights, next r'about straight on, then 3rd R (Elizabeth Drive) then 2nd L, then 3rd L.* Sun 23 July, Sun 20 Aug (10-4.30). Adm £3, chd free. Home-made teas. **Visits also by arrangement July & Aug, groups min 7.**

Plant lovers' small hidden oasis of unusual, tender, exotic and tropical plants in the midst of large housing estate. Trellis and archway festooned with climbers, colourful pots and hanging baskets. Herbaceous perennials, succulents, tree ferns, palms, bananas, pond and a decorative summerhouse.

GROUP OPENING

61 LITTLETHORPE GARDENS

Pottery Lane, Ripon, HG4 3LS. *1½m SE of Ripon. Off A61 bypass follow signs to Littlethorpe. Turn R at church. From Bishop Monkton follow signs to Ripon (Knaresborough Rd), turn R to Littlethorpe. The gardens are at least ¾m apart.* Sun 6 Aug (12-5). Combined adm £6, chd free. Home-made teas at Greencroft.

GREENCROFT
David & Sally Walden, 01765 602487, s.walden@talk21.com. **Visits also by arrangement, July to mid Aug. Refreshments available.**

KIRKELLA
Jacky Barber.

LITTLETHORPE HOUSE
Mr & Mrs James Hare.

Littlethorpe is a small village characterised by houses interspersed with fields. Greencroft is a ½ acre informal garden made by the owners. Special ornamental features incl gazebo, temple pavilions, formal pool, stone wall with mullions, and gate to rose pergola leading to a cascade water feature. Long herbaceous borders packed with colourful late flowering perennials, annuals and exotics culminate in circular garden with views through to large wildlife pond and surrounding countryside. Kirkella is a small garden recently created by plantswoman and flower arranger to give constant interest. Gravel garden to the front with Mediterranean feel. Densely planted hidden paved rear garden with decorative summerhouse; hostas, half-hardy perennials, salvias, succulents, desirable small shrubs, many in pots and containers. A willow hedge conceals a small productive vegetable plot. Opposite is Littlethorpe House with expansive lawns, clipped topiary and yew hedges, roses and large mixed herbaceous and shrub borders.

62 LITTLETHORPE MANOR

Littlethorpe Road, Littlethorpe, Ripon, HG4 3LG. Mr & Mrs J P Thackray, www.littlethorpemanor.com. *Outskirts of Ripon nr racecourse. Ripon bypass A61. Follow Littlethorpe Rd from Dallamires Lane r'about to stable block with clock tower. Map supplied on application.* Sun 10 Sept (1.30-5). Adm £6, chd free. Home-made teas.

11 acres. Walled garden based on cycle of seasons with box, herbaceous, roses, gazebo. Sunken garden with white rose parterre and herbs. Brick pergola with white wisteria, blue and yellow borders. Terraces with ornamental pots. Formal lawns with fountain pool, hornbeam towers and yew hedging. Box headed hornbeam drive with Aqualens water feature. Extensive perennial borders. Parkland with lake, late summer plantings and classical pavilion. Cut flower garden. Spring bulbs and winter garden. Tea, coffee, biscuits and cake £2.50 served in marquee. Wheelchair access - gravel paths, some steep steps.

63 LOW HALL

Dacre Banks, Nidderdale, HG3 4AA. Mrs P A Holliday, 01423 780230, pamela@pamelaholliday.co.uk. *10m NW of Harrogate. On B6451 between Dacre Banks & Darley.* Sun 14 May (1-5). Adm £4, chd free. Home-made teas. **Opening with Dacre Banks & Summerbridge Gardens on Sun 9 July. Visits also by arrangement May to Sept small groups of 3 or 4 and large groups up to 50. Teas by prior arrangement.**

Romantic walled garden set on differing levels designed to complement historic C17 family home (not open). Spring bulbs, rhododendrons; azaleas round tranquil water garden. Asymmetric rose pergola underplanted with auriculas and lithodora links orchard to the garden. Extensive herbaceous borders, shrubs and climbing roses give later interest. Bluebell woods and lovely countryside of the farm all round overlooking the R Nidd. 80% of garden can be seen from a wheelchair but access involves three stone steps.

64 LOW WESTWOOD GARDEN

Golcar, Huddersfield, HD7 4ER. Craig Limbert. *3½m W of Huddersfield off A62. R at T-lights in Linthwaite signed 'Titanic Spa'. Park on road by Spa. Garden is over canal bridge.* Sat 22 Apr (10.30-1.30). Sat 5 Aug (10.30-3.30). Light refreshments. Adm £3, chd free. Please note: refreshments are not available on 22 April.

With 110yds of canal frontage and recently landscaped, this garden of 1½ acres has both flat and steep sloping aspects with views across the Colne Valley. Mature lime tree walk, terraced herbacious beds, pond and vegetable plot contrasting shade and sunny sites. Spring bulbs followed by rhododendron, kniphofia, astrantia and hydrangea. Late summer colour is plentiful. Featured in Huddersfield Examiner. Partial wheelchair access into lower garden only.

65 LOWER CRAWSHAW

off Stringer House Lane, Emley,
Huddersfield, HD8 9SU. Mr &
Mrs Neil Hudson, 01924 840980,
janehudson42@btinternet.com.
*8m E of Huddersfield. Close to Emley
Moor TV mast. J39 off the M1 from
the N, J38 if from the S. Take Denby
Dale Rd turning R to Emley. 1m
beyond Emley village before TV mast
turn R along Stringer House Lane.*
**Visits by arrangement July to
Sept groups of 10+. Adm £4,
chd free. Light refreshments.**
Lovely large tranquil country garden,
hidden away down a farm lane, with
stunning views and surrounded by
open fields and farmland. 2 large
ponds fed by a natural stream form
the heart of the garden. Relaxed
and informal plantings of grasses
and colourful perennials, old roses
and rose arches, a small orchard, and
ornamental trees, shrubs and some
topiary. Partial wheelchair access.

& 🐴 ✿ ☕

66 MANOR FARM

North Leys Road, Hollym,
Withernsea, HU19 2QN. David
& Trish Smith. *2m S of Withernsea.
Enter Hollym on A1033 Hull to
Withernsea Rd. Turn E at Xrds.
Garden on R after double bend.
Strictly no roadside parking, please
park in grounds.* **Sun 25 June (11-
5). Adm £3.50, chd free.
Home-made teas.**
Quiet country garden near sea.
Borders generously planted with
choice perennials, roses, shrubs,
trees and exotics. Log arch to
shady hosta walk, emerging through
rose arch to large wildlife pond.
Specimen evergreens complement
box topiary and hedging. Gravel
garden with ornamental pond and
summerhouse. Through folly wall
clothed with clematis, to orchard
and bee/butterfly border. Plenty of
seating. Hosta walk too narrow for
wheelchairs but can be viewed from
entrance.

& 🐴 ✿ ☕ 🌱

67 THE MANOR HOUSE

Main Street, Heslington,
York, YO10 5EA. George
Smith & Brian Withill,
www.georgesmithflowers.com.
*2m S York City Centre. The garden will
supply a map on booking.* **Sun 18
June (2-5). Adm £15, chd free.
Pre-booking essential, please
visit www.ngs.org.uk or phone
01483 211535 for information
& booking. Adm includes
homemade teas.**
Home of the world renowned
flower arranger George Smith, this
3 acre garden reflects his painterly
style of planting. Sub-divided by
mellow walls it abounds with many
surprises as each area is colour
themed featuring herbaceous
perennials, especially hostas and
ferns. Exotic sheltered corners,
ponds and a shaded woodland
create a wildlife haven. The eye of
the artist abounds and the effect
is of a living flower arrangement
with careful attention to plant
associations. Refreshments with
George Smith will be served in
the tiled rustic loggia beneath his
Old Granary Studio. House not
open. Featured in Britain's Best
Gardens with Alan Titchmarsh and
numerous national and international
publications.

✿ ☕ 🌱

68 THE MANOR HOUSE

Main Street, Tollerton, York,
YO61 1QQ. Dr Weland & Audrey
Stone, 01347 838454. *10m N of
York off A19. Turn up Main Street
from village green. House is 200
yards on R.* **Visits by arrangement
June to Aug we can provide tea
and biscuits or wine for up to
approx 20. Adm £5, chd free.
Light refreshments.**
An acre in village centre, developed
over 45 years. Outbuildings and
barn of old brick are covered
with climbers. Various mixed
borders, shrub rose and geranium
bed, smaller areas of Hostas and
Heathers. Vegetable bed behind yew
hedge. Shaded front garden mainly
for spring, Rear lawn dominated by
fine Genista aetnensis in July. Lawns
and tarmac drive.

& 🐴 🚐 ☕

The National Garden Scheme is Hospice UK's largest single funder

69 MANSION COTTAGE

8 Gillus Lane, Bempton,
Bridlington, YO15 1HW. Polly
& Chris Myers, 01262 851404,
chrismyers0807@gmail.com. *2m
NE of Bridlington. From Bridlington
take B1255 to Flamborough. 1st
L at T lights - Bempton Lane, turn
1st R into Short Lane then L at end.
Continue - L fork at Church.* **Sat 5,
Sun 6 Aug (10-4). Adm £3.50,
chd free. Light refreshments.
Lunch on both Sat and Sun,
wide menu choice featuring
the best of local produce incl
teas and cakes. Visits also by
arrangement June to Aug,
groups of 10+.**
Exuberant, lush, vibrant perennial
planting highlighted with grasses in
this hidden, peaceful and surprising
garden offering many views and
features. Visitors book comments
'A truly lovely garden and a great
lunch', 'The garden is inspirational,
a veritable oasis!' Delicious home
made lunches, produce stalls and
hand made soaps. Areas include a
globe garden, mini hosta walk,
100 ft border, summerhouse,
vegetable plot, cuttery, late summer
hot border, bee and butterfly border,
bog garden and ponds, decking
areas and lawns. Wheelchair access
into the house involves steep steps.

🐴 ✿ ☕ 🌱

70 MARSTON GRANGE

Tockwith Road, Long Marston, York, YO26 7PL. David & Joanne Smakman, www.marstongrange.co.uk. *5m W of York 5m E of Wetherby. From B1224 in Long Marston turn towards Tockwith. ¾m after battlefield monument turn R down single track lane.* Sun 11 June (11-4). Adm £5, chd free. Light refreshments in the Education Barn at the end of the meadow. Lunches and light refreshments served throughout the day for NGS.

2 acre garden set on the Battlefield of Marston Moor and designed to blend into the arable landscape. Pond and topiary garden, traditional ha-ha, and small walled garden. Summerhouse and mature trees. Orchard with vegetables and cutting garden, ornamental trees, tree arbour, wildlife pond and themed island beds. Paths through a large perennial flower meadow with bee hives lead to the refreshment barn. Battle of Marston Moor 1644 guided battlefield tour begins 2pm taking 1hr 30mins. Rag rugging demonstration in the Summerhouse garden and children's Green Man hunt. Limited wheelchair access to some parts of the garden. Please ask for assistance when accessing the barn.

&♿ ✿ 🚗 ☕

71 MILLGATE HOUSE

Millgate, Richmond, DL10 4JN. Tim Culkin & Austin Lynch, 01748 823571, oztim@millgatehouse.demon.co.uk, www.millgatehouse.com. *Centre of Richmond. House located at bottom of Market Place opp Barclays Bank. Just off corner of Market Place. Park in the Market Place no restrictions on Sunday.* Sun 25 June (8-9), also open Swale Cottage. Sun 2 July (8-9). Adm £3.50, chd free.

SE walled town garden overlooking R Swale. Although small, the garden is full of character, enchantingly secluded with plants and shrubs. Foliage plants incl ferns and hostas. Old roses, interesting selection of clematis, small trees and shrubs. RHS associate garden. Immensely stylish, national award-winning

garden. Featured in GGG and on Alan Titchmarsh's Britain's Best Gardens. Specialist collections of ferns, hostas and roses. MANY STEPS AND STEEP SLOPES SLIPPERY SURFACES.

72 115 MILLHOUSES LANE

Sheffield, S7 2HD. Sue & Phil Stockdale. *Approx 4m SW of Sheffield City Centre. Follow A625 Castleton/Dore rd, 4th L after Prince of Wales PH, 2nd L. OR take A621 Baslow Rd; after Tesco garage take 2nd R, then 1st L.* Sun 28 May (12.30-5). Adm £3.50, chd free. Home-made teas.

Plantswoman's ⅓ acre south facing level cottage style garden, containing many choice and unusual perennials and bulbs, providing year round colour and interest. There is also a large collection of hostas, roses, peonies and clematis, together with unusual tender perennials - aeoniums, echeverias etc. Range of seating areas throughout the garden. Range of plants propagated by the owners for sale.

&♿ 🐄 ✿ ☕

73 23 MOLESCROFT ROAD

Beverley, HU17 7DX. Mr & Mrs D Bowden. *Located ½m N from edge of town centre Molescroft Rd connects A1033 on N & A1174 from E. Garden is ½ way between* Sun 4 June (12-5). Adm £3, chd free. Home-made teas.

A suburban garden facing SW, bordered by mature trees. Mixed borders and old herbaceous favourites. Several climbers, incl roses. The garden is terraced, on three different levels with lawns and seating areas providing different aspects of the garden. A paved patio area with three steps leads up to the lawn. The attractive summer house in one corner, enjoys views of the garden. A small productive area with fruit cage and greenhouse is screened from the rest of the garden. The lower area around the house has a paved area with rhododendrons and camellias. Sorry there is no wheelchair access, also note that the garden has steps

which some visitors may find difficult.

MR YORKE'S WALLED GARDEN

See North East

74 [NEW] MYTON GRANGE

Myton-On-Swale, York, YO61 2QU. Nick & Annie Ramsden. *15m N of York. From the N go through Helperby on York Rd. After ½m follow yellow signs towards Myton. From the S leave A19 through Tollerton & Flawith. Turn L at Xrds following yellow signs.* Sun 2 July (10-5). Adm £4, chd free. Light refreshments and wine.

This garden, attached to a Victorian farmhouse, once formed part of the Myton Estate. Extending to ¾ acre, the site is adjacent to the R Swale and includes a paved terrace garden, formal parterre; circular garden with mixed shrub and herbaceous border, lawn with topiary borders. There will also be guided tours throughout the day of the recently restored Victorian Stud Farm buildings.

☕

75 ♦ NEWBY HALL & GARDENS

Ripon, HG4 5AE. Mr R C Compton, 01423 322583, info@newbyhall.com, www.newbyhall.com. *4m SE of Ripon. (HG4 5AJ for Sat Nav). Follow brown tourist signs from A1(M) or from Ripon town centre.* For opening times and information, please phone, email or visit garden website.

40 acres of extensive gardens and woodland laid out in 1920s. Full of rare and beautiful plants. Formal seasonal gardens, stunning double herbaceous borders to R Ure and National Collection of Cornus. Miniature railway and adventure gardens for children. Sculpture exhibition (open June - Sept). Wheelchair map available Disabled parking Manual & electric wheelchairs available on loan, please call to reserve.

76 2 NEWLAY GROVE

Horsforth, Leeds, LS18 4LH. Kate & Chris van Heel, 01132 390191, vanheelk@me.com. *4m NW Leeds city centre. From Leeds follow A65. Turn L down Newlay Lane (just before pelican crossing), then 2nd R onto Newlay Grove. House is 25 metres on L, limited parking near house.* **Visits by arrangement July & Aug groups of 10+. Adm £3.50, chd free. Light refreshments.**

Large, rear family garden within a third of an acre plot in quiet conservation area close to R Aire. Landscaped over past 22 years, featuring late summer perennials, shrubs, pond and shade loving plants. Steps and slopes link lawns and paved terracing. Various seating areas allow viewing from different perspectives. Featured on BBC The Instant Gardener. Leeds in Bloom Gold Awards.

✿ ☕

77 ◆ NORTON CONYERS

Wath, Ripon, HG4 5EQ. Sir James & Lady Graham, 01765 640333, info@nortonconyers.org.uk, www.nortonconyers.org.uk. *4m NW of Ripon. Take Melmerby & Wath sign off A61 Ripon-Thirsk. Go through both villages to boundary wall. Signed entry 300 metres on R.* **For NGS: Sun 2 July (2-5). Adm £6, chd free. Tea. For other opening times and information, please phone, email or visit garden website.**

Romantic mid C18 walled garden of interest to garden historians. Lawns, herbaceous borders, yew hedges, and central Orangery with attractive pond. Small sales area specialising in unusual hardy plants. House: for opening dates and times see website. The garden retains the essential features of its original C18 design, combined with sympathetic replanting in the English style. There are borders of gold and silver plants, of old-fashioned peonies, and irises in season. Visitors frequently comment on its tranquil atmosphere. Most areas wheelchair accessible, gravel paths.

♿ 🐕 ✿ 🚌 ☕

78 THE NURSERY

15 Knapton Lane, Acomb, York, YO26 5PX. Tony Chalcraft & Jane Thurlow, 01904 781691, janeandtonyatthenursery@hotmail.co.uk. *2½m W of York. From A1237 take B1224 direction Acomb. At r'about turn L (Beckfield Ln.), after 150 metres Turn L.* **Sun 16 July (1-5); Wed 19 July (2-7). Adm £3, chd free. Home-made teas.**

Visits also by arrangement Apr to Oct.

Hidden, attractive and productive 1-acre organic garden behind suburban house (not open). Wide range of top and soft fruit with over 100 fruit trees, many in trained form. Many different vegetables grown both outside and under cover incl a large 20m greenhouse. Productive areas interspersed with informal ornamental plantings providing colour and habitat for wildlife. The extensive planting of different forms and varieties of fruit trees make this an interesting garden for groups to visit by appointment at blossom and fruiting times in addition to the main summer openings. Filmed by BBC Gardener's World.

☕

79 NUTKINS

72 Rolston Road, Hornsea, HU18 1UR. Alan & Janet Stirling, 01964 533721, ashornsea@aol.com. *12 NE of Beverley. On B1242 S-side of Hornsea between Freeport & golf course.* **Sun 28 May (11-4). Adm £4, chd free. Light refreshments.**

Visits also by arrangement May to Aug for groups.

The garden covers over ¾ acre with herbaceous borders, bog garden, streamside walk and woodland garden with features to bring a smile to your face. Pergolas, gazebo and plenty of seating to linger and enjoy different views of the garden and see light play on the many pieces of stained glass. Gravel and wood chip paths.

♿ 🚌 ☕ ☕

Devonshire Mill

80 OLD SLENINGFORD HALL

Mickley, nr Ripon, HG4 3JD. Jane & Tom Ramsden. *5m NW of Ripon. Off A6108. After N Stainley turn L, follow signs to Mickley. Gates on R after 1½m opp cottage.* Sat 3, Sun 4 June (12-4). Adm £5, chd free. Home-made teas.

A large English country garden and developing 'Forest Garden'. Early C19 house (not open) and garden with original layout; wonderful mature trees, woodland walk and Victorian fernery; romantic lake with islands, watermill, walled kitchen garden; beautiful long herbaceous border, yew and huge beech hedges. Award winning permaculture forest garden. Several plant and other stalls. Picnics very welcome. Reasonable wheelchair access to most parts of garden. Disabled WC at Old Sleningford Farm next to the garden.

🚜 🐄 🌼 ☕

81 THE OLD VICARAGE

Church Street, Whixley, YO26 8AR. Mr & Mrs Roger Marshall, biddymarshall@btinternet.com. *8m W of York, 8m E of Harrogate, 6m N of Wetherby. off A59 3m E of A1M Junction 47 (Postcode not for sat nav).* Visits by arrangement May to July groups of 15+.

This delightful ¾ acre walled flower garden overlooks the deer park. The walls, house and various structures within the garden are festooned with climbers. Mixed borders, old roses, hardy and half-hardy perennials, topiary, bulbs and many hellebores give interest all year. Gravel and old brick paths lead to hidden seating areas creating the atmosphere of a romantic English garden. Partial wheelchair access due to gravelled surfaces and some steps.

🐄 🌼 🚗 ☕

82 OMEGA

79 Magdalen Lane, Hedon, HU12 8LA. Mr & Mrs D Rosindale, 01482 897370, mavirosi@hotmail.co.uk. *6m E of Hull. Through to E Hull onto A1033. L into St Augustine's Gate through Market Place, immed R to Magdalen Gate, ahead to Magdalen Lane.* Sat 24, Sun 25 June (12.30-5). Adm £3.50, chd free. Home-made teas. Visits also by arrangement June & July group of 20+ incl quality cream tea. Afternoon tea (by prior arrangement).

An interesting box parterre surrounded by densely planted borders fills the front garden, leading through acers and ferns to a patio full of planted troughs. To the rear, herbaceous borders, a shady area and an arch lead to a small border and greenhouse and a thriving, newly planted willow dome. A full 'Afternoon Tea' can be booked in advance by telephone on or before the Wednesday prior to the open garden. Large range of perennial plants for sale including minature hostas and large selection of succulents. Wheelchair access to back garden only.

🐄 🌼 🚗 ☕

83 THE ORCHARD

4a Blackwood Rise, Cookridge, Leeds, LS16 7BG. Carol & Michael Abbott, 0113 2676764, michael.john.abbott@hotmail.co.uk. *5m N of Leeds centre. Off A660 (Leeds-Otley) N of A6120 Ring Rd. Turn L up Otley Old Rd. At top of hill turn L at T-lights (Tinshill Lane). Please park in Tinshill Lane.* Sun 4 June (12-4.30). Adm £3, chd free. Light refreshments. Pop up cafe and cover for inclement weather. Visits also by arrangement June & July, groups of 10+.

¾ acre plantswoman's hidden oasis. A wrap around garden of differing levels made by owners using stone found on site, planted for yr-round interest. Extensive rockery, unusual fruit tree arbour, oriental style seating area and Tea House, linked by grass paths, lawns and steps. Mixed perennials, hostas, ferns, shrubs, bulbs and pots amongst paved and pebbled areas. Best in area award Leeds in Bloom.

🌼 🚗 ☕

84 ORCHARD HOUSE

Sandholme Lane, Leven, Beverley, HU17 5LW. Mrs Frances Cooper, 01964 542359, francescooper1@gmail.com. *On outskirts of Leven village. In Leven turn between Hare & Hounds PH & PO. Continue for 400yds then onto Carr Lane picking up yellow signs to Orchard House.* Visits by arrangement Apr to July for groups of 2-30, adm £5, chd free adm incl refreshments.

A peaceful leafy, woodland garden. Amongst the many trees, there are several different areas which have been created including a new English rose garden. Hidden paths to tucked away spaces. Greenhouse. Bulging borders are a haven for the abundant wildlife. Some parts of the garden are accessible.

♿ ☕

85 ♦ PARCEVALL HALL GARDENS

Skyreholme, Skipton, BD23 6DE. Walsingham College, 01756 720311, parcevallhall@btconnect.com, www.parcevallhallgardens.co.uk. *9m N of Skipton. Signs from B6160 Bolton Abbey-Burnsall rd or off B6265 Grassington-Pateley Bridge & at A59 Bolton Abbey r'about.* For NGS: Wed 17 May (10-5). Adm £7, chd free. Light refreshments. For other opening times and information, please phone, email or visit garden website.

The only garden open daily in the Yorkshire Dales National Park. 24 acres in Wharfedale sheltered by mixed woodland; terrace garden, rose garden, rock garden, ponds. Mixed borders, spring bulbs, tender shrubs and autumn colour. Tea rooms (contact no. 01756 720630) at the foot of the gardens. There is no wheelchair access in the garden as it is set on a steep hillside with uneven paths.

🐄 🌼 ☕

86 PENNY PIECE COTTAGES

41/43 Piercy End, Kirkbymoorside, York, YO62 6DQ. Mick & Ann Potter, 07890 870551, skimmers@gmail.com. *Follow A170 to Kirkbymoorside at r'about turn up into Kirkby Main St approx 300yds on R. Street parking plus council car park at top of Main St.* Sun 11 June (12-5). Adm £4, chd free.

Home-made teas. **Visits also by arrangement Apr to Aug, groups 10+.**
Hidden away off the main street in Kirkbymoorside is a romantic cottage garden. Now fully matured it offers a sunny circular gravel garden incl lawns with island beds and mixed shrub and herbaceous borders. Gravel pathway leads to a brick garden, informal pond, bog garden and colourful herbaceous border. A rose arbour leads through to a wildlife pond and flower meadow. Featured in Daily Mail.

🐂 ☕

87 PILMOOR COTTAGES
Pilmoor, nr Helperby, YO61 2QQ. Wendy & Chris Jakeman, 01845 501848, cnjakeman@aol.com. *20m N of York. From A1M J48. N end B'bridge follow rd towards Easingwold. From A19 follow signs to Hutton Sessay then Helperby. Garden next to mainline railway.* **Wed 10 May, Wed 14 June, Sun 27 Aug (12-5). Adm £3.50, chd free.** Home-made teas. **Visits also by arrangement May to Sept.**
A year round garden for rail enthusiasts and garden visitors. A ride on the 7 1/4' gauge railway runs through 2 acres of gardens and gives you the opportunity to view the garden from a different perspective. The journey takes you across water, through a little woodland area, past flower filled borders, and through a tunnel behind the rockery and water cascade. 1½ acre wild flower meadow and pond. Clock-golf putting green.

🐂 🐕 ❀ ☕

ALLOTMENTS

88 QUEENSGATE & KITCHEN LANE ALLOTMENTS
Beverley, HU17 8NN. Beverley Town Council. *Outskirts of Beverley Town Centre. On A164 towards Cottingham, allotment site is before Victoria Rd, after double mini r'about & opp Beverley Grammar School.* **Sun 9 July (12-4). Adm £3, chd free. Refreshments.**

Varied allotment site of 85 plots, plus another 35 on Kitchen Lane, growing a wide variety of fruit, vegetables and flowers. Some allotment holders will be present to discuss their plots. Dogs on leads. Wide central grass pathway from which allotments can be viewed. Some can be accessed by wheelchairs.

🚻 🐕 ☕

---

89 THE RED HOUSE
17 Whin Hill Road, Bessacarr, Doncaster, DN4 7AF. Rosie Hamlin, www.pyjamagardenersyorks.com. *2m S of Doncaster. A638 South, L at T-lights for B1396, Whin Hill Rd is 2nd R. A638 North, R signed Branton B1396 onto Whin Hill.* **Sun 7 May (2-5). Combined adm with Tamarind £5, chd free. Home-made teas.**
Mature ⅔ acre garden. Dry shade a challenge but acid loving plants a joy. Fine acers, camellia, daphne, rhododendrons, kalmia and eucryphia. Terrace and rockery stepping stones lead past and through new wave and cloud pruned shrubs to lawn with modern orb-shaped rotating summerhouse and young trees. White border conceals pond, compost and hens.

❀ ☕

90 REWELA COTTAGE
Skewsby, YO61 4SG. John Plant & Daphne Ellis, 01347 888125, plantjohnsgarden@btinternet.com. *4m N of Sheriff Hutton, 15m N of York. After Sheriff Hutton, towards Terrington, turn L towards Whenby & Brandsby. Turn R just past Whenby to Skewsby. Turn L into village. 400yds on R.* **Sun 28 May, Sun 30 July (11-5). Adm £4, chd free.** Home-made teas, cakes, scones, refreshments incl BBQ. WC. **Visits also by arrangement May to July excluding June, min 15.**
¾ acre ornamental garden, designed by owner, featuring unusual trees, shrubs, and architectural plants. Pond, pergola, natural stone sunken garden, breeze house, plant nursery and outdoor kitchen. Specialist grower of heuchera, hosta

and penstemon. Many varieties also for sale. A very friendly welcome. Lovely surroundings, have lunch at the BBQ All unusual trees and shrubs have labels giving full descriptions, picture, and any cultivation notes incl propagation. Plant sales are specimens from garden. Many varieties of heuchera, heucherella and tiarellas, penstemon, hostas and herbs for sale. WC. Some gravel paths may be an effort for a wheelchair. Plenty of seats.

🚻 🐕 ❀ 🚗 ☕

91 ♦ RHS GARDEN HARLOW CARR
Crag Lane, Harrogate, HG3 1QB. Royal Horticultural Society, 01423 565418, harlowcarr@rhs.org.uk, www.rhs.org.uk/harlowcarr. *1½m W of Harrogate town centre. On B6162 (Harrogate - Otley).* **For NGS: Sun 7 May (9.30-5). Adm £11, chd £5.50. For other opening times and information, please phone, email or visit garden website.**
One of Yorkshire's most relaxing yet inspiring locations! Highlights include spectacular herbaceous borders, streamside garden, alpines, scented and kitchen gardens. Lakeside Gardens, woodland and wild flower meadows. Betty's Cafe Tearooms, gift shop, plant centre and childrens play area incl tree house and log ness monster. Wheelchairs and mobility scooters available, advanced booking recommended.

🚻 ❀ 🚗 ☕

The National Garden Scheme is the largest single funder of Macmillan

92 THE RIDINGS

South Street, Burton Fleming,
Driffield, YO25 3PE. Roy & Ruth
Allerston, 01262 470489. *11m NE
of Driffield. 11m SW of Scarborough.
7m NW of Bridlington. From Driffield
B1249, before Foxholes turn R to
Burton Fleming. From Scarborough
A165 turn R to Burton Fleming.* **Sun
21 May (1-5). Adm £3, chd free.
Sun 2 July (1-5). Home-made
teas. Visits also by arrangement
Apr to Aug.**
Secluded cottage garden with
colour-themed borders surrounding
neat lawns. Grass and paved paths
lead to formal and informal areas
through rose and clematis covered
pergolas and arbours. Box hedging
defines well stocked borders with
roses, herbaceous plants and trees.
Seating in sun and shade offer vistas
and views. Potager, greenhouse
and summerhouse. Terrace with
waterfeature and farming bygones.
Terrace, tea area and main lawn
accessible via ramp.

🐎 ✿ 🚗 ☕

Penny Piece Cottages

93 RIVELIN COTTAGE

1 Green Lane, Aston, Sheffield,
S26 2BD. Mr & Mrs S Pashley.
*J31 M1, Take A57 exit to Sheffield
(SE), 1st exit onto A57, travel approx
700 yds on Worksop Rd. Turn L onto
Green Lane, Parking at Yellow Lion
PH, Worksop Rd, Aston,.* **Sun 25
June (12-5). Adm £3.50, chd
free. Home-made teas.**
An English cottage garden with long
flowing borders filled with trees,
shrubs and perennials. Roses are a
passion for the owner and feature
throughout the garden. Pergolas,
arbour, water feature, box hedging
and box balls. Shabby chic shed.
Ornamental vegetable garden.
Inspirational use of space and wide
variety of plant interest. Featured
on Front Cover Period Living.
Wheelchair access to main garden
but steps to house and patio.

🚫 ✿ ☕

94 NEW ROSEMARY COTTAGE

163 High Street, Hook, Goole,
DN14 5PL. Justine Dixon,
www.rosemarycottagehook.co.uk.
*Between Goole, Howden & Airmyn,
close to M62 J36. Approach Hook
from Boothferry Rd r' about 300yds S
of Boothferry Bridge. Follow signs for
Hook. In Hook turn L at Xrds. Garden
is 550yds on L. Parking is just beyond.
Enter garden at rear from car park.*
**Sun 28 May (12-4). Adm £3, chd
free. Cream teas.**
Delightful quaint cottage garden -
combination of traditional cottage
garden theme planting linking the
individual garden 'rooms' to a small
orchard and herbaceous perennial
border overlooking open fields.
NGS day cake stall will also be in
aid of St Mary's Church. Featured in
Howdenshire Living Magazine, Goole
Times Newspaper. Wheelchair access
is available to most of the garden
(from rear carpark) albeit ground a
little uneven, one part of the garden
has stepped access.

🚫 🐕 ✿ 🚗 ☕

95 RUSTIC COTTAGE

Front Street, Wold Newton,
nr Driffield, YO25 3YQ.
Jan Joyce, 01262 470710,
janetmjoyce@icloud.com.

*13m N of Driffield. From Driffield
take B1249 to Foxholes (12m), take
R turning signed Wold Newton. Turn
L onto Front St, opp village pond,
continue up hill, garden on L.* **Visits
by arrangement 20 max. Adm
£4. Combined with Ridings adm
£6 . Refreshments at Ridings
when both gardens are open.
Adm £4, chd free.**
Plantswoman's cottage garden of
much interest with many choice and
unusual plants. Hellebores and bulbs
are treats for colder months. Old-
fashioned roses, fragrant perennials,
herbs and wild flowers, all grown
together provide habitat for birds,
bees, butterflies and small mammals.
It has been described as 'organised
chaos'! The owner's 2nd NGS
garden. Small dogs only.

🐎 ✿ ☕

96 ◆ SCAMPSTON WALLED GARDEN

Scampston Hall, Scampston,
Malton, YO17 8NG. The
Legard Family, 01944 759111,
info@scampston.co.uk,
www.scampston.co.uk/gardens.
*5m E of Malton. ½m N of A64, nr
the village of Rillington & signed
Scampston only.* **For opening times
and information, please phone,
email or visit garden website.**
An exciting modern garden
designed by Piet Oudolf. The 4-acre
walled garden contains a series of
hedged enclosures designed to
look good throughout the year.
The garden contains many unusual
species and is a must for any keen
plantsman. The Walled Garden is
set within the grounds and parkland
surrounding Scampston Hall. The
Hall opens to visitors for a short
period during the summer months.
A newly restored Richardson
conservatory at the heart of the
Walled Garden re-opened as a
Heritage and Learning Centre in
2015. The Walled Garden, Cafe
and facilities are accessible for the
disabled. Some areas of the Parkland
and the first floor of Hall are harder
to access.

🚫 ✿ 🚗 ☕

97 NEW SCAPE LODGE

11 Grand Stand, Scapegoat Hill, Golcar, Huddersfield, HD7 4NQ. Dr & Mrs David Smith. *5m W of Huddersfield. From J23 or 24 M62 follow signs to Rochdale. After Outlane village, 1st L. At top of hill, 2nd L. Parking at Scapegoat Hill Baptist Church (HD7 4N7) or in village. 5 mins walk to garden. 303/304 bus.* Sun 21 May (1-5.30); Sat 19 Aug (10.30-5.30). Adm £3, chd free. Home-made teas. *Donation to Mayor of Kirklees Charity.*

⅓ acre contemporary country garden at 1000ft in the Pennines. Steeply sloping site with far-reaching views over the Colne Valley and out towards the Peak District. Gravel paths lead between mixed borders on many levels. Naturalistic planting for year round colour, with interesting plants. Steps lead to terraced kitchen and cutting garden. Gazebo, pond, shade garden, deck and places to sit.

❀ ♥

98 NEW 1 SCHOOL LANE

Bempton, Bridlington, YO15 1JA. Mr Robert Tyas. *Close to the centre of the village. 3m N of Bridlington. From Brid take B1255 toward Flamborough. L at 1st T-lights. Follow Bempton Lane out of residential area then 2nd R onto Bolam Lane. Continue to end and garden is facing.* Sun 9 July (10-4). Adm £3.50, chd free. Home-made teas.

A previously formal garden recently transformed by current owner to provide interest all year. Front lawn edged by borders with interesting plants and trees. In the rear garden are many rare and unusual alpines displayed in a variety of ways incl the newly created crevice rockery. Small vegetable area designed to maximise the space while the fruit trees and other features provide additional interest. Crevice rockery. Greenhouse and alpine troughs display. Cottage style planting in front garden. Hand-crafted goods available. All areas of the garden can be viewed from the wheelchair.

&. 🐾 ❀ ♥

99 SERENITY

Arkendale Road, Ferrensby, nr Knaresborough, HG5 0QA. Mr & Mrs Smith, 01423 340062, geoffsmith269@gmail.com. *3m NE of Knaresborough, 4m SW of Boroughbridge. On A6055 between Boroughbridge & Knaresborough. A1M J47 follow A168 N, after 3m turn L to Arkendale & Ferrensby.* Wed 26, Sun 30 July (12-5). Adm £3.50, chd free. Home-made teas. **Visits also by arrangement July & Aug, groups of 15+, tours and coaches.**

After an extensive re-planting scheme Serenity is quickly establishing itself as a wonderful garden to visit for inspiration and ideas on how to bring your garden alive with colour. The garden is around a ¼ of an acre and has a cottage garden theme with large herbaceous beds, rockery, water features, circular brick feature in lawn, aviary, ornamental metal structures, and much more. Ample parking in nearby field. Featured in Amateur Gardening.

❀ 🚗 ♥

100 ◆ SHANDY HALL GARDENS

Coxwold, YO61 4AD. The Laurence Sterne Trust, 01347 868465, www.laurencesternetrust.org.uk/ shandy-hall-garden.php. *N of York. From A19, 7m from both Easingwold & Thirsk, turn E signed Coxwold.* **For NGS: Evening opening Fri 26 May, Fri 30 June (6.30-8). Adm £3, chd free. For other opening times and information, please phone or visit garden website.**

Home of C18 author Laurence Sterne. 2 walled gardens, 1 acre of unusual perennials interplanted with tulips and old roses in low walled beds. An old quarry, another acre of trees, shrubs, bulbs, climbers and wild flowers encouraging wildlife, incl. over 400 recorded species of moths. Moth trap, identification and release. Wildlife garden. Featured in The Telegraph, The English Garden and Living North. Wheelchair access to wild garden by arrangement.

&. 🐾 ❀ 🛏

GROUP OPENING

101 SHIPTONTHORPE GARDENS

Station Rd, Shiptonthorpe, York, YO43 3PQ. *2m NW of Market Weighton. Both gardens & VH are in the main village on the N of A1079.* Sat 3, Sun 4 June (11-5). Combined adm £5, chd free. Home-made teas in the village hall.

6 ALL SAINTS
Di Thompson.

WAYSIDE
Susan Sellars.

Two contrasting gardens offering different approaches to gardening style - 6 All Saints is an eclectic 'maze-like' garden with a mix of contemporary and cottage garden features; hidden corners, water features and pond. Wayside has interesting planting in different areas of the garden. Vegetable and fruit growing areas with greenhouse and poly tunnel. Proceeds for teas to go to the village hall and church. Wheelchairs possible with help at both gardens (narrow access and large gravel).

&. 🐾 ❀ 🚗 ♥

102 SION HILL HALL

Kirby Wiske, Thirsk, YO7 4EU. H W Mawer Trust, www.sionhillhall.co.uk. *6m S of Northallerton off A167 4m W of Thirsk, 6m E of A1 via A61.* Sat 24, Sun 25 June (11-4.30). Adm £5, chd free. Home-made teas.

The extensive 5 acre gardens surround an Arts and Crafts neo-Georgian house built in 1913, designed by Walter Brierley, York (house not open). The grounds have been designed and restored by Michael Mallaby, to include a formal parterre with Baroque statuary, clipped box and hornbeam, a Long Walk with yews, shrubs and herbaceous planting, a traditional kitchen garden, and centenary rose garden. Mostly level gravelled paths surround the parterre.

&. ❀ 🚗 ♥

103 SKIPWITH HALL

Skipwith, Selby, YO8 5SQ.
Mr & Mrs C D Forbes Adam,
01757 288381
rosalind@escrick.com
9m S of York, 6m N of Selby.
From York A19 Selby, L in Escrick,
4m to Skipwith. From Selby A19 York,
R onto A163 to Market Weighton,
then L after 2m to Skipwith. **Tue**
13 June (1-4). Adm £5, chd free.
Home-made teas. Visits also
by arrangement May & June,
groups of 10+.
4-acre walled garden of Queen
Anne house (not open). Extensive
mixed borders and lawns, walled
areas by renowned designer Cecil
Pinsent. Recreated working kitchen
garden with 15' beech hedge,
pleached fruit walks, herb maze
and pool. Woodland with specimen
trees and shell house. Decorative
orchard with espaliered and fan-
trained fruit on walls. Italian Garden
recently restored. Gravel paths.
& ✿ ☕ ☕

104 SLEIGHTHOLMEDALE LODGE

Fadmoor, YO62 7JG. Patrick &
Natasha James. *6m NE of Helmsley.*
Parking can be limited in wet
weather. Garden is the first property
in Sleightholmedale, 1m from
Fadmoor. **Wed 7 June, Sun 23 July**
(2-6). Adm £4, chd free.
Light refreshments.
Hillside garden, walled rose garden
and herbaceous borders with
delphiniums, roses, verbascums in
July. Species tulips and meconopsis
in early June. Views over peaceful
valley in N.Yorks Moors.
🐕 ☕

105 ♦ STILLINGFLEET LODGE

Stewart Lane, Stillingfleet, York,
YO19 6HP. Mr & Mrs J Cook,
01904 728506, vanessa.cook@
stillingfleetlodgenurseries.co.uk,
www.stillingfleetlodgenurseries.
co.uk. *6m S of York. From A19 York-*
Selby take B1222 towards Sherburn in
Elmet. In village turn opp church. **For**
NGS: Sun 14 May, Sun 10 Sept
(1-5). Adm £5, chd £1. Home-
made teas. For other opening
times and information, please phone,
email or visit garden website.
Organic, wildlife garden subdivided
into smaller gardens, each based
on colour theme with emphasis
on use of foliage plants. Wild
flower meadow and natural pond.
55yd double herbaceous borders.
Modern rill garden. Rare breeds of
poultry wander freely in garden.
Adjacent nursery. Wildlife Day
in June. Garden Courses run all
summer see website. Featured in
Country Living, Garden News and
Landlove. Winner of Visit York Small
attraction of the year. Gravel paths
and lawn. Ramp to cafe if needed.
No disabled WC.
& ✿ ☕ ☕

106 STONEFIELD COTTAGE

27 Nordham, North Cave, Brough,
HU15 2LT. Nicola Lyte. *15m W of*
Hull. M62 E, J38 towards N Cave.
Turn L towards N Cave Wetlands,
then R at LH bend. Stonefield
Cottage is on R, ¼m along Nordham.
Sat 22, Sun 23 July (12-5). Adm
£4, chd free. Home-made teas.
A hidden and surprising 1
acre garden, with an emphasis
throughout on strong, dramatic
colours and sweeping vistas. Rose
beds, mixed borders, vegetables, a
riotous hot bed, boggy woodland,
wildlife pond, jacquemontii under-
planted with red hydrangeas and a
Portmeirion garden. Collections of
Hellebores, Primulas, Ferns, Astilbes,
Hostas, Heucheras, Dahlias and
Hemerocallis.
✿ ☕

107 SUE PROCTOR PLANTS NURSERY GARDEN

69 Ings Mill Avenue, Clayton West,
Huddersfield, HD8 9QG. Sue &
Richard Proctor, 01484 866189,
hostas@sueproctorplants.co.uk,
www.sueproctorplants.co.uk.
9m NE of Holmfirth, 10m SW of
Wakefield. Off A636 Wakefield/
Holmfirth. From M1 J39 in Clayton
West Village turn L signed Clayton
West, High Hoyland, then R signed
Kaye's F & N School. Turn 1st R to
Ings Mill Avenue. **Sat 15, Sun 16**
July (11-4). Adm £3, chd free.
Light refreshments. Gluten
free available. **Visits also by**
arrangement May to Aug.
Small, mainly sloping, suburban
garden packed full of interest.
Summer highlights include over
300 varieties of hostas and close
plantings of flowering perennials
with some rare and unusual plants.
Shaded gravel and rock gardens
show off acers, ferns and hostas,
especially miniature hostas, the
nursery specialism. The garden is
close to the Kirklees Light Railway,
Cannon Hall Country Park and
Bretton Sculpture Park. A notable
feature is our collection of hostas,
one of the largest in the North
of England, including the smallest
miniature hostas, less than 4'
in height to the world's largest
'Empress Wu'. Partial wheelchair
access and a graded path to the top
of the garden.
🐕 ✿ ☕

GROUP OPENING

108 SUTTON GARDENS

Sutton Lane, Masham, HG4 4PB.
1½m W of Masham. From Masham
towards Leyburn (A6108) L into
Sutton Lane, single track tarmac rd
Low Sutton ¼m on L for parking &
entry tickets. **Sun 26 Feb (12-4);**
Sun 16 July (12-5). Combined
adm £5, chd free. Home-made
teas in July at Low Sutton.
Home made soup and rolls,
hot beverages and cakes for
Snowdrop Festival.

LOW SUTTON

Steve & Judi Smith,
01765 688565,
info@lowsutton.co.uk,
www.lowsutton.co.uk.
🛏

SUTTON GRANGE

Mr & Mrs Robert
Jameson, 01765 689068,
jameson3@btinternet.com,
www.themews-masham.com.
🛏

Set down a peaceful country lane
outside Masham, two contrasting
styles of gardens. Low Sutton set
within 6 acre smallholding, has a
circular colour wheel cottage garden

surrounded with scented roses and clematis. Wide variety of fruit and vegetables decoratively grown in raised beds, fruit cage, greenhouse and coldframe. Perennial border, grasses, fernery and courtyard with hostas surround the house. The old orchard that is newly planted with fruit trees has a rill and seasonal pond, and a walk on the wildside. Sutton Grange, 1½ acre established garden and orchard with woodland walk. Greenhouse with fig tree. Walled vegetable garden with cutting flower bed, gazebo, summerhouse, lawns surrounded by herbaceous borders with iris, roses, peonies, wisteria and clematis. Laburnum and honeysuckle arches and water features. Many places to sit and enjoy the views, or have a game of croquet or boules. Snowdrop Festival an abundance of naturalised snowdrops carpet the old orchard and hillside at Low Sutton and throughout the garden at Sutton Grange.

109 SUTTON UPON DERWENT SCHOOL

Main Street, Sutton On Derwent, York, YO41 4BN. Head - Angela Ekers. Garden - Annette Atkin. *7m SE of York on B1228. From A1079, at Barmby Moor turn S onto Sutton Lane. Follow rd to village, L at tennis courts. Blind corner, school on R.* **Sun 9 July (11-4). Adm £3.50, chd free.**

Sutton upon Derwent school is an RHS level 5 school garden. Grounds developed over the past 8yrs, have become the gardens which are now an integral part of school life; encouraging outdoor lessons in all areas of the curriculum. Outdoor learning spaces incl, sensory garden, wildlife area, extensive vegetable growing areas, greenhouse and poly tunnel. Children's crafts and wildlife activities free.

110 SWALE COTTAGE

Station Road, Richmond, DL10 4LU. Julie Martin & Dave Dalton, 01748 829452. *Richmond town centre. On foot, facing bottom of Market Place, turn L onto Frenchgate, then R onto Station Rd. House 1st on R.* **Sun 25 June (1-5). Adm £3.50, chd free. Home-made teas. Also open Millgate House. Visits also by arrangement May to Sept for groups of 10+.**

½ acre urban oasis on steep site, with sweeping views and hidden corners. Several enclosed garden rooms on different levels. Mature herbaceous, rose and shrub garden with some areas of recent improvement. Magnificent yew and cedar. Organic vegetables and soft fruit and pond. Adjacent orchard and paddock with sheep and hens.

111 TAMARIND

2 Whin Hill Road, Bessacarr, Doncaster, DN4 7AE. Ken & Carol Kilvington. *2m S of Doncaster. Through Lakeside, past Dome on R turn R at Bawtry Rd T-lights, through pedestrian crossing and T-lights then 1st L. A638 N from Bawtry to Doncaster turn R signed Cantley-Branton (B1396).* **Sun 7 May (1-5). Combined adm with The Red House £5, chd free. Sat 12, Sun 13 Aug (1-5). Adm £3.50, chd free. Light refreshments.**

A ⅔ acre garden is level at the front with acers and interesting varied planting. Round lawn leads to a steeply terraced rear garden full of colour and differing styles. White border with dovecote and doves; hot border, rose garden, herbaceous, embankment, fern garden and rhododendron garden. Stream with waterfalls, ponds, rockery and bog garden, thatched summerhouse, patio. Steep steps. The front garden and rear lower patio is accessible to wheelchairs, from which most of the rear garden can be viewed. Steps to the rest of the garden.

112 ◆ THORNYCROFT

Rainton, nr Thirsk, YO7 3PH. Martin & Jill Fish, 01845 577157, martin@martinfish.com, www.martinfish.com. *1m E of A1(M) between Ripon & Thirsk. Approx 6m N of Boroughbridge. Access to Rainton is from J48 or 50 of A1(M) or from A168 dual carriageway at Asenby or Topcliffe.* **For NGS: Sun 23 July (11-4.30). Adm £4, chd free. Home-made teas. For other opening times and information, please phone, email or visit garden website.**

A ¾ acre country garden created since 2009 comprising lawn areas, trees, shrubs and perennials and featuring some unusual plant specimens. Pergola, summerhouse and paved courtyard garden with container plants and raised beds. Orchard with mixture of heritage and modern varieties and an ornamental kitchen garden. Wooden greenhouse with decorative plants and productive poly-tunnel. BBC Radio York and BBC Radio Nottingham gardening expert Martin Fish will be on hand to answer your gardening questions. Features regularly in Kitchen Garden and Garden News magazines and used for outside radio broadcasts. Gravel drive and gravel paths in kitchen garden.

Hillbark

GROUP OPENING

113 TWO WALLED GARDENS OF BEVERLEY

Beverley, HU17 8DS. *On A1079 approx 100yds from North Bar (town gate) 6 York Rd is 100yds from North Bar opposite gates leading to Nether's Yard. Satnav does not recognise Willow Grove as it is an unadopted rd & not open to vehicles. Access to Willow Grove via Pasture Terrace from A1079/ via Tiger Lane, off North Bar Within. Houses are numbered starting at E end. No parking on York Rd. Parking on A164 inside & outside of the town walls.* **Sun 9 July (12-4.30). Combined adm £5, chd free. Home-made teas**

NEW 5 WILLOW GROVE
Tim Cartwright Taylor, 01482 882408, timct09@timct09.karoo.co.uk.
Visits also by arrangement June to Aug 20+.

6 YORK ROAD
Pamela Hopkins.
Visits also by arrangement June to Aug for groups of 20+.

These walled gardens have all been in existence for over a hundred years. 5 Willow Grove a charming small walled garden close to the centre of this lovely Georgian town. A hidden gem, no grass or sweeping lawns, but plenty of colour and interest to visitors. 6 York Road is a small town garden, with traditional front garden and walled garden to the rear. The design inspiration for the rear garden was taken from a trip to China, where the garden owner was informed that a circle signified heaven, and a square signified earth. Mixed borders and climbers and a bower in which to sit and enjoy the tranquil oasis. Wheelchair access: no access for wheelchairs

& ✿ ☕ ⬤

114 NEW VILLAGE FARM HOUSE

Main Street, Swine, Hull, HU11 4JE. Karl & Katrina Stephenson. *From A63 turn off towards Mount Pleasant, follow the road to Holderness Rd A165, at the T-lights turn R onto A165 & follow the road.* **Sun 23 July (11-5). Adm £3, chd free. Cream teas. Cakes, teas & coffee will be available as well as BBQ food on offer.**

We, Karl and Katrina welcome you to our garden which offers over 100+ different plants including camellias and magnolias as well as fruit trees, large vegetable plot, 2 Victorian wells and much more. We took over the property Nov 2015 and are new to gardening, we have established July as the best month and have added many unusual plants to the previously created garden and with time hope to create a Victorian garden.

& 🐕 ✿ ⬤ ☕

115 WARLEY HOUSE GARDEN

Stock Lane, Warley, Halifax, HX2 7RU. Dr & Mrs P J Hinton, 01422 831431, warleyhousegardens@outlook.com, www.warleyhousegardens.com.
2m W of Halifax. Take A646 (towards Burnley) from Halifax. Go through large intersection after approx 1m. After 1m take R turn up Windle Royd Lane. Signs will direct you from here. Disabled parking adjacent to the house limited to 4/5 vehicles. **Sun 14, Wed 17 May (1-5). Adm £4, chd free. Home-made teas. Visits also by arrangement May to July refreshments by arrangement with individual groups. 4 weeks notice please.**

Partly walled 2½ acre garden of demolished C18 House, renovated by the present owners. Rocky paths and Japanese style planting lead to lawns and lovely S-facing views. Alpine ravine planted with ferns and fine trees give structure to the developing woodland area. Drifts of shrubs, herbaceous plantings, wild flowers and heathers maintain constant seasonal interest. This is an historic garden, renovated after total neglect from 1945 to 1995. Spring planting is enhanced by many new rhododendrons and woodland planting. Partial wheelchair access to Japanese garden. Disabled access to WCs.

& ✿ ⬤ ☕

116 THE WHITE HOUSE

Husthwaite, YO61 4QA. Mrs A Raper, 01347 868688, audrey. husthwaite@btinternet.com. *5m S of Thirsk. Turn R off A19 signed Husthwaite. 1½m to centre of village opp parish church.* **Visits by arrangement any size group.** Meet an enthusiastic plantswoman. Exchange ideas and visit a 1-acre country garden. Walled garden, conservatory, herbaceous borders, fresh lavender and purple palette a late spring and hot summer border. Unusual plants and shrubs. Collections of pæonies, clematis and hemerocallis, landscaping, planting and bed of English and shrub roses in the old orchard. A garden for all seasons.

& ✿ ⬤ ☕

117 WHYNCREST

Bridlington Road, Hunmanby, Filey, YO14 9RS. Mrs Lieke Swann, 01723 890923, lieke@whyncrest.wanadoo.co.uk.
Between Hunmanby & Reighton Nursery off A165 between Hunmanby Gap & Reighton. Exit A165, junction signed Reigthon Nurseries & Hunmanby, follow this rd for 200 yds, Whyncrest is on R. Parking on grass verge outside. **Evening opening Thur 10 Aug (5.30-9). Adm £6, chd free. Wine. adm incl wine/ juice on arrival. Visits also by arrangement May to Sept.**

Elevated garden with fabulous views across Filey Bay and beyond. The garden has been carefully designed, creating micro climate 'rooms' taking you from jungle garden to a pond garden with tropical planting and a huge waterfall, herbaceous borders and topiary shrubs. The collection of plants is varied, giving an all year interest from early spring with all its bulbs all the way into late autumn. Dogs on leads welcome.

🐕 ✿ ⬤ ☕

118 WOODLANDS COTTAGE

Summerbridge, Nidderdale, HG3 4BT. Mr & Mrs Stark, 01423 780765, www.woodlandscottagegarden. co.uk. *10m NW of Harrogate. On the B6165 W of Summerbridge.*

Sun 14 May (1-5). Adm £3.50, chd free. Tea. Opening with Dacre Banks & Summerbridge Gardens on Sun 9 July. **Visits also by arrangement May to Aug.**

A one-acre country garden created by its owners and making full use of its setting, which includes natural woodland with wild bluebells and gritstone boulders. There are several gardens within the garden, from a wild flower meadow and woodland rock-garden to a formal herb garden and herbaceous areas; also a productive fruit and vegetable garden. Gravel paths with some slopes.

& ✿ ⌂ ⚏

119 WYEDALE
Ottringham Road, Keyingham, Hull, HU12 9RX. Mrs Angie & Mr J Woodmancy. *10m E of Hull. Enter Keyingham on A1033 Hull to Withernsea Rd, continue through village, garage on R, head towards mill. Parking on L at Eastend Nurseries, garden approx 70 yds on R.* Sun 2 July (11-5). Adm £3.50, chd free. Light refreshments.

An English Country garden, ¾ acre with far reaching views to Lincolnshire Wolds. Curved borders of herbaceous perennials, scented seating area with pinks, jasmin, philadelphus and herbs, wildlife pond. Gravel garden with grasses leading to pergola clothed in roses and clematis followed by cutting garden with interesting 'folly wall'. Wild life area with hedgehog houses leads to orchard.' Folly wall ' with window. All areas have wheelchair access.

& ✿ ⚏

120 ◆ YORK GATE
Back Church Lane, Adel, Leeds, LS16 8DW. Perennial, 0113 267 8240, yorkgate@perennial.org.uk, www.yorkgate.org.uk. *5m N of Leeds. N of Leeds 2¼m SE of Bramhope, signed from A660. Park in Church Lane in lay-by opp church & take public footpath through churchyard to garden.* **For opening times and information, please phone, email or visit garden website.**

A one-acre masterpiece and widely recognised as one of the most innovative small gardens of the period. A series of smaller gardens with different themes and in contrasting styles are linked by a succession of delightful vistas. Striking architectural features are found throughout the garden. White and Silver Borders, Pinetum and Arbour, Woodland Dell, Kitchen Gardens, Herb Garden and Summerhouse, Paved Garden, Nut Walk, Potting Shed, Pavement Maze, the Old Orchard, Alley and Sundial, Fern Border, Sybil's Garden, Scree Garden and Canal Garden. Steps and gravel paths make the garden unsuitable for wheelchairs.

✿ ⌂ ⚏

The National Garden Scheme is Marie Curie's largest single funder

121 YORKE HOUSE
Dacre Banks, Nidderdale, HG3 4EW. Tony & Pat Hutchinson, 01423 780456, pat@yorkehouse.co.uk, www.yorkehouse.co.uk. *4m SE of Pateley Bridge, 10m NW of Harrogate, 10m N of Otley. On B6451 near centre of Dacre Banks. Car park.* Sun 25 June (11-5). Adm £5, chd free. Cream teas. **Opening with Dacre Banks & Summerbridge Gardens on Sun 9 July. Visits also by arrangement June & July for groups of 10+.**

Award-winning English country garden in the heart of Nidderdale. Designed as a series of distinct areas which flow naturally through 2 acres of ornamental garden. Colour-themed borders, fragrant millennium garden, woodland sanctuary and secluded seating areas. Natural ponds and stream with delightful waterside plantings. Large collection of hostas. Orchard picnic area. 'Art in the Garden' event. Winner Harrogate's Glorious Gardens, Exhibition of paintings by local artists at 'Art in the Garden' event. Featured in 'Plants, Beds and Borders', on Radio York and Harrogate Advertiser. All main features accessible to wheelchair users.

& 🐎 ✿ ⌂ ☕ ⚏

122 ◆ THE YORKSHIRE ARBORETUM
Castle Howard, York, YO60 7BY. The Castle Howard Arboretum Trust, 01653 648598, visit@yorkshirearboretum.org, www.yorkshirearboretum.org. *15m NE of York. Off A64. Follow signs to Castle Howard then look for Yorkshire Arboretum signs at the obelisk r'about.* **For NGS: Sun 4 June (10-4.30). Adm £6, chd free. For other opening times and information, please phone, email or visit garden website.**

A glorious, 120 acre garden of trees from around the world set in a stunning landscape of parkland, lakes and ponds. With walks and lakeside trails, tours, family activities, a woodland playground, café and gift shop we welcome visitors of all ages wanting to enjoy the space, serenity and beauty of this sheltered valley as well as those interested in our extensive collection of trees and shrubs. Internationally renowned collection of trees in a beautiful setting, accompanied by a diversity of wild flowers, birds, insects and other wildlife. Children's playground, cafe and gift shop. Dogs on leads welcome. Not suitable for wheelchairs. Motorised all-terrain buggies are available on loan, please book 24hrs in advance on 01653 648598.

🐎 ⌂ ⚏

WALES

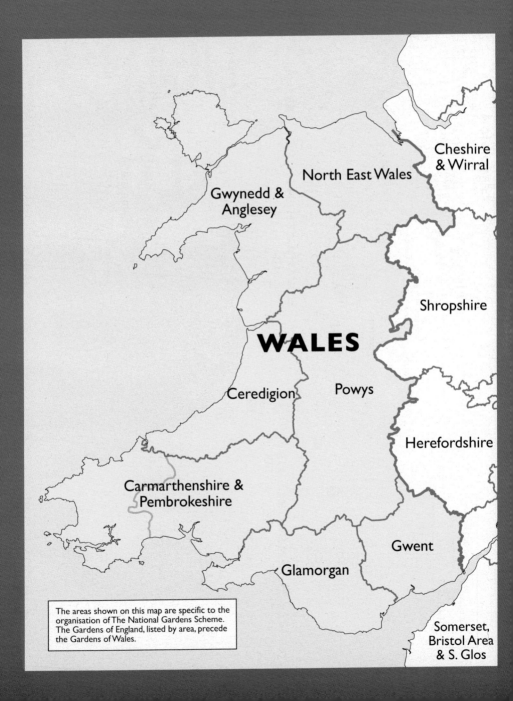

Cheshire & Wirral

North East Wales

Gwynedd & Anglesey

Shropshire

WALES

Ceredigion

Powys

Herefordshire

Carmarthenshire & Pembrokeshire

Gwent

Glamorgan

The areas shown on this map are specific to the organisation of The National Gardens Scheme. The Gardens of England, listed by area, precede the Gardens of Wales.

Somerset, Bristol Area & S. Glos

CARMARTHENSHIRE & PEMBROKESHIRE

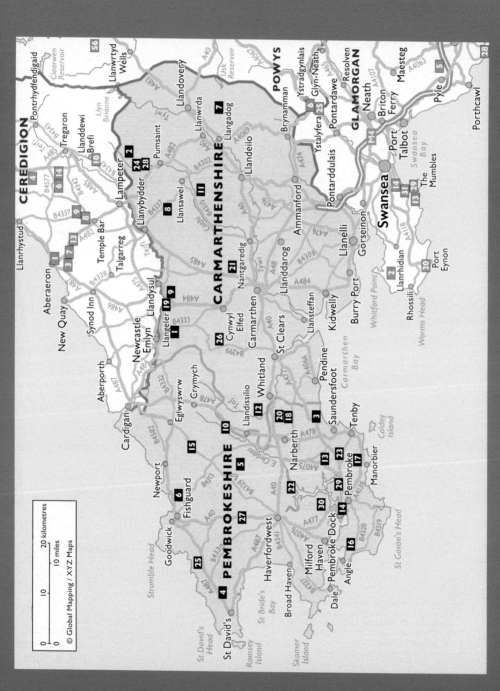

From the rugged Western coast and beaches to the foothills of the Brecon Beacons and Black Mountain, these counties offer gardens as varied as the topography and weather.

The remote and romantic gardens of Carmarthenshire, such as Lan Farm, Gelli Mydog and Gelli Uchaf also delight with superb views and borrowed landscape, whilst in the more moderate climes of the Pembrokeshire gardens such as Dyffryn Fernant, Treffgarne Hall, Picton Castle and a new garden, Vale Farmhouse, tender plants flourish. Each of our many gardens has something different to offer the visitor and many now welcome dogs as well as their owners!

Several fascinating gardens have restricted parking areas and so are only open 'By Arrangement'; the owners will be delighted to see you, but please do telephone first to arrange a visit. Mead Lodge, in Pembrokeshire, is part of the 'Quiet Garden Movement', and when not opening for the NGS, they offer their garden as a place of beauty and calm in a sometimes frantic world. They will be pleased to welcome you, but again, do call them first.

Most of our gardens also offer teas or light refreshments and what better way to enjoy an afternoon in a garden, where there is no weeding for you to do or washing up! We look forward to welcoming you to our counties.

Volunteers

County Organisers
Jackie Batty
01437 741115
bathole2000@aol.com

Jane Stokes
01558 823233
jane.h.stokes@btinternet.com

County Treasurer
Christine Blower
01267 253334
cheahnwood@toucansurf.com

Publicity
Liz & Paul O'Neill
01994 240717
lizpaulfarm@yahoo.co.uk

Jane Stokes
(as above)

Booklet Co-ordinator
Jane Stokes
(as above)

Assistant County Organisers
Liz & Paul O'Neill
(as above)

Ivor Stokes
01558 823233
ivor.t.stokes@btopenworld.com

Left: Pentresite

OPENING DATES

All entries subject to change. For latest information check www.ngs.org.uk

Extended openings are shown at the beginning of the month.

Map locator numbers are shown to the right of each garden name.

March

Sunday 26th
◆ Upton Castle
   Gardens   29

April

Sunday 16th
The Crystal Garden   4

Monday 17th
The Crystal Garden   4
Llwyngarreg   12

Sunday 30th
Treffgarne Hall   27

May

The Crystal Garden
(Every day from Sunday 7th to Sunday 21st)   4

Moorland Cottage Plants and Gardens
(Every Thursday to Tuesday from Monday 1st)   15

Sunday 7th
◆ Dyffryn Fernant   6

Saturday 13th
◆ Colby Woodland
   Garden   3

Sunday 14th
◆ Colby Woodland
   Garden   3

Saturday 20th
Glyn Bach Gardens   10

Sunday 21st
Glyn Bach Gardens   10
◆ Picton Castle &
   Gardens   22

90th Anniversary Weekend

Sunday 28th
Blaenfforest   1
Llwyngarreg   12
Panteg   20

Monday 29th
Llwyngarreg   12
Mandrake   13
NEW The Old Rectory   18

June

The Crystal Garden
(Every day from Thursday 1st to Wednesday 14th)   4

Moorland Cottage Plants and Gardens
(Every Thursday to Tuesday)   15

Saturday 10th
NEW Vale Farmhouse   30

Sunday 11th
Gelli Mydog   7
◆ Picton Castle &
   Gardens   22
NEW Vale Farmhouse   30

Saturday 17th
Glyn Bach Gardens   10

Sunday 18th
Glyn Bach Gardens   10
Llwyngarreg   12

Sunday 25th
Bwlchau Duon   2
Neath Farm   16
Sculptors Garden,
   The Old Post Office   24
Tradewinds   26

July

The Crystal Garden
(Every day from Saturday 1st to Friday 14th)   4

Moorland Cottage Plants and Gardens
(Every Thursday to Tuesday)   15

Saturday 1st
Glandwr   9

Sunday 2nd
Glandwr   9

Friday 7th
Mead Lodge   14

Saturday 8th
Mead Lodge   14

Sunday 9th
Mead Lodge   14
Pentresite   21

Monday 10th
Mead Lodge   14

Saturday 22nd
Glyn Bach Gardens   10

Sunday 23rd
Glyn Bach Gardens   10
Mandrake   13
Treffgarne Hall   27

August

The Crystal Garden
(Every day from Tuesday 1st to Thursday 10th)   4

Moorland Cottage Plants and Gardens
(Every Thursday to Tuesday)   15

Sunday 6th
◆ Dyffryn Fernant   6
Ty'r Maes   28

Sunday 20th
Tradewinds   26

Sunday 27th
Glyn Bach Gardens   10
Llwyngarreg   12

Monday 28th
Glyn Bach Gardens   10
Llwyngarreg   12

September

The Crystal Garden
(Every day from Sunday 3rd to Saturday 9th)   4

Moorland Cottage Plants and Gardens
(Every Thursday to Tuesday to Sunday 17th)   15

Sunday 3rd
◆ Dyffryn Fernant   6

By Arrangement

Blaenfforest   1
Bwlchau Duon   2
The Crystal Garden   4
Cwm Pibau   5
Gelli Uchaf   8
Glandwr   9
Glyn Bach Gardens   10
Lan Farm   11
Llwyngarreg   12
Mandrake   13
Mead Lodge   14
Moorland Cottage
   Plants and Gardens   15
Norchard   17
NEW The Old Rectory   18
The Old Vicarage   19
Panteg   20
Pentresite   21
Rosewood   23
Stable Cottage   25
Treffgarne Hall   27
Ty'r Maes   28

Gelli Mydog

THE GARDENS

1 BLAENFFOREST

Newcastle Emlyn, Carmarthenshire, SA38 9JD. Sally & Russell Jones, 01559 371264, enquiries@blaenfforest.co.uk, www.cottageholidayswales.com. *2m S of Newcastle Emlyn. From Newcastlle Emlyn take A484 to Carmarthen turn R on B4333. From Carmarthen take A484 to Cardigan, L on B4333 at Cynwyl Elfed. Follow brown tourist signs to Blaenfforest Cottages. NB: access is via uneven track, please take care.* **Sun 28 May** (11.30-4.30). **Adm £3.50, chd free. Light refreshments. Visits also by arrangement Apr to Aug, refreshments on request when booking.**

Relaxed and tranquil gardens incl stunning views from the terrace, lush planting by the wildlife ponds, interesting, tucked away corners, bees in the orchard and woodland walk, deep in the valley of the R Arad. Peacocks roam freely, but children to be supervised! A place to write poetry! Partial wheelchair access to parts of gardens.

2 BWLCHAU DUON

Ffarmers, Llanwrda, Carmarthenshire, SA19 8JJ. Brenda & Allan Timms, 01558 650187, brendatimmsuk@gmail.com, www.bwlchauduongardens.co.uk. *7m SE Lampeter, 8m NW Llanwrda. From A482 turn to Ffarmers. In Ffarmers, take lane opp Drovers Arms PH. Shortly after caravan site on L there is a very small Xrds, turn L into single track lane & follow NGS arrows.* **Sun 25 June** (2-6). **Combined adm with Sculptors Garden, The Old Post Office £5, chd free. Home-made teas. Visits also by arrangement June to Aug (Bwlchau Duon only).**

A 1 acre, ever evolving garden challenge, set in the foothills of the Cambrian Mountains at 1100ft. This is a plantaholics haven where borders are full of many unusual plants and lots of old favourites. There are raised vegetable gardens,

a 100ft herbaceous border, recently planted natural bog areas, winding pathways through semi-woodland and magnificent views over the Cothi valley. Rare breed turkeys, chickens, geese and rabbits!

> Your visit has already helped 600 more people gain access to a Parkinson's nurse

3 ◆ COLBY WOODLAND GARDEN

Amroth, Narberth, Pembrokeshire, SA67 8PP. National Trust, 01834 811885, www.nationaltrust.org.uk. *6m N of Tenby, 5m SE of Narberth. Follow brown tourist signs on coast rd & A477.* **For NGS: Sat 13, Sun 14 May** (10-5). **Adm £7, chd £3.50. Cream teas in the Bothy Tearoom. For other opening times and information, please phone or visit garden website.**

8 acre woodland garden in a secluded valley with fine collection of rhododendrons and azaleas. Wildflower meadow and stream with rope swings and stepping stones for children to explore and play. Ornamental walled garden incl unusual gazebo, designed by Wyn Jones, with internal tromp l'oeil. Incl in the *Register of Historic Parks and Gardens: Pembrokeshire.* Extensive play area for children incl

den building and log climbing. Free family activities incl duck racing, pond dipping, campfire lighting etc. Children under 5, free entry. Full range of refreshments incl lunches. Partial access for wheelchair users.

4 THE CRYSTAL GARDEN

Golwg yr Ynys, Carnhedryn, St Davids, Pembrokeshire, SA62 6XT. Mrs Sue Clark, 01437 721082, sueclark132@gmail.com, www.thecrystalgarden.org.uk. *4m E of St Davids, 11m SW of Fishguard, 2m N of Solva. Village of Carnhedryn, off A487 between Fishguard & St Davids.* **Sun 16, Mon 17 Apr** (1-5). **Daily Sun 7 May to Sun 21 May, Thur 1 June to Wed 14 June, Sat 1 July to Fri 14 July, Tue 1 Aug to Thur 10 Aug, Sun 3 Sept to Sat 9 Sept** (1-5). **Adm £3, chd free. Tea. Visits also by arrangement May to Sept. Teas on request when booking.**

¾ acre garden for plantaholics with yr-round floral colour and foliage interest. Intriguing layout of sheltered rooms full of surprises packed with unusual shrubs, perennials and garden favourites. Ever changing outer garden. The garden never stands still. Specialities incl hebes and hydrangeas. A warm welcome awaits. Art wall, glazed visitor room.

5 CWM PIBAU

New Moat, Clarbeston Road, Haverfordwest, Pembrokeshire, SA63 4RE. Mrs Duncan Drew, 01437 532454. *10m NE of Haverfordwest. 3m SW of Maenclochog. Off A40, take B4313 to Maenclochog, follow signs to New Moat, past church, then 2nd concealed drive on L, ½m rural drive.* **Visits by arrangement, please telephone first to ensure a welcome. Adm £3, chd free.**

5 acre woodland garden surrounded by old deciduous woodland and streams. Created in 1978, contains many mature, unusual shrubs and trees from Chile, New Zealand and Europe, set on S-facing hill. More conventional planting nearer house.

6 ◆ DYFFRYN FERNANT

Llanychaer, Fishguard, Pembrokeshire, SA65 9SP. Christina Shand & David Allum, 01348 811282, christina@dyffrynfernant.co.uk, www.dyffrynfernant.co.uk.
3m E of Fishguard, then ½ m inland. A487 E 2m from Fishguard turn R towards Llanychaer at garden signs. ½ m entrance is on L. Coming from direction of Dinas/Newport Pemb look for L turn off A487. For NGS: Sun 7 May, Sun 6 Aug, Sun 3 Sept (11-6). Adm £6, chd free. Home-made teas. For other opening times and information, please phone, email or visit garden website.
6 acres under the Preseli Hills, modern yet attached to the ancient past. Naturalistic in its planting as well as exotic and stylised in parts. Ornamental grasses, wild flower marsh, salvia collection, tropical planting and wide herbaceous borders. 'This is the very best of Atlantic Coast garden making… the essence of sense of place.' Noel Kingsbury. A Library for garden visitors incl a wide selection of books on gardening and art. Art exhibitions and events for 2017 Visit Wales Year of Legends. Home-made teas on NGS days and for pre-booked groups. Featured in print and online for Gardens Illustrated and on BBC Gardener's World.

7 GELLI MYDOG

Myddfai, Llandovery, Carmarthenshire, SA20 0JQ. Robert Lee & Barry Williams.
1.4m S of Myddfai. From Llandovery follow signs to Myddfai, approx 3m then follow yellow NGS signs. From Llangadog follow signs to Myddfai, approx 5m. Sun 11 June (12-5). Adm £3.50, chd free. Home-made teas.
Approx 2 acre garden set in 9 acre grounds. Garden incl immaculate sweeping lawns, formal and informal herbaceous and shrub borders containing wide variety of plants. Recently completed stream side and pond gardens adjacent to restored wildlife meadows. Places to relax and enjoy the extensive views across the upland landscape. Featured in Country Life magazine. All main areas accessible by wheelchair.

8 GELLI UCHAF

Rhydcymerau, Llandeilo, Carmarthenshire, SA19 7PY. Julian & Fiona Wormald, 01558 685119, thegardenimpressionists@gmail.com, www.thegardenimpressionists.com.
5m SE of Llanybydder. 1m NW of Rhydcymerau. In Rhydcymerau on B4337 turn up Mountain Rd for Llanllwni (by BT phone box). After about 300yds turn R up farm track (uneven surface 10mph max please), cont ½ m bearing R up hill at fork in track. Visits by arrangement Feb to May (Suns only) and Sat 1 July. Bookings times 10.30am or 2.30pm. Min 2 visitors. Adm £4, chd free. Home-made teas.
Complementing a C17 Longhouse and 11 acre smallholding this 1+ acre garden is mainly organic. Trees and shrubs are underplanted with

Colby Woodland Garden

collections of crocus, daffodils and snowdrops (150 cultivars). Diverse plantings inc colour filled perennial borders. Novel system for growing vegetables and 50+ fruit trees. Extensive views, seats to enjoy them. 6 acres of wildflower meadows, 2 ponds and stream. Snowdrop and daffodil open days; Open for National Meadows Day 1st July. A magical and inspirational garden. Featured in Amateur Gardening Magazine; Wales on Line: 10 Best Secret Gardens to Visit; S4C Wedi 3 TV; BBC Gardener's World - 1st Spring garden visited for 2016 season.

✿ ☕

9 GLANDWR

Pentrecwrt, Llandysul, Carmarthenshire, SA44 5DA. Mrs Jo Hicks, 01559 363729, leehicks@btinternet.com. *15m N of Carmarthen, 2m S of Llandysul, 7m E of Newcastle Emlyn. On A486. At Pentrecwrt village, take minor rd opp Black Horse PH. After bridge keep L for ¼ m. Glandwr is on R.* **Sat 1, Sun 2 July (11-5). Adm £3, chd free. Home-made teas. Visits also by arrangement, please phone first.** Delightful easily accessed 1 acre cottage garden, bordered by a natural stream. Incl a rockery and colour themed beds. Enter the mature woodland, now transformed into an adventurous wander with plenty of shade loving plants, ground cover, interesting trees, shrubs and many surprises. Dogs permitted on leads.

🐕 ☕

10 GLYN BACH GARDENS

Pont Hywel, Efailwen, Pembrokeshire, SA66 7JP. Peter & Carole Whittaker, 01994 419104, carole.whittaker7@btinternet.com, www.glynbachgardens.co.uk. *Efailwen 8m N of Narberth, 15m S of Cardigan. About 1m N of Efailwen turn W off A478 at Glandy Cross garage, follow signs for 1m towards Llangolman & Pont Hywel Bridge. Glyn Bach is situated on L before 'road narrows' sign.* **Sat 20 May (11-5); Sun 21 May (11-5.30); Sat 17, Sun 18 June, Sat 22, Sun 23 July, Sun 27, Mon 28 Aug (11-5). Adm £3.50, chd free.**

Home-made teas. Visits also by arrangement May to Aug. Groups 10+ welcome. Please arrange teas when booking. 2 acres of garden with numerous perennial borders, alpine walls, tropical beds, large pond, bog garden, rose garden, grass beds, raised vegetable beds, cottage garden, polytunnel, greenhouse and succulents, with emphasis on nectar rich plants for pollinators. Surrounded by 4 acres of mixed woodland and grassland; woodland walk with bluebells and wildflowers in spring. Activities for children. Holders of a National Collection of Monarda. Featured in RHS The Garden. Wheelchair access on grass pathways.

♿ 🐄 ✿ 🚐 NPC ☕

11 LAN FARM

Talley, Llandeilo, Carmarthenshire, SA19 7BQ. Karen & David Thomas, 07950 178333, davidhuw@gmail.com. *10m N of Llandeilo. Talley is on B4302 between Llandeilo & Crugybar. In Talley follow signs to Abbey, passing it on R. Cont on single track lane for 2m. Drive to Lan, ¼ m, on L, uneven surface, please take care.* **Visits by arrangement June to Aug, light refreshments available on request. Adm £3.50, chd free.** Extremely rural 2 acre SW facing garden oasis 900ft above sea level that has been sympathetically developed to augment the countryside. There are spectacular borrowed views in all directions. Interesting planting with plenty of surprises incl a wildflower meadow, utilisation of old farm buildings, bog and Mediterranean areas. There is also a small lake that attracts a variety of wildlife. A remote and romantic garden!

☕

12 LLWYNGARREG

Llanfallteg, Whitland, Carmarthenshire, SA34 0XH. Paul & Liz O'Neill, 01994 240717, lizpaulfarm@yahoo.co.uk, www.llwyngarreg.co.uk. *19m W of Carmarthen. A40 W from Carmarthen, turn R at Llandewi Velfrey, 2½ m to Llanfallteg. Go through village, garden ½ m further*

on: 2nd farm on R. Disabled car park in bottom yard on R. **Mon 17 Apr (1.30-6). Sun 28 May (1.30-6), also open Panteg. Mon 29 May (1.30-6), also open The Old Rectory. Sun 18 June, Sun 27, Mon 28 Aug (1.30-6). Adm £4, chd free. Home-made teas. Visits also by arrangement Apr to Aug, for other opening times please check website.** Llwyngarreg will delight the discerning plantsman with its many rarities incl species primulas, restios, many bamboos with roscoeas, hedychiums and salvias extending the season through to riotous autumn colour. Trees and rhododendrons have been underplanted with perennials. An extensive grass bed dominates the centre and three springs meet to form a stream around the main garden. This provides several bog garden opportunities – perfect for colour in May and June. Children will enjoy climbing the willow structures. Dogs welcomed. Wildlife ponds, twig piles for overwintering insects, composting, numerous living willow structures. Featured in Welsh Country Magazine. Partial wheelchair access.

♿ 🐄 ✿ 🚐 ☕

13 MANDRAKE

Lanes End, Cresselly, Kilgetty, Pembrokeshire, SA68 0SN. Brian Dawson & Barbara Pegg, 01646 651674. *On A477 take A4075 towards Carew, cont for approx 2m. Upon entering Cresselly take R turn to Jeffreyston, cont down lane for ½ mile. Mandrake on the L.* **Mon 29 May, Sun 23 July (12-5). Adm £3.50, chd free. Home-made teas. Visits also by arrangement May to Aug. Groups of 10 welcome after school hours, please request teas when booking.** An immaculately maintained 2 acre hill top garden incorporating an extensive collection of good sized deciduous specimen trees, shrubs, herbaceous perennials, conifers, grasses and exotic plants, cleverly integrated in long wide borders and island bed. Level access to lawns. Reopening again after 4 years.

♿ ✿ 🚐 ☕

14 MEAD LODGE

Imble Lane, Pembroke Dock, Pembrokeshire, SA72 6PN. John & Eileen Seal, 01646 682504, eileenseal@aol.com. *From A4139 between Pembroke & Pembroke Dock take B4322 signed Pennar & Leisure Centre. After ½ m turn L into Imble Lane. Mead Lodge is at the end.* **Fri 7, Sat 8, Sun 9, Mon 10 July (11-5). Adm £3.50, chd free. Home-made teas. Visits also by arrangement Apr to Sept, individuals or groups always welcome. Please request teas when booking.**
Unexpected, secluded country garden, a relaxing oasis on S-facing slope overlooking the Pembroke River estuary. Varied ¾ acre garden reflects the owners' keen interest in ferns, ornamental grasses and herbs. Incl terraces with Chinese and Mediterranean influences, colour themed beds, small arboretum underplanted for spring colour, fernery, vegetable garden, pond and bog garden. Wheelchair access to path around house and across lawn only.
& 🐂 ✿ 🚗 ☕

Donations
from the NGS
enable Perennial
to care for
horticulturalists

15 MOORLAND COTTAGE PLANTS AND GARDENS

Rhyd-y-Groes, Brynberian, Crymych, Pembrokeshire, SA41 3TT. Jennifer & Kevin Matthews, 01239 891363, jenny@moorlandcottageplants.co.uk, www.moorlandcottageplants.co.uk. *12m SW of Cardigan. 5m W of Crymych, 16m NE of Haverfordwest,* on B4329, ¾ m *downhill from cattlegrid (from Haverfordwest) & 1m uphill from signpost to Brynberian (from Cardigan).* **Every Thur to Tue 1 May to 17 Sept (10.30-4.30). Adm £5, chd £1.50. Visits also by arrangement May to Sept (Weds & evenings only). Refreshments available for groups 20+. Please request when booking.**
4 acres at 700ft on NE hillside overlooking miles of moorland and raised upland bog. Exuberant and diverse plantings provide propagating material for nursery. Secretive areas where carpets of spring flowers give way to jungly perennials, grasses, bamboos and ferns contrast with herbaceous borders, meadows and extensive shrubberies. Stunning mountain and moorland vistas. Mollusc proof plantings. New RHS Partner Garden. The adjoining nursery offers a wide range of outdoor grown hardy perennials, incl some rareties, most of which are propagated from the garden.
✿ 🚗 ⊜

16 NEATH FARM

Rhoscrowther, Pembroke, Pembrokeshire, SA71 5AB. Howell & Mary Woods. *6½ m W of Pembroke. B4320 from Pembroke towards Angle for 6½ m. Ignore 1st R turn signed Valero, Rhoscrowther, but turn R at next junction signed Rhoscrowther. Neath Farm ½ m on L.* **Sun 25 June (1-5). Adm £3.50, chd free. Home-made teas.**
1½ acre garden situated on coastal peninsula. Salt laden winds determine planting. Lawn and raised beds around house. Herbaceous borders, grass beds overlooking small lake which attracts wildlife; bordered by arum lilies and gunnera. Lavender edged path meanders around lake to secluded area with willows. Newly planted orchard. Children to be closely supervised please. Partial wheelchair access around house.
& 🐂 ✿ ☕

17 NORCHARD

The Ridgeway, Manorbier, Tenby, Pembrokeshire, SA70 8LD. Ms H E Davies, 07790 040278, h.norchard@hotmail.co.uk. *4m W of Tenby. From Tenby, take A4139 for Pembroke. ½ m after Lydstep, take R at Xrds. Proceed down lane for ¾ m. Norchard on R.* **Visits by arrangement Apr to June and September for groups 10+. Teas on request when booking. Adm £4, chd free.**
Historic gardens at medieval residence. Nestled in tranquil and sheltered location with ancient oak woodland backdrop. Strong structure with formal and informal areas incl early walled gardens with restored Elizabethan parterre and potager. 1½ acre orchard with old (many local) apple varieties. Mill and millpond. Extensive collections of roses, daffodils and tulips. Partial wheelchair access due to gravel paths. Access to potager via steps only.
& ☕

18 NEW THE OLD RECTORY

Lampeter Velfrey, Narberth, Pembrokeshire, SA67 8UH. Jane & Stephen Fletcher, 01834 831444, jane_e_fletcher@hotmail.com. *4m E of Narbeth. The Old Rectory is next to church in middle of Lampeter Velfrey. Parking in church car park.* **Mon 29 May (2-5). Adm £3, chd free. Home-made teas. Also open Llwyngarreg. Visits also by arrangement May to Aug. Home-made teas on request.**
Historic approx 2 acre garden, sympathetically redesigned and replanted since 2009 and still being restored. Many unique trees, some over 300yrs old, wide variety of planting and several unique, architecturally designed buildings. Formal beds, mature woodland surrounding an old quarry with recently planted terraces and rhododendron bank. Newly planted meadow and orchard.
🐂 🛏 ☕

19 THE OLD VICARAGE

Llangeler, Llandysul, Carmarthenshire, SA44 5EU. Mr & Mrs J C Harcourt, 01559 371168. *4m E of Newcastle Emlyn. 15m N of Carmarthen on A484. From N Emlyn turn down lane on L in Llangeler before church.* **Visits by arrangement May to Sept,**

Tradewinds

please request teas when booking. **Adm £3, chd free.**
A garden gem created since 1993. Less than 1 acre divided into 3 areas. Rose and shrub borders, semi formal pool with adjacent rose and clematis covered loggia. Extensive rose covered pergola, best late June, leads onto curved lawn area. Interesting collection of unusual herbaceous plants. Ever changing scene. Optimum colour, mid June onwards. Dogs permitted on leads. Gravel yard, temporary ramp available for wheelchair users.

20 PANTEG
Llanddewi Velfrey, Narberth, Pembrokeshire, SA67 8UU. Mr & Mrs D Pryse Lloyd, 01834 860081, d.pryselloyd@btinternet.com. *Situated off main A40 in village of Llanddewi Velfrey. A40 from Carmarthen, after garage take 1st L. At next T-junction turn L. On R gateway with stone gate pillars which is ½m drive to Panteg.* **Sun 28 May (11-5). Adm £3, chd free. Also open Llwyngarreg. Visits also by arrangement Mar to Sept, groups 6+.**
Approached down a woodland drive, this tranquil, S-facing, large garden, surrounding a Georgian house (not open), has been developed since early 1990s. Plantsman's garden set off by lawns on different levels. Walled garden, wisteria covered pergola. Vegetable garden, camellia and azalea bank, wildflower woodland. Many rare shrubs and plants incl *Embothrium, Eucryphia* and *Hoheria.*

21 PENTRESITE
Rhydargaeau Road, Carmarthen, SA32 7AJ. Gayle & Ron Mounsey, 01267 253928, gayle.mounsey@gmail.com. *4m N of Carmarthen. Take A485 heading N out of Carmarthen, once out of village of Peniel take 1st R to Horeb & cont for 1m. Turn R at NGS sign, 2nd house down lane.* **Sun 9 July (2-5). Adm £3.50, chd free. Home-made teas. Visits also by arrangement June to Sept.**
1¼ acre garden developed over the last 7yrs with extensive lawns, colour filled herbaceous and mixed borders, on several levels. A bog garden and magnificent views of the surrounding countryside. S-facing, catching the south westerly winds. Steep in places but possible for wheelchairs.

22 ◆ PICTON CASTLE & GARDENS
The Rhos, Haverfordwest, Pembrokeshire, SA62 4AS. Picton Castle Trust, 01437 751326, info@pictoncastle.co.uk, www.pictoncastle.co.uk. *3m E of Haverfordwest. On A40 to Carmarthen, signed off main rd.* **For NGS: Sun 21 May, Sun 11 June (10-5). Adm £7, chd £4. Lunches and teas at Maria's Courtyard Restaurant. For other opening times and information, please phone, email or visit garden website.**
Mature 40 acre woodland garden with unique collection of rhododendrons and azaleas, many bred over 42yrs, producing hybrids of great merit and beauty; rare and tender shrubs and trees incl *Magnolia*, myrtle, *Embothrium* and *Eucryphia.* Wild flowers abound. Walled garden with roses; fernery; herbaceous and climbing plants and large clearly labelled collection of herbs. Exciting art exhibitions and a wide range of seasonal events. Visit Maria's@Picton - our famous Spanish influenced restaurant. Some woodland walks unsuitable for wheelchair users.

Treffgarne Hall

23 ROSEWOOD

Redberth, Nr Tenby, Pembrokeshire, SA70 8SA. Jan & Keith Treadaway, 01646 651405, keithatredberth@btinternet.com.
3m WSW of Kilgetty. On W side of village on old A477, now bypassed. Parking in field opp if dry, or on verge by side of rd if wet. **Visits by arrangement Mar to Sept. Please request refeshments when booking. Adm £3.50, chd free.**
Intimate well maintained ¼ acre garden, cleverly designed in different areas with long season of interest. Abundant colourful mixed plantings with many exotic species and a collection of clematis in bloom all yr, but especially in summer. There is a pergola with clematis and other climbers, as well as a good collection of Hemerocallis, grasses and ferns. A pond and bog garden were added in 2016. Featured in local press. Partial wheelchair access.

&. ✳ 🚐 ☕

24 SCULPTORS GARDEN, THE OLD POST OFFICE

Ffarmers, Llanwrda, Carmarthenshire, SA19 8LQ. Mr Martin & Mrs Angela Farquharson-Duffy, www. farquharsonduffysculpture.com.
7m SE of Lampeter, 8m NW of Llanwrda. Turning to Ffarmers village off A482, garden in centre of village opp Drovers Arms PH. **Sun 25 June (2-6). Combined adm with Bwlchau Duon £5, chd free. Home-made teas.**
A compact courtyard garden with formal and informal planting on different levels, which has been created to form a backdrop for the garden sculptures created by the owners. Formal structured planting; herbaceous borders and water features, subtly blending into an informal shaded, damp area with a wide variety of ferns, hostas, acers, bamboo and gunnera. Figurative sculpture by international artists for sale with 10% of proceeds to NGS on open day.

25 STABLE COTTAGE

Rhoslanog Fawr, Mathry, Haverfordwest, Pembrokeshire, SA62 5HG. Mr Michael & Mrs Jane Bayliss, 01348 837712, michaelandjane1954@ michaelandjane.plus.com. *Rhoslanog, nr Mathry. Between Fishguard & St David's. Head W on A487 turn R at Square & Compass sign. ½m, past Chris Neale gallery, at hairpin take track L. Stable Cottage on L with block paved drive.* **Visits by arrangement May to Sept, very limited parking, max 5 cars. Refreshments available with prior notice. Adm £2.50, chd free.**
Garden extends to approx ⅓ of an acre. It is divided into several smaller garden types, with a seaside garden, small orchard and wildlife area, scented garden, small vegetable/kitchen garden, and two Japanese areas.

🐕 ✿ 🍵

26 TRADEWINDS

Ffynnonwen, Pen-y-Bont, nr Trelech, Carmarthenshire, SA33 6PX. Stuart & Eve Kemp-Gee. *10m NW of Carmarthen. From A40 W of Carmarthen, take B4298 to Meidrim, then R onto B4299 towards Trelech. After 5m turn R at Tradewinds sign.* **Sun 25 June, Sun 20 Aug (11-5). Adm £3.50, chd free. Home-made teas.**
2½ acre plantsman's garden with abundance of herbaceous perennials, shrubs and trees giving yr-round interest. Mixed borders, natural streams and pond. Picturesque garden in tranquil setting. 100ft grass, 100ft herbaceous and 80ft conifer borders. The arboretum incl *Quercus cerris* 'Argenteovariegata', *Salix fargesii, Catalpa, Decaisnea* plus numerous rhododendrons, azaleas and hydrangeas. Stream banks planted with many moisture loving plants. Many rare and unusual plants to be seen.

✿ 🚌 🍵

27 TREFFGARNE HALL

Treffgarne, Haverfordwest, Pembrokeshire, SA62 5PJ. Martin & Jackie Batty, 01437 741115, bathole2000@aol.com. *7m N of Haverfordwest, signed off A40. Proceed up through village & follow rd round sharply to L, Hall ¼m further on L.* **Sun 30 Apr, Sun 23 July (1-5). Adm £3.50, chd free. Home-made teas. Visits also by arrangement, teas on request when booking.**
Stunning hilltop location with panoramic views: handsome Grade II listed Georgian house (not open) provides formal backdrop to garden of 4 acres with wide lawns and themed beds. A walled garden, with double rill and pergolas, is planted with a multitude of borderline hardy exotics. Also large scale sculptures, summer broadwalk, meadow patch, gravel garden, heather bed and stumpery. Planted for yr-round interest. The planting schemes are the owner's, and seek to challenge the boundaries of what can be grown in Pembrokeshire!

🐕 ✿ 🚌 🍵

28 TY'R MAES

Ffarmers, Carmarthenshire, SA19 8JP. John & Helen Brooks, 01558 650541, johnhelen@ greystones140.freeserve.co.uk. *7m SE of Lampeter. 8m NW of Llanwrda. 1½m N of Pumsaint on A482, opp turn to Ffarmers.* **Sun 6 Aug (1-6). Adm £3.50, chd free. Home-made teas. Visits also by arrangement Apr to Sept, teas on request when booking.**
4 acre garden with splendid views. Herbaceous and shrub beds – formal design, exuberantly informal planting, full of cottage garden favourites and many unusual plants. Arboretum with over 200 types of tree; wildlife and lily ponds; pergola, gazebos, post and rope arcade covered in climbers. Gloriously colourful from early spring till late autumn. Craft, produce, book and jewellery stalls. Some gravel paths.

♿ 🐕 ✿ 🚌 🍵

29 ◆ UPTON CASTLE GARDENS

Cosheston, Pembroke Dock, Pembrokeshire, SA72 4SE. Prue & Stephen Barlow, 01646 689996, info@uptoncastle.com, www.uptoncastlegardens.com. *4m E of Pembroke Dock. 2m N of A477 between Carew & Pembroke Dock. Follow brown signs to Upton Castle Gardens through Cosheston.* **For NGS: Sun 26 Mar (10-4). Adm £4, chd free. Light refreshments. For other opening times and information, please phone, email or visit garden website.**
Lovely location in a tranquil valley leading to the upper reaches of the Cleddau estuary. 35 acres of mature gardens and arboretum; many rare trees and shrubs surrounding the C13 castle (not open) and C12 chapel. Spring flowering incl snowdrops, camellias, magnolias and rhododendrons. Also rose gardens, herbaceous borders, walled kitchen garden, wildflower meadow, woodland walks to estuary. Walk on the Wild Side: Woodland walks funded by C.C.W. and Welsh Assembly Government. Partial wheelchair access.

♿ 🐕 🚌 🚐 🍵

30 NEW VALE FARMHOUSE

Vale Road, Houghton, Milford Haven, Pembrokeshire, SA73 1NW. Mr & Mrs David & Sheila Camplin. *Approx 5m S of Haverfordwest, 1½m N of Cleddau Bridge. Turn off A4067 at Merlins Bridge r'about in H'west towards Burton. Cont until reaching Houghton. If crossing Cleddau Bridge, take 1st R to Burton & cont to Houghton. NGS signs in Houghton.* **Sat 10, Sun 11 June (11-4.30). Adm £3.50, chd free. Cream teas.**
⅓ acre traditional cottage garden with many interesting plants, trees and shrubs. Foliage plants incl ferns and hostas, perennials, roses and clematis offer plenty to enjoy as you wander through this pretty garden. A large pond with bog and wetland plants, wild flower and grassy areas with orchids offer a diverse habitat. A garden with a natural harmonious planting for shape and colour.

✿ 🍵

CEREDIGION

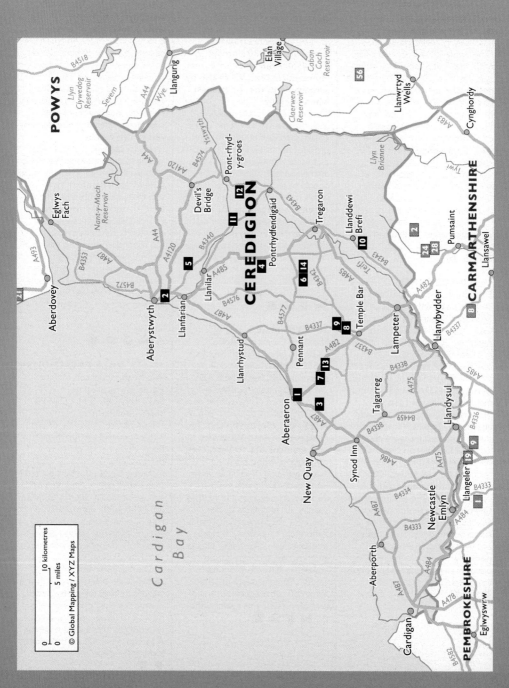

POWYS

CEREDIGION

CARMARTHENSHIRE

PEMBROKESHIRE

Cardigan Bay

Aberdovey

Aberystwyth

Llanfarian

Llanrhystud

Aberaeron

New Quay

Synod Inn

Aberporth

Cardigan

Newcastle Emlyn

Llangeler

Llandysul

Lampeter

Llanybydder

Pennant

Talgarreg

Temple Bar

Tregaron

Llanddewi Brefi

Pontrhydfendigaid

Llanilar

Devil's Bridge

Pont-rhyd-y-groes

Llangurig

Eglwys Fach

Elan Village

Llanwrtyd Wells

Cynghordy

Pumsaint

Llansawel

Eglwyswrw

Nant-y-Moch Reservoir

Llyn Clywedog Reservoir

Cabon Coch Reservoir

Claerwen Reservoir

Llyn Brianne

Severn

Wye

Ystwyth

Tywi

Teifi

0   10 kilometres
0   5 miles
© Global Mapping / XYZ Maps

Ceredigion is a rural county and the second most sparsely populated in Wales.

Much of the land is elevated, particularly towards the east of the county. There are steep-sided wooded valleys, fast flowing rivers and streams, acres of moorland and a dramatic coast line with some lovely sandy beaches. From everywhere in the county there are breath taking views of the Cambrian Mountains and from almost everywhere views of the sea and glimpses of the stunning Cardigan Bay are visible.

The gardens in Ceredigion reflect this natural beauty and sit comfortably in the rugged scenery. There are some gardens that have been created with great imagination and enterprise from the barren water-soaked moorland, others have sensitively enhanced and embellished steep stony hillsides. Rhododendrons, azaleas and camellias thrive in the acid soil, and from April till June the gardens are awash with their bright jewel-like blossoms.

We have two gardens which are particularly family-friendly; both Bwlch y Geuffordd and Ty Glyn Walled Garden will provide children of all ages with hours of fun and adventure. There are a number of dedicated vegetable growers, you can see the fruits of their labours in the allotments in Aberaeron and Aberystwyth and at Sky's Garden Nursery. In one small hilly, rock-strewn county, it is surprising how different the gardens are from each other, yet they have one thing in common; they are all created and tended with love, care and imagination.

Volunteers

County Organiser
Pat Causton
01974 272619
pat.causton@ngs.org.uk

County Treasurer
Steve Yeomans
01974 299370
s.j.yeomans@btinternet.com

Assistant County Organisers
Gay Acres
01974 251559
gayacres@aol.com

Lisa Raw-Rees
01545 570107
hywelrawrees@hotmail.com

Below: **Penybont**

OPENING DATES

All entries subject to change. For latest information check **www.ngs.org.uk**

Map locator numbers are shown to the right of each garden name.

February
Snowdrop Festival

Sunday 12th
◆ Ty Glyn Walled
Garden   13

May

Sunday 14th
Bwlch y Geuffordd   5

Sunday 21st
Ysgoldy'r Cwrt   14

90th Anniversary Weekend

Saturday 27th
Penybont   11

Sunday 28th
Arnant House   3
Penybont   11

Monday 29th
Penybont   11

June

Sunday 4th
NEW Cwrt Mawr
Garden   6

Thursday 22nd
◆ Llanerchaeron   7

Sunday 25th
Aberystwyth Allotments 2

July

Sunday 2nd
Ysgoldy'r Cwrt   14

Sunday 9th
Pantyfod   10

Sunday 30th
NEW Sky's Garden
Nursery   12

August

Sunday 6th
◆ Ty Glyn Walled
Garden   13

Sunday 20th
NEW Aberaeron
Allotments   1

By Arrangement

Arnant House   3
Bwlch y Geuffordd
Gardens   4
Llanllyr   8
Llwynbrain   9
Penybont   11
Ysgoldy'r Cwrt   14

LLanllyr

THE GARDENS

ALLOTMENTS

1 NEW ABERAERON ALLOTMENTS

Cae Ffynon Wyn, Dol Heulog, Aberaeron, SA46 0FP. Diana Mace. *In Aberaeron just off A482. Leave Aberaeron on A482 (towards Lampeter). At Vicarage Hill follow signs on R for Dol Heulog Lane.* Sun 20 Aug (10.30-6). Adm £3, chd free. Home-made teas.

Established in 2008. In the heart of Aberaeron our allotment site is situated on a gentle slope in a lovely wooded setting next to the R Aeron. We have 17 plots growing vegetables, soft fruit and flowers. Glasshouses, poly tunnels. Freshly harvested produce available with donations. For more information contact Diana Mace 07727 124218. Paved road to entrance of allotment site but inside there are grass paths.

&. 🍲

2 ABERYSTWYTH ALLOTMENTS

Caeffynnon, Penparcau, Aberystwyth, SY23 1RE. Ceredigion County Council. *On S side of R Rheidol on Aberystwyth by-pass. From N or E, take A4120 between Llanbadarn & Penparcau. Cross bridge then take 1st R into Minyddol. Allotments ¼m on R.* Sun 25 June (1-5). Adm £3.50, chd free. Home-made teas.

Group of 27 plots in lovely setting alongside R Rheidol close to Aberystwyth. Wide variety of produce grown, vegetables, soft fruit, top fruit, flowers. Sample tastings from allotment produce. Grass and gravel paths.

&. 🐄 🍲

3 ARNANT HOUSE

Llwyncelyn, Aberaeron, SA46 0HF. Pam & Ron Maddox, 01545 580083. *On A487, 2m S of Aberaeron. Next to Llwyncelyn Village Hall. Parking in lay-by opp house.* Sun 28 May (12-5). Adm £3.50, chd free. Light refreshments.

Also open Penybont. **Visits also by arrangement Apr to Aug.** Garden created 16yrs ago from derelict ground. 1 acre, in Victorian style and divided into rooms and themes. Laburnum arch, wildlife ponds, rotunda and tea house. Wide, long borders full of perennial planting with a good variety of species, numerous statues and oddities to be discovered. Many attractive ornamental shrubs incl acers, magnolias and rhododendrons in May, plus about 50 different types of clematis. Also a good selection of hellebores, primulas and fritillaries. Garden is level, but help may be needed on gravel paths.

&. 🐄 🍲 🚗 🍵

The National Garden Scheme is the largest single funder of the Queen's Nursing Institute

---

4 BWLCH Y GEUFFORDD GARDENS

Bronant, Aberystwyth, SY23 4JD. Mr & Mrs J Acres, 01974 251559, gayacres@aol.com, http://bwlch-y-geuffordd-gardens.myfreesites.net. *12m SE of Aberystwyth, 6m NW of Tregaron off A485. Take turning opp Bronant school for 1½m then L up ½m uneven track.* Visits by arrangement any time but advisable to phone first. Home-made teas available with 24hrs notice. Adm £4.50, chd £1.

1000ft high, 3 acre, constantly evolving wildlife garden featuring a lake and several pools. There are a number of themed gardens, incl Mediterranean, cottage garden, woodland, oriental, memorial and jungle. An adventure garden for children, incl pond dipping and treasure hunt. Plenty of seating.

Unique garden sculptures and buildings, incl a cave, temple, gazebo, jungle hut and willow den. Plus our wonderful Mad Hatters Tea Parties!! Please check website for more details. Featured in Western Mail, Gardeners World magazine. Short listed in Welsh Garden of the Year in Wales On Line.

🍲 🐄 🍵 🚗 🍵

5 BWLCH Y GEUFFORDD

New Cross, Aberystwyth, SY23 4LY. Manuel & Elaine Grande. *4½m SE of Aberystwyth. Off A487, take B4340 to New Cross. Garden 3m from turning on R at bottom of small dip. Park in lay-bys.* Sun 14 May (10.30-5). Adm £3.50, chd free. Home-made teas.

Lovely sloping 1½ acre garden, views of the Cambrian mountains. Embraces it's natural features with different levels, 2 ponds, unusual shade loving plants, borders, bog gardens merging into carefully managed informal areas. Banks of rhododendrons, azaleas. Full of colourful perennials, flowering shrubs, mature trees, bluebells and climbing roses scrambling up the walls of the old stone buildings. Plenty of seating. Partial wheelchair access, some steps and steep paths. Access to lower levels around house.

&. 🐄 🍲 🍵

6 NEW CWRT MAWR GARDEN

Tregaron, Llangeitho, SY25 6QJ. Pauline Gorissen. *From Llangeitho take rd to Aberystwyth past Three Horse Shoe PH. Take 1st L, drive for approx. ½m, Cwrt Mawr entrance is on R.* Sun 4 June (11-5). Adm £4, chd free. Light refreshments.

Beautiful gardens surround a listed Georgian manor in a wonderful rural setting. Centrepiece of the garden is a large stairway, bordered by terraced gardens full of seasonal colour. Newly planted flower beds mix with existing mature areas of rhododendrons, and forest paths wind through ancient woodland. 4 acres of flowing beds, ponds and interesting features make this garden unmissable.

🍲 🍵

7 ◆ LLANERCHAERON
Ciliau Aeron, Lampeter,
SA48 8DG. National
Trust, 01545 573029,
www.nationaltrust.org.uk.
*2½ m E of Aberaeron. On A482
Lampeter to Aberaeron. Brown sign
to Llanerchaeron gardens from
Aberaeron & opp turning off A487.*
For NGS: Evening opening
Thur 22 June (6-9). Adm £3.50,
chd free. Light refreshments.
For other opening times and
information, please phone or visit
garden website.
Llanerchaeron is a small C18 Welsh
gentry estate set in the beautiful
Dyffryn Aeron. The estate survived
virtually unaltered into the 20th
Century. 2 extensive restored
walled gardens produce home
grown vegetables, fruit and herbs
for sale. The kitchen garden sits at
the core of the estate with a John
Nash villa built in 1795 and home
farm, all virtually unaltered since its
construction. Music, refreshments,
plant and produce sales.
&. ✿ ⛟ ⛾

8 LLANLLYR
Talsarn, Lampeter, SA48 8QB. Mr
& Mrs Robert Gee, 01570 470900,
lgllanllyr@aol.com. *6m NW of
Lampeter. On B4337 to Llanrhystud.*
Visits by arrangement Apr to
Oct. Adm £4, chd free. Light
refreshments.
Large early C19 garden on site of
medieval nunnery, renovated and
replanted since 1989. Large pool,
bog garden, formal water garden,
rose and shrub borders, gravel
gardens, laburnum arbour, allegorical

labyrinth and mount, all exhibiting
fine plantsmanship. Yr-round appeal,
interesting and unusual plants.
&. ⛟ ⛾

9 LLWYNBRAIN
Talsarn, Lampeter, SA48 8QD.
Mrs Gillian Boyd, 01570 470557,
gboyd19@gmail.com, www.
ceredigiongrowersassociation.
co.uk. *6m N of Lampeter. 6m S of
Aberaeron. Turn at junction in Talsarn
onto B4342 (signed Llangeitho).
After 400yds turn L into small lane.
Llwynbrain is 500yds on L.* Visits by
arrangement May to Oct. Adm
£3.50, chd free. Tea.
One acre garden incorporating
an acer nursery, (open all year),
prairie border with collection of
grasses and perennials, a small
paddock planted with acers and
other trees. S-facing front garden
with Japanese themed corner area,
and mixed evergreen and perennial
beds with seating area. Artist studio.
Although garden is level, grass paths
makes some parts unsuitable for
wheelchairs if ground is soft.
&. ✿ ⛾

10 PANTYFOD
Llanddewi Brefi, Tregaron,
SY25 6PE. David & Susan Rowe,
www.pantyfodgarden.co.uk. *About
3m S of Tregaron. From Llanddewi
Brefi village square, take R fork
past Community Centre. Go up hill,
past Ffarmers turning on L, cont for
approx ¾ m. Pantyfod is on R.* Sun
9 July (12-6). Adm £4, chd free.
Home-made teas. Authentic
Italian pizzas cooked to order
in a wood-fired oven.

Peaceful well established 3½ acre
garden with lots of pathways
through a wide variety of perennials,
trees and shrubs, many unusual.
Varying habitats incl terraces,
woodland, mature trees, natural
ponds. Hardy geraniums, candelabra
primulas, Iris sibirica, grasses, rugosa
roses. Wildlife friendly. Stunning,
panoramic views of the Teifi Valley
and mountains beyond. Partial
wheelchair access due to gravel
paths, slopes and steps.
&. ✿ ⛾

11 PENYBONT
Llanafan, Aberystwyth,
SY23 4BJ. Norman & Brenda
Jones, 01974 261737,
blakeley@graphics.wanadoo.co.uk.
*9m SW of Aberystwyth. In Ystwyth
valley off B4340. From Aberystwyth,
stay on B4340 for 9m via Trawscoed.
R over stone bridge. ¼ m up hill,
turn R past row of cream houses.*
Sat 27, Sun 28, Mon 29 May
(11-5). Adm £3.50, chd free.
Light refreshments. Visits also
by arrangement May to Aug,
please phone or email first.
Penybont shows what can be
achieved from a green field sloping
site in just a few years. This exciting
and beautifully planted garden has
been designed to compliment the
modern building, its forest backdrop
and panoramic views. Country
location with stunning views of the
Ystwyth valley. Level around house,
but sloping ground, gravel paths and
lawn make much of garden difficult
for wheelchairs.
&. ⛾

**12 NEW SKY'S GARDEN
NURSERY**
Ysbyty Ystwyth, Ystrad
Meurig, Ceredigion,
SY25 6DB. Nathan Coates,
www.skysgardennursery.com. *On
unclassified road off B4343 just S of
Ysbyty Ystwyth. When approaching
Ysbyty Ystwyth from N on B4343,
take 1st R at end of village opp
housing estate. Sky's garden Nursery
150 metres on R.* Sun 30 July
(11.30-5). Adm £3.50, chd free.
Home-made teas.
Newly established nursery growing
ornamental perennial and bedding

Llanerchaeron

© David Dixon

Ty Glyn Walled Garden

plants, trees, fruit and vegetables. Everything is grown using organic methods and in sympathy with the environment. The growing site covers around 1 acre, but there is also an area of wetland supporting a variety of wildlife. Family-friendly with children's activities. Except for the wet area, grounds are flat so wheelchair access possible.

&. ✿ ☕

13 ◆ TY GLYN WALLED GARDEN

Ciliau Aeron, Lampeter, SA48 8DE. Ty Glyn Davis Trust, 07977 342836, tyglyngardener@yahoo.co.uk, www.tyglyndavistrust.co.uk. *3m SE of Aberaeron. Turn off A482 Aberaeron to Lampeter at Ciliau Aeron signed to Pennant. Entrance 700 metres on L.* For NGS: Sun 12 Feb (12-3). Home-made teas. Sun 6 Aug (1-5). Light refreshments. Adm £3.50, chd

free. For other opening times and information, please phone, email or visit garden website.
Secluded walled garden in beautiful woodland setting alongside R Aeron, developed specifically for special needs children. Terraced kitchen garden overlooks herbaceous borders, orchard and ponds with child orientated features and surprises amidst unusual shrubs and perennials. Planted fruit trees selected from former gardener's notebook of C19. Walled Garden, Children's play area. Refreshments in aid of Ty Hafan Childrens Hospice (Aug). Access paths, lower garden and woodland walk accessible to wheelchairs.

&. ✿ ☕

14 YSGOLDY'R CWRT

Llangeitho, Tregaron, SY25 6QJ. Mrs Brenda Woodley, 01974 821542. *1½ m N of*

Llangeitho. Llangeitho, turn L at school signed Penuwch. Garden 1½ m on R. From Cross Inn take B4577 past Penuwch Inn, R after brown sculptures in field. Garden ¾ m on L. Sun 21 May, Sun 2 July (11-5). Adm £4, chd free. Home-made teas. Visits also by arrangement May to Aug.
1 acre hillside garden, with 4 natural ponds which are a magnet for wildlife plus two new fish ponds. Areas of wildflower meadow, bog, dry and woodland gardens. Established rose walk. Rare trees, large herbaceous beds, acer collection, bounded by a mountain stream, with 2 natural cascades, and magnificent views. New shade bed with acers and azaleas. Large Iris ensata and Iris laevigata collections in a variety of colours. Steeply sloping ground.

✿ 🚗 ☕

GLAMORGAN

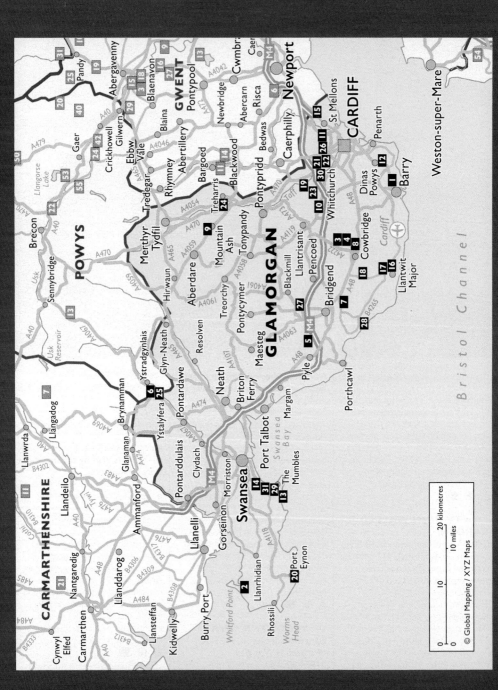

Glamorgan is a large county stretching from the Brecon Beacons in the north to the Bristol Channel in the south, and from the city of Cardiff in the east to the Gower Peninsula in the west. The area has a natural divide where the hills rise from the vale in a clear line of demarcation.

There are gardens opening for the NGS throughout the county, and in recent years the number of community openings has greatly increased and have been very successful.

A number of gardens open in villages or suburbs, often within walking distance of each other, providing a very pleasant afternoon for the visitors. Each garden has its own distinct character and the locality is full of hospitality and friendliness.

Gardens range from Mediterranean-style to gardens designed to encourage wildlife. Views from our coastal gardens are truly spectacular.

Our openings start around Easter with a woodland and spring bulbs garden and continue through to mid-September.

So just jump in the car – *Gardens to Visit* book in hand – and head west on the M4. The gardens in Wales are waiting for you!

Volunteers

County Organiser
Rosamund Davies
01656 880048
ros@sladewoodgarden.plus.com

County Treasurer
Trevor Humby
02920 512709
humbyt@cardiff.ac.uk

Publicity
Sara Bentley
02920 512709
sarajanebentley@googlemail.com

Booklet Co-ordinator
Lesley Sherwood
02920 890055
lesleywheeler@btinternet.com

Assistant County Organisers
Sol Blytt Jordens
01792 391676
solinge22@yahoo.co.uk

Frances Bowyer
02920 892264
frances5860@icloud.com

Melanie Hurst
01446 773659
melanie@hurstcreative.co.uk

Ceri Macfarlane
01792 404906
ceri@mikegravenor.plus.com

Left: The Old Post Office

OPENING DATES

All entries subject to change. For latest information check **www.ngs.org.uk**

Map locator numbers are shown to the right of each garden name.

April

Saturday 15th
Slade   28

Sunday 16th
Slade   28

May

Sunday 14th
9 Willowbrook
Gardens   31

Sunday 21st
19 Slade Gardens   29

Tuesday 23rd
◆ Bordervale Plants   3

90th Anniversary Weekend

Sunday 28th
NEW 110 Heritage
Park   15
Knightsbridge   16
The Old Post Office   19

Monday 29th
NEW 110 Heritage
Park   15
The Old Post Office   19

June

Saturday 3rd
Pontygwaith Farm   24

Sunday 4th
Creigiau Village
Gardens   10
Llanmaes Gardens   17
89 Pen y Dre   21
Pontygwaith Farm   24

Saturday 10th
NEW 4 Clyngwyn Road   6
Rhos y Bedw   25

Sunday 11th
NEW 4 Clyngwyn Road   6
Corntown Gardens   7
Llysworney Gardens   18
Rhos y Bedw   25

July

Tuesday 13th
◆ Bordervale Plants   3

Sunday 18th
Cefn Cribwr Garden
Club   5
Pentyrch Gardens
in June   23

Sunday 25th
Cyncoed and Penylan
Gardens   11
Overton and Port
Eynon Gardens   20

July

Saturday 1st
Dinas Powys   12

Sunday 2nd
Dinas Powys   12
Ty George Thomas   30

Sunday 9th
◆ Bordervale Plants   3

Sunday 16th
Big House Farm   2
Creigiau Village
Gardens   10
Rhydypenau
Allotments   26

Sunday 23rd
NEW 50 Pen y Dre   22

July (continued)

Saturday 29th
47 Aneurin Road   1

Sunday 30th
47 Aneurin Road   1
The Dingle   13

August

Sunday 6th
Knightsbridge   16

Monday 28th
◆ Bordervale Plants   3

September

Sunday 3rd
Rose Cottage   27

By Arrangement

Bryn-y-Ddafad   4
NEW The Corrie   8
The Cottage   9
The Dingle   13
16 Hendy Close   14
Pontygwaith Farm   24
Sydney House Farm,
Llysworney Gardens   18
9 Willowbrook
Gardens   31

THE GARDENS

1 47 ANEURIN ROAD

Barry, CF63 4PP. Dave Bryant. *Barry Town. Head to Barry Police Station & YMCA HUB on Gladstone Rd then follow yellow NGS signs.* **Sat 29, Sun 30 July (12-6). Adm by donation. Light refreshments.** Small town front garden with an ever changing canvas reflecting the seasons and flowering cycle of a wide and varied arrangement of plants, grown in containers and hanging baskets. A vertical arranged garden with substantial collections of clematis, fuchsias and geraniums and begonia's.

 ✿ ☕

2 BIG HOUSE FARM

Llanmadoc, Gower, Swansea, SA3 1DE. Mark & Sheryl Mead.

15m W of Swansea. M4 J47, L A483 for Swansea, 2nd r'about R, A484 Llanelli 3rd r'about L, B4296 Gowerton T-lights, R B4295, pass Bury Green R to Llanmadoc. **Sun 16 July (1-5.30). Adm £4.50, chd free. Home-made teas.** Award winning inspirational garden of just under an acre combines colour form and texture in this beautiful much loved Gower village, described by one visitor as 'the best I've seen this season'. Large variety of interesting plants and shrubs, with ambient cottage garden feel, Victorian glasshouse with rose garden pottager, beautiful views over the stunning surrounding area. Located on the Gower Peninsular, Britain's first designated Area of Outstanding Natural Beauty. Featured on TV and in Garden News. Majority of garden accessible to wheelchairs.

♿ 🐄 🚗 ☕ ☕

3 ◆ BORDERVALE PLANTS

Sandy Lane, Ystradowen, Cowbridge, CF71 7SX. Mrs Claire Jenkins, 01446 774036, bordervaleplants@gmail.com, www.bordervale.co.uk. *8m W of Cardiff. 10 mins from M4 or take A4222 from Cowbridge. Turn at Ystradowen postbox, then 3rd L & proceed ½ m, follow brown signs. Garden on R. Parking in rd.* **For NGS: Tue 23 May, Tue 13 June, Sun 9 July, Mon 28 Aug (11-4). Adm £3, chd free. For other opening times and information, please phone, email or visit garden website.** Within mature woodland valley (semi-tamed), with stream and bog garden, extensive mixed borders; mini wildflower meadow, providing diverse wildlife habitats. Children must be supervised. The Nursery specialises in unusual perennials and cottage garden plants. Nursery open: Fri - Sun (10-5), (and often open Mon - Thurs) Mar - Sept, when garden is also open mid May - Sept. Not for NGS. Awarded Silver Gilt Medal (for category) RHS Flower Show Cardiff. Wheelchair access to top third of garden as well as Nursery.

4 BRYN-Y-DDAFAD

Welsh St Donats, Cowbridge, CF71 7ST. Glyn & June Jenkins, 01446 774451, junejenkins@bydd.co.uk, www.bydd.co.uk/garden. *10m W of Cardiff. 3m E of Cowbridge. From A48 follow signs to Welsh St Donats village (for SatNav use CF71 7SS). Follow brown tourist signs from Xrds, Bryn-y-Ddafad is approx 1m from here.* **Visits by arrangement May to Sept, groups 8+. Adm £4.50, chd free. Home-made teas.**
A mature garden developed by the present owners from an overgrown state over a period of 40yrs. Areas of unusual plantings give interest through the seasons. Terraced rear garden, mature trees, numerous flowering shrubs and roses. Lily pond, pergola of clematis and wisteria, leading to a bridge crossing the natural stream and bog garden. To the front of the house is a raised courtyard garden. Most of garden accessible by wheelchair.

77 Gefn Road, Gefn Cribwr Garden Group

GROUP OPENING

5 CEFN CRIBWR GARDEN CLUB

Cefn Cribwr, Bridgend, CF32 0AP. *5m W of Bridgend on B4281.* **Sun 18 June (11-5). Combined adm £4.50, chd free. Light refreshments.**

6 BEDFORD ROAD
Carole & John Mason.

13 BEDFORD ROAD
Mr John Loveluck.

2 BRYN TERRACE
Alan & Tracy Birch.

CEFN CRIBWR GARDEN CLUB ALLOTMENTS
Cefn Cribwr Garden Club.

CEFN METHODIST CHURCH

77 CEFN ROAD
Peter & Veronica Davies & Mr Fai Lee.

25 EAST AVENUE
Mr & Mrs D Colbridge.

15 GREEN MEADOW
Tom & Helen.

6 TAI THORN
Mr Kevin Burnell.

Cefn Cribwr is an old mining village atop a ridge with views to Swansea in the west, Somerset to the south and home to Bedford Park and the Cefn Cribwr Iron Works. The village hall is at the centre with teas, cakes and plants for sale. The allotments are to be found behind the hall. Children, art and relaxation are just some of the themes to be found in the gardens besides the flower beds and vegetables. There are also water features, fish ponds, wildlife ponds, summerhouses and hens adding to the diverse mix. Themed colour borders, roses, greenhouses, recycling, composting and much more. The chapel grounds are peaceful with a woodland trail meandering off. There will also be craft stalls, games, raffles and a table top sale in the hall.

6 NEW 4 CLYNGWYN ROAD

Ystalyfera, Swansea, SA9 2AE.
Paul Steer, www.artinacorner.
blogspot.com. *Follow NGS signs
from Rhos y Bedw (combined
opener).* **Sat 10, Sun 11 June
(12-5). Combined adm with
Rhos y Bedw £3.50, chd free.
Light refreshments.**
The Coal Tip Cloister Garden is
a small personal space created in
order to help us unwind from our
work as nurses. Its main character
is enclosure and a sense of rest. It is
not a flowery garden but is formed
out of shrubs and trees - forming
a tapestry of hedging with arches
and niches being cut out in order
to place seats and sculpture and to
produce a visual rhythm.
  ♿ 🐕 ☕

GROUP OPENING

7 CORNTOWN GARDENS

Corntown, Bridgend, CF35 5BB.
*Take B4265 from Bridgend to
Ewenny. Take L in Ewenny on B4525
to Corntown follow yellow NGS signs
. From A48 take B4525 to Corntown.*
**Sun 11 June (11-4). Combined
adm £3.50, chd free. Home-
made teas.**

RHOS GELER

Bob Priddle & Marie D Robson.

Y BWTHYN

Mrs Joyce Pegg.

Y Bwythyn has had over 30yrs of
hard labour, some guesswork and
considerable good luck resulting
in a delightful garden. The area at
the front of the house is a mixture
of hot colour combinations whilst
at the rear of this modest sized
garden the themes are of a more
traditional cottage garden style
which incl colour themed borders
as well as soft fruit, herbs and
vegetables. Rhos Geler's garden has
a lavender hedge at the front and
subjects to attract butterflies. The
main garden area at the back of
the house is a long narrow garden
that is in a series of themed areas.
These incl an herbaceous border,
shade loving plants, an Elizabethan
style knot garden and a Japanese

influenced area. Containers hold a
range of subjects incl a collection
of sempervivums. As well as the
garden, visitors to Rhos Geler
are invited to view the owners
extensive collections. These incl
advertising tins, welsh studio pottery
and items connected with the
American Cowboy.
❀ ☕

8 NEW THE CORRIE

Pen-Y-Lan Road, Aberthin,
Cowbridge, CF71 7HB.
Jean Baker, 01446 773325,
jean@bakerlite.co.uk. *From
Cowbridge take A4222 Llantrisant Rd
to Aberthin. At sharp bend in Aberthin,
before Hare & Hounds, turn R then
immed R up Pen-y-Lan Rd. The Corrie
is 200 yrds on R. Limited on site
parking.* **Visits by arrangement
May to Sept. Adm £3, chd free.
Light refreshments.**
N-facing hillside garden on several
levels bordering open countryside.
Developed over the last 15yrs
by the keen plantaholic owner. It
incl herbaceous borders, S-facing
patio, woodland area with fernery.
There is also a small elevated front
garden with rockery. Large variety of
interesting plants and shrubs.

9 THE COTTAGE

Cwmpennar, Mountain Ash,
CF45 4DB. Helen & Hugh
Jones, 01443 472784,
hhjones1966@yahoo.co.uk.
*18m N of Cardiff. A470 from N or
S. Then follow B4059 to Mountain
Ash. Follow signs for Cefnpennar
then turn R before bus shelter
into village of Cwmpennar.* **Visits
by arrangement May to July,
groups 15 max. Adm £4, chd
free. Home-made teas.**
4 acres and 40yrs of amateur
muddling have produced what it
is hoped is an interesting garden
incl bluebell wood, rhododendron
and camellia shrubbery, herbaceous
borders, rose garden, small
arboretum, many uncommon trees
and shrubs. Garden slopes NE/SW.
❀ ☕

*National Garden
Scheme support
helps raise
awareness of
unpaid carers*

GROUP OPENING

10 CREIGIAU VILLAGE GARDENS

Maes Y Nant, Creigiau, CF15 9EJ.
*W of Cardiff (J34 M4). From M4
J34 follow A4119 to T-lights, turn R
by Castell Mynach PH, pass through
Groes Faen & turn L to Creigiau.
Follow NGS signs.* **Sun 4 June (2-5);
Sun 16 July (11-5). Combined
adm £5, chd free. Home-made
teas at 28 Maes-y-Nant and
Waunwyllt.**

28 MAES Y NANT

Mike & Lesley Sherwood.
Open on all dates

31 MAES Y NANT

Frances Bowyer.
Open on Sun 16 July

50 PARC-Y-BRYN

Bryan & Jan Thomas.
Open on Sun 4 June

PENYBRYN

Jen MacDonald.
Open on Sun 4 June

WAUNWYLLT

John Hughes & Richard Shaw.
Open on all dates

On the NW side of Cardiff and
with easy access from the M3 J34,
Creigiau Village Gardens incl five
vibrant and innovative gardens.
Each quite different, they combine
some of the best characteristics
of design and planting for modern
town gardens with the naturalism

of old fashioned cottage gardens. Each has its own forte; at Waunwyllt it is what has been achieved over 6yrs and the coloured themed rooms. At 28 Maes y Nant, cottage garden pastoralism reigns. This is in complete contrast to the strong architecture of 31 Maes y Nant, where the design coordinates water, the garden room and planting, incl a small scale prairie. Pen y Bryn is a large garden with colourful planting and incl a kitchen vegetable plot. 50 Parc y Bryn is planted for yr-round colour, and incl a greenhouse housing an amazing cacti and succulent display. Anyone looking for ideas for a garden in an urban setting will not go away disappointed; enjoy a warm welcome, home-made teas and plant sales.

✿ ☕ ♥

GROUP OPENING

11 CYNCOED AND PENYLAN GARDENS

Cyncoed, Cardiff, CF23 6SW. *From Hollybush Rd follow yellow NGS signs to Cyncoed Crescent & Danycoed Rd. 7 Cressy Rd is off Marlborough Rd, Penylan.* Sun 25 June (2-6). Combined adm £3.50, chd free. Home-made teas.

7 CRESSY ROAD
Victoria Thornton.

8 CYNCOED CRESCENT
Alistair & Teresa Pattillo.

22 DAN Y COED ROAD
Alan & Miranda Workman.

KINSLEY, 3 LLYSWEN ROAD
Ms Jill Davey.

This is a group of four, 1930's suburban gardens. Each one has its own individual style. They have been designed by the owners and are continually evolving to create an eclectic collection of climber, perennials and shrubs that reflect the interests of these gardeners. Garden structures and summerhouses are used to add interest and to create different viewpoints over the gardens. All are within walking distance from

each other except Penylan, which is a 5 mins drive away. Partial wheelchair access only.

🦽 ✿ ☕

GROUP OPENING

12 DINAS POWYS

Dinas Powys, CF64 4TL. *Approx 6m SW of Cardiff. Exit M4 at J33, follow A4232 to Leckwith, onto B4267 & follow to Merry Harrier T-lights. Turn R & enter Dinas Powys. Follow yellow NGS signs.* Sat 1, Sun 2 July (11-5). Combined adm £5, chd free. Home-made teas. *Donation to Dinas Powys Voluntary Concern.*

1 ASHGROVE
Sara Bentley, 02920 512709, sarajanebentley@gmail.com.
Open on all dates
🛏

BROOKLEIGH
Duncan & Melanie Syme.
Open on all dates

32 LONGMEADOW DRIVE
Julie Barnes.
Open on Sun 2 July

NIGHTINGALE COMMUNITY GARDENS
Mr Keith Hatton.
Open on all dates

THE POUND
Helen & David Parsons.
Open on all dates

WEST CLIFF
Jackie Hurley & Alan Blakoe.
Open on all dates

An inspiring and eclectic group of 6 gardens in this small friendly village, all with something different to offer. Attractions incl a garden based on permaculture principles, using perennials, shrubs and edibles together. There are ponds of all sizes and styles, planting in shade and sun, boggy areas, pergolas, child friendly attractions, mature shrubs and trees, vegetables and fruit, challenging terraced designs and wild areas. Plus we have our community gardens opening with lovely displays of vegetable and fruit. Our village church, St Peters, is also opening with displays of flowers, classic cars and other attractions. Lovely home-made teas will be served, incl gluten free options; wine served at Brookleigh. There are many restful and beautiful areas to sit and relax. Plant sales are also an attraction. Good wheelchair access at the community gardens. Partial access elsewhere.

🦽 ✿ ☕

4 Clyngwyn Road

13 THE DINGLE

Caswell, Swansea, SA3 4RT. Paul & Linda Griffiths, 01792 904420, the.spinney@hotmail.com. *4m W Swansea. Swansea A4067 to Mumbles. Mini r'bout in Mumbles R B4593 L at 2nd T-lights pass Church then follow yellow NGS signs. Park in Caswell Drive (road just before ours) or local public car parks.* **Sun 30 July (1.30-6). Adm £4, chd free. Tea. Visits also by arrangement Apr to Sept for groups 10+, please call or email.**

The Dingle is a secret garden in Caswell registered as a Historic Garden of Wales by CADW in 2015. We have spent the last 10yrs restoring the garden that was unmanaged for 50yrs and totally overgrown - it resembled a jungle. Today the garden is a real treasure.

14 16 HENDY CLOSE

Derwen Fawr, Swansea, SA2 8BB. Peter & Wendy Robinson, 07773 711973, robinsonpete1@hotmail.co.uk. *Approx 3m W of Swansea. A4067 Mumbles Rd follow sign for Singleton Hospital. Then R onto Sketty Lane at mini r'about, turn L then 2nd R onto Saunders Way. Follow yellow NGS signs. Please park on Saunders Way if possible.* **Visits by arrangement May to Sept, groups 10+. Adm £6 incl tea/coffee and slice of home-made cake.**

Originally the garden was covered with 40ft conifers. Cottage style, some unusual and mainly perennial plants which provide colour in spring, summer and autumn. Hopefully the garden is an example of how to plan for all seasons. Visitors say it is like a secret garden because there are a number of hidden places. Plants to encourage all types of wildlife in to the garden.

15 NEW 110 HERITAGE PARK

St Mellons, Cardiff, CF3 0DS. Sarah Boorman. *Leave A48 at St Mellons junction, take 2nd exit at r'about. Turn R to Willowdene Way & R to Willowbrook Drive. Heritage Park is 1st R. Park outside the cul-de-sac.* **Sun 28, Mon 29 May (11-5). Adm £3.**

An unexpected gem within a modern housing estate. Evergreen shrubs, herbaceous borders, box topiary and terracotta pots make for a mix between cottage garden and Italian style. With numerous seating areas and a few quirky surprises this small garden is described by neighbours as a calm oasis.

16 KNIGHTSBRIDGE

21 Monmouth Way, Boverton, Llantwit Major, CF61 2GT. Don & Ann Knight. *At Llanmaes rd T-lights turn onto Eagleswell Rd, next L into Monmouth Way, garden halfway down on R.* **Sun 28 May, Sun 6 Aug (11-5). Adm £3, chd free. Home-made teas.**

This is a Japanese garden with a Zen gate, Torri gate and Japanese lanterns featuring a large collection of Japanese style trees, which incl an English elm, oak, larch etc., a pagoda and 3 water features which incl the great Amazon waterfall along with large Buddha's head and new pond. Wheelchair access via rear garden.

GROUP OPENING

17 LLANMAES GARDENS

Llanmaes, Llantwit Major, CF61 2XR. *5m S of Cowbridge. From Mehefin & West Winds travel to Church via Gadlys Farm House & on to Brown Lion House, cont down lane for 1km to Old Froglands.* **Sun 4 June (12-5). Combined adm £5, chd free. Light refreshments at Old Froglands & Mehefin.**

Rhos y Bedw

BROWN LION HOUSE
Mrs Wendy Hewitt-Sayer.
🅓

GADLYS FARM HOUSE
Dot Williams.

MEHEFIN
Mrs Alison Morgan,
01446 793427,
bb@mehefin.com,
www.mehefin.com.
🛏

OLD FROGLANDS
Dorne & David Harris.

NEW WESTWINDS
Ms Jackie Simpson.

Llanmaes, 1m from Llantwit Major, is a pretty village with attractive village green, stream running through and C13 church. Old Froglands is an historic farmhouse with streams and woodland areas linked by bridges. Ducks swim and chickens roam free. The vegetable plot is now productive. Plantings are varied with interesting foliage. Brown Lion House is a newly renovated garden around mature trees and shrubs with patios and pathways. Gadlys Farm House is 1 acre of informal family garden surrounding a C17 farmhouse. Various sitting areas to relax amongst mature trees, herbaceous borders, summerhouse water feature and courtyard with planters. Mehefin is an enchanting garden with bursts of colour and West Winds a surprise in store!
⛓ ✿ ☕

GROUP OPENING

18 LLYSWORNEY GARDENS
Llysworney, Cowbridge,
CF71 7NQ. *2m SW of Cowbridge. W along A48 passing Cowbridge. Turn L at Pentre Meyrick on B4268 signed Llysworney & Llantwit Major.* **Sun 11 June (2-6). Combined adm £5, chd free. Home-made teas at Brocton House.**

BROCTON HOUSE
Peter & Colette Evans.

THE CHASE
Mr & Mrs David Gibson.

GREAT HOUSE
Mr David Scott-Coombes.

SYDNEY HOUSE FARM
Mrs Liz Rees, 01446 773132.
Visits also by arrangement June to Aug.

WOLF HOUSE
Martyn & Melanie Hurst.

Llysworney is a charming small rural village with church, duck pond children's play area and friendly people! Five gardens will be open. Wolf House has a walled cottage garden on two levels with a variety of perennials and roses. African summer house offers a quiet place to sit and ponder! Great House is C16 Grade II listed with terraced garden and a variety of trees, shrubs and perennials. Brocton House has a pretty terraced garden and large vegetable/fruit garden overlooking farmland with barn and wild flower area. Sydney House Farm is a wilflife friendly garden in over ½ acre bordering countryside. The garden is planted to encourage lots of wildlife. The Chase is a medium size informal garden full of herbaceous perennials, shrubs and roses with all yr-round colour. Refreshments to incl musical entertainment.
✿ ☕

19 THE OLD POST OFFICE
Main Road, Gwaelod-Y-Garth,
Cardiff, CF15 9HJ. Ms Christine Myant. *N of Cardiff nr Radyr & Pentyrch. Garden on L of rd, 4 houses pass PH. Parking in school car park further down hill.* **Sun 28, Mon 29 May (11-5). Adm £3, chd free. Home-made teas.**
Situated in the popular village of Gwaelod-y-Garth on the northern edge of Cardiff this informal terraced garden is entering its more mature stage and provides much to enjoy.
✿ ☕

GROUP OPENING

20 OVERTON AND PORT EYNON GARDENS
Overton Lane, Port Eynon,
Swansea, SA3 1NR. *16.8m W of Swansea on Gower Peninsula. From Swansea follow A4118 to Port Eynon. Parking in public car park in Port Eynon. Yellow NGS signs showing gardens. Maps of gardens locations available at both gardens on entry.* **Sun 25 June (2-5.30). Combined adm £4.50, chd free. Home-made teas at Box Boat Cottage.**

6 THE BOARLANDS
Robert & Annette Dyer.

BOX BOAT COTTAGE
Ms Christine Williams.

Overton offers breathtaking views of the Gower Peninsula. Port Eynon is the most southerly point on the Gower. Set in the heart of Port Eynon, Box Boat Cottage is a delight set with pretty borders and a riot of colour. 6 The Boarlands is a plantman's paradise! A gently sloping garden designed for yr-round interest lots of shrubs bulbs and perennials.
✿ ☕

21 89 PEN Y DRE
Cardiff, CF14 6EL. Lorraine & Emil Nelz. *Well signed from Rhiwbina Village by yellow NGS arrows. From M4 J36 follow directions to Whitchurch, turn L at Whitchurch Golf Club & R at mini r'about to Rhiwbina.* **Sun 4 June (11-5). Adm £3, chd free. Home-made teas.**
Small garden with lots of interesting plants, palms, tree ferns, seasonal perennials. Conservatory with many cacti and succulents. Selection of home-made savouries and cakes available.
⛓ ✿ ☕

22 NEW 50 PEN Y DRE
Rhiwbina, Cardiff, CF14 6EQ. Ann Franklin. *N Cardiff. M4 J32, A470 to Cardiff, 1st L to mini r'about, turn R. At T-lights in village, turn R to Pen-y-Dre.* **Sun 23 July (11-4.30). Adm £3, chd free. Home-made teas.**
Mixed mature borders in cottage garden style with many old favourites incl vegetable plot.
✿ ☕

GROUP OPENING

23 PENTYRCH GARDENS IN JUNE

Pentyrch, Cardiff, CF15 9QD. *2m N of Cardiff. M4 J32 - A470 to Merthyr. After ½m exit signed Taffs Well & Radyr. 1st exit at r'about onto B4262 signed Radyr, Gwaelod & Pentyrch. Next r'about R. Follow yellow NGS signs into Pentyrch.* **Sun 18 June (10.30-5.30). Combined adm £5, chd free. Home-made teas at Maes-y-Gof.**

NEW **1 FIELD TERRACE**
Del & Roma Beard.

9 HEOL Y PENTRE
Chris & Ken Rogers.

NEW **29 HEOL-Y-PENTRE**
Denise & Vince James.

MAES-Y-GOF
Jeanette & Chris Troughton.

SUNNY BANK
Chris & Dave Bilham.

Group of 5 gardens offering something to suit all interests. Maes-y-Gof: Medium sized cottage garden with exuberantly planted herbaceous borders, roses, clematis, ferns and palms. 9 Heol-y-Pentre: Corner plot with perennial borders and acers. Climbers and small gravel garden. Sunny Bank: 200yr old cottage with a wisteria covered veranda, formal terrace and informal garden. Pond with bridge leading to a summerhouse. Tries to be as organic as possible. 29 Heol-t-Pentre: Garden in development around new built house. Herbaceous borders, natural rockery, vegetable and fruit. 1 Field Terrace: A cottage garden being reclaimed from neglect. Newly planted fruit trees, productive vegetable plot, flower beds and seating area.

24 PONTYGWAITH FARM

Edwardsville, nr Treharris, CF46 5PD. Mrs D Cann, 07511 744976. *2m NW of Treharris. N from Cardiff on A470. At r'about take A4054 N towards Aberfan. 1m after Edwardsville turn sharp L by black bus shelter. Garden at bottom of hill.* **Sat 3, Sun 4 June (10-5). Adm £4, chd free. Light refreshments. Visits also by arrangement Apr to Aug, groups 10 max.**
Situated in a picturesque wooded valley is a truly magical garden with a surprise around every corner - New woodland walk, fish pond, perennial borders, vegetable patch, lakeside walk, rose garden, Japanese garden, Grade 2 listed humpback bridge, all surrounding C17 farmhouse adjacent to Trevithick's Tramway. Welcome to visitors on the Taff Trail (April - Sept, 10am - 5pm). Partial wheelchair access due to steep slope to river, gravel paths.

25 RHOS Y BEDW

4 Pen y Wern Rd, Ystalyfera, Swansea, SA9 2NH. Robert & Helen Davies. *13m N of Swansea. M4 J45 take A4067. Follow signs for Dan yr Ogof caves across 5 r'abouts. After T-lights follow yellow NGS signs. Parking above house on rd off to R.* **Sat 10, Sun 11 June (12-5). Combined adm with 4 Clyngwyn Road £3.50, chd free. Home-made teas.**
A haven of peace and tranquility with spectacular views, this glorious compact garden with its amazing array of planting areas is constantly evolving. Our diverse planting areas incl cottage, herb, and bog gardens also an array of roses and a knot garden are sure to provide inspiration. A garden with something different around every corner to be savored slowly, relax and enjoy. Home-made cakes available incl gluten free option.

ALLOTMENTS

26 RHYDYPENAU ALLOTMENTS

Heath Halt Road, Cyncoed, Cardiff, CF23 5QF. City of Cardiff Council. *Behind Heath Halt Rd & Lake Rd N. From M4 J32 go towards City Centre. After 1m look out for Xrds with T-lights & turn L. Cont straight through 2 junctions then turn L.* **Sun 16 July (1-6). Adm £4, chd free. Home-made teas.**
This group of over 100 allotments is a hidden oasis within a Cardiff suburb, with mature trees and bright communal areas and a variety of allotments, growing vegetables, fruit and flowers, one of which was winner of the most recent Cardiff in Bloom - Best Allotment. Plants and some produce available for sale. Most of the site is suitable for wheelchairs. However, entrance from rd is steep. Limited parking within gates.

27 ROSE COTTAGE

32 Blackmill Road, Bryncethin, Bridgend, CF32 9YN. Maria & Anne Lalic, www.marialalic.co.uk. *1m N of M4 J36 on A4061. Follow A4061 to Bryncethin. Straight on at mini r'about for approx 400 metres. Just past Used Car Garage, turn R onto side rd at grassed area.* **Sun 3 Sept (12-5). Adm £3.50, chd free. Home-made teas.**
If you want a proper garden with manicured borders and Latin plant names, Rose Cottage isn't the place for you. If you want to see how jumbled flower beds, a herb yard, seasonal growing of fruit and vegetables, ideas borrowed from Permaculture, NoDig, Companion Planting and old fashioned cottage gardening helps us with our simple, self reliant lifestyle, join us as we celebrate our Harvest. A raised terrace area alongside the conservatory allows viewing of the field where the goats, chickens and ducks graze. Our tea room sells tea, coffee and home-made cakes served on vintage china. Maria leads tours around the garden every 30 mins. Main path and gateways suitable for wheelchairs. Narrower, bark chip paths and grass paths are uneven and care should be taken.

28 SLADE

Southerndown, CF32 0RP. Rosamund & Peter Davies, 01656 880048, ros@sladewoodgarden.plus.com, www.sladeholidaycottages.co.uk.

5m S of Bridgend. M4 J35 Follow A473 to Bridgend. Take B4265 to St. Brides Major. Turn R in St. Brides Major for Southerndown, then follow yellow NGS signs. **Sat 15, Sun 16 Apr (2-5.30). Adm £4, chd free. Home-made teas.**
Set in 8 acres, Slade garden is an unexpected gem with established drifts of spring bulbs and a woodland plant collection. Ponds attract wildlife. The terraced lawns, mature specimen trees, living willow arbours, rose and clematis pergola, orchard and herbaceous borders, create a very natural garden. Extensive views over the Bristol Channel. Heritage Coast wardens will give guided tours of adjacent Dunraven Gardens with slide shows every hour from 2pm. Partial wheelchair access.

29 19 SLADE GARDENS
West Cross, Swansea, SA3 5QP. Norma & Peter Stephen. *5m SW of Swansea. At mini r'about on Mumbles Rd A4067 take 2nd exit (Fairwood Rd), 1st L onto West Cross Lane & follow yellow NGS signs.* **Sun 21 May (2-5). Adm £3, chd free. Home-made teas.**
A small enclosed front and rear garden designed to lead you around its informal planting of over 200 species. A garden to sit in! Narrow paths and steps make access difficult for less mobile visitors.

30 TY GEORGE THOMAS
Whitchurch Hospital Grounds, Park Road, Whitchurch, Cardiff, CF14 7BF. George Thomas Memorial Trust Ltd, www.gthc.org.uk. *Follow M4 to J32. Take A4054 signed Whitchurch. After 1m turn R through gates into Whitchurch Hospital, follow directions to George Thomas Hospice Care.* **Sun 2 July (2-5). Adm £3.50, chd free. Cream teas.**
Hospice garden of some 0.8 acres, designed with patient enjoyment and relaxation in mind. Hosts established trees, shrubs, and planting providing yr-round colour. Wildlife pond stocked with fish and aquatic plants and rock waterfall feature providing comforting sounds with natural woodland as a backcloth. Tended by volunteers, the paths and seating allow easy access for all.

31 9 WILLOWBROOK GARDENS
Mayals, Swansea, SA3 5EB. Gislinde Macpherson, 01792 403268, gislinde@willowgardens.idps. co.uk. *Nr Clyne Gardens. Go along Mumbles Rd to Blackpill. Turn R at Texaco garage up Mails Rd. 1st R along top of Clyne Park, at mini r'about into Westport Ave. 1st L into Willowbrook gardens.* **Sun 14 May (12.30-5). Adm £5, chd free. Home-made teas. Visits also by arrangement May to Sept, groups 25 max. (Min 7 days notice required).**
Informal ½ acre mature garden on acid soil, designed to give natural effect with balance of form and colour between various areas linked by lawns; unusual trees suited to small suburban garden, especially conifers and maples; rock and water garden. Sculptures, ponds and waterfall. Featured in South Wales Evening Post - Bay Magazine.

The Dingle

GWENT

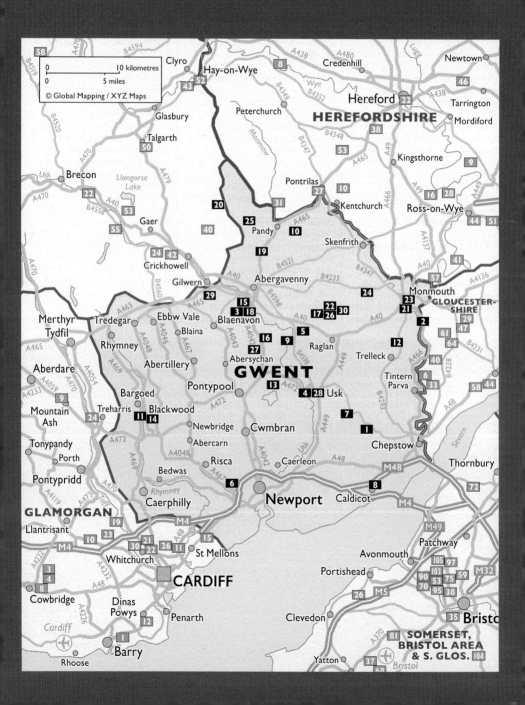

© Global Mapping / XYZ Maps

0 — 10 kilometres
0 — 5 miles

Clyro
Hay-on-Wye
Credenhill
Newtown
Glasbury
Peterchurch
Hereford
Tarrington
HEREFORDSHIRE
Mordiford
Talgarth
Kingsthorne
Brecon
Llangorse Lake
Pontrilas
Ross-on-Wye
Gaer
Pandy
Kentchurch
Crickhowell
Skenfrith
Gilwern
Abergavenny
Monmouth
GLOUCESTER-SHIRE
Merthyr Tydfil
Tredegar
Ebbw Vale
Blaenavon
Blaina
Raglan
Trelleck
Aberdare
Rhymney
Abertillery
Abersychan
Tintern Parva
Mountain Ash
Treharris
Bargoed
Pontypool
GWENT
Usk
Tonypandy
Porth
Blackwood
Newbridge
Cwmbran
Chepstow
Pontypridd
Abercarn
Thornbury
Risca
Caerleon
Bedwas
Caerphilly
Newport
Caldicot
GLAMORGAN
Llantrisant
Patchway
St Mellons
Avonmouth
Whitchurch
Portishead
CARDIFF
Cowbridge
Dinas Powys
Penarth
Clevedon
Bristol
SOMERSET, BRISTOL AREA & S. GLOS.
Barry
Rhoose
Yatton
Bristol

Gwent is a county of contrasts with the lush agricultural valley of the River Usk, a handful of stunning border castles, the wild Black Mountains and some of the old industrial heartlands of the South Wales Valleys.

The small town of Usk sits on either side of the river overlooked by the ruins of Usk Castle. The gardens of the castle gatehouse are partly in these romantic ruins opening with the Usk Open Gardens weekend and 'by arrangement'. Occasionally a cannon is discharged from the ramparts by the owners.

The Black Mountains are wild, sheep farming country with mountain ponies grazing on the tops and small stone farmhouses nestling in the shelter of the valleys.

The landscape of the South Wales Valleys has abundant evidence of the industrial past, and Big Pit National Coal Museum and ironworks in Blaenavon are working examples of this.

History, beauty, wilderness and water are all alive in Gwent.

Volunteers

County Organiser
Joanna Kerr
01873 840422
Joanna@amknet.com

County Treasurer
Ian Mabberley
01873 890219
ian.mabberley@ngs.org.uk

Publicity
Ian Mabberley
(as above)

Joanna Kerr
(as above)

Assistant County Organiser
Cathy Davies
01291 672625
cathy-davies@btconnect.com

Sue Torkington
01873 890045
sue@torkington.myzen.co.uk

Below: Nant y Bedd

OPENING DATES

All entries subject to change. For latest information check **www.ngs.org.uk**

Extended openings are shown at the beginning of the month.

Map locator numbers are shown to the right of each garden name.

April

Sunday 2nd
◆ Dewstow Gardens & Grottoes — 8
Llanover — 16

Sunday 23rd
The Old Vicarage — 22
Woodlands Farm — 30

Sunday 30th
Great Campston — 10
High Glanau Manor — 12

May

Sunday 14th
The Old Vicarage — 22
NEW Tandderwen — 26
Woodlands Farm — 30

90th Anniversary Weekend

Saturday 27th
Hillcrest — 14
Ty Boda — 27

Sunday 28th
Hillcrest — 14
Ty Boda — 27
Wenallt Isaf — 29

Monday 29th
Hillcrest — 14
Ty Boda — 27

June

Castle House
(Every day from Monday 26th to Friday 30th) — 4

Saturday 3rd
NEW The Alma — 1

Sunday 4th
NEW The Alma — 1
Castell Cwrt — 3
Middle Ninfa Farm & Bunkhouse — 18

Sunday 11th
Llanfoist Village Gardens — 15
Rockfield Park — 23

Saturday 17th
Glebe House — 9

Sunday 18th
Glebe House — 9

Saturday 24th
Castle House — 4
Usk Open Gardens — 28

Sunday 25th
Castle House — 4
Usk Open Gardens — 28

Friday 30th
Mione — 19

July

Sunday 2nd
Mione — 19

Friday 7th
Mione — 19

Saturday 8th
14 Gwerthonor Lane — 11

Sunday 9th
Birch Tree Well — 2
14 Gwerthonor Lane — 11
Mione — 19

Sunday 16th
NEW Hill House — 13

Sunday 23rd
Clytha Park — 5
Curlews — 7

Saturday 29th
◆ Nant y Bedd — 20
Tair-Ffynnon, 'The Garden in the Clouds' — 25

Sunday 30th
◆ Nant y Bedd — 20

September

Sunday 3rd
Croesllanfro Farm — 6

Sunday 10th
The Nelson Garden — 21

Saturday 23rd
Longhouse Farm — 17

Sunday 24th
Longhouse Farm — 17

October

Sunday 1st
◆ Dewstow Gardens & Grottoes — 8

Sunday 8th
Castell Cwrt — 3

By Arrangement

Birch Tree Well — 2
Castle House — 4
Croesllanfro Farm — 6
Glebe House — 9
Hillcrest — 14
Llanover — 16
Longhouse Farm — 17
Sunnyside — 24

THE GARDENS

and vegetable garden. Sunny terrace for teas.
🐕 ☕

1 NEW THE ALMA

Bully Hole Bottom, Usk Road, Shirenewton, NP16 6SA. Dr Pauline Ruth. *B4235 Usk to Chepstow signposted Bully Hole Bottom. Down hill over bridge up to T junction. Parking turn L and signposted. Disabled parking straight ahead on track to meadow on L.* **Sat 3, Sun 4 June (11-5.30). Adm £5, chd free. Home-made teas.**
New garden in development. Beautiful sheltered SW facing site previously randomly planted with uncommon trees and acid loving shrubs. Interesting original outbuildings and productive fruit

2 BIRCH TREE WELL

Upper Ferry Road, Penallt, Monmouth, NP25 4AN. Jill Bourchier, gillian.bourchier@btinternet.com. *4m SW of Monmouth. Approx 1m from Monmouth on B4293, turn L for Penallt & Trelleck. After 2m turn L to Penallt. On entering village turn L at Xrds & follow yellow signs.* **Sun 9 July (2-6). Adm £4, chd free. Home-made teas. Visits also by arrangement May to Sept, groups welcome but limited parking.**
Situated in the heart of the Lower Wye Valley, amongst the ancient habitat of woodland, rocks and

streams. These 3 acres are shared with deer, badger and fox. A woodland setting with streams and boulders which can be viewed from a lookout tower and a butterfly garden planted with specialist hydrangeas incl many plants to also attract bees and insects. Live music will be played (harp and cello). Children are very welcome (under supervision) with plenty of activities in the form of treasure hunts. Not all areas of garden suitable for wheelchairs but refreshments certainly are!
♿ ✿ ☕

3 CASTELL CWRT

Llanelen, Abergavenny, NP7 9LE. Lorna & John McGlynn. *1m S of Abergavenny. From Llanfoist B4629* signed Llanelen. ½m R up single track rd. Approx 500yds past canal, garden entrance 2nd on L. Disabled parking. On combined opening day (June) main parking at Castell Cwrt. **Sun 4 June (2-6). Combined adm with Middle Ninfa Farm & Bunkhouse £5, chd free. Sun 8 Oct (2-5). Adm £3.50, chd free. Home-made teas.**

Large informal wildlife friendly, family garden on 10 acre small holding with fine views overlooking Abergavenny. Lawns with established trees, shrubs and perennial borders. Soft fruit and vegetable gardens. Woodland and hay meadow walks, chickens and geese, bees, livestock in fields and family pets. Children very welcome, animals to see and space to let off steam. Farm Shop with own produce. Hay meadow in bloom in June. Some gravel paths.

&. ✿ ▣

4 CASTLE HOUSE
Castle Parade, Usk,
NP15 1SD. Mr & Mrs J H L
Humphreys, 01291 672563,
info@uskcastle.com,
www.uskcastle.com. *200yds NE from Usk centre. Footpath access signed to Usk Castle 300yds E from town square, opp Fire Station. Vehicles 400yds (next L) on Castle Parade in Usk.* **Sat 24 June, Sun 25 June (10-5), also open Usk Open Gardens. Daily Mon 26 June to Fri 30 June (10-5). Adm £4, chd free. Visits also by arrangement throughout the year. Refreshments for groups on request.**

Overlooked by the romantic ruins of Usk Castle which is also open, the gardens were established over 100 years ago, with yew hedges and topiary, long herbaceous border, croquet lawn and pond. The herb garden has plants that would have been used when the castle was last lived in c.1469. Most areas easily accessible to wheelchair users.

&. ⊨ ✿ ⌂ ▣

5 CLYTHA PARK
Abergavenny, NP7 9BW. Sir
Richard Hanbury-Tenison. *Between Abergavenny (5m) & Raglan (3m). On old A40 signed Clytha at r'abouts*

either end. **Sun 23 July (2-5). Adm £5, chd free. Home-made teas.**
Large C18/19 garden around lake with wide lawns and specimen trees, original layout by John Davenport, with C19 arboretum, and H. Avray Tipping influence. Visit the 1790 walled garden and the newly restored greenhouses. Some stalls. Gravel and grass paths.

&. ⊨ ✿ ▣

6 CROESLLANFRO FARM
Groes Road, Rogerstone,
Newport, NP10 9GP. Barry
& Liz Davies, 01633 894057,
lizplants@gmail.com. *3m W of Newport. From M4 J27 take B4591 towards Risca. Take 3rd R, Cefn Walk (also signed 14 Locks Canal Centre). Proceed over bridge, cont ½m to island in middle of rd.* **Sun 3 Sept (1.30-5). Adm £4.50, chd free. Home-made teas. Visits also by arrangement May to Sept for any size group.**

Two acres of informal, mass planted perennial borders. Spring and early summer is a tapestry of green concentrating on leaf form and texture. Late summer and early autumn brings the the garden to a finale with an explosion of colour. A barn stands in a large formal courtyard designed on 6 different levels. Children can explore the folly, grotto and try the treasure hunt! Co-author of Designing Gardens on Slopes. Some gravel paths and shallow steps to main area of garden.

&. ✿ ⌂ ▣

7 CURLEWS
Llangwm, Usk, NP15 1HD. Mr
& Mrs M Hatfield. *5m E of Usk. Midway between Usk (5m) & Chepstow (8m) on B4235. From Usk cont through Llangwm village for 1m.* **Sun 23 July (1-5). Adm £4, chd free. Home-made teas.**
Situated in open Monmouthshire countryside this 1½ acre garden offers delightful changes in perspective from the numerous ways it can be explored. Around a structure of mature trees and shrubs the varied planting reflects the owners wide ranging interest in plants. Recent lifting of tree

canopies, creating a new patio and rose beds has improved the perspective and integrated the whole structure. Plant stall, mature award winning cactus collection and 2 vintage cars. Sandwiches available from 1 to 2 pm only. Gravel paths and slopes so wheelchair access difficult in parts of garden.

&. ⊨ ✿ ▣

8 ◆ DEWSTOW GARDENS & GROTTOES
Caerwent, Caldicot, NP26 5AH.
John Harris, 01291 431020,
www.dewstowgardens.co.uk.
Dewstow House, 6m W of Chepstow. 8m E of Newport. A48 Newport to Chepstow rd, drive into village of Caerwent. Follow brown tourist daisy signs to Gardens. (1½m from Caerwent Village). **For NGS: Sun 2 Apr, Sun 1 Oct (10-4). Adm £6, chd free. Light refreshments. For other opening times and information, please phone or visit garden website.**

5 acre Grade I listed unique garden which was buried and forgotten after World War II and rediscovered in 2000. Created around 1895 by James Pulham & Sons, the garden contains underground grottoes, tunnels and ferneries and above ground stunning water features. You will not be disappointed. Various events throughout the season. No wheelchair access to underground areas. Partial access elsewhere.

&. ✿ ⌂ ▣

Visit a garden
and support
hospice care
in your local
community

9 GLEBE HOUSE

Llanvair Kilgeddin, Abergavenny, NP7 9BE. Mr & Mrs Murray Kerr, 01873 840422, joanna@amknet.com. *Midway between Abergavenny (5m) & Usk (5m) on B4598.* **Sat 17, Sun 18 June (12-6). Adm £5, chd free. Home-made teas. Visits also by arrangement Apr to July.** Summer borders bursting with colours, S-facing terrace, orchard, productive vegetable garden, wildflower meadow. Some topiary and formal hedging in 1½ acre garden set in beautiful Usk valley. Old rectory of St Mary's, Llanvair Kilgeddin which will be open to view famous Victorian Scraffito Murals. Some gravel and gently sloping lawns.

&. ✿ ☕

10 GREAT CAMPSTON

Campston Hill, Pandy, Abergavenny, NP7 8EE. Mr & Mrs C Dunn. *7m NE of Abergavenny. 13m SW of Hereford. 2½m towards Grosmont off A465 at Pandy. Drive on R just before brow of hill. 10m SW of Hereford on A465. Over bridge into Wales, L in Llangua follow rd for 4m. Drive on L.* **Sun 30 Apr (2-6). Adm £4.50, chd free. Home-made teas.** Pretty 3 acres set in wonderful surroundings with far reaching views, on the edge of the Breacon Beacons National Park. Lots of beautiful spring bulbs, wide variety of interesting plants and trees, a woodland walk with magnolias, rhododendrons and camellias, stone walls and summerhouse. Set 750ft above sea level on S-facing hillside with spring fed stream feeding pond. Wheelchair access to lower section of garden only.

✿ ☕

11 14 GWERTHONOR LANE

Gilfach, Bargoed, CF81 8JT. Suzanne & Philip George. *8m N of Caerphilly. A469 to Bargoed. Through T-lights next to School, then L filter lane at next T-lights to turn onto Cardiff Rd. Follow yellow NGS signs.* **Sat 8, Sun 9 July (11-6). Adm £3, chd free. Light refreshments.**

The garden has a beautiful panoramic view of the Rhymney Valley and is in a semi-rural setting. A real plantswoman's garden with over 600 varieties of perennials, annuals, bulbs, shrubs and trees. There are numerous rare and unusual plants combined with traditional and well loved favourites (many available for sale). A pond with a small waterfall adds to the tranquil feel of the garden.

✿ ☕

12 HIGH GLANAU MANOR

Lydart, Monmouth, NP25 4AD. Mr & Mrs Hilary Gerrish. *4m SW of Monmouth. Situated on B4293 between Monmouth & Chepstow. Turn R into Private Rd, ¼m after Craig-y-Dorth turn on B4293.* **Sun 30 Apr (2-6). Adm £6, chd free. Home-made teas.** Listed Arts and Crafts garden laid out by H Avray Tipping in 1922. Original features incl impressive stone terraces with far reaching views over the Vale of Usk to Blorenge, Skirrid, Sugar Loaf and Brecon Beacons. Pergola, herbaceous borders, Edwardian glasshouse, rhododendrons, azaleas, tulips, orchard with wild flowers. Originally open for the NGS in 1927. Garden guide by owner, Helena Gerrish, available to purchase. Featured in Gardener's World and Country Life magazines.

✿ 🚗 ☕

13 NEW HILL HOUSE

Church Lane, Glascoed, Pontypool, NP4 0UA. Susan & John Wright. *Between Usk & Pontypool. Approx 2m W of Usk via A472 turn L before Beaufort Arms into Glascoed Lane. Bear L up hill, Church Lane 1st turn on R. House at very end of narrow lane, do not turn off.* **Sun 16 July (12-5). Adm £4, chd free. Home-made teas.** Developing garden on ex-wasteland around modest farmhouse. Exposed hilltop site, fine views. Small orchard, reflecting pond, herbaceous borders, grasses, farmyard garden with standard parrotia and massed crocosmia, picket beds. Many seats. 30 mins walk through fields, steep

return climb. Some gravel paths. No disabled WC.

&. ☕

14 HILLCREST

Waunborfa Road, Cefn Fforest, Blackwood, NP12 3LB. Mr M O'Leary & Mr B Price, 01443 837029, bev.price@mclweb.net. *3m W of Newbridge. Follow A4048 to Blackwood town centre or A469 to Pengam (Glan-y-Nant) T-lights, then NGS signs.* **Sat 27, Sun 28, Mon 29 May (11-6). Adm £4, chd free. Cream teas. Visits also by arrangement Apr to Oct for groups 30 max. Refreshments on request.** A cascade of secluded gardens of distinct character, all within 1½ acres. Magnificent, unusual trees with interesting shrubs and perennials. With choices at every turn, visitors exploring the gardens are well rewarded as hidden delights and surprises are revealed. Well placed seats encourage a relaxed pace to fully appreciate the garden's treasures. Delicious cream teas to be enjoyed. Trees in their autumnal spendour. Parts of lower garden not accessible to wheelchairs.

&. 🐄 ✿ ☕

GROUP OPENING

15 LLANFOIST VILLAGE GARDENS

Llanfoist, Abergavenny, NP7 9NF. *1m SW of Abergavenny on B4246. Map provided with ticket. Most gardens within easy walking distance of village centre. Follow signs to Village Hall for parking close by.* **Sun 11 June (10-5). Combined adm £5, chd free. Light refreshments at Llanfoist Village Hall.** Make this a great day out. Visit around 15 exciting and contrasting village gardens, large and small, set just below the Blorenge Mountain on the edge of the Black Mountains. A number of new gardens opening along with many regulars. Also Allotments open for the first time. This is our 15th annual event. A variety of refreshments incl home-made cakes not to be missed. Plant stalls selling home grown plants at reasonable prices. St Faith's Parish Church and Llanfoist Allotments also open. Wheelchair access not available at all gardens.

♿ ❀ ⛾

---

16 LLANOVER

nr Abergavenny, NP7 9EF. Mr & Mrs M R Murray, 07753 423635, www.llanovergarden.co.uk. *4m S of Abergavenny, 15m N of Newport, 20m SW Hereford. On A4042 Abergavenny - Pontypool rd, in village of Llanover.* **Sun 2 Apr (2-5). Adm £5, chd free. Home-made teas. Visits also by arrangement Mar to Oct, groups min 15 for tours.** Stunning 15 acre garden laid out in C18. The Rhyd-y-Meirch stream tumbles through ponds and circular walled garden, over cascades and beneath flagstone bridges. Children can run on the lawns, play pooh-sticks along the streams or hide and seek amongst the trees. Home of Llanover Garden School where experienced gardeners share their knowledge. The House (not open) is the birthplace of Augusta Waddington, Lady Llanover, C19 patriot and supporter of the Welsh Language Descendants. The flock of Welsh Black Mountain Sheep which she introduced, can be seen grazing in the park. Historic listed garden laid with a Ha-Ha, circular garden and ponds. Featured in Country Life - Take me to the River by Helena Attlee and RHS The Garden magazine - article by Noel Kingsbury. Gravel and grass paths and lawns. No disabled WC.

♿ 🐇 ❀ ⛾

17 LONGHOUSE FARM

Penrhos, Raglan, NP15 2DE. Mr & Mrs M H C Anderson, 01600 780389, m.anderson666@btinternet.com. *Midway between Monmouth & Abergavenny. 4m from Raglan. Off Old Raglan/Abergavenny rd signed Clytha. At Bryngwyn/Great Oak Xrds turn towards Great Oak - follow yellow NGS signs from red phone box down narrow lane.* **Sat 23, Sun 24 Sept (2-6). Adm £4.50, chd free. Home-made teas. Visits also by**

arrangement May to Oct.
Hidden 2 acre garden with S-facing terrace, collection of pelargoniums, millrace wall, pond and spacious lawns with extensive views. Colourful and unusual plants in the borders, a malus avenue and a recently revamped productive vegetable garden. A woodland walk is being created with a stream, hidden ponds and massed bluebells in spring.

❀ ⛾

18 MIDDLE NINFA FARM & BUNKHOUSE

Llanelen, Abergavenny, NP7 9LE. Richard Lewis, 01873 854662, bookings@middleninfa.co.uk, www.middleninfa.co.uk. *2½m SSW Abergavenny. At A465/ B4246 junction, S for Llanfoist, L at mini r'about, B4269 towards Llanelen, ½m R turn up steep lane, over canal. ¾m to Middle Ninfa on R. Main parking at Castell Cwrt.* **Sun 4 June (2-6). Combined adm with Castell Cwrt £5, chd free.** Large terraced eco-garden on east slopes of the Blorenge mountain. Vegetable beds, polytunnel, 3 greenhouses, orchard, flower borders, wild flowers. Great

views, woodland walks, cascading water and ponds. Paths steep in places, unsuitable for less able. Campsite and small bunkhouse on farm. 5 mins walk uphill to scenic Punchbowl Lake and walks on the Blorenge.

🐇 ❀ 🛌

19 MIONE

Old Hereford Road, Llanvihangel Crucorney, Abergavenny, NP7 7LB. Yvonne & John O'Neil. *5m N of Abergavenny. From Abergavenny take A465 to Hereford. After 4.8m turn L - signed Pantygrli. Mione is ½m on L.* **Fri 30 June, Sun 2, Fri 7, Sun 9 July (10.30-6). Adm £3, chd free. Home-made teas.** Beautiful garden with a wide variety of established plants, many rare and unusual. Pergola with climbing roses and clematis. Wildlife pond with many newts, insects and frogs. Numerous containers with diverse range of planting. Several seating areas, each with a different atmosphere. Lovely home-made cakes, biscuits and scones to be enjoyed sitting in the garden or pretty summerhouse.

❀ ⛾

High Glanau manor

© Val Corbett

Llanover

20 ◆ NANT Y BEDD

Grwyne Fawr, Fforest Coal Pit, Abergavenny, NP7 7LY. Sue & Ian Mabberley, 01873 890219, garden@nantybedd.com, www.nantybedd.com. *In Grwyne Fawr valley. From A465 Llanv Crucorney, direction Llanthony, then L to Fforest Coal Pit. At grey telephone box cont for 4½ m towards Grwyne Fawr Reservoir.* **For NGS: Sat 29, Sun 30 July (11-5). Adm £5, chd free. Home-made teas. For other opening times and information, please phone, email or visit garden website.**
Blending wild and tame, 6½ acre garden described as 'Absolutely enchanting, of the place, so imaginative'. Set high in the Black Mountains by the Grwyne Fawr river with lots of places to sit and enjoy the tranquility. An inspiring mix of vegetables and fruit, mature trees and shrubs and water. A garden for everyone, loved by photographers. Productive organic vegetable and fruit gardens, stream, forest and river walk, wildflowers, natural swimming pond, tree sculpture, shepherd's hut and eco-features. Ducks, chickens, sheep, pigs, cats. Plants and garden accessories for sale. See www. nantybedd.com for details. No dogs please. Features in House & Garden and Country Homes & Interiors.
✿ ⊜ ☕

21 THE NELSON GARDEN

Monnow Street, Monmouth, NP25 3EE. Penny Thomas (Leader - Nelson Garden Gardening Group). *Garden accessed via Blestium St, follow yellow NGS signs. Also tourist signs indicating the Nelson Garden.* **Sun 10 Sept (1.30-5.30). Adm £4, chd free. Home-made teas.**
This ancient town garden was the site of a real tennis court in C17 and a bowling green by 1718. Roman and Norman remains lie deep beneath the lawn. Admiral Lord Nelson and his entourage took tea here on 19th August 1802. Planting throughout the garden is designed around species that would have been popular in informal gardens of the late C18, early C19.
&. ⛪ ☕

22 THE OLD VICARAGE

Penrhos, Raglan, Usk, NP15 2LE. Mrs Georgina Herrmann. *3m N of Raglan. From A449 take Raglan exit, join A40 & move immed into R lane & turn R across dual carriageway. Follow yellow NGS signs.* **Sun 23 Apr, Sun 14 May (2-6). Combined adm with Woodlands Farm £6.50, chd free. Home-made teas at Woodlands Farm Barns.**
The Old Vicarage has a series of skillfully crafted gardens surrounding a beautiful 150yr old (1867) Victorian Gothic house which

invites you to explore as the eye is drawn from one garden into the next. With sweeping lawns, a summer house and formal garden, two charming ponds and kitchen garden all enhanced by imaginatively placed pots, this gem is not one to be rushed and gets better each year. Plant stall.
✿ ☕

23 ROCKFIELD PARK

Rockfield, Monmouth, NP25 5QB. Mark & Melanie Molyneux. *On arriving in Rockfield village from Monmouth, turn R by phone box. After approx 400yds, church on L. Entrance to Rockfield Park on R, opp church, via private bridge over river.* **Sun 11 June (11-5). Adm £5, chd free. Home-made teas.**
Rockfield Park dates from C17 and is situated in the heart of the Monmouthshire countryside on the banks of the R Monnow. The extensive grounds comprise formal gardens, meadows and orchard, complemented by riverside and woodland walks. Possible to picnic on riverside walks. Main part of gardens can be accessed by wheelchair but not steep garden leading down to river.
&. 🐕 ✿ ☕

24 SUNNYSIDE

The Hendre, Monmouth, NP25 5HQ. Helen & Ralph Fergusson-Kelly, 01600 714928, helen_fk@hotmail.com. *4m W of Monmouth. On B4233 Monmouth to Abergavenny rd.* **Visits by arrangement for single visitors or groups 25 max (evenings and weekends). Adm £4.50, chd free.**
A sloping ⅓ acre garden on the old Rolls estate. There is much to be enjoyed throughout the yr with formal plant and topiary structure. The garden builds to a profusion of colour towards the end of the summer from russet tones of grasses then bold injections of scarlet, cerise, violet and gold from bulbs, perennials and trees. Quiet seating areas to enjoy views of the Monmouthshire countryside. Some gravel paths.
🐕 ✿ ☕

25 TAIR-FFYNNON, 'THE GARDEN IN THE CLOUDS'

Llanvihangel Crucorney, Abergavenny, NP7 7NR. Antony & Verity Woodward, www.thegardenintheclouds.com. *8m N of Abergavenny. Get to Llanvihangel Crucorney, then follow yellow lanes. DO NOT FOLLOW SATNAV. DO NOT GO TO CWMYOY. Challenging, steep single-track lanes - reversing may be necessary. If wet, parking 15 mins away.* **Sat 29 July (12.30-5.30). Adm £5, chd free. Home-made teas. Free cup of tea on arrival.**

'The Garden in the Clouds' of Antony Woodward's award-winning memoir. One of the highest in the NGS, this 6 acre smallholding in a mountain landscape reaching to over 1,800 ft sits on Offa's Dyke footpath in the Brecon Beacons National Park. For anyone who sees beauty in wild places: box balls rolling through upland flower meadows, fading poetry on wrinkly tin barns and gateways framing 70 mile views. 'The pinnacle of beauty' Sunday Times; 'Untamed but stunningly beautiful' Reader's Digest. Sensational 10 mins walk up Offa's Dyke footpath to Hatterrall Hill trig point, offering views to 11 counties, the Severn Estuary and across the Brecon Beacons. Cakes, sandwiches, tea, coffee, soft drinks and books for sale. Featured in The Gardens of England: Treasures of the National Garden Scheme, Sunday Times, Telegraph, Reader's Digest, South Wales Argus, Western Mail and on ITV Countrywise.

26 NEW TANDDERWEN

Penrhos, Raglan, NP15 2LE. Andrea Mallalieu & Matt Burhouse. *3m N of Raglan. From A449 take Raglan exit, join A40 & move into R lane & turn R across dual carriageway. Take the 1st L. Follow yellow NGS signs.* **Sun 14 May (2-6). Adm by donation. Also open The Old Vicarage.**

3 acre natural garden around an early pioneering Eco House. The garden is being developed with nature and the landscape in mind. Wooded areas with mature trees and wild native spring flowers, open spaces with views of the Black Mountains. A variety of old apple trees, areas of long grass, Summer House, wildlife pond, young orchard and small but established wildflower meadow. Child friendly.

27 TY BODA

Upper Llanover, Abergavenny, NP7 9EP. Mike & Mary Shooter. *Off A4042. Follow directions to Upper Llanover (coming from Abergavenny) or Pencroesoped (coming from Cwmbran), narrow lanes. Watch out for signs to Goose & Cuckoo PH. If you get there, you've past us!* **Sat 27, Sun 28, Mon 29 May (11-5). Adm £5. Home-made teas.**

A 4 acre hillside garden with stunning views out over the Vale of Usk. Wildlife pond, stream and winding paths through a meadow newly planted with fifteen hundred native trees. Medieval style medicinal herb garden, potager, fernery, orchard, rope swing, stone circle and roses, roses everywhere. Steep slopes and slippery steps, so come prepared! Scrumptious home-made cakes and tea.

GROUP OPENING

28 USK OPEN GARDENS

Twyn Square, Usk, NP15 1BH. UskOpenGardens@gmail.com, www.uskopengardens.com. *From M4 J24 take A449, proceed 8m N to Usk exit. Free parking in town. Blue badge car parking in main car parks & at Usk Castle. Map of gardens provided with ticket.* **Sat 24, Sun 25 June (10-5). Combined adm £7.50, chd free. Light refreshments in town (further details below).**

Winner of Wales in Bloom for over 30yrs, Usk is full of hanging baskets and boxes and a wonderful backdrop to around 20 gardens from small cottages packed with colourful and unusual plants to large gardens with brimming herbaceous borders. Romantic garden around the ramparts of Usk Castle. Gardeners' Market with interesting plants. Great day out for all the family with lots of places to eat and drink incl places to picnic. Various cafes, PH and restaurants available for refreshments, plus several volunteer groups offering teas and cakes; one garden has a pop up Pimms, Prosecco and ice cream bar with a picnic and children's play area by their lake. Usk Castle and school fully accessible but not all gardens/ areas of gardens fully wheelchair accessible. Accessibility noted on ticket.

29 WENALLT ISAF

Twyn Wenallt, Gilwern, Abergavenny, NP7 0HP. Tim & Debbie Field. *3m W of Abergavenny. From Gilwern r'about follow Yellow NGS signs.* **Sun 28 May (2-6). Adm £4, chd free. Home-made teas.**

2½ acre garden 650ft up on a N-facing hillside with magnificent views of the Black Mountains. Mature trees, flowering shrubs, borders, productive vegetable garden, small polytunnel, orchard, pigs, chickens, 2 bee hives and plenty of space to run about.

30 WOODLANDS FARM

Penrhos, NP15 2LE. Craig Loane & Charles Horsfield. *3m N of Raglan. From A449 take Raglan exit, join A40 & move immed into R lane & turn R across dual carriageway. Follow yellow NGS signs.* **Sun 23 Apr, Sun 14 May (2-6). Combined adm with The Old Vicarage £6.50, chd free. Home-made teas at Woodlands Farm Barns.**

Unique in its design and built to entertain with hidden nooks, paths and water feature that invite you into its hidden spaces. Acer walk, sculptures, a viewing platform within a modern ruin - all the easier to see the wonders below - the parterre garden, pavilion, striped bothy and eco credentials make the experience exceptional. This garden gives first time and returning visitors lots to enjoy.

GWYNEDD & ANGLESEY

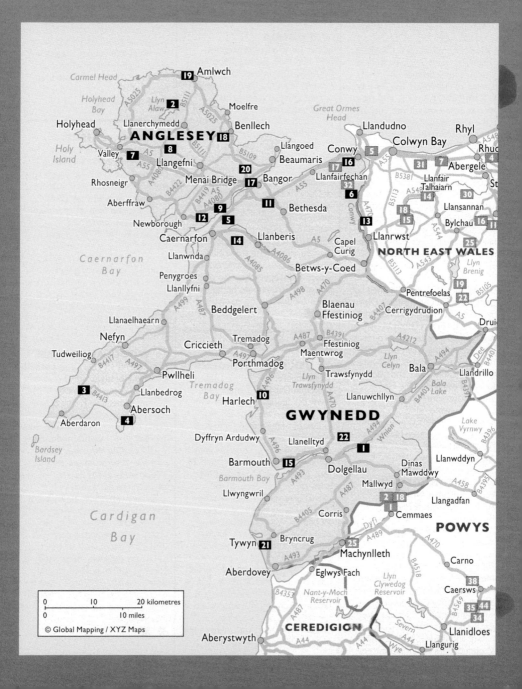

Gwynedd is a county rich in history and outstanding natural beauty. Bordered by the Irish Sea and home to Snowdonia National Park, Gwynedd can boast some of the most impressive landscapes in the UK.

The mountains in Gwynedd are world famous, and have attracted visitors for hundreds of years – the most famous perhaps, was Charles Darwin in 1831. As well as enjoying the tallest peaks in the UK, Gwynedd has fine woodland – from hanging oak forests in the mountains to lush, riverside woods.

Holiday-makers flock to Gwynedd and Anglesey to take advantage of the sandy beaches, and many can enjoy sightings of dolphins and porpoises off the coast.

The gardens of Gwynedd and Anglesey are just as appealing an attraction for visitors. A variety of gardens open for Gwynedd NGS, ranging from the harmonious two-acre garden of Llys-y-Gwynt with magnificent views of Snowdonia, to the glorious hillside garden of Pen y Bryn with panoramic views of the Mawddach Estuary.

So why not escape from the hustle and bustle of everyday life and relax in a beautiful Gwynedd garden? You will be assured of a warm welcome at every garden gate.

Volunteers

North Gwynedd & Anglesey
County Organiser
Grace Meirion-Jones
01286 831195

County Treasurer
Nigel Bond
01407 831354
nigel.bond@ngs.org.uk

Assistant County Organisers
Hazel Bond
01407 831354
nigel@cae-newydd.co.uk

Janet Jones
01758 740296
janetcoron@hotmail.co.uk

South Gwynedd
County Organiser
Hilary Nurse
01341 450255
antique_pete@btinternet.com

County Treasurer
Michael Bishton
01654 710882
m.bishton@btopenworld.com

Below: **Sunningdale**

OPENING DATES

All entries subject to change. For latest information check www.ngs.org.uk

Extended openings are shown at the beginning of the month.

Map locator numbers are shown to the right of each garden name.

April

Llyn Rhaeadr
(Every day from Friday 14th to Sunday 23rd) — 10

Saturday 22nd
Llanidan Hall — 9

Wednesday 26th
Plas Cadnant Hidden Gardens — 17

Sunday 30th
Llyn Rhaeadr — 10

May

Llyn Rhaeadr
(Every day from Sunday 28th) — 10

Monday 1st
Llyn Rhaeadr — 10

Sunday 7th
Gilfach — 6

Sunday 14th
Bryn Gwern — 1
Maenan Hall — 13
Sunningdale — 19

Monday 15th
Sunningdale — 19

Thursday 18th
Sunningdale — 19

Sunday 21st
Llys-y-Gwynt — 11
Pen y Bryn — 15

90th Anniversary Weekend

Saturday 27th
Cae Newydd — 2
◆ Crûg Farm — 5

Sunday 28th
Cae Newydd — 2
Ty Cadfan Sant — 21

Monday 29th
Cae Newydd — 2

June

Llyn Rhaeadr (Every day to Sunday 4th) — 10

Saturday 3rd
Gwaelod Mawr — 7

Ty Capel Ffrwd — 22

Sunday 4th
Gwaelod Mawr — 7
◆ Pensychnant — 16
Ty Capel Ffrwd — 22

Saturday 10th
Maen Hir — 12

Sunday 11th
Maen Hir — 12
Treffos School — 20

Saturday 17th
Crowrach Isaf — 4

Sunday 18th
Crowrach Isaf — 4
Rhosbach Cottage — 18

Saturday 24th
Llanidan Hall — 9

Sunday 25th
Llys-y-Gwynt — 11

July

Sunday 2nd
Gilfach — 6
Gwyndy Bach — 8

Saturday 8th
Llanidan Hall — 9

Sunday 23rd
◆ Pensychnant — 16
Sunningdale — 19

Saturday 29th
Coed Ty Mawr — 3

Sunday 30th
Bryn Gwern — 1
Coed Ty Mawr — 3
Ty Cadfan Sant — 21

August

Llyn Rhaeadr (Every day from Sunday 27th to Thursday 31st) — 10

Saturday 5th
Pant Ifan — 14

Sunday 13th
Maenan Hall — 13

September

Friday 1st
Llyn Rhaeadr — 10

Saturday 2nd
Llyn Rhaeadr — 10

Sunday 3rd
Llyn Rhaeadr — 10

By Arrangement

Garden	No.
Bryn Gwern	1
Cae Newydd	2
Coed Ty Mawr	3
Crowrach Isaf	4
Gilfach	6
Gwaelod Mawr	7
Gwyndy Bach	8
Llyn Rhaeadr	10
Llys-y-Gwynt	11
Maenan Hall	13
Rhosbach Cottage	18
Sunningdale	19
Ty Cadfan Sant	21
Ty Capel Ffrwd	22

> Macmillan and the National Garden Scheme, partners for more than 30 years

Plas Cadnant Hidden Gardens

© Carole Drake

THE GARDENS

BODYSGALLEN HALL & SPA
See North East Wales

1 BRYN GWERN
Llanfachreth, Dolgellau, Gwynedd, LL40 2DH. H O & P D Nurse, 01341 450 255, antique_pete@btinternet.com. *5m NE of Dolgellau. Do not go to Llanfachreth village, stay on A494 Bala-Dolgellau rd: 13m from Bala. Take 1st R Llanfachreth. From Dolgellau 4m Llanfachreth turn L, follow signs. Mini bus/coaches to park in lay-by on main rd* Sun 14 May, Sun 30 July (10-5). Adm £3.50, chd free. Cream teas. **Visits also by arrangement Apr to Oct.**
Sloping 2 acre garden in the hills overlooking Dolgellau with views to Cader Idris, originally wooded but redesigned to enhance its natural features with streams, ponds and imaginative and extensive planting and vibrant colour. The garden is now a haven for wildlife with hedgehogs and 27 species of birds feeding last winter as well as being home to ducks, dogs and cats. Stone mason at work and items for sale or orders taken. Wheelchair access to main area of garden but only when dry.
& 🐄 ❀ 🚗 ☕

2 CAE NEWYDD
Rhosgoch, Anglesey, LL66 0BG. Hazel & Nigel Bond, 01407 831354, nigel@cae-newydd.co.uk. *3m SW of Amlwch. A5025 from Benllech to Amlwch, follow signs for leisure centre & Lastra Farm. Follow yellow NGS signs (approx 3m), car park on L (no suitable parking for large coaches).* Sat 27, Sun 28, Mon 29 May (11-4). Adm £4, chd free. Light refreshments. **Visits also by arrangement June to Aug, groups 8+.**
Maturing country garden of 2½ acres which blends seamlessly into the open landscape with stunning views of Snowdonia and Llyn Alaw. Variety of shrubs, trees and herbaceous areas, large wildlife pond, polytunnel, greenhouses, raised vegetable beds and chicken run. Adjacent sheltered paddock garden and new pond. Patio area with formal pond and fountain. Rose garden with aquilegias, dianthus and lavender. Hay meadow. Lots of seating throughout the garden, visitors are welcome to bring a picnic. Garden area closest to house suitable for wheelchairs.
& ❀ ☕

CAEREUNI
See North East Wales

3 COED TY MAWR
Ty Mawr, Bryncroes, Pwllheli, LL53 8EH. Nonni & David Goadby, 01758 730359, nonni@goadby.net, www.coed-ty-mawr.co.uk. *12m W of Pwllheli. Take B4413 Llanbedrog to Aberdaron. 1¾m past Sarn Meyllteyrn. Turn R at Penygroeslon sign. From Nefyn take B4417, at Xrds with B4413 turn L.* Sat 29, Sun 30 July (10.30-5). Adm £4, chd free. Home-made teas. **Visits also by arrangement Mar to Sept.**
Outstanding 5 acre woodland garden created from wilderness and situated among some of the most beautiful scenery of Wales. Over 3,000 trees and shrubs incl growing collections of magnolia, rhododendron, hydrangea and cornus. Also large pond, orchard, fernery, vegetable, and sea view gardens. Plenty of seating. Sit on the raised deck, take in the sea views and enjoy a home-made tea. Grass paths.
& 🐄 ❀ 🚗 ☕

4 CROWRACH ISAF
Bwlchtocyn, LL53 7BY. Margaret & Graham Cook, 01758 712860, crowrach_isaf@hotmail.com. *1½m SW of Abersoch. Follow rd through Abersoch & Sarn Bach, L at sign for Bwlchtocyn for ½m until junction & no-through rd - TG Holiday Complex. Turn R, parking 50 metres on R.* Sat 17, Sun 18 June (1-5). Adm £4, chd free. Cream teas. **Visits also by arrangement in July, groups 20+.**
2 acre plot incl 1 acre fenced against rabbits, developed from 2000, incl island beds, windbreak hedges, vegetable garden, wild flower area and wide range of geraniums, shrubs and herbaceous perennials. Views over Cardigan Bay and Snowdonia. Grass and gravel paths, some gentle slopes.
& ❀ 🚗 ☕

5 ◆ CRÛG FARM
Griffiths Crossing, Caernarfon, LL55 1TU. Mr & Mrs B Wynn-Jones, 01248 670232, sue@crug-farm.co.uk, www.crug-farm.co.uk. *2m NE of Caernarfon. ¼m off main A487 Caernarfon to Bangor rd. Follow signs from r'about.* For NGS: Sat 27 May (10-4.30). Adm £3.50, chd free. Home-made teas. For other opening times and information, please phone, email or visit garden website.
3 acres; grounds to old country house (not open). Gardens filled with choice, unusual plants collected by the Wynn-Jones. Woodland garden with shade loving plants, many not seen in cultivation before. Walled garden with more wonderful collections growing. Chelsea Gold Medallists and winners of the President's Award among other many prestigious awards. Partial wheelchair access.
& ❀ 🚗 NPC ☕

FFRIDD-Y-GOG
See North East Wales

6 GILFACH
Rowen, Conwy, LL32 8TS. James & Isoline Greenhalgh, 01492 650216, isolinegreenhalgh@btinternet.com. *4m S of Conwy. At Xrds 100yds E of Rowen S towards Llanrwst, past Rowen School on L, turn up 2nd drive on L.* Sun 7 May, Sun 2 July (2-5.30). Adm £3.50, chd free. Home-made teas. **Visits also by arrangement Apr to Aug coffee/biscuits (am), tea/cake (pm). Groups 45 max.**
1 acre country garden on S-facing slope with magnificent views of the R Conwy and mountains; set in 35 acres of farm and woodland. Collection of mature shrubs is added to yearly; woodland garden, herbaceous border and small pool. Spectacular panoramic view of the Conwy Valley and the mountain range of the Carneddau. Classic cars. Large coaches can park at bottom of steep drive, disabled visitors can be driven to garden by the owner.
& ❀ 🚗 ☕

7 GWAELOD MAWR

Caergeiliog, Anglesey, LL65 3YL.
John & Tricia Coates,
01407 740080,
patriciacoates36@gmail.com. *6m
E of Holyhead. ½m E of Caergeiliog.
From A55 J4. r'about 2nd exit signed
Caergeiliog. 300yds, Gwaelod Mawr
is 1st house on L.* **Sat 3, Sun 4
June (11-5). Adm £4, chd free.
Home-made teas. Visits also by
arrangement May to Aug.**
2½ acre garden created by owners
over 20yrs with lake, large rock
outcrops and palm tree area.
Spanish style patio and laburnum
arch lead to sunken garden and
wooden bridge over lily pond with
fountain and waterfall. Peaceful
Chinese orientated garden offering
contemplation. Separate Koi carp
pond. Abundant seating throughout.
Mainly flat, with gravel and stone
paths, no wheelchair access to
sunken lily pond area.

8 GWYNDY BACH

Tynlon, Llandrygarn,
LL65 3AJ. Keith & Rosa
Andrew, 01407 720651,
keithandrew.art@gmail.com. *5m
W of Llangefni. From Llangefni take
B5109 towards Bodedern, cottage
exactly 5m out on L. Postcode good
for SatNav.* **Sun 2 July (11-4.30).
Adm £3, chd free. Home-made
teas. Visits also by arrangement
May to July.**
¾ acre artist's garden, set amidst
rugged Anglesey landscape.
Romantically planted in informal
intimate rooms with interesting
rare plants and shrubs, box and
yew topiary, old roses and Japanese
garden with large Koi pond (deep
water; children must be supervised).
National Collection of Rhapis
miniature Japanese palms. Gravel
entrance to garden.

9 LLANIDAN HALL

Brynsiencyn, LL61 6HJ.
Mr J W Beverley (Head
Gardener), 07759 305085,
Work.beverley@btinternet.com.
*5m E of Llanfair Pwll. From
Llanfair PG follow A4080 towards
Brynsiencyn for 4m. After Hooton's
farm shop on R take next L, follow
lane to gardens.* **Sat 22 Apr,
Sat 24 June, Sat 8 July (10-4).
Adm £3.50, chd free. Light
refreshments.** *Donation to CAFOD.*
Walled garden of 1¾ acres. Physic
and herb gardens, ornamental
vegetable garden, herbaceous
borders, water features and many
varieties of old roses. Sheep, rabbits
and hens to see. Children must
be kept under supervision. Well
behaved dogs on leads welcome.
Llanidan Church will be open for
viewing. The walled garden will be
open early in the season for viewing
of the spring bulbs. Hard gravel
paths, gentle slopes.

10 LLYN RHAEADR

15 Parc Bron-y-Graig, Centre of
Harlech, LL46 2SR. Mr D R Hewitt
& Miss J Sharp, 01766 780224.
*From A496 take B4573 into Harlech,
take turning to main car parks S
of town, L past overspill car park,
garden 75yds on R.* **Daily Fri 14
Apr to Sun 23 Apr. Sun 30 Apr,
Mon 1 May. Daily Sun 28 May
to Sun 4 June, Sun 27 Aug to
Thur 31 Aug. Fri 1, Sat 2, Sun
3 Sept (2-5). Adm £3.50, chd
free. Visits also by arrangement
Mar to Oct, most days (2-5).
Individual visitors welcome,
groups max 35.**
Hillside garden blending natural
wildlife areas with garden plants,
shrubs, vegetables and fruit. Small
lake with 20 species of waterfowl,
fish and wildlife ponds, waterfalls,
woodland, rockeries, lawns, borders,
snowdrops, daffodils, heathers,
bluebells, ferns, camellias, azaleas,
rhododendrons, wild flowers, views

Gwaelod Mawr

© Fiona Lea

of Tremadog Bay, Lleyn Peninsula. Good paths and seating with gazebos. Waterfowl collection.

🚐

II LLYS-Y-GWYNT

Pentir Road, Llandygai, Bangor, LL57 4BG. Jennifer Rickards & John Evans, 01248 353863. *3m S of Bangor. 300yds from Llandygai r'about at J11, A5 & A55, just off A4244. Follow signs for services (Gwasanaethau). No through rd sign, 50yds beyond. Do not use SatNav.* Sun 21 May, Sun 25 June (11-4). Adm £3.50, chd free. **Cream teas. Visits also by arrangement.** Interesting, harmonious and very varied 2 acre garden incl magnificent views of Snowdonia. An exposed site incl Bronze Age burial cairn. Winding paths and varied levels planted to create shelter, yr-round interest, microclimates and varied rooms. Ponds, waterfall, bridge and other features use local materials and craftspeople. Wildlife encouraged, well organised compost. Good family garden.

&. ✿ 🚐 ☕ ❧

I2 MAEN HIR

Dwyran, Anglesey, LL61 6UY. Mr & Mrs K T Evans. *6m SE of Llanfairpwll. From Llanfair P.G (Anglesey) follow A4080 through village Brynsiencyn. Cont on this rd for approx 2m. Maen Hir on R.* Sat 10, Sun 11 June (11-5). Adm £4, chd free. Home-made teas. Set in 7 acres incl beautiful walled garden with gazebo, old roses and mixed herbaceous borders replanted 2007. Courtyard, outer garden, woodland walks, greenhouse, potting shed, cutting patch and hay meadow. Maen Hir enjoys magnificent views of Snowdonia range. Refreshments served on the front lawn.

&. 🐐 ✿ ☕

I3 MAENAN HALL

Maenan, Llanrwst, LL26 0UL. The Hon Mr & Mrs Christopher Mclaren, 01492 640441, cmmclaren@gmail.com. *2m N of Llanrwst. On E side of A470, ¼m S of Maenan Abbey Hotel.* Sun 14 May, Sun 13 Aug (10.30-5.30). Adm £4, chd £3 (under 10s free).

Cae Newydd

© Fiona Lea

Home-made teas. **Visits also by arrangement Mar to Oct for groups 8+.** *Donation to Wales Air Ambulance.* A superbly beautiful 4 hectares on the slopes of the Conwy Valley, with dramatic views of Snowdonia, set amongst mature hardwoods. Both the upper part, with sweeping lawns, ornamental ponds and retaining walls, and the bluebell carpeted woodland dell contain copious specimen shrubs and trees, many originating at Bodnant. Magnolias, rhododendrons, camellias, pieris, cherries and hydrangeas, amongst many others, make a breathtaking display. Treasure Hunt (£1) on both open days. Upper part of garden accessible but with fairly steep slopes.

&. 🐐 ✿ ☕

I4 PANT IFAN

Ceunant, Llanrug, Caernarfon, LL55 4HX. Mrs Delia Lanceley. *2m E of Caernarfon. From Llanrug take rd opp PO between Premier Store & Monumental Mason. Straight across at next Xrds. Then 3rd turn on L at Xrds. Pant Ifan 2nd house on L.* Sat 5 Aug (11-5). Adm £4, chd free. Home-made teas. 2 acre mix of formal and wildlife garden set around farmhouse and yard. Herbaceous borders, shrubs, vegetables, fruit, ponds and recently planted woodland. Field walks, sitting areas in the sun or shade. Poultry, ducks, geese, donkeys, horse and greenhouses. Deep water, children must be supervised at all times. Wheelchair users can access yard and teas.

&. ✿ ☕ ❧

Llanidan Hall

15 PEN Y BRYN

Glandwr, Barmouth, LL42 1TG.
Phil & Jenny Martin. *2m E of
Barmouth; 7m W of Dolgellau. On
A496 7m W of Dolgellau, 2m E of
Barmouth, situated on N side of
Mawddach Estuary. Park in or nr
layby & walk L up narrow lane.* Sun
21 May (11-5). Adm £3.50, chd
free. Cream teas. *Donation to
Gwynedd Hospice at Home.*
A glorious hillside garden with
panoramic views of The Mawddoch
Estuary. Woodland walks awash
with Bluebells in the spring. Lawns
on different levels with vibrant
rhododendrons and azaleas, arches
of clematis, honeysuckle and roses.
Heather filled natural rocks, unusual
conifer feature, a rock cannon and a
pond for wildlife.
✿ ☕ ☙

16 ◆ PENSYCHNANT

Sychnant Pass, Conwy, LL32 8BJ.
Pensychnant Foundation;
Wardens Julian Thompson &
Anne Mynott, 01492 592595,
jpt.pensychnant@btinternet.com,
www.pensychnant.co.uk. *2½m W
of Conwy at top of Sychnant Pass.
From Conwy: L into Upper Gate
St; after 2½m Pensychnant's drive
signed on R. From Penmaenmawr:
fork R, up pass, after walls U turn
L into drive.* For NGS: Sun 4
June, Sun 23 July (10-5). Adm
£3.50, chd free. Home-made
teas. For other opening times and
information, please phone, email or
visit garden website.
Wildlife Garden. Diverse herbaceous
cottage garden borders surrounded
by mature shrubs, banks of
rhododendrons, ancient and Victorian
woodlands. 12 acre woodland walks
with views of Conwy Mountain and
Sychnant. Woodland birds. Picnic
tables, archaelogical trail on mountain.
A peaceful little gem. Large Victorian
Arts and Crafts house (open) with
art exhibition. Partial wheelchair
access, please phone for advice.
ᕕ ✿ ☕

17 PLAS CADNANT HIDDEN GARDENS

Cadnant Road, Menai Bridge,
LL59 5NH. Mr Anthony
Tavernor, 01248 717174,
plascadnantgardens@gmail.com,
www.plascadnantgardens.co.uk. *½m
E of Menai Bridge. Take A545 & leave
Menai Bridge heading for Beaumaris,
then follow brown tourist information
signs.* Wed 26 Apr (12-5). Adm
£7, chd £2. Light refreshments
in traditional Tea Room. *Donation
to Wales Air Ambulance; Anglesey Red
Squirrel Trust; Menai Bridge Community
Heritage Trust.*
Early C19 picturesque garden
undergoing restoration since 1996.
Valley gardens with waterfalls,
large ornamental walled garden,
woodland and early pit house.
Recently created Alpheus water
feature and Ceunant (Ravine) which
gives visitors a more interesting
walk featuring unusual moisture
loving Alpines. Newly restored
area following flood damage. New
guidebook available. Tea room
serving home-made light lunches,
delicious home-made scones and
cakes. Visitor centre open. Recently
featured on S4C. Partial wheelchair
access to parts of gardens. Some
steps, gravel paths, slopes. Access
statement available. Accessible Tea
Room and WC.
ᕕ ✿ 🚌 🚗 ☕ ☙

18 RHOSBACH COTTAGE

Brynteg, LL78 8JY. Ena Green,
ena.bryan1@sky.com. *Brynteg,
Anglesey. 1.4m W of Benllech. Take
B5108 to Brynteg. Follow NGS signs
to limited parking on lane on L, extra
parking approx 50 metres further
along rd on R at Storws Wen Golf
Club.* Sun 18 June (1-4.30). Adm
£3.50, chd free. Home-made teas.
Gluten free options available.
Visits also by arrangement May
to July groups 8+.
Situated close to Cors Goch Nature
Reserve, a recently rejuvenated
garden full of country charm, a
blend of mature trees, shrubs and
wide, mixed borders planted to
attract wildlife. The garden gently
slopes with some steps, seating
areas, and a small pond.
🐕 ✿ ☙

19 SUNNINGDALE
Bull Bay Road, Bull Bay, Amlwch, LL68 9SD. Mike & Gill Cross, 01407 830753, mikeatbb@aol.com. *1½m NW of Amlwch. On A5025 through Amlwch towards Cemaes. No parking at house but parking will be signed.* Sun 14 May (1-5). Home-made teas. Evening opening Mon 15 May (6-8.30). Light refreshments. Thur 18 May (2-5); Sun 23 July (1-5). Home-made teas. Adm £3.50, chd free. **Visits also by arrangement May to July for groups 8+.**
An evolving seaside garden. Headland has cliffs, steps, wild flowers and seating, spectacular views and sheer drops! Front garden has raised pond and planting to cope with hostile weather. The relatively sheltered rear garden is cottage style; no large lawn here! Lots of different plants, paths, seats, pots and raised bed vegetable area. Star is the 50yr old laburnum. Wheelchair access to front garden only.
✿ 🚗 ☕

20 TREFFOS SCHOOL
Llansadwrn, Anglesey, LL59 5SD. Stuart & Joyce Humphreys. *2½m N of Menai Bridge. A5025 Amlwch/ Benllech exit from Britannia Bridge onto Anglesey. Approx 3m turn R towards Llansadwrn. Entrance to Treffos School 200yds on L.* Sun 11 June (12-3). Adm £3, chd free. Cream teas.
7 acres, child friendly garden, in rural location, surrounding C17 house now run as school. Garden consists of mature woodland, underplanted with spring flowering bulbs and rhododendrons, ancient beech avenue leading down to rockery, herbaceous borders and courtyards. Art and Craft activities for children, face painting. Partial wheelchair access.
♿ ✿ ☕

21 TY CADFAN SANT
National Street, Tywyn, LL36 9DD. Mrs Katie Pearce, 01654 712188, Katie@tycadfansant.co.uk. *A493 going S & W. L into one way, garden ahead. Bear R, parking 2nd L. A493 going N, 1st R in 30mph zone, L at bottom by garden, parking 2nd L.* Sun 28 May, Sun 30 July (10-4). Adm £4, chd free. Cream teas. **Visits also by arrangement Apr to Sept, refreshments available on request.**
Large eco friendly garden. In the front, shrubbery, mixed flower beds and roses surround a mature copper beech. Up six steps the largely productive back garden has chickens in the orchard, fruit, vegetables, flowers and a poly tunnel. Cream teas and home baked cakes, special diets also catered for. Seasonal produce, crafts. Partial wheelchair access due to steps to rear garden.
♿ ✿ ☕

Your visit helps Marie Curie work night and day in people's homes

22 TY CAPEL FFRWD
Llanfachreth, Dolgellau, LL40 2NR. Revs Mary & George Bolt, 01341 422006, georgebolt34@gmail.com. *4m NE of Dolgellau, 18m SW of Bala. From Dolgellau 4m up hill to Llanfachreth. Turn L at War Memorial. Follow lane ½m to chapel on R. Park & walk down lane past chapel to cottage.* Sat 3, Sun 4 June (11-5). Adm £3.50, chd free. Home-made teas. **Visits also by arrangement May to Aug, groups 10 max. Art groups and gardening clubs welcome.**
True cottage garden in Welsh mountains. Azaleas, rhododendrons, acers; large collection of aquilegia. Many different hostas give added strength to spring bulbs and corms. Stream flowing through the garden, 10ft waterfall and on through a small woodland bluebell carpet. For summer visitor's there is a continuous show of colour with herbaceous plants, roses, clematis and lilies, incl cardiocrinum giganteum. Harp will be played in the garden.
🐕 ✿ ☕

TY HWNT YR AFON
See North East Wales

Maenan Hall

© Carole Drake

NORTH EAST WALES

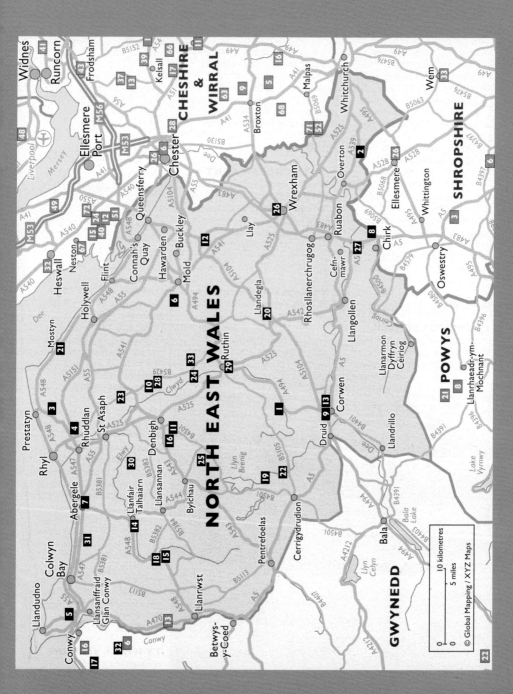

With its diversity of countryside from magnificent hills, seaside vistas and rolling farmland, North East Wales offers a wide range of gardening experiences.

Our gardens offer a wealth of designs and come in all shapes and sizes, ranging from abundant plantsmen's gardens to informal natural hillside planting. Visitors will have something to see from the frost-filled days of February through till the magnificent colourful days of autumn.

The majority of our gardens are within easy reach of North West England, and being a popular tourist destination make an excellent day out for all the family.

Come and enjoy the beauty and the variety of the gardens of North East Wales with the added bonus of a delicious cup of tea and a slice of cake. Our garden owners await your visit.

Volunteers

County Organiser
Jane Moore
07769 046317
jane.moore@ngs.org.uk

County Treasurer
Iris Dobbie
01745 886730
irisd@cactus5.freeserve.co.uk

Publicity
Trish Morris
01745 550121
trishmorris61@yahoo.co.uk

Booklet Co-ordinator
Roy Hambleton
01352 740206
royhambleton@btinternet.com

Assistant County Organisers
Fiona Bell
07813 087797
bell_fab@hotmail.com

Ann Knowlson
01745 832002
apk@slaters.com

Ann Rathbone
01244 532948
rathbone.ann@gmail.com

Carol Perkins
07808 988556
carolperkins24@yahoo.co.uk

Left: Tudor Cottage

OPENING DATES

All entries subject to change. For latest information check **www.ngs.org.uk**
Map locator numbers are shown to the right of each garden name.

February

Snowdrop Festival

Wednesday 15th
Clwydfryn 10

March

Wednesday 15th
Clwydfryn 10

April

Wednesday 5th
Aberclwyd Manor 1

Wednesday 12th
Clwydfryn 10

Wednesday 19th
Aberclwyd Manor 1

Sunday 30th
NEW Mostyn Hall 21
Ty Hwnt Yr Afon 32

May

Wednesday 3rd
Aberclwyd Manor 1

Wednesday 10th
Clwydfryn 10

Saturday 13th
Plas Nantglyn 25

Sunday 14th
Plas Nantglyn 25

Wednesday 17th
Aberclwyd Manor 1

90th Anniversary Weekend

Sunday 28th
Caereuni 9
Glog Ddu 15
Hafodunos Hall 18
NEW Scott House 29
Ty Hwnt Yr Afon 32

Monday 29th
Caereuni 9
Garthewin 14
NEW Scott House 29
Ty Hwnt Yr Afon 32

June

Sunday 4th
Isgaerwen 19

Wednesday 7th
Aberclwyd Manor 1

Saturday 10th
Caereuni 9

Ffridd-y-Gog 13

Sunday 11th
Caereuni 9
Ffridd-y-Gog 13

Wednesday 14th
Clwydfryn 10

Saturday 17th
33 Bryn Twr and Lynton 7

Sunday 18th
33 Bryn Twr and Lynton 7
Ty Hwnt Yr Afon 32

Wednesday 21st
Aberclwyd Manor 1

Saturday 24th
Gwel Yr Ynys 17
Plas Coch 24

Sunday 25th
The Beeches 2
Gwaenynog 16
Gwel Yr Ynys 17
Plas Coch 24
Queen Anne Cottage 27

Monday 26th
Bodysgallen Hall & Spa 5

July

Sunday 2nd
Llandegla Village Gardens 20

Wednesday 5th
Aberclwyd Manor 1

Sunday 9th
NEW 5 Birch Grove 3

Wednesday 12th
Clwydfryn 10

Saturday 15th
Tudor Cottage 31

Sunday 16th
Tudor Cottage 31

Wednesday 19th
Aberclwyd Manor 1

Sunday 23rd
Ruthin Town Gardens 28

Sunday 30th
Llandegla Village Gardens 20

August

Sunday 6th
Dove Cottage 12
Prices Lane Allotments 26

Wednesday 9th
Aberclwyd Manor 1

Wednesday 23rd
Aberclwyd Manor 1

Sunday 27th
Caereuni 9

Monday 28th
Caereuni 9

September

Wednesday 6th
Aberclwyd Manor 1

Thursday 7th
Brynkinalt Hall 8

Wednesday 20th
Aberclwyd Manor 1

By Arrangement

Aberclwyd Manor 1
Bryn Bellan 6
33 Bryn Twr and Lynton 7
Dolhyfryd 11
Dove Cottage 12
Ffridd-y-Gog 13
Garthewin 14
Gwel Yr Ynys 17
Isgaerwen 19
The Old Rectory 22
Pen Y Graig Bach 23
Queen Anne Cottage 27
Tal-y-Bryn Farm 30
Tudor Cottage 31
Ty Hwnt Yr Afon 32
Wylan 33

Ruthin Castle, Ruthin Town Gardens

© Jessie Williams

THE GARDENS

1 ABERCLWYD MANOR

Derwen, Corwen, LL21 9SF.
Miss Irene Brown & Mr G
Sparvoli, 01824 750431,
irene662010@live.com. *7m from
Ruthin. Travelling on A494 from
Ruthin to Corwen. At Bryn S.M service
station turn R, follow sign to Derwen.
Aberclwyd gates on L before Derwen.*
Weds 5, 19 Apr, 3, 17 May, 7,
21 June, 5, 19 July, 9, 23 Aug,
6, 20 Sept (11-4). Adm £3.50,
chd free. Cream teas. **Visits
also by arrangement Feb to
Oct for groups 10+, daytime or
evenings.**
4 acre garden on a sloping hillside
overlooking the Upper Clwyd Valley.
The garden has many mature trees
underplanted with snowdrops,
fritillaries and cyclamen. An Italianate
garden of box hedging lies below
the house and shrubs, ponds,
perennials, roses and an orchard
are also to be enjoyed within this
cleverly structured area. Mass of
cyclamen in Sept. Abundance of
Spring flowers. Snowdrops and
many spring flowering bulbs. Mostly
flat with some steps and slopes.

2 THE BEECHES

Vicarage Lane, Penley, Wrexham,
LL13 0NH. Stuart & Sue Hamon.
*Western edge of village. From
Overton turn 1st L after 30mph sign.
From Whitchurch go along A539
through village & turn R just after
church, signed to Adrefelyn. N.B.
SatNavs may show Vicarage Lane as
Hollybush Lane.* Sun 25 June (1-5).
Adm £3.50, chd free. Home-
made teas.
The garden surrounds an 1841
former vicarage and extends to 3½
acres. It has been redesigned to create
an attractive open garden laid mainly
to lawn with a mixture of mature and
younger specimen trees and shrubs.
There are shrub, rose and herbaceous
beds together with a productive
vegetable and fruit area. The walled
courtyard has tender plants incl many
varieties of agapanthus and hostas.
A mostly flat garden with gravelled

paths. Grass is usually firm allowing
easy access. Courtyard access has
three very shallow steps.

3 NEW 5 BIRCH GROVE

Prestatyn, LL19 9RH. Mrs Iris
Dobbie. *From A548 turn up The
Avenue, Woodland Park. Take care,
just after railway bridge if coming
from Rhuddlan. 10 mins walk from
town centre - at top of high st, turn
R.* Sun 9 July (1-5). Adm £3, chd
free.
A small well established town garden
on three sides of this property.
The gardens consist of a variety of
borders incl grass, herbaceous, alpine,
shrub, drought and a tropical type
border. Also two water features. The
front garden is lawn surrounded
by mixed colourful planting. A
small greenhouse is fully used for
propagation and storing tender
plants. Home-made compost. Winner
of both front and back garden
competitions at Prestatyn Flower
Show. Gravel drive, few steps.

5 BODYSGALLEN HALL & SPA

The Royal Welsh Way,
Llandudno, LL30 1RS. The
National Trust, 01492 584466,
info@bodysgallen.com,
www.bodysgallen.com. *2m from
Llandudno. Take A55 to intersection
with A470 (The Royal Welsh Way)
towards Llandudno. Proceed 1m,
hotel is 1m on R.* Mon 26 June
(1-4.30). Adm £4.50, chd £3.50.
Light refreshments in The Wynn
Rooms.
Garden is well known for box hedged
parterre. Stone walls surround
lower gardens with rose gardens
and herbaceous borders. Outside
walled garden is cascade over rocks.
Enclosed working fruit and vegetable
garden with espalier trained fruit trees,
hedging area for cut flowers with walls
covered in wineberry and Chinese
gooseberry. Restored Victorian
woodland, walks with stunning views
of Conwy and Snowdonia. Luncheon
available in the Main Hall. Booking in
advance recommended. Gravel paths
in places and steep slopes.

6 BRYN BELLAN

Bryn Road, Gwernaffield,
CH7 5DE. Gabrielle Armstrong
& Trevor Ruddle, 01352 741806,
gabriele@indigoawnings.co.uk.
*2m W of Mold. Leave A541 at Mold
on Gwernaffield rd (Dreflan), ½m
after Mold derestriction signs turn R
to Rhydymwyn & Llynypandy. After
200 yds park in field on R.* Visits by
arrangement May to Sept for
groups 8+. Adm £6, chd free.
Wine and nibbles available..
A late summer tranquil and elegant
garden which is perfect for a
relaxing evening visit. The garden
has been designed on two levels,
a partly walled upper garden with
circular sunken lawn, featuring
a Wellingtonia and structured
borders of a green and white colour
scheme with striking hydrangeas
and cyclamen. Lower garden, mainly
lawn, has an ornamental cutting and
vegetable garden with bijou potting
shed. Some gravel paths.

7 33 BRYN TWR AND LYNTON

Lynton, Highfield Park, Abergele,
LL22 7AU. Mr & Mrs Colin
Knowlson and Bryn Roberts
& Emma Knowlson-Roberts,
01745 832002 or 07712 623836,
apk@slaters.com. *From A55
heading W take slip rd into Abergele
town centre. Turn L at 2nd set of
T-lights signed Llanfair TH, 3rd rd on L.
For SatNav use LL22 8DD.* Sat 17,
Sun 18 June (1-5). Adm £4, chd
free. **Visits also by arrangement
for any size group.** Home-made
teas incl gluten free option.
More changes have been made
to the gardens for 2017, mixed
herbaceous and shrub borders,
some trees plus many unusual plants.
Lawn at Lynton replaced with slate
chips and more planting. Garage
with interesting fire engine; cars
and memorabilia; greenhouse over
water capture system; surrounding
planting coming along nicely, hens
now kept at Bryn Twr. Featured in
Amateur Gardens magazine. Partial
wheelchair access.

8 BRYNKINALT HALL

Brynkinalt, Chirk, Wrexham, LL14 5NS. Iain & Kate Hill-Trevor, www.brynkinalt.co.uk. *6m N of Oswestry, 10m S of Wrexham. Turn into Trevor Rd (beside St Mary's Church). Cont past houses on R. Turn R on bend into Estate Gates. Over 2 bridges. Straight on at fork. N.B. Do not use postcode for SatNav (uses tiny lane).* **Thur 7 Sept (2-5). Adm £4, chd free. Home-made teas.** 5 acre ornamental woodland shrubbery, overgrown until recently, now cleared and replanted, rhododendron walk, historic ponds, well, grottos, ha-ha and battlements, new stumpery, ancient redwoods and yews. Also 2 acre garden beside Grade II* house (see website for opening), with modern rose and formal beds, deep herbaceous borders, pond with shrub/mixed beds, pleached limes and hedge patterns. Home of the first Duke of Wellington's grandmother. Partial wheelchair access. Gravel paths in West Garden and grass paths and slopes in shrubbery.

🚗 ☕

9 CAEREUNI

Ffordd Ty Cerrig, Godre'r Gaer, Corwen, LL21 9YA. Mr S Williams. *1m N of Corwen. A5 Corwen to Bala rd, turn R at T-lights onto A494 to Chester. 1st R after lay by. House ¼m on L.* **Sun 28, Mon 29 May (2-5). Adm £3.50, chd free. Sat 10, Sun 11 June (2-5). Combined adm with Ffridd-y-Gog £5, chd free. Sun 27, Mon 28 Aug (2-5). Adm £3.50, chd free.** Plantsman's collection of rare trees, shrubs, plants, containers of tender plants and topiary set in a quirky themed garden. This approx ⅓ acre garden incls Japanese smoke water garden, old ruin, Spanish courtyard, Welsh gold mine, Chinese peace garden, Mexican chapel, 1950s petrol garage, woodman's lodge and jungle.

10 CLWYDFRYN

Bodfari, LL16 4HU. Keith & Susan Watson. *5m outside Denbigh. Halfway between Bodfari & Llandyrnog on B5429. Yellow signs at bottom of lane.* **Weds 15 Feb, 15 Mar, 12 Apr, 10 May, 14 June, 12 July (11-4). Adm £4, chd free. Home-made teas.** ¾ acre plantswoman's garden, well worth a visit any time of the year. Collection of snowdrops, epimediums, hellebores and daffodils in spring. Many unusual bulbs, shade loving plants and perennial borders in summer. Alpine house with sand plunge beds new in 2016 to house alpine plants and bulbs. Orchard and colourful cottage garden potager. Garden access to a paved area at back of house for wheelchair users.

♿ ☕

11 DOLHYFRYD

Lawnt, Denbigh, LL16 4SU. Captain & Mrs Michael Cunningham, 01745 814805, virginia@dolhyfryd.com. *1m SW of Denbigh. On B4501 to Nantglyn, from Denbigh - 1m from town centre.* **Visits by arrangement Jan to Nov. Light refreshments.** Established garden set in small valley of R Ystrad. Acres of crocuses in late Feb/early Mar. Paths through wildflower meadows and woodland of magnificent trees, shade loving plants and azaleas; mixed borders; walled kitchen garden - recently redesigned. Many woodland and riverside birds, incl dippers, kingfishers, grey wagtails. Many species of butterfly encouraged by new planting. Much winter interest, exceptional display of crocuses. Gravel paths, some steep slopes.

♿ 🐕 ✳ ☕

Your visit to a garden will help more people be cared for by a Parkinson's nurse

12 DOVE COTTAGE

Rhos Road, Penyffordd, Chester, CH4 0JR. Chris & Denise Wallis, 01244 547539, dovecottage@supanet.com. *6m SW of Chester. Leave A55 at J35 take A550 to Wrexham. Drive 2m, turn R onto A5104. From A541 Wrexham/Mold Rd in Pontblyddyn take A5104 to Chester. Garden opp train stn.* **Sun 6 Aug (2-5). Adm £3.50, chd free. Home-made teas. Visits also by arrangement June to Aug for groups 10+.** Approx 1½ acre garden, shrubs and herbaceous plants set informally around lawns. Established vegetable area, 2 ponds (1 wildlife), summerhouse and woodland planted area. Gravel paths.

♿ ✳ 🏠 ☕

13 FFRIDD-Y-GOG

Ffordd Ty Cerrig, Corwen, LL21 9YE. Mr & Mrs D Watkins, ffriddygog@hotmail.com. *1m out of Corwen. From A5 to Bala rd turn R at T-lights onto A494 to Chester, 1st R after lay-by. 1st L into Ffridd-y-Gog. Parking on Est Rd except for disabled. Turn L then R into drive.* **Sat 10, Sun 11 June (2-5). Combined adm with Caereuni £5, chd free. Home-made teas. Visits also by arrangement June & July for groups 10 - 25 max.** Old Welsh farmhouse set in ¾ acre of grounds. Organic kitchen garden growing fruit, vegetables and herbs. Greenhouse and polytunnel. Ornamental gardens with particular emphasis on perennials and alpines. Many container grown plants, mostly propagated and grown by the owners. A haven for wildlife and a peaceful and tranquil space to just sit and enjoy. All of garden accessible by wheelchair.

♿ 🐕 ✳ ☕

14 GARTHEWIN

Llanfairtalhaiarn, LL22 8YR. Mr Michael Grime, 01745 720288, michaelgrime12@btinternet.com. *6m S of Abergele & A55. From Abergele take A548 to Llanfair TH & Llanrwst. Entrance to Garthewin 300yds W of Llanfair TH on A548 to Llanrwst. SatNav misleading.* **Mon 29 May (2-6). Adm £4.50, chd** free. Home-made teas. **Visits also by arrangement Apr to Oct, groups 50 max. Regret, no coaches.**

Valley garden with ponds and woodland areas. Much of the 8 acres have been reclaimed and redesigned providing a younger garden with a great variety of azaleas, rhododendrons and young trees, all within a framework of mature shrubs and trees. Teas in old theatre. Chapel open. Some stalls to promote local arts, crafts and foods.

Bryn Twr and Lynton

15 GLOG DDU

Llangernyw, Abergele, LL22 8PS. Pamela & Anthony Harris. *1m S of Llangernyw. No parking at Glog Ddu. Park at Hafodunos Hall, LL22 8TY. Bus to within 250m of Glog Ddu. Then a walk down a steep lane unsuitable for those who have difficulty walking.* **Sun 28 May (11-5). Combined adm with Hafodunos Hall £7, chd free.** Approx 2½ acres designed to fit seamlessly into the spectacular landscape, consisting of rare trees and flowering shrubs, clematis, rhododendrons and azaleas, wildflower meadows, bluebells, tulips, naturalized camassias in abundance. Also has two ponds, herbaceous borders, arboretum and vegetable garden.

16 GWAENYNOG

Denbigh, LL16 5NU. Major & Mrs Tom Smith. *1m W of Denbigh. On A543, Lodge on L, ¼m drive.* **Sun 25 June (2-5.30). Adm £4. Cream teas.** *Donation to St James Church, Nantglyn.*

2 acres incl the restored walled garden where Beatrix Potter wrote and illustrated the Tale of the Flopsy Bunnies. Also a small exhibition of some of her work. C16 house (not open) visited by Dr Samuel Johnson during his Tour of Wales. Herbaceous borders some recently replanted, espalier fruit trees, rose pergola and vegetable area.

17 GWEL YR YNYS

Parc Moel Lus, Penmaenmawr, LL34 6DN. Mr Dafydd Lloyd-Borland, 07968 243119, garden@gwelyrynys.com, www.gwelyrynys.com. *Take J16 from A55. At Mountain View PH take sharp L onto Conwy Old Rd. In ½m take sharp R into Graiglwyd R. Parking at Ysgol Pen Cae. Disable parking available at garden, please enquire.* **Sat 24, Sun 25 June (11-4.30). Adm £3.50, chd free. Light refreshments. Visits also by arrangement Apr to July for groups min 10, max 20.**

A ¾ acre challenging hillside garden in an elevated position some 650ft above sea level. Full of trees, shrubs and much herbaceous prairie style planting. Featured in RHS Garden Magazine and BBC Gardeners World Magazine. Most areas accessible for wheelchair users.

18 HAFODUNOS HALL

Llangernyw, Abergele, Conwy, LL22 8TY. Dr Richard Wood, www.hafodunoshall.co.uk. *1m W of Llangernyw. Halfway between Abergele & Llanrwst on A548. Signed from opp Old Stag PH.* **Sun 28 May (11-5). Combined adm with Glog Ddu £7, chd free. Light refreshments.**

Historic garden undergoing restoration after 30yrs of neglect surrounds a Sir G G Scott Grade I Hall derelict after an arson attack. ½m treelined drive, formal terraces, woodland walks with ancient redwoods, laurels, yews, lake, streams, waterfalls and a gorge. Unique setting. Some uneven paths and steep steps. Children must be supervised by an adult at all times. Most areas around the hall accessible to wheelchairs by gravel pathways. Some gardens are set on slopes.

19 ISGAERWEN

Pentrellyncymer, Cerrigydrudion, Corwen, LL21 9TU. Michael Williams, 01490 420254, michael@isgaerwen.fsnet.co.uk. *10m W of Ruthin. From Ruthin take B5105 to Cerrigydrudion. After ½m turn R opp Cross Keys PH. Follow NGS signs 10m. From Cerrigydrudion take B4501. After 3m turn R to Pentrellyncymer then follow NGS signs 2½m.* **Sun 4 June (11-4). Adm £4, chd free. Cream teas incl dairy & gluten free options. Visits also by arrangement May to July for groups of 6+.**

Isolated with stunning views, possibly the highest garden in Wales. At 1500ft, the 2 acre garden balances the formal and informal: shubberies, copses, herbaceous and bog gardens, open spaces - all against the odds of wind, snow and a short growing season. Children very welcome - adventure play. Good wheelchair access however, whilst there are no steps, much of the garden is on a slope.

GROUP OPENING

20 LLANDEGLA VILLAGE GARDENS

Llandegla, LL11 3AP. *10m W of Wrexham. Please follow NGS signs for parking in Llandegla village. Minibus available from car park to take visitors to out-lying gardens as some have limited or no parking.* **Sun 2 July (1-5). Combined adm £6, chd free. Sun 30 July (1-5). Combined adm £5, chd free. Home-made teas at Plas yn Coed and The Gate House (2 July), Plas yn Coed (30 July).**

THE GATE HOUSE, RUTHIN ROAD
Rod & Shelagh Williams.
Open on Sun 2 July

11 MAES TEG
Mr & Mrs L Evans.
Open on all dates

13 MAES TEG
Phil & Joan Crawshaw.
Open on Sun 2 July

NEW 6 MAES TEG
Martin & Norma Weston.
Open on Sun 2 July

PLAS YN COED
Fraser & Helen Robertson,
www.plasyncoed.me.
Open on all dates

SWN Y GWYNT
Phil Clark.
Open on all dates

TY SIONED
Marco & Rachael Muia.
Open on Sun 2 July

Llandegla village lies on the banks of the R Alyn and nestles on the edge of the Clwydian Range, an area of outstanding natural beauty (AONB), in the NE corner of Wales. It offers the visitor a truly old fashioned village welcome in the most picturesque area of the county. Every part of the community appears to enjoy the busy atmosphere of the day when the gardens attract so many visitors to raise funds for the NGS charity. The garden owners work hard to get their gardens looking their best,

the bakers of the village supply tasty cakes for visitors to buy and enjoy in various venues and there are plenty of plants for sale. Perfect! Not all gardens accessible for wheelchair users due to steps and gravel paths.

21 NEW MOSTYN HALL
Mostyn, Holywell, CH8 9HN. Lord Mostyn, www.mostynestates.co.uk. *Use J31 A55 towards Tre Mostyn or A458 turning through Rhewl Mostyn.* **Sun 30 Apr (10-4). Adm £4, chd free. Home-made teas in Mostyn Kitchen Garden.** Mostyn Hall is set in approx 25 acres of gardens overlooking the Dee estuary. Large lawns lead to camellia and rhododendron lined walks among Victorian specimen trees. Other areas incl the rose garden, Japanese dell, herbaceous borders and 3 acre walled kitchen garden. Spectacular cherry blossom and daffodil displays may be in full flower. Generally accessible to wheelchairs with some gravel areas and slight gradients.

22 THE OLD RECTORY
Llanfihangel Glyn Myfyr, Corwen, LL21 9UN. Mr & Mrs E T Hughes, 01490 420568, elwynthomashughes@hotmail.com. *2½m NE of Cerrigydrudion. From Ruthin take B5105 SW for 12m. From Cerrigydrudion take B5105 for 3m.* **Visits by arrangement Feb to Sept. Please discuss refreshments when booking. Adm £4, chd free.** *Donation to Cancer Research U.K.* This 1 acre garden is in a beautiful setting along the Afon Alwen valley and has mixed borders; water, bog, and gravel gardens; walled garden with old roses, pergola, bower and garden of meditation. In early spring a number of different varieties of snowdrops may be seen together with hellebores, crocus and other spring flowers. Also hardy orchids, gentians, daffodils, rhododendrons and acers. Partial wheelchair access.

23 PEN Y GRAIG BACH
Tremeirchion, St Asaph, LL17 0UR. Roger Pawling & Christine Hoyle, 07875 642270, christinehoyle@gmail.com. *4m SE of St Asaph. Off A55 take J28/29/30 to Tremeirchion, then B5429 to Bodfari, go 0.7m (wide verge), turn L up hill, L at fork, cont to rd end. From Bodfari take B5429 take 2nd R (after 1¼m).* **Visits by arrangement Apr to Sept. Tea/coffee with biscuits/cake depending on numbers. Wine on request. Adm £3.50, chd free.**
2 acre wildlife friendly rural cottage garden. Succession of colour throughout the year. Box hedges and fruit trees enclose 5 plots of herbaceous perennials, unusual climbers, flowering shrubs, soft fruit and vegetables. Over 200 native and ornamental trees. 4 ponds and 3 paddocks which are managed organically for wild flowers and hay. Beehives. At 560ft with stunning views from sea to mountains. Partial wheelchair access, gravel paths between box hedges and grass paths.

24 PLAS COCH
Llanychan, Ruthin, LL15 1UF. Sir David & Lady Henshaw, 01824 790972, Enquiries@annedd.co.uk. *Llanychan. Situated on B5429 between villages of Llandyrnog & Llanbedr DC.* **Sat 24, Sun 25 June (11-4). Adm £3.50, chd free. Morning coffee, cakes, afternoon teas available.** Well established country garden with deep and varied herbaceous borders, vegetable garden and fruit trees with recently planted heritage variety small orchard. Other sections incl small yard garden, pond areas, three seater tybach (outside privy) MGTC 1949, all in the centre of the vale of Clwyd with extensive views towards the Clwydian Hills. Wheelchair access but gravel paths.

Bodysgallen Hall & Spa

25 PLAS NANTGLYN

Nantglyn, Denbigh, LL16 5PW. Janette & Richard Welch. *5m S of Denbigh. From Denbigh follow signs for Nantglyn in SW direction; nr phone box in Nantglyn straight over Xrds & bear R at fork, house 300yds on L. Map Reference SJ 003613.* Sat 13, Sun 14 May (2-5.30). Adm £4, chd free. Home-made teas. *Donation to Hope House and Ty Gobaith Children's Hospices.*

Large old established gardens with a collection of over 40 varieties of rhododendrons which should be at their best in May. Formal yew hedging and topiary enclose a rose garden and small vegetable plot beyond. Herbaceous borders and clematis. Fine trees incl some tall beeches along the drive and a cedar of Lebanon which is just reaching maturity. Pond, summerhouse, terrace and splendid views.

♿ ☕

ALLOTMENTS

26 PRICES LANE ALLOTMENTS

Prices Lane, Wrexham, LL11 2NB. Wrexham Allotment & Leisure Gardeners Association. *1m N of Wrexham town centre. Between A5152 Chester Rd & B5425 Rhosddu Rd. From J6 on A483 take A5152. From J5 take A541 to Wrexham, 1st exit B5101, cont 0.7m & at junction turn L onto B5425 then R into Prices Lane.* Sun 6 Aug (1-5). Adm £3, chd free. Light refreshments.

120 plus rented plots, growing a good variety of flowers, fruit and vegetables. Wide range of seasonal vegetables, fruit and flowers grown by the different plot-holders. WALGA shop full of different goods to meet all growing needs and staffed by volunteers with extensive personal knowledge and experience. Home-made cakes. Featured in local press. Site is all on one level, although the tracks are uneven and rather rough in places.

♿ ♿ ✿ ☕

27 QUEEN ANNE COTTAGE

Whitehurst Gardens, Chirk, LL14 5AS. Michael Kemp, 07958 670771, mikekemp40@yahoo.co.uk, www.fwg-heritage.org. *A5 from Chirk to Llangollen. 50 metres off Whitehurst r'about, opp Jewson`s Building Yard.* Sun 25 June (1-5). Adm £3.50, chd free. Home-made teas. **Visits also by arrangement May to Aug, phone to discuss refreshments.**

Queen Anne Cottage was the banqueting house of Whitehurst Gardens which were originally the walled garden of Chirk Castle. The garden was built in C17 for productive and ornamental purposes. Queen Anne Cottage and its near garden is now owned by a professional gardener who has made a tremendous effort to build and plant a beautiful garden around his unique home. BBC News - Chirk's Whitehurst Gardens secures restoration grant.

♿ ✿ ☕

GROUP OPENING

28 RUTHIN TOWN GARDENS

Ruthin, LL15 1DP. *Parking available in many car parks in town. Maps & ticket information available at all gardens. NO parking at Firgrove.* Sun 23 July (11-5). Combined adm £7, chd free. Home-made teas at Nantclwyd y Dre.

24 BORTHYN
Paul & Suzanne Simm.

FIRGROVE
Philip & Anna Meadway, 01824 702677, meadway@firgrovecountryhouse.co.uk, www.firgrovecountryhouse.co.uk.
🛌

NANTCLWYD Y DRE
Denbighshire County Council.

6 PARK ROAD
Mr & Mrs Glyn Jones.

RUTHIN CASTLE
Ruthin Castle Ltd, 01824 702664, debby.morris@ruthincastle.co.uk.
🛌

NEW SARUM HOUSE
Mr & Mrs John & Helen Roberts, 01824 703886, helenroberts48@hotmail.com, www.sarumhouseruthin.com.
🛌

The beautiful medieval town of Ruthin offers 6 contrasting gardens, ranging from the large garden of

Tal-y-Bryn Farm

Ruthin Castle, surrounded by ancient walls and picturesque grounds to beautiful little gardens hidden behind terraced cottages. One of the oldest timbered town house in Wales, Nantclwyd y Dre and the restored Lord`s garden beyond is a must see. Refreshments can be purchased here with proceeds going to the Friends of the property. 24 Borthyn and 6 Park Rd are pretty, cottage gardens both up the entry by the Chinese takeaway on Denbigh Rd and were a real hit with visitors in previous years. A new garden for this year, Sarum House, is through the archway on Record St hidden behind this large Georgian B&B and is so peaceful and elegant. For the first time a bus will be available to take visitors up to Firgrove, 10 mins away. This plantsmans garden has a collection of brugmansias and many unusual shrubs, and exotic plantings in containers. Wheelchair access to most gardens.

&. ✿ ☕

---

29 NEW SCOTT HOUSE

Corwen Road, Ruthin, LL15 2NP. Scott House Residents. *A494 Corwen Road. Disabled parking only at garden. Park in town, then walk from town square onto Castle St, garden 300m beyond Ruthin Castle Hotel, entrance on R.* **Sun 28, Mon 29 May (11-5). Adm £3.50, chd free. Home-made teas.** Redesigned 2½ acre shared garden surrounding a fine 1930s Arts and Crafts house former nurses home to Ruthin Castle hospital. Breathtaking open views of the Vale of Clwyd. Avenue of Limes and a magnificent Cedar of Lebanon stands sentinel over a newly planted arboretum. Long herbaceous borders planted for summer long interest. New highly scented rose garden and recently constructed vegetable plot. Partial wheelchair access due to steps and terraces.

✿ ☕

30 TAL-Y-BRYN FARM

Llannefydd, Denbigh, LL16 5DR. Mr & Mrs Gareth Roberts, 01745 540256, llaeth@villagedairy.co.uk,

www.villagedairy.co.uk. *3m W of Henllan. From Henllan take rd signed Llannefydd. After 2½m turn R signed Bont Newydd. Garden ½m on L.* **Visits by arrangement. Vintage home-made teas. Tours of the yoghurt dairy may also be booked. Adm £4, chd free.** *Donation to Elderly Committee of Llannefydd.* Medium sized working farmhouse cottage garden. Ancient farm machinery. Incorporating ancient privy festooned with honeysuckle, clematis and roses. Terraced arches, sunken garden pool and bog garden, fountains and old water pumps. Herb wheels, shrubs and other interesting features. Lovely views of the Clwydian range. Water feature, new rose tunnel, vegetable tunnel and small garden summer house.

&. ✿ 🛏 ☕

The National Garden Scheme and Perennial, helping gardeners when they are in need

---

31 TUDOR COTTAGE

Isallt Road, Llysfaen, Colwyn Bay, LL29 8LJ. Mr & Mrs C Manifold, 01492 518510, andrina50@outlook.com. *1½m SE of Old Colwyn. Turn S off A547 between Llandulas & Old Colwyn. Up Highlands Rd for ½m, R onto Tan-y-Graig, ignore SatNav, ¾m to swings. Take Isallt Rd on far R.* **Sat 15, Sun 16 July (2-5). Adm £4, chd free. Home-made teas. Visits also by arrangement July & Aug.** ¾ acre garden on different levels set amongst natural rock faces. Unusual and varied planting featuring cottage, scree, Japanese, shade and bog gardens. Display bedding, an abundance of colourful pots and baskets, together with quirky statues, ponds, bridges and a folly. Lovely

views from upper level. Some uneven paths and steep steps. Care required. Children must be supervised by an adult at all times please. Featured in Amateur Garden magazine.

✿ ☕

32 TY HWNT YR AFON

Rowen, Conwy, LL32 8YT. Ian & Margaret Trevette, 01492 650871, ian.trevette@btinternet.com. *Take B5106 from Conwy, R at Groes Inn. Follow signs. Park on rd below Ty Gwyn Hotel, garden 500yds thru village on L fork in rd. Disabled parking on drive.* **Sun 30 Apr, Sun 28, Mon 29 May, Sun 18 June (1-5). Adm £3.50, chd free. Home-made teas. Visits also by arrangement May to Aug.** ¾ acre garden relandscaped by owners over last 6yrs. With the backdrop of R Ro and preserved woodland beyond have used the gardens natural features of glacial stone, stream and springs to create an amphitheatre of garden shrubs and plants incl spring bulbs, acers, azaleas, camellias, rhododendrons and a multitude of other favourite perennials. Wheelchair access to view most of garden and for home-made teas on the sun terrace provided by Friends of ChildLine North Wales. Some steps.

&. ✿ ☕

33 WYLAN

Llangynhafal, Ruthin, LL15 1RU. John & Carol Perkins, 07808 988556, carolperkins24@yahoo.co.uk. *3m N of Ruthin. Take A494 from Ruthin to Llanbedr then B5429. After ½m turn R signed Llangynhafal 1½m. Entrance on R by large clump of trees.* **Visits by arrangement May to July, groups 25 max. Adm £3, chd free.** 1 acre garden designed by owners for all parts to be easily accessible. Magnificent panoramic views. Mature shrubs, mixed borders and water features. Pergola leading into sunken patio with colourful summer planted containers. Winner of Best Kept Country Garden in Ruthin Flower Show for 6 consecutive years. Gradual grass slope at end of front garden to access back garden.

&. 🐕

POWYS

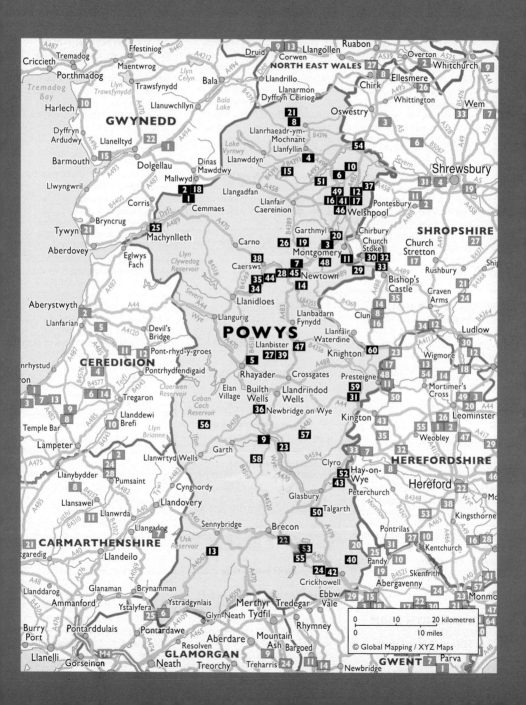

A three hour drive through Powys takes you through the spectacular and unspoilt landscape of Mid Wales, from the Berwyn Hills in the north to south of the Brecon Beacons.

Through the valleys and over the hills, beside rippling rivers and wooded ravines, you will see a lot of sheep, pretty market towns, half timbered buildings and houses of stone hewn from the land.

The stunning landscape is home to many of the beautiful NGS gardens of Powys. Some are clustered around the eastern side of the county, where Wales meets the Marches. There are a few in town centres, and the rest, both large and small, are scattered throughout this agricultural paradise.

Powis Castle, whose 18th century Italian terraces set the gold standard for the other gardens, owes much of its wealth to the farming and mining in the area. The Dingle is world-renowned for the dark, still lake at the centre of fantastic planting.

Here in Powys is the spectacular, the unusual, the peaceful and the enchanting, all opened by generous and welcoming garden owners.

Below: Hurdley Hall

Volunteers

North Powys County Organiser
Susan Paynton
01686 650531
susan.paynton@ngs.org.uk

County Treasurer
Gwyneth Jackson-Jones
01691 648578
gjacksonjones@icloud.com

Publicity
Annette Dowling
01938 820160
annette.dowling@ngs.org.uk

Social Media
Jude Boutle & Sue Cox
01597 840337
powys.socialmedia@ngs.org.uk

Booklet Co-ordinator
Carole Jones
01650 511176
carole.jones@ngs.org.uk

Assistant County Organisers
Penny Davies
01691 828373
digbydavies@aol.com

Group Captain Neil Bale
01691 648451
info@cyfiefarm.co.uk

Christine Scott
01691 780080
christine.scott@ngs.org.uk

South Powys County Organiser
Katharine Smith
01982 551308
katharinejsmith@hotmail.co.uk

County Treasurer
Steve Carrow
01591 620461
stevetynycwm@hotmail.co.uk

Assistant County Organisers
Christine Carrow
01591 620461
stevetynycwm@hotmail.co.uk

OPENING DATES

All entries subject to change. For latest information check **www.ngs.org.uk**

Map locator numbers are shown to the right of each garden name.

March

Sunday 19th
Oak Cottage   41

April

Sunday 9th
Maesfron Hall and Gardens   37

Sunday 16th
Oak Cottage   41

Monday 17th
Oak Cottage   41

Saturday 29th
Cartref   10

Sunday 30th
Cartref   10
Fraithwen   19
Oak Cottage   41

May

Monday 1st
Oak Cottage   41

Saturday 6th
◆ Dingle Nurseries & Garden   16

Sunday 7th
◆ Dingle Nurseries & Garden   16

Saturday 13th
1 Church Bank   12

Sunday 14th
1 Church Bank   12
Glanwye   23

Saturday 20th
NEW The Hymns   31
NEW Rock Mill   48

Sunday 21st
NEW The Hymns   31
Penmyarth House   42
NEW Rock Mill   48

90th Anniversary Weekend

Saturday 27th
Mill Cottage   39
NEW Vron   57
1 Ystrad House   60

Sunday 28th
Caer Beris Manor Hotel   9
Mill Cottage   39
The Rock House   47
1 Ystrad House   60

Monday 29th
Llysdinam   36
Mill Cottage   39

Wednesday 31st
◆ Grandma's Garden   25

June

Saturday 3rd
Hyssington, Gorsty House   32
Hyssington, The Old Barn   33

Sunday 4th
Aberangell, The Old Coach House   1
Aberangell, Pen Pentre   2
Gliffaes Country House Hotel   24
NEW ◆ The Hall at Abbey Cwm Hir   27
Hyssington, Gorsty House   32
Hyssington, The Old Barn   33
The Neuadd   40
The Rock House   47

Saturday 10th
Bryn y Llidiart   8

Sunday 11th
Bryn y Llidiart   8
◆ Gregynog Hall & Garden   26
NEW The Mill   38

Saturday 17th
NEW Hurdley Hall   30
Tremynfa   54

Sunday 18th
Cwm-Weeg   14
NEW Hurdley Hall   30
Pen-y-Maes   43
Tremynfa   54
Ty Cam   55
Tyn y Cwm   56

Wednesday 21st
◆ Powis Castle Garden   46

Saturday 24th
Cartref   10
Hyssington, Gorsty House   32
Hyssington, The Old Barn   33
Tinto House   52
1 Ystrad House   60

Sunday 25th
Cartref   10
Hyssington, Gorsty House   32
Hyssington, The Old Barn   33
Tinto House   52
1 Ystrad House   60

July

Saturday 1st
1 Church Bank   12
Ponthafren   45
Talgarth Mill   50

Sunday 2nd
1 Church Bank   12
Cwm-Weeg   14
Esgair Angell   18
Talgarth Mill   50
Treberfydd House   53

Cwm-Weeg

THE GARDENS

1 ABERANGELL, THE OLD COACH HOUSE
Aberangell, Machynlleth, SY20 9AB. Sue McKillop, www.theoldcoachhousecottage.co.uk. *On A470 midway beween Dolgellau & Machynlleth. From Mallwyd r'about to Cemmaes Rd, turn R after 3m just after turn for Aberangell village.* **Sun 4 June (11-4.30). Adm £2.50, chd free. Home-made teas. Also open Aberangell, Pen Pentre.** Nestled in the heart of the Dyfi Valley this small, cottage style garden is a haven for birds and pollinating insects. Narrow paths take you around the flower beds some raised, mini meadow and little pond. Planting is informal with mostly perennials and shrubs. Secluded seating areas allow the visitor to relax and enjoy different aspects of the garden with views down to the R Dyfi. Western Morning News featured our holiday cottage and garden. Garden featured in Welsh Country magazine. A gravel drive and cobbled area in front of the house leads to a grassy slope into

the garden. There are a few low steps within the garden.

2 ABERANGELL, PEN PENTRE
Aberangell, Machynlleth, SY20 9ND. Jacqueline Parsons. *From A470, follow signs for Aberangell. Past caravan park to Xrds. Turn R, Pen Pentre is 2nd house on R.* **Sun 4 June (11-4.30). Adm £2.50, chd free. Also open Aberangell, The Old Coach House. Home-made teas plus small selection of ice creams.** Delightful cottage garden built up around the old Aberangell railway station incorporating the station building, the railway platform and line. The station contains many old artefacts from a bygone era, and more are to be found around the garden itself. The borders are filled with colourful planting, attracting bees and butterflies. There are plenty of areas to sit, allowing different views. Featured in Welsh Country magazine.

3 ABERNANT
Garthmyl, SY15 6RZ. Mrs B M Gleave, 01686 640494, john.gleave@mac.com. *1½m S of Garthmyl. On A483 midway between Welshpool & Newtown (both 8m). Approached over steep humpback bridge with wooden statue of a workman to one side, then straight ahead.* **Visits by arrangement Apr to July, groups 5+. Home-made teas.** Approx 3 acres incl cherry orchard, roses, knot garden, lavender, box hedging, rockery, pond, shrubs, ornamental trees, raised specimen fern beds in natural setting. Examples of archaic sundials, fossilized wood and stone heads. Additional woodland of 9 acres, pond and stream with borrowed views of the Severn Valley. Late April - 90 cherry trees blossom; late June - roses. Picnics welcome.

The Queen's Nursing Institute founded the National Garden Scheme exactly 90 years ago

4 BACHIE UCHAF

Bachie Road, Llanfyllin, SY22 5NF.
Glyn & Glenys Lloyd. *S of Llanfyllin.*
Going towards Welshpool on A490
turn R onto Bachie Rd after Llanfyllin
primary school. Keep straight for
0.8m. Take drive R uphill at cottage
on L. **Sat 22, Sun 23 July (1.30-5).**
Adm £4.50, chd free. Home-
made teas.
Inspiring, colourful hillside country
garden. Gravel paths meander
around extensive planting and
over streams cascading down into
ponds. Specimen trees, shrubs
and vegetable garden. Enjoy the
wonderful views from one of
the many seats; your senses will
be rewarded. Featured in Welsh
Country magazine.

5 BEILI NEUADD

St Harmon, Rhayader, LD6 5NS.
Alison Parker, 01597 810211,
info@beilineuadd.co.uk,
www.beilneuadd.co.uk. *2m from*
Rhayader. Take A44 E from clock
tower. Leaving Rhayader fork L
(Abbey-Cwm-Hir, Brown sign Beili
Neuadd). After 1m turn L (brown
sign). Beili Neuadd 2nd property on
R. **Sun 16 July (1-5). Adm £3.50,**
chd free. Home-made teas.
Visits also by arrangement May
to Sept.
2 acre garden set within a 6 acre
small holding. Established ponds,
trees and stunning landscape, set
in the foothills of the Cambrian
Mountains, provides the framework
for an exciting, evolving garden with
herbaceous borders, ponds, streams
and wooded areas. A haven for birds
and wildlife along with our flock of
Shetland sheep, rare breed pigs and
hens.

6 BRONIARTH HALL

Pentrebeirdd, Guilsfield,
Welshpool, SY21 9DW. Mrs
Janet Powell, 01938 500639,
janet09br@hotmail.co.uk. *From*
Londis petrol station, Guilsfield, take
A490 towards Llanfyllin for approx
2m. Turn R through to Sarnau. After 1m
turn R for Broniarth Hall. **Sat 22,**
Sun 23 July (1.30-5). Adm £3.50,
chd free. Home-made teas.

Visits also by arrangement in
July groups of 10-15 with prior
arrangement.
Broniarth Hall is a C17 farm
house (not open) with bijou SE
facing cottage garden with 2 small
ponds, perennial filled beds and
aviary. Unique and quirky features
and containers incl a collection
of approx 70 heucheras. Stunning
views from patio areas with summer
bedding and foliage plants. Featured
in Welsh Country magazine.

7 BRYN TEG

Bryn Lane, Newtown, SY16 2DP.
Novlet Childs. *N side of Newtown.*
Lane on L before hospital on Llanfair
rd towards Bettws Cedewain. **Sun 30**
July (11-5). Adm £3, chd free.
Home-made teas at Cultivate
Community Garden.
An exciting walk through the jungle
in Newtown! High above the head
are banana leaves and colourful
climbers. An exotic Caribbean
garden planted to remind me of my
childhood in Jamaica. A winding path
from the front door around the side
of the house to the back door takes
you on a journey through another
land. Manual wheelchair access to
most of the garden. Not suitable for
mobility scooters.

8 BRYN Y LLIDIART

Cefn Coch, Llanrhaeadr
ym Mochnant, Oswestry,
SY10 0BP. Dr John & Mrs
Christine Scott, 01691 780080,
christine.scott@ngs.org.uk. *2m*
W of Llanrhaeadr ym Mochnant.
On rd between Llanrhaeadr village
& Penybontfawr. Follow yellow NGS
signs up hill on single track rd for 1m.
Sat 10, Sun 11 June (2-5). Adm
£4.50, chd free. Home-made
teas. Visits also by arrangement
June to Sept single visitors/large
groups.
Up the airy mountain you are in for
a big surprise! On S-facing lee of
Berwyns at 1100ft with spectacular
views, meander mown paths through
8 acres of wildflower meadows to
discover lush planting around house.
Stone walls, boulders, slate and shale
reflect the landscape. Extensive green

roof, sitouterie in Welsh orchard, bog
garden, wildlife pond and vegetables.
Good footwear required. Childrens'
Quiz. Featured on BBC2 Gardeners
World. Partial wheelchair access,
shale and rough grass paths, some
steps.

9 CAER BERIS MANOR HOTEL

Builth Wells, LD2 3NP.
Mr Peter & Mrs Katharine
Smith, 01982 552601,
caerberis@btconnect.com,
www.caerberis.com. *W edge Builth*
Wells. From Builth Wells town centre
take A483 signed Llandovery. Caer
Beris Manor is on L as you leave
Builth. **Sun 28 May (11-5). Adm**
£5, chd free. Sun 15 Oct (11-4).
Adm £4, chd free. Home-made
teas.
An original 1927 NGS pioneer
garden. 27 acres of mature
parklands, with the R Irfon bordering
the property. The grounds were
planted early C20 by the Vivien
family who were plant hunters.
Many varied specimen trees form
an Arboretum. Large displays of
rhododendrons at time of opening.
An Edwardian Rose archway has
been recently replanted with David
Austin roses. Concert by Builth
Wells Ladies Voice Choir: Sunday
lunches and afternoon teas available.
Lower parkland can be accessed by
car or wheelchair.

10 CARTREF

Sarnau, Arddleen, Llanymynech,
SY22 6QL. Neil & Stella Townsend.
8m N of Welshpool. Take A483 from
Welshpool towards Oswestry. Turn L
after 6m at Arddleen, bear R then
turn R towards Sarnau. Turn R after
1m. Cont for approx ½m. Cartref is
on L. **Sat 29, Sun 30 Apr, Sat 24,**
Sun 25 June (1-4.30). Adm £3,
chd free. Home-made teas.
1 acre modern cottage garden in
open countryside with an emphasis
on attracting wildlife. Spring bulbs
make the garden particularly
pretty in spring. Woodland, ponds,
perennial borders and a kitchen
garden give yr-round interest.
Meandering paths join areas and

give unexpected views within the garden. Children will love our ponds which are dragonfly, frog, toad and newt nurseries bordered by yellow, white and blue irises in June and full of pink, white and yellow water lilies.

11 CASTELL Y GWYNT

Llandyssil, Montgomery, SY15 6HR. John & Jacqui Wynn-Jones, 01686 668569, jacquiwj@btinternet.com. *2m out of Montgomery on the Sarn Rd, 1st R, 1st R.* **Visits by arrangement May to July single visitors/ small groups 30 max. Prior booking necessary as parking limited. Adm £5, chd free. Light refreshments.**

1½ acre garden at 900ft, set within 6 acres of land managed for wildlife. Native woodland corridors with mown rides surround hayfield/ wildflower meadow and pool with turf roofed summerhouse. Enclosed kitchen garden with boxed beds of vegetables, fruit and cutting flowers, greenhouse and orchard. Shrubberies, deep mixed borders and more formal areas close to house. Outstanding views of Welsh mountains. Circular path around the whole property which gives unique views of the house, garden and surrounding countryside. Bring good footwear and enjoy the walk.

12 1 CHURCH BANK

Welshpool, SY21 7DR. Mel & Heather Parkes, 01938 559112, melandheather@live.co.uk. *Centre of Welshpool. Church Bank leads onto Salop Rd from Church St. Follow one way system, use main car park then short walk. Follow yellow NGS signs.* **Sat 13, Sun 14 May, Sat 1, Sun 2 July (12-5). Adm £3.50, chd free. Home-made teas. Visits also by arrangement May to Aug for groups min 6, max 15.**

A jewel in the town. Explore the ground floor of this C17 barrel maker's cottage and walk into a large garden room which also houses a museum of tools from different trades. Mystic pool of smoke and sounds. Outside a Gothic arch and zig zag path leads

to a shell grotto and bonsai garden, fernery and many unusual features. Sounds of water fill the air and interesting plants fill the intimate space. Children's garden quiz. Museum of country life. Featured in County Times, Shropshire Star, Chronicle and Welsh Country Magazine.

GROUP OPENING

13 CRAI GARDENS

Crai, LD3 8YP. *13m SW of Brecon. Turn W off A4067 signed Crai. Village hall is 50yds straight ahead; park here for admission & information about gardens.* **Sun 13 Aug (2-5). Combined adm £5, chd free. Home-made teas in village hall.**

Set against the backdrop of Fan Gyhirych and Fan Brycheiniog, at 1000ft above sea level the Crai valley is a hidden gem, off the beaten track between Brecon and Swansea. Those in the know have long enjoyed visiting our serene valley, with its easy access to the hills and its fabulous views. In difficult climatic conditions, the Crai Gardens reflect a true passion for gardening. The gardens come in a wide variety of size, purpose and design, and incl a range of shrubs, perennials and annuals; organically grown vegetables and fruits; raised beds; polytunnels; water features; prolific

hanging baskets, patio containers and window boxes. Not to forget the chickens and ducks. And to complete your Sunday afternoon, come and enjoy the renowned hospitality of the Crai ladies by sampling their delicious home-made cakes in the village hall.

14 CWM-WEEG

Dolfor, Newtown, SY16 4AT. Dr W Schaefer & Mr K D George, www.cwmweeg.co.uk. *4½m SE of Newtown. Take A489 E from Newtown for 1½m, turn R towards Dolfor. After 2m turn L down farm track, signed at entrance. Do not rely on SatNav. Also signed from Dolfor village. Coaches (max 33 seater).* **Sun 18 June, Sun 2, Sun 30 July, Sun 27 Aug (2-5). Adm £5, chd free. Home-made teas.**

2½ acre garden set within 24 acres of wildflower meadows and bluebell woodland with stream centred around C15 farmhouse (open by prior arrangement). Formal garden in English landscape tradition with vistas, grottos, sculptures, lawns and extensive borders terraced with stone walls. Translates older garden vocabulary into an innovative C21 concept. Under cover area for refreshments if wet. Also open June - Sept (not for NGS), see website for details. Partial wheelchair access.

The Mill

15 CYFIE FARM

Llanfihangel, Llanfyllin, SY22 5JE. Group Captain Neil & Mrs Claire Bale, 01691 648451, info@cyfiefarm.co.uk, www.cyfiefarm.co.uk. *6m SE of Lake Vyrnwy. ½m N Llanfyllin on B490 turn L B4393 towards L Vrynwy. 4m turn L B4382 signed Llanfihangel go straight through, 1½m, 1st L, 3rd on L.* **Visits by arrangement Mar to Oct individuals/large groups. Adm £4, chd free. Cheese and nibbles or teas; alternative requirements on request.** Beautiful 1 acre hillside garden with spectacular views of Vyrnwy valley and Welsh hills. Linger over the roses or wander through the woodland garden with rhododendrons and bluebell banks. Many places to sit and contemplate the stunning views. Wildflower meadow and garden sculptures. Unusual garden statues. Spectacular views, peaceful setting. Finalist - Montgomeryshire Best Farm Garden. Partial wheelchair access.

16 ◆ DINGLE NURSERIES & GARDEN

Welshpool, SY21 9JD. Mr & Mrs D Hamer, 01938 555145, www.dinglenurseries.co.uk. *2m NW of Welshpool. Take A490 towards Llanfyllin & Guilsfield. After 1m turn L at sign for Dingle Nurseries & Garden.* **For NGS: Sat 6, Sun 7 May, Sat 14, Sun 15 Oct (9-5). Adm £3.50, chd free. Tea and coffee available. For other opening times and information, please phone or visit garden website.** RHS recommended 4½ acre garden on S-facing site, sloping down to lakes surrounded by yr-round interest. Beds mostly colour themed with a huge variety of rare and unusual trees, ornamental shrubs and herbaceous plants. Set in hills of mid Wales this beautiful and well known garden attracts visitors from Britain and abroad. Open all yr except 24 Dec - 2 Jan.

17 ELMHURST

Severn Road, Welshpool, SY21 7AR. Tony Solomon. *On Severn Rd between fire & police stations.* **Sat 15, Sun 16 July (2-5). Adm £4, chd free. Home-made teas.** Hidden Victorian house and garden dating from 1841. 3 acres lawns, rose and flower beds and very productive large Victorian partly walled vegetable garden with 3 glasshouses and orchard. Small woodland planted 35yrs ago and new small wood of native trees. Refreshments served on the lawn or in the old scullery. Flat gravel paths.

18 ESGAIR ANGELL

Aberangell, Machynlleth, SY20 9QJ. Carole Jones, 01650 511176, jonesey200@gmail.com, www.upperbarncottage.co.uk. *Midway between Dogellau & Machynlleth. Turn off A470 towards village of Aberangell, then signed.* **Sun 2 July (11-5). Adm £4, chd free. Home-made teas.** The garden extends to over 2 acres bounded by the R Angell, within the Dovey Forest and Snowdonia National Park. Around the central lake, which supports an abundance of plant and animal life, is a small wood, a wildlife meadow, vegetable garden and the aviaries that house our families of owls. Second lake and a circular walk through the neighbouring fields with spectacular views. Featured in Welsh Country magazine. Partial wheelchair access, mainly laid to lawn. Access on gravelled area above lake affording excellent views.

19 FRAITHWEN

Tregynon, SY16 3EW. Sydney Thomas, 01686 650307. *6m N of Newtown. On B4389 midway between villages of Bettws Cedewain & Tregynon.* **Sun 30 Apr, Sun 23 July (2-5). Adm £3.50, chd free. Home-made teas. Visits also by arrangement Feb to Oct single visitors/small groups - 30 max.** 1½ acre established garden with herbaceous borders, rockeries and ponds. Planted with rare plants for yr-round interest and for pollinators. Collector of unusual snowdrops. Plants in flower every day of the year: spring bulbs and alpines, alstroemeria collection, lilies in garden not pots, vegetable plot and pool. Featured in Welsh Country magazine. Partial wheelchair access. Some steps, gravel and slopes.

20 GARTHMYL HALL

Garthmyl, Montgomery, SY15 6RS. Julia Pugh, www.garthmylhall.co.uk. *On A483 midway between Welshpool & Newtown (both 8m). Turn R 200yds S of Nag's Head PH.* **Sun 16 July (12-5). Adm £3.50, chd free. Home-made teas served in summerhouse.** Grade II listed Georgian manor house (not open) surrounded by 5 acres of grounds currently under restoration. Over 100 metres newly planted herbaceous borders, newly restored 1 acre walled garden with gazebo, circular flowerbeds, lavender beds, two fire pits and gravel paths. Fountain, 3 magnificent Cedar of Lebanon and giant redwood. Partial wheelchair access. Accessible WC.

21 GLAN YR AFON

Commins, Llanrhaeadr Ym Mochnant, Oswestry, SY10 0BZ. Brian & Marian Jones, 01691 780479, riversideretreat@hotmail.com. *15m NW Welshpool, 15m W of Oswestry. From village of Llanrhaeadr YM, at Greatorex corner store drive 1.6m along Waterfall Rd. 1st L turn at white cottage, parking opp.* **Visits by arrangement June to Sept (Mons and Weds only 2-5) groups 10+. Limited parking. Adm £4.50, chd free. Home-made teas.** Situated in the Tanat valley stretching from the famous 240ft Pistyll Rhaeadr Waterfall to Llanrhaeadr Village. A tranquil, romantic location with the R Rhaeadr flowing through the length of the 2 acre garden. Lawn surrounded by cottage garden planting, with lavenders, salvias, roses and peonies, a gazebo by the river, rose swags, Sunray pergola, woodland path, riverside walk.

Vegetable garden. Shelter available if wet. WC. Disabled parking/access can be arranged. Most of garden accessible by wheelchair incl woodland gravel path.

 ♿ ❀ 🛏 ☕

22 GLANUSK

Llanfrynach, Brecon, LD3 7UY. Mike & Lorraine Lewis, 01874 665407, lorrainelewis595@gmail.com. *1½m SE of Brecon. Leave A40 signed Llanfrynach, Pencelli. Immed cross canal & cross narrow river bridge (R Usk), Signal R as you leave bridge, garden 1st entrance, 40 metres on R.* **Visits by arrangement May to Aug for 20 max. Adm £4, chd free. Light refreshments.**
2 acre garden on the R Usk. Steep bank has prairie and perennial planting criss-crossed with paths. Old orchard incl specimen trees, grass pattern, rose border and small woodland walk leading to stone circle. The formal garden incl borders, boxballs, rose pergola and beech hedge. Our water feature is the R Usk. Other features incl borders, small wood, roses, steep river bank planted with grasses and perennials. Tea, coffee and biscuits available.

🐄 ❀ ☕

23 GLANWYE

Builth Wells, LD2 3YP. Mr & Mrs H Kidston. *2m SE Builth Wells From Builth Wells on A470, after 2m R at Lodge Gate. From Llyswen on A470, after 6m L at Lodge Gate. Suggest not using SatNav as unreliable* **Sun 14 May (2-5). Adm £3.50, chd free. Home-made teas.**
Large Victorian garden, spectacular rhododendrons, azaleas. Herbaceous borders, extensive yew hedges, lawns, long woodland walk with bluebells and other woodland flowers. Magnificent views of upper Wye Valley

🐄 🛏 ☕

24 GLIFFAES COUNTRY HOUSE HOTEL

Gliffaes Rd, Crickhowell, NP8 1RH. Mrs N Brabner & Mr & Mrs J C Suter, 01874 730371, calls@gliffaeshotel.com, www.gliffaes.com. *3½m W of Crickhowell. 1m off A40, 2½ m W*

of Crickhowell. **Sun 4 June (2-5). Adm £5, chd free. Cream teas.**
The Gliffaes gardens lie in a dream position on a plateau 120ft above the spectacular fast flowing R Usk. As well as breath taking views of the Brecon Beacons and 33 acres of parkland and lawns, there are ancient and ornamental trees, fine maples, new tree plantings, spring bulbs, rhododendrons, azaleas, many shrubs and an ornamental pond. Gliffaes is a country house hotel and is open for lunch, bar snacks, afternoon tea and dinner to non residents and garden visitors. Wheelchair ramp to the west side of the hotel. In dry weather main lawns accessible, but more difficult if wet.

 ♿ 🐄 🛏 ☕

25 ◆ GRANDMA'S GARDEN

Dolguog Estates, Felingerrig, Machynlleth, SY20 8UJ. Richard Rhodes, 01654 702244, info@plasdolguog.co.uk, www.plasdolguog.co.uk. *1½m E of Machynlleth. Turn L off A489 Machynlleth to Newtown rd. Follow brown tourist signs to Plas Dolguog Hotel.* **For NGS: Wed 31 May (10.30-4.30). Adm £4, chd £1.50. Cream teas. For other opening times and information, please phone, email or visit garden website.**
Inspiration for the senses, unique, fascinating, educational and fun. Strategic seating, continuous new attractions, wildlife abundant, 9 acres of peace. Sculptures, poetry arboretum. Seven sensory gardens, wildlife pond, riverside boardwalk, stone circle, labyrinth. Azaleas and bluebells in May. Children welcome. Open every Sun and Wed (10.30-4.30). Plas Dolguog Hotel open their café in the conservatory - the hotel is the admission point - serving inside and out on patio overlooking gardens.

 ♿ 🐄 ❀ 🛏 ☕

26 ◆ GREGYNOG HALL & GARDEN

Tregynon, Newtown, SY16 3PW. Gregynog, 01686 650224, enquiries@gregynog.org, www.gregynog.org. *5m N of*

Newtown. *From main A483, take turning for Berriew. In Berriew follow sign for Bettws then for Tregynon (£2.50 car parking charge applies).* **For NGS: Sun 11 June, Sun 15 Oct (11-4). Adm £3, chd £1. Light refreshments at Courtyard Cafe. For other opening times and information, please phone, email or visit garden website.**
Grade I listed garden set within 750 acres of Gregynog Estate which was designated a National Nature Reserve in 2013. Fountains, lily lake and water garden. A mass display of rhododendrons and yew hedge create a spectacular backdrop to the sunken lawns. Azaleas and unusual trees. Fantastic autumn colour. Courtyard cafe serving morning coffee, light lunches and Welsh afternoon teas. As seen on BBC TV Antiques Roadshow. Some gravel paths.

 ♿ 🐄 🚗 🛏 ☕

27 NEW ◆ THE HALL AT ABBEY CWM HIR

Abbeycwmhir, Llandrindod Wells, LD1 6PH. Mr Paul Humperston, 01597 851727, info@abbeycwmhir.com, www.abbeycwmhir.com. *Nr Llandrindod-Wells. Go to Crossgates. Take A483 towards Newtown for ½m Follow village/brown signs for Abbey-Cwm-Hir. The Hall is on the R at entrance to village.* **For NGS: Sun 4 June (10.30-6.30). Adm £5, chd free. Home-made teas. For other opening times and information, please phone, email or visit garden website.**
The Hall is a Grade II* listed Gothic mansion. The 12 acre gardens are set above the ruins of the C12 Cistercian abbey. They incl a walled garden, lake, waterfall, woodlands, lawns, terraces and courtyards. The gardens contain climbers, conifers, acers, roses, rhododendra, azalea, shrubs and herbaceous plants. A garden of secrets opening out to stunning views along The Long Valley. The gardens are in one of the most spectacular settings in Wales. Featured on S4C programme Welsh Gardens. Also featured in the book The Finest Gardens in Wales.

🐄 🚗 ☕

28 HOLLY BUSH

Mochdre, Newtown,
SY16 4LB. Douglas & Jane
Wood, 01686 623154,
douglas_jane_wood@yahoo.co.uk.
*3m out of Newtown on A470 for
Llanidloes, over College r'about
for 1m turn L into narrow lane by
letterbox, NGS sign on post, house
at top of steep lane.* **Visits by
arrangement in June (Tues -
Sat), single visitors/groups 10
max. Parking for 6 cars max.
Please phone before coming.
Adm £3, chd free. Light
refreshments.**
A garden in the making, lawn and
flower beds surround the house,
with views NE over the Severn
valley, Steps to lower lawn, rose
bed, and day lilies. Field with young
specimen trees and pond: wet area
with mown path and wild orchids.
Fields with orchard and daffodils in
spring followed by bluebells. Good
footwear required.

🐕 ☕ 💬

29 HOLLY COTTAGE

Great Argoed, Mellington, nr
Churchstoke, SY15 6TH. Martin
& Allison Walter, 01588 620055,
allison.walter2@btinternet.com.
*On Powys/Shropshire border, 5m from
Bishops Castle & Montgomery. Take
minor rd off B4385 at Courthouse
Farm, Mellington. Follow NGS signs to
Great Argoed, approx 1m.* **Visits by
arrangement Apr to Aug, single
visitors/small groups (30 max)
welcome. Adm £4, chd free.
Home-made teas.**
Started in 2007, naturalistic garden
at 800' with spectacular views;
series of individual gardens with
different styles and planting incl 80m
perennial/wildflower border; fruit
and ornamental trees and wigloo;
massed spring bulbs; colourful
planting around house inc vertically
planted walled terrace. Fruit and
flower garden; slate garden; water
and wind features; new areas being
planted all the time. Featured in
Gardener's World magazine.

✿ ☕ 💬

30 NEW HURDLEY HALL

Hurdley, Churchstoke, SY15 6DY.
Simon Cain & Simon Quin, simon.
cain@westbourneconsulting.
com. *2m from Churchstoke. Take
turning for Hurdley off A489, 1m E
of Churchstoke. Garden is approx 1m
from here.* **Sat 17, Sun 18 June,
Sat 8, Sun 9 July (11-5). Adm
£4.50, chd free. Home-made
teas. Visits also by arrangement
Apr to Sept for groups 8+.**
2 acre garden set around C17
house with additional 18 acres
adjoining Roundton Hill National
Nature Reserve. Herbaceous and
mixed borders, orchard, ponds,
topiary and kitchen garden. Mown
paths lead to a 5 acre Coronation
Meadow, large newly planted
orchard, pastures and new and
ancient woodland with brook.
Uneven ground and steep slopes
give wide ranging views but may
restrict access Live music performed
by local orchestra on Sun 18 June
from 2pm and Swing Band on Sun 9
July from 2pm

🐕 🐕 ☕

31 NEW THE HYMNS

Walton, Presteigne, LD8 2RA.
E. Passey, 07958 762362,
thehymns@hotmail.com,
www.thehymns.co.uk. *5m W of
Kington. Take A44 W, then 1st R
for Kinnerton. After approx 1m, at
the top of small hill, turn L (W).*
**Sat 20, Sun 21 May (11-5.30).
Adm £3.50, chd free. Light
refreshments.**
In a beautiful setting in the heart
of the Radnor valley, the garden is
part of a restored C16 farmstead,
with long views to the hills, and
The Radnor Forest. It is a traditional
garden reclaimed from the wild,
using locally grown plants and seeds,
and with a herb patio, wildflower
meadows and a short woodland
walk. It is designed for all the senses:
sight, sound and smell.

♿ 🐕 ✿ 🚗 🅳 🛋 ☕

32 HYSSINGTON, GORSTY HOUSE

Hyssington, Montgomery,
SY15 6AT. Gary & Annie Frost.
*A488 N from Bishop's Castle. Approx
3½m, turn L (signed Churchstoke
& Hyssington), then follow yellow
NGS signs. Also signed A489 E from
Churchstoke. Please park at Village
Hall.* **Sat 3, Sun 4, Sat 24, Sun 25
June (2-6). Combined adm with
Hyssington, The Old Barn £5,
chd free. Home-made teas.**
A new renovation, started late in
2014, of a neglected garden. Just
over 2 acres, an acre of which is
wildflower meadow. We are planting
to attract wildlife, with wooded
and shady areas, herbaceous

Rock Mill

borders, new orchard, wildlife pond, and a secret garden, planted to encourage pollinators. Lovely views. A developing garden, with new planting being added all the time. Featured in Welsh Country magazine.

33 HYSSINGTON, THE OLD BARN

Hyssington, Montgomery, SY15 6AT. Avril & Stuart Dickinson. *A488 N from Bishop's Castle. Approx 3½m, turn L (signed Churchstoke & Hyssington), then follow yellow NGS signs. Also signed A489 E from Churchstoke. Please park at Village Hall.* **Sat 3, Sun 4, Sat 24, Sun 25 June (2-6). Combined adm with Hyssington, Gorsty House £5, chd free. Home-made teas at Gorsty House.**
A peaceful ½ acre hideaway with winding paths and archways leading to colourful mixed borders with evergreens and mature trees, incl a handkerchief tree. There is a wildlife pond, summerhouse and vegetable and soft fruit areas. Featured in Welsh Country magazine.

34 LLANDINAM, NEUADDLLWYD

Llandinam, SY17 5AU. Roger & Pat Scull. *Take A470 to Llandinam, turn off main rd over bridge by statue. Take 1st lane on L, follow track for ¾m. Garden on L. Do not use SatNav.* **Sat 29, Sun 30 July (1-5). Combined adm with Llandinam, Little House £5, chd free. Home-made teas.**
1 acre garden set within 4 acres of wildlife meadows around C19 Grade II listed farmhouse (not open). Shrub and herbaceous borders, lawn with magnificent Monkey Puzzle tree leading down to R Severn with glorious views to hills beyond. Cottage garden area with roses, old orchard, pond, water feature, wooded area and a small allotment used by Llandinam Village. Species Habitat Group will be in attendance to explain their work. Partial wheelchair access.

& ☕

35 LLANDINAM, LITTLE HOUSE

Llandinam, SY17 5BH. Peter & Pat Ashcroft, 07443 524128, littlehouse1692@gmail.com, http://www.littlehouse1692.uk/. *1m from Llandinam Lion Hotel. Cross river at statue of David Davies on A470 in Llandinam. Follow rd for just under 1m, Little House is black & white cottage on roadside. Limited parking.* **Sat 29, Sun 30 July (1-5). Combined adm with Llandinam, Neuaddllwyd £5, chd free. Teas at Neuaddllwyd. Visits also by arrangement May to July (Tues only). Single visitors/small groups (10 max).**
Little House is on a quiet lane surrounded by fields and woodland, bordered by a stream. Slate and bark paths give access to the many features in the ⅓ acre garden incl fish and wildlife ponds, woodland, conifer, azalea and mixed beds, vegetable garden and mini meadow. For 2017 we have added more plants and created a new sensory garden, grass bed, grotto water feature and 00 gauge railway. Featured in Welsh Country magazine.

36 LLYSDINAM

Newbridge-on-Wye, LD1 6NB. Sir John & Lady Venables-Llewelyn & Llysdinam Charitable Trust, 01597 860190, llethr@outlook.com, llysdinamgardens.co.uk. *5m SW of Llandrindod Wells. Turn W off A470 at Newbridge-on-Wye; turn R immed after crossing R Wye; entrance up hill.* **Mon 29 May (2-5). Adm £4, chd free. Cream teas. Visits also by arrangement. Conducted tours/refreshments for groups 15+.**
Llysdinam Gardens are among the loveliest in mid Wales, especially noted for a magnificent display of rhododendrons and azaleas in May. Covering some 6 acres in all, they command sweeping views down the Wye Valley. Successive family members have developed the gardens over the last 150yrs to incl woodland with specimen trees, large herbaceous and shrub borders and a water garden, all of which

provide varied and colourful planting throughout the yr. The Victorian walled kitchen garden and extensive greenhouses grow a wide variety of vegetables, hothouse fruit, and exotic plants. Gravel paths.

& 🐄 ❀ 🚗 ☕

37 MAESFRON HALL AND GARDENS

Trewern, Welshpool, SY21 8EA. Dr & Mrs TD Owen, www.maesfron.co.uk. *4m E of Welshpool. On N side of A458 Welshpool to Shrewsbury Rd.* **Sun 9 Apr, Sun 10 Sept (2-5). Adm £5, chd free. Home-made teas.**
Georgian house (partly open) built in Italian villa style set in 4 acres of S-facing gardens on lower slopes of Moel-y-Golfa with panoramic views of The Long Mountain. Terraces, walled kitchen garden, tropical garden, restored Victorian conservatories, tower, shell grotto and hanging gardens below tower. Hundreds of daffodils in spring. Explore the ground floor and outbuildings. Parkland walks with a wide variety of trees. Adjacent 3 acre Equestrian Centre. Teas served in the dining room or on the terrace. Featured in Welsh Country magazine. Some gravel, steps and slopes.

& 🐄 ☕

38 NEW THE MILL

Pontdolgoch, Caersws, SY17 5JE. Les & Kris George. *A470 2m from Caersws towards Carno.* **Sun 11 June, Sun 9 July (11-5). Adm £4, chd free. Home-made cakes and scones.**
S-facing ½ acre garden with beautiful herbaceous borders, roses, shrubs and trees creating a haven of peace and tranquillity. Sit and relax by Cornus controversa 'Variegata' (wedding cake tree) surrounded by roses with the sound of the river nearby. Raised beds, fruit trees and vegetable garden. Stunning mill pond with walk onto balcony over the old mill wheel. Pontdolgoch Water Mill was the last working watermill in Montgomeryshire. Inside view some of the workings and history of the Mill. Mostly wheelchair accessible apart from shady garden which has steps.

& 🐄 ☕

39 MILL COTTAGE
Abbeycwmhir, LD1 6PH. Mr & Mrs B D Parfitt, 01597 851935, nkmillcottage@yahoo.co.uk, www.abbeycwmhir.co.uk. *8m N of Llandrindod Wells. Turn L off A483 1m N of Crossgates r'about, then 3½m on L, signed Abbeycwmhir. Limited parking.* **Sat 27, Sun 28, Mon 29 May (12-6). Adm £3.50, chd free. Tea. Visits also by arrangement May to Sept. Please phone first or call in on passing.**
⅓ acre stream side garden in spectacular valley setting, close to Cwm Hir Abbey, on the Glyndwr Way, consisting mainly of mature, rare and unusual trees and shrubs, particularly interesting to the plantsman. Rockery with numerous ericaceous plants and interesting water feature. Beautiful church and Abbey ruins nearby on a national trail - Glyndwr`s Way.
✿ 🛏 ☕

With your support we can help raise awareness of Carers Trust and unpaid carers

40 THE NEUADD
Llanbedr, Crickhowell, NP8 1SP. Robin & Philippa Herbert, 01873 812164, philippahherbert@gmail.com. *1m NE of Crickhowell. Leave Crickhowell by Llanbedr Rd. At junction with Great Oak Rd bear L, cont up hill for approx 1m, garden on L. Ample parking.* **Sun 4 June (2-6). Adm £4.50, chd free. Home-made teas. Visits also by arrangement**

May to July, adequate parking spaces for cars/mini buses.
Robin and Philippa Herbert have worked on the restoration of the garden at The Neuadd since 1999 and have planted many unusual trees and shrubs in the dramatic setting of the Brecon Beacons National Park. One of the major features is the walled garden, which has both traditional and decorative planting of fruit, vegetables and flowers. There is also a woodland walk with ponds and streams and a formal garden with flowering terraces. Water and spectacular views. Garden featured in one of the Secret Gardens series in the Brecon and Radnor Express. The owner uses a wheelchair and most of the garden is accessible, but some steep paths.
♿ 🐑 ✿ ☕

41 OAK COTTAGE
23 High Street, Welshpool, SY21 7JP. Tony Harvey. *Entered from Bowling Green Lane which runs parallel to the High St in centre of Welshpool.* **Sun 19 Mar, Sun 16, Mon 17, Sun 30 Apr, Mon 1 May (2-5). Adm £3.50, chd free. Home-made teas.**
Revamped during the last 3yrs this is a plantsman's small and hidden garden providing an oasis of green in the town centre. Gravel paths and stepping stones meander through a wide variety of plants, incl unusual species. Alpines are still a favourite with more varieties for 2017. Period Wardian cabinet, alpine house and collection of insectivorous plants. Featured in Welsh Country magazine. Gravel paths and steep slope at entrance.
♿ ☕

42 PENMYARTH HOUSE
The Glanusk Estate, Crickhowell, NP8 1LP. Mrs Harry Legge-Bourke, 01873 810414, jo@glanuskestate.com, www.glanuskestate.com. *2m NW of Crickhowell. Please access open garden via main estate entrance off A40 & follow signs to car park.* **Sun 21 May (11-4). Adm £6.50, chd free. Home-made teas.**
The garden is adorned with many

established plant species such as rhododendrons, azaleas, acers, amelia, magnolia, prunus and dogwood giving a vast array of colour in the spring and summer months. Alongside the open garden, we will be holding the annual Estate Fayre, showcasing over 25 artisans and craftsmen with exhibits of works for sale. Penmyarth church, a short distance from the gardens, will be open. Updates about the Glanusk Estate Garden Fayre and NGS Open Gardens will be posted on this site as well as www. glanuskestate.com, and the Glanusk facebook and twitter pages. Home-made cakes, coffee, tea and gourmet catering.
♿ ✿ 🚗 🛏 ☕

43 PEN-Y-MAES
Hay-on-Wye, HR3 5PP. Shân Egerton, 01497 820423, penymaes.hay@gmail.com. *1m SW of Hay-on-Wye. On B4350 towards Hay from Brecon. 2½m from Glasbury.* **Sun 18 June (2-5). Adm £5, chd free. Home-made teas. Visits also by arrangement June to Sept.**
2 acre garden incl mixed and herbaceous borders; orchard, topiary; walled formal kitchen garden; shrub, modern and climbing roses, peony borders, espaliered pears. Fine mulberry. Beautiful dry stone walling and mature trees. Great double view of Black Mountains and the Brecon Beacons. Emphasis on foliage and shape. Artist's garden.
♿ 🐑 ✿ 🚗 ☕

44 PLAS DINAM
Llandinam, SY17 5DQ. Eldrydd Lamp, 07415 503554, eldrydd@plasdinam.co.uk, www.plasdinamcountryhouse.co.uk. *7½m SW Newtown. on A470.* **Visits by arrangement Mar to Nov for groups 10+ (weekdays only, excl school holidays). Home-made teas.**
12 acres of parkland, gardens, lawns and woodland set at the foot of glorious rolling hills with spectacular views across the Severn Valley. A host of daffodils followed by one of the best wildflower meadows in Montgomeryshire with 36 species

of flowers and grasses incl hundreds of wild orchids; Glorious autumn colour with parrotias, liriodendrons, cotinus etc. Millennium wood. From 1884 until recently the home of Lord Davies and his family (house not open).

 ♿ 🐄 🐕 🚗 🛏 ☕

45 PONTHAFREN
Long Bridge Street, Newtown, SY16 2DY. Janet Rogers (volunteer gardener), www.ponthafren.org. *Park in main car park in town centre, 5 mins walk. Turn L out of car park, turn L over bridge, garden on L. Limited disabled parking, please phone for details.* **Sat 1 July, Sat 5 Aug (11.30-3.30). Adm by donation. Light refreshments.** Ponthafren is a registered charity for people with mental health issues or those that feel lonely or isolated. Open door policy so everyone is welcome. Interesting community garden on banks of R Severn run and maintained totally by volunteers: sensory garden with long grasses, herbs, scented plants and shrubs. Productive vegetable plot. Lots of plants for sale. Covered seating areas positioned around the garden to enjoy the views. Featured in Glorious Gardens from Above. Partial wheelchair access.

 ♿ 🐕 ✿ 🚗 ☕

46 ◆ POWIS CASTLE GARDEN
Welshpool, SY21 8RF. National Trust, 01938 551929, powiscastle@nationaltrust.org. uk, www.nationaltrust.org.uk/ powis-castle-and-garden. *1m S of Welshpool. From Welshpool take A490 S towards Newtown. After ¾m turn R into Red Lane. Cont up lane for ¼m & turn R into property.* **For NGS: Wed 21 June (10-6). Adm £9.21, chd £4.60. Light refreshments. For other opening times and information, please phone, email or visit garden website.**
Laid out in early C18 the garden features the finest remaining examples of Italian terraces in Britain. Richly planted herbaceous borders; enormous yew hedges; lead statuary, orangery and large wild flower areas. One of the NT's finest gardens. National Collection of *Laburnum.* Short introductory talks about the castle and garden run throughout the day. Refreshments served in the Courtyard Restaurant and Garden Coffee Shop Step free route around the garden, gravel paths, due to steep slopes only 4 wheeled PMV's permitted.

 ♿ ✿ 🐕 🚾 NPC 🛏 ☕

47 THE ROCK HOUSE
Llanbister, LD1 6TN. Jude Boutle & Sue Cox. *10m N of Llandrindod Wells. Off B4356 just above Llanbister village.* **Sun 28 May, Sun 4 June (2-5). Adm £4, chd free. Home-made teas.**
An acre of informal hillside garden at 1000ft with sweeping views over Radnorshire Hills and managed using organic principles. The garden features hardy perennials and shrubs, raised beds, a walkway over a bog garden, dry shady border, wildlife ponds, grazed bluebell meadow, a laburnum arch and an epic greenhouse! Children's quiz to keep small people busy in the garden and meadow. Featured in Mid Wales Journal.

 ✿ ☕

48 NEW ROCK MILL
Abermule, Montgomery, SY15 6NN. Rufus & Cherry Fairweather. *1m S of Abermule on B4368 towards Kerry. Best approached from Abermule village as angled entrance into field for parking.* **Sat 20, Sun 21 May (2-5). Adm £4, chd free. Home-made teas.**
3 acre riverside garden in a wooded valley. Colourful borders and shrubberies, specimen trees, terraces, woodland walks, bridges, extensive lawns, fishponds, orchard, herb and vegetable gardens. Features incl beehives, dovecote, heather thatched roundhouse and remnants of industrial past (corn mill and railway line). Child friendly activities (supervision required) incl sunken trampoline, croquet and badminton, animal treasure hunt, interactive quiz, wilderness trails. Sensible shoes and a sense of adventure recommended.

 ✿ ☕

49 ROSE COTTAGE
Cloddiau, Welshpool, SY21 9JE. Peter & Frances Grassi, 01938 553723, effgrassi@gmail.com. *3m N of Welshpool. Take A490 towards Guilsfield & Llanfyllin. After 1m turn L at sign for Dingle Nurseries & follow yellow NGS signs.* **Visits by arrangement June to Sept. Single visitors/large groups welcome. Adm £4.50, chd free. Home-made teas.**
S-facing 1 acre garden set in wooded valley and bordered by farmland. Small stream meanders through garden, dammed to form pools teeming with wildlife. Stylish summerhouse at pool edge, elegant fruit cage, rustic floriferous archways, bespoke chicken hut all add extra interest to lush informal ribbon borders, raised beds, vegetable plots and cutting garden. Featured in Welsh Country magazine. Wheelchair access to most of garden with help. No access to WC.

 ♿ 🐕 ✿ 🚗 ☕

50 TALGARTH MILL
The Square, Talgarth, Brecon, LD3 0BW. Talgarth Mill, www.talgarthmill.com. *In centre of Talgarth. Park in free car park opp rugby club, turn L out of car park entrance, follow high st to end, cross bridge, the Mill is on your R.* **Sat 1, Sun 2 July (10-4). Adm £3.50, chd free. Refreshments available from The Bakers' Table.**
A pretty riverside garden, maintained by volunteers. Along the riverside there is mixed herbaceous planting, a shady area, and steps up to a productive garden with espalier fruit trees, vegetables, soft fruits and a wildlife area. Places to sit and watch the river and its bird life (dippers, wagtails, kingfishers, herons) and the mill wheel turning. Garden is part of a working water mill. Award winning cafe and bakery which champions local, seasonal produce, gourmet coffee and tea. Open 10-4pm. Garden can be accessed by lift. Wide, flat paths for wheelchair access.

 ♿ ✿ 🚗 ☕

51 TAN-Y-LLYN

Meifod, SY22 6YB. Callum Johnston & Brenda Moor, 01938 500370, admin@tanyllyn-nurseries.co.uk, www.tanyllyn-nursery.co.uk. *1m SE of Meifod. From Oswestry on A495 turn L in village, cross R Vyrnwy & climb hill for ½m. From Welshpool on A490 look for Meifod sign on L just past Groesllwyd.* **Visits by arrangement Apr to Oct. Single visitors/small groups (30 max). Adm by donation.**
The garden sits on the side of Broniarth Hill above the Vyrnwy Valley. Shrubs and perennials border the grass paths running along the contours: wild hedges are punctuated with porthole views before merging into the surrounding woodland. The garden hovers between clipped control and barely tamed nature. 550ft up, S-facing and sheltered; the soil is well drained, slightly acid clay loam.

52 TINTO HOUSE

13 Broad Street, Hay-on-Wye, HR3 5DB. Karen & John Clare, 01497 821556, tintohouse13@gmail.com, www.tinto-house.co.uk. *Tinto House faces the clocktower in the centre of Hay-on-Wye. Entrance to garden is through the coach arch.* **Sat 24, Sun 25 June (1.30-5.30). Adm £4, chd free. Cream teas. Visits also by arrangement Apr to Aug.**
Tinto House is a hidden treasure in Hay. Beyond the Georgian townhouse lies an extensive traditional English garden overlooking the R Wye. It is divided into different rooms, each with its own character, featuring a wide range of plants incl climbing and shrub roses, clematis, hardy perennials and annuals. The vegetable garden is stocked with a wide range of soft fruit and vegetables. Art gallery. Home-made afternoon tea served in the garden. Wheelchair users may require some assistance as entrance is via a cobble courtyard.
&♿ ⛊ ✿ 🛏 ☕

53 TREBERFYDD HOUSE

Llangasty, Bwlch, Brecon, LD3 7PX. David Raikes & Carla Rapoport, www.treberfydd.com. *6m E of Brecon. From Abergavenny on A40, turn R in Bwlch on B5460. Take 1st turning L towards Pennorth & cont 2m along lane. From Brecon, turn L off A40 towards Pennorth in Llanhamlach.* **Sun 2 July (1-5.30). Adm £3.50, chd free. Home-made teas.**
Grade I listed Victorian Gothic house with 10 acres of grounds designed by W A Nesfield. Magnificent Cedar of Lebanon, avenue of mature Beech, towering Atlantic Cedars, Victorian rockery, herbaceous border and manicured lawns ideal for a picnic. Wonderful views of the Black Mountains. Plants available from Commercial Nursery in grounds - Walled Garden Treberfydd. House tours every half hour (additional £2), last tour 4pm. Easy wheelchair access to areas around the house, but herbaceous border only accessible via steps.
&♿ ⛊ ✿ ☕

54 TREMYNFA

Carreghofa Lane, Llanymynech, SY22 6LA. Jon & Gillian Fynes. *Edge of Llanymynech village. From N leave Oswestry on A483 to Welshpool. In Llanymynech turn R at Xrds (car wash on corner). Take 2nd R then follow yellow NGS signs. 300 yds park signed field, limited disabled parking nr garden.* **Sat 17, Sun 18 June (1-5). Adm £4, chd free. Home-made teas.**
S-facing 1 acre garden developed over 10yrs. Old railway cottage set in herbaceous and raised borders, patio with many pots of colourful and unusual plants. Garden slopes to productive fruit and vegetable area, ponds, spinney, wild areas and peat bog. Patio and seats to enjoy extensive views incl Llanymynech Rocks. Pet ducks on site, Montgomery canal close by. 100s of home grown plants for sale. Featured Amateur Gardening magazine.
✿ ☕

55 TY CAM

Talybont-on-Usk, LD3 7JD. Harry & Ceri Chapman, www.facebook.com/tycamgarden. *7m E of Brecon off A40. Garden next door to White Hart PH! Also look out for mushrooms.* **Sun 18 June, Sun 16 July (2-6). Adm £2, chd free.**
Small garden of secret surprises imaginatively created on three levels with steps built into an old railway embankment. Attractive features incl patios, decks, pergola, pond and waterfalls. Many choice herbaceous plants, trees and shrubs. Woodturning workshop, craft gallery and chickens!

56 TYN Y CWM

Beulah, Llanwrtyd Wells, LD5 4TS. Steve & Christine Carrow, 01591 620461, stevetynycwm@hotmail.co.uk. *10m W of Builth Wells. On A483 at Beulah take rd towards Abergwesyn for 2m. Drive drops down to L.* **Sun 18 June, Sun 6 Aug (2-5.30). Adm £4, chd free. Home-made teas.**
Garden mainly started 15yrs ago, lower garden has spring/woodland area, raised beds mixed with vegetables, fruit trees, fruit and flowers. Perennial borders, summer house gravel paths through rose and clematis pergola. Upper garden, partly sloped, incl bog, winter, water gardens and perennial beds with unusual slate steps. Beautiful views. Property bounded by small river. Lower garden has wide gravel mainly level paths. Upper garden is grassed with slopes and not suitable for wheelchairs.
&♿ ✿ 🛏 ☕

57 NEW VRON

Cregrina, Llandrindod Wells, LD1 5SF. Ann West, 01982 50244, annwest@spamarrest.com. *Leave A481 at Hundred House & follow lane to Cregrina. Take R hand fork after 1m, the Vron is on L.* **Sat 27 May (10.30-4.30). Adm £3.50, chd free. Home-made teas. Visits also by arrangement May to Sept for groups 10 min, 20 max.**
The garden is a series of windows into the surrounding landscape of the Radnorshire hills with many interesting shrubs and specimen trees incl a beautiful

magnolia sieboldii which should be flowering at the end of April. Partial wheelchair access, slope which may prove difficult.

  ♿ ☕

58 ◆ WELSH LAVENDER

Cefnperfedd Uchaf, Maesmynis, Builth Wells, LD2 3HU. Nancy Durham & Bill Newton-Smith, 01982 552467, farmers@welshlavender.com, www.welshlavender.com. *Approx 4½m S of Builth Wells & 12m from Brecon Cathedral off B4520 The farm is 1.3m from turn signed FARMERS' Welsh Lavender.* **For NGS: Sun 30 July, Sat 5, Sun 6 Aug (11-6). Adm £3.50, chd free. Home-made teas. For other opening times and information, please phone, email or visit garden website.**

2016 saw Welsh Lavender renew ⅔ of their lavenders. The farm is situated at 1100ft in the hills of mid Wales where the growing season is short and challenging. Gardens around the farm are colourful. Swimming pond in idyllic setting. Spectacular views in all directions. Visitors are welcome to roam the lavender fields, learn how the distillation process works, and visit the farm shop to try body creams and balms made with lavender oil distilled on the farm. 10% of sales go to the NGS. Coffee, tea, wine and light refreshments available. Stories in Country Life, Country Living, Tatler, Saga Magazine, Sunday Times Style & on BBC TV, ITV and S4C. The farm is featured in Monocle's Made in Wales film which can be seen on line at: https://monocle.com/film/business/made-in-wales/. Partial wheelchair access. Large paved area adjacent to teas and shop area easy to negotiate.

  ♿ 🐕 ☕

59 ◆ THE WHIMBLE GARDEN

Park Road, Kinnerton, Presteigne, LD8 2PD. E Taylor, 01547 560413, whimble6@gmail.com, www.whimblegardens.co.uk. *5m W of Presteigne. B4356 W from Presteigne. After 1m, L for Discoed & Maes-Treylow, L onto B4357 then next R on B4372 to Kinnerton. From Kington*

take A44 W, at Walton take B4357, after 3m, L on B4372 to Kinnerton. **For NGS: Sat 5 Aug (10.30-5). Adm £5, chd free. Home-made teas. For other opening times and information, please phone, email or visit garden website.**

Magical garden with beautiful views of Radnor Valley. Garden incl parterre with stunning herbaceous planting. Fish ponds and wildlife pools. Clematis, vine and rose covered metal church. Paths through hay meadow to toposcope and nature reserve area. Easy walking with seats to take in the views. Delicious home-made cakes tea and coffee. Mostly wheelchair access but grass path through meadow may be difficult in wet weather.

  ♿ ✿ 🚗 ☕ ☕

60 ◆ YSTRAD HOUSE

1 Church Road, Knighton, LD7 1EB. John & Margaret Davis, 01547 528154, jamdavis@ystradhouse.plus.com. *At junction of Church Rd & Station Rd. 225yds along Station Rd (A488 Clun) opp Knighton Hotel. Yellow House at junction with Church Rd.* **Sat 27, Sun 28 May, Sat 24, Sun 25 June (2-5). Adm £4, chd free. Home-made teas. Visits also by arrangement June to Sept. Single visitors/small groups (max 30). Please call or email in advance.**

An unsuspected town garden hidden behind Ystrad House, a Regency villa of earlier origins. Developed over the last 10yrs with an emphasis on tranquillity and timelessness: having broad lawns and wide borders, mature trees and more intimate features adding interest and surprise. The formal areas merge with wooded glades leading to a riverside walk alongside the R Teme. Lawns and gravelled paths mostly flat except access to riverside walk.

  ♿ 🐕 ✿ 🚗 🛏 ☕ ☕

Tyn Y Cwm

Early Openings 2018

Plan your garden visiting well ahead – put these dates in your 2018 diary!

Gardens across the country open from early January onwards – before the next year's guide is published – with glorious displays of colour including hellebores, aconites, snowdrops and carpets of spring bulbs.

Cheshire & Wirral
Sun 25 February (1-3)
Bucklow Farm

**By arrangement
in February**
The Well House

Devon
**Fri 9, Fri 16, Sun 25 February
(2-5)**
Higher Cherubeer

Gloucestershire
**Sun 28 January, Sun 11
February (11-3)**
Home Farm

**Sun 11, Sun 18
February (11-5)**
Trench Hill

Hampshire
**Sun 18, Mon 19,
Sun 25, Mon 26
February (2-5)**
Little Court

Herefordshire
**Thurs 1, 8, 15, 22
February (9-4)**
Ivy Croft

Kent
Sun 18 February (12-4)
Copton Ash

Sat 3, Sun 4 February (11-3)
Knowle Hill Farm

**Sun 18, Sun 25
February (2-5)**
Mere House

**Sat 3, Sun 4, Wed 7
February (10-4)**
Spring Platt

Somerset, Bristol &
South Gloucestershire
Sun 17 February (10-5)
East Lambrook Manor Gardens

**Sun 11, Mon 12 February
(11-4)**
Sherborne Garden

**By arrangement Tue 7,
Wed 8, Thur 9 February
(10.30-2.30)**
Southfield Farm

Surrey
Sun 11 February (11-4)
Gatton Park

Sussex
By arrangement in February
Pembury House

Wiltshire
Sat 24 February (10.30-5.30)
Lacock Abbey Gardens

Yorkshire
Wed 21 February (12-4)
Austwick Hall

Sun 18 February (11-5)
Devonshire Mill

Sun 18 February (1.30-5.30)
Fawley House

Accommodation available at NGS Gardens

We feature here a list of NGS gardens offering accommodation, listed by county. You will find contact details in the garden listing. We are happy to provide this list to help you find accommodation, however please note:

The NGS has no statutory control over the establishments or their methods of operating. The NGS cannot become involved in legal or contractual matters and cannot get involved in seeking financial recompense. All liability for loss disappointment, negligence or other damage is hereby excluded.

Bedfordshire
Luton Hoo Hotel Golf & Spa

Berkshire
Field Farm Cottage
Rookwood Farm House

Buckinghamshire
Danesfield House
Glebe Farm
Magnolia House, Grange Drive
Wooburn
Nether Winchendon House
Westend House

Cambridgeshire
Cakebreade Cottage,
   Orwell Gardens
Ferrar House
39 Foster Road
Madingley Hall
Quercus, Burrough Green
   Gardens
5 The Crescent, Impington
   Gardens

**Carmarthenshire &
Pembrokeshire**
Blaenfforest
Dyffryn Fernant
The Old Rectory
The Old Vicarage
Picton Castle & Gardens
Upton Castle Gardens

Cheshire & Wirral
Tatton Park
Trustwood, Burton Village
   Gardens

Cornwall
Boconnoc
Bonython Manor
Carminowe Valley Garden
Creed House &
   Creed Lodge
Eden Project
Hidden Valley Gardens
The Homestead Woodland
   Garden
Meudon Hotel
Trereife Park
Trerose Manor

Cumbria
Askham Hall
Lakeside Hotel & Rocky Bank
Low Thackthwaite
Matson Ground
Rydal Hall
Swarthmoor Hall
Windy Hall

Derbyshire
Cascades Gardens
Tissington Hall

Devon
Avenue Cottage

Beachborough County House,
   Kentisbury Gardens
Fursdon
Higher Ash Farm, Ash Gardens
Hotel Endsleigh
Shapcott Barton Estate
Southcombe Gardens
Whitstone Bluebells
Whitstone Farm

Dorset
Deans Court
Domineys Yard
Marren
Old Down House
The Secret Garden

Essex
Green Island
Horkesley Hall

Glamorgan
1 Ashgrove, Dinas Powys
Bryn-y-Ddafad
Mehefin, Llanmaes Gardens
Slade

Gloucestershire
Barnsley House
Berrys Place Farm
Lindors Country House
Matara Gardens of Wellbeing
Oakwood Farm Plant Fair and
   Upper Minety Open Gardens

Snugborough Mill, Blockley
  Gardens
Wells Cottage

Gwent
Middle Ninfa Farm & Bunkhouse
Usk Open Gardens

Gwynedd & Anglesey
Plas Cadnant Hidden Gardens

Hampshire
12 Christchurch Road
Durmast House
Manor House
Tylney Hall Hotel

Herefordshire
Brobury House Gardens
Caves Folly Nurseries
Coddington Vineyard
Kentchurch Court, Kentchurch
  Gardens
Lawless Hill
Lower House Farm
Midland Farm
Montpelier Cottage
Oak House, Aulden Arts and
  Gardens
The Old Rectory
Perrycroft
Rhodds Farm
Wolferlow House

Hertfordshire
The White Cottage

Isle of Wight
Northcourt Manor Gardens

Kent
Boldshaves
Canterbury Cathedral Gardens
Falconhurst
Gleaners, Deal Gardens
Leeds Castle
Rock Farm
The Secret Gardens of
  Sandwich at The Salutation
Sissinghurst Castle Garden
Thatched Cottage

**Lancashire, Merseyside &
Greater Manchester**
111 Main Street, Warton
  Gardens
Mill Barn
The Ridges
The Secret Valley
Sefton Villa, Sefton Park Gardens

Leicestershire & Rutland
Tresillian House

Lincolnshire
Doddington Hall Gardens
Goltho House

Gunby Hall & Gardens
Hall Farm
Hope House
Manor House
Marigold Cottage

London
West Lodge Park

Norfolk
Bagthorpe Hall
Hindringham Hall
Manor House Farm, Wellingham
The Old Rectory, Ridlington
Oxnead Hall
Severals Grange

North East
Bichfield Tower
Crook Hall & Gardens
Fallodon Hall
Loughbrow House
Mindrum Garden
Mr Yorke's Walled Garden
Ushaw College
Westgate Village Gardens
Whalton Manor Gardens

North East Wales
Aberclwyd Manor
Bodysgallen Hall & Spa
Dove Cottage
Firgrove, Ruthin Town Gardens
Plas Coch
Ruthin Castle, Ruthin Town
  Gardens
Sarum House, Ruthin Town
  Gardens
Tal-y-Bryn Farm

Northamptonshire
Dale House, Spratton Gardens
Ellicar Gardens
Hodsock Priory Gardens
Wisteria House, Long Buckby
  Gardens

Oxfordshire
Monckton Cottage, Headington
  Gardens

Powys

Aberangell, The Old Coach House
Beili Neuadd
Caer Beris Manor Hotel
Cyfie Farm
Esgair Angell
Glan yr Afon
Glanwye
Gliffaes Country House Hotel
Grandma's Garden
Gregynog Hall & Garden
The Hymns
Mill Cottage
Penmyarth House
Plas Dinam
Powis Castle Garden
Tinto House
Tyn y Cwm
1 Ystrad House

Shropshire

Brownhill House
The Citadel
Goldstone Hall Gardens
Sambrook Manor
Shoothill House
Upper Shelderton House
Walcot Hall

Somerset, Bristol & South Gloucestershire

Bath Priory Hotel
Cherry Bolberry Farm
Church Farm House
Cothay Manor & Gardens
Hartwood House
Honeyhurst Farm
Model Farm
Penny Brohn Cancer Care
Sole Retreat
Stoberry Garden
Ston Easton Park

Staffordshire, Birmingham & West Midlands

Colour Mill
Grafton Cottage
The Trentham Estate

Suffolk

Bays Farm
Cattishall Farmhouse
Drinkstone Park

Surrey

Barnett Hill
7 Rose Lane

Sussex

Ashdown Park Hotel
The Beeches
Butlers Farmhouse
Dittons End
Follers Manor
Gravetye Manor
Ham Cottage
Holly House
King John's Lodge
Lordington House
Newtimber Place
South Grange
West Dean Gardens

Warwickshire

The Granary
Mallory Court Hotel
Whichford & Ascott Gardens

Wiltshire

Dauntsey Park, Dauntsey Gardens
The Manor House, Castle Combe

North Cottage
The Pound House
Stourhead Garden

Worcestershire

Chasewood, Hanley Swan NGS Gardens
The Dell House
Holland House
Meadow Bank, Hanley Swan NGS Gardens

Yorkshire

Austwick Hall
Basin Howe Farm
Cold Cotes
Devonshire Mill
Dowthorpe Hall & Horse Pasture Cottage
Fawley House
Goldsborough Hall
Greenwick Farm
Havoc Hall
Hillside
Low Hall, Dacre Banks & Summerbridge Gardens
Low Sutton, Sutton Gardens
Millgate House
Shandy Hall Gardens
Sutton Grange, Sutton Gardens
Thornycroft

Plant Heritage

National Council for the Conservation of Plants and Gardens

Over 70 gardens that open for The National Garden Scheme are guardians of a Plant Heritage National Plant Collection although this may not always be noted in the garden description. These gardens carry the NPC symbol.

Plant Heritage, 12 Home Farm, Loseley Park, Guildford, Surrey GU31HS. 01483447540 www.plantheritage.com

ACER (EXCL. PALMATUM CVS.)
Blagdon, North East

AGAPANTHUS - FAIRWEATHER NURSERY TRIALS COLLECTION (HORTICULTURAL)
Fairweather's Nursery, Hampshire

ALNUS
Blagdon, North East

ANEMONE NEMOROSA
Avondale Nursery, Warwickshire

Kingston Lacy, Dorset

ARALIACEAE
Meon Orchard, Hampshire

ARBUTUS
Barton House, Warwickshire

ARUNCUS
Windy Hall, Cumbria

ASPLENIUM SCOLOPENDRIUM
Sizergh Castle, Cumbria

ASTER & RELATED GENERA (AUTUMN FLOWERING)
The Picton Garden, Herefordshire

ASTER NOVAE-ANGLIAE
Avondale Nursery, Warwickshire

ASTER (SYMPHYOTRICHUM) NOVAE-ANGLIAE
Brockamin, Worcestershire

ASTILBE
Holehird Gardens, Cumbria

ASTILBE
Marwood Hill Garden, Devon

BRUNNERA
Hearns House, Oxfordshire

CAMELLIAS & RHODODENDRONS INTRODUCED TO HELIGAN PRE-1920
The Lost Gardens of Heligan, Cornwall

CARPINUS
Sir Harold Hillier Gardens, Hampshire

CARPINUS BETULUS CVS.
West Lodge Park, London

CATALPA
Barton House, Warwickshire

CEANOTHUS
Eccleston Square, London

CERCIDIPHYLLUM
Hodnet Hall Gardens, Shropshire

Sir Harold Hillier Gardens, Hampshire

CHRYSANTHEMUM (KOREAN, RUBELLUM & HARDY SPRAY)
Hill Close Gardens, Warwickshire

CODONOPSIS
Woodlands, Fotherby Gardens, Lincolnshire

CONVALLARIA
Kingston Lacy, Dorset

CORIARIA
Crûg Farm, Gwynedd & Anglesey

CORNUS
Sir Harold Hillier Gardens, Hampshire

CORNUS (EXCL. C. FLORIDA CVS.)
Newby Hall & Gardens, Yorkshire

CORYLUS
Sir Harold Hillier Gardens, Hampshire

COTINUS
Bath Priory Hotel, Somerset, Bristol & South Gloucestershire

COTONEASTER
Sir Harold Hillier Gardens, Hampshire

CYCLAMEN (EXCL. PERSICUM CVS.)
Higher Cherubeer, Devon

CYDONIA OBLONGA
Norton Priory Museum & Gardens, Cheshire & Wirral

CYSTOPTERIS
Sizergh Castle, Cumbria

DABOECIA
Holehird Gardens, Cumbria

DAHLIA
Varfell Farm, Cornwall

DESCHAMPSIA
The Walled Gardens of Cannington, Somerset, & South Gloucestershire

DICENTRA
Boundary Cottage, Yorkshire

DIERAMA SPP.
Yew Tree Cottage, Staffordshire

DRYOPTERIS
Sizergh Castle, Cumbria

EUCALYPTUS
Meon Orchard, Hampshire

EUCALYPTUS SPP.
The World Garden at Lullingstone Castle, Kent

EUCRYPHIA
Whitstone Farm, Devon

EUONYMUS (DECIDUOUS)
The Place for Plants, East Bergholt Place Garden, Suffolk

EUPHORBIA
University of Oxford Botanic Garden, Oxfordshire

EUPHORBIA (HARDY)
Firvale Allotment Garden, Yorkshire

FRAXINUS
The Lovell Quinta Arboretum, Cheshire & Wirral

GERANIUM SANGUINEUM, MACRORRHIZUM & X CANTABRIGIENSE
Brockamin, Worcestershire

GERANIUM SYLVATICUM & RENARDII - FORMS, CVS. & HYBRIDS
Wren's Nest, Cheshire & Wirral

GEUM
1 Brickwall Cottages, Kent

HAMAMELIS
Sir Harold Hillier Gardens, Hampshire

HEDERA
Ivybank, Pebworth Gardens, Warwickshire

HILLIERS (PLANTS RAISED BY)
Sir Harold Hillier Gardens, Hampshire

HOHERIA
Abbotsbury Gardens, Dorset

HOSTA
Cleave House, Devon

HOSTA (SMALL & MINIATURE)
Hogarth Hostas, Berkshire

HOSTA 'HALCYON' & SPORTS
Cleave House, Devon

HYPERICUM
Sir Harold Hillier Gardens, Hampshire

JUGLANS
Upton Wold, Gloucestershire

LABURNUM
Powis Castle Garden, Powys

LAPAGERIA ROSEA (& NAMED CVS.)
Roseland House, Cornwall

LEUCANTHEMUM X SUPERBUM (CHRYSANTHEMUM MAXIMUM)
Shapcott Barton Estate, Devon

LEWISIA
'John's Garden' at Ashwood Nurseries, Staffordshire

LIGUSTRUM
Sir Harold Hillier Gardens, Hampshire

LITHOCARPUS
Sir Harold Hillier Gardens, Hampshire

MALUS (CVS. FROM NOTTS & DERBY, LINCS, LEICS & YORKS)
Clumber Park Walled Kitchen Garden, Nottinghamshire

MALUS (ORNAMENTAL)
Barnards Farm, Essex

MECONOPSIS (LARGE PERENNIAL SPP. & HYBRIDS)
Holehird Gardens, Cumbria

METASEQUOIA
Sir Harold Hillier Gardens, Hampshire

MONARDA
Glyn Bach Gardens, Carmarthenshire & Pembrokeshire

Hole's Meadow, Devon

MUSCARI
16 Witton Lane, Norfolk

NEPETA
Hole's Meadow, Devon

NERINE - HARDY SPP., CVS., & HYBRIDS
Bickham Cottage, Devon

NERINE SARNIENSIS CVS
Bickham Cottage, Devon

OMPHALODES
Hearns House Oxfordshire

OSMUNDA
Sizergh Castle, Cumbria

PARIS
Crûg Farm, Gwynedd & Anglesey

PELARGONIUM
Ivybank, Pebworth Gardens, Warwickshire

PENNISETUM
Knoll Gardens, Dorset

PENSTEMON
Froggery Cottage,
Northamptonshire

PHLOMIS
Foamlea, Devon

PHOTINIA
Sir Harold Hillier Gardens,
Hampshire

PINUS (EXCL DWARF CVS.)
Sir Harold Hillier Gardens,
Hampshire

PINUS SPP.
The Lovell Quinta Arboretum,
Cheshire & Wirral

**PODOCARPUS & RELATED
PODOCARPACEAE**
Meon Orchard, Hampshire

POLYGONATUM
Crûg Farm, Gwynedd &
Anglesey

POLYSTICHUM
Holehird Gardens, Cumbria

PTEROCARYA
Upton Wold, Gloucestershire

QUERCUS
Sir Harold Hillier Gardens,
Hampshire

RHAPIS SPP. & CVS.
Gwyndy Bach, Gwynedd &
Anglesey

RHEUM (CULINARY CVS.)
Clumber Park Walled Kitchen
Garden, Nottinghamshire

**RHODODENDRON
(GHENT AZALEAS)**
Sheffield Park and Garden,
Sussex

**RHODODENDRON KURUME
AZALEA WILSON 50**
Trewidden Garden, Cornwall

RODGERSIA
The Gate House, Devon

**ROSA - HYBRID MUSK INTRO
BY PEMBERTON & BENTALL
1912-1939**
Dutton Hall, Lancashire

ROSA (RAMBLING)
Moor Wood, Gloucestershire

SANGUISORBA
Avondale Nursery, Warwickshire

SANTOLINA
The Walled Gardens of
Cannington, Somerset, Bristol &
South Gloucestershire

**SAXIFRAGA SECT.
LIGULATAE: SPP. & CVS.**
Waterperry Gardens,
Oxfordshire

**SAXIFRAGA SUBSECT.
KABSCHIA & ENGLERIA**
Waterperry Gardens,
Oxfordshire

**SIBERIAN IRIS CVS:
BRITISH, AWARD WINNERS
& HISTORICALLY
SIGNIFICANT**
Aulden Farm, Aulden Arts and
Gardens, Herefordshire

SORBUS
Blagdon, North East

Ness Botanic Gardens, Cheshire
& Wirral

**STERN, SIR F (PLANTS
SELECTED BY)**
Highdown Gardens, Sussex

STEWARTIA - ASIAN SPP.
High Beeches Woodland and
Water Garden, Sussex

**STYRACACEAE (INCL
HALESIA, PTEROSTYRAX,
STYRAX, SINOJACKIA)**
Holker Hall Gardens, Cumbria

TAXODIUM SPP. & CVS.
West Lodge Park, London

YUCCA
Renishaw Hall & Gardens,
Derbyshire

Society of Garden Designers

The Ⓓ symbol at the end of a garden description indicates that the garden has been designed by a Fellow, Member or Pre-Registered Member of the Society of Garden Designers.

Fellow of the Society of Garden Designers (FSGD) is awarded to Members for exceptional contributions to the Society or to the profession

Rosemary Alexander FSGD
Sally Court FSGD
Andrew Fisher Tomlin FSGD
Roderick Griffin FSGD
Ian Kitson FSGD
David Stevens FSGD
Robin Templar-Williams FSGD
Julie Toll FSGD

Member of the Society of Garden Designers (MSGD) is awarded after passing adjudication

Timothy Carless MSGD
Cheryl Cummings MSGD
Chris Eves MSGD
Jill Fenwick MSGD
Julia Fogg MSGD
Paul Harris MSGD
Paul Hensey MSGD
Joanna Herald MSGD
Barbara Hunt MSGD (retired)
Dawn Isaac MSGD
Arabella Lennox-Boyd MSGD
Robert Myers MSGD
Chris Parsons MSGD
Dan Pearson MSGD

Emma Plunket MSGD
Debbie Roberts MSGD
Charles Rutherfoord MSGD
Ian Smith MSGD
Tom Stuart-Smith MSGD
Sue Townsend MSGD
Jo Ward-Ellison MSGD
Cleve West MSGD
Rebecca Winship MSGD

Pre-Registered Member is a member working towards gaining Registered Membership

Joanne Bernstein
Tamara Bridge
Fiona Cadwallader
Wendy Cartwright

Kristina Clode
Helen Dolby
Anoushka Feiler
Fiona Green
Louise Hardwick
Sarah Murch
Angela Newman
Guy Petheram
Anne-Marie Powell
Faith Ramsay
Daniel Shea
Susan Summer
Helen Thomas
Virginia von Celsing
Alison Wear
Susan Young

Student
Suzanne Etherton

Acknowledgements

Each year the NGS receives fantastic support from the community of garden photographers who donate and make available images of gardens. The NGS would like to thank them for their generous donations. We also thank the garden owners who have kindly submitted images of their gardens.

Unless otherwise stated, photographs are kindly supplied by permission of the garden owner.

The 2017 Production Team: Elna Broe, Jack Claramunt, Linda Ellis, Louise Grainger, Rachel Hick, Kali Masure, George Plumptre, Jane Sennett, Sarah Turner, Georgina Waters, Anna Wili. With special thanks to our County Volunteers.

CONSTABLE

A CIP catalogue record for this book is available from the British Library.

ISBN: 978-1-47212-679-5

Designed by Level Partnership
Maps by Mary Spence © Global Mapping and XYZ Maps
Typeset in Gill Sans
Printed and bound in Italy by Rotolito Lombarda S.p.A.

Constable
An imprint of Little, Brown Book Group
Carmelite House, 50 Victoria Embankment,
London EC4Y 0DZ

An Hachette UK Company
www.hachette.co.uk www.littlebrown.co.uk

If you require this information in alternative formats, please telephone 01483 211535 or email ngs@ngs.org.uk